FORD | THUNDERBIRD/COUGAR 1983-97 REPAIR MANUAL

CHILTON'S

Covers all U.S. and Canadian models of Ford Thunderbird and Mercury Cougar

by **Eric Michael Mihalyi,** A.S.E., S.A.E., S.T.S.

CHILTON *Automotive Books*

PUBLISHED BY **HAYNES NORTH AMERICA. Inc.**

Manufactured in USA
© 1999 Haynes North America, Inc.
ISBN 0-8019-9133-1
Library of Congress Catalog Card No. 99-075917
3456789012 9876543210

Haynes Publishing Group
Sparkford Nr Yeovil
Somerset BA22 7JJ England

Haynes North America, Inc
861 Lawrence Drive
Newbury Park
California 91320 USA

ABCDE
FG

6E1

Contents

1 GENERAL INFORMATION AND MAINTENANCE

1-2 HOW TO USE THIS BOOK
1-2 TOOLS AND EQUIPMENT
1-4 SERVICING YOUR VEHICLE SAFELY
1-5 FASTENERS, MEASUREMENTS AND CONVERSIONS
1-7 SERIAL NUMBER IDENTIFICATION
1-12 ROUTINE MAINTENANCE AND TUNE-UP
1-35 FLUIDS AND LUBRICANTS
1-46 TOWING THE VEHICLE
1-47 JUMP STARTING A DEAD BATTERY
1-48 JACKING

2 ENGINE ELECTRICAL

2-2 FIRING ORDERS
2-3 IGNITION SYSTEMS
2-3 DURA SPARK II IGNITION SYSTEM
2-8 EEC-IV THICK FILM INTEGRATED (TFI) IGNITION SYSTEM
2-14 DISTRIBUTORLESS IGNITION SYSTEM (DIS)
2-17 CHARGING SYSTEM
2-21 STARTING SYSTEM

3 ENGINE AND ENGINE OVERHAUL

3-2 ENGINE MECHANICAL
3-57 EXHAUST SYSTEM
3-59 ENGINE RECONDITIONING

4 EMISSION CONTROLS

4-2 EMISSION CONTROLS
4-11 ELECTRONIC ENGINE CONTROLS
4-18 EEC-IV TROUBLE CODES
4-23 EEC-V TROUBLE CODES
4-28 VACUUM DIAGRAMS

5 FUEL SYSTEM

5-2 BASIC FUEL SYSTEM DIAGNOSIS
5-2 FUEL LINES AND FITTINGS
5-3 CARBURETED FUEL SYSTEM
5-7 CENTRAL FUEL INJECTION
5-11 MULTI-POINT INJECTION (EFI) AND SEQUENTIAL FUEL INJECTION (SFI)

6 CHASSIS ELECTRICAL

6-2 UNDERSTANDING AND TROUBLESHOOTING ELECTRICAL SYSTEMS
6-8 BATTERY CABLES
6-8 SUPPLEMENTAL RESTRAINT SYSTEM (AIR BAG)
6-11 HEATER
6-18 CRUISE CONTROL
6-20 ENTERTAINMENT SYSTEMS
6-23 WINDSHIELD WIPERS
6-25 INSTRUMENTS AND SWITCHES
6-30 LIGHTING
6-37 TRAILER WIRING
6-38 CIRCUIT PROTECTION
6-43 WIRING DIAGRAMS

Contents

7-2	MANUAL TRANSMISSION	7-25	DRIVELINE
7-4	CLUTCH	7-29	REAR AXLE
7-10	AUTOMATIC TRANSMISSION		

DRIVE TRAIN 7

| 8-2 | WHEELS | 8-16 | REAR SUSPENSION |
| 8-2 | FRONT SUSPENSION | 8-28 | STEERING |

SUSPENSION AND STEERING 8

9-2	BRAKE OPERATING SYSTEM	9-25	TEVES MARK II 4-WHEEL ANTI-LOCK BRAKE SYSTEM (ABS)
9-6	FRONT DISC BRAKES		
9-12	REAR DRUM BRAKES	9-32	TEVES MARK IV ANTI-LOCK BRAKE SYSTEM (ABS)
9-17	REAR DISC BRAKES		
9-20	PARKING BRAKE		

BRAKES 9

| 10-2 | EXTERIOR | 10-8 | INTERIOR |

BODY 10

| 10-21 | GLOSSARY |

GLOSSARY

| 10-25 | MASTER INDEX |

MASTER INDEX

SAFETY NOTICE

Proper service and repair procedures are vital to the safe, reliable operation of all motor vehicles, as well as the personal safety of those performing repairs. This manual outlines procedures for servicing and repairing vehicles using safe, effective methods. The procedures contain many NOTES, CAUTIONS and WARNINGS which should be followed, along with standard procedures to eliminate the possibility of personal injury or improper service which could damage the vehicle or compromise its safety.

It is important to note that repair procedures and techniques, tools and parts for servicing motor vehicles, as well as the skill and experience of the individual performing the work vary widely. It is not possible to anticipate all of the conceivable ways or conditions under which vehicles may be serviced, or to provide cautions as to all possible hazards that may result. Standard and accepted safety precautions and equipment should be used when handling toxic or flammable fluids, and safety goggles or other protection should be used during cutting, grinding, chiseling, prying, or any other process that can cause material removal or projectiles.

Some procedures require the use of tools specially designed for a specific purpose. Before substituting another tool or procedure, you must be completely satisfied that neither your personal safety, nor the performance of the vehicle will be endangered.

Although information in this manual is based on industry sources and is complete as possible at the time of publication, the possibility exists that some car manufacturers made later changes which could not be included here. While striving for total accuracy, the authors or publishers cannot assume responsibility for any errors, changes or omissions that may occur in the compilation of this data.

PART NUMBERS

Part numbers listed in this reference are not recommendations by Haynes North America, Inc. for any product brand name. They are references that can be used with interchange manuals and aftermarket supplier catalogs to locate each brand supplier's discrete part number.

SPECIAL TOOLS

Special tools are recommended by the vehicle manufacturer to perform their specific job. Use has been kept to a minimum, but where absolutely necessary, they are referred to in the text by the part number of the tool manufacturer. These tools can be purchased, under the appropriate part number, from your local dealer or regional distributor, or an equivalent tool can be purchased locally from a tool supplier or parts outlet. Before substituting any tool for the one recommended, read the SAFETY NOTICE at the top of this page.

ACKNOWLEDGMENTS

This publication contains material that is reproduced and distributed under a license from Ford Motor Company. No further reproduction or distribution of the Ford Motor Company material is allowed without the express written permission from Ford Motor Company.

HOW TO USE THIS BOOK 1-2
WHERE TO BEGIN 1-2
AVOIDING TROUBLE 1-2
MAINTENANCE OR REPAIR? 1-2
AVOIDING THE MOST COMMON
  MISTAKES 1-2
TOOLS AND EQUIPMENT 1-2
SPECIAL TOOLS 1-4
SERVICING YOUR VEHICLE SAFELY 1-4
DO'S 1-4
DON'TS 1-5
**FASTENERS, MEASUREMENTS AND
  CONVERSIONS 1-5**
BOLTS, NUTS AND OTHER THREADED
  RETAINERS 1-5
TORQUE 1-6
  TORQUE WRENCHES 1-6
  TORQUE ANGLE METERS 1-7
STANDARD AND METRIC
  MEASUREMENTS 1-7
SERIAL NUMBER IDENTIFICATION 1-7
VEHICLE 1-7
VEHICLE CERTIFICATION LABEL 1-7
ENGINE 1-10
TRANSMISSION 1-10
DRIVE AXLE 1-12
**ROUTINE MAINTENANCE AND
  TUNE-UP 1-12**
AIR CLEANER ELEMENT 1-12
  REMOVAL & INSTALLATION 1-12
FUEL FILTER 1-14
  REMOVAL & INSTALLATION 1-14
PCV VALVE 1-16
  REMOVAL & INSTALLATION 1-16
EVAPORATIVE CANISTER 1-18
  SERVICING 1-18
BATTERY 1-18
  PRECAUTIONS 1-18
  GENERAL MAINTENANCE 1-18
  BATTERY FLUID 1-18
  CABLES 1-19
  CHARGING 1-20
  REPLACEMENT 1-20
BELTS 1-20
  INSPECTION 1-20
  ADJUSTMENTS 1-20
  REMOVAL & INSTALLATION 1-22
TIMING BELTS 1-24
  INSPECTION 1-24
HOSES 1-25
  INSPECTION 1-25
  REMOVAL & INSTALLATION 1-25
CV BOOTS 1-26
  INSPECTION 1-26
SPARK PLUGS 1-26
  SPARK PLUG HEAT RANGE 1-27
  REMOVAL & INSTALLATION 1-27
  INSPECTION & GAPPING 1-27
SPARK PLUG WIRES 1-28
  TESTING 1-28
  REMOVAL & INSTALLATION 1-29
DISTRIBUTOR CAP AND ROTOR 1-29
  REMOVAL & INSTALLATION 1-29
  INSPECTION 1-29
IGNITION TIMING 1-30
  GENERAL INFORMATION 1-30
  INSPECTION & ADJUSTMENT 1-30
IDLE SPEED AND MIXTURE
  ADJUSTMENTS 1-31
AIR CONDITIONING SYSTEM 1-31
  SYSTEM SERVICE & REPAIR 1-31
  PREVENTIVE MAINTENANCE 1-32
  SYSTEM INSPECTION 1-32
WINDSHIELD WIPERS 1-32

ELEMENT (REFILL) CARE &
  REPLACEMENT 1-32
TIRES AND WHEELS 1-33
  TIRE ROTATION 1-33
  TIRE DESIGN 1-33
  TIRE STORAGE 1-34
  INFLATION & INSPECTION 1-34
FLUIDS AND LUBRICANTS 1-35
FLUID DISPOSAL 1-35
FUEL AND ENGINE OIL
  RECOMMENDATIONS 1-38
  FUEL 1-38
  OIL 1-38
  OIL LEVEL CHECK 1-39
  OIL AND FILTER CHANGE 1-39
MANUAL TRANSMISSION 1-40
  FLUID RECOMMENDATIONS 1-40
  LEVEL CHECK 1-40
  DRAIN AND REFILL 1-40
AUTOMATIC TRANSMISSIONS 1-40
  FLUID RECOMMENDATIONS 1-40
  LEVEL CHECK 1-40
  DRAIN AND REFILL 1-41
DRIVE AXLE 1-41
  FLUID RECOMMENDATIONS 1-41
  LEVEL CHECK 1-41
  DRAIN AND REFILL 1-42
COOLING SYSTEM 1-42
  FLUID RECOMMENDATIONS 1-42
  LEVEL CHECK 1-42
  DRAIN, FLUSH AND REFILL 1-42
  SYSTEM INSPECTION 1-43
  CHECKING SYSTEM PROTECTION 1-43
BRAKE MASTER CYLINDER 1-43
  FLUID RECOMMENDATIONS 1-43
  LEVEL CHECK 1-43
CLUTCH MASTER CYLINDER 1-44
  FLUID RECOMMENDATIONS 1-44
  LEVEL CHECK 1-44
POWER STEERING 1-44
  FLUID RECOMMENDATION 1-44
  LEVEL CHECK 1-44
CHASSIS GREASING 1-44
  BALL JOINTS 1-44
  TIE ROD ENDS 1-44
  CLUTCH LINKAGE 1-44
  AUTOMATIC TRANSMISSION
    LINKAGE 1-44
  PARKING BRAKE LINKAGE 1-44
BODY LUBRICATION AND
  MAINTENANCE 1-44
  CARE OF YOUR VEHICLE 1-44
  LOCK CYLINDERS 1-45
  DOOR HINGES & HINGE CHECKS 1-45
  TRUNK LID 1-45
  BODY DRAIN HOLES 1-45
FRONT WHEEL BEARINGS 1-45
  REMOVAL, REPACKING, &
    INSTALLATION 1-45
  ADJUSTMENT 1-46
TOWING THE VEHICLE 1-46
TOWING 1-46
JUMP STARTING A DEAD BATTERY 1-47
JUMP STARTING PRECAUTIONS 1-47
JUMP STARTING PROCEDURE 1-47
JACKING 1-48
JACKING PRECAUTIONS 1-49
SPECIFICATIONS CHARTS
  VEHICLE IDENTIFICATION CHART 1-8
  ENGINE IDENTIFICATION 1-10
  GENERAL ENGINE SPECIFICATIONS 1-11
  GENERAL ENGINE TUNE-UP
    SPECIFICATIONS 1-31
  MAINTENANCE SCHEDULES 1-49
  CAPACITIES 1-53

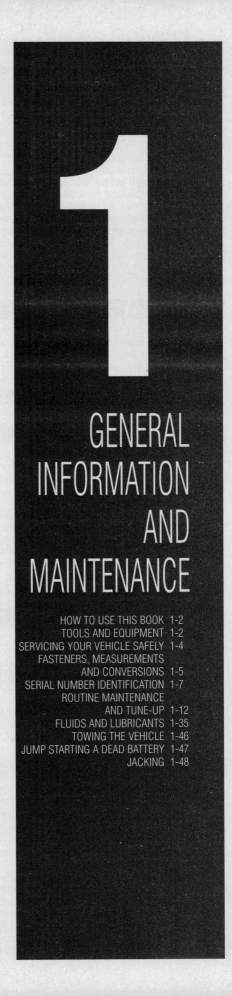

1

GENERAL INFORMATION AND MAINTENANCE

HOW TO USE THIS BOOK 1-2
TOOLS AND EQUIPMENT 1-2
SERVICING YOUR VEHICLE SAFELY 1-4
FASTENERS, MEASUREMENTS
AND CONVERSIONS 1-5
SERIAL NUMBER IDENTIFICATION 1-7
ROUTINE MAINTENANCE
AND TUNE-UP 1-12
FLUIDS AND LUBRICANTS 1-35
TOWING THE VEHICLE 1-46
JUMP STARTING A DEAD BATTERY 1-47
JACKING 1-48

HOW TO USE THIS BOOK

This Chilton's Total Car Care manual for the 1983–97 Ford Thunderbird and Mercury Cougar is intended to help you learn more about the inner workings of your vehicle while saving you money on its upkeep and operation.

The beginning of the book will likely be referred to the most, since that is where you will find information for maintenance and tune-up. The other sections deal with the more complex systems of your vehicle. Systems (from engine through brakes) are covered to the extent that the average do-it-yourselfer can attempt. This book will not explain such things as rebuilding a differential because the expertise required and the special tools necessary make this uneconomical. It will, however, give you detailed instructions to help you change your own brake pads and shoes, replace spark plugs, and perform many more jobs that can save you money and help avoid expensive problems.

A secondary purpose of this book is a reference for owners who want to understand their vehicle and/or their mechanics better.

Where to Begin

Before removing any bolts, read through the entire procedure. This will give you the overall view of what tools and supplies will be required. So read ahead and plan ahead. Each operation should be approached logically and all procedures thoroughly understood before attempting any work.

If repair of a component is not considered practical, we tell you how to remove the part and then how to install the new or rebuilt replacement. In this way, you at least save labor costs.

Avoiding Trouble

Many procedures in this book require you to "label and disconnect . . ." a group of lines, hoses or wires. Don't be think you can remember where everything goes—you won't. If you hook up vacuum or fuel lines incorrectly, the vehicle may run poorly, if at all. If you hook up electrical wiring incorrectly, you may instantly learn a very expensive lesson.

You don't need to know the proper name for each hose or line. A piece of masking tape on the hose and a piece on its fitting will allow you to assign your own label. As long as you remember your own code, the lines can be reconnected by matching your tags. Remember that tape will dissolve in gasoline or solvents; if a part is to be washed or cleaned, use another method of identification. A permanent felt-tipped marker or a metal scribe can be very handy for marking metal parts. Remove any tape or paper labels after assembly.

Maintenance or Repair?

Maintenance includes routine inspections, adjustments, and replacement of parts which show signs of normal wear. Maintenance compensates for wear or deterioration. Repair implies that something has broken or is not working. A need for a repair is often caused by lack of maintenance. for example: draining and refilling automatic transmission fluid is maintenance recommended at specific intervals. Failure to do this can shorten the life of the transmission/transaxle, requiring very expensive repairs. While no maintenance program can prevent items from eventually breaking or wearing out, a general rule is true: MAINTENANCE IS CHEAPER THAN REPAIR.

Two basic mechanic's rules should be mentioned here. First, whenever the left side of the vehicle or engine is referred to, it means the driver's side. Conversely, the right side of the vehicle means the passenger's side. Second, screws and bolts are removed by turning counterclockwise, and tightened by turning clockwise unless specifically noted.

Safety is always the most important rule. Constantly be aware of the dangers involved in working on an automobile and take the proper precautions. Please refer to the information in this section regarding SERVICING YOUR VEHICLE SAFELY and the SAFETY NOTICE on the acknowledgment page.

Avoiding the Most Common Mistakes

Pay attention to the instructions provided. There are 3 common mistakes in mechanical work:

1. Incorrect order of assembly, disassembly or adjustment. When taking something apart or putting it together, performing steps in the wrong order usually just costs you extra time; however, it CAN break something. Read the entire procedure before beginning. Perform everything in the order in which the instructions say you should, even if you can't see a reason for it. When you're taking apart something that is very intricate, you might want to draw a picture of how it looks when assembled in order to make sure you get everything back in its proper position. When making adjustments, perform them in the proper order. One adjustment possibly will affect another.

2. Overtorquing (or undertorquing). While it is more common for overtorquing to cause damage, undertorquing may allow a fastener to vibrate loose causing serious damage. Especially when dealing with aluminum parts, pay attention to torque specifications and utilize a torque wrench in assembly. If a torque figure is not available, remember that if you are using the right tool to perform the job, you will probably not have to strain yourself to get a fastener tight enough. The pitch of most threads is so slight that the tension you put on the wrench will be multiplied many times in actual force on what you are tightening.

There are many commercial products available for ensuring that fasteners won't come loose, even if they are not torqued just right (a very common brand is Loctite()). If you're worried about getting something together tight enough to hold, but loose enough to avoid mechanical damage during assembly, one of these products might offer substantial insurance. Before choosing a threadlocking compound, read the label on the package and make sure the product is compatible with the materials, fluids, etc. involved.

3. Crossthreading. This occurs when a part such as a bolt is screwed into a nut or casting at the wrong angle and forced. Crossthreading is more likely to occur if access is difficult. It helps to clean and lubricate fasteners, then to start threading the bolt, spark plug, etc. with your fingers. If you encounter resistance, unscrew the part and start over again at a different angle until it can be inserted and turned several times without much effort. Keep in mind that many parts have tapered threads, so that gentle turning will automatically bring the part you're threading to the proper angle. Don't put a wrench on the part until it's been tightened a couple of turns by hand. If you suddenly encounter resistance, and the part has not seated fully, don't force it. Pull it back out to make sure it's clean and threading properly.

Be sure to take your time and be patient, and always plan ahead. Allow yourself ample time to perform repairs and maintenance.

TOOLS AND EQUIPMENT

♦ See Figures 1 thru 15

Without the proper tools and equipment it is impossible to properly service your vehicle. It would be virtually impossible to catalog every tool that you would need to perform all of the operations in this book. It would be unwise for the amateur to rush out and buy an expensive set of tools on the theory that he/she may need one or more of them at some time.

The best approach is to proceed slowly, gathering a good quality set of those tools that are used most frequently. Don't be misled by the low cost of bargain tools. It is far better to spend a little more for better quality. Forged wrenches, 6 or 12-point sockets and fine tooth ratchets are by far preferable to their less expensive counterparts. As any good mechanic can tell you, there are few worse experiences than trying to work on a vehicle with bad tools. Your monetary savings will be far outweighed by frustration and mangled knuckles.

Begin accumulating those tools that are used most frequently: those associated with routine maintenance and tune-up. In addition to the normal assortment of screwdrivers and pliers, you should have the following tools:

• Wrenches/sockets and combination open end/box end wrenches in sizes from 1/8 –3/4 in. or 3–19mm, as well as a 13/16 in. or 5/8 in. spark plug socket (depending on plug type).

➡If possible, buy various length socket drive extensions. Universal-joint and wobble extensions can be extremely useful, but be careful when using them, as they can change the amount of torque applied to the socket.

• Jackstands for support.
• Oil filter wrench.

- Spout or funnel for pouring fluids.
- Grease gun for chassis lubrication (unless your vehicle is not equipped with any grease fittings)
- Hydrometer for checking the battery (unless equipped with a sealed, maintenance-free battery.)
- A container for draining oil and other fluids.
- Rags for wiping up the inevitable mess.

In addition to the above items there are several others that are not absolutely necessary, but handy to have around. These include an equivalent oil absorbent gravel, like cat litter, and the usual supply of lubricants, antifreeze and fluids. This is a basic list for routine maintenance, but only your personal needs and desire can accurately determine your list of tools.

After performing a few projects on the vehicle, you'll be amazed at the other tools and non-tools on your workbench. Some useful household items are: a large turkey baster or siphon, empty coffee cans and ice trays (to store parts), a ball of twine, electrical tape for wiring, small rolls of colored tape for tagging lines or hoses, markers and pens, a note pad, golf tees (for plugging vacuum lines), metal coat hangers or a roll of mechanic's wire (to hold things out of the way), dental pick or similar long, pointed probe, a strong magnet, and a small mirror (to see into recesses and under manifolds).

A more advanced set of tools, suitable for tune-up work, can be drawn up easily. While the tools are slightly more sophisticated, they need not be outrageously expensive. There are several inexpensive tach/dwell meters on the market that are every bit as good for the average mechanic as a professional model. Just be sure that it goes to a least 1200–1500 rpm on the tach scale and that it works on 4, 6 and 8-cylinder engines. The key to these purchases is to make them with an eye towards adaptability and wide range. A basic list of tune-up tools could include:

- Tach/dwell meter.
- Spark plug wrench and gapping tool.
- Feeler gauges for valve adjustment.
- Timing light.

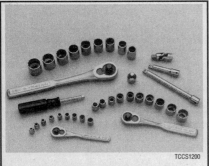

Fig. 1 All but the most basic procedures will require an assortment of ratchets and sockets

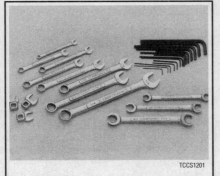

Fig. 2 In addition to ratchets, a good set of wrenches and hex keys will be necessary

Fig. 3 A hydraulic floor jack and a set of jackstands are essential for lifting and supporting the vehicle

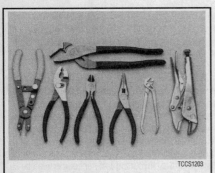

Fig. 4 An assortment of pliers, grippers and cutters will be handy for old rusted parts and stripped bolt heads

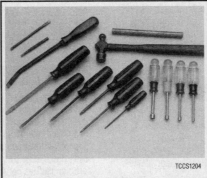

Fig. 5 Various drivers, chisels and prybars are great tools to have in your toolbox

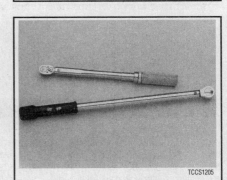

Fig. 6 Many repairs will require the use of a torque wrench to assure the components are properly fastened

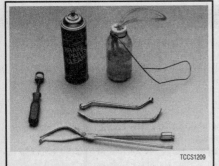

Fig. 7 Although not always necessary, using specialized brake tools will save time

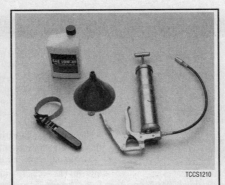

Fig. 8 A few inexpensive lubrication tools will make maintenance easier

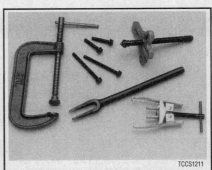

Fig. 9 Various pullers, clamps and separator tools are needed for many larger, more complicated repairs

Fig. 10 A variety of tools and gauges should be used for spark plug gapping and installation

TCCS1212

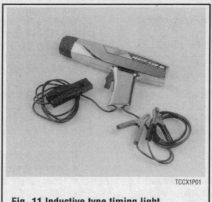

Fig. 11 Inductive type timing light

TCCX1P01

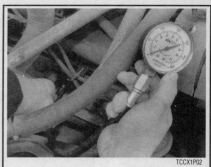

Fig. 12 A screw-in type compression gauge is recommended for compression testing

TCCX1P02

Fig. 13 A vacuum/pressure tester is necessary for many testing procedures

TCCX1P03

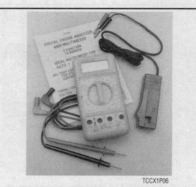

Fig. 14 Most modern automotive multimeters incorporate many helpful features

TCCX1P06

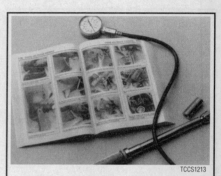

Fig. 15 Proper information is vital, so always have a Chilton Total Car Care manual handy

TCCS1213

The choice of a timing light should be made carefully. A light which works on the DC current supplied by the vehicle's battery is the best choice; it should have a xenon tube for brightness. On any vehicle with an electronic ignition system, a timing light with an inductive pickup that clamps around the No. 1 spark plug cable is preferred.

In addition to these basic tools, there are several other tools and gauges you may find useful. These include:

• Compression gauge. The screw-in type is slower to use, but eliminates the possibility of a faulty reading due to escaping pressure.

• Manifold vacuum gauge.

• 12V test light.

• A combination volt/ohmmeter

• Induction Ammeter. This is used for determining whether or not there is current in a wire. These are handy for use if a wire is broken somewhere in a wiring harness.

As a final note, you will probably find a torque wrench necessary for all but the most basic work. The beam type models are perfectly adequate, although the newer click types (breakaway) are easier to use. The click type torque wrenches tend to be more expensive. Also keep in mind that all types of torque wrenches should be periodically checked and/or recalibrated. You will have to decide for yourself which better fits your pocketbook, and purpose.

Special Tools

Normally, the use of special factory tools is avoided for repair procedures, since these are not readily available for the do-it-yourself mechanic. When it is possible to perform the job with more commonly available tools, it will be pointed out, but occasionally, a special tool was designed to perform a specific function and should be used. Before substituting another tool, you should be convinced that neither your safety nor the performance of the vehicle will be compromised.

Special tools can usually be purchased from an automotive parts store or from your dealer. In some cases special tools may be available directly from the tool manufacturer.

SERVICING YOUR VEHICLE SAFELY

▶ See Figures 16, 17 and 18

It is virtually impossible to anticipate all of the hazards involved with automotive maintenance and service, but care and common sense will prevent most accidents.

The rules of safety for mechanics range from "don't smoke around gasoline," to "use the proper tool(s) for the job." The trick to avoiding injuries is to develop safe work habits and to take every possible precaution.

Do's

• Do keep a fire extinguisher and first aid kit handy.

• Do wear safety glasses or goggles when cutting, drilling, grinding or prying, even if you have 20–20 vision. If you wear glasses for the sake of vision, wear safety goggles over your regular glasses.

• Do shield your eyes whenever you work around the battery. Batteries contain sulfuric acid. In case of contact with, flush the area with water or a mixture of water and baking soda, then seek immediate medical attention.

• Do use safety stands (jackstands) for any undervehicle service. Jacks are for raising vehicles; jackstands are for making sure the vehicle stays raised until you want it to come down.

• Do use adequate ventilation when working with any chemicals or hazardous materials. Like carbon monoxide, the asbestos dust resulting from some brake lining wear can be hazardous in sufficient quantities.

• Do disconnect the negative battery cable when working on the electrical system. The secondary ignition system contains EXTREMELY HIGH VOLTAGE. In some cases it can even exceed 50,000 volts.

• Do follow manufacturer's directions whenever working with potentially hazardous materials. Most chemicals and fluids are poisonous.

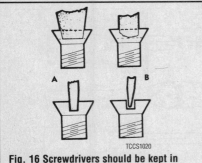

Fig. 16 Screwdrivers should be kept in good condition to prevent injury or damage which could result if the blade slips from the screw

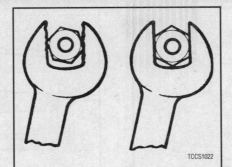

Fig. 17 Using the correct size wrench will help prevent the possibility of rounding off a nut

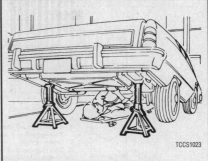

Fig. 18 NEVER work under a vehicle unless it is supported using safety stands (jackstands)

• Do properly maintain your tools. Loose hammerheads, mushroomed punches and chisels, frayed or poorly grounded electrical cords, excessively worn screwdrivers, spread wrenches (open end), cracked sockets, slipping ratchets, or faulty droplight sockets can cause accidents.

• Likewise, keep your tools clean; a greasy wrench can slip off a bolt head, ruining the bolt and often harming your knuckles in the process.

• Do use the proper size and type of tool for the job at hand. Do select a wrench or socket that fits the nut or bolt. The wrench or socket should sit straight, not cocked.

• Do, when possible, pull on a wrench handle rather than push on it, and adjust your stance to prevent a fall.

• Do be sure that adjustable wrenches are tightly closed on the nut or bolt and pulled so that the force is on the side of the fixed jaw.

• Do strike squarely with a hammer; avoid glancing blows.

• Do set the parking brake and block the drive wheels if the work requires a running engine.

Don'ts

• Don't run the engine in a garage or anywhere else without proper ventilation—EVER! Carbon monoxide is poisonous; it takes a long time to leave the human body and you can build up a deadly supply of it in your system by simply breathing in a little at a time. You may not realize you are slowly poisoning yourself. Always use power vents, windows, fans and/or open the garage door.

• Don't work around moving parts while wearing loose clothing. Short sleeves are much safer than long, loose sleeves. Hard-toed shoes with neoprene

soles protect your toes and give a better grip on slippery surfaces. Watches and jewelry is not safe working around a vehicle. Long hair should be tied back under a hat or cap.

• Don't use pockets for toolboxes. A fall or bump can drive a screwdriver deep into your body. Even a rag hanging from your back pocket can wrap around a spinning shaft or fan.

• Don't smoke when working around gasoline, cleaning solvent or other flammable material.

• Don't smoke when working around the battery. When the battery is being charged, it gives off explosive hydrogen gas.

• Don't use gasoline to wash your hands; there are excellent soaps available. Gasoline contains dangerous additives which can enter the body through a cut or through your pores. Gasoline also removes all the natural oils from the skin so that bone dry hands will suck up oil and grease.

• Don't service the air conditioning system unless you are equipped with the necessary tools and training. When liquid or compressed gas refrigerant is released to atmospheric pressure it will absorb heat from whatever it contacts. This will chill or freeze anything it touches.

• Don't use screwdrivers for anything other than driving screws! A screwdriver used as an prying tool can snap when you least expect it, causing injuries. At the very least, you'll ruin a good screwdriver.

• Don't use an emergency jack (that little ratchet, scissors, or pantograph jack supplied with the vehicle) for anything other than changing a flat! These jacks are only intended for emergency use out on the road; they are NOT designed as a maintenance tool. If you are serious about maintaining your vehicle yourself, invest in a hydraulic floor jack of at least a 1½ ton capacity, and at least two sturdy jackstands.

FASTENERS, MEASUREMENTS AND CONVERSIONS

Bolts, Nuts and Other Threaded Retainers

▶ **See Figures 19 and 20**

Although there are a great variety of fasteners found in the modern car or truck, the most commonly used retainer is the threaded fastener (nuts, bolts, screws, studs, etc.). Most threaded retainers may be reused, provided that they are not damaged in use or during the repair. Some retainers (such as stretch bolts or torque prevailing nuts) are designed to deform when tightened or in use and should not be reinstalled.

Whenever possible, we will note any special retainers which should be replaced during a procedure. But you should always inspect the condition of a retainer when it is removed and replace any that show signs of damage. Check all threads for rust or corrosion which can increase the torque necessary to achieve the desired clamp load for which that fastener was originally selected. Additionally, be sure that the driver surface of the fastener has not been compromised by rounding or other damage. In some cases a driver surface may become only partially rounded, allowing the driver to catch in only one direction. In many of these occurrences, a fastener may be installed and tightened, but the driver would not be able to grip and loosen the fastener again.

If you must replace a fastener, whether due to design or damage, you must ALWAYS be sure to use the proper replacement. In all cases, a retainer of the

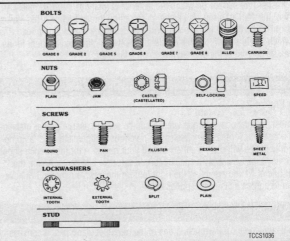

Fig. 19 There are many different types of threaded retainers found on vehicles

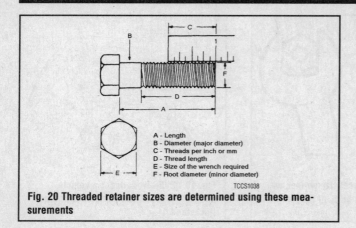

Fig. 20 Threaded retainer sizes are determined using these measurements

A - Length
B - Diameter (major diameter)
C - Threads per inch or mm
D - Thread length
E - Size of the wrench required
F - Root diameter (minor diameter)

TCCS1038

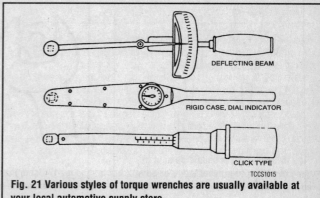

DEFLECTING BEAM

RIGID CASE, DIAL INDICATOR

CLICK TYPE

TCCS1015

Fig. 21 Various styles of torque wrenches are usually available at your local automotive supply store

same design, material and strength should be used. Markings on the heads of most bolts will help determine the proper strength of the fastener. The same material, thread and pitch must be selected to assure proper installation and safe operation of the vehicle afterwards.

Thread gauges are available to help measure a bolt or stud's thread. Most automotive and hardware stores keep gauges available to help you select the proper size. In a pinch, you can use another nut or bolt for a thread gauge. If the bolt you are replacing is not too badly damaged, you can select a match by finding another bolt which will thread in its place. If you find a nut which threads properly onto the damaged bolt, then use that nut to help select the replacement bolt.

✳✳ WARNING

Be aware that when you find a bolt with damaged threads, you may also find the nut or drilled hole it was threaded into has also been damaged. If this is the case, you may have to drill and tap the hole, replace the nut or otherwise repair the threads. NEVER try to force a replacement bolt to fit into the damaged threads.

Torque

Torque is defined as the measurement of resistance to turning or rotating. It tends to twist a body about an axis of rotation. A common example of this would be tightening a threaded retainer such as a nut, bolt or screw. Measuring torque is one of the most common ways to help assure that a threaded retainer has been properly fastened.

When tightening a threaded fastener, torque is applied in three distinct areas, the head, the bearing surface and the clamp load. About 50 percent of the measured torque is used in overcoming bearing friction. This is the friction between the bearing surface of the bolt head, screw head or nut face and the base material or washer (the surface on which the fastener is rotating). Approximately 40 percent of the applied torque is used in overcoming thread friction. This leaves only about 10 percent of the applied torque to develop a useful clamp load (the force which holds a joint together). This means that friction can account for as much as 90 percent of the applied torque on a fastener.

TORQUE WRENCHES

♦ See Figure 21

In most applications, a torque wrench can be used to assure proper installation of a fastener. Torque wrenches come in various designs and most automotive supply stores will carry a variety to suit your needs. A torque wrench should be used any time we supply a specific torque value for a fastener. Again, the general rule of "if you are using the right tool for the job, you should not have to strain to tighten a fastener" applies here.

Beam Type

The beam type torque wrench is one of the most popular types. It consists of a pointer attached to the head that runs the length of the flexible beam (shaft) to a scale located near the handle. As the wrench is pulled, the beam bends and the pointer indicates the torque using the scale.

Click (Breakaway) Type

Another popular design of torque wrench is the click type. To use the click type wrench you pre-adjust it to a torque setting. Once the torque is reached, the wrench has a reflex signaling feature that causes a momentary breakaway of the torque wrench body, sending an impulse to the operator's hand.

Pivot Head Type

♦ See Figure 22

Some torque wrenches (usually of the click type) may be equipped with a pivot head which can allow it to be used in areas of limited access. BUT, it must be used properly. To hold a pivot head wrench, grasp the handle lightly, and as you pull on the handle, it should be floated on the pivot point. If the handle comes in contact with the yoke extension during the process of pulling, there is a very good chance the torque readings will be inaccurate because this could alter the wrench loading point. The design of the handle is usually such as to make it inconvenient to deliberately misuse the wrench.

➡It should be mentioned that the use of any U-joint, wobble or extension will have an effect on the torque readings, no matter what type of wrench you are using. For the most accurate readings, install the socket directly on the wrench driver. If necessary, straight extensions (which hold a socket directly under the wrench driver) will have the least effect on the torque reading. Avoid any extension that alters the length of the wrench from the handle to the head/driving point (such as a crow's foot). U-joint or wobble extensions can greatly affect the readings; avoid their use at all times.

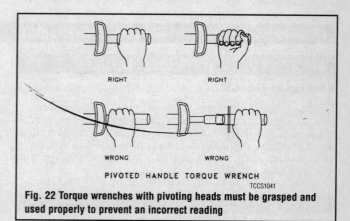

RIGHT

RIGHT

WRONG

WRONG

PIVOTED HANDLE TORQUE WRENCH

TCCS1041

Fig. 22 Torque wrenches with pivoting heads must be grasped and used properly to prevent an incorrect reading

Rigid Case (Direct Reading)

A rigid case or direct reading torque wrench is equipped with a dial indicator to show torque values. One advantage of these wrenches is that they can be held at any position on the wrench without affecting accuracy. These wrenches are often preferred because they tend to be compact, easy to read and have a great degree of accuracy.

TORQUE ANGLE METERS

Because the frictional characteristics of each fastener or threaded hole will vary, clamp loads which are based strictly on torque will vary as well. In most applications, this variance is not significant enough to cause worry. But, in certain applications, a manufacturer's engineers may determine that more precise clamp loads are necessary (such is the case with many aluminum cylinder heads). In these cases, a torque angle method of installation would be specified. When installing fasteners which are torque angle tightened, a predetermined seating torque and standard torque wrench are usually used first to remove any compliance from the joint. The fastener is then tightened the specified additional portion of a turn measured in degrees. A torque angle gauge (mechanical protractor) is used for these applications.

Standard and Metric Measurements

▶ See Figure 23

Throughout this manual, specifications are given to help you determine the condition of various components on your vehicle, or to assist you in their installation. Some of the most common measurements include length (in. or cm/mm), torque (ft. lbs., inch lbs. or Nm) and pressure (psi, in. Hg, kPa or mm Hg). In most cases, we strive to provide the proper measurement as determined by the manufacturer's engineers.

Though, in some cases, that value may not be conveniently measured with what is available in your toolbox. Luckily, many of the measuring devices which are available today will have two scales so the Standard or Metric measurements may easily be taken. If any of the various measuring tools which are available to you do not contain the same scale as listed in the specifications, use the accompanying conversion factors to determine the proper value.

The conversion factor chart is used by taking the given specification and multiplying it by the necessary conversion factor. For instance, looking at the first line, if you have a measurement in inches such as "free-play should be 2 in." but your ruler reads only in millimeters, multiply 2 in. by the conversion factor of 25.4 to get the metric equivalent of 50.8mm. Likewise, if the specification was given only in a Metric measurement, for example in Newton Meters (Nm), then look at the center column first. If the measurement is 100 Nm, multiply it by the conversion factor of 0.738 to get 73.8 ft. lbs.

CONVERSION FACTORS

LENGTH–DISTANCE				
Inches (in.)	x 25.4	= Millimeters (mm)	x .0394	= Inches
Feet (ft.)	x .305	= Meters (m)	x 3.281	= Feet
Miles	x 1.609	= Kilometers (km)	x .0621	= Miles
VOLUME				
Cubic Inches (in3)	x 16.387	= Cubic Centimeters	x .061	= in3
IMP Pints (IMP pt.)	x .568	= Liters (L)	x 1.76	= IMP pt.
IMP Quarts (IMP qt.)	x 1.137	= Liters (L)	x .88	= IMP qt.
IMP Gallons (IMP gal.)	x 4.546	= Liters (L)	x .22	= IMP gal.
IMP Quarts (IMP qt.)	x 1.201	= US Quarts (US qt.)	x .833	= IMP qt.
IMP Gallons (IMP gal.)	x 1.201	= US Gallons (US gal.)	x .833	= IMP gal.
Fl. Ounces	x 29.573	= Milliliters	x .034	= Ounces
US Pints (US pt.)	x .473	= Liters (L)	x 2.113	= Pints
US Quarts (US qt.)	x .946	= Liters (L)	x 1.057	= Quarts
US Gallons (US gal.)	x 3.785	= Liters (L)	x .264	= Gallons
MASS–WEIGHT				
Ounces (oz.)	x 28.35	= Grams (g)	x .035	= Ounces
Pounds (lb.)	x .454	= Kilograms (kg)	x 2.205	= Pounds
PRESSURE				
Pounds Per Sq. In. (psi)	x 6.895	= Kilopascals (kPa)	x .145	= psi
Inches of Mercury (Hg)	x .4912	= psi	x 2.036	= Hg
Inches of Mercury (Hg)	x 3.377	= Kilopascals (kPa)	x .2961	= Hg
Inches of Water (H₂O)	x .07355	= Inches of Mercury	x 13.783	= H₂O
Inches of Water (H₂O)	x .03613	= psi	x 27.684	= H₂O
Inches of Water (H₂O)	x .248	= Kilopascals (kPa)	x 4.026	= H₂O
TORQUE				
Pounds–Force Inches (in–lb)	x .113	= Newton Meters (N·m)	x 8.85	= in–lb
Pounds–Force Feet (ft–lb)	x 1.356	= Newton Meters (N·m)	x .738	= ft–lb
VELOCITY				
Miles Per Hour (MPH)	x 1.609	= Kilometers Per Hour (KPH)	x .621	= MPH
POWER				
Horsepower (Hp)	x .745	= Kilowatts	x 1.34	= Horsepower
FUEL CONSUMPTION*				
Miles Per Gallon IMP (MPG)	x .354	= Kilometers Per Liter (Km/L)		
Kilometers Per Liter (Km/L)	x 2.352	= IMP MPG		
Miles Per Gallon US (MPG)	x .425	= Kilometers Per Liter (Km/L)		
Kilometers Per Liter (Km/L)	x 2.352	= US MPG		

*It is common to covert from miles per gallon (mpg) to liters/100 kilometers (1/100 km), where mpg (IMP) x 1/100 km = 282 and mpg (US) x 1/100 km = 235.

TEMPERATURE	
Degree Fahrenheit (°F)	= (°C x 1.8) + 32
Degree Celsius (°C)	= (°F – 32) .56

TCCS1044

Fig. 23 Standard and metric conversion factors chart

SERIAL NUMBER IDENTIFICATION

Vehicle

▶ See Figure 24

The serial number contains seventeen or more digits or letters. The first three give the world manufacturer code. The fourth is the type of restraint system. The fifth will remain the letter P. The sixth and seventh are the car line, series and body type. The eighth is the engine type. The ninth is a check digit. The tenth is the model year. The eleventh is the assembly plant. The last 6 digits of the vehicle identification number indicates the consecutive unit number of each unit built at each assembly plant. The consecutive unit numbers begin as follows: 100 001 through 600 000: Ford division vehicles, 600 001 through 999 999: Lincoln/Mercury division vehicles.

There are two locations of the vehicle identification number. One is on the driver's door jam. This label also has many other codes; so be sure to specifically find the word VIN on the tag. The other location of the identification number is on the lower left driver's side dash. As you look through the windshield, there is a long thin tag with the VIN number stamped on it.

Vehicle Certification Label

▶ See Figures 25 and 26

This label is affixed on the left hand front door lock panel or door pillar. The upper half of the label contains the name of the manufacturer, month and year of the manufacture, Gross Vehicle Weight Rating (GVWR), Gross Axle Weight Rating (GAWR) and certification statement.

The vehicle certification label also contains a 17 character vehicle identification number. This number is used for warranty identification of the vehicle and

88181P01

Fig. 24 This 17 digit VIN is visible through the driver's side windshield

indicates: manufacturer, type of restraint system, line, series, body type, engine, model year and consecutive unit number.

The remaining information on this label consists of the following vehicle identification codes: color and body type, vinyl roof, molding and interior trim. Additional codes indicate vehicle equipped with air conditioning, radio type, sun roof type (if so equipped), as well as axle, transmission, spring, district sales office and special order codes.

VEHICLE IDENTIFICATION CHART

Model Year	VIN Code	Liters	Engine Code		Cu. In. (cc)	Cyl.	Fuel Sys.	Eng. Mfg.
1983	D	2.3	W	①	140 (2300)	4	MFI	Ford
		3.8	3		232 (3802)	6	BBL	Ford
		5.0	F		302 (4949)	8	BBL	Ford
1984	E	2.3	W	①	140 (2300)	4	MFI	Ford
		3.8	3		232 (3802)	6	BBL	Ford
		3.8	3		232 (3802)	6	CFI	Ford
		5.0	F		302 (4949)	8	BBL	Ford
		5.0	F		302 (4949)	8	CFI	Ford
1985	F	2.3	W	①	140 (2300)	4	MFI	Ford
		3.8	3		232 (3802)	6	BBL	Ford
		3.8	3		232 (3802)	6	CFI	Ford
		5.0	F		302 (4949)	8	CFI	Ford
1986	G	2.3	W	①	140 (2300)	4	MFI	Ford
		3.8	3		232 (3802)	6	BBL	Ford
		3.8	3		232 (3802)	6	CFI	Ford
		5.0	F		302 (4949)	8	CFI	Ford
1987	H	2.3	W	①	140 (2300)	4	MFI	Ford
		3.8	3		232 (3802)	6	CFI	Ford
		5.0	F		302 (4949)	8	CFI	Ford
1988	I	2.3	W	①	140 (2300)	4	MFI	Ford
		3.8	4		232 (3802)	6	CFI	Ford
		5.0	F		302 (4949)	8	MFI	Ford
1989	J	3.8	C		232 (3802)	6	MFI	Ford
		3.8	R	②	232 (3802)	6	MFI	Ford
		3.8	4		232 (3802)	6	SFI	Ford
1990	K	3.8	4		232 (3802)	6	SFI	Ford
		3.8	R	②	232 (3802)	6	MFI	Ford
1991	L	3.8	4		232 (3802)	6	SFI	Ford
		3.8	R	②	232 (3802)	6	MFI	Ford
		5.0	T		302 (4949)	8	MFI	Ford
1992	N	3.8	4		232 (3802)	6	SFI	Ford
		3.8	R	②	232 (3802)	6	SFI	Ford
		3.8	C	②	232 (3802)	6	SFI	Ford
		5.0	T		302 (4949)	8	MFI	Ford
1993	P	3.8	4		232 (3802)	6	SFI	Ford
		3.8	R	②	232 (3802)	6	SFI	Ford
		5.0	T		302 (4949)	8	MFI	Ford
1994	R	3.8	4		232 (3802)	6	SFI	Ford
		3.8	R	②	232 (3802)	6	SFI	Ford
		4.6	W	③	281 (4593)	8	SFI	Ford
1995	S	3.8	4		232 (3802)	6	SFI	Ford
		3.8	R	②	232 (3802)	6	SFI	Ford
		4.6	W	③	281 (4593)	8	SFI	Ford
1996	T	3.8	4		232 (3802)	6	SFI	Ford
		4.6	W	③	281 (4593)	8	SFI	Ford
1997	V	3.8	4		232 (3802)	6	SFI	Ford
		4.6	W	③	281 (4593)	8	SFI	Ford

BBL - Carburetor
CFI - Central fuel injection
MFI - Multipoint fuel injection
SFI - Sequential fuel injection
① Turbo
② Supercharged
③ (2V) 2 Valve

91331C03

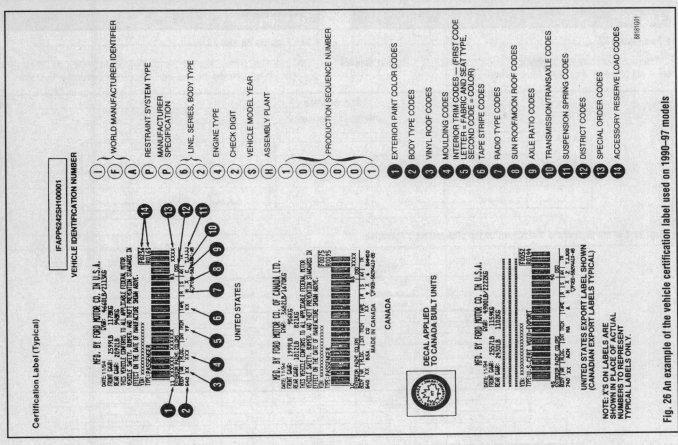

Fig. 26 An example of the vehicle certification label used on 1990-97 models

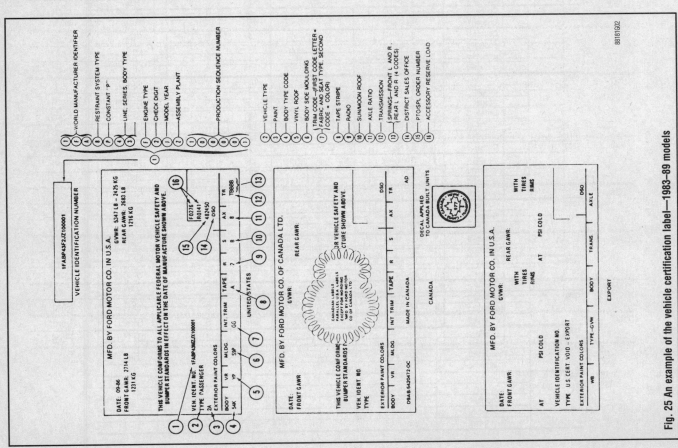

Fig. 25 An example of the vehicle certification label—1983-89 models

Engine

▶ **See Figure 27**

The engine identification number is located in the vehicle identification number. It will be the 8th digit of the serial number.

Transmission

▶ **See Figures 28 and 29**

The transmission identification tag is usually attached by the lower left extension attaching bolt or under the lower front intermediate servo cover bolt. The

VIN POSITION 8

1FAPP62 4 2SH100001

VIN Code	Displacement		Cylinders	Fuel	Manufacturer
	Liter	CID			
4	3.8 SFI	232	V-6	Gasoline	Ford
R	3.8 SFI SC	232	V-6	Gasoline	Ford
W	4.6 SFI (2V)	281	V-8	Gasoline	Ford

88181G05

Fig. 27 The 8th digit of the VIN identifies the size and type of engine

ENGINE IDENTIFICATION

Year	Model		Engine Displacement Liters (cc)	Engine Series (ID/VIN)	Fuel System	No. of Cylinders	Engine Type
1983	Cougar	①	2.3 (2300)	W	MFI	4	SOHC
	Cougar		3.8 (3802)	3	2BBL	6	OHV
	Cougar		5.0 (4949)	F	CFI	8	OHV
	Thunderbird	①	2.3 (2300)	W	MFI	4	SOHC
	Thunderbird		3.8 (3802)	3	2BBL	6	OHV
	Thunderbird		5.0 (4949)	F	CFI	8	OHV
1984	Cougar	①	2.3 (2300)	W	MFI	4	SOHC
	Cougar		3.8 (3802)	3	CFI	6	OHV
	Cougar		5.0 (4949)	F	CFI	8	OHV
	Thunderbird	①	2.3 (2300)	W	MFI	4	SOHC
	Thunderbird		3.8 (3802)	3	CFI	6	OHV
	Thunderbird		5.0 (4949)	F	CFI	8	OHV
1985	Cougar	①	2.3 (2300)	W	MFI	4	SOHC
	Cougar		3.8 (3802)	3	CFI	6	OHV
	Cougar		5.0 (4949)	F	CFI	8	OHV
	Thunderbird	①	2.3 (2300)	W	MFI	4	SOHC
	Thunderbird		3.8 (3802)	3	CFI	6	OHV
	Thunderbird		5.0 (4949)	F	CFI	8	OHV
1986	Cougar	①	2.3 (2300)	W	MFI	4	SOHC
	Cougar		3.8 (3802)	3	CFI	6	OHV
	Cougar		5.0 (4949)	F	CFI	8	OHV
	Thunderbird	①	2.3 (2300)	W	MFI	4	SOHC
	Thunderbird		3.8 (3802)	3	CFI	6	OHV
	Thunderbird		5.0 (4949)	F	CFI	8	OHV
1987	Cougar		3.8 (3802)	3	CFI	6	OHV
	Cougar		5.0 (4949)	F	CFI	8	OHV
	Thunderbird	①	2.3 (2300)	W	MFI	4	SOHC
	Thunderbird		3.8 (3802)	3	CFI	6	OHV
	Thunderbird		5.0 (4949)	F	CFI	8	OHV
1988	Cougar		3.8 (3802)	4	SFI	6	OHV
	Cougar		5.0 (4949)	F	MFI	8	OHV
	Thunderbird	①	2.3 (2300)	W	MFI	4	SOHC
	Thunderbird		3.8 (3802)	4	SFI	6	OHV
	Thunderbird		5.0 (4949)	F	MFI	8	OHV
1989	Cougar		3.8 (3802)	4	SFI	6	OHV
	Cougar	②	3.8 (3802)	C	MFI	6	OHV
	Cougar	②	3.8 (3802)	R	MFI	6	OHV
1989	Thunderbird		3.8 (3802)	4	SFI	6	OHV
	Thunderbird	②	3.8 (3802)	C	MFI	6	OHV
	Thunderbird	②	3.8 (3802)	R	MFI	6	OHV
1990	Cougar		3.8 (3802)	4	SFI	6	OHV
	Cougar XR7		3.8 (3802)	R	MFI	6	OHV
	Thunderbird		3.8 (3802)	4	SFI	6	OHV
	Thunderbird	②	3.8 (3802)	R	MFI	6	OHV
1991	Cougar		3.8 (3802)	4	SFI	6	OHV
	Cougar		5.0 (4943)	T	MFI	8	OHV
	Thunderbird		3.8 (3802)	4	SFI	6	OHV
	Thunderbird	②	3.8 (3802)	R	MFI	6	OHV
	Thunderbird		5.0 (4943)	T	MFI	8	OHV

91331C01

GENERAL ENGINE SPECIFICATIONS

Year	Engine ID/VIN	Engine Displacement Liters (cc)	Fuel System Type	Net Horsepower @ rpm	Net Torque @ rpm (ft. lbs.)	Net Bore x Stroke (in.)	Compression Ratio	Oil Pressure @ rpm
1983	W	2.3 (2300)	MFI-Turbo	145@4600	180@3600	3.78x3.13	8.0:1	40-60@2000
	3	3.8 (3802)	2 BBL	120@3400	250@1600	3.81x3.39	8.7:1	40-60@2000
	F	5.0 (4949)	2 BBL	132@3400	236@1800	4.00x3.00	8.4:1	40-60@2000
	F	5.0 (4949)	CFI	165@3200	250@1600	4.00x3.00	8.4:1	40-60@2000
1984	W	2.3 (2300)	MFI-Turbo	145@4600	180@3600	3.78x3.13	8.0:1	40-60@2000
	3	3.8 (3802)	2 BBL	120@3600	250@1600	3.81x3.39	8.7:1	40-60@2000
	F	5.0 (4949)	2 BBL	132@3400	236@1800	4.00x3.00	8.4:1	40-60@2000
	F	5.0 (4949)	CFI	165@3200	250@1600	4.00x3.00	8.4:1	40-60@2000
1985	W	2.3 (2300)	MFI-Turbo	145@4600	180@3600	3.78x3.13	8.0:1	40-60@2000
	3	3.8 (3802)	2 BBL	120@3600	250@1600	3.81x3.39	8.7:1	40-60@2000
	F	5.0 (4949)	2 BBL	132@3400	236@1800	4.00x3.00	8.4:1	40-60@2000
	F	5.0 (4949)	CFI	165@3200	250@1600	4.00x3.00	8.4:1	40-60@2000
1986	W	2.3 (2300)	MFI-Turbo	145@4600	180@3600	3.78x3.13	8.0:1	40-60@2000
	3	3.8 (3802)	2 BBL	120@3600	250@1600	3.81x3.39	8.7:1	40-60@2000
	3	3.8 (3802)	MFI	120@3600	250@1600	3.81x3.39	8.7:1	40-60@2000
	F	5.0 (4949)	2 BBL	150@3200	270@2000	4.00x3.00	8.9:1	40-60@2000
1987	W	2.3 (2300)	MFI-Turbo	145@4600	180@3600	3.78x3.13	8.0:1	40-60@2000
	3	3.8 (3802)	MFI	120@3600	250@1600	3.81x3.39	8.7:1	40-60@2000
	F	5.0 (4949)	MFI	165@3200	250@1600	4.00x3.00	8.4:1	40-60@2000
1988	W	2.3 (2300)	MFI-Turbo	145@4600	180@3600	3.78x3.13	8.0:1	40-60@2000
	4	3.8 (3802)	MFI	120@3600	205@1600	3.81x3.39	8.7:1	40-60@2000
	F	5.0 (4949)	MFI	165@3200	250@1600	4.00x3.00	8.4:1	40-60@2000
1989	4	3.8 (3802)	MFI	140@3800	215@2400	3.81x3.39	8.2:1	40-60@2000
	R ①	3.8 (3802)	MFI	210@2000	315@2600	3.81x3.39	8.2:1	40-60@2000
	C ①	3.8 (3802)	MFI	210@2000	315@2600	3.81x3.39	8.2:1	40-60@2000
1990	4	3.8 (3802)	MFI	120@3600	205@1600	3.81x3.39	8.7:1	40-60@2000
	R ①	3.8 (3802)	MFI	210@2000	315@2600	3.81x3.39	8.2:1	40-60@2000
1991	4	3.8 (3802)	MFI	140@3800	215@2400	3.81x3.39	8.2:1	40-60@2000
	R ①	3.8 (3802)	MFI	210@2000	315@3000	3.81x3.39	8.2:1	40-60@2000
1992	4	3.8 (3802)	MFI	140@3800	215@2400	3.81x3.39	8.2:1	40-60@2000
	R ①	3.8 (3802)	MFI	210@2000	315@2600	3.81x3.39	8.2:1	40-60@2000
	T	5.0 (4949)	MFI	200@4000	275@3000	4.00x3.00	9.0:1	40-60@2000
1993	4	3.8 (3802)	MFI	140@3800	215@2400	3.81x3.39	8.2:1	40-60@2000
	R ①	3.8 (3802)	MFI	210@2000	315@2600	3.81x3.39	8.2:1	40-60@2000
	T	5.0 (4949)	MFI	200@4000	275@3000	4.00x3.00	9.0:1	40-60@2000
1994	4	3.8 (3802)	SFI	140@3800	215@2400	3.81x3.39	8.2:1	40-60@2500
	W	4.6 (4593)	SFI	210@2000 ②	315@2600	3.55x3.54	9.0:1	40-60@2500
1995	4	3.8 (3802)	SFI	140@3800	215@2400	3.81x3.39	8.2:1	40-60@2500
	R ①	3.8 (3802)	SFI	210@2000	315@3000	4.00x3.39	9.0:1	20-45@2000
1996	4	3.8 (3802)	SFI	145@4000	215@2750	3.81x3.39	9.0:1	40-60@2500
	W	4.6 (4593)	SFI	205@4250	280@3000	3.55x3.54	9.0:1	20-45@1500
1997	4	3.8 (3802)	SFI	145@4000	215@2750	3.81x3.39	9.0:1	40-60@2500
	W	4.6 (4593)	SFI	205@4250	280@3000	3.55x3.54	9.0:1	20-45@1500

BBL - Barrel carburetor
MFI - Multiport fuel injection
CFI - Central fuel injection
SFI - Sequential fuel injection

① Supercharged
② Single exhaust: 190@4250 Dual exhaust: 210@4600
③ Single exhaust: 260@3200 Dual exhaust: 270@3400

91331C07

ENGINE IDENTIFICATION

Year	Model	Engine Displacement Liters (cc)	Engine Series (ID/VIN)	Fuel System	No. of Cylinders	Engine Type
1992	Cougar	3.8 (3802)	4	SFI	6	OHV
	Cougar	5.0 (4943)	T	MFI	8	OHV
	Thunderbird	3.8 (3802)	4	SFI	6	OHV
	Thunderbird ②	3.8 (3802)	C	SFI	6	OHV
	Thunderbird ②	5.0 (4943)	R	MFI	8	OHV
1993	Cougar	3.8 (3802)	4	SFI	6	OHV
	Cougar	5.0 (4943)	T	MFI	8	OHV
	Thunderbird	3.8 (3802)	4	SFI	6	OHV
	Thunderbird ②	3.8 (3802)	R	SFI	6	OHV
	Thunderbird	5.0 (4949)	T	MFI	8	OHV
1994	Cougar	3.8 (4593)	4	SFI	6	SOHC
	Cougar	4.6 (4593)	W	SFI	8	SOHC
	Thunderbird	3.8 (3802)	4	SFI	6	OHV
	Thunderbird ②	3.8 (3802)	R	SFI	6	OHV
	Thunderbird	4.6 (4593)	W	SFI	8	SOHC
1995	Cougar	3.8 (3802)	4	SFI	6	OHV
	Cougar	4.5 (4593)	W	SFI	8	SOHC
	Thunderbird	3.8 (3802)	4.	SFI	6	OHV
	Thunderbird ②	3.8 (3802)	R	SFI	6	OHV
	Thunderbird	4.6 (4593)	W	SFI	8	SOHC
1996	Cougar	3.8 (2802)	4	SFI	6	OHV
	Cougar	4.6 (4593)	W	SFI	8	SOHC
	Thunderbird	3.8 (3802)	4	SFI	6	OHV
	Thunderbird	4.6 (4593)	W	SFI	8	SOHC
1997	Cougar	3.8 (2802)	4	SFI	6	OHV
	Cougar	4.6 (4593)	W	SFI	8	SOHC
	Thunderbird	3.8 (3802)	4	SFI	6	OHV
	Thunderbird	4.6 (4593)	W	SFI	8	SOHC

Note: There are early models in 1992 with the Vin code of C

BBL - Barrel carburetor
MFI - Multiport fuel injection
SFI - Sequential fuel injection
CFI - Central fuel injection
SOHC - Single overhead camshaft
OHV - Overhead valve
① Turbo
② Supercharged

91331C02

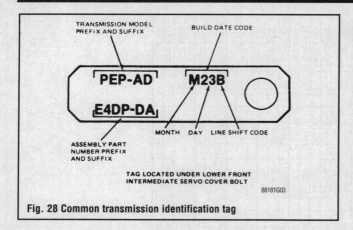

Fig. 28 Common transmission identification tag

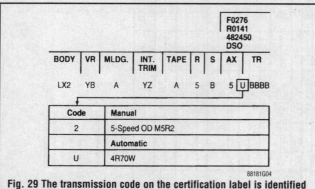

Fig. 29 The transmission code on the certification label is identified by the digits located under the TR of the label

transmission identification code number is found on the bottom of the vehicle certification label. The transmission tag shows the model prefix and suffix, assembly part numbers, and build date code. The first line on the tag shows the transmission model prefix and suffix. A number appearing after the suffix indicates that internal parts have been changed after the initial production start up. For example, a PEE-FL model transmission that has been changed internally would read PEE-FL1. Both transmissions are basically the same, but some service parts in the PEE-FL1 transmission are slightly different than the PEE-FL transmission. Therefore, it is important that the codes on the transmission identification tag be checked when ordering parts or making inquires about the transmission.

ROUTINE MAINTENANCE AND TUNE-UP

Proper maintenance and tune-up is the key to long and trouble-free vehicle life, and the work can yield its own rewards. Studies have shown that a properly tuned and maintained vehicle can achieve better gas mileage than an out-of-tune vehicle. As a conscientious owner and driver, set aside a Saturday morning, say once a month, to check or replace items which could cause major problems later. Keep your own personal log to jot down which services you performed, how much the parts cost you, the date, and the exact odometer reading at the time. Keep all receipts for such items as engine oil and filters, so that they may be referred to in case of related problems or to determine operating expenses. As a do-it-yourselfer, these receipts are the only proof you have that the required maintenance was performed. In the event of a warranty problem, these receipts will be invaluable.

The literature provided with your vehicle when it was originally delivered includes the factory recommended maintenance schedule. If you no longer have this literature, replacement copies are usually available from the dealer. A maintenance schedule is provided later in this section, in case you do not have the factory literature.

Drive Axle

▶ See Figures 30 and 31

The plant code on the axle identification tag is the official identifier. It is located under the cover-to-carrier bolt in the 12 o'clock position. The code for a particular axle assembly will not change as long as it never undergoes an external design change. If there is an internal change through the life of the axle, a suffix number will be added to the plant code.

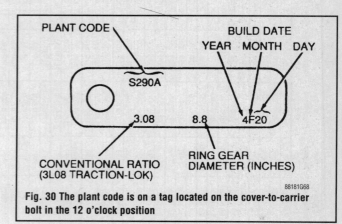

Fig. 30 The plant code is on a tag located on the cover-to-carrier bolt in the 12 o'clock position

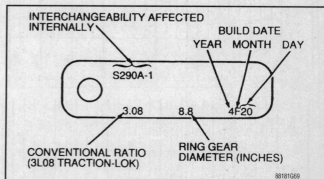

Fig. 31 A suffix is noted on the end of the plant code when an internal change is made to the axle

Air Cleaner Element

All engines are equipped with a dry type, replaceable air filter element. The element should be replaced at the recommended intervals shown on the Maintenance Chart in this section. If your vehicle is operated under severely dusty conditions or severe operating conditions, more frequent changes are necessary. Inspect the element at least twice a year. Early spring and at the beginning of fall are good times for the inspection.

REMOVAL & INSTALLATION

Carbureted Engines

▶ See Figure 32

1. Disconnect all hoses, ducts and vacuum tubes from the air cleaner assembly.

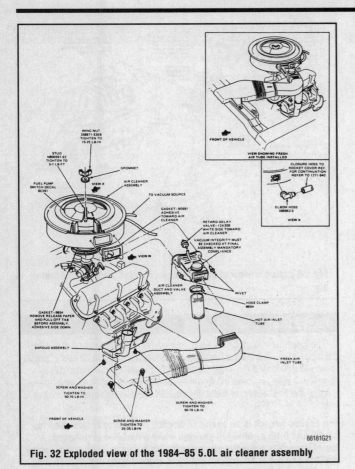

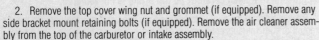

Fig. 32 Exploded view of the 1984–85 5.0L air cleaner assembly

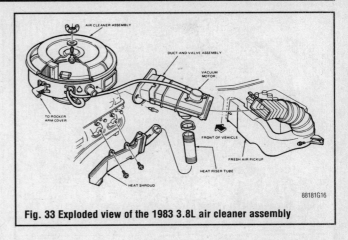

Fig. 33 Exploded view of the 1983 3.8L air cleaner assembly

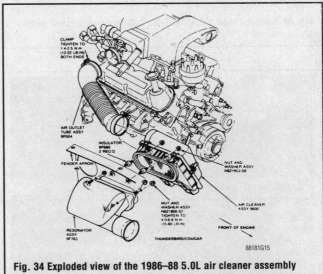

Fig. 34 Exploded view of the 1986–88 5.0L air cleaner assembly

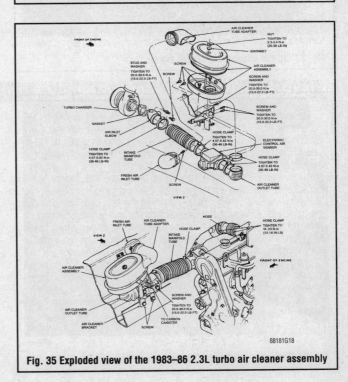

Fig. 35 Exploded view of the 1983–86 2.3L turbo air cleaner assembly

2. Remove the top cover wing nut and grommet (if equipped). Remove any side bracket mount retaining bolts (if equipped). Remove the air cleaner assembly from the top of the carburetor or intake assembly.

3. Remove the cover and the element, wipe clean all inside surfaces of the air cleaner housing and cover. Check the condition of the mounting gasket (cleaner base-to-carburetor). Replace the mounting gasket if it is worn or broken.

4. Check for holes in the filter. Check the cleaner housing for signs of dirt or dust that has leaked through the filter element. Place a light on the inside of the element and look through the filter at the light. If no glow of light can be seen through the element material, replace the filter. If holes in the filter are apparent or signs of dirt leakage through the filter are noticed, replace the filter.

To install:

5. Reposition the cleaner assembly, element and cover on the carburetor or intake assembly.

6. Reconnect all hoses, duct and vacuum hoses removed. Install the wing nut finger-tight.

Fuel Injected Engines

▶ **See Figures 33 thru 39**

1. Disconnect all hoses, ducts vacuum tubes and wiring from the air cleaner assembly.

2. On the early models, remove the top cover wing nut and grommet (if equipped), remove the cover.

3. On the later models, release the 2 hold-down clips from the cover and position the air cleaner lid aside.

4. Remove the air cleaner element, wipe clean all inside surfaces of the air cleaner housing and cover. Check the condition of the mounting gasket (if so equipped). Replace the mounting gasket if it is worn or broken.

To install:

5. Reposition the air cleaner assembly, element and cover.

6. Reconnect all hoses, duct, vacuum hoses and wiring that was removed. Install the wing nut finger-tight, if so equipped.

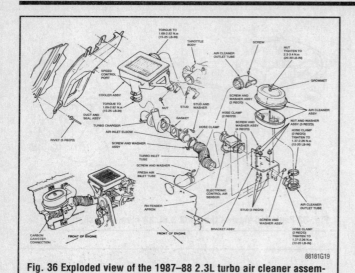

Fig. 36 Exploded view of the 1987–88 2.3L turbo air cleaner assembly

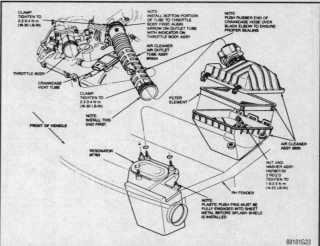

Fig. 39 Exploded view of the 3.8L supercharged air cleaner assembly

Fig. 37 Lift the clips up to release the lid

Fig. 38 Remove the lid and lift out the element

Fuel Filter

The fuel filter should be replaced, immediately, upon evidence of dirt in the fuel system. Regular replacement of the fuel filter should be every 30,000 miles (48,270 km). If the engine seems to be suffering from fuel starvation, remove the filter and blow through it to see if it is clogged. If air won't pass through the filter easily, or if dirt is visible in the inlet passage, replace the filter.

➡ **A backup wrench is an open end wrench of the proper size used to hold a fuel filter or fitting in position while a fuel line is removed. A flared wrench is a special hex wrench with a narrow open end allowing the fuel line nut to be gripped tightly. A regular open end wrench may be substituted if used carefully so the fitting is not rounded.**

The fuel filter on the carbureted models contains a screen to minimize the amount of contaminants entering the carburetor via the fuel system. The fuel filter is located in the carburetor.

The EFI model fuel filter provides extremely fine filtration to protect the small metering orifices of the injector nozzles. The filter is a one-piece construction which cannot be cleaned. If the filter becomes clogged or restricted, it should be replaced with a new filter.

An injector filter is located at the top of each injector and is not serviceable. If the injector screen becomes clogged, the complete injector assembly must be serviced.

REMOVAL & INSTALLATION

✱✱✱ CAUTION

Never smoke when working around gasoline! Avoid all sources of sparks or ignition. Gasoline vapors are EXTREMELY volatile!

Carbureted Engines

▶ **See Figure 40**

The screw in type filter is located on the carburetor.
1. Remove the air cleaner assembly.
2. Remove the hose clamps and rubber connector hose.
3. Place some absorbent rags under the inlet fitting. Unscrew the filter from the carburetor.
4. Discard the filter and clamps.
To install:
5. Coat the threads of the new filter with non-hardening, gasoline-proof sealer and screw it into place by hand. Tighten it snugly with the wrench.
6. Install new fuel line and clamps.
7. Start the engine and check for leaks.

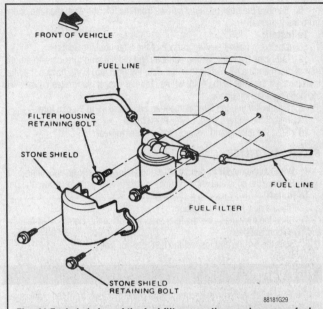

FUEL FILTER

SPRING CLAMP
380882 (2 REQ'D.)

STEEL
SUPPLY
LINE

APPLY ONE DROP
OF LOCTITE
HYDRAULIC
SEALANT NO. 069
(OR EQUIVALENT)
TO THREADS.

2.50-0.00 mm
(0.10-0.00 In.)

2.5-1.5 mm
(.10-.06 IN)

7.1-1.5 mm
(.28-.06 In.)

RUBBER
FUEL
HOSE

88181G28

Fig. 40 Proper installation of the screw-in type with hose connections

Fuel Injected Engines

♦ See Figures 41 thru 47

The filter used in these models is an in-line replaceable cartridge type. The filter has the capability of 50,000 miles (80,450 km) of maintenance free operation. Its function is to provide filtration to protect the small metering orifices of the injector nozzles. The filter is located downstream of the pump and is mounted on the chassis frame near the right rear wheel well. The filter and filter housing is protected by a metal stone shield.

Some models may use a secondary filter. It is a small serviceable in-line cylindrical unit located in the fuel supply line in the lower engine compartment area. There is approximately 14.5 inches (37 cm) of high pressure flexible line permanently attached to the filter. The line and filter are serviced as an assembly. This filter protects the injector nozzles from contaminates purged through the system during initial assembly or service operations. The secondary filter however, should never need replacement.

FRONT OF VEHICLE

FUEL LINE

FILTER HOUSING
RETAINING BOLT

STONE SHIELD

FUEL LINE

FUEL FILTER

STONE SHIELD
RETAINING BOLT

88181G29

Fig. 41 Exploded view of the fuel filter mounting used on some fuel injected models

88181P05

Fig. 42 Remove the clamp surrounding the stone shield

88181P06

Fig. 43 Unbolt the shield from the vehicle . . .

88181P07

Fig. 44 . . . then lower and remove it

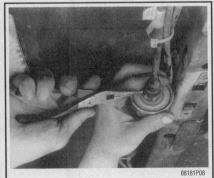

88181P08

Fig. 45 Remove the clamps retaining the lines to the filter

88181P09

Fig. 46 Slide the lines off the filter, watch for spillage

88181P10

Fig. 47 Use new clips when reinstalling the filter

PRIMARY FILTER

1. Raise and support the rear end on jackstands.
2. With the engine **OFF**, depressurize the fuel system. Refer to Section 5.
3. Remove the stone shield from in front of the filter.
4. On models with flare fittings, unscrew them at both ends of the filter.
5. Remove the filter retaining screws from the filter bracket, then the filter from the frame rail.

To install:

6. Clean the gasket sealing surface of the filter housing adapter.
7. Lubricate the filter sealing surfaces and the housing threads with a light film of clean engine oil. Screw the filter onto the housing. Hand tighten the filter, then back off the filter to the point where the filter gasket just makes contact with the housing sealing surface.
8. Finally, tighten the filter element an additional ⅝ to ¾ of a turn.
9. Install the stone shield. Lower the vehicle.
10. Start the engine and inspect the fuel filter for leaks.

SECONDARY FILTER

1. With the engine **OFF**, depressurize the fuel system. Refer to Section 5.
2. Remove the clips and slide the lines off of the filter ends to remove the unit.

To install:

3. Place a new filter into position.
4. Slide the fuel lines over the filter ends and place the clamps over the end/hose connections.
5. Start the engine and inspect the fuel filter for leaks.

PCV Valve

The PCV valve system vents combustion blow-by gases from the crankcase into the engine air intake where they are burned with the fuel and air mixture. The PCV valve system helps to keep the engine oil clean by ridding the crankcase of moisture and corrosive fumes. The PCV valve system consists of the PCV valve, its mounting grommet, the nipple in the air intake and the connecting hoses. On some engine applications, the PCV valve system is connected with the evaporative emission system.

The PCV valve controls the amount of vapors pulled into the intake manifold from the crankcase. It also acts as a check valve by preventing the flow of air from entering the crankcase in the opposite direction. The PCV valve limits the fresh air intake to suit the engine demand; it also serves to prevent combustion backfiring into the crankcase as well as protecting against crankcase explosions.

REMOVAL & INSTALLATION

PCV Valve

▶ **See Figures 48, 49 and 50**

1. On some models it may be necessary to remove the air cleaner outlet tube.
2. Disconnect the vacuum hose from the PCV valve.
3. Remove the PCV valve from its mounting grommet.

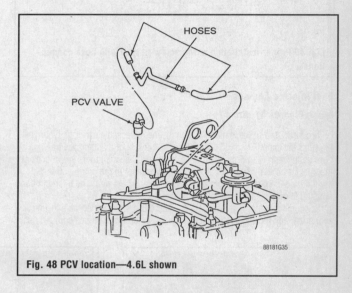

Fig. 48 PCV location—4.6L shown

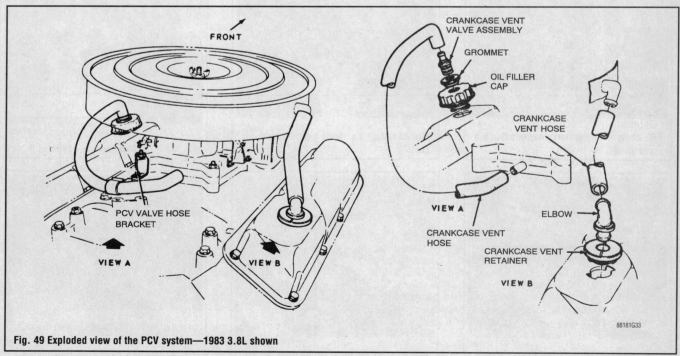

Fig. 49 Exploded view of the PCV system—1983 3.8L shown

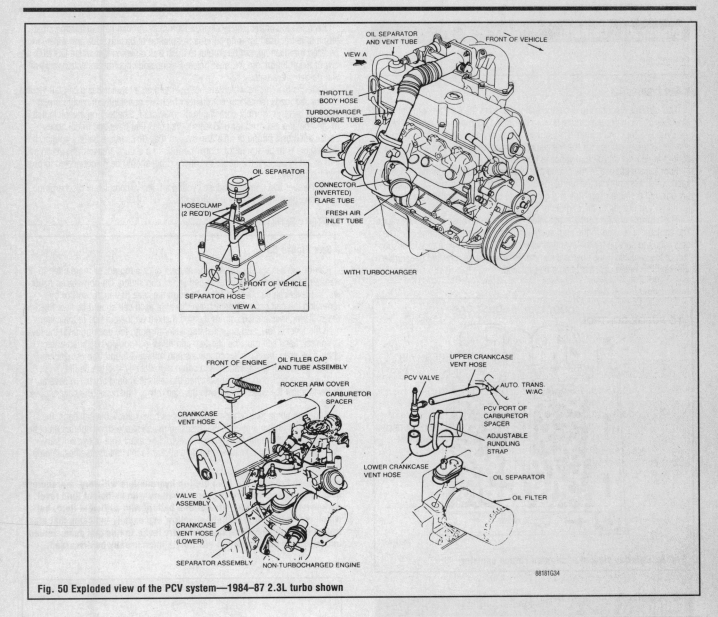

Fig. 50 Exploded view of the PCV system—1984–87 2.3L turbo shown

To install:

4. Inspect the mounting grommet and PCV hose, replace if necessary.

5. Place a small amount of clean engine oil onto the valve end portion to be inserted into the grommet. Then insert.

6. Place the PCV hose on the exposed valve end.

7. If removed, install the air cleaner outlet tube.

Crankcase Ventilation Filter

▶ See Figure 51

Replace or inspect cleaner mounted crankcase ventilation filter (on models equipped) at the same time the air cleaner filter element is serviced. To replace the filter, simply remove the air cleaner top cover and pull the filter from its housing. Push a new filter into the housing and install the air cleaner cover. If the filter and plastic holder need replacement, remove the clip mounting the feed tube to the air cleaner housing (hose already removed) and remove the assembly from the air cleaner. Installation is the reverse of removal.

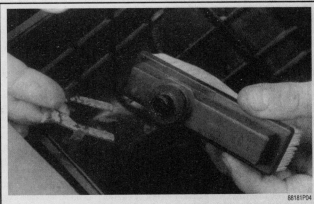

Fig. 51 To replace the holder and filter assembly, remove the clip mounting the feed tube

Evaporative Canister

SERVICING

♦ See Figure 52

The canister functions to cycle the fuel vapor from the fuel tank (and the float chamber on the carbureted models) into the intake manifold and eventually into the cylinders for combustion. The activated charcoal element within the canister acts as a storage device for the fuel vapor at times when the engine operating condition will not permit fuel vapor to burn efficiently.

Fuel vapors trapped in the sealed fuel tank are vented through the orifice's vapor valve assembly in the top of the tank. The vapors leave the valve assembly through a single vapor line and continue to the carbon canister for storage until they are purged to the engine for burning.

The carbon canister contains activated carbon, which absorbs the fuel vapor. The canister is located in the engine compartment or along the frame rail. The only required service for the evaporative emissions canister is a regular inspection of the canister. If the charcoal canister is gummed up, cracked or saturated with fuel, the entire canister should be replaced.

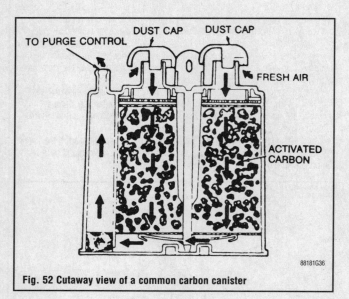

Fig. 52 Cutaway view of a common carbon canister

Battery

PRECAUTIONS

Always use caution when working on or near the battery. Never allow a tool to bridge the gap between the negative and positive battery terminals. Also, be careful not to allow a tool to provide a ground between the positive cable/terminal and any metal component on the vehicle. Either of these conditions will cause a short circuit, leading to sparks and possible personal injury.

Do not smoke or all open flames/sparks near a battery; the gases contained in the battery are very explosive and, if ignited, could cause severe injury or death.

All batteries, regardless of type, should be carefully secured by a battery hold-down device. If not, the terminals or casing may crack from stress during vehicle operation. A battery which is not secured may allow acid to leak, making it discharge faster. The acid can also eat away at components under the hood.

Always inspect the battery case for cracks, leakage and corrosion. A white corrosive substance on the battery case or on nearby components would indicate a leaking or cracked battery. If the battery is cracked, it should be replaced immediately.

GENERAL MAINTENANCE

Always keep the battery cables and terminals free of corrosion. Check and clean these components about once a year.

Keep the top of the battery clean, as a film of dirt can help discharge a battery that is not used for long periods. A solution of baking soda and water may be used for cleaning, but be careful to flush this off with clear water. DO NOT let any of the solution into the filler holes. Baking soda neutralizes battery acid and will de-activate a battery cell.

Batteries in vehicles which are not operated on a regular basis can fall victim to parasitic loads (small current drains which are constantly drawing current from the battery). Normal parasitic loads may drain a battery on a vehicle that is in storage and not used for 6–8 weeks. Vehicles that have additional accessories such as a phone or an alarm system may discharge a battery sooner. If the vehicle is to be stored for longer periods in a secure area and the alarm system is not necessary, the negative battery cable should be disconnected to protect the battery.

Remember that constantly deep cycling a battery (completely discharging and recharging it) will shorten battery life.

BATTERY FLUID

♦ See Figure 53

Check the battery electrolyte level at least once a month, or more often in hot weather or during periods of extended vehicle operation. On non-sealed batteries, the level can be checked either through the case (if translucent) or by removing the cell caps. The electrolyte level in each cell should be kept filled to the split ring inside each cell, or the line marked on the outside of the case.

If the level is low, add only distilled water through the opening until the level is correct. Each cell must be checked and filled individually. Distilled water should be used, because the chemicals and minerals found in most drinking water are harmful to the battery and could significantly shorten its life.

If water is added in freezing weather, the vehicle should be driven several miles to allow the water to mix with the electrolyte. Otherwise, the battery could freeze.

Although some maintenance-free batteries have removable cell caps, the electrolyte condition and level on all sealed maintenance-free batteries must be checked using the built-in hydrometer "eye." The exact type of eye will vary. But, most battery manufacturers, apply a sticker to the battery itself explaining the readings.

➡**Although the readings from built-in hydrometers will vary, a green eye usually indicates a properly charged battery with sufficient fluid level. A dark eye is normally an indicator of a battery with sufficient fluid, but which is low in charge. A light or yellow eye usually indicates that electrolyte has dropped below the necessary level. In this last case, sealed batteries with an insufficient electrolyte must usually be discarded.**

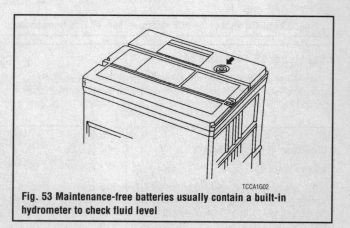

Fig. 53 Maintenance-free batteries usually contain a built-in hydrometer to check fluid level

Checking the Specific Gravity

♦ See Figures 54, 55 and 56

A hydrometer is required to check the specific gravity on all batteries that are not maintenance-free. On batteries that are maintenance-free, the specific gravity is checked by observing the built-in hydrometer "eye" on the top of the battery case.

Fig. 54 On non-sealed batteries, the fluid level can be checked by removing the cell caps

Fig. 55 If the fluid level is low, add only distilled water until the level is correct

Fig. 56 Check the specific gravity of the battery's electrolyte with a hydrometer

❊❊ CAUTION

Battery electrolyte contains sulfuric acid. If you should splash any on your skin or in your eyes, flush the affected area with plenty of clear water. If it lands in your eyes, get medical help immediately.

The fluid (sulfuric acid solution) contained in the battery cells will tell you many things about the condition of the battery. Because the cell plates must be kept submerged below the fluid level in order to operate, the fluid level is extremely important. And, because the specific gravity of the acid is an indication of electrical charge, testing the fluid can be an aid in determining if the battery must be replaced. A battery in a vehicle with a properly operating charging system should require little maintenance, but careful, periodic inspection should reveal problems before they leave you stranded.

At least once a year, check the specific gravity of the battery. It should be between 1.20 and 1.26 on the gravity scale. Most auto stores carry a variety of inexpensive battery hydrometers. These can be used on any non-sealed battery to test the specific gravity in each cell.

The battery testing hydrometer has a squeeze bulb at one end and a nozzle at the other. Battery electrolyte is sucked into the hydrometer until the float is lifted from its seat. The specific gravity is then read by noting the position of the float. If gravity is low in one or more cells, the battery should be slowly charged and checked again to see if the gravity has come up. Generally, if after charging, the specific gravity between any two cells varies more than 50 points (0.50), the battery should be replaced, as it can no longer produce sufficient voltage to guarantee proper operation.

CABLES

▶ **See Figures 57, 58, 59 and 60**

Once a year (or as necessary), the battery terminals and the cable clamps should be cleaned. Loosen the clamps and remove the cables, negative cable first. On top post batteries, the use of a puller specially made for this purpose is recommended. These are inexpensive and available in most parts stores. Side terminal battery cables are secured with a small bolt.

Clean the cable clamps and the battery terminal with a wire brush, until all corrosion, grease, etc., is removed and the metal is shiny. It is especially important to clean the inside of the clamp thoroughly (an old knife is useful here), since a small deposit of oxidation there will prevent a sound connection and inhibit starting or charging. Special tools are available for cleaning these parts, one type for conventional top post batteries and another type for side terminal batteries. It is also a good idea to apply some dielectric grease to the terminal, as this will aid in the prevention of corrosion.

After the clamps and terminals are clean, reinstall the cables, negative cable last; DO NOT hammer the clamps onto battery posts. Tighten the clamps securely, but do not distort them. Give the clamps and terminals a thin external coating of grease after installation, to retard corrosion.

Check the cables at the same time that the terminals are cleaned. If the cable insulation is cracked or broken, or if the ends are frayed, the cable should be replaced with a new cable of the same length and gauge.

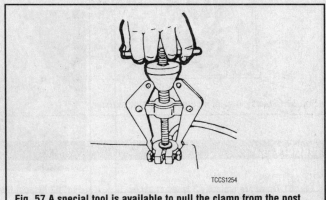

Fig. 57 A special tool is available to pull the clamp from the post

Fig. 58 The underside of this special battery tool has a wire brush to clean post terminals

Fig. 59 Place the tool over the battery posts and twist to clean until the metal is shiny

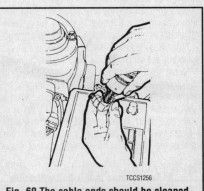

Fig. 60 The cable ends should be cleaned as well

CHARGING

The chemical reaction which takes place in all batteries generates explosive hydrogen gas. A spark can cause the battery to explode and splash acid. To avoid personal injury, be sure there is proper ventilation and take appropriate fire safety precautions when working with or near a battery.

A battery should be charged at a slow rate to keep the plates inside from getting too hot. However, if some maintenance-free batteries are allowed to discharge until they are almost "dead," they may have to be charged at a high rate to bring them back to "life." Always follow the charger manufacturer's instructions on charging the battery.

REPLACEMENT

When it becomes necessary to replace the battery, select one with an amperage rating equal to or greater than the battery originally installed. Deterioration and just plain aging of the battery cables, starter motor, and associated wires makes the battery's job harder in successive years. This makes it prudent to install a new battery with a greater capacity than

Belts

INSPECTION

▶ **See Figures 61 thru 66**

Inspect the belts for signs of glazing or cracking. A glazed belt will be perfectly smooth from slippage, while a good belt will have a slight texture of fabric visible. Cracks will usually start at the inner edge of the belt and run outward.

All worn or damaged drive belts should be replaced immediately. It is best to replace all drive belts at one time, as a preventive maintenance measure, during this service operation.

ADJUSTMENTS

Except Serpentine Belts

On models equipped with an electric cooling fan, disconnect the negative battery cable or fan motor wiring harness connector before replacing or adjusting drive belts. The fan may come on, under certain circumstances, even though the ignition is OFF.

Proper adjustment requires the use of the tension gauge. Since most people don't have the necessary gauge, a deflection method of adjustment is given. To assure proper belt tension, the following guidelines should be followed:
- Use belt tension gauge tool T63L–8620–A or equivalent.
- If a belt tension gauge is not obtainable, the belt deflection method may be used for conventional V and cogged V belts only.
- Locate a point on the belt midway between the two pulleys driven. Press firmly on the belt.

ALTERNATOR

▶ **See Figure 67**

1. Position the ruler perpendicular to the drive belt at its longest straight run. Test the tightness of the belt by pressing it firmly with your thumb. The deflection should not exceed ¼ in. (6mm).
2. If the deflection exceeds ¼ in. (6mm), loosen the alternator mounting and adjusting arm bolts.
3. Place a 1 in. open-end or adjustable wrench on the adjusting ridge cast on the body, and pull on the wrench until the proper tension is achieved.

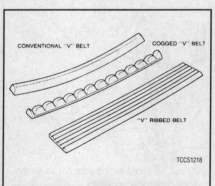

Fig. 61 There are typically 3 types of accessory drive belts found on vehicles today

Fig. 62 Inspect the belts for signs of glazing or cracking

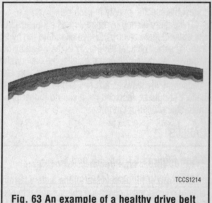

Fig. 63 An example of a healthy drive belt

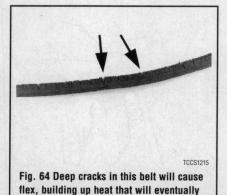

Fig. 64 Deep cracks in this belt will cause flex, building up heat that will eventually lead to belt failure

Fig. 65 The cover of this belt is worn, exposing the critical reinforcing cords to excessive wear

Fig. 66 Installing too wide a belt can result in serious belt wear and/or breakage

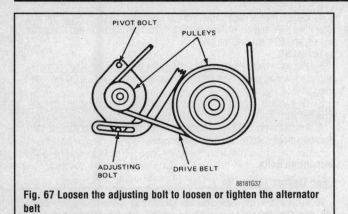

Fig. 67 Loosen the adjusting bolt to loosen or tighten the alternator belt

4. Holding the alternator in place to maintain tension, tighten the adjusting arm bolt. Recheck the belt tension. When the belt is properly tensioned, tighten the alternator mounting bolt.

POWER STEERING—2.3L ENGINE

1. Hold a ruler perpendicular to the drive belt at its longest run, test the tightness of the belt by pressing it firmly with your thumb. The deflection should not exceed ¼ in. (6mm).
2. To adjust the belt tension, loosen the adjusting and mounting bolts on the front face of the steering pump cover plate (hub side).
3. Using a prybar or broom handle on the pump hub, move the power steering pump toward or away from the engine until the proper tension is reached. Do not pry against the reservoir as it is relatively soft and easily deformed.
4. Holding the pump in place, tighten the adjusting arm bolt and then recheck the belt tension. When the belt is properly tensioned tighten the mounting bolts.

2. If the engine is equipped with an idler pulley, loosen the idler pulley adjusting bolt, insert a prybar between the pulley and the engine (or in the idler pulley adjusting slot), and adjust the tension accordingly. If the engine is not equipped with an idler pulley, the alternator must be moved to accomplish this adjustment, as outlined under Alternator Belt.
3. When the proper tension is reached, tighten the idler pulley adjusting bolt (if so equipped) or the alternator adjusting and mounting bolts.

AIR PUMP

▶ See Figure 70

1. Position a ruler perpendicular to the drive belt at its longest run. Test the tightness of the belt by pressing it firmly with your thumb. The deflection should be about ¼ in. (6mm).
2. To adjust the belt tension, loosen the adjusting arm bolt slightly. If necessary, also loosen the mounting belt slightly.
3. Using a prybar or broom handle, pry against the pump rear cover to move the pump toward or away from the engine as necessary.

※※ **CAUTION**

Do not pry against the pump housing itself, as damage to the housing may result.

4. Holding the pump in place, tighten the adjusting arm bolt and recheck the tension. When the belt is properly tensioned, tighten the mounting bolt.

Serpentine Belts

▶ See Figure 71

Most late models feature a single (some use a double), wide, ribbed V-belt that drives the water pump, alternator, and (on some models) the air conditioner compressor. These belts use an automatic belt tensioner.

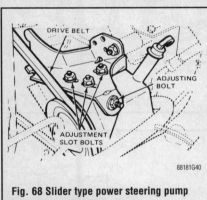

Fig. 68 Slider type power steering pump belt adjustment bolt locations

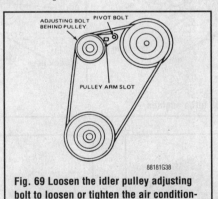

Fig. 69 Loosen the idler pulley adjusting bolt to loosen or tighten the air conditioning belt

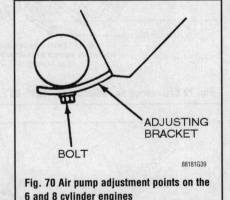

Fig. 70 Air pump adjustment points on the 6 and 8 cylinder engines

POWER STEERING—EXCEPT 2.3L ENGINES

▶ See Figure 68

1. Position a ruler perpendicular to the drive belt at its longest run. Test the tightness of the belt by pressing it firmly with your thumb. The deflection should be about ¼ in. (6mm).
2. To adjust the belt tension, loosen the three bolts in the three elongated adjusting slots at the power steering pump attaching bracket.
3. Turn the steering pump drive belt adjusting nut as required until the proper deflection is obtained. Turning the adjusting nut clockwise will increase tension and decrease deflection; counterclockwise will decrease tension and increase deflection.
4. Without disturbing the pump, tighten the three attaching bolts.

AIR CONDITIONING

▶ See Figure 69

1. Position a ruler perpendicular to the drive belt at its longest run. Test the tightness of the belt by pressing it firmly with your thumb. The deflection should not exceed ¼ in. (6mm).

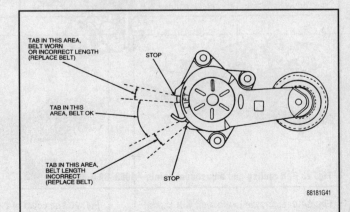

Fig. 71 Locate the area that the tab is on the adjuster to establish the life of the belt

The automatic belt tensioners are spring loaded devices which set and maintain the drive belt tension. The drive belt should not require tension adjustments for the life of the belt. All automatic belt tensioners have wear indicators on them. Check the indicator marks on the tensioner, if the mark is not between the indicator lines, the belt is worn or the wrong belt has been installed. Be sure to make the indicator mark inspection is done with the engine **OFF**.

REMOVAL & INSTALLATION

Except Serpentine Belts

♦ See Figure 72

If equipped with air conditioning and/or air pump it may be necessary to loosen and remove the drive belts before the fan drive belt can be removed.

1. Disconnect the negative battery cable.
2. Loosen the power steering pump at the mounting bracket and remove the drive belt.
3. On a vehicles with an air conditioner, remove the compressor drive belt.

4. Loosen the alternator mounting and adjusting arm bolts. Move the alternator toward the engine. Remove the belt(s) from the alternator and crankshaft pulleys, and lift them over the fan.

To install:

5. Place the belt(s) over the fan, insert the belt(s) in the water pump pulley, crankshaft pulley and alternator pulley grooves. Adjust the belt tension.
6. On a vehicle with an air conditioner, install and adjust the compressor drive belt tension.
7. Install the power steering pump drive belt and tighten the pump at the mounting bracket. Adjust the drive belt tension.

Serpentine Belts

♦ See Figures 73 thru 84

To install a new belt, loosen the bracket lockbolt and/or idler pulley lockbolt, retract the belt tensioner with a prybar and slide the old belt off of the pulleys. Slip on a new belt and release the tensioner and tighten the lockbolt. The automatic spring powered tensioner eliminates the need for periodic adjustments.

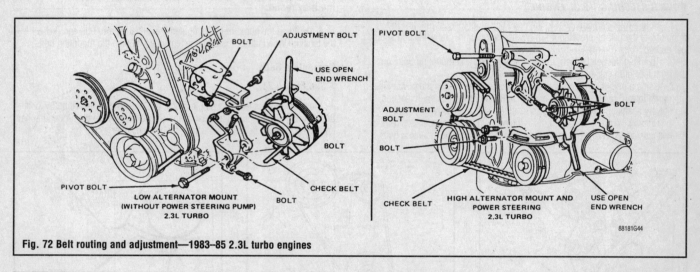

Fig. 72 Belt routing and adjustment—1983–85 2.3L turbo engines

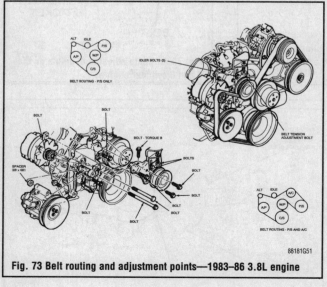

Fig. 73 Belt routing and adjustment points—1983–86 3.8L engine

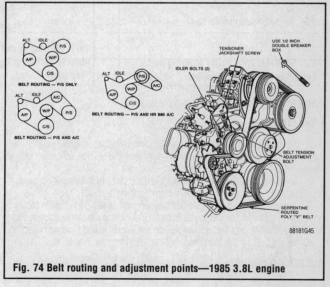

Fig. 74 Belt routing and adjustment points—1985 3.8L engine

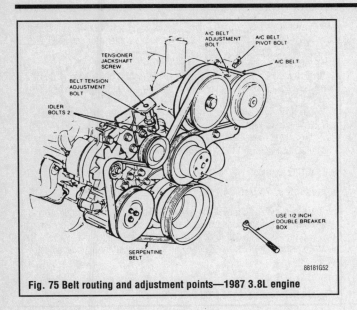

Fig. 75 Belt routing and adjustment points—1987 3.8L engine

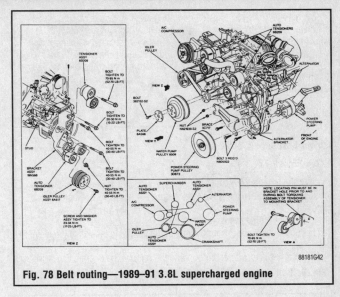

Fig. 78 Belt routing—1989–91 3.8L supercharged engine

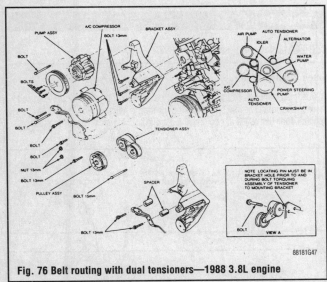

Fig. 76 Belt routing with dual tensioners—1988 3.8L engine

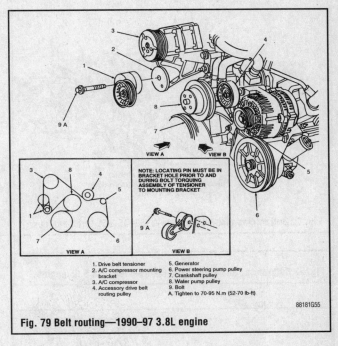

1. Drive belt tensioner
2. A/C compressor mounting bracket
3. A/C compressor
4. Accessory drive belt routing pulley
5. Generator
6. Power steering pump pulley
7. Crankshaft pulley
8. Water pump pulley
9. Bolt
A. Tighten to 70-95 N.m (52-70 lb-ft)

Fig. 79 Belt routing—1990–97 3.8L engine

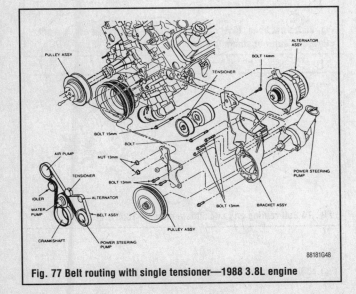

Fig. 77 Belt routing with single tensioner—1988 3.8L engine

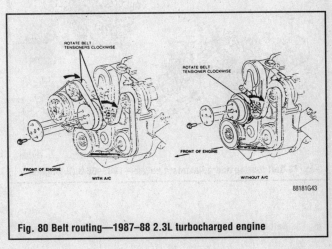

Fig. 80 Belt routing—1987–88 2.3L turbocharged engine

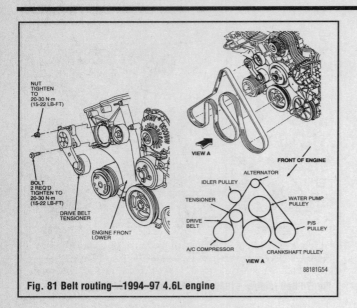

Fig. 81 Belt routing—1994–97 4.6L engine

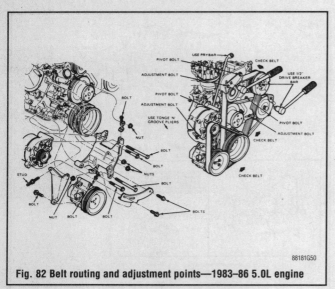

Fig. 82 Belt routing and adjustment points—1983–86 5.0L engine

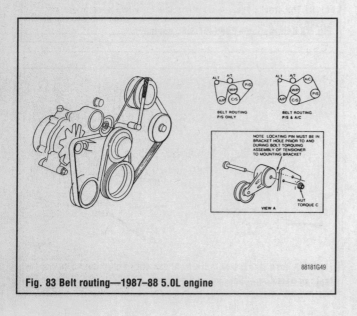

Fig. 83 Belt routing—1987–88 5.0L engine

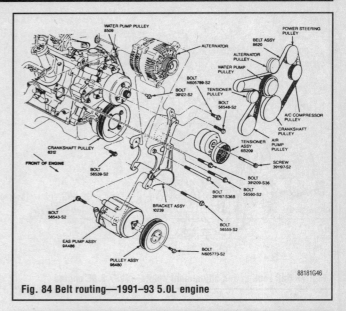

Fig. 84 Belt routing—1991–93 5.0L engine

Timing Belts

INSPECTION

▶ **See Figures 85 thru 90**

Ford recommends that the timing belt be replaced on vehicles that are used in extensive idling or low speed driving for long distances. Police, taxi and door-to-door deliveries are commonly used in this manner. The timing belt

Fig. 85 Do not bend, twist or turn the timing belt inside out. Never allow oil, water or steam to contact the belt

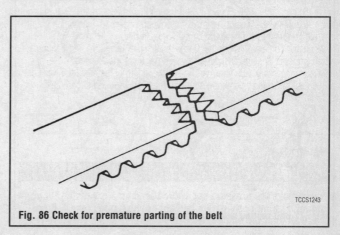

Fig. 86 Check for premature parting of the belt

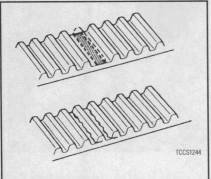

Fig. 87 Check if the teeth are cracked or damaged

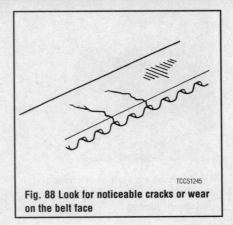

Fig. 88 Look for noticeable cracks or wear on the belt face

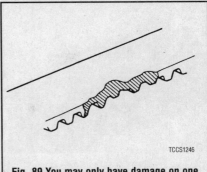

Fig. 89 You may only have damage on one side of the belt; if so, the guide could be the culprit

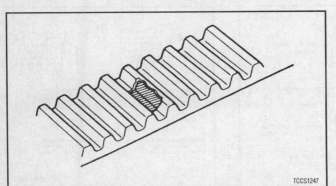

Fig. 90 Foreign materials can get in between the teeth and cause damage

should be replaced every 60,000 miles (96,000 km) in these cases. If your vehicle has high mileage, you may want to consider replacing the belt to prevent the possibility of having it snap. Or if your engine is being overhauled, inspect the belt for wear and replace if needed. In the event the belt does snap while you are driving, turn the engine **OFF** immediately. Section 3 has removal and installation procedures available.

Hoses

INSPECTION

▶ See Figures 91, 92, 93 and 94

Upper and lower radiator hoses along with the heater hoses should be checked for deterioration, leaks and loose hose clamps at least every 15,000 miles (24,000 km). It is also wise to check the hoses periodically in early spring and at the beginning of the fall or winter when you are performing other maintenance. A quick visual inspection could discover a weakened hose which might have left you stranded if it had remained unrepaired.

Whenever you are checking the hoses, make sure the engine and cooling system are cold. Visually inspect for cracking, rotting or collapsed hoses, and replace as necessary. Run your hand along the length of the hose. If a weak or swollen spot is noted when squeezing the hose wall, the hose should be replaced.

REMOVAL & INSTALLATION

1. Remove the radiator pressure cap.

❊❊ CAUTION

Never remove the pressure cap while the engine is running, or personal injury from scalding hot coolant or steam may result. If possible, wait until the engine has cooled to remove the pressure cap.

If this is not possible, wrap a thick cloth around the pressure cap and turn it slowly to the stop. Step back while the pressure is released from the cooling system. When you are sure all the pressure has been released, use the cloth to turn and remove the cap.

2. Position a clean container under the radiator and/or engine draincock or plug, then open the drain and allow the cooling system to drain to an appropriate level. For some upper hoses, only a little coolant must be drained. To remove hoses positioned lower on the engine, such as a lower radiator hose, the entire cooling system must be emptied.

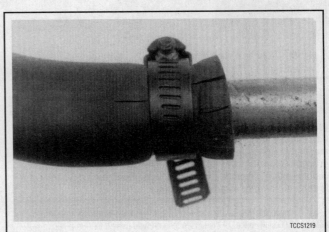

Fig. 91 The cracks developing along this hose are a result of age-related hardening

Fig. 92 A hose clamp that is too tight can cause older hoses to separate and tear on either side of the clamp

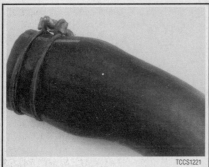

Fig. 93 A soft spongy hose (identifiable by the swollen section) will eventually burst and should be replaced

Fig. 94 Hoses are likely to deteriorate from the inside if the cooling system is not periodically flushed

Fig. 95 CV-Boots must be inspected periodically for damage

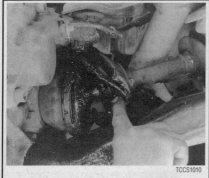

Fig. 96 A torn boot should be replaced immediately

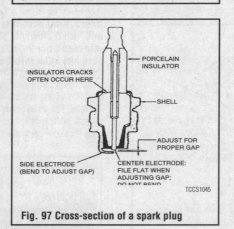

Fig. 97 Cross-section of a spark plug

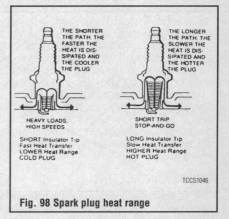

Fig. 98 Spark plug heat range

✳✳ CAUTION

When draining coolant, keep in mind that cats and dogs are attracted by ethylene glycol antifreeze, and are quite likely to drink any that is left in an uncovered container or in puddles on the ground. This will prove fatal in sufficient quantity. Always drain coolant into a sealable container. Coolant may be reused unless it is contaminated or several years old.

3. Loosen the hose clamps at each end of the hose requiring replacement. Clamps are usually either of the spring tension type (which require pliers to squeeze the tabs and loosen) or of the screw tension type (which require screw or hex drivers to loosen). Pull the clamps back on the hose away from the connection.

4. Twist, pull and slide the hose off the fitting, taking care not to damage the neck of the component from which the hose is being removed.

➥If the hose is stuck at the connection, do not try to insert a screwdriver or other sharp tool under the hose end in an effort to free it, as the connection and/or hose may become damaged. Heater connections especially may be easily damaged by such a procedure. If the hose is to be replaced, use a single-edged razor blade to make a slice along the portion of the hose which is stuck on the connection, perpendicular to the end of the hose. Do not cut deeply to prevent damaging the connection. The hose can then be peeled from the connection and discarded.

5. Clean both hose mounting connections. Inspect the condition of the hose clamps and replace them, if necessary.

To install:

6. Dip the ends of the new hose into clean engine coolant to ease installation.

7. Slide the clamps over the replacement hose, then slide the hose ends over the connections into position.

8. Position and secure the clamps at least ¼ in. (6.35mm) from the ends of the hose. Make sure they are located beyond the raised bead of the connector.

9. Close the radiator or engine drains and properly refill the cooling system with the clean drained engine coolant or a suitable mixture of ethylene glycol coolant and water.

10. If available, install a pressure tester and check for leaks. If a pressure tester is not available, run the engine until normal operating temperature is reached (allowing the system to naturally pressurize), then check for leaks.

✳✳ CAUTION

If you are checking for leaks with the system at normal operating temperature, BE EXTREMELY CAREFUL not to touch any moving or hot engine parts. Once temperature has been reached, shut the engine OFF, and check for leaks around the hose fittings and connections which were removed earlier.

CV Boots

INSPECTION

▶ See Figures 95 and 96

The CV (Constant Velocity) boots should be checked for damage each time the oil is changed and any other time the vehicle is raised for service. These boots keep water, grime, dirt and other damaging matter from entering the CV-joints. Any of these could cause early CV-joint failure which can be expensive to repair. Heavy grease thrown around the inside of the rear wheel(s) and on the brakes can be an indication of a torn boot. Thoroughly check the boots for missing clamps and tears. If the boot is damaged, have it replaced immediately.

Spark Plugs

▶ See Figure 97 and 98

A typical spark plug consists of a metal shell surrounding a ceramic insulator. A metal electrode extends downward through the center of the insulator and protrudes a small distance. Located at the end of the plug and attached to the side of the outer metal shell is the side electrode. The side electrode bends in at a 90° angle so that its tip is just past and parallel to the tip of the center electrode. The distance between these two electrodes (measured in thousandths of an inch or hundredths of a millimeter) is called the spark plug gap.

The spark plug does not produce a spark but instead provides a gap across which the current can arc. The coil produces anywhere from 20,000 to 50,000 volts (depending on the type and application) which travels through the wires to the spark plugs. The current passes along the center electrode and jumps the gap to the side electrode, and in doing so, ignites the air/fuel mixture in the combustion chamber.

SPARK PLUG HEAT RANGE

▶ **See Figure 98**

Spark plug heat range is the ability of the plug to dissipate heat. The longer the insulator (or the farther it extends into the engine), the hotter the plug will operate; the shorter the insulator (the closer the electrode is to the block's cooling passages) the cooler it will operate. A plug that absorbs little heat and remains too cool will quickly accumulate deposits of oil and carbon since it is not hot enough to burn them off. This leads to plug fouling and consequently to misfiring. A plug that absorbs too much heat will have no deposits but, due to the excessive heat, the electrodes will burn away quickly and might possibly lead to preignition or other ignition problems. Preignition takes place when plug tips get so hot that they glow sufficiently to ignite the air/fuel mixture before the actual spark occurs. This early ignition will usually cause a pinging during low speeds and heavy loads.

The general rule of thumb for choosing the correct heat range when picking a spark plug is: if most of your driving is long distance, high speed travel, use a colder plug; if most of your driving is stop and go, use a hotter plug. Original equipment plugs are generally a good compromise between the 2 styles and most people never have the need to change their plugs from the factory-recommended heat range.

REMOVAL & INSTALLATION

A non platinum set of spark plugs usually requires replacement after about 20,000–30,000 miles (32,000–48,000 km) depending on your style of driving. On the platinum spark plugs replace them at 60,000 miles (96,000 km). On normal operation plug gap increases about 0.001 in (0.025 mm) for every 2,500 miles (4000 km). As the gap increases, the plug's voltage requirement also increases. It requires a greater voltage to jump the wider gap and about two to three times as much voltage to fire the plug at high speeds than at idle. The improved air/fuel ratio control of modern fuel injection combined with the higher voltage output of modern ignition systems will often allow an engine to run significantly longer on a set of standard spark plugs, but keep in mind that efficiency will drop as the gap widens (along with fuel economy and power).

When you're removing spark plugs, work on one at a time. Don't start by removing the plug wires all at once, because, unless you number them, they may become mixed up. Take a minute before you begin and number the wires with tape.

1. Disconnect the negative battery cable, and if the vehicle has been run recently, allow the engine to thoroughly cool.
2. Carefully twist the spark plug wire boot to loosen it, then pull upward and remove the boot from the plug. Be sure to pull on the boot and not on the wire, otherwise the connector located inside the boot may become separated.

3. Using compressed air, blow any water or debris from the spark plug well to assure that no harmful contaminants are allowed to enter the combustion chamber when the spark plug is removed. If compressed air is not available, use a rag or a brush to clean the area.

➡**Remove the spark plugs when the engine is cold, if possible, to prevent damage to the threads. If removal of the plugs is difficult, apply a few drops of penetrating oil or silicone spray to the area around the base of the plug, and allow it a few minutes to work.**

4. Using a spark plug socket that is equipped with a rubber insert to properly hold the plug, turn the spark plug counterclockwise to loosen and remove the spark plug from the bore.

❊❊ WARNING

Be sure not to use a flexible extension on the socket. Use of a flexible extension may allow a shear force to be applied to the plug. A shear force could break the plug off in the cylinder head, leading to costly and frustrating repairs.

To install:
5. Inspect the spark plug boot for tears or damage. If a damaged boot is found, the spark plug wire must be replaced.
6. Using a wire feeler gauge, check and adjust the spark plug gap. When using a gauge, the proper size should pass between the electrodes with a slight drag. The next larger size should not be able to pass while the next smaller size should pass freely.
7. Carefully thread the plug into the bore by hand. If resistance is felt before the plug is almost completely threaded, back the plug out and begin threading again. In small, hard to reach areas, an old spark plug wire and boot could be used as a threading tool. The boot will hold the plug while you twist the end of the wire and the wire is supple enough to twist before it would allow the plug to crossthread.

❊❊ WARNING

Do not use the spark plug socket to thread the plugs. Always carefully thread the plug by hand or using an old plug wire to prevent the possibility of crossthreading and damaging the cylinder head bore.

8. Carefully tighten the spark plug. If the plug you are installing is equipped with a crush washer, seat the plug, then tighten about ¼ turn to crush the washer. If you are installing a tapered seat plug, tighten the plug to specifications provided by the vehicle or plug manufacturer.
9. Apply a small amount of silicone dielectric compound to the end of the spark plug lead or inside the spark plug boot to prevent sticking, then install the boot to the spark plug and push until it clicks into place. The click may be felt or heard, then gently pull back on the boot to assure proper contact.

INSPECTION & GAPPING

▶ **See Figures 99, 100, 101 and 102**

Check the plugs for deposits and wear. If they are not going to be replaced, clean the plugs thoroughly. Remember that any kind of deposit will decrease the

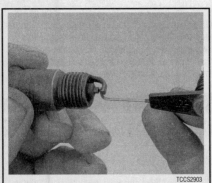

Fig. 99 Checking the spark plug gap with a feeler gauge

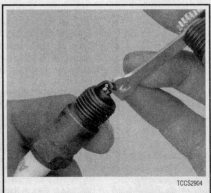

Fig. 100 Adjusting the spark plug gap

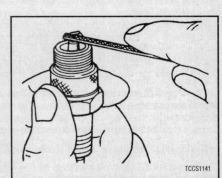

Fig. 101 If the standard plug is in good condition, the electrode may be filed flat—WARNING: do not file platinum plugs

A normally worn spark plug should have light tan or gray deposits on the firing tip.

A carbon fouled plug, identified by soft, sooty, black deposits, may indicate an improperly tuned vehicle. Check the air cleaner, ignition components and engine control system.

This spark plug has been **left in the engine too long,** as evidenced by the extreme gap- Plugs with such an extreme gap can cause misfiring and stumbling accompanied by a noticeable lack of power.

An oil fouled spark plug indicates an engine with worn poston rings and/or bad valve seals allowing excessive oil to enter the chamber.

A physically damaged spark plug may be evidence of severe detonation in that cylinder. Watch that cylinder carefully between services, as a continued detonation will not only damage the plug, but could also damage the engine.

A bridged or almost bridged spark plug, identified by a build-up between the electrodes caused by excessive carbon or oil build-up on the plug.

TCCA1P40

Fig. 102 Inspect the spark plug to determine engine running conditions

efficiency of the plug. Plugs can be cleaned on a spark plug cleaning machine, which can sometimes be found in service stations, or you can do an acceptable job of cleaning with a stiff brush. If the plugs are cleaned, the electrodes must be filed flat. Use an ignition points file, not an emery board or the like, which will leave deposits. The electrodes must be filed perfectly flat with sharp edges; rounded edges reduce the spark plug voltage by as much as 50%.

Check spark plug gap before installation. The ground electrode (the L-shaped one connected to the body of the plug) must be parallel to the center electrode and the specified size wire gauge (please refer to the Tune-Up Specifications chart for details) must pass between the electrodes with a slight drag.

➡**NEVER adjust the gap on a used platinum type spark plug.**

Always check the gap on new plugs as they are not always set correctly at the factory. Do not use a flat feeler gauge when measuring the gap on a used plug, because the reading may be inaccurate. A round-wire type gapping tool is the best way to check the gap. The correct gauge should pass through the electrode gap with a slight drag. If you're in doubt, try one size smaller and one larger.

The smaller gauge should go through easily, while the larger one shouldn't go through at all. Wire gapping tools usually have a bending tool attached. Use that to adjust the side electrode until the proper distance is obtained. Absolutely never attempt to bend the center electrode. Also, be careful not to bend the side electrode too far or too often as it may weaken and break off within the engine, requiring removal of the cylinder head to retrieve it.

Spark Plug Wires

TESTING

▶ **See Figures 103 and 104**

At every tune-up/inspection, visually check the spark plug cables for burns cuts, or breaks in the insulation. Check the boots and the nipples on the distributor cap and/or coil. Replace any damaged wiring.

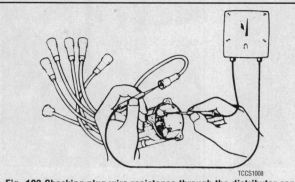

Fig. 103 Checking plug wire resistance through the distributor cap with an ohmmeter

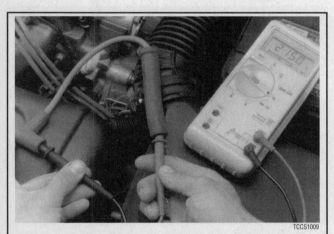

Fig. 104 Checking individual plug wire resistance with a digital ohmmeter

Every 50,000 miles (80,000 km) or 60 months, the resistance of the wires should be checked with an ohmmeter. Wires with excessive resistance will cause misfiring, and may make the engine difficult to start in damp weather.

To check resistance, remove the distributor cap, leaving the wires in place. Connect one lead of an ohmmeter to an electrode within the cap; connect the other lead to the corresponding spark plug terminal (remove it from the spark plug for this test). Replace any wire which shows a resistance over 30,000 ohms. The following resistance values are a function of length.

- 0-15 in. (0–38cm): 3000–10,000 ohms
- 15-25 in. (38–64cm): 4000–15,000 ohms
- 25-35 in. (64–89cm): 6000–20,000 ohms
- Over 35 in. (89cm): 25,000 ohms

It should be remembered that resistance is also a function of length; the longer the wire, the greater the resistance. Thus, if the wires on your car are longer than the factory originals, resistance will be higher, quite possibly outside these limits.

When installing new wires, replace them one at a time to avoid mixups. Start by replacing the longest one first. Install the boot firmly over the spark plug. Route the wire over the same path as the original. Insert the nipple firmly onto the tower on the distributor cap, then install the cap cover and latches to secure the wires.

REMOVAL & INSTALLATION

▶ See Figure 105

1. Before removing high tension wires from the spark plugs, distributor cap or coil, inspect them for visible damage such as cuts, pinches, cracks or torn boots. Replace only wires that are damaged.
2. Remove the wires from the spark plugs, using a suitable spark plug wire removal tool (T74P–6666–A or equivalent).

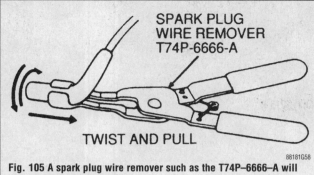

Fig. 105 A spark plug wire remover such as the T74P–6666–A will ease removal of the wires

3. Grasp and twist the spark plug wire boot back and forth, then pull the wire off the plug.

➡ Do not pull directly on the spark plug wire, or it may separate from its terminal inside the spark plug wire boot.

4. If it becomes necessary to remove the wires from the distributor cap or coil, grasp the boot by hand and remove with a twisting and pulling motion.

To install:

➡ Whenever an ignition wire is removed from a spark plug, ignition coil or distributor cap terminal, silicone compound must be applied to the spark plug wire boot before it is reconnected. Using a small clean tool, lightly coat the entire inner surface of the boot with Ford Silicone Dielectric Compound (D7AZ–19A331–A or equivalent).

5. When installing a new set of spark plug wires, replace the wires one at a time so there will be no mixup. Start by replacing the longest wire first. Install the boot firmly over the spark plug. Route the wire exactly the same as the original. Attach each wire to the proper terminal of the distributor cap. Check to ensure the wires are fully seated on the terminals. Repeat the process for each wire.
6. Remove the wire separators from the old wire set and install them on the new wire set in the same position.
7. Connect the wires to the proper spark plugs. Install the ignition coil wire. Check to ensure the wires are fully seated on the terminals.

Distributor Cap and Rotor

REMOVAL & INSTALLATION

▶ See Figures 106, 107 and 108

1. Disconnect the negative battery cable.
2. Label the spark plug wires.
3. Loosen the distributor cap hold-down screws or release the clamps.
4. Remove the cap by pulling it straight upwards. Avoid damaging the rotor points and spring.
5. If required, remove the rotor.

To install:

6. Position the rotor with the square and round locator pins matched to the distributor shaft plate.
7. Remove one wire at a time from the old cap and install onto the new cap in the correct position.
8. Position the distributor cap on the distributor base noting the square alignment locator.
9. Tighten the screws or engage the clamps as applicable.

INSPECTION

▶ See Figures 109 and 110

Clean the inside and outside of the cap surfaces with soap and water. Dry the cap with compressed air. Inspect it for cracks, broken carbon button or carbon tracks. Also inspect the terminals for dirt and corrosion.

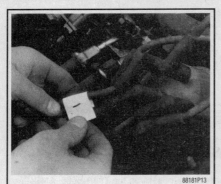

Fig. 106 If necessary for removal, label each wire for installation purposes

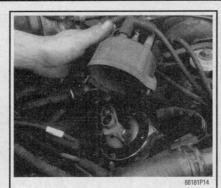

Fig. 107 Pull the cap upward to avoid damaging the rotor

Fig. 108 Pull the rotor straight up from the distributor shaft to remove

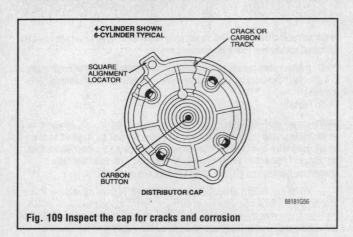

Fig. 109 Inspect the cap for cracks and corrosion

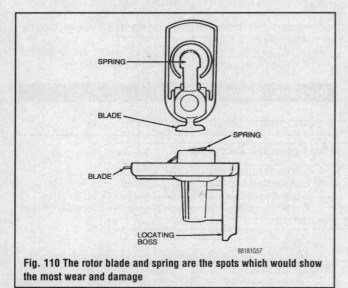

Fig. 110 The rotor blade and spring are the spots which would show the most wear and damage

Clean the distributor rotor with a soap and water solution. Dry the rotor with compressed air and inspect it for tip wear or damages.

✳✳ WARNING

Do not bend the rotor spring or file the tip.

Replace the cap and rotor if any signs of damage or wear are noticed. It is advisable to replace them both in a set.

Ignition Timing

GENERAL INFORMATION

Ignition timing is the measurement in degrees of crankshaft rotation at the instant the spark plug fires while the piston is on its compression stroke.

Ideally, the air/fuel mixture in the cylinder will be ignited by the spark plug and just beginning its rapid expansion as the piston passes Top Dead Center (TDC) of the compression stroke. If this happens, the piston will be beginning the power stroke just as the compressed air/fuel mixture starts to burn and expand. The expansion (explosion) of the air/fuel mixture will then force the piston down on the power stroke and turn the crankshaft.

It takes a fraction of a second for the spark from the plug to completely ignite the mixture in the cylinder. Because of this, the spark plug must fire before the piston reaches TDC, if the mixture is to be completely ignited as the piston passes TDC. This measurement is given in degrees of crankshaft rotation before the piston reaches top dead center (BTDC). If the ignition timing setting for your engine is ten (10°) BTDC, this means that the spark plug must fire at the time when the piston for that cylinder is 10° before reaching the top of its compression stroke. However, this only holds true while your engine is at idle speed.

As the engine accelerates from idle, the speed of the engine (rpm, or revolutions per minute) increases. The increase in rpm means that the pistons are now traveling up and down much faster. Because of this, the spark plugs will have to fire even sooner if the mixture is to be completely ignited as the piston passes TDC. To accomplish this, the distributor incorporates means to advance the timing of the spark as engine speed increases.

If ignition timing is set too far advanced (BTDC), the ignition and expansion of the air/fuel mixture in the cylinder will try to force the piston down in the cylinder while it is still traveling upward. This causes engine "ping", a sound which resembles marbles being dropped into an empty tin can. If the ignition timing is too far retarded (after, or ATDC), the piston will have already started down on the power stroke when the air/fuel mixture ignites. This will cause the piston to be forced down only a portion of its travel, resulting in poor engine performance and lack of power.

INSPECTION & ADJUSTMENT

Dura Spark II Ignition System

This system is used on the 3.8L carbureted engines.

➡️**If the following timing procedure differs from that found on the Vehicle's Emission Information label, use those found on the sticker. Always refer to the Vehicle Emission Information label for initial timing and spark plug specifications.**

1. Place the transmission in **P** or **N**.
2. Turn all accessories off (A/C, heater . . . etc.).
3. Remove vacuum hoses from the distributor vacuum advance connection and plug them.
4. Connect an inductive timing light and tachometer to the No. 1 cylinder ignition wire (following the manufactures instructions).

5. If equipped with a barometric pressure switch, disconnect it from the ignition module and place a jumper wire across the pins at the ignition module connector.

6. Start the engine and allow it to reach operating temperature.

7. With the engine at timing rpm, check/adjust initial timing to specifications.

8. Remove the test equipment.

9. Unplug and reconnect the vacuum hoses.

10. Remove the jumper from the ignition module connector and engage it.

EEC-IV Thick Film Ignition System

This system is used on the fuel injected engines.

1. Place the transmission in **P** or **N**.

2. Turn all accessories off (A/C, heater . . . etc.).

3. Connect an inductive timing light and tachometer to the No. 1 cylinder ignition wire (following the manufactures instructions).

4. Disconnect the single wire in-line Spout connector or remove the shorting bar from the double wire Spout connector.

5. Start the engine and allow it to reach operating temperature.

➡**Do not use a remote starter. Disconnecting the start wire at the starter relay will cause the TFI module to revert to start mode timing after the vehicle is started. Reconnecting the start wire after the vehicle is running will not correct the timing.**

6. With the engine at timing rpm, check/adjust initial timing to specifications.

7. Engage the single wire in-line Spout connector or the shorting bar to the double wire Spout connector. Check the timing advance to verify the distributor is advancing beyond the initial timing.

8. Remove the test equipment.

DIS Ignition System

On models equipped with the distributorless ignition system, the ignition timing is controlled by the Powertrain Control Module (PCM). No adjustments are necessary or possible.

Idle Speed and Mixture Adjustments

The idle speed and mixture adjustments are regulated by the computer control module. No routine adjustment is necessary. Refer to Section for any applicable adjustments.

Air Conditioning System

SYSTEM SERVICE & REPAIR

➡**It is recommended that the A/C system be serviced by an EPA Section 609 certified automotive technician utilizing a refrigerant recovery/recycling machine.**

GASOLINE ENGINE TUNE-UP SPECIFICATIONS

Year	Engine ID/VIN	Engine Displacement Liters (cc)	Spark Plugs Gap (in.)	Ignition Timing (deg.) MT	AT	Fuel Pump (psi)	Idle Speed (rpm) MT	AT	Valve Clearance In.	Ex.
1983	W	2.3 (2300) ①	0.034	10B	10B	36-42	750	750	HYD	HYD
	3	3.8 (3802)	0.044	10B	10B	6-8	600	600	HYD	HYD
	F	5.0 (4949)	0.050	-	10B	36-42	-	550	HYD	HYD
1984	W	2.3 (2300) ①	0.034	10B	10B	36-42	750	750	HYD	HYD
	3	3.8 (3802)	0.044	10B	10B	35-45	600	600	HYD	HYD
	F	5.0 (4949)	0.050	-	10B	6-8	-	550	HYD	HYD
1985	W	2.3 (2300) ①	0.034	10B	10B	36-42	750	750	HYD	HYD
	3	3.8 (3802)	0.044	10B	10B	35-45	600	600	HYD	HYD
	F	5.0 (4949)	0.050	-	10B	36-42	-	550	HYD	HYD
1986	W	2.3 (2300) ①	0.034	10B	10B	36-42	750	750	HYD	HYD
	3	3.8 (3802)	0.044	10B	10B	35-45	600	600	HYD	HYD
	F	5.0 (4949)	0.044	-	10B	36-42	-	550	HYD	HYD
1987	W	2.3 (2300) ①	0.034	10B	10B	36-42	750	750	HYD	HYD
	3	3.8 (3802)	0.044	10B	10B	35-45	600	600	HYD	HYD
	F	5.0 (4949)	0.044	-	10B	36-42	-	550	HYD	HYD
1988	W	2.3 (2300) ①	0.034	10B	10B	36-42	750	750	HYD	HYD
	4	3.8 (3802)	0.044	-	10B	35-45	550	550	HYD	HYD
	F	5.0 (4949)	0.044	-	10B	36-42	-	550	HYD	HYD
1989	4	3.8 (3802)	0.044	-	10B	35-45	550	550	HYD	HYD
	R	3.8 (3802)	0.054	10B	10B	35-45	550	550	HYD	HYD
1990	4	3.8 (3802)	0.054	10B	10B	35-45	550	550	HYD	HYD
	R	3.8 (3802)	0.054	10B	10B	35-45	550	550	HYD	HYD
1991	4	3.8 (3802)	0.054	10B	10B	35-45	550	550	HYD	HYD
	R	3.8 (3802)	0.054	10B	10B	35-45	550	550	HYD	HYD
	T	5.0 (4949)	0.054	-	10B	35-40	-	650	HYD	HYD
1992	4	3.8 (3802)	0.054	10B	10B	35-45	550	550	HYD	HYD
	R	3.8 (3802)	0.054	10B	10B	35-45	550	550	HYD	HYD
	T	5.0 (4949)	0.054	-	10B	35-40	-	650	HYD	HYD
1993	4	3.8 (3802)	0.054	10B	10B	35-45	550	550	HYD	HYD
	R	3.8 (3802)	0.054	②		35-45	550	550	HYD	HYD
	T	5.0 (4949)	0.054	-	10B	35-40	-	650	HYD	HYD
1994	4	3.8 (3802)	0.054	10B	10B	30-45	-	②	HYD	HYD
	R	3.8 (3802)	0.054	②	②	35-45	550	550	HYD	HYD
	W	4.6 (4593)	0.054	-	②	30-45	-	②	HYD	HYD
1995	4	3.8 (3802)	0.054	②	②	30-45	-	②	HYD	HYD
	R	3.8 (3802)	0.054	②	②	35-45	550	550	HYD	HYD
	W	4.6 (4593)	0.054	-	②	30-45	-	②	HYD	HYD
1996	4	3.8 (3802)	0.054	-	②	30-45	-	②	HYD	HYD
	W	4.6 (4593)	0.054	-	②	35-45	-	②	HYD	HYD
1997	4	3.8 (3802)	0.054	-	②	30-45	-	②	HYD	HYD
	W	4.6 (4593)	0.054	-	②	35-45	-	②	HYD	HYD

NOTE: The Vehicle Emission Control Information label often reflects specification changes made during production. The label figures must be used if they differ from those in this chart.

B - Before top dead center

HYD - Hydraulic

① Turbo

② Refer to Vehicle Emission Information label

91331C04

The do-it-yourselfer should not service his/her own vehicle's A/C system for many reasons, including legal concerns, personal injury, environmental damage and cost.

According to the U.S. Clean Air Act, it is a federal crime to service or repair (involving the refrigerant) a Motor Vehicle Air Conditioning (MVAC) system for money without being EPA certified. It is also illegal to vent R-12 and R-134a refrigerants into the atmosphere. State and/or local laws may be more strict than the federal regulations, so be sure to check with your state and/or local authorities for further information.

➡ **Federal law dictates that a fine of up to $25,000 may be levied on people convicted of venting refrigerant into the atmosphere.**

When servicing an A/C system you run the risk of handling or coming in contact with refrigerant, which may result in skin or eye irritation or frostbite. Although low in toxicity (due to chemical stability), inhalation of concentrated refrigerant fumes is dangerous and can result in death; cases of fatal cardiac arrhythmia have been reported in people accidentally subjected to high levels of refrigerant. Some early symptoms include loss of concentration and drowsiness.

➡ **Generally, the limit for exposure is lower for R-134a than it is for R-12. Exceptional care must be practiced when handling R-134a.**

Also, some refrigerants can decompose at high temperatures (near gas heaters or open flame), which may result in hydrofluoric acid, hydrochloric acid and phosgene (a fatal nerve gas).

It is usually more economically feasible to have a certified MVAC automotive technician perform A/C system service on your vehicle.

R-12 Refrigerant Conversion

If your vehicle still uses R-12 refrigerant, one way to save A/C system costs down the road is to investigate the possibility of having your system converted to R-134a. The older R-12 systems can be easily converted to R-134a refrigerant by a certified automotive technician by installing a few new components and changing the system oil.

The cost of R-12 is steadily rising and will continue to increase, because it is no longer imported or manufactured in the United States. Therefore, it is often possible to have an R-12 system converted to R-134a and recharged for less than it would cost to just charge the system with R-12.

If you are interested in having your system converted, contact local automotive service stations for more details and information.

PREVENTIVE MAINTENANCE

Although the A/C system should not be serviced by the do-it-yourselfer, preventive maintenance should be practiced to help maintain the efficiency of the vehicle's A/C system. Be sure to perform the following:
- The easiest and most important preventive maintenance for your A/C system is to be sure that it is used on a regular basis. Running the system for five minutes each month (no matter what the season) will help ensure that the seals and all internal components remain lubricated.

➡ **Some vehicles automatically operate the A/C system compressor whenever the windshield defroster is activated. Therefore, the A/C system would not need to be operated each month if the defroster was used.**

- In order to prevent heater core freeze-up during A/C operation, it is necessary to maintain proper antifreeze protection. Be sure to properly maintain the engine cooling system.
- Any obstruction of or damage to the condenser configuration will restrict air flow which is essential to its efficient operation. Keep this unit clean and in proper physical shape.

➡ **Bug screens which are mounted in front of the condenser (unless they are original equipment) are regarded as obstructions.**

- The condensation drain tube expels any water which accumulates on the bottom of the evaporator housing into the engine compartment. If this tube is obstructed, the air conditioning performance can be restricted and condensation buildup can spill over onto the vehicle's floor.

SYSTEM INSPECTION

Although the A/C system should not be serviced by the do-it-yourselfer, system inspections should be performed to help maintain the efficiency of the vehicle's A/C system. Be sure to perform the following:

The easiest and often most important check for the air conditioning system consists of a visual inspection of the system components. Visually inspect the system for refrigerant leaks, damaged compressor clutch, abnormal compressor drive belt tension and/or condition, plugged evaporator drain tube, blocked condenser fins, disconnected or broken wires, blown fuses, corroded connections and poor insulation.

A refrigerant leak will usually appear as an oily residue at the leakage point in the system. The oily residue soon picks up dust or dirt particles from the surrounding air and appears greasy. Through time, this will build up and appear to be a heavy dirt impregnated grease.

For a thorough visual and operational inspection, check the following:
- Check the surface of the radiator and condenser for dirt, leaves or other material which might block air flow.
- Check for kinks in hoses and lines. Check the system for leaks.
- Make sure the drive belt is properly tensioned. During operation, make sure the belt is free of noise or slippage.
- Make sure the blower motor operates at all appropriate positions, then check for distribution of the air from all outlets.

➡ **Remember that in high humidity, air discharged from the vents may not feel as cold as expected, even if the system is working properly. This is because moisture in humid air retains heat more effectively than dry air, thereby making humid air more difficult to cool.**

Windshield Wipers

ELEMENT (REFILL) CARE & REPLACEMENT

▸ **See Figures 111, 112 and 113**

For maximum effectiveness and longest element life, the windshield and wiper blades should be kept clean. Dirt, tree sap, road tar and so on will cause streaking, smearing and blade deterioration if left on the glass. It is advisable to wash the windshield carefully with a commercial glass cleaner at least once a

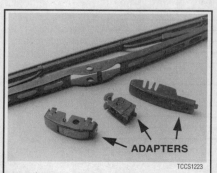

TCCS1223

Fig. 111 Most aftermarket blades are available with multiple adapters to fit different vehicles

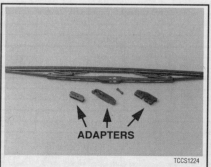

TCCS1224

Fig. 112 Choose a blade which will fit your vehicle, and that will be readily available next time you need blades

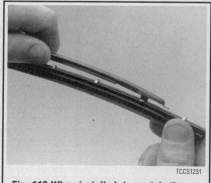

TCCS1231

Fig. 113 When installed, be certain the blade is fully inserted into the backing

month. Wipe off the rubber blades with the wet rag afterwards. Do not attempt to move wipers across the windshield by hand; damage to the motor and drive mechanism will result.

To inspect and/or replace the wiper blade elements, place the wiper switch in the **LOW** speed position and the ignition switch in the **ACC** position. When the wiper blades are approximately vertical on the windshield, turn the ignition switch to **OFF**.

Examine the wiper blade elements. If they are found to be cracked, broken or torn, they should be replaced immediately. Replacement intervals will vary with usage, although ozone deterioration usually limits element life to about one year. If the wiper pattern is smeared or streaked, or if the blade chatters across the glass, the elements should be replaced. It is easiest and most sensible to replace the elements in pairs.

If your vehicle is equipped with aftermarket blades, there are several different types of refills and your vehicle might have any kind. Aftermarket blades and arms rarely use the exact same type blade or refill as the original equipment.

Regardless of the type of refill used, be sure to follow the part manufacturer's instructions closely. Make sure that all of the frame jaws are engaged as the refill is pushed into place and locked. If the metal blade holder and frame are allowed to touch the glass during wiper operation, the glass will be scratched.

Tires and Wheels

Common sense and good driving habits will afford maximum tire life. Make sure that you don't overload the vehicle or run with incorrect pressure in the tires. Either of these will increase tread wear. Fast starts, sudden stops and sharp cornering are hard on tires and will shorten their useful life span.

➡**For optimum tire life, keep the tires properly inflated, rotate them often and have the wheel alignment checked periodically.**

Inspect your tires frequently. Be especially careful to watch for bubbles in the tread or sidewall, deep cuts or underinflation. Replace any tires with bubbles in the sidewall. If cuts are so deep that they penetrate to the cords, discard the tire. Any cut in the sidewall of a radial tire renders it unsafe. Also look for uneven tread wear patterns that may indicate the front end is out of alignment or that the tires are out of balance.

TIRE ROTATION

▶ **See Figure 114**

Tires must be rotated periodically to equalize wear patterns that vary with a tire's position on the vehicle. Tires will also wear in an uneven way as the front steering/suspension system wears to the point where the alignment should be reset.

Rotating the tires will ensure maximum life for the tires as a set, so you will not have to discard a tire early due to wear on only part of the tread. Regular rotation is required to equalize wear.

When rotating "unidirectional tires," make sure that they always roll in the same direction. This means that a tire used on the left side of the vehicle must not be switched to the right side and vice-versa. Such tires should only be rotated front-to-rear or rear-to-front, while always remaining on the same side of the vehicle. These tires are marked on the sidewall as to the direction of rotation; observe the marks when reinstalling the tire(s).

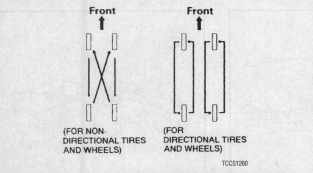

Fig. 114 Compact spare tires must NEVER be used in the rotation pattern

Some styled or "mag" wheels may have different offsets front to rear. In these cases, the rear wheels must not be used up front and vice-versa. Furthermore, if these wheels are equipped with unidirectional tires, they cannot be rotated unless the tire is remounted for the proper direction of rotation.

➡**The compact or space-saver spare is strictly for emergency use. It must never be included in the tire rotation or placed on the vehicle for everyday use.**

TIRE DESIGN

▶ **See Figure 115**

For maximum satisfaction, tires should be used in sets of four. Mixing of different brands or types (radial, bias-belted, fiberglass belted) should be avoided. In most cases, the vehicle manufacturer has designated a type of tire on which the vehicle will perform best. Your first choice when replacing tires should be to use the same type of tire that the manufacturer recommends.

When radial tires are used, tire sizes and wheel diameters should be selected to maintain ground clearance and tire load capacity equivalent to the original specified tire. Radial tires should always be used in sets of four.

✳✳ CAUTION

Radial tires should never be used on only the front axle.

When selecting tires, pay attention to the original size as marked on the tire. Most tires are described using an industry size code sometimes referred to as P-Metric. This allows the exact identification of the tire specifications, regardless of the manufacturer. If selecting a different tire size or brand, remember to check the installed tire for any sign of interference with the body or suspension while the vehicle is stopping, turning sharply or heavily loaded.

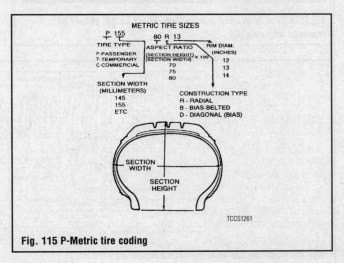

Fig. 115 P-Metric tire coding

Snow Tires

Good radial tires can produce a big advantage in slippery weather, but in snow, a street radial tire does not have sufficient tread to provide traction and control. The small grooves of a street tire quickly pack with snow and the tire behaves like a billiard ball on a marble floor. The more open, chunky tread of a snow tire will self-clean as the tire turns, providing much better grip on snowy surfaces.

To satisfy municipalities requiring snow tires during weather emergencies, most snow tires carry either an M + S designation after the tire size stamped on the sidewall, or the designation "all-season." In general, no change in tire size is necessary when buying snow tires.

Most manufacturers strongly recommend the use of 4 snow tires on their vehicles for reasons of stability. If snow tires are fitted only to the drive wheels, the opposite end of the vehicle may become very unstable when braking or turning on slippery surfaces. This instability can lead to unpleasant endings if the driver can't counteract the slide in time.

Note that snow tires, whether 2 or 4, will affect vehicle handling in all non-snow situations. The stiffer, heavier snow tires will noticeably change the turning and braking characteristics of the vehicle. Once the snow tires are installed, you must re-learn the behavior of the vehicle and drive accordingly.

➥**Consider buying extra wheels on which to mount the snow tires. Once done, the "snow wheels" can be installed and removed as needed. This eliminates the potential damage to tires or wheels from seasonal removal and installation. Even if your vehicle has styled wheels, see if inexpensive steel wheels are available. Although the look of the vehicle will change, the expensive wheels will be protected from salt, curb hits and pothole damage.**

TIRE STORAGE

If they are mounted on wheels, store the tires at proper inflation pressure. All tires should be kept in a cool, dry place. If they are stored in the garage or basement, do not let them stand on a concrete floor; set them on strips of wood, a mat or a large stack of newspaper. Keeping them away from direct moisture is of paramount importance. Tires should not be stored upright, but in a flat position.

INFLATION & INSPECTION

◗ **See Figures 116 thru 121**

The importance of proper tire inflation cannot be overemphasized. A tire employs air as part of its structure. It is designed around the supporting strength of the air at a specified pressure. For this reason, improper inflation drastically reduces the tire's ability to perform as intended. A tire will lose some air in day-to-day use; having to add a few pounds of air periodically is not necessarily a sign of a leaking tire.

Two items should be a permanent fixture in every glove compartment: an accurate tire pressure gauge and a tread depth gauge. Check the tire pressure

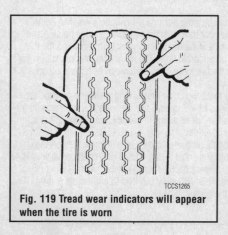

Fig. 116 Tires with deep cuts, or cuts which bulge, should be replaced immediately

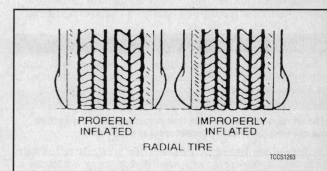

Fig. 117 Radial tires have a characteristic sidewall bulge; don't try to measure pressure by looking at the tire. Use a quality air pressure gauge

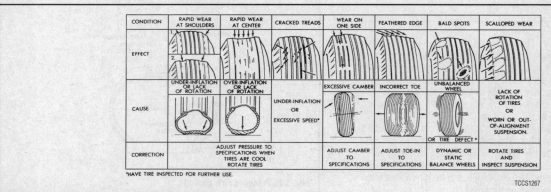

Fig. 118 Common tire wear patterns and causes

Fig. 119 Tread wear indicators will appear when the tire is worn

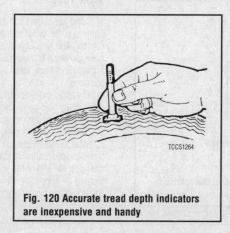

Fig. 120 Accurate tread depth indicators are inexpensive and handy

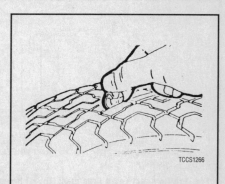

Fig. 121 A penny works well for a quick check of tread depth

(including the spare) regularly with a pocket type gauge. Too often, the gauge on the end of the air hose at your corner garage is not accurate because it suffers too much abuse. Always check tire pressure when the tires are cold, as pressure increases with temperature. If you must move the vehicle to check the tire inflation, do not drive more than a mile before checking. A cold tire is generally one that has not been driven for more than three hours.

A plate or sticker is normally provided somewhere in the vehicle (door post, hood, tailgate or trunk lid) which shows the proper pressure for the tires. Never counteract excessive pressure build-up by bleeding off air pressure (letting some air out). This will cause the tire to run hotter and wear quicker.

❊❊ CAUTION

Never exceed the maximum tire pressure embossed on the tire! This is the pressure to be used when the tire is at maximum loading, but it is rarely the correct pressure for everyday driving. Consult the owner's manual or the tire pressure sticker for the correct tire pressure.

Once you've maintained the correct tire pressures for several weeks, you'll be familiar with the vehicle's braking and handling personality. Slight adjustments in tire pressures can fine-tune these characteristics, but never change the cold pressure specification by more than 2 psi. A slightly softer tire pressure will give a softer ride but also yield lower fuel mileage. A slightly harder tire will give crisper dry road handling but can cause skidding on wet surfaces. Unless you're fully attuned to the vehicle, stick to the recommended inflation pressures.

All automotive tires have built-in tread wear indicator bars that show up as ½ in. (13mm) wide smooth bands across the tire when $\frac{1}{16}$ in. (1.5mm) of tread remains. The appearance of tread wear indicators means that the tires should be replaced. In fact, many states have laws prohibiting the use of tires with less than this amount of tread.

You can check your own tread depth with an inexpensive gauge or by using a Lincoln head penny. Slip the Lincoln penny (with Lincoln's head upside-down) into several tread grooves. If you can see the top of Lincoln's head in 2 adjacent grooves, the tire has less than $\frac{1}{16}$ in. (1.5mm) tread left and should be replaced. You can measure snow tires in the same manner by using the "tails" side of the Lincoln penny. If you can see the top of the Lincoln memorial, it's time to replace the snow tire(s).

FLUIDS AND LUBRICANTS

▶ **See Figures 122 thru 127**

Fluid Disposal

Used fluids such as engine oil, transmission fluid, antifreeze and brake fluid are hazardous wastes and must be disposed of properly. Before draining any fluids, consult with your local authorities; in many areas waste oil, etc. is being accepted as a part of recycling programs. A number of service stations and auto parts stores are also accepting waste fluids for recycling.

Be sure of the recycling center's policies before draining any fluids, as many will not accept different fluids that have been mixed together.

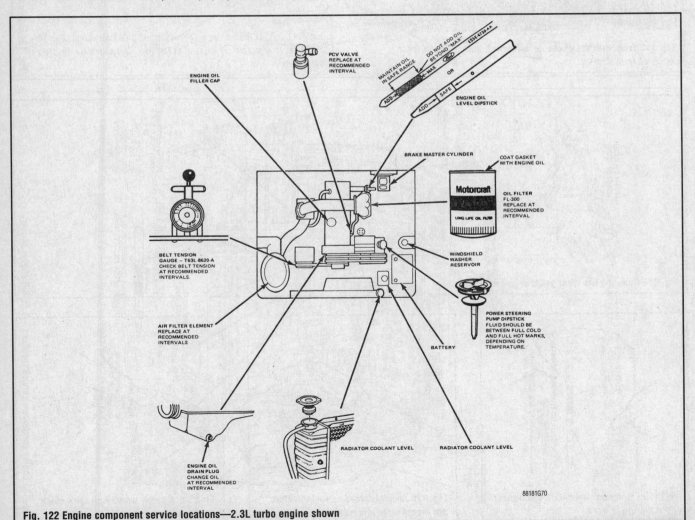

Fig. 122 Engine component service locations—2.3L turbo engine shown

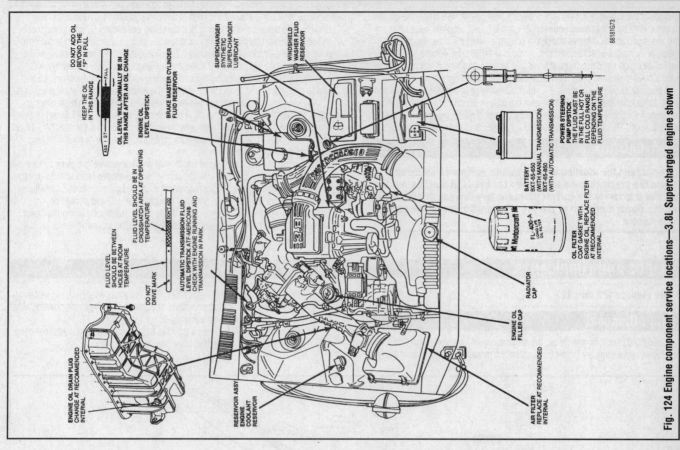

Fig. 124 Engine component service locations—3.8L Supercharged engine shown

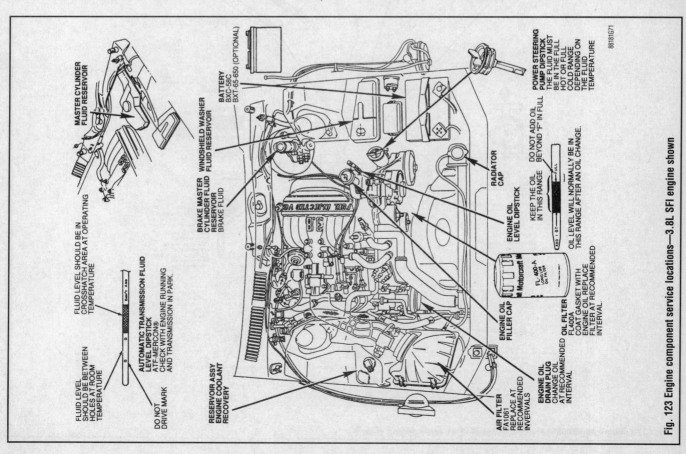

Fig. 123 Engine component service locations—3.8L SFI engine shown

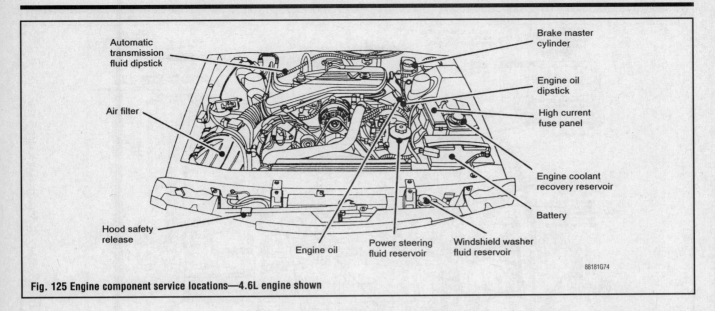

Fig. 125 Engine component service locations—4.6L engine shown

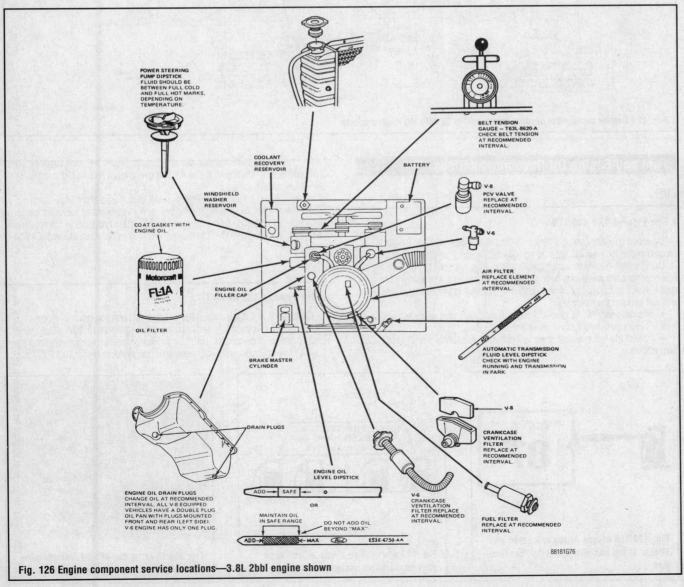

Fig. 126 Engine component service locations—3.8L 2bbl engine shown

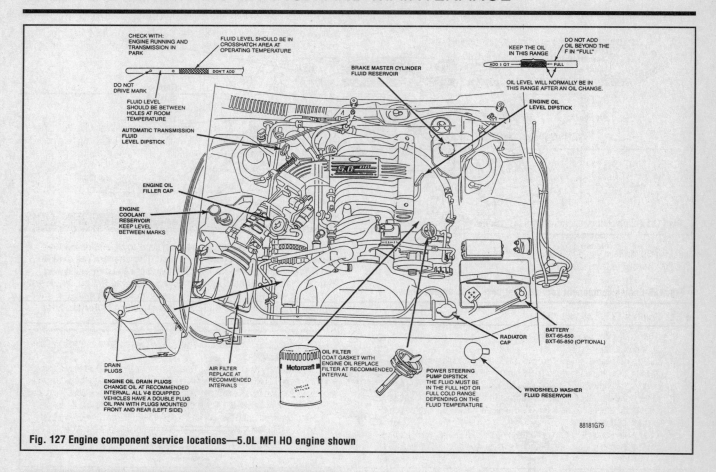

CHECK WITH:
ENGINE RUNNING AND
TRANSMISSION IN
PARK

FLUID LEVEL SHOULD BE IN
CROSSHATCH AREA AT
OPERATING TEMPERATURE

BRAKE MASTER CYLINDER
FLUID RESERVOIR

KEEP THE OIL
IN THIS RANGE

DO NOT ADD
OIL BEYOND THE
F IN "FULL"

DON'T ADD

DO NOT
DRIVE MARK

ADD 1 QT   FULL

OIL LEVEL WILL NORMALLY BE IN
THIS RANGE AFTER AN OIL CHANGE.

FLUID LEVEL
SHOULD BE BETWEEN
HOLES AT ROOM
TEMPERATURE

ENGINE OIL
LEVEL DIPSTICK

AUTOMATIC TRANSMISSION
FLUID
LEVEL DIPSTICK

ENGINE OIL
FILLER CAP

ENGINE
COOLANT
RESERVOIR
KEEP LEVEL
BETWEEN MARKS

BATTERY
BXT-65-650
BXT-65-850 (OPTIONAL)

RADIATOR
CAP

DRAIN
PLUGS

ENGINE OIL DRAIN PLUGS
CHANGE OIL AT RECOMMENDED
INTERVAL. ALL V-8 EQUIPPED
VEHICLES HAVE A DOUBLE PLUG
OIL PAN WITH PLUGS MOUNTED
FRONT AND REAR (LEFT SIDE)

AIR FILTER
REPLACE AT
RECOMMENDED
INTERVALS

OIL FILTER
COAT GASKET WITH
ENGINE OIL REPLACE
FILTER AT RECOMMENDED
INTERVAL

POWER STEERING
PUMP DIPSTICK
THE FLUID MUST BE
IN THE FULL HOT OR
FULL COLD RANGE
DEPENDING ON THE
FLUID TEMPERATURE

WINDSHIELD WASHER
FLUID RESERVOIR

88181G75

Fig. 127 Engine component service locations—5.0L MFI HO engine shown

Fuel and Engine Oil Recommendations

FUEL

▶ **See Figures 128 and 129**

Unleaded gasoline having a Research Octane Number (RON) of 87–91 is recommended for your car. Refer to your owners manual for the exact RON.

Using a high quality unleaded gasoline may help maintain the driveability, fuel economy and emissions performance of your vehicle. A properly formulated gasoline will be comprised of well refined hydrocarbons and chemical additives and will perform the following.

- Minimize varnish, lacquer and other induction system deposits.
- Prevent gum formation or other deterioration.
- Protect the fuel tank and other fuel system components from corrosion or degradation.

- Provide the correct seasonally and geographically adjusted volatility. This will provide easy starting in the winter and avoid vapor lock in the summer. Avoid fuel system icing.

In addition, the fuel will be free of water debris and other impurities. Some driveability deterioration on multi-port electronically fuel injected vehicles can be traced to continuous use of certain gasoline which may have insufficient amounts of detergent additives to provide adequate deposit control protection.

OIL

▶ **See Figures 130 and 131**

Oil meeting API classification SH or latest superceding grade is recommended for use in your vehicle. Viscosity grades 10W-30 or 10W-40 are recommended on 1983 models. On 1984 and later models it is recommended that you use 5W-30 if you drive your vehicle in temperatures below 100°F (37°C)

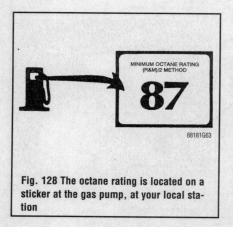

MINIMUM OCTANE RATING
(R&M)/2 METHOD

87

88181G63

Fig. 128 The octane rating is located on a sticker at the gas pump, at your local station

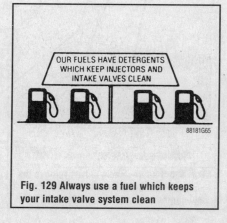

OUR FUELS HAVE DETERGENTS
WHICH KEEP INJECTORS AND
INTAKE VALVES CLEAN

88181G65

Fig. 129 Always use a fuel which keeps your intake valve system clean

API SERVICES SH/CD

SAE
10W-40

ENERGY CONSERVING

API SERVICES
SH/CD,SG,SF,CC

DON'T POLLUTE. CONSERVE RESOURCES.
RETURN USED OIL TO COLLECTION CENTERS

TCCS1235

Fig. 130 Look for the API oil identification label when choosing your engine oil

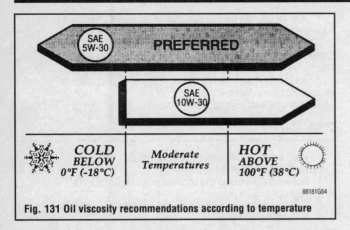

Fig. 131 Oil viscosity recommendations according to temperature

and 10W-30 for when you drive your vehicle in above 100°F (37°C) conditions. See the viscosity-to-temperature illustration in this section.

OIL LEVEL CHECK

▶ See Figures 132, 133 and 134

It is a good idea to check the engine oil each time or at least every other time you fill your gas tank.

1. Be sure your car is on level ground. Shut off the engine and wait for a few minutes to allow the oil to drain back into the oil pan.
2. Remove the engine oil dipstick and wipe clean with a rag.
3. Reinsert the dipstick and push it down until it is fully seated in the tube.
4. Remove the stick and check the oil level shown. If the oil level is below the lower mark, add one quart.
5. If you wish, you may carefully fill the oil pan to the upper mark on the dipstick with less than a full quart. Do not, however, add a full quart when it

would overfill the crankcase (level above the upper mark on the dipstick). The excess oil will generally be consumed at an excessive rate even if no damage to the engine seals occurs.

OIL AND FILTER CHANGE

▶ See Figures 135, 136, 137 and 138

The manufacturer recommends changing the engine oil and oil filter every 3 months or 3000 miles (5000 km). The engine oil and oil filter can be changed at 2000 miles (3200 km) or 2 month intervals if the driving conditions for your vehicle is done through severe dust and dirty conditions. Following these recommended intervals will help keep you car engine in good condition.

1. Make sure the engine is at normal operating temperature (this promotes complete draining of the old oil).

✳✳ CAUTION

The EPA warns that prolonged contact with used engine oil may cause a number of skin disorders, including cancer! You should make every effort to minimize your exposure to used engine oil. Protective gloves should be worn when changing the oil. Wash your hands and any other exposed skin areas as soon as possible after exposure to used engine oil. Soap and water, or waterless hand cleaner should be used.

2. Apply the parking brake and block the wheels or raise and support the car evenly on jackstands.
3. Place a drain pan of about a gallon and a half capacity under the engine oil pan drain plug (DO NOT DRAIN OIL ONTO THE GROUND). Using the proper size wrench, loosen and remove the plug. Allow all the old oil to drain. Wipe the pan and the drain plug with a clean rag. Inspect the drain plug gasket, replace if necessary.
4. Reinstall and tighten the drain plug to 15–25 ft. lbs. (20–34 Nm) on all engines excluding the 4.6L. On the 4.6L engine tighten to 9–11 ft. lbs. (11–16 Nm). DO NOT OVERTIGHTEN.

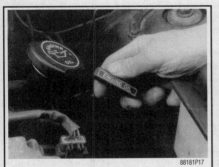

Fig. 132 The engine oil dipstick has the words imprinted on the handle on most vehicles

Fig. 133 To add oil, remove the filler cap . . .

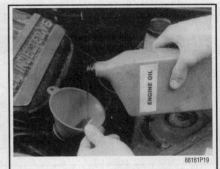

Fig. 134 . . . then using a funnel, top off with the correct type of oil to the crankcase

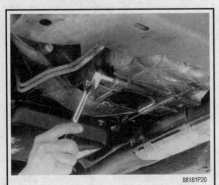

Fig. 135 Locate the oil drain plug and loosen

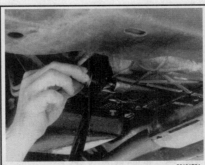

Fig. 136 Stepping back, slowly remove the plug from the oil pan to allow the oil to flow out

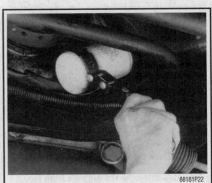

Fig. 137 Using a strap type filter wrench, loosen the old filter

Fig. 138 Before installing a new oil filter, lightly coat the rubber gasket with clean oil

5. Move the drain pan under the engine oil filter. Use a strap wrench and loosen the oil filter (do not remove), allow the oil to drain. Unscrew the filter the rest of the way by hand. Use a rag, if necessary, to keep from burning your fingers. When the filter comes loose from the engine, turn the mounting base upward to avoid spilling the remaining oil.

6. Wipe the engine filter mount clean with a rag. Coat the rubber gasket on the new oil filter with clean engine oil, applying it with a finger. Carefully start the filter onto the threaded engine mount. Turn the filter until it touches the engine mounting surface. Tighten the filter, by hand, ½ turn more or as recommended by the filter manufacturer.

7. Lower the vehicle to the ground. Refill the crankcase with the recommended amount of engine oil. Replace the filler cap and start the engine. Allow the engine to idle and check for oil leaks. Shut off the engine, wait for several minutes, then check the oil level with the dipstick. Add oil if necessary.

➡️**Used oil has been determined to be hazardous to the environment. Recycling oil is the best way for disposal. Check local laws and recycle whenever possible. Store the used oil in a container made for that purpose until you can find a service station or garage that accepts used oil for recycling.**

Manual Transmission

FLUID RECOMMENDATIONS

All of the Thunderbird and Cougar models use Dextrin®II or Mercian® type fluid. A 85W/90 gear oil may be used in the T50D transmission in very warm climates or if gear/bearing noise is excessive.

LEVEL CHECK

The fluid level should be checked every 6 months or 6000 miles (9654 km), whichever comes first.

1. Park the car on a level surface, turn off the engine, apply the parking brake and block the wheels.

2. Remove the filler plug from the side of the transmission case with a proper sized wrench. The fluid level should be even with the bottom of the filler hole.

3. If additional fluid is necessary, add it through the filler hole using a siphon pump or squeeze bottle.

4. Install the filler plug; do not overtighten.

DRAIN AND REFILL

1. Place a suitable drain pan under the transmission.
2. Remove the filler plug.
3. Remove the drain plug and allow the gear lube to drain out.
4. Replace the drain plug.
5. Fill the transmission to the proper level with the required fluid.
6. Reinstall the filler plug.

Automatic Transmissions

FLUID RECOMMENDATIONS

- 1983–86 C3—Dexron®II
- 1983–87 C5—Type H
- 1983–92 AOD—Mercon®/Dexron®II
- 1987–88 A4LD—Mercon®/Dexron®II
- 1994–97 4R70W—Mercon®/Dexron®II

LEVEL CHECK

▸ **See Figures 139, 140 and 141**

It is very important to maintain the proper fluid level in an automatic transmission. If the level is either too high or too low, poor shifting operation and internal damage are likely to occur. For this reason a regular check of the fluid level is essential.

1. Drive the vehicle for 15–20 minutes to allow the transmission to reach operating temperature.

2. Park the car on a level surface, apply the parking brake and leave the engine idling. Shift the transmission and engage each gear, then place the gear selector in **P** (PARK).

3. Wipe away any dirt in the areas of the transmission dipstick to prevent it from falling into the filler tube. Withdraw the dipstick, wipe it with a clean, lint-free rag and reinsert it until it seats.

4. Withdraw the dipstick and note the fluid level. It should be between the upper (FULL) mark and the lower (ADD) mark.

5. If the level is below the lower mark, use a funnel and add fluid in small quantities ½ pint (0.25L) through the dipstick filler neck. Keep the engine running while adding fluid and check the level after each small amount. Do not overfill.

Fig. 139 Withdraw the dipstick from the transmission filler tube

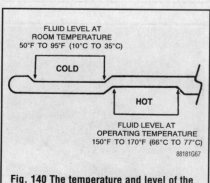

FLUID LEVEL AT
ROOM TEMPERATURE
50°F TO 95°F (10°C TO 35°C)

COLD

HOT

FLUID LEVEL AT
OPERATING TEMPERATURE
150°F TO 170°F (66°C TO 77°C)

Fig. 140 The temperature and level of the fluid determines where it will read on the dipstick

Fig. 141 If necessary, use a funnel to add fluid to the transmission

DRAIN AND REFILL

▶ **See Figures 142, 143, 144, 145 and 146**

1. Raise and safely support the vehicle.
2. Disconnect the fluid filler tube from the pan and allow the fluid to drain into an appropriate container.
3. Remove the transmission oil pan attaching bolts, pan and gasket. Allow the fluid to drain completely into an appropriate container before removing the pan.
4. Discard the old gasket.
5. Once the pan is removed, clean oil pan and mating surfaces.
6. Unscrew the filter from the valve body.
7. Remove the filter with both hands by pulling upwards on most models, then discard.
8. If equipped with a grommet, remove and discard.

➥**Always use a new filter and grommet. Never attempt to reuse or clean the old filter.**

9. Apply a new gasket to the pan.
10. Install a new filter and grommet on the valve body.
11. Attach the pan to the transmission, then tighten the bolts to 10–16 ft. lbs. (13–22 Nm).
12. Lower the vehicle.
13. Fill the transmission with the correct amount and type fluid.
14. Start the engine and move the gear selector through shift pattern. Allow the engine to reach normal operating temperature.
15. Check the transmission fluid. Add fluid, if necessary, to maintain correct level.

Drive Axle

FLUID RECOMMENDATIONS

Like the manual transmission, the rear axle fluid should be checked every six months or 6000 miles (9654 km). A filler plug is provided near the center of the rear cover or on the upper (driveshaft) side of the gear case. Add SAE 85W/90/95 gear lube as required.

LEVEL CHECK

▶ **See Figures 147, 148 and 149**

1. Remove the plug and check to ensure that the fluid level is even with the bottom of the filler hole.
2. Add SAE 85W/90/95 gear lube as required.
3. If the vehicle is equipped with a limited slip rear axle, add the required special fluid.
4. Install the filler plug but do not overtighten.

Fig. 142 Remove the oil pan mounting bolts

Fig. 143 Carefully pry the pan to break loose the seal

Fig. 144 Lower the pan and allow the fluid to drain

Fig. 145 Unscrew the filter from the transmission valve body

Fig. 146 Discard the old filter once removed

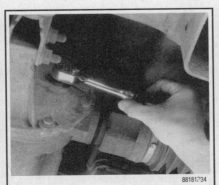

Fig. 147 Use a proper sized ratchet to loosen the filler plug

Fig. 148 If necessary, add the proper fluid through the filler hole

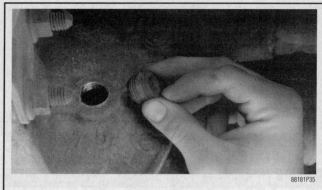

Fig. 149 When installing the plug, first thread it in by hand

88181P35

DRAIN AND REFILL

Normal maintenance does not require changing the rear axle fluid. However, to do so, remove the rear drain plug (models equipped), the lower two cover bolts, or the cover. Catch the drained fluid in a suitable container.

If the rear cover was removed, clean the mounting surfaces of the cover and rear housing. Install a new gasket (early models) or (on late models) apply a continuous bead of Silicone Rubber Sealant (D6AZ–19562–AA or BA or the equivalent) around the rear housing face inside the circle of bolt holes. Install the cover and tighten the bolts to specifications. Parts must be assembled within a half hour after the sealant is applied. If the fluid was drained by removing the two lower cover bolts, apply sealant to the bolts before reinstallation. Fill the rear axle through the filler hole with the proper lube. Add friction modifier to limited slip models if required.

Cooling System

FLUID RECOMMENDATIONS

When additional coolant is required to maintain the proper level, always add a 50/50 mixture of antifreeze/coolant and water.

LEVEL CHECK

▶ See Figures 150 and 151

✳✳ CAUTION

Exercise extreme care when removing the cap from a hot radiator. Wait a few minutes until the engine has time to cool somewhat, then wrap a thick towel around the radiator cap and slowly turn it counterclockwise to the first stop. Step back and allow the pressure

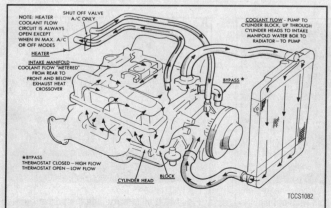

NOTE: HEATER
COOLANT FLOW
CIRCUIT IS ALWAYS
OPEN EXCEPT
WHEN IN MAX. A/C
OR OFF MODES

SHUT OFF VALVE
A/C ONLY

HEATER

INTAKE MANIFOLD
COOLANT FLOW "METERED"
FROM REAR TO
FRONT AND BELOW
EXHAUST HEAT
CROSSOVER

COOLANT FLOW - PUMP TO
CYLINDER BLOCK, UP THROUGH
CYLINDER HEADS TO INTAKE
MANIFOLD WATER BOX TO
RADIATOR - TO PUMP

BYPASS ★

★BYPASS
THERMOSTAT CLOSED – HIGH FLOW
THERMOSTAT OPEN – LOW FLOW

CYLINDER HEAD   BLOCK

TCCS1082

Fig. 150 Cutaway view of a typical cooling system flow

TCCS1083

Fig. 151 Cooling systems should be pressure tested for leaks periodically

to release from the cooling system. Then, when the steam has stopped venting, press down on the cap, turn it one more stop counterclockwise and remove the cap.

The coolant level in the radiator should be checked on a monthly basis, preferably when the engine is cold. On a cold engine, the coolant level should be maintained at one inch below the filler neck on vertical flow radiators, and 2½ in. (63.5mm) below the filler neck at the **COLD FILL** mark on crossflow radiators. On the Coolant Recovery System, the level is maintained at the **COLD LEVEL** mark in the translucent plastic expansion bottle. Top up as necessary with a mixture of 50% water and 50% ethylene glycol antifreeze, to ensure proper rust, freezing and boiling protection. If you have to add coolant more often than once a month or if you have to add more than one quart at a time, check the cooling system for leads. Also check for water in the crankcase oil, indicating a blown cylinder head gasket.

DRAIN, FLUSH AND REFILL

▶ See Figures 152, 153 and 154

✳✳ CAUTION

When draining the coolant, keep in mind that cats and dogs are attracted by the ethylene glycol antifreeze, and are quite likely to drink any that is left in an uncovered container or in puddles on the ground. This will prove fatal in sufficient quantity. Always drain the coolant into a sealable container. Coolant should be reused unless it is contaminated or several years old.

Completely draining and refilling the cooling system every two years at least will remove accumulated rust, scale and other deposits.

➡Use a good quality antifreeze with water pump lubricants, rust inhibitors and other corrosion inhibitors along with acid neutralizers. Use a permanent type coolant that meets specification ESE–M97B44A or the equivalent.

1. Remove the radiator cap to relieve the pressure.
2. Drain the existing antifreeze and coolant. Open the radiator and engine drain petcocks (models equipped), or disconnect the bottom radiator hose, at the radiator outlet. Set the heater temperature controls to the full HOT position.

➡Before opening the radiator petcock, spray it with some penetrating lubricant.

3. Close the petcock or reconnect the lower hose and fill the system with water.
4. Add a can of quality radiator flush. If applicable, be sure the flush is safe to use in engines having aluminum components.
5. Idle the engine until the upper radiator hose gets hot.
6. Drain the system again.
7. Repeat this process until the drained water is clear and free of scale.
8. Close all petcocks and connect all the hoses.
9. If equipped with a coolant recovery system, flush the reservoir with water and leave empty.

Fig. 152 Remove the radiator cap

88181P32

88181P31

Fig. 153 Slowly turn the petcock at the bottom of the radiator to release the water/coolant mixture

88181P33

Fig. 154 While the engine is running, top off the coolant level

10. Determine the capacity of your cooling system (see the capacity specification chart). Add a 50/50 mix of quality antifreeze (ethylene glycol) and water to provide the desired protection.

11. After adding the appropriate amount of coolant and water, start the engine. Add more fluid to top off while the engine is running.

SYSTEM INSPECTION

Most permanent antifreeze/coolant have a colored dye added which makes the solution an excellent leak detector. When servicing the cooling system, check for leakage at:

- All hoses and hose connections
- Radiator seams, radiator core, and radiator draincock
- All engine block and cylinder head freeze (core) plugs, and drain plugs
- Edges of all cooling system gaskets (head gaskets, thermostat gasket)
- Transmission fluid cooler
- Heating system components, water pump
- Check the engine oil dipstick for signs of coolant in the engine oil
- Check the coolant in the radiator for signs of oil in the coolant

Investigate and correct any indication of coolant leakage.

Check the Radiator Cap

▶ See Figure 155

While you are checking the coolant level, check the radiator cap for a worn or cracked gasket. If the cap doesn't seal properly, fluid will be lost and the engine will overheat.

A worn cap should be replaced with a new one.

Clean Radiator of Debris

▶ See Figure 156

Periodically clean any debris such as leaves, paper, insects, etc., from the radiator fins. Pick the large pieces off by hand. The smaller pieces can be washed away with water pressure from a hose.

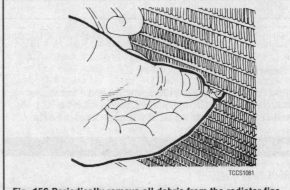

TCCS1081

Fig. 156 Periodically remove all debris from the radiator fins

Carefully straighten any bent radiator fins with a pair of needle nose pliers. Be careful, the fins are very soft. Don't wiggle the fins back and forth too much. Straighten them once and try not to move them again.

CHECKING SYSTEM PROTECTION

A 50/50 mix of coolant concentrate and water will usually provide protection to –35°F (–37°C). Freeze protection may be checked by using a cooling system hydrometer. Inexpensive hydrometers (floating ball types) may be obtained from a local department store (automotive section) or an auto supply store. Follow the directions packaged with the coolant hydrometer when checking protection.

Brake Master Cylinder

FLUID RECOMMENDATIONS

Use only Heavy Duty Brake Fluid meeting DOT 3 specifications on the brake master cylinder.

LEVEL CHECK

The fluid in the brake master cylinder should be checked every 6 months or 6000 miles (9600 km).

Cast Iron Reservoir

1. Park the vehicle on a level surface and open the hood.
2. Pry the retaining spring bar holding the cover onto the master cylinder to one side.
3. Clean any dirt from the sides and top of the cover before removal. Remove the master cylinder cover and gasket.
4. Add fluid, if necessary, to within ⅜ in. (10mm) of the top of the reservoir, or to the full level indicator (on models equipped).

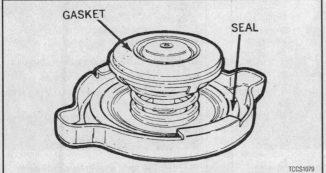

GASKET

SEAL

TCCS1079

Fig. 155 Be sure the rubber gasket on the radiator cap has a tight seal

5. Push the gasket bellows back into the cover. Reinstall the gasket and cover and position the retainer spring bar.

Plastic Reservoir

▶ See Figure 157

Check the fluid level on the side of the reservoir. If fluid is required, remove the filler cap and gasket from the reservoir. Fill the reservoir to the FULL line. Install the filler cap, making sure the gasket is properly seated in the cap.

Clutch Master Cylinder

FLUID RECOMMENDATIONS

Use only Heavy Duty Brake Fluid meeting DOT 3 specifications on the clutch master cylinder.

LEVEL CHECK

The fluid in the clutch master cylinder should be checked every 30,000 miles (50,000 km).

Plastic Reservoir

Check the fluid level on the side of the reservoir. If fluid is required, remove the filler cap and gasket from the reservoir. Fill the reservoir to the FULL line. Install the filler cap, making sure the gasket is properly seated in the cap.

Power Steering

FLUID RECOMMENDATION

Add power steering fluid; E6AZ-19582-AA or equivalent.

LEVEL CHECK

▶ See Figures 158 and 159

Check the power steering fluid level every 6 months or 6,000 miles (9600 km).
1. Park the vehicle on a level surface. Run the engine until normal operating temperature is reached.
2. Turn the steering all the way to the left and then all the way to the right several times. Center the steering wheel and shut off the engine.
3. Open the hood and check the power steering reservoir fluid level.
4. Remove the filler cap and wipe the dipstick attached clean.
5. Re-insert the dipstick and tighten the cap. Remove the dipstick and note the fluid level indicated on the dipstick.
6. The level should be at any point below the FULL mark, but not below the ADD mark.
7. Add fluid as necessary. Do not overfill.

Chassis Greasing

▶ See Figure 160

BALL JOINTS

Ford does not require the ball joints to be lubricated on these models.

TIE ROD ENDS

Apply a small amount of chassis grease to the tie rods ends and check for wear.

CLUTCH LINKAGE

On models so equipped, apply a small amount of chassis grease to the pivot points of the clutch linkage.

AUTOMATIC TRANSMISSION LINKAGE

On models so equipped, apply a small amount of 10W engine oil to the kick-down and shift linkage at the pivot points.

PARKING BRAKE LINKAGE

At yearly intervals or whenever binding is noticeable in the parking brake linkage, lubricate the cable guides, levers and linkage with a suitable chassis grease.

Body Lubrication and Maintenance

CARE OF YOUR VEHICLE

Glass Surfaces

All glass surfaces should be kept clean at all times for safe driving. You should use a window cleaner, the same cleaner you use on windows in your home. Use caution and never use an abrasive cleaners, this will cause scratching to the window surfaces.

Exterior Care

Your car is exposed to all kinds of corrosive effects from nature and chemicals. Some of these are road salt, oils, rain, hail and sleet just to name a few. To protect not only the paint and trim, but also the many exposed mounts and fixtures, it is important to wash your vehicle often and thoroughly. After washing, allow all surfaces to drain and dry before parking in a closed garage. Washing may not clean all deposits off your car, so you may need additional cleaners. When using professional cleaners, make sure they are suitable for enamel/acrylic painted surfaces, chrome, tires etc.. These supplies can be purchased in your local auto parts store. You also should wax and polish your vehicle every few months to keep the paint in good shape.

Fig. 157 Always use a funnel to avoid spilling the brake fluid

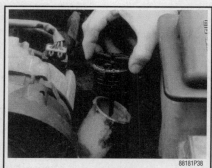

Fig. 158 Remove the filler cap and wipe the dipstick clean, then reinsert and read the level

Fig. 159 The level should be at any point below the FULL/MAX mark, but not below the ADD/MIN mark

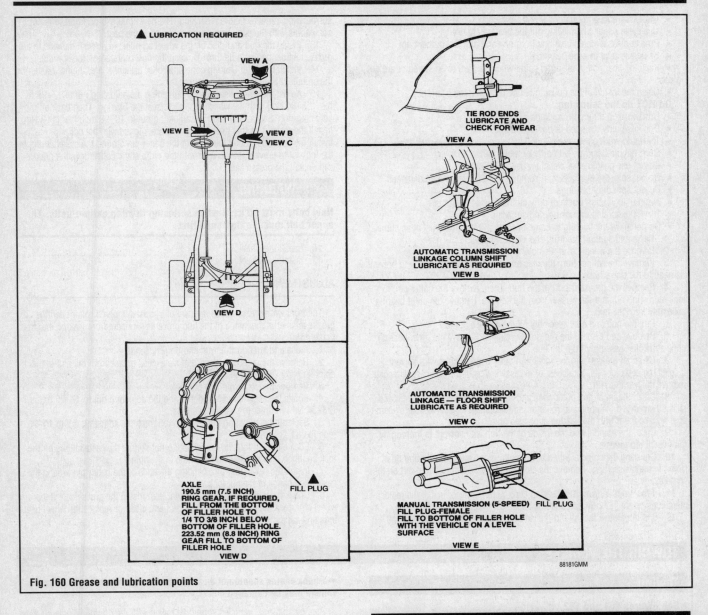

Fig. 160 Grease and lubrication points

LOCK CYLINDERS

Apply graphite lubricant sparingly through the key slot. Insert the key and operate the lock several times to be sure that the lubricant is worked into the lock cylinder.

DOOR HINGES & HINGE CHECKS

Spray a silicone lubricant on the hinge pivot points to eliminate any binding conditions. Open and close the door several times to be sure that the lubricant is evenly and thoroughly distributed.

TRUNK LID

Spray a silicone lubricant on all of the pivot and friction surfaces to eliminate any squeaks or binds. Work the trunk lid to distribute the lubricant

BODY DRAIN HOLES

Be sure that the drain holes in the doors and rocker panels are cleared of obstruction. A small screwdriver can be used to clear them of any debris.

Front Wheel Bearings

→On the 1989–97 models, the front wheel bearings are of an integral hub/bearing design and are pregreased, sealed and require no scheduled maintenance. The bearings are preset and cannot be adjusted. If a bearing replacement is required for any repair, the hub and bearing must be replaced as an assembly. The bearings cannot be disassembled from the hub and serviced separately. No individual service seals, roller or races are available. The hub nut torque of 225–254 ft. lbs. (305–345 Nm), restricts bearing/hub relative movement and maintains axial position of the hub. For more information on this hub assembly removal, refer to Section 8 of this manual.

REMOVAL, REPACKING, & INSTALLATION

Before handling the bearings, there are a few things that you should remember to do and not to do.
Remember to DO the following:
- Remove all outside dirt from the housing before exposing the bearing.
- Treat a used bearing as gently as you would a new one.
- Work with clean tools in clean surroundings.
- Use clean, dry canvas gloves, or at least clean, dry hands.

- Clean solvents and flushing fluids are a must.
- Use clean paper when laying out the bearings to dry.
- Protect disassembled bearings from rust and dirt. Cover them up.
- Use clean rags to wipe bearings.
- Keep the bearings in oil-proof paper when they are to be stored or are not in use.
- Clean the inside of the housing before replacing the bearing.

Do NOT do the following:

- Don't work in dirty surroundings.
- Don't use dirty, chipped or damaged tools.
- Try not to work on wooden work benches or use wooden mallets.
- Don't handle bearings with dirty or moist hands.
- Do not use gasoline for cleaning; use a safe solvent.
- Do not spin-dry bearings with compressed air. They will be damaged.
- Do not spin dirty bearings.
- Avoid using cotton waste or dirty cloths to wipe bearings.
- Try not to scratch or nick bearing surfaces.
- Do not allow the bearing to come in contact with dirt or rust at any time.

1. Raise and support the front end on jackstands.
2. Remove the wheel cover. Remove the wheel.
3. Remove the caliper from the disc and wire it to the underbody to prevent damage to the brake hose.
4. Remove the grease cap from the hub. Then, remove the cotter pin, nut lock, adjusting nut and flat washer from the spindle. Remove the outer bearing assembly from the hub.
5. Pull the hub and disc assembly off the wheel spindle.
6. Remove and discard the old grease retainer. Remove the inner bearing cone and roller assembly from the hub.
7. Clean all grease from the inner and outer bearing cups with solvent. Inspect the cups for pits, scratches, or excessive wear. If the cups are damaged, remove them with a drift.
8. Clean the inner and outer cone and roller assemblies with solvent and shake them dry. If the cone and roller assemblies show excessive wear or damage, replace them with the bearing cups as a unit.
9. Clean the spindle and the inside of the hub with solvent to thoroughly remove all old grease.
10. Covering the spindle with a clean cloth, brush all loose dirt and dust from the brake assembly. Remove the cloth carefully so as to not get dirt on the spindle.
11. If the inner and/or outer bearing cups were removed, install the replacement cups on the hub. Be sure that the cups seat properly in the hub.
12. It is imperative that all old grease be removed from the bearings and surrounding surfaces before repacking. The new lithium-based grease is not compatible with the sodium base grease used in the past.
13. Install the hub and disc on the wheel spindle. To prevent damage to the grease retainer and spindle threads, keep the hub centered on the spindle.
14. Install the outer bearing cone and roller assembly and the flat washer on the spindle. Install the adjusting nut.
15. Adjust the wheel bearings by tightening the adjusting nut to 17–25 ft. lbs. (23–34 Nm) with the wheel rotating to seat the bearing. Then back off the adjusting nut ½ turn. Retighten the adjusting nut to 10–28 inch lbs. (1–3 Nm). Install the locknut so that the castellations are aligned with the cotter pin hole. Install the cotter pin. Bend the ends of the cotter pin around the castellations of the locknut to prevent interference with the radio static collector in the grease cap. Install the grease cap.

❋❋ WARNING

New bolts must be used when servicing floating caliper units. The upper bolt must be tightened first.

16. Install the wheels.
17. Install the wheel cover.

ADJUSTMENT

The front wheels each rotate on a set of opposed, tapered roller bearings. The grease retainer at the inside of the hub prevents lubricant from leaking into the brake drum.

1. Raise and support the front end on jackstands.
2. Remove the grease cap and remove excess grease from the end of the spindle.
3. Remove the cotter pin and nut lock.
4. Rotate the assembly while tightening the adjusting nut to 17–25 ft. lbs. (23–34 Nm) in order to seat the bearings.
5. Back off the adjusting nut ½, then retighten the adjusting nut to 10–28 inch lbs. (1–3 Nm).
6. Locate the nut lock on the adjusting nut so that the castellations on the lock are lined up with the cotter pin hole in the spindle.
7. Install the new cotter pin, bending the ends of the cotter pin around the castellated flange of the nut lock.
8. Check the wheel for proper rotation, then install the grease cap. If the wheel still does not rotate properly, inspect and clean or replace the wheel bearings and cups.

TOWING THE VEHICLE

Towing

▶ **See Figures 161 and 162**

Whenever you are towing another vehicle, or being towed, make sure the chain or strap is sufficiently long and strong. Attach the chain securely at a point on the frame, shipping tie-down slots are provided on the front and rear of you car and should be used. Never attach a chain or strap to any steering or suspension part. Never try to start the vehicle when being towed, it might run into the back of the tow car. Do not allow too much slack in the tow line, the towed car could run over the line and damage to both cars could occur. If you car is being towed by a tow truck, the towing speed should be limited to 50 mph (80 km/h) with the driving wheels off the ground. If it is necessary to tow the car with the drive wheels on the ground, speed should be limited to no more then 35 mph (56 km/h) and the towing distance should not be greater than 50 miles (80 km).

Your vehicle may be towed by a wrecker from the front or rear as outlined in the following paragraphs. A 4 in. (102mm) x 4 in. (102mm) x 48 in. (122cm) wood pacer blocks and T-hook chains are required for proper towing to prevent damage to your vehicle. This equipment is commonly found on commercial wreckers. For flatbed towing, T-hook chains are required to prevent damage to the driveline or suspension components.

➡**J-hook chains should not be used under any circumstances or your vehicle may be damaged.**

As a general rule, vehicles should be towed with the driving wheels off the ground. To tow your vehicle in this manner, release the parking brake and place the transmission shift lever in the **NEUTRAL** position. Towing speed is limited to 50 mph (80 km/h) on smooth roads and 35 mph (56 km/h) on rough roads.

If it is necessary to tow a vehicle with an automatic transmission with the driving wheels on the ground, the transmission must be in proper working order. To tow your vehicle in this manner release the parking brake, place the shift lever in the **NEUTRAL** position and clamp the steering wheel in the straight ahead position with a steering wheel clamping device designed for towing service use. Do not exceed 35 mph (56 km/h) and a distance of 50 miles (80 km) or transmission damage could result.

If it is necessary to tow a vehicle with a manual transmission with the driving wheels on the ground, do not exceed 55 mph (88 km/h) but the distance is not limited. When ever towing from the rear, chains must not be attached forward of rear suspension arms or directly to the rear suspension arms. This could result in vehicle damage.

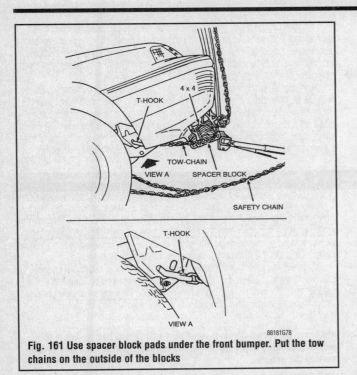

Fig. 161 Use spacer block pads under the front bumper. Put the tow chains on the outside of the blocks

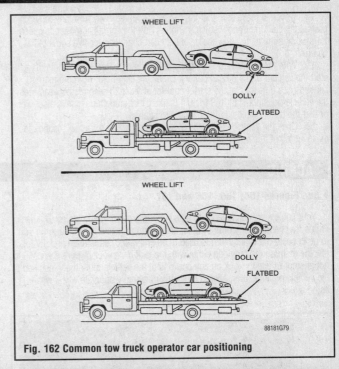

Fig. 162 Common tow truck operator car positioning

JUMP STARTING A DEAD BATTERY

▶ **See Figure 163**

Whenever a vehicle is jump started, precautions must be followed in order to prevent the possibility of personal injury. Remember that batteries contain a small amount of explosive hydrogen gas which is a by-product of battery charging. Sparks should always be avoided when working around batteries, especially when attaching jumper cables. To minimize the possibility of accidental sparks, follow the procedure carefully.

❈❈ CAUTION

NEVER hook the batteries up in a series circuit or the entire electrical system will go up in smoke, especially the starter!

Jump Starting Precautions

- Be sure that both batteries are of the same voltage. Vehicles covered by this manual and most vehicles on the road today utilize a 12 volt charging system.
- Be sure that both batteries are of the same polarity (have the same terminal, in most cases NEGATIVE grounded).
- Be sure that the vehicles are not touching or a short could occur.
- On serviceable batteries, be sure the vent cap holes are not obstructed.

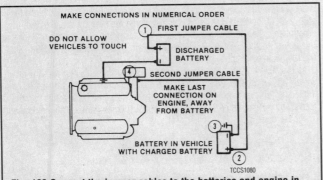

Fig. 163 Connect the jumper cables to the batteries and engine in the order shown

- Do not smoke or allow sparks anywhere near the batteries.
- In cold weather, make sure the battery electrolyte is not frozen. This can occur more readily in a battery that has been in a state of discharge.
- Do not allow electrolyte to contact your skin or clothing.

Jump Starting Procedure

1. Make sure that the voltages of the 2 batteries are the same. Most batteries and charging systems are of the 12 volt variety.
2. Pull the jumping vehicle (with the good battery) into a position so the jumper cables can reach the dead battery and that vehicle's engine. Make sure that the vehicles do NOT touch.
3. Place the transmissions/transaxles of both vehicles in **Neutral** (MT) or **P** (AT), as applicable, then firmly set their parking brakes.

➡ **If necessary for safety reasons, the hazard lights on both vehicles may be operated throughout the entire procedure without significantly increasing the difficulty of jumping the dead battery.**

4. Turn all lights and accessories OFF on both vehicles. Make sure the ignition switches on both vehicles are turned to the **OFF** position.
5. Cover the battery cell caps with a rag, but do not cover the terminals.
6. Make sure the terminals on both batteries are clean and free of corrosion or proper electrical connection will be impeded. If necessary, clean the battery terminals before proceeding.
7. Identify the positive (+) and negative (−) terminals on both batteries.
8. Connect the first jumper cable to the positive (+) terminal of the dead battery, then connect the other end of that cable to the positive (+) terminal of the booster (good) battery.
9. Connect one end of the other jumper cable to the negative (−) terminal on the booster battery and the final cable clamp to an engine bolt head, alternator bracket or other solid, metallic point on the engine with the dead battery. Try to pick a ground on the engine that is positioned away from the battery in order to minimize the possibility of the 2 clamps touching should one loosen during the procedure. DO NOT connect this clamp to the negative (−) terminal of the bad battery.

❈❈ CAUTION

Be very careful to keep the jumper cables away from moving parts (cooling fan, belts, etc.) on both engines.

10. Check to make sure that the cables are routed away from any moving parts, then start the donor vehicle's engine. Run the engine at moderate speed for several minutes to allow the dead battery a chance to receive some initial charge.

11. With the donor vehicle's engine still running slightly above idle, try to start the vehicle with the dead battery. Crank the engine for no more than 10 seconds at a time and let the starter cool for at least 20 seconds between tries. If the vehicle does not start in 3 tries, it is likely that something else is also wrong or that the battery needs additional time to charge.

12. Once the vehicle is started, allow it to run at idle for a few seconds to make sure that it is operating properly.

13. Turn ON the headlights, heater blower and, if equipped, the rear defroster of both vehicles in order to reduce the severity of voltage spikes and subsequent risk of damage to the vehicles' electrical systems when the cables are disconnected. This step is especially important to any vehicle equipped with computer control modules.

14. Carefully disconnect the cables in the reverse order of connection. Start with the negative cable that is attached to the engine ground, then the negative cable on the donor battery. Disconnect the positive cable from the donor battery and finally, disconnect the positive cable from the formerly dead battery. Be careful when disconnecting the cables from the positive terminals not to allow the alligator clips to touch any metal on either vehicle or a short and sparks will occur.

JACKING

♦ **See Figures 164, 165, 166 and 167**

Your vehicle was supplied with a jack for emergency road repairs. This jack is fine for changing a flat tire or other short term procedures not requiring you to go beneath the vehicle. If it is used in an emergency situation, carefully follow the instructions provided either with the jack or in your owner's manual. Do not attempt to use the jack on any portions of the vehicle other than specified by the vehicle manufacturer. Always block the diagonally opposite wheel when using a jack.

A more convenient way of jacking is the use of a garage or floor jack. You may use the floor jack at the specified points shown in following the illustrations.

Never place the jack under the radiator, engine or transmission components. Severe and expensive damage will result when the jack is raised. Additionally, never jack under the floorpan or bodywork; the metal will deform.

Whenever you plan to work under the vehicle, you must support it on jackstands or ramps. Never use cinder blocks or stacks of wood to support the vehicle, even if you're only going to be under it for a few minutes. Never crawl under the vehicle when it is supported only by the tire-changing jack or other floor jack.

➡**Always position a block of wood or small rubber pad on top of the jack or jackstand to protect the lifting point's finish when lifting or supporting the vehicle.**

Small hydraulic, screw, or scissors jacks are satisfactory for raising the vehicle. Drive-on trestles or ramps are also a handy and safe way to both raise

Fig. 164 Place a floor jack in the center under the rear axle to raise the rear end

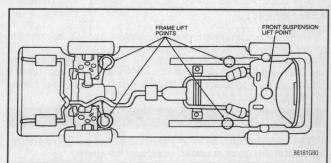

Fig. 166 These five area points are recommended to support the vehicle for jacking purposes

Fig. 165 A floor jack can also be placed on either side of the rear under the coil springs

Fig. 167 Using a safety stand in conjunction with a floor jack is highly recommended

and support the vehicle. Be careful though, some ramps may be too steep to drive your vehicle onto without scraping the front bottom panels. Never support the vehicle on any suspension member (unless specifically instructed to do so by a repair manual) or by an underbody panel.

Jacking Precautions

The following safety points cannot be overemphasized:
- Always block the opposite wheel or wheels to keep the vehicle from rolling off the jack.

- When raising the front of the vehicle, firmly apply the parking brake.
- When the drive wheels are to remain on the ground, leave the vehicle in gear to help prevent it from rolling.
- Always use jackstands to support the vehicle when you are working underneath. Place the stands beneath the vehicle's jacking brackets. Before climbing underneath, rock the vehicle a bit to make sure it is firmly supported.

1983-88 MAINTENANCE SCHEDULE

SCHEDULE 1 — UNIQUE DRIVING CONDITIONS — GASOLINE ENGINES

Follow this Schedule if your driving habits FREQUENTLY include:

- Operating when outside temperatures remain **below freezing** and most trips are less than 5 miles (8 km).
- Operating during HOT WEATHER (above 90°F, 32°C) and:
  — Driving continuously in excess of normal highway speeds;
  — Driving in stop-and-go "rush hour" traffic.
- Towing a trailer, using a camper or car-top carrier or otherwise carryng heavy loads.
- Operating in severe dust conditions.
- Extensive idling, such as police, taxi or door-to-door delivery use.

SERVICE INTERVAL Perform at the months or distances shown, whichever comes first. Miles × 1000 / Kilometers × 1000	3 / 4.8	6 / 9.6	9 / 14.4	12 / 19.2	15 / 24	18 / 28.8	21 / 33.6	24 / 38.4	27 / 43.2	30 / 48	33 / 52.8	36 / 57.6	39 / 62.4	42 / 67.2	45 / 72	48 / 76.8
EMISSION CONTROL SERVICE																
Change Engine Oil (every 3 months) or	X	X	X	X	X	X	X	X	X	X	X	X	X	X	X	X
Change Engine Oil Filter (every 3 months) or	X	X	X	X	X	X	X	X	X	X	X	X	X	X	X	X
Spark Plugs: Check/Regap (All)		X		X		X		X				X		X		X
Replace (Non-Turbo)										X						
Turbocharged Only-Replace					(X)					X					(X)	
Inspect Accessory Drive Belt(s)										X						
Check/Lube Exhaust Control Valve (if equipped)		(X)								(X)					(X)	
Replace Air Cleaner Filter (1)										X						
Replace Crankcase Emission Filter (1)										X						
Replace EGR Solenoid Filter (Six Cylinder 3.8L Engine Only)										X						
Check/Clean Choke Linkage — If Equipped										X						
Replace Engine Coolant, Check Hoses and Clamps EVERY 36 Months OR										X						
Check Engine Coolant Protection	ANNUALLY															
GENERAL MAINTENANCE																
Inspect Exhaust Heat Shields										X						
Change Automatic Transmission Fluid (2)										X						
Lubricate Steering and/or Suspension Linkage (All Cars)										X						
Lubricate Steering Linkage					X									X		

(1) If operating in severe dust, ask your dealer for proper replacement intervals.

(2) If your vehicle accumulates 5,000 miles (8 000 km) or more per month or is used in CONTINUOUS stop and go service, change every 30,000 miles (48 000 km) — not necessary for severe dust, short trips or extensive idling.

(X) All items with either a "X" or a "(X)" code are required t be performed in all states except California. For cars sold in California, only "X" items are REQUIRED to be performed. However, Ford recommends that you also perform maintenance on items designated by an "(X)" in order to achieve best vehicle operation.

88181C08

1983-88 MAINTENANCE SCHEDULE

SCHEDULE 2 — NORMAL DRIVING CONDITIONS — GASOLINE ENGINES

Follow this Schedule if, generally, you drive your vehicle on a daily basis for several miles and NONE OF THE UNIQUE DRIVING CONDITIONS SHOWN IN SCHEDULE I APPLY TO YOUR DRIVING HABITS.

SERVICE INTERVALS Perform at the months or distances shown, whichever comes first.	Miles x 1000	7.5	15	22.5	30	37.5	45	52.5	60
	Kilometers x 1000	12	24	36	48	60	72	84	96
EMISSIONS CONTROL SERVICE									
Four Cylinder Change Engine Oil (Every 12 Months) or		X	X	X	X	X	X	X	X
Change Oil Filter (Every 12 Months) or		X	X	X	X	X	X	X	X
Six and Eight Cylinders Change Engine Oil (Every 12 Months) or		X	X	X	X	X	X	X	X
Change Oil Filter (Every 12 Months) or		X		X		X		X	
Turbocharged Engines Change Spark Plugs			(X)		X		(X)		X
Change Oil and Filter		(EVERY 5,000 MILES (8 000 km))							
(ALL ENGINES)									
Replace Spark Plugs					X				X
Inspect Accessory Drive Belt(s) TURBOCHARGED ONLY					X				X
Inspect Accessory Drive Belt(s)					X				X
Replace EGR Vacuum Solenoid Filter 3.8L									X
Check/Lube Exhaust Control Valve (if equipped)		(X)			(X)		(X)		(X)
Change Crankcase Emission Filter					X				X
Replace Air Cleaner Filter					X				X
Check/Clean Choke Linkage					X				X
Change Engine Coolant Every 36 Months or					X				X
Check Engine Coolant Protection		ANNUALLY							
GENERAL MAINTENANCE									
Check Exhaust Heat Shields					X				X
Lube Steering and/or Suspension					X				X

(X) All items with either an "X" or an "(X)" code are required to be performed in all states except California. For cars sold in California, only "X" items are REQUIRED to be performed. However, Ford recommends that you also perform maintenance on items designated by an "(X)" in order to achieve best vehicle operation.

88181C55

1989-97 MAINTENANCE SCHEDULE

SCHEDULE A

Follow this Schedule if your driving habits MAINLY include one or more of the following conditions:

- Short trips of less than 16 km (10 miles) when outside temperatures remain below freezing.
- Operating during HOT WEATHER
  — Driving in stop-and-go "rush hour" traffic.
- Towing a trailer, using a car-top carrier.
- Operating in severe dust conditions.
- Extensive idling, such as police, taxi or door-to-door delivery service.

SERVICE INTERVAL Perform at the months or distances shown, whichever comes first.	Miles × 1000 Kilometers × 1000	3 4.8	6 9.6	9 14.4	12 19.2	15 24	18 28.8	21 33.6	24 38.4	27 43.2	30 48	33 52.8	36 57.6	39 62.4	42 67.2	45 72	48 76.8	51 81.6	54 86.4	57 91.2	60 96
EMISSION CONTROL SERVICE																					
Replace Engine Oil and Oil Filter Every 3 Months OR		X	X	X	X	X	X	X	X	X	X	X	X	X	X	X	X	X	X	X	X
Replace Spark Plugs											X										X
Replace Spark Plugs (Supercharged use Platinum Type)																					X
Check Supercharger Lubricant											X										X
Inspect Accessory Drive Belt(s)											X										X
Replace Air Cleaner Filter①											X										X
Replace Engine Coolant, EVERY 36 Months OR											X										X
Check Engine Coolant Protection, Hoses and Clamps		ANNUALLY																			
GENERAL MAINTENANCE																					
Lubricate Tie Rod Ends											X										X
Inspect Exhaust Heat Shields											X										X
Change Automatic Transmission Fluid②											X										X
Inspect Brake Pads and Rotors (front)③ (Front and Rear — Super Coupe/XR7)③											X										X
Inspect Brake Linings and Drums (Rear)③											X										X
Rotate Tires			X					X					X					X			

① If operating in severe dust, more frequent intervals may be required. Consult your dealer.
② Change automatic transmission fluid if your driving habits frequently include one or more of the following conditions:
   - Operation during hot weather (above 32°C (90°F)) carrying heavy loads and in hilly terrain.
   - Towing a trailer or using a car top carrier.
   - Police, taxi or door-to-door delivery service.
   - Vehicle accumulates 5,000 miles (8 000 km) or more per month or is used in CONTINUOUS stop-and-go service.
③ If your driving includes continuous stop-and-go driving or driving in mountainous areas, more frequent intervals may be required.
X All items designated by an X must be performed in all states.

88181CX1

1989-97 MAINTENANCE SCHEDULE

SCHEDULE B

Follow Maintenance Schedule B if, generally, you drive your vehicle on a daily basis for farther than 16 km (10 miles) and NONE OF THE DRIVING CONDITIONS SHOWN IN SCHEDULE A APPLY TO YOUR DRIVING HABITS.

SERVICE INTERVALS Perform at the months or distances shown, whichever comes first.	Miles x 1000	7.5	15	22.5	30	37.5	45	52.5	60
	Kilometers x 1000	12	24	36	48	60	72	84	96
EMISSIONS CONTROL SERVICE									
Supercharged Engines — Change Oil and Filter		As Indicated by the Vehicle Maintenance Monitor, But Not Beyond Every 5,000 Miles (8 000 km) or 6 Months, Whichever Comes First							
Replace Engine Oil and Oil Filter As Indicated by the Vehicle Maintenance Monitor (if equipped), But Not Beyond Every 6 Months or 7,500 Miles Whichever Occurs First — Except Supercharged		X	X	X	X	X	X	X	X
Replace Spark Plugs — Except Supercharged					X				X
Replace Spark Plugs — Platinum Type Supercharged									X
Check Supercharger Lubricant					X				X
Replace Crankcase Emission Filter①					X				X
Inspect Accessory Drive Belt(s)					X				X
Replace Air Cleaner Filter①					X				X
Replace Engine Coolant Every 36 Months OR					X				X
Check Engine Coolant Protection, Hoses and Clamps		ANNUALLY							
GENERAL MAINTENANCE									
Lubricate Tie Rod Ends					X				X
Check Exhaust Heat Shields					X				X
Inspect Disc Brake Pads and Rotors (Front and Rear Super Coupe/XR7)②					X				X
Inspect Brake Linings and Drums (Rear)②					X				X
Rotate Tires		X		X		X		X	

① If operating in severe dust, more frequent intervals may be required. Consult your dealer.
② If your driving includes continuous stop-and-go driving or driving in mountainous areas, more frequent intervals may be required.

88181CX2

CAPACITIES

Year	Model	Engine ID/VIN	Engine Displacement Liters (cc)	Engine Oil with Filter (qts.)	Transmission (pts.)			Transfer Case (pts.)	Drive Axle		Fuel Tank (gal.)	Cooling System (qts.)
					4-Spd	5-Spd	Auto.		Front (pts.)	Rear (pts.)		
1983	Cougar	W	2.3 (2300)	5.0	4.5	4.8	-	-	-	3.25	18.0	8.7
	Cougar	3	3.8 (3802)	5.0	-	-	22.0	-	-	3.25	21.0	10.7
	Cougar	F	5.0 (4949)	5.0	-	-	22.0	-	-	3.25	20.0	13.4
	Thunderbird	W	2.3 (2300)	5.0	4.5	4.8	-	-	-	3.25	18.0	8.7
	Thunderbird	3	3.8 (3802)	5.0	-	-	22.0	-	-	3.25	21.0	10.7
	Thunderbird	F	5.0 (4949)	5.0	-	-	22.0	-	-	3.25	20.0	13.4
1984	Cougar	W	2.3 (2300)	5.0	4.5	4.8	-	-	-	3.25	18.0	8.7
	Cougar	3	3.8 (3802)	5.0	-	-	22.0	-	-	3.25	21.0	10.7
	Cougar	F	5.0 (4949)	5.0	-	-	22.0	-	-	3.25	20.0	13.4
	Thunderbird	W	2.3 (2300)	5.0	4.5	4.8	-	-	-	3.25	18.0	8.7
	Thunderbird	3	3.8 (3802)	5.0	-	-	22.0	-	-	3.25	21.0	10.7
	Thunderbird	F	5.0 (4949)	5.0	-	-	22.0	-	-	3.25	20.0	13.4
1985	Cougar	W	2.3 (2300)	5.0	4.5	4.8	-	-	-	3.25	18.0	8.7
	Cougar	3	3.8 (3802)	5.0	-	-	22.0	-	-	3.25	21.0	10.7
	Cougar	F	5.0 (4949)	5.0	-	-	22.0	-	-	3.25	20.0	13.4
	Thunderbird	W	2.3 (2300)	5.0	4.5	4.8	-	-	-	3.25	18.0	8.7
	Thunderbird	3	3.8 (3802)	5.0	-	-	22.0	-	-	3.25	21.0	10.7
	Thunderbird	F	5.0 (4949)	5.0	-	-	22.0	-	-	3.25	20.0	13.4
1986	Cougar	W	2.3 (2300)	5.0	4.5	4.8	-	-	-	3.25	18.0	8.7
	Cougar	3	3.8 (3802)	5.0	-	-	22.0	-	-	3.25	21.0	10.7
	Cougar	F	5.0 (4949)	5.0	-	-	22.0	-	-	3.25	20.0	13.4
	Thunderbird	W	2.3 (2300)	5.0	4.5	4.8	-	-	-	3.25	18.0	8.7
	Thunderbird	3	3.8 (3802)	5.0	-	-	22.0	-	-	3.25	21.0	10.7
	Thunderbird	F	5.0 (4949)	5.0	-	-	22.0	-	-	3.25	20.0	13.4
1987	Cougar	3	3.8 (3802)	5.0	-	-	22.0	-	-	3.25	21.0	10.7
	Cougar	F	5.0 (4949)	5.0	-	-	22.0	-	-	3.25	20.0	13.4
	Thunderbird	W	2.3 (2300)	5.0	4.5	4.8	-	-	-	3.25	18.0	8.7
	Thunderbird	3	3.8 (3802)	5.0	-	-	22.0	-	-	3.25	21.0	10.7
	Thunderbird	F	5.0 (4949)	5.0	-	-	22.0	-	-	3.25	20.0	13.4
1988	Cougar	4	3.8 (3802)	5.0	-	-	22.0	-	-	3.25	21.0	11.8
	Cougar	F	5.0 (4949)	5.0	-	-	22.0	-	-	3.25	20.0	13.4
	Thunderbird	W	2.3 (2300)	5.0	4.8	4.8	16.0	-	-	3.25	18.0	10.0
	Thunderbird	4	3.8 (3802)	5.0	-	-	22.0	-	-	3.25	21.0	11.8
	Thunderbird	F	5.0 (4949)	5.0	-	-	22.0	-	-	3.25	20.0	13.4
1989	Cougar	4	3.8 (3802)	5.0	-	-	22.0	-	-	3.75	21.0	11.8
	Cougar	C	3.8 (3802)	5.0	-	-	22.0	-	-	3.75	21.0	12.0
	Cougar	R	3.8 (3802)	5.0	-	-	22.0	-	-	3.75	21.0	13.4
	Thunderbird	4	3.8 (3802)	5.0	-	-	22.0	-	-	3.25	21.0	11.8
	Thunderbird	R	3.8 (3802) ①	5.0	-	6.3	24.0	-	-	3.25	18.8	11.8
	Thunderbird	C	3.8 (3802) ①	5.0	-	6.3	24.0	-	-	3.25	28.8	11.8
1990	Cougar	4	3.8 (3802)	5.0	-	-	22.0	-	-	3.25	21.0	11.8
	Cougar	R	3.8 (3802)	5.0	-	6.3	24.0	-	-	3.25	18.8	11.8
	Thunderbird	4	3.8 (3802)	5.0	-	-	22.0	-	-	3.25	21.0	11.8
	Thunderbird	R	3.8 (3802) ①	5.0	-	6.3	24.0	-	-	3.25	18.8	11.8

91331C05

CAPACITIES

Year	Model	Engine ID/VIN	Engine Displacement Liters (cc)	Engine Oil with Filter (qts.)	Transmission (pts.)			Transfer Case (pts.)	Drive Axle		Fuel Tank (gal.)	Cooling System (qts.)
					4-Spd	5-Spd	Auto.		Front (pts.)	Rear (pts.)		
1991	Cougar	4	3.8 (3802)	5.0	-	-	22.0	-	-	3.25	21.0	11.8
	Cougar	R	3.8 (3802)	5.0	-	6.3	24.0	-	-	3.25	18.8	11.8
	Thunderbird	4	3.8 (3802)	5.0	-	-	22.0	-	-	②	21.0	11.8
	Thunderbird	R	3.8 (3802) ①	5.0	-	6.3	24.0	-	-	②	18.8	11.8
	Thunderbird	T	5.0 (4943)	5.0	-	-	24.6	-	-	②	19.0	14.1
1992	Cougar	4	3.8 (3802)	5.0	-	-	22.0	-	-	3.75	21.0	11.8
	Cougar	T	5.0 (4943)	5.0	-	-	24.6	-	-	3.75	19.0	14.1
	Thunderbird	4	3.8 (3802)	5.0	-	-	22.0	-	-	②	21.0	11.8
	Thunderbird	R	3.8 (3802) ①	5.0	-	6.3	24.0	-	-	②	18.8	11.8
	Thunderbird	T	5.0 (4943)	5.0	-	-	24.6	-	-	②	19.0	14.1
1993	Cougar	4	3.8 (3802)	5.0	-	-	22.0	-	-	②	21.0	11.8
	Cougar	T	5.0 (4943)	5.0	-	-	24.6	-	-	②	19.0	14.1
	Thunderbird	4	3.8 (3802)	5.0	-	-	22.0	-	-	②	21.0	11.8
	Thunderbird	R	3.8 (3802) ①	5.0	-	6.3	24.0	-	-	②	18.8	11.8
	Thunderbird	E	5.0 (4943)	5.0	-	-	24.6	-	-	②	19.0	14.1
1994	Cougar	4	3.8 (3802)	5.0	-	-	25.0	-	-	②	18.0	12.6
	Cougar	W	4.6 (4593)	5.0	-	-	25.0	-	-	②	18.0	14.1
	Thunderbird	4	3.8 (3802)	5.0	-	-	25.0	-	-	②	18.0	12.6
	Thunderbird	R	3.8 (3802) ①	5.0	-	6.3	25.0	-	-	②	18.0	12.5
	Thunderbird	W	4.6 (4593)	5.0	-	-	25.0	-	-	②	18.0	14.1
1995	Cougar	4	3.8 (3802)	5.0	-	-	27.2	-	-	②	18.0	12.6
	Cougar	W	4.6 (4593)	5.0	-	-	27.2	-	-	②	18.0	14.1
	Thunderbird	4	3.8 (3802)	5.0	-	-	27.2	-	-	②	18.0	12.6
	Thunderbird	R	3.8 (3802) ①	5.0	-	6.3	27.2	-	-	②	18.0	12.5
	Thunderbird	W	4.6 (4593)	5.0	-	-	27.2	-	-	②	18.0	14.1
1996	Cougar	4	3.8 (3802)	5.0	-	-	27.8	-	-	②	18.0	12.6
	Cougar	W	4.6 (4593)	5.3	-	-	27.8	-	-	②	18.0	14.1
	Thunderbird	4	3.8 (3802)	5.0	-	-	27.8	-	-	②	18.0	12.6
	Thunderbird	W	4.6 (4593)	5.3	-	-	27.8	-	-	②	18.0	14.1
1997	Cougar	4	3.8 (3802)	5.0	-	-	27.8	-	-	②	18.0	12.6
	Cougar	W	4.6 (4593)	5.3	-	-	27.8	-	-	②	18.0	14.1
	Thunderbird	4	3.8 (3802)	5.0	-	-	27.8	-	-	②	18.0	12.6
	Thunderbird	W	4.6 (4593)	5.3	-	-	27.8	-	-	②	18.0	14.1

① Supercharged
② 7.5" limited slip axle: 2.75 pts.
  7.50" axle: 3.0 pts.
  8.80" axle: 3.25 pts.

91331C06

2

ENGINE ELECTRICAL

FIRING ORDERS 2-2
IGNITION SYSTEMS 2-3
DURA SPARK II IGNITION
  SYSTEM 2-3
GENERAL INFORMATION 2-3
  PRIMARY CIRCUIT 2-3
  SECONDARY CIRCUIT 2-3
SYSTEM OPERATION 2-4
DIAGNOSIS AND TESTING 2-5
  SECONDARY SPARK TEST 2-5
  CYLINDER DROP TEST 2-5
IGNITION COIL 2-6
  TESTING 2-6
  REMOVAL & INSTALLATION 2-7
STATOR ASSEMBLY 2-7
  REMOVAL & INSTALLATION 2-7
VACUUM DIAPHRAGM ASSEMBLY 2-7
  REMOVAL & INSTALLATION 2-7
DISTRIBUTOR CAP AND ROTOR 2-7
  REMOVAL & INSTALLATION 2-7
DISTRIBUTOR 2-7
  REMOVAL 2-7
  INSTALLATION 2-8
EEC-IV THICK FILM INTEGRATED
  (TFI) IGNITION SYSTEM 2-8
GENERAL INFORMATION 2-8
  SYSTEM OPERATION 2-10
DIAGNOSIS AND TESTING 2-10
IGNITION COIL 2-10
  REMOVAL & INSTALLATION 2-10
TFI IGNITION MODULE 2-11
  REMOVAL & INSTALLATION 2-11
STATOR ASSEMBLY 2-12
  REMOVAL & INSTALLATION 2-12
DISTRIBUTOR 2-13
  REMOVAL & INSTALLATION 2-13
DISTRIBUTORLESS IGNITION
  SYSTEM (DIS) 2-14
GENERAL INFORMATION 2-14
  SYSTEM OPERATION 2-14
  SYSTEM COMPONENTS 2-15
DIAGNOSIS AND TESTING 2-15
  REMOVAL & INSTALLATION 2-15
DIS IGNITION MODULE/IGNITION
  CONTROL MODULE (ICM) 2-16
  REMOVAL & INSTALLATION 2-16
SYNCHRONIZER ASSEMBLY 2-16
  REMOVAL & INSTALLATION 2-16
CRANKSHAFT POSITION (CKP)
  SENSOR 2-17
  REMOVAL & INSTA17LLATION 2-17
CAMSHAFT POSITION (CMP)
  SENSOR 2-17
  REMOVAL & INSTALLATION 2-17
CHARGING SYSTEM 2-17
GENERAL INFORMATION 2-17
ALTERNATOR PRECAUTIONS 2-17
ALTERNATOR 2-17
  TESTING 2-17
  REMOVAL & INSTALLATION 2-18

VOLTAGE REGULATOR 2-20
  REMOVAL & INSTALLATION 2-20
STARTING SYSTEM 2-21
GENERAL INFORMATION 2-21
STARTER 2-21
  TESTING 2-21
  REMOVAL & INSTALLATION 2-21
  SOLENOID REPLACEMENT 2-23
SENDING UNITS AND SENSORS 2-24
  REMOVAL & INSTALLATION 2-24

FIRING ORDERS 2-2
IGNITION SYSTEMS 2-3
DURA SPARK II IGNITION SYSTEM 2-3
EEC-IV THICK FILM INTEGRATED
  (TFI) IGNITION SYSTEM 2-8
DISTRIBUTORLESS IGNITION
  SYSTEM (DIS) 2-14
CHARGING SYSTEM 2-17
STARTING SYSTEM 2-21

FIRING ORDERS

➡ To avoid confusion, remove and tag the wires one at a time, for replacement.

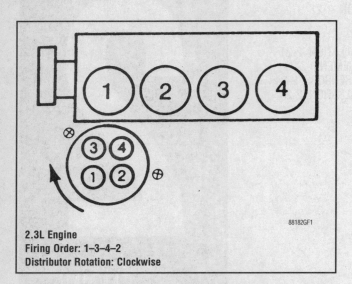

2.3L Engine
Firing Order: 1–3–4–2
Distributor Rotation: Clockwise

88182GF1

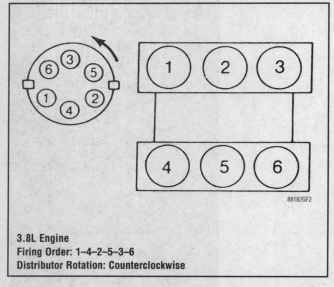

3.8L Engine
Firing Order: 1–4–2–5–3–6
Distributor Rotation: Counterclockwise

88182GF2

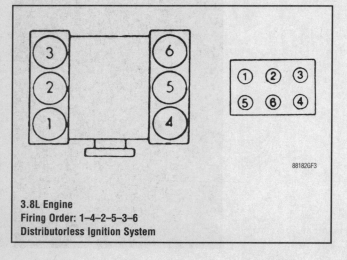

3.8L Engine
Firing Order: 1–4–2–5–3–6
Distributorless Ignition System

88182GF3

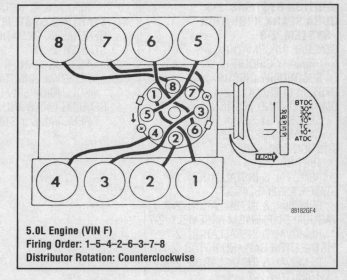

5.0L Engine (VIN F)
Firing Order: 1–5–4–2–6–3–7–8
Distributor Rotation: Counterclockwise

88182GF4

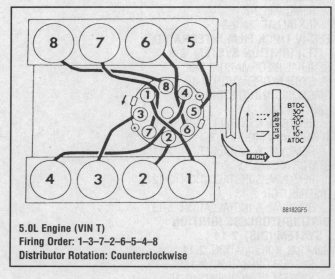

5.0L Engine (VIN T)
Firing Order: 1–3–7–2–6–5–4–8
Distributor Rotation: Counterclockwise

88182GF5

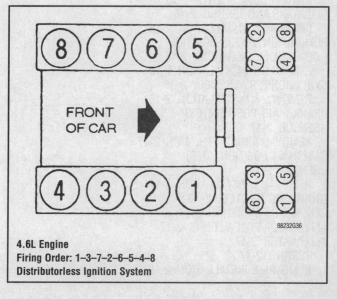

4.6L Engine
Firing Order: 1–3–7–2–6–5–4–8
Distributorless Ignition System

88232G36

IGNITION SYSTEMS

The ignition systems used on these vehicles are as follows:
- Dura Spark II Ignition System—used on 3.8L carbureted engines
- EEC-IV TFI Ignition System—used on 2.3L engines, 3.8L fuel injected engines (except SC) through 1995 and 5.0L engines
- Distributorless Ignition System (DIS)—used on 1996–97 3.8L (non-SC) and all 3.8L SC and 4.6L engines

DURA SPARK II IGNITION SYSTEM

General Information

▶ **See Figures 1 and 2**

The Dura Spark II ignition system was used on 3.8L carbureted vehicles. The Dura Spark II ignition system consists of the typical electronic primary and conventional secondary circuits, designed to carry higher voltages. The primary and secondary circuits consists of the following components:

PRIMARY CIRCUIT

- Battery
- Ignition switch
- Ballast resistor start bypass (wire)
- Ignition coil primary winding
- Ignition module
- Distributor stator assembly

SECONDARY CIRCUIT

- Battery
- Ignition switch
- Ignition coil secondary winding
- Distributor rotor
- Distributor cap
- Ignition wires

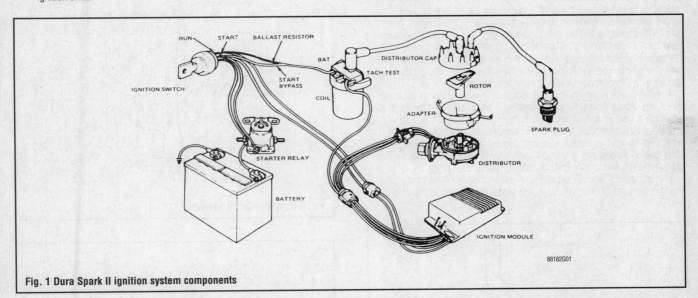

Fig. 1 Dura Spark II ignition system components

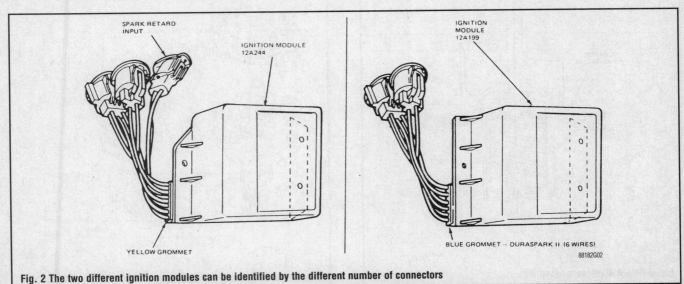

Fig. 2 The two different ignition modules can be identified by the different number of connectors

- Ballast resistor start bypass (wire)
- Spark plugs

The Dura Spark II system uses either a Dura Spark II module or the Universal Ignition Module (UIM).

The two different Duraspark II ignition modules can be identified by 2 connectors/blue grommet on the standard module and 3 connectors/yellow grommet on the UIM.

Both ignition modules perform the function of turning off current flow through the ignition coil in response to a control signal. In the Dura Spark II ignition system, this signal comes from the distributor stator assembly. Additionally, the Universal Ignition Module (UIM), can respond to another control signal from either an ignition barometric pressure switch or the Microprocessor Control Unit (MCU), depending upon the engine's calibration. In responding to this second control signal, the UIM provides additional spark timing control for certain operating conditions by turning off the ignition coil current flow at a different time than what would happen from just the distributor signal.

System Operation

▶ **See Figures 3, 4 and 5**

With the ignition switch in the **RUN** position, the primary circuit current is directed from the battery, through the ignition switch, the ballast resistor, the ignition coil (in the positive side, out the negative side), the ignition module and back to the battery through the ignition system ground in the distributor. This current flow causes a magnetic field to be built up in the ignition coil. When the poles on the armature and the stator assembly align, the ignition module turns the primary current flow off, collapsing the magnetic field in the ignition coil. The collapsing field induces a high voltage in the ignition coil secondary windings. The ignition coil wire then conducts the high voltage to the distributor where the cap and rotor distributes it to the appropriate spark plug.

A timing device in the ignition module turns the primary current back on after a very short period of time. High voltage is produced each time the magnetic field is built up and collapsed.

The red ignition module wire provides operating voltage for the ignition module for the ignition module electronic components in the run mode. The white ignition module wire and start bypass provide increased voltage for the ignition module and ignition coil, respectively, during start mode.

The distributor provides a signal to the ignition module, which controls the timing of the spark at the spark plugs. This signal is generated as the armature,

attached to the distributor shaft, rotates past the stator assembly. The rotating armature causes fluctuations in a magnetic field produced by the stator assembly magnet. These fluctuations induce a voltage in the stator assembly pick-up coil. The signal is connected to the ignition module by the vehicle wiring harness.

The occurrence of the signal to the ignition module, in relation to the initial spark timing, is controlled by centrifugal and vacuum advance mechanisms. The centrifugal advance mechanism controls spark timing in response to engine rpm. The vacuum advance mechanism controls spark timing in response to engine load.

The centrifugal advance mechanism varies the relationship of the armature to the stator assembly. The sleeve and plate assembly, on which the armature is mounted rotates in relation to the distributor shaft. This rotation is caused by centrifugal weights moving in response to the engine rpm. The movement of the centrifugal weights change the initial relationship of the armature to stator assembly ahead of its static position on the distributor shaft. This results in spark advance. The rate of movement of the centrifugal weights is controlled by calibrated springs.

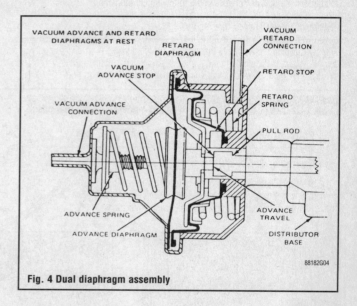

Fig. 4 Dual diaphragm assembly

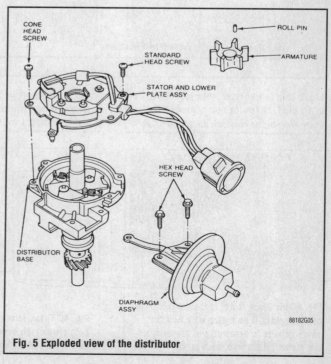

Fig. 5 Exploded view of the distributor

Fig. 3 Single diaphragm assembly

The vacuum spark control mechanism can provide spark advance if a single diaphragm assembly is used or spark advance and retard if a dual diaphragm assembly is used. The diaphragm assembly used depends on the engine calibration.

The single vacuum diaphragm assembly also varies the armature to stator assembly relationship. In this case the stator assembly positioned is changed by means of vacuum applied to the diaphragm assembly. The diaphragm assembly is attached to the stator assembly by the diaphragm rod. The stator assembly is mounted on the upper plate assembly. The vacuum applied to the diaphragm and attached diaphragm rod to move, compressing the advance spring, which controls the rate of spark advance. The rate of spark advance is controlled by a calibrated spring.

Spark advance is obtained with a dual diaphragm assembly in the same manner as with a single diaphragm assembly. In this case, vacuum applied to the vacuum advance port cause the advance diaphragm rod to move, other wise the action is the same. Spark retard is obtained by applying vacuum to the vacuum retard port. This causes the retard diaphragm to move, compressing the retard spring, which controls the rate of spark retard. Compressing the retard spring allows the diaphragm rod stop to move due to force applied by an advance spring pushing against the it by means of a diaphragm rod. The result is the diaphragm rod moves, causing the attached stator assembly to change position with respect to the armature. In this instance, the direction of the stator assembly movement is opposite that occurring during vacuum advance, resulting spark retard. It should be noted that vacuum applied to the advance port overrides any spark retard caused by vacuum applied to the retard port.

Diagnosis and Testing

SECONDARY SPARK TEST

▶ See Figures 6, 7, 8 and 9

The best way to perform this procedure is to use a spark tester (available at most automotive parts stores). Three types of spark testers are commonly available. The Neon Bulb type is connected to the spark plug wire and flashes with each ignition pulse. The Air Gap type must be adjusted to the individual spark plug gap specified for the engine. The last type of spark plug tester looks like a spark plug with a grounding clip on the side, but there is no side electrode for the spark to jump to. The last two types of testers allows the user to not only detect the presence of spark, but also the intensity (orange/yellow is weak, blue is strong).

1. Disconnect a spark plug wire at the spark plug end.
2. Connect the plug wire to the spark tester and ground the tester to an appropriate location on the engine.
3. Crank the engine and check for spark at the tester.
4. If spark exists at the tester, the ignition system is functioning properly.
5. If spark does not exist at the spark plug wire, perform diagnosis of the ignition system using individual component diagnosis procedures.

CYLINDER DROP TEST

▶ See Figures 10, 11 and 12

The cylinder drop test is performed when an engine misfire is evident. This test helps determine which cylinder is not contributing the proper power. The easiest way to perform this test is to remove the plug wires one at a time from the cylinders with the engine running.

1. Place the transmission in **P**, engage the emergency brake, and start the engine and let it idle.
2. Using a spark plug wire removing tool, preferably, the plier type, carefully remove the boot from one of the cylinders.

✳✳ WARNING

Make sure your body is free from touching any part of the car which is metal. The secondary voltage in the ignition system is high and although it cannot kill you, it will shock you and it does hurt.

3. The engine will sputter, run worse, and possibly nearly stall. If this happens reinstall the plug wire and move to the next cylinder. If the engine runs no differently, or the difference is minimal, shut the engine off and inspect the spark plug wire,

Fig. 6 This spark tester looks just like a spark plug, attach the clip to ground and crank the engine to check for spark

Fig. 7 This spark tester has an adjustable air-gap for measuring spark strength and testing different voltage ignition systems

Fig. 8 Attach the clip to ground and crank the engine to check for spark

Fig. 9 This spark tester is the easiest to use just place it on a plug wire and the spark voltage is detected and the bulb on the top will flash with each pulse

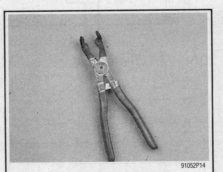
Fig. 10 These pliers are insulated and help protect the user from shock as well as the plug wires from being damaged

Fig. 11 To perform the cylinder drop test, remove one wire at a time and . . .

Fig. 12 . . . note the idle speed and idle characteristics of the engine. the cylinder(s) with the least drop is the non-contributing cylinder(s)

spark plug, and if necessary, perform component diagnostics as covered in this section. Perform the test on all cylinders to verify the which cylinders are suspect.

Ignition Coil

TESTING

▶ **See Figures 13 and 14**

1. Follow the coil wire from the center terminal on the distributor cap to the end at the ignition coil. Make sure that the transmission is in Park (AT) or Neutral (MT) and that the ignition is turned **OFF**.

2. Separate the wiring harness connector from the ignition module at the distributor. Inspect for dirt, corrosion and/or damage. Reconnect the harness if no problems are found.

3. Attach a 12 volt DC test light between the coil TACH terminal and an engine ground, then crank the engine. If the light flashes or is continuous:

    a. Turn the ignition switch **OFF**.

    b. Detach the ignition coil connector on top of the coil and inspect for dirt, corrosion and/or damage.

    c. Using an ohmmeter, measure the ignition coil primary resistance from the BATT to the TACH terminals.

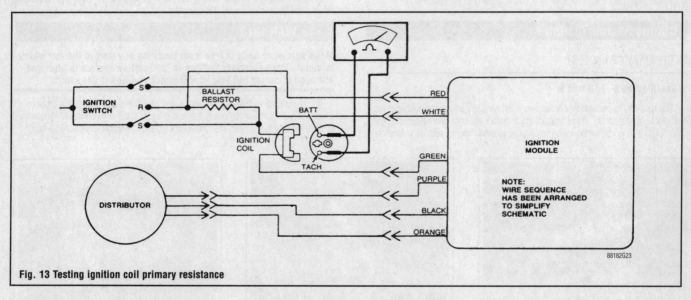

Fig. 13 Testing ignition coil primary resistance

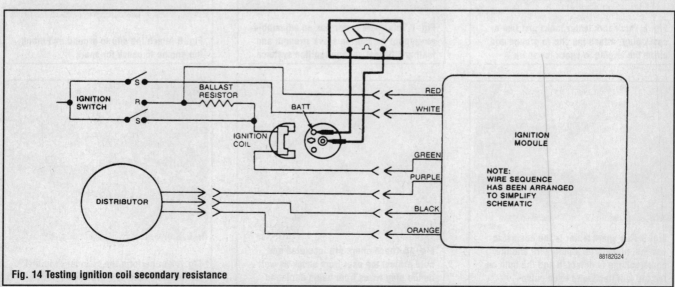

Fig. 14 Testing ignition coil secondary resistance

d. The ohmmeter reading should be 0.8–1.6 ohms. If the reading is less than 0.8 ohms or greater than 1.6 ohms, the ignition coil should be replaced.

e. Using an ohmmeter, measure the ignition coil secondary resistance from the BATT terminal to the high voltage terminal.

f. The resistance should be 7,700–10,500 ohms. If the resistance is less that 7,700 ohms or greater than 10,500 ohms, replace the ignition coil.

REMOVAL & INSTALLATION

1. Disconnect the negative battery cable.
2. Detach the coil electrical connector(s).
3. Unfasten the retainers, then remove the ignition coil from the vehicle.
4. Installation is the reverse of the removal procedure.

Stator Assembly

REMOVAL & INSTALLATION

1. Disconnect the negative battery cable.
2. Remove the distributor cap, rotor and adapter.
3. Separate the distributor connector from the wiring harness.
4. Using a small gear puller or 2 suitable pry bars, remove the armature from the sleeve and plate assembly. Use caution to avoid losing the roll pin.
5. Remove the two screws retaining the lower plate assembly and stator assembly to the distributor base. There are 2 different screws.
6. Remove the lower plate assembly and stator assembly from the distributor.
7. Remove the E-clip, flatwasher and wave washer securing the stator assembly to the lower plate assembly and separate the stator assembly from the lower plate assembly. Notice the installation of the wave washer.
   To install:
8. Place the stator assembly on the lower plate assembly and install the wave washer (OUTER EDGES UP), flatwasher and E-clip.
9. Install the stator/lower plate assembly on the distributor base, while aligning the pin on the stator assembly in the diaphragm rod.
10. Install the two retaining screws .
11. There are 2 locating notches in the armature and install on sleeve and plate assembly with unused notch and new roll pin.
12. Connect the distributor to the wiring harness.
13. Replace the distributor rotor and cap. Check to ensure the ignition wires are secured in the distributor cap and spark plugs.
14. Connect the negative battery cable. Check the ignition timing.

Vacuum Diaphragm Assembly

REMOVAL & INSTALLATION

1. Disconnect the diaphragm assembly vacuum hoses.
2. Remove the 2 diaphragm assembly attaching screws (Note screws location).
3. Disengage the diaphragm rod from the stator assembly pin and remove the diaphragm assembly.
   To install:
4. Adjust the new diaphragm assembly per manufacturer's instructions included with the new diaphragm.
5. Fit the diaphragm rod with the stator assembly pin.
6. Attach the diaphragm assembly and identification tag to the distributor base. Check to ensure the diaphragm rod is properly engaged with the stator assembly pin.
7. Connect the vacuum hoses.

Distributor Cap And Rotor

REMOVAL & INSTALLATION

▶ **See Figure 15**

1. Disconnect the negative battery cable.
2. If necessary for removal, tag and disconnect the spark plug wires from the distributor cap.

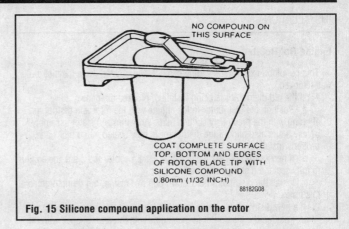

NO COMPOUND ON THIS SURFACE

COAT COMPLETE SURFACE TOP, BOTTOM AND EDGES OF ROTOR BLADE TIP WITH SILICONE COMPOUND 0.80mm (1/32 INCH)

88182G08

Fig. 15 Silicone compound application on the rotor

3. Loosen the distributor cap hold-down screws.
4. Remove the cap by pulling it cap straight up. Avoid damaging the rotor points and spring.
5. If required, remove the rotor by pulling it straight up.
   To install:
6. Apply a ⅟₃₂ in. (0.8mm) bead of a suitable silicone compound on the rotor as shown in the accompanying figure. Position the rotor with the square and round locator pins matched to the distributor shaft plate.
7. Position the distributor cap on the distributor base noting the square alignment locator. Tighten the hold-down screws to 17–23 inch lbs. (2.0–2.6 Nm).
8. If removed, attach the plug wires, noting the correct locations on the distributor cap.
9. Connect the negative battery cable, start the engine and check the timing. Adjust if necessary.

Distributor

REMOVAL

▶ **See Figure 16**

1. Disconnect the negative battery cable.

➡ **Make sure to tag the spark plug wires if it necessary to disconnect them from the distributor cap.**

2. Remove the distributor cap (if possible, DO NOT disconnect the wires from the cap) from the distributor and position it aside.
3. Disconnect and plug the vacuum hose at the vacuum diaphragm.
4. Separate the distributor connector from the wiring harness.
5. Rotate the engine to align the stator assembly pole and any armature pole.
6. Scribe a mark in the distributor body and the engine block to indicate position of the distributor in the engine and position the rotor.
7. Unfasten the distributor hold-down bolt and clamp, then carefully remove the distributor assembly from the engine. Be sure not to rotate the engine while the distributor is removed.

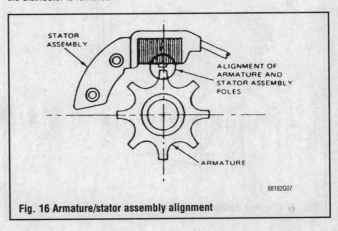

STATOR ASSEMBLY

ALIGNMENT OF ARMATURE AND STATOR ASSEMBLY POLES

ARMATURE

88182G07

Fig. 16 Armature/stator assembly alignment

INSTALLATION

Engine Not Rotated

This condition exists if the engine has not been rotated while the distributor was removed.

1. If the old distributor is being installed, proceed as follows:

a. Position the distributor in the engine with the rotor and distributor aligning with the previously scribed mark. Armature and stator assembly poles should also align if the distributor is fully seated in the block and properly installed.

b. If necessary, connect the negative battery cable, and crank the engine to fully seat the distributor in the block.

c. Install the distributor hold-down bolt and clamp, but do not tighten at this time.

2. If a new distributor is being installed, proceed as follows:

a. Position the distributor in the engine with the rotor aligned with the previously scribed mark. If necessary, connect the negative battery cable, then crank the engine to full seat the distributor.

b. Rotate the engine until the timing marks for correct initial timing align and the rotor is pointing at the No. 1 cap terminal.

c. Rotate the distributor in the block to align the armature and stator assembly poles.

d. Install the distributor hold-down bolt and clamp, but do not tighten at this time.

➡️**If the armature and stator assembly poles cannot be aligned by rotating the distributor in the block, pull the distributor up out of the block enough to disengage the distributor gear. Rotate the distributor shaft to engage a different gear tooth and install the distributor.**

3. Connect the distributor wiring harness. Install the distributor cap and tighten the mounting screws to 17–23 inch lbs., if so equipped. If necessary, attach the ignition wires as tagged during removal. Verify that the ignition wires are securely connected to the distributor cap and spark plugs.

4. Reconnect the negative battery cable and connect a suitable timing light and tachometer. Start the engine, letting it run until it reaches normal operating temperature.

5. Set the initial timing to the specifications given on the Vehicle Emission Control Information Decal located under the hood. Tighten down the distributor hold-down bolt to 17–25 ft. lbs. (23–34 Nm).

6. Recheck the initial timing and readjust as necessary.

7. Reconnect all vacuum lines and wire harness connectors. Reinstall and removed parts in the reverse order of the removal procedure.

Engine Rotated

This condition exists if the engine has been rotated with the distributor removed.

1. Rotate the engine until the No. 1 piston is on compression stroke.

2. Align the timing mark for correct initial timing.

3. Install the distributor with the rotor pointing at No. 1 terminal position in the cap and armature and stator assembly poles aligned.

4. Be sure that the oil pump intermediate shaft properly engages the distributor shaft. It may be necessary to crank the engine after the distributor gear is partially engaged in order to engage the oil pump intermediate shaft and fully seat the distributor in the engine block.

5. If it was necessary to crank the engine again, rotate the engine until the No. 1 piston is on top dead center of its compression stroke and align the timing marks for correct initial timing.

6. Rotate the distributor in the block to align the armature and stator assembly poles and verify that the rotor is pointing at the No. 1 terminal in the distributor cap.

7. Install the distributor hold-down bolt and clamp, but to not tighten at this time.

8. Connect the distributor wiring harness. Install the distributor cap and tighten the mounting screws to 17–23 inch lbs., if so equipped. If necessary, connect the ignition wires as tagged during removal. Verify that the ignition wires are securely connected to the distributor cap and spark plugs.

9. Reconnect the negative battery cable and connect a suitable timing light and tachometer. Start the engine letting it run until it reaches normal operating temperature.

10. Set the initial timing to the specifications given on the Vehicle Emission Control Information Decal located under the hood. Tighten down the distributor hold-down bolt to 17–25 ft. lbs. (23–34 Nm).

11. Recheck the initial timing and readjust as necessary.

12. Reconnect all vacuum lines and wire harness connectors.

EEC-IV THICK FILM INTEGRATED (TFI) IGNITION SYSTEM

General Information

▶ **See Figures 17 thru 24**

The TFI ignition system features a distributor which uses no vacuum or centrifugal advance. The distributor is conventionally mounted and incorporates a Hall Effect stator assembly. On vehicles through 1988, the TFI module is mounted on the distributor. On 1989–93 vehicles, the TFI module is mounted remotely on the radiator support bracket and on 1994–95 vehicles, it is mounted on the front fender apron.

There are 2 type of TFI systems, and are as follows:

• PUSH START: this first TFI system featured a "push start" mode which allow manual transmission vehicles to be push started. Automatic transmission vehicles must not be push started.

• COMPUTER CONTROLLED DWELL: this second TFI system features an EEC-IV controlled ignition coil charge time.

Both the PUSH START and COMPUTER CONTROLLED DWELL TFI systems operates in the same manner. The TFI module supplies voltage to the Profile

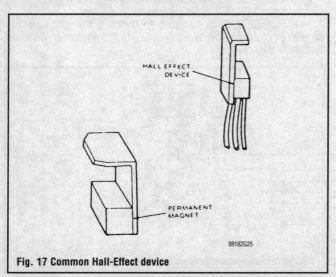

HALL EFFECT DEVICE

PERMANENT MAGNET

88182G25

Fig. 17 Common Hall-Effect device

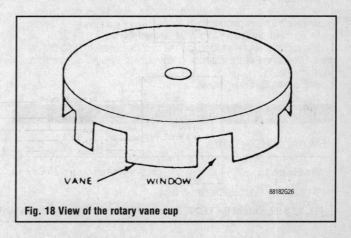

VANE   WINDOW

88182G26

Fig. 18 View of the rotary vane cup

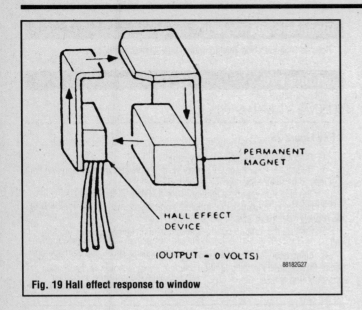

Fig. 19 Hall effect response to window

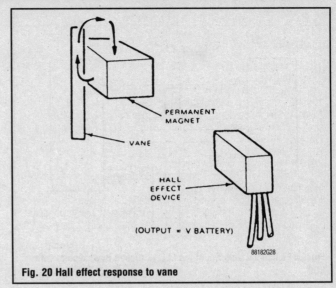

Fig. 20 Hall effect response to vane

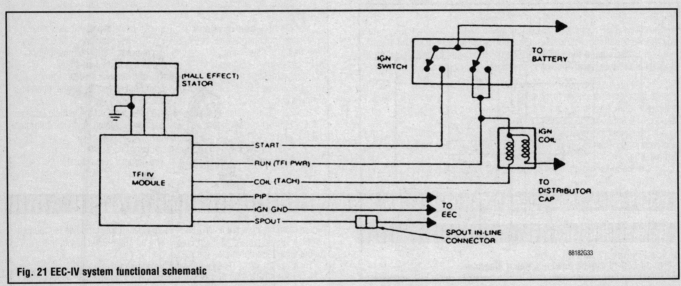

Fig. 21 EEC-IV system functional schematic

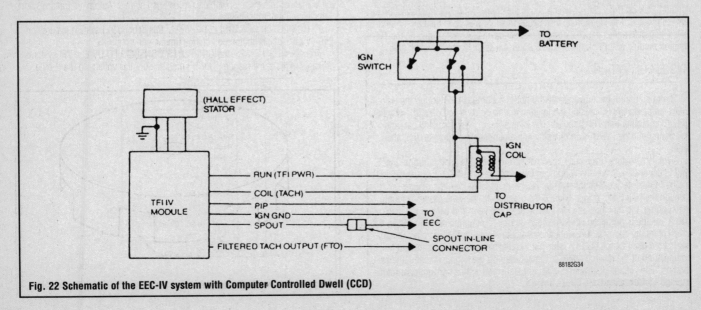

Fig. 22 Schematic of the EEC-IV system with Computer Controlled Dwell (CCD)

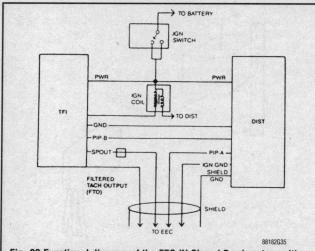

Fig. 23 Functional diagram of the EEC-IV Closed Bowl system with CCD

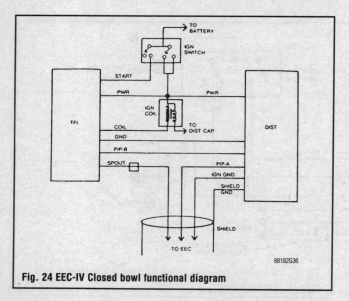

Fig. 24 EEC-IV Closed bowl functional diagram

Ignition Pick-up (PIP) sensor, which sends the crankshaft position information to the TFI module. The TFI module then sends this information to the EEC-IV module, which determines the spark timing and sends an electronic signal to the TFI ignition module to turn off the coil and produce a spark to fire the spark plug.

SYSTEM OPERATION

The operation of the universal distributor is accomplished through the Hall Effect stator assembly, causing the ignition coil to be switched off and on by the EEC-IV computer and TFI modules. The vane switch is encapsulated package consisting of a Hall sensor on one side and a permanent magnet on the other side.

A rotary armature (vane cup), made of ferrous metal, is used to trigger the Hall Effect switch. When the window of the armature is between the magnet and the Hall Effect device, a magnetic flux field is completed from the magnet through the Hall Effect device back to the magnet. As the vane passes through the opening, the flux lines are shunted through the vane and back to the magnet. A voltage is produced while the vane passes through the opening. When the vane clears the opening, the window causes the signal to go to 0 volts. The signal is then used by the EEC-IV system for crankshaft position sensing and the computation of the desired spark advance based on the engine demand and calibration. The voltage distribution is accomplished through a conventional rotor, cap and ignition wires.

Diagnosis and Testing

Refer to Diagnosis and Testing under Dura Spark II ignition system.

Ignition Coil

REMOVAL & INSTALLATION

♦ **See Figure 25**

1. Disconnect the negative battery cable.
2. Detach the engine control sensor wiring connector from the ignition coil and the radio ignition interference capacitor.
3. Tag and disconnect the ignition wires from the ignition coil.
4. Unfasten the ignition coil mounting bracket retaining bolts, then remove the bracket from the front side inner member.
5. Remove the ignition coil-to-bracket retaining screws and the ignition coil.
6. If necessary, unfasten the radio ignition interference capacitor retaining screw, then remove the radio ignition interference capacitor from the ignition coil mounting bracket.

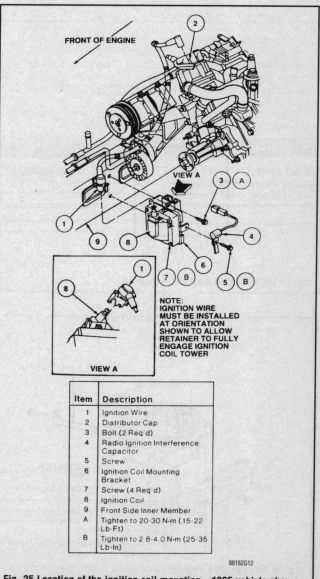

Item	Description
1	Ignition Wire
2	Distributor Cap
3	Bolt (2 Req'd)
4	Radio Ignition Interference Capacitor
5	Screw
6	Ignition Coil Mounting Bracket
7	Screw (4 Req'd)
8	Ignition Coil
9	Front Side Inner Member
A	Tighten to 20-30 N·m (15-22 Lb-Ft)
B	Tighten to 2.8-4.0 N·m (25-35 Lb-In)

Fig. 25 Location of the ignition coil mounting—1995 vehicle shown

To install:

7. Install the radio ignition interference capacitor to the mounting bracket and secure with the retaining screw. Tighten the screws to 25–35 inch lbs. (2.8–4.0 Nm).

8. Position the ignition coil, then install the ignition coil-to-bracket retaining screws and tighten to 25–35 inch lbs. (2.8–4.0 Nm).

9. Install the ignition coil mounting bracket on the front side inner member, then fasten with the retaining bolts and tighten to 15–22 ft. lbs. (20–30 Nm).

10. Connect the ignition wires to the coil, as tagged during removal.

11. Attach the engine control sensor wiring connector to the ignition coil and radio ignition interference capacitor.

12. Connect the negative battery cable.

TFI Ignition Module

REMOVAL & INSTALLATION

Vehicles Through 1988

▶ **See Figure 26**

1. Disconnect the negative battery cable.
2. Remove the distributor cap and position it aside with the wires attached.
3. Detach the TFI-ignition module electrical connector.
4. Remove the distributor from the engine and place on a workbench.
5. Remove the two ignition module retaining screws.
6. Slide the right side of the module down toward the distributor mounting flange and then back up. Then, slide the left side of the module down toward the distributor mounting flange and them back up. Continue alternating, side-to-side, until the module terminals are disengaged from the connector in the distributor base.
7. With the terminals completely disengaged, slide the module downward and gently pull the module away from the mounting surface.

> **⁂ WARNING**
>
> **Do not attempt to lift the module from the mounting surface before moving the entire module toward the distributor flange as you will break the pins at the distributor/module connector.**

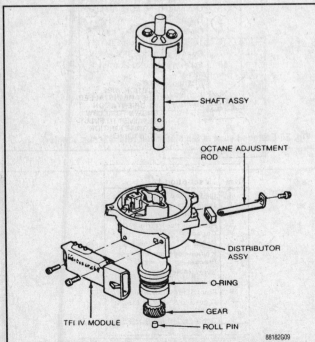

Fig. 26 Through 1988, then ignition module is mounted directly on the distributor assembly

To install:

8. Coat the metal base of the ignition module uniformly with suitable silicone compound, about ½₂ in. (0.79mm) thick.

9. Place the TFI-module on the distributor base.

10. Carefully slide the TFI module assembly toward the distributor connector pins until the connector engages and the module screw holes line up with the tapped holes on the base.

11. Install the two module mounting screws and tighten to 15–35 inch lbs. (1.7–4.0 Nm).

12. Install the distributor in the engine, as outlined later in this section.

13. Position the distributor cap and tighten the cap mounting screws to 17–23 inch lbs. (2.0–2.6 Nm).

14. Attach the TFI-module harness connector.

15. Connect the negative battery cable, then start the engine. Using a timing light, check the ignition timing and adjust, if necessary.

1989–95 Vehicles

▶ **See Figures 27 and 28**

1. Disconnect the negative battery cable
2. Detach the ignition module/ICM electrical connector.
3. Remove the screw(s) or bolts retaining the module heatsink/bracket assembly to the radiator support bracket for vehicles through 1993 or to the front fender apron for 1994–95 vehicles.
4. Unfasten the ignition module-to-heatsink retaining screws and remove the module.

To install:

5. Coat the baseplate of the ignition module uniformly with a ½₂ in. (0.8mm) of silicone dielectric compound WA-10 or equivalent.

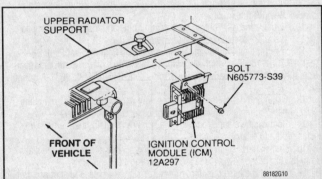

Fig. 27 The ignition module on 1989–93 vehicles, is located on the radiator support bracket

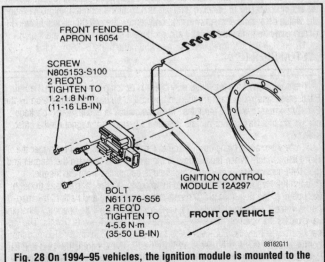

Fig. 28 On 1994–95 vehicles, the ignition module is mounted to the front fender apron

6. Position the ignition module on the heatsink/bracket and install the retaining screws. Tighten the screws to 15–35 inch lbs. (1.7–4.0 Nm) for 1989–93 vehicles or to 11–16 inch lbs. (1.2–1.8 Nm) for 1994–95 vehicles.

7. Install the module heatsink/bracket assembly to the radiator support bracket or front fender apron, as applicable. Secure with the retaining screw(s) or bolts. If retained with bolts, tighten them to 35–50 inch lbs. (4.0–5.6 Nm).

8. Attach the ignition module harness connector.

9. Connect the negative battery cable.

Stator Assembly

REMOVAL & INSTALLATION

▸ **See Figures 29, 30, 31 and 32**

1. Disconnect the negative battery cable.
2. Remove the distributor cap and position it aside with the wires attached.
3. For vehicles through 1988, detach the TFI module connector.
4. If necessary, detach the distributor from the engine control sensor.
5. Remove the distributor assembly from the engine.
6. Remove the rotor.
7. If equipped, unfasten the two retaining screws and remove the module from the base. Wipe the grease from the base and module, keeping the surfaces free of dirt.

➡ **Hold the gear to loosen the armature screws, do not hold the armature.**

8. Mark the armature and distributor gear for orientation during installation.
9. Hold the distributor drive gear and remove the armature retaining screws. Remove the armature.
10. Remove the distributor gear retaining pins and discard, if equipped.
11. If equipped, remove the gear and gear collar.
12. Invert the distributor and place in the Axle Bearing/Seal Plate D84L-950-A/T75L-1165-B or equivalent arbor press. Press off the distributor gear from the shaft, using bearing removal tool D84L-950-A/D79L-4621-A or equivalent.
13. Clean and polish the shaft with emery paper. Wipe clean so that the shaft slides out freely from the distributor base. Remove the shaft.
14. Remove the octane rod retaining screw and retain, then remove the octane rod and retain.
15. Unfasten the stator assembly retaining screws and remove the stator from the top of the bowl.
16. Inspect the base bushing for wear or signs of excess heat concentration. If damaged, replace the entire distributor. Inspect the base O-ring for damage and replace, if necessary.

To install:

17. Position the stator assembly over the bushing and press to seat. Place the stator connector in position. The tab should fit in the notch on the base and the fastening eyelets aligned with the screw holes. Be certain the wires are positioned away from moving parts.
18. Install the stator retaining screws and tighten to 15–35 inch lbs. (1.7–4.0 Nm).

19. Install the octane rod, inserting the rod through the base hole. Place the end of the octane rod onto the same post as the original stator. Only one post should fit easily in the rod hole. Firmly seat the octane rod seal into the housing.

20. Apply a light coat of engine oil to the distributor shaft (do NOT overlubricate), beneath the armature. Insert the shaft through the base bushing.

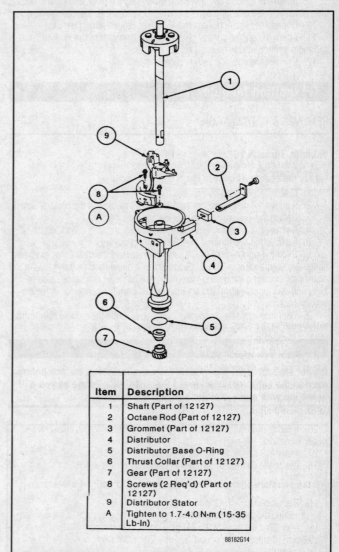

Item	Description
1	Shaft (Part of 12127)
2	Octane Rod (Part of 12127)
3	Grommet (Part of 12127)
4	Distributor
5	Distributor Base O-Ring
6	Thrust Collar (Part of 12127)
7	Gear (Part of 12127)
8	Screws (2 Req'd) (Part of 12127)
9	Distributor Stator
A	Tighten to 1.7–4.0 N·m (15-35 Lb-In)

88182G14

Fig. 30 Exploded view of the stator and related components

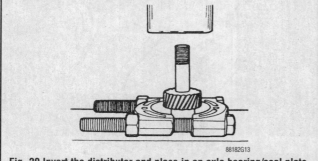

88182G13

Fig. 29 Invert the distributor and place in an axle bearing/seal plate, then press the gear from the shaft using a suitable bearing removal tool

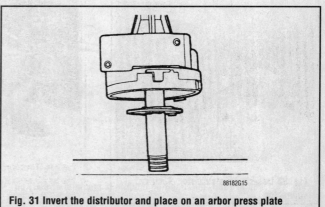

88182G15

Fig. 31 Invert the distributor and place on an arbor press plate

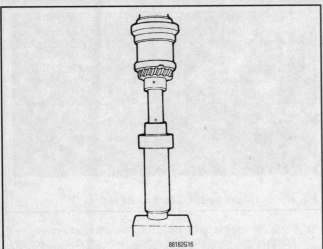

Fig. 32 Place a ⅝ in. deep well socket over the shaft and gear and press the gear to align with the retainer pin hole

21. Place the collar, if required, over the shaft and line up the mark on the armature and original drill hole. Use a drift punch to ensure proper alignment. If not present, go to step 24.

22. Insert a new roll pin through the collar and shaft. The pin should be flush with both sides of the collar when seated.

23. Position a ½ in. deep well socket over the shaft, invert and place in the arbor press.

24. Place the distributor gear on the shaft end. Make certain the mark on the armature align with the gear.

➡**The hole in the shaft and gear must be properly aligned to ensure ease of the roll pin.**

25. Place a ⅝ in. deep well socket over the shaft and gear and press the gear to align with the original drill hole.

➡**If the gear holes do not align, the gear must be removed and repressed on. A drift punch will not align the holes. As in the collar, the holes should align.**

26. Install a new roll pin through the gear and shaft. The pin should have proper extrusion.

27. Install the armature. Tighten the screws to 25–35 inch lbs. (2.8–40Nm).

28. Rotate the distributor shaft while checking for free movement.

➡**If the armature contacts the stator, replace the entire distributor.**

29. If equipped with TFI module, proceed as follows:
    a. Wipe the back of the module and its mounting surface in the distributor clean. Coat the base of the TFI ignition module uniformly with a 1/32 in. (0.8mm) of silicone compound (Silicone Dielectric Compound WA-10 or equivalent).

    b. Invert the distributor base so the stator connector is in full view. Then, insert the module. Be certain the 3 module pins are inserted into the stator connector.
    c. Install the module retaining screws and tighten to 15–35 inch lbs. (1.7–4.0 Nm).
30. Install the distributor assembly into the engine block.
31. If equipped, attach the distributor to the engine control sensor wiring.
32. For vehicles through 1988, connect the TFI module wiring harness.
33. Install the rotor and distributor cap. Tighten the cap mounting screws to 18–23 inch lbs. (2.0–2.6 Nm).
34. Connect the negative battery cable. Check the initial ignition timing and adjust if necessary.

Distributor

REMOVAL & INSTALLATION

♦ **See Figures 33, 34, 35, 36 and 37**

1. Rotate the engine until the No. 1 piston is on TDC of its compression stroke.
2. Disconnect the negative battery cable.
3. Before removing the distributor cap, mark the position of the No. 1 wire tower on the distributor base for future reference.
4. Loosen the distributor cap hold-down screws and remove the cap. Position the cap and wires out of the way.
5. Detach the distributor electrical connector.
6. If rotor removal is necessary, mark the position of the rotor to the distributor housing.
7. Scribe a mark in the distributor body and the engine block to indicate position of the distributor in the engine.
8. Remove the distributor hold-down bolt and clamp.
9. Remove the distributor assembly from the engine. Be sure not to rotate the engine while the distributor is removed.

To install:
10. Make sure that the engine it still at TDC of its compression stroke.

➡**If the crankshaft was rotated, while the distributor was removed, it will be necessary to remove the No. 1 spark plug and rotate the engine clockwise until No. 1 piston is on the compression stroke. Align the timing pointer with TDC on the crankshaft damper.**

11. Rotate the distributor shaft so the rotor points toward the mark on distributor housing, made previously.
12. Rotate the rotor slightly so the leading edge of the vane is centered in the vane switch stator assembly.
13. Rotate the distributor in the block to align the leading edge of the vane with the vane switch stator assembly. Make certain the rotor is pointing to the No. 1 mark on the distributor base.

➡**If the vane and vane switch stator cannot be aligned by rotating the distributor in the cylinder block, remove the distributor enough to just disengage the distributor gear from the camshaft gear. Rotate the rotor enough to engage the distributor gear on another tooth of the camshaft gear. Repeat Step 7, if necessary.**

Fig. 33 Detach the distributor electrical connector

Fig. 34 If removing the rotor, matchmark the position of the rotor to the distributor housing

Fig. 35 Unfasten the distributor hold-down bolt and clamp

Fig. 36 Carefully lift the distributor straight up, then . . .

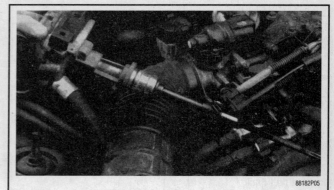

Fig. 37 . . . remove the distributor from the engine

14. Install the distributor hold-down clamp and bolt(s) and tighten slightly. Install the distributor cap and wires. Install the No. 1 spark plug, if removed.

15. Connect the negative battery cable. Check the initial ignition timing.
16. Tighten the hold-down clamp and recheck the timing. Adjust if necessary.

DISTRIBUTORLESS IGNITION SYSTEM (DIS)

General Information

The Distributorless Ignition System (DIS), also called the Electronic Ignition (EI) system, on later model vehicles, eliminates the conventional distributor and all its components, by using multiple ignition coils. Six cylinder engines use a six tower coil pack. Eight cylinder use two four tower coil packs. Each coil pack has 2 tach wires, 1 for each coil.

In the DIS ignition system, each coil fires 2 spark plugs at the same time. The plugs are paired so that the plug on the compression stroke fires, while the other plug is on its exhaust stroke. The next time the coil is fired, the plug that was on the exhaust will be on the compression and the one that was on the compression will be on the exhaust. The spark in the exhaust cylinder is wasted but little of the coil energy is lost.

The DIS ignition system consists of the following components:
• Crankshaft timing sensor
• Camshaft sensor
• DIS ignition module (vehicles through 1995)
• Ignition coil pack
• Spark angle portion of the EEC-IV module
• Powertrain Control Module (PCM)
• Related wiring

These engines use a camshaft and crankshaft sensor. These sensors are hall effect devices. A rotary vane cup (or wheel), made of ferrous metal is used to trigger the hall effect devices. The camshaft cup incorporates a single tooth and is driven by the camshaft. The signal from the camshaft sensor has 1 positive-going edge once every camshaft revolution. The crankshaft cup incorporates 3 teeth and causes the crankshaft sensor to generate 3 positive (PIP) edges every crankshaft revolution.

➡On 1996–97 vehicles, there is no longer a stand-alone Ignition Control Module (ICM). The ICM has been integrated into the PCM. The Profile Ignition Pickup (PIP), Spark Output (SPOUT), Ignition Ground (IGN GND), and Ignition Diagnostic Monitor (IDM) have also been enclosed in the PCM. The functionality of the ignition remains the same.

SYSTEM OPERATION

EEC-IV Vehicles Through 1995

In the DIS ignition system the EEC-IV processor determines the spark angle using the PIP signal to establish base timing. Spout is provided by the EEC-IV processor to the DIS module and serves 2 purposes. The leading edge fires the coil and the trailing edge controls the dwell time. This feature is referred to as Computer Control Dwell (CCD).

The DIS module incorporates an Ignition Diagnostic Monitor (IDM). This is an output signal that provides diagnostic information concerning the ignition system to the EEC-IV processor for self-test. It is also the input signal for the vehicle's tachometer.

If the CID circuit fails and an attempt to start the engine is made, the DIS module will randomly select 1 of the coils to fire. If hard starting results, turning the key **OFF** and trying to restart will result in another guess. Several attempts may be needed until the proper coil is selected, allowing the vehicle to be started and driven until repairs can be made. The Failure Mode Effects Management (FMEM) system will try to keep the vehicle driveable despite certain EEC-IV system failures that prevent the EEC-IV processor from providing spark angle or dwell commands. The EEC-IV processor opens the SPOUT line and the DIS module fires the coils directly from the PIP input. This condition will result in a fixed spark angle of 10 degrees and a fixed dwell.

The DIS ignition module receives the PIP signal from the crankshaft sensor, the CID signals from the camshaft sensor and the Spout (spark out) signal is from the EEC-IV control module. During normal operation the PIP signal is sent to the EEC-IV control module from the crankshaft timing sensor and provides base timing and rpm information. The CID signal provides the DIS module with the information required to synchronize the ignition coils so that they are fired in the proper sequence.

When the window of the vane cup is located between the magnet and hall effect device, a magnetic flux field is completed. At this time the magnetic field is allow to travel from the permanent magnet through the hall effect device and back to the magnetic. This condition creates a low (0 volts) output signal. When the vane tooth is located between the magnet and hall effect device, the flux field is shunted through the vane and back to the magnetic. The output signal, during this time, will change from a low (0 volts) to high (source volts).

1996–97 EEC-V Vehicles

In the EI system, the Crankshaft Position (CKP) sensor is used to indicate the crankshaft position and speed information to the PCM. By sensing a missing tooth on a trigger wheel mounted on the crankshaft damper, the CKP is also able to identify a specific point in the travel of piston 1. The PCM uses the information from the CKP sensor to generate an internal Profile Ignition Pickup (PIP) signal.

Once the PIP signal is generated, fuel and spark functions are enabled. The calculated spark target is used internally by the PCM as a pulse width modulated digital signal called the Spark Output (SPOUT). The PCM decodes the SPOUT signal and fires the next spark at the commanded spark target. The PIP signal is also used to supply a clean, inverted signal (PIP) for tachometer operation.

The PCM also serves as an electric switch for the coil primary circuit. When the switch closes, current flows and a magnetic field expands around the primary coil. When the switch opens, current flows and a magnetic field expands around the primary coil. When the switch opens, the field collapses and causes the secondary coil to fire the spark plugs at high voltage. In addition, and Ignition Diagnostic Monitor (IDM) signal is transmitted on each spark firing. This signal communicates information by pulse width modulation.

SYSTEM COMPONENTS

Crankshaft Timing Sensor

The crankshaft sensor, is a single hall effect magnetic device. Its provides base timing and rpm signals to by the DIS and EEC-IV modules.

Camshaft Sensor

The camshaft sensor, is a single hall effect magnetic device, which is activated by a single vane driven by the camshaft. This sensor provides CID information for the ignition coil and fuel synchronization. The sensor is in the location normally used for the distributor.

Ignition Coil Pack

The ignition coil pack contains six coil towers for 6-cylinder engine or two four tower coil packs for 8-cylinder engines. Each ignition coil fires 2 spark plugs simultaneously. The spark plug fired on the exhaust stroke uses very little of the ignition coil's stored energy.

DIS Ignition Module

On vehicles through 1995, the DIS ignition module receives the PIP signal from the crankshaft sensor. The CID signal provides the DIS ignition module with the information required to synchronize the ignition coils so that they are fired in the proper sequence.

1996–97 vehicles do not have an ignition control module. The PCM determines the ignition coil ON and OFF times and calculates the desired spark angle signal.

Diagnosis and Testing

Refer to Diagnosis and Testing under Dura Spark II ignition system.

REMOVAL & INSTALLATION

▸ **See Figures 38, 39 and 40**

1. Turn the ignition key **OFF** and disconnect the negative battery cable.
2. Detach the electrical harness connector(s) from the ignition coil pack and the radio ignition interference capacitors.
3. Disconnect the spark plug wires by squeezing the locking tabs and twisting while pulling upward to release the coil boot retainers.
4. Unfasten the ignition coil pack mounting screws, then remove the coil pack and radio ignition interference capacitors, if equipped.

➡**If equipped, save the radio ignition interference capacitors for reinstallation with the ignition coils.**

To install:

5. Position the coil pack and radio ignition interference capacitor (if equipped) to the mounting bracket. Secure with the retaining screws and tighten to 40–62 inch lbs. (5–7 Nm).

➡**Apply a suitable silicone dielectric compound to the spark plug wire boots before connecting them to the coil.**

6. Attach each spark plug wire to the ignition coil. Make sure the boots are properly seated.

7. Connect the engine control sensor wiring to the ignition coils and, if equipped, radio ignition interference capacitor.
8. Connect the negative battery cable.

➡**Be sure to place some dielectric compound into each spark plug boot prior to installation of the spark plug wire.**

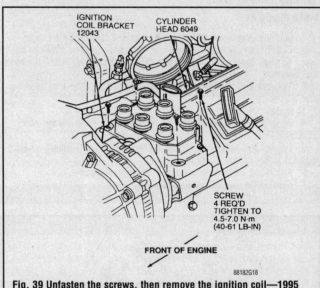

Fig. 39 Unfasten the screws, then remove the ignition coil—1995 3.8L SC engine shown

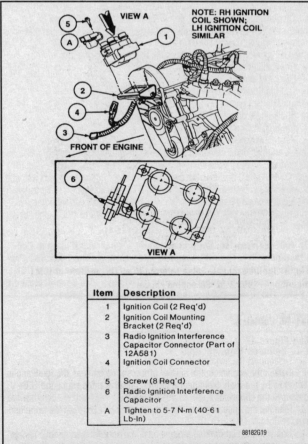

Item	Description
1	Ignition Coil (2 Req'd)
2	Ignition Coil Mounting Bracket (2 Req'd)
3	Radio Ignition Interference Capacitor Connector (Part of 12A581)
4	Ignition Coil Connector
5	Screw (8 Req'd)
6	Radio Ignition Interference Capacitor
A	Tighten to 5-7 N·m (40-61 Lb-In)

Fig. 40 Ignition coil location and mounting—1995 4.6L engine shown

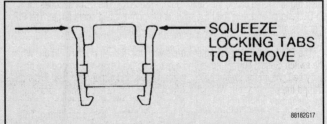

SQUEEZE LOCKING TABS TO REMOVE

Fig. 38 You must squeeze the locking tabs on the spark plug wires to remove them from the coil

DIS Ignition Module/Ignition Control Module (ICM)

REMOVAL & INSTALLATION

Vehicles Through 1993

♦ See Figure 41

1. Turn the ignition key **OFF** and disconnect the negative battery cable.
2. Detach both electrical connectors at the ignition module. It may be necessary to press down on the locking tabs (where it is stamped PUSH) to remove the connector.
3. Unfasten the ignition module mounting bolts, then remove the module from the vehicle.
To install:
4. Apply a uniform coat of about 1/32 in. (0.08mm) or silicone dielectric compound to the mounting surface of the ignition module.
5. Position the module, then install the mounting bolts. Tighten the mounting bolts to 22–30 inch lbs. (2.5–3.5 Nm).
6. Attach both electrical connectors to the ignition module.
7. Connect the negative battery cable.

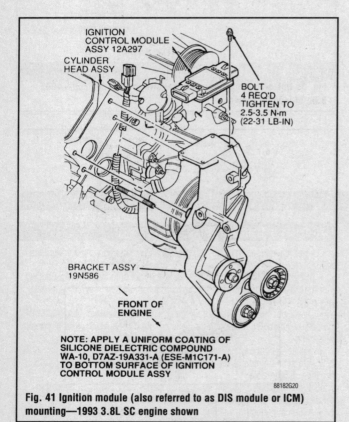

NOTE: APPLY A UNIFORM COATING OF SILICONE DIELECTRIC COMPOUND WA-10, D7AZ-19A331-A (ESE-M1C171-A) TO BOTTOM SURFACE OF IGNITION CONTROL MODULE ASSY

88182G20

Fig. 41 Ignition module (also referred to as DIS module or ICM) mounting—1993 3.8L SC engine shown

1994–95 Vehicles

♦ See Figure 42

1. Disconnect the negative battery cable.
2. Detach the engine control sensor wiring connector from the ignition control module by pressing down on the locking tab where it is stamped PUSH, and remove the connector.
3. Remove the ignition module and the module bracket from the front fender apron.
4. Unfasten the two ignition module retaining screws, then remove the ignition module form the module bracket.

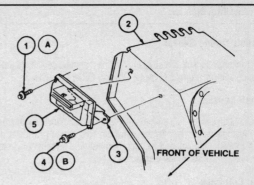

Item	Description
1	Screw (2 Req'd)
2	Front Fender Apron
3	Ignition Control Module Bracket
4	Bolt
5	Ignition Control Module
A	Tighten to 2.7-3.7 N·m (24-33 Lb-In)
B	Tighten to 4-5.6 N·m (35-50 Lb-In)

88182G21

Fig. 42 The ignition module on 1994–95 vehicles is mounted on the front fender apron

To install:
5. Install the ignition module onto the module bracket. Tighten the retaining screws to 24–33 inch lbs. (2.7–3.7 Nm).
6. Position the ignition module and bracket assembly onto the front fender apron. Secure with the retaining bolt and tighten to 35–50 inch lbs. (4–5.6 Nm).
7. Attach the engine control sensor wiring connector to the ignition module.
8. Connect the negative battery cable.

Synchronizer Assembly

REMOVAL & INSTALLATION

♦ See Figure 43

➡ Prior to starting this procedure, set the No. 1 cylinder to 26 degrees after top dead center of the compression stroke. Then take note of the position of the camshaft sensor electrical connector. The installation procedure requires that the connector be located in the same position.

1. Turn the ignition key **OFF** and disconnect the negative battery cable.
2. Remove the camshaft sensor.
3. Remove the synchronizer clamp (bolt and washer assembly).
4. Remove the synchronizer from the front of the engine cover assembly. Take note that the intermediate oil pump drive shaft should be removed with the synchronizer assembly.
To install:
If the replacement synchronizer does not contain a plastic locator cover tool, a special service tool such as synchro positioner T89P–12200–A or equivalent must be obtained prior to installation of the replacement synchronizer. Failure to follow this procedure will result in improper synchronizer alignment. This will result in the ignition system and fuel system being out of time with the engine, possibly causing engine damage.
5. If the replacement synchronizer does not contain a plastic locator cover tool, attach the synchro positioner tool T89P–12200–A or equivalent as follows:
    a. Engage the synchronizer vane into the radial slot of the tool. Rotate the tool on the synchronizer base until the tool boss engages the base notch.
    b. The cover tool should be square and in contact with the entire top surface of the synchronizer base.

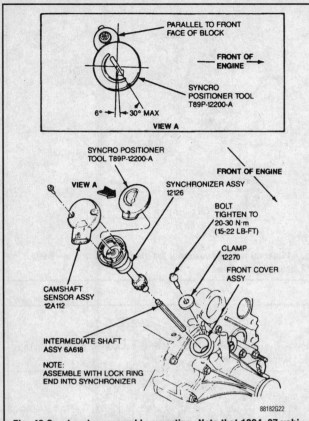

Fig. 43 Synchronizer assembly mounting. Note that 1994–97 vehicles do not utilize a synchronizer

6. Transfer the intermediate oil pump driveshaft from the old synchronizer to the new one.

7. Install the synchronizer assembly so that the gear engagement occurs when the arrow on the locator tool is pointed approximately 30 degrees counterclockwise from the front face of the engine block. This step will locate the camshaft sensor electrical connector in the pre-removal position.

8. Install the synchronizer base clamp, bolt and washer and torque the bolt to 15–22 ft. lbs. (20–30 Nm)

9. Remove the synchro positioner tool T89P–12200–A or equivalent.

10. Install the camshaft sensor.

➡**Make sure the camshaft sensor electrical connector is positioned properly (i.e. not contacting the A/C bracket or forward of the supercharger drive belt). Do not reposition the connector by rotating the synchronizer base. This will result in the ignition system and fuel system being out of time with the engine, possibly causing engine damage. Remove the synchronizer and repeat the installation procedure.**

11. Connect the negative battery cable.

Crankshaft Position (CKP) Sensor

REMOVAL & INSTALLATION

For removal and installation of the Crankshaft Position (CKP) sensor, please refer to Section 4 of this manual.

Camshaft Position (CMP) Sensor

REMOVAL & INSTALLATION

For removal and installation of the Camshaft Position (CMP) sensor, please refer to Section 4 of this manual.

CHARGING SYSTEM

General Information

The automobile charging system provides electrical power for operation of the vehicle's ignition and starting systems and all the electrical accessories. The battery serves as an electrical surge or storage tank, storing (in chemical form) the energy originally produced by the engine driven alternator. The system also provides a means of regulating generator output to protect the battery from being overcharged and to avoid excessive voltage to the accessories.

The storage battery is a chemical device incorporating parallel lead plates in a tank containing a sulfuric acid/water solution. Adjacent plates are slightly dissimilar, and the chemical reaction of the 2 dissimilar plates produces electrical energy when the battery is connected to a load such as the starter motor. The chemical reaction is reversible, so that when the generator is producing a voltage (electrical pressure) greater than that produced by the battery, electricity is forced into the battery, and the battery is returned to its fully charged state.

The vehicle's alternator is driven mechanically, by a belt(s) that is driven by the engine crankshaft. In an alternator, the field rotates while all the current produced passes only through the stator winding. The brushes bear against continuous slip rings rather than a commutator. This causes the current produced to periodically reverse the direction of its flow creating alternating current (A/C). Diodes (electrical one-way switches) block the flow of current from traveling in the wrong direction. A series of diodes is wired together to permit the alternating flow of the stator to be converted to a pulsating, but unidirectional flow at the alternator output. The alternator's field is wired in series with the voltage regulator.

The regulator consists of several circuits. Each circuit has a core, or magnetic coil of wire, which operates a switch. Each switch is connected to ground through one or more resistors. The coil of wire responds directly to system voltage. When the voltage reaches the required level, the magnetic field created by the winding of wire closes the switch and inserts a resistance into the generator field circuit, thus reducing the output. The contacts of the switch cycle open and close many times each second to precisely control voltage.

Alternator Precautions

Several precautions must be observed when performing work on alternator equipment.

• If the battery is removed for any reason, make sure that it is reconnected with the correct polarity. Reversing the battery connections may result in damage to the one-way rectifiers.

• Never operate the alternator with the main circuit broken. Make sure that the battery, alternator, and regulator leads are not disconnected while the engine is running.

• Never attempt to polarize an alternator.

• When charging a battery that is installed in the vehicle, disconnect the negative battery cable.

• When utilizing a booster battery as a starting aid, always connect it in parallel; negative to negative, and positive to positive.

• When arc (electric) welding is to be performed on any part of the vehicle, disconnect the negative battery cable and alternator leads.

• Never unplug the PCM while the engine is running or with the ignition in the **ON** position. Severe and expensive damage may result within the solid state equipment.

Alternator

TESTING

Voltage Test

1. Make sure the engine is **OFF**, and turn the headlights on for 15–20 seconds to remove any surface charge from the battery.

2. Using a DVOM set to volts DC, probe across the battery terminals.
3. Measure the battery voltage.
4. Write down the voltage reading and proceed to the next test.

No-Load Test

1. Connect a tachometer to the engine.

❋❋ CAUTION

Ensure that the transmission is in PARK and the emergency brake is set. Blocking a wheel is optional and an added safety measure.

2. Turn off all electrical loads (radio, blower motor, wipers, etc.)
3. Start the engine and increase engine speed to approximately 1500 rpm.
4. Measure the voltage reading at the battery with the engine holding a steady 1500 rpm. Voltage should have raised at least 0.5 volts, but no more than 2.5 volts.
5. If the voltage does not go up more than 0.5 volts, the alternator is not charging. If the voltage goes up more than 2.5 volts, the alternator is overcharging.

➡Usually under and overcharging is caused by a defective alternator, or its related parts (regulator), and replacement will fix the problem; however, faulty wiring and other problems can cause the charging system to malfunction. Further testing, which is not covered by this book, will reveal the exact component failure. Many automotive parts stores have alternator bench testers available for use by customers. An alternator bench test is the most definitive way to determine the condition of your alternator.

6. If the voltage is within specifications, proceed to the next test.

Load Test

1. With the engine running, turn on the blower motor and the high beams (or other electrical accessories to place a load on the charging system).
2. Increase and hold engine speed to 2000 rpm.
3. Measure the voltage reading at the battery.
4. The voltage should increase at least 0.5 volts from the voltage test. If the voltage does not meet specifications, the charging system is malfunctioning.

➡Usually under and overcharging is caused by a defective alternator, or its related parts (regulator), and replacement will fix the problem; however, faulty wiring and other problems can cause the charging system to malfunction. Further testing, which is not covered by this book, will reveal the exact component failure. Many automotive parts stores have alternator bench testers available for use by customers. An alternator bench test is the most definitive way to determine the condition of your alternator.

REMOVAL & INSTALLATION

Vehicles Through 1993

▶ **See Figures 44, 45, 46 and 47**

1. Disconnect the negative battery cable.
2. For all except side terminal alternators, disconnect the wire harness attachments from the integral alternator/regulator assembly.
3. Loosen the alternator pivot bolt, then remove the adjustment arm bolt from the alternator.
4. Disengage the alternator drive belt from the alternator pulley.
5. For side-terminal alternators, disconnect the wiring terminals from the back of the alternator. The stator and field wiring terminals are the push-on type. After depressing the lock tab, the push-on terminal should be pulled straight off the terminal to prevent damage.
6. Remove the alternator pivot bolt, then remove the alternator/regulator assembly.
7. If equipped, remove the alternator fan shield.
To Install:
8. Position the alternator/regulator assembly on the engine. Install the alternator pivot and adjuster arm bolts, but do not tighten the bolts until the belt is tensioned.

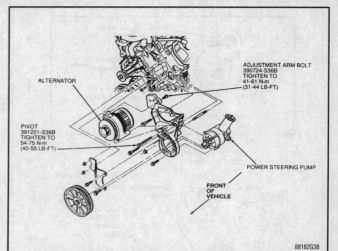
Fig. 44 Integral regulator/external fan alternator mounting—1992 3.8L base engine shown

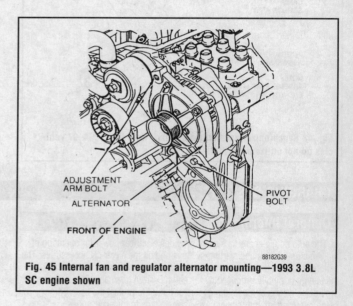
Fig. 45 Internal fan and regulator alternator mounting—1993 3.8L SC engine shown

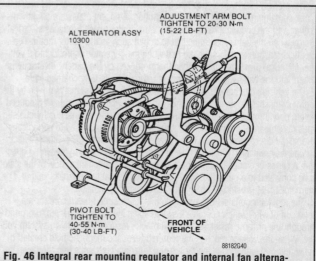
Fig. 46 Integral rear mounting regulator and internal fan alternator—1992 5.0L engine shown

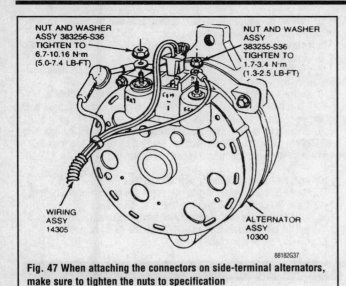

Fig. 47 When attaching the connectors on side-terminal alternators, make sure to tighten the nuts to specification

9. For side terminal alternators, connect the wiring terminals to the alternator. Tighten the nuts to the specifications shown in the accompanying figure.

10. Install the drive belt over the alternator pulley.

11. Adjust the belt tensioner, then tighten to the following specifications:
 a. 1983–88 vehicles: Tighten the adjusting bolt to 30–45 ft. lbs. (41–61 Nm) and the pivot bolt to 50–70 ft. lbs. (68–94 Nm).
 b. 1989–92 3.8L (base) engine: Tighten the adjustment arm bolt to 31–44 ft. lbs. (41–61 Nm) and the pivot bolt to 40–55 ft. lbs. (54–75 Nm).
 c. 1989–93 3.8L SC and 5.0L engines: Tighten the adjustment arm bolt to 15–22 ft. lbs. (20–30 Nm) and the pivot bolt to 30–40 ft. lbs. (40–55 Nm).
 d. 1993 3.8L (base) engine: Tighten the adjustment arm bolt to 23–31 ft. lbs. (30–43 Nm) and the pivot bolt to 45–56 ft. lbs. (61–77 Nm).

12. Check the belt tension using Belt Tensioner Gauge T63L-8620-A or equivalent. Apply pressure to the alternator front housing only when adjusting belt tension.

13. If not already done, connect the alternator wire harness.

14. If equipped, attach the alternator fan shield to the alternator assembly.

15. Connect the negative battery cable.

1994–97 Vehicles

♦ See Figures 48, 49 and 50

1. Disconnect the negative battery cable.

2. Detach the wire harness attachments to the alternator/voltage regulator assembly.

3. Disengage the drive belt from the alternator pulley.

4. On the 4.6L engine, unfasten the alternator mounting bolts, then remove the alternator mounting bracket. On the 3.8L (non-SC) engines, remove the alternator mounting bolt.

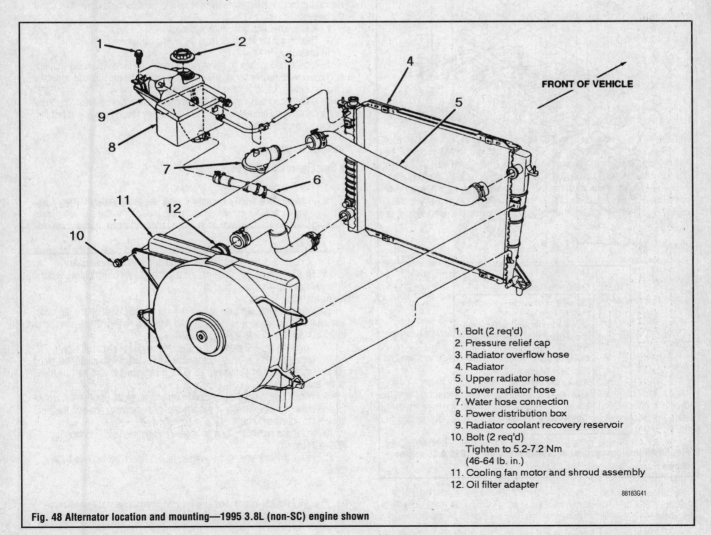

1. Bolt (2 req'd)
2. Pressure relief cap
3. Radiator overflow hose
4. Radiator
5. Upper radiator hose
6. Lower radiator hose
7. Water hose connection
8. Power distribution box
9. Radiator coolant recovery reservoir
10. Bolt (2 req'd)
   Tighten to 5.2-7.2 Nm
   (46-64 lb. in.)
11. Cooling fan motor and shroud assembly
12. Oil filter adapter

Fig. 48 Alternator location and mounting—1995 3.8L (non-SC) engine shown

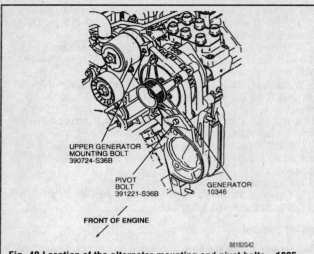

Fig. 49 Location of the alternator mounting and pivot bolts—1995 3.8L SC engine shown

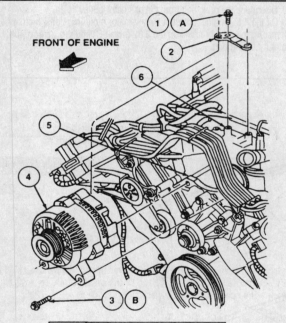

Item	Description
1	Generator Mounting Bracket Bolt (3 Req'd)
2	Generator Mounting Bracket
3	Generator Mounting Bolt (2 Req'd)
4	Generator
5	Cylinder Block
6	Intake Manifold
A	Tighten to 8-12 N·m (71-106 Lb-In)
B	Tighten to 20-30 N·m (15-22 Lb-Ft)

Fig. 50 Alternator/regulator assembly mounting—1995 4.6L engine shown

5. Remove the alternator mounting bolts or pivot bolt, as applicable, then remove the alternator from the vehicle.

To install:

6. Position the alternator on the engine.

7. On the 3.8L SC engine, install the alternator pivot and upper mounting bolts but do not tighten the bolts until the drive belt is installed.

8. On the 4.6L engine, install the mounting bolts. Tighten the bolts to 15–22 ft. lbs. (20–30 Nm). On the 3.8L (non-SC) engines, install the pivot bolt. Tighten the pivot bolt to 30–40 ft. lbs. (40–55 Nm).

9. On the 4.6L engine, install the alternator mounting bracket and retaining bolts. Tighten the bolts to 70–106 inch lbs. (8–12 Nm). On the 3.8L (non-SC) engine, install the alternator mounting bolt and tighten to 15–22 ft. lbs. (20–30 Nm).

10. Install the drive belt over the alternator pulley.

11. On the 3.8L SC engines, tighten the upper alternator mounting bolts to 30–40 ft. lbs. (40–55 Nm) and the pivot bolt to 40–53 ft. lbs.)

12. Attach the engine control sensor wiring to the alternator/voltage regulator. Tighten the output terminal nut to 80–97 inch lbs. (9–11 Nm).

13. Connect the negative battery cable.

Voltage Regulator

REMOVAL & INSTALLATION

Electronic Regulator

1. Remove the battery ground cable. On models with the regulator mounted behind the battery, it is necessary to remove the battery hold-down, and move the battery.

2. Remove the regulator mounting screws.

3. Disconnect the regulator from the wiring harness.

To install:

4. Mount the regulator to the regulator mounting plate. The radio suppression condenser mounts under one mounting screw; the ground lead under the other mounting screw. Tighten the mounting screws.

5. If the battery was moved to gain access to the regulator, position the battery and install the hold-down. Connect the battery ground cable, and test the system for proper voltage regulation.

Integral Regulator

▶ See Figures 51 thru 56

1. Disconnect the battery ground cable.

2. Remove the alternator from the engine as described previously.

3. Remove the four screws retaining the regulator to the alternator rear housing. Remove the regulator, with brush holder attached, from the alternator.

4. If necessary, hold the regulator in one hand and break off the tab covering the, **A** marked, screw head with you hand or a prytool, if necessary.

5. Remove two screws retaining the regulator to the brush holder. Separate the regulator from the brush holder.

To Install:

6. Wipe the regulator base plate with a clean cloth, position the regulator against the brush holder and install the two retaining screws. Tighten the screws to 20–30 inch lbs. (2.3–3.4 Nm).

7. Cover the head of the **A** terminal screw head with electrical tape.

8. Locate brushes in brush holder and hold in place with a thin, flat piece of steel, rubber band or equivalent. Loop the brush leads toward the brush end of the brush holder.

9. Wipe the alternator rear housing with a clean cloth. Position the regulator and brush holder assembly in the alternator rear housing and pull the piece of steel or rubberband out.

10. Install the regulator retaining screws and tighten to 25–35 inch lbs. (2.8–4.0 Nm).

11. Install the alternator in the vehicle, then connect the negative battery cable.

Fig. 51 Unfasten the retaining screws, then remove the regulator from the alternator housing

Fig. 52 Hold the regulator in one hand and break off the tab covering the, A-marked, screw head

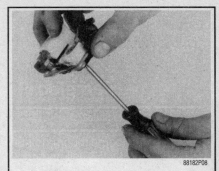

Fig. 53 Unfasten the two retaining screws, then separate the regulator from the brush holder

Fig. 54 Hold the brushes in place the brush holder with a rubber band, then position in the alternator housing

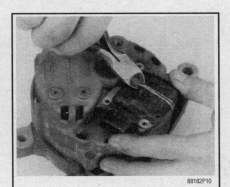

Fig. 55 Use a suitable tool to cut the rubber band, . . .

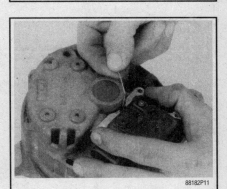

Fig. 56 . . . then pull the rubber band from the alternator housing

STARTING SYSTEM

General Information

The starting system includes the battery, starter motor, solenoid, ignition switch, circuit protection and wiring connecting the components. An inhibitor switch located in the Transmission Range (TR) sensor is included in the starting system to prevent the vehicle from being started with the vehicle in gear.

When the ignition key is turned to the **START** position, current flows and energizes the starter's solenoid coil. The solenoid plunger and clutch shift lever are activated and the clutch pinion engages the ring gear on the flywheel. The switch contacts close and the starter cranks the engine until it starts.

To prevent damage caused by excessive starter armature rotation when the engine starts, the starter incorporates an over-running clutch in the pinion gear.

Starter

TESTING

Voltage Drop Test

➡**The battery must be in good condition and fully charged prior to performing this test.**

1. Disable the ignition system by unplugging the coil pack. Verify that the vehicle will not start.
2. Connect a voltmeter between the positive terminal of the battery and the starter **B+** circuit.
3. Turn the ignition key to the **START** position and note the voltage on the meter.
4. If voltage reads 0.5 volts or more, there is high resistance in the starter cables or the cable ground, repair as necessary. If the voltage reading is ok proceed to the next step.

5. Connect a voltmeter between the positive terminal of the battery and the starter **M** circuit.
6. Turn the ignition key to the **START** position and note the voltage on the meter.
7. If voltage reads 0.5 volts or more, there is high resistance in the starter. Repair or replace the starter as necessary.

➡**Many automotive parts stores have starter bench testers available for use by customers. A starter bench test is the most definitive way to determine the condition of your starter.**

REMOVAL & INSTALLATION

Positive Engagement Type Starter

▸ **See Figure 57**

1. Disconnect the negative battery cable.
2. Raise and safely support the vehicle with jackstands.
3. Tag and disconnect the wiring at the starter.
4. If necessary, turn the front wheels fully to the right. On some later models it will be necessary to remove the frame brace. On many models, it will be necessary to remove the two bolts retaining the steering idler arm to the frame to gain access to the starter.
5. Unfasten the starter mounting bolts, then remove the starter from the vehicle.
   To install:
6. Position the starter motor to the engine, then secure with the retaining bolts. Tighten the mounting bolts to 12–15 ft. lbs. (16–20 Nm) on starters with 3 mounting bolts and 15–20 ft. lbs. (20–27 Nm) on starters with 2 mounting bolts.
7. If removed, tighten the idler arm retaining bolts to 28–35 ft. lbs. (38–47 Nm).

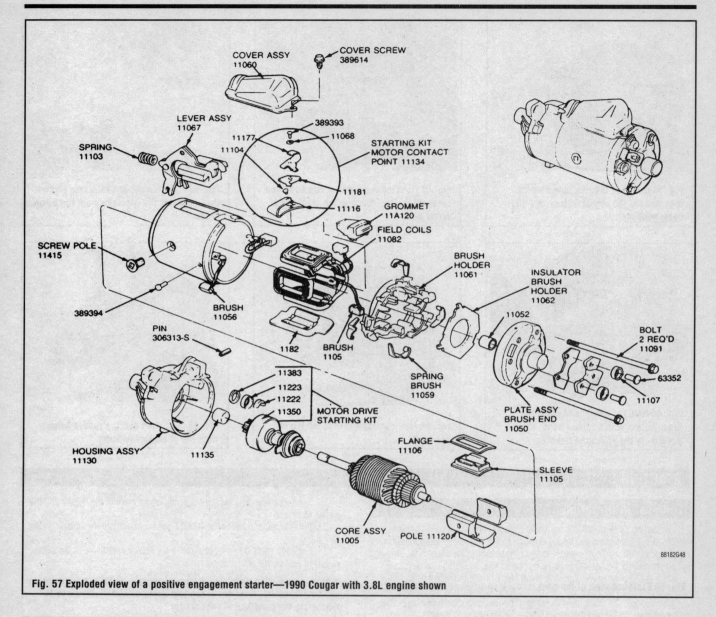

Fig. 57 Exploded view of a positive engagement starter—1990 Cougar with 3.8L engine shown

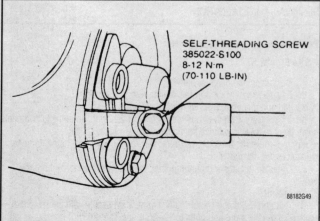

Fig. 58 Fasten the starter cable to the starter, then tighten to specification

8. Connect the starter cable to the motor. Tighten to 70–110 inch lbs. (8–12 Nm).
9. Carefully lower the vehicle.
10. Connect the negative battery cable.

Gear Reduced Permanent Magnet Starter

▶ See Figure 58 and 59

⁂ **CAUTION**

When servicing the starter or performing any work around the starter motor, note that the heavy gauge input lead connected to the starter solenoid is hot at all times. Make sure the protective cap is installed over the terminal and is replaced after service.

1. Disconnect the negative battery cable.
2. Raise and safely support the vehicle with jackstands.
3. Disconnect starter cable and the push-on relay connector from solenoid.
4. Unfasten the starter retaining bolts, then remove the starter from the vehicle.

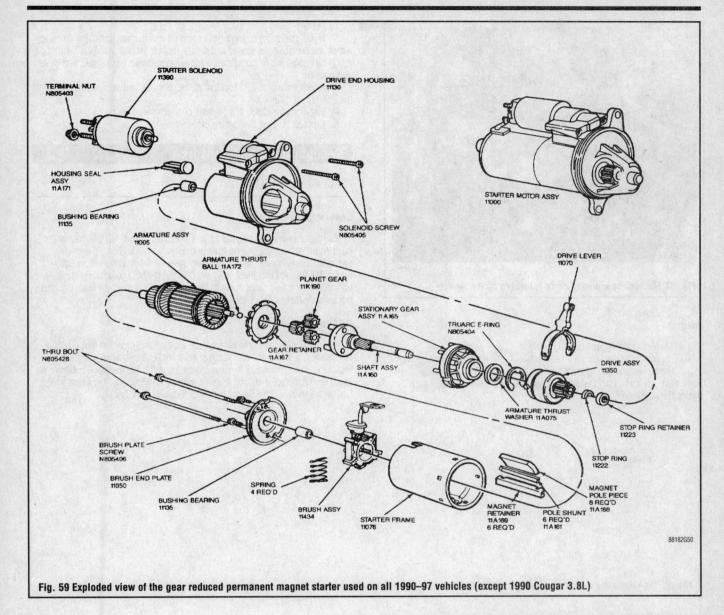

Fig. 59 Exploded view of the gear reduced permanent magnet starter used on all 1990–97 vehicles (except 1990 Cougar 3.8L)

To install:

5. Position the starter motor to the engine and install the upper and lower bolts finger-tight. Begin with the top most bolt and work down, tighten the bolts to 15–20 ft. lbs. (20–27 Nm).

6. Attach the starter solenoid connector. Be careful to push straight on and make sure the connector locks in positions with a notable click or detent.

7. Install the starter cable nut to the starter solenoid B-terminal. Tighten to 80–124 inch lbs. (9–14 Nm). Replace the red starter solenoid safety cap.

8. Carefully lower the vehicle, then connect the negative battery cable.

SOLENOID REPLACEMENT

Remote Mount

▶ **See Figures 60 and 61**

1. Disconect the negative battery cable.
2. Tag and disconnect all wires from the relay.
3. Unfasten the two mounting screws attaching relay to fender, then remove the relay from the vehicle.
4. Installation is the reverse of removal. Tighten the relay retaining bolts to 70–110 inch lbs. (8.0–12.4 Nm).

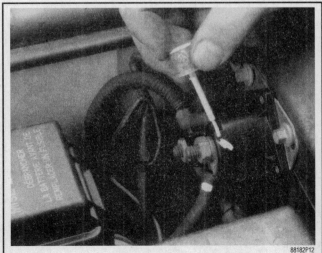

Fig. 60 Make sure to tag or mark the connectors before detaching

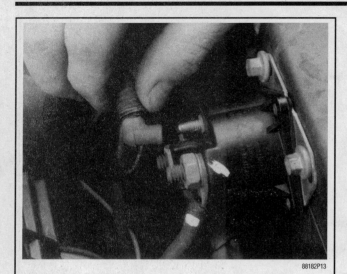

Fig. 61 The remote mounted relay is located on the fender

Integral

1. Disconnect the negative battery cable.
2. Remove the starter from the vehicle as outlined earlier in this section.
3. Detach the field coil connection from the solenoid motor terminal.
4. Remove the solenoid attaching screws, solenoid and plunger return spring. Rotate the solenoid 90° to remove it.

To install:

5. Install the return spring on the solenoid plunger and install the solenoid. Attach the two solenoid screws and tighten them to 84 inch lbs. (9.4 Nm). Apply a sealing compound to the junction of the solenoid case flange, gear and drive end housing.
6. Attach the motor field terminal to the solenoid, and tighten fasteners to 30 inch lbs. (3.4 Nm).
7. Install starter motor in vehicle as previously described.
8. Connect the negative battery cable.

Sending Units and Sensors

REMOVAL & INSTALLATION

Coolant Temperature

The coolant temperature sending unit is located on the, left side rear of the head on inline engines, and on front of the intake manifold on V6 and V8 engines. Disconnect the sensor wire and unscrew the sending unit, quickly thread the new unit into place (this will cause very little coolant fluid loss) tighten until the fluid stops leaking; to about 6–10 ft. lbs. (8–14 Nm). Connect the sensor wire and check for normal operation.

Oil Pressure

All Ford engines have the oil pressure sending unit mounted in the side of the engine block near the oil filter. A special socket is available to remove and install the unit. Disconnect the sensor wire, using the special socket remove the sending unit. Before installing the new sending unit, put Teflon® tape or equivalent on the threads, tighten unit to 10–15 ft. lbs. (14–20 Nm).

ENGINE MECHANICAL 3-2
ENGINE 3-7
  REMOVAL & INSTALLATION 3-7
ROCKER ARM (VALVE) COVER 3-13
  REMOVAL & INSTALLATION 3-13
ROCKER ARM (CAM FOLLOWER) AND
  HYDRAULIC LASH ADJUSTER 3-15
  REMOVAL & INSTALLATION 3-15
ROCKER ARM SHAFT/ROCKER
  ARMS 3-15
  REMOVAL & INSTALLATION 3-15
VALVE LASH 3-15
  ADJUSTMENTS 3-15
THERMOSTAT 3-16
  REMOVAL & INSTALLATION 3-16
INTAKE MANIFOLD 3-17
REMOVAL & INSTALLATION 3-17
EXHAUST MANIFOLD 3-22
  REMOVAL & INSTALLATION 3-22
TURBOCHARGER 3-26
  REMOVAL & INSTALLATION 3-26
SUPERCHARGER 3-27
  REMOVAL & INSTALLATION 3-27
RADIATOR 3-28
  REMOVAL & INSTALLATION 3-28
ELECTRIC COOLING FAN 3-29
  REMOVAL & INSTALLATION 3-29
BELT-DRIVEN COOLING FAN 3-30
  REMOVAL & INSTALLATION 3-30
WATER PUMP 3-30
  REMOVAL & INSTALLATION 3-30
CYLINDER HEAD 3-32
  REMOVAL & INSTALLATION 3-32
OIL PAN 3-38
  REMOVAL & INSTALLATION 3-38
OIL PUMP 3-42
  REMOVAL & INSTALLATION 3-42
CRANKSHAFT DAMPER 3-43
  REMOVAL & INSTALLATION 3-43
TIMING BELT COVER 3-43
  REMOVAL & INSTALLATION 3-43
TIMING CHAIN COVER AND SEAL 3-43
  REMOVAL & INSTALLATION 3-43
TIMING BELT 3-46
  REMOVAL & INSTALLATION 3-46
TIMING CHAIN 3-47
  REMOVAL & INSTALLATION 3-47
CAMSHAFT SPROCKET 3-50
  REMOVAL & INSTALLATION 3-50
CAMSHAFT 3-51
  REMOVAL & INSTALLATION 3-51
  INSPECTION 3-55
AUXILIARY SHAFT 3-55
  REMOVAL & INSTALLATION 3-55
REAR MAIN OIL SEAL 3-55
  REMOVAL & INSTALLATION 3-56
FLYWHEEL/FLEX PLATE AND RING
  GEAR 3-56
  REMOVAL & INSTALLATION 3-56

EXHAUST SYSTEM 3-57
INSPECTION 3-57
  REPLACEMENT 3-58
ENGINE RECONDITIONING 3-59
DETERMINING ENGINE CONDITION 3-59
  COMPRESSION TEST 3-59
  OIL PRESSURE TEST 3-59
BUY OR REBUILD? 3-60
ENGINE OVERHAUL TIPS 3-60
  TOOLS 3-60
  OVERHAUL TIPS 3-60
  CLEANING 3-60
  REPAIRING DAMAGED
    THREADS 3-61
ENGINE PREPARATION 3-62
CYLINDER HEAD 3-62
  DISASSEMBLY 3-62
  INSPECTION 3-65
  REFINISHING & REPAIRING 3-67
  ASSEMBLY 3-68
ENGINE BLOCK 3-69
  GENERAL INFORMATION 3-69
  DISASSEMBLY 3-69
  INSPECTION 3-70
  REFINISHING 3-72
  ASSEMBLY 3-72
ENGINE START-UP AND BREAK-IN 3-74
  STARTING THE ENGINE 3-74
  BREAKING IT IN 3-74
  KEEP IT MAINTAINED 3-74
SPECIFICATIONS CHARTS
  VALVE SPECIFICATIONS 3-2
  CAMSHAFT SPECIFICATIONS 3-3
  CRANKSHAFT AND CONNECTING ROD
    SPECIFICATIONS 3-4
  PISTON RING SPECIFICATIONS 3-5
  TORQUE SPECIFICATIONS 3-6

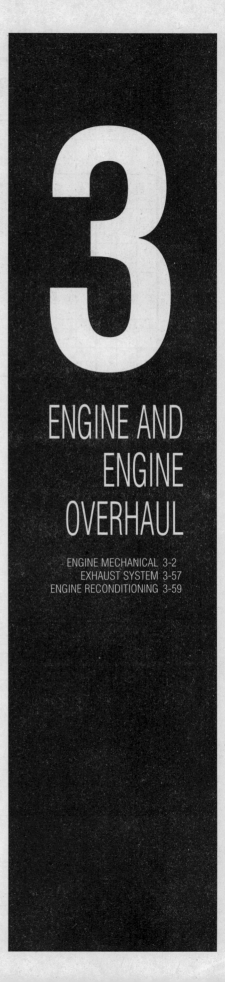

3

ENGINE AND ENGINE OVERHAUL

ENGINE MECHANICAL 3-2
EXHAUST SYSTEM 3-57
ENGINE RECONDITIONING 3-59

ENGINE MECHANICAL

VALVE SPECIFICATIONS

Year	Engine ID/VIN	Engine Displacement Liters (cc)	Seat Angle (deg.)	Face Angle (deg.)	Spring Test Pressure (lbs. @ in.)	Spring Installed Height (in.)	Stem-to-Guide Clearance (in.) Intake	Exhaust	Stem Diameter (in.) Intake	Exhaust
1991	4	3.8 (3802)	44.5	45.8	215@1.79	1.750	0.0010-0.0027	0.0015-0.0032	0.3420	0.3415
	R	3.8 (3802)	44.5	45.8	220@1.18	1.650	0.0010-0.0027	0.0015-0.0032	0.3420	0.3415
	T	5.0 (4949)	45	45	①	②	0.0010-0.0027	0.0015-0.0032	0.3420	0.3420
1992	4	3.8 (3802)	44.5	45.8	215@1.79	1.750	0.0010-0.0027	0.0015-0.0032	0.3420	0.3415
	R	3.8 (3802)	44.5	45.8	220@1.18	1.650	0.0010-0.0027	0.0015-0.0032	0.3420	0.3415
	T	5.0 (4949)	45	45	①	②	0.0010-0.0027	0.0015-0.0032	0.3420	0.3420
1993	4	3.8 (3802)	44.5	45.8	215@1.79	1.750	0.0010-0.0027	0.0015-0.0032	0.3420	0.3415
	R	3.8 (3802)	44.5	45.8	220@1.18	1.650	0.0010-0.0027	0.0015-0.0032	0.3420	0.3415
	T	5.0 (4949)	45	44	①	②	0.0010-0.0027	0.0015-0.0032	0.3420	0.3420
1994	4	3.8 (3802)	44.5	45.8	220@1.18	1.970	0.0010-0.0027	0.0015-0.0032	0.3415-0.3423	0.3410-0.3418
	R	3.8 (3802)	44.5	45.8	220@1.18	1.970	0.0010-0.0027	0.0015-0.0032	0.3415-0.3423	0.3410-0.3418
	W	4.6 (4593)	45	45.5	132@1.10	1.570	0.0008-0.0027	0.0018-0.0037	0.2746-0.2754	0.2736-0.2744
1995	4	3.8 (3802)	44.5	45.8	220@1.18	1.970	0.0010-0.0027	0.0015-0.0032	0.3415-0.3423	0.3410-0.3418
	R	3.8 (3802)	44.5	45.8	220@1.18	1.970	0.0010-0.0027	0.0015-0.0032	0.3415-0.3423	0.3410-0.3418
	W	4.6 (4593)	45	45.5	132@1.10	1.570	0.0008-0.0027	0.0018-0.0037	0.2746-0.2754	0.2736-0.2744
1996	4	3.8 (3802)	44.5	45.8	220@1.18	1.650	0.0010-0.0027	0.0015-0.0032	0.3415-0.3423	0.3410-0.3418
	W	4.6 (4593)	45	45.5	132@1.10	1.570	0.0008-0.0027	0.0018-0.0037	0.2746-0.2754	0.2736-0.2744
1997	4	3.8 (3802)	44.5	45.8	220@1.18	1.650	0.0010-0.0027	0.0015-0.0032	0.3415-0.3423	0.3410-0.3418
	W	4.6 (4593)	45	45.5	132@1.10	1.570	0.0008-0.0027	0.0018-0.0037	0.2746-0.2754	0.2736-0.2744

① Measure spring free length and out of square.
Maximum allowable out-of-square: 0.642.
Spring free length: Intake: 1.729, Exhaust: 1.847
② Intake 211-230@1.33
Exhaust: 200-226@1.15

91333C08

VALVE SPECIFICATIONS

Year	Engine ID/VIN	Engine Displacement Liters (cc)	Seat Angle (deg.)	Face Angle (deg.)	Spring Test Pressure (lbs. @ in.)	Spring Installed Height (in.)	Stem-to-Guide Clearance (in.) Intake	Exhaust	Stem Diameter (in.) Intake	Exhaust
1983	W	2.3 (2300)	45	44	154@1.12	1.563	0.0010-0.0027	0.0015-0.0032	0.3420	0.3415
	3	3.8 (3802)	44.5	45.8	215@1.79	1.750	0.0010-0.0027	0.0015-0.0032	0.3420	0.3415
	F	5.0 (4949)	45	45	205@1.36	1.750	0.0010-0.0027	0.0015-0.0032	0.3420	0.3420
1984	W	2.3 (2300)	45	44	154@1.12	1.563	0.0010-0.0027	0.0015-0.0032	0.3420	0.3415
	3	3.8 (3802)	44.5	45.8	215@1.79	1.750	0.0010-0.0027	0.0015-0.0032	0.3420	0.3415
	F	5.0 (4949)	45	45	205@1.36	1.750	0.0010-0.0027	0.0015-0.0032	0.3420	0.3420
1985	W	2.3 (2300)	45	44	154@1.12	1.563	0.0010-0.0027	0.0015-0.0032	0.3420	0.3415
	3	3.8 (3802)	44.5	45.8	215@1.79	1.750	0.0010-0.0027	0.0015-0.0032	0.3420	0.3415
	F	5.0 (4949)	45	45	205@1.36	1.750	0.0010-0.0027	0.0015-0.0032	0.3420	0.3420
1986	W	2.3 (2300)	45	44	154@1.12	1.563	0.0010-0.0027	0.0015-0.0032	0.3420	0.3415
	3	3.8 (3802)	44.5	45.8	215@1.79	1.750	0.0010-0.0027	0.0015-0.0032	0.3420	0.3415
	F	5.0 (4949)	45	45	205@1.36	1.750	0.0010-0.0027	0.0015-0.0032	0.3420	0.3420
1987	W	2.3 (2300)	45	44	154@1.12	1.563	0.0010-0.0027	0.0015-0.0032	0.3420	0.3415
	3	3.8 (3802)	44.5	45.8	215@1.79	1.750	0.0010-0.0027	0.0015-0.0032	0.3420	0.3415
	F	5.0 (4949)	45	45	205@1.36	1.750	0.0010-0.0027	0.0015-0.0032	0.3420	0.3420
1988	W	2.3 (2300)	45	44	154@1.12	1.563	0.0010-0.0027	0.0015-0.0032	0.3420	0.3415
	4	3.8 (3802)	44.5	45.8	215@1.79	1.750	0.0010-0.0027	0.0015-0.0032	0.3420	0.3415
	F	5.0 (4949)	45	45	205@1.36	1.750	0.0010-0.0027	0.0015-0.0032	0.3420	0.3420
1989	4	3.8 (3802)	44.5	45.8	215@1.79	1.750	0.0010-0.0027	0.0015-0.0032	0.3420	0.3415
	C	3.8 (3802)	44.5	45.8	220@1.18	1.660	0.0010-0.0027	0.0015-0.0032	0.3420	0.3415
	R	3.8 (3802)	44.5	45.8	220@1.18	1.660	0.0010-0.0027	0.0015-0.0032	0.3420	0.3415
1990	4	3.8 (3802)	44.5	45.8	220@1.18	1.660	0.0010-0.0027	0.0015-0.0032	0.3420	0.3415
	R	3.8 (3802)	44.5	45.8	220@1.18	1.660	0.0010-0.0027	0.0015-0.0032	0.3420	0.3415

91333C07

CAMSHAFT SPECIFICATIONS
All measurements given in inches.

Year	Engine ID/VIN	Engine Displacement Liters (cc)	Journal Diameter					Elevation		Bearing Clearance	Camshaft End Play
			1	2	3	4	5	In.	Ex.		
1983	W	2.3 (2300)	1.7713-1.7720	1.7713-1.7720	1.7713-1.7720	1.7713-1.7720	1.7713-1.7720	0.4000	0.4000	0.0010-0.0030	0.0010-0.0070
	3	3.8 (3802)	2.0505-2.0515	2.0505-2.0515	2.0505-2.0515	2.0505-2.0515	2.0505-2.0515	0.2400	0.2410	0.0010-0.0030	①
	F	5.0 (4949)	2.0805-2.0815	2.0655-2.0665	2.0505-2.0515	2.0355-2.0365	2.0205-2.0215	0.2780	0.2830	0.0010-0.0030	0.0010-0.0070
1984	W	2.3 (2300)	1.7713-1.7720	1.7713-1.7720	1.7713-1.7720	1.7713-1.7720	1.7713-1.7720	0.4000	0.4000	0.0010-0.0030	0.0010-0.0070
	3	3.8 (3802)	2.0505-2.0515	2.0505-2.0515	2.0505-2.0515	2.0505-2.0515	2.0505-2.0515	0.2400	0.2410	0.0010-0.0030	①
	F	5.0 (4949)	2.0805-2.0815	2.0655-2.0665	2.0505-2.0515	2.0355-2.0365	2.0205-2.0215	0.2780	0.2830	0.0010-0.0030	0.0010-0.0070
1985	W	2.3 (2300)	1.7713-1.7720	1.7713-1.7720	1.7713-1.7720	1.7713-1.7720	1.7713-1.7720	0.4000	0.4000	0.0010-0.0030	0.0010-0.0070
	3	3.8 (3802)	2.0505-2.0515	2.0505-2.0515	2.0505-2.0515	2.0505-2.0515	2.0505-2.0515	0.2400	0.2410	0.0010-0.0030	①
	F	5.0 (4949)	2.0805-2.0815	2.0655-2.0665	2.0505-2.0515	2.0355-2.0365	2.0205-2.0215	0.2780	0.2830	0.0010-0.0030	0.0010-0.0070
1986	W	2.3 (2300)	1.7713-1.7720	1.7713-1.7720	1.7713-1.7720	1.7713-1.7720	1.7713-1.7720	0.4000	0.4000	0.0010-0.0030	0.0010-0.0070
	3	3.8 (3802)	2.0505-2.0515	2.0505-2.0515	2.0505-2.0515	2.0505-2.0515	2.0505-2.0515	0.2400	0.2410	0.0010-0.0030	①
	F	5.0 (4949)	2.0805-2.0815	2.0655-2.0665	2.0505-2.0515	2.0355-2.0365	2.0205-2.0215	0.2780	0.2830②	0.0010-0.0030	0.0010-0.0070
1987	W	2.3 (2300)	1.7713-1.7720	1.7713-1.7720	1.7713-1.7720	1.7713-1.7720	1.7713-1.7720	0.4000	0.4000	0.0010-0.0030	0.0010-0.0070
	3	3.8 (3802)	2.0505-2.0515	2.0505-2.0515	2.0505-2.0515	2.0505-2.0515	2.0505-2.0515	0.2400	0.2410	0.0010-0.0030	①
	F	5.0 (4949)	2.0805-2.0815	2.0655-2.0665	2.0505-2.0515	2.0355-2.0365	2.0205-2.0215	0.2375	0.2474②	0.0010-0.0030	0.0010-0.0070
1988	W	2.3 (2300)	1.7713-1.7720	1.7713-1.7720	1.7713-1.7720	1.7713-1.7720	1.7713-1.7720	0.4000	0.4000	0.0010-0.0030	0.0010-0.0070
	3	3.8 (3802)	2.0505-2.0515	2.0505-2.0515	2.0505-2.0515	2.0505-2.0515	2.0505-2.0515	0.2400	0.2410	0.0010-0.0030	①
	F	5.0 (4949)	2.0805-2.0815	2.0655-2.0665	2.0505-2.0515	2.0355-2.0365	2.0205-2.0215	0.2375	0.2474②	0.0010-0.0030	0.0010-0.0070
1989	4	3.8 (3802)	2.0505-2.0515	2.0505-2.0515	2.0505-2.0515	2.0505-2.0515	2.0505-2.0515	0.2400	0.2410	0.0010-0.0030	①
	C	3.8 (3802)	2.0505-2.0515	2.0505-2.0515	2.0505-2.0515	2.0505-2.0515	2.0505-2.0515	0.2400	0.2410	0.0010-0.0030	①
	R	3.8 (3802)	2.0505-2.0515	2.0505-2.0515	2.0505-2.0515	2.0505-2.0515	2.0505-2.0515	0.2400	0.2410	0.0010-0.0030	①
1990	4	3.8 (3802)	2.0505-2.0515	2.0505-2.0515	2.0505-2.0515	2.0505-2.0515	2.0505-2.0515	0.2400-0.2450	0.2410-0.2490	0.0010-0.0030	①
	R	3.8 (3802)	2.0505-2.0515	2.0505-2.0515	2.0505-2.0515	2.0505-2.0515	2.0505-2.0515	0.2400-0.2450	0.2410-0.2590	0.0010-0.0030	①

91333C01

CAMSHAFT SPECIFICATIONS
All measurements given in inches.

Year	Engine ID/VIN	Engine Displacement Liters (cc)	Journal Diameter					Elevation		Bearing Clearance	Camshaft End Play
			1	2	3	4	5	In.	Ex.		
1991	4	3.8 (3802)	2.0505-2.0515	2.0505-2.0515	2.0505-2.0515	2.0505-2.0515	2.0505-2.0515	0.2400-0.2450	0.2410-0.2590	0.0010-0.0030	①
	R	3.8 (3802)	2.0505-2.0515	2.0505-2.0515	2.0505-2.0515	2.0505-2.0515	2.0505-2.0515	0.2400-0.2450	0.2410-0.2590	0.0010-0.0030	①
	T	5.0 (4949)	2.0805-2.0815	2.0655-2.0665	2.0505-2.0515	2.0355-2.0365	2.0205-2.0215	0.2780	0.2780	0.0010-0.0030	0.0050-0.0090
1992	4	3.8 (3802)	2.0505-2.0515	2.0505-2.0515	2.0505-2.0515	2.0505-2.0515	2.0505-2.0515	0.2400-0.2450	0.2410-0.2450	0.0010-0.0030	②
	C	3.8 (3802)	2.0505-2.0515	2.0505-2.0515	2.0505-2.0515	2.0505-2.0515	2.0505-2.0515	0.2400-0.2450	0.2410-0.2450	0.0010-0.0030	②
	R	3.8 (3802)	2.0505-2.0515	2.0505-2.0515	2.0505-2.0515	2.0505-2.0515	2.0505-2.0515	0.2400-0.2450	0.2410-0.2450	0.0010-0.0030	②
	T	5.0 (4949)	2.0805-2.0815	2.0655-2.0665	2.0505-2.0515	2.0355-2.0365	2.0205-2.0215	0.2780	0.2780	0.0010-0.0030	0.0050-0.0090
1993	4	3.8 (3802)	2.0505-2.0515	2.0505-2.0515	2.0505-2.0515	2.0505-2.0515	2.0505-2.0515	0.2400-0.2450	0.2410-0.2450	0.0010-0.0030	0.0010-0.0060
	R	3.8 (3802)	2.0505-2.0515	2.0505-2.0515	2.0505-2.0515	2.0505-2.0515	2.0505-2.0515	0.2400-0.2450	0.2410-0.2450	0.0010-0.0030	0.0010-0.0060
	T	5.0 (4949)	2.0805-2.0815	2.0655-2.0665	2.0505-2.0515	2.0355-2.0365	2.0205-2.0215	0.2780	0.2780	0.0010-0.0030	0.0010-0.0060
1994	4	3.8 (3802)	2.0505-2.0515	2.0505-2.0515	2.0505-2.0515	2.0505-2.0515	2.0505-2.0515	0.2400-0.2450	0.2410-0.2450	0.0010-0.0030	0.0010-0.0060
	R	3.8 (3802)	2.0505-2.0515	2.0505-2.0515	2.0505-2.0515	2.0505-2.0515	2.0505-2.0515	0.2400-0.2450	0.2410-0.2450	0.0010-0.0030	0.0010-0.0060
	W	4.6 (4593)	1.0605-1.0615	1.0605-1.0615	1.0605-1.0615	1.0605-1.0615	1.0605-1.0615	0.2540-0.2590	0.2540-0.2590	0.0010-0.0030	0.0010-0.0060
1995	4	3.8 (3802)	2.0505-2.0515	2.0505-2.0515	2.0505-2.0515	2.0505-2.0515	2.0505-2.0515	0.2400-0.2450	0.2410-0.2450	0.0010-0.0030	0.0010-0.0060
	R	3.8 (3802)	2.0505-2.0515	2.0505-2.0515	2.0505-2.0515	2.0505-2.0515	2.0505-2.0515	0.2400-0.2450	0.2410-0.2450	0.0010-0.0030	0.0010-0.0060
	W	4.6 (4593)	1.0605-1.0615	1.0605-1.0615	1.0605-1.0615	1.0605-1.0615	1.0605-1.0615	0.2590	0.2590	0.0010-0.0030	0.0010-0.0060
1996	4	3.8 (3802)	2.0505-2.0515	2.0505-2.0515	2.0505-2.0515	2.0505-2.0515	2.0505-2.0515	0.2400-0.2450	0.2410-0.2450	0.0010-0.0030	0.0010-0.0060
	W	4.6 (4593)	1.0605-1.0615	1.0605-1.0615	1.0605-1.0615	1.0605-1.0615	1.0605-1.0615	0.2590	0.2590	0.0010-0.0030	0.0065-0.0684
1997	4	3.8 (3802)	2.0505-2.0515	2.0505-2.0515	2.0505-2.0515	2.0505-2.0515	2.0505-2.0515	0.2400-0.2450	0.2540-0.2590	0.0010-0.0030	0.0010-0.0060
	W	4.6 (4593)	1.0605-1.0615	1.0605-1.0615	1.0605-1.0615	1.0605-1.0615	1.0605-1.0615	0.2590	0.2590	0.0010-0.0030	0.0065-0.0684

NA - Not Available
① Endplay is controlled by button and spring on camshaft end
② Front and rear journals: 0.0014-0.0030
   Center journals: 0.0026-0.0045

91333C02

CRANKSHAFT AND CONNECTING ROD SPECIFICATIONS
All measurements are given in inches.

Year	Engine ID/VIN	Engine Displacement Liters (cc)	Crankshaft Main Brg. Journal Dia.	Crankshaft Main Brg. Oil Clearance	Crankshaft Shaft End-play	Crankshaft Thrust on No.	Connecting Rod Journal Diameter	Connecting Rod Oil Clearance	Connecting Rod Side Clearance
1992	4	3.8 (3802)	2.5189-2.5190	0.0010-0.0014	0.0040-0.0080	3	2.3103-2.3111	0.0010-0.0014	0.0047-0.0114
	C	3.8 (3802)	2.5186-2.5194	0.0009-0.0026	0.0040-0.0080	3	2.4226-2.4274	0.0008-0.0026	0.0047-0.0114
	R	3.8 (3801)	①	②	0.0040-0.0080	3	2.3103-2.3111	0.0009-0.0027	0.0047-0.0140
1993	T	5.0 (4949)	2.2482-2.2490	0.0004-0.0015	0.0040-0.0080	3	2.1228-2.1236	0.0008-0.0015	0.0100-0.0200
	4	3.8 (3802)	2.5189-2.5190	0.0010-0.0015	0.0040-0.0080	3	2.3103-2.3111	0.0010-0.0014	0.0047-0.0114
	R	3.8 (3801)	2.5190 ①	0.0014 ②	0.0040-0.0080	3	2.3111	0.0014	0.0047-0.0140
1994	T	5.0 (4949)	2.2482-2.2490	0.0004-0.0015	0.0040-0.0080	3	2.1228-2.1236	0.0008-0.0015	0.0100-0.0200
	4	3.8 (3802)	2.5190-2.5198	0.0010-0.0014	0.0040-0.0080	3	2.3103-2.3111	0.0009-0.0027	0.0047-0.0140
	R	3.8 (3802)	2.5198 ①	0.0014 ②	0.0040-0.0080	3	2.3111	0.0027	0.0047-0.0140
1995	W	4.6 (4593)	2.6578-2.6598	0.0011-0.0025	0.0050-0.0100	5	2.0874-2.0891	0.0011-0.0027	0.0006-0.0177
	4	3.8 (3802)	2.5190-2.5198	0.0010-0.0014	0.0040-0.0080	3	2.3103-2.3111	0.0009-0.0027	0.0047-0.0140
	R	4.6 (4593)	2.6569-2.6576	0.0011-0.0026	0.0058-0.0119	5	2.0661-2.0867	0.0011-0.0027	0.0006-0.0177
1996	W	3.8 (3802)	2.5190-2.5198	0.0010-0.0024	0.0040-0.0080	3	2.3103-2.3111	0.0009-0.0027	0.0047-0.0140
	4	4.6 (4593)	2.6569-2.6576	0.0011-0.0026	0.0058-0.0119	5	2.0661-2.0867	0.0011-0.0027	0.0006-0.0177
1997	4	3.8 (3802)	2.5190-2.5198	0.0010-0.0024	0.0040-0.0080	3	2.3103-2.3111	0.0009-0.0027	0.0047-0.0140
	W	4.6 (4593)	2.6569-2.6676	0.0011-0.0026	0.0058-0.0119	5	2.0661-2.0867	0.0011-0.0027	0.0006-0.0177

① Nos. 1-3: 2.5190-2.5198 No. 4: 2.5096-2.5104
② Nos. 1-3: 0.0005-0.0023 No. 4: 0.0010-0.0028

91333C10

CRANKSHAFT AND CONNECTING ROD SPECIFICATIONS
All measurements are given in inches.

Year	Engine ID/VIN	Engine Displacement Liters (cc)	Crankshaft Main Brg. Journal Dia.	Crankshaft Main Brg. Oil Clearance	Crankshaft Shaft End-play	Crankshaft Thrust on No.	Connecting Rod Journal Diameter	Connecting Rod Oil Clearance	Connecting Rod Side Clearance
1983	W	2.3 (2300)	2.3990-2.3982	0.0008-0.0015	0.0040-0.0080	3	2.0464-2.0472	0.0008-0.0015	0.0035-0.0105
	3	3.8 (3802)	2.5190	0.0001-0.0010	0.0040-0.0080	3	2.3103-2.3111	0.0008-0.0026	0.0047-0.0114
	F	5.0 (4949)	2.2482-2.2490	0.0004-0.0015	0.0040-0.0150	3	2.1228-2.1236	0.0008-0.0015	0.0100-0.0200
1984	W	2.3 (2300)	2.3990-2.3982	0.0008-0.0015	0.0040-0.0080	3	2.0464-2.0472	0.0008-0.0015	0.0035-0.0105
	3	3.8 (3802)	2.5190	0.0001-0.0010	0.0040-0.0080	3	2.3103-2.3111	0.0008-0.0026	0.0047-0.0114
	F	5.0 (4949)	2.2482-2.2490	0.0004-0.0015	0.0040-0.0150	3	2.1228-2.1236	0.0008-0.0015	0.0100-0.0200
1985	W	2.3 (2300)	2.3990-2.3982	0.0008-0.0015	0.0040-0.0080	3	2.0464-2.0472	0.0008-0.0015	0.0035-0.0105
	3	3.8 (3802)	2.5190	0.0001-0.0010	0.0040-0.0080	3	2.3103-2.3111	0.0008-0.0026	0.0047-0.0114
	F	5.0 (4949)	2.2482-2.2490	0.0004-0.0015	0.0040-0.0150	3	2.1228-2.1236	0.0008-0.0015	0.0100-0.0200
1986	W	2.3 (2300)	2.3990-2.3982	0.0008-0.0015	0.0040-0.0080	3	2.0464-2.0472	0.0008-0.0015	0.0035-0.0105
	3	3.8 (3802)	2.5190	0.0001-0.0010	0.0040-0.0080	3	2.3103-2.3111	0.0008-0.0026	0.0047-0.0114
	F	5.0 (4949)	2.2482-2.2490	0.0004-0.0015	0.0040-0.0150	3	2.1228-2.1236	0.0008-0.0015	0.0100-0.0200
1987	W	2.3 (2300)	2.3982-2.3990	0.0008-0.0015	0.0040-0.0080	3	2.0464-2.0472	0.0008-0.0015	0.0035-0.0105
	3	3.8 (3802)	2.5190	0.0001-0.0010	0.0040-0.0080	3	2.3103-2.3111	0.0008-0.0026	0.0047-0.0114
	F	5.0 (4949)	2.2482-2.2490	0.0004-0.0015	0.0040-0.0150	3	2.1228-2.1236	0.0008-0.0015	0.0100-0.0200
1988	W	2.3 (2300)	2.3982-2.3990	0.0008-0.0015	0.0040-0.0080	3	2.0464-2.0472	0.0008-0.0015	0.0035-0.0105
	4	3.8 (3802)	2.5189-2.5190	0.0010-0.0014	0.0040-0.0080	3	2.3103-2.3111	0.0010-0.0014	0.0047-0.0114
	F	5.0 (4949)	2.2482-2.2490	0.0004-0.0015	0.0040-0.0150	3	2.1228-2.1236	0.0010-0.0020	0.0100-0.0200
1989	4	3.8 (3802)	2.5189-2.5190	0.0010-0.0014	0.0040-0.0080	3	2.3103-2.3111	0.0010-0.0014	0.0047-0.0114
	C	3.8 (3802)	2.5186-2.5194	0.0009-0.0026	0.0040-0.0080	3	2.4226-2.4274	0.0008-0.0026	0.0047-0.0114
	R	3.8 (3802)	2.5186-2.5194	0.0009-0.0026	0.0040-0.0080	3	2.4226-2.4274	0.0008-0.0026	0.0047-0.0114
1990	4	3.8 (3802)	2.5189-2.5190	0.0010-0.0014	0.0040-0.0080	3	2.3103-2.3111	0.0010-0.0014	0.0047-0.0114
	R	3.8 (3802)	2.5186-2.5194	0.0009-0.0026	0.0040-0.0080	3	2.4226-2.4274	0.0008-0.0026	0.0047-0.0114
1991	4	3.8 (3802)	2.5189-2.5190	0.0010 ②	0.0040-0.0080	3	2.3103-2.3111	0.0009-0.0027	0.0047-0.0140
	R	3.8 (3801)	①	0.0004-0.0015	0.0040-0.0080	3	2.3111	0.0009	0.0047-0.0140
	T	5.0 (4949)	2.2482-2.2490	0.0004-0.0015	0.0040-0.0150	3	2.1228-2.1236	0.0008-0.0015	0.0100-0.0200

91333C09

PISTON AND RING SPECIFICATIONS
All measurements are given in inches.

Year	Engine ID/VIN	Engine Displacement Liters (cc)	Piston Clearance	Ring Gap Top Compression	Ring Gap Bottom Compression	Ring Gap Oil Control	Ring Side Clearance Top Compression	Ring Side Clearance Bottom Compression	Ring Side Clearance Oil Control
1983	W	2.3 (2300)	0.0030-0.0038	0.0100-0.0200	0.0100-0.0200	0.0150-0.0550	0.0020-0.0040	0.0020-0.0040	SNUG
	3	3.8 (3802)	0.0014-0.0032	0.0100-0.0220	0.0100-0.0200	0.0150-0.0550	0.0020-0.0040	0.0020-0.0040	SNUG
	F	5.0 (4949)	0.0018-0.0026	0.0100-0.0200	0.0100-0.0200	0.0150-0.0550	0.0020-0.0040	0.0020-0.0040	SNUG
1984	W	2.3 (2300)	0.0030-0.0038	0.0100-0.0200	0.0100-0.0200	0.0150-0.0550	0.0020-0.0040	0.0020-0.0040	SNUG
	3	3.8 (3802)	0.0014-0.0032	0.0100-0.0220	0.0100-0.0200	0.0150-0.0550	0.0020-0.0040	0.0020-0.0040	SNUG
	F	5.0 (4949)	0.0018-0.0026	0.0100-0.0200	0.0100-0.0200	0.0150-0.0550	0.0020-0.0040	0.0020-0.0040	SNUG
1985	W	2.3 (2300)	0.0030-0.0038	0.0100-0.0200	0.0100-0.0200	0.0150-0.0550	0.0020-0.0040	0.0020-0.0040	SNUG
	3	3.8 (3802)	0.0014-0.0032	0.0100-0.0220	0.0100-0.0220	0.0150-0.0550	0.0020-0.0040	0.0020-0.0040	SNUG
	F	5.0 (4949)	0.0018-0.0026	0.0100-0.0200	0.0100-0.0200	0.0150-0.0550	0.0020-0.0040	0.0020-0.0040	SNUG
1986	W	2.3 (2300)	0.0030-0.0038	0.0100-0.0200	0.0100-0.0200	0.0150-0.0550	0.0020-0.0040	0.0020-0.0040	SNUG
	3	3.8 (3802)	0.0014-0.0032	0.0100-0.0220	0.0100-0.0220	0.0150-0.0550	0.0020-0.0040	0.0020-0.0040	SNUG
	F	5.0 (4949)	0.0018-0.0026	0.0100-0.0200	0.0100-0.0200	0.0150-0.0550	0.0020-0.0040	0.0020-0.0040	SNUG
1987	W	2.3 (2300)	0.0030-0.0038	0.0100-0.0200	0.0100-0.0200	0.0150-0.0550	0.0020-0.0040	0.0020-0.0040	SNUG
	3	3.8 (3802)	0.0014-0.0032	0.0100-0.0220	0.0100-0.0220	0.0150-0.0550	0.0020-0.0040	0.0020-0.0040	SNUG
	F	5.0 (4949)	0.0018-0.0026	0.0100-0.0200	0.0100-0.0200	0.0150-0.0550	0.0020-0.0040	0.0020-0.0040	SNUG
1988	W	2.3 (2300)	0.0030-0.0038	0.0100-0.0200	0.0100-0.0200	0.0150-0.0550	0.0020-0.0040	0.0020-0.0040	SNUG
	4	3.8 (3802)	0.0014-0.0032	0.0100-0.0220	0.0100-0.0220	0.0150-0.0550	0.0020-0.0040	0.0020-0.0040	SNUG
	F	5.0 (4949)	0.0018-0.0026	0.0100-0.0200	0.0100-0.0200	0.0150-0.0550	0.0020-0.0040	0.0020-0.0040	SNUG
1989	4	3.8 (3802)	0.0014-0.0032	0.0100-0.0220	0.0100-0.0220	0.0150-0.0550	0.0020-0.0040	0.0020-0.0040	SNUG
	C	3.8 (3802)	0.0014-0.0047	0.0602-0.0610	0.0602-0.0610	0.1582-0.0602	0.0016-0.0034	0.0016-0.0034	SNUG
	R	3.8 (3802)	0.0014-0.0032	0.0100-0.0220	0.0090-0.0200	0.0150-0.0550	0.0020-0.0040	0.0020-0.0040	SNUG
1990	4	3.8 (3802)	0.0014-0.0032	0.0110-0.0120	0.0090-0.0200	0.0150-0.0580	0.0016-0.0034	0.0016-0.0034	SNUG
	R	3.8 (3802)	0.0040-0.0045	0.0110-0.0120	0.0090-0.0200	0.0150-0.0580	0.0016-0.0034	0.0016-0.0034	SNUG

91333C05

PISTON AND RING SPECIFICATIONS
All measurements are given in inches.

Year	Engine ID/VIN	Engine Displacement Liters (cc)	Piston Clearance	Ring Gap Top Compression	Ring Gap Bottom Compression	Ring Gap Oil Control	Ring Side Clearance Top Compression	Ring Side Clearance Bottom Compression	Ring Side Clearance Oil Control
1991	4	3.8 (3802)	0.0014-0.0032	0.0100-0.0220	0.0100-0.0220	0.0150-0.0550	0.0020-0.0040	0.0020-0.0040	SNUG
	R	3.8 (3802)	0.0040-0.0045	0.0110-0.0120	0.0090-0.0200	0.0150-0.0580	0.0016-0.0034	0.0016-0.0034	SNUG
	T	5.0 (4949)	0.0030-0.0038	0.0100-0.0200	0.0100-0.0200	0.0150-0.0550	0.0020-0.0040	0.0020-0.0040	SNUG
1992	4	3.8 (3802)	0.0014-0.0032	0.0100-0.0200	0.0100-0.0200	0.0150-0.0550	0.0020-0.0040	0.0020-0.0040	SNUG
	C	3.8 (3802)	0.0014-0.0032	0.0602-0.0610	0.0602-0.0610	0.1582-0.0602	0.0016-0.0034	0.0016-0.0034	SNUG
	R	3.8 (3802)	0.0014-0.0047	0.0110-0.0120	0.0090-0.0200	0.0150-0.0580	0.0016-0.0034	0.0016-0.0034	SNUG
	T	5.0 (4949)	0.0030-0.0038	0.0100-0.0200	0.0100-0.0200	0.0150-0.0550	0.0020-0.0040	0.0020-0.0040	SNUG
1993	4	3.8 (3802)	0.0014-0.0032	0.0100-0.0200	0.0100-0.0200	0.0150-0.0550	0.0020-0.0040	0.0020-0.0040	SNUG
	R	3.8 (3802)	0.0040-0.0045	0.0110-0.0120	0.0090-0.0200	0.0150-0.0580	0.0016-0.0034	0.0016-0.0034	SNUG
	T	5.0 (4949)	0.0030-0.0038	0.0100-0.0200	0.0100-0.0200	0.0150-0.0550	0.0020-0.0040	0.0020-0.0040	SNUG
1994	4	3.8 (3802)	0.0014-0.0032	0.0100-0.0200	0.0100-0.0200	0.0150-0.0580	0.0016-0.0034	0.0016-0.0034	SNUG
	R	3.8 (3802)	0.0015-0.0032	0.0110-0.0120	0.0090-0.0200	0.0150-0.0580	0.0016-0.0034	0.0016-0.0034	SNUG
	W	4.6 (4593)	0.0003-0.0006	0.0090-0.0190	0.0090-0.0190	0.0060-0.0260	0.0016-0.0035	0.0012-0.0031	SNUG
1995	4	3.8 (3802)	0.0014-0.0032	0.0110-0.0120	0.0100-0.0200	0.0150-0.0580	0.0016-0.0034	0.0016-0.0034	SNUG
	R	3.8 (3802)	0.0004-0.0034	0.0110-0.0120	0.0090-0.0200	0.0150-0.0580	0.0016-0.0034	0.0016-0.0034	SNUG
	W	4.6 (4593)	0.0003-0.0006	0.0090-0.0190	0.0090-0.0190	0.0060-0.0260	0.0016-0.0035	0.0012-0.0031	SNUG
1996	4	3.8 (3802)	0.0014-0.0022	0.0110-0.0120	0.0100-0.0200	0.0150-0.0580	0.0016-0.0034	0.0016-0.0034	SNUG
	W	4.6 (4593)	0.0005-0.0010	0.0090-0.0190	0.0090-0.0190	0.0060-0.0260	0.0016-0.0035	0.0012-0.0031	SNUG
1997	4	3.8 (3802)	0.0014-0.0022	0.0110-0.0120	0.0100-0.0200	0.0150-0.0580	0.0016-0.0034	0.0012-0.0034	SNUG
	W	4.6 (4593)	0.0005-0.0010	0.0090-0.0190	0.0090-0.0190	0.0060-0.0260	0.0016-0.0035	0.0012-0.0031	SNUG

91333C06

TORQUE SPECIFICATIONS

All readings in ft. lbs.

Year	Engine ID/VIN	Engine Displacement Liters (cc)	Cylinder Head Bolts	Main Bearing Bolts	Rod Bearing Bolts	Crankshaft Damper Bolts	Flywheel Bolts	Manifold Intake	Manifold Exhaust	Spark Plugs	Lug Nut
1983	W	2.3 (2300)	①	②	③	100-120	54-64	14-21	16-23	5-10	95
	3	3.8 (3802)	④	65-81	31-36	85-100	75-85	⑤	15-22	5-11	95
	F	5.0 (4949)	65-72	60-70	19-24	70-90	75-85	23-25	18-24	10-15	95
1984	W	2.3 (2300)	①	②	③	100-120	54-64	14-21	16-23	5-10	95
	3	3.8 (3802)	④	65-81	31-36	85-100	75-85	⑤	15-22	5-11	95
	F	5.0 (4949)	65-72	60-70	19-24	70-90	75-85	23-25	18-24	10-15	95
1985	W	2.3 (2300)	①	②	③	100-120	54-64	14-21	16-23	5-10	95
	3	3.8 (3802)	④	65-81	31-36	85-100	75-85	⑤	15-22	5-11	95
	F	5.0 (4949)	65-72	60-70	19-24	70-90	75-85	23-25	18-24	10-15	95
1986	W	2.3 (2300)	①	②	③	100-120	54-64	14-21	16-23	5-10	95
	3	3.8 (3802)	⑥	65-81	31-36	85-100	75-85	⑤	15-22	5-11	95
	F	5.0 (4949)	65-72	60-70	19-24	70-90	75-85	23-25	18-24	10-15	95
1987	W	2.3 (2300)	①	②	③	100-120	54-64	⑦	16-23	5-10	95
	3	3.8 (3802)	⑥	65-81	31-36	85-100	75-85	⑤	15-22	5-11	95
	E	5.0 (4949)	65-72	60-70	19-24	70-90	75-85	23-25	18-24	10-15	95
1988	W	2.3 (2300)	①	②	③	100-120	54-64	⑦	16-23	5-10	95
	4	3.8 (3802)	⑥	65-81	31-36	85-100	75-85	⑤	15-22	5-11	95
	F	5.0 (4949)	65-72	60-70	19-24	70-90	75-85	23-25	18-24	10-15	95
1989	4	3.8 (3802)	⑥	65-81	31-36	85-100	75-85	⑤	15-22	5-11	95
	C	3.8 (3802)	⑥	65-81	31-36	85-100	75-85	⑧	15-22	5-11	95
	R	3.8 (3802)	⑥	65-81	31-36	85-100	75-85	⑧	15-22	5-11	95
1990	R	3.8 (3802)	⑩	65-81	31-36	103-132	54-64	⑧	15-22	5-11	95
	4	3.8 (3802)	⑥	65-81	31-36	85-100	75-85	⑨	15-22	5-11	95
1991	R	3.8 (3801)	⑩	65-81	31-36	103-132	54-64	①	15-22	5-11	95
	4	3. 8(3802)	⑥	65-81	31-36	85-100	75-85	⑨	15-22	5-11	95
	T	5.0 (4949)	65-72	60-70	19-24	70-90	75-85	23-25	18-24	10-15	95
1992	R	3.8 (3801)	⑩	65-81	31-36	103-132	54-64	①	15-22	5-11	95
	4	3.8 (3802)	⑥	65-81	31-36	85-100	75-85	⑨	15-22	5-11	95
	T	5.0 (4949)	65-72	60-70	19-24	70-90	75-85	23-25	18-24	10-15	95
1993	R	3.8 (3801)	⑩	65-81	31-36	103-132	54-64	①	15-22	5-11	95
	4	3.8 (3802)	⑥	65-81	31-36	85-100	75-85	⑨	15-22	5-11	95
	T	5.0 (4949)	65-72	60-70	19-24	70-90	75-85	23-25	18-24	10-15	95
1994	R	3.8 (3802)	⑫	65-81	31-36	103-132	54-64	⑩	15-22	7-15	95
	4	3.8 (3802)	⑫	65-81	31-36	103-132	54-64	⑩	15-22	7-15	95
	W	4.6 (4593)	⑬	⑮	⑮	114-121	54-64	15-22	15-22	7-15	95
1995	R	3.8 (3802)	⑩	65-81	31-36	103-132	54-64	⑫	15-22	7-15	95
	4	3.8 (3802)	⑬	65-81	31-36	103-132	54-64	⑫	15-22	7-15	95
	W	4.6 (4593)	⑭	⑮	⑮	114-121	54-64	15-22	15-22	7-15	95
1996	4	3.8 (3802)	⑬	82-88	⑰	103-132	54-64	⑫	23-26	7-15	95
	W	4.6 (4593)	⑬	⑮	⑯	114-121	54-64	15-22	14-16	7-15	95
1997	4	3.8 (3802)	⑬	82-88	⑰	103-132	54-64	⑫	23-26	7-15	95
	W	4.6 (4593)	⑱	⑮	⑯	114-121	54-64	15-22	14-16	7-15	95

NOTE: Always follow proper torque patterns.

NOTE: Stretch bolts are used in all procedures that require rotating the fastener a certain number of degrees. The bolts stretch and cannot be reused. For reassembly, replace with new fasteners.

91333C03

TORQUE SPECIFICATIONS

All readings in ft. lbs.

Year	Engine ID/VIN	Engine Displacement Liters (cc)	Cylinder Head Bolts	Main Bearing Bolts	Rod Bearing Bolts	Crankshaft Damper Bolts	Flywheel Bolts	Manifold Intake	Manifold Exhaust	Spark Plugs	Lug Nut

① Step 1: 50-60 ft. lbs.
Step 2: 80-90 ft. lbs.

② Step 1: 50-60 ft. lbs.
Step 2: 75-85 ft. lbs.

③ Step 1: 25-30 ft. lbs.
Step 2: 30-36 ft. lbs.

④ Step 1: 37 ft. lbs.
Step 2: 45 ft. lbs.
Step 3: 52 ft. lbs.
Step 4: 59 ft. lbs.

⑤ Step 1: 7 ft. lbs.
Step 2: 15 ft. lbs.
Step 3: 24 ft. lbs.

⑥ Step 1: 37 ft. lbs.
Step 2: 45 ft. lbs.
Step 3: 52 ft. lbs.
Step 4: 59 ft. lbs.

⑦ Step 1: 5-7 ft. lbs.
Step 2: 13-18 ft. lbs.

⑧ Step 1: 7.5 ft. lbs.
Step 2: 11 ft. lbs.

⑨ Step 1: 48-54 ft. lbs.
Step 2: 63-80 ft. lbs.

⑩ Step 1: 37 ft. lbs.
Step 2: 45 ft. lbs.
Step 3: 52 ft. lbs.
Step 4: 59 ft. lbs.
Step 5: Back off all bolts two to three turns
Step 6: Tighten to 48-55 ft.lbs.
Step 7: Rotate bolts and additional 90-110 degrees

⑪ Step 1: 11 ft. lbs.
Step 2: 18 ft. lbs.
Step 3: 24 ft. lbs.

⑫ Step 1: 22-26 ft. lbs.
Step 2: 33-36 ft. lbs.

⑬ Step 1: 15 ft. lbs.
Step 2: 29 ft. lbs.
Step 3: 37 ft. lbs.
Step 4: Loosen bolts and retorque as follows:
Long bolts: 11-18 ft. lbs.
Short bolts: 7-15 ft. lbs.
Step 5: Rotate 85-95 degrees

⑭ Step 1: 25-30 ft. lbs.
Step 2: Rotate each bolt 85-95 degrees
Step 3: Repeat Step 2

⑮ Step 1: Main bearing cap bolts: 22-25 ft. lbs.
Step 2: Rotate each bolts 85-95 degrees
Step 3: Main bearing cap adjusting screws:
4 ft. lbs. then 6.5-8.0 ft. lbs.
Step 4: Main bearing cap side bolts:
7 ft. lbs. then 14-17 ft. lbs.

⑯ Step 1: 12 ft. lbs.
Step 2: 85-95 degrees

⑰ 29 ft. lbs. plus 90-120 degrees

⑱ Step 1: 27-31 ft. lbs.
Step 2: Rotate 85-95 degrees
Step 3: Loosen bolts one turn
Step 4: 27-31 ft. lbs.
Step 5: Rotate 85-95 degrees
Step 6: Repeat Step 5

⑲ Step 1: Main bearing cap bolts: 27-31 ft. lbs.
Step 2: Rotate 85-95 degrees
Step 3: Main bearing cap adjusting screws:
4 ft. lbs. then 6.5-8.0 ft. lbs.
Step 4: Main beaing cap side bolts:
7 ft. lbs. then 14-17 ft. lbs.

91333C04

Engine

REMOVAL & INSTALLATION

In the process of removing the engine, you will come across a number of steps which call for the removal of a separate component or system, such as "disconnect the exhaust system" or "remove the radiator." In most instances, a detailed removal procedure can be found elsewhere in this manual.

It is virtually impossible to list each individual wire and hose which must be disconnected, simply because so many different model and engine combinations have been manufactured. Careful observation and common sense are the best possible approaches to any repair procedure.

Removal and installation of the engine can be made easier if you follow these basic points:

• If you have to drain any of the fluids, use a suitable container.
• Always tag any wires or hoses and, if possible, the components they came from before disconnecting them.
• Because there are so many bolts and fasteners involved, store and label the retainers from components separately in muffin pans, jars or coffee cans. This will prevent confusion during installation.
• After unbolting the transmission or transaxle, always make sure it is properly supported.
• If it is necessary to disconnect the air conditioning system, have this service performed by a qualified technician using a recovery/recycling station. If the system does not have to be disconnected, unbolt the compressor and set it aside.
• When unbolting the engine mounts, always make sure the engine is properly supported. When removing the engine, make sure that any lifting devices are properly attached to the engine. It is recommended that if your engine is supplied with lifting hooks, your lifting apparatus be attached to them.
• Lift the engine from its compartment slowly, checking that no hoses, wires or other components are still connected.
• After the engine is clear of the compartment, place it on an engine stand or workbench.
• After the engine has been removed, you can perform a partial or full teardown of the engine using the procedures outlined in this manual.

2.3L Engine

1. Raise and support the hood. In many cases, it may be easier to match-mark the hood hinges and remove the hood from the vehicle.
2. Properly drain the engine cooling system and the oil from the crankcase.
3. Disconnect the zip tube from the turbocharger inlet. Remove the ground strap on the turbocharger inlet elbow.
4. Remove the air cleaner and exhaust manifold shroud.
5. Disconnect the negative battery cable.
6. Detach the upper and lower radiator hoses.
7. Remove the radiator and fan assembly. On vehicles equipped with an electric cooling fan, detach the fan electrical connector, then remove the fan and shroud assembly.
8. Disconnect the heater hose from the water pump.
9. Detach the electrical connectors from the alternator and starter. Disconnect the accelerator cable from the throttle body.

✳✳ WARNING

When repositioning the compressor, DO NOT disconnect the refrigerant lines!

10. If equipped with A/C, remove the compressor from the mounting bracket and position it out of the way, leaving the refrigerant lines attached.
11. Disconnect and cap the power steering lines from the power steering pump.
12. Disconnect and plug the flexible fuel line at the fuel pump or fuel rail.
13. Detach the coil primary wire at the coil. Disconnect the oil pressure and water temperature sending unit wires from the units.
14. Remove the starter, as outlined in Section 2 of this manual.
15. Raise and safely support the vehicle.
16. Remove the flywheel or converter housing attaching bolts.
17. Disconnect the muffler inlet pipe at the turbocharger outlet pipe. Disconnect the engine right and left mounts at the No. 2 crossmember pedestals. Remove the flywheel or converter housing cover.

18. If equipped with a manual transmission, remove the flywheel housing lower attaching bolts.
19. If equipped with an automatic transmission, disconnect the converter from the flywheel. Disconnect the transmission oil cooler lines, if attached to the engine at the pan rail. Remove the converter housing cover lower attaching bolts.
20. Carefully lower the vehicle. Support the transmission and flywheel or converter housing with a jack.
21. Attach engine lifting hooks to the existing lifting brackets. Carefully lift the engine out of the engine compartment, using a suitable shop crane, then install the engine on a suitable work stand.
To install:
22. If removed, install the clutch. Carefully lower the engine into the engine compartment.
23. Make sure the studs on the turbocharger are aligned with the holes in the muffler inlet pipe.
24. If equipped with an automatic transmission, start the converter pilot into the crankshaft.
25. If equipped with a manual transmission, start the transmission main drive gear into the clutch disc. It may be necessary to adjust the position of the transmission in relation to the engine it the input shaft will not enter the clutch disc. If the engine hangs up after the shaft enters, turn the crankshaft in the clockwise direction slowly (transmission in gear) until the shaft splines mesh with the clutch disc splines.
26. Install the flywheel or converter housing upper attaching bolts. Remove the engine lifting sling hooks.
27. Carefully remove the jack from the transmission. Raise and safely support the vehicle.
28. Install the flywheel or converter housing lower attaching bolts.
29. If equipped with an automatic transaxle, attach the converter to the flexplate. Tighten the attaching nuts to 27–49 ft. lbs. (37–66 Nm).
30. Install the flywheel or converter housing dust cover.
31. Install the engine left and right mounts to the No. 2 crossmember pedestals. Tighten the nuts an bolts to 33–45 ft. lbs. (45–61 Nm).
32. Unplug the fuel line and connect it to the fuel pump or fuel rail. Install the turbocharger-to-muffler inlet pipe nuts.
33. Carefully lower the vehicle.
34. Connect the oil pressure and engine temperature sending unit wires. Attach the coil wires, then connect the accelerator cable.
35. Install the starter motor and attach the electrical connector. Connect the alternator wires and connect the heater hose to the water pump.
36. Connect the air inlet hose to the turbocharger. Connect the ground strap to the turbocharger inlet elbow.
37. Uncap and connect the power steering lines.
38. Install the pulley, fan and drive belt. Adjust the drive belt tension. If equipped with A/C, install the compressor on the mounting bracket and adjust the belt tension.
39. Install the fan and radiator. On vehicles equipped with an electric cooling fan, attach the electrical connector.
40. Attach the upper and lower radiator hoses. Fill and bleed the cooling system. Fill the crankcase with the proper grade and quantity of engine oil.
41. Connect the negative battery cable.
42. Start the engine and operate at fast idle. Inspect for fluid and/or vacuum leaks.
43. Either install or lower the hood assembly.

3.8L Engine

1983–87 VEHICLES (VIN 3 ENGINE)

1. Properly drain the engine cooling system.
2. Disconnect the negative battery cable.
3. If equipped with an underhood lamp, detach the wiring connector. Matchmark the hood hinges, then remove the hood.
4. Remove the air cleaner assembly, including the air intake duct and heat tube.
5. Unfasten the fan shroud attaching screws. Remove the fan/clutch assembly attaching bolts, then remove the fan/clutch assembly and shroud.
6. Loosen the accessory drive belt idler. Remove the drive belt and water pump pulley.
7. Disconnect the upper and lower radiator hoses at the radiator.
8. Detach the Thermactor hose from the downstream air tube check valve.

9. Remove the downstream air tube bracket attaching bolt at the rear of the right cylinder head.

10. Detach the coil secondary wire from the coil.

11. Remove the power steering pump mounting brackets' attaching bolts. Leave the hoses connected, then position the pump aside in a position to prevent the fluid from leaking out.

12. If equipped with A/C, remove the mounting bracket attaching bolts. Leaving the refrigerant lines attached, secure the compressor to the right shock tower.

13. Remove the alternator mounting bolts and position the alternator aside.

14. Disconnect the heater hoses from the heater tube and water pump.

15. If equipped with cruise control, disconnect the cable at the carburetor or fuel charging assembly, as applicable.

16. Tag and disconnect the necessary vacuum hoses.

17. Remove the screw attaching the engine ground strap to the dash panel.

18. Disconnect the transmission linkage at the carburetor or fuel charging assembly.

19. Disconnect the accelerator cable at the carburetor and remove the cable routing bracket attaching bolts from the intake manifold (two places).

20. Tag and detach any necessary electrical connectors.

21. Disconnect the fuel lines and PCV hose at the carburetor, or detach the flexible fuel lines from the steel lines over the rocker arm (valve) cover, as applicable.

22. Detach and plug the flexible fuel inlet line at the pump.

23. Remove the carburetor or fuel charging assembly, as applicable. Leaving the EGR spacer and phenolic gasket in place, install Engine Lifting Plate T75T-6000-A or equivalent over the carburetor/throttle body hold-down studs. Tighten the nuts securely.

✳✳ WARNING

Because the intake manifold is aluminum and of lightweight design, all studs must be used to secure the lifting plate. DO NOT remove the engine with the transmission attached when using the lifting plate.

24. Raise and safely support the vehicle. Properly drain the engine oil.

25. Remove the dust shield from the transmission converter housing.

26. Remove the flex plate-to-torque converter attaching nuts.

27. Disconnect the battery cable from the starter motor. Unfasten the starter motor attaching bolts, then remove the starter.

28. Remove the transmission oil cooler line routing clip.

29. Unfasten the exhaust inlet pipe-to-exhaust manifold attaching nuts.

30. Disconnect the exhaust heat control valve vacuum line and remove the valve from the exhaust manifold studs, if equipped.

31. Remove the transmission-to-engine lower attaching bolts. There are two on each side.

32. Remove the engine mount-to-crossmember through bolts.

33. Carefully lower the vehicle.

34. Position a jack under the transmission. Raise the jack just enough to support the weight of the transmission.

35. Remove the two transmission-to-engine upper attaching bolts.

36. Position a protective cover, such as ¼ in. (6.4mm) plywood, between the engine and the radiator to prevent damage to the radiator.

37. Using a suitable shop crane, raise the engine slightly and carefully pull it away from the transmission. Carefully lift the engine out of the engine compartment (avoid bending or damaging the rear cover plate or other components). Install the engine on a suitable work stand.

To install:

➡**Lightly oil all bolt and stud threads before installation except those specifying special sealant.**

38. With the EGR spacer and the phenolic gasket in position, install Engine Lifting plate T75T-6000-A or equivalent, over the carburetor/throttle body hold-down studs. Tighten the nuts securely.

✳✳ WARNING

Because the intake manifold is aluminum and of lightweight design, all studs must be used to secure the lifting plate. DO NOT remove the engine with the transmission attached when using the lifting plate.

39. Using a suitable shop crane, hoist the engine from the work stand and carefully lower it into the vehicle.

40. With the exhaust heat control valve in place, align the engine insulators, exhaust manifolds-to-exhaust inlet pipes, transmission converter housing-to-cylinder block dowels and transmission converter-to-flywheel stud bolts.

41. Install the transmission-to-engine upper attaching bolts. Remove the shop crane and transmission jack.

42. Raise and safely support the vehicle.

43. Install the transmission-to-engine lower attaching bolts.

44. Install the engine mount-to-crossmember through bolts and tighten to 33–45 ft. lbs. (45–61 Nm).

45. Install the flex plate-to-torque converter attaching nuts and tighten to 20–30 ft. lbs. (28–40 Nm).

46. Install the dust shield on the transmission converter housing.

47. Fasten the exhaust inlet pipe-to-exhaust manifold attaching nuts. Tighten to 16–24 ft. lbs. (21–32 Nm).

48. If equipped, connect the heat control vacuum line.

49. Install the transmission oil cooler line routing clip.

50. Position the starter motor, install the attaching bolts and tighten to 15–20 ft. lbs. (20–27 Nm).

51. Connect the battery cable to the starter motor.

52. Attach the flexible fuel inlet line to the fuel pump and tighten securely.

53. Carefully lower the vehicle.

54. Remove the engine lifting plate.

55. Install the carburetor or fuel charging assembly and tighten the hold-down nuts to 12–15 ft. lbs (16–20 Nm).

56. Connect the fuel lines to the carburetor or fuel charging assembly and secure. Connect the flexible fuel lines to the steel lines over the rocker arm cover.

57. Connect the PCV hose at the carburetor.

58. Attach the accelerator cable and tighten the mounting bracket attaching bolts to 15–22 ft. lbs. (20–30 Nm).

59. If equipped with cruise control, connect the speed control cable at the carburetor/fuel charging assembly.

60. Attach the transmission linkage at the carburetor or fuel charging assembly.

61. If equipped with A/C, position the compressor and mounting brackets, then secure with the attaching bolts.

62. If equipped with power steering, position the pump and mounting brackets and secure with the attaching bolts.

63. If fuel injected, connect the hose to the downstream air tube check valve and clamp securely.

64. Connect the heater and radiator hoses.

65. Position the alternator and install the attaching bolts.

66. Connect the necessary vacuum lines and electrical connectors, as tagged during removal.

67. Fasten the engine ground strap to the dash panel.

68. Connect the ignition coil secondary wires.

69. Position the accessory drive belt over the pulleys.

➡**Examine the fan for possible cracks, separation or damage before installation. Replace the fan if necessary.**

70. Install the water pump pulley, fan/clutch assembly and fan shroud. Cross-tighten the fan/clutch assembly retaining bolts to 12–18 ft. lbs. (16–24 Nm).

71. Place the fan shroud on the radiator, then install the attaching screws.

72. Position the accessory drive belt over the pump pulley and adjust the drive belt tension.

73. Fill the engine cooling system with the proper type and quantity of coolant. Fill the crankcase with the correct amount and type of engine oil.

74. Connect the negative battery cable, then install the hood assembly.

75. If equipped, connect the underhood light.

76. Start the engine and check for fluid and/or vacuum leaks.

77. Check the engine curb idle speed and adjust, if necessary.

78. Install the air cleaner assembly, including the air intake duct and heat tube.

1988–97 VEHICLES (VIN 4, C & R ENGINES)

➡**Supercharged engines require special procedures for removing and installing the charge air cooler/intercooler and tube assemblies.**

1. If equipped with A/C, have a repair shop recover the refrigerant using the proper equipment.

2. Properly drain the engine cooling system.

3. Disconnect the negative battery cable.

4. Detach the wiring connector from the engine compartment lamp, then matchmark the hood hinges and remove the hood assembly.

5. Remove the left side cowl vent screen and wiper module assembly.

6. For non-SuperCharged (SC) engines, disconnect the alternator-to-voltage regulator wiring.

7. If equipped with a supercharged engine, remove the charge air cooler/intercooler inlet tube at the supercharger and charge air cooler/intercooler. Remove the bolt retaining the charge air cooler inlet tube to the alternator mounting bracket and remove the tube.

8. Remove the radiator upper sight shield.

9. Release the belt tension, then remove the drive belt.

10. Detach the air cleaner outlet tube.

11. Disconnect the cooling fan motor. Remove the cooling fan motor, fan blade and fan shroud as an assembly.

12. Remove the upper radiator hose.

13. If equipped with an automatic transmission, disconnect the oil cooler inlet tube and oil cooler tube.

14. Disconnect the heater water hoses. Disconnect the lower radiator hose at the water pump.

15. Unfasten the radiator retaining bolts, then remove the radiator. On supercharged engines, it will also be necessary to remove the two push pins retaining the charge air cooler to the radiator.

16. Disconnect the power steering pressure hose. On non-supercharged engines, remove the power steering pump and power steering pump bracket and position aside.

17. Disconnect the fuel charge wiring from the A/C clutch.

18. Detach and cap the A/C compressor lines. Unfasten the retaining bolts, then remove the A/C compressor.

19. Remove the coolant recovery reservoir.

20. Remove the wiring shield.

21. Unfasten the accelerator cable bracket and position it aside.

22. Proper relieve the fuel system pressure. Disconnect the fuel supply hose, then the fuel return hose.

23. Disconnect the PCM from the engine control sensor wiring and fuel charging wiring.

24. Tag and detach all necessary vacuum hoses.

25. On non-SC 49 state engine vehicles, disconnect the ground wire assembly and the coil wire. On the SC and non-SC California vehicles, disconnect the Ignition Control Module (ICM) at the wiring connector.

26. For SC engines, remove the ignition coil retaining screws, then position the ignition coil aside.

27. For SC engines, remove the nuts retaining the charge air cooler outlet tube to the charge air cooler to intake manifold adapter and charge air cooler outlet tube bracket and remove the charge air cooler outlet tube retaining bolts and nut at the alternator mounting bracket.

28. For SC engines, unfasten the alternator mounting bracket bolts, disconnect the alternator wiring and remove the alternator.

29. If equipped with a supercharged engine, remove the power steering pump and bracket and position it aside.

30. Disconnect the fuel vapor hose.

31. Detach one end of the throttle valve control actuating cable.

32. Raise and safely support the vehicle. Properly drain the engine oil.

33. For SC engines, remove the two nuts retaining the charge air cooler and remove the charge air cooler and cooler outlet tube.

34. Remove the dual converter Y-pipe-to-exhaust manifold nuts and remove the left exhaust manifold shield.

35. Detach the heated oxygen sensors.

36. Remove the inspection plug from the engine rear plate and remove the torque converter bolts, if equipped with an automatic transaxle.

37. Remove the engine-to-transmission bolts.

38. Remove the front engine support insulator through bolts. On the SC engine, remove the left front engine support insulator retaining strap bolt.

➡️**If the crankshaft damper and pulley have to be separated, mark the damper and pulley so that they may be reassembled in the same relative position. This is important as the damper and pulley are initially balanced as a unit.**

39. Remove the pulley from the damper.

➡️**If the crankshaft damper is being replaced, check if the original crankshaft damper had balance pins installed on it. If so, new balance pins (EOSZ-6A328-A or equivalent) must be installed on the new crankshaft damper in the same position as the original crankshaft damper. The pulley must also be installed in the same relative position as originally installed.**

40. Remove the starter motor.

41. Remove the ground cable and remove the starter motor wire harness retainers (right and left sides).

42. For the SC, disconnect the low oil level sensor.

43. Partially lower the vehicle.

44. Disconnect the oil pressure sensor.

45. Position a suitable floor jack under the transmission. Position a shop crane and attach to the engine lifting eyes.

46. Remove the engine assembly from the vehicle and place it on a suitable work stand.

To install:

➡️**Lightly oil all bolt and stud bolt threads before installation except those specifying special sealant.**

47. Install engine lifting equipment to the engine lifting eyes and remove the engine assembly from the work stand.

48. Position the engine assembly in the vehicle. Install two engine-to-transmission bolts.

➡️**Seat the left side locating pin before seating the right side.**

49. Lower the engine onto the front engine support insulators and remove the shop crane.

50. Remove the floor jack from under the transmission. Tighten two engine-to-transmission bolts.

51. Attach the oil pressure sensor electrical connector.

52. Raise and safely support the vehicle.

53. Install the remaining engine-to-transmission bolts. Tighten all bolts to 40–50 ft. lbs. (55–68 Nm).

54. Install the torque converter bolts and tighten to 20–34 ft. lbs. (27–46 Nm). Install the inspection plug to the engine rear plate.

55. Install and tighten the front engine support insulator through bolts and the left front engine support insulator retaining strap bolt.

56. Install the starter motor, as outlined in Section 2 of this manual.

57. Fasten the starter motor wire harness retainer, ground cable and transmission oil cooler line bracket.

58. Install the dual converter Y-pipe-to-exhaust manifold retaining nuts.

59. Install the pulley to the crankshaft damper. Tighten the bolts to 20–28 ft. lbs. (26–38 Nm).

60. Attach the heated oxygen sensor(s) at the wiring connector.

61. Install the oil bypass filter.

62. For SC engines, connect the low oil level sensor.

63. Carefully lower the vehicle.

64. Connect the throttle valve control actuating cable.

65. Attach the fuel vapor hose.

66. For SC engines, install the charge air cooler outlet tube, charge air cooler and power steering pump and bracket.

67. If equipped with a SC engine, install the alternator, connect the wiring and install the alternator mounting bracket bolts.

68. If equipped with a SC engine, install the charge air cooler outlet tube bolts at the power steering bracket and install the nuts retaining the charge air cooler outlet tube to the charge air cooler outlet tube bracket and charge air cooler to the intake manifold adapter.

69. For SC engines, install the ignition coil and retaining bolts.

70. Install the coolant recovery reservoir.

71. Attach the alternator-to-voltage regulator electrical wiring.

72. Connect the vacuum hoses, as tagged during removal.

73. Attach the engine control sensor wiring and the fuel charging wiring.

74. On non-SC 49 state engine vehicles, connect the ground wire assembly and coil wire. On SC and non-SC California engines, attach the ignition control module at the wiring connector.

75. Unplug and connect the fuel supply and return lines.

76. Install the accelerator cable bracket.

77. Fasten the wiring shield.

78. If equipped, install the A/C compressor. Tighten the retaining bolts to 30–45 ft. lbs. (41–61 Nm). Unplug and connect the compressor lines.

79. If equipped, connect the fuel charging wiring to the A/C clutch.

80. For non-SC engines, install the power steering pump and bracket. Connect the power steering hoses.

81. Install the radiator and retaining bolts. On SC engines, install the charge air cooler to the radiator and secure with the retaining push pins.

82. Connect the lower radiator hose to the water pump. Install the heater water hoses.

83. If equipped with an automatic transmission, install the oil cooler inlet tube and oil cooler tube.

84. Attach the upper radiator hose.

85. Install the cooling fan motor, fan blade, and fan shroud as an assembly. For SC engines, attach the cooling fan motor.

86. Position the drive belts (accessory/supercharger).

87. Install the radiator upper sight shield.

88. For SC engines, install the charge air cooler tube and bolts retaining the tube to the power steering bracket. Install the charge air cooler tube to the supercharger and charge air cooler.

89. Install the cowl vent screen and wiper module.

90. Install the hood, using the marks make during removal for alignment purposes.

91. Attach the engine compartment lamp wiring.

92. Connect the negative battery cable.

93. Refill the crankcase to the proper level with the specified type of engine oil. Properly fill the engine cooling system.

94. Bleed the power steering system. Start the engine and check the fluid levels, and for fluid/vacuum leaks.

95. If equipped with A/C, take the car to a certified repair shop to have the system evacuated, charged and leak tested.

4.6L Engine

1. If equipped with A/C, have a repair shop recover the refrigerant using the proper equipment.

2. Disconnect the negative battery cable.

3. Properly drain the engine cooling system.

4. Remove the air cleaner outlet tube, then remove the air cleaner assembly.

5. Remove the cooling fan motor, blade and shroud as an assembly.

6. Properly relieve the fuel system pressure, then disconnect and plug the fuel lines.

7. Detach the fuel charging wiring 42-pin connector and 8-pin connector, then position out of the way.

8. Disconnect the accelerator cable and speed control actuator with a suitable prytool.

9. Detach the fuel charging wiring and front vapor hose from the evaporative emission canister purge valve.

10. Disconnect the positive battery cable from the power distribution box.

11. Detach the vacuum supply hose from the throttle body adapter vacuum port.

12. Disconnect the transmission oil cooler tubes from the oil cooler.

13. Unfasten the upper radiator hose from the radiator. Disconnect the heater supply and return hoses.

14. If equipped, disconnect the A/C compressor inlet and outlet hoses from the compressor using Spring Lock Coupling Disconnect tool T81P-19623-G1 (⅜ in.) and T81P-19623-G2 (½ in.), or equivalent tools.

15. Detach the engine-to-frame wire from the dash panel.

16. Partially raise and safely support the vehicle.

17. Remove the front wheel and tire assemblies.

18. Detach the right and left front anti-lock sensor and bracket wiring connectors.

19. Remove the right and left front disc brake caliper bolts. Remove the calipers and support from the body using a piece of wire. DO NOT let the calipers hang by the brake hose.

20. Disconnect the right and left front suspension upper control arms.

21. Detach the front spring and shocks from the front suspension lower control arms.

22. Raise and safely support the vehicle. Properly drain the engine oil into a suitable container.

23. Disconnect the dual converter Y-pipe from the right and left exhaust manifolds and resonator.

24. Detach the shift cable and bracket.

25. Index the driveshaft centering socket yoke to the rear axle universal joint flange.

26. Remove the four bolts connecting the driveshaft centering socket yoke to the rear axle universal joint flange. Support the rear axle assembly with a jackstand.

27. Remove the two nut and bolt assemblies retaining the front of the rear axle to the rear sub-frame.

28. Loosen the rear differential bracket-to-body bolts, then lower.

29. Slide the driveshaft rearward until it is free of the extension housing.

30. Disconnect the lower hose from the radiator.

31. Loosen the spring clamps and remove the power steering hoses from the power steering oil cooler.

32. Detach the wiring connector bulkhead.

33. Support the front sub/frame using Rotunda Powertrain Lift 014-00765 and Adapter 014-00341 or equivalent.

34. Remove the rear engine support insulator retaining bolts.

35. Disconnect the steering coupling at the pinch bolt joint.

36. Remove the eight front sub-frame retaining bolts, then lower the engine and transmission from the vehicle.

37. Disconnect the power steering pressure and return hoses from the power steering pump.

38. Remove the engine wire harness retainers from the front sub-frame.

39. Remove the left and right front engine support insulator through bolts.

40. Install Rotunda Engine Lift Bracket Set 014-00334 or equivalent on the side of the left cylinder head as the front, as shown in the accompanying figure. Attach Rotunda Engine Lift Bracket Set 014-00334 or equivalent using two M-12 x 1.75 x 20mm bolts. Install Rotunda Engine Lift Bracket Set on the side of right cylinder head at the rear.

41. Connect a shop crane, to the lift brackets.

42. Raise the engine and transmission assembly and carefully separate the engine from the front sub-frame.

43. Remove the starter, as outlined in Section 2 of this manual.

44. Disconnect the transmission oil cooler tubes.

45. Remove the retaining nut from the transmission line stud-to-cylinder block.

46. Remove the transmission housing cover from the cylinder block to gain access to the torque converter retaining nuts. Rotate the crankshaft until each of the four nuts is accessible, then remove the nuts.

47. Lower the engine and transmission assembly to a level, stationary surface.

48. Detach the transmission wire harness connectors at the transmission.

49. Remove the six engine-to-transmission retaining bolts, then separate the engine from the transmission.

50. Position the engine on a suitable work stand, then remove the engine lifting equipment.

To install:

51. Install the Rotunda Engine Lifting Bracket set 014-00334 in the position described earlier in this procedure.

52. Connect a suitable shop crane to the lifting brackets, then remove the engine from the work stand.

53. Carefully lower the engine and align it to the transmission.

➥**Make sure the studs on the torque converter align with the holes in the flywheel.**

54. Start the torque converter pilot into the flywheel and align the paint marks on the flywheel and torque converter.

55. Fully engage the engine to the transmission, then install the six retaining bolts. Tighten the bolts to 30–44 ft. lbs. (40–60 Nm).

➥**Rotate the crankshaft until each of the four nuts is accessible.**

56. Install the four torque converter retaining nuts, then tighten to 22–25 ft. lbs. (30–35 Nm).

57. Fasten the transmission housing cover to the cylinder block.

58. Install the starter motor, as outlined in Section 2 of this manual.

59. Position the transmission case to the cylinder block bracket, then install the three bolts and one stud. Tighten the bolts and stud to 18–31 ft. lbs. (25–43 Nm).

60. Position the transmission oil cooler tube bracket to the transmission case-to-cylinder block bracket stud and install the retaining nut. Tighten the nut to 15–22 ft. lbs. (20–30 Nm).

61. Connect the transmission oil cooler tubes to the transmission. Attach the transmission wire harness connector to the transmission.

62. Raise the engine and transmission assembly with a suitable shop crane.

63. Carefully lower the engine and transmission assembly onto the front sub-frame.

64. Install the left and right front engine support insulator through bolts. Tighten the bolts to 15–22 ft. lbs. (20–30 Nm).

65. Fasten the engine wire harness retainers to the front sub-frame.

66. Connect the power steering pressure and return hoses to the power steering pump.

67. Remove the lift bracket from the cylinder heads.

68. Raise the engine, transmission and front sub-frame using Rotunda Powertrain Lift 014-00765 and Adapter 014-00341 or equivalent, into the vehicle.

69. Align the front sub-frame with the body and install the retaining bolts. Tighten to 70–96 ft. lbs. (95–130 Nm).

70. Connect the steering coupling at the pinch bolt joint.

71. Install the rear engine support insulator retaining bolts. Tighten to 15–22 ft. lbs. (20–30 Nm).

72. Remove the powertrain lift and position it out of the way.

73. Install the driveshaft to the transmission.

74. Lift the rear axle assembly into position.

75. Install the two nut and bolts assemblies retaining front of the rear axle assembly to the rear sub-frame. Tighten to 72–89 ft. lbs. (98–120 Nm).

76. Tighten the two rear axle differential insulator nuts to 75–94 ft. lbs. (102–127 Nm).

77. Align the driveshaft centering socket yoke to the rear axle universal joint flange, then install the four retaining bolts. Tighten to 70–96 ft. lbs. (95–130 Nm).

78. Connect the transmission shift linkage.

79. Position the front suspension lower arms to the front spring and shock and install the retaining bolt. Tighten to 118–162 ft. lbs. (160–220 Nm).

80. Connect the upper radiator hose.

81. Attach the power steering hoses to the power steering oil cooler.

82. Connect the engine-to-frame wire to the dash panel.

83. Install the dual converter Y-pipe.

84. Connect the front suspension upper arms to the front wheel knuckles. Tighten to 50–68 ft. lbs. (68–92 Nm).

85. Attach the front anti-lock sensor and bracket wiring connectors.

86. Install the disc brake calipers.

87. Install the front wheel and tire assemblies.

88. Carefully lower the vehicle.

89. Attach the A/C lines to the compressor.

90. Connect the transmission oil cooler tubes to the transmission fluid cooler.

91. Attach the upper radiator hose to the radiator.

92. Connect the heater supply and return hoses.

93. Attach the vacuum supply hose to the throttle body adapter vacuum port.

94. Connect the positive battery cable to the power distribution box.

95. Connect the fuel charging wiring and front vapor hose to the evaporative emission canister purge valve.

96. Attach the accelerator cable and cruise control actuator to the throttle body.

97. Fasten the 42-pin and 8-pin fuel charging wire connectors.

98. Connect the fuel lines.

99. Install the cooling fan motor, blade and shroud.

100. Install the air cleaner outlet tube and the engine air cleaner assembly.

101. Fill and bleed the engine cooling system.

102. Connect the negative battery cable.

103. Fill the crankcase with the proper type and amount of engine oil.

104. Start the engine and check for fluid and/or vacuum leaks.

105. If equipped, take the car to a certified repair shop to have the A/C system evacuated, charged and leak tested.

5.0L Engine

1983–88 VEHICLES (VIN F ENGINES)

The engine removal and installation procedures are for the engine only, without the transmission attached. Remove or disconnect parts of Thermactor system that will interfere with the removal or installation of the engine.

1. If equipped with A/C, have a repair shop recover the refrigerant using the proper equipment.

2. Disconnect the negative battery cable.

3. Properly drain the cooling system and crankcase.

4. Properly relieve the fuel system pressure.

5. Scribe a matchmark around the hood hinges, for installation purposes, then remove the hood.

6. Disconnect the battery ground cables from the engine block.

7. Remove the air intake duct assembly.

8. Disconnect the upper radiator hose from the coolant outlet housing and the lower radiator hose from the water pump.

9. If equipped, disconnect the transmission oil cooler lines from the radiator.

10. Unfasten the bolts attaching the fan shroud to the radiator, then remove the radiator. Remove the fan, spacer, belt pulley and shroud.

11. Remove the alternator bolts, then position the alternator out of the way.

12. Disconnect the oil pressure sending unit wire from the sending unit. Disconnect the low oil level sensor wire, if equipped, at the middle of the rear oil sump on the left side of the oil pan and the flexible fuel lines at the fuel tank line. Plug the fuel tank line.

13. Disconnect the accelerator cable from the throttle body. On automatic transmissions, disconnect the TV rod. If equipped, disconnect the cruise control cable.

14. If equipped, disconnect the throttle valve vacuum line from the intake manifold. Remove the transmission filler tube bracket from the cylinder block.

15. If equipped with A/C, remove the compressor.

16. Disconnect the power steering pump bracket from the cylinder head. Position the power steering pump out of the way and in a position that will prevent the fluid from leaking out.

17. Disconnect the brake vacuum line from the intake manifold.

18. Disconnect the heater hoses from the engine mounted heater tubes and intake manifold. Detach the coolant temperature sending unit wire from the unit.

19. Remove the flywheel or converter housing-to-engine upper bolts.

20. Detach the wiring harness at the two 10-pin connectors.

21. Raise and safely support the front of the vehicle.

22. Detach the starter electrical connector, then remove the starter from the vehicle.

23. Disconnect the muffler inlet pipes from the exhaust manifolds. Disconnect the engine support insulators from the chassis. If equipped detach the downstream Thermactor tubing and check valve from the right exhaust manifold stud.

24. Detach the transmission cooler lines from the retainer and remove the converter housing inspection cover. Disconnect the flywheel from the converter. Secure the converter assembly in the housing. Remove the remaining converter housing-to-engine bolts.

25. Carefully lower the vehicle, then support the transmission with a suitable jack. Attach a suitable shop crane to the lifting brackets on the exhaust manifolds.

26. Raise the engine slightly and carefully pull it from the transmission. Carefully lift the engine out of the engine compartment (avoid bending or damaging the rear cover plate or other components). Install the engine on a suitable work stand.

To install:

27. Attach the engine lifting sling and lifting brackets to the exhaust manifold. Carefully hoist the engine from the work stand.

28. Lower the engine carefully into the engine compartment. Make sure the exhaust manifolds are properly aligned with the muffler inlet pipes. Start converter pilot into the crankshaft. Align the paint mark on the flywheel with the mark on the torque converter.

29. Install the flywheel or converter housing upper bolts. Make sure the dowels in the cylinder block engage the converter housing.

30. Install the engine support insulator to the chassis attaching fasteners.

31. Raise and safely support the front of the vehicle. Connect both muffler inlet pipes to the exhaust manifolds.

32. Install the starter, then attach the starter electrical connector.

33. Remove the retainer holding the converter in the housing. Attach the converter to the flex plate. Install the converter housing inspection cover. Install the remaining converter housing attaching bolts.

34. Remove the support from the transmission, then lower the vehicle.

35. Attach the wiring harness at the two 10-pin connectors.

36. Connect the coolant temperature sending unit wire. Connect the heater hose to the intake manifold. Connect the low oil sensor wire. Attach the metal heater tubes at the ECT, ACT and EGO sensors, if equipped.

37. Install the transmission filler tube bracket. Connect the manual shift rod and connect the retracting spring. If equipped, connect the throttle valve vacuum line.

38. Unplug the fuel tank line and connect the fuel line and oil pressure sending unit wire.

39. Install the pulley, belt, spacer and fan.

40. Position the alternator, then install the retaining bolts. Attach the alternator and battery ground connections. Adjust the belt tension to specifications.

41. If equipped with A/C, install the compressor.

42. Install the drive belt and power steering pump bracket. Install the bracket attaching bolts. Adjust the belt tension to specifications.

43. Connect the brake vacuum line.

44. Place the radiator shroud over the fan, if equipped. Connect the radiator upper and lower hoses. If equipped with an automatic transmission, connect the transmission fluid cooler lines. If equipped, install the shroud bolts and tighten to 24–48 inch lbs. (3–5 Nm).

45. Connect the heater hoses to the heater tubes.

46. Fill and bleed the engine cooling system. Fill the crankcase with the proper grade and amount of engine oil.

47. Adjust the transmission throttle linkage.

48. Connect the negative battery cable, then start the engine and run at a fast idle. Check the fluid levels and inspect for any fluid and/or vacuum leaks.

49. Install the air intake duct assembly.

50. Install the hood assembly.

51. If equipped, take the car to a certified repair shop to have the A/C system evacuated, charged and leak tested.

1991–93 VEHICLES (VIN T AND E ENGINES)

1. If equipped with A/C, have a repair shop recover the refrigerant using the proper equipment.

2. Properly drain the engine cooling system.

3. Disconnect the negative battery cable. Detach the underhood lamp wiring connector.

4. Remove the engine oil dipstick.

5. Scribe a matchmark around the hood hinges for installation reference, then remove the hood.

6. If equipped, disconnect and cap or plug the A/C compressor lines.

7. Detach the compressor clutch electrical connector and the power steering pressure switch.

8. Disconnect the alternator wiring harness from the alternator and position the harness aside.

9. Remove the fan shroud and fan assembly.

10. Disconnect the upper radiator hose.

11. Remove the air cleaner-to-throttle body tube assembly.

12. Disconnect the transmission oil cooler inlet and outlet tubes.

13. Detach the throttle and kickdown cables from the throttle body and remove the cable bracket retaining bolts. Position the cable and bracket assembly out of the way.

14. Tag and disconnect the following vacuum lines:
  • Upper intake manifold vacuum tee
  • A/C control panel vacuum supply hose
  • Secondary air injection valve
  • EGR external pressure valve (vacuum and electrical connections)

15. Remove the upper intake manifold, as outlined in this section.

16. Detach the main engine wiring harness at the dash panel (right side).

17. Disconnect the heater hoses at the engine.

18. Position the engine wiring harness so it can be removed with the engine.

19. Disconnect the wiring harness form the coil and distributor and position it out of the way.

20. Properly relieve the fuel system pressure. For details, please refer to Section 5 of this manual.

21. Disconnect and plug the fuel inlet and return hoses from the fuel supply manifold.

22. Detach the lower radiator hose from the water pump.

23. Unfasten the radiator retaining bolts, then remove the radiator.

24. Raise and safely support the vehicle, then properly drain the engine oil and remove the oil filter.

25. Remove the starter, as outlined in Section 2 of this manual.

26. Disconnect the heated O_2 sensor from the right and left catalytic converters.

27. Detach the battery ground cable from the left side of the engine.

28. On the right side of the engine, disconnect the bracket for the transmission cooler lines, engine-to-body ground straps and the starter motor wiring harness.

29. Remove the torque converter inspection cover and mark one of the converter studs to the flywheel for alignment during reassembly.

30. Remove the torque converter retaining nuts.

31. Remove the exhaust manifold heat shield at the left manifold flange and disconnect the exhaust pipe from the flange.

32. Disconnect the right side exhaust manifold flange.

33. Loosen the transmission mount retaining nut.

34. Remove the converter housing-to-engine bolts.

35. Remove the engine mount through bolts.

➡ It may be helpful to drain the power steering fluid before removing the lines.

36. Carefully lower the vehicle, then disconnect and plug the power steering fluid lines.

37. Support the transmission with a suitable floor jack.

38. Install a suitable engine lifting sling on the engine lifting eyes.

39. Using a shop crane, lift the engine assembly clear of the engine mounts and remove the engine assembly from the vehicle. Place the engine on a suitable work stand.

To install:

40. Install a suitable engine lifting sling on the engine lifting eyes and lift the engine from the work stand.

41. Carefully lower the engine into the engine compartment. Make sure the exhaust manifolds are properly aligned with the muffler inlet pipes.

42. Start the converter pilot into the crankshaft. Align the mark on the flywheel to the mark on the torque converter.

43. Position the retaining clip for the left side O_2 sensor wiring near the left side upper transmission-to-engine bolt.

44. Install the converter housing upper bolts. Make sure the dowels in the cylinder block engage the converter housing.

45. Raise and safely support the vehicle, then install the housing bolts.

46. Install the engine mount through bolts and tighten to 35–50 ft. lbs. (47–68 Nm).

47. Tighten the transmission mount retaining nut to 65–85 ft. lbs. (88–115 Nm).

48. Connect the right side exhaust manifold flange.

49. Attach the exhaust pipe to the left side exhaust manifold flange, then install the exhaust manifold heat shield.

50. Install the torque converter, then install the converter inspection cover.

51. On the right side of the engine, install the bracket for the transmission cooler lines, engine-to-body ground strap and the starter motor wiring harness.

52. Connect the battery ground cable to the left side of the engine.

53. Attach the O_2 sensors for the right and left catalytic converters.

54. Install the starter, as outlined in Section 2 of this manual.

55. Install a new engine oil filter, and install the drain plug, if still removed.

56. Carefully lower the vehicle, then unplug and connect the power steering lines.

57. Install the radiator. Attach the coolant overflow hose to the radiator.

58. Connect the lower radiator hose to the water pump.

59. Uncap and connect the fuel inlet and return hoses to the fuel supply manifold.

60. Position and connect the engine wiring harness for the coil and distributor.

61. Attach the engine wiring harness to the coil.

62. Connect the heater hoses at the engine.

63. Attach the main engine wiring harness connectors at the dash panel (right side).

64. Install the upper intake manifold.

65. Connect the following vacuum lines:
  • Upper intake manifold vacuum tee
  • A/C control panel vacuum supply hose
  • Secondary air injection valve
  • EGR external pressure valve (vacuum and electrical connections)

66. Connect the throttle and kickdown cables to the throttle body and install the cable bracket retaining bolts.

67. Attach the transmission oil cooler inlet and outlet tubes.

68. Install the upper radiator hose.

69. Install the fan assembly and fan shroud.

70. Connect the air cleaner-to-throttle body tube.

71. Position and connect the wiring harness for the alternator.

72. Attach the compressor clutch electrical connector.

73. If equipped, unplug and connect the A/C compressor lines.

74. Install the hood, using the marks made during removal for alignment purposes.

75. Attach the wiring connector for the underhood lamp.

76. Connect the negative battery cable.

77. Fill and bleed the engine cooling system and crankcase.

78. Fill and bleed the power steering fluid with the proper type and amount of fluid.

79. Install the oil dipstick.

80. Start the engine and check the fluid levels. Inspect for fluid and/or vacuum leaks.

81. If equipped, take the car to a certified repair shop to have the A/C system evacuated, charged and leak tested.

Rocker Arm (Valve) Cover

REMOVAL & INSTALLATION

2.3L Engine

1. Disconnect the negative battery cable..

2. Detach the air intake tube at the throttle body by disconnecting the metal tube from the turbocharger (there are two retaining bolts) and remove the clamp from the throttle body end.

3. Disconnect the PCV hose from the rear of the rocker arm cover.

4. Remove the throttle body assembly, as outlined in Section 5 of this manual.

5. Remove the eight retaining bolts, then remove the rocker arm (valve) cover. Clean all old gasket material from the cover and cylinder head gasket surfaces.

To install:

6. Coat the gasket surfaces of the rocker arm cover and cylinder head with Gasket and Seal Contact Adhesive D7AZ-19B508-A or equivalent. Allow to dry past the "wet" stage.

7. Install the guide pins, the position the rocker arm cover over the pins. Hand start two bolts, then remove the guide pins. Hand start the remaining bolts. Tighten the rocker arm cover bolts to 62–97 inch lbs. (7–11 Nm).

8. Install the throttle body, as outlined in Section 5 of this manual.

9. Attach the PCV hose to the rear of the rocker arm cover.

10. Connect the air intake tube.

11. Connect the negative battery cable, then start the engine and check for leaks.

3.8L Engine

♦ See Figures 1, 2, 3 and 4

1. Disconnect the negative battery cable.

2. Tag and disconnect the spark plug wires. Remove the ignition wire routing clips from the valve cover retaining bolt studs.

3. If the left side valve cover is being removed, proceed as follows:
   a. Remove the oil filler cap.
   b. For SC engines, remove the charge air cooler/intercooler tubes.
   c. Remove the crankcase ventilation tube.
   d. For SC engines, disconnect the engine oil cooler inlet tube and hose.

4. If the right side valve cover is being removed, proceed as follows:
   a. Remove the PCV valve.
   b. For SC engines, remove the air cleaner outlet tube.
   c. For SC engines, remove the throttle body.

5. Unfasten the valve cover retaining screws/bolts, then remove the cover from the vehicle. Remove and discard the old gasket. Use a suitable solvent to carefully clean the old gasket material and/or dirt from the sealing surfaces.

To install:

➡Lightly oil all bolt and stud threads before installation.

6. Position a new gasket into the groove on the valve cover.

7. Place the cover on the cylinder head and install the retaining bolts. Note the location of the spark plug wire routing clip stud bolts. Tighten the retaining bolts to 7–9 ft. lbs. (9–12 Nm).

8. If the left side valve cover is being installed, proceed as follows:
   a. For SC engines, connect the engine oil cooler inlet tube and hose.
   b. Connect the crankcase ventilation tube.
   c. For SC engines, install the charge air cooler/intercooler tubes.
   d. Install the oil filler cap.

9. If the right side valve cover is being installed, proceed as follows:
   a. For SC engines, install the throttle body.
   b. For SC engines, connect the air cleaner outlet tube.
   c. Install the PCV valve.

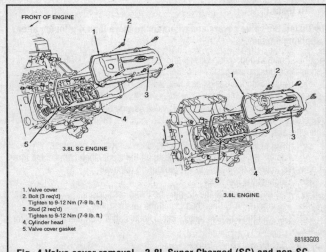

FRONT OF ENGINE

3.8L SC ENGINE

3.8L ENGINE

1. Valve cover
2. Bolt (3 req'd)
   Tighten to 9-12 Nm (7-9 lb. ft.)
3. Stud (2 req'd)
   Tighten to 9-12 Nm (7-9 lb. ft.)
4. Cylinder head
5. Valve cover gasket

88183G03

Fig. 4 Valve cover removal—3.8L Super Charged (SC) and non-SC engines

88183P01

Fig. 1 Unfasten the retaining bolts, then . . .

88183P02

Fig. 2 . . . remove the valve cover from the engine

88183P03

Fig. 3 Remove the old gasket and replace with a new one during installation

10. Install the spark plug wire routing clips, then connect the spark plug wires, as tagged during removal.

11. Connect the negative battery cable, then start the engine and check for leaks.

4.6L Engine

▶ See Figure 5

RIGHT SIDE

1. Disconnect the negative battery cable.
2. Remove the air cleaner outlet tube.
3. Detach the 42-pin connector and the 8-pin connector leading to the Mass Air Flow (MAF) sensor and Intake Air Temperature (IAT) sensor.
4. Remove the nut retaining the A/C line to the right front fender apron.
5. Lift the A/C line and feed the 42-pin connector under the line. Position the connector out of the way.
6. Properly relieve the fuel system pressure, as outlined in Section 5 of this manual. Disconnect the fuel lines.

➡ **Do NOT pull on the ignition wires, as the wire may separate from the connector in the wire boot.**

7. Tag and disconnect the ignition wires from the spark plugs.
8. Remove the ignition wires and the ignition wire separators from the valve cover studs, then position the wires out of the way.
9. Disconnect the PCV valve from the crankcase ventilation grommet, then position it out of the way.
10. Unfasten the bolts and stud bolts retaining the valve cover to the cylinder, then remove the valve cover. Remove and discard the gasket. Thoroughly clean and dry the gasket mating surfaces using Metal Surface Cleaner F4AZ-19A536-RA or equivalent.

To install:

➡ **Install the valve covers and retainers no more than 4 minutes after applying sealant.**

11. Position and, using Gasket and Trim Adhesive D7AZ-19B508-B or equivalent, glue a new gasket into the valve cover.
12. Apply Silicone Gasket and Sealer F1AZ-19562-B or equivalent, in both places where the engine front cover meets the cylinder head.
13. Install the valve cover gaskets, valve covers, bolts and stud bolts. Tighten the stud bolts and bolts to 71–106 inch lbs. (8–12 Nm) no more than 4 minutes after applying sealer.
14. Install the PCV valve into the crankcase ventilation grommet.
15. Fasten the ignition wire separators on the studs, then connect the ignition wires to the spark plugs, as tagged during removal.
16. Connect the fuel lines.
17. Position and attach the 42-pin and 8-pin connectors.
18. Position the A/C line, then install the retaining nut.
19. Connect the negative battery cable, then start the engine and check for leaks.

LEFT SIDE

1. Disconnect the negative battery cable.
2. Remove the air cleaner outlet tube.
3. Disconnect the speed control actuator from the throttle body, then position the actuator out of the way.
4. Detach the fuel charging wiring from the Electronic Variable Orifice (EVO) sensor and oil pressure sensor. Position the fuel charging wiring out of the way.

➡ **Do NOT pull on the ignition wires, as the wire may separate from the connector in the wire boot.**

5. Tag and disconnect the ignition wires from the spark plugs.
6. Remove the ignition wires and the ignition wire separators from the valve cover studs, then position the wires out of the way.
7. Unfasten the bolts and stud bolts retaining the valve cover to the cylinder head, then remove the valve cover.
Remove and discard the gasket. Thoroughly clean and dry the gasket mating surfaces using Metal Surface Cleaner F4AZ-19A536-RA or equivalent.

To install:

➡ **Install the valve covers and retainers no more than 4 minutes after applying sealant.**

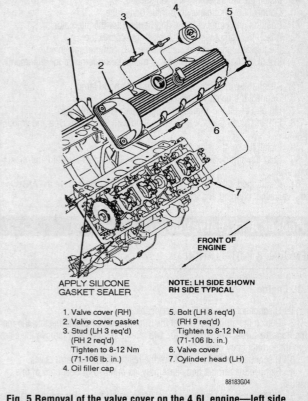

APPLY SILICONE GASKET SEALER

NOTE: LH SIDE SHOWN RH SIDE TYPICAL

1. Valve cover (RH)
2. Valve cover gasket
3. Stud (LH 3 req'd)
   (RH 2 req'd)
   Tighten to 8-12 Nm
   (71-106 lb. in.)
4. Oil filler cap
5. Bolt (LH 8 req'd)
   (RH 9 req'd)
   Tighten to 8-12 Nm
   (71-106 lb. in.)
6. Valve cover
7. Cylinder head (LH)

88183G04

Fig. 5 Removal of the valve cover on the 4.6L engine—left side shown, right side similar

8. Position and, using Gasket and Trim Adhesive D7AZ-19B508-B or equivalent, glue a new gasket into the valve cover.
9. Apply Silicone Gasket and Sealer F1AZ-19562-B or equivalent, in both places where the engine front cover meets the cylinder head.
10. Install the valve cover gaskets, valve covers, bolts and stud bolts. Tighten the stud bolts and bolts to 71–106 inch lbs. (8–12 Nm) no more than 4 minutes after applying sealer.
11. Fasten the ignition wire separators on the studs, then connect the ignition wires to the spark plugs, as tagged during removal.
12. Position and connect the fuel charging wiring to the EVO sensor and oil pressure sensor.
13. Position and attach the speed control actuator.
14. Connect the negative battery cable, then start the engine and check for leaks.

5.0L Engine

1. Disconnect the negative battery cable.
2. Remove the air cleaner assembly.
3. To remove the right side valve cover:
   a. Remove the PCV valve and hose from the valve cover. Disconnect the EGR vacuum hoses.
   b. Remove the Thermactor®/secondary air injection bypass valve and air supply hoses as necessary to gain clearance.
   c. Tag and disconnect the spark plug wires from the plugs, using tool T74P-666-A or equivalent, with a twisting pulling motion. Twist and pull on the boots only, never on the wire. Position the wires and mounting bracket out of the way.
4. To remove the left side valve cover:
   a. Remove the spark plug wires and bracket.
   b. Remove the wiring harness and any vacuum hose from the bracket.
   c. Remove the upper intake manifold.
   d. Remove the valve cover mounting bolts and valve cover.
5. Remove the upper intake manifold.
6. Unfasten the valve cover mounting bolts, then remove the valve cover.

7. Clean all old gasket material from the valve cover and cylinder head mounting surfaces.

To install:

8. Use oil resistant sealing compound and a new valve cover gasket. Position a new valve cover gasket, making sure all the gasket tangs are engaged into the cover notches provided.

9. Position the valve cover(s) on the cylinder head. On the left side cover, install the bolts and wire loom clips. For vehicles through 1988, the cover is tightened in two steps. Tighten the bolts to 3–5 ft. lbs. (4–7 Nm) for vehicles through 1985, to 6–9 ft. lbs. (8–12 Nm) for 1986–88 vehicles or to 10–13 ft. lbs. (14–18 Nm) for 1991–92 vehicles, then two minutes later, tighten the bolts to the same specification. For 1993 vehicles, tighten the bolts to 12–15 ft. lbs. (16–20 Nm).

10. Install the upper intake manifold.

11. Install the crankcase ventilation hoses in the cover(s).

12. Install the spark plugs wires and bracket assembly on the rocker arm cover attaching stud. Connect the spark plug wires, as tagged during removal.

13. Install the air cleaner and intake duct assembly.

14. Install the Thermactor bypass valve and air supply hoses.

15. Connect the negative battery cable.

Rocker Arm (Cam Follower) and Hydraulic Lash Adjuster

REMOVAL & INSTALLATION

2.3L Engine

➡ **A special tool is required to compress the lash adjuster.**

1. Remove the valve cover and associated parts as required.

2. Rotate the camshaft so that the base circle of the cam is against the cam follower you intend to remove.

3. Remove the retaining spring from the cam follower, if so equipped.

4. Using special tool T74P–6565–B or a valve spring compressor tool, collapse the lash adjuster and/or depress the valve spring, as necessary, and slide the cam follower over the lash adjuster and out from under the camshaft.

5. Install the cam follower in the reverse order of removal. Make sure that the lash adjuster is collapsed and released before rotating the camshaft.

Rocker Arm Shaft/Rocker Arms

REMOVAL & INSTALLATION

V6 and V8 Engines

1. Disconnect the negative battery cable.

2. Remove the rocker arm (valve) cover, as outlined earlier in this section.

3. Remove the rocker arm stud nut or bolt, fulcrum seat and rocker arm.

4. Lubricate all parts with heavy engine oil before installation.

5. When installing, rotate the crankshaft until the lifter is on the base of the cam circle (all the way down) and assemble the rocker arm.

6. Tighten the nut or bolt to 17–23 ft. lbs. (23–31 Nm).

➡ **Some later engines use RTV sealant instead of valve cover gaskets.**

Valve Lash

ADJUSTMENTS

2.3L Engine

▸ **See Figure 6**

The 2.3L engine is an overhead cam engine with hydraulic lash adjusters. These units are placed at the fulcrum point of the cam followers (rocker arms). Their action are similar to hydraulic tappets used in pushrod engines and are serviced in the same manner.

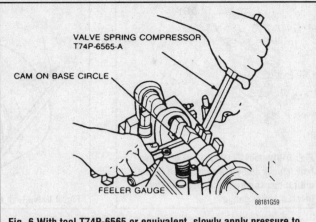

Fig. 6 With tool T74P-6565 or equivalent, slowly apply pressure to the cam follower until the lash adjuster is completely collapsed. Then insert a feeler gauge

➡ **Valve Arrangement (Front to Rear) . . . E-I-E-I-E-I-E-I**

1. Position the camshaft so that the base circle of the lobe is facing the cam follower of the valve to be checked.

2. Using the appropriate tool (T74P-6565 or equivalent), slowly apply pressure to the cam follower until the lash adjuster is completely collapsed. Hold the follower in this position and insert the proper size feeler gauge between the base circle of the cam and the follower.

3. If the clearance is excessive, remove the cam follower and inspect for damage.

4. If the cam follower appears to be intact and not excessively worn, measure the valve spring assembled height to be sure the valve is not sticking.

5. If the valve spring assembled height is correct, check the dimensions of the camshaft.

6. If the camshaft dimensions are within specifications, remove, clean and test the lash adjuster.

7. Reinstall the lash adjuster and check the clearance. Replace any damaged or worn parts, as necessary.

3.8L and 4.6L Engines

The 3.8L and 4.6L engines are equipped with hydraulic tappets, providing automatic lash adjustment.

5.0L Engine

EXCEPT HIGH OUTPUT

▸ **See Figures 7 and 8**

1. Install an auxiliary starter switch.

➡ **Turn the ignition switch OFF and remove the ignition key while performing this procedure.**

2. Crank the engine until the No. 1 piston is on TDC after the compression stroke.

3. With the crankshaft in the positions designated in Steps 4, 5 and 6, position the tappet compressor tool (T71P-6513-B or equivalent) on the rocker arm.

    a. Slowly apply pressure to bleed down the tappet until the plunger is completely bottomed. Hold the tappet in this position and check the available clearance between the rocker arm and the valve stem tip with a feeler gauge.

    b. If the clearance is less than specified, install a shorter pushrod.

    c. If the clearance is greater than specified, install a longer pushrod.

4. With the No. 1 piston on TDC at the end of the compression stroke (POSITION 1), check the following valves:

    a. No. 1 Intake & No. 1 Exhaust

    b. No. 7 Intake & No. 5 Exhaust

    c. No. 8 Intake & No. 4 Exhaust

5. Rotate the crankshaft (POSITION 2) and check the following valves.

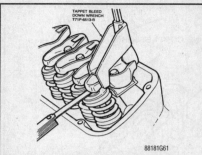

Fig. 7 With tool T71P–6513–B or equivalent, slowly apply pressure to the tappet until it has completely bottomed. Then insert a feeler gauge

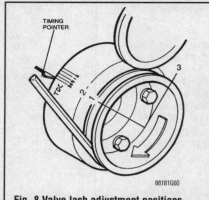

Fig. 8 Valve lash adjustment positions

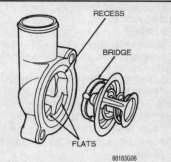

Fig. 9 Turn the thermostat clockwise to lock it in position on the flats cast into the connection

   a. No. 5 Intake & No. 2 Exhaust
   b. No. 4 Intake & No. 6 Exhaust
6. Rotate the crankshaft (POSITION 3) and check the following valves.
   a. No. 2 Intake & No. 7 Exhaust
   b. No. 3 Intake & No. 3 Exhaust
   c. No. 6 Intake & No. 8 Exhaust

HIGH-OUTPUT

1. Disconnect the "I terminal" and the "S terminal" from the starter relay.
2. Install an auxiliary starter switch between the battery and S terminals of the starter relay.

➡**Turn the ignition switch OFF and remove the ignition key while performing this procedure.**

3. Crank the engine until the No. 1 piston is on TDC after the compression stroke.
4. With the crankshaft in the positions designated in Steps 5, 6 and 7, position the tappet compressor tool (T71P-6513-B or equivalent) on the rocker arm.
   a. Slowly apply pressure to bleed down the tappet until the plunger is completely bottomed. Hold the tappet in this position and check the available clearance between the rocker arm and the valve stem tip with a feeler gauge.
   b. If the clearance is less than specified, install a shorter pushrod.
   c. If the clearance is greater than specified, install a longer pushrod.
5. With the No. 1 piston on TDC at the end of the compression stroke (POSITION 1), check the following valves:
   a. No. 1 Intake & No. 1 Exhaust
   b. No. 4 Intake & No. 3 Exhaust
   c. No. 8 Intake & No. 7 Exhaust
6. Rotate the crankshaft (POSITION 2) and check the following valves.
   a. No. 3 Intake & No. 2 Exhaust
   b. No. 7 Intake & No. 6 Exhaust
7. Rotate the crankshaft (POSITION 3) and check the following valves.
   a. No. 2 Intake & No. 4 Exhaust
   b. No. 5 Intake & No. 5 Exhaust
   c. No. 6 Intake & No. 8 Exhaust

Thermostat

REMOVAL & INSTALLATION

❄❄ CAUTION

When draining the coolant, keep in mind that cats and dogs are attracted by the ethylene glycol antifreeze, and are quite likely to drink any that is left in an uncovered container or in puddles on the ground. This will prove fatal in sufficient quantity. Always drain the coolant into a sealable container. Coolant should be reused unless it is contaminated or several years old.

Except 2.3L Engine

▶ **See Figure 9**

1. Partially drain the cooling system so the coolant level is below the thermostat.
2. Disconnect the upper radiator hose at the thermostat housing.
3. Unfasten the two water outlet connection/thermostat housing retaining bolts, the remove the thermostat housing, thermostat and gasket or O-ring, as applicable.
  To install:
4. Clean the mating surfaces of the housing and the engine to remove all old gasket material and sealer.

➡**To prevent incorrect installation of the thermostat, the hose/housing connection on all engine contains a locking recess into the thermostat is turned and locked. Install the thermostat with the bridge section in the connection. Turn the thermostat clockwise to lock it in position on the flats cast into the connection.**

5. Position the thermostat, gasket or O-ring and connection on the intake manifold. Install the retaining bolts and tighten to 15–22 ft. lbs. (20–30 Nm).
6. Connect the upper radiator hose to the housing/hose connection. Position a new hose clamp on the connection. Make sure the clamp is between the alignment marks on the hose.
7. Properly fill the cooling system with the correct type and quantity of coolant. Run the engine at operating temperature and check for leaks. Recheck the coolant level.

2.3L Engine

▶ **See Figure 10**

1. Partially drain the engine cooling system to a level below the thermostat.
2. Disconnect the heater return hose at the thermostat housing located on the left front lower side of the engine.
3. Unfasten the coolant outlet housing retaining bolts. Pull the housing

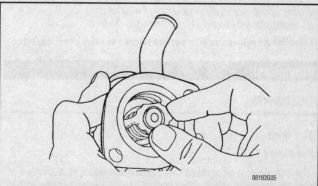

Fig. 10 On the 2.3L engine, rotate the thermostat counterclockwise to remove

away from the cylinder head or manifold sufficiently to provide access to the thermostat.

4. Remove the thermostat by rotating counterclockwise in the housing until the thermostat becomes free. Do not pry on the thermostat. Remove the gasket.

To install:

➡ **To prevent incorrect installation of the thermostat, the hose/housing connection on all engine contains a locking recess into the thermostat is turned and locked. Install the thermostat with the bridge section in the connection. Turn the thermostat clockwise to lock it in position on the flats cast into the connection.**

5. Clean the mating surfaces of the outlet elbow and the engine to remove all old gasket material and sealer. Using an adhesive-type gasket cement, glue the gasket to the engine outlet. Coat the gasket surfaces of the outlet housing with gasket sealer. Position the thermostat in the outlet housing. The thermostat must be rotated clockwise to lock it in position. Be sure the full width of the heater outlet tube is visible within the thermostat port.

6. Position the coolant outlet elbow, then install the retaining bolts. Tighten the bolts to 12–15 ft. lbs. (16–20 Nm).

7. Connect the heater hoses to the thermostat housing.

8. Properly fill the cooling system with the correct type and quantity of coolant. Run the engine at operating temperature and check for leaks. Recheck the coolant level.

Intake Manifold

REMOVAL & INSTALLATION

❋❋ CAUTION

When draining the coolant, keep in mind that cats and dogs are attracted by the ethylene glycol antifreeze, and are quite likely to drink any that is left in an uncovered container or in puddles on the ground. This will prove fatal in sufficient quantity. Always drain the coolant into a sealable container. Coolant should be reused unless it is contaminated or several years old.

2.3L Engine

◆ **See Figure 11**

UPPER INTAKE MANIFOLD

1. Properly relieve the fuel system pressure.
2. Disconnect the negative battery cable.
3. Remove the air cleaner and duct assembly.
4. Tag and detach the wiring at the Throttle Position (TP) sensor, air bypass valve, Knock Sensor (KS) and EGR valve.
5. Tag and disconnect all vacuum lines at the manifold.
6. Disconnect the throttle, speed control and kickdown cables. Unbolt the bracket and position it out of the way.
7. Detach the air intake and crankcase vent hoses.
8. Separate the cast tube from the turbocharger.
9. Remove the EGR tube.
10. Unfasten the 4 upper intake manifold mounting bolts and left off the manifold/throttle body assembly.

To install:

11. Clean all mating surfaces thoroughly. Take great care to avoid damaging the machined surfaces!
12. Place a new gasket on the lower manifold assembly, then tighten the bolts to 15–22 ft. lbs. (20–30 Nm).
13. Install the EGR tube. Tighten to 6–9 ft. lbs. (8–12 Nm).
14. Connect the cast tube to the turbocharger.
15. Attach the air intake manifold crankcase vent hoses.
16. Position the bracket, then connect the kickdown, speed control and throttle cables.
17. Connect the vacuum lines as tagged during removal.
18. Attach the wiring at the EGR valve, Knock sensor, air bypass valve and TP sensor.
19. Install the air cleaner and duct assembly.
20. Connect the negative battery cable.

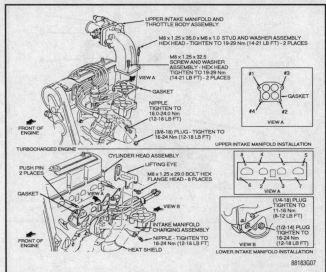

Fig. 11 Upper and lower intake manifold removal and installation— 2.3L engine

LOWER INTAKE MANIFOLD

1. Properly relieve the fuel system pressure.
2. Disconnect the negative battery cable.
3. Properly drain the engine cooling system into a suitable container.
4. Remove the upper intake manifold/throttle body assembly.
5. Disconnect the coolant hose at the lower intake manifold.
6. Remove the fuel injector pulse dampening bracket.
7. Detach the fuel supply line quick-connect fitting.
8. Disconnect the fuel return line.
9. Detach the injector wiring.
10. Unfasten the 2 bolts and lift off the fuel supply manifold.
11. Remove the 8 retaining bolts, then lift off the lower intake manifold.

To install:

12. Clean all mating surfaces thoroughly. Take great care to avoid damaging the machined surfaces!
13. Position a new gasket, then install the lower manifold. Tighten the retaining bolts to 14–21 ft. lbs. (19–28 Nm).
14. Install the fuel supply manifold, then tighten the 2 bolts to 15–22 ft. lbs. (20–30 Nm).
15. Attach the injector wiring. Connect the fuel return line. Attach the fuel supply line quick-connect fitting.
16. Install the fuel injector pulse dampening bracket. Tighten the nuts to 15–22 ft. lbs. (20–30 Nm).
17. Attach the coolant hose at the lower intake manifold.
18. Install the upper intake manifold, as outlined in this section.
19. Properly fill the engine cooling system.
20. Connect the negative battery cable, then start the engine and check for leaks.

3.8L Engine

◆ **See Figures 12 thru 21**

1. Disconnect the negative battery cable.
2. Remove the air cleaner assembly including the air intake duct and heat tube.
3. Disconnect the accelerator cable from the carburetor or throttle body, as applicable. If equipped, also disconnect the speed control cable.
4. Detach the transmission linkage at the carburetor or fuel charging assembly, as applicable.
5. Unfasten the retaining bolts from the accelerator cable bracket, then position the cables aside.
6. If equipped with an SC engine, remove the supercharger as follows:
   a. Remove the cowl vent screens.
   b. Tag and disconnect the right side spark plug wires from the ignition coil and move out of the way. Detach the fuel charging wiring connectors at

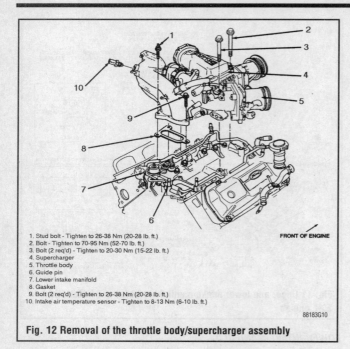

1. Stud bolt - Tighten to 26-38 Nm (20-28 lb. ft.)
2. Bolt - Tighten to 70-95 Nm (52-70 lb. ft.)
3. Bolt (2 req'd) - Tighten to 20-30 Nm (15-22 lb. ft.)
4. Supercharger
5. Throttle body
6. Guide pin
7. Lower intake manifold
8. Gasket
9. Bolt (2 req'd) - Tighten to 26-38 Nm (20-28 lb. ft.)
10. Intake air temperature sensor - Tighten to 8-13 Nm (6-10 lb. ft.)

FRONT OF ENGINE

88183G10

Fig. 12 Removal of the throttle body/supercharger assembly

the Idle Air Control (IAC) valve, Throttle Position (TP) sensor, and Intake Air Temperature (IAT) sensor.

c. Tag and disconnect the vacuum lines from the supercharger bypass valve actuator and fuel pressure regulator. Detach the crankcase ventilation tube.

d. Disconnect the EGR valve-to-exhaust manifold tubes from the EGR valve.

e. Remove the EGR transducer.

f. Remove the supercharger drive belt.

g. Remove the charge air cooler inlet tube and outlet tube.

h. Unfasten the three charge air cooler-to-intake manifold adapter retaining bolts.

i. Remove the three supercharger retaining bolts, then lift the supercharger and charge air cooler-to-intake manifold adapter from the vehicle as a unit. Remove and discard the gasket, then clean all mating surfaces.

7. If equipped, disconnect the Thermactor air supply hose at the check valve. The valve is located at the back of the intake manifold.

8. Disconnect and plug the fuel lines from the carburetor or fuel charging assembly, as applicable.

9. Detach the upper radiator hose at the thermostat housing.

10. Disconnect the coolant bypass hose at the intake manifold.

11. Disconnect the heater tube at the intake manifold. Remove the heater hose at the rear of the heater tube. Loosen the hose clamp at the heater elbow and remove the heater tube with the hoses attached. On fuel injected engines, remove the heater tube with the fuel lines attached and position the assembly aside.

12. Tag and disconnect the vacuum lines at the carburetor/fuel charging assembly and the intake manifold.

13. Tag and detach all necessary electrical connectors.

14. If equipped with A/C, remove the compressor mounting bracket.

15. Disconnect one crankcase ventilation tube at the upper intake manifold and at the PCV valve. Remove the second crankcase ventilation tube from the left valve cover.

16. Remove the carburetor or throttle body assembly, as applicable. If equipped with a carburetor, remove and discard the phenolic gasket.

17. Remove the EGR valve from the upper intake manifold.

18. Unfasten the retaining nut and remove the wiring retainer bracket located at the left front of the intake manifold and set aside with the spark plug wires.

19. Unfasten the upper intake manifold retaining bolts and stud bolts, then remove the upper intake manifold from the vehicle. Remove and discard the gasket and thoroughly clean all mating surfaces.

20. Remove the fuel injectors and the fuel injection supply manifold.

21. Remove the heater water outlet tube.

22. Disconnect the upper radiator hose from the water hose connection.

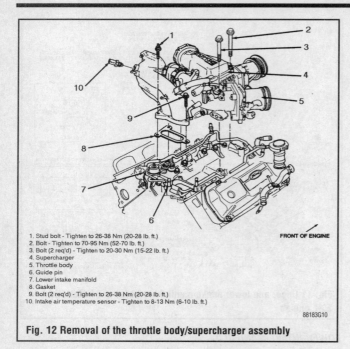

88183P04

Fig. 13 Unfasten the upper manifold bolts, then . . .

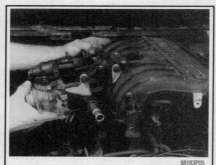

88183P05

Fig. 14 . . . remove the upper intake manifold (and throttle body) assembly—3.8L non-SC engine shown

88183P06

Fig. 15 Remove the upper intake manifold gasket, then clean the mating surfaces

88183P17

Fig. 16 Unfasten the lower intake manifold retaining bolts, then . . .

88183P18

Fig. 17 . . . remove the lower manifold from the vehicle

88183P19

Fig. 18 Remove and discard the lower manifold gasket, then thoroughly clean the gasket mating surfaces

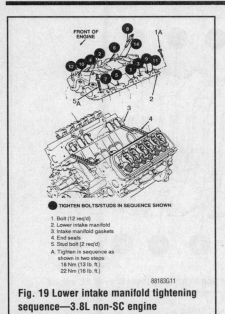

TIGHTEN BOLTS/STUDS IN SEQUENCE SHOWN

1. Bolt (12 req'd)
2. Lower intake manifold
3. Intake manifold gaskets
4. End seals
5. Stud bolt (2 req'd)
A. Tighten in sequence as shown in two steps:
   18 Nm (13 lb. ft.)
   22 Nm (16 lb. ft.)

88183G11

Fig. 19 Lower intake manifold tightening sequence—3.8L non-SC engine

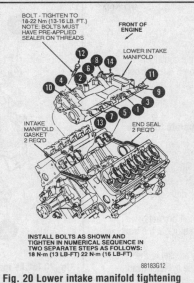

BOLT - TIGHTEN TO 18-22 Nm (13-16 LB. FT.) NOTE: BOLTS MUST HAVE PRE-APPLIED SEALER ON THREADS

LOWER INTAKE MANIFOLD

INTAKE MANIFOLD GASKET 2 REQ'D

END SEAL 2 REQ'D

INSTALL BOLTS AS SHOWN AND TIGHTEN IN NUMERICAL SEQUENCE IN TWO SEPARATE STEPS AS FOLLOWS:
18 N·m (13 LB-FT) 22 N·m (16 LB-FT)

88183G12

Fig. 20 Lower intake manifold tightening sequence—3.8L SC engine

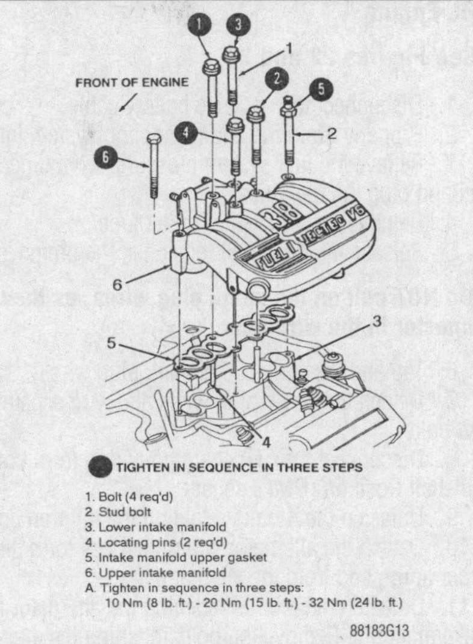

FRONT OF ENGINE

TIGHTEN IN SEQUENCE IN THREE STEPS

1. Bolt (4 req'd)
2. Stud bolt
3. Lower intake manifold
4. Locating pins (2 req'd)
5. Intake manifold upper gasket
6. Upper intake manifold
A. Tighten in sequence in three steps:
   10 Nm (8 lb. ft.) - 20 Nm (15 lb. ft.) - 32 Nm (24 lb. ft.)

88183G13

Fig. 21 Non-SC engine upper intake manifold tightening sequence

✳✳ WARNING

The intake manifold is sealed at each end with silicone sealer. To break the seal, it may be necessary to pry on the front of the intake manifold with a suitable prybar. If this is necessary, be careful not to damage the machined surfaces or engine oil and coolant leakage may occur.

23. Unfasten the lower intake manifold retaining bolts and stud bolts. Remove the lower intake manifold. Remove and discard the gasket and end seals and thoroughly clean all mating surfaces.

24. If the lower manifold is to be disassembled, perform the following:
  a. Remove the water hose connection and thermostat.
  b. Remove the ECT sensor.
  c. Remove the heater elbow.
  d. Remove all vacuum and electrical fittings.

To install:

➡**Lightly oil all retaining bolt and stud bolt threads before installation.**

25. If the intake manifold was disassembled, perform the following:
  a. Apply a coat of Pipe Sealant with Teflon® D8AZ-19554-A or equivalent to the threads of the EGR sensor, all vacuum fittings and heater elbows, if equipped.
  b. Install the thermostat and water hose connection gasket. Install the water hose connection and tighten the retaining bolts to 15–22 ft. lbs. (20–30 Nm).

➡**Before applying sealer, clean the mating surfaces with Metal Surface Cleaner F4AZ-19A536-A or equivalent.**

➡**The SC engine uses a graph-oil type intake manifold gasket.**

26. Apply a dab of Gasket and Trim Adhesive D7AZ-19B508-B or equivalent to each cylinder head mating surface. Press new intake manifold gasket into place, using location pins as necessary to aid in alignment.

➡**When using silicone rubber sealer, assembly must occur within 15 minutes after application or the sealer may start to set.**

27. Apply a ¾ in (3–4mm) bead of Silicone Rubber D6AZ-19562-BA or equivalent, at each corner where the cylinder head joins the block. Install new front and rear intake manifold seals.

28. Carefully lower the lower intake manifold into position on the block and cylinder heads. Install the retainers in the original locations. Tighten in sequence to the following specifications, in two steps:
- Step 1: 13 ft. lbs. (18 Nm)
- Step 23: 16 ft. lbs. (22 Nm)

29. Install the heater water outlet tube so that the mounting bracket sits over the lower intake manifold stud bolt. Tighten the nut on the stud bolt to 15–22 ft. lbs. (20–30 Nm). Install and tighten the retaining bolt on the water pump to 6–8 ft. lbs. (8–11 Nm).

30. Install the fuel injectors and fuel supply manifold.

31. Connect the upper radiator hose to the water hose connection and tighten the clamp securely.

32. For non SC engines, position a new upper intake manifold upper gasket and upper intake manifold on top of the lower intake manifold. Install the bolts and stud bolts in their original locations, then tighten in the sequence shown to the following specifications:
  a. Step 1: 8 ft. lbs. (15 Nm)
  b. Step 2: 15 ft. lbs. (20 Nm)
  c. Step 3: 24 ft. lbs. (32 Nm)

33. For SC engines, install the supercharger as follows:
  a. Position a new gasket on the lower intake manifold.
  b. Install the supercharger and charge air cooler to the intake manifold as a unit.
  c. Tighten the two 8mm bolts to 15–22 ft. lbs. (20–30 Nm). Tighten the 12mm bolt to 52–70 ft. lbs. (70–95 Nm).
  d. Install the three charge air cooler-to-intake manifold adapter retaining bolts. Tighten to 20–28 ft. lbs. (26–38 Nm).
  e. Install the charge air cooler inlet tube and outlet tube as outlined.
  f. Attach the EGR valve-to-exhaust manifold tube to the EGR valve.
  g. Install the EGR transducer.
  h. Install the accelerator cable bracket, then connect the accelerator cable. Tighten the bolt to 10–15 ft. lbs. (14–20 Nm).
  i. Connect the vacuum lines to the supercharger bypass valve actuator and fuel pressure regulator.
  j. Attach the right side spark plug wires, as tagged during removal.
  k. Connect the fuel charging wiring connectors at the Idle Air Control (IAC) valve, Throttle Position (TP) sensor, and Intake Air Temperature (IAT) sensor.
  l. Install the cowl vent screens.

34. Install the throttle body. Tighten the retaining nuts in a criss-cross pattern to 15–22 ft. lbs. (20–30 Nm).

35. Connect the rear crankcase ventilation tube at the positive crankcase ventilation valve on the upper intake manifold.

36. For non-SC engines, if equipped, install the A/C compressor mounting bracket. Tighten the retaining nut to 15–22 ft. lbs. (20–30 Nm).

37. If equipped, connect the speed control actuator cable.

38. Attach the throttle valve control actuating cable at the upper intake manifold.

39. For SC engines, install the supercharger and charge air cooler tubes.

40. Connect the negative battery cable.

41. Properly fill the engine cooling system.

4.6L Engine

▶ **See Figures 22 and 23**

1. Disconnect the negative battery cable.
2. Properly drain the engine cooling system into a suitable container.
3. Relieve the fuel system pressure, as outlined in Section 5, then disconnect and plug the fuel lines.
4. Remove the air cleaner outlet tube.
5. Release the drive belt tensioner, then remove the belt.

➡**Do NOT pull on the spark plug wires, as they may separate from the connector in the wire boot.**

6. Tag and disconnect the spark plug wires.
7. Detach the spark plug wires and wire separators from the valve cover stud bolts.
8. Disconnect the fuel charging wiring from both ignition coils and Camshaft Position (CMP) sensor.
9. Unfasten the 4 bolts retaining the ignition coil to the coil brackets.
10. Detach the alternator wiring harness form the junction block at the front fender apron and from the alternator.
11. Unfasten the 4 bolts retaining the alternator mounting bracket to the intake manifold. Remove the bolts retaining the alternator to the cylinder head, then remove the alternator from the vehicle.
12. Raise and safely support the vehicle.
13. Disconnect the fuel charging wiring from the oil pressure sensor and EVO sensor, then position the wiring out of the way.
14. Disconnect the EGR valve-to-exhaust manifold tube from the right side exhaust manifold.
15. Carefully lower the vehicle.
16. Disconnect the accelerator cable and speed control actuator from the throttle body using a suitable pry tool.
17. Remove the accelerator cable bracket from the intake manifold and position it out of the way.
18. Disconnect the vacuum hose from the throttle body adapter vacuum port.
19. Disconnect the heater water hose.
20. Remove the 2 bolts retaining the water hose connection to the intake manifold and position the upper radiator hose and water hose connection out of the way.
21. Unfasten the 9 bolts retaining the intake manifold to the cylinder head, then remove the manifold. Remove and discard the gasket. Thoroughly clean the intake manifold and cylinder head mating surfaces.

To install:

➡**If a new intake manifold is being installed, transfer all necessary components onto the new manifold.**

22. Position new intake manifold gaskets on the cylinder heads, then place the intake manifold on the heads. Install and tighten the 9 retaining bolts, in the sequence shown in the accompanying figure, to 15–22 ft. lbs. (20–30 Nm).

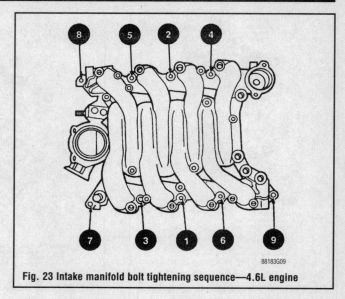

Fig. 23 Intake manifold bolt tightening sequence—4.6L engine

23. Replace the O-ring seal on the water hose connection. Position the water hose connection and upper radiator hose, and the 2 retaining bolts. Tighten the bolts to 15–22 ft. lbs. (20–30 Nm). Attach the heater water hose.
24. Connect the vacuum hose to the throttle body adapter vacuum port.
25. Install the accelerator cable bracket on the intake manifold, then connect the accelerator cable and speed control actuators to the throttle body.
26. Raise and safely support the vehicle.
27. Connect the EGR valve-to-exhaust manifold tube to the right side exhaust manifold, then tighten the nut to 26–33 ft. lbs. (35–45 Nm).
28. Attach the fuel charging wiring to the EVO sensor and oil pressure sensor.
29. Carefully lower the vehicle.
30. Position the alternator, then install the 2 retaining bolts. Tighten the bolts to 15–22 ft. lbs. (20–30 Nm).
31. Install the 2 bolts retaining the alternator rear mounting bracket to the intake manifold and tighten to 71–106 inch lbs. (8–12 Nm). Connect the alternator wiring harness to the alternator, right side front fender apron and junction block.
32. Position the spark plug wires and wire separators on the engine, then install the bolts retaining the ignition coil to the coil bracket. Tighten the bolts to 71–106 ft. lbs. (8–12 Nm). Connect the spark plug wires to the spark plugs, as tagged during removal. Attach the spark plug wire separators on the valve cover studs.
33. Connect the fuel charging wiring to both ignition coils and CMP sensor.
34. Install the drive belt.
35. Connect the air cleaner outlet tube.
36. Unplug and attach the fuel lines.
37. Connect the negative battery cable. Fill and bleed the engine cooling system. Check the engine oil level, and add if necessary. Start the engine and check for fluid and/or vacuum leaks.

5.0L Engine

▶ **See Figures 24, 25, 26, 27 and 28**

1. Disconnect the negative battery cable.
2. Properly drain the cooling system into a suitable container. Relieve the fuel system pressure, as outlined in Section 5 of this manual.
3. Remove the air intake duct assembly and crankcase vent hose.
4. Disconnect the accelerator cable and speed control linkage (if equipped) from the throttle body. Disconnect the TV cable from the accelerator cable bracket.
5. Tag and disconnect the vacuum lines at the intake manifold fitting.
6. Tag and disconnect the spark plug wires from the spark plugs by pulling on the boots. Do NOT pull on the wires. Remove the wires and bracket assembly from the rocker arm (valve) cover attaching stud. Remove the distributor cap, adapter and spark plug wire assembly.
7. Disconnect and cap the fuel supply and return lines.

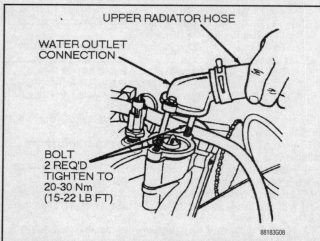

Fig. 22 Unfasten the two bolts, then remove the water hose connection and position aside

UPPER RADIATOR HOSE

WATER OUTLET CONNECTION

BOLT 2 REQ'D TIGHTEN TO 20-30 Nm (15-22 LB FT)

88183G08

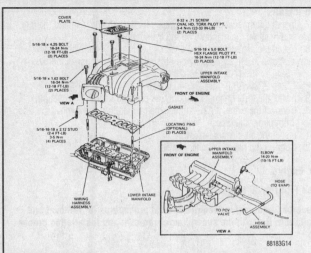

Fig. 24 Unfasten the retaining bolts, remove the cover, then remove the upper intake manifold

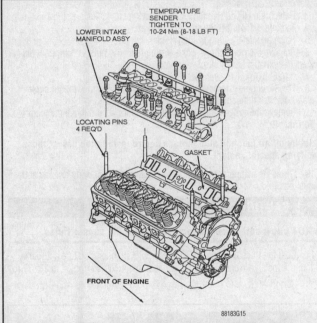

Fig. 25 Installing the lower intake manifold—1993 5.0L engine shown

8. Detach the distributor wiring connector. Unfasten the distributor hold-down bolt, then remove the distributor.

9. Disconnect the radiator upper hose form the coolant outlet housing, and the water temperature sending unit wire at the sending unit. Disconnect the 2 throttle body cooler hoses.

10. Loosen the clamp on the water pump bypass hose at the coolant outlet housing and slide the hose off the outlet housing.

11. Tag and detach the wires at the ECT sensor, IAT sensor, TP sensor, IAC valve and EGR sensors. Disconnect the fuel charging assembly wiring.

12. Pull the PCV valve out of the grommet at the rear of the lower intake manifold or the rocker arm cover. Disconnect the fuel evaporative purge hose from the plastic connector at the front of the upper intake manifold.

13. Unfasten the upper intake manifold cover plate retaining screws/bolts, then remove the cover. Remove the upper intake manifold from the vehicle.

14. Remove the heater tube assembly from the lower intake manifold.

➡ **It may be necessary to pry the intake manifold away from the cylinder head(s). Be careful to avoid damage to the gasket sealing surfaces.**

15. Remove the lower intake manifold. Remove and discard the gaskets and seals and clean all gasket mating surfaces.

16. If necessary, remove the ignition coil and temperature sending unit. Transfer parts to the new manifold.

To install:

17. If the intake manifold was disassembled, install the temperature sending unit (threads coated with electrical conductive sealer). Position the thermostat in the coolant outlet housing. Coat the thermostat gasket with suitable sealer and position it on the coolant outlet housing. Install the coolant outlet housing. Install the ignition coil, if necessary.

18. Make sure the mating surfaces of the manifold and intake manifold are clean, then apply a ⅛ in. (3.2mm) bead of Silicone Rubber D6AZ-19562-AA or equivalent at the points shown in the accompanying figure.

➡ **This sealer sets up in 15 minutes, so it's important that assembly take place swiftly. Do NOT drip any sealer into the engine valley.**

19. Position new seals on the cylinder block and new gaskets on the cylinder heads with the gaskets interlocked with the seal tabs. Make sure the holes in the gaskets are aligned with the holes in the cylinder heads.

20. Apply a ¹⁄₁₆ in. (1.6mm) bead of sealer to the outer end of each intake manifold seal for the full width of the seal (four places).

21. Using guide pins ease installation, carefully lower the intake manifold into position on the block and heads. After the manifold is in place, run a finger around the seal area to be sure the seals are in place. If not, remove the manifold and reposition the seals.

22. Make sure the holes in the manifold gaskets and intake manifold are aligned. Remove the guide pins. Install the intake manifold retaining bolts, then tighten in sequence to the following specifications:
- Step 1: 8 ft. lbs. (11 Nm)
- Step 2: 16 ft. lbs. (22 Nm).
- Step 3: 23–25 ft. lbs. (31–34 Nm).

23. Install the heater tube assembly to the lower intake manifold.

24. Install the water pump bypass hose on the coolant outlet housing. Slide the clamp into position and tighten the clamp. Connect the hoses to the heater tubes, then tighten the clamps.

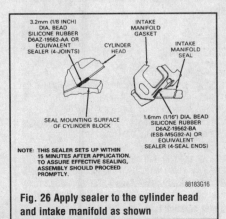

Fig. 26 Apply sealer to the cylinder head and intake manifold as shown

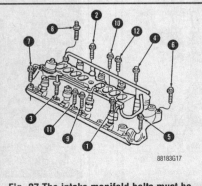

Fig. 27 The intake manifold bolts must be tightened in sequence

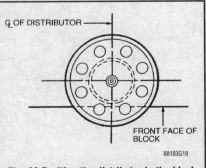

Fig. 28 Position the distributor in the block with the rotor at the No. 1 firing position, then install the hold-down bolt/clamp

25. Attach the upper radiator hose. Connect the heater hose at the intake manifold.

26. Uncap and connect the fuel lines.

27. Rotate the crankshaft until the No. 1 piston is on TDC at the end of the compression stroke. Align the correct initial timing mark on the damper with the pointer. Position the distributor in the block with the rotor at the No. 1 firing position, then install the hold-down bolt/clamp.

28. Install the distributor cap. Position the spark plug wires in the harness brackets on the valve cover attaching stud, then connect the wires to the spark plugs as tagged earlier.

29. Install the upper intake manifold.

30. Connect the PCV/crankcase vent tube.

31. Attach the accelerator cable and cable bracket. Connect the TV cable and speed control (if equipped) to the throttle body.

32. Attach all electrical connections, as tagged during removal.

33. Connect any vacuum lines that were disconnected from the manifold. Connect the coolant hoses to the EGR spacer.

34. Properly fill and bleed the engine cooling system.

35. Connect the negative battery cable. Start the engine, then check and adjust (if necessary) the ignition timing.

36. Operate the engine at fast idle and check all hose connections and gaskets for leaks. When the engine has warmed up, check the intake manifold bolt torques.

37. Install the air intake duct assembly and crankcase vent hose.

Exhaust Manifold

➡Although, in most cases, the engine does not have exhaust manifold gaskets installed by the factory, aftermarket gaskets are available from parts stores.

REMOVAL & INSTALLATION

2.3L Engine

◆ See Figure 29

1. Disconnect the negative battery cable.
2. Remove the air cleaner assembly.
3. Remove the heat shroud from the exhaust manifold.
4. Remove the turbocharger, as outlined later in this section.
5. Place a block of wood under the exhaust pipe and disconnect the exhaust pipe from the exhaust manifold.
6. Unfasten the exhaust manifold attaching nuts/bolts, then remove the manifold.

To install:

7. Install a light coat of graphite grease on the exhaust manifold mating surface and position the manifold on the cylinder head.

8. Install the exhaust manifold attaching nuts and tighten them in the sequence shown in the accompanying illustration in two steps, as follows:
   - Step 1: 15–17 ft. lbs. (20–23 Nm).
   - Step 2: 20–30 ft. lbs. (27–40.5 Nm).

9. Install the turbocharger assembly, as outlined later in this section.

10. Connect the exhaust pipe to the exhaust manifold and remove the wood support from under the pipe.

11. Install the air cleaner assembly.

12. Connect the negative battery cable.

3.8L Engine

◆ See Figures 30 thru 35

➡Supercharged engines require special procedures for removal and installation. Refer to the supercharger removal and installation procedure.

LEFT SIDE

1. Disconnect the negative battery cable.
2. For fuel injected engines, remove the oil level dipstick tube support bracket or tube, as necessary.
3. Detach the HEGO/HO₂ sensor at the wiring connector.
4. Tag and disconnect the spark plug wires.
5. Raise and safely support the vehicle.
6. Remove the manifold-to-exhaust pipe retaining nuts. If equipped, disconnect the exhaust heat control valve vacuum line.
7. Carefully lower the vehicle.
8. For SC engines, remove the intercooler tubes. Remove the oil cooler tube and dipstick tube support brackets from the studs.
9. Remove the exhaust manifold retaining bolts, then remove the manifold.

To install:

➡Lightly oil all bolt and stud threads before installation except those specifying special sealant.

10. Clean the mating surfaces of the exhaust manifold, cylinder head and exhaust pipe.

✳✳ CAUTION

Do NOT allow anti-seize compound to enter the sensor flutes.

11. Coat the threads of the HEGO sensor with high temperature anti-seize compound. Install the sensor into the exhaust manifold and tighten to 28–33 ft. lbs. (37–45 Nm).

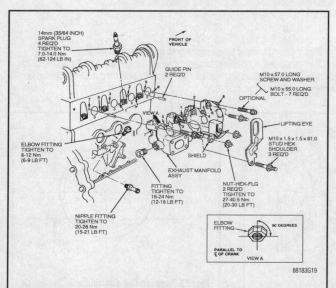

Fig. 29 Exhaust manifold installation and tightening sequence—2.3L engine

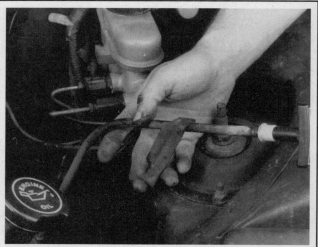

Fig. 30 Remove the oil level dipstick tube

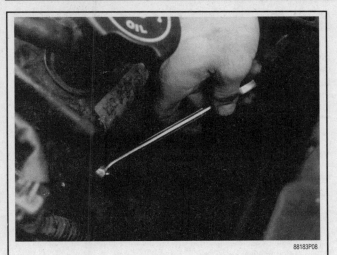

Fig. 31 Using a suitable sized wrench, unfasten the retaining bolts, then . . .

Fig. 32 . . . remove the exhaust manifold from the vehicle.

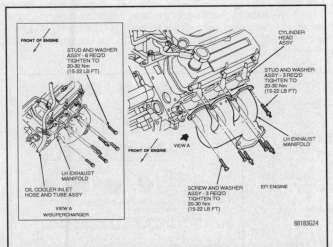

Fig. 33 Exhaust manifold removal—1992 3.8L engine shown

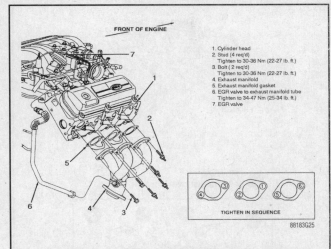

1. Cylinder head
2. Stud (4 req'd)
   Tighten to 30-36 Nm (22-27 lb. ft.)
3. Bolt (2 req'd)
   Tighten to 30-36 Nm (22-27 lb. ft.)
4. Exhaust manifold
5. Exhaust manifold gasket
6. EGR valve to exhaust manifold tube
   Tighten to 34-47 Nm (25-34 lb. ft.)
7. EGR valve

TIGHTEN IN SEQUENCE

Fig. 34 On 1996–97 3.8L engines, the exhaust manifold bolts must be tightened in sequence—left side shown

12. Position the exhaust manifold on the cylinder head. Install the pilot bolt (lower front bolt hole on No. 5 cylinder.

➡For 1996–97 vehicles, tighten the retaining bolts in the sequence shown in the accompanying figure.

13. Install the remaining manifold retaining bolts. Tighten the bolts to 15–22 ft. lbs. (20–30 Nm).

❉❉ WARNING

A slight warpage in the exhaust manifold may cause a misalignment between the bolt holes in the head and the manifold. Elongate the holes in the manifold as necessary to correct the misalignment. Do NOT, however, elongate the lower front No. 5 cylinder hole on the left side, nor the lower rear No. 2 cylinder hole on the right side. These holes are used as alignment pilots.

14. For SC engines, install the dipstick tube and oil cooler tube support brackets to the studs. Tighten the nuts to 15–22 ft. lbs. (20–30 Nm). Install the intercooler tubes.
15. Raise and safely support the vehicle.
16. If equipped, connect the exhaust heat control valve to the manifold. Connect the exhaust pipe to the manifold. Tighten the retaining nuts to 16–23 ft. lbs. (21–32 Nm).
17. Carefully lower the vehicle.
18. Connect the spark plug wires as tagged during removal.
19. Attach the HEGO sensor.
20. Install the dipstick tube support bracket retaining nut. Tighten to 15–22 ft. lbs. (20–30 Nm).
21. Connect the negative battery cable, then start the engine and check for exhaust leaks.

RIGHT SIDE

1. Disconnect the negative battery cable.
2. For SC engines, remove the air cleaner inlet tube.
3. If equipped with CFI, disconnect the Thermactor hose form the downstream air tube check valve.
4. Disconnect the coil secondary wire from the coil, then tag and disconnect the wires from the spark plugs.
5. Remove the spark plugs. For fuel injected engines, remove the outer heat shroud.
6. Raise and safely support the vehicle.
7. Disconnect the EGR tube.
8. If equipped with an automatic transmission, remove the transmission dipstick tube.
9. If equipped with CFI, remove the Thermactor downstream air tube. Use

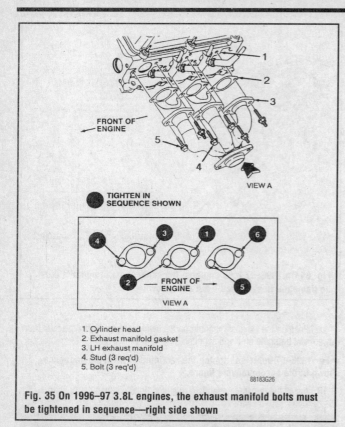

TIGHTEN IN SEQUENCE SHOWN

FRONT OF ENGINE

VIEW A

1. Cylinder head
2. Exhaust manifold gasket
3. LH exhaust manifold
4. Stud (3 req'd)
5. Bolt (3 req'd)

88183G26

Fig. 35 On 1996–97 3.8L engines, the exhaust manifold bolts must be tightened in sequence—right side shown

EGR Clamp Cutter and Crimping tool T78P-9481-A or equivalent to cut the tube clamp at the underbody catalyst.

10. Remove the manifold-to-exhaust pipe retaining nuts.
11. Carefully lower the vehicle.
12. Unfasten the exhaust manifold retaining bolts, then remove the manifold assembly.

To install:

➡Lightly oil all bolt and stud threads before installation except those specifying special sealant.

13. Clean the mating surfaces of the exhaust manifold, cylinder head and exhaust pipe.
14. Position the inner half of the heat shroud and exhaust manifold on the cylinder head. Start two retaining bolts.

➡For 1996–97 vehicles, tighten the retaining bolts in the sequence shown in the accompanying figure.

15. Install the remaining retaining bolts. Tighten to 15–22 ft. lbs. (20–30 Nm).

✳✳ WARNING

A slight warpage in the exhaust manifold may cause a misalignment between the bolt holes in the head and the manifold. Elongate the holes in the manifold as necessary to correct the misalignment. Do NOT, however, elongate the lower front No. 5 cylinder hole on the left side, nor the lower rear No. 2 cylinder hole on the right side. These holes are used as alignment pilots.

16. Raise and safely support the vehicle.
17. Connect the exhaust pipe to the manifold. Tighten the retaining nuts to 16–23 ft. lbs. (21–32 Nm).
18. For CFI engines, position the Thermactor downstream air tube. Clamp the tube to the under body catalyst fitting using EGR Clamp Cutter and Crimping tool T78P-9481-A or equivalent.
19. If equipped with an automatic transmission, install the transmission dipstick tube.
20. Carefully lower the vehicle.
21. Install the spark plugs, then connect the wires to the spark plugs as tagged during removal.
22. On fuel injected engines, connect the coil secondary wire to the coil.
23. Attach the EGR tube.
24. If equipped, connect the Thermactor hose to the downstream air tube, and clamp securely.
25. For SC engines, install the air cleaner inlet tube.
26. Connect the negative battery cable, then start the engine and check for exhaust leaks. Check the transmission fluid level.

4.6L Engine

♦ See Figures 36, 37, 38 and 39

1. Disconnect the negative battery cable.
2. If removing the left side exhaust manifold, remove the bolt retaining the oil level indicator tube.
3. Raise and safely support the vehicle.
4. Detach the fuel charging wiring from both heated oxygen sensors.
5. Remove the EGR valve-to-exhaust manifold tube line nut from the right side exhaust manifold and remove the EGR valve-to-exhaust manifold tube.
6. Detach the three-way catalytic converter from the right and left side exhaust manifolds.
7. Lower the three-way catalytic converter and secure to the crossmember with wire as shown in the accompanying figure.
8. If removing the left side exhaust manifold, disconnect the steering shaft and position it out of the way.
9. Remove the eight nuts retaining the left side exhaust manifold, then remove the manifold and two gaskets.
10. For the right side exhaust manifold, unfasten the eight retaining nuts, then remove the exhaust manifold and gaskets from the vehicle.

To install:

11. If the exhaust manifolds are being replaced, transfer the heated oxygen sensors to the replacement manifolds and tighten to 27–33 ft. lbs. (37–45 Nm). For the right side exhaust manifold, transfer the EGR valve tube to manifold connector and tighten to 33–48 ft. lbs. (45–65 Nm).

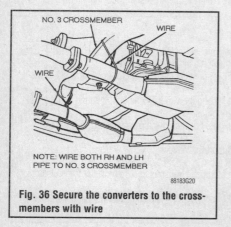

NO. 3 CROSSMEMBER

WIRE

WIRE

NOTE: WIRE BOTH RH AND LH PIPE TO NO. 3 CROSSMEMBER

88183G20

Fig. 36 Secure the converters to the crossmembers with wire

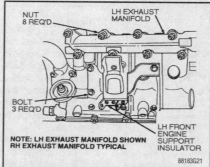

NUT 8 REQ'D

LH EXHAUST MANIFOLD

BOLT 3 REQ'D

LH FRONT ENGINE SUPPORT INSULATOR

NOTE: LH EXHAUST MANIFOLD SHOWN RH EXHAUST MANIFOLD TYPICAL

88183G21

Fig. 37 Unfasten the left side exhaust manifold retaining nuts, then remove the manifold from the vehicle

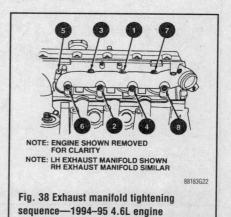

NOTE: ENGINE SHOWN REMOVED FOR CLARITY
NOTE: LH EXHAUST MANIFOLD SHOWN RH EXHAUST MANIFOLD SIMILAR

88183G22

Fig. 38 Exhaust manifold tightening sequence—1994–95 4.6L engine

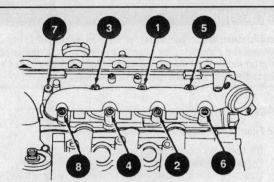

NOTE: **ENGINE SHOWN REMOVED FOR CLARITY**

NOTE: **LH EXHAUST MANIFOLD SHOWN RH EXHAUST MANIFOLD SIMILAR**

88183G23

Fig. 39 Exhaust manifold tightening sequence—1996–97 4.6L engine

12. Thoroughly clean the mating surfaces of the exhaust manifolds and cylinder heads.

13. Position the exhaust manifold gaskets and right side exhaust manifold to the cylinder head and studs, then install the eight retaining nuts. Tighten, in the sequence shown in the accompanying figures, to 13–16 ft. lbs. (18–22 Nm).

14. Position the gaskets and the left side exhaust manifold to the cylinder head and studs, then install the eight retaining nuts. Tighten, in the sequence shown in the accompanying figures, to 13–16 ft. lbs. (18–22 Nm).

15. Position and connect the steering shaft.

16. Loosen the line nut at the EGR valve before installing the assembly into the vehicle. This will allow enough movement to align the EGR valve retaining bolts. Position and connect the EGR valve-to-exhaust tube to the exhaust manifold. Tighten the line nut to 26–33 ft. lbs. (35–45 Nm).

➡**Two through bolts are required on the left front engine support insulator and one through bolt is required on the right side from engine support insulator. Make sure the exhaust system clears the No. 3 crossmember.**

17. Remove the wire, then position the three-way catalytic converter. Install the four nuts, then tighten to 20–30 ft. lbs. (27–41 Nm).

18. Connect the fuel charging wiring to the heated oxygen sensors.

19. Carefully lower the vehicle.

20. Connect the negative battery cable, then start the engine and check for leaks.

5.0L Engine

▶ **See Figures 40, 41, 42 and 43**

1. Disconnect the negative battery cable.

2. For the left side manifold, remove the oil level dipstick tube retaining nut, then pull the bracket off the manifold stud.

3. Raise and safely support the vehicle.

4. Remove the oil level dipstick tube assembly by carefully tapping upward on the tube.

5. For the left manifold, detach the HO2S connector from the manifold.

6. Disconnect the exhaust manifolds from the muffler inlet pipe(s).

7. Carefully lower the vehicle.

8. Detach the electrical connector from the MAF sensor located on the air cleaner assembly.

9. Remove the air cleaner and inlet duct assembly.

10. Unfasten the nuts attaching the alternator rear brace to the exhaust manifold, then remove the brace.

11. Tag and disconnect the spark plug wires.

12. On the exhaust manifold, remove the Secondary Air Injection hose assembly and EGR valve-to-exhaust manifold tube.

13. Remove the retaining nuts and washers attaching the engine lifting eyes to the exhaust manifolds.

➡**The exhaust manifolds are removed from the vehicle out through the top of the engine compartment.**

14. Unfasten the retaining bolts and washers and remove the exhaust manifolds.

To install:

15. Clean the mating surfaces of the manifolds and cylinder head(s). Clean the mounting flange of the exhaust manifold and muffler inlet pipe.

16. Position the exhaust manifold on the cylinder head with a new exhaust manifold gasket. Install the attaching bolts and washers, and working from the center to the ends, tighten the bolts to 26–32 ft. lbs. (32–43 Nm).

17. Attach the engine lifting eyes to the exhaust manifold studs and tighten.

18. Install the oil level dipstick tube in the engine block and position the tube bracket to the exhaust manifold stud. Install the retaining nut.

19. Connect the spark plug wires, as tagged during removal.

20. On the right side exhaust manifold; install the secondary air injection control valve hose assembly, alternator rear brace and EGR valve-to-exhaust manifold tube.

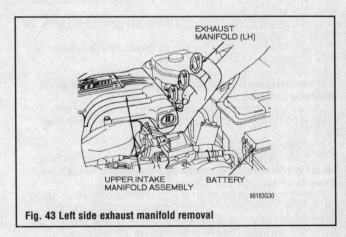

88183G30

Fig. 43 Left side exhaust manifold removal

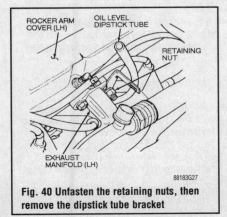

88183G27

Fig. 40 Unfasten the retaining nuts, then remove the dipstick tube bracket

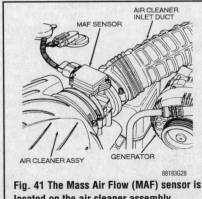

88183G28

Fig. 41 The Mass Air Flow (MAF) sensor is located on the air cleaner assembly

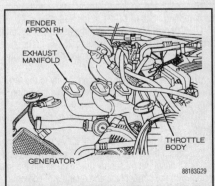

88183G29

Fig. 42 Removing the right side exhaust manifold

21. Install the air cleaner and inlet duct assembly.
22. Attach the electrical connector to the MAF sensor on the air cleaner.
23. Raise the vehicle. Install the muffler inlet pipes.
24. On the left side, install the HO2S wiring connector.
25. Carefully lower the vehicle.
26. Connect the negative battery cable, then start the engine and check for leaks.

Turbocharger

➡Do not confuse a turbocharger with a supercharger. They operate differently and no parts are interchangeable. The turbocharger and supercharger are serviced by replacement only.

REMOVAL & INSTALLATION

➡Before starting removal/service procedures, clean the area around the turbocharger with a non-caustic solution. Cover the openings of component connections to prevent the entry of dirt and foreign materials. Exercise care when handling the turbocharger not to nick, bend or in any way damage the compressor wheel blades.

1983–85 2.3L Engines

1. Disconnect the negative battery cable.
2. Properly drain the cooling system into a suitable container.
3. Loosen the upper clamp on the turbocharger inlet hose. Remove the two bolts mounting the throttle body discharge tube to the turbo.
4. Tag and disconnect all of the turbocharger vacuum hoses and tubes.
5. Disconnect the PCV tube from the turbo air inlet elbow. Remove the throttle body discharge tube and hose as an assembly.
6. Detach the ground wire from the air inlet elbow. Remove (disconnect) the water outlet connection (and fitting if a new turbo unit is to be installed) from the turbo center housing.
7. Remove the turbo oil supply feed line. Detach the oxygen sensor connector at the turbocharger.
8. Raise and support the front of the vehicle on jackstands. Disconnect the exhaust pipe from the turbocharger.
9. Disconnect the oil return line from the bottom of the turbocharger. Be careful not to damage or kink the line.
10. Detach the water inlet tube at the turbo center housing.
11. Remove the lower turbo mounting bracket-to-engine bolt. Lower the vehicle from the stands.
12. Unfasten the lower front mounting nut. Remove the three remaining mounting nuts evenly while sliding the turbocharger away from its mounting.
To install:
13. Position a new turbocharger mounting gasket in position with the bead side facing outward. Install the turbocharger in position over the four mounting studs.
14. Position the lower mounting bracket over the two bottom studs. Using new nuts, start the two lower then the two upper mountings. Do not tighten them completely at this time; allow for slight turbo movement.
15. Raise and support the front of the vehicle on jackstands.
16. Install and tighten the lower gasket and connect the return line. Tighten the mounting bolts to 14–21 ft. lbs. (19–28 Nm).
17. Connect the water inlet tube assembly. Install the exhaust pipe on the turbo. Tighten the mounting nuts to 25–35 ft. lbs. (34–47 Nm).
18. Lower the vehicle. Tighten the turbo mounting nut to 28–40 ft. lbs. (38–54 Nm).
19. Connect the water outlet assembly to the turbocharger, tighten the fasteners to 11–14 ft. lbs. (15–19 Nm). Hold the fitting with a wrench when tightening the line.
20. Install the air inlet tube to the turbo inlet elbow, then tighten the clamp.
21. Connect the PCV tube and all vacuum lines.
22. Attach the oxygen sensor and other wiring and lines.
23. Connect the oil supply line, then attach the intake tube. Fill the cooling system with the correct type and quantity of coolant.
24. Connect the negative battery cable. Start the engine and check for coolant leaks. Check vehicle operation.

✵✵ WARNING

When installing the turbocharger, or after an oil and filter change, disconnect the distributor feed harness and crank the engine with the starter motor until the oil pressure light on the dash goes out. Oil pressure must be up before starting the engine.

1986–88 2.3L Engines

▶ See Figures 44 thru 50

1. Disconnect the negative battery cable.
2. Properly drain the cooling system into a suitable container.
3. Loosen the upper and lower clamps securing the hoses to the intercooler.
4. Disconnect the aspirator hoses at the intercooler and remove the nut securing the bracket to the engine.
5. Remove the intercooler by first lifting then pulling it out.
6. Tag and disconnect all of the vacuum hoses and tubes from the turbocharger. Detach the oxygen sensor connector.
7. Disconnect the PCV tube from the turbocharger air inlet elbow.
8. Loosen the clamp, then disconnect the air inlet tube from the inlet elbow.
9. Detach the ground wire from the turbocharger air inlet elbow, then remove the air inlet elbow.
10. Remove the water connections and fittings from the turbo center housing. Note that some coolant may drain from the engine block.
11. Remove the turbocharger oil supply feed line. Plug the oil inlet hole, to avoid debris from entering.
12. Detach the oxygen sensor connector from the turbocharger.
13. Raise and safely support the vehicle on jackstands. Disconnect the exhaust pipe from the turbocharger by removing the two bolts.
14. Unfasten the two bolts from the oil return line located below the turbocharger. Be careful not to damage or kink the line as it is being removed.
15. Remove the lower turbocharger bracket-to-block stud.
16. Carefully lower the vehicle.
17. Remove the front lower turbocharger mounting nut. Simultaneously remove the three remaining mounting nuts evenly while sliding the turbocharger off the studs. Remove the turbocharger from the vehicle.
To install:
18. Apply pipe sealant with Teflon® D8AZ-19554-A or equivalent. Install the water inlet connector fittings into the turbocharger center housing. Tighten to 6–8 ft. lbs. (8–11 Nm) and rotate clockwise so that the fitting is within 5 degrees of vertical, pointing down.
19. Position a new turbocharger mounting gasket in position with the bead side facing outward. Install the turbocharger in position over the four mounting studs.
20. Install the turbocharger bracket on the two lower studs. Using new nuts, start the two lower then the two upper mountings. Do not tighten them completely at this time; allow for slight turbo movement.
21. Raise and safely support the vehicle on jackstands.
22. Install the lower bracket-to-block bolt. Tighten to 28–40 ft. lbs. (38–54 Nm).
23. Position a new oil return line gasket. Attach the oil return line to the turbocharger. Tighten the bolt to 14–21 ft. lbs. (19–29 Nm).
24. Connect the water inlet tube assembly to the inlet fitting at the turbocharger assembly. Tighten the hose clamp to 12–20 inch lbs. (1.4–2.3 Nm).
25. Attach the exhaust pipe to the turbocharger. Tighten the mounting nuts to 25–35 ft. lbs. (34–47 Nm).
26. Lower the vehicle.
27. Using four new nuts, tighten the turbocharger-to-exhaust manifold nuts to 28–40 ft. lbs. (38–54 Nm).
28. Connect the water tube assemblies to the fitting on the turbocharger, then tighten the fasteners to 8–12 ft. lbs. (11–16 ft. lbs.) using a backup wrench to hold the fitting while tightening the line.
29. Position a new gasket, then install the compressor inlet elbow. Tighten the bolts to 14–21 ft. lbs. (19–29 Nm).
30. Fasten the air inlet tube to the turbocharger inlet elbow. Tighten the hose clamp to 1.2–1.6 ft. lbs. (1.7–2.3 Nm).
31. Install the PCV tube fitting, then tighten the clamp to 15–20 inch lbs. (1.7–2.2 Nm).

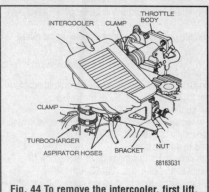

Fig. 44 To remove the intercooler, first lift, then pull the assembly out

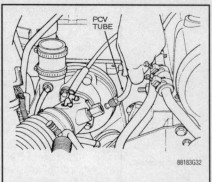

Fig. 45 Detach the PCV tube from the air inlet elbow

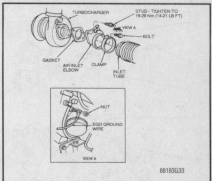

Fig. 46 Unfasten the clamp and remove the air inlet tube and elbow

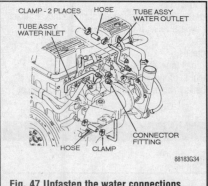

Fig. 47 Unfasten the water connections and fittings

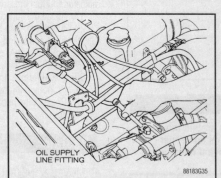

Fig. 48 After disconnect the oil supply feed line, plug it to avoid debris from entering

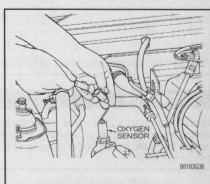

Fig. 49 Detach the oxygen sensor connector from the turbocharger

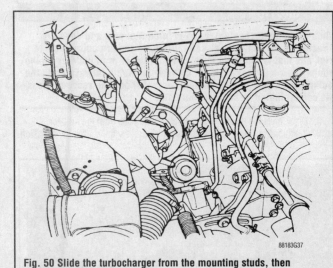

Fig. 50 Slide the turbocharger from the mounting studs, then remove from the vehicle

32. Attach all vacuum lines, as tagged during removal.
33. Connect the oxygen sensor.
34. Attach the electrical ground wire to the air inlet elbow attaching stud.
35. Unplug the oil inlet hole. Connect the oil supply line. Tighten the fitting to 9–16 ft. lbs. (12–22 Nm).
36. Install the intercooler assembly. Tighten the clamps to 25–35 inch lbs. (2.9–3.9 Nm) and tighten the nut to 20–30 ft. lbs. (27–41 Nm).
37. Properly fill and bleed the cooling system.

38. Connect the negative battery cable. Start the engine and check for coolant leaks. Check vehicle operation.

✳✳ WARNING

When installing the turbocharger, or after an oil and filter change, disconnect the distributor feed harness and crank the engine with the starter motor until the oil pressure light on the dash goes out. Oil pressure must be up before starting the engine.

Supercharger

➡Do not confuse the turbocharger with the supercharger, they operate differently and no parts are interchangeable. The turbocharger and supercharger are serviced by replacement only.

REMOVAL & INSTALLATION

3.8L (VIN C and R) Engines

▶ See Figure 51

➡The supercharger is not a bolt-on option. It is part of an integrated engine system. Many components of the supercharged engine are not interchangeable with similar parts from a non-supercharged engine.

The supercharger has a self-contained oiling system that does not require a fluid change for the life of the vehicle. The fluid level should be checked at 30,000 mile intervals, or if visual signs of leakage occur. To check the oil, remove the Allen head plug located at the front of the supercharger. The oil should be at the bottom of the fill plug threads when cold. If the fluid level is low, add a synthetic supercharger fluid that meets or exceeds Ford specification ESE–M99C115–A

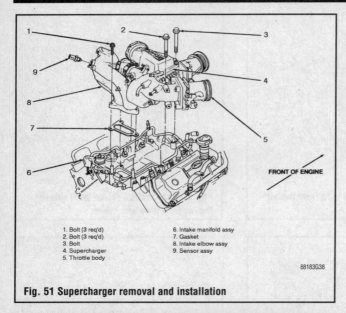

1. Bolt (3 req'd)
2. Bolt (3 req'd)
3. Bolt
4. Supercharger
5. Throttle body
6. Intake manifold assy
7. Gasket
8. Intake elbow assy
9. Sensor assy

88183G38

Fig. 51 Supercharger removal and installation

✳✳ CAUTION

Before any supercharger service, clean the areas around the supercharger assembly. Cover all openings of the engine and supercharger while the supercharger is removed to prevent damage by foreign material.

1. Disconnect the negative battery cable.
2. Remove throttle body air inlet tube/air cleaner outlet tube.
3. Remove cowl vent screens.
4. Partially drain cooling system.

✳✳ CAUTION

When draining the coolant, keep in mind that cats and dogs are attracted by the ethylene glycol antifreeze, and are quite likely to drink any that is left in an uncovered container or in puddles on the ground. This will prove fatal in sufficient quantity. Always drain the coolant into a sealable container. Coolant should be reused unless it is contaminated or several years old.

5. Tag and disconnect the right side spark plug wires at the ignition coil assembly, and position out of the way. Detach electrical connections at the air bypass valve, Idle Air Control (IAC) valve, Throttle Position (TP) sensor and air charger temperature/Intake Air Temperature sensors.
6. Tag and disconnect the vacuum lines from the inlet/plenum assembly/supercharger bypass valve actuator and fuel pressure regulator Detach the crankcase ventilation tube.
7. Disconnect the EGR valve-to-exhaust manifold tubes from the EGR valve. Remove EGR transducer from bracket and disconnect vacuum line (If so equipped).
8. Disconnect the throttle linkage at throttle body. Remove linkage bracket attaching bolts and position bracket out of the way. If equipped, disconnect the speed control cable.
9. If necessary, remove two EGR valve attaching bolts and move EGR valve away from the intake assembly.
10. Disconnect coolant hoses from throttle body.
11. Remove the supercharger drive belt.
12. Remove intercooler/charge air cooler inlet and outlet tubes.
13. Unfasten the three charge air cooler-to-intake manifold adapter retaining bolts.
14. Remove the three supercharger retaining bolts.
15. Lift the supercharger and charge air cooler/intercooler-to-intake manifold adapter from the vehicle as a unit.

To install:

16. Clean and inspect the sealing surfaces of the supercharger outlet adapter, intake elbow, and intercooler/charge air cooler.
17. Position new gasket on intake manifold using guide pins, if available.
18. Install supercharger, throttle body and charger air cooler to the intake manifold as an assembly.
19. Tighten the two 8mm bolts to 15–22 ft. lbs. (20–30 Nm). Tighten the 12mm bolt to 52–70 ft. lbs. (70–95 Nm).
20. Install three intake elbow/charger air cooler-to-intake manifold adapter retaining nuts/bolts and tighten to 20–28 ft. lbs. (26–38 Nm).
21. Connect the charger air cooler inlet and outlet tubes.
22. Fasten the EGR valve-to-exhaust manifold tube to the EGR valve. Install the EGR transducer. Tighten the retainers to 6–9 ft. lbs. (8–13 Nm).
23. Attach the coolant hoses to throttle body.
24. Connect EGR valve with new gasket to supercharger inlet elbow (if equipped). Tighten retaining bolts to 15–22 ft. lbs. (20–30 Nm).
25. Install throttle linkage/accelerator cable bracket and connect the throttle linkage/cable. Tighten to 10–15 ft. lbs. (14–20 Nm).
26. Connect vacuum lines to inlet assembly/supercharger bypass valve actuator and fuel pressure regulator. Connect the PCV tube.
27. Install the supercharger drive belt.
28. Attach the right side spark plug wires, as tagged during removal. Attach the electrical connectors at air bypass valve, IAC valve, TP sensor and air charge temperature/IAT sensors.
29. Install the cowl vent screens.
30. Install throttle body air inlet tube/air cleaner outlet tube.
31. Properly refill the coolant to proper level.
32. Connect the negative battery cable. Start engine and check for proper operation.

Radiator

REMOVAL & INSTALLATION

▶ **See Figures 52, 53, 54 and 55**

1. Properly drain the cooling system into a suitable container.

✳✳ CAUTION

When draining the coolant, keep in mind that cats and dogs are attracted by the ethylene glycol antifreeze, and are quite likely to drink any that is left in an uncovered container or in puddles on the ground. This will prove fatal in sufficient quantity. Always drain the coolant into a sealable container. Coolant should be reused unless it is contaminated or several years old.

2. Disconnect the upper, lower and overflow hoses from the radiator.
3. If equipped with an automatic transmission, disconnect the transmission

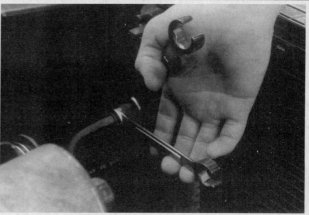

88183P10

Fig. 52 If equipped with an automatic transmission, you must disconnect the oil cooler lines; you must use a backup wrench to avoid stripping the fittings

Fig. 53 Unfasten the fan shroud retaining bolts

Fig. 54 Remove the rest of the shroud or mounting bolts, then . . .

Fig. 55 . . . lift and remove the radiator from the vehicle

oil cooler inlet and outlet lines from the radiator. Plug the fittings/lines to prevent contamination of the transmission oil cooling system.

4. Depending on the model, remove the two top mounting bolts and remove the radiator and shroud assembly, remove the shroud mounting bolts and position the shroud out of the way, or remove the side mounting bolts. If the A/C condenser is attached to the radiator, remove the retaining bolts and position the condenser out of the way. DO NOT disconnect the refrigerant lines.

5. If equipped with an SC engine, remove the two bolts retaining the top of the air duct to the charge air cooler.

6. Unfasten the radiator attaching bolts or top brackets, then lift out the radiator.

To install:

7. If a new radiator is to be installed, transfer the petcock from the old radiator to the new one. If equipped with an automatic transmission, transfer the oil cooler line intermediate fittings to the new radiator, using Pipe Sealant with Teflon®.

8. Position the radiator and install the upper brackets, if equipped and tighten the mounting bolts securely.

9. If equipped with an SC engine, cut the retaining strap from the charge air cooler air duct. The duct should spring out from the radiator support assembly. Lift the top of the duct and insert the tabs into the bottom of the duct into the clips at the bottom of the charge air cooler. Install the two bolts that retaining the top of the duct to the charger air cooler.

10. On cars equipped with automatic transmissions, unplug and connect the oil cooler lines using a backup wrench. If equipped, tighten the tube nut on the line to 18–21 ft. lbs. (24.4–28.5 Nm).

11. Install the cooling fan motor, blade and/or shroud as necessary.

※ CAUTION

Make sure the clamps are beyond the bead and place in the center of the clamping surface of the connections. New screw-type hose clamps must be installed inside the hose alignment marks.

12. Connect the radiator upper and lower and the overflow hoses. Position the clamps at least 2 in. (50mm) from each end of the hose and slide the hose on the connections. Tighten the clamps to 20–30 inch lbs. (2.2–3.4 Nm).

13. Close the radiator petcock. Fill and bleed the cooling system with a 50/50 mix of the proper type and quantity of coolant and clean water.

14. Start the engine and bring it to operating temperature. Check for leaks.

15. On cars equipped with automatic transmissions, check the cooler lines for leaks and interference. Check the transmission fluid level.

16. Turn the engine off, then check the radiator and radiator coolant recovery reservoir fluid levels. Add if necessary.

Electric Cooling Fan

REMOVAL & INSTALLATION

♦ See Figures 56, 57 and 58

Various models, are equipped with a bracket-mounted electric cooling fan that replaces the conventional water pump mounted fan.

Operation of the fan motor is dependent on engine coolant temperature and air conditioner compressor clutch engagement. The fan will run only when the coolant temperature is approximately 180° or higher, or when the compressor clutch is engaged. The fan, motor and mount can be removed as an assembly after disconnecting the wiring harnesses and mounting bolts.

※ CAUTION

The cooling fan is automatic and may come on at any time without warning even if the ignition is switched OFF. To avoid possible injury, always disconnect the negative battery cable when working near the electric cooling fan.

1. Disconnect the negative battery cable.
2. Detach the fan motor wire connector at the side of the fan shroud. Remove the male terminal connector retaining clip from the fan shroud mounting tab.

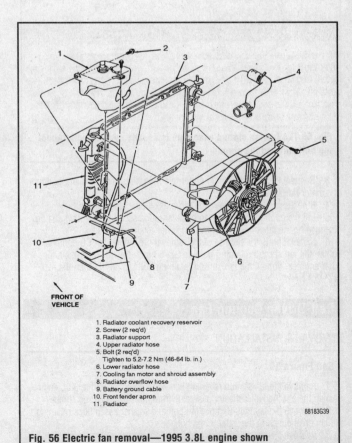

FRONT OF VEHICLE

1. Radiator coolant recovery reservoir
2. Screw (2 req'd)
3. Radiator support
4. Upper radiator hose
5. Bolt (2 req'd)
   Tighten to 5.2-7.2 Nm (46-64 lb. in.)
6. Lower radiator hose
7. Cooling fan motor and shroud assembly
8. Radiator overflow hose
9. Battery ground cable
10. Front fender apron
11. Radiator

Fig. 56 Electric fan removal—1995 3.8L engine shown

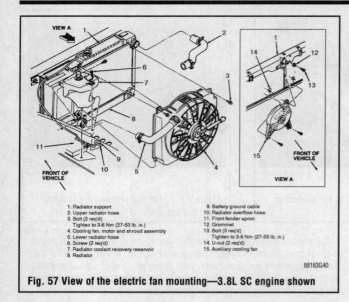

1. Radiator support
2. Upper radiator hose
3. Bolt (2 req'd)
   Tighten to 3-6 Nm (27-53 lb. in.)
4. Cooling fan, motor and shroud assembly
5. Lower radiator hose
6. Screw (2 req'd)
7. Radiator coolant recovery reservoir
8. Radiator
9. Battery ground cable
10. Radiator overflow hose
11. Front fender apron
12. Grommet
13. Bolt (3 req'd)
    Tighten to 3-6 Nm (27-53 lb. in.)
14. U-nut (2 req'd)
15. Auxiliary cooling fan

Fig. 57 View of the electric fan mounting—3.8L SC engine shown

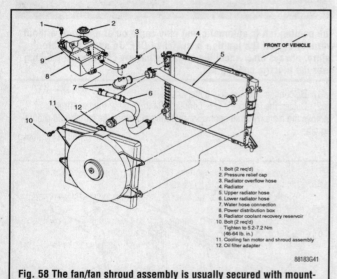

1. Bolt (2 req'd)
2. Pressure relief cap
3. Radiator overflow hose
4. Radiator
5. Upper radiator hose
6. Lower radiator hose
7. Water hose connection
8. Power distribution box
9. Radiator coolant recovery reservoir
10. Bolt (2 req'd)
    Tighten to 5.2-7.2 Nm
    (46-64 lb. in.)
11. Cooling fan motor and shroud assembly
12. Oil filter adapter

Fig. 58 The fan/fan shroud assembly is usually secured with mounting bolts around the shroud

3. Remove the two fan shroud upper retaining bolts at the radiator support of radiator tanks.

4. If necessary, remove the mounting bracket attaching screws.

5. Lift the cooling fan motor/fan blade/shroud assembly past the radiator, disengaging the fan shroud from the two lower retaining clips.

6. Installation is the reverse of the removal procedure. On SC engines, tighten the fan shroud retaining bolts to 27–53 inch lbs. (3–6 Nm). On all other engines, tighten the fan shroud retaining bolts to 46–64 inch lbs. (5.2–7.2 Nm).

Belt-Driven Cooling Fan

REMOVAL & INSTALLATION

▶ **See Figure 59**

1. Remove the fan shroud retaining screws. If equipped with a 5.0L engine, unsnap the attached air deflector assembly from the subframe cross brace.

2. Remove the fan belt. Remove the bolt and washer assemblies retaining the fan drive clutch to the water pump hub.

3. Remove the fan drive clutch and fan as an assembly at the same time

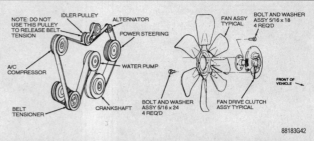

Fig. 59 Exploded view of the belt drive fan assembly—1992 vehicle shown

removing the fan shroud and deflector assembly. Unfasten the retaining bolts and washer assemblies, then separate the fan from the drive clutch.

To install:

4. Position the fan on the drive clutch. Install the bolt and washer assemblies, then tighten to 12–17 ft. lbs. (16–24 Nm).

5. Position the fan drive clutch, fan assembly and fan shroud, then bolt the fan and clutch assembly to the water pump hub. Install and tighten the clutch retaining bolt and water pump assemblies evenly and alternately to 15–22 ft. lbs. (20–30 Nm) for the 3.8L engine or to 36–47 ft. lbs. (48–65 Nm) for the 5.0L engine.

6. Install the fan belt. Align the fan shroud and adjust for equal fan-to-shroud radiator clearance but maintaining a minimum of 0.38 inch clearance to the fan tip on 5.0L engines.

7. Install and tighten the shroud retaining screws. On 5.0L engines, snap the air deflector assembly to the sub-frame cross brace.

Water Pump

REMOVAL & INSTALLATION

2.3L Engine

▶ **See Figure 60**

1. Disconnect the negative battery cable.

2. Properly drain the cooling system into a suitable container.

3. Unfasten the four bolts retaining the pulley to the water pump shaft. Remove the fan and shroud.

4. Remove the A/C (if equipped) and power steering belts. Remove the water pump pulley.

5. Disconnect the heater hose from the water pump, then remove the lower radiator hose.

6. Remove the timing belt outer cover bolt, release the interlocking tabs, then remove the cover.

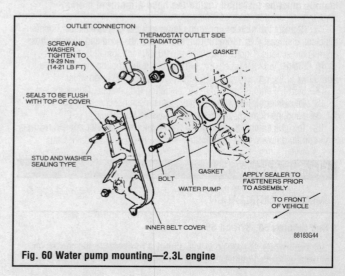

Fig. 60 Water pump mounting—2.3L engine

Fig. 61 Unfasten the retaining bolts, then . . .

Fig. 62 . . . remove the water pump from the vehicle

Fig. 63 When cleaning the gasket surfaces be careful not to gouge the surfaces, which may cause leakage

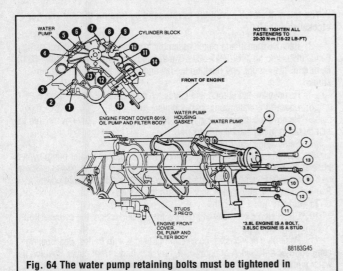

Fig. 64 The water pump retaining bolts must be tightened in sequence to prevent possible coolant leakage

7. Unfasten the water pump retaining bolts, then remove the water pump from the vehicle.

To install:

8. Installation is the reverse of the removal procedure. Clean all gasket mating surfaces prior to installation. Apply pipe sealant to the water pump bolts, then tighten to 15–21 ft. lbs. (20–30 Nm). Tighten the pulley retaining bolts to 15–22 ft. lbs. (20–30 Nm).

9. Fill and bleed the cooling system.

10. Connect the negative battery cable.

11. Start and run the engine until normal operating temperature has been reached, then check for leaks. Check the coolant level, and add if necessary.

3.8L Engine

▶ **See Figures 61, 62, 63 and 64**

1. Disconnect the negative battery cable.

2. Properly drain the cooling system into a suitable container.

3. Remove the cooling fan and fan shroud, as outlined earlier in this section.

4. Release the belt tensioner, then remove the accessory drive belt(s).

5. If the vehicle is equipped with air conditioning, remove the idler pulley bracket and air conditioner drive belt.

6. On engines with a Thermactor®, remove the belt.

7. Unfasten the bolts retaining the water pump pulley to the water pump, then remove the pulley.

8. Remove the power steering pump pulley and remove the water pump-to-power steering pump brace.

➥**On some supercharged models, it may be necessary to remove the charge air cooler to gain access to the power steering pump pulley.**

9. Detach the water bypass hose at the water pump.

10. Disconnect the heater hose at the water pump and disconnect the lower radiator hose. On SC models, disconnect the oil cooler inlet tube and hose.

11. On SC vehicles, remove the Crankshaft Position (CKP) sensor upper shield.

12. Unfasten the bolts retaining the water pump to the engine, then remove the water pump from the vehicle.

To install:

13. Clean any gasket material from the pump mating surfaces. On engines equipped with a water pump backing plate, remove the plate, clean the gasket surfaces, install a new gasket and plate on the water pump.

14. Coat both sides of the new gasket with a water-resistant sealer, then position the gasket on the water pump housing.

➥**The use of gasket adhesive is recommended.**

15. Install the water pump, then tighten the retaining bolts, in the sequence shown in the accompanying figure, to 15–22 ft. lbs. (20–30 Nm).

16. On SC vehicles, install the CKP sensor upper shield.

17. Connect the water bypass hose at the water pump, then tighten the clamps (and oil cooler inlet tube and hose).

18. Attach the heater hose at the water pump and connect the lower radiator hose and tighten the clamps.

19. Install the power steering pump pulley and water pump-to-power steering pump brace. If removed, install the charge air cooler.

20. Install the water pump pulley and tighten the retaining bolts to 15–22 ft. lbs. (20–30 Nm).

21. On engines with a Thermactor®, install the belt.

22. If the vehicle is equipped with air conditioning, install the idler pulley bracket and air conditioner drive belt.

23. Install the accessory drive belt(s).

24. Install the cooling fan and shroud, as outlined earlier in this section.

25. Fill the engine cooling system with the proper type and quantity of coolant. Connect the negative battery cable.

26. Start and run the engine and inspect for leaks. Check the coolant level, and add if necessary.

4.6L Engine

▶ **See Figure 65**

1. Disconnect the negative battery cable.

2. Properly drain the engine cooling system into a suitable container.

3. Remove the cooling fan/motor/blade assembly, as outlined in this section.

4. Release the drive belt tension, then remove the belt.

5. Unfasten the four bolts retaining the water pump pulley to the water pump, then remove the pulley.

6. Unfasten the four retaining bolts, then remove the water pump from the vehicle.

To install:

7. Replace the O-ring type water pump housing gasket and clean the sealing surfaces of the cylinder block

8. Lubricate the water pump housing gasket with a suitable coolant. Position the water pump on the engine and install the four retaining bolts. Tighten the bolts to 15–22 ft. lbs. (20–30 Nm).

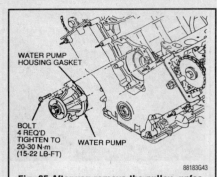

Fig. 65 After you remove the pulley, unfasten the bolts and remove the water pump from the vehicle

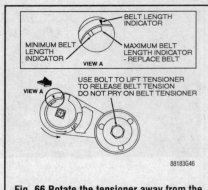

Fig. 66 Rotate the tensioner away from the belt to remove the drive belt

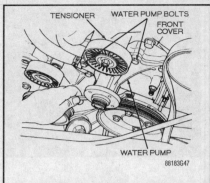

Fig. 67 Unfasten the retaining bolts, then remove the water pump from the vehicle

9. Place the water pump pulley on the water pump, then secure with the four retaining bolts. Tighten the bolts to 15–22 ft. lbs. (20–30 Nm).

10. Install the drive belt.

11. Install the cooling fan motor/blade/shroud assembly, then fill the cooling system with a 50/50 mix of suitable coolant and clean water.

12. Connect the negative battery cable, then start the engine and check for leaks. Check the coolant level, and add if necessary.

5.0L Engine

1983–88 VEHICLES

1. Disconnect the negative battery cable.
2. Properly drain the cooling system into a suitable container.
3. If equipped, remove the air inlet tube.
4. Unfasten the fan shroud attaching bolts, then position the shroud over the fan. Remove the fan and clutch assembly from the water pump shaft. Remove the shroud.
5. If equipped remove the A/C drive belt and the idler pulley bracket. Remove the alternator drive belt.
6. Remove the power steering drive belt and the power steering pump. Do NOT disconnect the power steering pump lines.
7. Remove all accessory brackets which attach to the water pump. Remove the water pump pulley.
8. Disconnect the radiator lower hose, heater hose, and water pump bypass hose at the water pump.
9. Unfasten the bolts that attach the pump to the cylinder front cover. Remove the pump and gasket. Discard the gasket.

To install:

10. Clean all gasket material from the mounting surfaces of the cylinder front cover and water pump.

11. Position a new gasket, coated on both sides with Perfect Seal sealing compound B5A-19554-A or equivalent, on the cylinder front cover. Position the water pump, then install the retaining bolts. Tighten the bolts to 12–18 ft. lbs. (16–24 Nm).

12. Connect the radiator hose, heater hose and water pump bypass hose at the water pump.

13. Install all the accessory brackets which attach to the water pump. Place the water pump pulley on the water pump shaft.

14. Install the power steering pump and drive belt. Install the alternator and drive belt. If equipped install the A/C idler pulley bracket and drive belt.

15. Position the fan shroud over the water pump pulley and install the fan drive clutch and fan. Install the shroud attaching bolts.

16. Adjust the drive belts to the specified belt tension.

17. Fill and bleed the cooling system. Connect the negative battery cable.

18. Start and run the engine until it reaches normal operating temperature, then inspect for leaks. Check the coolant level and add if necessary.

1991–93 VEHICLES

▶ See Figures 66 and 67

1. Disconnect the negative battery cable.
2. Properly drain the cooling system into a suitable container.

➡The fan and clutch assembly is removed by turning the nut counterclockwise.

3. Remove the fan and clutch assembly from the water pump shaft using Fan Clutch Holding Tool T84T-6312-C and Fan Clutch Nut Wrench T84T-6312-D, or equivalent tools, and position the fan and clutch assembly in the fan shroud.

4. Remove the fan shroud and fan/clutch as an assembly.

5. Loosen the water pump pulley bolts.

6. Remove the accessory drive belt by rotating the tensioner away from the belt by using pulley retaining bolts only.

7. Remove the water pump pulley.

8. Disconnect the lower radiator hose, heater hose and water pump bypass hose at the water pump.

9. Unfasten the bolts that attach the pump to the cylinder front cover. Remove the pump and gasket, then discard the gasket.

To install:

10. Clean all gasket material from the mating surfaces of the cylinder front cover and the water pump.

11. Position a new gasket, coated on both sides with Perfect Seal sealing compound B5A-19554-A or equivalent, on the cylinder front cover. Position the water pump, then install the retaining bolts. Tighten the bolts to 12–18 ft. lbs. (16–24 Nm).

12. Connect the radiator hose, heater hose and water pump bypass hose at the water pump.

13. Install the water pump pulley and tighten the bolts hand-tight.

14. Install the accessory drive belt and tighten the water pump pulley bolts.

15. Position the fan and clutch assembly in the fan shroud, then install the shroud.

16. Install the fan drive clutch and fan using Fan Clutch Holding tool T84T-6312-C and Fan Clutch Nut Wrench T84T-6312-D, or equivalent tools.

17. Connect the upper radiator hose.

18. Fill and bleed the cooling system. Connect the negative battery cable.

19. Start and run the engine until it reaches normal operating temperature, then inspect for leaks. Check the coolant level and add if necessary.

Cylinder Head

REMOVAL & INSTALLATION

2.3L Engine

▶ See Figure 68

➡Set the engine at TDC position for No. 1 piston, if possible prior to head removal.

1. Disconnect the negative battery cable.
2. Properly drain the cooling system into a suitable container.
3. Remove the air cleaner assembly.
4. Disconnect the water outlet elbow from the cylinder head with the hose attached.

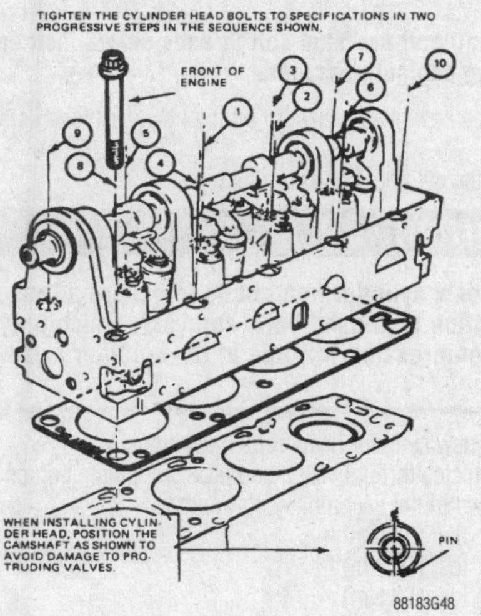

Fig. 68 Cylinder head bolt tightening sequence—2.3L engine

5. Remove the valve cover, as outlined in this section. Note the location of the valve cover attaching screws that have rubber grommets.
6. Remove the turbocharger. For details, please refer to the procedure located in this section.
7. Remove the intake and exhaust manifolds from the head, as outlined in this section.
8. Remove the camshaft drive belt cover. Note the location of the belt cover attaching screws that have rubber grommets.
9. Loosen the drive belt tensioner and remove the belt.
10. Unfasten the cylinder head attaching bolts, then remove the cylinder head from the engine. Remove and discard the gasket.
11. Clean all gaskets material and carbon from the top of the cylinder block and pistons and from the bottom of the cylinder head.

To install:

12. Position a new cylinder head gasket on the engine. Rotate the camshaft so that the head locating pin is at the five o'clock position to avoid damage to the valves and pistons.
13. If they are available, cut the heads off of two old cylinder head bolts to use as guide studs. Thread the studs into the engine block at opposite corners.
14. Fit the gasket onto the block, then set the head into place. Remove the guide studs. Apply a non-hardening gasket sealer to the bolt threads, then install the bolts finger tight.
15. Using a torque wrench, tighten the head bolts, in the sequence shown in the illustration, first to 50–60 ft. lbs. (68–81 Nm), then to 80–90 ft. lbs. (108–122 Nm).
16. Install the camshaft drive belt.
17. Install the camshaft drive belt cover and its attaching bolts. Make sure the rubber grommets are installed on the bolts. Tighten the bolts to 6–13 ft. lbs. (8–18 Nm).
18. Install the water outlet elbow and a new gasket on the engine and tighten the attaching bolts to 12–15 ft. lbs. (16–20 Nm).
19. Install the intake and exhaust manifolds and the turbocharger.
20. Install the air cleaner and the valve cover.
21. Fill the cooling system.
22. Connect the negative battery cable, then start and run the engine and inspect for leaks. Check the coolant level and add if necessary.

3.8L Engine

➧ See Figures 69 thru 74

➡Cylinder head bolts must be replaced any time they are removed. The bolts are designed to stretch when tightened to the proper angle torque and may break or loosen if torqued a second time. Do NOT use the old bolts over again.

1. Disconnect the negative battery cable.

✲✲ CAUTION

Fuel injection systems remain under pressure, even after the engine has been shut OFF. The fuel system pressure must be relieved before disconnecting any fuel lines. Failure to do so may result in fire and/or personal injury.

2. Properly relieve the fuel system pressure. Drain the cooling system into a suitable container.
3. Remove the air cleaner assembly including the air intake duct and heat tube.
4. Loosen the accessory drive belt idler. Remove the drive belt.
5. If the left cylinder head is being removed:
   a. For SC engines, remove the charge air cooler and charge air cooler tubes.
   b. Remove the oil fill cap.
   c. Remove the power steering pump front mounting bracket attaching bolts.
   d. Remove the alternator assembly and accessory drive belt main idler.
   e. Remove the power steering pump/alternator bracket retaining bolts.
   f. Leaving the hoses connected, place the power steering pump/alternator bracket aside in a position to prevent fluid from leaking out.
6. If the right cylinder head is being removed:
   a. If equipped, disconnect the Thermactor® tube support bracket from the rear of the cylinder head. Remove the Thermactor® pump pulley, then remove the pump.
   b. If equipped, remove the A/C compressor belt and main drive belt.
   c. If equipped, remove the compressor mounting bracket retaining bolts. Leave the hoses connected, then position the compressor aside.
   d. Remove the PCV valve.
7. For non-SC engines, remove the upper intake manifold, as follows:
   a. Tag and detach the electrical connectors at the idle air bypass valve, throttle position sensor and EGR position sensor.
   b. Disconnect the throttle and transmission linkage from the throttle body. Remove the cable bracket from the manifold and position the bracket and cables aside.

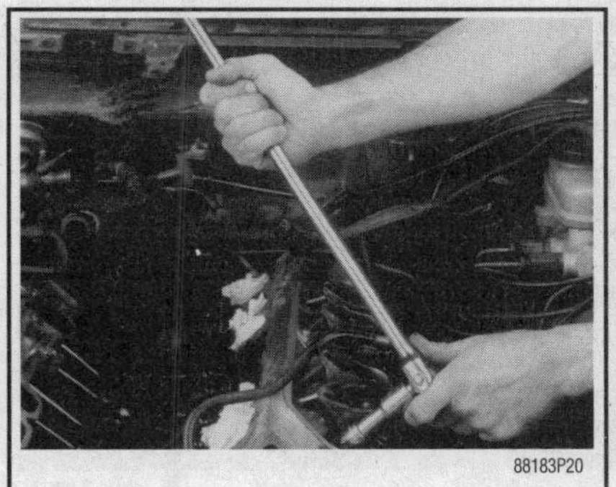

Fig. 69 Unfasten and discard the cylinder head bolts, then . . .

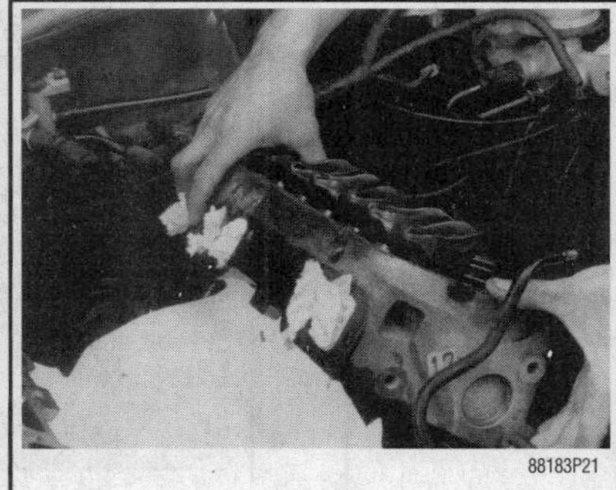

Fig. 70 . . . remove the head from the vehicle

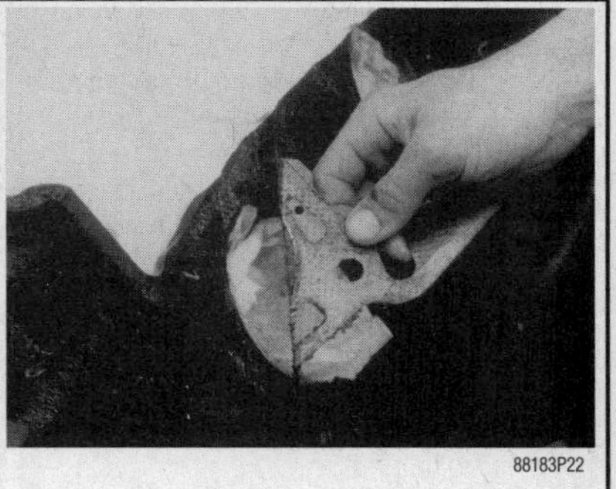

Fig. 71 Remove and discard the cylinder head gasket

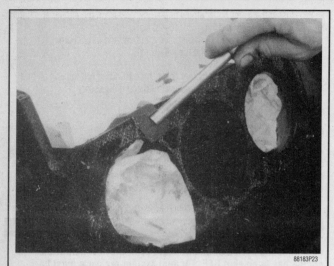

Fig. 72 Use a suitable gasket scraper to clean the mating surfaces

c. Tag and disconnect the vacuum lines at the upper manifold vacuum tree, EGR valve and fuel pressure regulator.

d. Detach the PCV hose from the fitting at the rear of the upper manifold.

e. Unfasten the retaining bolts, then remove the upper intake manifold.

8. For SC engines, remove the supercharger, as outlined in this section.

9. Remove the valve (rocker arm) cover attaching screws. Loosen the silicone rubber gasketing material by inserting a putty knife under the cover flange. Work the cover loose and remove. The plastic rocker arm covers will break if excessive prying is applied.

10. Remove the fuel rail and lower intake manifold.

11. Remove the exhaust manifold(s).

12. Loosen the rocker arm fulcrum attaching bolts enough to allow the rocker arm to be lifted off the pushrod and rotated to one side.

13. Remove the pushrods. Make sure to identify the position of each rod. They must be installed in their original position during assembly.

14. Unfasten the cylinder head attaching bolts and discard.

15. Remove the cylinder head(s). Remove and discard the old cylinder head gasket(s). Clean all gasket mating surfaces.

16. Check the flatness of the cylinder head gasket surface using a straight-edge and a feeler gauge. The allowable warpage is 0.003 in. for every 6.0 inches. Do not machine more than 0.010 in.

To install:

➡Lightly oil all bolt and stud bolt threads before installation except those entering coolant passages.

17. Position new head gasket(s) on the cylinder block using the dowels for alignment.

18. Place the cylinder heads on the block.

✳✳ CAUTION

Always use new cylinder head bolts to assure a leak-tight assembly. Torque retention with used bolts can vary, which may result in coolant or compression leakage at the cylinder head mating surface area.

19. Install new cylinder head bolts hand-tight.

20. For vehicles through 1992 and all SC engines, tighten the bolts, in the sequence shown in the accompanying figure to:
   a. 37 ft. lbs. (50 Nm)
   b. 45 ft. lbs. (60 Nm)
   c. 52 ft. lbs. (70 Nm)
   d. 59 ft. lbs. (80 Nm)

21. For 1993–97 vehicles, except SC engines, tighten the bolts, in the sequence shown in the accompanying figure to:
   a. 15 ft. lbs. (20 Nm)
   b. 29 ft. lbs. (40 Nm)
   c. 37 ft. lbs. (50 Nm)

➡**Do NOT loosen more than one bolt at a time.**

22. For non SC engines, loosen each bolt in the torque sequence, on at a time, 2–3 turns, then :
   a. Tighten each long bolt to 11–18 ft. lbs. (15–25 Nm), then rotate an additional 90 degrees.
   b. Tighten each short bolt to 7–15 ft. lbs. (10–20 Nm), then rotate an additional 90 degrees.

23. For SC engines, loosen each bolt in sequence 2–3 turns, then torque to 48–55 ft. lbs. (67–75 Nm). Rotate each bolt in sequence an additional 90–110 degrees.

➡**When the cylinder head attaching bolts have been tightened using the above sequential procedure, it is not necessary to retighten the bolts after extended engine operation. However, the bolts can be checked for tightness if desired.**

24. Lubricate each pushrod in heavy engine oil and install them in their original positions. Rotate the rocker arm into position.

25. For each valve, rotate the crankshaft until the lifter rests on the base circle of the camshaft lobe (pushrod all the way down), then tighten the fulcrum bolt to 43 inch lbs. (5 Nm). The fulcrum must be fully seated and the pushrod must be seated in the rocker arm socket before final tightening.

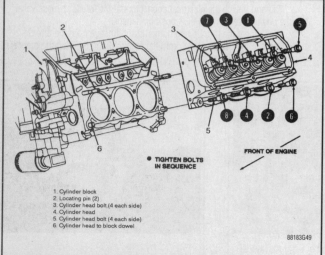

Fig. 73 The cylinder head bolts may NOT be reused and must be tightened in sequence—3.8L engine

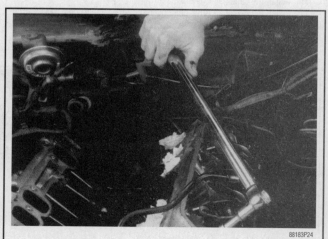

Fig. 74 The head bolts must be tightened to the correct sequence to prevent leakage

✳✳ WARNING

Fulcrums must be fully seated in cylinder head and pushrods must be seated in rocker arm sockets prior to final tightening.

26. Lubricate all rocker arm assemblies with heavy engine oil, then tighten the fulcrum bolts to 19–25 ft. lbs. (25–35 Nm). For final tightening, the camshaft may be in any position.

➡ **If the original valve train components are being installed, a valve clearance check is not required. If a component has been replaced, perform a valve clearance check.**

27. Install the exhaust manifold(s).
28. Install the lower intake manifold and the fuel rail.
29. Position a new gasket and the valve cover on the cylinder head, then install the attaching bolts. Note the location of the spark plug routing clip stud bolts. Tighten the attaching bolts to 80–106 inch lbs. (9–12 Nm).
30. Install the upper intake manifold or the supercharger, as applicable.
31. If removed, install the spark plugs. Connect the spark plug wires to the spark plugs.
32. If the left cylinder head is being installed:
    a. Install the oil fill cap.
    b. Install the alternator/power steering pump mounting bracket.
    c. Install the alternator assembly,.
    d. Install the main accessory drive belt tensioner assembly.
    e. Install the power steering pump assembly.
    f. Install the power steering pump support bracket.
    g. If equipped with an SC engine, install the charge air cooler tubes and charge air cooler.
33. If the right cylinder head is being installed:
    a. Install the PCV valve.
    b. If equipped with A/C, install the compressor mounting and support brackets and install the compressor.
    c. If equipped, install the Thermactor® pump and pump pulley.
    d. If equipped, install the accessory drive belt idler pulley.
    e. If equipped, install the Thermactor air control valve or idle air bypass hose. Tighten the clamps securely to the air pump assembly.
34. Install the accessory drive belt. If equipped, attach the Thermactor tube(s) support bracket to the rear of the cylinder head. Tighten the attaching bolts to 30–40 ft. lbs. (40–55 Nm).
35. Connect the cable to the battery negative terminal.
36. Fill and bleed the cooling system with the specified coolant.

✳✳ WARNING

This engine has an aluminum cylinder head and requires a compatible coolant formulation to avoid radiator damage.

37. Start the engine and check for coolant, fuel, and oil leaks.
38. Check and, if necessary, adjust the curb idle speed.
39. Install the air cleaner assembly including the air intake duct and heat tube.

4.6L Engines

▶ **See Figures 75 thru 80**

✳✳ CAUTION

Fuel injection systems remain under pressure, even after the engine has been turned OFF. The fuel system pressure must be relieved before disconnecting any fuel lines. Failure to do so may result in fire and/or personal injury.

➡ **The cylinder head bolts are a torque-to-yield design and cannot be reused. Before beginning this procedure, make sure new cylinder head bolts are available.**

1. Disconnect the negative battery cable.
2. Properly drain the cooling system into a suitable container.
3. Remove the cooling fan and shroud assembly.
4. Relieve the fuel system pressure as follows:
    a. Remove the fuel tank fill cap to relieve the pressure in the fuel tank.
    b. Remove the cap from the Schrader valve located on the fuel injection supply manifold.
    c. Attach Fuel Pressure Gauge T80L-9974-B or equivalent, to the Schrader valve and drain the fuel through the drain tube into a suitable container.
    d. After the fuel system pressure is relieved, remove the fuel pressure gauge and install the cap on the Schrader valve.
5. Remove the engine air cleaner outlet tube.
6. Remove the windshield wiper governor (module).
7. Release the drive belt tensioner and remove the accessory drive belt.
8. Tag and disconnect the ignition wires from the spark plugs. Disconnect the ignition wire brackets from the cylinder head cover studs and are move the two bolts retaining the ignition wire tray to the ignition coil brackets.
9. Remove the bolt retaining the A/C pressure line to the right-hand ignition coil bracket.
10. Disconnect the wiring to both ignition coils and the Camshaft Position (CMP) sensor.
11. Remove the nuts retaining the ignition coil brackets to the engine front cover. Slide the ignition coil brackets ignition wire assemblies off the mounting studs and remove from the vehicle.
12. Remove the water pump pulley.
13. Disconnect the alternator wiring harness from the junction block, fender apron and alternator. Unfasten the bolts retaining the alternator to the intake manifold and cylinder block, then remove the alternator.
14. Disconnect the positive battery cable at the power distribution box. Remove the retaining bolt from the positive battery cable bracket located on the side of the right-hand cylinder head.
15. Detach the vent hose from the canister purge solenoid and position the positive battery cable out of the way. Disconnect the canister purge solenoid vent hose from the PCV valve and remove the PCV valve from the cylinder head cover.
16. Remove and disconnect the engine and transmission harness connectors from the retaining bracket on the power brake booster.

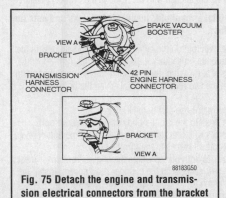

Fig. 75 Detach the engine and transmission electrical connectors from the bracket on the brake booster

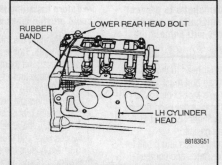

Fig. 76 Use a rubber band to hold the lower rear head bolt away from the cylinder block

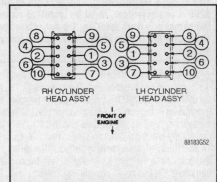

Fig. 77 Cylinder head bolt torque sequence—4.6L engine

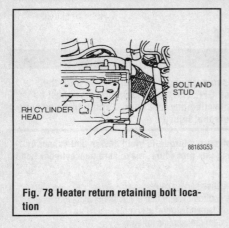

Fig. 78 Heater return retaining bolt location

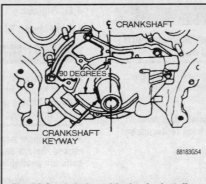

Fig. 79 Crankshaft positioning for installation of the cylinder heads

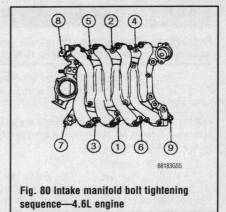

Fig. 80 Intake manifold bolt tightening sequence—4.6L engine

17. Detach the Crankshaft Position (CKP) sensor, A/C compressor clutch and canister purge solenoid electrical connectors.

18. Raise and safely support the vehicle.

19. Remove the bolts retaining the power steering pump to the cylinder block and engine front cover. The front lower bolt on the power steering pump will not come all the way out. Wire the power steering pump out of the way.

20. Remove the engine oil pan and oil pan gasket.

21. Remove the crankshaft pulley retaining bolts and remove the pulley, using Damper Remover T58P-6316-D or equivalent.

22. Detach the power steering control valve actuator and oil pressure sensor wiring connector and position out of the way.

23. Disconnect the EGR tube from the right hand exhaust manifold.

24. Detach the exhaust pipes from the exhaust manifolds. Lower the exhaust pipes and hang with wire from the crossmember.

25. Remove the bolt retaining the starter wiring harness to the rear of the right-hand cylinder head.

26. Carefully lower the vehicle.

27. Unfasten the bolts and stud bolts retaining the cylinder head covers to the cylinder head and remove the covers.

28. Disconnect the accelerator and cruise control cables. Remove the accelerator cable bracket from the intake manifold and position out of the way.

29. Tag and disconnect the vacuum hose from the throttle body elbow vacuum port, both Heated Oxygen Sensors (HO2S) and the heater water hose.

➡The two thermostat housing bolts also retain the intake manifold.

30. Unfasten the two bolts retaining the thermostat housing to the intake manifold and position the upper hose and thermostat housing out of the way.

31. Unfasten the 9 bolts retaining the intake manifold to the cylinder heads and remove the intake manifold and gaskets.

32. Remove the 7 stud bolts and 4 bolts retaining the engine front cover to the engine, then remove the front cover.

33. Remove both timing chains.

❊❊ WARNING

This is not a freewheeling engine. Cam Positioning Tools T92P-6256-A or equivalent, must be installed on the camshafts to prevent the camshafts from rotating. Do not rotate the camshafts or crankshaft with the timing chains removed or the valves will contact the pistons.

34. Unfasten the 10 bolts retaining the left-hand cylinder head to the cylinder block and remove the head. The lower rear cylinder head bolt must stay in the cylinder head until the cylinder head is removed due to a lack of clearance for removal in the vehicle. Use a rubber band to secure the cylinder head bolt in the cylinder head during removal and installation of the cylinder head and to prevent the bolt from damaging the cylinder block or head gasket.

35. Clean all gasket mating surfaces. Check the cylinder heads and block for flatness. Check the head for scratches near the coolant passages and combustion chambers that could provide leak paths.

To install:

36. Rotate the crankshaft counterclockwise 45 degrees. The crankshaft keyway should be at the 9 o'clock position viewed from the front of the engine. This ensures that all pistons are below the top of the engine block deck face.

37. Rotate the camshaft to a stable position where the valves do not extend below the head face.

38. Position new cylinder head gaskets on the block. Install new bolts in the lower rear bolt holes on both cylinder heads and retain with rubber bands, as explained during the removal procedure.

➡New cylinder head bolts must be used whenever the cylinder head is removed and reinstalled. The cylinder head bolts are a torque-to-yield design and cannot be reused.

39. Position the cylinder heads on the cylinder block dowels, being careful not to score the surface of the head face. Apply clean oil to the new cylinder head bolts, remove the rubber bands from the lower rear bolts and install all bolts hand-tight.

40. Tighten the new cylinder head bolts as follows:
    a. Torque the bolts in sequence, to 22–30 ft. lbs. (30–40 Nm).
    b. Rotate each bolt in sequence 85–95 degrees.
    c. Rotate each bolt in sequence and additional 85–95 degrees.

41. Position the heater return hose, then install the 2 retaining bolts.

42. Rotate the camshafts using the flats matched at the center of the camshaft until both are in time. Install Cam Positioning Tools T91P-6256-A or equivalent, on the flats of the camshaft to keep them from rotating.

43. Rotate the crankshaft clockwise 45 degrees to position the crankshaft at TDC for the No. 1 cylinder.

➡The crankshaft MUST be rotated in the clockwise direction any only as far as TDC.

44. Install both timing chains.

45. Install a new engine front cover and gasket. Apply silicone sealer to the lower corners of the cover where it meets the junction of the engine oil pan and cylinder block and to the points where the cover contacts the junction of the cylinder block and the heads.

46. Install the engine front cover and the stud bolts and bolts. Tighten to 15–22 ft. lbs. (20–30 Nm).

47. Position new intake manifold gaskets on the cylinder heads. Make sure the alignment tabs on the gaskets are aligned with the holes in the cylinder heads.

➡Before installing the intake manifold, inspect it for nicks and cuts that could provide leaks paths.

48. Position the intake manifold on the cylinder heads and secure with the retaining bolts. Tighten the bolts, in sequence, to 15–22 ft. lbs. (20–30 Nm).

49. Install the thermostat and O-ring, then position the thermostat housing and upper hose and install the two retaining bolts. Tighten the bolts to 15–22 ft. lbs. (20–30 Nm).

50. Connect the heater water hose and both HO2S sensors.

51. Attach the vacuum hose to the throttle body adapter vacuum port.

52. Install the accelerator cable bracket on the intake manifold and connect the accelerator and cruise control cables to the throttle body.

53. Apply silicone sealer to both places where the engine front cover meets the cylinder heads. Install new gaskets on the cylinder head covers. Install the bolts and stud bolts and tighten to 71–106 inch lbs. (8–12 Nm).

54. Raise and safely support the vehicle.

55. Place the starter motor wiring harness on the right hand cylinder head and install the retaining bolt.

56. Fit the exhaust pipes to the exhaust manifold. Install and tighten the 4 nuts to 20–30 ft. lbs. (27–41 Nm).

➡**Make sure the exhaust system clears No. 3 crossmember. Adjust as necessary.**

57. Connect the EGR tube to the right-hand exhaust manifold and tighten the line nut to 26–33 ft. lbs. (35–45 Nm).

58. Attach the power steering control valve actuator and oil pressure sensor electrical connectors.

59. Apply a small amount of silicone sealer in the rear of the keyway on the crankshaft pulley. Position the pulley on the crankshaft, making sure the crankshaft key and keyway are aligned.

60. Using Damper Installer T74P-6316-B or equivalent, install the crankshaft pulley. Install the pulley bolt and washer and tighten to 114–121 ft. lbs. (155–165 Nm).

61. Install the engine oil pan and a new gasket.

62. Place the power steering pump in position on the cylinder block and install 4 retaining bolts. Tighten the bolts to 15–22 ft. lbs. (20–30 Nm).

63. Carefully lower the vehicle.

64. Attach the A/C compressor, CKP sensor and canister purge solenoid electrical connectors.

65. Connect the engine and transmission harness connectors install on the retaining bracket on the power brake booster.

66. Install the PCV valve in the right hand cylinder head cover and connect the canister purge solenoid vent hose.

67. Position the positive battery cable harness on the right-hand cylinder head and install the bolt retaining the cable bracket to the cylinder head. Connect the positive battery cable at the power distribution box and battery.

68. Position the alternator and install the two retaining bolts. Tighten the bolts to 15–22 ft. lbs. (20–30 Nm). Install the 2 bolts retaining the alternator brace to the intake manifold and tighten to 6–8 ft. lbs. (8–12 Nm).

69. Install the water pump pulley and tighten the bolts to 15–22 ft. lbs. (20–30 Nm).

70. Position the ignition coil brackets and ignition wire assemblies onto the mounting studs. Install the 7 nuts retaining the ignition coil brackets to the engine front cover and tighten to 15–22 ft. lbs. (20–30 Nm).

71. Install the 2 bolts retaining the ignition wire tray to the ignition coil bracket and tighten to 71–106 inch lbs. (8–12 Nm). Attach both ignition coil and CMP sensor harness connectors.

72. Place the A/C pressure line on the right-hand ignition coil bracket and install the retaining bolt. Connect the ignition wires to the spark plugs and install the bracket onto the cylinder head cover studs.

73. Install the accessory drive belts and the windshield wiper governor.

74. Attach the fuel supply and return lines.

75. Install the cooling fan and shroud.

76. Fill the engine cooling system, then install the engine air cleaner outlet tube.

77. Connect the negative battery cable.

78. Check all fluid levels. Replace the engine oil and filter if the oil is contaminated.

79. Start the engine and bring to normal operating temperature while checking for leaks.

80. Road test the vehicle and check for proper engine operation.

5.0L Engine

▶ **See Figure 81**

1. If equipped, have the A/C system discharged at a reputable repair shop.

2. Disconnect the negative battery cable.

3. Properly drain the cooling system into a suitable container.

4. Relieve the fuel system pressure as follows:

   a. Remove the fuel tank fill cap to relieve the pressure in the fuel tank.

   b. Remove the cap from the Schrader valve located on the fuel injection supply manifold.

   c. Attach Fuel Pressure Gauge T80L-9974-B or equivalent, to the Schrader valve and drain the fuel through the drain tube into a suitable container.

   d. After the fuel system pressure is relieved, remove the fuel pressure gauge and install the cap on the Schrader valve.

5. Remove the upper and lower intake manifold and throttle body assembly.

6. If the A/C compressor is in the way of a cylinder head that is to be removed, proceed as follows:

   a. Disconnect and plug the refrigerant lines at the compressor. Cap the openings on the compressor.

   b. Detach the electrical connector from the compressor.

   c. Remove the compressor and necessary mounting brackets.

7. If the left cylinder head is to be removed, disconnect the power steering pump bracket from the cylinder head and remove the drive belt from the pump pulley. Position the pump out of the way in a position that will prevent the oil from draining out.

8. Disconnect the oil level dipstick tube bracket from the exhaust manifold stud, if necessary.

9. If the right cylinder head is to be removed, on some vehicles it is necessary to disconnect the alternator mounting bracket from the cylinder head.

10. Remove the Thermactor crossover tube from the rear of the cylinder heads. If equipped, remove the fuel lines from the clip at the front of the right cylinder head.

11. Raise and safely support the vehicle. Disconnect the exhaust manifolds from the muffler inlet pipes. Carefully lower the vehicle.

12. Remove the rocker arm fulcrum bolts and the pushrods. Keep these in order; they must be installed into their original locations.

13. Unfasten the cylinder head attaching bolts, then remove the cylinder heads. Only if necessary, remove the exhaust manifolds to gain access to the lower bolts. Remove and discard head gaskets.

14. Clean all gasket mating surfaces. Check the flatness of the cylinder head using a straight-edge and a feeler gauge. The cylinder head must not be warped any more than 0.003 in any 6.0 inch span; 0.006 overall.

To install:

15. Position the new cylinder head gasket over the dowels on the block. Position the cylinder heads on the block and install the attaching bolts.

16. Tighten the bolts in sequence in 2 steps, first to 55–65 ft. lbs. (75–88 Nm), then to 65–72 ft. lbs. (88–97 Nm).

➡**When the cylinder head bolts have been tightened following this procedure, it is not necessary to retighten the bolts after extended operation.**

17. If removed, install the exhaust manifolds with new gaskets and tighten the bolts to 18–24 ft. lbs. (24–32 Nm).

18. Clean the pushrods, making sure the oil passages are clean. Check the ends of the pushrods for warpage. Visually check the pushrods straightness or check for run-out using a dial indicator. Replace pushrods as necessary.

19. Apply lithium grease to the ends of the pushrods and install them in their original locations. Position the rocker arms over the pushrods and the valves.

20. Before tightening each fulcrum bolt, make sure the lifter is on the base circle of the camshaft (pushrod all the way down by rotating the crankshaft as needed. Tighten the fulcrum bolt to 18–25 ft. lbs. (24–32 Nm).

➡**If all the original valve train parts are reinstalled, a valve clearance check is not necessary. If any valve train components are replaced, a valve clearance check must be performed.**

21. Install new rocker arm cover gaskets on the cover, then install the covers on the cylinder heads.

22. Raise and safely support the vehicle. Connect the exhaust manifolds to the muffler inlet pipes. Carefully lower the vehicle.

23. If necessary, install the A/C compressor and brackets. Unplug and connect the refrigerant lines and electrical connector to the compressor.

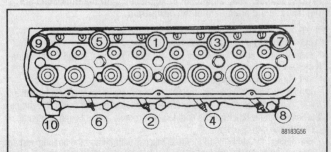

88183G56

Fig. 81 Cylinder head bolt tightening sequence—5.0L engine

24. If necessary, install the alternator bracket.

25. If the left cylinder head was removed, install the power steering pump.

26. Install the drive belts. Install the Thermactor tube at the rear of the cylinder heads.

27. Install the intake manifold. Fill and bleed the cooling system.

28. Connect the negative battery cable, start the engine and bring to normal operating temperature. Inspect for leaks, and check all fluid levels.

29. If necessary, take the vehicle to a reputable repair shop the have the A/C system evacuated and charged.

Oil Pan

REMOVAL & INSTALLATION

☀ CAUTION

The EPA warns that prolonged contact with used engine oil may cause a number of skin disorders, including cancer! You should make every effort to minimize your exposure to used engine oil. Protective gloves should be worn when changing the oil. Wash your hands and any other exposed skin areas as soon as possible after exposure to used engine oil. Soap and water, or waterless hand cleaner should be used. Recycle used engine oil; check local laws.

2.3L Engine

1. Disconnect the negative battery cable.

2. Raise and safely support the vehicle.

3. Drain the crankcase into a suitable container. If equipped, detach the low oil level sensor.

4. Remove the right and left engine support bolts and nuts or through-bolts.

5. Using a jack, raise the engine as far as it will go. Place blocks of wood between the mounts and the No. 2 crossmember pedestal brackets. Remove the jack.

6. Remove the steering gear retaining nuts and bolts. Unfasten the bolt retaining the steering flex coupling to the steering gear. Position the steering gear forward and down.

7. Remove the shake brace.

8. Disconnect the starter cable, then remove the starter.

9. Remove the engine rear support-to-crossmember nuts.

10. Position a jack under the transmission and raise it.

11. Unfasten the oil pan retaining bolts and reinforcements. Remove the oil pump and lay it in the oil pan. Remove the oil pan. Clean the pan mating surfaces.

To install:

12. Remove and clean the oil pickup tube and screen assembly. After cleaning, reinstall.

13. Position a new oil pan gasket to the oil pan with gasket and Seal Contact Adhesive D7AZ-19B508-A or equivalent.

14. Place the pump in the oil pan, then install the pump when the pan is in position. Position the oil pan to the cylinder block. Place the reinforcements and install the retaining bolts. Tighten to 90–120 inch lbs. (10–13.5 Nm).

15. Lower the jack under the transmission and install the crossmember nuts. Remove the jack.

➥**Crossmember nuts should not be tightened until the front bolts are tightened to aid alignment of the powertrain.**

16. Replace the oil filter.

17. If equipped, attach the low oil level sensor.

18. Position the flex coupling on the steering gear and install the retaining bolt.

19. Install the steering gear.

20. Install the shake brace. Install the starter and connect the starter cable.

21. Raise the engine enough to remove the wood blocks. Lower the engine and remove the jack. Install the engine support bolts and nuts and tighten to 33–45 ft. lbs. (45–61 Nm).

22. Lower the vehicle and fill the crankcase with oil and the cooling system with coolant.

23. Connect the negative battery cable. Start the engine and check for leaks.

3.8L Engine

1983–88 VEHICLES

◗ See Figure 82

1. Disconnect the negative battery cable.

2. Remove the air cleaner assembly including the air intake duct.

3. Unfasten the fan shroud attaching bolts, then position the shroud back over the fan.

4. Remove the oil level dipstick. If equipped with a low oil level sensor, remove the retainer clip at the sensor. Detach the electrical connector from the sensor.

5. Raise and safely support the vehicle.

6. Remove the exhaust manifold-to-exhaust pipe attaching nuts.

7. Drain the crankcase into a suitable container, then remove the oil filter.

8. Remove the bolts attaching the shift linkage bracket to the transmission bell housing. If necessary, remove the starter motor for more clearance.

9. Disconnect the transmission cooler lines at the radiator.

10. Unfasten the four converter cover retaining bolts, then remove the cover.

11. Disconnect the steering flex coupling. Unfasten the two bolts attaching the steering gear to the main crossmember, then let the steering gear rest on the frame away from the oil pan.

12. Remove the through bolts attaching the front engine insulator to the chassis.

13. Remove the nut and washer assembly attaching the front engine insulator to the chassis.

14. Raise the engine 2–3 in. (50–80mm) and insert wood blocks between the engine mounts and the vehicle frame.

➥**It may be necessary to raise the engine as much as 5 inches (127mm) to provide adequate pan-to-crossmember clearance. When raising the engine, watch the clearance between the transmission dipstick tube and the Thermactor® downstream air tube. If the tubes contact before adequate pan-to-crossmember clearance is provided, lower the engine and remove the transmission dipstick tube and the downstream air tube. Manual Clamp Cutter T78P-9481-A or equivalent, will be needed to disconnect the tube from the catalyst.**

15. Remove the oil pan attaching bolts. Work the oil pan loose, then remove it from the vehicle.

16. Lower the oil pan onto the crossmember. Remove the oil pickup tube attaching nut. Lower the pickup tube/screen assembly into the pan and remove the oil pan through the front of the vehicle.

17. Remove the oil pan gasket and discard.

To install:

➥**When using silicone rubber sealer, assembly must occur within 15 minutes after sealer application. After this time, the sealer may start to set-up, and its sealing effectiveness may be reduced.**

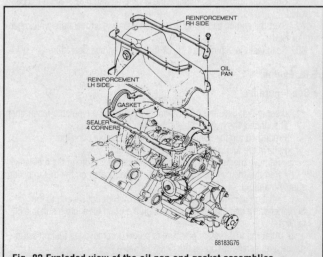

88183G76

Fig. 82 Exploded view of the oil pan and gasket assemblies— 1983–88 3.8L engine

18. Clean the gasket surfaces on the cylinder block, oil pan and oil pick-up tube.

19. Trial fit the oil pan to the cylinder block. Ensure enough clearance has been provided to allow the oil pan to be installed without the sealant being scraped off when the pan is positioned under the engine. Remove the oil pan.

✳✳ CAUTION

Make sure to use adequate ventilation when applying the gasket adhesive.

20. Install the oil pan gasket as follows:

a. Apply a thin film of GE pressure sensitive adhesive PSA-6574 or equivalent to the block rails front cover, rear bearing cap and block side of gasket.

➡ **The gasket taps go to the block side.**

b. Allow the adhesive to become tacky, then apply a ⅛ in. (3–4mm) bead of Silicone Rubber D6AZ-19562-A or equivalent to the joints between the front cover and the block.

c. Apply a ⅛ in. (4–5mm) bead of Silicone Rubber D6AZ-19562-A or equivalent, into the groove where the main bearing cap meets the block.

d. Immediately position the oil pan gasket against the engine block and press into position, being careful not to press out the sealant beads applied in Step c.

21. Install the oil pan, as follows:

a. Place the oil pickup tube/screen assembly in the oil pan.

b. Position the oil pan.

c. Position the oil pickup tube/screen with a new gasket. Install the tube attaching bolts and support bracket attaching nut. Tighten the attaching bolt to 15–22 ft. lbs. (20–30 Nm) and support bracket nut to 30–40 ft. lbs. (40–55 Nm).

d. Install the left and right side oil pan reinforcements and retaining bolts. Tighten the pan bolts to 80–105 inch lbs. (9–12 Nm).

22. Raise the engine, remove the wood blocks supporting the engine.

23. Install the front mount and damper attaching bolts. Tighten to 33–45 ft. lbs. (45–61 Nm).

24. Position the steering gear on the main crossmember. Install two attaching bolts. Connect the steering flex coupling and tighten the retaining nuts.

25. Position the shift linkage bracket and install the attaching bolts.

26. Connect the transmission cooler lines at the radiator.

27. If removed, install the transmission dipstick tube and the Thermactor® downstream air tube. Clamp cutter and Crimping tool T78P-9481-A or equivalent will be needed to connect the air tube to the catalyst.

28. Raise and safely support the vehicle.

29. Install a new oil filter.

30. Attach the exhaust manifold to the exhaust pipe and tighten the retaining nuts.

31. Carefully lower the vehicle.

32. If equipped, attach the low level oil sensor connector, then install the sensor with the retaining clip.

33. Position the fan shroud on the radiator and install the retaining bolts.

34. Connect the negative battery cable.

35. Fill the crankcase with the proper type and amount of oil.

36. Start the engine and check the fluid levels in the transmission. Check for engine oil, and transmission fluid leaks.

37. Install the air cleaner assembly, including the air intake duct.

1989–97 VEHICLES

▶ **See Figure 83**

1. Disconnect the negative battery cable.

2. Remove the air cleaner outlet tube.

3. Unfasten the two bolts retaining the radiator upper sight shield, then position the shield aside.

4. Remove hood weather seal.

5. Remove the wiper pivot arms.

6. Remove LH cowl vent screen and wiper module.

7. On SC engines, remove intercooler/charge air cooler tubes.

8. Install Three Bar Engine Lifting Support D88L-6000-A or equivalent.

9. Raise and safely support the vehicle.

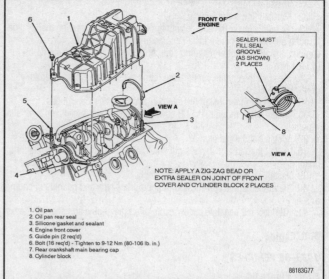

FRONT OF ENGINE

SEALER MUST FILL SEAL GROOVE (AS SHOWN) 2 PLACES

VIEW A

VIEW A

NOTE: APPLY A ZIG-ZAG BEAD OR EXTRA SEALER ON JOINT OF FRONT COVER AND CYLINDER BLOCK 2 PLACES

1. Oil pan
2. Oil pan rear seal
3. Silicone gasket and sealant
4. Engine front cover
5. Guide pin (2 req'd)
6. Bolt (16 req'd) - Tighten to 9-12 Nm (80-106 lb. in.)
7. Rear crankshaft main bearing cap
8. Cylinder block

88183G77

Fig. 83 Exploded view of the oil pan mounting—1995 3.8L engine shown

10. Remove the front engine support insulator through bolt. On SC, also remove LH front engine support/mount retaining strap bolt.

11. Partially lower the vehicle. Raise the engine with the lifting support tool.

12. Raise and safely support the vehicle. Remove the starter motor assembly.

13. Position a drain pan, drain the engine oil, then remove the filter.

14. Remove the starter motor wire, ground strap and oil cooler inlet tube (automatic transmission only).

15. Unfasten oil pan-to-bell housing bolts and Crankshaft Position (CKP) sensor lower shield retaining bolts (if equipped).

16. Remove the remaining oil pan retaining bolts.

17. Remove steering shaft pinch bolts and separate steering shaft.

18. Position transmission jack under front of the front subframe. Remove the six rearward bolts on front of subframe, then loosen the two forward subframe bolts.

19. Remove lower shock absorber-to-control arm bolts and nuts (both sides).

➡ **It is necessary to remove the front wheels, brake calipers, anti-lock sensors, power steering pressure lines and all wiring harness clips from subframe to allow lowering of subframe.**

20. Lower the front subframe.

21. Remove oil pan then empty any residual oil from the pan.

To install:

22. Clean mating surfaces of oil pan and cylinder block.

23. Apply a bead of RTV silicone gasket sealer to oil pan.

➡ **When using silicone rubber (RTV) sealer, assembly must occur within 15 minutes after sealer application. After this time, the sealer may start to set up, and its sealing effectiveness may be reduced.**

24. Fit oil pan to block to ensure enough clearance has been provided, to allow oil pan to be installed without sealant being scraped off, under cylinder block assembly.

25. Install oil pan retaining bolts at cylinder block, bell housing and install lower crankshaft sensor shield (if equipped). Tighten to 80–106 inch lbs. (9–12 Nm).

26. Raise subframe into position.

27. Install the lower shock absorber-to-front suspension lower arm bolts. Tighten to 103–144 ft. lbs. (140–195 Nm).

28. Install the two forward front sub-frame bolts and six bolts at the rear of the subframe.

29. Connect the steering column input shaft coupling, install the pinch bolt and tighten to 30–42 ft. lbs. (41–57 Nm).

30. If equipped with an automatic transaxle, install the oil cooler inlet tube and the oil cooler tube, the starter wire harness and the ground strap.

31. Install oil filter.

32. Partially lower the vehicle.

33. Carefully lower the engine with the engine support, seating the LH side locating pin before RH side. Install engine mount through bolts, (on SC engines, install LH mount retaining strap bolt), and tighten to 34–44 ft. lbs. (45–61 Nm).

34. Remove the engine support and lifting eyes, or equivalent. Carefully lower the vehicle.

35. On SC engines, install the intercooler/charge air cooler tubes.

36. Install wiper module, the LH cowl vent screen and the left and right side wipers.

37. Install hood weather seal.

38. Install the radiator upper sight shield and secure with the two retaining bolts.

39. Install air cleaner outlet tube assembly.

40. Refill the engine crankcase with appropriate type and quantity of engine oil.

41. Connect the negative battery cable. Start the engine and check for leaks.

5.0L Engine

1983–88 VEHICLES

♦ **See Figure 84**

❈❈ WARNING

On vehicles equipped with a dual sump oil pan, both drain plugs must be removed to thoroughly drain the crankcase. When raising the engine for oil pan removal clearance, drain the cooling system, disconnect the hoses, check the fan-to-radiator clearance when jacking. Remove the radiator if clearance is inadequate.

1. Disconnect the negative battery cable.

2. Remove the oil level indicator from the left side of the cylinder block.

3. Remove the air cleaner tube assembly.

4. Remove the fan shroud retaining bolts, then position the shroud over the fan.

5. Raise and safely support the vehicle. Properly drain the engine oil.

6. Remove the starter motor retaining bolts and electrical connections, then remove the starter from the vehicle.

7. Remove the exhaust catalyst converter and muffler inlet pipes.

8. Unfasten the engine mount-to-no. 2 crossmember attaching bolts or nuts. Remove the no. 3 crossmember and the rear insulator support assemblies.

9. Remove the steering gear attaching bolts, then position the gear forward, out of the way.

10. Raise and safely support the engine in a position which allows for oil pan removal.

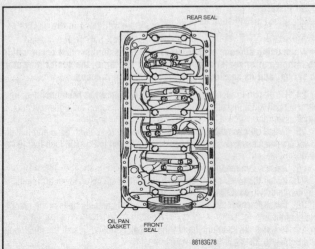

Fig. 84 After applying sealer to the mating surfaces, position the gasket(s) and/or seal(s)—1988 5.0L engine shown

11. Remove the oil pan attaching bolts and lower the oil pan on the frame, remove the oil pan from the vehicle.

To install:

12. Clean the gasket mounting surfaces thoroughly. Coat the gasket mating surfaces on the block and pan with sealer. Position the pan gaskets and/or seals.

13. Install the oil pan, then tighten the retaining bolts to 6–9 ft. lbs. (9–12 Nm).

14. Lower the engine onto the engine insulators, then install the engine mount-to-no. 2 crossmember attaching bolts or nuts. Tighten to 33–45 ft. lbs. (45–61 Nm).

15. Position the steering gear on the main crossmember. Install the two attaching bolts and tighten them to specification.

16. Install the starter motor and attach the electrical connections.

17. If equipped, connect the transmission oil cooler lines.

18. Install the rear insulator and the no. 3 crossmember.

19. Install the exhaust catalyst converter and the muffler inlet pipes.

20. Partially lower the vehicle.

21. Position the fan shroud in place, then secure with the attaching screws.

22. Install the oil level dipstick and tube assembly. Fill crankcase with the proper type and amount of engine oil.

23. Install the air cleaner assembly.

24. Connect the negative battery cable.

25. Apply the parking brake and while holding a foot on the brake, start the engine and allow to run for a few minutes. Turn the engine OFF and check for oil leaks.

1991–93 VEHICLES

♦ **See Figures 85 thru 93**

1. Disconnect the negative battery cable.

2. Remove the oil level dipstick.

3. Detach the air filter cover retaining clips to allow free movement when the engine is raised.

4. Unfasten the two bolts retaining the radiator, then pull the shroud loose from the lower retaining clips.

5. Install Engine Support Fixture D88L-6000-A or equivalent.

6. Raise and safely support the vehicle.

➡**It is recommended to use an engine hoist to lift the engine. Although wooden blocks and a jack will work, it may not provide enough room to remove the subframe and oil pan safely.**

7. Properly drain the engine oil, then remove the oil filter.

8. Unfasten the engine mount through bolts.

9. Loosen the transmission mount nut to allow the mount to move the when the engine is raised.

10. Partially lower the vehicle.

11. Carefully raise the engine, about two inches, with the support fixture.

12. Raise and safely support the vehicle.

13. Remove the power steering cooler line retaining clips.

14. Remove the bolt securing the transmission lines to the engine block (right hand side).

15. If equipped, detach the electrical connector from the low oil level sensor.

16. Unfasten the oil pan retaining bolts.

17. Remove the steering shaft pinch bolt, then separate the shaft from the power steering rack assembly.

18. Position two jackstands under the engine support subframe.

19. Unfasten the lower strut-to-control arm bolts and nuts on both sides.

20. While supporting the engine subframe on the jackstands, remove the six rearward bolts on the subframe. Loosen the two forward bolts on the subframe, then lower the subframe.

➡**It is necessary to remove the front wheels, brake calipers, anti-lock sensors, power steering pressure lines and all wiring harness clips from subframe to allow lowering of subframe.**

21. Remove oil pan. Empty any residual oil from the oil pan.

To install:

22. Clean mating surfaces of oil pan and cylinder block.

➡**The following procedure allows the gasket to stick to the engine block to insure correct gasket position during assembly. Do NOT apply and**

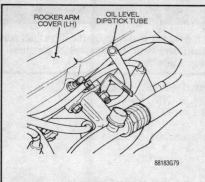

Fig. 85 Remove the oil dipstick, which is located near the left side valve cover

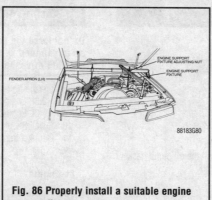

Fig. 86 Properly install a suitable engine support fixture

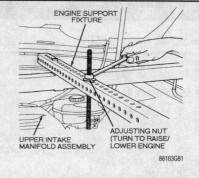

Fig. 87 Using the support fixture, raise the engine about two inches

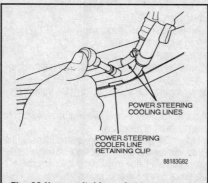

Fig. 88 Use a suitable socket to remove the power steering line clips

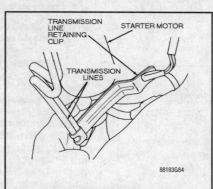

Fig. 89 Unfasten the bolt holding the transmission lines to the engine block

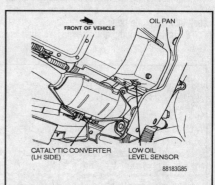

Fig. 90 Detach the connector from the low oil level sensor

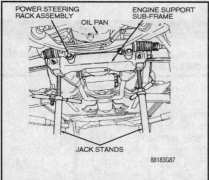

Fig. 91 Put two jackstands or transmission jacks under the front of the subframe

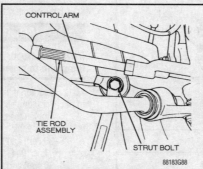

Fig. 92 Use an open-ended wrench to remove the lower strut-to-control arm bolts and nuts

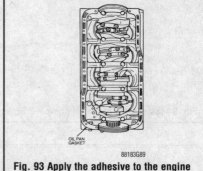

Fig. 93 Apply the adhesive to the engine block, NOT to the oil pan or pan side of the gasket

adhesive to the oil pan, or the oil pan side of the gasket. If adhesive is applied too thick, it will take longer to dry.

23. Apply a thin coat of Silicone Gasket Adhesive E6AZ-19562-A or equivalent, to the engine block and to the engine block side of a new oil pan gasket. Allow the adhesive to set-up for about 5 minutes, before positioning the gasket to the engine.

24. Position the oil pan to the engine. Install all the pan bolts hand tight, then tighten the ¼ inch pan bolt to 80–120 inch lbs. and the ⁵⁄₁₆ inch oil pan bolts to 12–18 ft. lbs. (16–24 Nm).

25. If equipped, attach the electrical connector to the lower oil level sensor located in the oil pan.

26. Raise the subframe into position while supporting the subframe with jackstands, install the six rearward bolts loosely on the subframe. Align the subframe and tighten the bolts.

27. Install lower strut-to-control arm bolts and nuts, then tighten to 103–144 ft. lbs. (140–195 Nm).

28. Remove the two jackstands used for installing the subframe.

29. Connect the steering shaft and install the steering shaft pinch bolt, then tighten to 30–42 ft. lbs. (41–57 Nm).

30. Secure the power steering cooler line retaining clips.

31. Carefully lower the vehicle.

32. Lower the engine onto the engine mounts, then remove the support fixture.

33. Raise and safely support the vehicle.

34. Tighten the transmission mount nut to 65–85 ft. lbs. (88–115 Nm).

35. Install the engine mount through-bolts and tighten.

36. Install a new engine oil filter.

37. Carefully lower the vehicle.

38. Position the radiator fan shroud into the lower retaining clips, then install the two bolts retaining the shroud to the radiator.

39. Attach the air filter cover retaining clips.

40. Fill the engine with the proper type and quantity of oil. Install the engine oil dipstick.

41. Connect the negative battery cable. Start engine and check for leaks.

Oil Pump

REMOVAL & INSTALLATION

2.3L and 5.0L Engines

▶ **See Figures 94 and 95**

1. Disconnect the negative battery cable.
2. Remove the oil pan.
3. Remove the oil pump inlet tube and screen assembly.
4. Unfasten the oil pump attaching bolts, then remove the oil pump gasket and the intermediate shaft.

To install:

5. Prime the oil pump by filling the inlet and outlet ports with engine oil and rotating the shaft of pump to distribute it.
6. Position the intermediate driveshaft into the distributor socket.
7. Place a new gasket on the pump body and insert the intermediate driveshaft into the pump body.
8. Install the pump and intermediate shaft as an assembly.

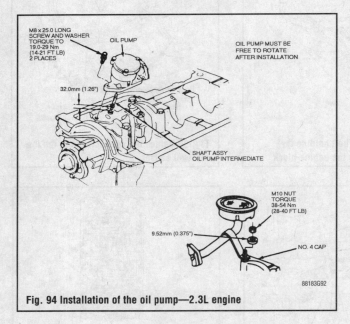

Fig. 94 Installation of the oil pump—2.3L engine

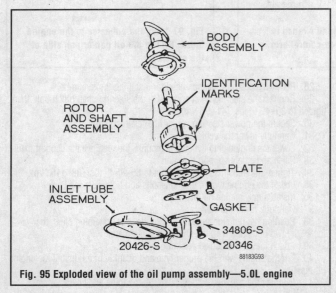

Fig. 95 Exploded view of the oil pump assembly—5.0L engine

Do not force the pump if it does not seat readily. The driveshaft may be misaligned with the distributor shaft. To align, rotate the intermediate driveshaft into a new position.

9. Install and tighten the oil pump attaching screws to:
   • 2.3L Engine: 12–15 ft. lbs. (16–20 Nm)
   • 5.0L Engine: 22–32 ft. lbs. (30–43 Nm)
10. Install the oil pan.
11. Connect the negative battery cable, then start the engine and check for leaks.

3.8L Engine

▶ **See Figure 96**

➡**The oil pump is mounted in the front cover assembly. Oil pan removal is necessary for pick-up tube/screen replacement or service.**

1. Disconnect the negative battery cable.
2. Raise and safely support the vehicle on jackstands.
3. Drain the engine oil, then remove the oil filter.
4. If necessary, remove the oil cooler.
5. Unfasten the oil pump-to-front cover retaining bolts, then remove the pump from the front cover.
6. Lift the two pump gears from their mounting pocket in the front cover.
7. Clean all gasket mounting surfaces.
8. Inspect the mounting pocket for wear. If excessive wear is present, complete timing cover assembly replacement is necessary.
9. Inspect the cover/filter mounting gasket-to-timing cover surface for flatness. Place a straightedge across the flat and check the clearance with a feeler gauge. If the measured clearance exceeds 0.004 in. (0.10mm), replace the cover/filter mount. Replace the pump gears if wear is excessive.

To install:

10. Lightly pack the gear pocket with petroleum jelly or coat all gear surfaces with Oil Conditioner D9AZ-19579-CA or equivalent, then install the pump gears in the cover pocket. Make sure the petroleum jelly fills all voids between the gears and pockets.

Failure to properly coat the oil pump gears may result in failure of the pump to prime when the engine is started.

11. Position the pump body O-ring seal and install the pump body to the front cover using alignment dowels on the front cover.
12. Tighten the pump retaining bolts as follows
   a. For vehicles through 1993, tighten the M8 bolts to 18–22 ft. lbs. (25–30 Nm) and the M10 bolts to 30–40 ft. lbs. (40–55 Nm).
   b. For 1994–97 vehicles, tighten the four smaller bolts to 15–22 ft. lbs. (20–30 Nm) and the two larger retaining bolts to 6–11 ft. lbs. (8–15 Nm).
13. If removed, install the engine oil cooler. Install the oil filter.

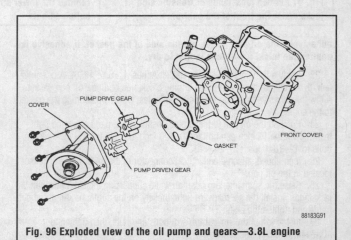

Fig. 96 Exploded view of the oil pump and gears—3.8L engine

14. Carefully lower the vehicle, then refill the engine crankcase with the correct type and amount of engine oil.

15. Connect the negative battery cable, then start the engine and check for leaks.

4.6L Engine

▶ See Figure 97

1. Disconnect the negative battery cable.
2. Remove the valve covers, engine front cover and the oil pan.
3. Remove the timing chains.
4. Remove the 2 bolts retaining the oil pickup tube to the oil pump and remove the bolt retaining the oil pickup tube to the main bearing stud spacer. Remove the pickup tube.
5. Unfasten the 4 bolts retaining the oil pump to the cylinder block, then remove the oil pump.

To install:

6. Rotate the inner rotor of the oil pump to align with the flats on the crankshaft and install the oil pump flush with the cylinder block.
7. Install the four retaining bolts, then tighten to 71–106 inch lbs. (8–12 Nm).
8. Clean the oil pickup tube and replace the O-ring.
9. Place the pickup tube on the oil pump and hand-start the 2 retaining bolts. Install the bolt retaining the pickup tube to the main bearing stud spacer hand-tight. Tighten the pick-up tube-to-oil pump bolts to 72–106 inch lbs. (8–12 Nm). Tighten the pickup tube-to-main bearing stud spacer bolt to 15–22 ft. lbs. (20–30 Nm).
10. Install a new oil filter.
11. Install the timing chains.
12. Install the oil pan, engine front cover, and valve covers.
13. Fill the crankcase with the proper type and quantity of engine oil.
14. Connect the negative battery cable, then start the engine and check for leaks.

Crankshaft Damper

REMOVAL & INSTALLATION

▶ See Figures 98 and 99

1. Disconnect the negative battery cable.
2. Remove the fan shroud, as required.
3. If necessary, drain the cooling system and remove the radiator.
4. Remove drive belts from pulley.
5. On those engines with a separate pulley, remove the retaining bolts and separate the pulley from the vibration damper.
6. Remove the vibration damper/pulley retaining bolt from the crankshaft end.
7. Using a puller, remove the damper/pulley from the crankshaft.

To install:

8. Align the key slot of the pulley hub to the crankshaft key.
9. Complete the assembly in the reverse order of removal. Tighten the retaining bolts to specifications, as follows:

a. 2.3L engines: 100–120 ft. lbs. (136–162 Nm).
b. 3.8L engines: 103–132 ft. lbs. (140–180 Nm)
c. 5.0L engines: 70–90 ft. lbs. (95–122 Nm).

10. Connect the negative battery cable, then start the engine and check for proper engine operation.

Timing Belt Cover

REMOVAL & INSTALLATION

2.3L Engine

1. Disconnect the negative battery cable.
2. Properly drain the engine cooling system.
3. Unfasten the four water pump pulley bolts.
4. Remove the automatic belt tensioner and accessory drive belt(s).
5. Disconnect the upper radiator hose.
6. Unfasten the crankshaft pulley bolt, then remove the pulley.
7. Remove the thermostat housing and gasket.
8. Remove the timing belt outer cover retaining bolt(s). Release the cover interlocking tabs, if equipped, then remove the cover from the vehicle.

To install:

9. Position the timing belt front cover. If equipped, snap the interlocking tabs into place. Install the outer cover retaining bolts, then tighten to 71–106 inch lbs. (8–12 Nm).
10. Using a new gasket, install the thermostat housing.
11. Connect the upper radiator hose.
12. Install the crankshaft pulley and retaining bolt. Tighten the bolt to 103–133 ft. lbs. (140–180 Nm).
13. Install the water pump pulley.
14. Install the accessory drive belt(s) and the tensioner.
15. Fill the cooling system with the correct type and amount of coolant.
16. Connect the negative battery cable, then start the engine and check for leaks.

Timing Chain Cover and Seal

REMOVAL & INSTALLATION

3.8L Engine

▶ See Figure 100

1. Disconnect the negative battery cable
2. Properly drain the cooling system into a suitable container.
3. Remove the air cleaner and air cleaner outlet tube/duct assemblies.
4. Remove the electric cooling fan motor, fan blade and fan shroud as an assembly. For details, please refer to the procedure located in this section.
5. Remove all drive belts and the water pump pulley.
6. Remove the power steering pump bracket retaining bolts, then, with the

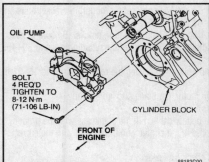

Fig. 97 Position the pump flush with the cylinder block, then install and tighten the retaining bolts—4.6L engine

Fig. 98 Use a suitable puller to remove the damper from the crankshaft—1990 3.8L engine shown

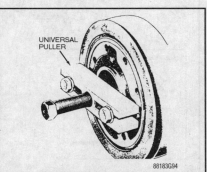

Fig. 99 There are several types of pullers to remove the crankshaft (vibration) damper from the crankshaft

hoses attached, position the pump and bracket aside. Be sure to keep the pump upright to prevent fluid leakage.

7. If equipped with A/C, remove the compressor front mounting bracket. It is not necessary to remove the compressor.

8. On non-SC engines, disconnect the heater water outlet tube and the water bypass hose from the water pump.

9. Disconnect the upper radiator hose at the thermostat housing.

10. Detach the ignition coil wire from the distributor cap and remove the cap with the ignition wires attached.

11. For non-SC engines, remove the hold-down clamp and lift the distributor out of the engine front cover. For SC engines, remove the hold-down clamp and remove the Camshaft Position (CMP) sensor from the engine front cover.

12. If equipped with a tripminder, remove the fuel flow meter support bracket. The fuel lines will support the flow meter.

13. Raise and safely support the vehicle using jackstands.

➡️ If the crankshaft damper and pulley have to be separated, mark the damper and pulley so that they may be reassembled in the same relative position. This is important as the damper and pulley are initially balanced as a unit.

14. Remove the crankshaft damper using Crankshaft Damper Remover T58P-6316-D and Vibration Damper Remover Adapter T82L-6316-B or equivalent pullers.

15. For carbureted vehicles, remove the fuel pump shield. disconnect the fuel line from the carburetor at the fuel pump. Remove the mounting bolts and the fuel pump. Position pump out of the way with tank line still attached.

16. Drain the engine oil and remove the oil filter and the oil cooler (if equipped).

17. Disconnect the lower radiator hose at the water pump.

18. Unfasten the oil pan mounting bolts and remove the oil pan.

➡️ The front cover cannot be removed without lowering the oil pan, or possible engine oil leakage may occur.

19. Carefully lower the car from the jackstands.

20. Remove the front cover mounting bolts. It is not necessary to remove the water pump from the engine front cover.

➡️ Do not overlook the engine front cover retaining bolt, located behind the oil pump and filter body. The engine front cover will break if pried upon and all retaining bolts are not removed.

21. Remove the engine front cover and water pump as an assembly. Remove and discard the front cover gasket.

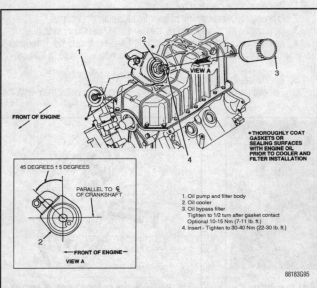

Fig. 100 Remove the oil filter and oil cooler (if equipped)

To install:

➡️ Lightly oil all bolt and stud bolt threads before installation except those specifying special sealant.

22. Clean all gasket surfaces on the front cover, cylinder block, fuel pump and oil pan.

23. If reusing the engine front cover, install a new front cover oil seal. If a new front cover is to be installed:

a. Install the oil pump, oil filter adapter and intermediate shaft from the old cover.

b. Remove the water pump from the old cover.

c. Clean the mounting surface, install a new mounting gasket and the pump on the new front cover. Tighten the water pump attaching bolts to 15-22 ft. lbs. (20–30 Nm).

➡️ Gasket and trim adhesive D7AZ-19B508-B or equivalent is recommended to hold the new front cover gasket in position while the front cover is installed.

24. Position a new front cover gasket on the front of the engine and install the cover and water pump assemblies, using the dowels for proper alignment. Tighten the front cover bolts to 15–22 ft. lbs. (20–30 Nm).

25. Raise and safely support the vehicle. Install the oil pan.

26. Connect the lower radiator hose to the water pump. Make sure to tighten the clamp securely.

27. Install the oil filter.

28. If equipped with a carbureted engine, install the fuel pump, then connect the fuel line at the carburetor and at the fuel pump.

❊❊ WARNING

When installing the fuel pump, turn the crankshaft 180° to position the fuel pump drive eccentric away from the fuel pump arm. Failure to turn the drive eccentric away from the pump arm can cause stress on the pump mounting threads and strip them out when installing the pump.

29. Coat the crankshaft front seal sealing surface with clean engine oil. Apply a small amount of Silicone Gasket and Sealant F1AZ-19562-A or equivalent, to the crankshaft keyway.

30. Position the crankshaft key in the crankshaft keyway. Install the crankshaft damper using Damper Front Cover Seal Replacer T82L-6316-A or equivalent. Install the damper retaining washer and bolt, then tighten the bolt to 103–132 ft. lbs. (140–180 Nm).

31. Fasten the pulley to the damper, then tighten the retaining bolts to 20–28 ft. lbs. (26–38 Nm).

32. Install the fuel pump shield.

33. Carefully lower the vehicle.

34. If equipped with an SC engine, connect the water bypass hose. Tighten the clamp securely. On non-SC engines, install the heater water outlet tube to the water pump. Tighten the retaining bolt to 6–8 ft. lbs. (8–11 Nm).

35. On non-SC engines, install the distributor with the rotor pointing at the No. 1 distributor cap tower. On SC engines, install the CMP sensor.

36. Install the distributor cap and connect the ignition coil wire.

37. Connect the upper radiator hose at the water hose connection. Tighten the clamp securely.

38. If equipped, install the front A/C compressor mounting bracket bolts and tighten to 30–45 ft. lbs. (41–61 Nm).

39. Install the power steering pump and mounting bracket. Be sure to keep the pump upright to prevent fluid leakage. Tighten the retaining bolts to 30–45 ft. lbs. (40–62 Nm).

40. Install the water pump pulley and tighten the retaining bolts to 16–21 ft. lbs. (21–29 Nm).

41. Install the cooling fan motor, fan blade and fan shroud.

42. Install the drive belt(s).

43. Connect the negative battery cable. Fill the crankcase with the proper type and amount of engine oil. Fill the engine cooling system with the correct quantity and type of coolant.

44. Start the engine and check for leaks.

45. Check the ignition timing and adjust as required. If equipped, tighten the distributor hold-down clamp to 15–22 ft. lbs. (20–30 Nm).

46. Install the air cleaner and air duct assemblies.

4.6L Engine

▶ **See Figures 101, 102 and 103**

1. Disconnect the negative battery cable.

➡ **The valve covers, oil pan and oil pan gasket must be removed prior to the engine front cover or possible engine damage and/or leakage may occur upon reassembly.**

2. Remove the cooling fan motor/fan blade and shroud assembly.
3. Loosen the water pump pulley bolts.
4. Remove the drive belt and the water pump pulley.
5. Raise and safely support the vehicle.
6. Remove the bolts retaining the power steering pump to the cylinder block and engine front cover. Note that the front lower bolt on the pump will not come all the way out. Wire the power steering pump out of the way. DO NOT disconnect the fluid lines.
7. Remove the oil pan and gasket, as outlined in this section.
8. Remove the crankshaft pulley retaining bolt and washer from the crankshaft.
9. Install Crankshaft Damper Remover T58P-6316-D on the crankshaft pulley, then pull the pulley from the crankshaft.
10. Carefully lower the vehicle.
11. Unfasten the bolts retaining the power steering fluid reservoir of the left side coil bracket, then position the reservoir out of the way.
12. Remove the right and left side valve covers, as outlined in this section.
13. Detach the fuel charging wiring from both ignition coils and Camshaft Position (CMP) sensor.
14. Unfasten the three bolts retaining the right side ignition coil bracket to the engine front cover.
15. Remove the left side ignition coil from the bracket, then lay it on the top of the engine.
16. Unfasten the three nuts retaining the left side ignition coil bracket to the engine front cover.
17. Slide the right side ignition coil bracket and ignition wires off the mounting studs and lay the assembly on top of the engine. Remove the bolts and retaining belt idler pulley, then remove the pulley.
18. Detach the fuel charging wiring from the Crankshaft Position (CKP) sensor.
19. Unfasten the seven stud bolts and four bolts retaining the engine front cover, then remove the cover from the vehicle.

To install:

20. Clean all dirt, oil and/or sealant from the engine front cover, cylinder heads and cylinder block sealing surfaces. The surfaces must be clean and dry before applying sealant.
21. Replace the crankshaft front seal and engine front cover gasket (three each).
22. Apply a 0.32–0.47 inch (8–12mm) bead of Silicone Gasket Sealant F1AZ-19562-B or equivalent, to the locations shown in the accompanying illustration. Install the engine front cover and retainers in no more than four minutes after applying sealer.
23. Install the studs and bolts retaining the engine front cover to the engine in the locations shown in the accompanying figure. Tighten to 15–22 ft. lbs. (20–30 Nm) no more than four minutes after applying sealer.
24. Connect the fuel charging wiring to the CKP sensor.

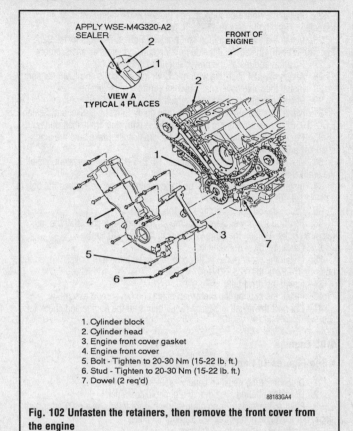

1. Cylinder block
2. Cylinder head
3. Engine front cover gasket
4. Engine front cover
5. Bolt - Tighten to 20-30 Nm (15-22 lb. ft.)
6. Stud - Tighten to 20-30 Nm (15-22 lb. ft.)
7. Dowel (2 req'd)

88183GA4

Fig. 102 Unfasten the retainers, then remove the front cover from the engine

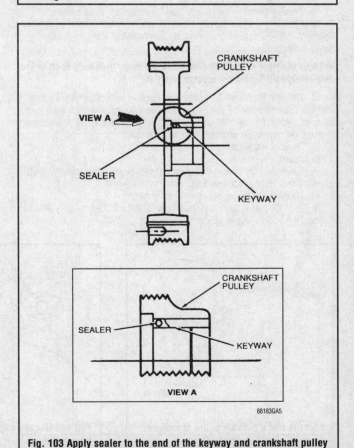

88183GA5

Fig. 103 Apply sealer to the end of the keyway and crankshaft pulley

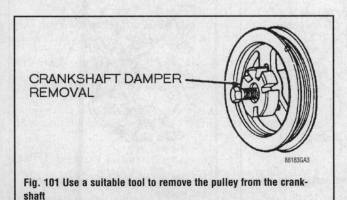

88183GA3

Fig. 101 Use a suitable tool to remove the pulley from the crankshaft

25. Install the right side ignition coil bracket and ignition wires as an assembly. Tighten the nuts to 15–22 ft. lbs. (20–30 Nm).

26. Install the left side ignition coil bracket. Tighten the nuts to 15–22 ft. lbs. (20–30 Nm). Install the left side ignition coil and wires as an assembly.

27. Position and install the power steering fluid reservoir.

28. Attach the fuel charging wiring to both ignition coils and CMP sensors.

29. Install the valve covers, as outlined earlier in this section.

30. Raise and safely support the vehicle.

31. Make sure the surfaces is clean, then apply Silicone Gasket and Sealant F1AZ-19562-B or equivalent to the end of the keyway and crankshaft pulley.

32. Position the crankshaft pulley on the crankshaft. Make sure the crankshaft key and keyway are aligned.

33. Using Crankshaft Damper Replacer T47P-6316-B or equivalent, install the crankshaft pulley.

34. Install the crankshaft pulley bolt and retaining washer. Tighten the bolt to 114–121 ft. lbs. (155–165 Nm).

35. Install the oil pan as outlined in this section.

36. Position the power steering pump on the engine, then install the four retaining bolts. Tighten the bolts to 15–22 ft. lbs. (20–30 Nm).

37. Carefully lower the vehicle.

38. Install the water pump pulley and secure with the four bolts. Tighten the bolts to 15–22 ft. lbs. (20–30 Nm).

39. Install the drive belt.

40. Install the cooling fan motor/fan blade and fan shroud assembly.

41. Connect the negative battery cable, then start the engine and check for leaks.

5.0L Engines

▶ **See Figures 104 and 105**

1. Disconnect the negative battery cable.

2. Drain the cooling system into a suitable container.

3. Refer to the Water Pump removal procedure in this section. Perform all steps, but leave the pump attached to the front cover.

4. Drain the oil from the crankcase.

5. Remove the crankshaft pulley from the crankshaft vibration damper. Remove the damper attaching capscrew and washer. Install Crankshaft Damper Remover T58P-6316-D, or equivalent, on the crankshaft vibration damper. Remove the damper.

➡**Cover the front oil pan opening while the cover assembly is off to prevent foreign material from entering the pan.**

6. Unfasten the oil pan-to-front cover attaching bolts. Carefully separate the front cover from the oil pan gasket. Remove the front cover and water pump as an assembly. If a new front cover is to be installed, remove the water pump from the old front cover and transfer to the new cover.

7. Remove and discard the front cover gasket.

To install:

8. Clean the front cover and mating surfaces of old gasket material. Install a new oil seal in the cover. Use a seal driver tool, if available.

9. Lubricate the timing chain with engine oil.

10. Coat the gasket surface of the oil pan gasket with sealer. Apply Silicone Rubber D6AZ-19562-AA or BB at the corners.

➡**Gasket and Trim Adhesive D7AZ-19B508-AA is recommended to hold the gasket in position during assembly.**

11. Coat the gasket surfaces of the block and cover with Perfect Seal Sealing Compound B5A-19554-A or equivalent and position a new gasket on the block.

12. Position the front cover on the cylinder block. Use care when installing the cover to avoid seal damage or possible gasket mislocation.

13. It may be necessary to force the cover downward to slightly compress the pan gasket. This operation can be facilitated by using Front Cover Aligner T61P-6019-B at the front cover attaching locations.

14. Coat the threads of the attaching screws with oil resistant Pipe Sealant with Teflon® and install the screws. While pushing on the alignment tool, tighten the oil pan-to-cover attaching screws to 12–18 ft. lbs. (16–24 Nm).

15. Tighten the cover-to-block attaching screws to 12–18 ft. lbs. (16–24 Nm). Remove the pilot.

16. Apply a suitable multi-purpose grease to the oil seal rubbing surface of the vibration damper inner hub to prevent damage to the seal. Apply Silicone Gasket and Sealant F1AZ-19562-A or equivalent to the keyway before installing on the crankshaft.

17. Line up the crankshaft vibration damper keyway with the key on the crankshaft. Install the vibration damper on the crankshaft using Crankshaft Sprocket and Damper replacer T52L-6306-AEE. Install the capscrew and washer. Tighten the screw to 70–90 ft. lbs. (95–122 Nm).

18. Install the crankshaft pulley.

19. Install the water pump, as outlined in this section.

20. Connect the negative battery cable.

21. Refill the cooling system and the crankcase.

22. Start the engine and operate it at fast idle.

23. Check for leaks, install the air cleaner. Adjust the ignition timing and make all final adjustments.

Timing Belt

REMOVAL & INSTALLATION

▶ **See Figures 106 and 107**

1. Set the engine to TDC as described in the troubleshooting section. The crankshaft and camshaft timing marks should align with their respective pointers and the distributor rotor should point to the No. 1 plug tower.

2. Disconnect the negative battery cable, then properly drain the engine cooling system.

3. Remove the timing belt front cover, as outlined in this section.

4. Loosen the belt tensioner adjustment screw, position belt tensioner tool T74P-6254-A or equivalent, on the tension spring roll pin and release the belt tensioner. Tighten the adjustment screw to hold the tensioner in the released position.

5. Remove the crankshaft pulley, hub and belt guide. Remove the timing belt. If the belt is to be reused, mark the direction of rotation so it may be reinstalled in the same direction.

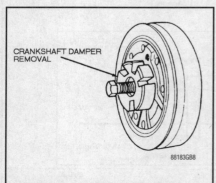

Fig. 104 Use a suitable puller to remove the crankshaft (vibration) damper

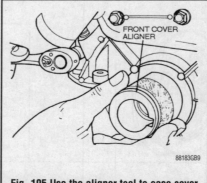

Fig. 105 Use the aligner tool to ease cover installation

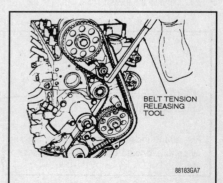

Fig. 106 Use the suitable tool to release belt tension

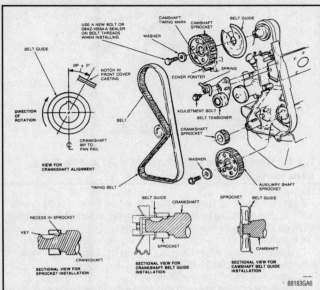

Fig. 107 Exploded view of the timing belt, sprockets and related components—2.3L engine

To install:

6. Position the crankshaft sprocket to align with the TDC mark and the camshaft sprocket to align wit the camshaft timing pointer.

7. Install the timing belt over the crankshaft sprocket, then counterclockwise over the auxiliary shaft and the camshaft sprockets. Align the belt fore-and-aft so that it is centered on the sprockets.

8. Loosen the tensioner adjustment bolt to allow the tensioner to move against the belt. If the spring does not have enough tension to move the roller against the belt, it may be necessary to manually push the roller against the belt and tighten the bolt.

9. To make sure the belt does not jump time during rotation in the next step, remove a spark plug from each cylinder.

10. Rotate the crankshaft two complete turns in the direction of normal rotation to remove any slack from the belt. Tighten the tensioner adjustment to 29–40 ft. lbs. (40–55 Nm) and pivot bolts to 14–22 ft. lbs. (20–30 Nm). Check the alignment of the timing marks.

11. Install the crankshaft belt guide. Install the crankshaft pulley and tighten the retaining bolt.

12. Install the timing belt front cover, spark plugs and remaining components.

13. Fill the cooling system, then connect the negative battery cable. Start the engine and check for proper operation. Check the coolant level and add if necessary. Check and adjust the ignition timing, if necessary.

Timing Chain

REMOVAL & INSTALLATION

3.8L Engine

1983–87 VEHICLES

▶ See Figures 108, 109 and 110

1. Disconnect the negative battery cable.
2. Remove the timing chain front cover, as outlined earlier in this section.
3. Remove the timing indicator. Remove the front cover and water pump assembly.
4. Remove the camshaft thrust button and spring from the end of the camshaft. Remove the camshaft sprocket attaching bolts.
5. Remove the camshaft sprocket, crankshaft sprocket and timing chain by pulling forward evenly on both sprockets. If the crankshaft sprocket is difficult to remove, position two small prybars, one on each side, behind the sprocket and pry forward.

To install:

6. Clean all gasket surfaces on the front cover, cylinder block, fuel pump and oil pan.
7. Install a new front cover oil seal. If a new front cover is to be installed:
   a. Install the oil pump, oil filter adapter and intermediate shaft from the old cover.
   b. Remove the water pump from the old cover.
   c. Clean the mounting surface, install a new mounting gasket and the pump on the new front cover. Pump attaching bolt torque is 13–22 ft. lbs.
8. Rotate the crankshaft, if necessary, to bring No. 1 piston to TDC with the crankshaft keyway at the 12 o'clock position.
9. Lubricate the timing chain with motor oil. Install the chain over the two gears making sure the marks on both gears are positioned across from each other. Install the gears and chain on the cam and crankshaft. Install the camshaft mounting bolts. Tighten the bolts to 15–22 ft. lbs. (20–30 Nm).
10. Install the camshaft thrust button and spring. Lubricate the thrust button with polyethylene grease before installation.

❉❉ WARNING

The thrust button and spring must be bottomed in the camshaft seat and must not be allowed to fall out during front cover installation.

11. Position a new cover gasket on the front of the engine and install the cover and water pump assemblies. Install the timing indicator. Torque the front cover bolts to 15–22 ft. lbs. (20–30 Nm).
12. Install the remaining components as outlined under the Timing Chain Front Cover procedure, located in this section.
13. Connect the negative battery cable. Fill the crankcase with the proper

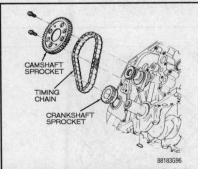

Fig. 108 Remove the sprockets and chain by pulling forward evenly on both sprockets

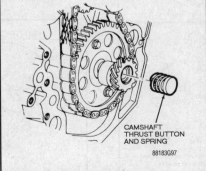

Fig. 109 Lubricate, then install the camshaft thrust button and spring

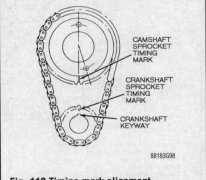

Fig. 110 Timing mark alignment—1983–87 3.8L engines

type and amount of engine oil. Fill the engine cooling system with the correct quantity and type of coolant.

14. Start the engine and check for leaks.

1988–97 VEHICLES

▶ See Figures 111, 112 and 113

1. Disconnect the negative battery cable.
2. Remove the timing chain front cover, as outlined earlier in this section.
3. Unfasten the camshaft sprocket retainer bolt and washer from the end of the camshaft.
4. Remove the distributor drive gear.
5. Remove the camshaft and crankshaft sprockets and the timing chain by pulling forward evenly on both sprockets. If the crankshaft sprocket is difficult to remove, position two small prybars, one on each side, behind the sprocket and pry forward.

➡The engine front cover contains the oil pump gears and water pump. If a new engine front cover is to be installed, remove the water pump and oil pump gears from the oil engine front cover.

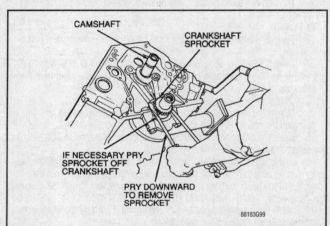

Fig. 111 If the crankshaft sprocket is difficult to remove, pry the sprocket off the shaft using a pair of prytools positioned on both sides of the crankshaft sprocket

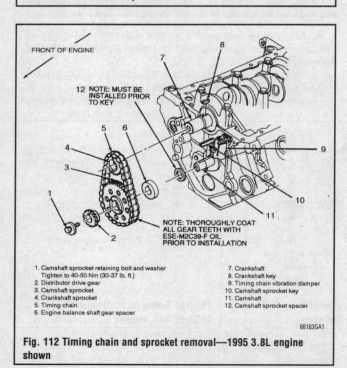

1. Camshaft sprocket retaining bolt and washer
   Tighten to 40-50 Nm (30-37 lb. ft.)
2. Distributor drive gear
3. Camshaft sprocket
4. Crankshaft sprocket
5. Timing chain
6. Engine balance shaft gear spacer
7. Crankshaft
8. Crankshaft key
9. Timing chain vibration damper
10. Camshaft sprocket key
11. Camshaft
12. Camshaft sprocket spacer

Fig. 112 Timing chain and sprocket removal—1995 3.8L engine shown

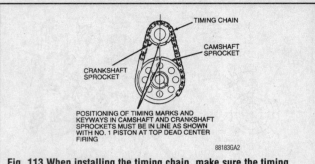

Fig. 113 When installing the timing chain, make sure the timing marks line up across from each other

6. Remove the timing chain vibration damper from the front of the cylinder block. This requires pulling back on the ratcheting mechanism, then install the pin through the hole in the bracket to relieve tension.

To install:

7. Rotate the crankshaft, as necessary to bring No. 1 piston to TDC with the crankshaft keyway at the 12 o'clock position.
8. Lubricate the timing chain with motor oil.
9. Install the camshaft and crankshaft sprockets and the timing chain. Make sure the timing marks line up across from each other.
10. Install the bolt and washer assembly at the end of the camshaft. Tighten the bolt to 30–37 ft. lbs. (41–50 Nm).
11. Install the remaining components as outlined under the Timing Chain Front Cover procedure, located in this section.
12. Connect the negative battery cable. Fill the crankcase with the proper type and amount of engine oil. Fill the engine cooling system with the correct quantity and type of coolant.
13. Start the engine and check for leaks.

4.6L Engine

▶ See Figures 114 thru 122

❋❋ WARNING

At no time, when the timing chain(s) are removed and the cylinder head installed, may the crankshaft and/or camshafts be rotated. Failure to heed this warning will result in valve and/or piston damage.

Because this is not a free-wheeling engine, if it has "jumped free" there will be damage to the valves and/or pistons and will require the removal of the cylinder heads. The camshaft sprockets should only be disassembled from the camshafts when one of the components is being replaced.

1. Disconnect the negative battery cable.
2. Remove the valve covers, oil pan and timing chain front cover, as outlined in this section.
3. Remove the Crankshaft Position (CKP) sensor pulse wheel.
4. Rotate the engine to No. 1 Top Dead Center (TDC).

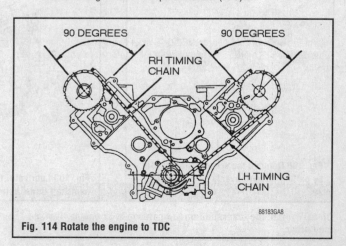

Fig. 114 Rotate the engine to TDC

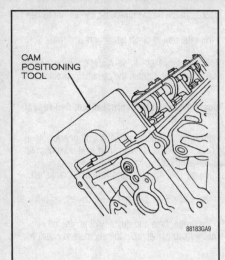

CAM POSITIONING TOOL

88183GA9

Fig. 115 These tools MUST be installed to prevent accidental rotation of the camshafts

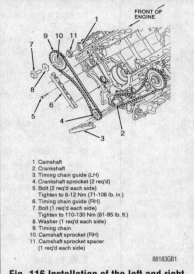

FRONT OF ENGINE

1. Camshaft
2. Crankshaft
3. Timing chain guide (LH)
4. Crankshaft sprocket (2 req'd)
5. Bolt (2 req'd each side)
   Tighten to 8-12 Nm (71-106 lb. in.)
6. Timing chain guide (RH)
7. Bolt (1 req'd each side)
   Tighten to 110-130 Nm (81-95 lb. ft.)
8. Washer (1 req'd each side)
9. Timing chain
10. Camshaft sprocket (RH)
11. Camshaft sprocket spacer
    (1 req'd each side)

88183GB1

Fig. 116 Installation of the left and right side timing chains and guides

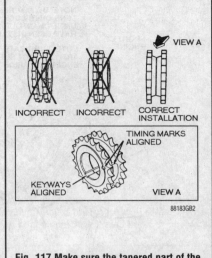

INCORRECT   INCORRECT   CORRECT INSTALLATION

VIEW A

TIMING MARKS ALIGNED

KEYWAYS ALIGNED

VIEW A

88183GB2

Fig. 117 Make sure the tapered part of the crankshaft sprocket faces away from the cylinder block

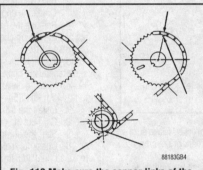

NOTE: WITH EITHER CHAIN POSITIONED AS SHOWN, MARK EACH END AND USE MARKS AS TIMING MARKS

88183GB3

Fig. 118 If the copper links of the timing chain are not visible, split both timing chains in half and mark the the opposing links

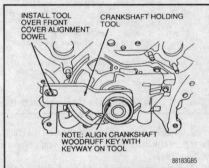

88183GB4

Fig. 119 Make sure the copper links of the timing chains line up with the timing marks of the crankshaft and camshaft sprockets

INSTALL TOOL OVER FRONT COVER ALIGNMENT DOWEL

CRANKSHAFT HOLDING TOOL

NOTE: ALIGN CRANKSHAFT WOODRUFF KEY WITH KEYWAY ON TOOL

88183GB5

Fig. 120 To position the crankshaft, position the holding tool over the crankshaft and engine front cover alignment dowel

➡This will prevent accidental rotations of the camshafts.

5. Install Cam Positioning Tool Adapters T92P-6256-A and Cam Positioning Tools T91P-6256-A on the flats of the camshafts.

6. Unfasten the two bolts retaining the right-side timing chain tensioner to the cylinder, then remove the tensioner.

7. Remove the right-side timing chain tensioner arm.

8. Remove the two bolts retaining the right-side timing chain guide to the cylinder head and remove the timing chain guide.

9. Remove the right-side timing chain from the camshaft and crankshaft sprockets.

➡Cam Positioning Tool Adapters T92P-6256-A and Cam Positioning Tools T91P-6256-A MUST be installed on the camshaft to prevent it from turning.

10. Remove the two bolts retaining the left-side timing chain tensioner to the cylinder head, then remove the timing chain tensioner.

11. Remove the left-side timing chain tensioner arm.

12. Unfasten the two bolts retaining the left-side timing chain guide to the cylinder head and remove the timing chain guide.

13. Remove the left-side timing chain from the camshaft and crankshaft sprockets.

14. If necessary, remove the camshaft and crankshaft sprockets.

✲✲ WARNING

Do NOT rotate the crankshaft and/or camshafts or engine damage may occur.

15. Inspect the plastic running face on the timing chain tensioner arms and timing chain guides. If worn or damaged, remove and clean the oil pan and oil pump screen cover and tube.

➡If the engine has "jumped time", make sure that all repairs to the engine components and/or valve train have been made. Then, rotate the engine counterclockwise 45 degrees. This will position all pistons below the top of the deck face. Install the cylinder heads as outlined.

To install:

➡Cam Positioning Tool Adapters T92P-6256-A and Cam Positioning Tools T91P-6256-A MUST be installed on the camshaft to prevent it from turning.

16. Install the timing chain guides (both sides) and secure with the retaining bolts. Tighten the bolts to 71–106 inch lbs. (8–12 Nm).

17. If removed, position the left-side camshaft sprocket spacer and sprocket on the camshaft.

18. Install the washer and the camshaft sprocket retaining bolt, but do not tighten at this time.

19. If removed, position the right-side camshaft sprocket spacer and sprocket on the camshaft.

20. Install the washer and the camshaft sprocket retaining bolt, but do not tighten at this time.

➡Crankshaft sprockets are identical. They may be installed only one way. Refer to the accompanying illustration for proper crankshaft sprocket installation.

21. If removed, install the left-side crankshaft sprocket.

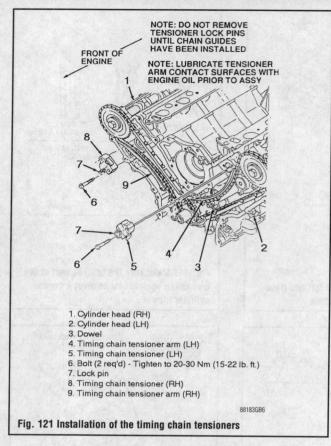

NOTE: DO NOT REMOVE TENSIONER LOCK PINS UNTIL CHAIN GUIDES HAVE BEEN INSTALLED

NOTE: LUBRICATE TENSIONER ARM CONTACT SURFACES WITH ENGINE OIL PRIOR TO ASSY

FRONT OF ENGINE

1. Cylinder head (RH)
2. Cylinder head (LH)
3. Dowel
4. Timing chain tensioner arm (LH)
5. Timing chain tensioner (LH)
6. Bolt (2 req'd) - Tighten to 20-30 Nm (15-22 lb. ft.)
7. Lock pin
8. Timing chain tensioner (RH)
9. Timing chain tensioner arm (RH)

Fig. 121 Installation of the timing chain tensioners

22. Install the left-side timing chain on the crankshaft sprocket. Make sure the copper link of the timing chain lines up with the timing mark of the crankshaft sprocket.

23. If removed, install right-side crankshaft sprocket. Install the right-side timing chain on the camshaft sprocket. Make sure the copper link of the timing chain lines up with the timing mark of the camshaft sprocket.

24. Install the right-side timing chain on the crankshaft sprocket. Make sure the copper link of the timing chain lines up with the timing mark of the crankshaft sprocket.

25. Install the right and left-side tensioners and secure with two bolts on each. Tighten the bolts to 15–22 ft. lbs. (20–30 Nm).

26. Install Crankshaft Holding Tool T93P-6303-A over the crankshaft and engine front cover alignment dowel, to position the crankshaft.

27. Lubricate the timing chain tensioner arm contact surfaces with clean engine oil and install the right and left-side timing chain tensioner arms on their dowels.

28. With a suitable C-clamp around the timing chain tensioner arm and tim-

ing chain guide. remove all slack from the timing chain. Be careful not to bend the timing chain guide.

29. Remove the lock pins from the timing chain tensioners and make sure all timing marks are aligned.

30. Using Cam Position Tool Adapters T92P-6256-A and Cam Positioning Tool T91P-6256-A, align the camshaft, then tighten the camshaft sprocket bolt to 81–95 ft. lbs. (110–130 Nm).

➡ **If not at maximum lift, loosen the camshaft sprocket bolt and repeat steps 26–29.**

31. Install Rotunda Dial Indicator with Bracketry 014-00282 or equivalent, ins cylinder No. 1 spark plug hole. Check that the camshaft is at maximum lift for the intake valve at 114 degrees after TDC.

32. Remove the Cam Positioning Tool Adapters and Tool and Crankshaft Holding Tool.

33. Install the timing chain front cover, oil pan and valve covers, as outlined in this section.

34. Fill the crankcase with the proper type and quantity of engine oil.

35. Connect the negative battery cable, then start the engine and check for leaks and proper operation.

5.0L Engine

▶ **See Figures 123 and 124**

1. Disconnect the negative battery cable.
2. Remove the timing chain front cover, as outlined earlier in this section.
3. Crank the engine until the timing marks on the sprockets are positioned.
4. Remove the camshaft sprocket capscrew and washer. Slide both sprockets and the timing chain forward, and remove then as an assembly.

To install:

5. Position the sprockets and timing chain on the camshaft and crankshaft simultaneously. Make sure the timing marks on the sprockets are positioned.

6. Install the washer and camshaft sprocket capscrew. Tighten the capscrew to 40–45 ft. lbs. (54–61 Nm).

7. Install the front cover as outlined earlier in this section.
8. Connect the negative battery cable.
9. Start the engine and operate it at fast idle.
10. Check for leaks, install the air cleaner. Adjust the ignition timing and make all final adjustments.

Camshaft Sprocket

REMOVAL & INSTALLATION

2.3L Engine

▶ **See Figures 125 and 126**

1. Disconnect the negative battery cable.
2. Remove the drive belt(s).
3. Remove the timing belt cover and the timing belt, as outlined in this section.
4. Using Cam Holding/Removing tool T74P-6256-B, or equivalent to hold

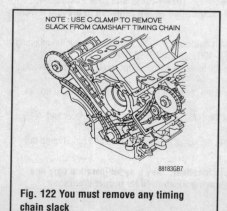

NOTE : USE C-CLAMP TO REMOVE SLACK FROM CAMSHAFT TIMING CHAIN

Fig. 122 You must remove any timing chain slack

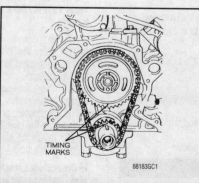

TIMING MARKS

Fig. 123 Crank the engine until the timing marks on the sprockets are positioned

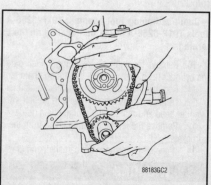

Fig. 124 Carefully slide the timing chain and sprockets off as an assembly

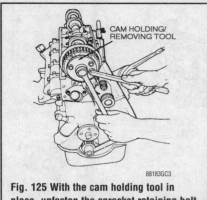

Fig. 125 With the cam holding tool in place, unfasten the sprocket retaining bolt

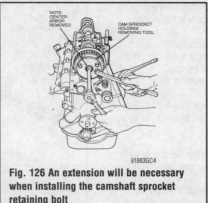

Fig. 126 An extension will be necessary when installing the camshaft sprocket retaining bolt

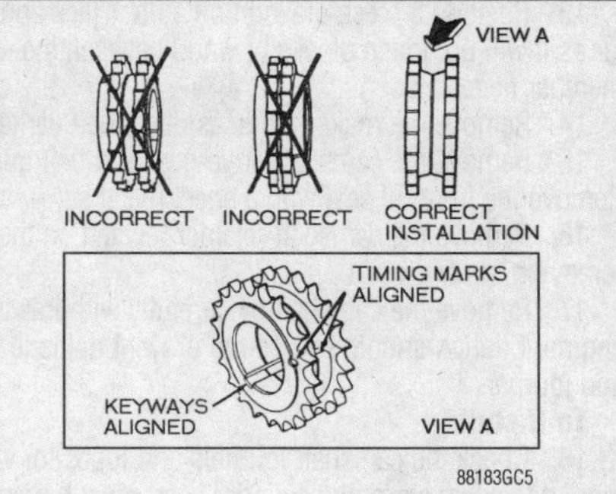

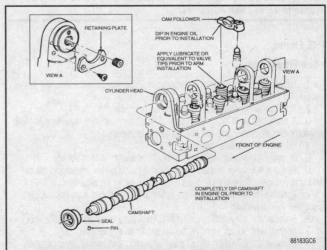

Fig. 127 Correct crankshaft sprocket installation

the camshaft in position, unfasten the bolts, then remove the camshaft sprocket from the vehicle.

To install:

5. Position the camshaft sprocket, then use Cam Holding/Removing tool T74P-6256-B, or equivalent to install the sprocket retaining bolt. Tighten the bolt to 52–70 ft. lbs. (70–95 Nm).

6. Install the timing belt and cover, as outlined earlier in this section.

7. Install the drive belt(s).

8. Connect the negative battery cable.

4.6L Engine

▶ See Figure 127

1. Disconnect the negative battery cable.

2. Remove the timing chains and tensioners as outlined earlier in this section.

3. If necessary, remove the crankshaft sprockets from the crankshaft.

➡ Cam Positioning Tool Adapters T92P-6256-A and Cam Positioning Tool T91P-6256-A MUST be installed on the camshafts to prevent them from turning.

4. Remove the camshaft sprocket retaining bolts, washers, camshaft sprockets and sprocket spacers from the vehicle.

✳✳ WARNING

Do not rotate the crankshaft or camshafts as possible damage to the engine may occur.

5. Inspect the sprockets for wear and/or damage and replace if necessary.

To install:

➡ Cam Positioning Tool Adapters T92P-6256-A and Cam Positioning Tool T91P-6256-A MUST be installed on the camshafts to prevent them from turning.

6. Position the camshaft sprocket spacers and sprockets on the camshafts.

7. Install the washers and camshaft sprocket retaining bolts, but do not tighten at this time.

➡ Crankshaft sprockets are identical and may be installed in only one way.

8. Install the crankshaft sprockets onto the crankshaft.

9. Install the timing chains and tensioners, as outlined earlier in this section.

10. Connect the negative battery cable.

Camshaft

REMOVAL & INSTALLATION

✳✳ CAUTION

When draining the coolant, keep in mind that cats and dogs are attracted by the ethylene glycol antifreeze, and are quite likely to drink any that is left in an uncovered container or in puddles on the

ground. **This will prove fatal in sufficient quantity. Always drain the coolant into a sealable container. Coolant should be reused unless it is contaminated or several years old.**

2.3L Engine

▶ See Figure 128

➡ The following procedure covers camshaft removal and installation with the cylinder head on or off the engine. If the cylinder head has been removed start at Step 9.

1. Properly drain the cooling system into a suitable container.

2. Remove the air cleaner assembly and disconnect the negative battery cable.

3. Tag and disconnect the spark plug wires from the plugs, detach the retainer from the valve cover, then position the wires out of the way.

4. Label and disconnect the rubber vacuum lines as necessary.

5. Remove all drive belts.

6. Unfasten the alternator mounting bracket-to-cylinder head mounting bolts, then position the bracket and alternator out of the way.

7. Disconnect the upper radiator hose. Remove the radiator shroud.

8. Remove the fan blades and water pump pulley and fan shroud. Remove the cam belt and valve covers.

9. Align the engine timing marks at TDC. Remove the timing belt, as outlined earlier in this section.

10. Raise and safely support the vehicle on jackstands.

11. Remove the front engine mount bolts.

12. Disconnect the lower radiator hose from the radiator. If equipped, disconnect and plug the automatic transmission cooler lines.

Fig. 128 Exploded view of the camshaft removal and related components

13. Position a piece of wood on a floor jack and carefully raise the engine as far as it will go. Place blocks of wood between the engine mounts and crossmember pedestals.

14. Remove the rocker arms, as described earlier in this section.

15. Remove the camshaft drive gear and belt guide using a suitable puller. Remove the front oil seal with a sheet metal screw and slide hammer.

16. Remove the camshaft retainer located on the rear mounting stand, by removing the two bolts.

17. Remove the camshaft by carefully withdrawing it toward the front of the engine. Caution should be used to prevent damage to the cam bearings, lobes and journals.

To install:

18. Check the camshaft journals and lobes for wear. Inspect the cam bearings. If they are worn, the cylinder head must be removed for new bearings to be installed by a machine shop.

19. Install the camshaft. Caution should be used to prevent damage to the cam bearings, lobes and journals. Coat the camshaft with heavy clean engine oil before sliding it into the cylinder head.

20. Install the camshaft retainer located on the rear mounting stand.

21. Install a new front oil seal.

22. Install the camshaft drive gear and belt guide. Apply a coat of sealer or Teflon® tape to the cam drive gear bolt before installation.

23. Install the rocker arms, as described earlier in this section.

24. Remove the blocks of wood between the engine mounts and crossmember pedestals and carefully lower the engine onto the mounts.

25. Carefully lower the vehicle.

26. Install the front engine mount bolts.

27. Connect the lower radiator hose at the radiator.

28. Unplug and connect the automatic transmission cooler lines.

29. Align the engine timing marks at TDC.

30. Install the cam drive belt.

31. Install the cam belt and valve covers.

32. Install the fan blades and water pump pulley and fan shroud.

33. Connect the upper radiator hose.

34. Install the alternator and mounting bracket on the cylinder head.

35. Install all drive belts.

36. Attach the spark plug wires to the plugs, as tagged during removal.

37. Fasten the plug wires to the retainer on the valve cover.

38. Connect the rubber vacuum lines, as labeled during removal.

39. Fill the cooling system with the correct type and amount of coolant.

40. Install the air cleaner assembly.

41. Connect the negative battery cable, then start the engine and check for leaks and/or proper operation.

❊❊ WARNING

After any procedure requiring removal of the rocker arms, each lash adjuster must be fully collapsed after assembly, then released. This must be done before the camshaft is turned. See Valve Clearance—Hydraulic Valve Lash Adjusters.

3.8L Engine

▶ **See Figure 129**

1. Disconnect the negative battery cable. Properly drain the cooling system and engine oil into suitable containers.

2. Remove or reposition the radiator, as necessary.

3. If equipped with A/C, remove the A/C condenser core, auxiliary cooling fan motor/fan assembly and fan shroud as an assembly.

4. Remove the radiator grille.

5. Remove the intake manifold, as outlined earlier in this section.

6. Remove the valve tappets, valve tappet guide plates and tappet guide plate and retainer. Make sure to keep all parts in order for reassembly.

7. Remove the timing chain front cover and timing chain as previously described in this section.

8. Remove the camshaft sprocket and engine balance shaft gear spacer.

9. As outlined earlier, remove the oil pan from the vehicle.

10. Remove the camshaft thrust plate or button and spring, then carefully remove the camshaft by pulling toward the front of the engine. Be careful not to damage the camshaft bearing surfaces and lobes.

11. Inspect the camshaft for damage and replace if necessary.

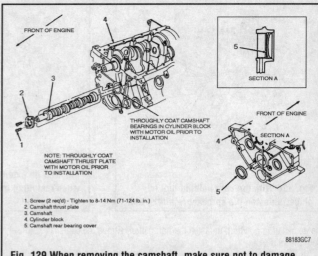

1. Screw (2 req'd) - Tighten to 8–14 Nm (71–124 lb. in.)
2. Camshaft thrust plate
3. Camshaft
4. Cylinder block
5. Camshaft rear bearing cover

88183GC7

Fig. 129 When removing the camshaft, make sure not to damage the bearing surfaces or cam lobes

To install:

➡ **Lightly oil all bolt and stud bolt threads before installation, except those specifying special sealant.**

12. Inspect the camshaft rear bearing cover for damage or leakage and replace if necessary.

13. Before installing, lubricate the camshaft lobes and bearing surfaces with Engine Assembly Lubricant D9AZ-19579, or equivalent.

14. Install the camshaft, being careful not to damage the bearing surfaces and lobes while sliding it into position.

15. Position the camshaft thrust plate with the groove towards the cylinder block. Tighten the bolts to 71–124 inch lbs. (8–14 Nm).

16. Install the engine balance shaft gear spacer, timing chain, camshaft sprocket and timing chain front cover.

17. Install the oil pan, as outlined earlier in this section.

18. Install the valve tappet guide plate and retainer, valve tappet guide plates and valve tappets.

19. As outlined in this section, install the intake manifold.

20. Install the radiator grille.

21. If equipped with A/C, install the A/C condenser core.

22. Install the radiator and cooling fan motor/blade and fan shroud assembly.

23. Fill the crankcase and cooling system to the proper levels with the correct type of fluids.

24. Connect the negative battery cable, then start the engine and check for leaks and/or proper operation. Check the fluid levels and add if necessary.

4.6L Engine

▶ **See Figures 130 thru 136**

1. Disconnect the negative battery cable.

2. Remove the cooling fan motor/fan blade and fan shroud assembly.

3. Properly relieve the fuel system pressure, as outlined in Section 5 of this manual.

4. Disconnect the fuel lines.

5. Remove the air cleaner outlet tube.

6. Release the tensioner, then remove the drive belt.

❊❊ WARNING

Do NOT pull on the spark plug wire, as it may separate from the connector in the wire boot.

7. Tag and disconnect the spark plug wires from the plugs. Detach the spark plug wire and brackets from the valve cover studs.

8. Unfasten the two bolts retaining the spark plug wire separator to the ignition coil bracket.

9. Disconnect the fuel charging wiring from both ignition coils and Camshaft Position (CMP) sensor.

Fig. 130 Use the correct tool to pull the crankshaft pulley from the crankshaft

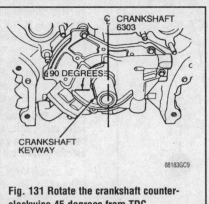

Fig. 131 Rotate the crankshaft counter-clockwise 45 degrees from TDC.

Fig. 132 Install a suitable valve spring compressor

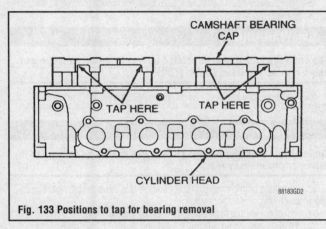

Fig. 133 Positions to tap for bearing removal

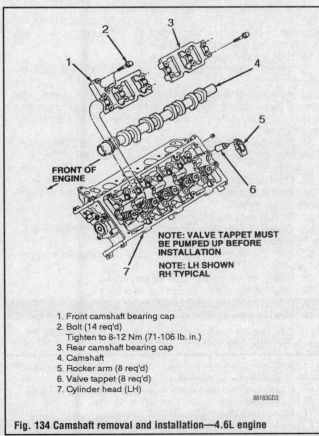

1. Front camshaft bearing cap
2. Bolt (14 req'd)
   Tighten to 8-12 Nm (71-106 lb. in.)
3. Rear camshaft bearing cap
4. Camshaft
5. Rocker arm (8 req'd)
6. Valve tappet (8 req'd)
7. Cylinder head (LH)

Fig. 134 Camshaft removal and installation—4.6L engine

10. Remove the three nuts retaining the right side ignition coil bracket to the engine front cover. Remove the ignition coil bracket, ignition coil and wires from the vehicles as an assembly.

11. Unfasten the bolts retaining the power steering oil reservoir to the left side ignition coil bracket and position the reservoir out of the way.

12. Remove the left side ignition coil from the bracket and remove from the vehicle as an assembly with the wires.

13. Unfasten the three nuts retaining the left side ignition coil bracket to the engine front cover, then remove the bracket.

14. Remove the water pump pulley.

15. Remove the PCV valve from the valve cover and position out of the way.

16. Detach the fuel charging wiring at the 42-pin connector and 8-pin connect leading to the Mass Air Flow (MAF) sensor.

17. Remove the nut retaining the A/C line to the right front fender apron.

18. Lift the A/C line and feed the 42-pin connector under the line. Position the connector aside.

19. Disconnect the fuel charging wiring from the Crankshaft Position (CKP) sensor, A/C clutch and EVAP canister purge valves.

20. Raise and safely support the vehicle.

➡**The front lower bolt on the power steering pump will not come all the way out.**

21. Remove the bolts retaining the power steering pump to the cylinder block and engine front cover.

22. Wire the power steering pump out of the way.

23. Remove the oil pan and gasket as outlined.

24. Remove the crankshaft pulley bolt and retaining washer from the crankshaft.

25. Install Crankshaft Damper Remover T58P-6316-D on the crankshaft pulley and pull the crankshaft pulley from the crankshaft.

26. Position a suitable drain pan under the oil filter, then remove the filter.

27. Disconnect the fuel charging wiring from the EVO sensor and oil pressure sensor.

28. Remove the oil filter adapter and position the fuel charging wiring out of the way.

29. Unfasten the nine bolts and two stud bolts retaining the right side valve cover to the cylinder head and remove the valve cover.

30. Unfasten the eight bolts and three stud bolts retaining the left side valve cover to the cylinder head, then remove the valve cover.

31. Remove the timing chain cover and timing chains, as outlined earlier in this section.

✷✷ WARNING

Crankshaft must be in this position prior to rotating camshafts or damage to the pistons and/or valve train will result.

32. Rotate the crankshaft counterclockwise 45 degrees from TDC.

➡**This ensures that all pistons are below the top of the cylinder block deck face.**

33. Install Valve Spring Compressor T91P-6565-A under the camshaft and on the top of the valve spring retainer.

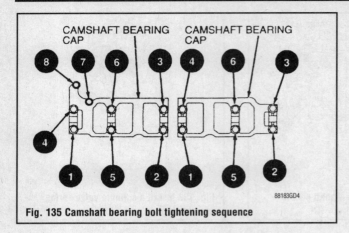

Fig. 135 Camshaft bearing bolt tightening sequence

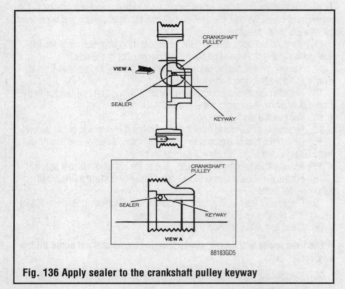

Fig. 136 Apply sealer to the crankshaft pulley keyway

➡**Valve Spring Spacer T91P-6565-AH must be installed between valve spring coils. The camshaft must be at base circle before compressing the valve spring. Rotate the camshafts as required until all rocker arms are removed.**

34. Compress the valve spring enough to remove the rocker arm.
35. Repeat the previous two steps until all rocker arms are removed.
36. Unfasten the 14 bolts retaining the camshaft bearing caps to the cylinder head.
37. Tap upward on the camshaft bearing caps at the position shown in the figure and gradually lift the camshaft bearing caps from the cylinder head.
38. Remove the camshaft by lifting it straight upward to avoid damage to the bearings.
39. If both camshafts are to be removed, repeat steps 33–38 to remove the other camshaft.
    To install:
40. Clean and inspect the valve cover, engine front cover and cylinder head sealing surfaces.

➡**Steps 41–48 will install only one camshaft. If both camshafts are being serviced, repeat steps 41–48 to install the other camshaft.**

41. Position the camshaft on the cylinder head. Apply oil to the journals and lobed of the camshaft.
42. Install and seat the camshaft bearing caps. Hand-start the 14 bolts.

➡**Each camshaft bearing bolt is tightened individually.**

43. Tighten the camshaft bearing bolts, in sequence to 71–106 inch lbs. (8–12 Nm). Loosen the 14 bolts about two turns or until the head of the bolt is

free. The camshaft should turn freely with a slight drag. Retighten all bolts, in sequence, to 71–106 inch lbs. (8–12 Nm).
44. Check camshaft end-play using Rotunda Dial Indicator with Bracketry 014-00282 or equivalent.
45. If necessary, install Camshaft Position Tool Adapters T92P-6256-A and Cam Position Tool T91P-6256-A on the flats of the camshaft and install the camshaft sprocket spacer and camshaft sprocket. Install the bolt and washer and tighten to 81–95 ft. lbs. (110–130 Nm).

➡**Valve Spring Spacer T91P-6565-AH must be installed between the valve spring coils and the camshaft MUST be at base circle prior to compressing the valve spring. Rotate the camshaft as necessary until all rocker arms are installed.**

46. Install Valve Spring Compressor T91P-6565-A under the camshaft and on top of the valve spring retainer. Install the valve tappet.
47. Compress the valve spring far enough to install the rocker arm.
48. Repeat steps 45–47 until all rocker arms are installed. Remove the valve spring spacer.

❋❋ **WARNING**

The crankshaft must only be rotated in the clockwise direction and only as far as Top Dead Center (TDC).

49. Rotate the crankshaft clockwise 45 degrees to position the crankshaft at TDC.

❋❋ **WARNING**

Timing chain procedures must be followed exactly or damage to the valves or pistons may result.

50. Install the timing chains. Inspect and replace the crankshaft front seal and engine front cover as necessary.
51. Install the engine front cover, as outlined earlier in this section.
52. Position and, using Silicone Gasket and Sealant F1AZ-19562-B or equivalent, secure the gaskets into the valve covers.
53. Using sealant, install the right side, then the left side valve covers and secure with the bolts and stud bolts. Tighten the 71–106 inch lbs. (8–12 Nm), no more than four minutes after applying sealer.
54. Raise and safely support the vehicle.
55. Connect the fuel charging wiring to the EVO sensor and oil pressure sensor.
56. Apply Silicone Gasket and Sealant F1AZ-19562-B or equivalent, in the keyway of the crankshaft pulley as shown in the accompanying figure. position the crankshaft pulley on the crankshaft. Make sure the crankshaft key and keyway are aligned.
57. Using Crankshaft Damper Replacer, T74P-6316-B, install the crankshaft pulley. Install the pulley bolt and washer, then tighten to 114–121 ft. lbs. (155–165 Nm).
58. Install the oil pan, using a new gasket.
59. Position the power steering pump on the engine and install the four retaining bolts. Tighten to 15–22 ft. lbs. (20–30 Nm).
60. Carefully lower the vehicle.
61. Connect the fuel charging wiring to the A/C clutch, CKP sensor and EVAP purge valves.
62. Position and connect the 42-pin engine harness connector and 8-pin connector.
63. Position the A/C line and install the retaining nut.
64. Install the PCV valve in the right side valve cover.
65. Connect the vent hose to the EVAP canister purge valve.
66. Install the water pump pulley and tighten the bolts to 15–22 ft. lbs. (20–30 Nm).
67. Position the right side ignition coil bracket, spark plug wires and wire separators onto the mounting studs.
68. Install the three nuts retaining the ignition coil bracket to the front cover. Tighten to 15–22 ft. lbs. (20–30 Nm).
69. Install the left side ignition coil and wires as an assembly.
70. Position and install the power steering oil reservoir.
71. Connect both ignition coils and CMP sensor.

72. Attach the spark plug wires to the plugs, as tagged during removal, then install the brackets on the valve cover studs.

73. Install the drive belt.

74. Connect the fuel lines.

75. Install the cooling fan motor/blade and fan shroud assembly.

76. Fill the cooling system. Install the air cleaner outlet tube.

77. Connect the negative battery cable.

78. Start the engine and check for leaks. Check the fluid levels and add as necessary.

5.0L Engine

1. Remove or reposition the radiator, A/C condenser and grille components as necessary to provide clearance to remove the camshaft.

2. Remove the timing chain/cylinder front cover and timing chain as previously described in this section.

3. Remove the intake manifolds and related parts described earlier in this section.

4. Remove the crankcase ventilation valve and tubes from the valve rocker covers. Remove the EGR cooler, if so equipped.

5. Remove the rocker arm covers and loosen the valve rocker arm fulcrum bolts and rotate the rocker arms to the side.

6. Remove the valve pushrods and identify them so that they can be installed in their original positions.

7. Remove the valve lifters and place them in a rack so that they can be installed in their original bores.

8. Remove the camshaft thrust plate or button and spring and carefully remove the camshaft by pulling toward the front of the engine. Be careful not to damage the camshaft bearings.

To install:

9. Before installing, oil the camshaft journals with heavy engine oil SG and apply Lubriplate® or equivalent to the lobes. Carefully slide the camshaft through the bearings.

10. Install the camshaft thrust plate with the groove towards the cylinder block.

11. Lubricate the lifters with heavy SG engine oil and install in their original bores.

12. Apply Lubriplate® or equivalent to the valve stem tips and each end of the pushrods. Install the pushrods in their original position.

13. Lubricate the rocker arms and fulcrum seats with heavy SG engine oil and position the rocker arms over the push rods.

14. Install all other parts previously removed.

15. Fill the crankcase and cooling system and adjust the timing.

INSPECTION

Degrease the camshaft using safe solvent, clean all oil grooves. Visually inspect the cam lobes and bearing journals for excessive wear. If a lobe is questionable, check all lobes and journals with a micrometer.

Measure the lobes from nose to base and again at 90°. The lift is determined by subtracting the second measurement from the first. If all exhaust lobes and all intake lobes are not identical, the camshaft must be reground or replaced. Measure the bearing journals and compare to specifications. If a journal is worn there is a good chance that the cam bearings are worn too, requiring replacement.

If the lobes and journals appear intact, place the front and rear cam journals in V-blocks and rest a dial indicator on the center journal. Rotate the camshaft to check for straightness. If deviation exceeds 0.001 in. (0.025mm), replace the camshaft.

Auxiliary Shaft

REMOVAL & INSTALLATION

2.3L Engine

▶ See Figure 137

1. Disconnect the negative battery cable.

2. Remove the camshaft drive belt cover.

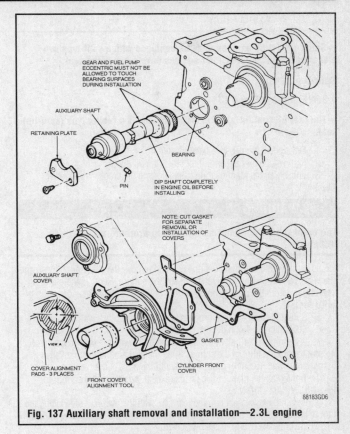

Fig. 137 Auxiliary shaft removal and installation—2.3L engine

3. Remove the drive belt. Remove the auxiliary shaft sprocket. A puller may be necessary to remove the sprocket.

4. Remove the distributor and fuel pump.

5. Remove the auxiliary shaft cover and thrust plate.

6. Withdraw the auxiliary shaft from the block.

❋❋ WARNING

The distributor drive gear and the fuel pump eccentric on the auxiliary shaft must not be allowed to touch the auxiliary shaft bearings during removal and installation. Completely coat the shaft with oil before sliding it into place.

To install:

7. Slide the auxiliary shaft into the housing and insert the thrust plate to hold the shaft.

8. Install a new gasket and auxiliary shaft cover.

➡The auxiliary shaft cover and cylinder front cover share a gasket. Cut off the old gasket around the cylinder cover and use half of the new gasket on the auxiliary shaft cover.

9. Fit a new gasket on the fuel pump and install the pump.

10. Insert the distributor and install the auxiliary shaft sprocket.

11. Align the timing marks and install the drive belt.

12. Install the drive belt cover.

13. Connect the negative battery cable.

14. Check the ignition timing.

Rear Main Oil Seal

Replacing a rear main seal can be a formidable task. Before replacing the seal, care should be taken in determining the exact source of the leak. Various manufacturers produce a fluorescent dye oil additive which can be added to your crankcase. The engine is run, allowing the dyed oil to leak from the same source, then a black light is used to illuminate the leak so it can be traced.

REMOVAL & INSTALLATION

➡Some 1983 3.8L engines, may be equipped with a split-type two piece rear main seal. All other engines have a one piece seal.

Split-Type Seal

♦ See Figures 138 and 139

➡The rear oil seal installed in these engines is a rubber type (split-lip) seal.

1. Disconnect the negative battery cable.
2. Remove the oil pan, and, if required, the oil pump.
3. Loosen all the main bearing caps allowing the crankshaft to lower slightly.

✳✳ WARNING

The crankshaft should not be allowed to drop more than 1/32 in. (0.8mm).

4. Remove the rear main bearing cap and remove the seal from the cap and block. Be very careful not to scratch the sealing surface. Remove the old seal retaining pin from the cap, if equipped. It is not used with the replacement seal.

To install:
5. Carefully clean the seal grooves in the cap and block with solvent.
6. Soak the new seal halves in clean engine oil.
7. Install the upper half of the seal in the block with the undercut side of the seal toward the front of the engine. Slide the seal around the crankshaft journal until 3/8 in. (9.5mm) protrudes beyond the base of the block.
8. Tighten all the main bearing caps (except the rear main bearing) to 65–81 ft. lbs. (88–110 Nm).
9. Install the lower seal into the rear cap, with the undercut side facing the front of the engine. Allow 3/8 in. (9.5mm) of the seal to protrude above the surface, at the opposite end from the block seal.
10. Squeeze a 1/16 in. (1.6mm) bead of silicone sealant onto the areas shown in the accompanying figure.
11. Install the rear main bearing cap, secure with the retaining bolts and tighten to 65–81 ft. lbs. (88–110 Nm).
12. Install the oil pump and pan.
13. Fill the crankcase with oil, the connect the negative battery cable.
14. Start the engine and inspect for leaks. Check the oil level, and add if necessary.

One-Piece Seal

♦ See Figure 140

1. Disconnect the negative battery cable.
2. Remove the transmission, clutch and flywheel or driveplate after referring to the appropriate section for instructions.
3. Punch two holes in the crankshaft rear oil seal on opposite sides of the crankshaft just above the bearing cap to the cylinder block split line. Install a sheet metal screw in each of the holes or use a small slide hammer, and pry the crankshaft rear main oil seal from the block.

✳✳ WARNING

Use extreme caution not to scratch the crankshaft oil seal surface.

To install:
4. Clean the oil seal recess in the cylinder block and main bearing cap.
5. Coat the seal and all of the seal mounting surfaces with oil and install the seal in the recess, driving it into place with an oil seal installation tool or a large socket.
6. Install the driveplate or flywheel and clutch, and transmission in the reverse order of removal.
7. Connect the negative battery cable.

Flywheel/Flex Plate and Ring Gear

REMOVAL & INSTALLATION

➡The ring gear is replaceable only on engines mated with a manual transmission. Engines with automatic transmissions have ring gears which are welded to the flex plate.

1. Remove the transmission, as outlined in Section 7 of this manual.
2. Remove the clutch, if equipped, or torque converter from the flywheel. The flywheel bolts should be loosened a little at a time in a cross pattern to avoid warping the flywheel. On cars with manual transmissions, replace the pilot bearing in the end of the crankshaft if removing the flywheel.
3. The flywheel should be checked for cracks and glazing. It can be resurfaced by a machine shop.
4. If the ring gear is to be replaced, drill a hole in the gear between two teeth, being careful not to contact the flywheel surface. Using a cold chisel at this point, crack the ring gear and remove it.

To install:
5. Polish the inner surface of the new ring gear and heat it in an oven to about 600°F (316°C). Quickly place the ring gear on the flywheel and tap it into place, making sure that it is fully seated.

✳✳ WARNING

Never heat the ring gear past 800°F (426°C), or the tempering will be destroyed.

6. Position the flywheel on the end of the crankshaft. Most flywheels will only attach to the crankshaft in one position, as the bolt holes are unevenly spaced and/or the crankshaft is fitted with a dowel pin. Install the bolts and tighten to specification using a criss-cross pattern.
7. Install the clutch or torque converter.
8. Install the transmission and transfer case.

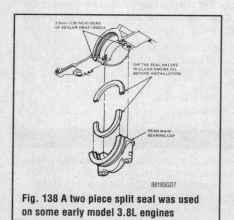

Fig. 138 A two piece split seal was used on some early model 3.8L engines

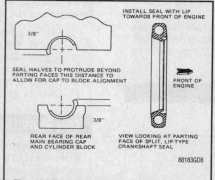

Fig. 139 Proper installation of the split-type rear main oil seal

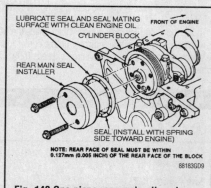

Fig. 140 One piece rear main oil seal installation—2.3L engine shown

EXHAUST SYSTEM

Inspection

▶ See Figures 141 thru 147

☞Safety glasses should be worn at all times when working on or near the exhaust system. Older exhaust systems will almost always be covered with loose rust particles which are more than a nuisance and could injure your eye.

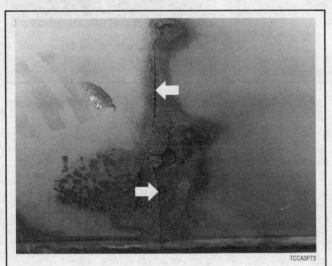

Fig. 141 Cracks in the muffler are a guaranteed leak

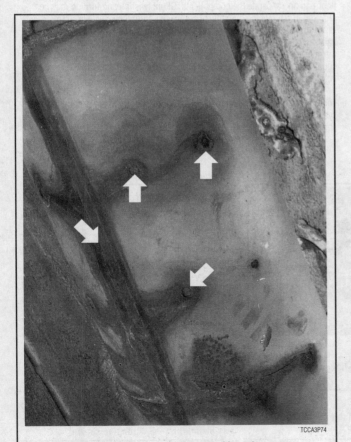

Fig. 142 Check the muffler for rotted spot welds and seams

✳✳ CAUTION

DO NOT perform exhaust repairs or inspection with the engine or exhaust hot. Allow the system to cool completely. Exhaust systems are noted for sharp edges, flaking metal and rusted bolts. Gloves and eye protection are required. A healthy supply of penetrating oil and rags is highly recommended.

Your vehicle must be raised and supported safely at four points to inspect the exhaust system properly. Start the inspection at the exhaust manifold where the header pipe is attached and work your way to the back of the vehicle. On dual exhaust systems, remember to inspect both sides of the vehicle. Check the complete exhaust system for open seams, holes, loose connections, or other deterioration which could permit exhaust fumes to seep into the passenger compartment. Inspect all mounting brackets and hangers for deterioration, some may have rubber O-rings that can become overstretched and non-supportive (and should be replaced if worn). Many technicians use a pointed tool to poke up into the exhaust system at rust spots to see whether or not they crumble. Most models have heat shield(s) covering certain parts of the exhaust system, it is often necessary to remove these shields to visually inspect those components.

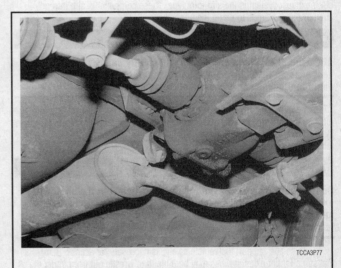

Fig. 143 Make sure the exhaust does contact the body or suspension

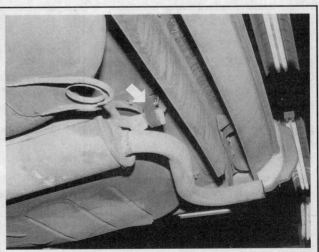

Fig. 144 Check for overstretched or torn exhaust hangers

Fig. 145 Example of a badly deteriorated exhaust pipe

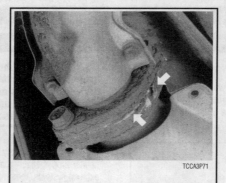

Fig. 146 Inspect flanges for gaskets that have deteriorated and need replacement

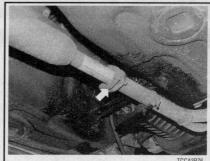

Fig. 147 Some systems, like this one, use large O-rings (donuts) in between the flanges

REPLACEMENT

▶ See Figures 148, 149 and 150

There are basically two types of exhaust systems. One is the flange type where the component ends are attached with bolts and a gasket in-between. The other exhaust system is the slip joint type. These components slip into one another using clamps to retain them together.

✳✳ CAUTION

Allow the exhaust system to cool sufficiently before spraying a solvent exhaust fasteners. Some solvents are highly flammable and could ignite when sprayed on hot exhaust components.

Before removing any component of the exhaust system, ALWAYS squirt a liquid rust dissolving agent onto the fasteners for ease of removal. A lot of knuckle skin will be saved by following this rule. It may even be wise to spray the fasteners and allow them to sit overnight.

✳✳ CAUTION

Do NOT perform exhaust repairs or inspection with the engine or exhaust hot. Allow the system to cool. Exhaust systems are noted for sharp edges, flaking metal and rusted bolts. Gloves and eye protection are required.

1. Raise and support the vehicle safely, as necessary for access. Remember that some longer exhaust pipes may be difficult to wrestle out from under the vehicle if it is not supported high enough.

2. If you haven't already, apply a generous amount of penetrating oil or solvent to any rusted fasteners.

3. On flange joints, carefully loosen and remove the retainers at the flange. If bolts or nuts are difficult to break loose, apply more penetrating liquid and give it some additional time to set. If the fasteners still will not come loose an impact driver may be necessary to jar it loose (and keep the fastener from breaking).

➡**When unbolting the headpipe from the manifold, make sure that the bolts are free before trying to remove them. If you snap a stud in the exhaust manifold, the stud will have to be removed with a bolt extractor, which often means removal of the manifold itself.**

4. On slip joint components, remove the mounting U-bolts from around the exhaust pipe you are extracting from the vehicle. Don't be surprised if the U-bolts break while removing the nuts.

5. Loosen the exhaust pipe from any mounting brackets retaining it to the floor pan and separate the components. Slight twisting and turning may be required to remove the component completely from the vehicle. You may need to tap on the component with a rubber mallet to loosen it. If all else fails, use a hacksaw to separate the parts. An oxy-acetylene cutting torch may be faster but the sparks are DANGEROUS near the fuel tank, and at the very least, accidents could happen, resulting in damage to the under-vehicle parts, not to mention yourself.

6. When installing exhaust components, you should loosely position all components before tightening any of the joints. Once you are certain that the system is run correctly, begin tightening the fasteners at the front of the vehicle and work your way back.

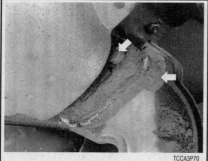

Fig. 148 Nuts and bolts will be extremely difficult to remove when deteriorated with rust

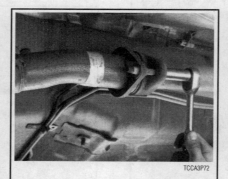

Fig. 149 Example of a flange type exhaust system joint

Fig. 150 Example of a common slip joint type system

ENGINE RECONDITIONING

Determining Engine Condition

Anything that generates heat and/or friction will eventually burn or wear out (for example, a light bulb generates heat, therefore its life span is limited). With this in mind, a running engine generates tremendous amounts of both; friction is encountered by the moving and rotating parts inside the engine and heat is created by friction and combustion of the fuel. However, the engine has systems designed to help reduce the effects of heat and friction and provide added longevity. The oiling system reduces the amount of friction encountered by the moving parts inside the engine, while the cooling system reduces heat created by friction and combustion. If either system is not maintained, a break-down will be inevitable. Therefore, you can see how regular maintenance can affect the service life of your vehicle. If you do not drain, flush and refill your cooling system at the proper intervals, deposits will begin to accumulate in the radiator, thereby reducing the amount of heat it can extract from the coolant. The same applies to your oil and filter; if it is not changed often enough it becomes laden with contaminates and is unable to properly lubricate the engine. This increases friction and wear.

There are a number of methods for evaluating the condition of your engine. A compression test can reveal the condition of your pistons, piston rings, cylinder bores, head gasket(s), valves and valve seats. An oil pressure test can warn you of possible engine bearing, or oil pump failures. Excessive oil consumption, evidence of oil in the engine air intake area and/or bluish smoke from the tailpipe may indicate worn piston rings, worn valve guides and/or valve seals. As a general rule, an engine that uses no more than one quart of oil every 1000 miles is in good condition. Engines that use one quart of oil or more in less than 1000 miles should first be checked for oil leaks. If any oil leaks are present, have them fixed before determining how much oil is consumed by the engine, especially if blue smoke is not visible at the tailpipe.

COMPRESSION TEST

◆ See Figure 151

A noticeable lack of engine power, excessive oil consumption and/or poor fuel mileage measured over an extended period are all indicators of internal engine wear. Worn piston rings, scored or worn cylinder bores, blown head gaskets, sticking or burnt valves, and worn valve seats are all possible culprits. A check of each cylinder's compression will help locate the problem.

➡A screw-in type compression gauge is more accurate than the type you simply hold against the spark plug hole. Although it takes slightly longer to use, it's worth the effort to obtain a more accurate reading.

1. Make sure that the proper amount and viscosity of engine oil is in the crankcase, then ensure the battery is fully charged.

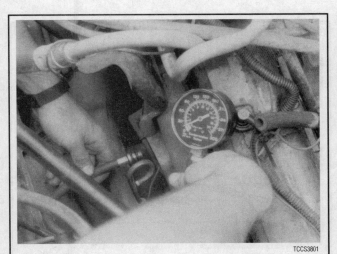

TCCS3801

Fig. 151 A screw-in type compression gauge is more accurate and easier to use without an assistant

2. Warm-up the engine to normal operating temperature, then shut the engine **OFF**.
3. Disable the ignition system.
4. Label and disconnect all of the spark plug wires from the plugs.
5. Thoroughly clean the cylinder head area around the spark plug ports, then remove the spark plugs.
6. Set the throttle plate to the fully open (wide-open throttle) position. You can block the accelerator linkage open for this, or you can have an assistant fully depress the accelerator pedal.
7. Install a screw-in type compression gauge into the No. 1 spark plug hole until the fitting is snug.

✳✳ WARNING

Be careful not to crossthread the spark plug hole.

8. According to the tool manufacturer's instructions, connect a remote starting switch to the starting circuit.
9. With the ignition switch in the **OFF** position, use the remote starting switch to crank the engine through at least five compression strokes (approximately 5 seconds of cranking) and record the highest reading on the gauge.
10. Repeat the test on each cylinder, cranking the engine approximately the same number of compression strokes and/or time as the first.
11. Compare the highest readings from each cylinder to that of the others. The indicated compression pressures are considered within specifications if the lowest reading cylinder is within 75 percent of the pressure recorded for the highest reading cylinder. For example, if your highest reading cylinder pressure was 150 psi (1034 kPa), then 75 percent of that would be 113 psi (779 kPa). So the lowest reading cylinder should be no less than 113 psi (779 kPa).
12. If a cylinder exhibits an unusually low compression reading, pour a tablespoon of clean engine oil into the cylinder through the spark plug hole and repeat the compression test. If the compression rises after adding oil, it means that the cylinder's piston rings and/or cylinder bore are damaged or worn. If the pressure remains low, the valves may not be seating properly (a valve job is needed), or the head gasket may be blown near that cylinder. If compression in any two adjacent cylinders is low, and if the addition of oil doesn't help raise compression, there is leakage past the head gasket. Oil and coolant in the combustion chamber, combined with blue or constant white smoke from the tailpipe, are symptoms of this problem. However, don't be alarmed by the normal white smoke emitted from the tailpipe during engine warm-up or from cold weather driving. There may be evidence of water droplets on the engine dipstick and/or oil droplets in the cooling system if a head gasket is blown.

OIL PRESSURE TEST

Check for proper oil pressure at the sending unit passage with an externally mounted mechanical oil pressure gauge (as opposed to relying on a factory installed dash-mounted gauge). A tachometer may also be needed, as some specifications may require running the engine at a specific rpm.

1. With the engine cold, locate and remove the oil pressure sending unit.
2. Following the manufacturer's instructions, connect a mechanical oil pressure gauge and, if necessary, a tachometer to the engine.
3. Start the engine and allow it to idle.
4. Check the oil pressure reading when cold and record the number. You may need to run the engine at a specified rpm, so check the specifications.
5. Run the engine until normal operating temperature is reached (upper radiator hose will feel warm).
6. Check the oil pressure reading again with the engine hot and record the number. Turn the engine **OFF**.
7. Compare your hot oil pressure reading to specification. If the reading is low, check the cold pressure reading against the chart. If the cold pressure is well above the specification, and the hot reading was lower than the specification, you may have the wrong viscosity oil in the engine. Change the oil, making sure to use the proper grade and quantity, then repeat the test.

Low oil pressure readings could be attributed to internal component wear, pump related problems, a low oil level, or oil viscosity that is too low. High oil pressure readings could be caused by an overfilled crankcase, too high of an oil viscosity or a faulty pressure relief valve.

Buy or Rebuild?

Now if you have determined that your engine is worn out, you must make some decisions. The question of whether or not an engine is worth rebuilding is largely a subjective matter and one of personal worth. Is the engine a popular one, or is it an obsolete model? Are parts available? Will it get acceptable gas mileage once it is rebuilt? Is the car it's being put into worth keeping? Would it be less expensive to buy a new engine, have your engine rebuilt by a pro, rebuild it yourself or buy a used engine from a salvage yard? Or would it be simpler and less expensive to buy another car? If you have considered all these matters, and have still decided to rebuild the engine, then it is time to decide how you will rebuild it.

➡The editors at Chilton feel that most engine machining should be performed by a professional machine shop. Think of it as an assurance that the job has been done right the first time. There are many expensive and specialized tools required to perform such tasks as boring and honing an engine block or having a valve job done on a cylinder head. Even inspecting the parts requires expensive micrometers and gauges to properly measure wear and clearances. A machine shop can deliver to you clean, and ready to assemble parts, saving you time and aggravation. Your maximum savings will come from performing the removal, disassembly, assembly and installation of the engine and purchasing or renting only the tools required to perform these tasks.

A complete rebuild or overhaul of an engine involves replacing all of the moving parts (pistons, rods, crankshaft, camshaft, etc.) with new ones and machining the non-moving wearing surfaces of the block and heads. Unfortunately, this may not be cost effective. For instance, your crankshaft may have been damaged or worn, but it can be machined undersize for a minimal fee.

So although you can replace everything inside the engine, it is usually wiser to replace only those parts which are really needed, and, if possible, repair the more expensive ones. Later in this section, we will break the engine down into its two main components: the cylinder head and the engine block. We will discuss each component, and the recommended parts to replace during a rebuild on each.

Engine Overhaul Tips

Most engine overhaul procedures are fairly standard. In addition to specific parts replacement procedures and specifications for your individual engine, this section is also a guide to acceptable rebuilding procedures. Examples of standard rebuilding practice are given and should be used along with specific details concerning your particular engine.

Competent and accurate machine shop services will ensure maximum performance, reliability and engine life. In most instances it is more profitable for the do-it-yourself mechanic to remove, clean and inspect the component, buy the necessary parts and deliver these to a shop for actual machine work.

Much of the assembly work (crankshaft, bearings, piston rods, and other components) is well within the scope of the do-it-yourself mechanic's tools and abilities. You will have to decide for yourself the depth of involvement you desire in an engine repair or rebuild.

TOOLS

The tools required for an engine overhaul or parts replacement will depend on the depth of your involvement. With a few exceptions, they will be the tools found in a mechanic's tool kit (see Section 1 of this manual). More in-depth work will require some or all of the following:
• A dial indicator (reading in thousandths) mounted on a universal base
• Micrometers and telescope gauges
• Jaw and screw-type pullers
• Scraper
• Valve spring compressor
• Ring groove cleaner
• Piston ring expander and compressor
• Ridge reamer
• Cylinder hone or glaze breaker
• Plastigage®
• Engine stand

The use of most of these tools is illustrated in this section. Many can be rented for a one-time use from a local parts jobber or tool supply house specializing in automotive work.

Occasionally, the use of special tools is called for. See the information on Special Tools and the Safety Notice in the front of this book before substituting another tool.

OVERHAUL TIPS

Aluminum has become extremely popular for use in engines, due to its low weight. Observe the following precautions when handling aluminum parts:
• Never hot tank aluminum parts (the caustic hot tank solution will eat the aluminum.)
• Remove all aluminum parts (identification tag, etc.) from engine parts prior to the tanking.
• Always coat threads lightly with engine oil or anti-seize compounds before installation, to prevent seizure.
• Never overtighten bolts or spark plugs especially in aluminum threads.

When assembling the engine, any parts that will be exposed to frictional contact must be prelubed to provide lubrication at initial start-up. Any product specifically formulated for this purpose can be used, but engine oil is not recommended as a prelube in most cases.

When semi-permanent (locked, but removable) installation of bolts or nuts is desired, threads should be cleaned and coated with Loctite® or another similar, commercial non-hardening sealant.

CLEANING

▶ See Figures 152 thru 155

Before the engine and its components are inspected, they must be thoroughly cleaned. You will need to remove any engine varnish, oil sludge and/or carbon deposits from all of the components to insure an accurate inspection. A crack in the engine block or cylinder head can easily become overlooked if hidden by a layer of sludge or carbon.

Most of the cleaning process can be carried out with common hand tools and readily available solvents or solutions. Carbon deposits can be chipped away using a hammer and a hard wooden chisel. Old gasket material and varnish or sludge can usually be removed using a scraper and/or cleaning solvent. Extremely stubborn deposits may require the use of a power drill with a wire brush. If using a wire brush, use extreme care around any critical machined surfaces (such as the gasket surfaces, bearing saddles, cylinder bores, etc.). USE OF A WIRE BRUSH IS NOT RECOMMENDED ON ANY ALUMINUM COMPONENTS. Always follow any safety recommendations given by the manufacturer of the tool and/or solvent.

✳✳ CAUTION

Always wear eye protection during any cleaning process involving scraping, chipping or spraying of solvents.

TCCS3132

Fig. 152 Use a gasket scraper to remove the old gasket material from the mating surfaces

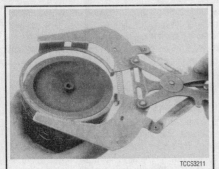

Fig. 153 Before cleaning and inspection, use a ring expander tool to remove the piston rings

Fig. 154 Clean the piston ring grooves using a ring groove cleaner tool, or . . .

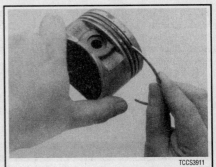

Fig. 155 . . . use a piece of an old ring to clean the grooves. Be careful, the ring can be quite sharp

An alternative to the mess and hassle of cleaning the parts yourself is to drop them off at a local garage or machine shop. They should have the necessary equipment to properly clean all of the parts for a nominal fee.

Remove any oil galley plugs, freeze plugs and/or pressed-in bearings and carefully wash and degrease all of the engine components including the fasteners and bolts. Small parts such as the valves, springs, etc., should be placed in a metal basket and allowed to soak. Use pipe cleaner type brushes, and clean all passageways in the components.

Use a ring expander and remove the rings from the pistons. Clean the piston ring grooves with a special tool or a piece of broken ring. Scrape the carbon off of the top of the piston. You should never use a wire brush on the pistons. After preparing all of the piston assemblies in this manner, wash and degrease them again.

✳✳ WARNING

Use extreme care when cleaning around the cylinder head valve seats. A mistake or slip may cost you a new seat.

When cleaning the cylinder head, remove carbon from the combustion chamber with the valves installed. This will avoid damaging the valve seats.

REPAIRING DAMAGED THREADS

◗ **See Figures 156, 157, 158, 159 and 160**

Several methods of repairing damaged threads are available. Heli-Coil® (shown here), Keenserts® and Microdot® are among the most widely used. All involve basically the same principle—drilling out stripped threads, tapping the hole and installing a prewound insert—making welding, plugging and oversize fasteners unnecessary.

Two types of thread repair inserts are usually supplied: a standard type for most inch coarse, inch fine, metric course and metric fine thread sizes and a spark lug type to fit most spark plug port sizes. Consult the individual tool manufacturer's catalog to determine exact applications. Typical thread repair kits will contain a selection of prewound threaded inserts, a tap (corresponding to the

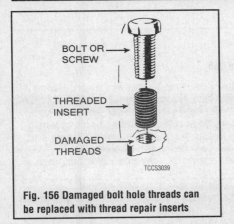

Fig. 156 Damaged bolt hole threads can be replaced with thread repair inserts

Fig. 157 Standard thread repair insert (left), and spark plug thread insert

Fig. 158 Drill out the damaged threads with the specified size bit. Be sure to drill completely through the hole or to the bottom of a blind hole

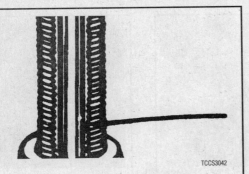

Fig. 159 Using the kit, tap the hole in order to receive the thread insert. Keep the tap well oiled and back it out frequently to avoid clogging the threads

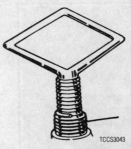

Fig. 160 Screw the insert onto the installer tool until the tang engages the slot. Thread the insert into the hole until it is ¼–½ turn below the top surface, then remove the tool and break off the tang using a punch

outside diameter threads of the insert) and an installation tool. Spark plug inserts usually differ because they require a tap equipped with pilot threads and a combined reamer/tap section. Most manufacturers also supply blister-packed thread repair inserts separately in addition to a master kit containing a variety of taps and inserts plus installation tools.

Before attempting to repair a threaded hole, remove any snapped, broken or damaged bolts or studs. Penetrating oil can be used to free frozen threads. The offending item can usually be removed with locking pliers or using a screw/stud extractor. After the hole is clear, the thread can be repaired as shown in the kit manufacturer's instructions.

Engine Preparation

To properly rebuild an engine, you must first remove it from the vehicle, then disassemble and diagnose it. Ideally you should place your engine on an engine stand. This affords you the best access to the engine components. Remove the flywheel or flexplate before installing the engine to the stand.

Now that you have the engine on a stand, and assuming that you have drained the oil and coolant from the engine, it's time to strip it of all but the necessary components. Before you start disassembling the engine, you may want to take a moment to draw some pictures, or fabricate some labels or containers to mark the locations of various components and the bolts and/or studs which fasten them. Modern day engines use a lot of little brackets and clips which hold wiring harnesses and such, and these holders are often mounted on studs and/or bolts that can be easily mixed up. The manufacturer spent a lot of time and money designing your vehicle, and they wouldn't have wasted any of it by haphazardly placing brackets, clips or fasteners on the vehicle. If it's present when you disassemble it, put it back when you assemble, you will regret not remembering that little bracket which holds a wire harness out of the path of a rotating part.

You should begin by unbolting any accessories still attached to the engine, such as the water pump, power steering pump, alternator, etc. Then, unfasten any manifolds (intake or exhaust) which were not removed during the engine removal procedure. Finally, remove any covers remaining on the engine such as the rocker arm, front or timing cover and oil pan. Some front covers may require the vibration damper and/or crank pulley to be removed beforehand. The idea is to reduce the engine to the bare necessities of cylinder head(s), valve train, engine block, crankshaft, pistons and connecting rods, plus any other ëin blockí components such as oil pumps, balance shafts and auxiliary shafts.

Finally, remove the cylinder head(s) from the engine block and carefully place on a bench. Disassembly instructions for each component follow later in this section.

Cylinder Head

There are two basic types of cylinder heads used on today's automobiles: the Overhead Valve (OHV) and the Overhead Camshaft (OHC). The latter can also be broken down into two subgroups: the Single Overhead Camshaft (SOHC) and the Dual Overhead Camshaft (DOHC). Generally, if there is only a single camshaft on a head, it is just referred to as an OHC head. Also, an engine with an OHV cylinder head is also known as a pushrod engine.

Most cylinder heads these days are made of an aluminum alloy due to its light weight, durability and heat transfer qualities. However, cast iron was the material of choice in the past, and is still used on many vehicles. Whether made from aluminum or iron, all cylinder heads have valves and seats. Some use two valves per cylinder, while the more hi-tech engines will utilize a multi-valve configuration using 3, 4 and even 5 valves per cylinder. When the valve contacts the seat, it does so on precision machined surfaces, which seals the combustion chamber. All cylinder heads have a valve guide for each valve. The guide centers the valve to the seat and allows it to move up and down within it. The clearance between the valve and guide can be critical. Too much clearance and the engine may consume oil, lose vacuum and/or damage the seat. Too little, and the valve can stick in the guide causing the engine to run poorly if at all, and possibly causing severe damage. The last component all automotive cylinder heads have are valve springs. The spring holds the valve against its seat. It also returns the valve to this position when the valve has been opened by the valve train or camshaft. The spring is fastened to the valve by a retainer and valve locks (sometimes called keepers). Aluminum heads will also have a valve spring shim to keep the spring from wearing away the aluminum.

An ideal method of rebuilding the cylinder head would involve replacing all of the valves, guides, seats, springs, etc. with new ones. However, depending on how the engine was maintained, often this is not necessary. A major cause of valve, guide and seat wear is an improperly tuned engine. An engine that is running too rich, will often wash the lubricating oil out of the guide with gasoline, causing it to wear rapidly. Conversely, an engine which is running too lean will place higher combustion temperatures on the valves and seats allowing them to wear or even burn. Springs fall victim to the driving habits of the individual. A driver who often runs the engine rpm to the redline will wear out or break the springs faster then one that stays well below it. Unfortunately, mileage takes it toll on all of the parts. Generally, the valves, guides, springs and seats in a cylinder head can be machined and re-used, saving you money. However, if a valve is burnt, it may be wise to replace all of the valves, since they were all operating in the same environment. The same goes for any other component on the cylinder head. Think of it as an insurance policy against future problems related to that component.

Unfortunately, the only way to find out which components need replacing, is to disassemble and carefully check each piece. After the cylinder head(s) are disassembled, thoroughly clean all of the components.

DISASSEMBLY

OHV Heads

▶ See Figures 161 thru 166

Before disassembling the cylinder head, you may want to fabricate some containers to hold the various parts, as some of them can be quite small (such as keepers) and easily lost. Also keeping yourself and the components organized will aid in assembly and reduce confusion. Where possible, try to maintain a components original location; this is especially important if there is not going to be any machine work performed on the components.

1. If you haven't already removed the rocker arms and/or shafts, do so now.
2. Position the head so that the springs are easily accessed.
3. Use a valve spring compressor tool, and relieve spring tension from the retainer.

TCCS3137

Fig. 161 When removing an OHV valve spring, use a compressor tool to relieve the tension from the retainer

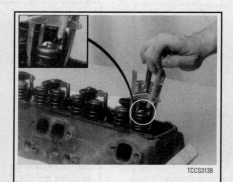

TCCS3138

Fig. 162 A small magnet will help in removal of the valve locks

TCCS3139

Fig. 163 Be careful not to lose the small valve locks (keepers)

Fig. 164 Remove the valve seal from the valve stem—O-ring type seal shown

Fig. 165 Removing an umbrella/positive type seal

Fig. 166 Invert the cylinder head and withdraw the valve from the valve guide bore

➡**Due to engine varnish, the retainer may stick to the valve locks. A gentle tap with a hammer may help to break it loose.**

4. Remove the valve locks from the valve tip and/or retainer. A small magnet may help in removing the locks.

5. Lift the valve spring, tool and all, off of the valve stem.

6. If equipped, remove the valve seal. If the seal is difficult to remove with the valve in place, try removing the valve first, then the seal. Follow the steps below for valve removal.

7. Position the head to allow access for withdrawing the valve.

➡**Cylinder heads that have seen a lot of miles and/or abuse may have mushroomed the valve lock grove and/or tip, causing difficulty in removal of the valve. If this has happened, use a metal file to carefully remove the high spots around the lock grooves and/or tip. Only file it enough to allow removal.**

8. Remove the valve from the cylinder head.

9. If equipped, remove the valve spring shim. A small magnetic tool or screwdriver will aid in removal.

10. Repeat Steps 3 though 9 until all of the valves have been removed.

OHC Heads

▸ **See Figures 167 and 168**

Whether it is a single or dual overhead camshaft cylinder head, the disassembly procedure is relatively unchanged. One aspect to pay attention to is careful labeling of the parts on the dual camshaft cylinder head. There will be an intake camshaft and followers as well as an exhaust camshaft and followers and they must be labeled as such. In some cases, the components are identical and could easily be installed incorrectly. DO NOT MIX THEM UP! Determining which is which is very simple; the intake camshaft and components are on the same side of the head as was the intake manifold. Conversely, the exhaust camshaft and components are on the same side of the head as was the exhaust manifold.

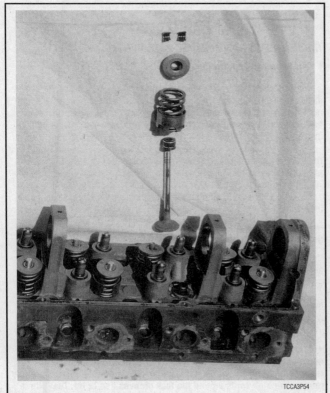

Fig. 167 Exploded view of a valve, seal, spring, retainer and locks from an OHC cylinder head

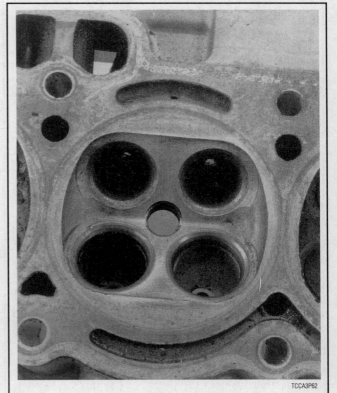

Fig. 168 Example of a multi-valve cylinder head. Note how it has 2 intake and 2 exhaust valve ports

CUP TYPE CAMSHAFT FOLLOWERS

♦ **See Figures 169, 170 and 171**

Most cylinder heads with cup type camshaft followers will have the valve spring, retainer and locks recessed within the follower's bore. You will need a C-clamp style valve spring compressor tool, an OHC spring removal tool (or equivalent) and a small magnet to disassemble the head.

1. If not already removed, remove the camshaft(s) and/or followers. Mark their positions for assembly.
2. Position the cylinder head to allow use of a C-clamp style valve spring compressor tool.

➡**It is preferred to position the cylinder head gasket surface facing you with the valve springs facing the opposite direction and the head laying horizontal.**

3. With the OHC spring removal adapter tool positioned inside of the follower bore, compress the valve spring using the C-clamp style valve spring compressor.
4. Remove the valve locks. A small magnetic tool or screwdriver will aid in removal.
5. Release the compressor tool and remove the spring assembly.
6. Withdraw the valve from the cylinder head.
7. If equipped, remove the valve seal.

➡**Special valve seal removal tools are available. Regular or needlenose type pliers, if used with care, will work just as well. If using ordinary pliers, be sure not to damage the follower bore. The follower and its bore are machined to close tolerances and any damage to the bore will effect this relationship.**

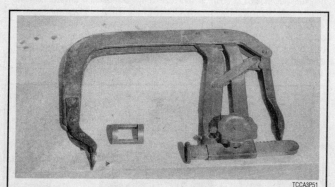

Fig. 169 C-clamp type spring compressor and an OHC spring removal tool (center) for cup type followers

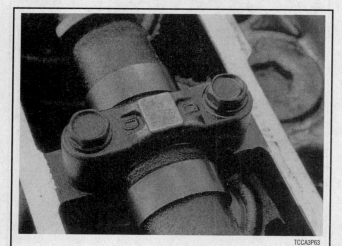

Fig. 170 Most cup type follower cylinder heads retain the camshaft using bolt-on bearing caps

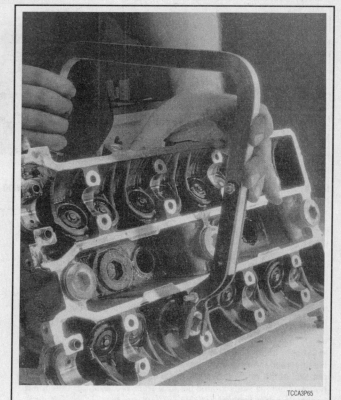

Fig. 171 Position the OHC spring tool in the follower bore, then compress the spring with a C-clamp type tool

8. If equipped, remove the valve spring shim. A small magnetic tool or screwdriver will aid in removal.
9. Repeat Steps 3 through 8 until all of the valves have been removed.

ROCKER ARM TYPE CAMSHAFT FOLLOWERS

♦ **See Figures 172 thru 180**

Most cylinder heads with rocker arm-type camshaft followers are easily disassembled using a standard valve spring compressor. However, certain models may not have enough open space around the spring for the standard tool and may require you to use a C-clamp style compressor tool instead.

1. If not already removed, remove the rocker arms and/or shafts and the camshaft. If applicable, also remove the hydraulic lash adjusters. Mark their positions for assembly.
2. Position the cylinder head to allow access to the valve spring.
3. Use a valve spring compressor tool to relieve the spring tension from the retainer.

➡**Due to engine varnish, the retainer may stick to the valve locks. A gentle tap with a hammer may help to break it loose.**

4. Remove the valve locks from the valve tip and/or retainer. A small magnet may help in removing the small locks.
5. Lift the valve spring, tool and all, off of the valve stem.
6. If equipped, remove the valve seal. If the seal is difficult to remove with the valve in place, try removing the valve first, then the seal. Follow the steps below for valve removal.
7. Position the head to allow access for withdrawing the valve.

➡**Cylinder heads that have seen a lot of miles and/or abuse may have mushroomed the valve lock grove and/or tip, causing difficulty in removal of the valve. If this has happened, use a metal file to carefully remove the high spots around the lock grooves and/or tip. Only file it enough to allow removal.**

8. Remove the valve from the cylinder head.

Fig. 172 Example of the shaft mounted rocker arms on some OHC heads

Fig. 173 Another example of the rocker arm type OHC head. This model uses a follower under the camshaft

Fig. 174 Before the camshaft can be removed, all of the followers must first be removed . . .

Fig. 175 . . . then the camshaft can be removed by sliding it out (shown), or unbolting a bearing cap (not shown)

Fig. 176 Compress the valve spring . . .

Fig. 177 . . . then remove the valve locks from the valve stem and spring retainer

Fig. 178 Remove the valve spring and retainer from the cylinder head

Fig. 179 Remove the valve seal from the guide. Some gentle prying or pliers may help to remove stubborn ones

Fig. 180 All aluminum and some cast iron heads will have these valve spring shims. Remove all of them as well

9. If equipped, remove the valve spring shim. A small magnetic tool or screwdriver will aid in removal.

10. Repeat Steps 3 though 9 until all of the valves have been removed.

INSPECTION

Now that all of the cylinder head components are clean, itís time to inspect them for wear and/or damage. To accurately inspect them, you will need some specialized tools:

- A 0–1 in. micrometer for the valves
- A dial indicator or inside diameter gauge for the valve guides
- A spring pressure test gauge

If you do not have access to the proper tools, you may want to bring the components to a shop that does.

Valves

▶ See Figures 181 and 182

The first thing to inspect are the valve heads. Look closely at the head, margin and face for any cracks, excessive wear or burning. The margin is the best place to look for burning. It should have a squared edge with an even width all around the diameter. When a valve burns, the margin will look melted and the edges rounded. Also inspect the valve head for any signs of tulipping. This will show as a lifting of the edges or dishing in the center of the head and will usually not occur to all of the valves. All of the heads should look the same, any that seem dished more than others are probably bad. Next, inspect the valve lock grooves and valve tips. Check for any burrs around the lock grooves, especially if you had to file them to remove the valve. Valve tips should appear flat, although slight rounding with high mileage engines is normal. Slightly worn valve tips will need to be machined flat. Last, measure the valve stem diameter with the micrometer.

Measure the area that rides within the guide, especially towards the tip where most of the wear occurs. Take several measurements along its length and compare them to each other. Wear should be even along the length with little to no taper. If no minimum diameter is given in the specifications, then the stem should not read more than 0.001 in. (0.025mm) below the unworn portion of the stem. Any valves that fail these inspections should be replaced.

Springs, Retainers and Valve Locks

▶ See Figures 183 and 184

The first thing to check is the most obvious, broken springs. Next check the free length and squareness of each spring. If applicable, insure to distinguish between intake and exhaust springs. Use a ruler and/or carpenterís square to measure the length. A carpenterís square should be used to check the springs for squareness. If a spring pressure test gauge is available, check each springs rating and compare to the specifications chart. Check the readings against the specifications given. Any springs that fail these inspections should be replaced.

The spring retainers rarely need replacing, however they should still be checked as a precaution. Inspect the spring mating surface and the valve lock retention area for any signs of excessive wear. Also check for any signs of cracking. Replace any retainers that are questionable.

Valve locks should be inspected for excessive wear on the outside contact area as well as on the inner notched surface. Any locks which appear worn or broken and its respective valve should be replaced.

Cylinder Head

There are several things to check on the cylinder head: valve guides, seats, cylinder head surface flatness, cracks and physical damage.

VALVE GUIDES

▶ See Figure 185

Now that you know the valves are good, you can use them to check the guides, although a new valve, if available, is preferred. Before you measure any-thing, look at the guides carefully and inspect them for any cracks, chips or breakage. Also if the guide is a removable style (as in most aluminum heads), check them for any looseness or evidence of movement. All of the guides should appear to be at the same height from the spring seat. If any seem lower (or higher) from another, the guide has moved. Mount a dial indicator onto the spring side of the cylinder head. Lightly oil the valve stem and insert it into the cylinder head. Position the dial indicator against the valve stem near the tip and zero the gauge. Grasp the valve stem and wiggle towards and away from the dial indicator and observe the readings. Mount the dial indicator 90 degrees from the initial point and zero the gauge and again take a reading. Compare the two readings for an out of round condition. Check the readings against the specifications given. An Inside Diameter (I.D.) gauge designed for valve guides will give you an accurate valve guide bore measurement. If the I.D. gauge is used, compare the readings with the specifications given. Any guides that fail these inspections should be replaced or machined.

VALVE SEATS

A visual inspection of the valve seats should show a slightly worn and pitted surface where the valve face contacts the seat. Inspect the seat carefully for severe pitting or cracks. Also, a seat that is badly worn will be recessed into the cylinder head. A severely worn or recessed seat may need to be replaced. All cracked seats must be replaced. A seat concentricity gauge, if available, should be used to check the seat run-out. If run-out exceeds specifications the seat must be machined (if no specification is available given use 0.002 in. or 0.051mm).

CYLINDER HEAD SURFACE FLATNESS

▶ See Figures 186 and 187

After you have cleaned the gasket surface of the cylinder head of any old gasket material, check the head for flatness.

Place a straightedge across the gasket surface. Using feeler gauges, determine the clearance at the center of the straightedge and across the cylinder head at several points. Check along the centerline and diagonally on the head sur-

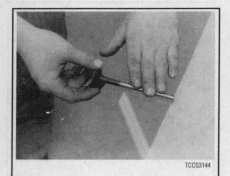

TCCS3144

Fig. 181 Valve stems may be rolled on a flat surface to check for bends

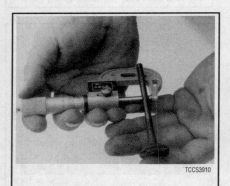

TCCS3910

Fig. 182 Use a micrometer to check the valve stem diameter

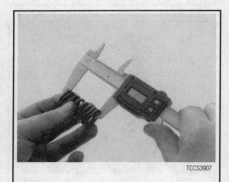

TCCS3907

Fig. 183 Use a caliper to check the valve spring free-length

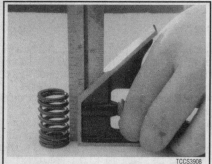

TCCS3908

Fig. 184 Check the valve spring for squareness on a flat surface; a carpenterís square can be used

TCCS3142

Fig. 185 A dial gauge may be used to check valve stem-to-guide clearance; read the gauge while moving the valve stem

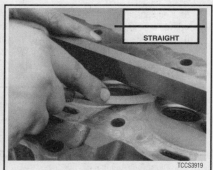

STRAIGHT

TCCS3919

Fig. 186 Check the head for flatness across the center of the head surface using a straightedge and feeler gauge

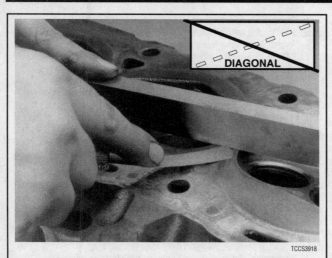

TCCS3918

Fig. 187 Checks should also be made along both diagonals of the head surface

face. If the warpage exceeds 0.003 in. (0.076mm) within a 6.0 in. (15.2cm) span, or 0.006 in. (0.152mm) over the total length of the head, the cylinder head must be resurfaced. After resurfacing the heads of a V-type engine, the intake manifold flange surface should be checked, and if necessary, milled proportionally to allow for the change in its mounting position.

CRACKS AND PHYSICAL DAMAGE

Generally, cracks are limited to the combustion chamber, however, it is not uncommon for the head to crack in a spark plug hole, port, outside of the head or in the valve spring/rocker arm area. The first area to inspect is always the hottest: the exhaust seat/port area.

A visual inspection should be performed, but just because you donít see a crack does not mean it is not there. Some more reliable methods for inspecting for cracks include Magnaflux®, a magnetic process or Zyglo®, a dye penetrant. Magnaflux® is used only on ferrous metal (cast iron) heads. Zyglo® uses a spray on fluorescent mixture along with a black light to reveal the cracks. It is strongly recommended to have your cylinder head checked professionally for cracks, especially if the engine was known to have overheated and/or leaked or consumed coolant. Contact a local shop for availability and pricing of these services.

Physical damage is usually very evident. For example, a broken mounting ear from dropping the head or a bent or broken stud and/or bolt. All of these defects should be fixed or, if unrepairable, the head should be replaced.

Camshaft and Followers

Inspect the camshaft(s) and followers as described earlier in this section.

REFINISHING & REPAIRING

Many of the procedures given for refinishing and repairing the cylinder head components must be performed by a machine shop. Certain steps, if the inspected part is not worn, can be performed yourself inexpensively. However, you spent a lot of time and effort so far, why risk trying to save a couple bucks if you might have to do it all over again?

Valves

Any valves that were not replaced should be refaced and the tips ground flat. Unless you have access to a valve grinding machine, this should be done by a machine shop. If the valves are in extremely good condition, as well as the valve seats and guides, they may be lapped in without performing machine work.

It is a recommended practice to lap the valves even after machine work has been performed and/or new valves have been purchased. This insures a positive seal between the valve and seat.

LAPPING THE VALVES

➥Before lapping the valves to the seats, read the rest of the cylinder head section to insure that any related parts are in acceptable enough condition to continue. Also, remember that before any valve seat machining and/or lapping can be performed, the guides must be within factory recommended specifications.

1. Invert the cylinder head.
2. Lightly lubricate the valve stems and insert them into the cylinder head in their numbered order.
3. Raise the valve from the seat and apply a small amount of fine lapping compound to the seat.
4. Moisten the suction head of a hand-lapping tool and attach it to the head of the valve.
5. Rotate the tool between the palms of both hands, changing the position of the valve on the valve seat and lifting the tool often to prevent grooving.
6. Lap the valve until a smooth, polished circle is evident on the valve and seat.
7. Remove the tool and the valve. Wipe away all traces of the grinding compound and store the valve to maintain its lapped location.

✳✷ WARNING

Do not get the valves out of order after they have been lapped. They must be put back with the same valve seat with which they were lapped.

Springs, Retainers and Valve Locks

There is no repair or refinishing possible with the springs, retainers and valve locks. If they are found to be worn or defective, they must be replaced with new (or known good) parts.

Cylinder Head

Most refinishing procedures dealing with the cylinder head must be performed by a machine shop. Read the sections below and review your inspection data to determine whether or not machining is necessary.

VALVE GUIDE

➥If any machining or replacements are made to the valve guides, the seats must be machined.

Unless the valve guides need machining or replacing, the only service to perform is to thoroughly clean them of any dirt or oil residue.

There are only two types of valve guides used on automobile engines: the replaceable-type (all aluminum heads) and the cast-in integral-type (most cast iron heads). There are four recommended methods for repairing worn guides.
- Knurling
- Inserts
- Reaming oversize
- Replacing

Knurling is a process in which metal is displaced and raised, thereby reducing clearance, giving a true center, and providing oil control. It is the least expensive way of repairing the valve guides. However, it is not necessarily the best, and in some cases, a knurled valve guide will not stand up for more than a short time. It requires a special knurlizer and precision reaming tools to obtain proper clearances. It would not be cost effective to purchase these tools, unless you plan on rebuilding several of the same cylinder head.

Installing a guide insert involves machining the guide to accept a bronze insert. One style is the coil-type which is installed into a threaded guide. Another is the thin-walled insert where the guide is reamed oversize to accept a split-sleeve insert. After the insert is installed, a special tool is then run through the guide to expand the insert, locking it to the guide. The insert is then reamed to the standard size for proper valve clearance.

Reaming for oversize valves restores normal clearances and provides a true valve seat. Most cast-in type guides can be reamed to accept an valve with an oversize stem. The cost factor for this can become quite high as you will need to purchase the reamer and new, oversize stem valves for all guides which were reamed. Oversizes are generally 0.003–0.030 in. (0.076–0.762mm), with 0.015 in. (0.381mm) being the most common.

To replace cast-in type valve guides, they must be drilled out, then reamed to accept replacement guides. This must be done on a fixture which will allow centering and leveling off of the original valve seat or guide, otherwise a serious guide-to-seat misalignment may occur making it impossible to properly machine the seat.

Replaceable-type guides are pressed into the cylinder head. A hammer and a stepped drift or punch may be used to install and remove the guides. Before removing the guides, measure the protrusion on the spring side of the head and record it for installation. Use the stepped drift to hammer out the old guide from the combustion chamber side of the head. When installing, determine whether or not the guide also seals a water jacket in the head, and if it does, use the recommended sealing agent. If there is no water jacket, grease the valve guide and its bore. Use the stepped drift, and hammer the new guide into the cylinder head from the spring side of the cylinder head. A stack of washers the same thickness as the measured protrusion may help the installation process.

VALVE SEATS

➡**Before any valve seat machining can be performed, the guides must be within factory recommended specifications. If any machining occurred or if replacements were made to the valve guides, the seats must be machined.**

If the seats are in good condition, the valves can be lapped to the seats, and the cylinder head assembled. See the valves section for instructions on lapping.

If the valve seats are worn, cracked or damaged, they must be serviced by a machine shop. The valve seat must be perfectly centered to the valve guide, which requires very accurate machining.

CYLINDER HEAD SURFACE

If the cylinder head is warped, it must be machined flat. If the warpage is extremely severe, the head may need to be replaced. In some instances, it may be possible to straighten a warped head enough to allow machining. In either case, contact a professional machine shop for service.

➡**Any OHC cylinder head that shows excessive warpage should have the camshaft bearing journals align bored after the cylinder head has been resurfaced.**

✳✳ WARNING

Failure to align bore the camshaft bearing journals could result in severe engine damage including but not limited to: valve and piston damage, connecting rod damage, camshaft and/or crankshaft breakage.

CRACKS AND PHYSICAL DAMAGE

Certain cracks can be repaired in both cast iron and aluminum heads. For cast iron, a tapered threaded insert is installed along the length of the crack. Aluminum can also use the tapered inserts, however welding is the preferred method. Some physical damage can be repaired through brazing or welding. Contact a machine shop to get expert advice for your particular dilemma.

ASSEMBLY

The first step for any assembly job is to have a clean area in which to work. Next, thoroughly clean all of the parts and components that are to be assembled. Finally, place all of the components onto a suitable work space and, if necessary, arrange the parts to their respective positions.

OHV Engines

1. Lightly lubricate the valve stems and insert all of the valves into the cylinder head. If possible, maintain their original locations.
2. If equipped, install any valve spring shims which were removed.
3. If equipped, install the new valve seals, keeping the following in mind:
   • If the valve seal presses over the guide, lightly lubricate the outer guide surfaces.
   • If the seal is an O-ring type, it is installed just after compressing the spring but before the valve locks.

4. Place the valve spring and retainer over the stem.
5. Position the spring compressor tool and compress the spring.
6. Assemble the valve locks to the stem.
7. Relieve the spring pressure slowly and insure that neither valve lock becomes dislodged by the retainer.
8. Remove the spring compressor tool.
9. Repeat Steps 2 through 8 until all of the springs have been installed.

OHC Engines

▶ **See Figure 188**

CUP TYPE CAMSHAFT FOLLOWERS

To install the springs, retainers and valve locks on heads which have these components recessed into the camshaft follower's bore, you will need a small screwdriver-type tool, some clean white grease and a lot of patience. You will also need the C-clamp style spring compressor and the OHC tool used to disassemble the head.

1. Lightly lubricate the valve stems and insert all of the valves into the cylinder head. If possible, maintain their original locations.
2. If equipped, install any valve spring shims which were removed.
3. If equipped, install the new valve seals, keeping the following in mind:
   • If the valve seal presses over the guide, lightly lubricate the outer guide surfaces.
   • If the seal is an O-ring type, it is installed just after compressing the spring but before the valve locks.
4. Place the valve spring and retainer over the stem.
5. Position the spring compressor and the OHC tool, then compress the spring.
6. Using a small screwdriver as a spatula, fill the valve stem side of the lock with white grease. Use the excess grease on the screwdriver to fasten the lock to the driver.
7. Carefully install the valve lock, which is stuck to the end of the screwdriver, to the valve stem then press on it with the screwdriver until the grease squeezes out. The valve lock should now be stuck to the stem.
8. Repeat Steps 6 and 7 for the remaining valve lock.
9. Relieve the spring pressure slowly and insure that neither valve lock becomes dislodged by the retainer.
10. Remove the spring compressor tool.
11. Repeat Steps 2 through 10 until all of the springs have been installed.
12. Install the followers, camshaft(s) and any other components that were removed for disassembly.

ROCKER ARM TYPE CAMSHAFT FOLLOWERS

1. Lightly lubricate the valve stems and insert all of the valves into the cylinder head. If possible, maintain their original locations.
2. If equipped, install any valve spring shims which were removed.
3. If equipped, install the new valve seals, keeping the following in mind:

TCCA3P64

Fig. 188 Once assembled, check the valve clearance and correct as needed

- If the valve seal presses over the guide, lightly lubricate the outer guide surfaces.
- If the seal is an O-ring type, it is installed just after compressing the spring but before the valve locks.

4. Place the valve spring and retainer over the stem.

5. Position the spring compressor tool and compress the spring.

6. Assemble the valve locks to the stem.

7. Relieve the spring pressure slowly and insure that neither valve lock becomes dislodged by the retainer.

8. Remove the spring compressor tool.

9. Repeat Steps 2 through 8 until all of the springs have been installed.

10. Install the camshaft(s), rockers, shafts and any other components that were removed for disassembly.

Engine Block

GENERAL INFORMATION

A thorough overhaul or rebuild of an engine block would include replacing the pistons, rings, bearings, timing belt/chain assembly and oil pump. For OHV engines also include a new camshaft and lifters. The block would then have the cylinders bored and honed oversize (or if using removable cylinder sleeves, new sleeves installed) and the crankshaft would be cut undersize to provide new wearing surfaces and perfect clearances. However, your particular engine may not have everything worn out. What if only the piston rings have worn out and the clearances on everything else are still within factory specifications? Well, you could just replace the rings and put it back together, but this would be a very rare example. Chances are, if one component in your engine is worn, other components are sure to follow, and soon. At the very least, you should always replace the rings, bearings and oil pump. This is what is commonly called a "freshen up".

Cylinder Ridge Removal

Because the top piston ring does not travel to the very top of the cylinder, a ridge is built up between the end of the travel and the top of the cylinder bore.

Pushing the piston and connecting rod assembly past the ridge can be difficult, and damage to the piston ring lands could occur. If the ridge is not removed before installing a new piston or not removed at all, piston ring breakage and piston damage may occur.

➡It is always recommended that you remove any cylinder ridges before removing the piston and connecting rod assemblies. If you know that new pistons are going to be installed and the engine block will be bored oversize, you may be able to forego this step. However, some ridges may actually prevent the assemblies from being removed, necessitating its removal.

There are several different types of ridge reamers on the market, none of which are inexpensive. Unless a great deal of engine rebuilding is anticipated, borrow or rent a reamer.

1. Turn the crankshaft until the piston is at the bottom of its travel.

2. Cover the head of the piston with a rag.

3. Follow the tool manufacturers instructions and cut away the ridge, exercising extreme care to avoid cutting too deeply.

4. Remove the ridge reamer, the rag and as many of the cuttings as possible. Continue until all of the cylinder ridges have been removed.

DISASSEMBLY

▶ See Figures 189 and 190

The engine disassembly instructions following assume that you have the engine mounted on an engine stand. If not, it is easiest to disassemble the engine on a bench or the floor with it resting on the bell housing or transmission mounting surface. You must be able to access the connecting rod fasteners and turn the crankshaft during disassembly. Also, all engine covers (timing, front, side, oil pan, whatever) should have already been removed. Engines which are seized or locked up may not be able to be completely disassembled, and a core (salvage yard) engine should be purchased.

TCCS3803

Fig. 189 Place rubber hose over the connecting rod studs to protect the crankshaft and cylinder bores from damage

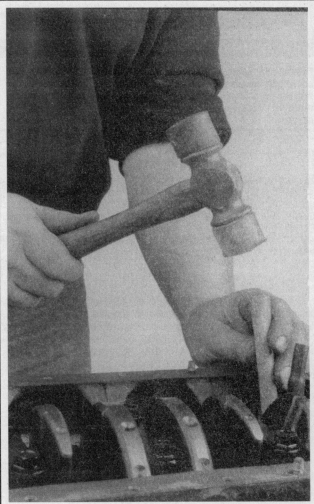

TCCS3804

Fig. 190 Carefully tap the piston out of the bore using a wooden dowel

Pushrod Engines

If not done during the cylinder head removal, remove the pushrods and lifters, keeping them in order for assembly. Remove the timing gears and/or timing chain assembly, then remove the oil pump drive assembly and withdraw the camshaft from the engine block. Remove the oil pick-up and pump assembly. If equipped, remove any balance or auxiliary shafts. If necessary, remove the cylinder ridge from the top of the bore. See the cylinder ridge removal procedure earlier in this section.

OHC Engines

If not done during the cylinder head removal, remove the timing chain/belt and/or gear/sprocket assembly. Remove the oil pick-up and pump assembly and, if necessary, the pump drive. If equipped, remove any balance or auxiliary shafts. If necessary, remove the cylinder ridge from the top of the bore. See the cylinder ridge removal procedure earlier in this section.

All Engines

Rotate the engine over so that the crankshaft is exposed. Use a number punch or scribe and mark each connecting rod with its respective cylinder number. The cylinder closest to the front of the engine is always number 1. However, depending on the engine placement, the front of the engine could either be the flywheel or damper/pulley end. Generally the front of the engine faces the front of the vehicle. Use a number punch or scribe and also mark the main bearing caps from front to rear with the front most cap being number 1 (if there are five caps, mark them 1 through 5, front to rear).

✳✳ WARNING

Take special care when pushing the connecting rod up from the crankshaft because the sharp threads of the rod bolts/studs will score the crankshaft journal. Insure that special plastic caps are installed over them, or cut two pieces of rubber hose to do the same.

Again, rotate the engine, this time to position the number one cylinder bore (head surface) up. Turn the crankshaft until the number one piston is at the bottom of its travel, this should allow the maximum access to its connecting rod. Remove the number one connecting rods fasteners and cap and place two lengths of rubber hose over the rod bolts/studs to protect the crankshaft from damage. Using a sturdy wooden dowel and a hammer, push the connecting rod up about 1 in. (25mm) from the crankshaft and remove the upper bearing insert. Continue pushing or tapping the connecting rod up until the piston rings are out of the cylinder bore. Remove the piston and rod by hand, put the upper half of the bearing insert back into the rod, install the cap with its bearing insert installed, and hand-tighten the cap fasteners. If the parts are kept in order in this manner, they will not get lost and you will be able to tell which bearings came form what cylinder if any problems are discovered and diagnosis is necessary. Remove all the other piston assemblies in the same manner. On V-style engines, remove all of the pistons from one bank, then reposition the engine with the other cylinder bank head surface up, and remove that banks piston assemblies.

The only remaining component in the engine block should now be the crankshaft. Loosen the main bearing caps evenly until the fasteners can be turned by hand, then remove them and the caps. Remove the crankshaft from the engine block. Thoroughly clean all of the components.

INSPECTION

Now that the engine block and all of its components are clean, it's time to inspect them for wear and/or damage. To accurately inspect them, you will need some specialized tools:

• Two or three separate micrometers to measure the pistons and crankshaft journals
• A dial indicator
• Telescoping gauges for the cylinder bores
• A rod alignment fixture to check for bent connecting rods

If you do not have access to the proper tools, you may want to bring the components to a shop that does.

Generally, you shouldn't expect cracks in the engine block or its components unless it was known to leak, consume or mix engine fluids, it was severely overheated, or there was evidence of bad bearings and/or crankshaft damage. A visual inspection should be performed on all of the components, but just because you don't see a crack does not mean it is not there. Some more reliable methods for inspecting for cracks include Magnaflux®, a magnetic process or Zyglo®, a dye penetrant. Magnaflux® is used only on ferrous metal (cast iron). Zyglo® uses a spray on fluorescent mixture along with a black light to reveal the cracks. It is strongly recommended to have your engine block checked professionally for cracks, especially if the engine was known to have overheated and/or leaked or consumed coolant. Contact a local shop for availability and pricing of these services.

Engine Block

ENGINE BLOCK BEARING ALIGNMENT

Remove the main bearing caps and, if still installed, the main bearing inserts. Inspect all of the main bearing saddles and caps for damage, burrs or high spots. If damage is found, and it is caused from a spun main bearing, the block will need to be align-bored or, if severe enough, replacement. Any burrs or high spots should be carefully removed with a metal file.

Place a straightedge on the bearing saddles, in the engine block, along the centerline of the crankshaft. If any clearance exists between the straightedge and the saddles, the block must be align-bored.

Align-boring consists of machining the main bearing saddles and caps by means of a flycutter that runs through the bearing saddles.

DECK FLATNESS

The top of the engine block where the cylinder head mounts is called the deck. Insure that the deck surface is clean of dirt, carbon deposits and old gasket material. Place a straightedge across the surface of the deck along its centerline and, using feeler gauges, check the clearance along several points. Repeat the checking procedure with the straightedge placed along both diagonals of the deck surface. If the reading exceeds 0.003 in. (0.076mm) within a 6.0 in. (15.2cm) span, or 0.006 in. (0.152mm) over the total length of the deck, it must be machined.

CYLINDER BORES

▶ See Figure 191

The cylinder bores house the pistons and are slightly larger than the pistons themselves. A common piston-to-bore clearance is 0.0015–0.0025 in. (0.0381mm–0.0635mm). Inspect and measure the cylinder bores. The bore should be checked for out-of-roundness, taper and size. The results of this inspection will determine whether the cylinder can be used in its existing size and condition, or a rebore to the next oversize is required (or in the case of removable sleeves, have replacements installed).

The amount of cylinder wall wear is always greater at the top of the cylinder than at the bottom. This wear is known as taper. Any cylinder that has a taper of

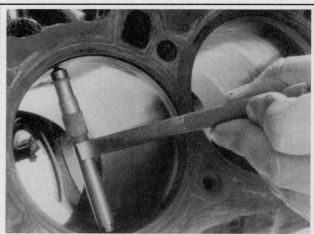

TCCS3209

Fig. 191 Use a telescoping gauge to measure the cylinder bore diameter—take several readings within the same bore

0.0012 in. (0.305mm) or more, must be rebored. Measurements are taken at a number of positions in each cylinder: at the top, middle and bottom and at two points at each position; that is, at a point 90 degrees from the crankshaft centerline, as well as a point parallel to the crankshaft centerline. The measurements are made with either a special dial indicator or a telescopic gauge and micrometer. If the necessary precision tools to check the bore are not available, take the block to a machine shop and have them mike it. Also if you donít have the tools to check the cylinder bores, chances are you will not have the necessary devices to check the pistons, connecting rods and crankshaft. Take these components with you and save yourself an extra trip.

For our procedures, we will use a telescopic gauge and a micrometer. You will need one of each, with a measuring range which covers your cylinder bore size.

1. Position the telescopic gauge in the cylinder bore, loosen the gauges lock and allow it to expand.

➥**Your first two readings will be at the top of the cylinder bore, then proceed to the middle and finally the bottom, making a total of six measurements.**

2. Hold the gauge square in the bore, 90 degrees from the crankshaft centerline, and gently tighten the lock. Tilt the gauge back to remove it from the bore.

3. Measure the gauge with the micrometer and record the reading.

4. Again, hold the gauge square in the bore, this time parallel to the crankshaft centerline, and gently tighten the lock. Again, you will tilt the gauge back to remove it from the bore.

5. Measure the gauge with the micrometer and record this reading. The difference between these two readings is the out-of-round measurement of the cylinder.

6. Repeat steps 1 through 5, each time going to the next lower position, until you reach the bottom of the cylinder. Then go to the next cylinder, and continue until all of the cylinders have been measured.

The difference between these measurements will tell you all about the wear in your cylinders. The measurements which were taken 90 degrees from the crankshaft centerline will always reflect the most wear. That is because at this position is where the engine power presses the piston against the cylinder bore the hardest. This is known as thrust wear. Take your top, 90 degree measurement and compare it to your bottom, 90 degree measurement. The difference between them is the taper. When you measure your pistons, you will compare these readings to your piston sizes and determine piston-to-wall clearance.

Crankshaft

Inspect the crankshaft for visible signs of wear or damage. All of the journals should be perfectly round and smooth. Slight scores are normal for a used crankshaft, but you should hardly feel them with your fingernail. When measuring the crankshaft with a micrometer, you will take readings at the front and rear of each journal, then turn the micrometer 90 degrees and take two more readings, front and rear. The difference between the front-to-rear readings is the journal taper and the first-to-90 degree reading is the out-of-round measurement. Generally, there should be no taper or out-of-roundness found, however, up to 0.0005 in. (0.0127mm) for either can be overlooked. Also, the readings should fall within the factory specifications for journal diameters.

If the crankshaft journals fall within specifications, it is recommended that it be polished before being returned to service. Polishing the crankshaft insures that any minor burrs or high spots are smoothed, thereby reducing the chance of scoring the new bearings.

Pistons and Connecting Rods

PISTONS

▶ **See Figure 192**

The piston should be visually inspected for any signs of cracking or burning (caused by hot spots or detonation), and scuffing or excessive wear on the skirts. The wrist pin attaches the piston to the connecting rod. The piston should move freely on the wrist pin, both sliding and pivoting. Grasp the connecting rod securely, or mount it in a vise, and try to rock the piston back and forth along the centerline of the wrist pin. There should not be any excessive play evident between the piston and the pin. If there are C-clips retaining the pin in the piston then you have wrist pin bushings in the rods. There should not be any excessive play between the wrist pin and the rod

Fig. 192 Measure the pistonís outer diameter, perpendicular to the wrist pin, with a micrometer

bushing. Normal clearance for the wrist pin is approx. 0.001–0.002 in. (0.025mm–0.051mm).

Use a micrometer and measure the diameter of the piston, perpendicular to the wrist pin, on the skirt. Compare the reading to its original cylinder measurement obtained earlier. The difference between the two readings is the piston-to-wall clearance. If the clearance is within specifications, the piston may be used as is. If the piston is out of specification, but the bore is not, you will need a new piston. If both are out of specification, you will need the cylinder rebored and oversize pistons installed. Generally if two or more pistons/bores are out of specification, it is best to rebore the entire block and purchase a complete set of oversize pistons.

CONNECTING ROD

You should have the connecting rod checked for straightness at a machine shop. If the connecting rod is bent, it will unevenly wear the bearing and piston, as well as place greater stress on these components. Any bent or twisted connecting rods must be replaced. If the rods are straight and the wrist pin clearance is within specifications, then only the bearing end of the rod need be checked. Place the connecting rod into a vice, with the bearing inserts in place, install the cap to the rod and torque the fasteners to specifications. Use a telescoping gauge and carefully measure the inside diameter of the bearings. Compare this reading to the rods original crankshaft journal diameter measurement. The difference is the oil clearance. If the oil clearance is not within specifications, install new bearings in the rod and take another measurement. If the clearance is still out of specifications, and the crankshaft is not, the rod will need to be reconditioned by a machine shop.

➥**You can also use Plastigage® to check the bearing clearances. The assembling section has complete instructions on its use.**

Camshaft

Inspect the camshaft and lifters/followers as described earlier in this section.

Bearings

All of the engine bearings should be visually inspected for wear and/or damage. The bearing should look evenly worn all around with no deep scores or pits. If the bearing is severely worn, scored, pitted or heat blued, then the bearing, and the components that use it, should be brought to a machine shop for inspection. Full-circle bearings (used on most camshafts, auxiliary shafts, balance shafts, etc.) require specialized tools for removal and installation, and should be brought to a machine shop for service.

Oil Pump

➥**The oil pump is responsible for providing constant lubrication to the whole engine and so it is recommended that a new oil pump be installed when rebuilding the engine.**

Completely disassemble the oil pump and thoroughly clean all of the components. Inspect the oil pump gears and housing for wear and/or damage. Insure that the pressure relief valve operates properly and there is no binding or sticking due to varnish or debris. If all of the parts are in proper working condition, lubricate the gears and relief valve, and assemble the pump.

REFINISHING

▶ **See Figure 193**

Almost all engine block refinishing must be performed by a machine shop. If the cylinders are not to be rebored, then the cylinder glaze can be removed with a ball hone. When removing cylinder glaze with a ball hone, use a light or penetrating type oil to lubricate the hone. Do not allow the hone to run dry as this may cause excessive scoring of the cylinder bores and wear on the hone. If new pistons are required, they will need to be installed to the connecting rods. This should be performed by a machine shop as the pistons must be installed in the correct relationship to the rod or engine damage can occur.

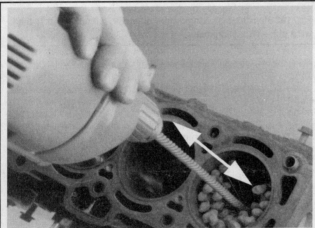

Fig. 193 Use a ball type cylinder hone to remove any glaze and provide a new surface for seating the piston rings

Pistons and Connecting Rods

▶ **See Figure 194**

Only pistons with the wrist pin retained by C-clips are serviceable by the home-mechanic. Press fit pistons require special presses and/or heaters to remove/install the connecting rod and should only be performed by a machine shop.

Fig. 194 Most pistons are marked to indicate positioning in the engine (usually a mark means the side facing the front)

All pistons will have a mark indicating the direction to the front of the engine and the must be installed into the engine in that manner. Usually it is a notch or arrow on the top of the piston, or it may be the letter F cast or stamped into the piston.

ASSEMBLY

Before you begin assembling the engine, first give yourself a clean, dirt free work area. Next, clean every engine component again. The key to a good assembly is cleanliness.

Mount the engine block into the engine stand and wash it one last time using water and detergent (dishwashing detergent works well). While washing it, scrub the cylinder bores with a soft bristle brush and thoroughly clean all of the oil passages. Completely dry the engine and spray the entire assembly down with an anti-rust solution such as WD-40® or similar product. Take a clean lint-free rag and wipe up any excess anti-rust solution from the bores, bearing saddles, etc. Repeat the final cleaning process on the crankshaft. Replace any freeze or oil galley plugs which were removed during disassembly.

Crankshaft

▶ **See Figures 195, 196, 197 and 198**

1. Remove the main bearing inserts from the block and bearing caps.
2. If the crankshaft main bearing journals have been refinished to a definite undersize, install the correct undersize bearing. Be sure that the bearing inserts and bearing bores are clean. Foreign material under inserts will distort bearing and cause failure.

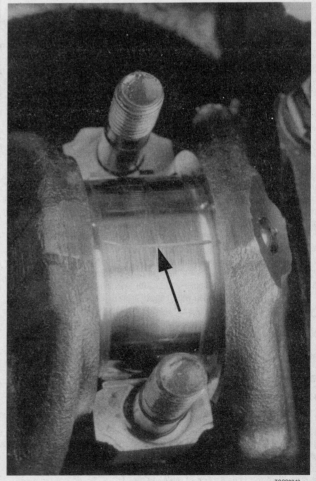

Fig. 195 Apply a strip of gauging material to the bearing journal, then install and torque the cap

Fig. 196 After the cap is removed again, use the scale supplied with the gauging material to check the clearance

Fig. 197 A dial gauge may be used to check crankshaft end-play

Fig. 198 Carefully pry the crankshaft back and forth while reading the dial gauge for end-play

3. Place the upper main bearing inserts in bores with tang in slot.

➡The oil holes in the bearing inserts must be aligned with the oil holes in the cylinder block.

4. Install the lower main bearing inserts in bearing caps.
5. Clean the mating surfaces of block and rear main bearing cap.
6. Carefully lower the crankshaft into place. Be careful not to damage bearing surfaces.
7. Check the clearance of each main bearing by using the following procedure:

   a. Place a piece of Plastigage® or its equivalent, on bearing surface across full width of bearing cap and about ¼ in. off center.

   b. Install cap and tighten bolts to specifications. Do not turn crankshaft while Plastigage® is in place.

   c. Remove the cap. Using the supplied Plastigage® scale, check width of Plastigage® at widest point to get maximum clearance. Difference between readings is taper of journal.

   d. If clearance exceeds specified limits, try a 0.001 in. or 0.002 in. undersize bearing in combination with the standard bearing. Bearing clearance must be within specified limits. If standard and 0.002 in. undersize bearing does not bring clearance within desired limits, refinish crankshaft journal, then install undersize bearings.

8. Install the rear main seal.
9. After the bearings have been fitted, apply a light coat of engine oil to the journals and bearings. Install the rear main bearing cap. Install all bearing caps except the thrust bearing cap. Be sure that main bearing caps are installed in original locations. Tighten the bearing cap bolts to specifications.
10. Install the thrust bearing cap with bolts finger-tight.
11. Pry the crankshaft forward against the thrust surface of upper half of bearing.
12. Hold the crankshaft forward and pry the thrust bearing cap to the rear. This aligns the thrust surfaces of both halves of the bearing.
13. Retain the forward pressure on the crankshaft. Tighten the cap bolts to specifications.
14. Measure the crankshaft end-play as follows:

    a. Mount a dial gauge to the engine block and position the tip of the gauge to read from the crankshaft end.

    b. Carefully pry the crankshaft toward the rear of the engine and hold it there while you zero the gauge.

    c. Carefully pry the crankshaft toward the front of the engine and read the gauge.

    d. Confirm that the reading is within specifications. If not, install a new thrust bearing and repeat the procedure. If the reading is still out of specifications with a new bearing, have a machine shop inspect the thrust surfaces of the crankshaft, and if possible, repair it.

15. Rotate the crankshaft so as to position the first rod journal to the bottom of its stroke.

Pistons and Connecting Rods

▸ See Figures 199, 200, 201 and 202

1. Before installing the piston/connecting rod assembly, oil the pistons, piston rings and the cylinder walls with light engine oil. Install connecting rod

bolt protectors or rubber hose onto the connecting rod bolts/studs. Also perform the following:

   a. Select the proper ring set for the size cylinder bore.

   b. Position the ring in the bore in which it is going to be used.

   c. Push the ring down into the bore area where normal ring wear is not encountered.

   e. Measure the gap between the ends of the ring with a feeler gauge. Ring gap in a worn cylinder is normally greater than specification. If the ring gap is greater than the specified limits, try an oversize ring set.

   f. Check the ring side clearance of the compression rings with a feeler gauge inserted between the ring and its lower land according to specification. The gauge should slide freely around the entire ring circumference without binding. Any wear that occurs will form a step at the inner portion of the lower land. If the lower lands have high steps, the piston should be replaced.

2. Unless new pistons are installed, be sure to install the pistons in the

Fig. 199 Checking the piston ring-to-ring groove side clearance using the ring and a feeler gauge

Fig. 200 The notch on the side of the bearing cap matches the tang on the bearing insert

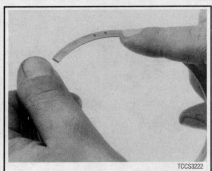

Fig. 201 Most rings are marked to show which side of the ring should face up when installed to the piston

Fig. 202 Install the piston and rod assembly into the block using a ring compressor and the handle of a hammer

cylinders from which they were removed. The numbers on the connecting rod and bearing cap must be on the same side when installed in the cylinder bore. If a connecting rod is ever transposed from one engine or cylinder to another, new bearings should be fitted and the connecting rod should be numbered to correspond with the new cylinder number. The notch on the piston head goes toward the front of the engine.

3. Install all of the rod bearing inserts into the rods and caps.

4. Install the rings to the pistons. Install the oil control ring first, then the second compression ring and finally the top compression ring. Use a piston ring expander tool to aid in installation and to help reduce the chance of breakage.

5. Make sure the ring gaps are properly spaced around the circumference of the piston. Fit a piston ring compressor around the piston and slide the piston and connecting rod assembly down into the cylinder bore, pushing it in with the wooden hammer handle. Push the piston down until it is only slightly below the top of the cylinder bore. Guide the connecting rod onto the crankshaft bearing journal carefully, to avoid damaging the crankshaft.

6. Check the bearing clearance of all the rod bearings, fitting them to the crankshaft bearing journals. Follow the procedure in the crankshaft installation above.

7. After the bearings have been fitted, apply a light coating of assembly oil to the journals and bearings.

8. Turn the crankshaft until the appropriate bearing journal is at the bottom of its stroke, then push the piston assembly all the way down until the connecting rod bearing seats on the crankshaft journal. Be careful not to allow the bearing cap screws to strike the crankshaft bearing journals and damage them.

9. After the piston and connecting rod assemblies have been installed, check the connecting rod side clearance on each crankshaft journal.

10. Prime and install the oil pump and the oil pump intake tube.

11. Install the auxiliary/balance shaft(s)/assembly(ies).

OHV Engines

CAMSHAFT, LIFTERS AND TIMING ASSEMBLY

1. Install the camshaft.
2. Install the lifters/followers into their bores.
3. Install the timing gears/chain assembly.

CYLINDER HEAD(S)

1. Install the cylinder head(s) using new gaskets.
2. Assemble the rest of the valve train (pushrods and rocker arms and/or shafts).

OHC Engines

CYLINDER HEAD(S)

1. Install the cylinder head(s) using new gaskets.
2. Install the timing sprockets/gears and the belt/chain assemblies.

Engine Covers and Components

Install the timing cover(s) and oil pan. Refer to your notes and drawings

made prior to disassembly and install all of the components that were removed. Install the engine into the vehicle.

Engine Start-up and Break-in

STARTING THE ENGINE

Now that the engine is installed and every wire and hose is properly connected, go back and double check that all coolant and vacuum hoses are connected. Check that your oil drain plug is installed and properly tightened. If not already done, install a new oil filter onto the engine. Fill the crankcase with the proper amount and grade of engine oil. Fill the cooling system with a 50/50 mixture of coolant/water.

1. Connect the vehicle battery.
2. Start the engine. Keep your eye on your oil pressure indicator; if it does not indicate oil pressure within 10 seconds of starting, turn the vehicle **OFF**.

✳✳ WARNING

Damage to the engine can result if it is allowed to run with no oil pressure. Check the engine oil level to make sure that it is full. Check for any leaks and if found, repair the leaks before continuing. If there is still no indication of oil pressure, you may need to prime the system.

3. Confirm that there are no fluid leaks (oil or other).
4. Allow the engine to reach normal operating temperature (the upper radiator hose will be hot to the touch).
5. At this point any necessary checks or adjustments can be performed, such as ignition timing.
6. Install any remaining components or body panels which were removed.

BREAKING IT IN

Make the first miles on the new engine, easy ones. Vary the speed but do not accelerate hard. Most importantly, do not lug the engine, and avoid sustained high speeds until at least 100 miles. Check the engine oil and coolant levels frequently. Expect the engine to use a little oil until the rings seat. Change the oil and filter at 500 miles, 1500 miles, then every 3000 miles past that.

KEEP IT MAINTAINED

Now that you have just gone through all of that hard work, keep yourself from doing it all over again by thoroughly maintaining it. Not that you may not have maintained it before, heck you could have had one to two hundred thousand miles on it before doing this. However, you may have bought the vehicle used, and the previous owner did not keep up on maintenance. Which is why you just went through all of that hard work. See?

EMISSION CONTROLS 4-2
CRANKCASE VENTILATION
 SYSTEM 4-2
  OPERATION 4-2
  COMPONENT TESTING 4-2
  REMOVAL & INSTALLATION 4-3
EVAPORATIVE EMISSION
 CONTROLS 4-3
  OPERATION 4-3
  SYSTEM INSPECTION 4-3
  REMOVAL & INSTALLATION 4-3
THERMACTOR® AIR INJECTOR
 SYSTEM 4-4
  OPERATION 4-4
  SYSTEM INSPECTION 4-5
  REMOVAL & INSTALLATION 4-6
HEATED AIR INTAKE SYSTEM 4-6
  OPERATION 4-6
  COMPONENT TESTING 4-6
  REMOVAL & INSTALLATION 4-7
EXHAUST GAS RECIRCULATION
 SYSTEM 4-7
  OPERATION 4-7
  REMOVAL & INSTALLATION 4-8
EMISSION SERVICE LIGHTS 4-10
  RESETTING 4-10
**ELECTRONIC ENGINE
 CONTROLS 4-11**
ELECTRONIC ENGINE CONTROL
 (EEC) 4-11
POWERTRAIN CONTROL MODULE
 (PCM) 4-11
  OPERATION 4-11
  REMOVAL & INSTALLATION 4-11
OXYGEN SENSORS 4-11
  OPERATION 4-11
  TESTING 4-11
  REMOVAL & INSTALLATION 4-12
IDLE AIR CONTROL (IAC) VALVE 4-12
  OPERATION 4-12
  TESTING 4-12
  REMOVAL & INSTALLATION 4-12
ENGINE COOLANT TEMPERATURE (ECT)
 SENSOR 4-12
  OPERATION 4-12
  TESTING 4-12
  REMOVAL & INSTALLATION 4-13
INTAKE AIR TEMPERATURE (IAT)
 SENSOR 4-13
  OPERATION 4-13
  TESTING 4-13
  REMOVAL & INSTALLATION 4-13
MASS AIR FLOW (MAF) SENSOR 4-13
  OPERATION 4-13
  TESTING 4-13
  REMOVAL & INSTALLATION 4-14
THROTTLE POSITION (TP)
 SENSOR 4-14
  OPERATION 4-14
  TESTING 4-14

  REMOVAL & INSTALLATION 4-15
CAMSHAFT POSITION (CMP)
 SENSOR 4-15
  OPERATION 4-15
  TESTING 4-15
  REMOVAL & INSTALLATION 4-16
BAROMETRIC/MANIFOLD ABSOLUTE
 PRESSURE SENSORS (B/MAP) 4-16
  OPERATION 4-16
  TESTING 4-16
  REMOVAL & INSTALLATION 4-17
CRANKSHAFT POSITION (CP)
 SENSOR 4-17
  OPERATION 4-17
  TESTING 4-17
  REMOVAL & INSTALLATION 4-17
KNOCK SENSOR (KS) 4-17
  OPERATION 4-17
  TESTING 4-17
  REMOVAL & INSTALLATION 4-17
EGR VALVE POSITION (EVP)
 SENSOR 4-17
  OPERATION 4-17
  TESTING 4-18
  REMOVAL & INSTALLATION 4-18
EEC-IV TROUBLE CODES 4-18
GENERAL INFORMATION 4-18
  VEHICLE PREPARATION 4-18
  READING CODES 4-18
  CLEARING CODES 4-19
EEC-V TROUBLE CODES 4-23
GENERAL INFORMATION 4-23
DATA LINK CONNECTOR (DLC) 4-23
READING CODES 4-23
CLEARING CODES 4-24
  PCM RESET 4-24
  KEEP ALIVE MEMORY (KAM)
  RESET 4-24
VACUUM DIAGRAMS 4-28
TROUBLESHOOTING CHARTS
  TROUBLE CODES 4-19

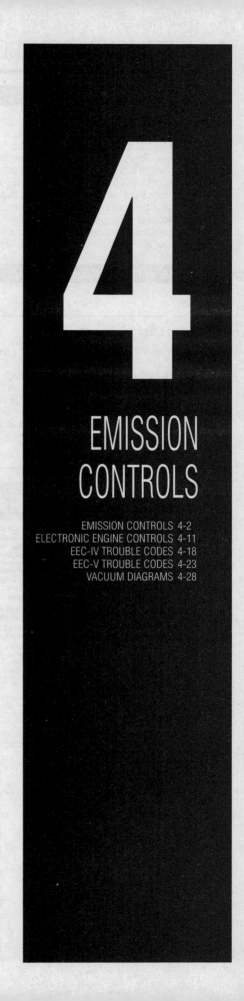

4

EMISSION CONTROLS

EMISSION CONTROLS 4-2
ELECTRONIC ENGINE CONTROLS 4-11
EEC-IV TROUBLE CODES 4-18
EEC-V TROUBLE CODES 4-23
VACUUM DIAGRAMS 4-28

EMISSION CONTROLS

▶ See Figure 1

There are three basic sources of automotive pollution in the modern internal combustion engine. They are the crankcase with its accompanying blow-by vapors, the fuel system with its evaporation of unburned gasoline, and the combustion chambers with their resulting exhaust emissions. Pollution arising from the incomplete combustion of fuel generally falls into three categories: hydrocarbons (HC), carbon monoxide (CO), and oxides of nitrogen (NOx).

All vehicles (covered in this book) have an Emissions Control Information Decal, mounted on the radiator support or possibly on the air cleaner housing. Always refer to this decal when performing service to the emission controls.

Crankcase Ventilation System

OPERATION

▶ See Figures 2 and 3

All models covered in this book are equipped with a positive crankcase ventilation (PCV) system. The system vents harmful combustion blow-by fumes from the crankcase into the engine air intake for burning with the fuel/air mixture. The PCV valve prevents combustion backfiring into the crankcase and serves the engine upon demand by limiting the fresh air intake. The PCV valve also controls the amount of blow-by vapors that are allowed into the intake manifold from the crankcase. The PCV valve also acts as a one-way check valve and prevents air from entering the crankcase in the opposite direction. The PCV

valve system maximizes oil cleanliness by venting moisture and corrosive fumes from the crankcase. The PCV valve system is connected with the evaporative emission system on some vehicles. Do not remove the PCV valve system from the engine. Doing so will adversely affect fuel economy and engine ventilation and may result in shortened engine life.

COMPONENT TESTING

PCV Valve

▶ See Figure 4

1. Remove the PCV valve from the grommet and shake the valve. If the valve rattles when shaken, reinstall and proceed to the next step. If it does not rattle, it is sticking and should be replaced.
2. Start the engine and bring it to normal operating temperature.
3. Disconnect the hose from the remote air cleaner or air outlet tube.
4. Place a stiff piece of paper over the hose end and wait 1 minute. If the vacuum holds the paper in place, the system is okay. Reconnect the hose. If the paper is not held in place, the system is plugged or the Evaporative Emission Valve is leaking (if equipped). If valve is suspected of leaking, proceed to the next step.
5. Disconnect the evaporative hose, if equipped and cap the connector.
6. Place a stiff piece of paper over the hose end/nipple and wait 1 minute. If the vacuum holds the paper in place, proceed to the evaporative emission system testing.
7. If the paper is not held in place, check the system for vacuum leaks or

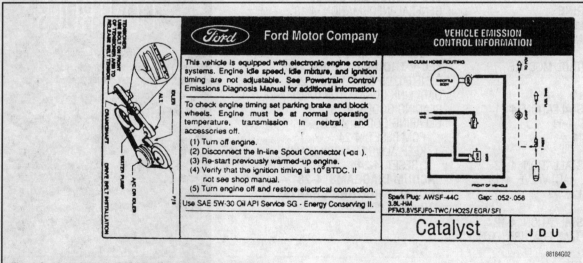

Fig. 1 Common Vehicle Emission Control Information decal

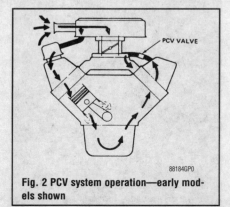

Fig. 2 PCV system operation—early models shown

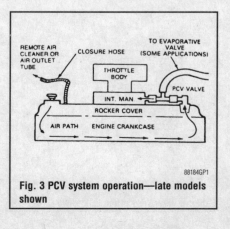

Fig. 3 PCV system operation—late models shown

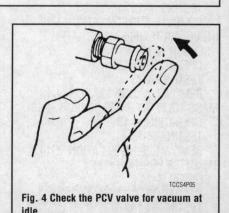

Fig. 4 Check the PCV valve for vacuum at idle

obstructions. Inspect the oil cap, PCV valve, hoses, grommets and valve cover for bolt tighten/gasket leak.

REMOVAL & INSTALLATION

PCV Valve

▶ **See Figures 5 and 6**

1. On some engines it may be necessary to remove the air cleaner outlet tube.
2. Remove the PCV valve from the mounting grommet in the valve cover.
3. Disconnect the hose from the valve and remove the valve from the vehicle.
4. Inspect the hoses and grommet for deterioration. Replace if necessary.

To install:
5. Install a new PCV valve into the valve cover grommet.
6. Attach the hose to the valve.
7. If removed, install the air cleaner outlet tube.

Ventilation Filter

▶ **See Figure 7**

1. Disconnect the PCV hose at the air cleaner by unsnapping the elbow from the retainer clip or sliding off the hose from the PCV filter adapter.
2. Remove the air cleaner body top.
3. Remove the ventilation filter retainer clip and filter retainer from the air cleaner body.
4. Remove the filter from the retainer and clean out the retainer.

To install:
5. Install a new filter into the filter retainer pack.
6. Position the filter assembly into the air cleaner body with the retainer clip.
7. Attach the hose to the air cleaner assembly.
8. Place the air cleaner cap on the air cleaner body and secure.

Evaporative Emission Controls

OPERATION

▶ **See Figure 8**

The evaporative emission control system prevents the escape of fuel vapors to the atmosphere under hot soak and engine off conditions by diverting the vapors to and storing them in a carbon canister. When the engine is running and reaches the proper temperature, the system purges the vapors from the canister to the engine where they are efficiently burned.

The evaporative emission control system consists of the carbon canister, the CANP purge control solenoid(s), purge valve(s), the fuel tank vapor hose, and the fuel vapor return line.

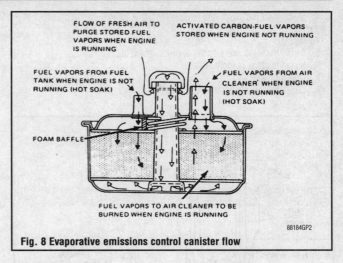

Fig. 8 Evaporative emissions control canister flow

SYSTEM INSPECTION

1. Inspect the canister hose and inlet nipple for blockage.
2. Inspect fuel evaporative emission system for blockage.
3. Inspect the vapor tube and the hoses for kinks or pinched areas.
4. Inspect the vapor hose routing between the fuel tank and the body for kinks or pinched areas.

REMOVAL & INSTALLATION

Carbon Canister

The carbon canister stores the fuel vapor by absorbing it until it is returned to the engine to be burned. There should be no liquid in the canister.
1. Disconnect the canister purge hose from the air cleaner fitting.
2. Loosen the canister retaining bracket and lift out the canister.

To install:
3. Attach the canister to the retaining bracket.
4. Connect the purge hose to the air cleaner fitting.

Fuel Tank Vapor Valve

▶ **See Figures 9 and 10**

The fuel tank vapor valve vents the fuel vapor from the tank to the carbon canister for storage. The valve is located in the upper area of the fuel tank.
1. Disconnect the negative battery cable.
2. Raise and safely support the vehicle.
3. Remove the fuel tank from the vehicle.

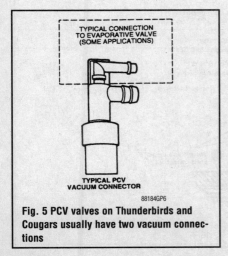

Fig. 5 PCV valves on Thunderbirds and Cougars usually have two vacuum connections

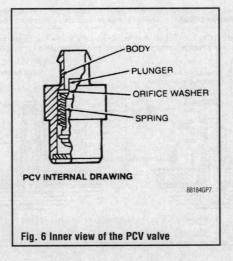

Fig. 6 Inner view of the PCV valve

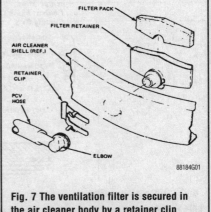

Fig. 7 The ventilation filter is secured in the air cleaner body by a retainer clip

4. Disconnect the hoses and remove the vapor valve from the grommet in the fuel tank.

To install:

5. Install the vapor valve to the tank and attach the hoses.
6. Install the tank in the vehicle.
7. Check for leaks.
8. Lower the vehicle. Connect the negative battery cable.

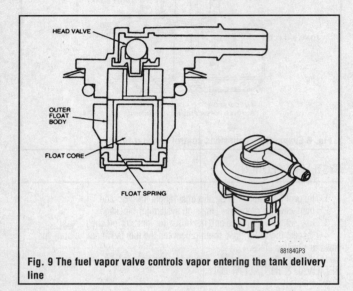

Fig. 9 The fuel vapor valve controls vapor entering the tank delivery line

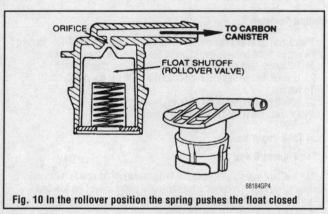

Fig. 10 In the rollover position the spring pushes the float closed

Ported Vacuum Switch (PVS)

▶ **See Figure 11**

The Ported Vacuum Switch (PVS) turns the purge vacuum valve on as the engine warms up. It also allows the purge valve to close when the engine is turned off and the vacuum is lost.

Vapor Management (VMV) Valve

▶ **See Figure 12**

The Vapor Management (VMV) valve is the part of the emissions system that is controlled by the PCM. This valve controls the flow of vapors purging from the carbon canister to the intake manifold during various engine operating modes. The VMV is normally a closed valve.

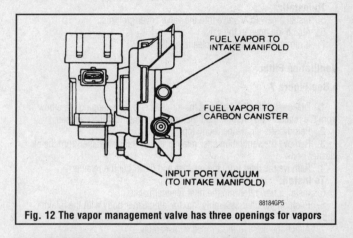

Fig. 12 The vapor management valve has three openings for vapors

Thermactor® Air Injector System

OPERATION

▶ **See Figures 13, 14 and 15**

This system is found in most models sold in the 50 states.

The Thermactor® emission control system makes use of a belt-driven air pump to inject fresh air into the hot exhaust stream through the engine exhaust ports. The result is the extended burning of those fumes which were not completely ignited in the combustion chamber, and the subsequent reduction of some of the hydrocarbon and carbon monoxide content of the exhaust emissions into harmless carbon dioxide and water.

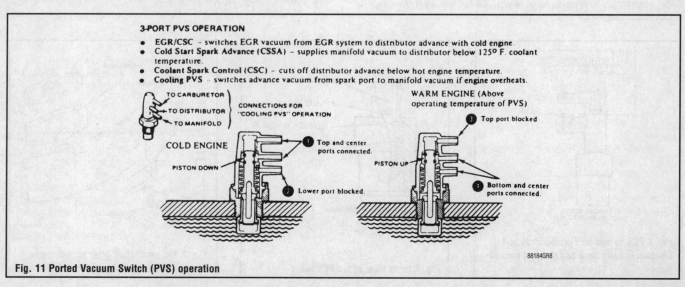

Fig. 11 Ported Vacuum Switch (PVS) operation

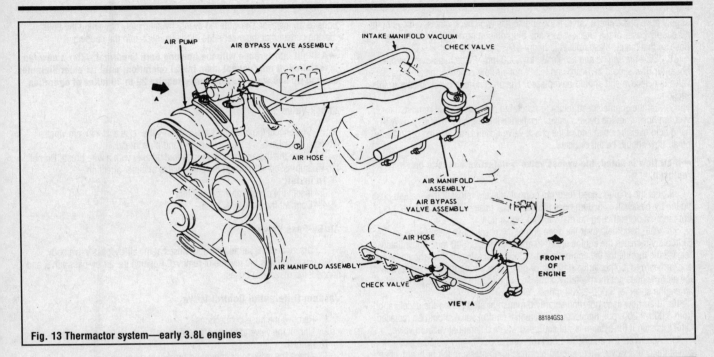

Fig. 13 Thermactor system—early 3.8L engines

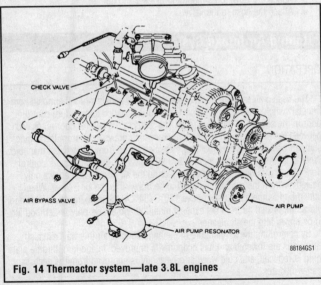

Fig. 14 Thermactor system—late 3.8L engines

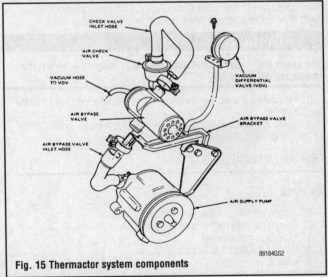

Fig. 15 Thermactor system components

The Thermactor® system is composed of the following components:
1. Air supply pump (belt-driven)
2. Air by-pass valve
3. Check valves
4. Air manifolds (internal or external)
5. Air supply tubes (on external manifolds only).

Air for the Thermactor® system is cleaned by means of a centrifugal filter fan mounted on the air pump driveshaft. The air filter does not require a replaceable element.

To prevent excessive pressure, the air pump is equipped with a pressure relief valve which uses a replaceable plastic plug to control the pressure setting.

The Thermactor® air pump has sealed bearings which are lubricated for the life of the unit, and preset rotor vane and bearing clearances, which do not require any periodic adjustments.

The air supply from the pump is controlled by the air by-pass valve, sometimes called a dump valve. During deceleration, the air by-pass valve opens, momentarily diverting the air supply through a silencer and into the atmosphere, thus preventing backfires within the exhaust system.

A check valve is incorporated in the air inlet side of the air manifolds. Its purpose is to prevent exhaust gases from backing up into the Thermactor® system. This valve is especially important in the event of drive belt failure, and during deceleration, when the air by-pass valve is dumping the air supply.

The air manifolds and air supply tubes channel the air from the Thermactor® air pump into the exhaust ports of each cylinder, thus completing the cycle of the Thermactor® system.

SYSTEM INSPECTION

The entire Thermactor® system should be checked periodically. Use the following procedure to determine if the system is functioning properly.
1. Remove air cleaner, if necessary.
2. Inspect all components of the Thermactor® system for any loose connections or other abnormal conditions. Repair or replace them as necessary.
3. Inspect the air pump drive belt for wear and tension. Adjust or replace them as necessary.
4. With the transmission in neutral or park and the parking brake on, start engine and bring to normal operating temperature.
5. Stop the engine. Connect a tachometer to the engine. Remove the air

supply hose at the check valve. If the engine has two check valves, remove both air supply hoses at the check valves and plug off one hose. Position the open hose so that the air blast emitted is harmlessly dissipated.

6. Start the engine and accelerate to 1,500 rpm. Place hand over the open hose. Air flow should be heard and felt. If not air flow is noted, the air bypass valve is defective and should be replaced. The procedure is outlined later in this section.

7. Let the engine speed return to normal idle. Pinch off and remove the vacuum hose from the bypass valve. Accelerate the engine to 1,500 rpm. With hand held over the open end of the check valve hose (same as Step 6), virtually no air flow should be felt or heard.

➡️**If air flow is noted, the bypass valve is defective and is to be replaced.**

8. Let the engine speed return to normal idle and reinstall the vacuum hose on the by-pass valve vacuum hose nipple. Check hose routing to be sure it is not pinched or restricting normal vacuum signal flow.

9. With hand held over the open end of the check valve hose (same as Step 6), rapidly increase the engine speed to approximately 2,500 rpm. Immediately release the throttle for the engine to return to normal idle. Air flow should be felt and/or heard to momentarily diminish or go to zero during the deceleration. If the air flow does not momentarily diminish or go to zero repeat the above using an engine speed of 3,000-3,200 rpm.

10. If air flow does not momentarily diminish or stop during the deceleration from 3,000-3,200 rpm, the vacuum differential control valve should be replaced. Omit this step if the system is not equipped with a differential vacuum valve.

11. Accelerate the engine to 1,500 rpm and check for any exhaust gas leakage at the check valve. There should be virtually no pressure felt or heard when hand is held over the open end of the check valve for approximately 15 seconds. If excessive leakage is noted, replace the check valve(s).

✳ CAUTION

The check valve may be hot and capable of causing a burn if the hands are not protected.

12. If the engine is equipped with two check valves, repeat step 10 on the second valve.

13. Stop the engine and remove all the test equipment. Reconnect all the related components. Reinstall the air cleaner, if removed.

REMOVAL & INSTALLATION

Air Pump

1. Disconnect the air outlet hose at the air pump.
2. Loosen the pump belt tension adjuster.
3. Disengage the drive belt.
4. Remove the mounting bolt and air pump.
To install:
5. Position the air pump on the mounting bracket and install the mounting bolt.
6. Place drive belt in pulleys and attach the adjusting arm to the air pump.
7. Adjust the drive belt tension to specifications and tighten the adjusting arm and mounting bolts.
8. Connect the air outlet hose to the air pump.

Air Pump Filter Fan

1. Loosen the air pump adjusting arm bolt and mounting bracket bolt to relieve drive belt tension.
2. Remove the drive pulley attaching bolts and pull the drive pulley off the air pump shaft.
3. Pry the outer disc loose, then pull off the centrifugal filter fan with slip-joint pliers.

✳ CAUTION

Do not attempt to remove the metal drive hub.

To install:
4. Install a new filter fan by drawing it into position, using the pulley and

bolts as an installer. Draw the fan evenly by alternately tightening the bolts, making certain that the outer edge of the fan slips into the housing.

➡️**A slight interference with the housing bore is normal. After a new fan is installed, it may squeal upon initial operation, until its outer diameter sealing lip has worn in, which may require 20 to 30 miles of operation.**

Check Valve

1. Disconnect the air supply hose at the valve. Use a 1¼ in. crowfoot wrench, the valve has a standard, right hand pipe thread.
2. Clean the threads on the air manifold adapter with a wire brush. Do not blow compressed air through the check valve in either direction.
To install:
3. Install the check valve and tighten.
4. Connect the air supply hose.

Air By-Pass Valve

1. Disconnect the air and vacuum hoses at the air by-pass valve body.
2. Installation is the reverse of removal. Position the air by-pass valve, and connect the respective hoses.

Vacuum Differential Control Valve

1. Remove the hose connections.
2. Unbolt the valve at its mounting bracket.
To install:
3. Attach the valve to its mounting bracket and tighten.
4. Attach the hose to the valve.

Heated Air Intake System

OPERATION

The heated air intake portion of the air cleaner consists of a thermostat, or bimetal switch and vacuum motor, and a spring-loaded temperature control door in the snorkel of the air cleaner. The temperature control door is located between the end of the air cleaner snorkel which draws in air from the engine compartment and the duct that carries heated air up from the exhaust manifold. When underhood temperature is below 90°F (32°C), the temperature control door blocks off underhood air from entering the air cleaner and allows only heated air from the exhaust manifold to be drawn into the air cleaner. When underhood temperature rises above 130°F (54°C), the temperature control door blocks off heated air from the exhaust manifold and allows only underhood air to be drawn into the air cleaner.

By controlling the temperature of the engine intake air this way, exhaust emissions are lowered and fuel economy is improved. In addition, throttle plate icing is reduced, and cold weather driveability is improved from the necessary leaner mixtures.

COMPONENT TESTING

Duct and Valve Assembly

1. Either start with a cold engine or remove the air cleaner from the engine for at least half an hour. While cooling the air cleaner, leave the engine compartment hood open.
2. Tape a thermometer, of known accuracy, to the inside of the air cleaner so that is near the temperature sensor unit. Install the air cleaner on the engine but do not fasten its securing nut.
3. Start the engine. With the engine cold and the outside temperature less than 90°F (32°C), the door should in the **HEAT ON** position (closed to outside air).
4. Operate the throttle lever rapidly to ½-¾ of its opening and release it. The air door should open to allow outside air to enter and then close again.
5. Allow the engine to warm up to normal temperature. Watch the door. When it opens to the outside air, remove the cover from the air cleaner. The temperature should be over 90°F (32°C) and no more than 130°F (54°C); 105°F (41°C) is about normal. If the door does not work within these temperature ranges, or fails to work at all, check for linkage or door binding.

If binding is not present and the air door is not working, proceed with the vacuum tests given below. If these indicate no faults in the vacuum motor and the door is not working, the temperature sensor is defective and must be replaced.

Vacuum Motor

➡Be sure that the vacuum hose that runs between the temperature switch and the vacuum motor is not pinched by the retaining clip under the air cleaner. This could prevent the air door from closing.

1. Check all the vacuum lines and fittings for leaks. Correct any leaks. If none are found, proceed with the test.
2. Remove the hose which runs from the sensor to the vacuum motor. Run a hose directly from the manifold vacuum source to the vacuum motor.
3. If the motor closes the air door, it is functioning properly and the temperature sensor is defective.
4. If the motor does not close the door and no binding is present in its operation, the vacuum motor is defective and must be replaced.

➡If an alternator vacuum source is applied to the motor, insert a vacuum gauge in the line by using a T-fitting. Apply at least 9 in.Hg of vacuum in order to operate the motor.

REMOVAL & INSTALLATION

Temperature Operated Duct and Valve Assembly

1. Remove the hex-head cap screws which secure the air intake duct and valve assembly to the air cleaner.
2. Remove the air intake duct and valve assembly from the engine.
3. If inspection reveals that the valve plate is sticking or the thermostat is malfunctioning, remove the thermostat and valve plates as follows:
    a. Detach the valve plate tension spring from the valve plate using long-nose pliers.
    b. Loosen the thermostat locknut and unscrew the thermostat from the mounting bracket.
    c. Grasp the valve plate and withdraw it from the cut.
To install:
4. Install the air intake duct and valve assembly on the shroud tube.
5. Connect the air intake duct and valve assembly the air cleaner and tighten the hex-head retaining cap screws.
6. If it was necessary to disassemble the thermostat and air duct and valve, assembly the unit as follows: Install the locknut on the thermostat, and screw the thermostat into the mounting bracket. Install the valve plate tension spring on the valve plate and duct.
7. Install the vacuum override motor (if applicable) and check for proper operation.

Vacuum Operated Duct and Valve Assembly

1. Disconnect the vacuum hose at the vacuum motor.
2. Remove the hex-head cap screws which secure the air intake duct and valve assembly to the air cleaner.
3. Remove the duct and valve assembly from the engine.
To install:
4. Position the duct and valve assembly to the air cleaner and heat stove tube. Install the attaching cap screws.
5. Connect the vacuum line at the vacuum motor.

Exhaust Gas Recirculation System

OPERATION

▶ See Figures 16, 17 and 18

All models are equipped with an exhaust gas recirculation (EGR) system which reintroduces the exhaust gas into the combustion cycle. This process lowers the combustion temperatures and reduces the formation of oxides of nitrogen. There are several systems that are utilized on the Thunderbird and the Cougar.

One of the systems used is the Pressure Feedback Electronic (PFE) system. The PFE is a subsonic closed loop system that controls the EGR flow rate by monitoring the pressure drop across a remotely mounted sharp edged orifice. A pressure transducer serves as the feedback device. Controlled pressure is varied by valve modulation using vacuum output of the EGR Vacuum Regulator (EVR) solenoid. In the PFE system the EGR valve serves only as a pressure regulator rather than a flow metering device.

Another system used is the Electronic EGR (EEGR) valve system. This system is required in EEC systems where the EGR flow is controlled according to the demands made by the computer through the EGR Valve Position (EVP) sensor attached to the valve. The valve is operated by a vacuum signal from the electronic vacuum regulator. The regulator actuates the valve diaphragm as supply vacuum overcomes the spring load. This in turn lifts the pintle off of it's seat which allows the exhaust gas to recirculate. The amount of flow is proportional to the pintle position. The EVP sensor on the valve sends a signal of its position to the PCM.

The ported EGR valve is operated by a vacuum signal which in turn actuates the valve diaphragm. As the vacuum increases sufficiently to overcome the

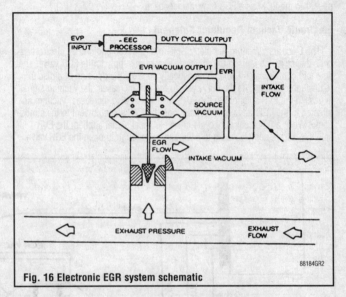

Fig. 16 Electronic EGR system schematic

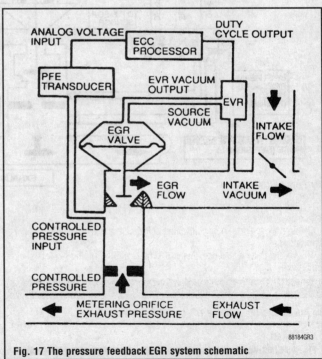

Fig. 17 The pressure feedback EGR system schematic

power spring, the valve opens to allow EGR flow. The vacuum that reaches the EGR valve is controlled by the EGR Vacuum Regulator (EVR) or the Pressure Feedback EGR transducer (PFE), depending on the system application.

The Differential Pressure Feedback EGR (DPFE) system is continuously monitored by the On Board Diagnostic II (OBDII) system for component integrity. The systems functionally faults that can cause the emission levels to exceed the Federal regulations. When the OBDII monitor determines that a failure had occurred, the Malfunction Indicator Lamp (MIL) illuminates to warn the driver and a trouble code is stored in the memory.

Differential Pressure Feedback (DPFE) Sensor

The DPFE sensor is a ceramic capacitive type pressure transducer which monitors the differential pressure across a metering orifice located in the orifice tube assembly. The sensor receives this signal through two hoses called the downstream pressure hose (REF SIGNAL) and the upstream pressure hose HI SIGNAL). The HI and REF signals are marked on the DPFE sensor outputs a voltage proportional to the pressure drop across the metering orifice and supplies it to the PCM as a EGR flow rate feedback.

Electronic Vacuum Regulator Solenoid

The Electronic Vacuum Regulator Solenoid (EVR) solenoid is an electromagnetic device which is used to regulate the vacuum supply to the EGR valve. The solenoid contains a coil which magnetically controls the position of a disc to regulate the vacuum. As the duty cycle to the coil increases, the vacuum signal is passed the EVR solenoid to the EGR valve which also increases. Vacuum not directed to the EGR valve is vented through the EVR solenoid vent to the atmosphere. When a 0 percent duty cycle or no electrical signal applied, the EVR solenoid allows some vacuum to pass, but not enough to open the EGR valve.

REMOVAL & INSTALLATION

Ported EGR

◗ See Figure 19

1. Disconnect the negative battery cable.
2. Tag and disconnect the vacuum line from the EGR valve.
3. Remove the mounting bolts and remove the EGR valve.
4. Scrape the old gasket off of the engine mating area.

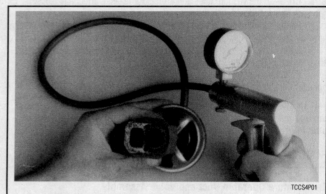

TCCS4P01

Fig. 19 Some EGR valves may be tested using a vacuum pump by watching for diaphragm movement

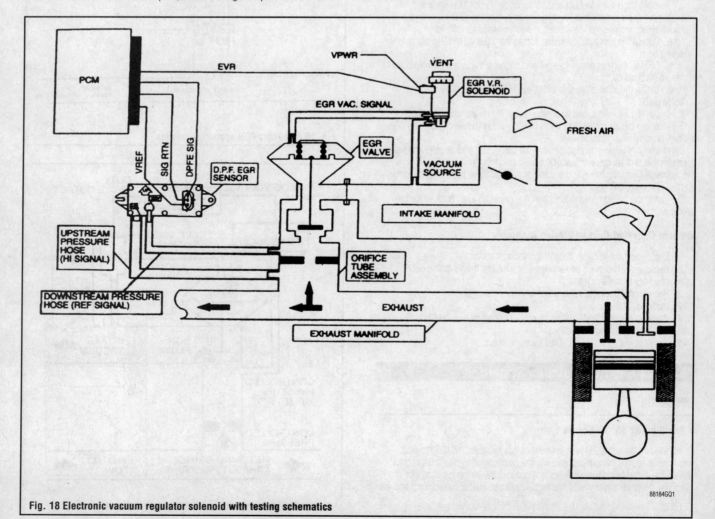

Fig. 18 Electronic vacuum regulator solenoid with testing schematics

88184GQ1

To install:
5. Attach the EGR valve with a new gasket and tighten.
6. Attach the vacuum lines to the valve.
7. Connect the negative battery cable.

Electronic EGR

The electronic EGR valve is vacuum operated. When the vacuum signal becomes strong enough, the pintle is lifted off of it's seat which allows the exhaust gas to recirculate. The main difference between the ported EGR valve and the electronic EGR valve is that there is a EGR valve position sensor mounted on top of the electronic EGR valve. The EVP sensor must be serviced separately from the EGR valve. The electronic EGR valve is not serviceable.
1. Disconnect the negative battery cable.
2. Disconnect the vacuum line from the EGR valve.
3. Remove the mounting bolts and remove the EGR valve.
4. Remove the EVP sensor from the EGR valve.
5. Remove any old gasket material from the engine mating area.

To install:
6. Attach the EVP sensor to the EGR valve.
7. Install the EGR valve to the engine with a new gasket and tighten.
8. Attach the vacuum line to the valve.
9. Connect the negative battery cable.

Pressure Feedback Electronic (PFE) Transducer

The PFE EGR transducer converts exhaust pressure into proportional voltage which is digitized by the PCM. The PCM utilizes the signal from the PFE to maintain optimum EGR flow.
1. Disconnect the negative battery cable.

2. Detach the electrical connector and exhaust pressure line from the transducer.
3. Remove the transducer from the vehicle.

To install:
4. Attach the transducer to the engine and tighten the mounting bolt.
5. Attach the electrical connector and exhaust pressure line to the transducer.

Differential Pressure Feedback EGR

3.8L ENGINE

▶ See Figure 20

1. Disconnect the negative battery cable.
2. Disconnect the PCV hose from the air cleaner.
3. Remove the air cleaner outlet tube from the throttle body and mass air flow sensor.
4. Disconnect the emission vacuum control hose from the valve.
5. Separate the fuel charging wiring from the EGR pressure sensor.
6. Disconnect the EGR pressure sensor hose(s) from the valve-to-exhaust manifold tube.
7. Remove the transducer mounting bracket retainers. Remove the pressure sensor and transducer mounting bracket from the engine.
8. Disconnect the EGR valve-to-exhaust manifold tube from the EGR valve.
9. Remove the valve bolts and valve from the vehicle.
10. Discard the old gasket and clean the mating areas.

To install:
11. Apply a heat resistant sealer on the gasket and mating areas of the valve.
12. Attach the valve with gasket on the engine and tighten the mounting bolts to 15–22 ft. lbs. (20–30 Nm).

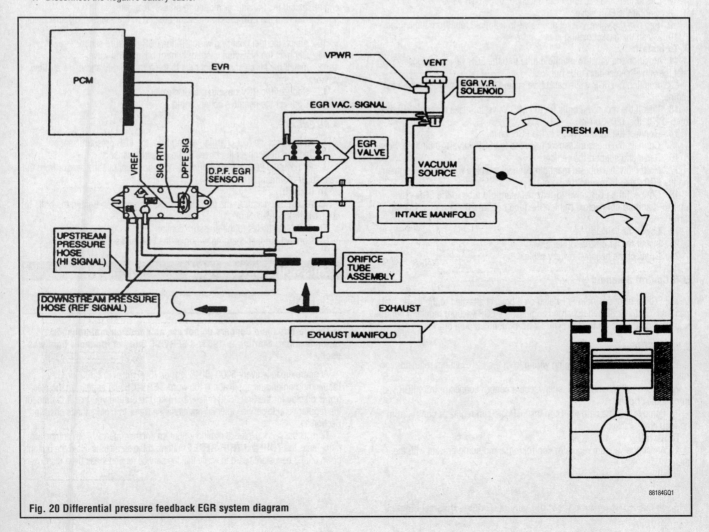

Fig. 20 Differential pressure feedback EGR system diagram

13. Attach the EGR valve-to-exhaust manifold tube to the EGR valve and tighten the bolts to 26–33 ft. lbs. (35–45 Nm).

14. Attach the pressure sensor and transducer mounting bracket to the engine. Install the transducer mounting bracket retainers.

15. Connect the EGR pressure sensor hose(s) to the valve-to-exhaust manifold tube.

16. Attach the fuel charging wiring to the EGR pressure sensor.

17. Connect the emission vacuum control hose to the valve.

18. Install the air cleaner outlet tube to the throttle body and mass air flow sensor.

19. Connect the PCV hose to the air cleaner.

20. Connect the negative battery cable.

4.6L ENGINE

➡️**On this procedure it will be necessary to raise and lower the vehicle several times.**

1. Disconnect the negative battery cable.
2. Raise and safely support the vehicle on a hoist.
3. Remove the air cleaner outlet tube.

➡️**Be careful not to damage the EGR valve tube-to-manifold connection. Hold the valve tube-to manifold connector with a wrench while disconnecting the EGR valve-to manifold tube.**

4. Disconnect the EGR valve-to-manifold tube from the EGR valve and valve tube-to manifold connector.

5. Lower the vehicle.

6. Disconnect the EGR pressure sensor hoses from the EGR valve-to manifold tube.

7. Disconnect the vacuum hose attached to the EGR valve.

8. Unbolt the EGR valve.

9. Remove the valve, gasket and valve-to manifold tube from the engine.

10. Clean the gasket mating areas.

To install:

11. Position the valve-to manifold tube into the EGR valve and loosely connect the valve-to-manifold tube nut.

12. Position the EGR valve gasket, valve and valve-to-manifold nut on the engine.

13. Install the mounting bolts for the EGR valve-to intake manifold. Tighten to 15–22 ft. lbs. (20–30 Nm).

14. Connect the vacuum hose to the EGR valve.

15. Connect the pressure sensor hoses to the EGR valve-to-manifold.

16. Raise and support the vehicle.

17. Hold the valve tube-to manifold connector with a wrench while tightening the EGR valve-to manifold tube nut.

18. Connect the EGR valve-to-exhaust manifold tube to the EGR valve tube-to-manifold connector. Tighten the tube nuts to 26–33 ft. lbs. (35–45 Nm).

19. Lower the vehicle.

20. Install the air cleaner outlet tube.

21. Connect the negative battery cable.

EGR Control Solenoid

The EGR control solenoid is located on a bracket attached to the lower intake manifold. On the 3.8L supercharged engines, the EGR vacuum regulator control is located on the rear of the left cylinder head mounted on a bracket.

3.8L ENGINE

1. Disconnect the fuel charging wiring from the EGR vacuum regulator control.

2. Disconnect the main emission vacuum control connector from EGR vacuum regulator control.

3. Remove the retaining nuts and the EGR vacuum regulator control from the mounting bracket.

To install:

4. Attach the vacuum regulator control to the mounting bracket with the nuts.

5. Connect the main emission vacuum control connector to the EGR vacuum regulator control.

6. Attach the fuel wiring to the EGR vacuum regulator control.

4.6L ENGINE

1. Disconnect the fuel charging wiring from the EGR vacuum regulator control.

2. Disconnect the emission vacuum control connector from the EGR vacuum regulator control

3. Remove the retaining nut and EGR vacuum regulator control from the transducer mounting bracket located at the rear of the lower intake manifold.

4. Reverse to install. Tighten the retaining nut for the EGR vacuum regulator to 40–61 inch lbs. (5–7 Nm).

EGR Pressure Sensor

3.8L ENGINE

1. Disconnect the negative battery cable.
2. Disconnect the PCV hose from the air cleaner.
3. Remove the air cleaner outlet tube from the throttle body and mass air flow sensor.
4. Disconnect the emission vacuum control hose from the valve.
5. Separate the fuel charging wiring from the EGR pressure sensor.
6. Disconnect the EGR pressure sensor hose(s) from the valve-to-exhaust manifold tube.
7. Remove the transducer mounting bracket retainers. Remove the pressure sensor and transducer mounting bracket from the engine.

To install:

8. Attach the pressure sensor and transducer mounting bracket to the engine. Install the transducer mounting bracket retainers.

9. Connect the EGR pressure sensor hose(s) to the valve-to-exhaust manifold tube.

10. Attach the fuel charging wiring to the EGR pressure sensor.

11. Connect the emission vacuum control hose to the valve.

12. Install the air cleaner outlet tube to the throttle body and mass air flow sensor.

13. Connect the PCV hose to the air cleaner.

14. Connect the negative battery cable.

4.6L ENGINE

1. Disconnect the fuel charging wiring from the EGR pressure sensor.

2. Tag and disconnect the hoses at the pressure sensor.

3. Remove the EGR sensor mounting bolts and separate the sensor from the transducer mounting bracket.

To install:

4. Attach the sensor to the transducer mounting bracket, tighten the bolts to 40–61 inch lbs. (5–7 Nm).

5. Attach the hoses to the pressure sensor.

6. Connect the fuel charging wiring to the EGR pressure sensor.

Emission Service Lights

RESETTING

➡️**Thunderbirds and Cougars do not use an emission maintenance reminder light. Starting in 1985, a SERVICE interval reminder light was used.**

At approximately every 5000 (8046 km) or 7500 miles (12,070 km), (depending on engine application) the word **SERVICE** will appear on the electronic display for the first 1500 miles (2414 km) to remind you that it is time for the regular vehicle service interval maintenance (refer to maintenance chart in Section 1).

To reset the service interval reminder light for another interval. With engine running, press the **TRIP** and **TRIP RESET** buttons at the same time. Hold the buttons down until 3 beeps are heard to verify that the service reminder has been reset.

ELECTRONIC ENGINE CONTROLS

Electronic Engine Control (EEC)

All CFI and MFI engines use the EEC system. The heart of the EEC system is a micro-processor called an Powertrain Control Module (PCM). The PCM receives data from a number of sensors and other electronic components (switches, relay, etc.). Based on information received and information programmed in the PCM's memory, it generates output signals to control various relay, solenoids and other actuators. The PCM in the EEC system has calibration modules located inside the assembly that contain calibration specifications for optimizing emissions, fuel economy and drive ability. The calibration module is called a PROM.

A potentiometer senses the position of the vane airflow meter in the engine's air induction system and generates a voltage signal that varies with the amount of air drawn into the engine. A sensor in the area of the vane airflow meter measures the temperature of the incoming air and transmits a corresponding electrical signal. Another temperature sensor inserted in the engine coolant tells if the engine is cold or warmed up. And a switch that senses throttle plate position produces electrical signals that tell the control unit when the throttle is closed or wide open.

A special probe (oxygen sensor) in the exhaust manifold measures the amount of oxygen in the exhaust gas, which is in indication of combustion efficiency, and sends a signal to the control unit. The sixth signal, crankshaft position information, is transmitted by a sensor integral with the new-design distributor.

The EEC microcomputer circuit processes the input signals and produces output control signals to the fuel injectors to regulate fuel discharged to the injectors. It also adjusts ignition spark timing to provide the best balance between driveability and economy.

➡️**Because of the complicated nature of the Ford system, special tools and procedures are necessary for testing and troubleshooting.**

Powertrain Control Module (PCM)

OPERATION

The Powertrain Control Module (PCM) performs many functions on your car. The module accepts information from various engine sensors and computes the required fuel flow rate necessary to maintain the correct amount of air/fuel ratio throughout the entire engine operational range.

Based on the information that is received and programmed into the PCM's memory, the PCM generates output signals to control relays, actuators and

solenoids. The PCM also sends out a command to the fuel injectors that meters the appropriate quantity of fuel. The module automatically senses and compensates for any changes in altitude when driving your vehicle.

REMOVAL & INSTALLATION

1. Disconnect the negative battery cable.
2. Remove the right cowl trim panel.
3. Disconnect the module wiring leading to the unit.
4. Remove the control unit from the bracket by pulling the unit downwards.

To install:
5. Attach the module to the bracket.
6. Attach the wiring to the module.
7. Install the right cowl trim panel.
8. Connect the negative battery cable.

Oxygen Sensors

OPERATION

▶ See Figure 21

The oxygen sensor supplies the computer with a signal which indicates a rich or lean condition during engine operation. The input information assists the computer in determining the proper air/fuel ratio. The oxygen sensor is threaded into the exhaust manifold or exhaust pipes on all vehicles. Heated oxygen sensors are used on some models to allow the engine to reach the closed loop faster.

TESTING

▶ See Figure 22

1. Disconnect the Oxygen Sensor (O_2S).
2. On heated O_2S sensors, measure the resistance between PWR and GND terminals of the sensor. If the reading is about 6 ohms at 68°F (20°C). the sensor's heater element is okay.
3. With the O_2S connected and engine running, measure voltage with DVOM between terminals O_2S and **SIG RTN** (GND) of the oxygen sensor connector. If the voltage readings are about equal to those in the table, the sensor is okay.

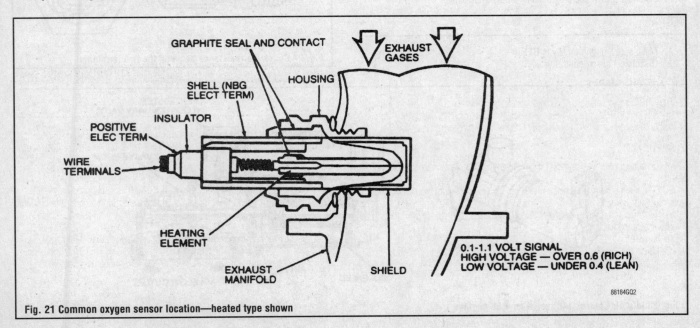

Fig. 21 Common oxygen sensor location—heated type shown

88184GQ2

Condition	Voltage—Between Terminals HO2S and SIG RTN
Ignition ON, engine OFF	0V
Idle (cold)	0V
Idle (warm)	0–1.0V
Acceleration	0.5–1.0V
Deceleration	0–0.5V

88184GZA

Fig. 22 The heated oxygen sensor voltage table

REMOVAL & INSTALLATION

➡**The 4.6L engine uses four heated oxygen sensors for the engine control system. The heated sensors are located in the dual converter and pipe. On the 3.8L engines, there are two sensors, one is located in the left exhaust manifold and the other in the dual converter Y pipe.**

1. Disconnect the negative battery cable.
2. Raise and safely support the vehicle.
3. Disconnect the heated oxygen sensor from the engine control sensor wiring.

➡**If excessive force is needed to remove the sensors, lubricate the sensors with penetrating oil prior to removal.**

4. Remove the sensors from the Y pipe or left manifold with a sensor removal tool T94P-9472-A or equivalent.
To install:
5. Install the sensor in its correct location, tighten to 26–34 ft. lbs. (36–46 Nm).
6. Connect the sensor electrical wiring.
7. Lower the vehicle.
8. Connect the negative battery cable.

Idle Air Control (IAC) Valve

OPERATION

▶ **See Figure 23**

The Idle Air Control (IAC) valve control the engine idle speed and dashpot functions. The valve is located on the throttle body on the 2.3L, 3.8L and 5.0L engines, and on the intake manifold on the 4.6L engines. This valve allows air to bypass the throttle plate. The amount of air is determined by the Powertrain Control Module (PCM) and controlled by a duty cycle signal.

TESTING

1. Make sure the ignition key is **OFF**.
2. Disconnect the air control valve.

3. Use an ohmmeter to measure the resistance between the terminals of the valve solenoid.

➡**Due to the diode in the solenoid, place the ohmmeter positive lead on the VPWR pin and the negative lead on the ISC pin.**

4. If the resistance is not 7–13 ohms replace the air control valve.

REMOVAL & INSTALLATION

1. Disconnect the negative battery cable.
2. Disconnect the engine wiring to the IAC sensor.
3. Remove the two retaining screws for the valve.
4. Remove the IAC valve and discard of the old gasket.
To install:
5. Clean the area of old gasket material.
6. Using a new gasket, attach the IAC valve to the engine. Tighten the retaining screws to 71–102 inch lbs. (8–12 Nm) on the 2.3L, 3.8L and 5.0L engines and 7 ft. lbs. (10 Nm) on the 4.6L engines.
7. Connect the IAC valve wiring to the unit.
8. Connect the negative battery cable.

Engine Coolant Temperature (ECT) Sensor

OPERATION

The engine coolant temperature sensor changes the resistance in response to the engine coolant temperature. The sensor decreases the resistance as the surrounding temperature increases. This provides a signal to the PCM that indicates the engine coolant temperature.

TESTING

▶ **See Figures 24 and 25**

1. Disconnect the temperature sensor.
2. Connect an ohmmeter between the sensor terminals and set the ohmmeter scale on 200,000 ohms.

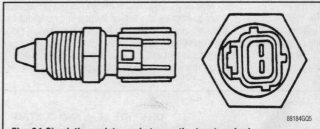

88184GQ5

Fig. 24 Check the resistance between the two terminals

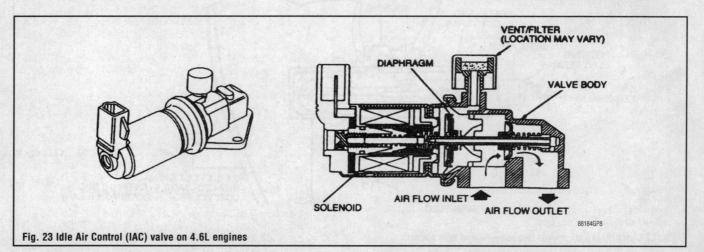

Fig. 23 Idle Air Control (IAC) valve on 4.6L engines

Labels in Fig. 23: VENT/FILTER (LOCATION MAY VARY), DIAPHRAGM, VALVE BODY, AIR FLOW INLET, AIR FLOW OUTLET, SOLENOID

88184GP8

Temperature		Engine Coolant/Air Charge Temperature Sensor Values	
°F	°C	Voltage (volts)	Resistance (K ohms)
248	120	.27	1.18
230	110	.35	1.55
212	100	.46	2.07
194	90	.60	2.80
176	80	.78	3.84
158	70	1.02	5.37
140	60	1.33	7.70
122	50	1.70	10.97
104	40	2.13	16.15
86	30	2.60	24.27
68	20	3.07	37.30
50	10	3.51	58.75

88184GZP

Fig. 25 ACT, IAT and ECT temperature sensor value chart

3. Measure the resistance with the engine off and cool and with the engine running and warmed up. Compare the resistance values obtained with the chart.

4. Replace the sensor if the readings are incorrect.

REMOVAL & INSTALLATION

1. Drain the engine cooling system slightly.
2. Disconnect the negative battery cable.
3. Detach the wiring connection from the sensor.
4. Remove the coolant temperature sensor from the intake manifold.
5. Clean the sensor area of any debris.

To install:

6. Install a new sensor into the intake manifold. Tighten the 6–14 ft. lbs. (8–19 Nm).
7. Attach the sensor wiring to the unit.
8. Connect the negative battery cable.
9. Fill the engine cooling system with a 50/50 coolant water mixture.
10. Start the engine and top off the cooling system.

Intake Air Temperature (IAT) Sensor

OPERATION

The Intake Air Temperature (IAT) sensor changes the resistance in response to the intake air temperature. The sensor resistance decreases as the surrounding air temperature increases. This provides a signal to the PCM indicating the temperature of the incoming air intake.

TESTING

♦ **See Figures 25 and 26**

Except 2.3L Engines

With ignition **OFF**, disconnect the IAT sensor. Measure the resistance across the sensor connector terminals. If the reading for a given temperature is about that shown in the table, the IAT sensor is okay.

2.3L Engines

1. Disconnect the vane air flow meter connector.
2. Access the sensor in the meter.
3. Monitor the temperature near the sensor.

➥ **If using a hot air gun to heat the sensor, be careful not to melt any plastic or rubber components.**

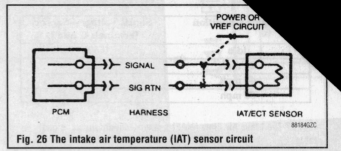

Fig. 26 The intake air temperature (IAT) sensor circuit

4. Measure the resistance between the meter black/white terminal and the meter pink/black terminal and record.
5. Compare the resistance readings with the chart. If the readings are incorrect, replace the sensor.

REMOVAL & INSTALLATION

2.3L Engines

The air temperature sensor is an integral component of the vane air flow meter. If the temperature sensor is defective, the vane air flow meter must be replaced.

3.8L and 5.0L Engines

1. Disconnect the negative battery cable.
2. Disconnect the wiring to the IAT.
3. Remove the sensor from the intake manifold.

To install:

4. Clean the sensor area. Install the sensor into the intake manifold and tighten to 6–8 ft. lbs. (8–13 Nm).
5. Attach the wiring to the unit.
6. Connect the negative battery cable.

4.6L Engine

1. Disconnect the negative battery cable.
2. Disconnect the wiring to the IAT.
3. Remove the sensor from the air cleaner cover.

To install:

4. Clean the sensor area. Install the sensor into the air cleaner cover.
5. Attach the wiring to the unit.
6. Connect the negative battery cable.

Mass Air Flow (MAF) Sensor

OPERATION

The Mass Air Flow (MAF) sensor directly measures the mass of the air flowing into the engine. The sensor output is an analog signal ranging from about 0.5–5.0 volts. The signal is used by the PCM to calculate the injector pulse width. The sensing element is a thin platinum wire wound on a ceramic bobbin and coated with glass. This "hot wire" is maintained at 392°F (200°C) above the ambient temperature as measured by a constant "cold wire". The MAF sensor is located in the outlet side of the air cleaner lid assembly on all models except the 1995–97 4.6L and 1996–97 3.8L engines. On the 1995–97 4.6L and 1996–97 3.8L engines, the sensor is located between the air cleaner and the throttle body.

TESTING

♦ **See Figure 27**

Except 1995–97 4.6L and 1996–97 3.8L Engines

1. With engine running, use DVOM to verify there is at least 10.5 volts between terminals A and B of the MAF sensor connector. This indicates the power input to the sensor is okay.

CONTROLS

Signal Voltage—Sensor Terminals C and D
0.60V
1.10V
1.70V
2.10V

88184GZK

Fig. 27 The Mass Air Flow (MAF) sensor—conditions vs. signal table

2. With engine running, use DVOM to measure voltage between MAF sensor connector terminals C and D. If the readings are about as indicated in the table, the sensor is okay. The readings may vary based on vehicle load and temperature.

1995–97 4.6L and 1996–97 3.8L Engines

▶ **See Figures 28 and 29**

1. With engine running, use DVOM to verify there is at least 10.5 volts between terminals A and B of the MAF sensor connector. This indicates the power input to the sensor is okay.

2. With engine running, use DVOM to measure voltage between MAF sensor connector terminals C and D. If the reading is about 0.34–1.96 volts at idle, the sensor is okay.

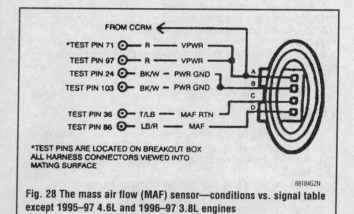

88184GZN

Fig. 28 The mass air flow (MAF) sensor—conditions vs. signal table except 1995–97 4.6L and 1996–97 3.8L engines

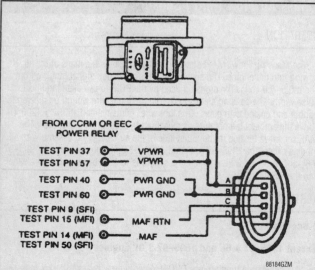

88184GZM

Fig. 29 The mass air flow (MAF) sensor connector—1995–97 4.6L and 1996–97 3.8L engines

REMOVAL & INSTALLATION

✳✳ CAUTION

The mass air flow sensor hot wire sensing element and housing are calibrated as a unit and must be serviced as a complete assembly. Do not damage the sensing element or possible failure of the sensor may occur.

1. Disconnect the negative battery cable.
2. Disconnect the engine control sensor wiring from the MAF sensor.
3. Loosen the engine air cleaner outlet tube clamps and the engine air cleaner cover.
4. Disconnect the mass air flow sensor.
   To install:
5. Install the MAF sensor to the vehicle.
6. Install the air cleaner cover and tighten the outlet tube clamps to 12–22 inch lbs. (1–3 Nm).
7. Attach the engine control sensor wiring to the sensor.
8. Connect the negative battery cable.

Throttle Position (TP) Sensor

OPERATION

▶ **See Figure 30**

The Throttle Position (TP) sensor is a potentiometer that provides a signal to the PCM that is directly proportional to the throttle plate position. The TP sensor is mounted on the side of the throttle body and is connected to the throttle plate shaft.

The TPS is mounted on the right side of the throttle body, directly connected to the throttle shaft. The TPS senses the throttle movement and position and transmits an appropriate electrical signal to the PCM. These signals are used by the PCM to adjust the air/fuel mixture, spark timing and EGR operation according to engine load at idle, part throttle, or full throttle. The TPS is nonadjustable.

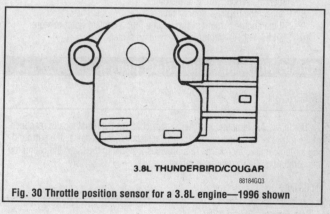

3.8L THUNDERBIRD/COUGAR

88184GQ3

Fig. 30 Throttle position sensor for a 3.8L engine—1996 shown

TESTING

1. Disconnect the negative battery cable.
2. Remove the PCM and connect a breakout box to the PCM and harness.
3. Probe terminals 89 and 90 with an ohmmeter.
4. Slowly rotate the throttle shaft and monitor the ohmmeter for a continuous change in resistance. Any sudden changes in resistance indicates an open or substrate sensor.
5. Reconnect the negative battery cable.
6. Turn the ignition switch **ON** and using a voltmeter, measure the voltage between terminals 89 and 90 of the breakout box. The specification is 0.8 volts on the 2.3L, 3.8L and 5.0L engines or 0.9 volts on the 4.6L engine.
7. If the voltage is outside the standard value or if it does not change smoothly, inspect the circuit wiring and/or replace the throttle position sensor.

REMOVAL & INSTALLATION

2.3L and 3.8L (Except SC) Engines

EXCEPT 1996–97

1. Disconnect the throttle position sensor from the wiring harness.
2. Matchmark the sensor and throttle body.
3. Remove the two retaining screws.
4. Remove the throttle position sensor.

To install:

5. Align the matchmarks and install the sensor.
6. Tighten the sensor screws 11–16 inch lbs. (1–2 Nm).

➡This throttle position sensor is not adjustable.

3.8L (SC) Engine

EXCEPT 1996–97

1. Disconnect the negative battery cable.
2. Disconnect the idle bypass valve wiring.
3. Remove the lower IBV bolt and loosen the upper. Rotate the valve out of the way to gain access to the TPS bolts.
4. Disconnect the TPS wiring and remove the bolts.
5. Remove the sensor.

To install:

6. Attach the sensor and tighten the screws to 26 inch lbs. (3 Nm).; and the IBV bolts to 70-100 inch lbs. (8–11 Nm).
7. Attach the wiring to the sensor.
8. Connect the negative battery cable.

3.8L and 4.6L Engines

1995–97 4.6L AND 1996–97 3.8L ENGINES

1. Disconnect the negative battery cable.
2. Detach the wiring leading to the sensor.
3. Remove the two screws retaining the sensor to the throttle body.
4. Remove the TP sensor.

To install:

5. Install the sensor with the retaining screws. Tighten the screws to 25–34 inch lbs. (3–4 Nm).
6. Attach the wire to the sensor.
7. Connect the negative battery cable.

5.0L Engines

1. Disconnect the TPS wiring harness.
2. Matchmark the TPS and throttle body.

3. Remove the 2 retaining screws and the sensor.

To install:

4. If the sensor had a bushing, it must be reused. Install the bushing with the larger diameter facing outwards.
5. Install the TPS on the throttle shaft and rotate the sensor 10-20° counter-clockwise to align the bolt holes.
6. Install the bolts and tighten them to 11-15 inch lbs. (1–2 Nm).
7. Cycle the throttle to the wide open position. It should return without interference.
8. Connect the wiring.
9. Connect the negative battery cable.

Camshaft Position (CMP) Sensor

OPERATION

The distributor stator or Camshaft Position Sensor, is a single Hall effect magnetic switch. This is activated by a single vane. This is driven by the camshaft.

The distributor stator or Camshaft Position sensor provides the camshaft position information. The sensor also provides what is called the CMP signal. This signal is used by the powertrain control module (PCM) for fuel synchronization.

On the 4.6L engines, the Camshaft Position (CMP) sensor is a variable reluctance sensor that is triggered by the high-point mark on the camshaft sprocket.

TESTING

▶ See Figures 31 and 32

Three Wire Sensors

1. With the ignition **OFF**, disconnect the CMP sensor. With the ignition **ON** and the engine **OFF**, measure the voltage between sensor harness connector VPWR and PWR GND terminals (refer to the figure). If the reading is greater than 10.5 volts, the power circuit to the sensor is okay.
2. With the ignition **OFF**, install breakout box. Connect CMP sensor and ECM. Using DVOM on AC and scale set to monitor less than 5 volts, measure voltage between breakout box terminals 24 and 40 with the engine running at varying RPM. If the voltage reading varies more than 0.1 volt AC, the sensor is okay.

Two Wire Sensors

1. With the ignition **OFF**, install breakout box.
2. Connect CMP sensor and ECM.

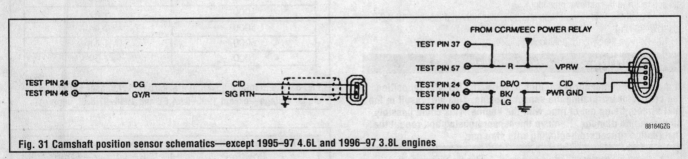

Fig. 31 Camshaft position sensor schematics—except 1995–97 4.6L and 1996–97 3.8L engines

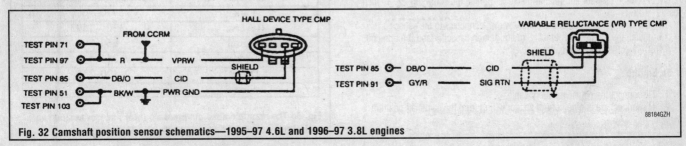

Fig. 32 Camshaft position sensor schematics—1995–97 4.6L and 1996–97 3.8L engines

3. Using DVOM on AC scale and set to monitor less than 5 volts, measure voltage between breakout box terminals 24 and 46 with the engine running at varying RPM. If the voltage reading varies more than 0.1 volt AC, the sensor is okay.

REMOVAL & INSTALLATION

Except 4.6L Engines

✳✳ CAUTION

Prior to removing the camshaft position sensor, set the No. 1 cylinder to 26° after top dead center of the compression stroke. Note the position of the sensor electrical connection. When installing the sensor, the connection must be in the exact position on installation.

1. Disconnect the negative battery cable.
2. Remove the ignition coil, radio capacitor and ignition coil bracket.
3. Remove the camshaft position sensor retaining screw and sensor.
4. Remove the retaining bolt and hold-down clamp.
5. The oil pump intermediate shaft should be removed with the camshaft sensor housing. Remove the housing from the front engine cover.

To install:

✳✳ CAUTION

If the camshaft position sensor housing does not contain a plastic locator cover tool, a special service tool such as T89P–12200–A or equivalent must be obtained prior to installation. Failure to follow this procedure may result in improper stator alignment. This will result in the fuel system being out of time with the engine, possibly causing engine damage.

➡If the plastic locator cover is not attached to the replacement camshaft position sensor, attach a synchro positioning tool T89P–12200–A or equivalent. To do so perform the following.

6. Engage the sensor housing vane into the radial slot of the tool.
   a. Rotate the tool on the camshaft sensor housing until the tool boss engages notch in the sensor housing.
   b. The cover tool should be square and in contact with the entire top surface of the camshaft position sensor housing.
7. Transfer the oil pump intermediate shaft from the old camshaft position sensor housing to the replacement sensor housing.
8. Install the camshaft sensor housing so that the drive gear engagement occurs when the arrow on the locator tool is pointed approximately 30° counterclockwise from the face of the cylinder block. This will locate the sensor electrical connector in the removal procedure.
9. Install the hold-down clamp and bolt, then tighten the bolt to 15–22 ft. lbs. (20–30 Nm).
10. Remove the synchro positioning tool.

✳✳ CAUTION

If the sensor connector is positioned correctly, DO NOT reposition the connector by rotating the sensor housing. This will result in the fuel system being out of time with the engine. This could possibly cause engine damage. Remove the sensor housing and repeat the installation procedure beginning with step one.

11. Install the sensor and retaining screws, tighten the screws to 22–31 inch lbs. (2–4 Nm).
12. Connect the engine control sensor wiring connector to the sensor.
13. Install the ignition coil bracket, radio ignition capacitor and ignition coil.
14. Connect the negative battery cable.

4.6L Engine

1. Disconnect the negative battery cable.
2. Disconnect the engine control sensor wiring from the camshaft position sensor.

3. Remove the sensor retaining screw and the sensor from the front of the engine front cover.

To install:

4. Make sure the camshaft position sensor mounting surface is clean and the O-ring is positioned correctly.
5. Position the sensor, then install the retaining screw and tighten to 71–106 inch lbs. (8–12 Nm).

✳✳ CAUTION

Do not overtighten the screw.

6. Connect the sensor wiring to the sensor.
7. Connect the negative battery cable.

Barometric/Manifold Absolute Pressure Sensors (B/MAP)

OPERATION

The B/MAP sensor used on 3.8L engines is separate from the barometric sensor and is located on the left fender panel in the engine compartment. The barometric sensor signals the PCM of changes in atmospheric pressure and density to regulate calculated air flow into the engine. The MAP sensor monitors and signals the PCM of changes in intake manifold pressure which result from engine load, speed and atmospheric pressure changes.

The Manifold Absolute Pressure (MAP) sensor measures the pressure in the intake manifold and sends a variable frequency signal to the Powertrain Control Module (PCM). When the ignition is **ON** and the engine **OFF**, the MAP sensor will indicate the barometric pressure in the intake manifold.

TESTING

▶ **See Figures 33, 34 and 35**

1. Connect **MAP/BARO** tester to sensor connector and sensor harness connector. With ignition **ON** and engine **OFF**, use DVOM to measure voltage

Approximate Altitude (Feet)	Signal Voltage (±0.04V)
0	1.59
1000	1.56
2000	1.53
3000	1.50
4000	1.47
5000	1.44
6000	1.41
7000	1.39

88184GZD

Fig. 33 The manifold absolute pressure (MAP) sensor altitude vs. signal voltage—except 1995–97 4.6L and 1996–97 3.8L engines

Transmission Range Position	Resistance—Ohms
Park	3770–4607
Reverse	1304–1593
Neutral	660–807
Overdrive	361–442
Drive	190–232
First	78–95

88184GZE

Fig. 34 The manifold absolute pressure (MAP) sensor position vs. resistance—1995–97 4.6L and 1996–97 3.8L engines

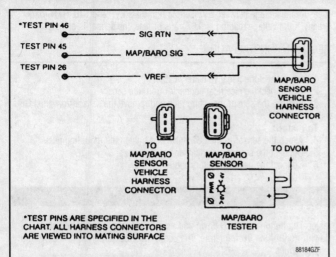

*TEST PINS ARE SPECIFIED IN THE CHART. ALL HARNESS CONNECTORS ARE VIEWED INTO MATING SURFACE

Fig. 35 Barometric/Manifold Absolute Pressure Sensors (B/MAP) circuit and tester—except 1995–97 4.6L and 1996–97 3.8L engines

across tester terminals. If the tester's 4-6 volts indicator is ON, the reference voltage input to the sensor is okay.

2. If the DVOM voltage reading is as indicated in the table, the sensor is okay.

REMOVAL & INSTALLATION

1. Disconnect the negative battery cable.
2. Disconnect the electrical wiring and the vacuum line from the sensor.
3. Remove the sensor mounting bolts and remove the sensor.
To install:
4. Install the sensor with the mounting bolts and tighten.
5. Attach the electrical wiring lead to the sensor.
6. Attach the vacuum line to the sensor.
7. Connect the negative battery cable.

Crankshaft Position (CP) Sensor

OPERATION

▶ **See Figure 36**

The Crankshaft Position (CP) sensor, located inside the front cover is used to determine crankshaft position and crankshaft rpm.

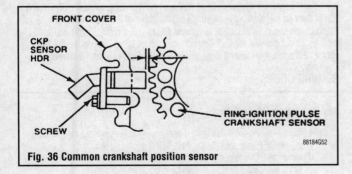

Fig. 36 Common crankshaft position sensor

TESTING

▶ **See Figure 37**

Using DVOM on the AC scale and set to monitor less than 5 volts, measure voltage between the sensor Cylinder Identification (CID) terminal and ground.

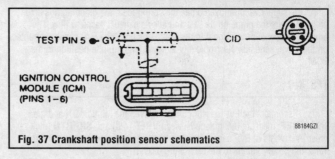

Fig. 37 Crankshaft position sensor schematics

The sensor is okay if the voltage reading varies more than 0.1 volt AC with the engine running at varying RPM.

REMOVAL & INSTALLATION

1. Disconnect the negative battery cable.
2. Loosen the water pump pulley bolts, then remove the accessory drive belt is necessary.
3. Disconnect the wiring to the crankshaft position sensor. Remove the sensor mounting bolt, then remove the sensor.
To install:
4. Install the sensor and connect the wiring. Tighten the mounting bolt to 71–106 inch lbs. (8–12 Nm).
5. Install the accessory drive belt if removed. Tighten the water pump pulley bolts as described in Section 1.
6. Connect the negative battery cable.

Knock Sensor (KS)

OPERATION

This sensor is used on various models equipped with the 3.8L engine. It is attached to the intake manifold in front of the ACT sensor. The KS detects engine vibrations caused by preignition or detonation and provides information to the PCM, which then retards the timing to eliminate detonation.

TESTING

1. With ignition **ON** and engine **OFF**, measure voltage between KS connector terminals. If voltage reading is 2.4-2.6 volts, the circuit between the ECM and KS is okay.
2. With engine running at idle and 3000 rpm, measure voltage using a DVOM on the AC setting between the KS terminals. If the AC voltage reading increases as the rpm increases, the sensor is okay.

REMOVAL & INSTALLATION

1. Disconnect the negative battery cable.
2. Disconnect the electrical wiring from the sensor.
3. Remove the sensor from the front of the ACT sensor.
To install:
4. Attach the KS to the front of the ACT sensor.
5. Attach the electrical connector to the sensor.
6. Connect the negative battery cable.

EGR Valve Position (EVP) Sensor

OPERATION

The EGR Valve Position (EVP) system uses an electronic EGR valve to control the flow of exhaust gases. The Powertrain Control Module (PCM) monitors the flow by means of an EVP sensor and regulates the electronic EGR valve accordingly. The valve is operated by a vacuum signal from the EGR Vacuum Regulator (EVR) solenoid which actuates the valve diaphragm.

As the supply vacuum overcomes the spring load, the diaphragm is actuated. This lifts the pintle off its seat and allows exhaust gases to flow. The amount of flow is proportional to the pintle position. The EVP sensor, mounted on the valve, sends an electronic signal representing pintle position to the ECM.

TESTING

1. Disconnect the EVP sensor connector. With the ignition **ON** and the engine **OFF**, measure the voltage between **VREF** (red) and **SIG RTN** (dark green) terminals of EVP sensor harness connector. If the voltage is 4.0–6.0 volts, the power circuits to the sensor are okay.
2. Reconnect the EVP sensor. With the ignition **ON** and the engine **OFF**, measure the voltage between EVP sensor terminals EVP and **SIG RTN** (dark green). If the voltage reading is 0.67 volts or less, the sensor is okay.

REMOVAL & INSTALLATION

1. Disconnect the negative battery cable.
2. Disconnect the electrical connector from the sensor.
3. Remove the sensor mounting nuts and remove the sensor from the EGR valve.

To install:
4. Attach the sensor to the EGR valve and tighten the mounting nuts.
5. Connect the sensor electrical lead to the sensor.
6. Connect the negative battery cable.

EEC-IV TROUBLE CODES

• These procedures apply only to vehicles equipped with fourth generation Electronic Engine Controls (EEC-IV). This is found on all models except 1995–97 4.6L and 1996–97 3.8L engines
• The Key On Engine Off and Engine Running self tests detect faults that are present at the time of testing. Intermittent faults that have occurred in the last 80 (40 for some applications) warm-up cycles are detected during continuous self test and stored in the EEC-IV memory
• Vehicles with a Malfunction Indicator Light (MIL) concern must run quick test and address all service codes present
• If all phases of the quick test result in a Pass, it is likely that the problem is non EEC-IV related and will be found elsewhere
• After service, rerun quick test to ensure that service was effective

General Information

All vehicles have self-diagnostic capabilities. Malfunctions in the engine control system are found through the Self-Test procedure. Vehicles using the EEC-IV system use a Self-Test divided into 3 specialized tests: Key On Engine Off Self-Test, Engine Running Self-Test and Continuous Self-Test. The Self-Test is not a conclusive test by itself, but is used as a part of a functional Quick Test diagnostic procedure. The PCM stores the Self-Test program in its permanent memory. When activated, it checks the EEC-IV system by testing it's memory integrity and processing capability and verifies that various sensors and actuators are connected and operating properly. The Key On Engine Off and Engine Running Self-Tests are functional tests which only detect faults present at the time of the Self-Test. Continuous Self-Test is an ongoing test that stores fault information in Keep Alive Memory (KAM) for retrieval at a later time.

Fault information is communicated through the Self-Test service codes. These service codes are 2-digit or 3-digit numbers representing the results of the Self-Test. The 3-digit numbers start in the 1991 models. The service codes are transmitted on the Self-Test output line found in the vehicle Self-Test connector. They are in the form of timed pulses and are read on a voltmeter, STAR or SUPER STAR II tester and the malfunction indicator light.

VEHICLE PREPARATION

1. Apply the parking brake, place the transaxle shift lever firmly into **P** on automatic transaxle or neutral on manual transaxles and block the drive wheels.
2. Turn all electrical loads such as the radio, lights, blower fan, etc. OFF.

Using The Star Or Super Star II Tester

➡The STAR tester cannot be used to read 3-digit service codes. If the STAR tester is used on a 3-digit service code application, the display will be blank. The SUPER STAR II tester must be used to read 3-digit service codes.

After hooking up the STAR tester and turning on it's power switch, the tester will run a display check and the numerals **88** will begin to flash in the display window. A steady **00** will then appear, indicating that the STAR tester is ready. To receive service codes, press the button on the front of the STAR tester. The button will latch down and a colon will appear in the display window in front of the **00** numerals. The colon must be displayed to receive the service codes.

If it is desired to clear the display window during the Self-Test, turn **OFF** the vehicle's engine, press the tester's button once to unlatch it, then press the button again to latch down the button.

Connect the STAR or SUPER STAR II tester as follows:
1. Turn the ignition key **OFF**.
2. Connect the color coded adapter cable to the STAR tester.
3. Connect the adapter cable leads to the proper Self-Test connectors.
4. Ground the adapter cable for vehicles using the SUPER STAR II tester.
5. Slide the SUPER STAR II tester switch to the EEC-IV position, according to the vehicle system.

Using The Analog Voltmeter

Service codes will be represented by pulsing or sweeping movements of the voltmeter's needle across the dial face of the voltmeter. Therefore, a single digit number of 3 will be reported by 3 needle sweeps. However, a service code is represented by a 2-digit or 3-digit number, such as 23. As a result, the Self-Test service code of 23 will appear on the voltmeter as 2 needle sweeps, then after a 2 second pause, the needle will sweep 3 times.

Connect the analog voltmeter as follows:
1. Turn the ignition key **OFF**.
2. Set the voltmeter on a DC voltage range to read from 0–20 volts.
3. On all EEC-IV vehicles, connect the voltmeter from the battery positive post to the Self-Test output pin of the large Self-Test connector. On all others Connect the positive voltmeter lead to the EEC STO line and the negative lead to engine ground and jumper the EEC STI to ground.

Using The Indicator Light

During the Self-Test a service code is reported by the malfunction indicator light. It will represent itself as a flash on the CHECK ENGINE or SERVICE ENGINE SOON light on the dash panel. A single digit number of 3 will be reported by 3 flashes. However, a service code is represented by a 2-digit or 3-digit number, such as 23. As a result, the Self-Test service code of 23 will appear on the MIL light as 2 flashes, then, after a 2 second pause, the light will flash 3 times.

READING CODES

Key On Engine Off Self-Test

Start the engine and let it run until it reaches normal operating temperature. Turn the engine **OFF** and activate the Self-Test.
1. If using the STAR tester, proceed as follows:
   a. Latch the center button in the down position.
   b. Place the ignition key in the **ON** position.
   c. Record all service codes displayed.
2. If using the SUPER STAR II tester, proceed as follows:
   a. Latch the center button in the **TEST** position.
   b. Turn the ignition key **ON**.
   c. Turn the tester **ON**, the tester will sound and **888** will be displayed for 2 seconds.

d. Unlatch and relatch the center test button. After all codes are received, unlatch the center button to review all codes retained in tester memory.

➡**The SUPER STAR II tester has a mode switch. The tester will only display 3-digit service codes in fast code mode. If slow code mode is used on 3-digit service code applications, the display will be blank.**

3. If using the analog voltmeter jumper the STI to the SIG RTN at the Self-Test connectors and turn the ignition key and the voltmeter **ON**. Observe the needle for any code indications and record.

4. If using the malfunction indicator light connect the jumper wire from STI to the SIG RTN at the Self-Test connectors and turn the ignition switch **ON**. Service codes will be flashed on the MIL light.

Engine Running Self-Test

1. Deactivate the Self-Test.
2. Start and run the engine at 2000 rpm for 2 minutes.
3. Turn the engine **OFF** and wait 10 seconds.
4. Activate the Self-Test.
5. Start the engine.
6. Record all service codes displayed.

➡**Engine identification codes are issued at the beginning of the Engine Running Self-Test and are 1-digit numbers represented by the number of pulses sent out. The engine identification code is equal to ½ the number of engine cylinders. Two pulses equals 4 cylinders. The identification codes are used to verify that the proper processor is installed and that the Self-Test has been entered.**

CLEARING CODES

➡**Do not disconnect the battery to clear continuous memory codes. This will erase the Keep Alive Memory (KAM) information which may cause a driveability concern.**

1. Run the Key On Engine Off Self-Test.
2. When the service codes begin to be displayed, deactivate the Self-Test as follows:

a. STAR tester: unlatch the center button to the UP position.

b. Analog voltmeter, MIL, Continental message center: remove the jumper wire from between the Self-Test Input (STI) connector and the signal return pin of the Self-Test connector.

c. The continuous memory codes will be erased from the PCM memory.

TEST STEP	RESULT ▶	ACTION TO TAKE
1.0 VISUAL CHECK		
• Check vacuum hoses for damage and proper connection.	Yes ▶	GO to Quick Test Step **2.0**.
• Check EEC-IV system wiring harness for proper connections.	No ▶	SERVICE as necessary.
• Are all visual checks OK?		
2.0 VEHICLE PREPARATION AND EQUIPMENT HOOKUP		
• Apply parking brake.	Yes ▶	GO to Quick Test Step **3.0**.
• Place shift lever firmly in PARK (NEUTRAL for manual transmissions).	No ▶	REPEAT this test step.
• Block drive wheels.		
• Turn off all electrical loads.		
• Connect appropriate test equipment to the Self-Test connector in order to run Self-Test.		
• Is vehicle prepared to run Self-Test?		

88184C10

TEST STEP	RESULT ▶	ACTION TO TAKE
3.0 PERFORM KOEO SELF-TEST		
• Start engine and idle until vehicle is at operating temperature. NOTE: If engine does not start or stalls after starting, continue to perform KOEO Self-Test.	Yes ▶	If Malfunction Indicator Light (MIL) is on: GO to Continuous Memory code charts.
• Key off, wait 10 seconds. • Activate Self-Test. • Key on, engine off.		If engine runs rough or idles rough: GO to Pinpoint Test Step **S2**, except DIS/EDIS vehicles, GO to Quick Test Step **3.1**.
• Record all KOEO and Continuous Memory Codes received. • Is a PASS code "11" or "111" present in KOEO? (11/111-10-any code)		If engine is a no start: GO to Pinpoint Test Step **A1**, except EDIS vehicles, GO to Pinpoint Test Step **AA1**.
		If these symptoms are not present: GO to Quick Test Step **4.0**, except 7.3L diesel, GO to Quick Test Step **5.0**.
	No ▶	If KOEO service codes are received: GO to KOEO code charts.
		If no service codes are received: GO to Pinpoint Test Step **QA1**.

88184C11

TEST STEP	RESULT ▶	ACTION TO TAKE
3.1 CHECK FOR CONTINUOUS MEMORY SERVICE CODES 45, 46, 48, 215, 216, 217, 232, OR 238		
• For DIS/EDIS vehicles only. • Were Continuous Memory service codes 45, 46, 48, 215, 216, 217, 232 or 238 received during KOEO Self-Test?	Yes ▶	GO to DIS or EDIS diagnostics.
	No ▶	GO to Pinpoint Test Step **S2**.
4.0 COMPUTED TIMING CHECK		
• Key off, wait 10 seconds. • Activate Engine Running Self-Test. • Start engine. NOTE: If additional information is required for Engine Running Self-Test, refer to Quick Test	Yes ▶	Go to Quick Test Step **5.0**.
	No ▶	For EDIS: GO to Pinpoint Test Step **PC2**.
If engine starts but stalls or stalls during Self-Test, GO to Pinpoint Test Step **S1**.		For DIS: Go to Pinpoint Test Step **PB2**.
Engine Running Service Code 98/998 indicates vehicle is in Failure Mode Effects Management (FMEM) and DID NOT PASS KOEO On-Demand/Continuous Memory Self-Test. Engine Running Self-Test cannot be performed while in FMEM. Rerun KOEO Self-Test, Quick Test Step **3.0**.		For TFI: Go to Pinpoint Test Step **PA2**.
• Check computed timing after the last service code has been displayed. The timing will remain fixed for two minutes, unless Self-Test is deactivated. NOTE: Computed timing is equal to base timing plus 20 degrees BTDC with 3 degrees tolerance. See vehicle decal for correct base timing. • Is computed timing within specs?		

88184C12

TEST STEP	RESULT ▶	ACTION TO TAKE
5.0 PERFORM ENGINE RUNNING SELF-TEST		
• Deactivate Self-Test.	Yes ▶	If any Continuous Memory service codes were received in Quick Test Step 3.0:
• Start engine and idle until vehicle is at operating temperature.		
• Turn engine off.		GO to Continuous Memory code charts
• Activate Engine Running Self-Test.		
• Start engine.		
		If a Continuous Memory PASS Code (11/111) was received in Quick Test Step 3.0 and no symptoms are present: EEC-IV diagnostic testing is complete.
• Record all service codes displayed.		
NOTE: Engine Running Service Code 98/998 indicates vehicle is in Failure Mode Effects Management (FMEM) and DID NOT PASS KOEO On-Demand/Continuous Memory Self-Test. Engine Running Self-Test cannot be performed while in FMEM. Rerun KOEO Self-Test, Quick Test Step 3.0.		If a Continuous Memory PASS Code (11/111) was received in Quick Test Step 3.0 and symptoms are present: GO to Diagnosis By Symptom chart Quick Test Step 12.0
• Is a PASS Code (11 or 111) received during Engine Running Self-Test?		
	No ▶	If Engine Running service codes are received: GO to Engine Running code charts, Quick
		If no service codes are received: GO to Pinpoint Test Step QA1.

88184C14

12.0 DIAGNOSIS BY SYMPTOM
SPECIAL NOTES:
• Verify that a Pass Code 11/111 was received in Key On Engine Off, Engine Running and Continuous Self-Tests before continuing with this test.
• If a symptom is present and the EEC system is suspected, Go to Diagnosis By Symptom charts. If the EEC system is not suspected, GO to Diagnostic Routines.

88184C15

1984-88 2.3L EFI TURBOCHARGED ENGINE SERVICE CODES

Code		Explanation
11	O/R/C	System pass
12	R	Rpm unable to reach upper test limit
13	R	Rpm unable to reach lower test limit
14	C	PIP circuit failure
15	O	ROM test failure
15	C	Power interrupted to keep alive memory
18	C	Loss of tach input to ECU, spout grounded
21	O/R	ECT sensor input out of test range
22	O/R/C	BP sensor input out of test range
23	O/R	TP sensor input out of test range
24	O/R	VAT sensor input out of test range
25	R	KS sensor not detected during test
26	O/R	VAF sensor input out of self-test range
34	R	Insufficient EGR flow
35	R	Rpm too low for EGR test
41	R	EGO/HEGO circuit shows system lean
41	C	No EGO/HEGO switching detected, system lean
42	R	EGO/HEGO shows system rich
42	C	No EGO/HEGO switching detected, system rich
51	O/C	ECT sensor input exceeds test maximum
53	O/C	TP sensor input exceeds test maximum
54	O/C	VAT sensor input exceeds test maximum
61	O/C	ECT test sensor input below test minimum
63	O/C	TP sensor below test minimum
64	O/C	VAT sensor input below test minimum
66	O/C	VAF sensor input below test minimum
67	O	Neutral drive switch open. A/C input high
67	C	Clutch switch circuit failure
71	C	Software re-initialization detected
72	C	Power interrupt detected
73	R	Insufficient TP output change during test
76	R	Insufficient VAF output change during test
77	R	Wide open throttle not sensed during test
Ko Code		Unable to run self-test or output codes ¹
Code not listed		Does not apply to vehicle being tested ¹

O—Key On, Engine Off
R—Engine running
C—Continuous Memory
1 Refer to system diagnostics

88184C16

1984-87 3.8L CFI ENGINE SERVICE CODES

Code		Explanation
11	O/R/C	System pass
12	R	Rpm unable to reach upper test limit
13	R	Rpm unable to reach lower test limit
14	C	PIP circuit failure
15	O	ROM test failure
15	C	Power interrupted to keep alive memory
18	C	Loss of tach input to ECU, spout grounded
18	R	Spout circuit open
19	O	Failure of EEC power supply
21	O/R	ECT sensor input out of test range
22	O/R/C	MAP sensor input out of test range
23	O/R	TP sensor input out of test range
24	O/R	ACT sensor input out of test range
29	C	Insufficient input from vehicle speed sensor
31	O/R/C	PFE circuit below minimum voltage
32	R/C	EGR valve not seated
33	R/C	EGR valve not opening
34	O	Defective PFE sensor
34	R/C	Excess exhaust back pressure
35	O/R/C	PFE circuit above maximum voltage
39	C	AXOD by-pass clutch not applying properly
41	R	EGO/HEGO circuit shows system lean (right side HEGO)
41	C	No EGO/HEGO switching detected, system lean (right side HEGO)
42	R	EGO/HEGO shows system rich (right side HEGO)

88184C17

1984-87 3.8L CFI ENGINE SERVICE CODES

Code		Explanation
51	O/C	ECT sensor input exceeds test maximum
52	O	PSPS circuit open
52	R	PSPS always open or always closed
53	O/C	TP sensor input exceeds test maximum
54	O/C	ACT sensor input exceeds test maximum
57	C	AXOD neutral pressure switch failed open
59	C	AXOD 4/3 pressure switch failed open
59	O	AXOD 4/3 pressure switch failed closed
61	O/C	ECT test sensor input below test minimum
63	O/C	TP sensor below test minimum
64	O/C	ACT sensor input below test minimum
67	O	Neutral drive switch open. A/C input high
67	O	AXOD neutral pressure switch failed closed
68	O/R/C	AXOD temperature switch failed open
69	C	AXOD 3/4 pressure switch failed open
69	O	AXOD 3/2 pressure switch failed closed
70	C	EEC-IV data transmission link failed
71	C	Cluster control assembly circuit failed
72	C	Message center control circuit failed
74	R	Brake on/off circuit open, not on during test
79	O	A/C on during self-test
83	O	High speed electro drive fan circuit failure
84	O	EGR VAC regulator circuit failure
85	O	Canister purge circuit failure
87	O/C	Fuel pump primary circuit failure
88	O	Electro drive fan circuit failure
89	O	AXOD lock-up solenoid circuit failure
91	R	HEGO sensor circuit shows system lean (left side HEGO)
91	C	No HEGO switching sensed (left side HEGO)
92	R	HEGO sensor circuit shows system rich
95	O/C	Fuel pump secondary circuit failure

88184C18

1986-87 5.0L SEFI ENGINE SERVICE CODES

Code		Explanation
12	R	Rpm unable to reach upper test limit
13	R	Rpm unable to reach lower test limit
14	C	PIP circuit failure
15	O/C	Power interrupted to keep alive memory
16	R	Rpm too low to perform test
18	C	Loss of ignition signal to ECU—ignition grounded, spout, PIP, IDM
19	O	Failure of EEC power supply
21	O/R	ECT sensor input out of test range
22	O/R/C	MAP sensor input out of test range
23	O/R	TP sensor input out of test range
24	O/R	ACT sensor input out of test range
29	C	Insufficent input from vehicle speed sensor
31	O/R/C	EVP circuit below minimum voltage
32	O/R/C	EVP voltage below closed limit
33	R/C	EGR valve not opening
34	O/R/C	EVP voltage above closed limit
35	O/R/C	EVP circuit above maximum voltage
41	R	EGO/HEGO circuit shows system lean (right side HEGO)
42	R	EGO/HEGO shows system rich (right side HEGO)
44	R	Thermactor air system inoperative (cyl. 1–4)
45	R	Thermactor air upstream during self-test
46	R	Thermactor air not bypassed during self-test
51	O/C	ECT sensor input exceeds test maximum
53	O/C	TP sensor input exceeds test maximum
54	O/C	ACT sensor input exceeds test maximum
61	O/C	ECT test sensor input below test minimum
63	O/C	TP sensor below test minimum
64	O/C	ACT sensor input below test minimum
67	O	Neutral drive switch open. A/C input high

88184C1A

1986–87 5.0L SEFI ENGINE SERVICE CODES (CONTINUED)

Code		Explanation
81	O	Air management 2 circuit failure
82	O	Air management 1 circuit failure
84	O	EGR VAC regulator circuit failure
85	O	Canister purge circuit failure
87	O	Fuel pump primary circuit failure
91	R	HEGO sensor circuit shows system lean (left side HEGO)
92	R	HEGO sensor circuit shows system rich (left side HEGO)
94	R	Thermactor air system inoperative (cyl. 5–8)
98	R	Hard fault is present
No Code		Unable to run self-test or output codes [1]
Code not listed		Does not apply to vehicle being tested [1]

O — Key On, Engine Off
R — Engine running
C — Continuous Memory
1 Refer to system diagnostics

88184C1B

1988 5.0L SEFI ENGINE SERVICE CODES

Code		Explanation
11	O/R/C	System pass
12	R	Rpm unable to reach upper test limit
13	R	Rpm unable to reach lower test limit
14	C	PIP circuit failure
15	O	ROM test failure
15	C	Power interrupted to keep alive memory
16	R	Rpm too low to perform test
18	C	Loss of tach input to ECU, spout grounded
18	R	Spout circuit open
19	O	Failure of EEC power supply
21	O/R	ECT sensor input out of test range
22	O/R/C	MAP sensor input out of test range
23	O/R	TP sensor input out of test range
24	O/R	ACT sensor input out of test range
29	C	Insufficent input from vehicle speed sensor
31	O/R/C	EVP circuit below minimum voltage
32	O/R/C	EVP voltage below closed limit
33	R/C	EGR valve not opening
34	O/R/C	EVP voltage above closed limit
35	O/R/C	EVP circuit above maximum voltage
41	R	EGO/HEGO circuit shows system lean (right side HEGO)
41	C	No EGO/HEGO switching detected, system lean (right side HEGO)
42	R	EGO/HEGO shows system rich (right side HEGO)
44	R	Thermactor air system inoperative (cyl. 1–4)
45	R	Thermactor air upstream during self-test
46	R	Thermactor air not bypassed during self-test
51	O/C	ECT sensor input exceeds test maximum
53	O/C	TP sensor input exceeds test maximum
54	O/C	ACT sensor input exceeds test maximum
61	O/C	ECT test sensor input below test minimum
63	O/C	TP sensor below test minimum
64	O/C	ACT sensor input below test minimum
67	O	Neutral drive switch open. A/C input high
74	R	Brake on/off circuit open, not on during test
75	R	Brake on/off circuit closed, always high
79	O	A/C on during self-test
81	O	Air management 2 circuit failure
82	O	Air management 1 circuit failure
84	O	EGR VAC regulator circuit failure
85	O	Canister purge circuit failure
87	O/C	Fuel pump primary circuit failure
91	R	HEGO sensor circuit shows system lean (left side HEGO)
91	C	No HEGO switching sensed (left side HEGO)
92	R	HEGO sensor circuit shows system rich (left side HEGO)
94	R	Thermactor air system inoperative (cyl. 5–8)
98	R	Hard fault is present
No Code		Unable to run self-test or output codes [1]
Code not listed		Does not apply to vehicle being tested [1]

O — Key On, Engine Off
R — Engine running
C — Continuous Memory
1 Refer to system diagnostics

88184C20

1989–90 3.8L SEFI ENGINE SERVICE CODES

Code		Explanation
11	O/R/C	System pass
12	R	Rpm unable to reach upper test limit
13	R	Rpm unable to reach lower test limit
14	C	PIP circuit failure
15	O	ROM test failure
15	C	Power interrupted to keep alive memory
18	C	Loss of tach input to ECU, spout grounded
18	R	Spout circuit open
19	O	Failure of EEC power supply
21	O/R	ECT sensor input out of test range
22	O/R/C	MAP sensor input out of test range
23	O/R/C	TP sensor input out of test range
24	O/R	ACT sensor input out of test range
29	C	Insufficient input from vehicle speed sensor
31	O/R/C	PFE circuit below minimum voltage
32	R/C	EGR valve not seated
33	R/C	EGR valve not opening
34	O	Defective PFE sensor
34	R/C	Excess exhaust back pressure
35	O/R/C	PFE circuit above maximum voltage
41	R	EGO/HEGO circuit shows system lean (right side HEGO)
41	C	No EGO/HEGO switching detected, system lean (right side HEGO)
42	R	EGO/HEGO shows system rich (right side HEGO)
51	O/C	ECT sensor input exceeds test maximum
53	O/C	TP sensor input exceeds test maximum
54	O/C	ACT sensor input exceeds test maximum
61	O/C	ECT test sensor input below test minimum
63	O/C	TP sensor below test minimum
64	O/C	ACT sensor input below test minimum
74	R	Brake on/off circuit open, not on during test
79	O	A/C on during self-test
84	C	EGR VAC regulator circuit failure
85	O	Canister purge circuit failure
87	O/C	Fuel pump primary circuit failure
91	R	HEGO sensor circuit shows system lean (left side HEGO)
91	C	No HEGO switching sensed (left side HEGO)
92	R	HEGO sensor circuit shows system rich (left side HEGO)
95	O/C	Fuel pump secondary circuit failure
96	O/C	Fuel pump secondary circuit failure
98	R	Hard fault is present
No Code		Unable to run self-test or output codes [1]
Code not listed		Does not apply to vehicle being tested [1]

O — Key On, Engine Off
R — Engine running
C — Continuous Memory
1 Refer to system diagnostics

88184C21

1989–90 3.8L SEFI SUPERCHARGED ENGINE SERVICE CODES

Code		Explanation
11	O/R/C	System pass
12	R	Rpm unable to reach upper test limit
13	R	Rpm unable to reach lower test limit
14	C	PIP circuit failure
15	O	ROM test failure
15	C	Power interrupted to keep alive memory
18	C	Loss of tach input to ECU, spout grounded
18	R	Spout circuit open
19	C	CID sensor input failed
21	O/R	ECT sensor input out of test range
22	O/R/C	BP sensor input out of test range
23	O/R	TP sensor input out of test range
24	O/R	ACT sensor input out of test range
25	R	KS sensor input out of self-test range
26	O/R	MAF sensor input out of self-test range
29	C	Insufficent input from vehicle speed sensor
31	O/R/C	PFE circuit below minimum voltage
32	R/C	EGR valve not seated
33	R/C	EGR valve not opening
34	O	Defective PFE sensor
34	R/C	Excess exhaust back pressure
35	O/R/C	PFE circuit above maximum voltage
41	R	EGO/HEGO circuit shows system lean (right side HEGO)
41	C	No EGO/HEGO switching detected, system lean (right side HEGO)
42	R	EGO/HEGO shows system rich (right side HEGO)
45	C	DIS coil Pack 3 circuit failure
46	C	DIS coil Pack 1 circuit failure
48	C	DIS coil Pack 2 circuit failure
49	C	Spout signal defaulted to 10 degrees BTDC
51	O/C	ECT sensor input exceeds test maximum
52	O	PSPS circuit failure
52	R	PSPS always open or always closed
53	O/C	TP sensor input exceeds test maximum
54	O/C	ACT sensor input exceeds test maximum
56	O/C	MAF sensor input exceeds test maximum
61	O/C	ECT test sensor input below test minimum
63	O/C	TP sensor below test minimum
64	O/C	ACT sensor input below test minimum
66	C	MAF sensor input below test minimum
67	O	Neutral drive switch open. A/C input high
67	C	Clutch switch circuit failure
72	R	Insufficient BP change during test
73	R	Insufficient TP output change during test
74	R	Brake on/off circuit open, not on during test

88184C22

1989–90 3.8L SEFI SUPERCHARGED ENGINE SERVICE CODES

77	R	Wide open throttle not sensed during test
79	O	A/C on during self-test
82	O	Supercharger bypass circuit failure
83	O	High speed electro drive fan circuit failure
84	O	EGR VAC regulator circuit failure
85	O	Canister purge circuit failure
87	O/C	Fuel pump primary circuit failure
88	O	Electro drive fan circuit failure
91	R	HEGO sensor circuit shows system lean (left side HEGO)
91	C	No HEGO switching sensed (left side HEGO)
92	R	HEGO sensor circuit shows system rich (left side HEGO)
96	O/C	Fuel pump secondary circuit failure
98	R	Hard fault is present
No Code		Unable to run self-test or output codes [1]
Code not listed		Does not apply to vehicle being tested [1]

O—Key On, Engine Off
R—Engine running
C—Continuous Memory
1 Refer to system diagnostics

88184C23

1991–92 3.8L SEFI SUPERCHARGED ENGINE SERVICE CODES

SERVICE CODE			SERVICE CODE DEFINITION
111	orc	▶	System PASS
112	oc	▶	Air Charge Temp (ACT) sensor circuit below minimum voltage/ 254°F indicated
113	oc	▶	Air Charge Temp (ACT) sensor circuit above maximum voltage/ – 40°F indicated
114	or	▶	Air Charge Temp (ACT) higher or lower than expected during KOEO, KOER
116	or	▶	Engine Coolant Temp (ECT) higher or lower than expected during KOEO, KOER
117	oc	▶	Engine Coolant Temp (ECT) sensor circuit below minimum voltage/ 254°F indicated
118	oc	▶	Engine Coolant Temp (ECT) sensor circuit above maximum voltage/ – 40°F indicated
121	orc	▶	Closed throttle voltage higher or lower than expected
122	oc	▶	Throttle Position (TP) Sensor circuit below minimum voltage
123	oc	▶	Throttle Position (TP) Sensor circuit above maximum voltage
124	c	▶	Throttle Position (TP) Sensor voltage higher than expected
125	c	▶	Throttle Position (TP) Sensor voltage lower than expected
126	orc	▶	BP sensor higher or lower than expected
129	r	▶	Insufficient Mass Air Flow (MAF) change during Dynamic Response Test
136	r	▶	Lack of Oxygen Sensor (HEGO) switches, indicates lean (LEFT SIDE)
137	r	▶	Lack of Oxygen Sensor (HEGO) switches, indicates rich (LEFT SIDE)
139	c	▶	No Oxygen Sensor (HEGO) switches detected (LEFT SIDE)
144	c	▶	No Oxygen Sensor (HEGO) switches detected (RIGHT SIDE)
157	c	▶	Mass Air Flow (MAF) sensor circuit below minimum voltage
158	oc	▶	Mass Air Flow (MAF) sensor circuit above maximum voltage
159	or	▶	Mass Air Flow (MAF) higher or lower than expected during KOEO, KOER
167	r	▶	Insufficient throttle position change during Dynamic Response Test
171	rc	▶	Fuel system at adaptive limits, Oxygen Sensor (HEGO) unable to switch (RIGHT SIDE)
172	rc	▶	Lack of Oxygen Sensor (HEGO) switches, indicates lean (RIGHT SIDE)
173	rc	▶	Lack of Oxygen Sensor (HEGO) switches, indicates rich (RIGHT SIDE)
175	c	▶	Fuel system at adaptive limits, Oxygen Sensor (HEGO) unable to switch (LEFT SIDE)
176	c	▶	Lack of Oxygen Sensor (HEGO) switches, indicates lean (LEFT SIDE)
177	c	▶	Lack of Oxygen Sensor (HEGO) switches, indicates rich (LEFT SIDE)
179	c	▶	Fuel system at lean adaptive limit at part throttle, system rich (RIGHT SIDE)
181	c	▶	Fuel system at rich adaptive limit at part throttle, system lean (RIGHT SIDE)
182	c	▶	Fuel system at lean adaptive limit at idle, system rich (RIGHT SIDE)
183	c	▶	Fuel system at rich adaptive limit at idle, system lean (RIGHT SIDE)
184	c	▶	Mass Air Flow (MAF) higher than expected
185	c	▶	Mass Air Flow (MAF) lower than expected
186	c	▶	Injector pulse width higher than expected
187	c	▶	Injector pulse width lower than expected
188	c	▶	Fuel system at lean adaptive limit at part throttle, system rich (LEFT SIDE)
189	c	▶	Fuel system at rich adaptive limit at part throttle, system lean (LEFT SIDE)
191	c	▶	Fuel system at lean adaptive limit at idle, system rich (LEFT SIDE)
192	c	▶	Fuel system at rich adaptive limit at idle, system lean (LEFT SIDE)
211	c	▶	Profile Ignition Pickup (PIP) circuit fault
212	oc	▶	Loss of Ignition Diagnostic Monitor (IDM) input to EEC processor/SPOUT circuit grounded
213	r	▶	SPOUT circuit open
214	c	▶	Cylinder Identification (CID) circuit failure
215	c	▶	EEC processor detected coil 1 primary circuit failure
216	c	▶	EEC processor detected coil 2 primary circuit failure
217	c	▶	EEC processor detected coil 3 primary circuit failure
219	c	▶	Spark timing defaulted to 10 degrees-SPOUT circuit open
225	r	▶	Knock not sensed during Dynamic Response Test
341	o	▶	Octane adjust service pin in use
411	r	▶	Cannot control rpm during KOER low rpm check
412	r	▶	Cannot control rpm during KOER high rpm check
452	c	▶	Insufficient input from Vehicle Speed Sensor (VSS)
511	o	▶	EEC Processor Read Only Memory (ROM) test failure
512	c	▶	EEC Processor Keep Alive Memory (KAM) test failure
522	o	▶	Vehicle not in PARK or NEUTRAL during KOEO
525	o	▶	Indicates vehicle in gear / AC ON
528	c	▶	Clutch switch circuit failure
536	rc	▶	Brake On/Off (BOO) circuit failure / not actuated during KOER
538	r	▶	Insufficient rpm change during KOER Dynamic Response Test
539	o	▶	AC On/Defrost On during KOEO
542	oc	▶	Fuel pump secondary circuit failure
543	oc	▶	Fuel pump secondary circuit failure
556	oc	▶	Fuel pump relay primary circuit failure
558	o	▶	EGR Vacuum Regulator (EVR) circuit failure
563	o	▶	High Speed-Electro Drive Fan (HEDF) circuit failure
564	o	▶	Electro-Drive Fan (EDF) circuit failure
565	o	▶	Canister Purge (CANP) circuit failure
998	r	▶	Hard fault present****FMEM mode****

KEY: o = Key On Engine Off (KOEO) r = Engine Running (ER) c = Continuous Memory

88184C24

1991–92 3.8L SEFI ENGINE SERVICE CODES

SERVICE CODE			SERVICE CODE DEFINITION
111	orc	▶	System Pass
112	oc		Air Charge Temp (ACT) Sensor circuit below minimum voltage/ 254°F indicated
113	oc		Air Charge Temp (ACT) Sensor circuit above maximum voltage/ – 40°F indicated
114	or		Air Charge Temp (ACT) higher or lower than expected during KOEO, KOER
116	oc		Engine Coolant Temp (ECT) higher or lower than expected during KOEO, KOER
117	oc		Engine Coolant Temp (ECT) sensor circuit below minimum voltage/ 254°F indicated
118	oc		Engine Coolant Temp (ECT) Sensor circuit above maximum voltage/ – 40°F indicated
121	orc		Closed throttle voltage higher or lower than expected
122	oc		Throttle Position (TP) Sensor circuit below minimum voltage
123	oc		Throttle Position (TP) Sensor circuit above maximum voltage
124	c		Throttle Position (TP) Sensor voltage higher than expected
125	c		Throttle Position (TP) Sensor voltage lower than expected
129	r	▶	Insufficient Mass Air Flow (MAF) change during Dynamic Response Test
136	r	▶	Lack of Oxygen Sensor (HEGO) switches, indicates lean (LEFT SIDE)
137	r	▶	Lack of Oxygen Sensor (HEGO) switches, indicates lean (LEFT SIDE)
139	c	▶	No Oxygen Sensor (HEGO) switches detected (LEFT SIDE)
144	c	▶	No Oxygen Sensor (HEGO) Switches detected (RIGHT SIDE)
157	c	▶	Mass Air Flow (MAF) sensor circuit below minimum voltage
158	oc	▶	Mass Air Flow (MAF) sensor circuit above maximum voltage
159	or	▶	Mass Air Flow (MAF) higher or lower than expected during KOEO, KOER
167	r	▶	Insufficient throttle position change during Dynamic Response Test
171	c	▶	Fuel system at adaptive limits, Oxygen Sensor (HEGO) unable to switch (RIGHT SIDE)
172	rc	▶	Lack of Oxygen Sensor (HEGO) switches, indicates lean (RIGHT SIDE)
173	rc	▶	Lack of Oxygen Sensor (HEGO) switches, indicates rich (RIGHT SIDE)
175	c	▶	Fuel system at adaptive limits, Oxygen Sensor (HEGO) unable to switch (LEFT SIDE)
176	c	▶	Lack of Oxygen Sensor (HEGO) switches, indicates lean (LEFT SIDE)
177	c	▶	Lack of Oxygen Sensor (HEGO) switches, indicates rich (LEFT SIDE)
179	c	▶	Fuel system at lean adaptive limit at part throttle, system rich (RIGHT SIDE)
181	c	▶	Fuel system at rich adaptive limit at part throttle, system lean (RIGHT SIDE)
182	c	▶	Fuel system at lean adaptive limit at idle, system rich (RIGHT SIDE)
183	c	▶	Fuel system at rich adaptive limit at idle, system lean (RIGHT SIDE)
184	c	▶	Mass Air Flow (MAF) higher than expected
185	c	▶	Mass Air Flow (MAF) lower than expected
186	c	▶	Injector pulse width higher or MAF lower than expected
187	c	▶	Injector pulse width lower or MAF higher than expected
188	c	▶	Fuel system at lean adaptive limit at part throttle, system rich (LEFT SIDE)
189	c	▶	Fuel system at rich adaptive limit at part throttle, system lean (LEFT SIDE)
191	c	▶	Fuel system at lean adaptive limit at idle, system rich (LEFT SIDE)
192	c	▶	Fuel system at rich adaptive limit at idle, system lean (LEFT SIDE)
211	c	▶	Profile Ignition Pickup (PIP) circuit fault
212	c	▶	Loss of Ignition Diagnostic Monitor (IDM) input to EEC processor/SPOUT circuit grounded
213	r	▶	SPOUT circuit open
326	rc	▶	PFE circuit voltage higher than expected
327	orc	▶	PFE circuit below minimum voltage
332	rc	▶	Insufficient EGR flow detected
335	o	▶	PFE sensor voltage lower than expected during KOEO
336	rc	▶	Exhaust Pressure high/PFE circuit voltage higher than expected
337	orc	▶	PFE circuit above maximum voltage
411	r	▶	Cannot control RPM during KOER low RPM check
412	r	▶	Cannot control RPM during KOER high RPM check
452	c	▶	Insufficient input from Vehicle Speed Sensor (VSS)
511	o	▶	EEC processor Read Only Memory (ROM) test failure
512	o	▶	EEC processor Keep Alive Memory (KAM) test failure
522	o	▶	Vehicle not in PARK or NEUTRAL during KOEO
525	o	▶	Indicates vehicle in gear / AC on
536	oc	▶	Brake On/Off (BOO) circuit failure / not actuated during KOER
538	r	▶	Insufficient RPM change during KOER Dynamic Response Test
539	o	▶	AC ON/Defrost ON during KOEO
542	oc	▶	Fuel pump secondary circuit failure
543	oc	▶	Fuel pump secondary circuit failure
556	or	▶	Fuel pump relay primary circuit failure
558	o	▶	EGR Vacuum Regulator (EVR) circuit failure
565	o	▶	Canister Purge (CANP) circuit failure
998	r	▶	Hard fault present****FMEM Mode****

KEY: o = Key On Engine Off (KOEO)   r = Engine Running (ER)   c = Continuous Memory

88184C25

1991–92 5.0L SEFI ENGINE SERVICE CODES

SERVICE CODE			SERVICE CODE DEFINITION
111	orc	▶	System PASS
112	oc	▶	ACT indicated 254°F/circuit grounded
113	oc	▶	ACT indicated – 40°F/circuit open
114	or		ACT out of Self-Test range
116	or		ECT out of Self-Test range
117	oc		ECT indicated 254°F/circuit grounded
118	oc	▶	ECT indicated – 40°F/circuit open
121	orc		TP out of Self-Test range
122	oc	▶	TP circuit below minimum voltage
123	oc	▶	TP circuit above maximum voltage
124	c		TP circuit output higher than expected
125	c		TP circuit output lower than expected
129	r		Insufficient MAF change during Dynamic Response Test
136	r	▶	HEGO sensor indicates system lean (Left Side)
137	r	▶	HEGO sensor indicates system rich (Left Side)
139	c	▶	No HEGO switching detected (Left Side)
144	c	▶	No HEGO switching detected (Right Side)
157	c	▶	MAF circuit below minimum voltage
158	oc	▶	MAF circuit above maximum voltage
159	or	▶	MAF out of Self-Test range
167	r	▶	Insufficient TP change during Dynamic Response Test
171	c	▶	No HEGO switching detected/adaptive fuel at limit (Right Side)
172	rc	▶	HEGO sensor indicates system lean (Right Side)
173	rc	▶	HEGO sensor indicates system rich (Right Side)
174	c	▶	HEGO switching time is slow (Right Side)
175	c	▶	No HEGO switching detected/adaptive fuel at limit (Left Side)
176	c	▶	HEGO sensor indicates system lean (Left Side)
177	c	▶	HEGO sensor indicates system rich (Left Side)
178	c	▶	HEGO switching time is slow (Left Side)
179	c	▶	Adaptive fuel lean limit is reached (Right Side)
181	c	▶	Adaptive fuel rich limit is reached (Right Side)
182	c	▶	Adaptive fuel lean limit is reached at idle (Right Side)
183	c	▶	Adaptive fuel rich limit is reached at idle (Right Side)
184	c	▶	MAF circuit output higher than expected
185	c	▶	MAF circuit output lower than expected
186	c	▶	Injector pulsewidth higher than expected
187	c	▶	Injector pulsewidth lower than expected
188	c	▶	Adaptive fuel lean limit is reached (Left Side)
189	c	▶	Adaptive fuel rich limit is reached (Left Side)
191	c	▶	Adaptive fuel lean limit is reached at idle (Left Side)
192	c	▶	Adaptive fuel rich limit is reached at idle (Left Side)
211	c	▶	PIP circuit failure
212	c	▶	IDM circuit failure/SPOUT circuit grounded
213	r	▶	SPOUT circuit open
311	r	▶	Thermactor air system inoperative (Right Side)
313	r	▶	Thermactor air not bypassed during Self-Test
314	r	▶	Thermactor air system inoperative (Left Side)
327	orc	▶	EVP circuit output below minimum
328	orc	▶	EVP voltage below closed limit
332	rc	▶	EGR valve opening not detected (SONIC)
334	orc	▶	EVP voltage above closed limit (SONIC)
337	orc	▶	EVP circuit above maximum voltage
411	r	▶	Cannot control rpm during Self-Test low rpm check
412	r	▶	Cannot control rpm during Self-Test high rpm check
452	c	▶	Insufficient input from the Vehicle Speed Sensor (VSS)
511	o	▶	EEC processor Read Only Memory (ROM) test failed
512	o	▶	EEC processor Keep Alive Memory (KAM) test failed
513	o	▶	Failure in EEC processor internal voltage
522	o	▶	Indicates vehicle in gear
538	r	▶	Operator error (Dynamic response/Cylinder Balance Test)
539	o	▶	A/C on/Defrost on during Self-Test
542	oc	▶	Fuel pump secondary circuit failure
543	oc	▶	Fuel pump secondary circuit failure
552	o	▶	Air Management 1 (AM1) circuit failure
556	oc	▶	Fuel pump primary circuit failure
558	o	▶	EGR Vacuum Regulator (EVR) circuit failure
565	o	▶	Canister Purge Solenoid (CANP) circuit failure
998	r	▶	Hard fault is present – FMEM mode
NO CODES		▶	Unable to initiate Self-Test or unable to output Self-Test codes
CODES NOT LISTED		▶	Service codes displayed are not applicable to the vehicle being tested

KEY: o = Key On Engine Off (KOEO)   r = Engine Running (ER)   c = Continuous Memory

88184C26

EEC-V TROUBLE CODES

General Information

Ford developed the EEC-V system on the 1995–97 models in response to the increased diagnostic requirements for the California Air Resource Board. The regulations developed by the Environmental Protection Agency are designated as the OBD II system.

The OBDII is similar to the OBD I system but not identical. The OBD I requires that the malfunction indicator lamp (MIL) illuminates to inform the driver when an emissions component or monitored system fails. The MIL also lights up to indicate when the PCM is operating in hardware limiting operating strategy (HLOS).

The EEC-V is a evolutionary development from the EEC-IV. None of the components involved are actually new, only the applications have changed.

The only component that has been added is another heated Oxygen Sensor (HO2S located behind the catalyst. These downstream sensors are called the Catalyst Monitor sensors (CSM). This means that there are four sensors instead of two.

Data Link Connector (DLC)

▶ See Figure 38

The DLC on the EEC-V is located on the passenger's side of the vehicle, beneath the instrument panel, and the right of the console.

The DLC is rectangular in design and capable of allowing access to 16 terminals. The connector has keying features that allow easy connection. The test equipment and the DLC have a latching feature to ensure a good mated connection.

Reading Codes

When diagnosing the OBD II EEC-V system, the New Generation Star (NGS) tester or generic scan tool may be used to retrieve codes, view the system operating specifications or test the system components.

1994 4.6L 2V THUNDERBIRD/COUGAR

DLC

88184G53

Fig. 38 The data link connector is located on the passengers side of the vehicle, beneath the instrument panel

Clearing Codes

PCM RESET

The PCM reset mode allows the scan tool to clear any emission related diagnostic information from the PCM. When resetting the PCM, a DTC P1000 will be stored until all OBD II system monitors or components have been tested to satisfy a Trip without any other faults occurring.

The following items occur when the PCM Reset is performed:
- The DTC is cleared
- The freeze frame data is cleared
- The oxygen sensor test data is cleared
- The status of the OBD II system monitors is reset
- A DTC P1000 code is set

PCM fault codes may be cleared by using the scan tool or disconnecting the negative battery cable for a minimum of 15 seconds.

KEEP ALIVE MEMORY (KAM) RESET

The Keep Alive Memory (KAM) contains the adaptive factors used by the processor to compensate for component tolerances and wear. It should not be routinely cleared during diagnosis. If and emissions related part is replaced during repair, the KAM must be cleared. Failure to clear the KAM may cause severe driveability problems since the correction factor for the old component will be applied to the new component.

To clear the KAM disconnect the negative battery cable for at least 5 minuets. After the memory is cleared and the battery is reconnected, the vehicle must be driven a couple of miles so that the PCM may relearn the needed correction factors. The distance to be driven depends on the engine and vehicle, but all drives should include steady throttle cruise on the open roads. Certain driveability problems may be noted during the drive because the adaptive factors are not yet functioning.

Key On Engine Off (KOEO)

A series of characters must be entered into the scan tool to perform this test. The codes are listed below and must be entered as such to perform the test correctly. See the manufacture of the scan tool for any additional instructions.

1. Perform the necessary vehicle preparation and visual inspection.
2. Connect the scan tool to the DLC.
3. Turn the ignition to the ON position but DO NOT start the engine.
4. Verify that the scan tool is connected and communicating correctly by entering the OBD II system readiness test. All scan tools are required to automatically enter this test once communication is established between the tool and the PCM.

5. Enter the following string of information to initiate the KOEO self test.
6. Enter the four strings separately and in the order shown. All of the string ID numbers must match in the order shown.

   a. 04, 31, 21, C4 103381, 9E 00 445443287329 20 8042 20 8062 20 8082 A851 FF, 2E

   b. 03, 32, 22FF, C4 10220202, 9E 00 434E54 20 8061 A961 00 04, EA

   c. 02, 32, 21, C4 10328100, 9E 00 574149 54 20 8081 A181 61 03, 5E

   d. 01, 32, 21, C4 103181, 9E 00 53544155254 20 8081 A 181 00 02, 54

7. Turn the ignition OFF to end the test cycle.

Key On Engine Running (KOER)

A series of characters must be entered into the scan tool to perform this test. The codes are listed below and must be entered as such to perform the test correctly. See the manufacture of the scan tool for any additional instructions.

1. Perform the necessary vehicle preparation and visual inspection.
2. Connect the scan tool to the DLC.
3. Turn the ignition to the ON position and start the engine.
4. Verify that the scan tool is connected and communicating correctly by entering the OBD II system readiness test. All scan tools are required to automatically enter this test once communication is established between the tool and the PCM.
5. Enter the following string of information to initiate the KOEO self test.
6. Enter the four strings separately and in the order shown. All of the string ID numbers must match in the order shown.
7. After the test begins, cycle the brake and Transmission Control (TCS) switches if equipped.

   a. 08, 31, 21, C4103382, 9E 00 445443287329 20 8042 20 8062 20 8082 A851 FF, 33

   b. 07, 32, 22FF, C410220202, 9E 00 434E54 20 8061 A961 00 08, F2

   c. 06, 32, 21, C4 10328200, 9E 00 574149 54 20 8081 A181 61 07, 67

   d. 05, 32, 21, C4 103182, 9E 00 5354415254 20 8081 A181 00 06, 5D

8. Turn the ignition OFF to end the test cycle.

Continuous Memory

1. Perform the necessary vehicle preparation and visual inspection.
2. Connect the scan tool to the DLC.
3. Turn the key to the **ON** position or start the vehicle. This may depend on the pinpoint manual instructions for the type of data requested.
4. Verify the tool is connected properly and communicating.
5. Enter the following string of characters to retrieve all the continuous DTC's (DTC CNT).

   a. 09, 2C, 21, C4 10 13,, 9E 00 44 54 43 20 43 4E 54 20 8B 44, B2

6. The scan tool will display all the continuous DTC's.

Diagnostic Trouble Code (DTC) Definitions

DTC	Definitions
P0102	Mass Air Flow (MAF) sensor circuit low input
P0103	Mass Air Flow (MAF) sensor circuit high input
P0106	Barometric Pressure (BP) sensor circuit performance
P0107	Barometric Pressure (BP) sensor circuit low input
P0108	Barometric Pressure (BP) sensor circuit high input
P0112	Intake Air Temperature (IAT) sensor circuit low input
P0113	Intake Air Temperature (IAT) sensor circuit high input
P0117	Engine Coolant Temperature (ECT) sensor circuit low input
P0118	Engine Coolant Temperature (ECT) sensor circuit high input
P0121	In-range operating Throttle Position (TP) sensor circuit failure
P0122	Throttle Position (TP) sensor circuit low input
P0123	Throttle Position (TP) sensor circuit high input
P0125	Insufficient coolant temperature to enter closed loop fuel control
P0131	Upstream Heated Oxygen Sensor (HO2S 11) circuit out of range low voltage (Bank #1)
P0133	Upstream Heated Oxygen Sensor (HO2S 11) circuit slow response (Bank #1)
P0135	Upstream Heated Oxygen Sensor Heater (HTR 11) circuit malfunction (Bank #1)
P0136	Downstream Heated Oxygen Sensor (HO2S 12) circuit malfunction (Bank #1)
P0141	Downstream Heated Oxygen Sensor Heater (HTR 12) circuit malfunction (Bank #1)
P0151	Upstream Heated Oxygen Sensor (HO2S 21) circuit out of range low voltage (Bank #2)
P0153	Upstream Heated Oxygen Sensor (HO2S 21) circuit slow response (Bank #2)
P0155	Upstream Heated Oxygen Sensor Heater (HTR 21) circuit malfunction (Bank #2)
P0156	Downstream Heated Oxygen Sensor (HO2S 22) circuit malfunction (Bank #2)
P0161	Downstream Heated Oxygen Sensor Heater (HTR 22) circuit malfunction (Bank #2)
P0171	System (adaptive fuel) too lean (Bank #1)
P0172	System (adaptive fuel) too rich (Bank #1)
P0174	System (adaptive fuel) too lean (Bank #2)
P0175	System (adaptive fuel) too rich (Bank #2)
P0176	Fuel Composition sensor (FCS) circuit malfunction
P0182	Fuel Temperature sensor A circuit low input
P0183	Fuel Temperature sensor A circuit high input
P0187	Fuel Temperature sensor B circuit low input
P0188	Fuel Temperature sensor B circuit high input
P0191	Injector Pressure sensor circuit performance
P0192	Injector Pressure sensor circuit low input
P0193	Injector Pressure sensor circuit high input
P0222	Throttle Position Sensor B (TP-B) circuit low input
P0223	Throttle Position Sensor B (TP-B) circuit high input
P0230	Fuel Pump primary circuit malfunction
P0231	Fuel Pump secondary circuit low
P0232	Fuel Pump secondary circuit high
P0300	Random Misfire detected
P0301	Cylinder #1 Misfire detected
P0302	Cylinder #2 Misfire detected
P0303	Cylinder #3 Misfire detected

EEC-V Diagnostic Trouble Codes—1995–97 vehicles only

89694G37

Diagnostic Trouble Code (DTC) Definitions

DTC	Definitions
P0304	Cylinder #4 Misfire detected
P0305	Cylinder #5 Misfire detected
P0306	Cylinder #6 Misfire detected
P0307	Cylinder #7 Misfire detected
P0308	Cylinder #8 Misfire detected
P0320	Ignition Engine Speed (Profile Ignition Pickup (PIP)) input circuit malfunction
P0325	Knock Sensor (KS) 1 circuit malfunction
P0326	Knock Sensor (KS) 1 circuit performance
P0331	Knock Sensor (KS) 2 circuit malfunction
P0331	Knock Sensor (KS) 2 circuit performance
P0340	Camshaft Position (CMP) sensor circuit malfunction (CID)
P0350	Ignition Coil primary circuit malfunction
P0351	Ignition Coil A primary circuit malfunction
P0352	Ignition Coil B primary circuit malfunction
P0353	Ignition Coil C primary circuit malfunction
P0354	Ignition Coil D primary circuit malfunction
P0385	Crankshaft Position (CKP) sensor malfunction
P0400	Exhaust Gas Recirculation (EGR) flow malfunction
P0401	Exhaust Gas Recirculation (EGR) flow insufficient detected
P0402	Exhaust Gas Recirculation (EGR) flow excess detected
P0411	Secondary Air Injection system incorrect upstream flow detected
P0412	Secondary Air Injection system switching valve A malfunction
P0413	Secondary Air Injection system switching valve A circuit open
P0414	Secondary Air Injection system switching valve A circuit shorted
P0416	Secondary Air Injection system switching valve B circuit open
P0417	Secondary Air Injection system switching valve B circuit shorted
P0420	Catalyst system efficiency below threshold (Bank #1)
P0430	Catalyst system efficiency below threshold (Bank #2)
P0440	Evaporative emission control system malfunction (Probe)
P0442	Evaporative emission control system small leak detected
P0443	Evaporative emission control system purge control solenoid or vapor management valve circuit malfunction
P0446	Evaporative emission control system Canister Vent (CV) solenoid control malfunction
P0452	Evaporative emission control system Fuel Tank Pressure (FTP) sensor low input
P0453	Evaporative emission control system Fuel Tank Pressure (FTP) sensor high input
P0455	Evaporative emission control system control system leak detected (gross leak)
P0500	Vehicle Speed Sensor (VSS) malfunction
P0503	Vehicle Speed Sensor (VSS) circuit intermittent
P0505	Idle Air Control (IAC) system malfunction
P0552	Power Steering Pressure (PSP) sensor circuit low input
P0553	Power Steering Pressure (PSP) sensor circuit high input
P0603	Powertrain Control Module (PCM) - Keep Alive Memory (KAM) test error
P0605	Powertrain Control Module (PCM) - Read Only Memory (ROM) test error
P0703	Brake On/Off (BOO) switch input malfunction

EEC-V Diagnostic Trouble Codes—1995–97 vehicles only (continued)

89694G38

Diagnostic Trouble Code (DTC) Definitions

DTC	Definitions
P0704	Clutch Pedal Position (CPP) switch input circuit malfunction
P0707	Transmission Range (TR) sensor circuit low input
P0708	Transmission Range (TR) sensor circuit high input
P0712	Transmission Fluid Temperature (TFT) sensor circuit low input
P0713	Transmission Fluid Temperature (TFT) sensor circuit high input
P0715	Turbine Shaft Speed (TSS) sensor circuit malfunction
P0720	Output Shaft Speed (OSS) sensor circuit malfunction
P0721	Output Shaft Speed (OSS) sensor performance (noise)
P0731	Incorrect ratio for first gear
P0732	Incorrect ratio for second gear
P0733	Incorrect ratio for third gear
P0734	Incorrect ratio for fourth gear
P0736	Reverse incorrect gear ratio
P0741	Torque Converter Clutch (TCC) mechanical system performance
P0743	Torque Converter Clutch (TCC) electrical system malfunction
P0746	Electronic Pressure Control (EPC) solenoid performance
P0750	Shift Solenoid #1 (SS1) circuit malfunction
P0751	Shift Solenoid #1 (SS1) performance
P0755	Shift Solenoid #2 (SS2) circuit malfunction
P0756	Shift Solenoid #2 (SS2) performance
P0760	Shift Solenoid #3 (SS3) circuit malfunction
P0761	Shift Solenoid #3 (SS3) performance
P0781	1 to 2 shift error
P0782	2 to 3 shift error
P0783	3 to 4 shift error
P0784	4 to 5 shift error
P1000	OBD II Monitor Testing not complete
P1001	Key On Engine Running (KOER) Self-Test not able to complete. KOER aborted
P1100	Mass Air Flow (MAF) sensor intermittent
P1101	Mass Air Flow (MAF) sensor out of Self-Test range
P1112	Intake Air Temperature (IAT) sensor intermittent
P1116	Engine Coolant Temperature (ECT) sensor out of Self-Test range
P1117	Engine Coolant Temperature (ECT) sensor intermittent
P1120	Throttle Position (TP) sensor out of range low
P1121	Throttle Position (TP) sensor inconsistent with MAF Sensor
P1124	Throttle Position (TP) sensor out of Self-Test range
P1125	Throttle Position (TP) sensor circuit intermittent
P1127	Exhaust not warm enough, downstream Heated Oxygen Sensors (HO2Ss) not tested
P1128	Upstream Heated Oxygen Sensors (HO2Ss) swapped from bank to bank
P1129	Downstream Heated Oxygen Sensors (HO2Ss) swapped from bank to bank
P1130	Lack of upstream Heated Oxygen Sensor (HO2S 11) switch, adaptive fuel at limit (Bank #1)
P1131	Lack of upstream Heated Oxygen Sensor (HO2S 11) switch, sensor indicates lean (Bank #1)
P1132	Lack of upstream Heated Oxygen Sensor (HO2S 11) switch, sensor indicates rich (Bank #1)

89694G39

Diagnostic Trouble Code (DTC) Definitions

DTC	Definitions
P1137	Lack of downstream Heated Oxygen Sensor (HO2S 12) switch, sensor indicates lean (Bank #1)
P1138	Lack of downstream Heated Oxygen Sensor (HO2S 12) switch, sensor indicates rich (Bank #1)
P1150	Lack of upstream Heated Oxygen Sensor (HO2S 21) switch, adaptive fuel at limit (Bank #2)
P1151	Lack of upstream Heated Oxygen Sensor (HO2S 21) switch, sensor indicates lean (Bank #2)
P1152	Lack of upstream Heated Oxygen Sensor (HO2S 21) switch, sensor indicates rich (Bank #2)
P1157	Lack of downstream Heated Oxygen Sensor (HO2S 22) switch, sensor indicates lean (Bank #2)
P1158	Lack of downstream Heated Oxygen Sensor (HO2S 22) switch, sensor indicates rich (Bank #2)
P1220	Series Throttle Control system malfunction
P1224	Throttle Position Sensor B (TP-B) out of Self-Test range
P1230	Fuel Pump low speed malfunction
P1231	Fuel Pump secondary circuit low with high speed pump on
P1232	Low speed Fuel Pump primary circuit malfunction
P1233	Fuel Pump Driver Module disabled or offline
P1234	Fuel Pump Driver Module disabled or offline
P1235	Fuel Pump control out of Self-Test range
P1236	Fuel Pump control out of Self-Test range
P1237	Fuel Pump secondary circuit malfunction
P1238	Fuel Pump secondary circuit malfunction
P1260	THEFT detected - engine disabled
P1270	Engine RPM or vehicle speed limiter reached
P1285	Cylinder Head over temperature sensed
P1288	Cylinder Head Temperature (CHT) sensor out of Self-Test range
P1289	Cylinder Head Temperature (CHT) sensor circuit high input
P1290	Cylinder Head Temperature (CHT) sensor circuit low input
P1299	Engine over temperature condition
P1351	Ignition Diagnostic Monitor (IDM) circuit input malfunction
P1356	PIPs occurred while IDM pulsewidth indicates engine not turning
P1357	Ignition Diagnostic Monitor (IDM) pulsewidth not defined
P1358	Ignition Diagnostic Monitor (IDM) signal out of Self-Test range
P1359	Spark output circuit malfunction
P1390	Octane Adjust (OCT ADJ) out of Self-Test range
P1400	Differential Pressure Feedback EGR (DPFE) sensor circuit low voltage detected
P1401	Differential Pressure Feedback EGR (DPFE) sensor circuit high voltage detected
P1405	Differential Pressure Feedback EGR (DPFE) sensor upstream hose off or plugged
P1406	Differential Pressure Feedback EGR (DPFE) sensor downstream hose off or plugged
P1408	Exhaust Gas Recirculation (EGR) flow out of Self-Test range
P1409	Electronic Vacuum Regulator (EVR) control circuit malfunction
P1411	Secondary Air Injection system incorrect downstream flow detected
P1413	Secondary Air Injection system monitor circuit low voltage
P1414	Secondary Air Injection system monitor circuit high voltage

89694G40

Diagnostic Trouble Code (DTC) Definitions

DTC	Definitions
P1442	Evaporative emission control system small leak detected
P1443	Evaporative emission control system - vacuum system, purge control solenoid or vapor management valve malfunction
P1444	Purge Flow (PF) Sensor circuit low input
P1445	Purge Flow (PF) Sensor circuit high input
P1449	Evaporative emission control system unable to hold vacuum (Probe)
P1450	Unable to bleed up fuel tank vacuum
P1452	Unable to bleed up fuel tank vacuum
P1455	Evaporative emission control system control leak detected (gross leak)
P1460	Wide Open Throttle Air Conditioning Cut-off (WAC) circuit malfunction
P1461	Air Conditioning Pressure (ACP) sensor circuit low input
P1462	Air Conditioning Pressure (ACP) sensor circuit high input
P1463	Air Conditioning Pressure (ACP) sensor insufficient pressure change
P1464	Air condition (A/C) demand out of Self-Test range
P1469	Low air conditioning cycling period
P1473	Fan secondary high with fan(s) off
P1474	Low Fan Control primary circuit malfunction
P1479	High Fan Control primary circuit malfunction
P1480	Fan secondary low with low fan on
P1481	Fan secondary low with high fan on
P1483	Power to fan circuit overcurrent
P1484	Open power ground to Variable Load Control Module (VLCM)
P1500	Vehicle Speed Sensor (VSS) circuit intermittent
P1501	Vehicle Speed Sensor (VSS) out of Self-Test range
P1504	Idle Air Control (IAC) circuit malfunction
P1505	Idle Air Control (IAC) system at adaptive clip
P1506	Idle Air Control (IAC) overspeed error
P1507	Idle Air Control (IAC) underspeed error
P1512	Intake Manifold Runner Control (IMRC) malfunction (Bank # 1 stuck closed)
P1513	Intake Manifold Runner Control (IMRC) malfunction (Bank # 2 stuck closed)
P1516	Intake Manifold Runner Control (IMRC) input error (Bank # 1)
P1517	Intake Manifold Runner Control (IMRC) input error (Bank # 2)
P1518	Intake Manifold Runner Control (IMRC) malfunction (stuck open)
P1519	Intake Manifold Runner Control (IMRC) malfunction (stuck closed)
P1520	Intake Manifold Runner Control (IMRC) circuit malfunction
P1530	Air Condition (A/C) clutch circuit malfunction
P1537	Intake Manifold Runner Control (IMRC) malfunction (Bank # 1 stuck open)
P1538	Intake Manifold Runner Control (IMRC) malfunction (Bank # 2 stuck open)
P1539	Power to Air Condition (A/C) clutch circuit overcurrent
P1550	Power Steering Pressure (PSP) sensor out of Self-Test range
P1605	Powertrain Control Module (PCM) - Keep Alive Memory (KAM) test error
P1625	B(+) supply to Variable Load Control Module (VLCM) fan circuit malfunction
P1626	B(+) supply to Variable Load Control Module (VLCM) Air Condition (A/C) circuit malfunction
P1650	Power Steering Pressure (PSP) switch out of Self-Test range

EEC-V Diagnostic Trouble Codes—1995–97 vehicles only (continued)

89694G41

Diagnostic Trouble Code (DTC) Definitions

DTC	Definitions
P1651	Power Steering Pressure (PSP) switch input malfunction
P1701	Reverse engagement error
P1703	Brake On/Off (BOO) switch out of Self-Test range
P1705	Transmission Range (TR) Sensor out of Self-Test range
P1709	Park or Neutral Position (PNP) switch is not indicating neutral during KOEO Self-Test
P1711	Transmission Fluid Temperature (TFT) sensor out of Self-Test range
P1728	Transmission slip fault
P1729	4x4 Low switch error
P1741	Torque Converter Clutch (TCC) control error
P1742	Torque Converter Clutch (TCC) solenoid failed on (turns on MIL)
P1743	Torque Converter Clutch (TCC) solenoid failed on (turns on TCIL)
P1744	Torque Converter Clutch (TCC) system mechanically stuck in off position
P1746	Electronic Pressure Control (EPC) solenoid open circuit (low input)
P1747	Electronic Pressure Control (EPC) solenoid short circuit (high input)
P1749	Electronic Pressure Control (EPC) solenoid failed low
P1751	Shift Solenoid # 1 (SS1) performance
P1754	Coast Clutch Solenoid (CCS) circuit malfunction
P1756	Shift Solenoid # 2 (SS2) performance
P1761	Shift Solenoid # 3 (SS3) performance
P1780	Transmission Control switch (TCS) circuit out of Self-Test range
P1781	4x4 Low switch out of Self-Test range
P1783	Transmission overtemperature condition
P1788	3-2 Timing/Coast Clutch Solenoid (3-2/CCS) circuit open
P1789	3-2 Timing/Coast Clutch Solenoid (3-2/CCS) circuit shorted
U1021	SCP indicating the lack of Air Condition (A/C) clutch status response
U1039	SCP indicating the vehicle speed signal missing or incorrect
U1051	SCP indicating the brake switch signal missing or incorrect
U1073	SCP indicating the lack of engine coolant fan status response
U1131	SCP indicating the lack of Fuel Pump status response
U1135	SCP indicating the ignition switch signal missing or incorrect
U1256	SCP indicating a communications error
U1451	Lack of response from Passive Anti-Theft system (PATS) module - engine disabled

EEC-V Diagnostic Trouble Codes—1995–97 vehicles only (continued)

89694G42

VACUUM DIAGRAMS

Following are vacuum diagrams for most of the engine and emissions package combinations covered by this manual. Because vacuum circuits will vary based on various engine and vehicle options, always refer first to the vehicle emission control information label, if present. Should the label be missing, or should vehicle be equipped with a different engine from the vehicle's original equipment, refer to the diagrams below for the same or similar configuration.

If you wish to obtain a replacement emissions label, most manufacturers make the labels available for purchase. The labels can usually be ordered from a local dealer.

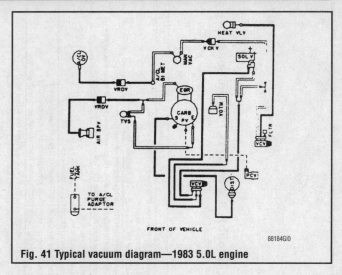

Fig. 41 Typical vacuum diagram—1983 5.0L engine

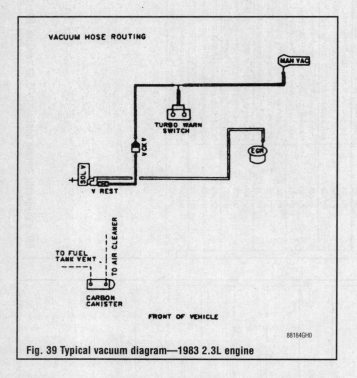

Fig. 39 Typical vacuum diagram—1983 2.3L engine

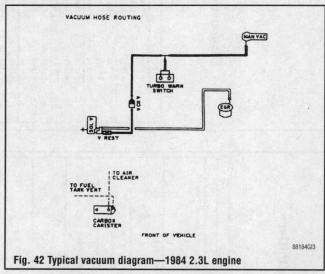

Fig. 42 Typical vacuum diagram—1984 2.3L engine

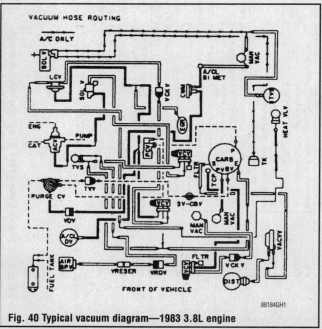

Fig. 40 Typical vacuum diagram—1983 3.8L engine

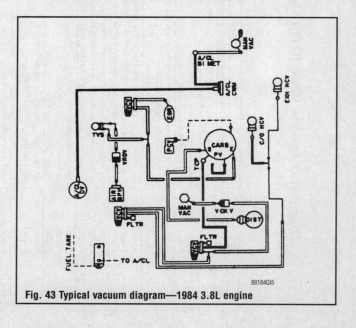

Fig. 43 Typical vacuum diagram—1984 3.8L engine

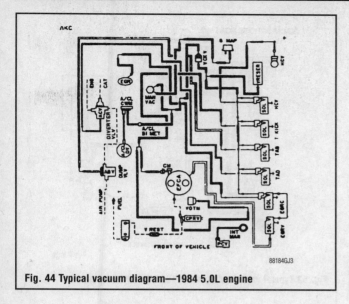

Fig. 44 Typical vacuum diagram—1984 5.0L engine

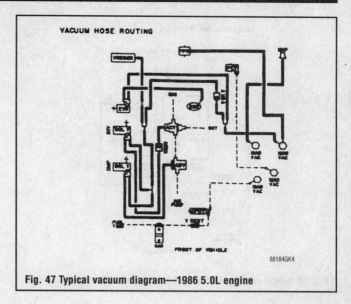

Fig. 47 Typical vacuum diagram—1986 5.0L engine

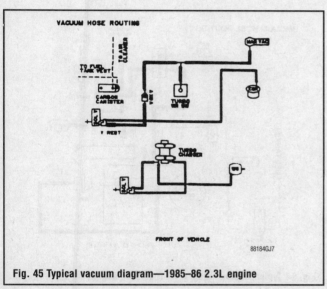

Fig. 45 Typical vacuum diagram—1985–86 2.3L engine

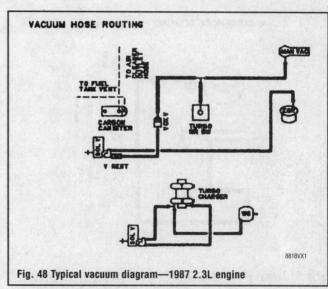

Fig. 48 Typical vacuum diagram—1987 2.3L engine

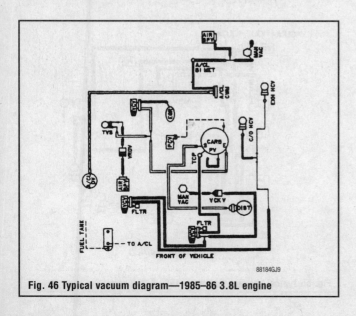

Fig. 46 Typical vacuum diagram—1985–86 3.8L engine

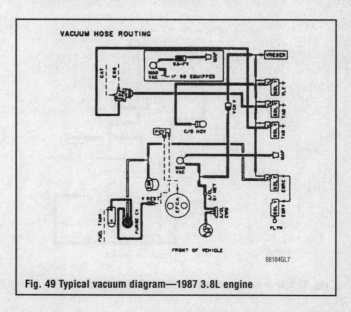

Fig. 49 Typical vacuum diagram—1987 3.8L engine

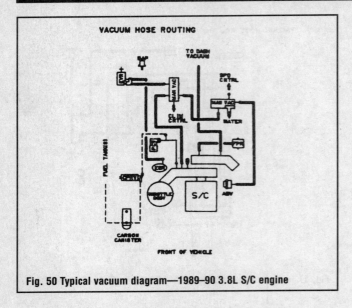

Fig. 50 Typical vacuum diagram—1989–90 3.8L S/C engine

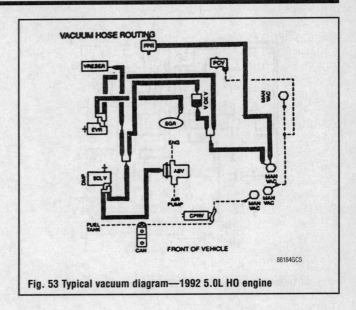

Fig. 53 Typical vacuum diagram—1992 5.0L HO engine

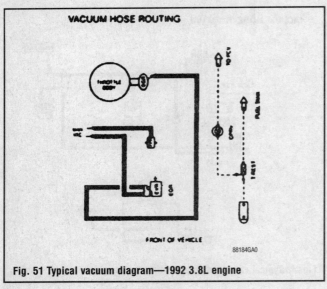

Fig. 51 Typical vacuum diagram—1992 3.8L engine

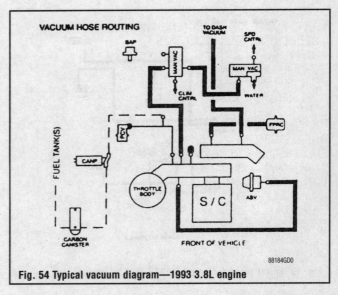

Fig. 54 Typical vacuum diagram—1993 3.8L engine

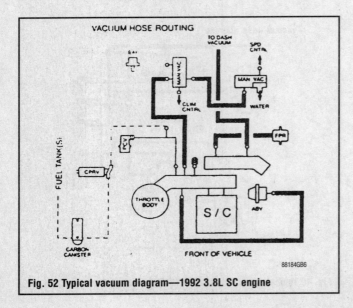

Fig. 52 Typical vacuum diagram—1992 3.8L SC engine

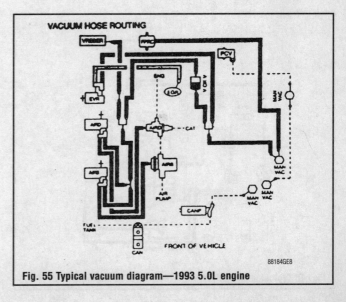

Fig. 55 Typical vacuum diagram—1993 5.0L engine

**BASIC FUEL SYSTEM
DIAGNOSIS 5-2**
FUEL LINES AND FITTINGS 5-2
QUICK-CONNECT FUEL LINE
FITTINGS 5-2
REMOVAL & INSTALLATION 5-2
CARBURETED FUEL SYSTEM 5-3
MECHANICAL FUEL PUMP 5-3
REMOVAL & INSTALLATION 5-3
TESTING 5-4
CARBURETORS 5-4
ADJUSTMENTS 5-4
CENTRAL FUEL INJECTION 5-7
GENERAL INFORMATION 5-7
RELIEVING FUEL SYSTEM
PRESSURE 5-7
ELECTRIC FUEL PUMP 5-7
REMOVAL & INSTALLATION 5-7
TESTING 5-11
THROTTLE BODY 5-11
REMOVAL & INSTALLATION 5-11
**MULTI-POINT INJECTION (EFI) AND
SEQUENTIAL FUEL INJECTION
(SEFI) 5-11**
GENERAL INFORMATION 5-11
RELIEVING FUEL SYSTEM
PRESSURE 5-11
ELECTRIC FUEL PUMP 5-12
REMOVAL & INSTALLATION 5-12
PRESSURE TESTING 5-12
FUEL PRESSURE REGULATOR 5-12
REMOVAL & INSTALLATION 5-12
FUEL INJECTOR MANIFOLD
ASSEMBLY 5-13
REMOVAL & INSTALLATION 5-13
PRESSURE RELIEF VALVE 5-13
REMOVAL & INSTALLATION 5-13
AIR INTAKE THROTTLE BODY 5-14
REMOVAL & INSTALLATION 5-14
FUEL INJECTOR 5-15
REMOVAL & INSTALLATION 5-15
FUEL TANK 5-17
REMOVAL & INSTALLATION 5-17

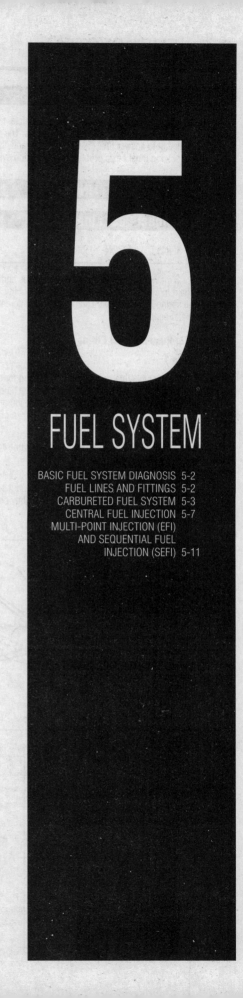

5

FUEL SYSTEM

BASIC FUEL SYSTEM DIAGNOSIS 5-2
FUEL LINES AND FITTINGS 5-2
CARBURETED FUEL SYSTEM 5-3
CENTRAL FUEL INJECTION 5-7
MULTI-POINT INJECTION (EFI)
AND SEQUENTIAL FUEL
INJECTION (SEFI) 5-11

BASIC FUEL SYSTEM DIAGNOSIS

When there is a problem starting or driving a vehicle, two of the most important checks involve the ignition and the fuel systems. The questions most mechanics attempt to answer first, "is there spark?" and "is there fuel?" will often lead to solving most basic problems. For ignition system diagnosis and testing, please refer to the information on engine electrical components and ignition systems found earlier in this manual. If the ignition system checks out (there is spark), then you must determine if the fuel system is operating properly (is there fuel?).

FUEL LINES AND FITTINGS

Quick-Connect Fuel Line Fittings

REMOVAL & INSTALLATION

There are 3 methods used to connect the fuel lines and fuel system components: the hairpin clip push connect fitting, the duck bill clip push connect fitting and the spring lock coupling. Each requires a different procedure to disconnect and connect.

Hairpin Clip Push Connect Fitting

▶ **See Figure 1**

1. Inspect the visible internal portion of the fitting for dirt accumulation. If more than a light coating of dust is present, clean the fitting before disassembly.
2. Some adhesion between the seals in the fitting and the tubing will occur with time. To separate, twist the fitting on the tube, then push and pull the fitting until it moves freely on the tube.

➡ **Use care when separating 90 degree elbow connectors, as excessive side loading could break the connector body.**

3. Remove the hairpin clip from the fitting by first bending and breaking the shipping tab. Next, spread the 2 clip legs by hand about ⅛ in. each to disengage the body and push the legs into the fitting. Lightly pull the triangular end of the clip and work it clear of the tube and fitting.

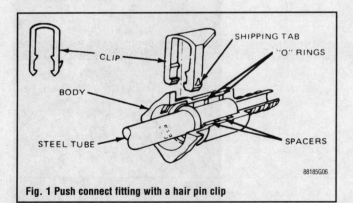

Fig. 1 Push connect fitting with a hair pin clip

➡ **Do not use hand tools to complete this operation.**

4. Grasp the fitting and pull in an axial direction to remove the fitting from the tube.
5. After disassembly, inspect and clean the tube end sealing surfaces. The tube end should be free of scratches and corrosion that could provide leak paths. Inspect the inside of the fitting for any internal parts such as O-rings and spacers that may have been dislodged from the fitting. Replace any damaged connector.

To connect:

6. Install a new connector if damage was found. Insert a new clip into any 2 adjacent openings with the triangular portion pointing away from the fitting opening. Install the clip until the legs of the clip are locked on the outside of the body. Piloting with an index finger is necessary.
7. Before installing the fitting on the tube, wipe the tube end with a clean cloth. Inspect the inside of the fitting to make sure it is free of dirt and/or obstructions.
8. Apply a light coating of engine oil to the tube end. Align the fitting and tube axially and push the fitting onto the tube end. When the fitting is engaged, a definite click will be heard. Pull on the fitting to make sure it is fully engaged.

Duck Bill Clip Push Connect Fitting

▶ **See Figures 2, 3 and 4**

1. Inspect the visible internal portion of the fitting for dirt accumulation. If more than a light coating of dust is present, clean the fitting before disassembly.
2. Some adhesion between the seals in the fitting and the tubing will occur with time. To separate, twist the fitting on the tube, then push and pull the fitting until it moves freely on the tube.
3. Align the slot on push connect disassembly tool T82L–9600–AH or equivalent, with either tab on the clip, 90 degrees from the slots on the side of the fitting and insert the tool. This disengages the duck bill retainer from the tube.
4. Holding the tool and the tube with one hand, pull the fitting away from the tube.

➡ **Use hands only. Only moderate effort is required if the tube has been properly disengaged.**

5. After disassembly, inspect and clean the tube end sealing surfaces. The tube end should be free of scratches and corrosion that could provide leak paths. Inspect the inside of the fitting for any internal parts such as O-rings and spacers that may have been dislodged from the fitting. Replace any damaged connector.

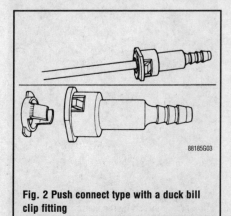

Fig. 2 Push connect type with a duck bill clip fitting

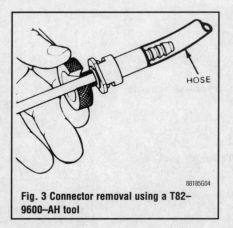

Fig. 3 Connector removal using a T82–9600–AH tool

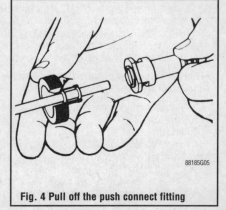

Fig. 4 Pull off the push connect fitting

6. Some fuel tubes have a secondary bead which aligns with the outer surface of the clip. These beads can make tool insertion difficult. If there is extreme difficulty, use the following disassembly method:

  a. Using pliers with a jaw width of 0.2 in. (5mm) or less, align the jaws with the openings in the side of the fitting case and compress the portion of the retaining clip that engages the fitting case. This disengages the retaining clip from the case. Often one side of the clip will disengage before the other. The clip must be disengaged from both openings.

  b. Pull the fitting off the tube by hand only. Only moderate effort is required if the retaining clip has been properly disengaged.

  c. After disassembly, inspect and clean the tube end sealing surfaces. The tube end should be free of scratches and corrosion that could provide leak paths. Inspect the inside of the fitting for any internal parts such as O-rings and spacers that may have been dislodged from the fitting. Replace any damaged connector.

  d. The retaining clip will remain on the tube. Disengage the clip from the tube bead and remove.

To connect:

7. Install a new connector if damage was found. Install the new replacement clip into the body by inserting 1 of the retaining clip serrated edges on the duck bill portion into one side of the window openings. Push on the other side until the clip snaps into place.

8. Before installing the fitting on the tube, wipe the tube end with a clean cloth. Inspect the inside of the fitting to make sure it is free of dirt and/or obstructions.

9. Apply a light coating of engine oil to the tube end. Align the fitting and tube axially and push the fitting onto the tube end. When the fitting is engaged, a definite click will be heard. Pull on the fitting to make sure it is fully engaged.

Spring Lock Coupling

▶ **See Figures 5, 6 and 7**

The spring lock coupling is a fuel line coupling held together by a garter spring inside a circular cage. When the coupling is connected together, the flared end of the female fitting slips behind the garter spring inside the cage of the male fitting. The garter spring and cage then prevent the flared end of the female fitting from pulling out of the cage. As an additional locking feature, most vehicles have a horseshoe shaped retaining clip that improves the retaining reliability of the spring lock coupling.

Fig. 5 Remove the clip retaining the hose to the line

Fig. 6 Separate the line from the hose

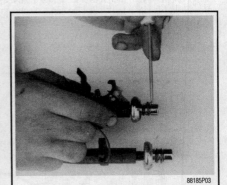

Fig. 7 Replace the O-rings from the fuel line fittings

CARBURETED FUEL SYSTEM

Mechanical Fuel Pump

REMOVAL & INSTALLATION

▶ **See Figure 8**

➡**Before removing the pump, rotate the engine so that the low point of the cam lobe is against the pump arm. This can be determined by rotating the engine with the fuel pump mounting bolts loosened slightly. When tension (resistance) is removed from the arm, proceed.**

1. Loosen the threaded fuel line connection(s) with the proper size flared nut wrench, then retighten snugly. Do not remove the lines at this time.

2. Loosen the mounting bolts one to two turns. Apply force with your hands to loosen the fuel pump if the gasket is stuck. Rotate the engine, by nudging the starter, until the pump cam lobe is near its low position. The tension on the pump will be greatly reduced at the low cam position.

➡**The outlet line is pressurized. Disconnect the fuel pump inlet line, the outlet vapor return line, if so equipped.**

3. Remove the pump attaching bolts, then the pump and gasket. Clean the mating areas well.

To Install:

4. Install the attaching bolts into the pump, then install a new gasket on the bolts. Position the pump to the mounting pad. Turn the bolts alternately and evenly, then tighten to 12–15 ft. lbs. (16–20 Nm).

5. Install the fuel outlet line. If it is a threaded connection, start fitting by hand to avoid any crossthreading. Tighten the fitting to 20–24 ft. lbs. (15–18 Nm).

6. Install the inlet line and fuel vapor return line, if removed. Using new clamps, install the fuel hose. Inspect and replace any cracked or damaged fuel hoses.

7. Check that all connections are intact, then start the engine and inspect for leaks. Run the engine for approximately 2 minutes.

8. Stop the engine and check all the pump and fuel line connections for any leaks. Inspect for any oil leaks at the pump mounting pad.

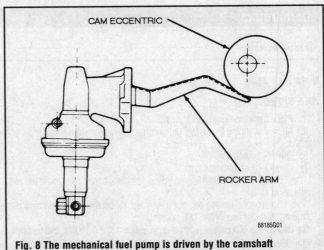

Fig. 8 The mechanical fuel pump is driven by the camshaft

TESTING

▶ **See Figure 9**

No adjustments may be made to the fuel pump. Before removing and replacing the old fuel pump, the following test may be made while the pump is still installed on the engine.

1. If a fuel pressure gauge is available, connect the gauge to the engine and operate the engine until the pressure stops rising. Stop the engine and take the reading. If the reading is within the specifications given in the Tune-Up Specifications chart in Section 2, the malfunctions is not in the fuel pump. Also check the pressure drop after the engine is stopped. A large pressure drop below the minimum specification indicates leaky valves. If the pump proves to be satisfactory, check the tank and inlet line.

2. If a fuel pressure gauge is not available, disconnect the fuel line at the pump outlet, place a vessel beneath the pump outlet, and crank the engine. A good pump will force the fuel out of the outlet in steady spurts. One pint in 25–30 seconds is a good flow. A worn diaphragm spring may not provide proper pumping action.

3. As a further test, disconnect and plug the fuel line from the tank at the pump, and hold your thumb over the pump inlet. If the pump is functioning properly, a suction indicates that the pump diaphragm is leaking, or that the diaphragm linkage is worn.

4. Check the crankcase for gasoline. A ruptured diaphragm may leak fuel into the engine.

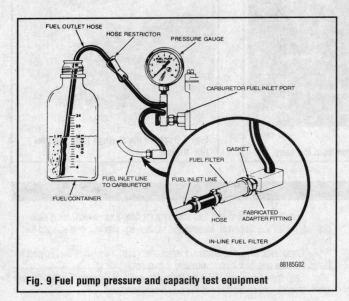

Fig. 9 Fuel pump pressure and capacity test equipment

Carburetors

ADJUSTMENTS

Motorcraft 2150

IDLE SPEED

1. Place the transmission in **P** or **N**.
2. Allow the engine to operate until normal operating temperature is reached.
3. Turn all accessories off.
4. Check/adjust curb idle rpm:
    a. On non-air conditioning equipped vehicles, adjust the saddle bracket adjusting screw.
    b. On air conditioning equipped vehicles, adjust the hex head screw protruding from the rear of the TSP housing.
5. Slightly rev the engine momentarily. Recheck the curb idle and readjust, if required.

FAST IDLE

▶ **See Figure 10**

1. Place the transmission in Neutral or Park position.
2. Bring the engine to normal operating condition.
3. Disconnect the vacuum hose at the EGR valve and plug.
4. Place the fast idle cam adjustment on the specified step of the fast idle cam. Check and adjust the fast idle rpm to specification.
5. Rev the engine momentarily, place the fast idle on the specified step and then recheck the fast idles RPM.
6. Remove the plug from the EGR vacuum hose, then reconnect.

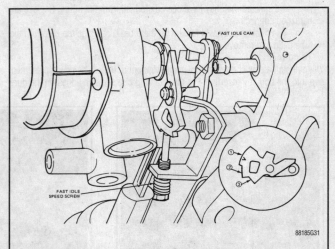

Fig. 10 Fast idle adjustment screw location on the 2150 model carburetor

IDLE MIXTURE

1. Set the parking brake and block the drive wheels.
2. Connect a tachometer (Rotunda 20362 or equivalent).
3. If equipped with a Hot Idle Compensator (HIC), insure that it remains in closed position throughout the test. Idle the vehicle on the kickdown step of the fast idle cam for 3 minutes to ensure the HIC valve is closed.
4. Disconnect the fuel evaporative purge return hose at the engine and air cleaner, if equipped. Plug the connections.
5. Disconnect the flexible fresh air tube from the air cleaner duct or adapter. Using a propane enrichment tool (Rotunda T75L-9600 or equivalent), insert the tool hose approximately ¾ of the way into the duct or fresh air tube. If necessary, secure the hose with tape.
6. On vehicles equipped with thermactor system, revise the dump valve vacuum hoses as follows:
    a. For dump valves with 2 vacuum fittings, disconnect and plug the hoses.
    b. For dump valves with 1 fitting or combination air bypass/air control valve, remove the hose at the dump valve and plug it. Connect a slave hose from the dump valve vacuum fitting to an intake manifold vacuum fitting.

➡Leave all vacuum signal hoses attached to the air cleaner assembly when relocating the assembly to perform carburetor adjustments. The air cleaner assembly must be in place, however, when measuring engine speeds.

✳✳ CAUTION

Prolonged engine idling can result in catalyst overheating and excessive underbody temperatures.

7. Verify the ignition timing and curb idle is set to specifications.
8. Remove the PCV valve from the grommet and allow it to draw underhood air during the idle mixture check. Locate the crankcase vent hose and disconnect it at the air cleaner, allowing the in-line fixed orifice to vent to underhood air.

9. With the transmission in **N**, run the engine at approximately 2500 rpm for 15 seconds before each mixture check.

10. Gradually open the propane tool valve and watch for engine speed gain, if any, on the tachometer. When the engine speed reaches a maximum and then begins to drop off, note the amount of speed gain. The propane cartridge must be in vertical position.

➡**If the engine speed will not drop off, check the propane cartridge gas supply. If necessary, repeat Steps 9 and 10 with a new cartridge. If the measured speed gain is 0 rpm (no rpm rise) and the minimum speed gain specification is 0 rpm, go to Step 13.**

11. If the measured speed gain is higher than the speed gain specification, turn the mixture screws counter clockwise (rich) in equal amounts while simultaneously repeating the mixture adjustment, until the measured speed rise meets the reset rpm specification.

12. Reinstall the PCV valve in the grommet and adjust the curb idle.

13. Reinstall the tamper resistant feature.

CHOKE PLATE PULLDOWN CLEARANCE

▶ **See Figure 11**

1. Remove the air cleaner assembly.
2. Set the throttle on the stop step of the fast idle cam.
3. Noting the position of the choke housing cap, loosen the retaining screws and rotate the cap 90° in the rich (closing) direction.
4. Activate the pulldown motor by manually forcing the pulldown control diaphragm link in the direction of applied vacuum or by applying vacuum to the external vacuum tube.
5. Using a drill gauge of the specified diameter, measure the clearance between the choke plate and the center of the air horn wall nearest the fuel bowl.
6. To adjust, reset the diaphragm stop on the end of the choke pulldown diaphragm.
7. After adjusting, reset the choke housing cap to the specified notch. Check and reset fast idle speed, if necessary. Install the air cleaner.

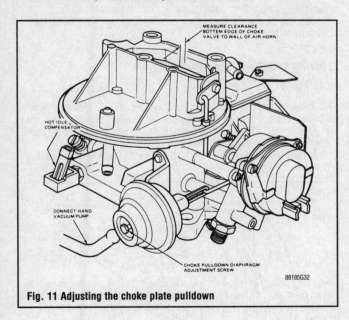

Fig. 11 Adjusting the choke plate pulldown

FLOAT LEVEL ADJUSTMENT—DRY

▶ **See Figures 12 and 13**

This preliminary setting of the float level adjustment must be done with the carburetor removed from the engine.

1. Remove the air horn and see that the float is raised and the fuel inlet needle is seated. Check the distance between the top surface of the main body (with the gasket removed) and the top surface of the float. Depress the float tab to seat the fuel inlet needle. Take a measurement near the center of the float, at a point ⅛ in. (3mm) from the free end. If you are using a prefabricated float gauge,

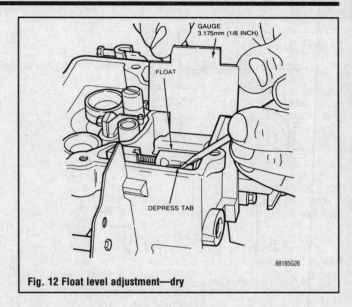

Fig. 12 Float level adjustment—dry

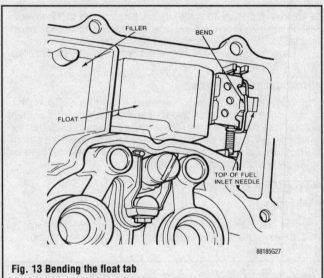

Fig. 13 Bending the float tab

place the gauge in the corner of the enlarged end section of the fuel bowl. The gauge should touch the float near the end, but not on the end radius.

2. If necessary, bend the tab on the end of the float to bring the setting within the specified limits.

FLOAT LEVEL ADJUSTMENT—WET

▶ **See Figure 14**

1. Bring the engine to its normal operating temperature, park the car on as nearly level a surface as possible, and stop the engine.
2. Remove the air cleaner assembly from the carburetor.
3. Remove the air horn retaining screws and the carburetor identification tag. Leave the air horn and gasket in position on the carburetor main body. Start the engine, let it idle for several minutes, rotate the air horn out of the way, and remove the gasket to provide access to the float assembly.
4. With the engine idling, use a standard depth scale to measure the vertical distance from the top machined surface of the carburetor main body to the level of the fuel in the fuel bowl. This measurement must be made at least ¼ in. (6mm) away from any vertical surface in order to assure an accurate reading.
5. Stop the engine before making any adjustment to the float level. Adjustment is accomplished by bending the float tab (with contacts the fuel inlet valve) up or down as required to raise or lower the fuel level. After making an adjust-

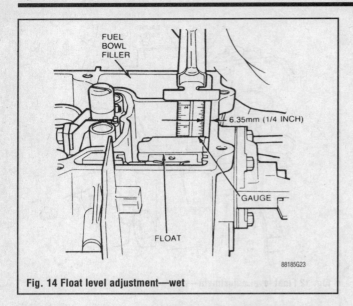

Fig. 14 Float level adjustment—wet

ment, start the engine, and allow it to idle for several minutes before repeating the fuel level check. Repeat as necessary until the proper fuel level is attained.

6. Reinstall the air horn with a new gasket and secure it with the screw. Include the installation of the identification tag in its proper location.

7. Check the idle speed, fuel mixture, and dashpot adjustments. Install the air cleaner assembly.

AUTOMATIC CHOKE HOUSING

By rotating the spring housing of the automatic choke, the reaction of the choke to engine temperature can be controlled. To adjust, remove the air cleaner assembly, loosen the thermostatic spring housing retaining screws and set the spring housing to the specified index mark. The marks are shown in the accompanying illustration. After adjusting the setting, tighten the retaining screws and replace the air cleaner assembly to the carburetor.

ACCELERATOR PUMP STROKE ADJUSTMENT

♦ See Figure 15

In order to keep the exhaust emission level of the engine within the specified limits, the accelerating pump stroke has been preset at the factory. The addi-

tional holes are provided for differing engine-transmission-body applications only. The primary throttle shaft lever (overtravel lever) has four holes to control the pump stroke. The accelerating pump operating rod should be in the overtravel lever hole number listed in the Carburetor Specifications chart, and in the inboard hole (hole closest to the pump plunger) in the accelerating pump link. If the pump stroke has been changed from the specified settings, use the following procedure to correct the stroke.

1. Release the operating rod from the retaining clip by pressing the tab end of the clip toward the rod while pressing the rod away from the clip until it disengages.

2. Position the clip over the specified hole (see Carburetor Specifications chart) in the overtravel lever. Press the ends of the clip together and insert the operating rod through the clip and the overtravel lever. Release the clip to engage the rod.

ANTI-STALL DASHPOT ADJUSTMENT

Having made sure that the engine idle speed and mixture are correct and that the engine is at normal operating temperature, loosen the anti-stall dashpot locking nut (see accompanying illustration). With the throttle held closed, depress the plunger with a screwdriver blade and measure the clearance between the throttle lever and the plunger tip. If the clearance is not as specified in the Carburetor Specifications chart, turn the dashpot until the proper clearance is obtained between the throttle lever and the plunger tip. After tightening the locking nut, recheck the adjustment.

KICKER SET SPEED

1. Place the transmission in the Neutral or Park position.
2. Bring the engine to the normal operating temperature.
3. Place the A/C-heater selector in the OFF position.
4. Disconnect and plug the vacuum hose at the VOTM kicker.
5. Connect the external vacuum source providing a minimum of 33.7 kPA (10 in-Hg) to the VOTM kicker.
6. Place the transmission selector in the specified position.
7. Check and adjust the VOTM kicker on the rpm, if the adjustment is required. Adjust the VOTM saddle bracket adjustment screw.
8. Remove the external vacuum source, remove the plug from the VOTM kicker hose and reconnect.
9. Reset the curb idle.

ELECTRIC CHOKE—OPERATIONAL TEST

♦ See Figures 16, 17 and 18

All carbureted models use an electrically assisted choke to reduce exhaust emissions of carbon monoxide during warm-up. The system consists of a choke cap, a thermostatic spring, a bimetal sensing disc (switch) and a ceramic positive temperature coefficient (PTC) heater.

The choke is powered from the center tap of the alternator, so that current is

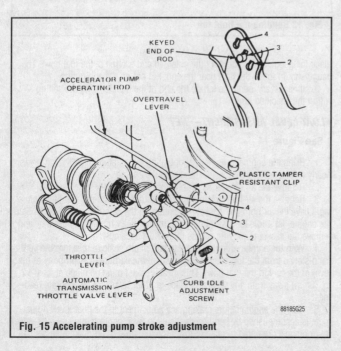

Fig. 15 Accelerating pump stroke adjustment

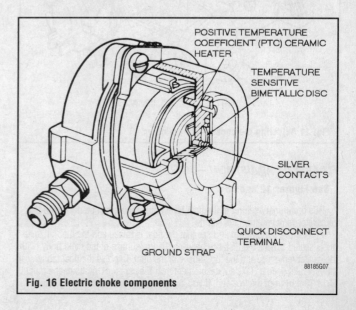

Fig. 16 Electric choke components

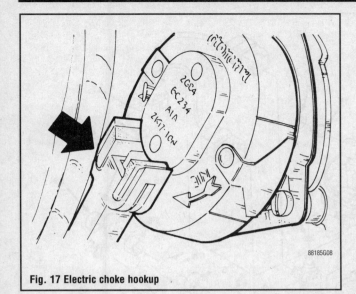

Fig. 17 Electric choke hookup

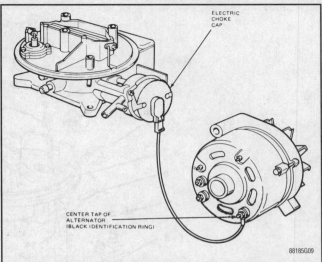

Fig. 18 The electric choke has wiring that attaches to the alternator

constantly applied to the temperature sensing disc. The system is grounded through the carburetor body. At temperatures below approximately 60°F (16°C), the switch is open and no current is supplied to the ceramic heater, thereby resulting in normal unassisted thermostatic spring choke action. When the temperature rises above 60°F (16°C), the temperature sensing disc closes and current is supplied to the heater, which in turn, acts on the thermostatic spring. Once the heater starts, it causes the thermostatic spring to pull the choke plate(s) open within 1½ minutes, which is sooner than it would open if non-assisted.

1. Detach the electrical lead from the choke cap.
2. Use a jumper lead to connect the terminal on the choke cap and the wire terminal, so that the electrical circuit is still completed.
3. Start the engine.
4. Hook up a test light between the connector on the choke lead and ground.
5. The test light should glow. If it does not, current is not being supplied to the electrically assisted choke.
6. Connect the test light between the terminal on the alternator and the terminal on the choke cap. If the light now glows, replace the lead, since it is not passing current to the choke assist.

✳✳ CAUTION

Do not ground the terminal on the alternator while performing Step 6.

7. If the light still does not glow, the fault lies somewhere in the electrical system. Check the system out. If the electrically assisted choke receives power but still does not appear to be functioning properly, reconnect the choke lead and proceed with the rest of the test.
8. Tape the bulb end of the thermometer to the metallic portion of the choke housing.
9. If the electrically assisted choke operates below 55°F (13°C), it is defective and must be replaced.
10. Allow the engine to warm up to 80–100°F (27–38°C); at these temperatures the choke should operate for about 1½ minutes.
11. If it does not operate for this length of time, check the bimetallic spring to see if it is connected to the tang on the choke lever.
12. If the spring is connected and the choke is not operating properly, replace the cap assembly.

CENTRAL FUEL INJECTION

General Information

▶ See Figures 19, 20, 21 and 22

Central Fuel Injection (CFI) is a throttle body injection system in which two fuel injectors are mounted in a common throttle body, spraying fuel down through the throttle valves at the bottom of the body and into the intake manifold.

Fuel is supplied from the fuel tank by a high pressure, in-tank fuel pump. The fuel passes through a filter and is sent to the throttle body where a regulator keeps the fuel delivery pressure at a constant 39 psi. The two fuel injectors are mounted vertically above the throttle plates and are connected in line with the fuel pressure regulator. Excess fuel supplied by the pump, but not needed by the engine, is returned to the fuel tank by a steel fuel return line.

The fuel injection system is linked with and controlled by the Electronic Engine Control (EEC) system.

Relieving Fuel System Pressure

Fuel supply lines on all fuel injected engines will remain pressurized for some period of time after the engine is shut **OFF**. This pressure must be relieved before servicing the fuel system. Pressure is relieved through the fuel pressure relief valve. To relieve the fuel system pressure, first remove the fuel tank cap to relieve pressure in the tank, then remove the cap on the fuel pressure relief valve, located on the fuel rail. Attach fuel pressure gauge T80L–9974–A or equivalent, and drain the system through the drain tube into a suitable container. Remove the fuel pressure gauge and replace the cap on the relief valve.

Electric Fuel Pump

REMOVAL & INSTALLATION

Models equipped with a high output injected or turbocharged injected engine are equipped with two electric pumps. A low pressure pump is mounted in the tank and a high pressure pump is externally mounted.

All other models are equipped with a single, in-tank, high pressure fuel pump.

✳✳ CAUTION

Before servicing any part of the fuel injection it is necessary to depressurize the system. A special tool is available for testing and bleeding the system.

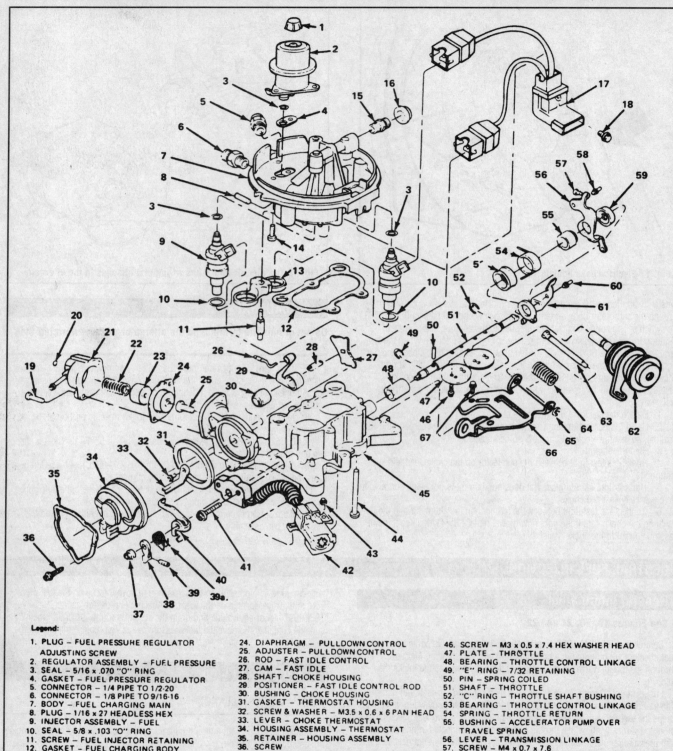

Legend:

1. PLUG – FUEL PRESSURE REGULATOR ADJUSTING SCREW
2. REGULATOR ASSEMBLY – FUEL PRESSURE
3. SEAL – 5/16 x .070 "O" RING
4. GASKET – FUEL PRESSURE REGULATOR
5. CONNECTOR – 1/4 PIPE TO 1/2-20
6. CONNECTOR – 1/8 PIPE TO 9/16-16
7. BODY – FUEL CHARGING MAIN
8. PLUG – 1/16 x 27 HEADLESS HEX
9. INJECTOR ASSEMBLY – FUEL
10. SEAL – 5/8 x .103 "O" RING
11. SCREW – FUEL INJECTOR RETAINING
12. GASKET – FUEL CHARGING BODY
13. RETAINER – FUEL INJECTOR
14. SCREW M5.0 x 20.0 PAN HEAD
15. VALVE ASSEMBLY – DIAGNOSTIC VALVE
16. CAP – FUEL PRESSURE RELIEF VALVE
17. WIRING ASSEMBLY – FUEL CHARGING
18. SCREW – M3.5 x 1.27 x 12.7 PAN HEAD
19. SCREW & WASHER – M4 x 7.0 20.00
20. BALL – LEAD SHOT .26 - .24 DIA.
21. COVER ASSEMBLY – CONTROL DIAPHRAGM
22. SPRING – CONTROL MODULATOR
23. RETAINER – PULLDOWN DIAPHRAGM

24. DIAPHRAGM – PULLDOWN CONTROL
25. ADJUSTER – PULLDOWN CONTROL
26. ROD – FAST IDLE CONTROL
27. CAM – FAST IDLE
28. SHAFT – CHOKE HOUSING
29. POSITIONER – FAST IDLE CONTROL ROD
30. BUSHING – CHOKE HOUSING
31. GASKET – THERMOSTAT HOUSING
32. SCREW & WASHER – M3.5 x 0.6 x 6 PAN HEAD
33. LEVER – CHOKE THERMOSTAT
34. HOUSING ASSEMBLY – THERMOSTAT
35. RETAINER – HOUSING ASSEMBLY
36. SCREW
37. NUT & WASHER ASSEMBLY - .7-6H HEX
38. LEVER – FAST IDLE CAM ADJUSTER
39. SCREW – NO. 10 - 32 x .50 SET SLOTTED HEAD
39a. FAST IDLE PICK-UP LEVER RETURN SPRING
40. LEVER – FAST IDLE
41. SCREW & WASHER – M4.07 x 22.0 PAN HEAD
42. THROTTLE POSITION SENSOR
43. SCREW – M4 x .7 14.0 HEX WASHER TAP
44. SCREW – M5 x .7 x 55.0
45. BODY – FUEL CHARGING – THROTTLE

46. SCREW – M3 x 0.5 x 7.4 HEX WASHER HEAD
47. PLATE – THROTTLE
48. BEARING – THROTTLE CONTROL LINKAGE
49. "E" RING – 7/32 RETAINING
50. PIN – SPRING COILED
51. SHAFT – THROTTLE
52. "C" RING – THROTTLE SHAFT BUSHING
53. BEARING – THROTTLE CONTROL LINKAGE
54. SPRING – THROTTLE RETURN
55. BUSHING – ACCELERATOR PUMP OVER TRAVEL SPRING
56. LEVER – TRANSMISSION LINKAGE
57. SCREW – M4 x 0.7 x 7.6
58. PIN – TRANSMISSION LINKAGE LEVER
59. SPACER – THROTTLE SHAFT
60. BALL – THROTTLE LEVER
61. LEVER – THROTTLE
62. POSITIONER ASSEMBLY – THROTTLE
63. SCREW – 1/4 - 28 x 2.53 HEX HEAD ADJUSTING
64. SPRING – THROTTLE POSITIONER RETAINING
65. "E" RING – RETAINING
66. BRACKET – THROTTLE POSITIONER
67. SCREW – M5 x 8 x 14.0 HEX WASHER TAP

Fig. 19 Exploded view of the CFI system components

88185G40

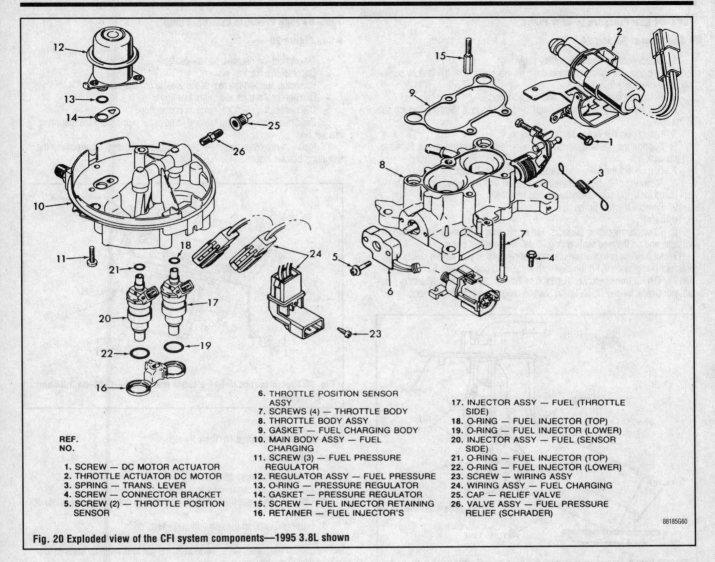

**REF.
NO.**

1. SCREW — DC MOTOR ACTUATOR
2. THROTTLE ACTUATOR DC MOTOR
3. SPRING — TRANS. LEVER
4. SCREW — CONNECTOR BRACKET
5. SCREW (2) — THROTTLE POSITION
   SENSOR

6. THROTTLE POSITION SENSOR
   ASSY
7. SCREWS (4) — THROTTLE BODY
8. THROTTLE BODY ASSY
9. GASKET — FUEL CHARGING BODY
10. MAIN BODY ASSY — FUEL
    CHARGING
11. SCREW (3) — FUEL PRESSURE
    REGULATOR
12. REGULATOR ASSY — FUEL PRESSURE
13. O-RING — PRESSURE REGULATOR
14. GASKET — PRESSURE REGULATOR
15. SCREW — FUEL INJECTOR RETAINING
16. RETAINER — FUEL INJECTOR'S

17. INJECTOR ASSY — FUEL (THROTTLE
    SIDE)
18. O-RING — FUEL INJECTOR (TOP)
19. O-RING — FUEL INJECTOR (LOWER)
20. INJECTOR ASSY — FUEL (SENSOR
    SIDE)
21. O-RING — FUEL INJECTOR (TOP)
22. O-RING — FUEL INJECTOR (LOWER)
23. SCREW — WIRING ASSY
24. WIRING ASSY — FUEL CHARGING
25. CAP — RELIEF VALVE
26. VALVE ASSY — FUEL PRESSURE
    RELIEF (SCHRADER)

88185G60

Fig. 20 Exploded view of the CFI system components—1995 3.8L shown

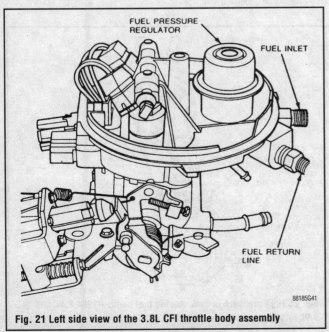

88185G41

Fig. 21 Left side view of the 3.8L CFI throttle body assembly

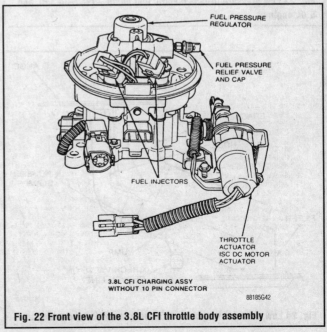

3.8L CFI CHARGING ASSY
WITHOUT 10 PIN CONNECTOR

88185G42

Fig. 22 Front view of the 3.8L CFI throttle body assembly

1983–84 Low Pressure In-Tank Pump

◆ **See Figures 23 and 24**

1. Disconnect the negative battery cable.
2. Depressurize the system and drain as much gas from the tank by pumping out through the filler neck.
3. Raise and support the rear end on jackstands.
4. Disconnect the fuel supply, return and vent lines at the right and left side of the frame.
5. Disconnect the wiring to the fuel pump.
6. Support the gas tank, loosen and remove the mounting straps. Remove the gas tank.
7. Disconnect the lines and harness at the pump flange.
8. Clean the outside of the mounting flange and retaining ring. Turn the fuel pump lock ring counterclockwise and remove.
9. Remove the fuel pump.

To Install:

10. Clean the mounting surfaces. Put a light coat of grease on the mounting surfaces and on the new sealing ring. Install the new fuel pump.
11. Installation is in the reverse order of removal. If you have a single high pressure pump system, fill the tank with at least 10 gals. of gas. Turn the ignition key **ON** for three seconds. Repeat 6 or 7 times until the fuel system is pressurized. Check for any fitting leaks. Start the engine and check for leaks.

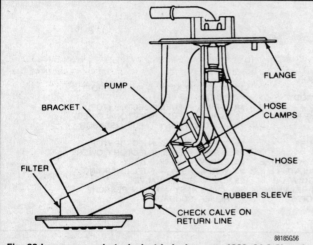

Fig. 23 Low pressure in-tank electric fuel pump—1983–84 3.8L and 5.0L engines

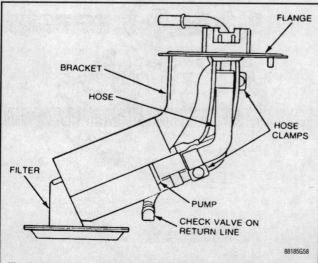

Fig. 24 Low pressure in-tank electric fuel pump—2.3 turbo engine

1983–84 High Pressure External Pump

◆ **See Figure 25**

1. Disconnect the negative battery cable.
2. Depressurize the fuel system.
3. Raise and support the rear of the vehicle on jackstands.
4. Disconnect the inlet and outlet fuel lines.
5. Disconnect the electrical harness connection.
6. Bend down the retaining tab and remove the pump from the mounting bracket ring.
7. Install in reverse order, make sure the pump is indexed correctly in the mounting bracket insulator.

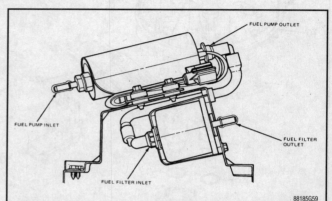

Fig. 25 High pressure in-line electric fuel pump—1983–84 3.8L and 5.0L engines

1985–87 High Pressure In-Tank Pump

◆ **See Figure 26**

1. Depressurize the system.
2. Disconnect the negative battery cable.
3. Drain as much gas from the tank by pumping out through the filler neck as possible.
4. Raise and support the rear end on jackstands.
5. Disconnect the filler hose, fuel supply, return and vent lines at the right and left side of the frame. On some models the gas tank must be lowered to gain access to the fuel and vent lines.

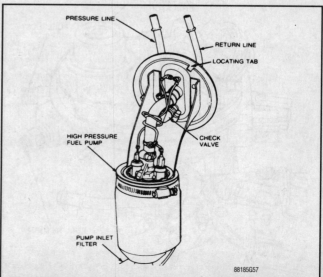

Fig. 26 High pressure in-tank electric fuel pump—1984 3.8L and 5.0L engines

6. Disconnect the wiring to the fuel pump.

7. Support the gas tank, loosen and remove the mounting straps. Remove the gas tank. On some models the exhaust pipe and shield must be removed first.

8. Disconnect the lines and harness at the pump flange.

9. Clean the outside of the mounting flange and retaining ring. Turn the fuel pump lock ring counterclockwise and remove.

10. Remove the fuel pump.

To install:

11. Clean the mounting surfaces. Put a light coat of grease on the mounting surfaces and on the new sealing ring. Install the new fuel pump.

12. Installation is in the reverse order of removal. If you have a single high pressure pump system, fill the tank with at least 10 gals. of gas. Turn the ignition key **ON** for three seconds. Repeat 6 or 7 times until the fuel system is pressurized. Check for any fitting leaks. Start the engine and check for leaks.

TESTING

1. Check the fuel tank for the adequate fuel supply.

2. Check for any fuel leakage at the fittings and lines.

3. Check for continuity at the pump:

a. Locate the pump power feed wire as it comes through the grommet in the trunk. Attach a VOM between there and the chassis ground.

b. With the key in the **OFF** position, measure the resistance to ground, if the resistance is 5 ohms or less, go to step C. if not proceed. Refer to the appropriate wiring diagram and attach the ground lead of the VOM to the ground lead of the pump circuit, then check the continuity. If this is OK, then check the pump body ground or wiring between the pump and body ground. If the resistance is still not within the limits then the tank must be removed to check for a bad connection at the fuel pump connector or if the pump is defective. Remove the tank and check for continuity across the pump terminals. If the resistance is within the limits, the continuity is OK. Check the wiring. If the resistance is still bad, proceed to the next step.

c. Set the meter to read the voltage and turn the ignition **ON**. The voltage should rise to 10 volts or more for one second, then return to 0. If the voltage is not within specification, check the electrical circuit and service as needed.

4. Check the fuel pump pressure and flow:

a. Attach a pressure gage tool T80L–9974–A or equivalent to the fuel diagnostic valve.

b. As a primary check, turn the ignition **ON**, and check the pressure gage reading. The gage should read between 30–40 psi (2.7–275 kPa). If the pump is operating properly and other system components are OK, continue.

c. Disconnect the fuel return line at the fuel rail.

d. Connect a hose from the rail fitting to a calibrated container of at least one quart.

e. Locate and replace with the modified relay. Take the ground lead to a convenient location of the vehicle and ground it. This should make the pump run. Energize the pump for ten seconds.

f. Allow the fuel to drain from the return hose into the container, then observe the volume.

g. The pump is operating properly if:

• The pressure reaches 35–45 psi (241–310 kPa)

• Fuel flow is a minimum of 5.6 oz. (170ml) in 10 seconds

• The fuel pressure remains a minimum of 30 psi (207 kPa) immediately after de-energization

h. If all three conditions are met, the pump is operating normally. Check the engine and possible electrical problems.

i. If the pressure is met but the flow is not, check for a clogged fuel filter and/or supply hoses. After correcting any of these problems and the conditions are still not met, replace the pump.

j. If both pressure and flow are good but the pressure will not remain after de-energization, check for leaking injectors or regulator. If both check OK, then replace the pump.

k. If no flow or pressure is seen, the fuel system should be checked as in step i. If no trouble is found, replace the pump.

Throttle Body

REMOVAL & INSTALLATION

1. Remove the air cleaner assembly.

2. Release the pressure from the fuel system at the diagnostic valve on the throttle body using SST T80L–9974–A or equivalent.

3. Disconnect the throttle cable and transmission valve lever.

4. Disconnect the fuel, vacuum and electrical connections.

➡**Either the multi or single ten pin connections may be encountered. To disconnect the electrical ten pin connectors, push in or squeeze on the right side lower locking tab while pulling up on the connection. Multi connectors disconnect by pulling apart. The ISC connector tab must be moved out while pulling them apart.**

5. Remove the throttle body assembly retaining nuts, then remove the unit.

6. Remove the mounting gasket from the intake manifold.

To install:

7. Clean the gasket mounting surfaces and place a spacer and gaskets on the intake manifold. Position the throttle body assembly on the spacer and gasket.

8. Secure the throttle body assembly with the retaining nut, tighten to 10 ft. lbs. (14 Nm). To prevent any leakage, distortion or damage to the throttle body flange, snug the nuts, then in an alternately fashion; tighten each nut in a criss-cross pattern.

9. Connect the fuel line, electrical connections, throttle cable and all emission lines.

10. Start the engine, check for leaks. Adjust the engine idle if necessary.

MULTI-POINT INJECTION (EFI) AND SEQUENTIAL FUEL INJECTION (SEFI)

General Information

The Electronic Fuel Injector System (EFI) is classified as a multi-point, pulse time, mass air flow (EFI) or speed density control (SEFI) fuel injection system.

An on board vehicle electronic engine control (EEC) computer accepts inputs from various engine sensors to compute the required fuel flow rate necessary to maintain a prescribed air/fuel ratio throughout the entire engine operational range. The computer then outputs a command to the fuel injectors to meter the approximate quantity of fuel.

The fuel charging manifold assembly incorporates electrically actuated fuel injectors directly above each of the engine's intake ports. The injectors, when energized, spray a metered quantity of fuel into the intake air stream.

A constant fuel pressure drop is maintained across the injector nozzles by a pressure regulator. The regulator is connected in series with the fuel injectors and positioned down stream from them. Excess fuel supplied by the pump, but not required by the engine, passes through the regulator and returns to the fuel tank through a fuel return line.

All injectors are energized simultaneously, once every crankshaft revolution. The period of time that the injectors are energized (injector on-time or the pulse width) is controlled by the vehicles' Engine Electronic Control (EEC) computer.

Relieving Fuel System Pressure

Fuel supply lines on all fuel injected engines will remain pressurized for some period of time after the engine is shut **OFF**. This pressure must be relieved before servicing the fuel system. Pressure is relieved through the fuel pressure relief valve. To relieve the fuel system pressure, first remove the fuel tank cap to relieve pressure in the tank, then remove the cap on the fuel pressure relief valve, located on the fuel rail. Attach fuel pressure gauge T80L–9974–A or equivalent, and drain the system through the drain tube into a suitable container. Remove the fuel pressure gauge and replace the cap on the relief valve.

Electric Fuel Pump

REMOVAL & INSTALLATION

Non-Supercharged

1. Disconnect the negative battery cable and properly relieve the fuel system pressure.
2. Remove the fuel tank and place it on a bench.
3. Remove any dirt that has accumulated around the fuel pump retaining flange so it will not enter the tank during pump removal and installation.
4. Turn the fuel pump locking ring counterclockwise and remove the locking ring.
5. Remove the fuel pump and bracket assembly. Remove and discard the seal ring.

To install:

6. Clean the fuel pump mounting flange, fuel tank mounting surface and seal ring groove.
7. Apply a light coating of grease on a new seal ring to hold it in place during assembly and install in the seal ring groove.
8. Install the fuel pump and bracket assembly carefully to ensure the filter is not damaged. Make sure the locating keys are in the keyways and the seal ring remains in the groove.
9. Hold the pump assembly in place and install the locking ring finger-tight. Make sure all the locking tabs are under the tank lock ring tabs.
10. Rotate the locking ring clockwise until the ring is against the stops.
11. Install the fuel tank in the vehicle. Add a minimum of 10 gallons of fuel to the tank and check for leaks.
12. Install a suitable fuel pressure gauge on the valve on the fuel rail.
13. Turn the ignition switch from **OFF** to **ON** for 3 seconds. Repeat this procedure 5–10 times until the pressure gauge shows at least 35 psi. Check for fuel leaks.
14. Remove the pressure gauge, start the engine and check for leaks.

PRESSURE TESTING

1. Relieve the fuel system pressure and connect a fuel pressure gauge to the valve on the fuel rail.
2. Ground the fuel pump lead of the self-test connector through a jumper wire at the **FP** lead.
3. Turn the ignition key to the **RUN** position to operate the fuel pump.
4. Observe the fuel pressure gauge. The indicated pressure should be 35–40 psi.
5. Remove the fuel pressure gauge and the jumper wire.

Fuel Pressure Regulator

REMOVAL & INSTALLATION

▶ See Figures 27, 28, 29, 30 and 31

The fuel pressure regulator is attached to the fuel supply manifold assembly downstream of the fuel injectors. It regulates the fuel pressure supplied to the injectors. The regulator is a diaphragm operated relief valve in which one side of the diaphragm senses fuel pressure and the other side is subjected to intake manifold pressure. The nominal fuel pressure is established by a spring preload applied to the diaphragm. Balancing one side of the diaphragm with manifold pressure maintains a constant fuel pressure drop across the injectors. Fuel, in excess of that used by the engine, is bypassed through the regulator and returns to the fuel tank.

✳✳ WARNING

Before attempting this procedure, depressurize the fuel system.

1. Remove the vacuum line at the pressure regulator.
2. Remove the three Allen retaining screws from the regulator housing.
3. Remove the pressure regulator, gasket and O-ring. Discard the gasket and inspect the O-ring for deterioration.

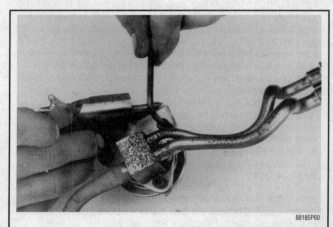

Fig. 27 Separate the pressure regulator from the fuel rail

Fig. 28 Lift the regulator off of the mating surface . . .

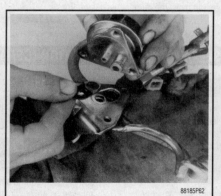

Fig. 29 . . . remove the gasket . . .

Fig. 30 . . . then the O-ring

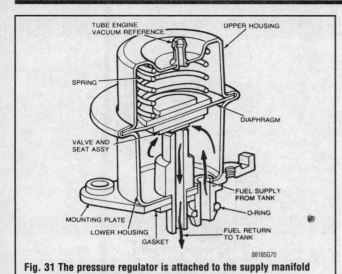

Fig. 31 The pressure regulator is attached to the supply manifold downstream of the injectors on the 5.0L engine

Fig. 32 Fuel injection manifold with injectors attached

☀☀ WARNING

If scraping is necessary be careful not to damage the gasket surface.

4. Lubricate the O-ring with light oil prior to installation.
5. Ensure the gasket surfaces of the fuel pressure regulator and fuel rail assembly are clean.
6. Install the new O-ring and gasket on the regulator.
7. Using new allen head screws, install the pressure regulator on the fuel rail assembly, tighten the screws 27–40 inch lbs. (3–4 Nm).
8. Install the vacuum line to the regulator.
9. With the injector wiring disconnected, turn the ignition system to **RUN** and allow the system to pressurize. Check for leaks. Connect the wiring, run the engine at idle for 2 minutes. Turn the engine off and check for leaks.

Fuel Injector Manifold Assembly

REMOVAL & INSTALLATION

The fuel supply manifold assembly is the component that delivers high pressure fuel from the vehicle fuel supply line to the fuel injectors. The assembly consists of a single preformed tube or stamping with four injector connector, a mounting flange for the fuel pressure regulator, a pressure relief valve for diagnostic testing or field service fuel system pressure bleed down and mounting attachments which locate the fuel manifold assembly and provide fuel injector retention.

2.3L Engine

1. Remove the fuel tank cap. Release the pressure from the fuel system.
2. Disconnect the fuel supply and return lines.
3. Disconnect the wiring harness from the injectors.
4. Disconnect the vacuum line from the fuel pressure regulator valve.
5. Remove the two fuel injector manifold retaining bolts.
6. Carefully disengage the manifold from the fuel injectors. Remove the manifold.
7. Installation is the reverse of removal. Tighten the fuel manifold bolts 15–22 ft. lbs. (20–30 Nm).

3.8L, Exc. SC and 5.0L Engines

▶ **See Figure 32**

1. Remove the fuel tank cap and relieve the fuel system pressure.
2. Remove the upper intake manifold.

3. Disconnect the fuel inlet and return quick-disconnect couplings.
4. Remove the fuel pressure regulator.
5. Remove the retaining bolts and injection manifold with the injectors attached.
   To install:
6. Position the injection manifold making sure all injectors are pushed into a fully seated position.
7. Install the retaining bolts while holding the injection manifold down and tighten the bolts to 87 inch lbs. (9 Nm) on the 3.8L; 71-106 inch lbs. (8–12 Nm) on the 5.0L.
8. Install all remaining parts. With the injector wiring disconnected, turn the ignition system to **RUN** and allow the system to pressurize. Check for leaks. Connect the wiring, run the engine at idle for 2 minutes. Turn the engine off and check for leaks.

3.8L SC Engine

1. Remove the fuel tank cap and relieve the fuel system pressure.
2. Remove the supercharger/throttle body assembly, intercooler tubes, intercooler and intake elbow.
3. Disconnect the fuel inlet and return quick-disconnect couplings.
4. Remove the fuel pressure regulator.
5. Remove the retaining bolts and injection manifold with the injectors attached.
   To install:
6. Position the injection manifold making sure all injectors are pushed into a fully seated position.
7. Install the retaining bolts while holding the injection manifold down and tighten the bolts to 71-97 inch lbs. (8–11 Nm).
8. Install all remaining parts. With the injector wiring disconnected, turn the ignition system to **RUN** and allow the system to pressurize. Check for leaks. Connect the wiring, run the engine at idle for 2 minutes. Turn the engine off and check for leaks.

Pressure Relief Valve

REMOVAL & INSTALLATION

▶ **See Figure 33**

1. If the fuel charging assembly is mounted on the engine, the fuel system must be depressurized.
2. Using an open end wrench or suitable deep well socket, remove the pressure relief valve from the injection manifold.
3. Install the pressure relief valve and cap. Tighten the valve 48–84 inch lbs. (5–9 Nm). Tighten the cap to 4–6 inch lbs. (0.5–0.7 Nm).

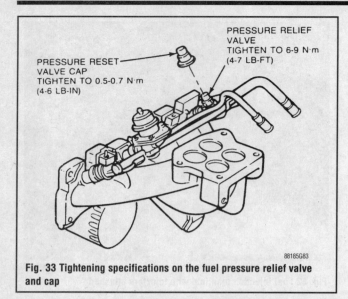

Fig. 33 Tightening specifications on the fuel pressure relief valve and cap

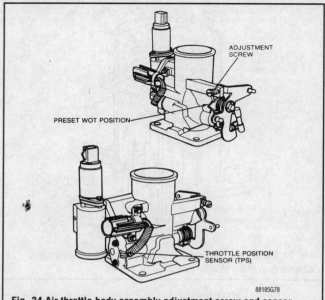

Fig. 34 Air throttle body assembly adjustment screw and sensor locations—2.3L engine

Air Intake Throttle Body

REMOVAL & INSTALLATION

The throttle body assembly controls air flow to the engine through a single butterfly-type valve. The throttle position is controlled by conventional cable/cam throttle linkage. The body is a single piece die casting made of aluminum. It has a single bore with an air bypass channel around the throttle plate. This by-pass channel controls both cold and warm engine idle air flow control as regulated by an air bypass valve assembly mounted directly to the throttle body. The valve assembly is an electromechanical device controlled by the EEC computer. It incorporates a linear actuator which positions a variable area metering valve.

Other features of the air throttle body assembly include:
- An adjustment screw to set the throttle plate at a minimum idle airflow position.
- A preset stop to locate the WOT position.
- A throttle body mounted throttle position sensor.
- A PCV fresh air source (4 and 8-cylinder) located upstream of the throttle plate.
- Individual ported vacuum taps (as required) for PCV and EVAP control signals.

2.3L Engine

▶ See Figures 34 and 35

1. Remove the four throttle body nuts. Make sure that the throttle position sensor connector and the air by-pass valve connector have been disconnected from the harness. Disconnect the air cleaner outlet tube.
2. Identify and disconnect the vacuum hoses.
3. Remove the throttle bracket.
4. Carefully separate the throttle body from the upper intake manifold.
5. Remove and discard the gasket between the throttle body and the upper intake manifold.

❊❊ WARNING

If scraping is necessary, be careful not to damage the gasket surfaces, or allow any material to drop into the manifold.

6. Installation is the reverse of removal. Tighten the throttle body-to-upper intake manifold nuts 12–15 ft. lbs. (16–20 Nm).

3.8L Engine Except SC

1. Remove the air inlet duct.
2. Disconnect the throttle position sensor and idle bypass wiring.
3. Remove the 4 throttle body retaining nuts.

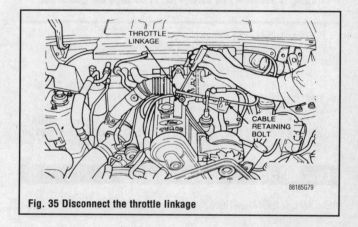

Fig. 35 Disconnect the throttle linkage

4. Carefully separate the throttle body from the intake manifold.
5. Discard the gasket.

To install:
6. Thoroughly clean the gasket mating surfaces. If scraping is necessary, take great care to avoid dropping gasket material into the manifold. DO NOT SCRATCH THE MATING SURFACES!
7. Position the new gasket and throttle body. Tighten the nuts to 15-22 ft. lbs. (20–29 Nm).
8. Connect the wiring.

3.8L SC Engine

1. Remove the air inlet duct.
2. Disconnect the throttle cable.
3. Disconnect the throttle position sensor and idle bypass wiring.
4. Remove the 4 throttle body retaining nuts.
5. Carefully separate the throttle body from the intake manifold.
6. Discard the gasket.

To install:
7. Thoroughly clean the gasket mating surfaces. If scraping is necessary, take great care to avoid dropping gasket material into the manifold. DO NOT SCRATCH THE MATING SURFACES!
8. Position the new gasket and throttle body. Tighten the nuts to 15-22 ft. lbs. (20–29 Nm).
9. Connect the wiring.

5.0L Engine

1. Remove the air inlet duct.
2. Disconnect the TPS and air bypass valve wiring.
3. Remove the PCV vent closure hose from the throttle body.
4. Remove the 4 throttle body nuts.
5. Carefully remove the throttle body from the EGR spacer and discard the gasket.

To install:

6. Clean the gasket mating surfaces thoroughly. If scraping is necessary, take great care to avoid dropping gasket material into the manifold. DO NOT SCRATCH THE MATING SURFACES!
7. Position the new gasket and throttle body. Tighten the nuts to 12-17 ft. lbs. (16–23 Nm).
8. Connect the PCV hose.
9. Connect the wiring.

Fuel Injector

REMOVAL & INSTALLATION

▶ **See Figures 36 and 37**

The fuel injector nozzles are electromechanical devices which both meter and atomize fuel delivered to the engine. The injectors are mounted in the lower intake manifold and are positioned so that their tips are directing fuel just ahead of the engine intake valves. The injector bodies consist of a solenoid actuated pintle and needle valve assembly. An electrical control signal from the Electronic Engine Control unit activates the injector solenoid causing the pintle to move inward off the seat, allowing fuel to flow. Since the injector flow orifice is fixed and the fuel pressure drop across the injector tip is constant, fuel flow to the engine is regulated by how long the solenoid is energized. Atomization is obtained by contouring the pintle at the point where the fuel separates.

2.3L Engine

▶ **See Figure 38**

✳✳ WARNING

The fuel system must be depressurized prior to starting this procedure.

1. Disconnect the negative battery cable.
2. Remove the fuel tank cap and relieve the fuel system pressure.
3. Disconnect the air intake, electrical connectors, throttle linkage, vacuum lines and EGR tube from the upper intake manifold and throttle body. Tag the electrical connectors and vacuum lines prior to removal for installation reference.
4. Remove the upper intake manifold retaining bolts and remove the upper intake manifold and throttle body assembly.
5. Disconnect the electrical connectors from the injectors.
6. Disconnect the fuel lines from the fuel supply manifold.

7. Remove the fuel supply manifold retaining bolts, carefully disengage the manifold and fuel injectors from the engine and remove the manifold and injectors.
8. Remove the fuel injectors from the manifold.

To install:

9. Lubricate new O-rings with clean light grade oil and install 2 on each injector.

➡ **Never use silicone grease as it will clog the injectors.**

10. Install the fuel supply manifold and injectors into the intake manifold. Push the fuel rail down to make sure all the fuel injector O-rings are fully seated in the fuel rail cups and intake manifold.
11. Install the fuel manifold assembly retaining bolts and tighten to 15–22 ft. lbs. (20–30 Nm) while holding the assembly down.
12. Connect the fuel lines to the manifold assembly.
13. After the fuel rail assembly has been installed and before the fuel injector wire connectors have been connected, connect the negative battery cable and turn the key to the **ON** position. This will cause the fuel pump to run for 2–3 seconds and pressurize the system.
14. Check for fuel leaks, especially where the fuel injector is installed into the fuel rail.
15. Disconnect the negative battery cable.
16. Install the upper intake manifold in the reverse order of removal. Tighten the retaining bolts, in sequence, to 15–22 ft. lbs. (20–30 Nm).
17. Connect the fuel injector wire connectors.
18. Connect the negative battery cable. Start the engine and let it idle.
19. Turn the engine **OFF** and check for fuel leaks.

3.8L Engine

EXCEPT SUPERCHARGED ENGINE

1. Disconnect the negative battery cable.
2. Remove the fuel tank cap and relieve the fuel system pressure.
3. Disconnect the electrical connectors at the idle air bypass valve, TP sensor and EGR position sensor.
4. Disconnect the throttle linkage at the throttle ball and the transmission linkage from the throttle body.
5. Remove the 2 bolts securing the bracket to the intake manifold and position the bracket with the cables aside.
6. Disconnect all the vacuum lines and PCV from the upper intake manifold and throttle assembly. Tag all lines prior to removal for ease of reinstallation.
7. Remove the upper intake manifold retaining bolts and remove the upper intake manifold and throttle body assembly.
8. Disconnect the fuel lines from the fuel rail assembly.
9. Remove the fuel pressure regulator.
10. Disconnect the electrical connectors from the fuel injectors. Remove the injector retaining clips, as required.
11. Remove the fuel rail retaining bolts. Carefully disengage the fuel rail from the fuel injectors and remove the fuel rail.

➡ **It may be easier to remove the injectors with the fuel rail as an assembly.**

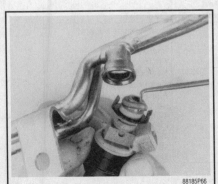

Fig. 36 Remove the O-ring from the lower portion of the injector

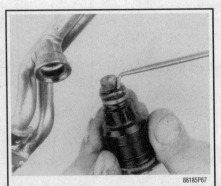

Fig. 37 Remove the O-ring from the upper portion of the injector

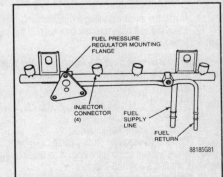

Fig. 38 Exploded view of the fuel supply manifold assembly—2.3L engine

12. Grasping the injector body, pull while gently rocking the injector from side-to-side to remove the injector from the fuel rail or the intake manifold.

13. Inspect the pintle protection cap (plastic hat) and washer for signs of deterioration. Replace the complete injector, as required. If the cap is missing, look for it in the intake manifold.

➡**The pintle protection cap is not available as a separate part.**

To install:

14. Lubricate new O-rings with light grade oil and install 2 on each injector.

➡**Never use silicone grease as it will clog the injectors.**

15. Install the injectors in the intake manifold using a light, twisting pushing motion.

16. Install the fuel rail, pushing it down to ensure all injector O-rings are fully seated in the fuel rail cups and intake manifold.

17. Install the retaining bolts while holding the fuel rail down and tighten to 87 inch lbs. (10 Nm). Reinstall the injector retaining clips, as required.

18. Install the fuel pressure regulator retaining bolt and tighten to 15–22 ft. lbs. (20–30 Nm).

19. Connect the fuel lines to the fuel rail.

20. With the injector wiring disconnected, connect the negative battery cable and turn the ignition to the **RUN** position to allow the fuel pump to pressurize the system. Check for fuel leaks.

21. Disconnect the negative battery cable.

22. Connect the fuel injector wiring harness.

23. Install the upper intake manifold and throttle body assembly by reversing the removal procedure. Tighten the upper intake manifold retaining bolts to 24 ft. lbs. (32 Nm).

24. Connect the negative battery cable, start the engine and check for fuel leaks.

SUPERCHARGED ENGINE

1. Disconnect the negative battery cable.

2. Remove the fuel tank cap and relieve the fuel system pressure.

3. Remove the supercharger assembly.

4. Disconnect the fuel lines from the fuel rail assembly.

5. Remove the 4 fuel rail assembly retaining bolts and remove the fuel pressure regulator bracket retaining bolt.

6. Disconnect the electrical connectors from the injectors.

7. Carefully disengage the fuel rail from the fuel injectors and remove the fuel rail.

➡**It may be easier to remove the injectors with the fuel rail as an assembly.**

8. Grasping the injector body, remove the injector from the fuel rail or intake manifold by pulling while gently rocking the injector from side-to-side.

9. Inspect the pintle protection cap (plastic hat) and washer for signs of deterioration. Replace the complete injector, as required. If the cap is missing, look for it in the intake manifold.

➡**The pintle protection cap is not available as a separate part.**

To install:

10. Lubricate new O-rings with light grade oil and install 2 on each injector.

➡**Never use silicone grease as it will clog the injectors.**

11. Install the injectors, using a light, twisting, pushing motion.

12. Place the fuel rail assembly over each of the injectors and seat the injectors into the fuel rail.

➡**It may be easier to seat the injectors in the fuel rail and then seat the entire assembly in the lower intake manifold.**

13. Install the fuel rail assembly retaining bolts and tighten to 70–97 inch lbs. (8–11 Nm). Install the fuel pressure regulator bracket retaining bolt and tighten to 15–22 ft. lbs. (20–30 Nm).

14. Install the supercharger assembly.

15. Connect the negative battery cable. Turn the ignition from **OFF** to **ON** several times without starting the engine to check for fuel leaks. Check all connections at the fuel rail and injectors.

16. Start the engine and warm to operating temperature. Check for fuel or coolant leaks.

4.6L Engine

▶ **See Figure 39**

1. Disconnect the negative battery cable.

2. Remove the fuel tank cap and relieve the fuel system pressure.

3. Disconnect the vacuum line at the pressure regulator.

4. Disconnect the fuel lines from the fuel rail.

5. Disconnect the electrical connectors from the injectors.

6. Remove the fuel rail assembly retaining bolts.

7. Carefully disengage the fuel rail from the fuel injectors and remove the fuel rail.

➡**It may be easier to remove the injectors with the fuel rail as an assembly.**

8. Grasping the injector body, pull while gently rocking the injector from side-to-side to remove the injector from the fuel rail or intake manifold.

9. Inspect the pintle protection cap and washer for signs of deterioration. Replace the complete injector, as required. If the cap is missing, look for it in the intake manifold.

➡**The pintle protection cap is not available as a separate part.**

To install:

10. Lubricate new O-rings with light grade oil and install 2 on each injector.

➡**Never use silicone grease as it will clog the injectors.**

11. Install the injectors using a light, twisting, pushing motion.

12. Install the fuel rail, pushing it down to ensure all injector O-rings are fully seated in the fuel rail cups and intake manifold.

13. Install the retaining bolts while holding the fuel rail down and tighten to 71–106 inch lbs. (8–12 Nm).

14. Connect the fuel lines to the fuel rail and the vacuum line to the pressure regulator.

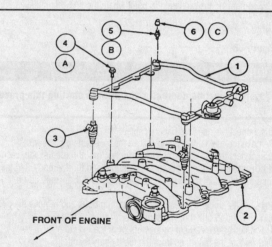

FRONT OF ENGINE

Item	Part Number	Description
1	9F792	Fuel Injection Supply Manifold
2	9424	Intake Manifold
3	9F593	Fuel Injector
4	N804394-S8M	Bolt (4 Req'd)
5	9H321	Fuel Pressure Relief Valve
6	9H323	Fuel Pressure Relief Valve Cap
A	—	Tighten to 8-12 N·m (71-106 Lb-In)
B	—	Tighten to 7.75 N·m (69 Lb-In)
C	—	Tighten to 0.6 N·m (5.3 Lb-In)

88185G87

Fig. 39 Fuel rail assembly—4.6L engine

15. With the injector wiring disconnected, connect the negative battery cable and turn the ignition switch to the **RUN** position to allow the fuel pump to pressurize the system.

16. Check for fuel leaks.

17. Disconnect the negative battery cable.

18. Connect the electrical connectors to the fuel injectors.

19. Connect the negative battery cable and start the engine. Let it idle for 2 minutes.

20. Turn the engine **OFF** and check for leaks.

5.0L Engine

▶ **See Figures 40, 41 and 42**

1. Disconnect the negative battery cable.

2. Remove the fuel tank cap and relieve the fuel system pressure.

3. Partially drain the cooling system into a suitable container.

4. Disconnect the electrical connectors at the idle air bypass valve, TP sensor and EGR sensor.

5. Disconnect the throttle linkage at the throttle ball and transmission linkage from the throttle body. Remove the 2 bolts securing the bracket the bracket to the intake manifold and position the bracket with the cables aside.

6. Disconnect the upper intake manifold vacuum fitting connections by disconnecting all vacuum lines to the vacuum tree, vacuum lines to the EGR valve, vacuum line to the fuel pressure regulator and canister purge line.

7. Disconnect the PCV system by disconnecting the hose from the fitting on the rear of the upper manifold and disconnect the PCV vent closure tube at the throttle body.

8. Remove the 2 EGR coolant lines from the fittings on the EGR spacer.

9. Remove the 6 upper intake manifold retaining bolts.

10. Remove the upper intake and throttle body as an assembly from the lower intake manifold.

11. Disconnect the fuel lines from the fuel rail.

12. Remove the 4 fuel rail assembly retaining bolts.

13. Disconnect the electrical connectors from the injectors.

14. Carefully disengage the fuel rail from the fuel injectors.

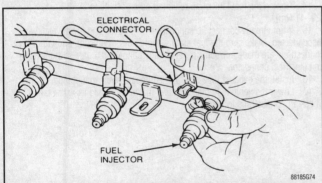

Fig. 40 Carefully remove the electrical harness from the individual injectors

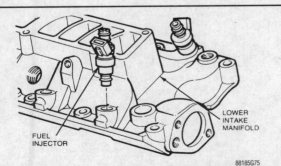

Fig. 41 Grasping the injector body, pull up while gently rocking the injector from side-to-side to remove the injector from the fuel rail or intake manifold

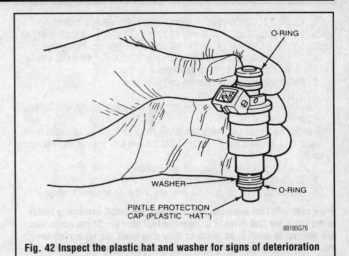

Fig. 42 Inspect the plastic hat and washer for signs of deterioration

➡ **It may be easier to remove the injectors with the fuel rail as an assembly.**

15. Grasping the injector body, pull up while gently rocking the injector from side-to-side to remove the injector from the fuel rail or intake manifold.

16. Inspect the pintle protection cap (plastic hat) and washer for signs of deterioration. Replace the complete injector, as required. If the cap is missing, look for it in the intake manifold.

➡ **The pintle protection cap is not available as a separate part.**

To install:

17. Lubricate new O-rings with light grade oil and install 2 on each injector.

➡ **Never use silicone grease as it will clog the injectors.**

18. Install the injectors using a light, twisting, pushing motion.

19. Install the fuel rail, pushing it down to ensure all the injector O-rings are fully seated in the fuel rail cups and intake manifold.

20. Install the retaining bolts while holding the fuel rail down and tighten to 70–105 inch lbs. (8–12 Nm).

21. Connect the fuel lines to the fuel rail.

22. With the injector wiring disconnected, connect the negative battery cable and turn the ignition switch to the **RUN** position to allow the fuel pump to pressurize the system.

23. Check for fuel leaks.

24. Disconnect the negative battery cable.

25. Connect the electrical connectors to the injectors.

26. Install the upper intake manifold and throttle body assembly by reversing the removal procedure. Tighten the retaining bolts to 12–17 ft. lbs. (16–24 Nm).

27. Refill the cooling system and connect the negative battery cable.

28. Start the engine and let it idle for 2 minutes. Turn the engine **OFF** and check for leaks.

Fuel Tank

✳✳ WARNING

NEVER SMOKE AROUND OR NEAR GASOLINE! GASOLINE VAPORS ARE EXTREMELY FLAMMABLE! EVEN THE PROXIMITY OF LIGHTED SMOKING MATERIAL CAN CAUSE AN EXPLOSION AND FIRE!

REMOVAL & INSTALLATION

1983–92 Models

➡ **Before disconnecting any fuel line, relieve the pressure from the fuel system. On 3.8L and 5.0L engines with CFI, relieve the system pressure at the pressure relief valve mounted on the throttle body. Special tool T80L–9974–A, or its equivalent, is needed for this procedure.**

1. On the 2.3L turbocharged engines with EFI this valve is located in the flexible fuel supply tube approximately 12 inches (305mm) back from where it connects to the engine fuel rail on the left side of the engine compartment.

2. On the 3.8L and 5.0L with EFI, the valve is located in the metal engine fuel line at the right front corner of the engine.

3. Before opening the fuel system on EFI engines:

   a. Remove the fuel tank cap.

   b. Disconnect the vacuum hose from the fuel pressure regulator located on the engine fuel rail.

   c. Using a hand vacuum pump, apply about 25 in.Hg to the pressure regulator. Fuel pressure will be released into the fuel tank through the fuel return hose.

4. Raise and support the rear end on jackstands.

5. Disconnect the battery ground cable.

6. Siphon off as much gasoline as possible into an approved container.

➡**On cars with fuel injection, the fuel tank has small reservoirs inside to maintain the fuel level at or near the fuel pick-up. These reservoirs are difficult to drain in as much as they may block the siphoning hose. You'll have to try different angle and repeated attempts with the siphoning hose. Be patient.**

7. Place a pan under the fuel fill hose and disconnect the fuel filler hose at the tank. Pour any drained fuel into an approved container.

➡**On 1989–92 models the exhaust pipe and exhaust shields must be removed from car first, refer to Engine section for proper removal and installation procedures**

8. Place a floor jack, cushioned with a length of wood, under the fuel tank.

9. Remove the fuel tank strap nuts and lower the fuel tank just enough to disconnect the fuel liquid and vapor lines, and the fuel sending unit wire.

10. Remove the air deflector from the tank retaining straps. The deflector is retained with pop rivets.

11. On cars equipped with a metal retainer which fastens the filler pipe to the tank, remove the screw attaching the retainer to the fuel tank flange.

12. Continue lowering the tank once all lines are disconnected, and remove it from the car.

13. Installation is the reverse of removal. The fuel vapor line should be retaped in position in the ribbed channel atop the tank.

1993–97 Models

1. Disconnect the negative battery cable and relieve the fuel system pressure.

2. Siphon or pump as much fuel as possible out through the fuel filler pipe.

➡**All vehicles have reservoirs inside the fuel tank to maintain fuel near the fuel pickup during cornering and under low fuel operating conditions. These reservoirs could block siphon tubes or hoses from reaching the bottom of the fuel tank. Repeated attempts using different hose orientations can overcome this obstacle.**

3. Raise and safely support the vehicle.

4. Remove the exhaust pipe and exhaust shield, if equipped. Disconnect the fuel fill and vent hoses connecting the filler pipe to the tank. Disconnect one end of the vapor crossover hose at the rear over the driveshaft.

5. If equipped with a metal retainer that fastens the filler pipe to the fuel tank, remove the screw attaching the retainer to the fuel tank flange.

6. Disconnect the fuel lines and the electrical connector to the fuel tank sending unit. On some vehicles, these are inaccessible on top of the tank. In these cases they must be disconnected with the tank partially removed.

7. Place a safety support under the fuel tank and remove the bolts from the fuel tank straps. Allow the straps to swing out of the way. Be careful not to deform the fuel tank.

8. Partially remove the tank and disconnect the fuel lines and electrical connector from the sending unit, if required.

9. Remove the tank from the vehicle.

To install:

10. Raise the fuel tank into position in the vehicle. Connect the fuel lines and sending unit electrical connector if it is necessary to connect them before the tank is in the final installed position.

11. Lubricate the fuel filler pipe with water base tire mounting lubricant and install the tank onto the filler pipe, then bring the tank into final position. Be careful not to deform the tank.

12. Bring the fuel tank straps around the tank and start the retaining nut or bolt. Align the tank with the straps. If equipped, make sure the fuel tank shields are installed with the straps and are positioned correctly on the tank. Align the tank with the driveshaft.

13. Check the hoses and wiring mounted on the tank top to make sure they are correctly routed and will not be pinched between the tank and body. Make sure the fuel vent hose is positioned above the vent retainer and not contacting the driveshaft.

14. Tighten the fuel tank strap retaining nuts or bolts to 22–30 ft. lbs. (29–41 Nm).

15. If not already connected, connect the fuel hoses and lines which were disconnected. Make sure the fuel supply, fuel return, if present, and vapor vent connections are made correctly. If not already connected, connect the sending unit electrical connector.

16. Install the exhaust pipe shield, if equipped, and exhaust pipe.

17. Lower the vehicle. Replace the fuel that was drained from the tank. Check all connections for leaks.

UNDERSTANDING AND
TROUBLESHOOTING ELECTRICAL
SYSTEMS 6-2
BASIC ELECTRICAL THEORY 6-2
   HOW DOES ELECTRICITY WORK:
     THE WATER ANALOGY 6-2
   OHM'S LAW 6-2
ELECTRICAL COMPONENTS 6-2
   POWER SOURCE 6-2
   GROUND 6-3
   PROTECTIVE DEVICES 6-3
   SWITCHES & RELAYS 6-3
   LOAD 6-4
   WIRING & HARNESSES 6-4
   CONNECTORS 6-4
TEST EQUIPMENT 6-5
   JUMPER WIRES 6-5
   TEST LIGHTS 6-5
   MULTIMETERS 6-5
TROUBLESHOOTING ELECTRICAL
  SYSTEMS 6-6
TESTING 6-6
   OPEN CIRCUITS 6-6
   SHORT CIRCUITS 6-6
   VOLTAGE 6-6
   VOLTAGE DROP 6-7
   RESISTANCE 6-7
WIRE AND CONNECTOR REPAIR 6-7
BATTERY CABLES 6-8
**SUPPLEMENTAL RESTRAINT
  SYSTEM (AIR BAG) 6-8**
GENERAL INFORMATION 6-8
   SYSTEM OPERATION 6-8
   SYSTEM COMPONENTS 6-9
AIR BAG DIAGNOSTIC
  MONITOR 6-10
SENSORS 6-10
   SERVICE PRECAUTIONS 6-10
   DISARMING THE SYSTEM 6-10
   ARMING THE SYSTEM 6-11
HEATER 6-11
BLOWER MOTOR 6-11
   REMOVAL & INSTALLATION 6-11
HEATER CORE 6-12
   REMOVAL & INSTALLATION 6-12
CONTROL PANEL 6-15
   REMOVAL & INSTALLATION 6-15
BLOWER SWITCH 6-17
   REMOVAL & INSTALLATION 6-17
   PRESET & ADJUSTMENT 6-17
AIR CONDITIONING COMPONENTS 6-18
   REMOVAL & INSTALLATION 6-18
CRUISE CONTROL 6-18
CONTROL SWITCHES 6-18
   REMOVAL & INSTALLATION 6-18
SPEED SENSOR 6-19
   REMOVAL & INSTALLATION 6-19
AMPLIFIER 6-19
   REMOVAL & INSTALLATION 6-19

SERVO 6-19
   REMOVAL & INSTALLATION 6-19
VACUUM DUMP VALVE 6-19
   REMOVAL & INSTALLATION 6-19
ENTERTAINMENT SYSTEMS 6-20
RADIO RECEIVER 6-20
   REMOVAL & INSTALLATION 6-20
SPEAKERS 6-22
   REMOVAL & INSTALLATION 6-22
WINDSHIELD WIPERS 6-23
WIPER BLADE AND ARM 6-23
   REMOVAL & INSTALLATION 6-23
WINDSHIELD WIPER MOTOR 6-23
   REMOVAL & INSTALLATION 6-23
WASHER PUMP AND RESERVOIR 6-25
   REMOVAL & INSTALLATION 6-25
**INSTRUMENTS AND
  SWITCHES 6-25**
INSTRUMENT CLUSTER 6-25
   REMOVAL & INSTALLATION 6-25
GAUGES 6-28
   REMOVAL & INSTALLATION 6-28
WINDSHIELD WIPER SWITCH 6-28
   REMOVAL & INSTALLATION 6-28
HEADLIGHT SWITCH 6-29
   REMOVAL & INSTALLATION 6-29
BACK-UP LIGHT SWITCH 6-29
   REMOVAL & INSTALLATION 6-29
LIGHTING 6-30
HEADLIGHTS 6-30
   REMOVAL & INSTALLATION 6-30
   AIMING 6-31
SIGNAL AND MARKER LIGHTS 6-31
   REMOVAL & INSTALLATION 6-31
TRAILER WIRING 6-37
CIRCUIT PROTECTION 6-38
FUSES 6-38
   REPLACEMENT 6-38
FUSIBLE LINKS AND CIRCUIT
  BREAKERS 6-38
   REPLACEMENT 6-38
FLASHERS 6-39
   REPLACEMENT 6-39
WIRING DIAGRAMS 6-43
SPECIFICATIONS CHARTS
  BULB SPECIFICATIONS 6-36
  FUSE PANEL DESCRIPTION 6-39

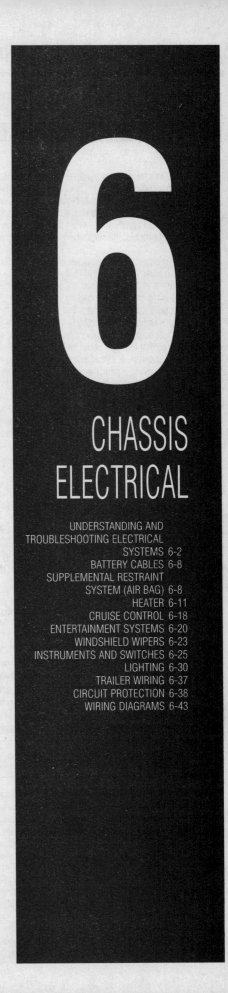

6

CHASSIS ELECTRICAL

UNDERSTANDING AND
TROUBLESHOOTING ELECTRICAL
SYSTEMS 6-2
BATTERY CABLES 6-8
SUPPLEMENTAL RESTRAINT
SYSTEM (AIR BAG) 6-8
HEATER 6-11
CRUISE CONTROL 6-18
ENTERTAINMENT SYSTEMS 6-20
WINDSHIELD WIPERS 6-23
INSTRUMENTS AND SWITCHES 6-25
LIGHTING 6-30
TRAILER WIRING 6-37
CIRCUIT PROTECTION 6-38
WIRING DIAGRAMS 6-43

UNDERSTANDING AND TROUBLESHOOTING ELECTRICAL SYSTEMS

Basic Electrical Theory

▶ See Figure 1

For any 12 volt, negative ground, electrical system to operate, the electricity must travel in a complete circuit. This simply means that current (power) from the positive (+) terminal of the battery must eventually return to the negative (−) terminal of the battery. Along the way, this current will travel through wires, fuses, switches and components. If, for any reason, the flow of current through the circuit is interrupted, the component fed by that circuit will cease to function properly.

Perhaps the easiest way to visualize a circuit is to think of connecting a light bulb (with two wires attached to it) to the battery—one wire attached to the negative (−) terminal of the battery and the other wire to the positive (+) terminal. With the two wires touching the battery terminals, the circuit would be complete and the light bulb would illuminate. Electricity would follow a path from the battery to the bulb and back to the battery. It's easy to see that with longer wires on our light bulb, it could be mounted anywhere. Further, one wire could be fitted with a switch so that the light could be turned on and off.

The normal automotive circuit differs from this simple example in two ways. First, instead of having a return wire from the bulb to the battery, the current travels through the frame of the vehicle. Since the negative (−) battery cable is attached to the frame (made of electrically conductive metal), the frame of the vehicle can serve as a ground wire to complete the circuit. Secondly, most automotive circuits contain multiple components which receive power from a single circuit. This lessens the amount of wire needed to power components on the vehicle.

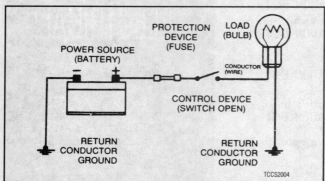

Fig. 1 This example illustrates a simple circuit. When the switch is closed, power from the positive (+) battery terminal flows through the fuse and the switch, and then to the light bulb. The light illuminates and the circuit is completed through the ground wire back to the negative (−) battery terminal. In reality, the two ground points shown in the illustration are attached to the metal frame of the vehicle, which completes the circuit back to the battery

HOW DOES ELECTRICITY WORK: THE WATER ANALOGY

Electricity is the flow of electrons—the subatomic particles that constitute the outer shell of an atom. Electrons spin in an orbit around the center core of an atom. The center core is comprised of protons (positive charge) and neutrons (neutral charge). Electrons have a negative charge and balance out the positive charge of the protons. When an outside force causes the number of electrons to unbalance the charge of the protons, the electrons will split off the atom and look for another atom to balance out. If this imbalance is kept up, electrons will continue to move and an electrical flow will exist.

Many people have been taught electrical theory using an analogy with water. In a comparison with water flowing through a pipe, the electrons would be the water and the wire is the pipe.

The flow of electricity can be measured much like the flow of water through a pipe. The unit of measurement used is amperes, frequently abbreviated as amps (a). You can compare amperage to the volume of water flowing through a pipe.

When connected to a circuit, an ammeter will measure the actual amount of current flowing through the circuit. When relatively few electrons flow through a circuit, the amperage is low. When many electrons flow, the amperage is high.

Water pressure is measured in units such as pounds per square inch (psi); The electrical pressure is measured in units called volts (v). When a voltmeter is connected to a circuit, it is measuring the electrical pressure.

The actual flow of electricity depends not only on voltage and amperage, but also on the resistance of the circuit. The higher the resistance, the higher the force necessary to push the current through the circuit. The standard unit for measuring resistance is an ohm. Resistance in a circuit varies depending on the amount and type of components used in the circuit. The main factors which determine resistance are:

• Material—some materials have more resistance than others. Those with high resistance are said to be insulators. Rubber materials (or rubber-like plastics) are some of the most common insulators used in vehicles as they have a very high resistance to electricity. Very low resistance materials are said to be conductors. Copper wire is among the best conductors. Silver is actually a superior conductor to copper and is used in some relay contacts, but its high cost prohibits its use as common wiring. Most automotive wiring is made of copper.

• Size—the larger the wire size being used, the less resistance the wire will have. This is why components which use large amounts of electricity usually have large wires supplying current to them.

• Length—for a given thickness of wire, the longer the wire, the greater the resistance. The shorter the wire, the less the resistance. When determining the proper wire for a circuit, both size and length must be considered to design a circuit that can handle the current needs of the component.

• Temperature—with many materials, the higher the temperature, the greater the resistance (positive temperature coefficient). Some materials exhibit the opposite trait of lower resistance with higher temperatures (negative temperature coefficient). These principles are used in many of the sensors on the engine.

OHM'S LAW

There is a direct relationship between current, voltage and resistance. The relationship between current, voltage and resistance can be summed up by a statement known as Ohm's law.

Voltage (E) is equal to amperage (I) times resistance (R): $E = I \times R$

Other forms of the formula are $R = E/I$ and $I = E/R$

In each of these formulas, E is the voltage in volts, I is the current in amps and R is the resistance in ohms. The basic point to remember is that as the resistance of a circuit goes up, the amount of current that flows in the circuit will go down, if voltage remains the same.

The amount of work that the electricity can perform is expressed as power. The unit of power is the watt (w). The relationship between power, voltage and current is expressed as:

Power (w) is equal to amperage (I) times voltage (E): $W = I \times E$

This is only true for direct current (DC) circuits; The alternating current formula is a tad different, but since the electrical circuits in most vehicles are DC type, we need not get into AC circuit theory.

Electrical Components

POWER SOURCE

Power is supplied to the vehicle by two devices: The battery and the alternator. The battery supplies electrical power during starting or during periods when the current demand of the vehicle's electrical system exceeds the output capacity of the alternator. The alternator supplies electrical current when the engine is running. Just not does the alternator supply the current needs of the vehicle, but it recharges the battery.

The Battery

In most modern vehicles, the battery is a lead/acid electrochemical device consisting of six 2 volt subsections (cells) connected in series, so that the unit is capable of producing approximately 12 volts of electrical pressure. Each sub-section consists of a series of positive and negative plates held a short distance apart in a solution of sulfuric acid and water.

The two types of plates are of dissimilar metals. This sets up a chemical reaction, and it is this reaction which produces current flow from the battery when its positive and negative terminals are connected to an electrical load. The power removed from the battery is replaced by the alternator, restoring the battery to its original chemical state.

The Alternator

On some vehicles there isn't an alternator, but a generator. The difference is that an alternator supplies alternating current which is then changed to direct current for use on the vehicle, while a generator produces direct current. Alternators tend to be more efficient and that is why they are used.

Alternators and generators are devices that consist of coils of wires wound together making big electromagnets. One group of coils spins within another set and the interaction of the magnetic fields causes a current to flow. This current is then drawn off the coils and fed into the vehicles electrical system.

GROUND

Two types of grounds are used in automotive electric circuits. Direct ground components are grounded to the frame through their mounting points. All other components use some sort of ground wire which is attached to the frame or chassis of the vehicle. The electrical current runs through the chassis of the vehicle and returns to the battery through the ground (−) cable; if you look, you'll see that the battery ground cable connects between the battery and the frame or chassis of the vehicle.

➡**It should be noted that a good percentage of electrical problems can be traced to bad grounds.**

PROTECTIVE DEVICES

▶ **See Figure 2**

It is possible for large surges of current to pass through the electrical system of your vehicle. If this surge of current were to reach the load in the circuit, the surge could burn it out or severely damage it. It can also overload the wiring, causing the harness to get hot and melt the insulation. To prevent this, fuses, circuit breakers and/or fusible links are connected into the supply wires of the electrical system. These items are nothing more than a built-in weak spot in the system. When an abnormal amount of current flows through the system, these protective devices work as follows to protect the circuit:

• Fuse—when an excessive electrical current passes through a fuse, the

fuse "blows" (the conductor melts) and opens the circuit, preventing the passage of current.

• Circuit Breaker—a circuit breaker is basically a self-repairing fuse. It will open the circuit in the same fashion as a fuse, but when the surge subsides, the circuit breaker can be reset and does not need replacement.

• Fusible Link—a fusible link (fuse link or main link) is a short length of special, high temperature insulated wire that acts as a fuse. When an excessive electrical current passes through a fusible link, the thin gauge wire inside the link melts, creating an intentional open to protect the circuit. To repair the circuit, the link must be replaced. Some newer type fusible links are housed in plug-in modules, which are simply replaced like a fuse, while older type fusible links must be cut and spliced if they melt. Since this link is very early in the electrical path, it's the first place to look if nothing on the vehicle works, yet the battery seems to be charged and is properly connected.

❊❊ CAUTION

Always replace fuses, circuit breakers and fusible links with identically rated components. Under no circumstances should a component of higher or lower amperage rating be substituted.

SWITCHES & RELAYS

▶ **See Figures 3 and 4**

Switches are used in electrical circuits to control the passage of current. The most common use is to open and close circuits between the battery and the various electric devices in the system. Switches are rated according to the amount of amperage they can handle. If a sufficient amperage rated switch is not used in a circuit, the switch could overload and cause damage.

Some electrical components which require a large amount of current to operate use a special switch called a relay. Since these circuits carry a large amount of current, the thickness of the wire in the circuit is also greater. If this large wire were connected from the load to the control switch, the switch would have to carry the high amperage load and the fairing or dash would be twice as large to accommodate the increased size of the wiring harness. To prevent these problems, a relay is used.

Relays are composed of a coil and a set of contacts. When the coil has a current passed though it, a magnetic field is formed and this field causes the contacts to move together, completing the circuit. Most relays are normally open, preventing current from passing through the circuit, but they can take any electrical form depending on the job they are intended to do. Relays can be considered "remote control switches." They allow a smaller current to operate devices that require higher amperages. When a small current operates the coil, a larger current is allowed to pass by the contacts. Some common circuits which may use relays are the horn, headlights, starter, electric fuel pump and other high draw circuits.

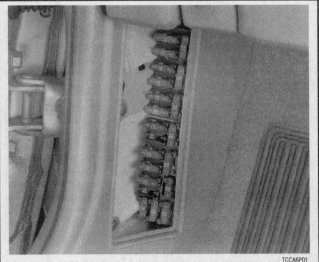

TCCA6P01

Fig. 2 Most vehicles use one or more fuse panels. This one is located on the driver's side kick panel

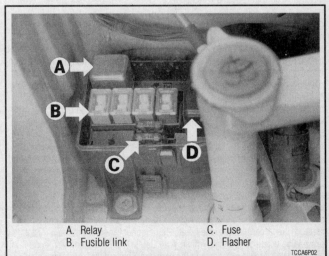

A. Relay
B. Fusible link
C. Fuse
D. Flasher

TCCA6P02

Fig. 3 The underhood fuse and relay panel usually contains fuses, relays, flashers and fusible links

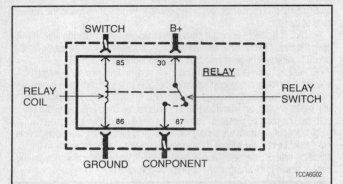

Fig. 4 Relays are composed of a coil and a switch. These two components are linked together so that when one operates, the other operates at the same time. The large wires in the circuit are connected from the battery to one side of the relay switch (B+) and from the opposite side of the relay switch to the load (component). Smaller wires are connected from the relay coil to the control switch for the circuit and from the opposite side of the relay coil to ground

LOAD

Every electrical circuit must include a "load" (something to use the electricity coming from the source). Without this load, the battery would attempt to deliver its entire power supply from one pole to another. This is called a "short circuit" All this electricity would take a short cut to ground and cause a great amount of damage to other components in the circuit by developing a tremendous amount of heat. This condition could develop sufficient heat to melt the insulation on all the surrounding wires and reduce a multiple wire cable to a lump of plastic and copper.

WIRING & HARNESSES

The average vehicle contains meters and meters of wiring, with hundreds of individual connections. To protect the many wires from damage and to keep them from becoming a confusing tangle, they are organized into bundles, enclosed in plastic or taped together and called wiring harnesses. Different harnesses serve different parts of the vehicle. Individual wires are color coded to help trace them through a harness where sections are hidden from view.

Automotive wiring or circuit conductors can be either single strand wire, multi-strand wire or printed circuitry. Single strand wire has a solid metal core and is usually used inside such components as alternators, motors, relays and other devices. Multi-strand wire has a core made of many small strands of wire twisted together into a single conductor. Most of the wiring in an automotive electrical system is made up of multi-strand wire, either as a single conductor or grouped together in a harness. All wiring is color coded on the insulator, either as a solid color or as a colored wire with an identification stripe. A printed circuit is a thin film of copper or other conductor that is printed on an insulator backing. Occasionally, a printed circuit is sandwiched between two sheets of plastic for more protection and flexibility. A complete printed circuit, consisting of conductors, insulating material and connectors for lamps or other components is called a printed circuit board. Printed circuitry is used in place of individual wires or harnesses in places where space is limited, such as behind instrument panels.

Since automotive electrical systems are very sensitive to changes in resistance, the selection of properly sized wires is critical when systems are repaired. A loose or corroded connection or a replacement wire that is too small for the circuit will add extra resistance and an additional voltage drop to the circuit.

The wire gauge number is an expression of the cross-section area of the conductor. Vehicles from countries that use the metric system will typically describe the wire size as its cross-sectional area in square millimeters. In this method, the larger the wire, the greater the number. Another common system for expressing wire size is the American Wire Gauge (AWG) system. As gauge number increases, area decreases and the wire becomes smaller. An 18 gauge wire is smaller than a 4 gauge wire. A wire with a higher gauge number will carry less current than a wire with a lower gauge number. Gauge wire size refers to

the size of the strands of the conductor, not the size of the complete wire with insulator. It is possible, therefore, to have two wires of the same gauge with different diameters because one may have thicker insulation than the other.

It is essential to understand how a circuit works before trying to figure out why it doesn't. An electrical schematic shows the electrical current paths when a circuit is operating properly. Schematics break the entire electrical system down into individual circuits. In a schematic, usually no attempt is made to represent wiring and components as they physically appear on the vehicle; switches and other components are shown as simply as possible. Face views of harness connectors show the cavity or terminal locations in all multi-pin connectors to help locate test points.

CONNECTORS

▶ See Figures 5 and 6

Three types of connectors are commonly used in automotive applications—weatherproof, molded and hard shell.

• Weatherproof—these connectors are most commonly used where the connector is exposed to the elements. Terminals are protected against moisture and dirt by sealing rings which provide a weathertight seal. All repairs require the use of a special terminal and the tool required to service it. Unlike standard blade type terminals, these weatherproof terminals cannot be straightened once they are bent. Make certain that the connectors are properly seated and all of the sealing rings are in place when connecting leads.

• Molded—these connectors require complete replacement of the connector if found to be defective. This means splicing a new connector assembly into

Fig. 5 Hard shell (left) and weatherproof (right) connectors have replaceable terminals

Fig. 6 Weatherproof connectors are most commonly used in the engine compartment or where the connector is exposed to the elements

the harness. All splices should be soldered to insure proper contact. Use care when probing the connections or replacing terminals in them, as it is possible to create a short circuit between opposite terminals. If this happens to the wrong terminal pair, it is possible to damage certain components. Always use jumper wires between connectors for circuit checking and NEVER probe through weatherproof seals.

• Hard Shell—unlike molded connectors, the terminal contacts in hard-shell connectors can be replaced. Replacement usually involves the use of a special terminal removal tool that depresses the locking tangs (barbs) on the connector terminal and allows the connector to be removed from the rear of the shell. The connector shell should be replaced if it shows any evidence of burning, melting, cracks, or breaks. Replace individual terminals that are burnt, corroded, distorted or loose.

Test Equipment

Pinpointing the exact cause of trouble in an electrical circuit is most times accomplished by the use of special test equipment. The following describes different types of commonly used test equipment and briefly explains how to use them in diagnosis. In addition to the information covered below, the tool manufacturer's instructions booklet (provided with the tester) should be read and clearly understood before attempting any test procedures.

JUMPER WIRES

✳✳ CAUTION

Never use jumper wires made from a thinner gauge wire than the circuit being tested. If the jumper wire is of too small a gauge, it may overheat and possibly melt. Never use jumpers to bypass high resistance loads in a circuit. Bypassing resistances, in effect, creates a short circuit. This may, in turn, cause damage and fire. Jumper wires should only be used to bypass lengths of wire or to simulate switches.

Jumper wires are simple, yet extremely valuable, pieces of test equipment. They are basically test wires which are used to bypass sections of a circuit. Although jumper wires can be purchased, they are usually fabricated from lengths of standard automotive wire and whatever type of connector (alligator clip, spade connector or pin connector) that is required for the particular application being tested. In cramped, hard-to-reach areas, it is advisable to have insulated boots over the jumper wire terminals in order to prevent accidental grounding. It is also advisable to include a standard automotive fuse in any jumper wire. This is commonly referred to as a "fused jumper". By inserting an in-line fuse holder between a set of test leads, a fused jumper wire can be used for bypassing open circuits. Use a 5 amp fuse to provide protection against voltage spikes.

Jumper wires are used primarily to locate open electrical circuits, on either the ground (–) side of the circuit or on the power (+) side. If an electrical component fails to operate, connect the jumper wire between the component and a good ground. If the component operates only with the jumper installed, the ground circuit is open. If the ground circuit is good, but the component does not operate, the circuit between the power feed and component may be open. By moving the jumper wire successively back from the component toward the power source, you can isolate the area of the circuit where the open is located. When the component stops functioning, or the power is cut off, the open is in the segment of wire between the jumper and the point previously tested.

You can sometimes connect the jumper wire directly from the battery to the "hot" terminal of the component, but first make sure the component uses 12 volts in operation. Some electrical components, such as fuel injectors or sensors, are designed to operate on about 4 to 5 volts, and running 12 volts directly to these components will cause damage.

TEST LIGHTS

▶ See Figure 7

The test light is used to check circuits and components while electrical current is flowing through them. It is used for voltage and ground tests. To use a 12 volt test light, connect the ground clip to a good ground and probe wherever necessary with the pick. The test light will illuminate when voltage is detected.

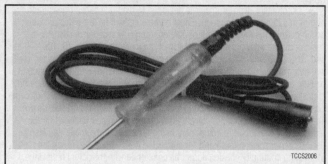

TCCS2006

Fig. 7 A 12 volt test light is used to detect the presence of voltage in a circuit

This does not necessarily mean that 12 volts (or any particular amount of voltage) is present; it only means that some voltage is present. It is advisable before using the test light to touch its ground clip and probe across the battery posts or terminals to make sure the light is operating properly.

✳✳ WARNING

Do not use a test light to probe electronic ignition, spark plug or coil wires. Never use a pick-type test light to probe wiring on computer controlled systems unless specifically instructed to do so. Any wire insulation that is pierced by the test light probe should be taped and sealed with silicone after testing.

Like the jumper wire, the 12 volt test light is used to isolate opens in circuits. But, whereas the jumper wire is used to bypass the open to operate the load, the 12 volt test light is used to locate the presence of voltage in a circuit. If the test light illuminates, there is power up to that point in the circuit; if the test light does not illuminate, there is an open circuit (no power). Move the test light in successive steps back toward the power source until the light in the handle illuminates. The open is between the probe and a point which was previously probed.

The self-powered test light is similar in design to the 12 volt test light, but contains a 1.5 volt penlight battery in the handle. It is most often used in place of a multimeter to check for open or short circuits when power is isolated from the circuit (continuity test).

The battery in a self-powered test light does not provide much current. A weak battery may not provide enough power to illuminate the test light even when a complete circuit is made (especially if there is high resistance in the circuit). Always make sure that the test battery is strong. To check the battery, briefly touch the ground clip to the probe; if the light glows brightly, the battery is strong enough for testing.

➡**A self-powered test light should not be used on any computer controlled system or component. The small amount of electricity transmitted by the test light is enough to damage many electronic automotive components.**

MULTIMETERS

Multimeters are an extremely useful tool for troubleshooting electrical problems. They can be purchased in either analog or digital form and have a price range to suit any budget. A multimeter is a voltmeter, ammeter and ohmmeter (along with other features) combined into one instrument. It is often used when testing solid state circuits because of its high input impedance (usually 10 megaohms or more). A brief description of the multimeter main test functions follows:

• Voltmeter—the voltmeter is used to measure voltage at any point in a circuit, or to measure the voltage drop across any part of a circuit. Voltmeters usually have various scales and a selector switch to allow the reading of different voltage ranges. The voltmeter has a positive and a negative lead. To avoid damage to the meter, always connect the negative lead to the negative (–) side of the circuit (to ground or nearest the ground side of the circuit) and connect the positive lead to the positive (+) side of the circuit (to the power source or the nearest power source). Note that the negative voltmeter lead will always be black and that the positive voltmeter will always be some color other than black (usually red).

• Ohmmeter—the ohmmeter is designed to read resistance (measured in ohms) in a circuit or component. Most ohmmeters will have a selector switch which permits the measurement of different ranges of resistance (usually the selector switch allows the multiplication of the meter reading by 10, 100, 1,000 and 10,000). Some ohmmeters are "auto-ranging" which means the meter itself will determine which scale to use. Since the meters are powered by an internal battery, the ohmmeter can be used like a self-powered test light. When the ohmmeter is connected, current from the ohmmeter flows through the circuit or component being tested. Since the ohmmeter's internal resistance and voltage are known values, the amount of current flow through the meter depends on the resistance of the circuit or component being tested. The ohmmeter can also be used to perform a continuity test for suspected open circuits. In using the meter for making continuity checks, do not be concerned with the actual resistance readings. Zero resistance, or any ohm reading, indicates continuity in the circuit. Infinite resistance indicates an opening in the circuit. A high resistance reading where there should be none indicates a problem in the circuit. Checks for short circuits are made in the same manner as checks for open circuits, except that the circuit must be isolated from both power and normal ground. Infinite resistance indicates no continuity, while zero resistance indicates a dead short.

✳✳ WARNING

Never use an ohmmeter to check the resistance of a component or wire while there is voltage applied to the circuit.

• Ammeter—an ammeter measures the amount of current flowing through a circuit in units called amperes or amps. At normal operating voltage, most circuits have a characteristic amount of amperes, called "current draw" which can be measured using an ammeter. By referring to a specified current draw rating, then measuring the amperes and comparing the two values, one can determine what is happening within the circuit to aid in diagnosis. An open circuit, for example, will not allow any current to flow, so the ammeter reading will be zero. A damaged component or circuit will have an increased current draw, so the reading will be high. The ammeter is always connected in series with the circuit being tested. All of the current that normally flows through the circuit must also flow through the ammeter; if there is any other path for the current to follow, the ammeter reading will not be accurate. The ammeter itself has very little resistance to current flow and, therefore, will not affect the circuit, but it will measure current draw only when the circuit is closed and electricity is flowing. Excessive current draw can blow fuses and drain the battery, while a reduced current draw can cause motors to run slowly, lights to dim and other components to not operate properly.

Troubleshooting Electrical Systems

When diagnosing a specific problem, organized troubleshooting is a must. The complexity of a modern automotive vehicle demands that you approach any problem in a logical, organized manner. There are certain troubleshooting techniques, however, which are standard:
• Establish when the problem occurs. Does the problem appear only under certain conditions? Were there any noises, odors or other unusual symptoms? Isolate the problem area. To do this, make some simple tests and observations, then eliminate the systems that are working properly. Check for obvious problems, such as broken wires and loose or dirty connections. Always check the obvious before assuming something complicated is the cause.
• Test for problems systematically to determine the cause once the problem area is isolated. Are all the components functioning properly? Is there power going to electrical switches and motors. Performing careful, systematic checks will often turn up most causes on the first inspection, without wasting time checking components that have little or no relationship to the problem.
• Test all repairs after the work is done to make sure that the problem is fixed. Some causes can be traced to more than one component, so a careful verification of repair work is important in order to pick up additional malfunctions that may cause a problem to reappear or a different problem to arise. A blown fuse, for example, is a simple problem that may require more than another fuse to repair. If you don't look for a problem that caused a fuse to blow, a shorted wire (for example) may go undetected.

Experience has shown that most problems tend to be the result of a fairly simple and obvious cause, such as loose or corroded connectors, bad grounds or damaged wire insulation which causes a short. This makes careful visual inspection of components during testing essential to quick and accurate troubleshooting.

Testing

OPEN CIRCUITS

♦ **See Figure 8**

This test already assumes the existence of an open in the circuit and it is used to help locate the open portion.
1. Isolate the circuit from power and ground.
2. Connect the self-powered test light or ohmmeter ground clip to the ground side of the circuit and probe sections of the circuit sequentially.
3. If the light is out or there is infinite resistance, the open is between the probe and the circuit ground.
4. If the light is on or the meter shows continuity, the open is between the probe and the end of the circuit toward the power source.

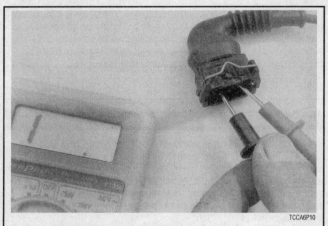

TCCA6P10

Fig. 8 The infinite reading on this multimeter indicates that the circuit is open

SHORT CIRCUITS

➡**Never use a self-powered test light to perform checks for opens or shorts when power is applied to the circuit under test. The test light can be damaged by outside power.**

1. Isolate the circuit from power and ground.
2. Connect the self-powered test light or ohmmeter ground clip to a good ground and probe any easy-to-reach point in the circuit.
3. If the light comes on or there is continuity, there is a short somewhere in the circuit.
4. To isolate the short, probe a test point at either end of the isolated circuit (the light should be on or the meter should indicate continuity).
5. Leave the test light probe engaged and sequentially open connectors or switches, remove parts, etc. until the light goes out or continuity is broken.
6. When the light goes out, the short is between the last two circuit components which were opened.

VOLTAGE

This test determines voltage available from the battery and should be the first step in any electrical troubleshooting procedure after visual inspection. Many electrical problems, especially on computer controlled systems, can be caused by a low state of charge in the battery. Excessive corrosion at the battery cable terminals can cause poor contact that will prevent proper charging and full battery current flow.
1. Set the voltmeter selector switch to the 20V position.
2. Connect the multimeter negative lead to the battery's negative (–) post or terminal and the positive lead to the battery's positive (+) post or terminal.
3. Turn the ignition switch **ON** to provide a load.
4. A well charged battery should register over 12 volts. If the meter reads below 11.5 volts, the battery power may be insufficient to operate the electrical system properly.

VOLTAGE DROP

▶ **See Figure 9**

When current flows through a load, the voltage beyond the load drops. This voltage drop is due to the resistance created by the load and also by small resistances created by corrosion at the connectors and damaged insulation on the wires. The maximum allowable voltage drop under load is critical, especially if there is more than one load in the circuit, since all voltage drops are cumulative.

1. Set the voltmeter selector switch to the 20 volt position.
2. Connect the multimeter negative lead to a good ground.
3. Operate the circuit and check the voltage prior to the first component (load).
4. There should be little or no voltage drop in the circuit prior to the first component. If a voltage drop exists, the wire or connectors in the circuit are suspect.
5. While operating the first component in the circuit, probe the ground side of the component with the positive meter lead and observe the voltage readings. A small voltage drop should be noticed. This voltage drop is caused by the resistance of the component.
6. Repeat the test for each component (load) down the circuit.
7. If a large voltage drop is noticed, the preceding component, wire or connector is suspect.

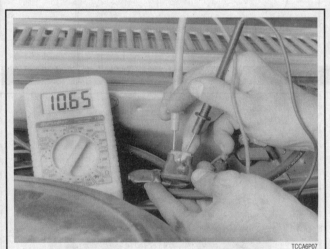

Fig. 9 This voltage drop test revealed high resistance (low voltage) in the circuit

RESISTANCE

▶ **See Figures 10 and 11**

❊❊❊ WARNING

Never use an ohmmeter with power applied to the circuit. The ohmmeter is designed to operate on its own power supply. The normal 12 volt electrical system voltage could damage the meter!

1. Isolate the circuit from the vehicle's power source.
2. Ensure that the ignition key is **OFF** when disconnecting any components or the battery.
3. Where necessary, also isolate at least one side of the circuit to be checked, in order to avoid reading parallel resistances. Parallel circuit resistances will always give a lower reading than the actual resistance of either of the branches.
4. Connect the meter leads to both sides of the circuit (wire or component) and read the actual measured ohms on the meter scale. Make sure the selector switch is set to the proper ohm scale for the circuit being tested, to avoid misreading the ohmmeter test value.

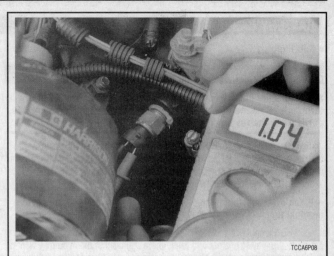

Fig. 10 Checking the resistance of a coolant temperature sensor with an ohmmeter. Reading is 1.04 kilohms

Wire and Connector Repair

Almost anyone can replace damaged wires, as long as the proper tools and parts are available. Wire and terminals are available to fit almost any need. Even the specialized weatherproof, molded and hard shell connectors are now available from aftermarket suppliers.

Be sure the ends of all the wires are fitted with the proper terminal hardware and connectors. Wrapping a wire around a stud is never a permanent solution and will only cause trouble later. Replace wires one at a time to avoid confusion. Always route wires exactly the same as the factory.

➡**If connector repair is necessary, only attempt it if you have the proper tools. Weatherproof and hard shell connectors require special tools to release the pins inside the connector. Attempting to repair these connectors with conventional hand tools will damage them.**

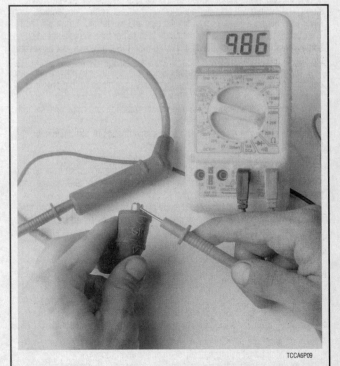

Fig. 11 Spark plug wires can be checked for excessive resistance using an ohmmeter

BATTERY CABLES

▶ See Figure 12

✳✳ WARNING

Make sure the battery cables are connected to the correct battery terminals. Reverse polarity will damage the electrical components, particularly the (expensive) engine control module.

In most cases to work on many portions of your vehicle, it ids necessary to disconnect the battery cables from the terminals so not to damage any components or cause harm to yourself with a jolt of electricity.

1. Start by making sure the ignition is **OFF**.

➡**When disconnecting the battery cables, always remove the negative terminal first.**

2. Use the correct size wrenches to loosen the terminal hardware. If this is not done you may strip a nut and cause more aggravation than you may want on a Sunday evening!

3. If necessary, use a puller tool which is designed to remove the terminal from the battery post.

4. Lift the negative terminal off the battery post, then the positive.

✳✳ CAUTION

Do not allow the battery cables to touch during or after removal!

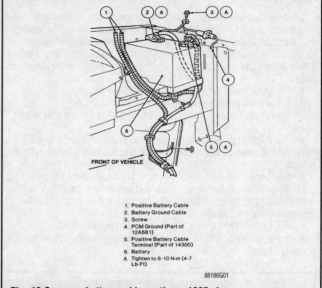

1. Positive Battery Cable
2. Battery Ground Cable
3. Screw
4. PCM Ground (Part of 12A581)
5. Positive Battery Cable Terminal (Part of 14300)
6. Battery
A. Tighten to 6-10 N·m (4-7 Lb-Ft)

88186G01

Fig. 12 Common battery cable routing—1995 shown

SUPPLEMENTAL RESTRAINT SYSTEM (AIR BAG)

General Information

SYSTEM OPERATION

▶ See Figures 13, 14 and 15

The air bag system is designed to operate in frontal or front angled collisions. The system will activate in a crash with severe frontal deceleration, more sever than hitting a parked car of similar size and weight at 28 mph (45 km/h). The system will sense the severity of the crash rather than vehicle speed so some frontal collisions at speeds above 28 mph (45 km/h) may not be severe enough to require inflation.

The Supplemental Air Bag Restraint System is designed to provide increased collision protection for the front seat occupants in addition to that provided by the three-point seat belt system.

The seat belts are used to obtain the best protection and to receive the full advantages of the supplemental air bag.

The Supplemental Air Bag Restraint System consists of two basic subsystems:

• Drivers and passenger's side air bag module assemblies
• Electrical system, including the left and right primary crash front air bag sensor and bracket, left kick panel safing rear air bag sensor and bracket and the air bag diagnostic monitor.

The air bag system is powered directly by the battery. The system can function with the ignition switch in any position, including **OFF** and **LOCK**. The system can also function when the driver's and passenger's side seats are unoccupied. The system performs three main functions:

• Detects on impact
• Carries electrical current to the igniters
• Monitors the system to determine the readiness

The air bag electrical system components are as follows:

• Air bag diagnostic monitor with integrated back-up power supply
• Air bag warning indicator
• Wiring harness and air bag sliding contact
• Left and right primary crash front air bag sensors with brackets
• Left kick panel safing rear air bag sensor and bracket
• An igniter within the driver's and passenger's side air bag modules

Fig. 13 Air bag warning labels are very important for your own personal safety

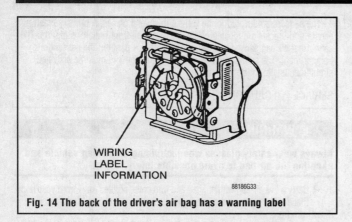

WIRING
LABEL
INFORMATION

88186G33

Fig. 14 The back of the driver's air bag has a warning label

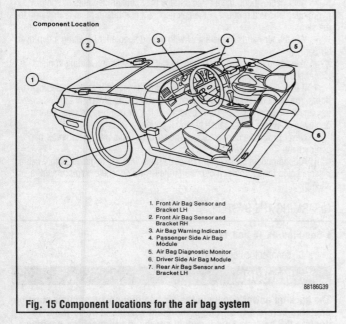

Component Location

1. Front Air Bag Sensor and Bracket LH
2. Front Air Bag Sensor and Bracket RH
3. Air Bag Warning Indicator
4. Passenger Side Air Bag Module
5. Air Bag Diagnostic Monitor
6. Driver Side Air Bag Module
7. Rear Air Bag Sensor and Bracket LH

88186G39

Fig. 15 Component locations for the air bag system

SYSTEM COMPONENTS

Driver's Side

AIR BAG MODULE

▶ **See Figure 16**

The driver's side air bag module is serviced as an assembly. It is mounted in the center of the steering wheel. The module consists of the following components:

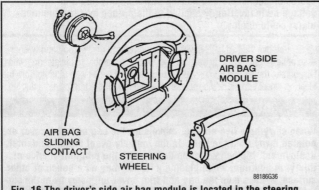

DRIVER SIDE
AIR BAG
MODULE

AIR BAG
SLIDING
CONTACT

STEERING
WHEEL

88186G36

Fig. 16 The driver's side air bag module is located in the steering wheel front cover

- Inflator
- Air bag
- Mounting plate and retainer ring
- Steering wheel trim cover

INFLATOR

The inflator assembly is not a serviceable item.

When the sensors close, signaling a crash, the electrical current flows to the air bag inflator. Inside the inflator, an igniter converts the electrical energy to thermal energy (heat). This causes the ignition of the inflator gas generant.

This ignition reaction combusts the sodium azide/copper oxide gas generant in the inflator, producing nitrogen gas, which in turn inflates the air bag.

AIR BAG

The driver's side air bag is constructed of neoprene coated nylon and is 26.5 inches (673mm) in diameter. The air bag fills to a volume of about 1.94 cubic feet (0.059 cubic meters) in approximately 40 milliseconds. The air bag assembly is not a serviceable item. You must replace it with a new one when involved in any type of crash whether it has inflated or not.

STEERING WHEEL TRIM COVER

The steering wheel trim cover encases the driver's side air bag module. The trim has molded-in tear seams that separate to allow inflation of the air bag. The trim cover is a component of the air bag module and is not a serviceable item.

Passenger's Side

AIR BAG MODULE

▶ **See Figure 17**

The passenger's side air bag module is serviced as an assembly. It is mounted in the right position of the instrument panel above the glove compartment. The module consists of the following components:

- Inflator
- Air bag
- Reaction housing with mounting hardware
- Trim cover

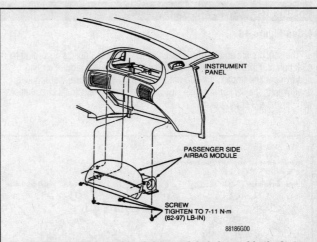

INSTRUMENT
PANEL

PASSENGER SIDE
AIRBAG MODULE

SCREW
TIGHTEN TO 7-11 N·m
(62-97) LB-IN)

88186G00

Fig. 17 The passenger's side air bag module is located in the instrument panel

INFLATOR

The inflator assembly is not a serviceable item. Inside the inflator, an igniter converts the electrical energy to thermal energy (heat). This causes the gas generant to ignite, as with the driver's side. This ignition reaction combusts the sodium azide/copper oxide gas generant in the inflator, producing nitrogen gas, which in turn inflates the air bag.

Since the passenger's side air bag module is much larger than the driver's side module, it contains more gas generant in a different inflator configuration to produce more nitrogen gas.

AIR BAG

The passenger's side air bag is constructed of ripstop nylon. The air bag fills to a volume of 8 cubic feet (0.227 cubic meters). The air bag assembly is not a serviceable item. You must replace it with a new one when involved in any type of crash whether it has inflated or not.

REACTION HOUSING

The steel reaction housing supplies support for the inflator. The housing provides a reaction surface for the passenger's side air bag module. It is used to attach the trim cover. The reaction housing contains mounting brackets that attach the passenger's air bag module to the instrument panel. This is not a serviceable item.

TRIM COVER

The thermo-plastic trim cover is textured and painted to match the surface of the instrument panel. It is constructed with a molded-in tear seam that separates when the air bag is inflated and hinges out of the way during deployment. The trim cover retains the air bag in the reaction housing during the operation of the vehicle and is not a serviceable item.

Air Bag Diagnostic Monitor

The air bag diagnostic monitor continually monitors all air bag system components and wiring connections for possible faults in the system. The monitor will display a diagnostic trouble code on the air bag warning indicator if it detects a fault in the air bag system while the ignition switch is in the **RUN** position.

The monitor performs system diagnostics which is its main function. The air bag diagnostic monitor does not deploy the air bags in the event of a crash! Crash sensors are hard wired to the air bags and, therefore, the sensors determine when to deploy the bags.

The air bag diagnostic monitor illuminates the air bag warning light for approximately six seconds when the ignition switch is turned to **RUN** and then turns off. This indicates that the air bag warning indicator is operational. If the air bag warning light does not illuminate or if it stays on or flashes at any time, a fault has been detected by the air bag diagnostic monitor.

Sensors

▶ **See Figure 18**

The sensors are an electrical switch which reacts to impacts according to direction and force. It discriminates between impacts that require air bag deployment and impacts that do not . When an impact occurs that requires deployment, the sensor contacts close, completing the electrical circuit necessary for the system to operate.

The sensors are located in the vehicle in several places. A primary crash sensor and bracket are located on the left and right front radiator supports. The safing rear air bag sensor is located in the left kick panel in the passenger's compartment. The safing and one of the primary sensors must be activated simultaneously to inflate the air bag.

SERVICE PRECAUTIONS

✳✳ WARNING

Always wear safety glasses when servicing an air bag vehicle and handling the air bag to avoid possible injury.

- Carry a live air bag with the bag and trim cover pointed away from your body.
- Place a live air bag on a bench or other surface with the trim cover up, away from the surface.
- After deployment, the air bag surface may contain deposits of sodium hydroxide. This is a product of the gas generant combustion that is irritating to the skin.
- Wash your hands immediately with a mild soap after handling a deployed air bag.
- You can only replace, NOT service the crash sensors, sliding contact, diagnostic monitor and air bag modules.
- If the air bag module has a discolored or damaged trim cover deployment door, it must be replaced. Do not attempt to paint it, as any paint applied may damage the cover material. This could affect the air bag performance during deployment, which could cause personal injury.
- Never probe the connectors on the air bags. This may result in air bag deployment.
- All component replacement must be done with the negative battery cable disconnected for a minimum of one minute before service or replacement is attempted.

DISARMING THE SYSTEM

▶ **See Figures 16 and 17**

1. Disconnect the negative battery cable.

✳✳ WARNING

The back-up power supply in the air bag diagnostic monitor must be depleted before any air bag component service is performed. To deplete the back-up power supply energy, disconnect the positive battery cable and wait a minimum of one minute before service or replacement is attempted.

2. Disconnect the positive battery cable and wait at least one minute.

✳✳ CAUTION

Whenever working near air bag system wiring or components, as an extra safety precaution, it is recommended that the air bag module(s) also be disconnected and removed. Even with the battery cables disconnected and backup power supply depleted, should voltage be inadvertently applied to the air bag system, the module(s) could deploy.

3. Remove the two back cover plugs and remove the two bolt and washer assemblies retaining the driver's air bag module assembly to the steering wheel. Disconnect the air bag harness at the bag. Remove the air bag module from the steering wheel and place the module on a bench with the trim cover facing up.

✳✳ CAUTION

When carrying a live air bag, make sure the bag and trim cover are pointed away from the body. In the unlikely event of an accidental deployment, the bag will then deploy with the minimal chance of injury. In addition, when placing a live air bag on a bench or other surface, always face the bag and trim cover up, away from the surface. This will reduce the motion of the unit if it is accidentally deployed.

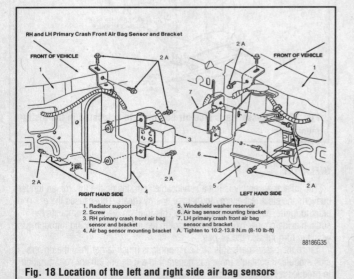

RH and LH Primary Crash Front Air Bag Sensor and Bracket

FRONT OF VEHICLE

FRONT OF VEHICLE

RIGHT HAND SIDE

LEFT HAND SIDE

1. Radiator support
2. Screw
3. RH primary crash front air bag sensor and bracket
4. Air bag sensor mounting bracket
5. Windshield washer reservoir
6. Air bag sensor mounting bracket
7. LH primary crash front air bag sensor and bracket
A. Tighten to 10.2-13.8 N.m (8-10 lb-ft)

88186G35

Fig. 18 Location of the left and right side air bag sensors

4. If so equipped, also remove the passenger's side air bag module assembly as follows:

a. Open the glove compartment.

b. Disconnect the damping rod on the right-hand side of the glove compartment with a small screwdriver.

c. Pull the left-hand side of the glove compartment inward and lower the glove compartment toward the floor.

d. Remove the 2 or 3 screws that attach the two-piece air duct. Unfasten the center bolt, then remove both pieces of the air duct.

e. Remove the 2 vertically driven bolts on both sides of the bottom of the air bag module.

f. Remove the 2 fore-aft driven bolts that attach the air bag tabs to the instrument panel steel.

g. Gently push the air bag module back out of the instrument panel opening enough to access the electrical connector, then detach the connector.

h. Remove the passenger side air bag module and place it on a bench with the trim cover facing up.

❊❊ CAUTION

When carrying a live air bag, make sure the bag and trim cover are pointed away from the body. In the unlikely event of an accidental deployment, the bag will then deploy with the minimal chance of injury. In addition, when placing a live air bag on a bench or other surface, always face the bag and trim cover up, away from the surface. This will reduce the motion of the unit if it is accidentally deployed.

ARMING THE SYSTEM

◆ See Figures 16 and 17

1. If applicable, reconnect the driver's side air bag module assembly, then position the module on the steering wheel and secure with the two bolts and washers. Tighten the bolt and washer assemblies to 8–10 ft. lbs. (10–14 Nm).

2. If applicable, reconnect and install the passenger's side air bag module assembly Tighten the module retaining bolts to 62–97 inch lbs. (7–11 Nm).

3. Connect the positive and then the negative battery cables.

4. Turn the ignition switch from **OFF** to **RUN** and visually monitor the air bag warning indicator. The light will illuminate continuously for approximately six seconds and then turn off. If a fault occurs, the air bag indicator will either fail to light, remain lighted continuously or flash. The flashing may not occur until approximately 16 seconds after the ignition switch has been turned from **OFF** to **RUN**. This is the time needed for the air bag diagnostic monitor to complete testing the system. If the air bag indicator is inoperative, an air bag system fault exists, a tone will sound in a pattern of five sets of five beeps. If this occurs, the air bag indicator will need to be serviced before further diagnostics can be done.

HEATER

Blower Motor

REMOVAL & INSTALLATION

1983–88 Models

◆ **See Figure 19**

1. Disconnect the negative battery cable.

2. Remove the glove compartment and disconnect the hose from the outside-recirculation door vacuum motor.

3. Remove the lower instrument panel right side to cowl attaching bolt.

4. Remove the screw attaching the support brace to the top of the air inlet duct.

5. Disconnect the blower motor power lead at the wire connector.

6. Remove the nut retaining the blower housing lower support bracket to the evaporator (heater) case.

7. Remove the screw attaching the top of the air inlet duct to the heater assembly.

8. Move the air duct and blower housing assembly down and away from the heater case.

9. Remove the air inlet duct and blower housing assembly from the vehicle.

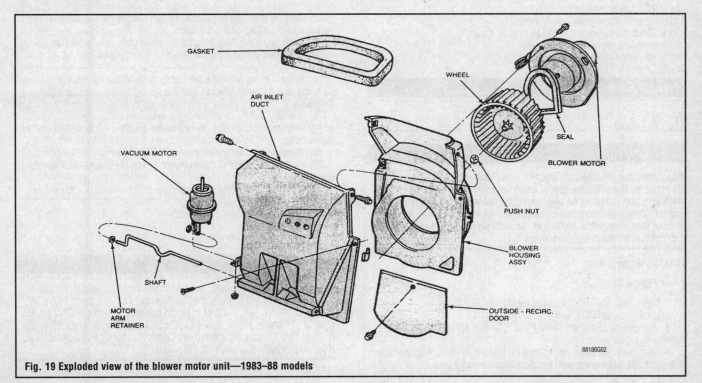

Fig. 19 Exploded view of the blower motor unit—1983–88 models

88186G02

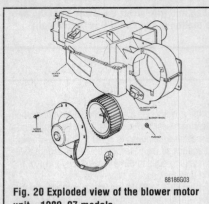

Fig. 20 Exploded view of the blower motor unit—1989–97 models

Fig. 21 Disconnect the wiring attached to the blower motor

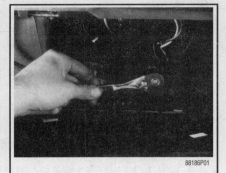

Fig. 22 Remove the retaining screws that mount the motor to the heater unit

10. Remove the blower motor mounting plate screws and remove the blower motor and wheel assembly from the housing.
11. Service as necessary. Installation is the reverse of removal.
12. Check the operation of the system.

1989–97 Models

♦ See Figures 20, 21 and 22

1. Disconnect the negative battery cable.
2. Remove the glove box liner.
3. Use a small flat bladed tool to remove the clip retaining the hydraulic damper strut.
4. Disconnect the wires at the blower motor.
5. Remove the four retaining screws and pull the blower motor from the heater case.
6. Remove the pushnuts and slide the blower wheel from the shaft.
To install:
7. Using a new seal, position the blower motor and motor wheel assembly to the motor housing with the flat side of the flange near motor switch resistor.
8. Install the four retaining screws.
9. Tape the blower motor power lead to the air inlet duct to keep the wire away from the blower outlet during installation.
10. Install the blower motor and motor wheel assembly into the vehicle.
11. Attach the blower motor wiring.
12. Connect the negative battery cable.
13. Check the blower motor operation in all speeds.
14. Install the glove compartment liner.
15. Check the operation of the system.

Heater Core

REMOVAL & INSTALLATION

✳✳ CAUTION

When draining the coolant, keep in mind that cats and dogs are attracted by the ethylene glycol antifreeze, and are quite likely to drink any that is left in an uncovered container or in puddles on the ground. This will prove fatal in sufficient quantity. Always drain the coolant into a sealable container. Coolant should be reused unless it is contaminated or several years old.

1983–88 Without A/C

♦ See Figure 23

1. Disconnect the negative battery cable.
2. Drain the cooling system.
3. Remove the instrument panel. Refer to Section 10, Instrument Panel Removal and Installation.
4. Disconnect the heater hoses from the heater core tubes. Plug the heater hoses and core tubes to prevent coolant spillage during removal.

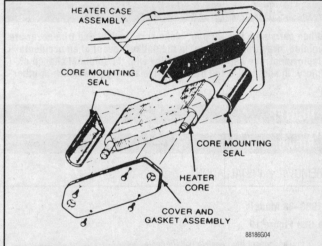

Fig. 23 Exploded view of the heater core on vehicles without A/C—1983–88 models

5. Working under the hood at the firewall, remove the two nuts retaining the evaporator (heater) case to the dash.
6. From under the dash, remove the screws attaching the heater assembly support bracket and air inlet duct support bracket to the top cowl panel.
7. Remove the nut retaining the bracket at the left end of the heater assembly to the dash panel, and the nut retaining the bracket below the case to the dash panel.
8. Carefully pull the heater assembly away from the dash panel to gain access to the screws that retain the heater core access cover to the evaporator (heater) case.
9. Remove the cover retaining screws and the cover.
10. Lift the heater core and seals from the case. Remove the seals from the core tubes.
11. Install the heater core in the reverse order of removal. Fill the system with the correct coolant mix.
12. Check the operation of the system.

1983–88 Air Conditioned Models

✳✳ CAUTION

When draining the coolant, keep in mind that cats and dogs are attracted by the ethylene glycol antifreeze, and are quite likely to drink any that is left in an uncovered container or in puddles on the ground. This will prove fatal in sufficient quantity. Always drain the coolant into a sealable container. Coolant should be reused unless it is contaminated or several years old.

WITH MANUAL AIR CONDITIONING

▶ See Figure 24

➡Heater core removal requires instrument panel and heater/evaporator case assembly removal.

1. Disconnect the negative battery cable.
2. Remove the instrument panel. Refer to Section 10, Instrument Panel Removal and Installation.

❊❊ WARNING

Removal of the heater/air conditioner (evaporator) housing, if necessary, requires evacuation of the air conditioner refrigerant. This operation requires special tools and a thorough familiarity with automotive refrigerant systems. Failure to follow proper safety precautions may cause personal injury. If you are not familiar with these systems, it is recommended that discharging and charging of the A/C system be performed by an experienced professional mechanic.

3. Discharge the air conditioning system at the service access gauge port locate on the suction line. See the WARNING notice.
4. Once the air conditioning system has been discharged, remove the high and low pressure hoses. Use a second wrench to hold the fittings when loosening the lines. Plug the hose openings to prevent dirt and moisture from entering.
5. Drain the cooling system and remove the heater hoses from the heater core tubes. Plug the hoses and the heater core tubes.
6. Remove the screw that attaches the air inlet duct and blower housing support brace to the cowl top panel under the dash.
7. Disconnect the vacuum supply hose from the inline vacuum check valve in the engine compartment.
8. Disconnect the blower motor wiring connector.
9. From under the hood, remove the two nuts retaining the evaporator case to the firewall.
10. From under the dash, remove the screw attaching the evaporator case support bracket to the cowl top panel.

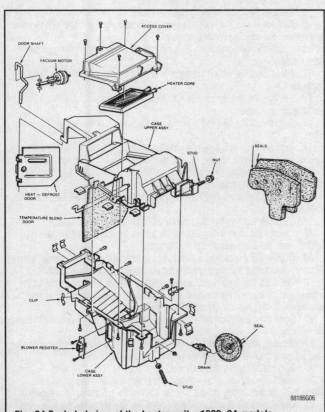

Fig. 24 Exploded view of the heater unit—1983–84 models

88186G06

11. Remove the nut that retains the bracket below the evaporator case to the dash panel.
12. Carefully pull the evaporator case away from the dash panel and remove the case from the vehicle.
13. Remove the heater core access cover from the evaporator case.
14. Remove the heater core and seals from the case. Remove the seals from the core fitting tubes.
15. Service as required. Install in the reverse order of removal. Fill the cooling system with the correct coolant mix. Have the air conditioning system charged. See the WARNING notice.

WITH AUTOMATIC TEMPERATURE CONTROL

➡Core removal requires instrument panel and evaporator case assembly removal.

1. Disconnect the negative battery cable.
2. Remove the instrument panel. Refer to Section 10, Instrument Panel Removal and Installation.
3. Discharge the air conditioning system at the service access gauge port located on the suction line. See the WARNING notice.
4. Once the air conditioning system has been discharged, remove the high and low pressure hoses. Use a second wrench to hold the receiver fittings when loosening the lines. Plug the hose openings to prevent dirt and moisture from entering.
5. Drain the cooling system and remove the heater hoses from the heater core tubes. Plug the hoses and heater core tubes.
6. Remove the screw attaching the air inlet duct and blower housing assembly support brace to the top cowl panel under the dash.
7. Disconnect the vacuum supply hose from the inline vacuum check valve and the vacuum hose from the TBL (Thermal Blower Lockout Switch) in the engine compartment.
8. Disconnect the blower motor wiring connector.
9. From under the hood, remove the two nuts retaining the evaporator case to the firewall.
10. From under the dash, remove the screw attaching the evaporator case support bracket to the cowl top panel.
11. Remove the screw retaining the bracket below the evaporator case and dash panel.
12. Carefully pull the evaporator case assembly away from the dash panel and remove the assembly from the vehicle.
13. Remove the heater core access cover screws and the cover.
14. Lift the heater core and seals from the case assembly.
15. Remove the seals from the core.
16. Service as required. Install in the reverse order of removal. Fill the cooling system with the correct mixture of coolant. Have the air conditioning system recharged. See WARNING notice!

1989–93 Models

▶ See Figure 25

➡The instrument panel must be removed to remove the heater assembly.

1. Disconnect the negative battery cable.
2. Disconnect the underhood wiring at the left side of dash panel.
3. Disengage the wiring connector from the dash panel and push the wiring harness into the passenger compartment.
4. Remove the steering column lower trim cover by removing the three screws at the bottom, one screw on the left side, and pull to disengage the five snap-in retainers across top.
5. Remove the six screws retaining steering column lower opening reinforcement, and remove it from the instrument panel.
6. Remove the steering column upper and lower shrouds, and disconnect the wiring from the steering column.
7. Remove the shift interlock switch.
8. Disconnect the steering column lower universal joint.
9. Support the steering column and remove the four nuts retaining column to the support bracket. Remove the column from the vehicle.
10. Remove the one screw retaining the left side of the instrument panel to the parking brake bracket.
11. Reinstall the steering column lower opening reinforcement using only four screws (one in each corner).

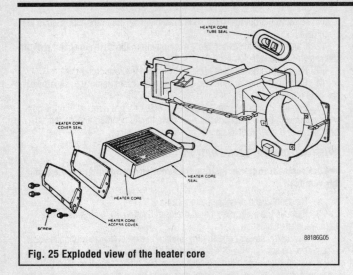

Fig. 25 Exploded view of the heater core

➡**Reinforcement prevents instrument panel from twisting when being removed from vehicle.**

12. Remove the right and left cowl side trim panels.
13. To remove the console assembly from vehicle:
   a. Open the console door and remove the container and mat to gain access to the two console-to-floorpan retaining screws. Then remove the screws.
   b. Remove the gear shift knob on the 5-speed transmission only.
   c. Remove the two rear finish panel retaining screws. Tilt the finish panel forward, disconnect the electrical connectors and remove the panel.
   d. Remove the two front console-to-instrument panel retaining screws and remove the console.
14. Remove the two nuts retaining the center of instrument panel to the floor (tunnel).
15. Open the glove compartment, squeeze the sides of the bin and lower it to the full open position.
16. From underneath the instrument panel and through glove compartment opening, disconnect the wiring, heater, A/C vacuum lines and control cables.
17. Remove the two screws at the right and left side retaining the instrument panel to the cowl sides.
18. Remove the right and left upper finish panels by pulling up to disengage the snap-in retainers. Three on the right and four on the left sides.
19. Remove the four screws retaining the instrument panel to the cowl top. Remove the right and left roof rail trim panel and the door frame weatherstrip.
20. Carefully pull the instrument panel away from the cowl. Disconnect any remaining wiring controls and remove from the vehicle.

➡**If instrument panel is being replaced, transfer all components, wiring and hardware to new panel.**

21. Remove the right side instrument panel brace located above the heater case and attached to the cowl.
22. Drain the engine coolant from the cooling system and remove the hoses from the heater core. Plug the hoses and the core.
23. Disconnect the vacuum supply hose (black) from the inline vacuum check valve in the engine compartment.
24. Disconnect the blower motor wire harness from the resistor and motor lead.
25. Working under the hood, remove the three nuts retaining the heater assembly to the firewall.
26. In the passenger compartment, remove the screw attaching the heater assembly support bracket to the cowl top panel.
27. Remove the one screw retaining the bracket below the heater assembly to the dash panel.
28. Carefully pull the heater assembly away from the dash panel and remove the assembly from vehicle.
29. Remove the four heater core access cover attaching screws, and the access cover from the case.
30. Remove the seal from the heater core tubes.
31. Inspect all of the seals for proper fit, replace if they are worn or cracked.
To install:
32. Replace the heater core tube seal when installing the heater core.
33. Install the heater core access plate and tighten the screws.

34. Place the heater assembly into vehicle.
35. Install the retaining bracket and tighten the screw.
36. Install and tighten the screws attaching heater assembly support brace to the cowl top panel.
37. Replace and tighten the three nuts that secure the heater assembly to the firewall.
38. Connect the blower motor wires.
39. Connect the vacuum supply line.
40. Connect the heater hoses and tighten clamps. If possible, pressure check the cooling system before installing the instrument panel.
41. Install the instrument panel and steering column. Before installing the final trim pieces, connect the battery cables and make sure all systems function properly.
42. Refill cooling system using proper engine coolant.

1994–97 Models

➡**The instrument panel and steering column must be removed to remove the heater assembly. Two people are required to remove the assembly from the vehicle.**

1. Disconnect negative battery cable. Disconnect positive battery cable and wait one minute for air bag diagnostic monitor to deplete the backup power supply.
2. Loosen main wiring connector bolt in the engine compartment at the left side of dash panel and separate connectors.
3. Remove radio antenna stanchion and disconnect cable from base of the radio antenna stanchion.
4. Remove both the right hand and left hand windshield side garnish mouldings.

➡**Do not remove safety belt retaining bolts in next step.**

5. Remove the screws retaining both the right and left front door scuff plates and remove the front door opening weather-strips from body flanges.
6. Remove the right and left cowl side trim panels.
7. Remove the steering column cover by removing the three screws along the bottom and pull on the cover to unsnap the three clips across the top of the instrument panel steering column cover.
8. Remove the ignition switch lock cylinder.
9. Remove the four screws retaining the steering column shrouds together and remove the steering column shrouds.
10. Install the ignition switch lock cylinder to prevent the steering wheel from turning.
11. Disconnect the wiring connectors at the turn signal and windshield wiper switch.
12. Remove the one screw and A/C evaporator register duct from under the steering column tube.
13. Disconnect the wiring connectors at the bottom of the steering column tube.
14. Remove the pinch bolt attaching the steering column tube to the steering column lower yoke and slightly spread the joint with a screwdriver.
15. While supporting the steering column tube, remove the four steering column tube retaining nuts.
16. Remove the interlock cable retaining screws and shift actuator cable fitting.
17. Carefully remove the steering column tube from the vehicle.
18. Loosen the main wiring connector bolt at the left side of the steering column opening and separate the connectors.
19. Disconnect the stoplight switch wiring connector. On the manual transmission, disconnect the clutch pedal position switch wiring connector.
20. Pull back the floor carpet as required on the left and right sides of the vehicle and disconnect the window regulator safety relay switch wiring, and the powertrain control module from the main wiring.
21. Open the glove compartment to the stop, unsnap the hydraulic lift from the right side.
22. Remove the three screws at the bottom retaining the glove compartment door hinge and glove compartment to the instrument panel.
23. Remove the glove compartment.
24. Reach through the glove compartment opening and disconnect the wiring and vacuum hoses/connector from the heater-A/C evaporator housing.
25. Disconnect the wiring connector from the speed control amplifier and bracket assembly.

26. Remove floor console panel:

    a. Open the console panel glove compartment door to access screws to console finish panel.

    b. Remove the two screws, and lift the rear of the console finish panel to unsnap retainers.

    c. Reach under the console finish panel and disconnect wires to fog lamp and ride control switches (if equipped) and cigar lighter socket and retainer.

    d. Lift the rear of the console finish panel and slide rearward to release the two front locating tabs, remove console finish panel.

    e. With the console panel door open, remove the console glove compartment mat.

    f. Remove the center screw from the console (rear of shifter) bin, then lift the bin from the console panel. Disconnect the luggage compartment door release switch and fuel filler door lock switch (if equipped).

    g. Remove the two screws from the bottom of the console panel bin to floor pan.

    h. Remove the two cups and screws. Remove the floor console panel.

    i. Remove the two screws retaining the front of the floor console panel to the instrument panel. Disconnect the remaining wires (main jumper wire) and main wiring, then lift the console panel from the vehicle.

➡**Protect the instrument panel surface during next step.**

27. Using a putty knife or similar tool, insert under the left or right corner of the instrument panel upper finish panel and pry up on the instrument panel upper finish panel to release one snap clip.

28. Unsnap the remaining four clips pulling up by hand, working toward the opposite side of the vehicle.

29. Remove the two nuts retaining the left side of the instrument panel to the cowl side.

30. Remove the two nuts and one bolt retaining the instrument panel to the console bracket.

31. Remove the nut attaching the right side of the instrument panel to cowl side.

➡**The following steps require two people.**

32. Remove the six bolts retaining the top of the instrument panel to the dash panel.

33. Carefully pull the instrument panel away from the windshield glass while checking for and disconnecting any remaining wiring connectors. Disengage the antenna wire grommet from the sheet metal and pull the radio antenna lead in cable through.

34. Remove the right side instrument panel brace located above the heater case and attached to the cowl.

35. Drain the engine coolant from the cooling system, then remove the hoses from the heater core. Plug the hoses and the core.

36. Properly discharge the air conditioning system into freon recovery equipment.

37. Disconnect the vacuum supply hose (black) from the inline vacuum check valve in the engine compartment.

38. Disconnect the blower motor wire harness from the resistor and motor lead.

39. Working under the hood, remove the three nuts retaining the heater assembly to the firewall.

40. In the passenger compartment, remove the screw attaching the heater assembly support bracket to the cowl top panel.

41. Remove the one screw retaining the bracket below the heater assembly to the dash panel.

42. Carefully pull the heater assembly away from the dash panel and remove the assembly from vehicle.

43. Remove the four heater core access cover attaching screws, and the access cover from the case.

44. Remove the seal from the heater core tubes.

45. Inspect all seals for proper fit, replace if worn or cracked.

To install:

46. Replace the heater core tube seal.

47. Install the heater core and the access plate, then tighten the screws.

48. Place the heater assembly into vehicle.

49. Install the retaining bracket and tighten screw.

50. Install and tighten the screws attaching the heater assembly support brace to the cowl top panel.

51. Replace and tighten the three nuts that secure the heater assembly to the firewall.

52. Connect the blower motor wires.

53. Connect the vacuum supply line.

54. Connect the heater hoses and tighten the clamps. Pressure test the cooling system to check the heater core installation.

55. Carefully place instrument panel to windshield glass while connecting wiring connectors.

56. Install the six bolts retaining the top of the instrument panel to dash panel.

57. Install the nut attaching the right side of the instrument panel to cowl side.

58. Install the two nuts and one bolt retaining the instrument panel to the console bracket.

59. Install the two nuts retaining the left side of the instrument panel to cowl side.

60. Snap the clips in place, working toward the opposite side of the vehicle.

61. Install the floor console panel.

62. Connect the wiring harness to the speed control amplifier and bracket assembly.

63. Reach through the glove compartment opening and connect the wiring and vacuum hoses/connector from the heater-A/C evaporator housing.

64. Install the glove compartment.

65. Install the three screws at the bottom retaining the glove compartment door hinge and glove compartment to the instrument panel.

66. Open the glove compartment to the stop, snap in the hydraulic lift from the right side.

67. Connect the window regulator safety relay switch wiring and the powertrain control module from the main wiring.

68. Attach the stoplight switch wiring connector and on manual transmission. Connect the clutch pedal position switch wiring.

69. Carefully install the steering column tube into the vehicle.

70. Install the interlock cable retaining screws and shift actuator cable fitting.

71. While supporting the steering column tube, install the four steering column tube retaining nuts.

72. Install the pinch bolt attaching the steering column tube to steering column lower yoke.

73. Connect the wiring at the bottom of the steering column tube.

74. Install the one screw and A/C evaporator register duct from under the steering column tube.

75. Connect the wiring at the turn signal and windshield wiper switch.

76. Remove the ignition switch lock cylinder which was temporarily installed to prevent the steering wheel from turning.

77. Install the four screws retaining the steering column shrouds together, then install the steering column shrouds.

78. Install the ignition switch lock cylinder.

79. Install the steering column.

80. Install the right and left cowl side trim panels.

81. Install the screws retaining both right and left front door scuff plates, then install the front door opening weather-strips to body flanges.

82. Install both the right hand and left hand windshield side garnish mouldings.

83. Install the radio antenna stanchion and connect cable to base of the radio antenna stanchion.

84. Connect the main wiring and tighten bolt.

85. Connect the battery cables.

86. Refill the cooling system using proper engine coolant.

87. Evacuate and recharge the air conditioning system.

Control Panel

REMOVAL & INSTALLATION

1983 Models

▸ **See Figure 26**

1. Disconnect the negative battery cable.
2. Remove the 4 control assembly-to-instrument panel screws.
3. Pull the control panel towards you.
4. Disconnect the wiring from the panel connectors.

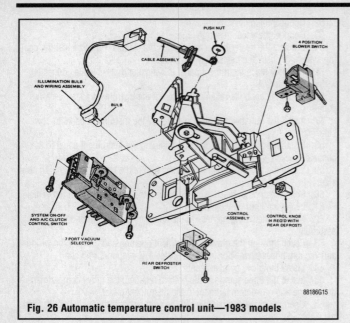

Fig. 26 Automatic temperature control unit—1983 models

5. Disconnect the vacuum harness and the temperature control cable from the control panel.

To install:

6. Attach the vacuum harness and control cables to the unit.

➡**Push on the vacuum harness retaining nut, DO NOT TRY TO SCREW IT ON!**

7. Connect the wiring to the control assembly.
8. Insert the unit into the dash, tighten the four mounting screws.
9. Connect the negative battery cable.
10. Adjust the cables as necessary.

1984–88 Models

◗ **See Figures 27 and 28**

1. Disconnect the negative battery cable.
2. Remove the temperature control knob from the lever shaft (on 1985 and later models only).
3. Remove the instrument cluster opening finish panel.
4. Remove the 4 screws attaching the control panel to the instrument panel.
5. Pull the control panel out and disconnect the wiring from the control panel.
6. Disconnect the vacuum harness and the temperature control cable from the control panel.

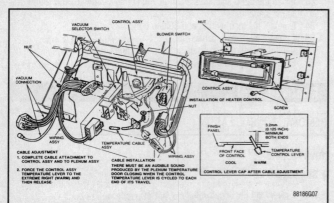

Fig. 27 Exploded view of the heater control assembly with associated components—1984–88 models

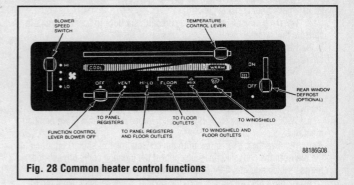

Fig. 28 Common heater control functions

To install:

7. Attach the vacuum harness and temperature control cable to the control panel.

➡**Remember that the vacuum harness nut is a pushnut. It does not screw on.**

8. Connect the wiring to the control unit.
9. Insert the unit into the dash, tighten the four screws to retain the unit in the vehicle.
10. Install the instrument cluster opening finish panel.
11. Install the knob if removed.
12. Connect the negative battery cable.
13. Check the operation of the control assembly.

1989–97 Models

◗ **See Figures 29 thru 35**

1. Disconnect the negative battery cable.
2. Insert the radio removing tool T87P–19061–A or equivalent in the retaining clip.
3. Apply a side load away from the control to disengage the clips.
4. Pull the semi-automatic A/C control from the instrument panel opening and disconnect the wiring harness from the control assembly.
5. Disconnect the vacuum harness.

To install:

6. Connect the wiring harness and vacuum harness to the control assembly.
7. Position the control assembly into the instrument panel opening. Engage it into the track in the instrument panel, then push the unit in until it latches firmly into place.
8. Connect the negative battery cable.
9. Check the system for proper operation.

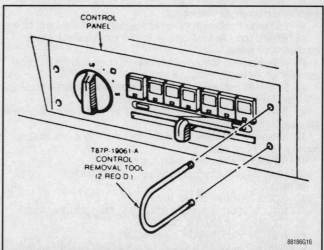

Fig. 29 Use the T87P–19061–A tool to remove the control unit from the dash—1989–93 shown

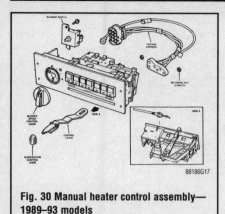

Fig. 30 Manual heater control assembly—
1989–93 models

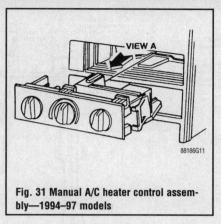

Fig. 31 Manual A/C heater control assembly—1994–97 models

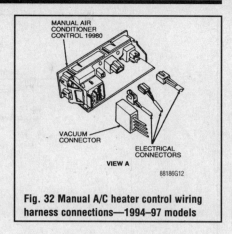

Fig. 32 Manual A/C heater control wiring harness connections—1994–97 models

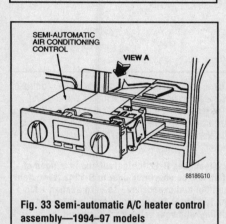

Fig. 33 Semi-automatic A/C heater control assembly—1994–97 models

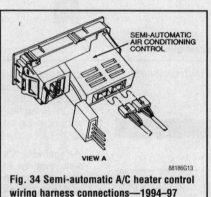

Fig. 34 Semi-automatic A/C heater control wiring harness connections—1994–97 models

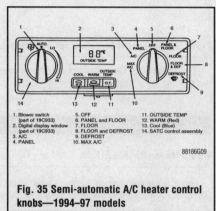

Fig. 35 Semi-automatic A/C heater control knobs—1994–97 models

Blower Switch

REMOVAL & INSTALLATION

Without Climate Control

1. Disconnect the negative battery cable.
2. Remove the control assembly from the instrument panel.
3. Remove the switch knob.
4. Remove the screw from the underside of the control assembly, attaching the switch to the control assembly.
5. Disconnect the wire connector from the switch and remove the switch.

To Install:

6. Position the switch in the control assembly making sure the pins are inserted into the holes of the switch mounting plate.
7. Install the screw to attach the switch to the control assembly.
8. Connect the wire harness connector to the switch.
9. Install the control assembly in the instrument panel.
10. Place the switch knob on the switch shaft and push the knob all the way on.
11. Check the system for proper operation.

With Climate Control

1. Remove the climate control assembly.
2. Place the blower motor switch in the **LO** position, then pull the knob off of the switch shaft.
3. Detach the wiring connector from the heater blower motor switch.
4. Remove the circuit board cover.
5. Remove the one screw that retains the blower motor switch to the manual A/C control assembly.
6. Rotate the blower motor switch to disengage the locking tab. Pull the blower motor switch away from the housing, disengaging the knob.

To install:

7. Position the blower motor switch in the manual A/C control assembly. Ensure that the switch is correctly rotated into place.
8. Install the screw that attaches the switch to the manual A/C control assembly.
9. Place the switch knob on the switch shaft in the **LO** position, then push the knob all the way on.
10. Connect the wiring harness to the blower motor switch.
11. Install the circuit board cover.
12. Install the manual A/C control assembly into the instrument panel.
13. Check the system operation.

PRESET & ADJUSTMENT

▶ See Figure 36

Before Installation

1. Insert the blade of a small tool into the wire end loop (crank arm end) of the control cable.
2. Grip the self adjusting clip with a pair of pliers, then slide it down the control wire away from the loop approximately 1 inch (25mm).
3. Install the cable assembly.
4. Rapidly move the control lever to the extreme right of the slot (WARM) to position the self adjusting clip.
5. Check for proper operation.

After Installation

1. Move the control lever to the COOL position.
2. Hold the crank arm firmly into position, then insert the blade of a small flatbladed tool into the wire loops, and pull the cable wire through the self adjusting clip until there is a space of approximately 1 inch (25mm) between the clip and the wire end loop.

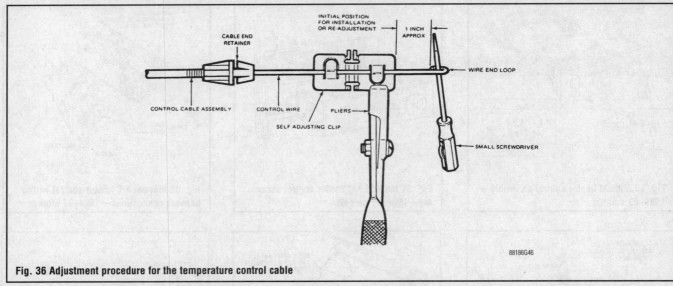

Fig. 36 Adjustment procedure for the temperature control cable

3. Rapidly move the control lever to the extreme right of the slot (WARM) to position the self adjusting clip.
4. Check for proper operation.

Air Conditioning Components

REMOVAL & INSTALLATION

Repair or service of air conditioning components is not covered by this manual, because of the risk of personal injury or death, and because of the legal ramifications of servicing these components without the proper EPA certification and experience. Cost, personal injury or death, environmental damage, and legal considerations (such as the fact that it is a federal crime to vent refrigerant into the atmosphere), dictate that the A/C components on your vehicle should be serviced only by a Motor Vehicle Air Conditioning (MVAC) trained, and EPA certified automotive technician.

➡️ **If your vehicle's A/C system uses R-12 refrigerant and is in need of recharging, the A/C system can be converted over to R-134a refrigerant (less environmentally harmful and expensive). Refer to Section 1 for additional information on R-12 to R-134a conversions, and for additional considerations dealing with your vehicle's A/C system.**

CRUISE CONTROL

Control Switches

REMOVAL & INSTALLATION

Without Air Bags

1. Disconnect the negative battery cable.
2. Remove the steering wheel horn cover and pad assembly.
3. Disconnect the harness connector from the speed control and horn contact plate terminal.
4. On vehicles equipped with the base model steering wheel, pry the speed control switches from the steering wheel using finger pressure.
5. On vehicles with the sport steering wheel, remove the 4 screws attaching the speed control switches to the steering wheel.
6. Remove the speed control switch and harness assembly.

To install:

7. On vehicles equipped with the base model steering wheel, position the speed control switches into the steering wheel and snap into place.
8. On vehicles with the sport steering wheel, position the speed control switches into the steering wheel and install the 4 attaching screws.
9. Connect the wire harness to the terminal on the contact plate.
10. Connect the horn wires to the terminals on the horn cover and press the horn cover onto the steering wheel.

➡️**Ensure that the wire harness does not interfere with cover installation.**

11. Position the pad and cover assembly and snap into place.
12. Connect the negative battery cable and check system operation.

With Air Bags

1. Disconnect the negative battery cable.
2. Disconnect the positive battery cable and wait one minute for the backup power supply to deplete its stored energy.

3. Remove the two back cover plugs. Remove the two screw and washer assemblies retaining the driver's side air bag module to the steering wheel.
4. Disconnect the air bag electrical connection from the air bag sliding contact connector.

❋❋ WARNING

Place the air bag module on a bench with the trim cover facing up.

5. Remove the driver's side air bag module from the steering wheel.
6. Disconnect the harness connector from the speed control.
7. Disconnect the horn switch wire.
8. Remove the retaining screws from the cruise control actuator switch.
9. Carefully pry away the right side of the steering wheel back cover to allow enough clearance to remove the right speed control switch wiring from the steering wheel. Repeat for the left side., then remove the actuator switch.

To install:

10. Position the cruise control actuator switch onto the steering wheel, then install the screws.

❋❋ CAUTION

Make sure that the wires are positioned so that there is no interference when installing the air bag module.

11. Connect all of the harness wiring, then route them into the steering wheel cavity. Install the wire organizer.
12. Position the driver's side air bag module on the steering wheel, then connect the air bag sliding contact.
13. Install the driver's side air bag module on the steering wheel, and install the screws and washers assemblies. Tighten to 8–10 ft. lbs. (10–14 Nm).
14. Install the two back cover plugs.
15. Connect the positive battery cable.

16. Connect the negative battery cable.
17. Check the operation of the cruise control actuator switch.
18. Prove out the air bag system.

Speed Sensor

REMOVAL & INSTALLATION

▶ **See Figure 37**

1. Raise and safely support vehicle on jackstands.
2. Loosen the retaining nut holding the sensor in the transmission.
3. Remove the driven gear with the sensor from the transmission.
4. Disconnect the electrical connector from the speed sensor.
5. Disconnect the speedometer cable by pulling it out of the speed sensor.

➡**Do not attempt to remove the spring retainer clip with the speedometer in the sensor.**

To install:

6. Position the driven gear on the speed sensor. Install the gear retainer.
7. Connect the electrical connector.
8. Ensure that the internal O-ring is properly seated in the sensor housing. Snap the speedometer cable into the sensor housing.
9. Insert the sensor assembly into the transmission housing and tighten the retaining nut to 36–54 inch lbs. (4–6 Nm). Lower the vehicle and check system operation.

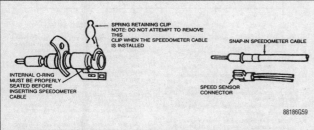

Fig. 37 The speed sensor is a vital part in the cruise control system

Amplifier

REMOVAL & INSTALLATION

The amplifier is located on the brake pedal on some models, and behind the glove box, under the evaporator housing on others.
1. Disconnect the negative battery cable.
2. Remove the amplifier assembly hardware.
3. Disconnect the 2 amplifier assembly electrical connectors.
4. Remove the amplifier assembly from the its mounting area.

To Install:

5. Place the amplifier assembly into position and connect the electrical connectors.
6. Install the amplifier assembly hardware. Tighten the amplifier to its mounting bracket to 12–21 inch lbs. (1–3 Nm).
7. Connect the negative battery cable.

Servo

REMOVAL & INSTALLATION

▶ **See Figure 38**

1. Disconnect the negative battery cable.
2. Disconnect the actuator cable from the accelerator cable.
3. Disconnect the servo wire at wiring harness connector near the radiator support.
4. Raise and safely support the left front side of vehicle on jackstands.

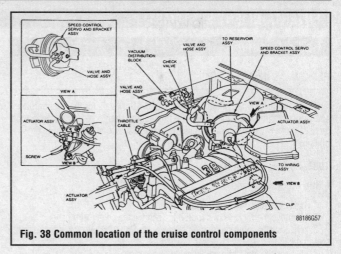

Fig. 38 Common location of the cruise control components

5. Remove the left front wheel and inner fender splash shield.
6. Remove the vacuum hoses from the servo assembly.
7. Remove the screws holding the servo mounting bracket to the brace.
8. Remove the nuts from the actuator cable cover at the servo. Remove the cable, cover and rubber boot.
9. Remove the nuts attaching the servo to the mounting bracket.

To install:

10. Attach the bolt assemblies two the front of the servo.
11. Attach the servo to mounting bracket with the nuts and tighten to 45–65 inch lbs. (5–7 Nm).
12. Install the servo rubber boot.
13. Attach the actuator cable to the servo plunger. Attach the cable cover to the servo with the nuts and tighten to 45–65 inch lbs. (5–7 Nm).
14. Attach the servo and bracket to the brace with screws.
15. Attach the vacuum hoses to the servo. Ensure that the vacuum hoses are connected in the correct position. Adjust the servo boot to protect the servo.
16. Install the inner fender splash shield, install the wheel and lower the vehicle.
17. Connect the servo wire harness connector near the radiator support.
18. Connect the speed control actuator cable to the accelerator cable.
19. Connect the negative battery cable and check system operation.

Vacuum Dump Valve

REMOVAL & INSTALLATION

▶ **See Figure 39**

1. Remove the vacuum hose from valve.
2. Remove the valve from the bracket.

To install:

3. Attach the valve to the bracket.
4. Attach the hose to the valve.
5. Adjust the vacuum dump valve so that it is closed (no vacuum leak) when the brake pedal is up (brakes released) and open when brake pedal is depressed.

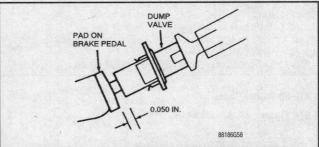

Fig. 39 The vacuum dump valve needs to be adjusted to allow no vacuum leaks in the system

ENTERTAINMENT SYSTEMS

Radio Receiver

REMOVAL & INSTALLATION

There are many types of radio, cassette and CD models for the Thunderbird and Cougars throughout the years. The procedures should be pretty standard on most of these types of units. However it is impossible to show you all of the units themselves.

1983–85 exc. Digital Radio

▶ See Figures 40 and 41

1. Disconnect the negative battery cable.
2. Remove the radio knobs (pull off). Remove the center trim panel.
3. Remove the radio mounting plate screws. Pull the radio towards the front seat to disengage it from the lower bracket.
4. Disconnect the radio and antenna connections.
5. Remove the radio. Remove the nuts and washers as necessary.
6. The rest of installation is the reverse of removal.

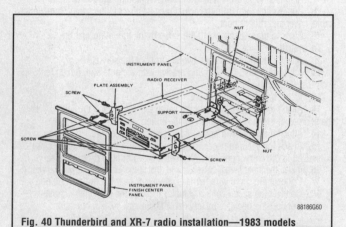

Fig. 40 Thunderbird and XR-7 radio installation—1983 models

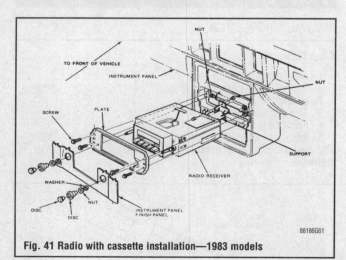

Fig. 41 Radio with cassette installation—1983 models

1983–88 Digital Radio

▶ See Figures 42, 43 and 44

1. Disconnect the negative battery cable.
2. Remove the center instrument trim panel.
3. Remove the 4 screws retaining the radio and mounting bracket to the instrument panel.

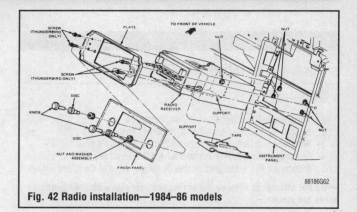

Fig. 42 Radio installation—1984–86 models

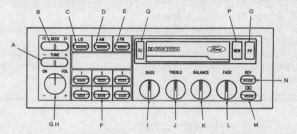

The features described are identical on all the radios (where applicable).

A. **Tune** up or down to the next channel (.2 mHz in FM, 10 kHz in AM).

B. **Seek** up or down to the next listenable station.

C. **LOCAL/DISTANT:** Toggles between local and Distant mode. Only displays LOC in Local mode (Distant mode not displayed). Local mode is for use in metropolitan areas and only on strong signal stations.

D. Pushing **AM** enables AM mode. AM will be displayed. Six AM memories.

E. Pushing **FM** enables FM mode. Pushing FM again will toggle between FM1 and FM2. Six FM memories in FM1 and another six in FM2. FM1 or FM2 will be displayed.

F. To store a station depress **MEMORY** button and hold for two seconds (sound will disappear and come back after two seconds). To recall a station, depress MEMORY button and release.

G. **VOLUME/ON-OFF:** (Thunderbird/Cougar), Push to turn on, push again to turn off. Turn control clockwise to increase volume.

H. **VOLUME/ON-OFF/CLOCK CONTROL:** (Mustang), Rotate to turn on radio and increase volume. Push to change display mode or push and hold to set time. Refer to clock operation.

I. **BASS:** Rotate clockwise for more bass and counterclockwise for less bass.

J. **TREBLE:** Rotate clockwise for more treble and counterclockwise for less treble.

K. **BALANCE:** Adjusts sound between LH side and RH side of vehicle.

L. **FADE:** Adjusts sound between front and rear of vehicle.

M. **DOLBY:** Press for playing tapes recorded using the Dolby® System. Press again to deactivate.

N. **REVERSE:** Press to change direction of cassette tape.

O. **FAST FORWARD:** Press to fast advance the program being played.

P. **FAST REWIND:** Press to change direction of tape and fast rewind.

Q. **EJECT:** Press to eject cassette.

Fig. 43 Electronic radio with cassette—1988 shown

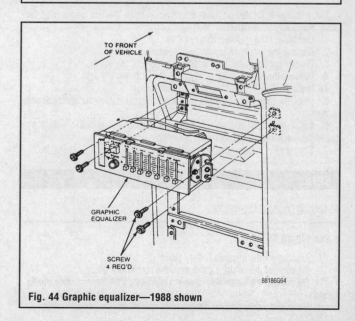

Fig. 44 Graphic equalizer—1988 shown

4. Push the radio forward and raise the back end slightly to clear the clip in the panel. Pull the radio out slowly.

5. Disconnect the antenna and wiring.

To install:

6. Attach the antenna and wiring to back of the unit..

7. Insert the radio into the dash, tighten the mounting screws to the bracket to retain the unit.

8. Connect the negative battery cable.

9. Test the unit for proper operation

10. If the system works well, install the center trim panel.

1989–97 Radio and Tape Player

▶ **See Figures 45 thru 50**

➡ **A special tool, number T87P–19061–A or equivalent, must be used in order to remove radio components with out damage to unit.**

1. Disconnect negative battery cable.

2. Insert two removal tools T87P–19061–A or equivalent into the radio face plates holes, until tension of spring clips is felt.

3. Flex outward on both sides simultaneously and pull radio out.

4. Disconnect wiring connectors and antenna cable.

To install:

5. Attach the antenna and wiring to back of the unit..

6. Insert the radio into the dash, then push on the radio until the clips "click".

7. Connect the negative battery cable.

8. Test the unit for proper operation

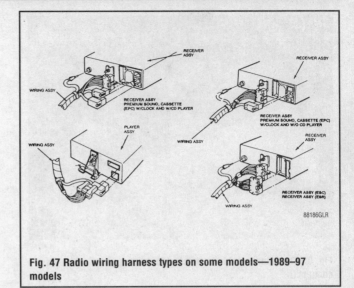

Fig. 47 Radio wiring harness types on some models—1989–97 models

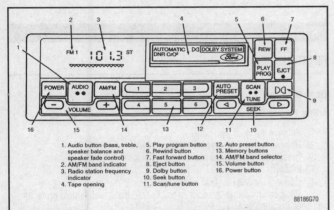

1. Audio button (bass, treble, speaker balance and speaker fade control)
2. AM/FM band indicator
3. Radio station frequency indicator
4. Tape opening
5. Play program button
6. Rewind button
7. Fast forward button
8. Eject button
9. Dolby button
10. Seek button
11. Scan/tune button
12. Auto preset button
13. Memory buttons
14. AM/FM band selector
15. Volume button
16. Power button

Fig. 45 Premium Analog Cassette (PAC) and CCDJ radio chassis assembly—1995 models

Fig. 48 Using the special radio removal tool, detach the unit from the dash

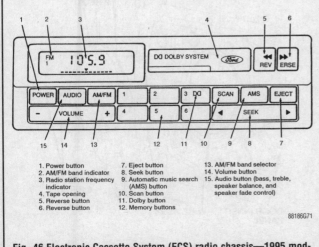

1. Power button
2. AM/FM band indicator
3. Radio station frequency indicator
4. Tape opening
5. Reverse button
6. Reverse button
7. Eject button
8. Seek button
9. Automatic music search (AMS) button
10. Scan button
11. Dolby button
12. Memory buttons
13. AM/FM band selector
14. Volume button
15. Audio button (bass, treble, speaker balance, and speaker fade control)

Fig. 46 Electronic Cassette System (ECS) radio chassis—1995 models

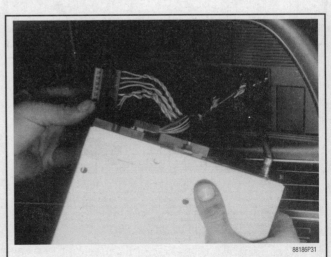

Fig. 49 Pull the electrical harness from the back of the radio assembly

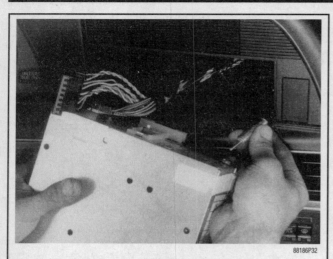

Fig. 50 The antenna cable is attached to the rear of the radio, disconnect it

CD Player

DASH MOUNTED

▶ See Figures 51 and 52

1. Disconnect negative battery cable.

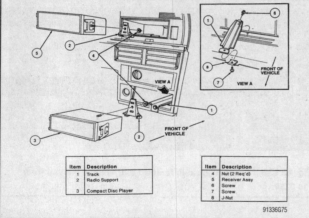

Item	Description
1	Track
2	Radio Support
3	Compact Disc Player

Item	Description
4	Nut (2 Req'd)
5	Receiver Assy
6	Screw
7	Screw
8	J-Nut

91336G75

Fig. 51 CD, radio, tape player assembly mounted in the dash—1989–93 models

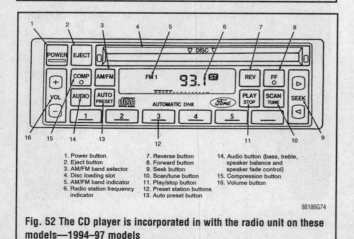

1. Power button
2. Eject button
3. AM/FM band selector
4. Disc loading slot
5. AM/FM band indicator
6. Radio station frequency indicator
7. Reverse button
8. Forward button
9. Seek button
10. Scan/tune button
11. Play/stop button
12. Preset station buttons
13. Auto preset button
14. Audio button (bass, treble, speaker balance and speaker fade control)
15. Compression button
16. Volume button

88186G74

Fig. 52 The CD player is incorporated in with the radio unit on these models—1994–97 models

2. Insert two removal tools T87P–19061–A or equivalent into holes, until tension of spring clips is felt.
3. Flex outward on both sides simultaneously and pull CD player out.
4. Disconnect wiring connectors and ground strap.
5. Remove rear support

➡**If gear shift on console interferes with removal and installation, set parking brake and place in L1 or L2 for automatic transmission and 2nd or 4th gear for manual transmission.**

To install:
6. Install the rear support.
7. Connect the wiring and ground strap for the radio unit.
8. Insert the radio/CD player unit into the dash, until the clips "click".
9. Connect the negative battery cable.
10. Test the system.

TRUNK MOUNTED

1. Remove the luggage compartment trim covers.
2. Remove the bolts, nuts and washers retaining the digital CD player bracket-to-body.
3. Disconnect the wiring and remove the CD player and bracket assembly.
To install:
4. Connect the wiring and install the CD player and bracket assembly to the vehicle.
5. Install the bolts, nuts and washers retaining the digital CD player bracket-to-body.
6. Install the luggage compartment trim covers.
7. Test the system.

Speakers

REMOVAL & INSTALLATION

Door Mounted

▶ See Figure 53

1. Remove the door trim panel.
2. Remove the four speaker retaining screws.
3. Disconnect the speaker lead wire connector and remove speaker.
To Install:
4. Connect the speaker lead wire connector.
5. Position speaker to the door panel. Ensure that a watershield protector has been installed first.
6. Install attaching screws.
7. Install door panel on door and check speaker operation.

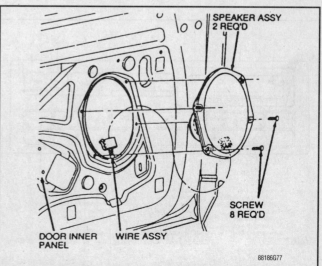

Fig. 53 Door mounted speakers are typically the same on most models

Rear Quarter Mounted

▶ **See Figures 54 and 55**

1. Remove the screws or unsnap retaining speaker grille cover and remove the cover.
2. Remove the screws retaining the speaker to mount.
3. Disconnect the speaker lead wire connector and remove speaker.

To install:

4. Connect the speaker lead to the unit.
5. Insert the speaker into the quarter panel, then tighten the mounting screws to 24–32 inch lbs. (2–4 Nm).
6. Place the speaker cover into position and snap shut or screw tight.
7. Check the operation of the speaker.

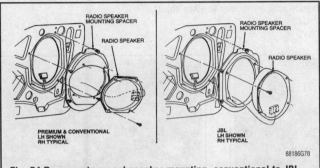

Fig. 54 Rear quarter panel speaker mounting, conventional to JBL types

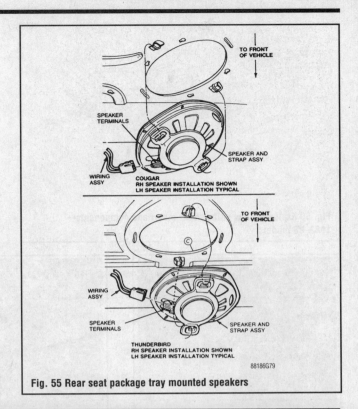

Fig. 55 Rear seat package tray mounted speakers

WINDSHIELD WIPERS

Wiper Blade and Arm

REMOVAL & INSTALLATION

▶ **See Figures 56, 57 and 58**

➡ **To prevent damage, do not pry arm from pivot with metal or sharp tool.**

Raise the blade end of the arm off the windshield and move the slide latch away from the pivot shaft. This will unlock the wiper arm from the pivot shaft and hold the blade end of the arm off of the glass at the same time. The wiper arm can now be pulled off of the pivot shaft without the aid of any tools.

To install, position the auxiliary arm over the pivot pin, (on 1989 and later models align the keyway on the pivot shaft) hold it down and push the main arm head over the pivot shaft. Ensure pivot shaft is in position, and that the blade assembly is positioned to the correct dimension. Hold the main arm head onto the pivot shaft while raising the blade end of the wiper arm and push the slide latch into the lock under the pivot shaft. Then, lower the blade to the windshield.

If the blade does not touch the windshield, the slide latch is not completely in place.

Windshield Wiper Motor

REMOVAL & INSTALLATION

1983–88 Models

▶ **See Figure 59**

1. Turn the ignition switch to the **ON** position. Turn the wiper switch on. When the blades are straight up on the windshield, turn the key switch **OFF**.
2. Disconnect the negative battery cable. Remove the arm and blade assemblies.
3. Remove the left side leaf guard screen or cowl assembly. Disconnect the linkage drive arm from the wiper motor after removing the retaining clip.
4. Disconnect the electrical wiring harness connector from the wiper motor. Remove the wiper motor mounting bolts and the motor.

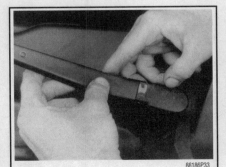

Fig. 56 Raise the wiper arm off of the windshield

Fig. 57 Move the slide latch away from the pivot shaft. This will unlock the wiper arm from the pivot shaft

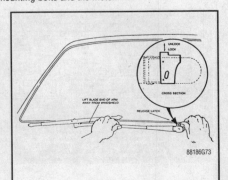

Fig. 58 Removing the wiper arm and blade from the pivot shaft with the release latch

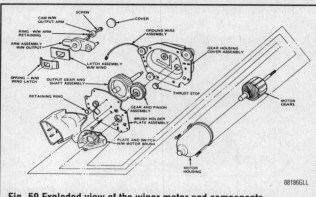

Fig. 59 Exploded view of the wiper motor and components—1983–88 models

5. Install in the reverse order of removal. Before installing the arm and blade assemblies, turn on the key and allow the motor to cycle. Turn the wiper control switch off so that the drives and motor will stop in the park position. Install the arm and blade assemblies.

6. Check the operation of the system.

1989–97 Models

▶ See Figures 60 thru 69

1. Disconnect the negative battery cable. With the wipers in the **PARK** position remove the arm and blade assemblies.

➡The internal permanent magnets used in the wiper motor are a ceramic (glass-like) material. Care must be exercised in handling the motor to avoid damaging the magnets. The motor must not be struck or tapped with a hammer or other object.

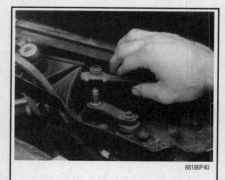

Fig. 60 Remove the cowl vent seal if necessary

Fig. 61 Unscrew the cowl vent screen

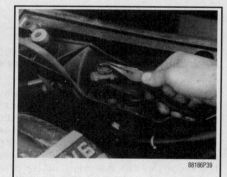

Fig. 62 Detach the vacuum lines from the wiper module

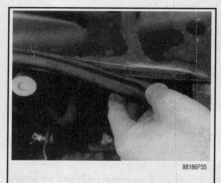

Fig. 63 Unbolt the wiper module . . .

Fig. 64 . . . then remove the wiper module from the vehicle

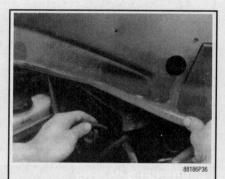

Fig. 65 Remove the wiper linkage clip from the crank arm

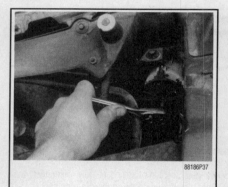

Fig. 66 Lift the linkage off the shaft

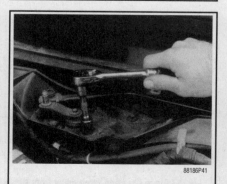

Fig. 67 Unbolt the motor

Fig. 68 Detach the wiring harness from the motor . . .

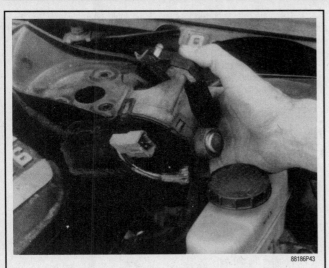

Fig. 69 . . . then lift the motor out of the engine compartment

2. Remove the cowl vent screens. On some models it may be necessary to remove the cowl top extension-to-hood seal.

3. Remove vacuum manifolds from wiper module.

4. Disconnect wiring connections.

5. Remove the screws and nut from wiper module, then remove the wiper module.

6. Disconnect the linkage drive arm from the motor crankpin after removing the clip.

7. Remove the wiper motor's three attaching nuts. Pull the motor from the opening.

➡ **Before installing the arm and blade assembly on the pivot shaft, cycle motor and turn off switch to ensure that it is in PARK position.**

To install:

8. Position the wiper in the cowl, then install the retaining bolts and nuts. Tighten the bolts to 91–122 inch lbs. (10–14 Nm).

9. Connect the windshield wiper mounting arm and pivot shaft to the windshield wiper motor. Ensure the clip is on the motor mounting arm and pivot shaft and is then secured to the motor. Install the mounting arm and pivot shaft by pulling until the clip snaps into place.

10. Installation is reverse of removal. Check the operation of the system.

Washer Pump and Reservoir

REMOVAL & INSTALLATION

1. Remove the washer pump retaining screws.
2. Remove the reservoir hose to drain the fluid.
3. Disconnect the electrical connection.
4. Remove the washer reservoir from the vehicle.
5. Remove the pump from the reservoir.

To install:

6. Install the pump into the grommet. Check for deterioration of the grommet.
7. Secure the reservoir to the vehicle.
8. Connect the electrical wiring to the pump and attach the hose.
9. Check the operation of the unit.

INSTRUMENTS AND SWITCHES

Instrument Cluster

REMOVAL & INSTALLATION

✳✳ WARNING

Extreme care must be exercised during the removal and installation of the instrument cluster and dash components to avoid damage or breakage. Wooden paddles should be used to separate dash components, if required. Tape or cover dash areas that may be damaged by the removal and installation of the dash components.

During the removal and installation procedures, slight variations may be required from the general outline, to facilitate the removal and installation of the instrument panel and cluster components, due to slight changes from model year to model year.

1983 Models

STANDARD CLUSTER

▸ **See Figure 70**

1. Disconnect the negative battery cable.
2. Disconnect the speedometer cable.
3. Remove the instrument panel trim cover and steering column lower shroud.
4. Remove the attaching screw holding the transmission indicator quadrant cable bracket to the steering column. Disconnect the cable loop from the pin on the steering column.
5. Remove the cluster retaining screws.
6. Remove the cluster from the instrument panel.
7. Reverse the removal procedure to install.

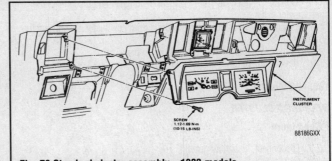

Fig. 70 Standard cluster assembly—1983 models

ELECTRONIC CLUSTER

▸ **See Figure 71**

1. Disconnect the negative battery cable.
2. Remove the instrument panel trim cover and steering column lower shroud.
3. Remove the cluster retaining screws.
4. Remove the attaching screw holding the transmission indicator quadrant cable bracket to the steering column. Disconnect the cable loop from the pin on the steering column.
5. Pull the cluster away from the instrument panel and disconnect the speedometer cable.
6. Disconnect the electrical connections from the cluster. Disconnect the ground wire.
7. Remove the cluster from the instrument panel.
8. Reverse the removal procedure to install.

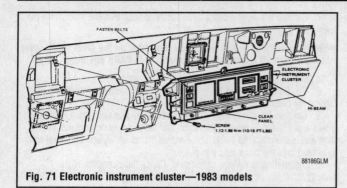

Fig. 71 Electronic instrument cluster—1983 models

1984 Models

STANDARD CLUSTER

1. Disconnect the battery ground.
2. Remove the steering column shroud.
3. Remove the 4 cluster trim retaining screws and lift off the trim.
4. Remove the 6 cluster-to-instrument panel screws.
5. Pull the cluster out and disconnect the speedometer cable.
6. Disconnect the electrical connectors and remove the cluster.
7. Installation is the reverse of removal.

ELECTRONIC CLUSTER

1. Disconnect the negative battery cable.
2. Remove the 4 lower instrument panel trim cover screws.
3. Remove the steering column cover.
4. Remove the 6 cluster trim panel retaining screws.
5. Remove the 4 cluster-to-instrument panel attaching screws.
6. Remove the attaching screw from the transmission selector cable bracket. Disconnect the cable loop from the pin on the steering column.
7. Pull the cluster away from the instrument panel and disconnect the speedometer cable.
8. Disconnect the electrical connections from the cluster. Disconnect the ground wire.
9. Remove the cluster from the instrument panel.
10. Reverse the removal procedure to install.

1985–88 Models

STANDARD CLUSTER

▶ See Figure 72

1. Disconnect the battery ground.
2. Remove the 2 lower trim covers.
3. Remove the steering column cover.

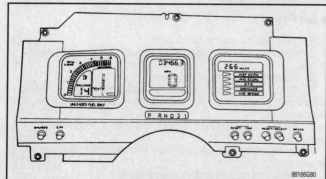

Fig. 72 Base electronic instrument cluster non-turbo coupe—1984–88

4. Disconnect the shift selector bracket and cable assembly from the column.
5. Move the shift lever and remove the cluster trim panel.
6. Remove the 4 cluster mounting screws.
7. Pull the bottom of the cluster toward the steering wheel.
8. Reach behind the cluster and unplug the 2 connectors.
9. Swing the bottom of the cluster out and remove the cluster.
10. Install the components in the reverse order of removal.
11. Check the operation of the system.

TURBO COUPE CLUSTER

▶ See Figure 73

1. Disconnect the battery ground.
2. Remove the steering column shroud.
3. Remove the 10 cluster trim screws and lift off the trim.
4. Remove the 4 cluster-to-instrument panel screws and pull the cluster out slightly.
5. Disconnect the cluster connectors.
6. Pull the boost gauge rubber tube off of the gauge nipple.
7. Remove the cluster.

To install:

8. Install the cluster in the dash.
9. Attach the boost gauge rubber tube onto the gauge nipple.
10. Attach the cluster connectors.
11. Secure the 4 cluster-to-instrument panel screws.
12. Tighten the 10 cluster trim screws.
13. Install the steering column shroud.
14. Connect the battery ground.
15. Check the operation of the system.

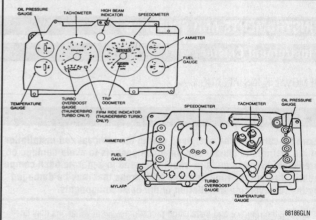

Fig. 73 Analog Thunderbird Coupe and Cougar/Thunderbird with 5.0L—1988

ELECTRONIC CLUSTER

▶ See Figure 74

1. Disconnect the negative battery cable.
2. Remove the 2 lower instrument panel trim covers.
3. Remove the steering column cover.
4. Disconnect the shift selector bracket and cable at the column.
5. Move the shift lever and remove the cluster trim panel.
6. Remove the 4 cluster-to-instrument panel attaching screws.
7. Pull the bottom of the cluster toward the steering wheel.
8. Reach behind the cluster and disconnect the electrical connections.
9. Swing the bottom of the cluster out and away from the instrument panel.
10. Installation is the reverse of removal.

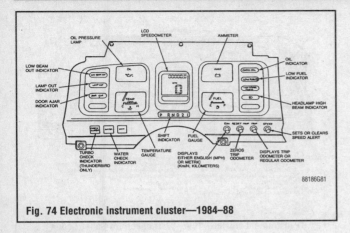

Fig. 74 Electronic instrument cluster—1984–88

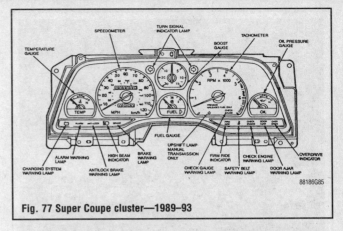

Fig. 77 Super Coupe cluster—1989–93

1989–93 Models

STANDARD CLUSTER

▶ **See Figures 75 thru 80**

1. Disconnect negative battery cable.
2. Remove two retaining screws from cluster trim panel and remove panel.
3. Remove four cluster mounting screws, and pull bottom of cluster toward steering wheel.
4. Reaching behind and underneath cluster, unplug two connectors. For Super Coupe and XR-7 disconnect vacuum line for boost gauge.

5. Swing bottom of cluster out to clear top of steering column shroud and remove.
6. Installation is reverse of removal by inserting top of cluster, under crash pad leaving the bottom out, first.

ELECTRONIC CLUSTER

➡**The electronics with in the cluster are not serviceable. The cluster should be disassembled only to repair plastic defects or servicing other components where the cluster has to be removed to gain access to the component(s).**

1. Disconnect negative battery cable.
2. Remove headlamp knob.
3. Remove cluster finish panel by removing two screws on upper inside surface.
4. Carefully pull away finish panel while detaching spring clips surrounding the finish panel.
5. Unplug connector on rear of switch assembly. If equipped, disconnect autolamp module.

➡**To prevent scratching and or damage to cluster assembly and steering column shroud, place a clean, soft cloth over steering column shroud, and lens of cluster assembly.**

6. Remove the four cluster retaining screws, and pull bottom of cluster towards steering wheel.
7. Reaching behind and underneath cluster unplug two connectors.

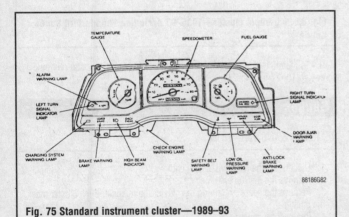

Fig. 75 Standard instrument cluster—1989–93

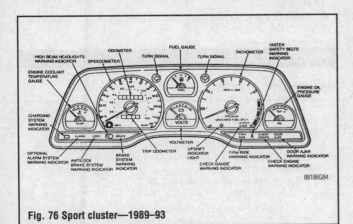

Fig. 76 Sport cluster—1989–93

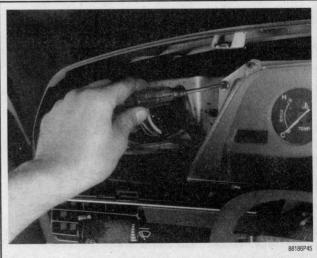

Fig. 78 Remove the attaching screws for the instrument cluster

Fig. 79 Lift the instrument cluster from the dash

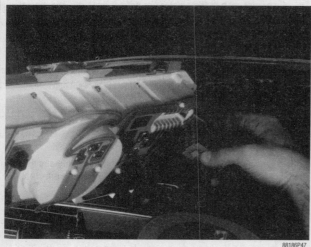

Fig. 80 Detach the harnesses in the back of the instrument cluster

8. Swing bottom of cluster out to clear top from crash pad and remove.

9. Installation is reverse of removal by inserting top of cluster, under crash pad leaving the bottom out, first.

1994–97 Models

▶ **See Figures 81 and 82**

1. Disconnect the negative battery cable.
2. Remove the screws holding the instrument panel reinforcement.
3. Remove the screws holding the instrument panel lower shield.
4. Remove the fasteners that hold the steering wheel column. Gently lower the steering column.
5. Remove the fasteners that hold the instrument panel finish panel, then gently pry it off.
6. Remove the four cluster retaining screws. Do not remove the screws from the instrument panel main lens and cluster mask.
7. Slide the cluster to the right of the panel opening and unhook the panel harness from the back of the cluster.
8. Remove the instrument cluster from the panel.

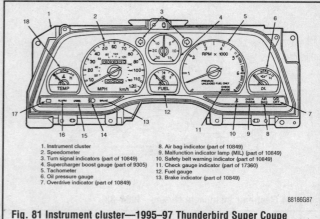

1. Instrument cluster
2. Speedometer
3. Turn signal indicators (part of 10849)
4. Supercharger boost gauge (part of 9305)
5. Tachometer
6. Oil pressure gauge
7. Overdrive indicator (part of 10849)
8. Air bag indicator (part of 10849)
9. Malfunction indicator lamp (MIL) (part of 10849)
10. Safety belt warning indicator (part of 10849)
11. Check gauge indicator (part of 17360)
12. Fuel gauge
13. Brake indicator (part of 10849)

Fig. 81 Instrument cluster—1995–97 Thunderbird Super Coupe

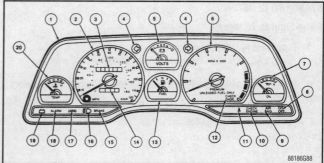

Fig. 82 Instrument cluster—1995–97 excluding Thunderbird Super Coupe

9. To install, reverse the removal procedure, Tighten the cluster retaining screws to 18–27 inch lbs. (2–3 Nm).

Gauges

REMOVAL & INSTALLATION

1. Disconnect the negative battery cable.
2. Remove the instrument cluster assembly.
3. Remove the screws retaining the cluster main lens and the cluster mask on the cluster.
4. Remove the gauge.

To install:

5. Install the components in the reverse order of removal.
6. Check the operation of the gauge.

Windshield Wiper Switch

REMOVAL & INSTALLATION

1. Disconnect the negative battery cable.
2. Remove the split steering column cover retaining screws.
3. Separate the two halves and remove the wiper switch retaining screws.
4. Disconnect the wire connector and remove the wiper switch.

To install:

5. Attach the wire connector to the wiper switch.
6. Attach the wiper switch to the column unit with the mounting screws.

7. Install the split steering column.
8. Connect the negative battery cable.

Headlight Switch

REMOVAL & INSTALLATION

1983–84 Models

1. Disconnect the negative battery cable.
2. Pull the switch to the full **ON** position.
3. Reach up under the instrument panel and, while depressing the release button, pull the knob out of the switch.
4. Unscrew the switch bezel and pull the switch from the instrument panel.
5. Unplug the wiring.
6. Installation is the reverse of removal.

1985–88 Models

▶ **See Figure 83**

1. Disconnect the negative battery cable.
2. Remove the headlamp switch lens screws and lift off the lens.
3. Remove the switch attaching screws and pull the switch out from the instrument panel.

➡ **On cars equipped with Auto Lamp/Auto Dimmer, remove the control.**

4. Disconnect the wiring and remove the switch.
To install:
5. Attach the wiring to the switch assembly.
6. Install the switch to the instrument panel with the retaining screws.
7. Install the headlamp switch lens.
8. Connect the negative battery cable.

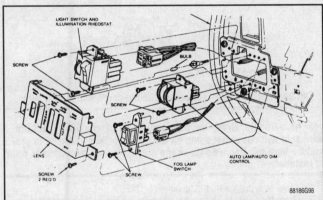

Fig. 83 Exploded view of the headlamp switch and associated components—1987 shown

1989–92 Models

▶ **See Figure 84**

1. Disconnect the negative battery cable.
2. Remove the two cluster finish panel retaining screws.
3. Pull off the headlamp switch knob.
4. Remove the cluster finish panel. It snaps off. Disconnect electrical connector to dimmer sensor assembly.

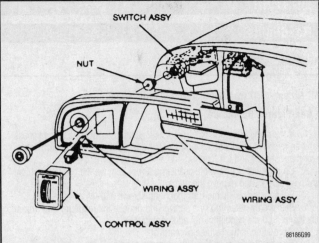

Fig. 84 The headlamp switch is mounted on the driver's side of the instrument panel—1988–92 models

5. Using the opening in the instrument panel, depress the shaft release button on switch and remove shaft.
6. Remove headlamp switch retaining nut and pull switch through opening to disconnect the wiring connector.
7. Installation is the reverse of removal.

Back-up Light Switch

REMOVAL & INSTALLATION

➡ **Before replacing a back-up light switch, be sure to check the condition of the bulbs first.**

Since all back-up light switches are operated by the transmission shift lever, replacement procedures differ according to mounting location of the selector lever and type of transmission used.

Column Mounted Automatic Transmission

1. Disconnect the back-up light switch wires at the plug connector. On vehicles so equipped, disconnect the two parking brake release vacuum hoses.
2. Remove the two screws, securing the back-up light switch to the steering column and lift the switch from the column.
3. Check column to ensure that the metal switch actuator is secured to the shift tube and that it is seated as far forward against the shift tube bearing as possible. Also check for a broken or damaged actuator.

➡ **Before installing a new switch, check to see that the drive position gauge is inserted in the drive pinning hole. If the pin is missing, align the two holes on top of switch and install a No. 43 drill or a 0.092–0.093 in. (2.34–2.36mm) gauge pin.**

4. While holding the selector lever against the stop in the drive detent position, place the switch on the column and install the two attaching screws.
5. Remove the gauge pin (or equivalent). Connect switch wires to plug connector and connect the two parking brake release vacuum hoses (if equipped).

Manual Transmission

Refer to Section 7.

LIGHTING

Headlights

REMOVAL & INSTALLATION

All Except 1987 and Later Aerodynamic Headlamps

▶ See Figures 85 and 86

1. If the car is equipped with movable headlamp covers, close the bypass valve to raise the headlamp covers. The valve is located in the vacuum lines near the reservoir and left fender.
2. On cars without movable headlamp doors, remove the headlamp door retaining screws and remove the doors.
3. Remove the headlamp trim mounting screws and remove the trim.
4. Remove the retaining ring screws and remove the retaining ring from the headlamp. Pull the headlamp out and unplug it.
5. Installation is the reverse of removal.
6. Turn the lights on to check for proper operation.

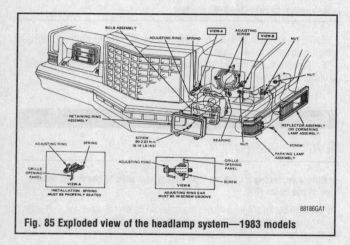

Fig. 85 Exploded view of the headlamp system—1983 models

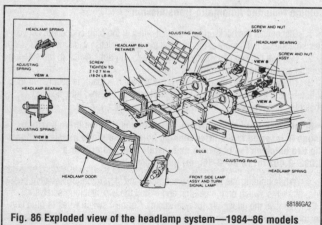

Fig. 86 Exploded view of the headlamp system—1984–86 models

1987–97 Aerodynamic Headlamps

BULB ASSEMBLY

▶ See Figures 87 and 88

✶✶ CAUTION

The halogen bulb contains pressurized gas. If the bulb is dropped or scratched it will shatter. Also, avoid touching the bulb glass with

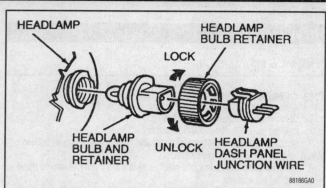

Fig. 87 The headlamp bulb on the aerodynamic type is retained with a bulb retainer ring

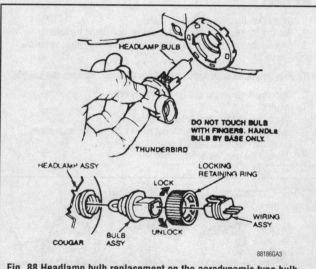

Fig. 88 Headlamp bulb replacement on the aerodynamic type bulb

your bare fingers. Grasp the bulb only by its plastic base. Oil from bare skin will cause hot spots on the glass surface and lead to premature burnout. If you do touch the glass, clean it with alcohol prior to installation.

1. Make sure that the headlamp switch is **OFF**.
2. Raise the hood. The bulb protrudes from the rear of the headlamp assembly.
3. Unplug the electrical connector from the bulb.
4. Rotate the bulb retaining ring ⅛ turn counterclockwise and remove it.
5. Pull the bulb straight back out of its socket. Don't rotate it.
To install:
6. When installing the bulb, push it into position, turning it slightly right or left to align the grooves in the forward part of the base with the tabs in the socket. When they are aligned, push the bulb firmly into position until the mounting flange on the base contacts the rear face of the socket.

➡When servicing the headlamp bulb, energize the bulb only while it is contained within the headlamp body.

7. Slip the bulb retaining ring over the plastic base until it contacts the rear of the socket. Lock the ring into the socket by rotating it clockwise until you feel a stop.
8. Push the connector onto the bulb until it snaps into position.
9. Turn the headlamps on and make sure that they work properly. If the headlamp was correctly aimed before replacement, you should not need to adjust it.

1988 MODELS

♦ See Figure 89

1. Make sure that the headlamp switch is **OFF**.
2. Raise the hood. The bulb protrudes from the rear of the headlamp assembly.
3. Unplug the electrical connector from the bulb.
4. Remove the 3 nuts and washers from the rear of the headlamp.
5. Push forward on the headlamp at the bulb socket. It may be necessary to loosen the parking lamp and cornering lamp fasteners.
6. Remove the 3 clips which attach the headlamp to the black ring by prying them out from the base with a flat-bladed screwdriver.
7. Installation is the reverse of removal. Make sure that the black rubber shield is securely crimped on the headlamp.
8. Turn the lights on to check for proper operation.

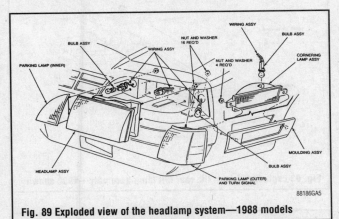

Fig. 89 Exploded view of the headlamp system—1988 models

1989–97 MODELS

♦ See Figure 90

1. Make sure the headlamp switch and time delay switch are in the off position.
2. Raise hood and disconnect wiring from each of the two bulbs.
3. Using snapring pliers, spread the three metal retainers attaching lamp assembly to grille opening panel, from the rear of panel. Pull straight upward to disengage and remove metal retainers.
4. Remove the lamp assembly from vehicle, then remove the bulbs. Reverse the procedure to install.
5. Turn the lights on to check for proper operation.

➡A correctly aimed headlamp normally need not be re-aimed after installation of a new bulb. A burned out bulb should not be removed from the headlamp until just before a replacement bulb is to be installed. Removal of bulb for an extended period of time may allow contaminants such as, dust, moisture, smoke, etc. to enter the headlamp body and affect performance of the headlamp.

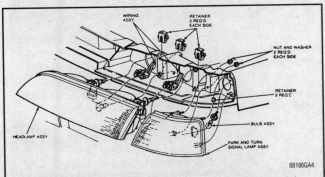

Fig. 90 Exploded view of the headlamp system—1989–97 models

AIMING

The headlights must be properly aimed to provide the best, safest road illumination. The lights should be checked for proper aim and adjusted as necessary. Certain state and local authorities have requirements for headlight aiming; these should be checked before adjustment is made.

Headlight adjustment may be temporarily made using a wall, as described below, or on the rear of another vehicle. When adjusted, the lights should not glare in oncoming car or truck windshields, nor should they illuminate the passenger compartment of vehicles driving in front of you. These adjustments are rough and should always be fine-tuned by a repair shop which is equipped with headlight aiming tools. Improper adjustments may be both dangerous and illegal.

For most vehicles, horizontal and vertical aiming of each sealed beam unit is provided by two adjusting screws which move the retaining ring and adjusting plate against the tension of a coil spring. There is no adjustment for focus; this is done during headlight manufacturing.

➡Because the composite headlight assembly is bolted into position, no adjustment should be necessary or possible. Some applications however may be bolted to an adjuster plate or may be retained used adjusting screws. If so, follow this procedure when adjusting the lights, BUT always have the adjustment checked by a reputable shop.

Before removing the headlight bulb or disturbing the headlamp in any way, note the current settings in order to make adjusting the headlights upon reassembly easier. If the high or low beam setting of the old lamp still works, this can be done using the wall of a garage or a building:

1. Park the vehicle on a level surface, with the fuel tank no more than ½ full and with the vehicle empty of all extra cargo (unless normally carried). The vehicle should be facing a wall which is no less the 6 feet high and 12 feet wide. The front of the vehicle should be about 25 feet from the wall.

➡The vehicle's fuel tank should be about half full when adjusting the headlights. Tires should be properly inflated.

2. If this is be performed outdoors, it is advisable to wait until dusk in order to properly see the headlight beams on the wall. If done in a garage, darken the area around the wall as much as possible by closing shades or hanging cloth over the windows.
3. Turn the headlights **ON** and mark the wall at the center of each light's low beam, then switch on the brights and mark the center of each light's high beam. A short length of masking tape which is visible from the front of the vehicle may be used. Although marking all 4 positions is advisable, marking 1 position from each light should be sufficient.
4. If neither beam on 1 side of the vehicle is working, park another like-sized vehicle in the exact spot where the car was and mark the beams using the same side light on that vehicle. Then switch the vehicle's so the car is back in the original spot. The vehicle must be parked no closer to or farther away from the wall than the second vehicle.
5. Perform the necessary repairs, but make sure the vehicle is not moved or is returned to the exact spot from which the lights were marked. Turn the headlights **ON** and adjust the beams to match the marks on the wall.
6. Have the headlight adjustment checked as soon as possible by a reputable repair shop.

Signal and Marker Lights

REMOVAL & INSTALLATION

Front Parking and Turn Signal Lamps

♦ See Figure 91

1. Remove the nuts that retain the lamp on the back of the fender.
2. Pull the lamp forward and remove the socket assembly. Slide the lamp from the vehicle.

To install:

3. Place the lamp socket into the lens assembly.
4. Insert the lamp assembly on the vehicle and tighten the mounting nuts.
5. Turn the lights on to check for proper operation.

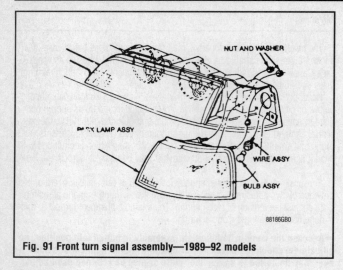

Fig. 91 Front turn signal assembly—1989–92 models

BULBS

To replace the bulbs on the 1983 XR-7, reach behind the bumper and remove the socket from the lamp to replace the bulb. On the 1983 Thunderbird, reach behind the lamp and remove the 4 attaching nuts. Pull the lamp out and remove the screw from the parking lamp and the nut from the headlamp cover. Replace the bulb. On the 1984–87 models, reach behind the fender and remove the 2 nuts securing the assembly to the fender, pull out the assembly and replace the bulb.

Rear Turn Signal, Brake and Parking Lamps

BUTYL SEAL TYPE

To remove the rear tail lamp lens on some models, you need to only carefully pry off the lens from the lamp body. These types of lenses are attached with a butyl seal. When you remove the lens, be sure to clean all of the old seal from the lamp body prior to applying more sealer. Once the new sealer is applied, press the lens on the body firmly and hold for approximately 10–20 seconds. Do not apply pressure to the middle of the lens, this could cause the lens to break from the pressure.

RETAINED TYPE

▶ See Figures 92 thru 98

1. Remove the luggage compartment front cover as necessary.
2. Remove the nuts that attach the rear lamp to the lower back panel.
3. Remove the lamp from the vehicle.

To install:

4. Place the lamp into position. Tighten the nuts to 3–5 ft. lbs. (4–7 Nm).
5. Install the luggage compartment front cover.
6. Turn the lights on to check for proper operation.

All bulb sockets can be accessed from inside the trunk. In some models, the trunk trim panel will have to be removed first. To remove lamp assembly, remove retaining nuts from inside luggage compartment pull out all bulb sockets and remove assembly. Check sealant gaskets before reinstallation of assembly.

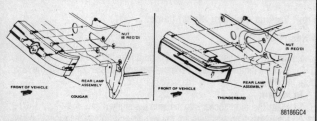

Fig. 92 Exploded view of the rear tail lamp assembly—1983–87 models

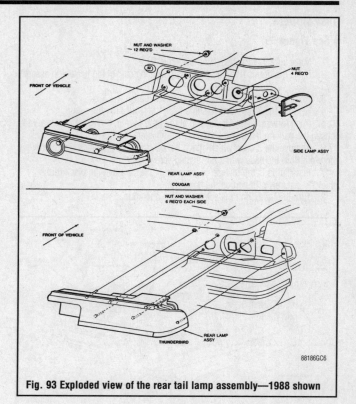

Fig. 93 Exploded view of the rear tail lamp assembly—1988 shown

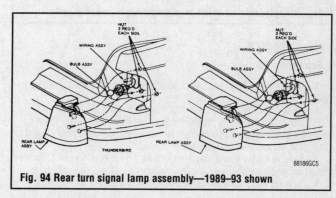

Fig. 94 Rear turn signal lamp assembly—1989–93 shown

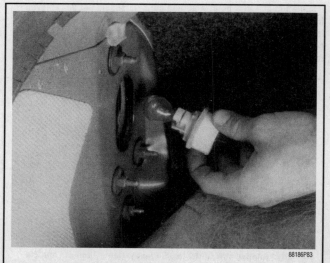

Fig. 95 Turn the rear bulb socket to release it from the lamp unit

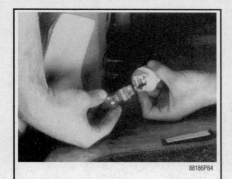

Fig. 96 Pull the bulb from the socket to replace

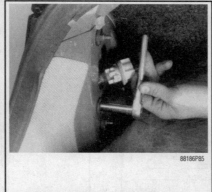

Fig. 97 Unbolt the rear side marker . . .

Fig. 98 . . . pull the lamp from the outside of the vehicle to remove

High Mount Stop Light

1986–88 MODELS

▶ See Figures 99 and 100

1. Using a thin-bladed screwdriver, remove the lamp screw covers.
2. Remove the 2 lamp retaining screws.

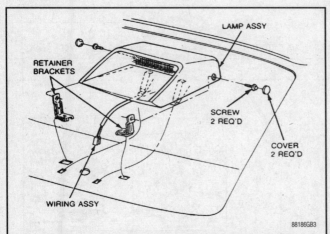

Fig. 99 Exploded view of the high mount lamp system—1986–88 Thunderbird

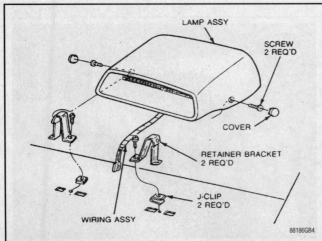

Fig. 100 Exploded view of the high mount lamp system—1986–88 Cougar

3. Lift the lamp up and out of the brackets.
4. To replace the bulb, turn the socket 45° counterclockwise.
5. Turn the lights on to check for proper operation.

1989–97 MODELS

▶ See Figure 101

1. Slide cover away from back window and remove cover.

➡If only bulb replacement is necessary, base removal is not required, go to step No. 4.

2. Remove one screw attaching lamp base.
3. Lift edge of base and pull away from back window.
4. Rotate and remove the two bulb and socket assemblies from lamp base.
5. Installation is the reverse of removal.
6. Turn the lights on to check for proper operation.

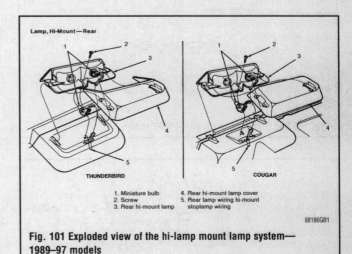

Fig. 101 Exploded view of the hi-lamp mount lamp system—1989–97 models

Fog Lamps

▶ See Figures 102, 103, 104 and 105

1. Disconnect the headlamp dash panel junction wire from the fog lamp assembly.
2. Remove the two screws that retain the fog lamps.
3. Pull the fog lamps from the front bumper.

To install:

4. Install the fog lamp to the front bumper, tighten the screws to 13–20 ft. lbs. (17–27 Nm).
5. Attach the junction wire to the lamp assembly.
6. Turn the lights on to check for proper operation.

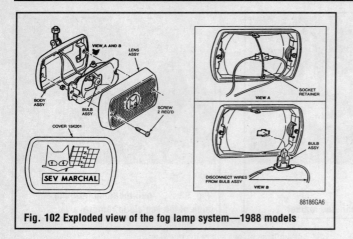

Fig. 102 Exploded view of the fog lamp system—1988 models

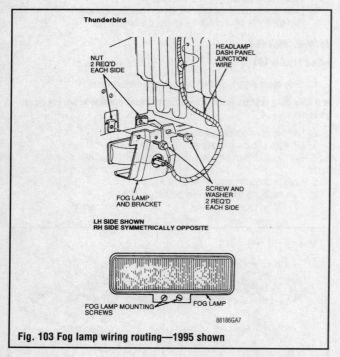

Fig. 103 Fog lamp wiring routing—1995 shown

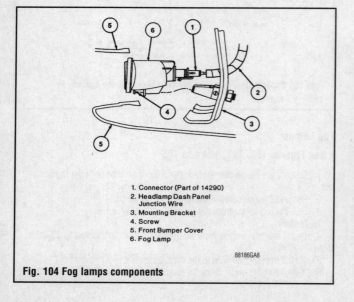

1. Connector (Part of 14290)
2. Headlamp Dash Panel Junction Wire
3. Mounting Bracket
4. Screw
5. Front Bumper Cover
6. Fog Lamp

Fig. 104 Fog lamps components

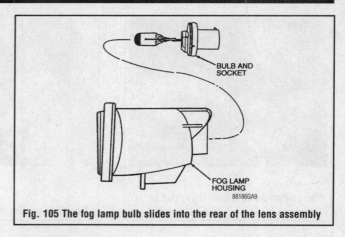

Fig. 105 The fog lamp bulb slides into the rear of the lens assembly

Dome/Map Lamp

CEILING MOUNTED

▶ See Figures 106, 107 and 108

1. Carefully squeeze the lens inwards to release the locking tabs.
2. Remove the lens from the lamp body.

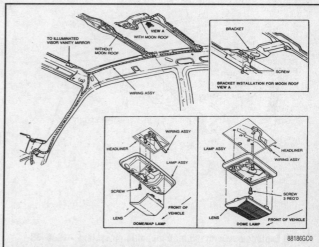

Fig. 106 Exploded view of the dome lamp with and without map light—1983–88 models

Fig. 107 Unsnap the lens off of the ceiling mounting area

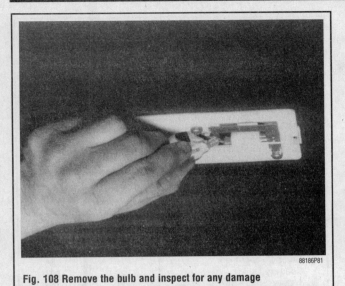

Fig. 108 Remove the bulb and inspect for any damage

3. Pull the wedge base bulb directly out of its socket.
4. Remove the screws that retain the lamp assembly to its mounting area.
5. Lower the lamp assembly, then replace the bulbs from the rear of the lamp.
6. Install in the reverse order of removal.
7. Check the operation of the lamp for proper operation.

WITHOUT MAP LIGHTS

1. Carefully remove the dome lamp lens from the housing.
2. Remove the lamp screws retaining the unit to the body of the vehicle.
3. Replace the bulb if necessary.
To install:
4. Install the lamp unit to the ceiling of the vehicle and tighten the mounting screws.
5. Install the lens to the housing.

WITHOUT SLIDING ROOF

▶ **See Figure 109**

1. Carefully pry the pillar/dome lamp lens from the lamp using a flatbladed tool.
2. Remove the screws retaining the lamp to the roof panel.
3. Lower the lamp, then remove the reflector heatshield and miniature bulb from the rear of the lamp.

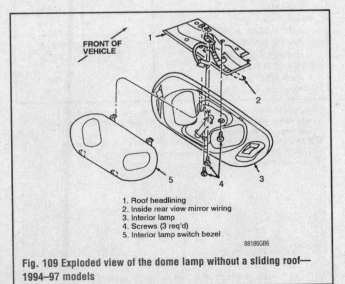

FRONT OF VEHICLE

1. Roof headlining
2. Inside rear view mirror wiring
3. Interior lamp
4. Screws (3 req'd)
5. Interior lamp switch bezel

Fig. 109 Exploded view of the dome lamp without a sliding roof—1994–97 models

To install:
4. Install a new bulb if required, then attach the reflector heatshield to the lamp assembly.
5. Install the lamp assembly to the roof panel.
6. Place the lens into position and carefully snap it in.
7. Check the operation of the lamp.

WITH SLIDING ROOF

▶ **See Figure 110**

1. Carefully pry the pillar/dome lamp lens from the lamp using a flatbladed tool.
2. Carefully pry the switch bezel from the lamp assembly.
3. Remove the screws retaining the lamp to the interior roof.
4. Lower the lamp, then remove miniature bulb from the rear of the lamp.
To install:
5. Install a new bulb if required.
6. Install the lamp assembly on the roof panel. Install the switch bezel on the lamp assembly.
7. Place the lens into position and carefully snap it in.
8. Check the operation of the lamp.

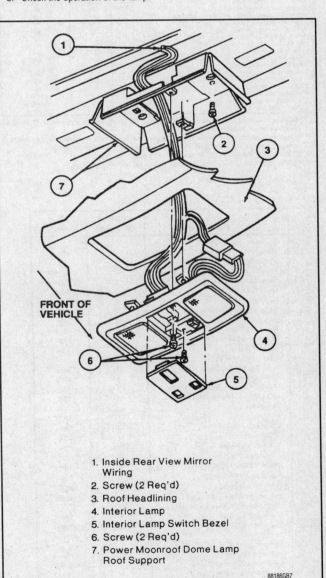

FRONT OF VEHICLE

1. Inside Rear View Mirror Wiring
2. Screw (2 Req'd)
3. Roof Headlining
4. Interior Lamp
5. Interior Lamp Switch Bezel
6. Screw (2 Req'd)
7. Power Moonroof Dome Lamp Roof Support

Fig. 110 Exploded view of the dome lamp with a sliding roof—1994–97 models

Table 1 (88186C50)

Function	Number of Bulbs	Trade Number
Exterior Illumination		
Headlamps — Lo Beam	2	H4656**
Headlamps — Hi Beam	2	H4651
Front Park/Turn	2	1157
Front Side Marker	2	194
Rear Side Marker	2	194
Back-Up Light	2	1156
High Mount Stop Lamp	2	912
License Plate	2	194
Tail/Stop/Turn	4	157
Cornering (Opt.)	2	1156
Ornament (Coach) (Opt.)	2	Electro Panel
Interior Illumination		
Turn Signal Indicator	2	194
Fan Nomenclature	1	1892
Heater Control Nomenclature	1	161
A/C Control Nomenclature	1	161
Electric Rear Window Defroster	1	2162
Glove Compartment (Opt.)	1	1816
Ashtray	1	1892
Instrument Panel Clock	1	194
High Beam Indicator	1	194
Warning Lamps — All	(1 each)	194
Instrument Cluster Illumination		
Standard Cluster	6	194
Standard Cluster	2	Halogen #2033*
Turbo Cluster	6	194
Electronic Cluster	1	Mini #37
Electronic Cluster	6	194
Electronic Cluster	6	Halogen #2033*
Dome Lamp	1	906
Dome/Map Lamp	1/2	912/105
Trunk Compartment (Opt.)	1	89
Engine Compartment (Opt.)	1	89
Automatic Transmission ''PRND21'' Indicator	1	1893
Anti-Theft Warning Lamp	1	***
Armrest Courtesy Lamp	2	904
Radio Lamps		
AM/FM Stereo		
General Illumination	6	7152
Dial Illumination	1	936
AM/FM Stereo Cassette		
General Illumination	6	7152
Dial Illumination	1	936
Pilot (Dial Illumination)		
AM/FM/Stereo	1	1893
AM/FM/Stereo/Cassette	2	1893
Stereo Indicator Lamp	N/A	—

*Replace with Ford Part Number D20B-18C622-AB or equivalent, if available (Bulb is an integral part of assembly).

**Substitution of headlamp bulbs other than original equipment or equivalent may result in false warning or no warning in the lamp outage warning indicator system.

***E3SB-10C915-AA — RPO (Throw away unit) (Bulb not replaceable)

****E5SF-13B765-CB — Requires cleaning only — no handling of glass.

88186C50

Table 2 (88186C51)

FUNCTION	NUMBER OF BULBS	TRADE NUMBER
Exterior Illumination		
Headlamps — Lo Beam, Hi Beam	2	9004[1]
Foglamps (Turbo Coupe)	2	H3
Front Park/Turn	2	2357NA
Park Lamp	2	2458NA
Rear Side Marker	2	904
Backup Lamp	2	1156
High Mount Brakelamp	2	912
License Plate	2	194
Tail/Stop/Turn	4	2458
Cornering Lamp (Opt.)	2	1156
Taillamp Only	2	194
Interior Illumination		
Turn Signal Indicator	2	194/37[4]
Fan Nomenclature	1	1892
Heater Control Nomenclature	1	161
A/C Control Nomenclature Defroster	1	161
Ashtray	1	161
Courtesy Lamps	2	904
Door	2	194
Floor Console	2	194
Instrument Panel	2	89
Visor Vanity Light	4	168
Keyless Entry Switch	3	731
High Beam Indicator	1	194/37[4]
Warning Lights — All (Opt.)	(1 each)	194/37[4]
Instrument Cluster Illumination		
Standard Cluster	6	194
Standard Cluster	2	Halogen #2033[2]
Performance Cluster Sport Turbo Coupe	6	194
Electronic Cluster (Opt.)	9	Mini #37
Electronic Cluster (Opt.)	4	194
Electronic Cluster (Opt.)	6	Halogen #2033[3]

88186C51

Table 3 (88186C52)

FUNCTION	NUMBER OF BULBS	TRADE NUMBER
Exterior Illumination		
Headlamps — Lo Beam/Hi Beam	2	9006/9005[1]
Foglamps (Super Coupe)	2	H3
Front Park/Turn/Side Marker	2	2458NA
Backup Lamp	2	2456
High Mount Stoplamp	2	921
License Plate	2	194
Tail/Stop/Turn/Side Marker	2	2458
Cornering Lamp	2	2456
Interior Illumination	2	194
Turn Signal Indicator	2	194/37[4]
Fan Nomenclature	1	1892
Heater Control Nomenclature	1	161
A/C Control Nomenclature	1	161
EATC	2	37
Ashtray	1	161
Glove Compartment	1	194
Courtesy Lamps	2	904
Door	2	168
Floor Console	1	T1895
Instrument Panel	2	89
Keyless Entry Switch	3	731
High Beam Indicator	1	194/37[4]
Warning Lights — All (Opts)	(1 each)	194/37[4]
Instrument Cluster Illumination		
Standard Cluster	6	1904
Standard Cluster	2	Xenon A7742 [3]
Performance Cluster (Sport and Super Coupe)	6	194
Electronic Cluster (Opt.)	9	Mini #37
Electronic Cluster (Opt.)	4	194
Electronic Cluster (Opt.)	6	Xenon A7742[3]

88186C52

Table 4 (88186C53)

FUNCTION	NUMBER OF BULBS	TRADE NUMBER
Dome Lamp	1	906
Dome/Map Lamp (Opt.)	1/2	912/105[4]
Trunk Compartment	1	98
Engine Compartment (Opt.)	1	98
Automatic Transmission Indicator	1	1893
Radio Pilot Light		
AM/FM/MPX (ESR)	6	7152
AM/FM/CASS (ESR)	6	7152
Graphic Equalizer	2	7373
Radio LCD Backlight		
AM/FM/MPX (ESR)	1	936
AM/FM/CASS (ESR)	1	936

[1] Substitution of headlamp bulbs other than original equipment or equivalent may result in false warning or no warning in the lamp outage warning indicator system.

[2] E3SB-10C915-AA — RPO (Throw away unit). (Bulb not replaceable.)

[3] E5SF-13B765-CB — Refer bulb replacement to dealer

[4] Optional Replacement Bulb

88186C53

Function	Trade number
Exterior lights	
Rear	
Tail lamp, brakelamp, turn lamp side marker	3157
Front	
Parklamp, turn lamp, side marker	3157NA**
Backup lamp	3156
Fog lamp (Super Coupe)	880
License plate lamp	194
High-mounted brakelamp	921
Headlamps	
Lo beam/Hi beam	9007
Interior lights	
Luggage compartment lamp	912
Dome lamp	912
Dome/map lamp	
Dome	912
Map	105
Courtesy lamps	98
Door courtesy lamp	168
Floor console storage bin lamp	T-1865
Engine compartment lamp (opt.)	906
Visor vanity	194
Instrument panel lights	
Glove compartment	194
Instrument courtesy lights	89
High beam indicator	194
Floor console ashtray lamp	1893
Floor console cigar lighter lamp	161
Radio illumination	•
Warning lights (all)	194
Turn signal indicator	194
Fan	1892
"PRND21" bulb	194
Heater or Heater A/C	37
Automatic climate control	37
Keyless entry switch	713
Instrument cluster lights	
Standard	194/37
Performance (sport and super coupe)	194

**NA means Natural Amber
• Refer bulb replacement to a Ford authorized radio service center.

88186C54

Function	Trade number
Exterior lights	
Rear	
Tail lamp, brakelamp, turn lamp side marker	3157
Front	
Parklamp, turn lamp, side marker	3157NA**
Backup lamp	3156
License plate lamp	194
High-mounted brakelamp	921
Headlamps	
Lo beam/Hi beam	9007
Interior lights	
Luggage compartment lamp	912
Dome lamp	912
Dome/map lamp	
Dome	912
Map	105
Courtesy lamps	98
Door courtesy lamp	168
Floor console storage bin lamp	T1865
Floor console ashtray lamp	1893
Visor vanity lamp (opt.)	194
Engine compartment lamp (opt.)	906
Instrument panel lights	
Glove compartment	194
High beam indicator	194
Cigar lighter lamp	161
Radio illumination	•
Warning lights (all)	194
Turn signal indicator	194
Fan	1892
"PRND21" bulb	194
Heater or Heater A/C	37
Semi automatic climate control	37
Instrument cluster lights	
Mechanical	194/37

**NA means Natural Amber
• Refer bulb replacement to a Ford authorized radio service center.

88186C55

TRAILER WIRING

Wiring the vehicle for towing is fairly easy. There are a number of good wiring kits available and these should be used, rather than trying to design your own.

All trailers will need brake lights and turn signals as well as tail lights and side marker lights. Most areas require extra marker lights for overwide trailers. Also, most areas have recently required back-up lights for trailers, and most trailer manufacturers have been building trailers with back-up lights for several years.

Additionally, some Class I, most Class II and just about all Class III trailers will have electric brakes. Add to this number an accessories wire, to operate trailer internal equipment or to charge the trailer's battery, and you can have as many as seven wires in the harness.

Determine the equipment on your trailer and buy the wiring kit necessary. The kit will contain all the wires needed, plus a plug adapter set which includes the female plug, mounted on the bumper or hitch, and the male plug, wired into, or plugged into the trailer harness.

When installing the kit, follow the manufacturer's instructions. The color coding of the wires is usually standard throughout the industry. One point to note: some domestic vehicles, and most imported vehicles, have separate turn signals. On most domestic vehicles, the brake lights and rear turn signals operate with the same bulb. For those vehicles without separate turn signals, you can purchase an isolation unit so that the brake lights won't blink whenever the turn signals are operated.

One, final point, the best kits are those with a spring loaded cover on the vehicle mounted socket. This cover prevents dirt and moisture from corroding the terminals. Never let the vehicle socket hang loosely; always mount it securely to the bumper or hitch.

CIRCUIT PROTECTION

Fuses

REPLACEMENT

▶ See Figures 111 and 112

A fuse panel is used to house the numerous fuses protecting the various branches of the electrical system and is normally the most accessible. The mounting of the fuse panel is either on the left side of the passenger compartment, under the dash, on the side kick panel or on the firewall to the left of the steering column. Certain models will have the fuse panel exposed while other models will have it covered with a removable trim cover.

Fuses are simply snapped in and out for replacement. Always replace a fuse with one of the same amp rating. On plug type fuses, the color will also be the same.

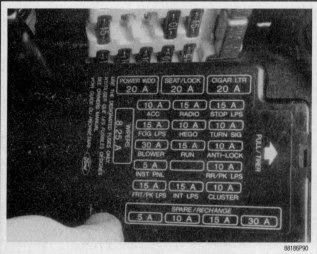

Fig. 111 Unsnap the fuse box cover from the housing

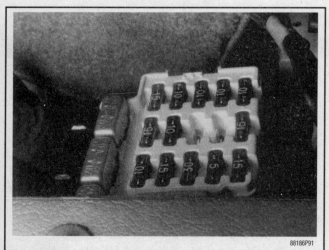

Fig. 112 Be sure to replace the fuse that is bad with the correct size fuse!!

Fusible Links and Circuit Breakers

REPLACEMENT

▶ See Figures 113 and 114

A fuse link is a short length of insulated wire, integral with the engine compartment wiring harness. It is several wire gauges smaller than the circuit

Fig. 113 There is another fuse box located near the battery. This may contain your flashers and circuit breakers

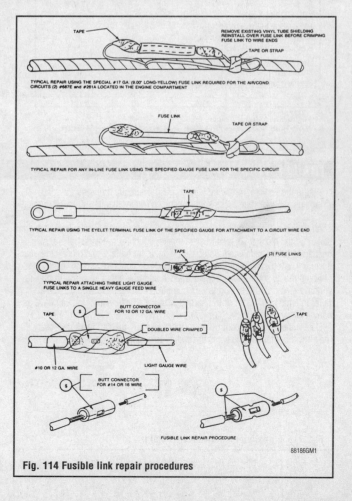

Fig. 114 Fusible link repair procedures

it protects and is located inline directly from the positive terminal of the battery.

When heavy current flows or when a short to ground occurs in the wiring harness, the fuse link burns out and protects the alternator or wiring. Production fuse links are color coded:

- 12 gauge: Gray
- 14 gauge: Dark Green
- 16 gauge: Black
- 18 gauge: Brown
- 20 gauge: Dark Blue

➡ **Replacement fuse link color coding may vary from production fuse link color coding.**

Circuit breakers are used on certain electrical components requiring high amperage, such as the headlamp circuit, electrical seats and/or windows to name a few. The advantage of the circuit breaker is its ability to open and close the electrical circuit as the lead demands, rather than the necessity of a part replacement, should the circuit be opened with another protective device in line.

Flashers

REPLACEMENT

▸ **See Figure 115**

The flasher unit can be found under the dash panel attached to a bracket on the right side steering column opening reinforcement. On some models, the flasher plugs into the fuse panel.

The flasher can be removed by pressing the plastic retaining clip and pulling straight rearward. Align the new flasher housing with bracket and push forward until it snaps into the bracket

➡ **Never unplug or plug in a flasher unit while it is in the ON mode. Damage could occur to fuses, light bulbs, and/or the flasher unit being installed.**

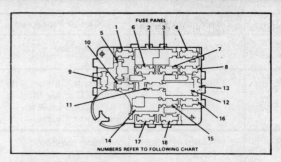

Fuse Panel Description

Position	Description	Color	Circuit Protected
1	15 Amp. Fuse	Light Blue	Stop Lamps, Hazard Warning Lamps, Speed Control Module and Cornering Lamp Relays
2	6 Amp. C.B.	—	Windshield Wiper, Windshield Washer Pump, Interval Wiper
3	Spare	—	(Not Used)
4	15 Amp. Fuse	Light Blue	Taillamps, Parking Lamps, Side Marker Lamps, Instrument Cluster Illumination Lamps, License Lamps, A/C and Heater Illumination, Radio Illumination, Digital Clock Illumination, Autolamp Relay

88186C57

Position	Description	Color	Circuit Protected
5	15 Amp. Fuse	Light Blue	Turn Signal Lamps, Back-Up Lamps, Illumination Entry, Keyless Entry Module
6	20 Amp. Fuse	Yellow	A/C Clutch, Heated Backlite Relay Timer, Trunk Lid Release, Speed Control Module, Electronic Digital Clock Display, Graphic Warning Display Module, Illuminated Entry, AntiTheft Module
7	15 Amp. Fuse	—	Fog Lamps (Turbo Only)
8	15 Amp. Fuse	Light Blue	Courtesy Lamps, Key Warning Buzzer, Illuminated Entry Module, Analog Clock
9	30 Amp. Fuse	Light Green	A/C Heater Blower Motor
10	20 C.B.	—	Horn, Cigar Lighter
11	20 Amp. Fuse	Yellow	Radio, Tape Player, Premium Sound, Power Antenna
12	20 Amp. C.B.	—	Power Seat, Power Locks, Keyless Entry Fuel Filler Door
13	5 Amp. Fuse	Tan	Instrument Cluster Illumination Lamps, Radio, Climate Control
14	20 Amp. C.B.	—	Power Windows
15	10 Amp. Fuse	Red	On cars with optional Lamp Outage System, Taillamps, Rear Side Markers, License Lamps

88186C58

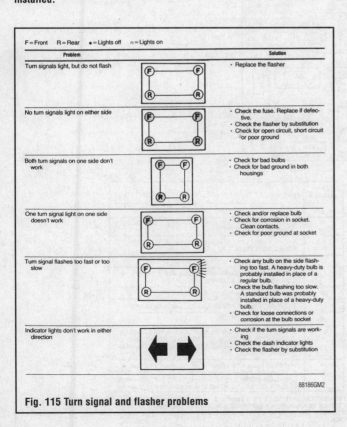

Fig. 115 Turn signal and flasher problems

F = Front   R = Rear   ● = Lights off   ○ = Lights on

Problem	Solution
Turn signals light, but do not flash	• Replace the flasher
No turn signals light on either side	• Check the fuse. Replace if defective. • Check the flasher by substitution • Check for open circuit, short circuit or poor ground
Both turn signals on one side don't work	• Check for bad bulbs • Check for bad ground in both housings
One turn signal light on one side doesn't work	• Check and/or replace bulb • Check for corrosion in socket. Clean contacts. • Check for poor ground at socket
Turn signal flashes too fast or too slow	• Check any bulb on the side flashing too fast. A heavy-duty bulb is probably installed in place of a regular bulb. • Check the bulb flashing too slow. A standard bulb was probably installed in place of a heavy-duty bulb. • Check for loose connections or corrosion at the bulb socket
Indicator lights don't work in either direction	• Check if the turn signals are working • Check the dash indicator lights • Check the flasher by substitution

88186GM2

Position	Description	Color	Circuit Protected
16	20 Amp. Fuse	Yellow	Flash-to-Pass
17	15 Amp. Fuse	Light Blue	Electronic Cluster, Tripminder Display Module Fuel Gauge on Non-Electronic Cluster
18	10 Amp. Fuse	Red	Warning Indicator Lamps, Throttle Solenoid Positioner, Low Fuel Module, Dual Timer Chime, Tachometer, Washer Fluid Level Indicator

3 fuses for optional anti-theft system located in the luggage compartment near the package tray in fuse holders:
- 20 amp fuse to protect headlamps wiring.
- 20 amp fuse to protect horn circuit & feed circuit to module.
- 15 amp fuse to protect marker & taillamp wiring.

88186C59

Circuit	Circuit Protection Rating	Location
Lamp Feed	16 GA Fuse Link	Near Starter Motor Relay
Ignition Feed	16 GA Fuse Link	Near Starter Motor Relay
Charging Circuit	14 GA Fuse Link	Near Starter Motor Relay
Heated Backlite	16 GA Fuse Link	Near Starter Motor Relay
Engine Compartment Lamp	20 GA Fuse Link	Near Starter Motor Relay
Electric Cooling Fan	20 GA Fuse Link	Near Starter Motor Relay
Electric Fan Control Unit	20 GA Fuse Link	Near Starter Motor
Windshield Wiper/Washer	6 Amp. C.B.	Fuse Panel
Headlights, High Beam Indicator	22 Amp. C.B.	Part of Headlight Switch
Power Door Locks and Power Seats	20 Amp. C.B.	Fuse Panel
Power Window (2-Dr.)	20 Amp. C.B.	Fuse Panel
Horn, Cigar Lighter	20 Amp. C.B.	Fuse Panel

Turn Signal Flasher	Hazard Flasher
Connected to front side of fuse panel.	Connected to rear side of fuse panel.

NOTE—To replace turn signal or hazard flasher, disengage flasher units from the fuse panel.

88186C60

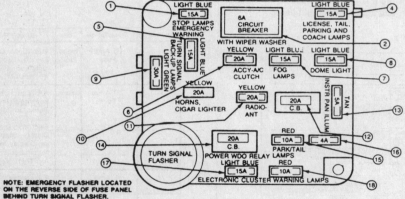

NOTE: EMERGENCY FLASHER LOCATED ON THE REVERSE SIDE OF FUSE PANEL BEHIND TURN SIGNAL FLASHER.

CAVITY NUMBER	SYSTEMS
1	STOP LAMPS, HAZARD WARNING LAMPS, SPEED CONTROL MODULE, CORNERING LAMP RELAY
2	WINDSHIELD WIPER, WINDSHIELD WASHER PUMP, INTERVAL WIPER MODULE
4	TAILLAMPS, PARKING LAMPS, SIDE MARKER/COACH LAMPS, CLUSTER ILLUMINATION LAMPS, LICENSE LAMPS, DIGITAL CLOCK ILLUMINATOR, A/C AND HEATER ILLUMINATION, RADIO ILLUMINATION
5	TURN SIGNAL LAMPS, BACK-UP LAMPS, ILLUMINATE/KEYLESS ENTRY/DAY/NIGHT MIRRORS, TURBO BUZZER
6	HEATED BACKLIGHT CONTROL DECK LID RELEASE, ELECTRONIC CHIMES MODULE, LAMP OUTAGE AND CORNERING LAMPS/ELECTRONIC DIGITAL CLOCK DISPLAY, TRIPMINDER, ILLUMINATED ENTRY, ANTI-THEFT MODULE, RADIO AND CLUSTER ILLUMINATION, REAR READING LAMPS
7	FOG LAMPS (TURBO ONLY)
8	COURTESY LAMPS, KEY WARNING BUZZER, ILLUMINATED ENTRY MODULE, REMOTE ELECTRIC MIRRORS, ELECTRONIC RADIO MEMORY, CLOCK, CLUSTER MEMORY, GLOVE COMPARTMENT LAMP, ANTI-THEFT RELAY

CAVITY NUMBER	SYSTEMS
9	A/C-HEATER BLOWER MOTOR
10	HORN, CIGAR LIGHTER, FLASH-TO-PASS, FUEL FILLER DOOR, SPEED CONTROL
11	RADIO, TAPE PLAYER, POWER ANTENNA, PREMIUM SOUND AMPLIFIER
12	POWER SEAT, DOOR LOCKS, KEYLESS ENTRY
13	INSTRUMENT CLUSTER, RADIO, CLIMATE CONTROL, INSTRUMENT PANEL ILLUMINATION
14	POWER WINDOWS, POWER MOON ROOF
15	TAIL/PARK LAMPS, COACH LAMPS, LICENSE LAMPS
16	EATC MEMORY
17	ELECTRONIC CLUSTER TRIPMINDER DISPLAY MODULE, FUEL GAUGE ON NON-ELECTRONIC CLUSTER, A/C CLUTCH, SPEED CONTROL MODULE, GRAPHIC WARNING DISPLAY MODULE
18	WARNING INDICATOR LAMPS, AUTO LAMP SYSTEM ELECTRONIC CHIMES; LOW WASHER FLUID LEVEL LAMP, LOW FUEL MODULE/THROTTLE SOLENOID POSITIONER, LOW OIL RELAY, TACHOMETER, FLASH-TO-PASS RELAY

*THE VISOR MIRROR USES TWO FUSES: A 15-AMP FUSE LOCATED IN THE FUSE PANEL AND A 2-AMP FUSE LOCATED IN THE VISOR ASSEMBLY. THE GARAGE DOOR OPENER IS NOT FUSED WITHIN THE VISOR.

88186C61

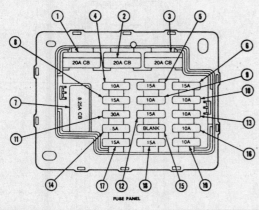

FUSE PANEL

88186C62

Cavity Number	Systems
1	Deck lid solenoid, RH power window, LH power window, moon roof motor
2	Fuel door release solenoid, RH power seat, LH power seat, LH power door lock, RH power door lock
3	Cigar lighter, high beam
4	Radio LCD, autolamp dimmer control, anti-theft module, chime
5	Radio, power antenna motor
6	Stoplamps, hi-mount stoplamps, EEC module
7	Wiper motor, washer motor, IWW module
8	Fog lamps
9	HEGO sensors
10	Backup lamps, flasher
11	Blower motor
12	A/C clutch, heated rear window switch, VMM module, engine coolant level sensor, EIC feed, EVO test, steering sensor, ride control mode switch, ride control module, ride control relay, washer level sensor, auto day/nite mirror, parking brake illumination, keyless entry illumination module, daytime running lamps, performance cluster ride control lamp
13	Anti-lock motor relay coil
14	PRNDL lamp, VMM, EIC switch, EIC, rear defrost switch, A/C/heat selector switch, radio, radio LCD, compact disc LCD
15	Not used
16	Rear park lamps, license lamps
17	Chime, front park lamps, LCD illumination relay (coil)
18	Instrument panel courtesy lamp, glove box lamp, anti-theft lamp in cluster, daytime running lamps module, engine compartment lamp, map lamp, console lamp, power mirrors, keyless entry module, vanity lamps, luggage compartment lamp, door courtesy lamp, C-pillar courtesy lamp, dome lamp
19	Chime, autolamp lite sensor, chime, anti-lock module, cluster

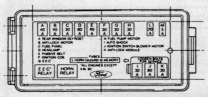

HIGH CURRENT FUSE PANEL

THE HIGH CURRENT FUSE PANEL IS LOCATED IN THE ENGINE COMPARTMENT ON THE LH FENDER APRON.

WARNING — ALWAYS DISCONNECT THE BATTERY BEFORE SERVICING HIGH CURRENT FUSES. FORD RECOMMENDS THAT HIGH CURRENT FUSES BE REPLACED BY A QUALIFIED TECHNICIAN.

CAVITY	FUSE RATING	COLOR	CIRCUIT PROTECTED
A	40 Amp	Green	Rear Window Defroster
B	40 Amp	Green	Anti-Lock Motor
C	40 Amp	Green	Fuse Panel
D	60 Amp	Yellow	Headlamp
E	40 Amp	Green	Passive Restraints
F	30 Amp	Pink	Ignition Coil
G	30 Amp	Pink	Electronic Engine Control
H	30 Amp	Pink	Fuel Pump Motor
I	30 Amp	Pink	Auto Shock
J	60 Amp	Black	Ignition Switch/Blower Motor
K	30 Amp	Pink	Anti-Lock Module
L	20 Amp	Yellow	Horn/Hazard
M	5 Amp	Tan	Memory

88186C63

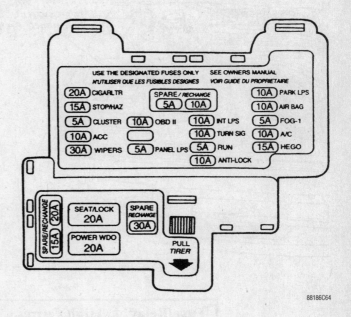

88186C64

Fuse/CB Location	Fuse Amp Rating	Description
Run	5A	• Cluster • Defrost switch • Coolant level sensor • Washer level sensor • DRL module • EVO test • EVO steering sensor • ARC (EVO) module • ARC switch • Hard ride relay • Soft ride relay • Auto mirror • EATC blend door • Air bag module • Overdrive cancel switch • Brake shift solenoid
Anti-Lock	10A	• Main ABS relay • ABS module
OBD-II	10A	• OBD-II test connector
Panel Lps.	5A	• Cluster illumination • Phone switch illumination • Rear defrost switch illumination • A/C switch-manual illumination • PRND21 illumination • Ashtray light • EATC illumination • Clock illumination • Radio illumination
Cigar Ltr.	20A	• Lighter • Flash to pass
Stop/Haz.	15A	• Speed control module • ABS module • Brake shift interlock • High mount brake lamp • Stop lamps • Flashers
Cluster	5A	• Cluster (gauges) • Cluster (ABS) • Cluster (air bags) • Chime • Autolamp sensor

88186C65

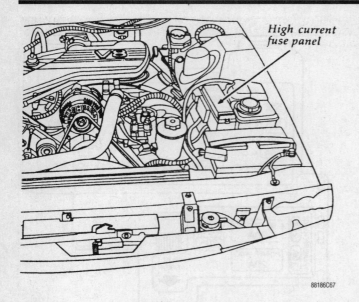

High current fuse panel

88186C67

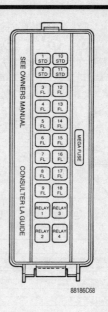

88186C68

Fuse/Relay Location	High Current Fuse Amp Rating	Description
1 STD	15A	• DRL module fog lamps
2 STD	5A	• Memory
3 FL	20A	• Ignition coil
4 FL	20A	• Autoshock
5 FL	60A	• Engine fan
6 FL	40A	• ABS motor
7 FL	60A	• Headlamps
8 FL	20A	• ABS module
9 FL	60A	• Ignition switch
10 STD	15A	• Horn
11 STD	15A	• Generator
12 FL	40A	• Fuse panel
13 FL	20A	• Fuel pump
14 FL	40A	• Rear defrost
15 FL	20A	• Electronic engine control (EEC) module
16 FL	30A	• Pusher fan
17 FL	60A	• Blower motor
18 FL	—	Not Used
Relay 1	—	Not Used
Relay 2	—	• Horn
Relay 3	—	Not Used
Relay 4	—	• ABS
Mega Fuse	175A	• Power distribution box

88186C69

WIRING DIAGRAMS

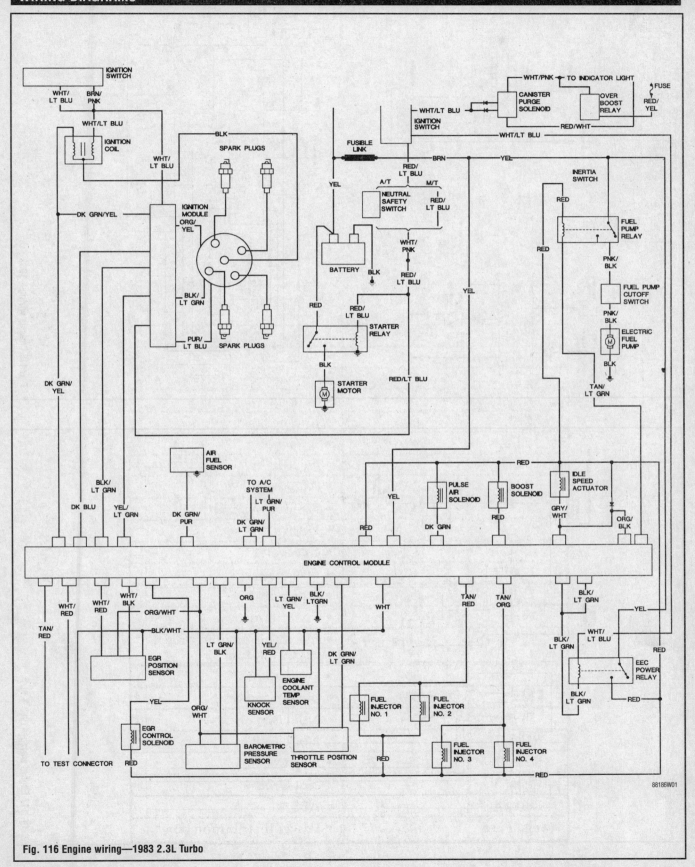

Fig. 116 Engine wiring—1983 2.3L Turbo

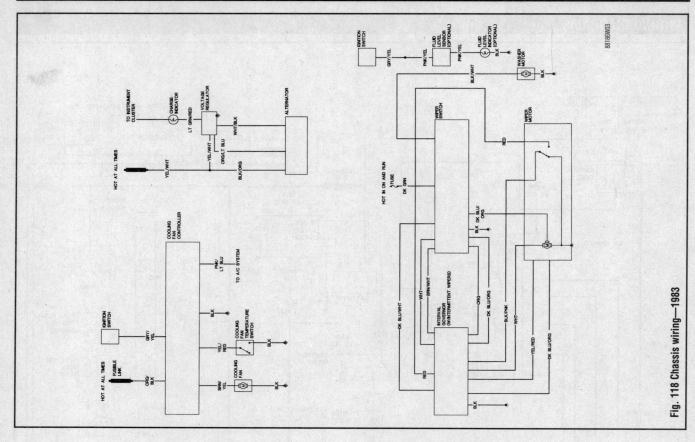

Fig. 118 Chassis wiring—1983

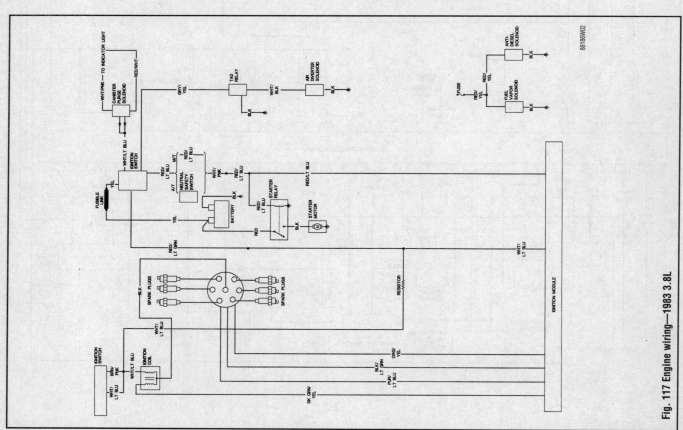

Fig. 117 Engine wiring—1983 3.8L

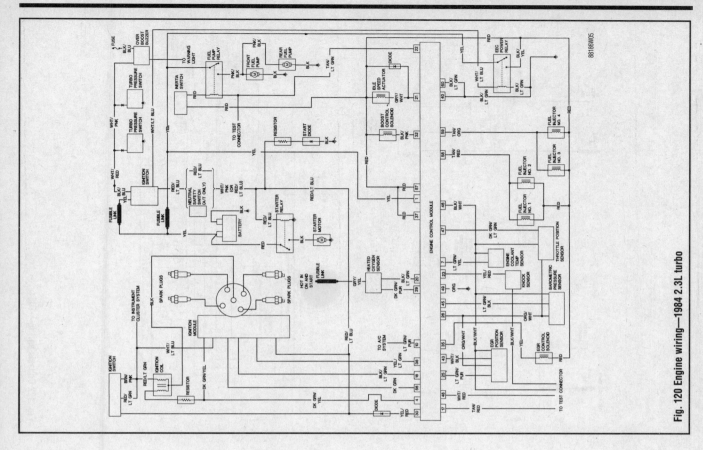

Fig. 120 Engine wiring—1984 2.3L turbo

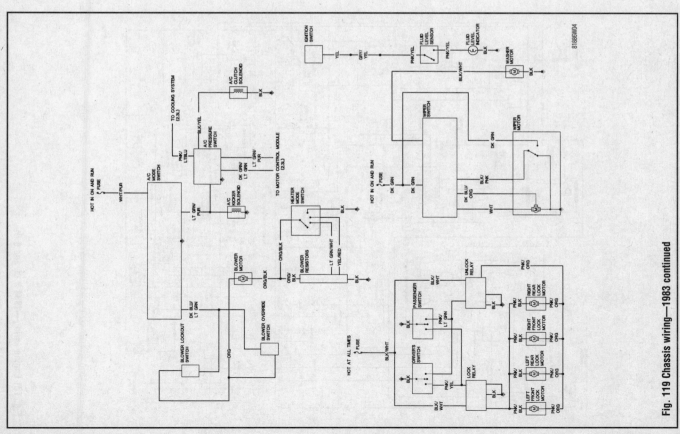

Fig. 119 Chassis wiring—1983 continued

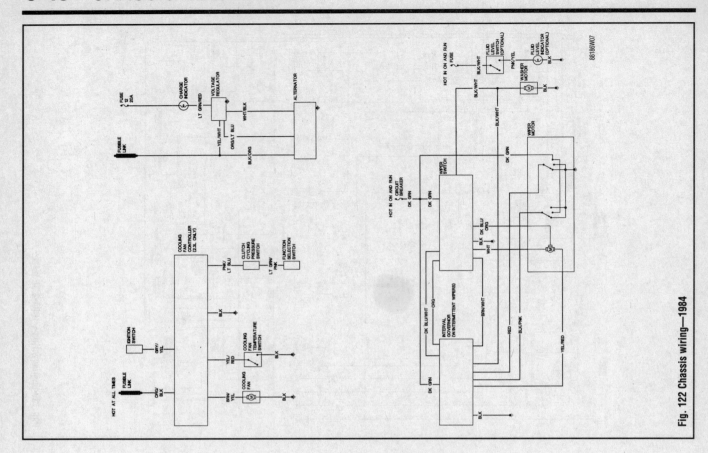

Fig. 122 Chassis wiring—1984

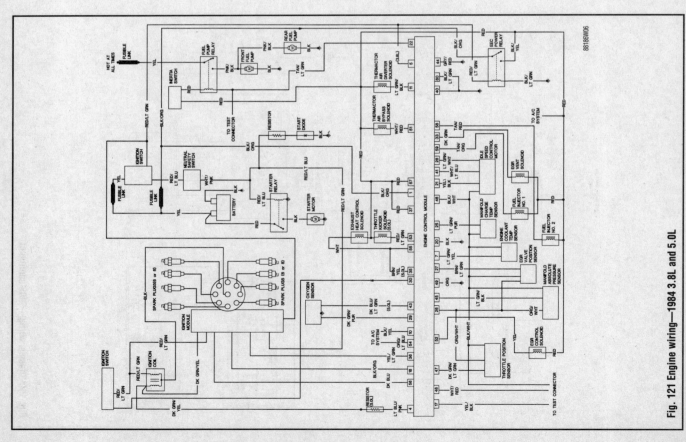

Fig. 121 Engine wiring—1984 3.8L and 5.0L

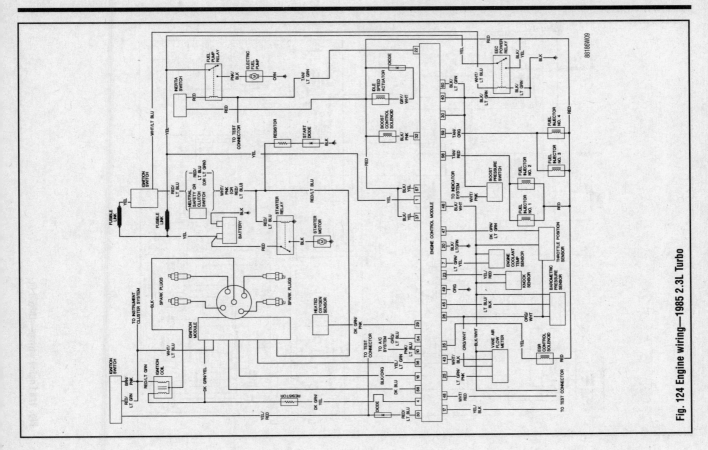

Fig. 124 Engine wiring—1985 2.3L Turbo

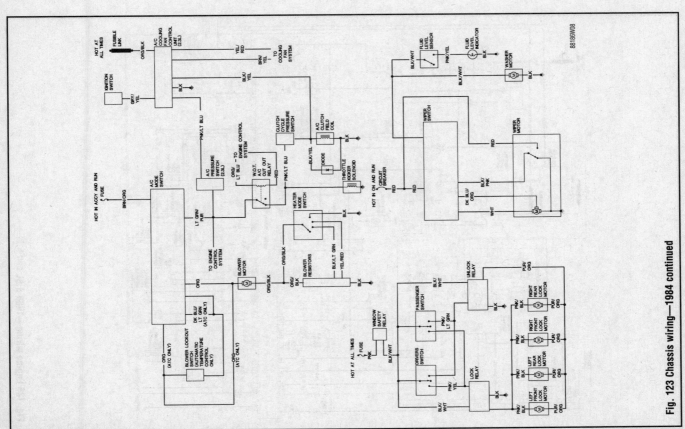

Fig. 123 Chassis wiring—1984 continued

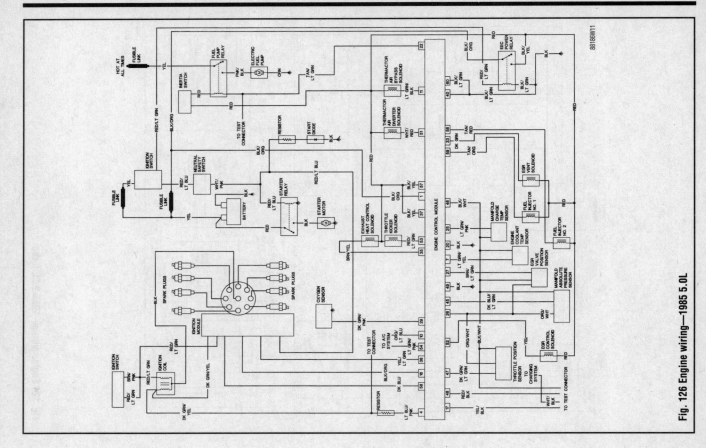

Fig. 126 Engine wiring—1985 5.0L

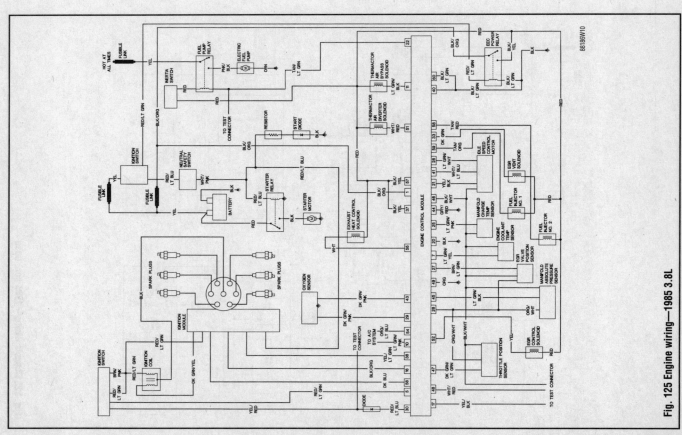

Fig. 125 Engine wiring—1985 3.8L

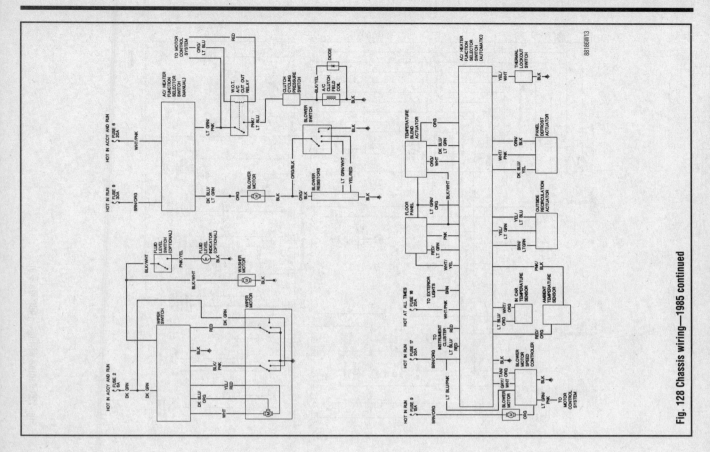

Fig. 128 Chassis wiring—1985 continued

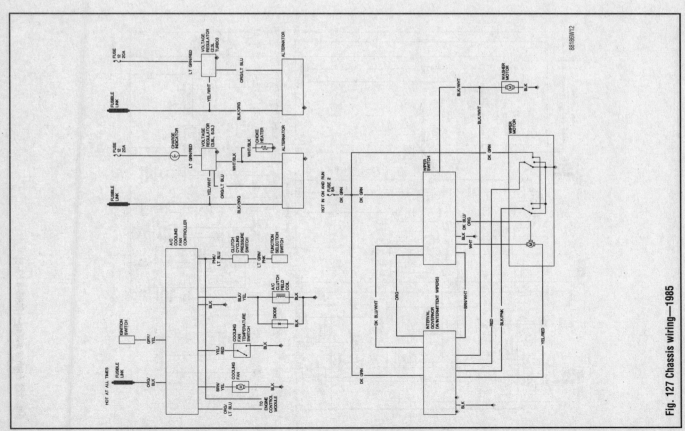

Fig. 127 Chassis wiring—1985

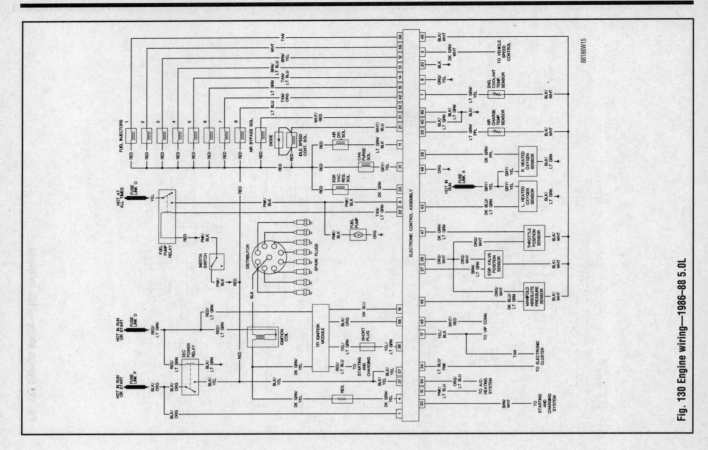

Fig. 130 Engine wiring—1986-88 5.0L

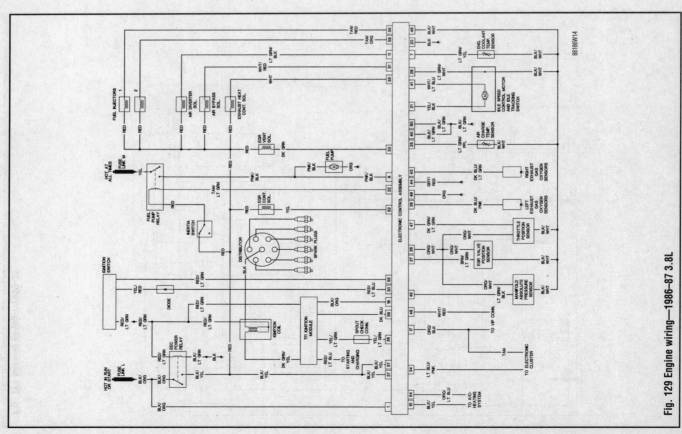

Fig. 129 Engine wiring—1986-87 3.8L

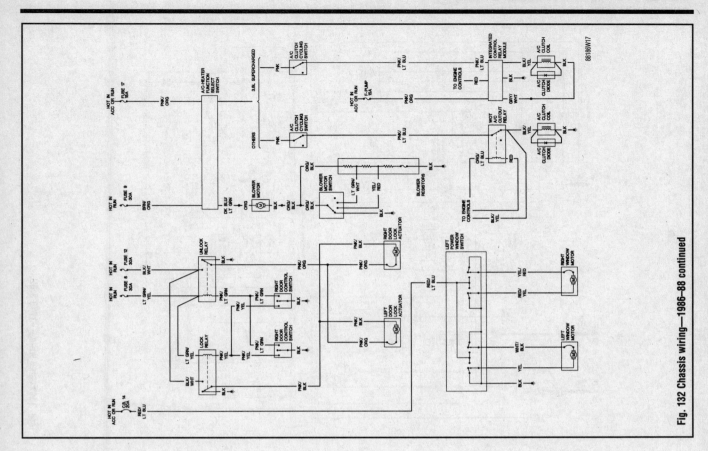

Fig. 132 Chassis wiring—1986-88 continued

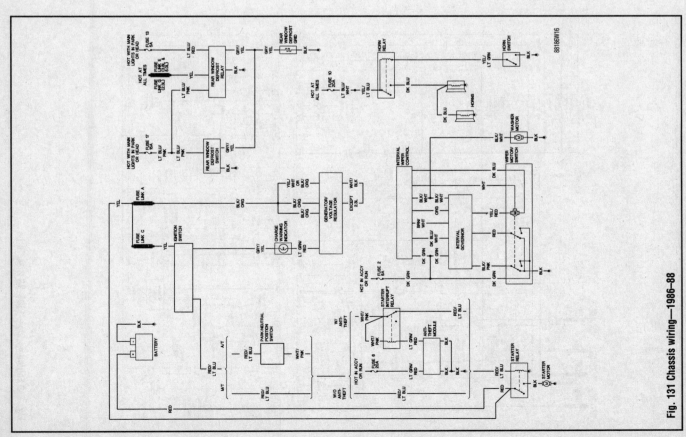

Fig. 131 Chassis wiring—1986-88

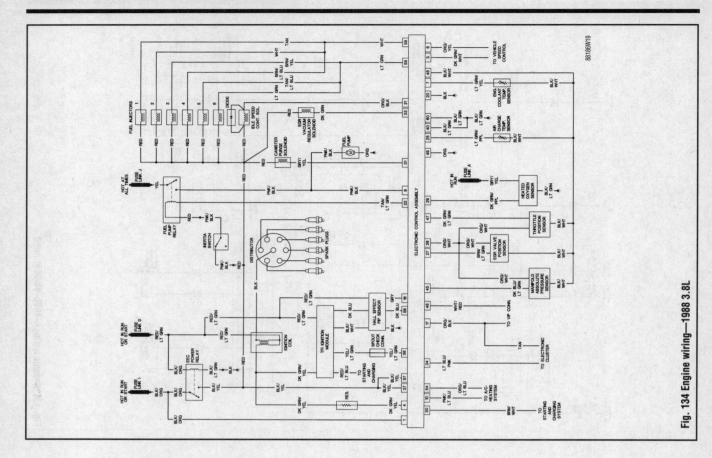

Fig. 134 Engine wiring—1988 3.8L

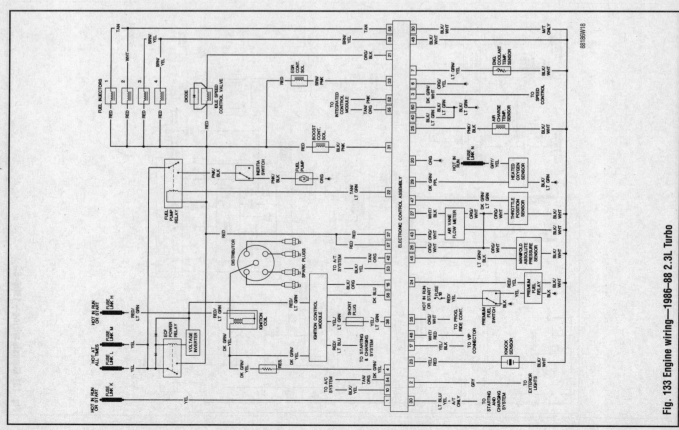

Fig. 133 Engine wiring—1986–88 2.3L Turbo

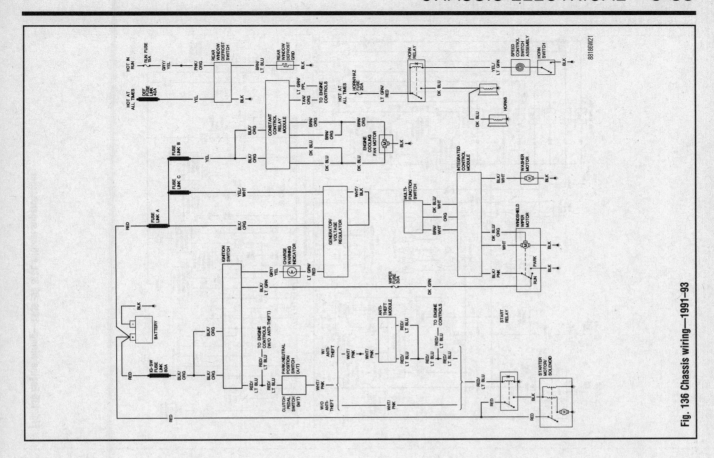

Fig. 136 Chassis wiring—1991-93

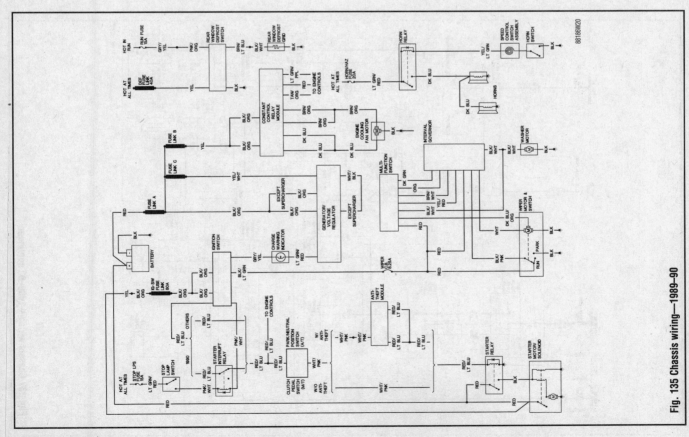

Fig. 135 Chassis wiring—1989-90

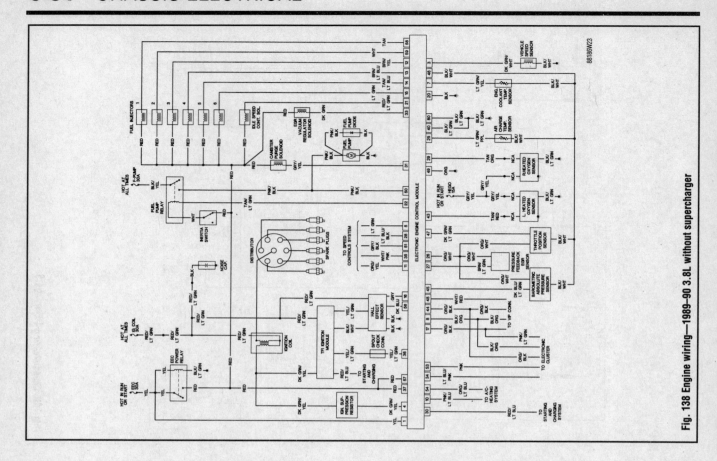

Fig. 138 Engine wiring—1989–90 3.8L without supercharger

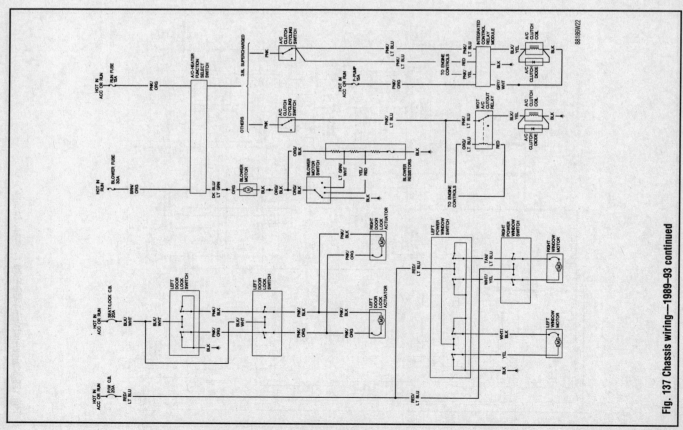

Fig. 137 Chassis wiring—1989–93 continued

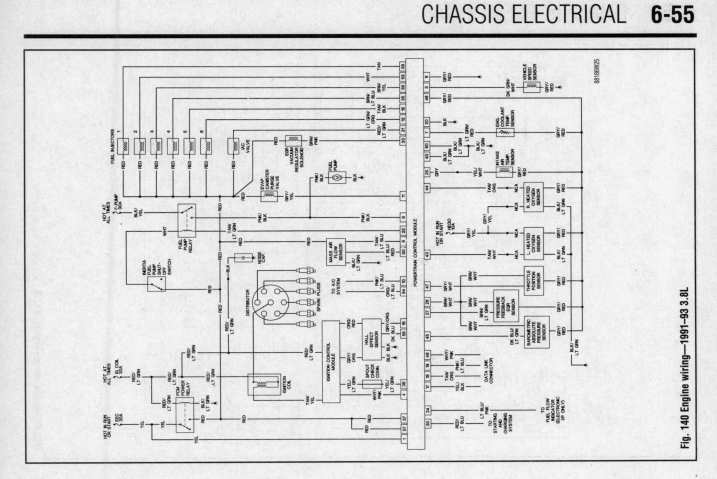

Fig. 140 Engine wiring—1991-93 3.8L

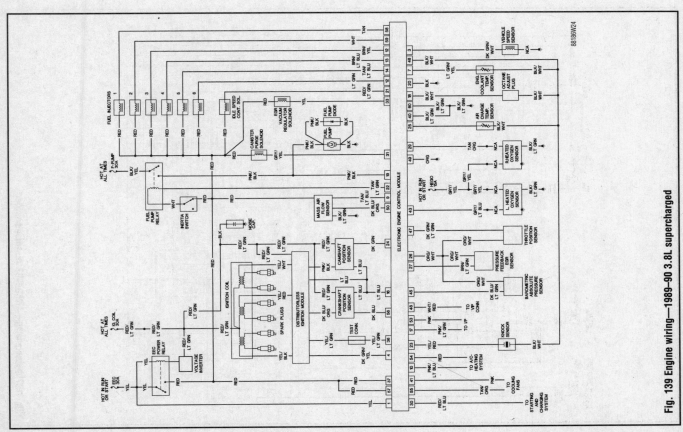

Fig. 139 Engine wiring—1989-90 3.8L supercharged

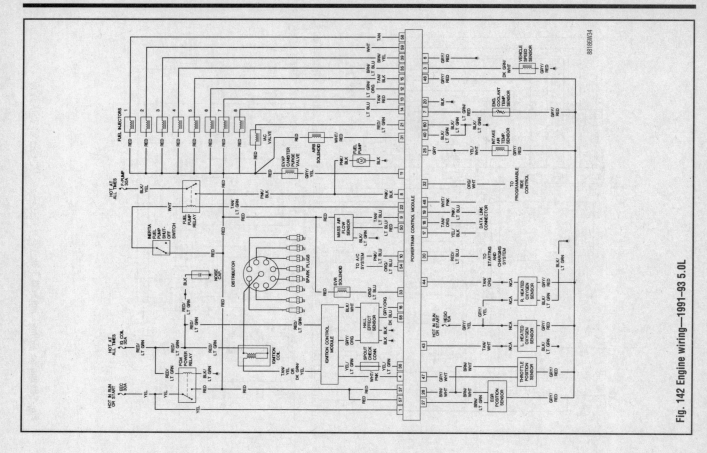

Fig. 142 Engine wiring—1991–93 5.0L

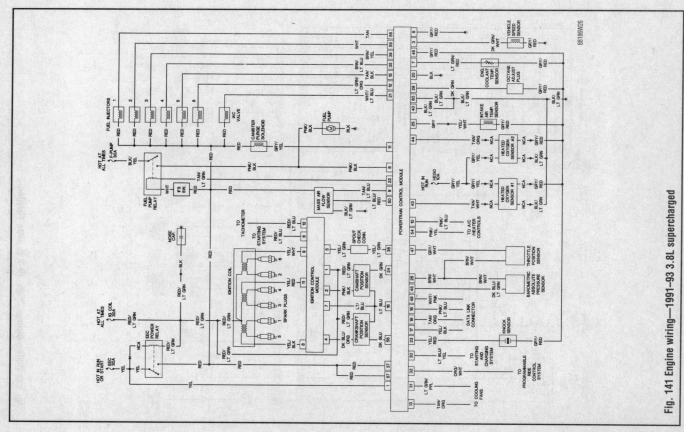

Fig. 141 Engine wiring—1991–93 3.8L supercharged

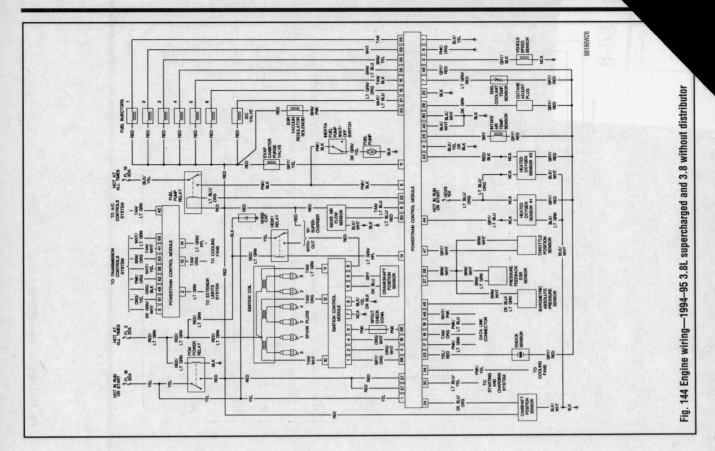

Fig. 144 Engine wiring—1994–95 3.8L supercharged and 3.8 without distributor

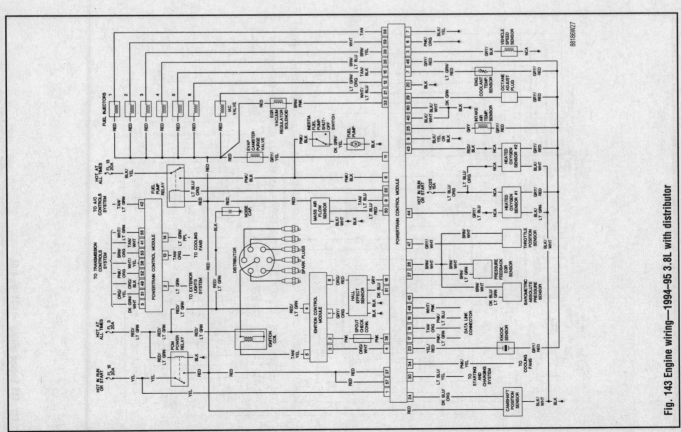

Fig. 143 Engine wiring—1994–95 3.8L with distributor

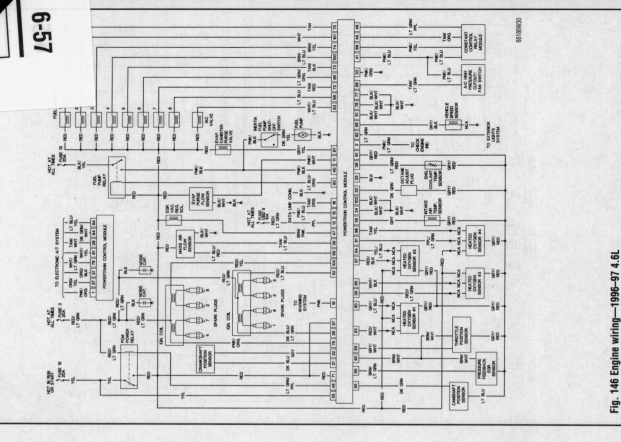

Fig. 146 Engine wiring—1996-97 4.6L

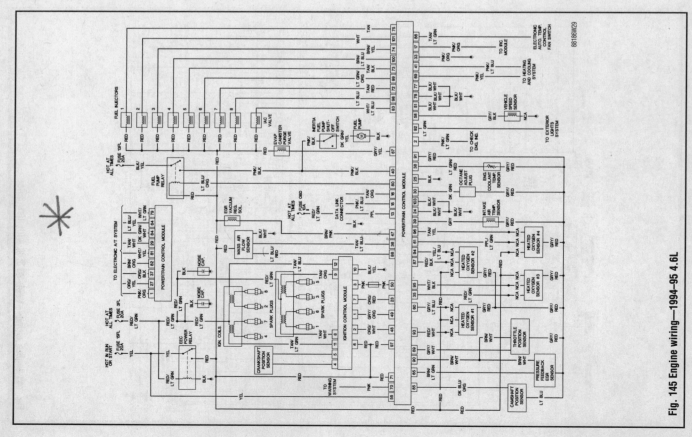

Fig. 145 Engine wiring—1994-95 4.6L

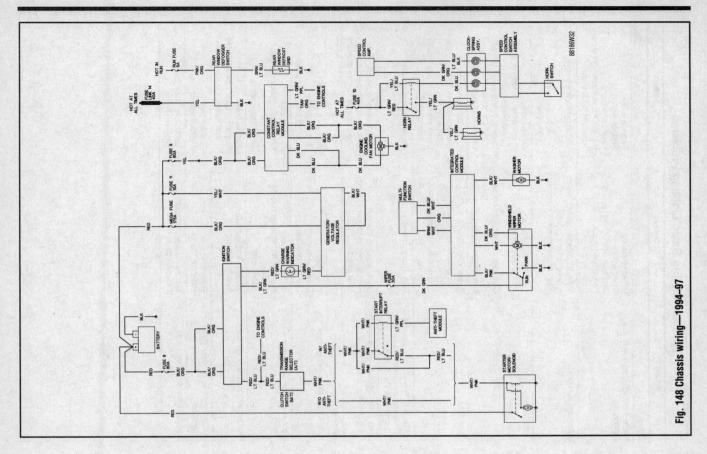

Fig. 148 Chassis wiring—1994–97

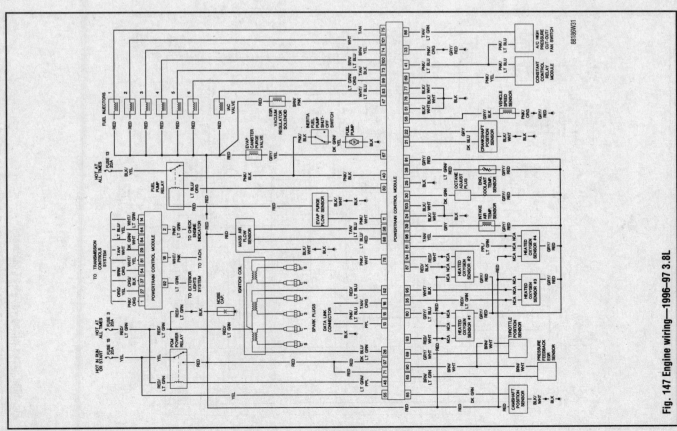

Fig. 147 Engine wiring—1996–97 3.8L

Troubleshooting Basic Lighting Problems

Problem	Cause	Solution
Lights		
One or more lights don't work, but others do	• Defective bulb(s) • Blown fuse(s) • Dirty fuse clips or light sockets • Poor ground circuit	• Replace bulb(s) • Replace fuse(s) • Clean connections • Run ground wire from light socket housing to car frame
Lights burn out quickly	• Incorrect voltage regulator setting or defective regulator • Poor battery/alternator connections	• Replace voltage regulator • Check battery/alternator connections
Lights go dim	• Low/discharged battery • Alternator not charging • Corroded sockets or connections • Low voltage output	• Check battery • Check drive belt tension; repair or replace alternator • Clean bulb and socket contacts and connections • Replace voltage regulator
Lights flicker	• Loose connection • Poor ground • Circuit breaker operating (short circuit)	• Tighten all connections • Run ground wire from light housing to car frame • Check connections and look for bare wires
Lights "flare"—Some flare is normal on acceleration—if excessive, see "Lights Burn Out Quickly"	• High voltage setting	• Replace voltage regulator
Lights glare—approaching drivers are blinded	• Lights adjusted too high • Rear springs or shocks sagging • Rear tires soft	• Have headlights aimed • Check rear springs/shocks • Check/correct rear tire pressure
Turn Signals		
Turn signals don't work in either direction	• Blown fuse • Defective flasher • Loose connection	• Replace fuse • Replace flasher • Check/tighten all connections
Right (or left) turn signal only won't work	• Bulb burned out • Right (or left) indicator bulb burned out • Short circuit	• Replace bulb • Check/replace indicator bulb • Check/repair wiring
Flasher rate too slow or too fast	• Incorrect wattage bulb • Incorrect flasher	• Flasher bulb • Replace flasher (use a variable load flasher if you pull a trailer)
Indicator lights do not flash (burn steadily)	• Burned out bulb • Defective flasher	• Replace bulb • Replace flasher
Indicator lights do not light at all	• Burned out indicator bulb • Defective flasher	• Replace indicator bulb • Replace flasher

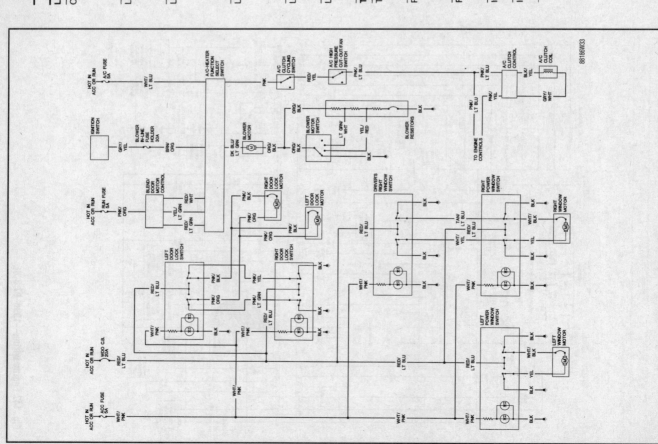

Fig. 149 Chassis wiring—1994–97 continued

Troubleshooting Basic Dash Gauge Problems

Problem	Cause	Solution
Coolant Temperature Gauge		
Gauge reads erratically or not at all	• Loose or dirty connections	• Clean/tighten connections
	• Defective sending unit	• Bi-metal gauge: remove the wire from the sending unit. Ground the wire for an instant. If the gauge registers, replace the sending unit.
	• Defective gauge	• Magnetic gauge: disconnect the wire at the sending unit. With ignition ON gauge should register COLD. Ground the wire; gauge should register HOT.
Ammeter Gauge—Turn Headlights ON (do not start engine). Note reaction		
Ammeter shows charge	• Connections reversed on gauge	• Reinstall connections
Ammeter shows discharge	• Ammeter is OK	• Nothing
Ammeter does not move	• Loose connections or faulty wiring	• Check/correct wiring
	• Defective gauge	• Replace gauge
Oil Pressure Gauge		
Gauge does not register or is inaccurate	• On mechanical gauge, Bourdon tube may be bent or kinked	• Check tube for kinks or bends preventing oil from reaching the gauge
	• Low oil pressure	• Remove sending unit. Idle the engine briefly. If no oil flows from sending unit hole, problem is in engine.
	• Defective gauge	• Remove the wire from the sending unit and ground it for an instant with the ignition ON. A good gauge will go to the top of the scale.
	• Defective wiring	• Check the wiring to the gauge. If it's OK and the gauge doesn't register when grounded, replace the gauge.
	• Defective sending unit	• If the wiring is OK and the gauge functions when grounded, replace the sending unit
All Gauges		
All gauges do not operate	• Blown fuse	• Replace fuse
	• Defective instrument regulator	• Replace instrument voltage regulator
All gauges read low or erratically	• Defective or dirty instrument voltage regulator	• Clean contacts or replace
	• Loss of ground between instrument voltage regulator and car	• Check ground
All gauges pegged	• Defective instrument regulator	• Replace regulator

88186C71

Troubleshooting Basic Dash Gauge Problems

Problem	Cause	Solution
Warning Lights		
Light(s) do not come on when ignition is ON, but engine is not started	• Defective bulb	• Replace bulb
	• Defective wire	• Check wire from light to sending unit
	• Defective sending unit	• Disconnect the wire from the sending unit and ground it. Replace the sending unit if the light comes on with the ignition ON
Light comes on with engine running	• Problem in individual system	• Check system
	• Defective sending unit	• Check sending unit (see above)

88186C72

Troubleshooting the Heater

Problem	Cause	Solution
Blower motor will not turn at any speed	• Blown fuse	• Replace fuse
	• Loose connection	• Inspect and tighten
	• Defective ground	• Clean and tighten
	• Faulty switch	• Replace switch
	• Faulty motor	• Replace motor
	• Faulty resistor	• Replace resistor
Blower motor turns at one speed only	• Faulty switch	• Replace switch
	• Faulty resistor	• Replace resistor
Blower motor turns but does not circulate air	• Intake blocked	• Clean intake
	• Fan not secured to the motor shaft	• Tighten security
Heater will not heat	• Coolant does not reach proper temperature	• Check and replace thermostat if necessary
	• Heater core blocked internally	• Flush or replace core if necessary
	• Heater core air-bound	• Purge air from core
	• Blend-air door not in proper position	• Adjust cable
Heater will not defrost	• Control cable adjustment incorrect	• Adjust control cable
	• Defroster hose damaged	• Replace defroster hose

88186C73

Troubleshooting Basic Windshield Wiper Problems

Problem	Cause	Solution
Electric Wipers		
Wipers do not operate— Wiper motor heats up or hums	• Internal motor defect • Bent or damaged linkage • Arms improperly installed on linking pivots	• Replace motor • Repair or replace linkage • Position linkage in park and reinstall wiper arms
Electric Wipers		
Wipers do not operate— No current to motor	• Fuse or circuit breaker blown • Loose, open or broken wiring • Defective switch • Defective or corroded terminals • No ground circuit for motor or switch	• Replace fuse or circuit breaker • Repair wiring and connections • Replace switch • Replace or clean terminals • Repair ground circuits
Wipers do not operate— Motor runs	• Linkage disconnected or broken	• Connect wiper linkage or replace broken linkage
Vacuum Wipers		
Wipers do not operate	• Control switch or cable inoperative • Loss of engine vacuum to wiper motor (broken hoses, low engine vacuum, defective vacuum/fuel pump) • Linkage broken or disconnected • Defective wiper motor	• Repair or replace switch or cable • Check vacuum lines, engine vacuum and fuel pump • Repair linkage • Replace wiper motor
Wipers stop on engine acceleration	• Leaking vacuum hoses • Dry windshield • Oversize wiper blades • Defective vacuum/fuel pump	• Repair or replace hoses • Wet windshield with washers • Replace with proper size wiper blades • Replace pump

88186C74

MANUAL TRANSMISSION 7-2
ADJUSTMENTS 7-2
  LINKAGE 7-2
SHIFT LEVER AND BOOT ASSEMBLY 7-2
  REMOVAL & INSTALLATION 7-2
BACK-UP LIGHT SWITCH 7-2
  REMOVAL & INSTALLATION 7-2
EXTENSION HOUSING SEAL 7-2
  REMOVAL & INSTALLATION 7-2
TRANSMISSION 7-3
  REMOVAL & INSTALLATION 7-3
CLUTCH 7-4
ADJUSTMENT 7-4
CLUTCH CABLE ASSEMBLY 7-4
  REMOVAL & INSTALLATION 7-4
DRIVEN DISC AND PRESSURE
  PLATE 7-4
  REMOVAL & INSTALLATION 7-4
MASTER CYLINDER 7-7
  REMOVAL & INSTALLATION 7-7
SLAVE CYLINDER 7-8
  REMOVAL & INSTALLATION 7-8
  HYDRAULIC SYSTEM BLEEDING 7-9
AUTOMATIC TRANSMISSION 7-10
FLUID PAN 7-10
ADJUSTMENTS 7-10
  BAND ADJUSTMENTS 7-10
  SHIFT LINKAGE ADJUSTMENT 7-10
  DOWNSHIFT (THROTTLE) LINKAGE
    ADJUSTMENT 7-14
  AOD IDLE SPEED
    ADJUSTMENT 7-14
NEUTRAL START SWITCH 7-16
  REMOVAL & INSTALLATION 7-16
TRANSMISSION 7-17
  REMOVAL & INSTALLATION 7-17
DRIVELINE 7-25
DRIVESHAFT AND U-JOINTS 7-25
  REMOVAL AND INSTALLATION 7-25
  U-JOINT REPLACEMENT 7-28
REAR AXLE 7-29
AXLE SHAFT, BEARING AND SEAL 7-29
  REMOVAL & INSTALLATION 7-29
PINION OIL SEAL 7-30
  REMOVAL & INSTALLATION 7-30
AXLE HOUSING ASSEMBLY 7-32
  REMOVAL & INSTALLATION 7-32
DIFFERENTIAL CARRIER 7-32
  REMOVAL & INSTALLATION 7-32

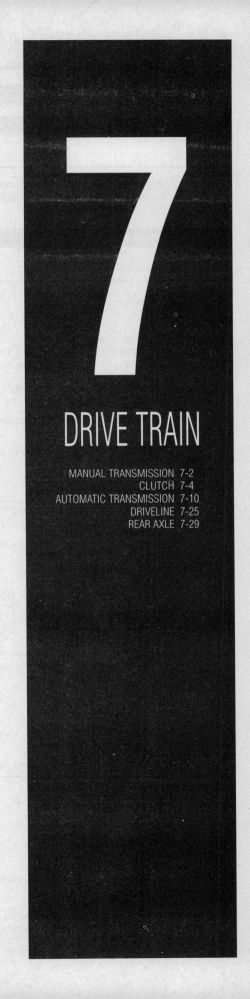

7
DRIVE TRAIN

MANUAL TRANSMISSION 7-2
CLUTCH 7-4
AUTOMATIC TRANSMISSION 7-10
DRIVELINE 7-25
REAR AXLE 7-29

MANUAL TRANSMISSION

Adjustments

LINKAGE

Neither of these units has any adjustment points. However, on some models when the shifter becomes loose or sloppy feeling, the shifter insert bushing can be replaced to tighten the feel of the shifter.

Shift Lever and Boot Assembly

REMOVAL & INSTALLATION

T5OD Manual Transmission

▶ **See Figure 1**

1. Disconnect the negative battery cable.
2. Remove the four bolts attaching the shift boot to the floorpan.
3. Remove the two bolts attaching the shift lever to the transmission.
To install:
4. Install the two bolts attaching the shift lever to the transmission. Tighten the bolts to 23–32 ft. lbs. (31–43 Nm).

➡**The shift lever bolts must only be install in one direction; from the left side of the shift lever.**

5. Install the four bolts attaching the shift boot to the floor pan, then tighten to 3–7 ft. lbs. (4.1–9.5 Nm).
6. Connect the negative battery cable.

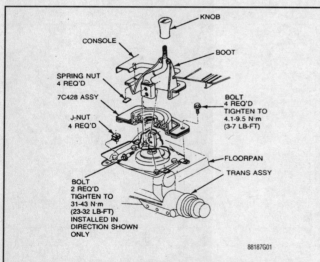

Fig. 1 The shift boot and lever are secured to the floorpan with bolts

M5R2 Manual Transmission

▶ **See Figure 2**

1. Disconnect the negative battery cable.
2. Unscrew the gearshift lever knob.
3. Remove the center console panels.
4. Unfasten the console retaining clip from the underside of the upper gearshift lever boot.
5. Remove the upper gearshift lever boot.
6. Unfasten the two retaining screws, then remove the gearshift lever.
7. Remove the four retaining screws, then remove the lower gearshift lever boot.

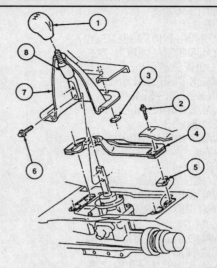

1. Gearshift lever knob
2. Lower dust boot retaining screw
3. Upper dust boot retaining clip
4. Lower gearshift lever boot
5. Retaining clip
6. Gearshift lever retaining screw
7. Upper gearshift lever boot
8. Gearshift lever

Fig. 2 View of the gear shift lever and boot assembly mounting—1995 M5R2 transmission shown

To install:
8. Position the lower gearshift lever boot and secure with the four retaining screws.
9. Install the gearshift lever and the two retaining screws.
10. Fasten the upper gearshift lever boot.
11. Install the console retaining clip from the underside of the upper gearshift lever boot.
12. Install the center console panels.
13. Install the gearshift lever knob by hand-tightening clockwise, then turn the gearshift lever knob 180 degrees to lock, and line up shift pattern.

Back-Up Light Switch

REMOVAL & INSTALLATION

1. Place the shift lever in neutral.
2. Raise and safely support the car on jackstands.
3. Unplug the electrical connector at the switch.
4. Unscrew the switch from the transmission extension housing.
To install:
5. Screw the new switch into place on the extension housing, then tighten it to 60 inch lbs. (6.7 Nm).
6. Attach the electrical wiring to the switch.
7. Carefully lower the vehicle.
8. Connect the negative battery cable, then check the switch for proper operation.

Extension Housing Seal

REMOVAL & INSTALLATION

1. Raise and safely support vehicle on jack stands.
2. Place a suitable container under the rear end of the transmission. Remove the propeller drive shaft.

3. Using an extension housing seal removal tool No. T74P-77248-A, remove the rear seal.

To install:

4. Using a seal installing tool No. T61L-7657-A, install the new seal.

5. Install the propeller driveshaft. Check fluid level in transmission fill as necessary.

6. Lower vehicle and check for leaks.

Transmission

REMOVAL & INSTALLATION

✳✳ CAUTION

The clutch driven disc contains asbestos, which has been determined to be a cancer causing agent. Never clean clutch surfaces with compressed air! Avoid inhaling any dust from any clutch surface! When cleaning clutch surfaces, use a commercially available brake cleaning fluid.

T5OD 5-Speed Transmission

1. Disconnect the negative battery cable.
2. Raise and support the vehicle safely.
3. Matchmark the driveshaft for reassembly in the same relative position.
4. Disconnect the driveshaft from the rear U-joint flange. Slide the driveshaft off the transmission output shaft and install an extension housing seal installation tool into the extension housing to prevent lubricant from leaking out.
5. Unfasten the four retaining bolts, then remove the catalytic converter.
6. Remove the 2 nuts attaching the rear transmission support to the crossmember. Remove the bolts.

➡ **On the Thunderbird Coupe with the 2.3L turbocharged engine, remove the catalytic converter and inlet pipe.**

7. Using a suitable jack, support the engine and transmission.
8. Remove the 2 nuts from the crossmember bolts. Remove the bolts, raise the jack slightly and remove the crossmember.
9. Lower the transmission to expose the 2 bolts securing the shift handle to the shift tower. Remove the 2 nuts and bolts, then remove the shift handle.
10. Disconnect the wiring harness from the backup lamp switch. On the 5.0L engine, disconnect the neutral sensing switch.
11. Remove the bolt from the speedometer cable retainer and remove the speedometer driven gear from the transmission.
12. Remove the 4 bolts that secure the transmission to the flywheel housing.
13. Move the transmission and jack rearward until the transmission input shaft clears the flywheel housing. If necessary, lower the engine enough to obtain clearance for removing the transmission.

➡ **Do not depress the clutch while the transmission is removed.**

To install:

14. Make sure the mounting surface of the transmission and flywheel housing are clean and free of dirt, paint and burrs.
15. Install 2 guide pins in the flywheel housing lower mounting bolt holes. Raise the transmission and move forward on the guide pins until the input shaft splines enter the clutch hub splines and the case is positioned against the flywheel housing.
16. Install the 2 upper transmission-to-flywheel housing mounting bolts snug and remove the 2 guide pins. Install the 2 lower mounting bolts and tighten all the bolts to 45–65 ft. lbs. (61–88 Nm).
17. Raise the transmission with a jack until the shift handle can be secured to the shift tower. Install and tighten the attaching bolts and washers to 23–32 ft. lbs. (31–43 Nm).
18. Connect the speedometer cable to the extension housing and tighten the attaching screw to 36–54 inch lbs. (4–6 Nm).
19. Raise the rear of the transmission with the jack and install the transmission support. Install and tighten the attaching bolts to 36–50 ft. lbs. (48–68 Nm).
20. With the transmission extension housing resting on the engine rear support, install the attaching bolts and tighten to 25–35 ft. lbs. (38–48 Nm).

21. Connect the backup lamp switch wiring harness. On the 5.0L engine, connect the neutral sensing switch to the wiring harness.
22. Install the catalytic converter. Tighten the attaching bolts to 20–30 ft. lbs. (27–41 Nm).
23. Remove the extension housing installation tool and slide the forward end of the driveshaft over the transmission output shaft. Connect the driveshaft to the rear U-joint flange. Make sure the matchmarks align. Tighten the U-bolt nuts to 42–57 ft. lbs. (56–77 Nm).
24. Fill the transmission with the proper type and quantity of fluid.
25. Lower the vehicle. Check the shift and crossover motion for full shift engagement and smooth crossover operation.

M5R2 5-Speed

▶ **See Figures 3, 4 and 5**

1. Disconnect the negative battery cable.
2. Shift transmission into the Neutral position.
3. Remove the gearshift lever knob.
4. Remove the console top cover.
5. Remove the two shift control selector lever and housing retaining bolts, then remove the shift lever.
6. Raise and safely support the vehicle with jackstands.
7. Remove the drain plug, then drain the oil from the transmission into a suitable container.
8. Remove the body reinforcement in front of the axle.
9. Disconnect the rear exhaust assembly from the resonator.

➡ **If not marked, mark the rear driveshaft centering socket yoke and circular companion flange so that the driveshaft can be installed in its original position.**

10. Remove the four bolts retaining the driveshaft axle to the circular companion flange.
11. Position a suitable jackstand under the front of the axle housing and remove the forward retaining nuts, and bushings.

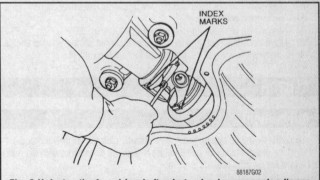

Fig. 3 Unfasten the four driveshaft axle-to-circular companion flange bolts

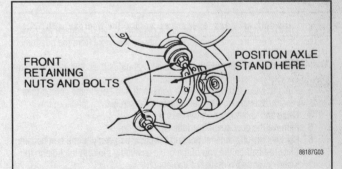

Fig. 4 With an axle stand under the front of the housing, remove the front nuts and bolts

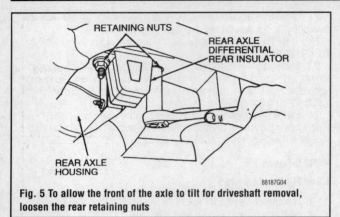

RETAINING NUTS

REAR AXLE
DIFFERENTIAL
REAR INSULATOR

REAR AXLE
HOUSING

88187G04

Fig. 5 To allow the front of the axle to tilt for driveshaft removal, loosen the rear retaining nuts

12. Loosen the rear retaining nuts to allow the axle to tilt for driveshaft removal.
13. Pull the vent tube from the hole in the subframe.
14. Lower the front of the axle housing with the axle stand and slide the driveshaft out of the transmission above the axle housing. Let the driveshaft rest on the front driveshaft support and axle assembly.

❊❊ WARNING

Be very careful when positioning the driveshaft so as not to nick, burr or contaminate the driveshaft yoke or companion flange.

15. Remove the catalytic converter assembly.
16. Disconnect the hydraulic clutch line.
17. Detach the electrical connectors.
18. Remove the starter. For details, please refer to the procedure in Section 2 of this manual.
19. With the full weight of the transmission on the crossmember, remove the transmission mount nut using a 21mm socket.
20. Position a suitable transmission jack under the transmission.
21. Remove the crossmember.
22. Remove the bellhousing-to-engine bolts.
23. Move the transmission to the rear until the input shaft clears the engine flywheel, then carefully lower the transmission from the vehicle.

To install:
24. Secure the transmission assembly on the transmission jack. Install the guide studs in the engine block and raise the transmission until the input shaft splines are aligned with the clutch disc splines.
25. Slide the transmission forward on the guide studs until it is positioned in the vehicle.
26. Install the bellhousing/flywheel-to-engine retaining bolts. Tighten to 28–38 ft. lbs. (38–51 Nm).
27. Install the crossmember. Tighten the bolts to 35–50 ft. lbs. (47–68 Nm).
28. Remove the transmission jack.
29. Attach the electrical connectors.
30. Connect the hydraulic clutch line.
31. Install the starter, as outlined in Section 2 of this manual.
32. Install the catalytic converter assembly.
33. Slide the driveshaft into transmission.

➡**Lubricate the yoke splines with Premium Long-Life Grease C1AZ–19590–E (ESA–MIC75–B) or equivalent.**

34. Raise the axle housing with the axle stand and install the bushings and retaining nuts. Tighten the retaining nuts to 68–100 ft. lbs. (92–136 Nm). Remove the axle stand.
35. Position the vent tube in hole of subframe.
36. Align the driveshaft centering socket yoke and circular companion flange, then install the retaining bolts. Tighten to 71–95 ft. lbs. (95–129 Nm).
37. Connect the exhaust pipe/muffler assembly to the resonator.
38. Add 5 ounces of Additive Friction Modifier C8AZ-19B546-A or equivalent, and fill to a total of 6.3 pts. (3L) with Synthetic MERCON® transmission fluid E6AZ-19582-B or equivalent.

➡**Apply Pipe Sealant with Teflon® to the fill plug threads in a clockwise position before installing the plug.**

39. Install the transmission case plug, and fill/drain plug gasket. Tighten to 29–43 ft. lbs. (40–58 Nm) using a 24mm socket.
40. Carefully lower the vehicle.
41. Position the shifter and install the retaining bolts. Tighten to 18–24 ft. lbs. (24–33 Nm).
42. Install the console top cover.
43. Install the shifter knob.
44. Connect the battery ground cable.

CLUTCH

Adjustment

Since the hydraulic system provides automatic clutch adjustment, no adjustment of the clutch linkage or pedal height is required on vehicles with the master and slave cylinder actuator system.

Clutch Cable Assembly

REMOVAL & INSTALLATION

1. Lift the clutch pedal to its upward most position to disengage the pawl and quadrant. Push the quadrant forward, unhook the cable from the quadrant and allow to slowly swing rearward.
2. Open the hood and remove the screw that holds the cable assembly isolator to the dash panel.
3. Pull the cable through the dash panel and into the engine compartment. On 2.3L and 5.0L engines, remove cable bracket screw from fender apron.
4. Raise and safely support the vehicle.
5. Remove the dust cover from the bell housing.
6. Remove the clip retainer holding the cable assembly to the bell housing.
7. Slide the ball on the end of the cable assembly through the hole in the clutch release lever and remove the cable.
8. Remove the dash panel isolator from the cable.
To install:
9. Install the dash panel isolator on the cable assembly.
10. Insert the cable through the hole in the bell housing and through the

hole in the clutch release lever. Slide the ball on the end of the cable assembly away from the hole in the clutch release lever.
11. Install the clip retainer that holds the cable assembly to the bell housing.
12. Install the dust shield on the bell housing.
13. Push the cable assembly into the engine compartment and lower the vehicle. On 2.3L and 5.0L engines, install cable bracket screw in fender apron.
14. Push the cable assembly into the hole in the dash panel and secure the isolator with a screw.
15. Install the cable assembly by lifting the clutch pedal to disengage the pawl and quadrant, then, pushing the quadrant forward, hook the end of the cable over the rear of the quadrant.
16. Depress clutch pedal several times to adjust cable.

Driven Disc and Pressure Plate

➡**Models through 1986 employ a mechanically actuated clutch. Clutch release is accomplished through a cable linkage system. 1987 and later models use a hydraulically actuated clutch with a master cylinder, plastic reservoir, and slave cylinder**

REMOVAL & INSTALLATION

▶ **See Figures 6, 7, 8, 9 and 10**

1. Disconnect the negative battery cable.
2. If equipped with a hydraulic clutch system, disconnect the master cylinder from the clutch pedal.

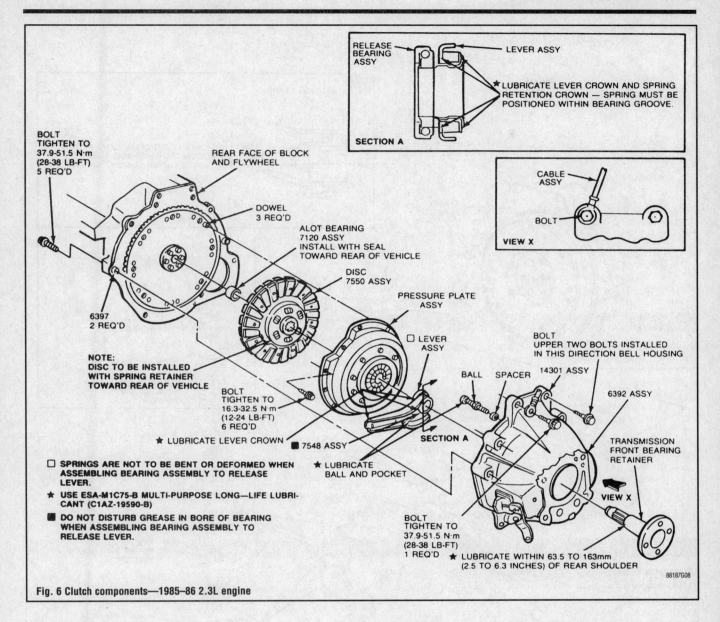

Fig. 6 Clutch components—1985–86 2.3L engine

3. Raise and safely support the vehicle.

4. Remove the starter, as outlined in

5. If equipped with a hydraulic clutch, disconnect the hydraulic coupling at the transmission with Clutch Coupling Tool T88T-70522-A, or equivalent, by sliding the white plastic sleeve. Slide the sleeve toward the clutch slave cylinder and apply a slight tug on the tube.

6. Remove the transmission, as outlined earlier in this section.

7. Mark the cover and flywheel to facilitate reassembly in the same position. Loosen the six pressure plate cover attaching bolts evenly to release the spring pressure.

➡️The pressure plate is held in place with only the retaining bolts. Support the pressure plate before removing the last retaining bolt.

8. Remove the six attaching bolts while holding the pressure plate cover. Remove the pressure plate and clutch disc.

✳️ WARNING

Do not depress the clutch pedal while the transmission is removed.

To install

9. Before installing the clutch, clean the flywheel surface and pressure plate with a suitable commercial alcohol base solvent. Do NOT use cleaners with a petroleum base. Inspect the flywheel and pressure plate for wear, scoring, or burn marks (blue color). Light scoring and wear may be cleaned up with emery paper; heavy wear may require refacing of the flywheel or replacement of the damaged parts.

➡️The clutch disc must be assembled so that the **FW SIDE** or **FLYWHEEL SIDE** stamped notation is facing toward the engine. The three clutch pressure plate-to-flywheel dowels and the flywheel must be properly aligned with the pressure plate.

10. Position the clutch disc on the flywheel so that Clutch Aligner T74P-7137-K or equivalent, can enter the pilot bearing and align the clutch disc.

11. When reinstalling the original clutch pressure plate and cover, align the assembly and flywheel according to the marks made during removal. Position the pressure plate and cover assembly on the flywheel, align the pressure plate and disc and install the retaining bolts that fasten the assembly to the flywheel. To avoid pressure plate cover distortion, alternately tighten the cover bolts in

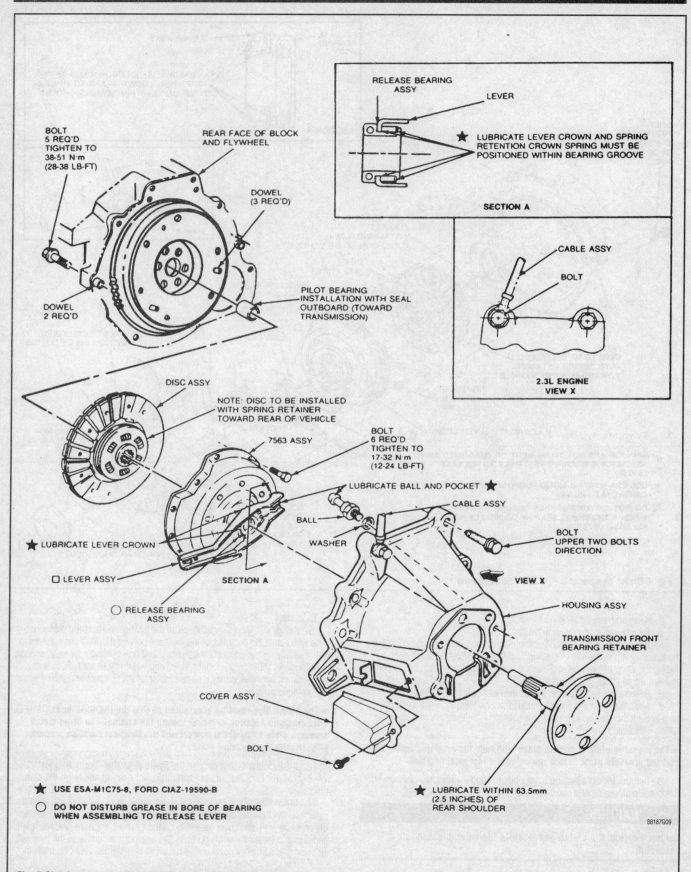

BOLT
5 REQ'D
TIGHTEN TO
38-51 N·m
(28-38 LB-FT)

REAR FACE OF BLOCK
AND FLYWHEEL

DOWEL
(3 REQ'D)

DOWEL
2 REQ'D

PILOT BEARING
INSTALLATION WITH SEAL
OUTBOARD (TOWARD
TRANSMISSION)

RELEASE BEARING
ASSY

LEVER

★ LUBRICATE LEVER CROWN AND SPRING
RETENTION CROWN SPRING MUST BE
POSITIONED WITHIN BEARING GROOVE

SECTION A

CABLE ASSY

BOLT

2.3L ENGINE
VIEW X

DISC ASSY

NOTE: DISC TO BE INSTALLED
WITH SPRING RETAINER
TOWARD REAR OF VEHICLE

7563 ASSY

BOLT
6 REQ'D
TIGHTEN TO
17-32 N·m
(12-24 LB-FT)

LUBRICATE BALL AND POCKET ★

BALL

WASHER

CABLE ASSY

BOLT
UPPER TWO BOLTS
DIRECTION

★ LUBRICATE LEVER CROWN

□ LEVER ASSY

SECTION A

VIEW X

HOUSING ASSY

○ RELEASE BEARING
ASSY

TRANSMISSION FRONT
BEARING RETAINER

COVER ASSY

BOLT

★ USE ESA-M1C75-8, FORD CIAZ-19590-B

○ DO NOT DISTURB GREASE IN BORE OF BEARING
WHEN ASSEMBLING TO RELEASE LEVER

★ LUBRICATE WITHIN 63.5mm
(2.5 INCHES) OF
REAR SHOULDER

88187G09

Fig. 7 Clutch removal and installation on 1987–88 2.3L engines

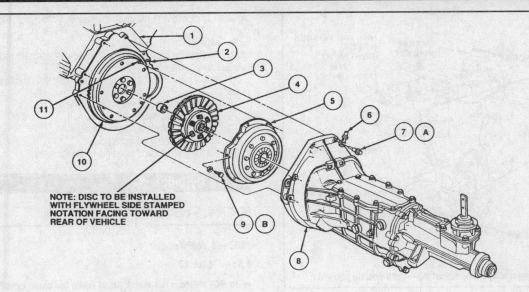

NOTE: DISC TO BE INSTALLED
WITH FLYWHEEL SIDE STAMPED
NOTATION FACING TOWARD
REAR OF VEHICLE

1. Cylinder block
2. Flywheel housing to block dowel (2 req'd)
3. Pilot bearing
4. Clutch disc
5. Clutch pressure plate
6. Dash panel ground cable
7. Bolt (6 req'd)
8. Transmission
9. Bolt and washer assembly (6 req'd)
10. Flywheel
11. Clutch pressure plate-to-flywheel dowel
A. Tighten to 54-64 Nm (40-49 lb-ft)
B. Tighten to 27-39 Nm (20-28 lb-ft)

88187G10

Fig. 8 Clutch components—1995 vehicle shown

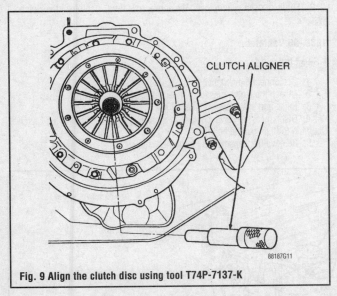

CLUTCH ALIGNER

88187G11

Fig. 9 Align the clutch disc using tool T74P-7137-K

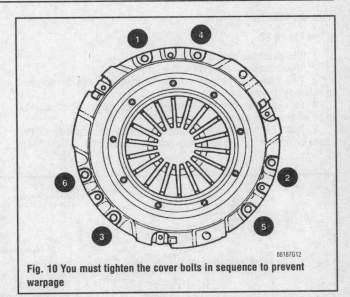

88187G12

Fig. 10 You must tighten the cover bolts in sequence to prevent warpage

sequence as shown until fully seated. Then, tighten the bolts to 29 ft. lbs. (39 Nm) in the sequence shown in the accompanying figure.

12. Remove the clutch alignment tool.
13. Align the clutch disc with the pilot bushing. Torque cover bolts to 12–14 ft. lbs. (16–19 Nm).
14. Install the transmission assembly.
15. If equipped, connect the coupling by pushing the male coupling into the slave cylinder female coupling. Connect the hydraulic clutch master cylinder push rod to the clutch pedal.
16. If necessary, bleed the clutch hydraulic system.
17. Connect the negative battery cable.

Master Cylinder

REMOVAL & INSTALLATION

1987–88 Vehicles

◆ See Figure 11

1. Disconnect the negative battery cable.
2. Remove the slave cylinder as outlined later in this section.

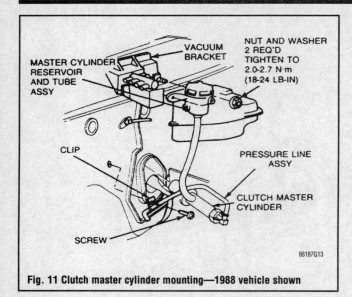

Fig. 11 Clutch master cylinder mounting—1988 vehicle shown

3. Unfasten the two retaining nuts, then remove the master cylinder reservoir.

4. Disengage the pushrod from the clutch pedal.

5. Remove the master cylinder by carefully turning it 45° clockwise and gently pulling it out.

6. If necessary, remove the hydraulic pressure line.

To install:

7. Installation is the reverse of the removal procedure.

8. Fill the clutch master cylinder with the fresh clean DOT 3 brake fluid.

9. If the pressure line was removed, bleed the hydraulic system.

10. Connect the negative battery cable.

1989–95 Vehicles

▶ See Figure 12

1. Disconnect the negative battery cable.

2. Disconnect the clutch pedal from the pushrod.

3. Detach the clutch hydraulic line (slave cylinder-to-master cylinder tube) as outlined in this section.

4. Remove the two push pins retaining the clutch master cylinder reservoir to the left side shock tower.

5. Rotate the master cylinder 45° counterclockwise, then carefully pull the master cylinder through the dash panel. Note the routing of the hydraulic line to the slave cylinder before removing the master cylinder from the engine compartment.

To install:

6. Position the master cylinder in the engine compartment, then route the hydraulic line to the slave cylinder.

7. Install the master cylinder on the dash panel by turning it 45° clockwise to seat.

8. Install the master cylinder fluid reservoir.

9. Connect the hydraulic line.

10. Attach the pushrod to the clutch pedal.

11. Connect the negative battery cable.

12. Fill the reservoir and bleed the hydraulic system.

Slave Cylinder

REMOVAL & INSTALLATION

1987–88 Vehicles

▶ See Figure 13

➡ Do NOT depress the clutch pedal while the slave cylinder is removed from the clutch housing.

1. Disconnect the negative battery cable.

2. Remove the self-tapping screw, then remove the slave cylinder dust cover.

3. Unlatch the slave cylinder from the transmission housing bracket.

4. Place a drip pan under the cylinder and disconnect and cap the fluid line.

To install:

5. Uncap and connect the hydraulic line to the slave cylinder.

6. Attach the slave cylinder to the transmission housing bracket.

7. Position the slave cylinder dust cover, then secure with the self-tapping screw.

8. Connect the negative battery cable.

9. Fill the master cylinder with the appropriate fluid, then bleed the clutch system.

1989–95 Vehicles

▶ See Figure 14

1. Disconnect the negative battery cable.

2. Detach the clutch master cylinder pushrod from the clutch pedal.

3. Raise and safely support the vehicle.

4. Disconnect the slave cylinder-to-master cylinder tube using the Clutch Coupling tool, as outlined earlier.

5. Remove the transmission from the vehicle.

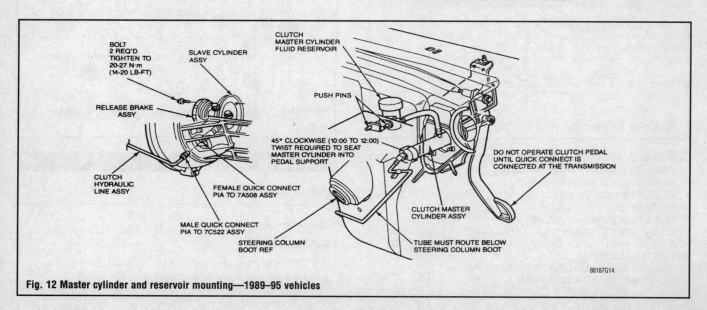

Fig. 12 Master cylinder and reservoir mounting—1989–95 vehicles

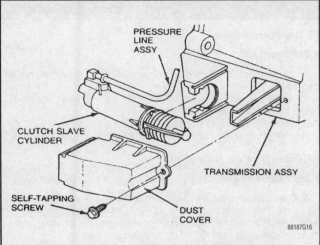

Fig. 13 The slave cylinder on 1987–88 vehicles is mounted on the transmission, under a dust cover

6. Unfasten the slave cylinder retaining bolts, then remove the slave cylinder from the vehicle.

To install:

7. Position the slave cylinder over the input shaft, aligning the bleeder screw and line coupling with the holes in the transmission housing.

8. Install the slave cylinder retaining bolts and tighten to 15–19 ft. lbs. (20–27 Nm).

9. Install the transmission.

10. Attach the slave cylinder-to-master cylinder hydraulic tube/line.

11. Carefully lower the vehicle.

12. Connect the master cylinder pushrod to the clutch pedal.

13. Connect the negative battery cable, then bleed the clutch system.

HYDRAULIC SYSTEM BLEEDING

▶ **See Figure 15**

➡ Be sure to pump the clutch pedal at least 30 times to make sure that no air is in the system. If the slave cylinder is pushed off the clutch plate, a similar pedal feel may occur. Pumping the clutch pushes fluid from the clutch reservoir into the slave cylinder, pushing it out to meet the clutch plate.

✳✳ CAUTION

Carefully clean the top and sides of the reservoir before opening to prevent contamination of the system. Remove the reservoir diaphragm when checking or adding fluid.

1. Remove the reservoir cap and diaphragm and top off with clean, fresh DOT 3 or equivalent heavy duty brake fluid.

2. Raise and safely support vehicle on jack stands.

3. Attach a hose to the bleeder valve at slave cylinder. Clear (Tygon) hose is recommended by the manufacturer to observe all air bubbles.

➡ Keep the clutch master cylinder full at all times; this will prevent air from being pulled into the hydraulic system.

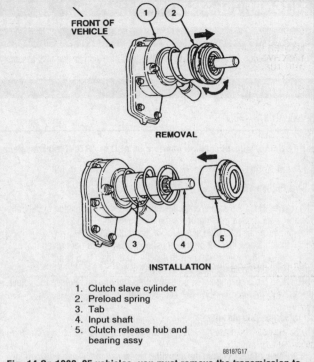

INSTALLATION

1. Clutch slave cylinder
2. Preload spring
3. Tab
4. Input shaft
5. Clutch release hub and bearing assy

Fig. 14 On 1989–95 vehicles, you must remove the transmission to access the slave cylinder

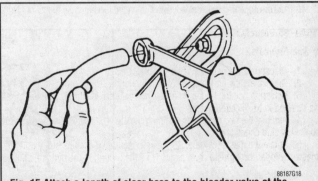

Fig. 15 Attach a length of clear hose to the bleeder valve at the slave cylinder

4. While the clutch pedal is being depressed, slightly open the bleeder valve. Observe air bubbles in clutch fluid at end of hose.

5. Close the bleeder valve before releasing the clutch pedal.

6. Repeat the previous two steps as many times as necessary until no air bubbles can be seen in the reservoir.

7. Carefully lower the vehicle and top off the reservoir. Install the diaphragm and reservoir cap.

8. Road test the vehicle for proper operation. If hard shifting, low reserve, or weak pedal are noticed, repeat the bleeding procedure.

AUTOMATIC TRANSMISSION

Fluid Pan

Refer to Section 1 for removal and installation of the fluid pan and filter assembly.

Adjustments

BAND ADJUSTMENTS

➡**No external adjustments are possible on AOD or 4R70W transmissions.**

C3 Front Band

▶ **See Figure 16**

1. Wipe clean the area around the adjusting screw on the side of the transmission, near the left front corner of the transmission.
2. Remove the adjusting screw locknut and discard it.
3. Install a new locknut on the adjusting screw but do not tighten it.
4. Tighten the adjusting screw to exactly 10 ft. lbs. (13.5 Nm).
5. Back off the adjusting screw exactly 2 turns.
6. Hold the adjusting screw so that it does not turn and tighten the adjusting screw locknut to 35–45 ft. lbs. (47–61 Nm).

C5 Intermediate Band

▶ **See Figure 17**

1. Clean all the dirt from the adjusting screw and remove and discard the locknut.
2. Install a new locknut on the adjusting screw. Using a torque wrench, tighten the adjusting screw to 10 ft. lbs. (13.5 Nm).
3. Back off the adjusting screw exactly 4¼ turns.
4. Hold the adjusting screw steady and tighten the locknut to 35 ft. lbs. (47 Nm).

C5 Low-Reverse Band

▶ **See Figure 18**

1. Clean all dirt from around the band adjusting screw, and remove and discard the locknut.
2. Install a new locknut of the adjusting screw. Using a torque wrench, tighten the adjusting screw to 10 ft. lbs. (13.5 Nm).
3. Back off the adjusting screw exactly 3 full turns.
4. Hold the adjusting screw steady and tighten the locknut to 35 ft. lbs. (47 Nm).

A4LD Overdrive and Intermediate Band

▶ **See Figures 19 and 20**

Both band adjustment screws are located on the left side of transmission, the front being the overdrive band and the rear being the intermediate band adjustment screw. Both adjustment screws use the same procedure for adjustment.

1. Remove and discard locking nut from adjustment screw.
2. Install a new locking nut but do not tighten.
3. Using a torque wrench, tighten the adjusting screw to 10 ft. lbs. (13.5 Nm).
4. Back off adjusting screw exactly 2 turns.
5. Hold adjusting screw from turning. Tighten locknut to 35–45 ft. lbs. (47–61 Nm).

SHIFT LINKAGE ADJUSTMENT

Column Shift

▶ **See Figures 21, 22, 23 and 24**

1. With the engine off, place the gear selector in the D (Drive) position, or OD (Overdrive) position (AOD). Either hang a weight on the shifter or have an assistant sit in the car and hold the selector against the stop.

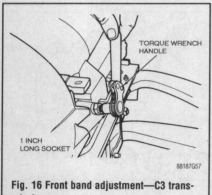

Fig. 16 Front band adjustment—C3 transmissions

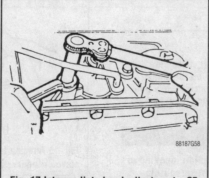

Fig. 17 Intermediate band adjustment—C5 transmissions

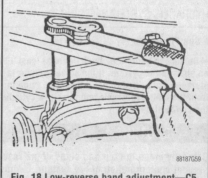

Fig. 18 Low-reverse band adjustment—C5 transmissions

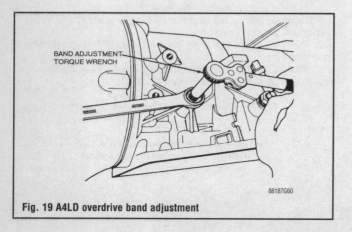

Fig. 19 A4LD overdrive band adjustment

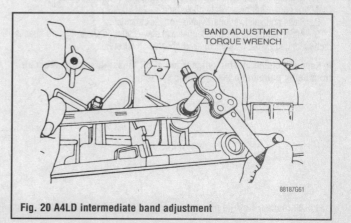

Fig. 20 A4LD intermediate band adjustment

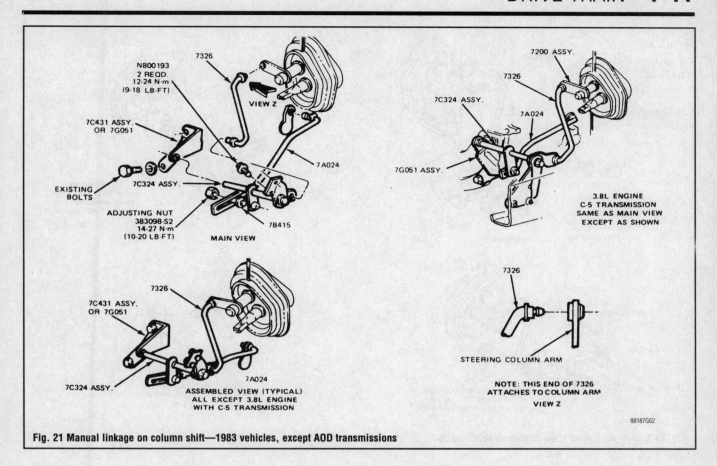

Fig. 21 Manual linkage on column shift—1983 vehicles, except AOD transmissions

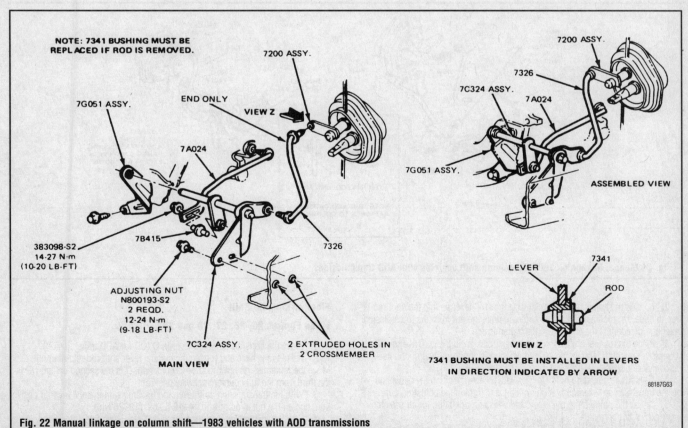

Fig. 22 Manual linkage on column shift—1983 vehicles with AOD transmissions

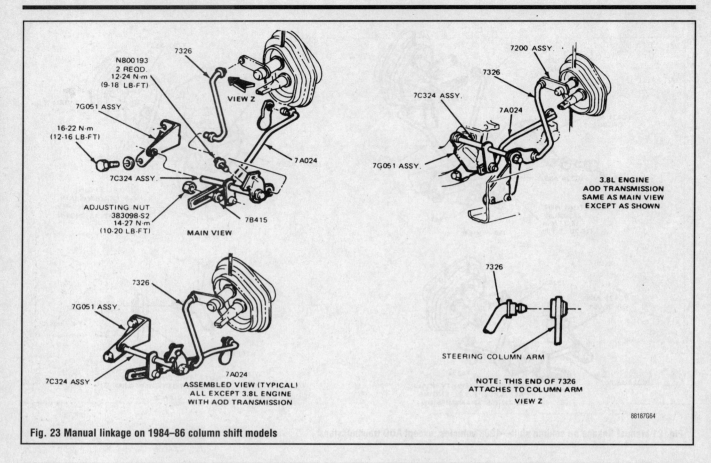

Fig. 23 Manual linkage on 1984–86 column shift models

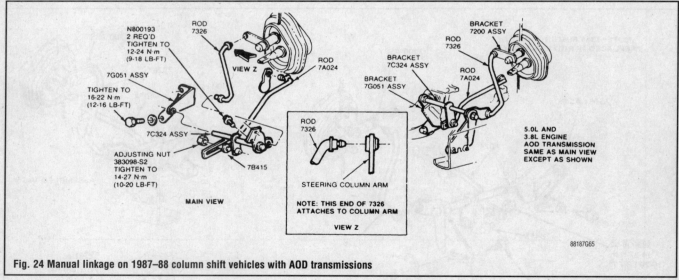

Fig. 24 Manual linkage on 1987–88 column shift vehicles with AOD transmissions

2. Loosen the adjusting nut or clamp at the shift lever so that the shift rod is free to slide. On models with a shift cable, remove the nut from the transmission lever and disconnect the cable from the transmission.

3. Place the manual shift lever on the transmission in the D (Drive) or OD (Overdrive) position. This is the second detent position from the full counterclockwise position.

4. Tighten the adjusting bolt. On cars with a cable, position the cable end on the transmission lever stud, aligning the flats. Tighten the adjusting nut.

5. Check the pointer alignment and transmission operation for all selector positions. If not correct, adjust linkage.

Floor or Console Shift

▶ **See Figures 25, 26, 27, 28 and 29**

1. Place the transmission shift lever in D (OD for AOD transmission).

2. Raise the vehicle and loosen the manual lever shift rod retaining nut. Move the transmission lever to D or OD position. D is the second detent, OD is the third from the full counterclockwise position.

3. With the transmission shift lever and transmission manual lever in position, tighten the nut at point A to 14–19 ft. lbs. (19–26 Nm).

4. Check transmission operation for all selector lever detent positions.

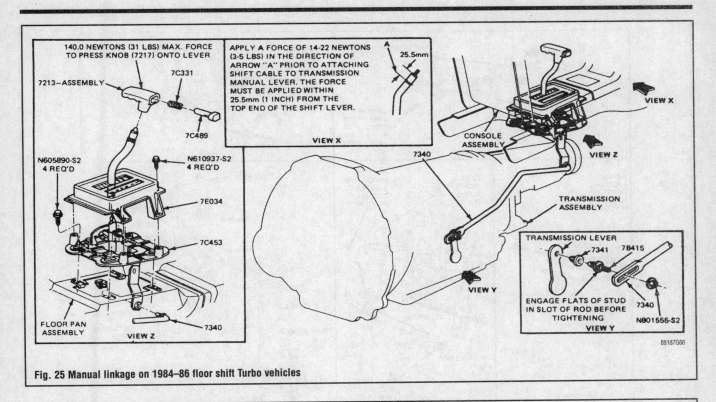

Fig. 25 Manual linkage on 1984–86 floor shift Turbo vehicles

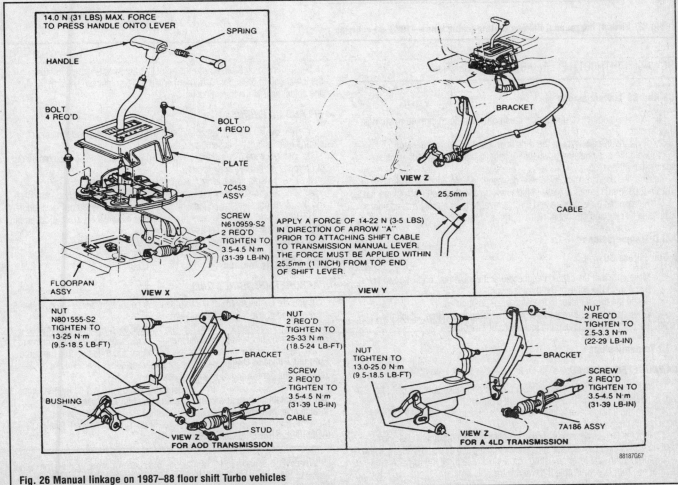

Fig. 26 Manual linkage on 1987–88 floor shift Turbo vehicles

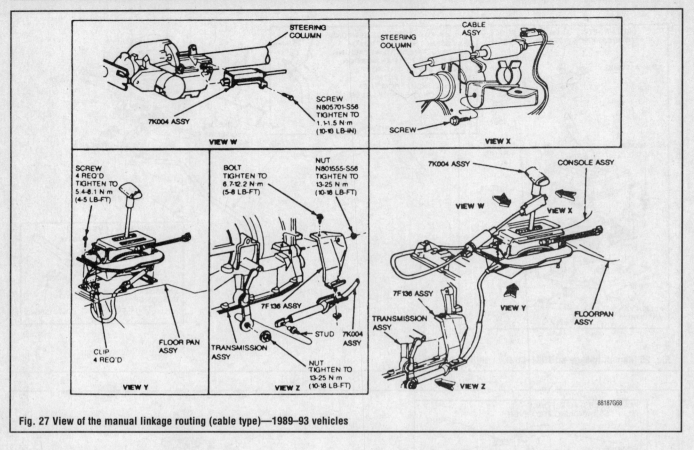

Fig. 27 View of the manual linkage routing (cable type)—1989–93 vehicles

DOWNSHIFT (THROTTLE) LINKAGE ADJUSTMENT

C3 And C5 Transmissions

1. With the engine off, disconnect the throttle and downshift return springs, if equipped.
2. Hold the throttle lever in the wide open position against the stop.
3. Hold the transmission downshift linkage in the full downshift position against the internal stop.
4. Turn the adjustment screw on the downshift lever to obtain 0.010–0.080 in. (0.254–2.032mm) clearance between the screw tip and the throttle shaft lever tab.
5. Release the transmission and throttle lever to their normal free positions. Install the throttle and downshift return springs, if removed.

A4LD Transmissions

▶ See Figure 30

1. Make sure that the cable is connected at the transmission kickdown lever.
2. Disconnect the cable at the throttle lever.
3. Rotate the throttle lever to the wide open position.
4. While holding the throttle lever in the wide open position, attach the cable, install the clip and push the locking lever into place.

AOD Transmissions

CARBURETED ENGINES

1. With the engine off, remove the air cleaner and make sure the fast idle cam is released; the throttle lever must be at the idle stop.
2. Turn the linkage lever adjusting screw counterclockwise until the end of the screw is flush with the face of the lever.
3. Turn the linkage adjustment screw in until there is a maximum clearance of 0.005 in. (0.127mm) between the throttle lever and the end of the adjustment screw.
4. Turn the linkage lever adjusting screw clockwise three full turns. A minimum of one turn is permissible if the screw travel is limited.

5. If it is not possible to turn the adjusting screw at least one full turn or if the initial gap of 0.005 in. (0.127mm) could not be obtained, perform the linkage adjustment at the transmission.

EFI AND SC ENGINES

1. Remove air cleaner cover and inlet tube from throttle body inlet to access throttle lever and cable assembly.
2. Using a wide blade screw driver, pry grooved pin on cable assembly out of grommet on throttle body lever.
3. Using a small screwdriver, push out white locking tab.
4. Check to ensure plastic block with pin and tab slides freely on notched rod. If it does not slide freely, the white tab may not be pushed out far enough.
5. While holding throttle lever firmly against its idle stop, push grooved pin into grommet on throttle lever as far as it will go.
6. Install air cleaner cover and air inlet tube.

AOD Alternate Method

CARBURETED ENGINES ONLY

If you are unable to adjust the throttle valve control linkage at the carburetor, as described above, proceed as follows.

1. At the transmission, loosen the 8 mm bolt on the throttle (TV) control rod sliding trunnion block. Make sure the trunnion block slides freely on the control rod.
2. Push up on the lower end of the TV control rod to insure that the carburetor linkage lever is held against the throttle lever. When the pressure is released, the control rod must stay in position.
3. Force the TV control lever on the transmission against its internal stop. While maintaining pressure tighten the trunnion block bolt. Make sure the throttle lever is at the idle stop.

AOD IDLE SPEED ADJUSTMENT

Whenever it is necessary to adjust the idle speed by more than 50 rpm either above or below the factory specifications, the adjustment screw on the linkage

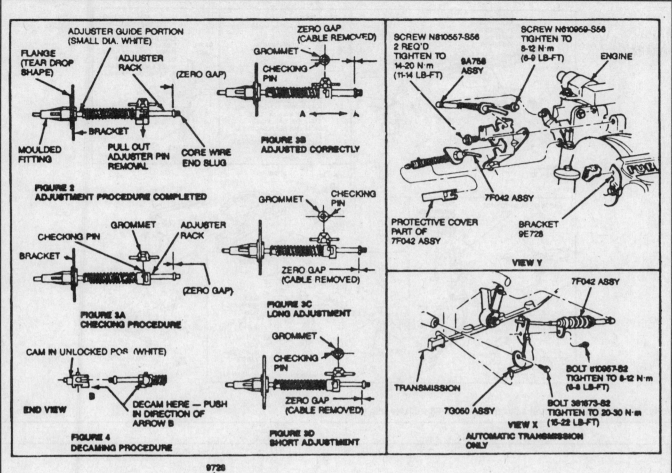

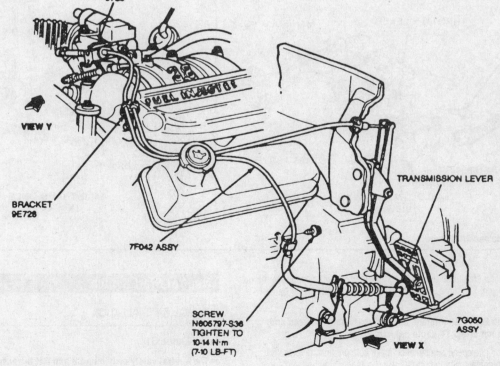

Fig. 28 Automatic shift control adjustment—1989–93 vehicles with the 3.8L engine

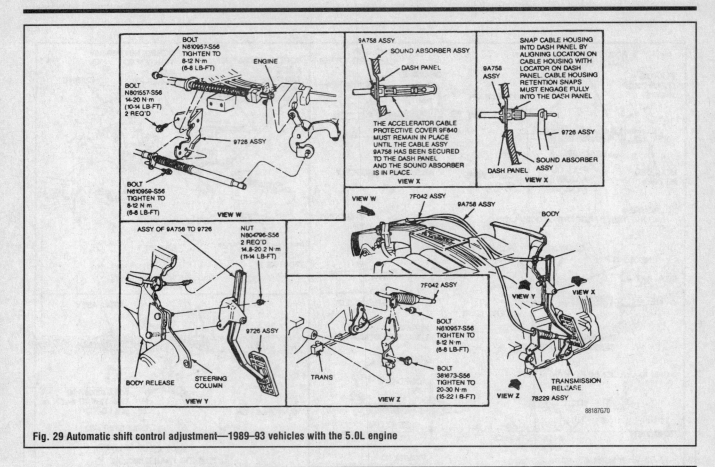

Fig. 29 Automatic shift control adjustment—1989–93 vehicles with the 5.0L engine

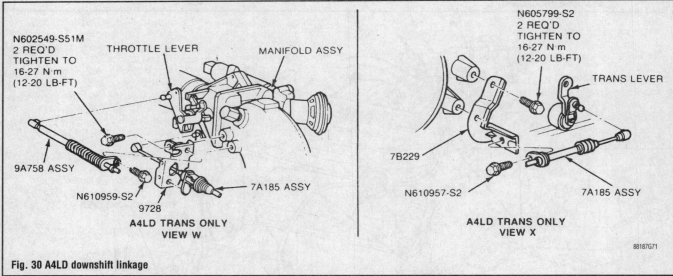

Fig. 30 A4LD downshift linkage

lever at the carburetor should be used. 1½ turns either way will change the idle speed by 50–100 rpm; 2½ turns either way will change the idle speed by 100–150 rpm.

➡ **On models with EFI or SC engines an Air Bypass valve is used and idle setting does not effect TV cable adjustment**

After making any idle speed adjustments, make sure the linkage lever and throttle lever are in contact with the throttle lever at its idle stop and verify that the shift lever is in N (neutral).

Neutral Start Switch

REMOVAL & INSTALLATION

♦ **See Figure 31**

➡ **The neutral safety switch on C3 and A4LD transmission is non-adjustable.**

1983–84 C5 With Floor Mounted Shifter

1. Raise and support the front end on jackstands.
2. Remove the downshift linkage rod from the transmission downshift lever.
3. Apply penetrating oil to the downshift lever shaft and nut. Remove the transmission downshift outer lever retaining nut and lever.
4. Remove the 2 switch attaching screws.
5. Unplug the connector and remove the switch.

To install:

6. Position the new switch on the transmission and install the bolts loosely.
7. Place the transmission lever in NEUTRAL, rotate the switch until the hole in the switch aligns with the depression in the case and insert a No. 43 drill bit through the hole and into the depression. Make sure the drill bit is fully inserted. Tighten the switch bolts to 60 inch lbs. Remove the gauge pin.
8. The remainder of installation is the reverse of removal. Torque the shaft nut to 20 ft. lbs.

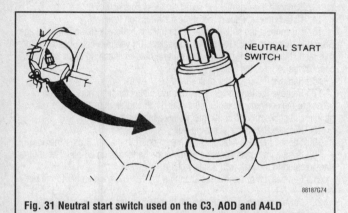

Fig. 31 Neutral start switch used on the C3, AOD and A4LD

1985–87 C5 With Floor Mounted Shifter

◆ **See Figure 32**

1. Disconnect the negative battery cable.
2. Raise and support the front end on jackstands.
3. Remove the downshift linkage rod from the transmission downshift lever.
4. Apply penetrating oil to the downshift lever shaft and nut. Remove the transmission downshift outer lever retaining nut and lever.
5. Remove the 2 switch attaching screws.
6. Unplug the connector and remove the switch.

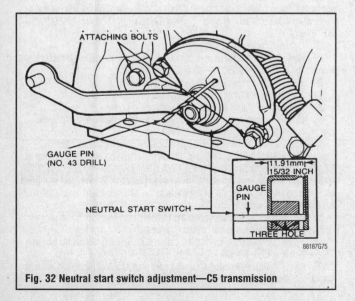

Fig. 32 Neutral start switch adjustment—C5 transmission

To install:

7. Position the new switch on the transmission and install the bolts loosely.
8. Place the transmission lever in NEUTRAL, rotate the switch until the hole in the switch aligns with the depression in the case and insert a No. 43 drill bit through the hole and into the depression. Make sure the drill bit is fully inserted. Tighten the switch bolts to 60 inch lbs. (7.3 Nm). Remove the gauge pin.
9. The remainder of installation is the reverse of removal. Tighten the shaft nut to 20 ft. lbs. (27 Nm).
10. Connect the negative battery cable.

1985–93 AOD With Floor Mounted Shifter

1. Place the selector lever in the MANUAL LOW position.
2. Disconnect the negative battery cable.
3. Raise and support the car on jackstands.
4. Disconnect the switch harness by pushing the harness straight up off the switch with a long screwdriver underneath the rubber plug section.
5. Using special tool socket T74P–77247–A, or equivalent, on a ratchet extension at least 9½ in. (241mm) long, unscrew the switch. Once the tool is on the switch, reach around the rear of the transmission over the extension housing.
6. Installation is the reverse of removal. Use a new O-ring. Tighten the switch to 11 ft. lbs. (15 Nm).

Transmission

REMOVAL & INSTALLATION

C3 Transmission

1. Disconnect the negative battery cable.
2. Raise and safely support the vehicle.
3. Place a drain pan under the transmission fluid pan. Starting at the rear of the pan and working toward the front, loosen the attaching bolts and allow the fluid to drain. Then remove all of the pan attaching bolts except two at the front, to allow the fluid to further drain. After all the fluid has drained, install two bolts on the rear side of the pan to temporarily hold it in place.
4. Remove the converter drain plug access cover and adapter plate bolts from the lower end of the converter housing.
5. Remove the four flexplate-to-converter attaching nuts. Crank the engine to turn the converter to gain access to the nuts, using a wrench on the crankshaft pulley attaching bolt. On 2.3L engines, never turn the engine backwards.
6. Crank the engine until the converter drain plug is accessible and remove the plug. Place a drain pan under the converter to catch the fluid. After all the fluid has been drained from the converter, reinstall the plug and tighten to 20–30 ft. lbs. (28–40 Nm).
7. Remove the driveshaft and install the extension housing seal replacer tool in the extension housing.
8. Remove the speedometer cable from the extension housing.
9. Disconnect the shift rod at the transmission manual lever using Shift Linkage Grommet Remover T84P-7341-A or equivalent. Disconnect the downshift rod at the transmission downshift lever.
10. Remove the starter-to-converter housing attaching bolts and position the starter out of the way.
11. Disconnect the neutral start switch wires from the switch.
12. Remove the vacuum line from the transmission vacuum unit.
13. Position a transmission jack under the transmission and raise it slightly.
14. Remove the engine rear support-to-crossmember nut.
15. Remove the crossmember-to-frame side support attaching bolts and remove the crossmember.
16. Remove the inlet pipe steady rest from the inlet pipe and rear engine support; then disconnect the muffler inlet pipe at the exhaust manifold and secure it.
17. Lower the jack under the transmission and allow the transmission to hang.
18. Position a jack to the front of the engine and raise the engine to gain access to the two upper converter housing-to-engine attaching bolts.
19. Disconnect the oil cooler lines at the transmission. Plug all openings to keep out dirt.

20. Remove the lower converter housing-to-engine attaching bolts.
21. Remove the transmission filter tube.
22. Secure the transmission to the jack with a safety chain.
23. Remove the two upper converter housing-to-engine attaching bolts. Move the transmission to the rear and down to remove it from under the vehicle.

To install:

24. Tighten the converter drain plug to 20–30 ft. lbs. (28–40 Nm). if not previously done.
25. Position the converter to the transmission making sure the converter hub is fully engaged in the pump gear. The dimension given in the accompanying illustration is for guidance only. It does not indicate engagement.
26. With the converter properly installed, place the transmission on the jack and secure with safety chain.
27. Rotate the converter so the drive studs and drain plug are in alignment with their holes in the flexplate.
28. With the transmission mounted on a transmission jack, move the converter and transmission assembly forward into position being careful not to damage the flexplate and the converter pilot.
29. During this move, to avoid damage, do not allow the transmission to get into a nosed down position as this will cause the converter to move forward and disengage from the pump gear. The converter must rest squarely against the flexplate. This indicates that the converter pilot is not binding in the engine crankshaft.
30. Install the two upper converter housing-to-engine attaching bolts and tighten to 28–38 ft. lbs.
31. Remove the safety chain from the transmission.
32. Insert the filler tube in the stub tube and secure it to the cylinder block with the attaching bolt. Tighten the bolt to 28–38 ft. lbs. If the stub tube is loosened or dislodged, it should be replaced.
33. Install the oil cooler lines in the retaining clip at the cylinder block. Connect the lines to the transmission case.
34. Remove the jack supporting the front of the engine.
35. Position the muffler inlet pipe support bracket to the converter housing and install the four lower converter housing-to-engine attaching bolts. Tighten the bolts to 28–38 ft. lbs. (38–51 Nm).
36. Raise the transmission. Position the crossmember to the frame side supports and install the attaching bolts. Tighten the bolts to 30–40 ft. lbs. (41–54 Nm).
37. Lower the transmission and install the rear engine support-to-crossmember nut. Tighten the nut to 30–40 ft. lbs. (41–54 Nm).
38. Remove the transmission jack.
39. Install the vacuum hose on the transmission vacuum unit. Install the vacuum line into the retaining clip.
40. Connect the neutral start switch plug to the switch.
41. Install the starter and tighten the attaching bolts.
42. Install the four flexplate-to-converter attaching nuts.
43. Install the converter drain plug access cover and adaptor plate bolts. Tighten the bolts to 15–20 ft. lbs. (20–30 Nm).
44. Connect the muffler inlet pipe to the exhaust manifold.
45. Connect the transmission shift rod to the manual lever.
46. Connect the downshift rod to the downshift lever.
47. Connect the speedometer cable to the extension housing.
48. Install the driveshaft. Tighten the companion flange U-bolt attaching nuts to 30 ft. lbs. (41 Nm).
49. Adjust the manual and downshift linkage as required.
50. Carefully lower the vehicle, then connect the negative battery cable.
51. Fill the transmission to the proper level with Dexron®II. Pour in 5 qts. (4.7L) of fluid; then run the engine and add fluid as required.
52. Check the transmission, converter assembly and oil cooler lines for leaks.

C5 Transmission

1. Open the hood and install protective covers on the fenders.
2. Disconnect the battery negative cable.
3. On Cougars equipped with a 3.8L engine, remove the air cleaner assembly.
4. Remove the fan shroud attaching bolts and position the shroud back over the fan.
5. On Cougars equipped with a 3.8L engine, loosen the clamp and disconnect the Thermactor® air injection hose at the catalytic converter check valve.

The check valve is located on the right side of the engine compartment near the dash panel.

6. On Cougars equipped with a 3.8L engine, remove the two transmission-to-engine attaching bolts located at the top of the transmission bell housing. These bolts are accessible from the engine compartment.
7. Raise and safely support the vehicle.
8. Remove the driveshaft.
9. Disconnect the muffler inlet pipe from the catalytic converter outlet pipe. Support the muffler/pipe assembly by wiring it to a convenient underbody bracket.
10. Remove the nuts attaching the exhaust pipe(s) to the exhaust manifold(s).
11. Pull back on the catalytic coverts to release the converter hangers from the mounting bracket.
12. Remove the speedometer clamps bolt and pull the speedometer out of the extension housing.
13. Separate the neutral start switch harness connector.
14. Detach the kick down rod at the transmission lever.
15. Disconnect the shift linkage at the linkage bellcrank using Shift Linkage Grommet Remover T84P-7341-A or equivalent. On vehicles equipped with floor mounted shift, remove the shift cable routing bracket attaching bolts and disconnect the cable at the transmission lever.
16. Remove the converter dust shield.
17. Remove the torque converter to drive plate attaching nuts. To gain access to the converter nuts, turn the crankshaft and drive plate using a ratchet handle and socket on the crankshaft pulley attaching bolt.
18. Remove the starter attaching bolts.
19. Loosen the nuts attaching the rear support to the No. 3 crossmember.
20. Position a transmission jack under the transmission oil pan. Secure the transmission to the jack with a safety chain.
21. Remove the through bolts attaching the No. 3 crossmember to the body brackets.
22. Lower the transmission enough to allow access to the cooler line fittings. Disconnect the cooler lines.
23. On Cougars, remove the (4) remaining transmission-to-engine attaching bolts (2 each side). On all models, remove the (6) transmission-to-engine attaching bolts.
24. Pull the transmission back to disengage the converter studs from the drive plate. Lower the transmission out of the vehicle.

To install:

25. Raise the transmission into the vehicle. As the transmission is being slowly raised into position, rotate the torque converter until the studs and drain plug are aligned with the holes in the drive plate.
26. Move the converter/transmission assembly forward against the back of the engine. Make sure the converter studs engage the drive plate and that the transmission dowels on the back of the engine engage the bolts holes in the bellhousing.
27. On Cougars equipped with a 3.8L engine, install four transmission-to-engine attaching bolts (2 each side). On all other models, install the (6) transmission-to-engine attaching bolts. Tighten the attaching bolts to 40–50 ft. lbs. (55–67 Nm).
28. Connect the cooler lines.
29. Raise the transmission and install the No. 3 crossmember through bolts. Tighten the attaching nuts to 20–30 ft. lbs. (30–41 Nm).
30. Remove the safety chain and transmission jack.
31. Tighten the rear support attaching nuts to 30–50 ft. lbs. (41–68 Nm).
32. Position the starter and install the attaching bolts.
33. Install the torque converter to drive plate attaching nuts. Tighten the attaching nuts to 20–30 ft. lbs. (30–41 Nm).
34. Position the dust shield and on vehicles with column mounted shift, position the linkage bellcrank bracket. Install the attaching bolts and tighten to 12–16 ft. lbs. (16–22 Nm).
35. Connect the shift linkage to the linkage bellcrank. On vehicles equipped with floor mounted shift, connect the cable to the shift lever and install the routing bracket attaching bolt.
36. Connect the kick down rod to the transmission lever.
37. Connect the neutral start switch harness.
38. Install the speedometer and the clamp bolt. Tighten the clamp bolt to 35–54 inch lbs. (3.9–6.1 Nm).
39. Install the catalytic converts using new seal(s) at the pipe(s) to exhaust manifold connection(s).

40. Install the pipe(s) to exhaust manifold attaching nuts. Do not tighten the attaching nuts.

41. Remove the wire supporting the muffler/pipe assembly and connect the pipe to the converter outlet. Do not tighten the attaching nuts.

42. Align the exhaust system and tighten the manifold and converter outlet attaching nuts.

43. Install the driveshaft.

44. Check and if necessary, adjust the shift linkage.

45. Carefully lower the vehicle.

46. On Cougars equipped with a 3.8L engine, install the two transmission-to-engine attaching bolts located at the top of the transmission bellhousing.

47. On Cougars equipped with a 3.8L engine, connect the Thermactor® air injection hose to the converter check valve.

48. Position the fan shroud and install the attaching bolts.

49. On Cougars equipped with a 3.8L engine, install the air cleaner assembly.

50. Connect the battery negative cable.

51. Start the engine. Make sure the engine cranks only when the selector lever is positioned in the neutral (N) or Park (P) detent.

52. Fill the transmission with type H fluid.

53. Raise the vehicle and inspect for fluid leaks.

Automatic Overdrive (A4LD) Transmission

▶ See Figures 33 thru 41

1. Disconnect the negative battery cable.

2. Raise and safely support the vehicle.

3. Place a drain pan under transmission fluid pan. Starting at the rear of pan and working toward front, loosen attaching bolts and allow fluid to drain. Finally remove all the pan attaching bolts except two at the front, to allow the fluid to further drain. With fluid drained install to bolts on the rear side of the pan to temporarily hold it in place.

4. Remove the converter access cover and adapter plate bolts from the lower left side of converter housing.

5. Remove the four flexplate-to-converter attaching nuts by placing a 22mm socket and breaker bar on the crankshaft pulley attaching (center) bolt. Rotate pulley clockwise (as viewed from front) to gain access to each of the nuts.

➡**Never rotate a 2.3L engine in the counterclockwise direction (as viewed from the front) serious engine damage can occur!**

6. Scribe a mark indexing the driveshaft to axle flange, disconnect the driveshaft from the rear axle and slide shaft rearward from the transmission. Install Extension Housing Seal Replacer T74P-77052-A or equivalent in the extension housing to prevent fluid leakage.

7. Disconnect and remove speedometer sensor from extension housing.

8. Disconnect shift cable from transmission manual lever and retainer bracket (mounted at extension housing). Disconnect downshift cable at transmission downshift lever. Depress tab on cable downshift retainer and remove downshift cable from bracket.

9. Remove starter-to-converter housing attaching bolts and position out of the way.

10. Tag and detach the neutral start switch wires, converter clutch solenoid and the 3–4 shift solenoid connector.

11. Remove vacuum line from transmission vacuum modulator.

12. Position a transmission jack under transmission and raise it slightly.

13. Remove the engine rear support-to-crossmember bolts.

➡**Certain models require the removal of some or all exhaust system components, before transmission can be removed from vehicle. Check for clearance and remove exhaust pipe or catalytic converter before removing crossmember.**

14. Remove crossmember-to-frame side support attaching bolts. Remove crossmember insulator support and damper.

15. Lower jack under transmission and allow transmission to hang.

16. Position a jack under the front of the engine. Raise engine to gain access to two upper converter housing-to-engine attaching bolts.

17. Disconnect oil cooler lines from fittings at transmission and plug all openings to keep dirt out.

18. Remove the lower converter housing-to-engine attaching bolts and remove transmission filler tube.

19. Secure transmission to the jack with a safety chain or strap.

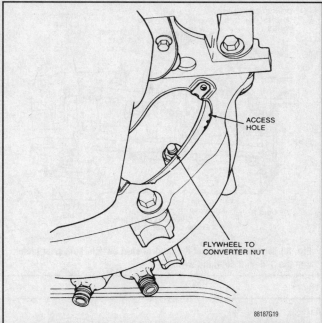

Fig. 33 Rotate the pulley clockwise to access each flexplate-to-converter nut

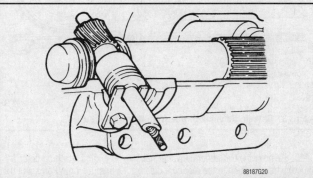

Fig. 34 Remove the driveshaft and install a suitable seal installation tool to prevent fluid from leaking out

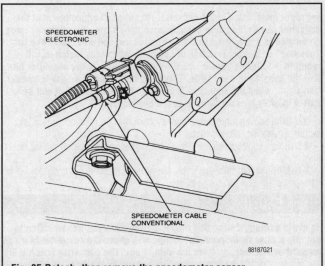

Fig. 35 Detach, then remove the speedometer sensor

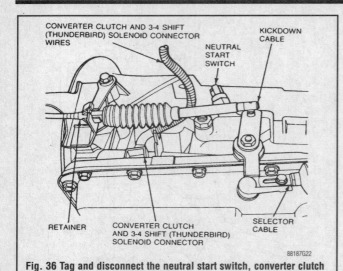

Fig. 36 Tag and disconnect the neutral start switch, converter clutch and the 3–4 shift solenoid wiring

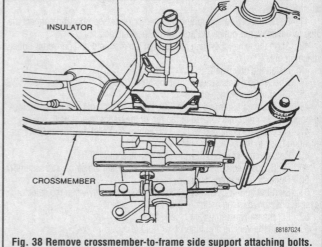

Fig. 38 Remove crossmember-to-frame side support attaching bolts. Remove crossmember insulator support and damper

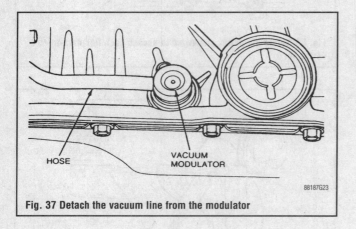

Fig. 37 Detach the vacuum line from the modulator

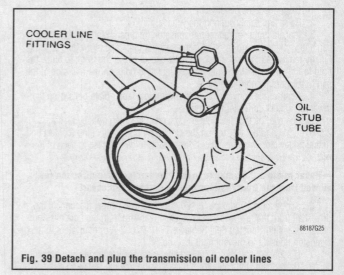

Fig. 39 Detach and plug the transmission oil cooler lines

20. Remove the two upper converter housing-to-engine attaching bolts. Slide the transmission to the rear so it disengages from the dowel pins and the converter is disengaged from the flexplate.

21. Lower and remove transmission from vehicle. If necessary, remove the torque converter from vehicle.

To install:

➡ Proper installation of the converter requires full engagement of the converter hub in the pump gear. To accomplish this, the converter must be pushed in and at the same time rotated through what feels like two "notches" or bumps. Rotation of converter when fully installed will result in a "clicking" noise heard which is caused by the converter hitting the housing-to-case bolts. This is an indication of proper installation since, when the converter is attached to the flexplate, it will be pulled slightly forward away from the bolt heads.

22. With converter properly installed, place the transmission on jack and secure with a safety chain or strap.

23. Rotate converter so drive studs are aligned with there holes in the flexplate.

24. Move transmission assembly forward into position, being careful not to damage flexplate and converter pilot.

✳✳ CAUTION

To avoid damage during this move, do not allow the transmission to get into a nose down position, as this will cause the converter to move forward and disengage from the pump gear. The converter housing is

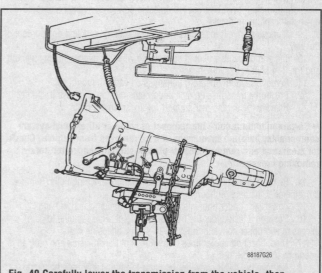

Fig. 40 Carefully lower the transmission from the vehicle, then . . .

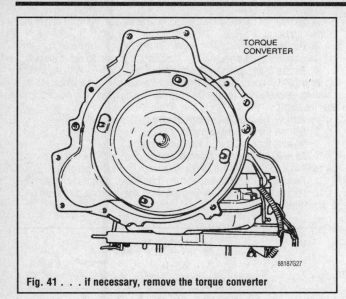

Fig. 41 . . . if necessary, remove the torque converter

piloted into position by dowels in the rear of the engine block. The converter must rest squarely against the flexplate. This indicates that the converter pilot is not binding in the end of the crankshaft.

25. Install two converter housing-to-engine attaching bolts at the engine dowel locations and tighten to 28–38 ft. lbs. (38–51 Nm).

26. Install the remaining housing-to-engine attaching bolts and tighten to 28–38 ft. lbs. (38–51 Nm).

27. Remove the safety chain or strap from the transmission.

28. Insert the filler tube into the stub tube and secure it to cylinder block with attaching bolt and tighten to 28–38 ft. lbs. (38–51 Nm).

➡**If stub tube becomes loose or dislodged, it should be replaced.**

29. Install the fluid cooler lines into the retaining clip at cylinder block. connect fittings to the transmission case.

30. Raise the transmission. Position the crossmember, insulator, support and damper to frame side supports. Install attaching bolts and tighten to 20–30 ft. lbs. (30–41 Nm).

31. Align and lower transmission to install rear engine support nut and tighten to 60–80 ft. lbs. (81–108 Nm).

32. Install vacuum hose onto vacuum unit and into retaining clip.

33. Connect plug to neutral start switch. Connect converter clutch solenoid wires and 3–4 shift solenoid wires.

34. Install starter and tighten attaching bolts to 15–20 ft. lbs. (20–27 Nm).

35. Install the four flexplate-to-converter attaching nuts and tighten to 20–34 ft. lbs. (27–46 Nm).

36. Install the converter access cover, adapter plate bolts and tighten to 12–16 ft. lbs. (16–22 Nm).

37. Reconnect any exhaust system components that were disconnected for transmission removal.

38. Position selector cable in bracket on transmission extension housing. Press the end of cable onto ball stud on lower portion of selector lever and install retaining clip on bracket.

39. Connect downshift cable to downshift lever. Install speedometer sensor and connect wiring.

40. Align the scribe marks on driveshaft to the rear axle companion flange and tighten attaching nuts to 70–95 ft. lbs. (95–129 Nm).

41. Adjust manual and downshift linkage as required. Lower vehicle.

42. Fill the transmission to the correct level with Mercon® or equivalent fluid. Start the engine and shift the transmission to all ranges, then recheck the fluid level.

Automatic Overdrive (AOD) Transmission

1983–89 VEHICLES

▶ See Figure 42

1. Disconnect the negative battery cable.

2. Raise and safely support the vehicle.

3. Place a suitable drain pan under the transmission fluid pan. Starting at the rear of the pan and working toward the front, loosen the attaching bolts and allow the fluid to drain. Finally remove all of the pan attaching bolts except two at the front, to allow the fluid to further drain. With fluid drained, install two bolts on the rear side of the pan to temporarily hold it in place.

4. Remove the converter drain plug access cover from the lower end of the converter housing.

5. Remove the converter-to-flexplate attaching nuts. place a wrench on the crankshaft pulley attaching bolt to turn the converter to gain access to the nuts.

6. Place a drain pan under the converter to catch the fluid. With the wrench on the crankshaft pulley attaching bolts, turn the converter to gain access to the converter drain plug and remove the plug. After the fluid has been drained, reinstall the plug.

7. Scribe a mark indexing the driveshaft to axle flange, disconnect the driveshaft from the rear axle and slide shaft rearward from the transmission. Install a seal installation tool in the extension housing to prevent fluid leakage.

8. Disconnect the cable from the terminal on the starter motor. Remove the three attaching bolts and remove the starter motor. Disconnect the neutral start switch wires at the plug connector.

9. Remove the rear mount-to-crossmember attaching bolts and the two crossmember-to-frame attaching bolts.

10. Remove the two engine rear support-to-extension housing attaching bolts.

11. Disconnect the TV linkage rod from the transmission TV lever. Disconnect the manual rod from the transmission manual lever at the transmission.

12. Remove the two bolts securing the bellcrank bracket to the converter housing.

13. Raise the transmission with a transmission jack to provide clearance to remove the crossmember. Remove the rear mount from the crossmember and remove the crossmember from the side supports.

14. Lower the transmission to gain access to the oil cooler lines.

15. Disconnect each oil line from the fittings on the transmission using Cooler Line Disconnect Tool T86P-77265-AH or equivalent.

16. Disconnect the speedometer cable from the extension housing.

17. Remove the bolt that secures the transmission fluid filler tube to the cylinder block. Lift the filler tube and the dipstick from the transmission.

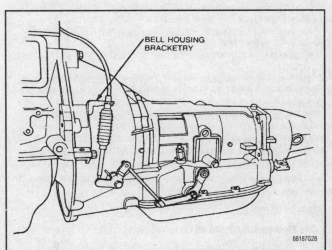

Fig. 42 Unfasten the two bellcrank bracket-to-converter housing bolts

18. Secure the transmission to the jack with the chain.

19. Remove the converter housing-to-cylinder block attaching bolts.

20. Carefully move the transmission and converter assembly away from the engine and, at the same time, lower the jack to clear the underside of the vehicle.

21. Remove the converter and mount the transmission in Bench Mounted Holding Fixture T57L-500-B, or equivalent holding fixture.

To install:

22. Tighten the converter drain plug to 8–28 ft. lbs. (11–38 Nm).

23. Position the converter on the transmission, making sure the converter drive flats are fully engaged in the pump gear by rotating the converter.

24. With the converter properly installed, place the transmission on the jack. Secure the transmission to the jack with a chain.

25. Rotate the converter until the studs and drain plug are in alignment with the holes in the flexplate.

✵✵ WARNING

Lubricate the pilot bushing with a suitable chassis grease.

26. Align the yellow balancing marks on converter and flexplate.

27. Move the converter and transmission assembly forward into position, using care not to damage the flexplate and the converter pilot. The converter must rest squarely against the flexplate. This indicates that the converter pilot is not binding in the engine crankshaft.

28. Install and tighten the converter housing-to-engine attaching bolts to 40–50 ft. lbs. (55–68 Nm), making sure that the vacuum tube retaining clips are properly positioned.

29. Remove the safety chain from around the transmission.

30. Install a new O-ring on the lower end of the transmission filler tube. Insert the tube in the transmission case and secure the tube to the engine with the attaching bolts.

31. Connect the speedometer cable to the extension housing.

32. Connect the oil cooler lines to the right side of the transmission case. Tighten the lines to 24–31 Nm).

33. Position the crossmember on the side supports. Position the rear mount on the crossmember and install the attaching bolt and nut.

34. Secure the engine rear support to the extension housing and tighten the bolts to 35–40 ft. lbs. (47–54 Nm).

35. Lower the transmission and remove the jack.

36. Secure the crossmember to the side supports with the attaching bolts and tighten them to 70–100 ft. lbs. (95–136 Nm).

37. Position the bellcrank to the converter housing and install the two attaching bolts.

38. Connect the TV linkage rod to the transmission TV lever. Connect the manual linkage rod to the manual lever at the transmission.

39. Secure the converter-to-flexplate attaching nuts and tighten them to 20–30 ft. lbs. (27–41 Nm).

40. Install the converter housing access cover and secure it with the attaching bolts.

41. Secure the starter motor in place with the attaching bolts. Connect the cable to the terminal on the starter. Connect the neutral start switch wires at the plug connector.

42. Align the scribe marks and connect the driveshaft to the rear axle.

43. Adjust the shift linkage as required.

44. Adjust the throttle linkage.

45. Carefully lower the vehicle, then connect the negative battery cable.

46. Fill the transmission to the correct level with Mercon® or equivalent fluid. Start the engine and shift the transmission to all ranges, then recheck the fluid level.

1990–93 VEHICLES

▶ **See Figures 43, 44 and 45**

1. Disconnect the negative battery cable.

2. Raise and safely support the vehicle.

3. Place the drain pan under the transmission fluid pan. Starting at the rear of the pan and working toward the front, loosen the attaching bolts and allow the fluid to drain. Finally remove all of the pan attaching bolts except two at the front, to allow the fluid to further drain. With fluid drained, install two bolts on the rear side of the pan to temporarily hold it in place.

4. Remove the converter drain plug access cover from the lower end of the converter housing.

5. Remove the converter-to-flexplate attaching nuts. place a wrench on the crankshaft pulley attaching bolt to turn the converter to gain access to the nuts.

6. Place a drain pan under the converter to catch the fluid. With the wrench on the crankshaft pulley attaching bolts, turn the converter to gain access to the converter drain plug and remove the plug. After the fluid has been drained, reinstall the plug.

7. Remove the catalytic converter assembly.

8. Remove the body reinforcement.

9. Remove the exhaust pipe and muffler assembly.

10. To maintain balance, matchmark the rear driveshaft yoke and the companion flange so the driveshaft can be installed in its original position.

11. Remove the four bolts retaining the driveshaft to the companion flange.

12. Loosen the differential housing assembly rear mounting nuts about 0.25 inch (6.4mm).

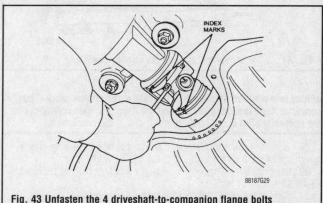

Fig. 43 Unfasten the 4 driveshaft-to-companion flange bolts

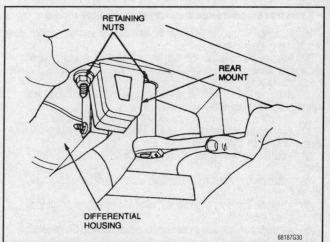

Fig. 44 Loosen the differential housing assembly rear nuts approximately ¼ inch

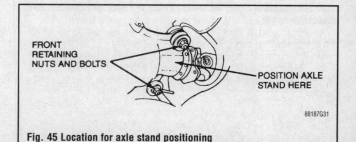

Fig. 45 Location for axle stand positioning

13. Position a suitable jackstand stand under the front of the differential housing and remove the forward mounting nuts and bushings. Pull the tube from the vent hole in the subframe.

➡**Use care when positioning the driveshaft so not to nick, burr of contaminate the driveshaft yoke and companion flange.**

14. Lower the front of the differential housing with the axle stand and slide the driveshaft out of the transmission above the axle housing. Let the driveshaft rest on the front driveshaft support and axle assembly.

15. Disconnect the cable from the terminal on the starter motor. Unfasten the three retaining bolts, then remove the starter motor. Detach the neutral start switch wires at the plug connector.

16. Remove the rear mount-to-crossmember retaining bolts and the two crossmember-to-frame retaining bolts.

17. Remove the two engine rear support-to-extension housing retaining bolts.

18. Disconnect the TV linkage rod or cable from the transmission TV lever ball stud. Disconnect the cable from the bellcrank lever stud and remove the self-tapping bolt from the bell housing bracketry.

19. Carefully disconnect the manual cable form the transmission manual lever at the transmission. Remove the cable mounting bracket from the case using Grommet Remover T84P-7341-A or equivalent.

20. Remove the two bolts retaining the bellcrank bracket to the converter housing.

➡**Disconnect and remove any interfering exhaust system components.**

21. Raise the transmission with a transmission jack to provide clearance to remove the crossmember. Remove the rear mount from the crossmember and remove the crossmember from the side supports.

22. Lower the transmission for access to the oil cooler lines. Detach and plug each oil line from the fittings on the transmission.

23. Disconnect the speedometer cable from the extension housing.

24. Remove the bolt that retains the transmission fluid filler tube to the cylinder block. Lift the filler tube and the dipstick from the transmission.

25. Secure the transmission to the jack with a chain.

26. Remove the converter housing-to-cylinder block retaining bolts.

27. Carefully move the transmission and converter assembly away from the engine and, at the same time, lower the jack to clear the underside of the vehicle.

28. Remove the converter and mount the transmission in Bench Mounted Holding Fixture T57L-500-B, or equivalent holding fixture.

To install:

29. Tighten the converter drain plug to 8–28 ft. lbs. (11–38 Nm).

➡**Lubricate the pilot with suitable chassis grease.**

30. Position the converter on the transmission, making sure the converter drive flats are fully engaged in the pump gear by rotating the converter.

31. With the converter properly installed, place the transmission on the jack. Secure the transmission to the jack with a chain.

32. Rotate the converter until the studs and drain plug are in alignment with the holes in the flexplate.

33. Align the orange balancing marks on converter stud and flexplate bolt hole if balancing marks are present.

➡**Before installing the torque converter on the flexplate retaining nut, a check should be made to ensure that the converter is properly seated. The converter should move freely with respect to the flexplate. Grasp the stud. Movement back and forth should result in a metallic clank noise if the converter is properly seated. If the converter will not move, the transmission must be removed and the converter repositioned so that the impeller hub is properly engaged in the pump gear.**

34. Move the converter and transmission assembly forward into position, using care not to damage the flexplate and the converter pilot. The converter must rest squarely against the flexplate. This indicates that the converter pilot is not binding in the engine crankshaft.

35. Install and tighten the converter housing-to-engine attaching bolts to 40–50 ft. lbs. (55–68 Nm).

36. Remove the safety chain from around the transmission.

37. Install a new O-ring on the lower end of the transmission filler tube. Insert the tube in the transmission case and secure the tube to the engine with the attaching bolts.

38. Connect the speedometer cable to the extension housing.

39. Connect the oil cooler lines to the right side of the transmission case. Tighten the lines to 12–18 ft. lbs. (16–24 Nm).

40. Position the crossmember on the side supports. Position the rear mount on the crossmember and install the attaching bolt and nut. Tighten the nut to 65–84 ft. lbs. (88–115 Nm).

41. Secure the engine rear support to the extension housing and tighten the bolts to 51–70 ft. lbs. (68–95 Nm).

42. Lower the transmission and remove the jack.

43. Secure the crossmember to the side supports with the attaching bolts and tighten them to 70–100 ft. lbs. (95–136 Nm).

44. Connect the TV linkage rod to the transmission TV lever. Connect the manual linkage rod to the manual lever at the transmission.

45. Secure the converter-to-flexplate attaching nuts and tighten them to 12–16 ft. lbs. (16–22 Nm).

46. Install the converter housing access cover and secure it with the attaching bolts. Tighten the bolts to 12–16 ft. lbs. (16–22 Nm).

47. Secure the starter motor in place with the attaching bolts. Connect the cable to the terminal on the starter. Connect the neutral start switch wires at the plug connector.

48. Slide the driveshaft into the transmission.

49. Raise the differential housing with the axle stand and install the bushings and retaining nuts. Tighten to 68–100 ft. lbs. (92–136 Nm). Remove the axle stand.

50. Tighten the differential assembly rear retaining nuts to 122–156 ft. lbs. (165–211 Nm).

51. Position the vent tube in the hole of the subframe.

➡**Lubricate the yoke splines with Premium Long Life Grease, or equivalent.**

52. Align the driveshaft yoke and companion flange and install the retaining bolts. Tighten to 70–95 ft. lbs. (95–129 Nm).

53. Install the catalytic converter, exhaust pipe and muffler and the body reinforcement.

54. Carefully lower the vehicle, then connect the negative battery cable.

55. Fill the transmission to the correct level with Mercon® or equivalent fluid. Start the engine and shift the transmission to all ranges, then recheck the fluid level.

56. Adjust the manual shift linkage as required. Adjust the TV linkage.

4R70W Transmission

1994–95 VEHICLES

◆ See Figure 46

1. Disconnect the negative battery cable.

2. Raise and safely support the vehicle.

3. Disconnect the driveshaft from the rear axle assembly and slide the shaft rearward from the transmission. To maintain driveshaft balance, mark the rear driveshaft yoke and rear axle universal joint flange so the driveshaft can be installed in its original position.

4. Remove the exhaust system.

5. Place a suitable drain pan under the transmission oil pan. Starting at the rear of the pan and working forward, loosen the retaining bolts and allow the fluid to drain. Finally remove all of the transmission pan retaining bolts except the two at the front, to allow the fluid to further drain. With the fluid drained, install two bolts on the rear side of the transmission pan to temporarily hold it in place.

6. Remove the converter drain plug access cover from the lower end of the converter housing.

7. Remove the torque converter-to-flexplate retaining nuts. Place a wrench on the crankshaft pulley retaining bolt to turn the torque converter to gain access to the nuts.

8. Place a suitable drain pan under the torque converter. With the wrench on the crankshaft pulley retaining bolts, turn the torque converter to gain access to the converter housing plug and remove the converter housing access plug. After the fluid has been drained, install the converter housing access plug.

9. Disconnect the cable from the terminal on the starter motor. Unfasten the retaining bolts, then remove the starter. Detach the park/neutral position start switch wires at the plug connector.

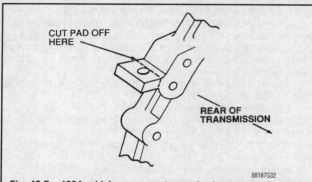

Fig. 46 For 1994 vehicles, you must use a hacksaw to cut the transmission pad off the left side of the converter housing

10. Remove the rear mount-to-crossmember retaining bolts and the two crossmember-to-frame retaining bolts.

11. Remove the two engine rear support-to-extension housing retaining bolts.

12. Carefully disconnect the shift cable from the transmission manual control lever at the transmission by removing the adjusting nut.

13. Detach the wiring connectors from the wiring harness assembly.

14. Raise the transmission with a suitable jack to provide clearance to remove the rear engine support. Remove the rear engine support insulator from the rear engine support and remove the rear support from the side support.

15. Carefully lower the transmission to gain access to the transmission oil cooler inlet tube.

16. Disconnect the transmission oil cooler inlet tube from the fittings on the transmission.

17. Detach the vehicle speed sensor from the extension housing.

18. Remove the bolt that retains the oil filler tube to the cylinder block. Lift the oil filler tube and the oil lever indicator from the transmission.

19. Secure the transmission to the jack with a chain.

20. Remove the converter housing-to-cylinder block retaining bolts.

21. For 1994 vehicles, remove the transmission pad from the left side of the converter housing using a hacksaw.

22. Carefully move the transmission and torque converter away from the engine and, at the same time, lower the jack to clear the underside of the vehicle.

To install:

23. Tighten the converter housing plug to 21–23 ft. lbs. (28–30 Nm).

➡**Make sure the lubricate the pilot with chassis grease.**

24. Position the torque converter on the transmission, ensuring the converter drive flats are fully engaged in the pump gear by rotating the torque converter.

25. With the torque converter properly installed, place the transmission on a jack. Secure the transmission to the jack with a chain.

26. Rotate the torque converter until the studs and converter housing access plug are in alignment with the holes in the flexplate.

27. If present, align the orange balancing marks on the converter stud and flexplate bolt hole.

28. Move the torque converter and transmission assembly forward into position, using care not to damage the flexplate and the converter pilot. The torque converter face must rest squarely against the flexplate. This indicates that the converter pilot is not binding in the engine crankshaft.

➡**Before installing the crankshaft to the flexplate retaining nut, a check should be make to ensure that the torque converter is properly seated. The torque converter should move freely with respect to the flexplate. Grasp the stud. Movement back and forth should result in a metallic clank noise if the torque converter is properly seated. If the torque converter will not move, the transmission must be removed and the torque converter repositioned so that the impeller hub is properly engaged in the pump gear.**

29. Connect the EGR tube to the torque converter assembly.

30. Position the transmission to the engine and install the retaining bolts. Tighten the bolts to 40–50 ft. lbs. (50–68 Nm).

31. Install the nuts retaining the torque converter to the flexplate. Tighten the nuts to 20–34 ft. lbs. (27–46 Nm).

32. Install the starter and the oil fill tube.

33. Connect the transmission shift selector mounting bracket.

34. Install the transmission rear engine support assembly. Tighten the bolts to 64–81 ft. lbs. (87–110 Nm).

35. Install the vehicle speed sensor and electrical connector.

36. Remove the transmission jack from under the vehicle.

37. Position the driveshaft yoke inside the extension housing.

38. Connect both transmission oil cooler inlet tube and oil cooler tube. Tighten to 15–19 ft. lbs. (20–26 ft. lbs.).

39. Raise the rear axle housing, then install the retaining nuts.

40. Install the driveshaft and secure with the retaining bolts.

41. Install the exhaust system components.

42. Carefully lower the vehicle, then connect the negative battery cable.

43. Fill the transmission with the proper type and amount of fluid.

44. Start the engine and check transmission operation.

1996–97 VEHICLES

1. Disconnect the negative battery cable.

2. Raise and safely support the vehicle.

3. Properly drain the transmission fluid.

4. Remove any exhaust system components necessary for transmission removal.

5. Remove the converter access cover and adapter plate bolts from the engine oil pan.

⁂ WARNING

Be careful not to damage the cooler lines.

➡**Never rotate the crankshaft pulley in a counterclockwise direction.**

6. Remove the four flexplate-to-converter retaining nuts by placing a 22mm socket and breaker bar on the crankshaft pulley retaining bolt. Rotate the crankshaft pulley clockwise to gain access to each of the nuts.

7. Remove the driveshaft.

8. Disconnect and remove the vehicle speed sensor from the extension housing.

9. Place a suitable drain pan under the torque converter. With the wrench on the crankshaft pulley retaining bolt, turn the torque converter to gain access to the converter housing access plug and remove. After the fluid has been drained, install the converter housing access plug.

10. Carefully disconnect the shift cable form the transmission manual control lever at the transmission by removing the adjusting nut.

11. Detach the wiring harness electrical connectors.

12. Unfasten the starter-to-converter housing retaining bolts, then position the starter out of the way.

13. Position a transmission jack under the transmission and raise it slightly.

14. Remove the engine rear support-to-crossmember bolts.

15. Remove the crossmember-to-frame side support retaining bolts and remove the engine and transmission support insulator and engine and transmission support and engine damper mounting body bracket.

16. Lower the jack under the transmission and allow the transmission to hang.

17. Position a jack to the front of the engine and raise the engine to gain access to the two upper converter housing-to-engine retaining bolts.

18. Disconnect and plug the transmission cooler lines form the transmission.

19. Remove the lower converter housing-to-engine retaining bolts.

20. Remove the transmission fluid filler tube.

21. Secure the transmission to the jack with a safety chain.

➡**If the transmission is to be removed for a period of time, support the engine with a safely stand and wood block.**

22. Remove the two upper converter housing-to-engine retaining bolts. Move the transmission to the rear so it disengages from the dowel pins and the

torque converter is disengaged from the flexplate. Carefully lower the transmission from the vehicle.

23. Remove the torque converter from the transmission.

To install:

24. Tighten the converter housing drain plug to 21–22 ft. lbs. (28–30 Nm).

25. Proper installation of the torque converter requires full engagement of the converter hub in the pump gear. To accomplish this, the converter must be pushed and at the same time rotated through what feels like two "notches" or bumps.

26. With the torque converter properly installed, place the transmission on a jack and secure with safety chain.

27. Rotate the torque converter so the drive studs and converter housing access plug are in alignment with their holes in the flexplate.

✳✳ WARNING

During this move, to avoid damage, do not allow the transmission to get into a nose-down position as this will cause the torque converter to move forward and disengage from the pump gear. The converter housing is piloted into position by dowels in the rear of the engine block. The torque converter must rest squarely against the flexplate. This indicates that the converter pilot is not binding in the engine crankshaft.

28. If present, align the orange balancing marks on the converter stud and flexplate bolt hole.

29. With the transmission mounted on a transmission jack, move the torque converter and transmission assembly forward into position, being careful not to damage the flexplate and the converter pilot. The torque converter face must rest squarely against the flexplate. This indicates that the converter pilot is not binding in the engine crankshaft.

➡ **Before installing the torque converter housing-to-flexplate retaining nut, a check should be make to ensure that the torque converter is properly seated. The torque converter should move freely with respect to the flexplate. Grasp the stud. Movement back and forth should result in a**

metallic clank noise if the torque converter is properly seated. If the torque converter will not move, the transmission must be removed and the torque converter repositioned so that the impeller hub is properly engaged in the pump gear.

30. Install two converter housing-to-engine retaining bolts at the engine dowel locations and tighten to 40–50 ft. lbs. (50–68 Nm).

31. Install the remaining converter housing-to-engine retaining bolts and tighten to 40–50 ft. lbs. (50–68 Nm).

32. Remove the safety chain from the transmission.

33. Install the fluid filler tube and secure it to the cylinder block with the retaining bolt. Tighten the bolt to 28–38 ft. lbs. (38–51 Nm). If the fluid filler tube is loose in the case, it should be replaced.

34. Unplug and connect the cooler lines to the transmission case. Tighten the lines to 15–19 ft. lbs. (20–26 Nm).

35. Remove the jack supporting the front of the engine.

36. Raise the transmission. Position the engine and transmission support insulator and engine and transmission support and engine damper mounting body bracket to the frame side support and install the retaining bolts.

37. Lower the transmission and install the rear engine support-to-crossmember nut.

38. Remove the transmission jack.

39. Attach the transmission wiring harness.

40. Install the starter motor.

41. Install the four flexplate-to-converter retaining nuts. Tighten to 20–33 ft. lbs. (27–46 Nm).

42. Install the converter access cover and cover plate bolts on the engine oil pan. Tighten to 12–16 ft. lbs. (16–22 Nm).

43. Install any exhaust system components that were removed.

44. Install the vehicle speed sensor, then connect the wiring.

45. Install the driveshaft.

46. Remove the safety stands and carefully lower the vehicle.

47. Connect the negative battery cable.

48. Fill the transmission with the proper type and amount of fluid.

49. Start the engine and check transmission operation. Inspect for transmission, torque converter assembly and oil cooler lines for leaks.

DRIVELINE

Driveshaft and U-Joints

The driveshaft is the means by which the power from the engine and transmission (in the front of the car) is transferred to the differential and rear axles, and finally to the rear wheels.

The driveshaft assembly incorporates two universal joints, one at each end, and a slip yoke at the front end of the assembly, which fits into the back of the transmission.

All driveshafts are balanced when installed in a car. It is therefore imperative that before applying undercoating to the chassis, the driveshaft and universal joint assembly be completely covered to prevent the accidental application of undercoating to the surfaces, and the subsequent loss of balance.

The universal joints are of a lube-for-life design, on 1989–92 models. The universal joints are equipped with a nylon thrust washer at the base of the bearing cup. This thrust washer controls end play, positions the needle bearings and improves grease movement in the bearing chamber.

➡ **Other type universal joints should not be used in place of this type. Driveshaft imbalance and vibration will result.**

REMOVAL AND INSTALLATION

1983–88 Vehicles

◆ **See Figure 47**

The procedure for removing the driveshaft assembly, complete with universal joint and slip yoke, is as follows:

1. Raise and safely support the vehicle.

2. Mark the relationship of the rear driveshaft yoke and the drive pinion flange of the axle. If the original yellow alignment marks are visible, there is

no need for new marks. The purpose of this marking is to facilitate installation of the assembly in its exact original position, thereby maintaining proper balance.

3. Remove the four bolts or U-clamps which hold the rear universal joint to the pinion flange. Wrap tape around the loose bearing caps in order to prevent them from falling off the spider.

4. Pull the driveshaft toward the rear of the vehicle until the slip yoke clears the transmission housing and the seal. Plug the hole at the rear of the transmission housing or place a container under the opening to catch any fluid which might leak.

5. Carefully inspect the rubber seal on the output shaft and the seal in end of the transmission extension housing. Replace them if they are damaged.

6. Examine the lugs on the axle pinion flange and replace the flange if the lugs are shaved or distorted.

To install:

7. Coat the yoke spline with special-purpose lubricant. The Ford part number for this lubricant if B8A–19589–A.

8. Remove the plug from the rear of the transmission housing.

9. Insert the yoke into the transmission housing and onto the transmission output shaft. Make sure that the yoke assembly does not bottom on the output shaft with excessive force.

10. Locate the marks which you made on the rear driveshaft yoke and the pinion flange prior to removal of the driveshaft assembly. Install the driveshaft assembly with the marks properly aligned.

11. Install the U-bolts and nuts or bolts which attach the universal joint to the pinion flange. Tighten the U-bolt nuts to 8–15 ft. lbs. (11–20 Nm). Tighten the flange bolts to 70–95 ft. lbs. (95–129 Nm).

12. Carefully lower the vehicle.

➡ **Always check transmission fluid levels after removal and installation of driveshaft.**

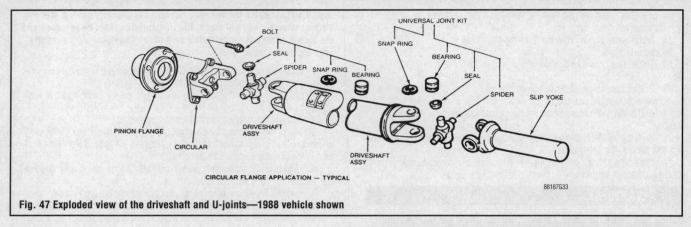

Fig. 47 Exploded view of the driveshaft and U-joints—1988 vehicle shown

1989–97 Vehicles

♦ See Figures 48 thru 61

1. Disconnect the negative battery cable.
2. Properly drain the fuel tank into a suitable container.
3. Raise and safely support vehicle on jack stands.
4. Remove the crossmember/fuel tank modification shield and pipe kit on the forward side of the fuel tank.
5. Disconnect the outlet pipe from the muffler. Lower the pipe and support with wire.
6. Remove the exhaust hanger insulator from exhaust pipe hanger stud.
7. Remove the muffler rear insulator from the hanger stud, lower the exhaust and remove the complete system from the vehicle.
8. Remove the driveshaft safety hoop/sub-frame crossmember at the rear side of fuel tank.
9. Remove the fuel tank filler tube retaining bolt from the right side of frame rail.

✳✳ CAUTION

Use care not to damage the fuel tank to prevent a fuel leak.

10. Being careful not to damage the fuel tank, place a transmission jack under tank.
11. Remove the sub-frame center support on the forward side of fuel tank. Remove the fuel tank support straps, then carefully lower the fuel tank approximately 6 inches (15cm).
12. Mark the relationship of the rear driveshaft yoke and the drive pinion flange of the axle. If the original yellow alignment marks are visible, there is no need for new marks. The purpose of this marking is to facilitate installation of the assembly in its exact original position, thereby maintaining proper balance.
13. Remove the four driveshaft retaining bolts.
14. Pull the driveshaft toward the rear of the vehicle until the slip yoke clears the transmission extension housing and seal. Factory made paint marks

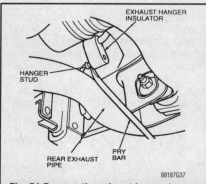

Fig. 48 Unfasten the retaining bolts, then remove the crossmember from the forward side of the fuel tank

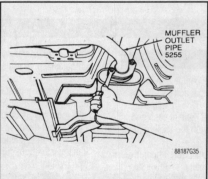

Fig. 49 Remove the exhaust pipe from the muffler, then . . .

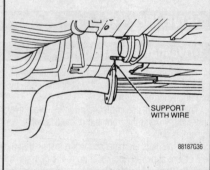

Fig. 50 . . . lower the pipe and secure it with a piece of wire

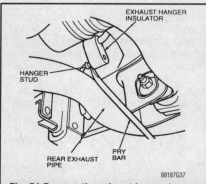

Fig. 51 Remove the exhaust hanger insulator from exhaust pipe hanger stud

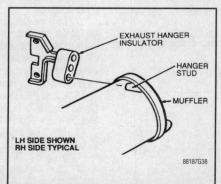

Fig. 52 Carefully lower and remove the complete exhaust system from the vehicle

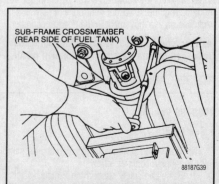

Fig. 53 Remove the sub-frame crossmember from the rear side of the fuel tank

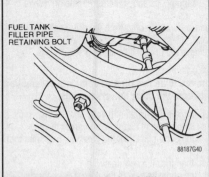

Fig. 54 Unfasten the fuel tank filler tube bolt

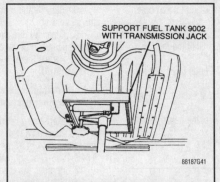

Fig. 55 When supporting the fuel tank, be very careful not to damage the fuel tank

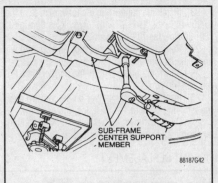

Fig. 56 Remove the sub-frame center support from the forward side of the fuel tank

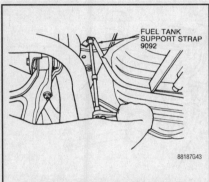

Fig. 57 Remove the fuel tank straps, then carefully lower the tank about 6 inches

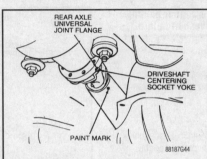

Fig. 58 If there are no factory-made marks, mark the relationship between the rear driveshaft yoke and the drive pinion flange of the axle

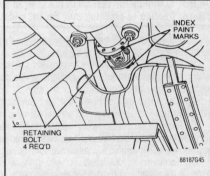

Fig. 59 Unfasten and remove the driveshaft retaining bolts

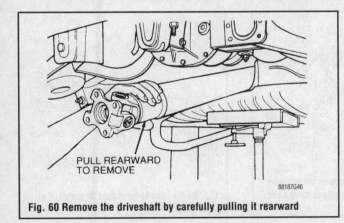

Fig. 60 Remove the driveshaft by carefully pulling it rearward

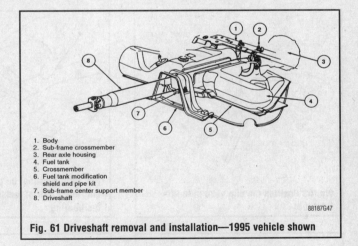

1. Body
2. Sub-frame crossmember
3. Rear axle housing
4. Fuel tank
5. Crossmember
6. Fuel tank modification shield and pipe kit
7. Sub-frame center support member
8. Driveshaft

Fig. 61 Driveshaft removal and installation—1995 vehicle shown

are on the end of the transmission output shaft and the driveshaft front yoke weld. If factory made paint marks are not visible, mark the driveshaft slip yoke in relation to the transmission output shaft. Plug the hole at the rear of the transmission housing or place a container under the opening to catch any fluid which might leak.

15. Carefully inspect the rubber seal on the output shaft and the seal in end of the transmission extension housing. Replace them if they are damaged.

16. Examine the lugs on the axle pinion flange and replace the flange if the lugs are shaved or distorted.

To install:

17. Lubricate the driveshaft slip yoke splines with Premium Long Life Grease XG-1-C or equivalent. Remove the plug from the transmission extension. Inspect the housing seal for damage and replace if necessary.

18. Align the slip yoke marks on the driveshaft with the transmission output shaft and install. Do not allow the driveshaft slip yoke to bottom on the output shaft with excessive force.

➡When installing a new driveshaft, align the factory make yellow paint mark at the rear of the driveshaft tube with the factory made yellow paint mark on the outside diameter of the rear axle universal joint flange.

19. Align the match marks on the rear of the driveshaft centering socket yoke with the rear axle universal joint flange. Install the retaining bolts and tighten to 71–95 ft. lbs. (95–130 Nm).

20. Carefully raise the fuel tank, then install the support straps and tighten the retaining bolts to 21–30 ft. lbs. (29–41 Nm).

21. Install the fuel tank fill tube retaining bolt and tighten to 24–32 inch lbs. (2.7–3.7 Nm).

22. Install the driveshaft safety hoop/sub-frame crossmember, then tighten the retaining bolts to 30–44 ft. lbs. (41–60 Nm) for vehicles through 1992 or to 14–22 ft. lbs. (20–30 Nm) for 1993–97 vehicles.

23. Install the support on the forward side of the fuel tank and tighten bolts to 30–44 ft. lbs. (41–60 Nm) for vehicles through 1992 or to 14–22 ft. lbs. (20–30 Nm) for 1993–97 vehicles.

24. Raise the muffler outlet pipe and support with wire. Install the muffler and exhaust pipe insulators on the hanger studs.

25. Attach the outlet pipe to the muffler, then tighten the bolts to 21–29 ft. lbs. (28–40 Nm).

26. Install the crossmember on the forward side of the fuel tank and tighten the retaining bolts to 12–17 ft. lbs. (16–24 Nm).

27. Carefully lower the vehicle, refill the fuel tank, connect the negative battery cable and check for proper operation.

U-JOINT REPLACEMENT

▶ See Figures 62 thru 68

✳✳ WARNING

Do NOT clamp the driveshaft in the jaws of a vise or similar holding fixture. Denting or cracking may result, causing driveshaft failure.

1. Remove the driveshaft from the vehicle and place on a suitable work bench. Be careful not to damage the tube.

2. Before disassembly, mark the positions of the driveshaft components relative to the driveshaft tube. All components must be reassembled in the same relationship for proper balance.

3. Clamp U-Joint tool T74P-4635, or equivalent in a vise.

4. Remove the four snaprings which retain the bearings.

5. Position the driveshaft slip yoke in U-Joint tool T74P-4635-C or equivalent, then press out the bearing. If the bearing cup cannot be pressed all the way out, remove it with vise grips, or suitable locking pliers.

6. Reposition the driveshaft slip yoke in the U-Joint tool 180 degrees to press on the spider and remove the remaining bearing cup from the opposite side.

7. Remove the driveshaft slip yoke from the spider.

8. Remove the remaining bearing cups and spiders from the driveshaft in the same way.

9. Clean all dirt, debris and/or foreign matter from the driveshaft slip yoke area at each end of the driveshaft.

10. Repeat Steps 1–9 to remove the driveshaft centering socket yoke.

To install:

➡**Universal joint service kits are to be installed as complete assemblies only. Do not mix components from the other universal joints.**

11. Start a new bearing cup into the driveshaft slip yoke of a the driveshaft.

12. Position a new spider in the driveshaft slip yoke and press the new bearing cup ¼ in. (6mm) below the outer surface of the yoke using U-Joint tool T74P-4635-C or equivalent.

13. Remove the U-joint tool, then install a new snapring.

14. Start a new bearing into the opposite side of the yoke. Check the needles for proper position.

15. Position the driveshaft in U-Joint tool T74P-4635-C, then press on the

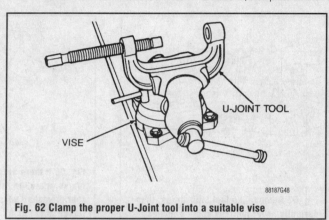

Fig. 62 Clamp the proper U-Joint tool into a suitable vise

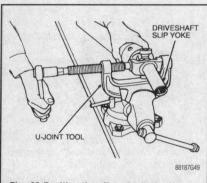

Fig. 63 Position the slip yoke in the U-joint tool

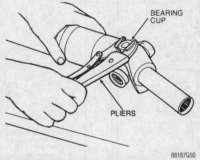

Fig. 64 If it cannot be pressed all the way out, use a pair of locking pliers to remove the bearing

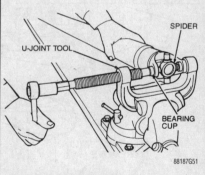

Fig. 65 Use the U-joint tool to press in a new bearing cup

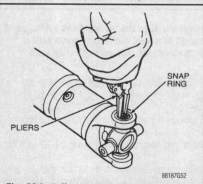

Fig. 66 Install a new snapring using suitable pliers

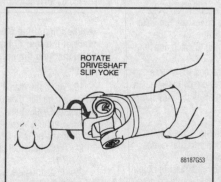

Fig. 67 Check the driveshaft for any binding before installing it in the vehicle

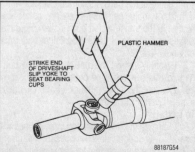

Fig. 68 To properly seat the bearing cups, use a brass or plastic hammer to sharply rap the side of the yoke. Do NOT hit the bearings themselves

bearing until the opposite bearing cup, which you have just installed, contacts the inner surface of the snapring.

➡**Assemble the rear axle shaft universal joint using the yellow snap rings supplied in the kit. If difficulty is encountered with the yellow snap rings, install the black rings supplied with the kit.**

16.   Remove the U-joint tool, then install a new snapring on the second bearing. Check the snapring for proper seating.

17.   Install the driveshaft slip yoke, remaining bearing cups, spider, driveshaft centering socket yoke and snaprings in the same manner.

REAR AXLE

Axle Shaft, Bearing and Seal

➡**The axle type and ratio are stamped on a plate attached to a rear housing cover bolt. All 1983–88 axles are C-lock type axles. All 1989–97 axles are halfshaft type axles.**

REMOVAL & INSTALLATION

➡**Bearings must be pressed on and off the shaft with an arbor press. Unless you have access to one, it is inadvisable to attempt any repair work on the axle shaft bearing assemblies.**

1983–88 Vehicles

▶ **See Figures 69, 70, 71 and 72**

1.   Raise and safely support the rear of the vehicle.
2.   Remove the wheels and tire assembly.
3.   Remove the brake drum or disc brake caliper, as applicable.
4.   If equipped, remove the anti-lock speed sensor.
5.   Clean all dirt from around the axle housing cover. Place a suitable drain pan under the housing cover . Remove the axle housing cover and allow the rear axle lubricant to drain.

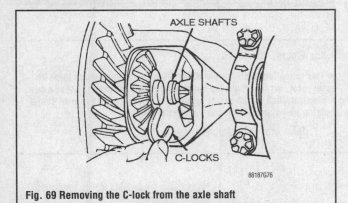

Fig. 69 Removing the C-lock from the axle shaft

18.   Check the rear axle shaft universal joints for freedom of movement. If misalignment of any part is causing a bind, a sharp rap on the side of the yoke with a brass or plastic hammer should seat the bearing needle and provide the desired freedom of movement. Care should be exercised to firmly support the shaft end during this operation, as well as to prevent blows to the bearings themselves. Make sure the rear axle shaft universal joints are free to rotate easily without binding before installing the driveshaft.

19.   Repeat steps 11–19 to install the driveshaft centering socket yoke.
20.   Install the driveshaft in the vehicle.

6.   Remove the housing cover and gasket, if used.

7.   Position jackstands under the rear frame member and lower the axle housing. This is done to give easy access to the inside of the differential.

8.   Working through the opening in the differential case, remove the side gear pinion shaft lockbolt and the side gear pinion shaft.

9.   Push the axle shafts inward and remove the C-locks from the inner end of the axle shafts. Temporarily replace the shaft and lockbolt to retain the differential gears in position.

10.   Remove the axle shaft from the housing.

11.   Place Bearing Remover T85L-1225-AH or equivalent, into the axle shaft housing bore and position the tangs behind the axle bearing. Remove the axle bearing and axle seal as an assembly with a slide hammer installed on the bearing removal tool. Be sure the seal is not damaged by the splines on the axle shaft.

➡**Two types of bearings are used on some axles, one with a press fit and the other a slip fit. A loose fitting bearing does not necessarily indicate excessive wear.**

12.   Inspect the axle shaft housing and axle shafts for burrs or other irregularities. Replace any worn or damaged parts. A light yellow color on the bearing journal of the axle shaft is normal, and does not require replacement of the axle shaft. Slight pitting and wear is also normal.

To install:

13.   Lightly coat the wheel bearing rollers with axle lubricant. Install the bearings in the axle housing bore using Bearing Installer T78P-1225-A, or equivalent. Make sure the bearing seats firmly against the shoulder in the housing.

14.   Wipe all lubricant from the oil seal bore, before installing the seal. Inspect the original seals for wear. If necessary, these may be replaced with new seals, which are prepacked with lubricant and do not require soaking. If the seals are dry, apply a suitable wheel bearing grease between the lips of the axle seal.

15.   Install the axle seal using Seal Installer T78P-1177-A or equivalent.

➡**Installation of the seal without the proper tool can cause distortion and seal leakage. Seals may be color coded for side identification. Do not interchange seals from side to side, if they are coded.**

16.   Remove the lock bolt/pin and pinion shaft. Carefully slide the axle shafts into place. Be careful that you do not damage the seal with the splined end of

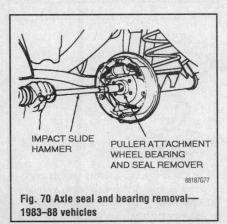

IMPACT SLIDE HAMMER

PULLER ATTACHMENT WHEEL BEARING AND SEAL REMOVER

Fig. 70 Axle seal and bearing removal— 1983–88 vehicles

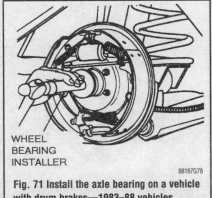

WHEEL BEARING INSTALLER

Fig. 71 Install the axle bearing on a vehicle with drum brakes—1983–88 vehicles

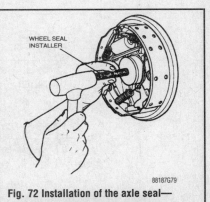

WHEEL SEAL INSTALLER

Fig. 72 Installation of the axle seal— 1983–88 vehicles with drum brakes

the axle shaft. Engage the splined end of the shaft with the differential side gears.

17. Install the axle shaft C-locks on the bottom end of the axle shaft splines and seat the C-lock in the counterbore of the differential side gears by pulling the axle shaft in an outward direction.

18. Rotate the differential pinion gears until the differential pinion shaft can be installed. Apply a suitable thread locking compound to the threads on the lock pin and install the lock pin securing the differential pinion shaft. Tighten to 15–30 ft. lbs. (20–41 Nm).

19. Check the rear axle housing vent, making sure it is not plugged. A plugged vent can cause excessive pressure to build in the axle housing and leaking seals will result.

20. Clean the axle housing cover and the housing mating surface.

21. Apply a bead of silicone sealer to the axle housing cover and install the cover and retaining bolts. Tighten the bolts to 18–28 ft. lbs. (24–38 Nm).

➡Some axle housing covers use a gasket instead of silicone sealer. Use the same type of gasket as removed.

22. Add a suitable rear axle lubricant to bring the level to approximately ½ in. (13mm) below the fill hole. For traction-lock equipped vehicles, a suitable friction modifier must also be added.

23. Install the brake drum or disc brake rotor and caliper, as applicable.

24. If equipped, install the anti-lock brake sensor.

25. Install the wheel and tire assembly.

26. If the brake system was opened, bleed the rear brakes.

27. Carefully lower the vehicle.

28. Road test the vehicle and check for leaks and proper operation.

1989–97 Vehicles

◗ See Figures 73 and 74

➡The bearings must be pressed on and off the shaft using an arbor press.

1. Raise and safely support the rear of the vehicle with jackstands.

2. Remove the wheel, tire, and brake drum. With disc brakes, remove the caliper, retainer, nuts and rotor. New anchor plate bolts will be needed for reassembly.

3. Remove the nuts holding the retainer plate in the backing plate, or axle shaft retainer bolts from the housing. Disconnect the brake line with drum brakes.

4. Remove the retainer and install nuts, finger-tight, to prevent the brake backing plate from being dislodged.

5. Pull out the axle shaft and bearing assembly, using a slide hammer.

6. On models with a tapered roller bearing, the tapered cup will normally remain in the axle housing when the shaft is removed. The cup must be removed from the housing to prevent seal damage when the shaft is reinstalled. The cup can be removed with a slide hammer and an expanding puller.

7. Using a chisel, nick the bearing retainer in 3 or 4 places. The retainer does not have to be cut, but merely collapsed sufficiently to allow the bearing retainer to be slid from the shaft.

To install:

8. Press off the bearing and install the new one by pressing it into position. With tapered bearings, place the lubricated seal and bearing on the axle shaft (cup rib ring facing the flange). make sure that the seal is the correct length. Disc brake seal rims are black, drum brake seal rims are grey. Press the bearing and seal onto the shaft.

9. Press on the new retainer.

➡Do not attempt to press the bearing and the retainer on at the same time.

10. To replace the seal on ball bearing models:

   a. Remove the seal from the housing with an expanding cone type puller and a slide hammer. The seal must be replaced whenever the shaft is removed.

   b. Wipe a small amount of sealer onto the outer edge of the new seal before installation; do not put sealer on the sealing lip.

   c. Press the seal into the housing with a seal installation tool.

11. Assemble the shaft and bearing in the housing, being sure that the bearing is seated properly in the housing. On ball bearing models, be careful not to damage the seal with the shaft. With tapered bearings, first install the tapered cup on the bearing, and lubricate the outer diameter of the cup and the seal with axle lube. Then install the shaft and bearing assembly into the housing.

12. Install the retainer, drum or rotor and caliper, wheel and tire. Bleed the brakes.

Pinion Oil Seal

REMOVAL & INSTALLATION

◗ See Figures 75 and 76

➡This procedure disturbs the pinion bearing preload which must be reset for a correct repair. Do not attempt this procedure without a new pinion nut, inch pound torque wrench, rear axle universal joint flange holding tool and a pinion seal installation tool.

1. Raise and safely support the vehicle.

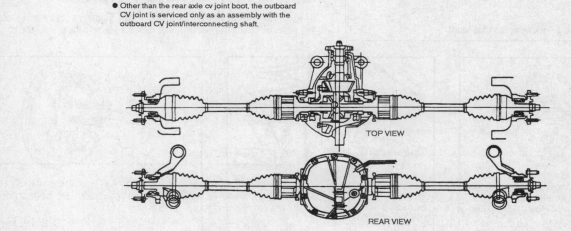

● Other than the rear axle cv joint boot, the outboard CV joint is serviced only as an assembly with the outboard CV joint/interconnecting shaft.

TOP VIEW

REAR VIEW

88187G80

Fig. 73 Rear axle housing and halfshafts—1989–97 vehicles

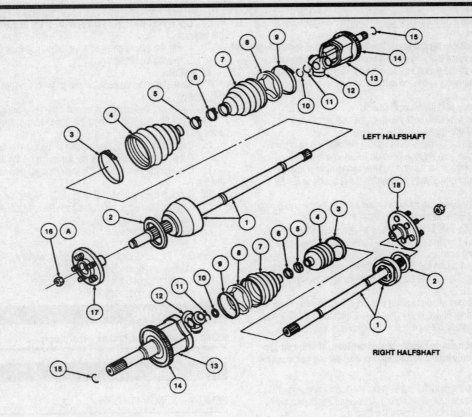

1. Outboard CV joint/interconnecting shaft
2. Halfshaft dust seal
3. Boot clamp(large outboard)
4. Rear axle CV joint boot(outboard)
5. Boot clamp(small inboard)
6. Boot clamp(small inboard)
7. Rear axle CV joint boot(inboard)
8. TriLobe insert
9. Boot clamp(large inboard)
10. Rear axle shaft joint assy retaining ring
11. Rear axle shaft retaining u-washer
12. Tripod assy
13. Inboard CV joint stub shaft pilot bearing housing
14. Rear brake anti-lock sensor indicator
15. "C" clip
16. Axle nut
17. Hub left shaft
18. Hub right shaft

88187G81

Fig. 74 Exploded view of the rear axle shaft assembly—1989–97 vehicles

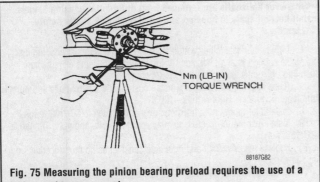

Nm (LB-IN)
TORQUE WRENCH

88187G82

Fig. 75 Measuring the pinion bearing preload requires the use of a inch pound torque wrench

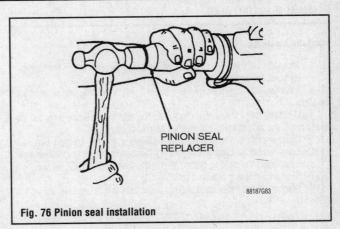

PINION SEAL
REPLACER

88187G83

Fig. 76 Pinion seal installation

2. Place jackstands under the rear axle housing.
3. Remove both wheel and tire assemblies.
4. Remove the brake drums or calipers, as applicable.
5. Mark the driveshaft and yoke for reassembly in the same location.
6. Disconnect the driveshaft from the rear yoke.
7. Place an inch pound (Nm) torque wrench with a suitable socket on the pinion nut. Record the torque required to maintain rotation of the pinion through several revolutions.

8. Install Flange Holding Tool T78P-4851-A or equivalent on the rear axle universal joint flange. Remove the pinion nut while holding the flange stationary. Discard the pinion nut.
9. Clean the area around the pinion seal. Place a suitable drain pan under the pinion seal.
10. Mark the pinion shaft in relationship to the axle joint flange for assembly reference.

11. Remove the rear axle joint flange using Companion Flange Remover T65L-4851-B or equivalent.

12. Carefully place a suitable prytool under the flange of the pinion seal and strike with a hammer to wedge the prying tool between the seal and the axle housing. Pry on the flange of the pinion seal to raise the flange enough the grasp with suitable gripping pliers and remove the pinion seal.

To install:

13. Clean the seal seating area in the axle housing.

14. Before installing the new seal, coat the lip of the seal with a suitable wheel bearing grease, if not pre-greased.

15. Place the pinion seal on Pinion Seal Installer T79P-4676-A or equivalent and install the pinion seal into the axle housing using a hammer.

16. Check the axle universal joint flange for burrs and remove if found.

17. Apply a small amount of rear axle lubricant to the rear axle universal joint flange splines.

18. Align the index marks made on the axle universal joint flange and pinion shaft, then install the flange onto the shaft.

19. Install Flange Holding Tool T78P-4851-A or equivalent, on the rear axle universal joint flange. Rotate the pinion shaft while tightening the pinion nut the ensure proper pinion bearing seating.

20. Take frequent pinion bearing torque preload readings until the original recorded reading is reached. Tighten the nut in small increments to avoid over-tightening.

21. If the originally recorded pinion bearing preload is less than 8–14 inch lbs. (0.9–1.6 Nm) with original pinion bearing or 16–29 inch lbs. (1.8–3.2 Nm) with new pinion bearings, tighten the pinion nut to these readings.

➡**Never back off the pinion nut to reduce pinion preload. If reduced preload is required, a new collapsible pinion spacer and pinion nut must be installed.**

22. Install the driveshaft, aligning the index marks made during disassembly.

23. Add the proper rear axle lubricant to bring the level to approximately ½ in. (13mm) below the fill hole, if needed. Install the fill plug.

24. Check the rear axle housing vent, making sure it is not plugged. A plugged vent can cause excessive pressure to build in the axle housing and leaking seals may result.

25. Install the rear brake drums or calipers, as applicable.

26. Install the wheel and tire assemblies. Tighten the lug nuts in a star pattern to 85–105 ft. lbs. (115–142 Nm).

27. If the brake system was opened, bleed the rear brakes.

28. Remove the jackstands, then carefully lower the vehicle.

29. Road test the vehicle and check for leaks and proper operation.

Axle Housing Assembly

REMOVAL & INSTALLATION

1983–88 Vehicles

1. Raise the vehicle and support it on jackstands placed under the frame.

2. Remove the rear wheels.

3. Place an indexing mark on the rear yoke and driveshaft, and disconnect the shaft.

4. Disconnect the shock absorbers from the axle tubes. Disconnect the stabilizer bar at the axle bracket, on vehicles so equipped.

5. Disconnect the brake hose from the tee fitting on the axle housing. Disconnect the brake lines at the clips on the housing. Disconnect the vent tube at the axle.

6. Disconnect the parking brake cable at the frame mounting.

7. Support the rear axle with a jack.

8. Disconnect the lower control arms at the axle and swing them down out of the way.

9. Disconnect the upper control arms at the axle and swing them up out of the way.

10. Lower the axle slightly, remove the coil springs and insulators.

11. Lower the axle housing.

To install:

12. Raise the axle into position and connect the lower arms. Don't tighten the bolts yet.

13. Lower the axle slightly and install the coil springs and insulators.

14. Raise the axle and connect the upper control arms. Don't tighten the bolts yet.

15. Connect the parking brake cable at the frame mounting.

16. Connect the brake hose at the tee fitting on the axle housing.

17. Connect the vent tube at the axle. Apply thread locking compound to the threads.

18. Connect the stabilizer bar at the axle bracket, on vehicles so equipped.

19. Connect the shock absorbers from the axle tubes.

20. Connect the driveshaft.

21. Install the rear wheels.

22. Lower the vehicle.

23. Once the car is back on its wheels, observe the following torques:
   - Lower arm bolts: 100 ft. lbs.
   - Lower shock absorber nuts: 55 ft. lbs.
   - Upper arm bolts: 100 ft. lbs.

✳✳ WARNING

Bleed and adjust the brakes accordingly.

Differential Carrier

REMOVAL & INSTALLATION

1989–97 Vehicles

1. Raise and support vehicle, remove driveshaft and only the right side halfshaft.

2. Using a transmission jack to support differential housing, remove the rear mount retaining bolts and remove rear mount from the housing cover.

3. Remove the front retaining nuts, bolts, bushings and washers.

4. Using a halfshaft removal tool, T89P-3514-A or equivalent, push tool towards carrier to release CV joint stub shaft from gear.

5. While lowering axle assembly, move assembly to the right to disengage stub shaft from housing and install plug tool T89P-4850-B or equivalent into left side of housing.

To install:

➡**Whenever halfshafts are removed from differential housing always install new oil seals in housing and circlips on stub shafts before reassembly.**

6. Lightly lubricate left side stub shaft. Position differential housing on jack, raise enough to align left side CV joint stub shaft. Using extreme care push into differential side gear until circlip engages.

7. Raise housing into position. Install bushings, washers, bolts and nuts in front mounting holes. Tighten to 68–100 ft. lbs.

8. Install rear mount onto housing cover and tighten to 80–100 ft. lbs.

9. Install rear mount-to-crossmember retaining bolts and nuts. Tighten to 122–156 ft. lbs.

10. Replace the driveshaft and right side halfshaft using the procedures outlined previously.

11. Check differential oil level, fill as necessary.

WHEELS 8-2
WHEELS 8-2
  REMOVAL & INSTALLATION 8-2
WHEEL LUG STUDS 8-2
  REMOVAL AND INSTALLATION 8-2
FRONT SUSPENSION 8-2
COIL SPRINGS 8-2
  REMOVAL & INSTALLATION 8-2
MACPHERSON STRUT 8-5
  REMOVAL & INSTALLATION 8-5
UPPER BALL JOINT 8-6
  INSPECTION 8-6
  REMOVAL & INSTALLATION 8-6
LOWER BALL JOINT 8-6
  INSPECTION 8-6
  REMOVAL & INSTALLATION 8-6
STABILIZER BAR 8-7
  REMOVAL & INSTALLATION 8-7
UPPER CONTROL ARM 8-9
  REMOVAL & INSTALLATION 8-9
  CONTROL ARM BUSHING
  REPLACEMENT 8-10
LOWER CONTROL ARM 8-10
  REMOVAL & INSTALLATION 8-10
  CONTROL ARM BUSHING
  REPLACEMENT 8-11
SPINDLE/KNUCKLE 8-12
  REMOVAL & INSTALLATION 8-12
FRONT WHEEL BEARINGS 8-13
  REMOVAL & INSTALLATION 8-13
FRONT HUB AND BEARING 8-14
  REMOVAL & INSTALLATION 8-14
WHEEL ALIGNMENT 8-15
  CASTER 8-15
  CAMBER 8-15
  TOE 8-15
REAR SUSPENSION 8-16
COIL SPRINGS 8-16
  REMOVAL & INSTALLATION 8-16
SHOCK ABSORBER 8-20
  REMOVAL & INSTALLATION 8-20
UPPER CONTROL ARMS 8-22
  REMOVAL & INSTALLATION 8-22
LOWER CONTROL ARMS 8-23
  REMOVAL & INSTALLATION 8-23
STABILIZER BAR 8-23
  REMOVAL & INSTALLATION 8-23
REAR WHEEL BEARINGS AND HUB 8-23
  REMOVAL & INSTALLATION 8-23
STEERING 8-28
STEERING WHEEL 8-28
  REMOVAL & INSTALLATION 8-28
TURN SIGNAL SWITCH 8-29
  REMOVAL & INSTALLATION 8-29
MULTI-FUNCTION SWITCH 8-29
  REMOVAL & INSTALLATION 8-29
IGNITION SWITCH 8-30
  REMOVAL & INSTALLATION 8-30
IGNITION LOCK CYLINDER 8-31
  REMOVAL & INSTALLATION 8-31

STEERING LINKAGE 8-33
  REMOVAL & INSTALLATION 8-33
POWER RACK AND PINION STEERING
 GEAR 8-34
  REMOVAL & INSTALLATION 8-34
POWER STEERING PUMP 8-35
  REMOVAL & INSTALLATION 8-35
  BLEEDING 8-39

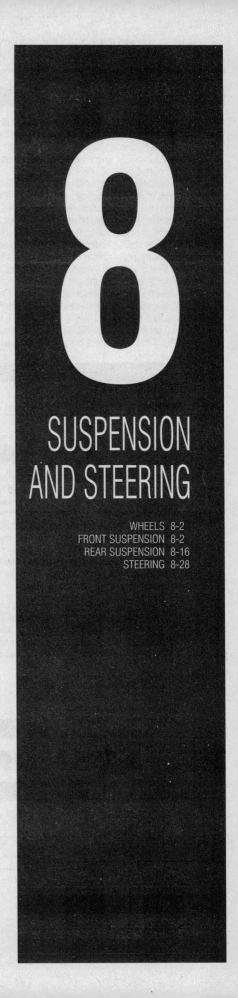

8

SUSPENSION AND STEERING

WHEELS 8-2
FRONT SUSPENSION 8-2
REAR SUSPENSION 8-16
STEERING 8-28

WHEELS

Wheels must be replaced when they are bent, dented, heavily rusted, have air leaks or enlongated bolt holes. Replacement wheels must be equal to the original equipment wheels in load capacity, diameter, width, offset and mounting configuration. An improper wheel may affect wheel bearing life, ground and tire clearance, speedometer and odometer misreadings.

Corrosion buildup can result in wheels sticking to the axle or rotor flange. To help prevent this from happening, spray wheel center and wheel stud nuts with a good penetrating oil. Once the wheel has been removed, clean the axle/rotor flange and wheel bore with a wire brush, steel wool or other suitable material. Spread a thin coat of disc brake caliper grease on the wheel bore, but do not put grease on the wheel studs. Use spray penetrating lubricant on the wheel studs.

• To avoid injury from vehicles with a Traction-Lok® axle, NEVER run the engine with only one wheel off the ground, such as changing a tire. The wheel still on the ground could cause the vehicle to move.

• Never allow hoists or jacks to contact the axle housing, halfshafts or CV joints.

• Do not attempt to use jack pressure on either front or rear bumpers of any Unitized Bodied vehicle.

• The mini spare is provided only for temporary emergency use. Do not use as a regular tire. Service or replace the regular tire as soon as possible.

Wheels

REMOVAL & INSTALLATION

▶ See Figure 1

✳✳ CAUTION

The service jack provided with the vehicle is only intended to be used in an emergency, for changing a deflated tire. Never use the service jack to hoist the vehicle for any other service.

1. Using the end of the lug wrench, either remove the wheel cover or carefully pry off the wheel cover applique, as applicable.
2. If equipped, remove the wheel locking nut.
3. Loosen the remaining lug nuts with the wheel on the ground, then raise and safely support the vehicle. If you are working at home (not on a roadside emergency) support the car safely using jackstand(s).
4. Remove the lug nuts, then remove the wheel and tire assembly.

➡**If the wheel is stuck or rusted on the hub, make all the lug nuts finger-tight, then back each one off 2 turns. Put the car back on the ground and rock it side to side. Get another person to help, if necessary. This is far safer than hitting a stuck wheel with the vehicle on a jack or jackstands.**

To install:
5. Clean the wheel bore and bolt holes as necessary.
6. Position wheel and tire assembly onto the axle or hub.

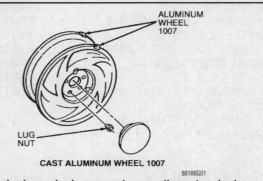

Fig. 1 On aluminum wheels, you must remove the center wheel cover to access the lug nuts

7. Install the lug nuts hand-tight.
8. Carefully lower the vehicle, then tighten the lug nuts in a rotation, skipping every other one. Always use a torque wrench to avoid uneven tightening. Tighten the lug nuts (including the locking nut, if so equipped) to 80–105 ft. lbs. (115–142 Nm).
9. Install the wheel cover, ensuring that the valve stem is positioned correctly, if so equipped.

Wheel Lug Studs

REMOVAL AND INSTALLATION

1. Raise and support the vehicle safely.
2. Remove the wheel.
3. Remove the brake assembly. On disc brake systems remove the rotor.
4. For vehicles equipped with disc brake systems, place the rotor in a press and remove the stud. On drum brake systems, use a portable press or a soft faced hammer to remove the stud.

To Install:
5. For disc brake systems, press the stud into place. Install the rotor.
6. On drum brake systems, use several washers and the lug nut to draw the stud into place.
7. Ensure that the head of the stud is seated tightly against the back of the hub or rotor.
8. Install the brake assembly and wheel. Tighten lug nuts to 80–105 ft. lbs. (115–142 Nm).
9. Lower vehicle and test drive. Check lug nut torque after driving vehicle a short distance.

FRONT SUSPENSION

Coil Springs

✳✳ CAUTION

Always use extreme caution when working with coil springs. Make sure the vehicle is supported safely.

REMOVAL & INSTALLATION

▶ See Figures 2, 3, 4, 5 and 6

1983–88 Vehicles

1. Raise the front of the vehicle and place safety stands under both sides of the jack pads just back of the lower control arms so the lower control arms hang free.

2. Remove the wheel and tire assembly.
3. Remove the brake caliper and support out of the way with a piece of wire.
4. Disconnect the tie rod from the steering spindle, using Tie Rod End Remover Tool-3290-D or equivalent.
5. Detach the stabilizer bar link from the lower control arm.
6. Unfasten the steering gear bolts, if necessary, and move the steering gear out of the way so that the suspension arm bolt can be removed.
7. Use Spring Compressor Tool T82P-5310-A or equivalent, to place the upper plate in position into the spring pocket cavity on the crossmember. The hooks on the plate should be facing the center of the vehicle.
8. Install the compression rod into the lower arm spring pocket hole, through the coil spring, into the upper plate.
9. Install the lower plate, lower ball nut, thrust washer and bearing, and forcing nut onto the compression rod.
10. Tighten the forcing nut on the compression tool until a drag on the nut is felt.

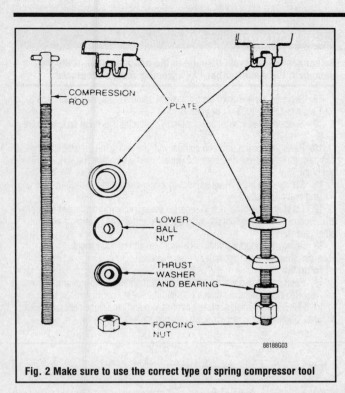

Fig. 2 Make sure to use the correct type of spring compressor tool

COMPRESSION ROD

PLATE

LOWER BALL NUT

THRUST WASHER AND BEARING

FORCING NUT

88188G03

11. Remove the suspension arm-to-crossmember nuts and bolts. The compressor tool forcing nut may have to be tightening or loosened for easy bolt removal.

➡If a new spring is to be installed, mark the position of the upper and lower plates on the spring with chalk. Measure the compressed length of the spring as well as the amount of the spring curvature to assist in the compressing and installation of a new spring.

12. Loosen the compression rod forcing nut until the spring tensioner is relieved, then remove the forcing nut.

13. Remove the compression rod and the coil spring from the vehicle.

To install:

14. Place the insulator on the top of the spring. Position the spring into the lower arm spring pocket.

➡Make sure the spring pigtail is positioned between the two holes in the lower arm spring pocket.

15. Position the spring into the upper spring seat in the crossmember.

16. Insert the compression rod through the control arm and spring, then hook it to the upper plate. The upper plate is installed with the hooks facing the center of the vehicle.

17. Tighten the forcing nut, position the lower arm into the crossmember, then install new lower arm-to-crossmember bolts and nuts, but do not tighten at this time.

18. Remove the spring compressor tool from the vehicle.

19. With a suitable jack, raise the suspension arm to a normal position. Tighten the lower arm-to-crossmember attaching nuts to 110–150 ft. lbs. (149–203 Nm). Remove the jack.

20. Install the steering gear-to-crossmember bolts and nuts, if removed. Hold the bolts, then tighten to nuts to 90–100 ft. lbs. (122–136 Nm).

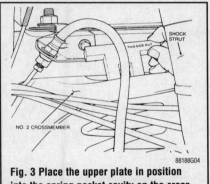

Fig. 3 Place the upper plate in position into the spring pocket cavity on the crossmember

88188G04

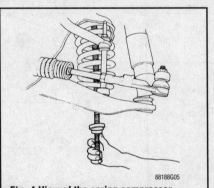

Fig. 4 View of the spring compressor inserted through the control arm

88188G05

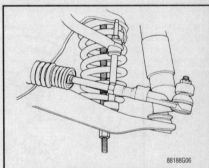

Fig. 5 View of the spring compressor with the control arm and spring in position after tension is relieved

88188G06

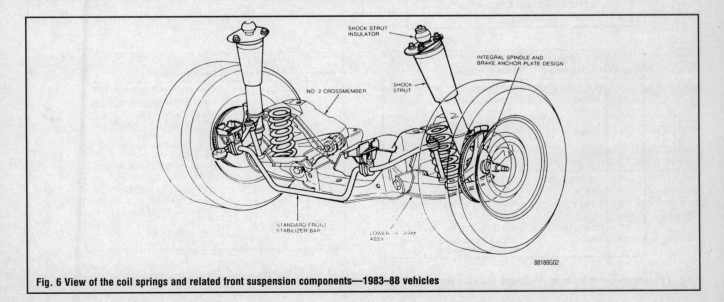

Fig. 6 View of the coil springs and related front suspension components—1983–88 vehicles

88188G02

21. Connect the stabilizer bar link to the lower suspension arm. Tighten the attaching nut to 8–12 ft. lbs. (12–16 Nm).

22. Position the tie rod assembly into the steering spindle, then install the retaining nut. Tighten the nut to 35 ft. lbs. (47 Nm), and continue tightening the nut to align the next castellation with the cotter pin hole in the stud. Install a new cotter pin.

23. Install the wheel and tire assembly, then carefully lower the vehicle.

1989–97 Vehicles

▶ See Figures 7, 8 and 9

➡ **The following procedures are used for removal and installation of the coil springs and MacPherson struts, since they are removed together; one can not be removed without the other.**

1. If equipped, remove plastic front shock cover cup at the front shock absorber mounting bracket.

2. If equipped, remove the electronic automatic ride actuator and actuator mounting washer at top strut mount in engine compartment.

3. Unfasten the three upper shock retaining nuts and collar plate/seal from the mounting studs in the engine compartment.

4. Raise and safely support the vehicle with jackstands.

5. Remove the tire and wheel assembly.

6. Remove the lower strut mounting bolt and nut.

7. Remove nut at the stabilizer link upper mounting stud.

✳✳ WARNING

Be very careful to avoid damage to the ball joint seal. If the seal is damaged, the stabilizer bar link assembly must be replaced.

8. Separate the link from the front wheel spindle using Ball Joint Separator/Remover D88L–3006–A, or equivalent.

9. Support lower control arm assembly with a transmission jack, or equivalent.

10. Raise the control arm and spindle with the jack, until the stabilizer link can be completely separated from the wheel spindle. Position the stabilizer link out of the way.

11. Remove the front wheel spindle-to-upper control arm ball joint attaching nut and bolt and discard.

12. Carefully lower the jack to separate the spindle from the upper control arm. Do not allow the spindle to hang free, support it with a piece of wire or other means.

13. Remove support from lower control arm and remove shock absorber/strut and spring assembly from vehicle.

To install:

14. Position the shock absorber and upper mount assembly over the lower control arm. Insert the lower shock bolt into the lower control arm.

15. Using a jack, raise the lower control arm and strut/shock absorber into position, aligning the upper strut mounting studs with the holes.

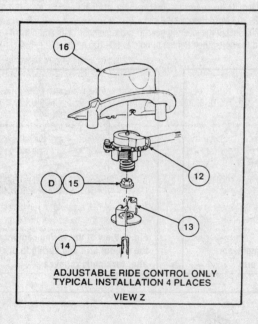

**ADJUSTABLE RIDE CONTROL ONLY
TYPICAL INSTALLATION 4 PLACES**

VIEW Z

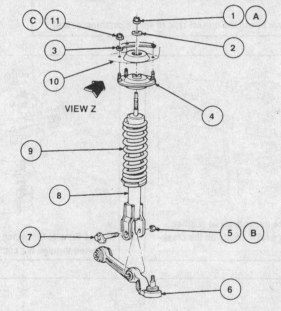

VIEW Z

Item	Part Number	Description
1	N805377-S100	Nut (2 Req'd)
2	18041	Washer (2 Req'd)
3	18T003	Shock Absorber Housing Seal (2 Req'd)
4	18183	Upper Front Shock Absorber Mounting Bracket (2 Req'd)
5	N805476-S160	Nut (2 Req'd)
6	3079	Front Suspension Lower Arm
7	N806798-S56	Bolt (2 Req'd)
8	18124	Front Shock Absorber
9	5310	Front Coil Spring (2 Req'd)
10	—	Body (Ref)
11	N801310-S100	Nut (6 Req'd)
12	18B012	Shock Absorber Electronic Actuator (2 Req'd)

Item	Part Number	Description
13	18171	Actuator Washer (4 Req'd)
14	18124	Front Shock Absorber
15	N805377-S100	Nut (2 Req'd for Base Vehicles) (4 Req'd for Ride Control Vehicles)
16	18A179	Front Shock Absorber Strut Cover Cup
A	—	Tighten to 50-71 N·m (37-52 Lb-Ft)
B	—	Tighten to 170-230 N·m (125-170 Lb-Ft)
C	—	Tighten to 22-31 N·m (17-22 Lb-Ft)
D	—	Tighten to 37-54 N·m (28-39 Lb-Ft)

88188G09

Fig. 7 Exploded view of the front strut/shock absorber and spring removal—1989–97 vehicles

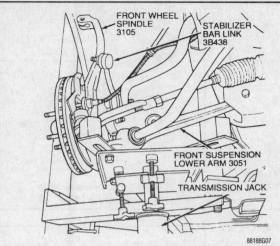

Fig. 8 Use a suitable jack to raise the control arm and spindle so the stabilizer link can be removed

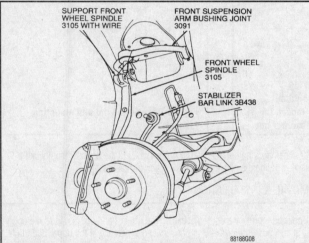

Fig. 9 Support the spindle with a piece of wire; do NOT let it hang free

16. Remove the wire holding the spindle and position the spindle to the upper control arm. Raise the lower control arm with the jack and attach the spindle to the upper control arm ball joint using a new attaching bolt and nut. Tighten the nut to 50–68 ft. lbs. (68–92 Nm).

17. Position the stabilizer bar link and lower spindle assembly until link is in position to install the nut onto link. Tighten to 30–39 ft. lbs. (40–55 Nm).

18. Remove the jack from the lower control arm.

19. Install the lower strut nut, but do not tighten at this time.

20. Install tire and wheel assembly, then tighten the lug nuts to 85–105 ft. lbs. (115–142 Nm), using a torque wrench.

21. Carefully lower the vehicle, making sure the upper strut mounting studs are aligned with holes.

22. Install the shock absorber housing seal and three nuts to the upper mounting studs. Tighten to 17–22 ft. lbs. (22–31 Nm).

23. Install the washer, nut and install the electronic actuator, if equipped. Tighten the nut to 28–39 ft. lbs. (37–54 Nm).

24. Install the plastic shock absorber/strut cover cup, if equipped.

�֎ WARNING

To prevent front suspension lower arm strut bushing wind-up, the lower shock nut must be tightened with the vehicle weight on the wheels.

25. Neutralize the lower control arm bushings by pushing down on the front of the vehicle and releasing. Tighten the lower shock absorber/strut nut to 125–170 ft. lbs. (170–230 Nm).

MacPherson Strut

REMOVAL & INSTALLATION

1983–88 Vehicles

▶ **See Figures 10 thru 15**

➡ **The bolts used in this procedure are made to metric specifications and require the use of metric tools.**

1. Disconnect the negative battery cable.

2. Place the ignition key in the unlock position to permit free movement of the front wheels. Raise the hood.

3. For Thunderbird Turbo Coupes, proceed as follows:

   a. Detach the actuator connector from the wiring harness connector.

   b. Remove the actuator protective cover. The cover snaps off.

   c. Slide the actuator connector off the protective cover.

   d. Unfasten the two screws retaining the actuator to the mounting bracket.

   e. Remove the actuator by lifting it off.

   f. Grasp the actuator mounting bracket with water pump pliers and hold firmly.

   g. Loosen the nut retaining the mounting bracket to the shock absorber, then remove the nut and mounting bracket.

   h. Install the nut onto the shock absorber.

✖✖ WARNING

DO NOT move or raise the vehicle after removing the bracket retaining nut. If the shock absorber must be removed, install the nut onto the shock.

4. Raise the vehicle by the lower control arms until the wheels are just off the ground. From the engine compartment, remove and discard the three 12mm upper mount retaining nuts.

✖✖ WARNING

The vehicle should not be driven with these nuts removed. Do NOT remove the pop-rivet holding the camber plate in position.

5. If the upper mount is to be replaced, loosen the 16mm strut rod nut.

6. Continue to raise the front of the vehicle by the lower control arms, then position safety stands under the frame jacking pads, behind the wheels.

7. Remove the tire and wheel assembly.

8. Remove the brake caliper, and rotate out of position.

9. Remove the two lower nuts attaching the strut to the spindle, leaving the bolts in place. Carefully remove both spindle-to-strut bolts, push the bracket free of the spindle, then remove the strut.

10. Compress the strut to clear the upper mount of the body mounting pad. Lift the strut up from the spindle to compress the rod, then pull down and remove the strut.

11. If necessary, remove the upper mount and jounce bumper from the strut.

To install:

12. If removed, install the upper mount and jounce bumper on the strut.

13. Position the three upper mount studs into the body mounting pad and camber plate, then start three new nuts.

14. With the rod half extended, place the rod through the upper mount and hand start the mount as soon as possible.

15. Extend the strut and position into the spindle.

16. Install two new lower mounting bolts and hand start the nuts. Remove the suspension load from the lower control arms by carefully lowering the vehicle. Tighten the lower mounting nuts to 140–200 ft. lbs. (190–271 Nm).

17. Raise the suspension control arms, then tighten the three new upper mounting nuts inside the engine compartment to 50–70 ft. lbs. (68–102 Nm).

18. For Thunderbird Turbo Coupes, perform the following:

   a. Install the actuator mounting bracket on the shock absorber. Make sure the flats on the bracket and shock absorber line up.

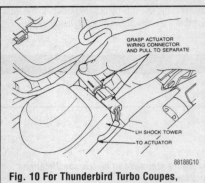

Fig. 10 For Thunderbird Turbo Coupes, detach the connector from the actuator wiring harness

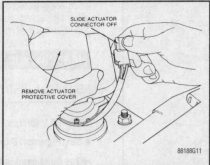

Fig. 11 Remove the protective cover, then slide the actuator connector from the cover

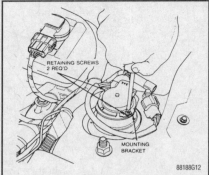

Fig. 12 Unfasten the two actuator-to-mounting bracket screws, then . . .

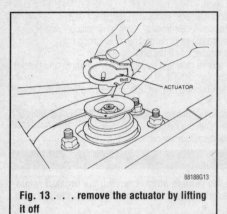

Fig. 13 . . . remove the actuator by lifting it off

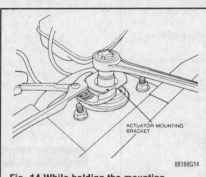

Fig. 14 While holding the mounting bracket with suitable pliers, loosen the mounting bracket-to-shock absorber nut

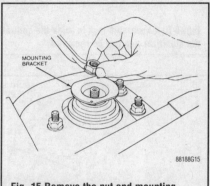

Fig. 15 Remove the nut and mounting bracket

b. Rotate the mounting bracket to align with the inner edge of the fender.

c. Install the retaining nut onto the shock absorber.

d. Grasp the mounting bracket with water pump pliers and hold firmly.

e. Tighten the nut to 60–75 ft. lbs. (81–102 Nm). Make sure the alignment of the mounting bracket to the fender is maintained while tightening the nut.

f. Install the actuator on the mounting bracket. Make sure the flats of the actuator and shock absorber are aligned.

g. Rotate the actuator to align the screw attaching holes in the mounting bracket.

h. Install the two actuator-to-mounting bracket attaching screws. Tighten the screws to 10–14 inch lbs. (1.1–1.6 Nm).

i. Fasten the actuator wiring connector onto the protective cover.

j. Position the actuator wiring in front of and under the actuator.

k. Install the wiring in the cutout in the protective cover.

19. If necessary, tighten the 16mm strut rod nut to 55–92 ft. lbs. (75–125 Nm).

20. Install the brake caliper and the tire and wheel assembly.

21. Remove the safety stands, then carefully lower the vehicle.

22. Connect the negative battery cable.

1989–97 Vehicles

Strut removal and installation procedures are the same as for front coil spring. Refer to the Coil Spring removal procedure located earlier in this section.

Upper Ball Joint

INSPECTION

1. Support the vehicle in normal driving position with ball joints loaded.

2. Wipe the grease fitting and checking surface, so they are free of dirt and grease. The checking surface is the round boss into which the grease fitting is threaded.

3. The checking surface should project outside the cover. If the checking surface is inside the cover, replace the lower arm assembly.

REMOVAL & INSTALLATION

Upper ball joints are not replaceable. The upper ball joint is part of the upper control arm bushing joint and is not serviced separately. If the upper ball joints are found to be defective, the entire upper control arm bushing joint assembly must be replaced.

Lower Ball Joint

INSPECTION

1. Support the vehicle in normal driving position with ball joints loaded.

2. Wipe the grease fitting and checking surface, so they are free of dirt and grease. The checking surface is the round boss into which the grease fitting is threaded.

3. The checking surface should project outside the cover. If the checking surface is inside the cover, replace the lower arm assembly.

REMOVAL & INSTALLATION

▶ See Figures 16 and 17

1. Raise and safely support the vehicle.

2. Remove the lower control arm as outlined later in this section.

3. Remove and discard the ball joint boot seal.

4. Clamp the lower control arm in a suitable vise.

5. Press out the lower control arm ball joint using Ball Joint Remover D89P-3010-A, Receiving Cup D84P-3395-A4, and U-Joint Tool T74P-4635-C, or equivalents. A suitable press may be used in place of the U-Joint tool, to press the ball joint out.

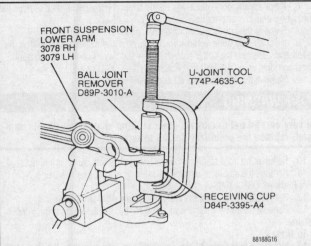

Fig. 16 You must use the correct tool to press the ball joint out from the lower control arm

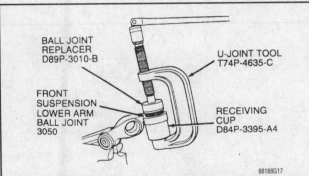

Fig. 17 Installation of the lower ball joint. Note that several special tools are needed for this job

To install:

➡When installing a new lower ball joint, it is advisable that the protective cover be left in place during installation to protect the ball joint seal. It may be necessary to cut off the end of the cover to allow it to pass through the receiving cup.

6. Install the ball joint with a Ball Joint Replacer D89P-3010-A, Receiving Cup D84P-3395-A4 and U-Joint Tool T74P-4635-C. A press may be used instead of the U-Joint tool.

7. Discard the protective cover and check the ball joint to make sure that it is fully seated in the control arm.

8. Inspect the ball seal and ensure that it is free of cuts or tears.

9. Install the lower control arm as outlined in this Section.

10. Carefully lower the vehicle.

11. Have the wheel alignment checked by a reputable repair shop.

Stabilizer Bar

REMOVAL & INSTALLATION

1983–88 Vehicles

1. Raise and safely support the front end of the vehicle with jackstands.

2. Disconnect the stabilizer bar from each stabilizer link and both stabilizer insulator attaching clamps. Remove the stabilizer bar assembly.

3. Remove the adapter brackets from the clamps.

4. Cut the worn insulators form the stabilizer bar.

To install:

5. Coat the necessary parts of the stabilizer bar and the inside diameter of the stabilizer bar insulator with Rubber Lubricant E25Y-19553-A or equivalent and slide the insulators onto the stabilizer bar.

6. Install the adapter brackets on the clamps.

7. Using a new nut and bolt, secure each end of the stabilizer bar to the lower suspension arm. Tighten the nuts to 6–12 ft. lbs. (8–16 Nm).

8. Using new bolts, clamp the stabilizer bar to the attaching brackets on the side rail. Tighten the retaining bolts to 37–50 ft. lbs. (50–68 Nm).

9. Carefully lower the vehicle.

1989–93 Vehicles

1. Remove the air inlet tube.

2. Remove the stabilizer bar retaining bracket bolts and retaining brackets.

3. Remove the serpentine drive belt.

4. Raise and safely support vehicle on jackstands.

5. Remove the front tire and wheel assemblies.

6. Remove the crankshaft vibration damper pulley.

7. Remove the cotter pins and castellated nuts from the outer tie rod ends. Separate the tie rod ends from the spindle using a tie rod end removal tool.

8. Remove transmission oil cooler line bracket.

9. Remove the stabilizer bar retaining nuts from the lower link.

10. Remove the bar link from the stabilizer bar using joint separator D88L–3006–A or equivalent.

❊❊ CAUTION

Use extreme care when separating the link from the sway bar as not to damage the ball joint seal. If seal becomes damaged, the link assembly must be replaced

11. Remove the stabilizer bar from the vehicle, through the right wheel opening and remove bushings from bar.

To install:

12. Install the bushings onto the stabilizer bar and position bar into vehicle through the right side wheel opening.

13. Attach the stabilizer links to the bar and tighten the retaining nuts to 40–55 ft. lbs. (54–74 Nm).

14. Install the transmission oil cooler line bracket.

15. Install the tie rod ends to the spindles. Tighten the nuts to 35–53 ft. lbs. (47–72 Nm) and install new cotter pins.

16. Install the crankshaft damper.

17. Install front tires and wheels and lower vehicle off the jackstands.

18. Install the stabilizer bar brackets and retaining nuts, tighten to 40–55 ft. lbs. (54–74 Nm).

19. Install the serpentine belt and air inlet tube.

1994–97 Vehicles

♦ See Figures 18, 19, 20 and 21

MOUNTING BRACKET INSULATOR

1. Disconnect the negative battery cable.

2. For 1995–97 vehicles, remove the front subframe, as follows:

    a. Install Engine Lifting Brackets D91P-6001-A or equivalent.

    b. Install Three Bar Engine Support D88L-6000-A or equivalent to the engine lifting brackets.

    c. Raise and safely support the vehicle.

    d. Remove the front engine support insulator through bolts.

❊❊ WARNING

Raise the engine carefully so as not to damage the lines and hoses at the rear of the engine.

    e. Raise the engine and support it with Three Bar Engine Support D88L-6000-A, or equivalent.

    f. Remove the front wheel and tire assemblies.

    g. Remove the tie rod end from the front wheel spindles.

    h. Remove the stabilizer bar link from the front wheel spindles.

    i. Remove the lower front shock absorber retaining bolts.

j. Remove the front suspension lower arm strut from the front suspension lower arms.

k. Remove the front suspension the front suspension lower arm inner pivot-to-front subframe retainer bolts.

l. Remove the steering coupling pinch bolt and disconnect the steering coupling.

m. Drain the power steering fluid into a suitable container.

n. Disconnect and cap the power steering return line and pressure hoses.

o. Remove the power steering oil cooler from the body side rail.

p. Remove the wire harnesses and/or the wire harness clips from the front subframe.

q. Safely support the front subframe with adjustable jacks at the four points.

r. Remove the 8 front subframe-to-body retaining bolts.

s. With the help of an assistant, carefully lower the adjustable jacks and allow the front subframe to lower.

t. If replacing the subframe, place the subframe on the floor or a bench and transfer the power steering rack, front suspension lower arm struts, front suspension lower arms and the front stabilizer bar to the new subframe. Also, transfer the reinforcement rod and tighten to 72–97 ft. lbs. (97–132) to the new subframe.

3. Remove the air cleaner outlet tube.

4. Remove the stabilizer bar bracket bolts and the stabilizer bar brackets.

5. Remove the drive belt.

6. If not already done, raise and safely support the vehicle, then remove the front wheel and tire assemblies.

7. Remove the crankshaft vibration damper.

8. If not already done, remove the cotter pins and castellated nuts from the tie rod ends. Discard the cotter pins. Separate the tie rod ends from the front wheel spindles using Tie Rod End Puller TOOL-3290-D or equivalent.

9. Remove the transmission oil cooler line clip.

✳✳ WARNING

Be very careful not to damage the ball joint seal. If the seal is damaged, replace the stabilizer link kit assembly.

10. Remove the front stabilizer bar-to-lower stabilizer bar retaining nuts.

11. Remove the stabilizer bar link from the front stabilizer bar using Ball Joint Remover D88L-3006-A or equivalent.

12. Remove the front stabilizer bar through the right wheel opening.

13. Remove the lower control arm stabilizer bar insulators from the front stabilizer bar.

To install:

14. Install the lower control arm stabilizer bar insulators onto the front stabilizer bar.

15. Position the front stabilizer bar into the vehicle.

16. Attach the stabilizer bar link to the front stabilizer bar. Tighten the retaining nuts to 29–39 ft. lbs. (40–55 Nm).

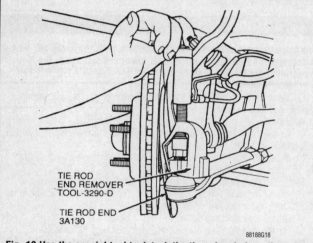

Fig. 18 Use the special tool to detach the tie rod ends from the spindles

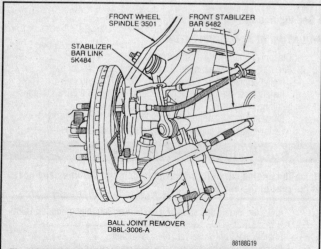

Fig. 19 Unfasten the stabilizer bar link from the bar using a ball joint removal tool

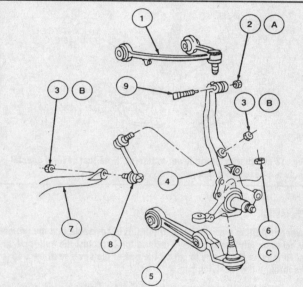

Item	Part Number	Description
1	3085	Upper Front Suspension Arm Bushing Joint
2	N805475-S150	Nut (2 Req'd)
3	N807145-S7	Nut (2 Req'd)
4	3105	Front Wheel Spindle
5	3079	Front Suspension Lower Arm
6	N805477-S1050-C	Nut (2 Req'd)
7	5482	Front Stabilizer Bar
8	5K484	Stabilizer Bar Link (2 Req'd)
9	N806579-S150	Bolt (2 Req'd)
A	—	Tighten to 68-92 N·m (50-68 Lb-Ft)
B	—	Tighten to 40-55 N·m (29-39 Lb-Ft)
C	—	Tighten to 113-153 N·m (83-113 Lb-Ft)

Fig. 20 Exploded view of the stabilizer bar and related components—1996 vehicle shown

17. Install the stabilizer bar brackets and retaining bolts. Tighten to 39–53 ft. lbs. (53–72 Nm).

18. Install the transmission oil cooler line clip.

19. For 1994 vehicles, attach the tie rod ends to the front wheel spindles. Tighten the nuts to 39–53 ft. lbs. (53–73 Nm). Install new cotter pins.

20. Install the crankshaft vibration damper.

21. For 1994 vehicles, install the front wheel and tire assemblies. Tighten the lug nuts to 85–105 ft. lbs. (115–142 Nm).

22. For 1994 vehicles, carefully lower the vehicle.

23. Install the serpentine drive belt.

24. Install the air cleaner outlet tube.

25. If removed, install the front subframe, as follows:

   a. With the help of an assistant, position the front subframe to the body and hand start the 8 retaining bolts into the mating body cage nuts.

➡Do not tighten the front subframe-to-body bolts at this time as the subframe must be aligned to the body before tightening the retainers.

   b. Using an adjustable jack, carefully raise the subframe into contact with the bottom of the body side rails.

   c. Install a ¾ in. (19mm) outside diameter pipe into body front left and right front subframe and body alignment holes. Tighten one bolt at each corner.

   d. Remove the alignment tools, then tighten the 8 bolts to 72–97 ft. lbs. (97–132 Nm).

   e. Install the wire harness clips and/or harnesses to the front subframe.

   f. Install the power steering oil cooler on the body side rail. Uncap and connect the power steering pressure hose and return line hoses.

   g. Connect the steering coupling and install the pinchbolt. Tighten the bolt to 21–30 ft. lbs. (28–40 Nm).

   h. Attach the stabilizer bar links to the spindles and tighten to 41–55 ft. lbs. (55–75 Nm).

   i. Install the tie rod end to the to the wheel spindles and tighten to 39–54 ft. lbs. (53–73 Nm).

   j. Install the front suspension lower arm pivots onto the subframe. Tighten to 92–125 ft. lbs. (125–170 Nm).

   k. Install the front suspension lower arm struts onto the left and right side front suspension lower arms and tighten to 89–118 ft. lbs. (120–160 Nm).

   l. Connect the front shock absorber of the right and left front suspension lower arm and tighten to 103–144 ft. lbs. (140–195 Nm).

   m. Install the tire and wheel assemblies.

   n. Carefully lower the vehicle partway.

➡The left side front engine support insulator (with locating pin) must seat first.

   o. Lower the engine onto the front engine support insulators, then raise and safely support the vehicle.

   p. Install the front engine support insulator through bolts. On 3.8L engines, tighten to 35–50 ft. lbs. (47–68 Nm). On 4.6L engines, tighten the bolts to 35–46 ft. lbs. (47–63 Nm).

   q. Carefully lower the vehicle, then remove the engine support and lifting bracket.

   r. Check and fill the power steering fluid. Bleed the power steering system, as outlined in this section.

26. Connect the negative battery cable. Have the front end alignment checked at a reputable repair shop.

BAR LINK ASSEMBLY

1. Raise and safely support the vehicle.
2. Remove the nuts from the stabilizer bar link.

❈❈ WARNING

Be very careful not to damage the ball joint seal. If the seal is damaged, replace the stabilizer link kit assembly.

3. Separate the link studs from the front steering knuckle/spindle and front stabilizer bar using Ball Joint Remover D88L-3006-A or equivalent.

   To install:

4. Install the stabilizer bar link to the front wheel spindle/knuckle and front stabilizer bar. Tighten the retaining nuts to 29–39 ft. lbs. (40–55 Nm).

5. Carefully lower the vehicle.

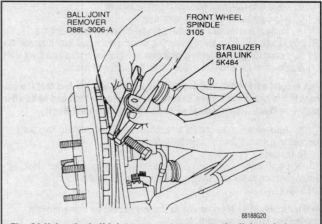

Fig. 21 Using the ball joint remover to separate the link studs from the steering knuckle

Upper Control Arm

REMOVAL & INSTALLATION

1989–97 Vehicles

♦ See Figure 22

➡The following procedure is the same for both the right and left side upper control arm.

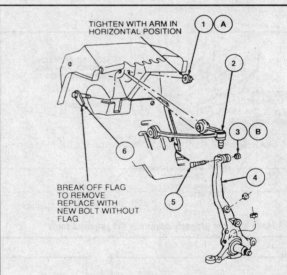

Item	Part Number	Description
1	N805470-S160	Nut (4 Req'd)
2	3085	Upper Front Suspension Arm Bushing Joint
3	N805475-S150	Nut (2 Req'd)
4	3105	Front Wheel Spindle
5	N806579-S150	Bolt (2 Req'd)
6	N805461-S150	Bolt (4 Req'd)
A	—	Tighten to 88-119 N·m (65-88 Lb-Ft)
B	—	Tighten to 68-92 N·m (50-68 Lb-Ft)

Fig. 22 Upper control arm, also referred to as the upper front suspension arm bushing joint, removal

1. Raise and safely support vehicle on jackstands.
2. Remove the tire and wheel assembly.
3. Remove and discard the upper spindle-to-ball joint bolt and nut.
Slightly spread spindle at the slot opening to remove the ball joint from spindle.
4. Lower vehicle enough to gain access to the upper control arm pivot bolts.
5. Break off the small metal flags from the pivot bolt heads.

➥**A 6-point socket must be used on the bolts due to the fact that the corners of the heads have been shaved off. Discard the nuts and bolts after removing them. Replacement bolts do not require metal flags.**

6. Remove the upper control arm/upper control arm bushing joint bolts, then remove the control arm from the vehicle.

To install:
7. Position the upper control arm and install new bolts and nuts. Holding the control arm in the horizontal position, tighten the nuts to 65–87 ft. lbs. (113–153 Nm).

➥**If nuts cannot be torqued due to limited access on some models, tighten the bolts to 81–88 ft. lbs.**

8. Raise and safely support the vehicle.
9. Attach spindle to the upper control arm/arm bushing joint. Install a new bolt and nut (install the bolt through front to rear), and tighten nut to 50–68 ft. lbs. (68–92 Nm).
10. Install tire and wheel assembly, then carefully lower the vehicle.

CONTROL ARM BUSHING REPLACEMENT

1989–93 Vehicles

▶ **See Figures 23, 24, 25 and 26**

1. Remove the upper control arm as outlined previously.
2. Assemble Collets T89P-5638-C1, Bushing Installer T89P-5638-C3, Bushing Remover T89P-5638-D and Forcing Screw T78P-5638-A1, or equivalent, on the control arm over the bushing.

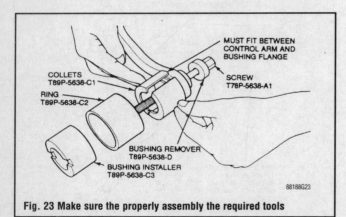

Fig. 23 Make sure the properly assembly the required tools

3. Assemble the tools so that the bushing will be forced outward (away from the head of the forcing screw).
4. Ensure the collet fits between the bushing flange and control arm surface.
5. Tighten the screw to force bushing out of the control arm.

To Install:
6. Position the Forcing Screw, Bushing Remover, Bushing Installer (T89P-5638-E) and the new bushing on the outer side of the control arm. Position the Bushing Installer T89P-5638-C3 on the inside of the control arm, lining up the grooves in the installer with the ridge on the control arm.
7. Tighten the screw until the halves of the installer bottom out against each other.
8. Install the upper control arm as outlined previously.

1994–97 Vehicles

The upper control arm bushings on these vehicles are part of the upper control arm bushing joint. Replacement of the bushings require replacement of the complete upper control arm/bushing joint assembly.

Lower Control Arm

REMOVAL & INSTALLATION

1983–88 Vehicles

1. Raise the front of the vehicle and position safety stands under both sides of the jack pads, just to the rear of the lower arms.
2. Remove the wheel and tire assembly.
3. Disconnect the stabilizer bar link from the lower arm.
4. If necessary for access, remove the disc brake caliper and wire it out of the way, then remove the rotor and dust shield.
5. Disconnect the tie rod assembly from the steering spindle/knuckle using Tie Rod End Remover TOOL-3290-D or equivalent.
6. Remove the steering gear bolts and position out of the way so the control arm bolt my be removed.
7. Remove and discard the cotter pin from the ball joint stud nut, and loosen the ball joint nut one or two turns. Do NOT remove the nut at this time.
8. Tap the spindle/knuckle boss sharply to relieve the stud pressure.
9. Use Spring Compressor Tool T82P-5310-A or equivalent to place the upper plate in position into the spring pocket cavity on the crossmember. The hooks on the plate should be facing toward the center of the vehicle.
10. Install the compression rod into the lower arm spring pocket hole, through the coil spring, into the upper plate.
11. Install the lower plate, lower ball nut, thrust washer and bearing, and forcing nut, onto the compression rod.
12. Tighten the forcing nut onto the compressor tool until a drag on the nut is felt.
13. Remove and discard the ball joint stud nut, and raise the entire stud and spindle/knuckle assembly. Wire it out of the way to obtain working room.
14. Remove and discard the control arm-to-crossmember retaining nuts and bolts. The compressor tool may have to be tightened or loosened for easy bolt removal.

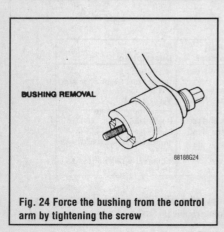

Fig. 24 Force the bushing from the control arm by tightening the screw

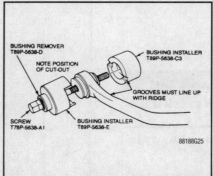

Fig. 25 Install the tools and new control arm bushing as shown

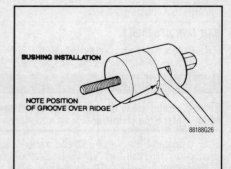

Fig. 26 Tighten the screw until the halves of the bushing installer bottom out against one another

15. Loosen the compression rod forcing nut until spring tension is relieved, then remove the forcing nut, lower control arm and coil spring.

To install:

16. Place the insulator on the top of the spring. Position the spring into the lower arm spring pocket.

➡**Make sure the spring pigtail is positioned between the two holes in the lower arm spring pocket.**

17. Position the spring and lower control arm onto the compression rod.

18. Tighten the forcing nut and position the lower control arm into the crossmember.

19. Install new lower control arm-to-crossmember bolts and nuts, but do not tighten yet.

20. Remove the wire from the strut and spindle/knuckle assembly, pull the assembly down and attach to the ball joint stud. Install a new ball joint stud nut, but do not tighten yet.

21. With a suitable jack, raise the control arm to a normal attitude position. Remove the compressor tool.

22. With the jack still in place, tighten the lower arm-to-crossmember attaching nuts to 110–150 ft. lbs. (149–203 Nm).

23. Tighten the ball joint stud nut to 100–120 ft. lbs. (149–203 Nm). Tighten the nut to align the holes, then install a new cotter pin. Carefully lower the vehicle and remove the jack.

24. Install the brake dust shield, rotor and caliper, if removed.

25. Install the steering gear-to-crossmember bolts and nuts, if removed. Hold the bolts and tighten them to 90–100 ft. lbs. (122–135 Nm).

26. Position the tie rod assembly into the steering spindle, then install the retaining nut. Tighten the nut to 35 ft. lbs. (47 Nm) and continue tightening the nut to align the next castellation with the cotter pin hole in the stud. Install a new cotter pin.

27. Connect the stabilizer bar link to the lower control arm. Tighten the attaching nut to 9–12 ft. lbs. (12–16 Nm).

28. Install the wheel and tire assembly.

29. Remove the safety stands and carefully lower the vehicle.

1989–97 Vehicles

◆ **See Figure 27**

1. Raise and safely support vehicle on jackstands.

2. Remove the tire and wheel assembly.

3. Loosen the lower ball joint nut 3 or 4 turns.

4. Rap on spindle with a heavy hammer, just enough to separate the ball joint from the spindle. Leave the nut on the ball joint.

5. Support the spindle by a wire or other means to prevent excessive sagging of the upper control arm.

6. Matchmark the position of the camber adjustment cam.

✳✳ WARNING

Do not hold tension strut, with a wrench on any curved part of strut. Use only the flat spots, as damage to the tension strut may result.

7. Hold the lower control arm strut by the flats with a wrench, then remove the nut retaining the lower control arm strut to the control arm bushing joint and discard.

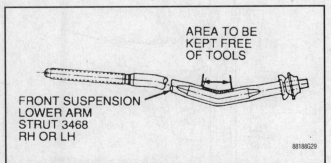

AREA TO BE
KEPT FREE
OF TOOLS

FRONT SUSPENSION
LOWER ARM
STRUT 3468
RH OR LH

88188G29

Fig. 27 Do not hold the strut, with a wrench on the curved part of the strut

8. Remove the lower shock attaching bolt and nut.

9. Remove the pivot (camber) bolt and nut.

10. Remove the nut from the lower ball joint, then remove lower control arm.

To install:

11. Position the lower control arm in vehicle and loosely install the pivot (camber) bolt and nut.

12. Install the tension strut insulator bushings and loosely install the attaching nut.

13. Install the ball joint nut loosely.

14. Install the lower shock bolt and nut but do not tighten at this time.

15. Tighten the ball joint nut to 83–113 ft. lbs. (113–153 Nm) and install a new cotter pin.

16. Tighten the tension strut control arm nut to 83–113 ft. lbs. (113–153 Nm).

✳✳ CAUTION

Do not hold tension strut, with a wrench on any curved part of strut. Use only the flat spots, as damage to the tension strut may result.

17. Remove the wire or other type of support holding the spindle.

18. Install the tire and wheel assembly. Tighten the lug nuts, with a torque wrench, to 85–105 ft. lbs. (115–142 Nm).

19. Carefully lower the vehicle.

20. Push down on the front of the vehicle and release to neutralize the suspension. Tighten the lower shock nut to 125–170 ft. lbs. (170–230 Nm).

21. Align the camber marks at the pivot bolt and tighten nut to 83–113 ft. lbs. (113–153 Nm).

➡**If the lower control arm was replaced, the alignment must be checked.**

CONTROL ARM BUSHING REPLACEMENT

◆ **See Figures 28 and 29**

1. Remove the lower control arm as outlined previously.

2. Press out the lower control arm mounting bolt bushing with Bushing Remover T78P-5638-A5, Receiving Cup T78P-5638-A4 and Forcing Screw T78P-5638-A1.

To install:

3. Install a new lower control arm bushing into the lower control arm from the front of the control arm using Bushing Replacers T78P-5638-A and T89P-5493-B, Forcing Screw T78P-5638-A1 and Forcing Screw Washer T79P-5638-A6. Turn the Forcing Screw until it bottoms.

4. Install the lower control arm, as outlined earlier in this section.

5. Have the front alignment checked by a reputable repair shop.

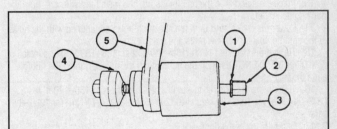

Item	Part Number	Description
1	T78P-5638-A6	Forcing Screw Washer
2	T78P-5638-A1	Forcing Screw
3	T78P-5638-A4	Receiving Cup
4	T78P-5638-A5	Bushing Remover
5	3051	Front Suspension Lower Arm

88188G27

Fig. 28 Use the specified tools to press the bushing out

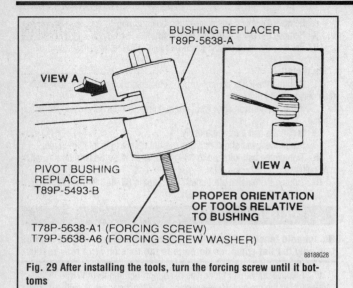

Fig. 29 After installing the tools, turn the forcing screw until it bottoms

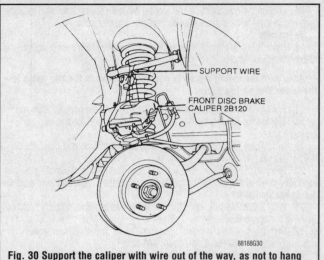

Fig. 30 Support the caliper with wire out of the way, as not to hang by the brake line

Spindle/Knuckle

REMOVAL & INSTALLATION

1983–88 Vehicles

1. Raise and safely support the front end of the vehicle on jackstands under the frame.
2. Remove the wheel and tire assembly.
3. Remove the caliper and suspend it out of the way, with wire.
4. Remove the hub and rotor.
5. Remove the rotor dust shields.
6. Unbolt the stabilizer link from the lower control arm.
7. Using a separator, disconnect the tie rod ends from the spindle.
8. Remove and discard the cotter pin from the ball joint stud nut, and loosen the ball joint stud nut a few turns. Don't remove it at this time!
9. Using a hammer, tap the spindle boss sharply to relieve stud pressure.
10. Support the lower control arm with a floor jack, compress the coil spring and remove the stud nut.
11. Remove the two bolts and nuts attaching the spindle to the shock strut. Compress the shock strut until working clearance is obtained.
12. Remove the spindle assembly.
To install:
13. Place the spindle on the ball joint stud, and install the stud nut, but don't tighten it yet.
14. Lower the shock strut until the attaching holes are aligned with the holes in the spindle. Install two new bolts and nuts.
15. Tighten the ball stud nut to 100–120 ft. lbs. (136–163 Nm) and install a new cotter pin. Do NOT back off the nut to align the holes. Tighten the nut to align the holes.
16. Tighten the shock strut-to-spindle attaching nuts to 150–180 ft. lbs. (203–244 Nm) for 1983–85 cars; 140–200 ft. lbs. (190–271 Nm) for 1986–88 cars.
17. Carefully lower the floor jack.
18. Install the stabilizer links. Tighten the nuts to 6–12 ft. lbs. (8–16 Nm).
19. Attach the tie rod ends and tighten the nuts to 35–47 ft. lbs. (47–64 Nm).
20. The remainder of installation is the reverse of the removal procedure.
21. Have the alignment checked at a reputable repair shop.

1989–97 Vehicles

▶ See Figures 30, 31 and 32

1. Raise and safely support the vehicle on jackstands.
2. Remove tire and wheel assembly.
3. Mark the brake rotor and wheel hub bolt so the rotor can be install in

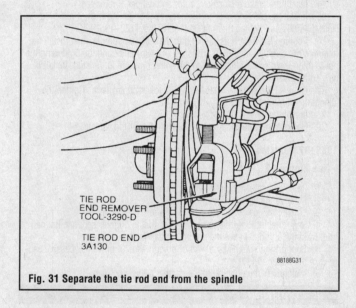

Fig. 31 Separate the tie rod end from the spindle

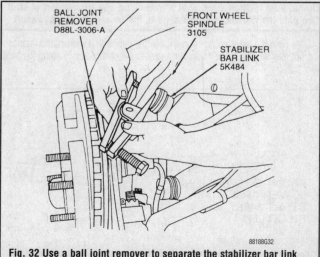

Fig. 32 Use a ball joint remover to separate the stabilizer bar link from the spindle

the same position as original for rotor runout. Remove the brake caliper and support with wire, then remove the rotor.

➡ **Do not disconnect the brake fluid line. Support brake caliper with wire. Do not let the caliper hang by, or bend the fluid line.**

4. Remove the hub and bearing assembly.
5. If equipped, remove the anti-lock brake sensor and position out of the way.
6. Remove the cotter pin and loosen the castellated nut from the tie rod end. Using a tie rod removal tool, separate the tie rod end from spindle and remove nut.

❊❊ WARNING

Be very careful to avoid damage to the ball joint seal. If the seal is damaged, the stabilizer bar link must be replaced.

7. Remove the stabilizer bar link from spindle using a joint separator D88L–3006–A or equivalent.
8. Loosen the lower ball joint nut three to four turns, then rap on the spindle with a hammer to separate ball joint from spindle and remove and discard the nut.
9. Remove the upper spindle-to-upper control arm bolt and nut. Discard the bolt and nut.
10. Spread the upper slot enough to remove the spindle from vehicle.
To install:
11. Position the spindle on the lower control arm and attach the upper control arm to the spindle.
12. Install a new bolt and nut (front to back) into spindle to hold the upper control arm and tighten to 50–65 ft. lbs. (68–88 Nm).
13. Install a new nut onto the lower ball joint and tighten to 83–113 ft. lbs. (113–153 Nm).
14. Install the hub and bearing assembly and hand-tighten.
15. Install the brake rotor and caliper assembly. For details, please refer to Section 9 of this manual.
16. Install and adjust the anti-lock brake sensor. For details, please refer to Section 9 of this manual.
17. Install the stabilizer bar link to the spindle and tighten nut to 29–39 ft. lbs. (40–55 Nm).
18. Attach the tie rod end to the spindle and install the nut. Tighten the nut to 39–53 ft. lbs. (53–73 Nm). If the nut does not line up with the holes, continue to tighten the nut until the nut lines up with the holes. Install a new cotter pin.
19. Install the tire and wheel assembly, then carefully lower the vehicle.
20. Tighten the wheel hub retainer to 236–250 ft. lbs. (320–340 Nm). Install a new hub grease cap, using a suitable tool as not to distort or damage the cap.

Front Wheel Bearings

REMOVAL & INSTALLATION

1983–88 Vehicles

◆ **See Figures 33, 34, 35, 36 and 37**

Each front hub has an inner and outer bearing, with a grease retainer (seal) on the inside of hub. The outer bearing is held in place by nut and retainer washer with a cotter pin. Both inner and outer bearings are replaceable.

1. Loosen the wheel lug nuts.
2. Raise and safely support vehicle on jackstands.
3. Remove tire and wheel assembly.
4. Remove the disc brake caliper assembly. Tie the caliper assembly out of the way, do NOT let assembly hang by the brake line.
5. Remove the grease cap from center of hub.
6. Remove the cotter pin, nut locking ring, adjusting nut and washer. Wipe off all excess grease from spindle.
7. Wiggle rotor assembly back and forth, enough for the outer bearing to slide out and remove.
8. Pull the hub and rotor off the spindle.
9. Remove the grease retainer using removal tool Tool–1175–AC or equivalent. Discard grease retainer.
10. Remove inner bearing cone and roller assembly. Thoroughly clean both roller assemblies, and inspect for damage or worn parts. Replace parts as necessary.
11. Clean and inspect the bearing cups inside hub assembly. If the cups are to be replaced use bearing cup puller T77F–1102–A or equivalent. Be sure to seat the new cups properly into the hub assembly.

➡ **When removing or installing bearing cups on rotor, use a block of wood to rest the rotor on. This will prevent damage to the wheel studs.**

To install:
12. Pack the bearing cone and roller assemblies with Long Life Multi-purpose grease, C1AZ–19590–B or equivalent with a bearing packer. If a bearing packer is not available, pack as much grease as possible by hand into bearing assembly and grease the cup surfaces also.
13. Place the inner bearing assembly into rotor onto cup. Apply a light film of grease to the lip of the new grease retainer seal and install into rotor assembly. Be sure that the seal is seated flush with back of the rotor hub.

➡ **When installing the grease retainer, use a block of wood to rest the rotor on. This will prevent damage to the wheel studs.**

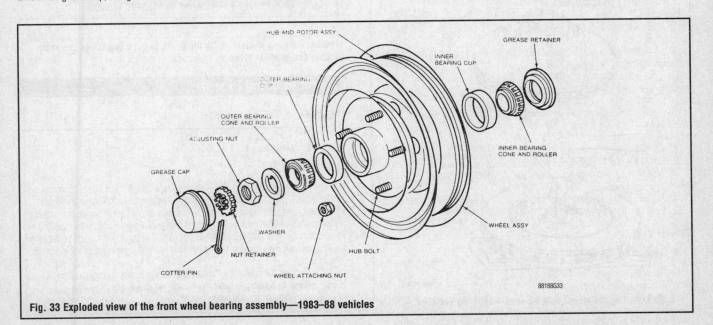

Fig. 33 Exploded view of the front wheel bearing assembly—1983–88 vehicles

88188G33

14. Install the hub and rotor assembly onto the spindle, keeping the hub centered to prevent damage to the retainer and spindle threads.

15. Install the outer bearing assembly and flat washer. Install the adjusting nut finger tight.

16. While rotating the hub tighten the adjusting nut to 17–25 ft. lbs. (23–34 Nm). Back the nut off ½ turn, using an inch pound torque wrench, tighten adjusting nut to 10–28 inch lbs. (1.1–3.2 Nm).

17. Place the nut locking ring on adjusting nut aligning the castellated flange with the cotter pin hole in spindle.

18. Install a new cotter pin, bending the ends around spindle and install the center hub dust cap.

19. Install the brake caliper, the tire and wheel assembly, then lower the vehicle.

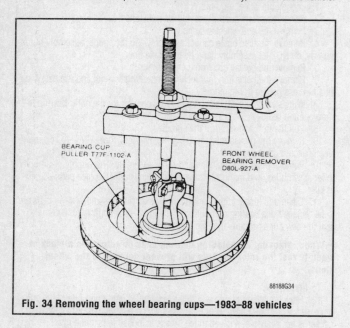

Fig. 34 Removing the wheel bearing cups—1983–88 vehicles

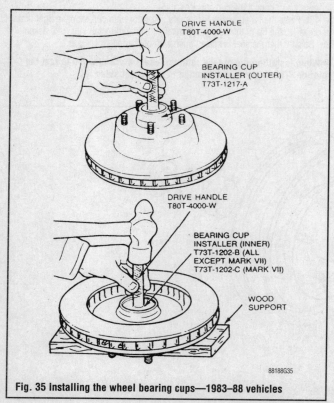

Fig. 35 Installing the wheel bearing cups—1983–88 vehicles

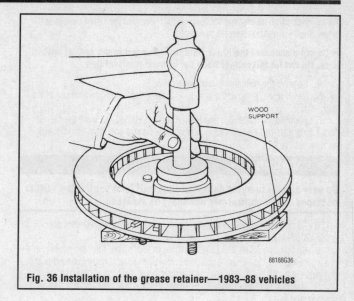

Fig. 36 Installation of the grease retainer—1983–88 vehicles

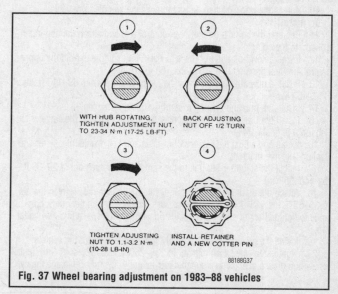

Fig. 37 Wheel bearing adjustment on 1983–88 vehicles

➡ Before driving vehicle pump the brake pedal a few times to ensure proper brake pedal pressure to brakes.

Front Hub And Bearing

REMOVAL & INSTALLATION

1989–97 Vehicles

▶ See Figure 38

The front wheel bearings are of the hub type design. The bearings are an integral part of the hub assembly and are pregreased for the life of the bearing. There are no adjustments to be made and they are not serviceable. If a bearing is suspected of being worn or damaged, the hub assembly must be replaced as a unit. Whenever a hub nut has been backed off or removed it must be replaced with a new nut. Never reuse an old nut and never use an impact tool to install the new nut.

1. Remove the center grease cap and loosen hub nut about 2–3 turns.
2. Raise and safely support the vehicle on jackstands.
3. Remove the tire and wheel assembly.
4. Remove the brake caliper, then suspend out of the way with a piece of wire.

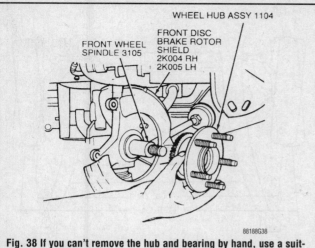

Fig. 38 If you can't remove the hub and bearing by hand, use a suitable hub puller

➡ **Do NOT let the brake caliper assembly hang by the fluid hose.**

5. Matchmark the rotor and wheel hub bolt to assure the parts are installed in the proper location. Remove the push-on nuts from the wheel stud, then remove the rotor.

6. Remove and discard the hub nut.

7. Remove the wheel hub and bearing assembly by pulling it straight off the studs. If the assembly cannot be removed by hand, use Front Hub Remover T81P–1104–C, to remove the hub and bearing assembly.

To install:

8. Install hub and bearing assembly and a new hub nut. Only hand-tighten the nut at this time.

9. Install the rotor and push-on nuts. Make sure the rotor marks line up with the hub bolt marks.

10. Install brake caliper assembly. For details, please refer to the procedure located in Section 9 of this manual.

11. Install the tire and wheel assembly. Tighten the wheel lug nuts to 85–105 ft. lbs. (115–142 Nm) using a torque wrench.

12. Carefully lower the vehicle.

13. Tighten the center hub nut to 238–250 ft. lbs. and install a new hub grease cap, using a suitable tool as not to distort of damage the cap.

➡ **Once torque has been applied to hub nut, do not back off the nut for any reason. The hub nut must be replaced with a new nut each time the nut has been loosened. Serious damage and or personal injury will occur if the hub nut is not replaced.**

Wheel Alignment

If the tires are worn unevenly, if the vehicle is not stable on the highway or if the handling seems uneven in spirited driving, the wheel alignment should be checked. If an alignment problem is suspected, first check for improper tire inflation and other possible causes. These can be worn suspension or steering components, accident damage or even unmatched tires. If any worn or damaged components are found, they must be replaced before the wheels can be properly aligned. Wheel alignment requires very expensive equipment and involves minute adjustments which must be accurate; it should only be performed by a trained technician. Take your vehicle to a properly equipped shop.

Following is a description of the alignment angles which are adjustable on most vehicles and how they affect vehicle handling. Although these angles can apply to both the front and rear wheels, usually only the front suspension is adjustable.

CASTER

▶ **See Figure 39**

Looking at a vehicle from the side, caster angle describes the steering axis rather than a wheel angle. The steering knuckle is attached to a control arm or strut at the top and a control arm at the bottom. The wheel pivots around the line between these points to steer the vehicle. When the upper point is tilted back, this is described as positive caster. Having a positive caster tends to make the wheels self-centering, increasing directional stability. Excessive positive caster makes the wheels hard to steer, while an uneven caster will cause a pull to one side. Overloading the vehicle or sagging rear springs will affect caster, as will raising the rear of the vehicle. If the rear of the vehicle is lower than normal, the caster becomes more positive.

CAMBER

▶ **See Figure 40**

Looking from the front of the vehicle, camber is the inward or outward tilt of the top of wheels. When the tops of the wheels are tilted in, this is negative camber; if they are tilted out, it is positive. In a turn, a slight amount of negative camber helps maximize contact of the tire with the road. However, too much negative camber compromises straight-line stability, increases bump steer and torque steer.

TOE

▶ **See Figure 41**

Looking down at the wheels from above the vehicle, toe angle is the distance between the front of the wheels, relative to the distance between the back of the wheels. If the wheels are closer at the front, they are said to be toed-in or to have negative toe. A small amount of negative toe enhances directional stability and provides a smoother ride on the highway.

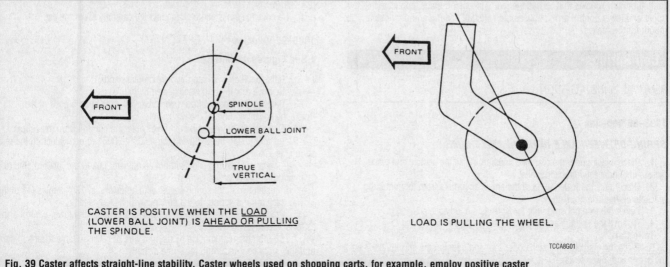

Fig. 39 Caster affects straight-line stability. Caster wheels used on shopping carts, for example, employ positive caster

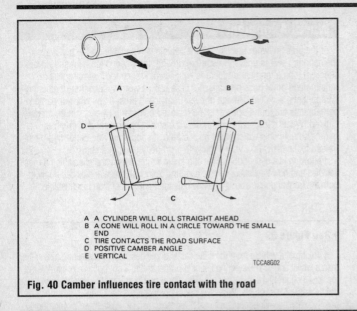

A A CYLINDER WILL ROLL STRAIGHT AHEAD
B A CONE WILL ROLL IN A CIRCLE TOWARD THE SMALL END
C TIRE CONTACTS THE ROAD SURFACE
D POSITIVE CAMBER ANGLE
E VERTICAL

TCCA8G02

Fig. 40 Camber influences tire contact with the road

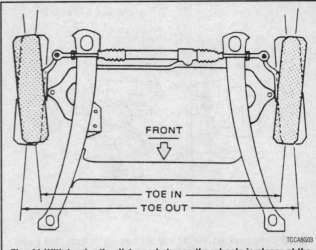

FRONT

TOE IN
TOE OUT

TCCA8G03

Fig. 41 With toe-in, the distance between the wheels is closer at the front than at the rear

REAR SUSPENSION

▶ **See Figures 42, 43 and 44**

All models through 1988 use a 4-link coil spring suspension. The axle housing is suspended from the frame by an upper and lower trailing arm and a shock absorber at each side of the vehicle. These arms pivot in the frame members and the rear axle housing brackets. Each coil spring is mounted between a lower seat which is welded to the axle housing or lower arm and an upper seat which is integral with the frame. The shock absorbers are bolted to the spring upper seats at the top and brackets mounted on the axle housing at the bottom. The upper trailing arms are attached to the frame crossmember brackets at the front and brackets located near the outer ends of the axle housing at the rear. Both lower arms attach similarly to the frame side members and the axle housing brackets. A rear stabilizer bar attached to the frame side rail brackets and the two axle housing brackets is available as optional equipment.

All 1989–97 models use a fully independent coil spring suspension system which is mounted on a rubber isolated subframe. Large lower control arms (H-arm configuration) are used to oppose torque reaction on braking and acceleration. A toe compensator link controls toe-out during braking. The upper control arm provides camber control. Epoxy coated, variable rate, steel coil springs are used on all models. Insulators are used on either end of the spring for added isolation. Although the springs are mounted in the same manner on both the Base and the Super Coupe/XR-7 models, unique spring load/rate provisions are used to suit the particular model. The suspension also features a cast aluminum knuckle that carries the rear suspension loads, connects the upper and lower control arms, houses the halfshaft bearing and provides a mount for the brakes.

Coil Springs

REMOVAL & INSTALLATION

1983–88 Vehicles

SPRING BETWEEN AXLE HOUSING AND FRAME

1. Place a jack under the rear axle housing. Raise the vehicle and place jackstands under the frame side rails.
2. Disconnect the lower studs of the shock absorbers from the mounting brackets on the axle housing.
3. Lower the axle housing until the springs are fully seated.
4. Remove the springs and insulators from the vehicle.
To install:
5. Place the insulators in each upper seat and position the springs between the upper and lower seats.
6. With the springs in position, raise the axle housing until the lower studs

of the rear shock absorbers reach the mounting brackets on the axle housing. Connect the lower studs and install the attaching nuts.
7. Remove the jackstands and carefully lower the vehicle.

SPRING BETWEEN LOWER CONTROL ARM AND FRAME

➡**If one spring must be replaced, the other should be replaced also. If the car is equipped with a rear stabilizer bar, the bar must be removed first.**

1. Raise and safely support the car at the rear crossmember, while supporting the axle with a jack.
2. Lower the axle until the shocks are fully extended.
3. Place a jack under the lower arm pivot bolt. Remove the pivot bolt and nut. Carefully and slowly lower the arm until the spring load is relieved.
4. Remove the spring and insulators.
To install:
5. Tape the insulator in place in the frame, and place the lower insulator in place on the arm. Install the internal damper in the spring.
6. Position the spring in place and slowly raise the jack under the lower arm. Install the pivot bolt and nut, with the nut facing outwards. Do not tighten the nut yet.
7. Raise the axle to curb height, and tighten the lower pivot bolt to 70–100 ft. lbs. (95–135 Nm).
8. If removed, install the stabilizer bar and tighten it to 20–27 ft. lbs. (27–37 Nm).
9. Remove the crossmember stands, then carefully lower the car.

1989–97 Vehicles

▶ **See Figures 45 thru 52**

1. Raise and safely support vehicle on jackstands.
2. Remove rear tire and wheel assembly.
3. Remove the rear stabilizer (sway) bar link nuts at both ends of bar. Rotate the bar up and out of the way.
4. Disconnect the rear parking brake cable and conduit from the caliper.
5. Install three Rotunda Spring Cages 086–00031 or equivalent, to the rear spring, as follows:
    a. Install one spring cage without an adjuster link to the inboard side (the innermost "bend" of the spring).
    b. Install two more spring cages, with adjusters, at 120° angles (⅓ of the way each around spring) to the previously installed cage.
6. Place a transmission jack or suitable stand under the lower control arm as far outboard as possible.
7. Support the rear knuckle by using a wire or other suitable means to support the upper control arm to the frame or body.
8. Remove the lower strut/shock mounting bolt, washer and nut.

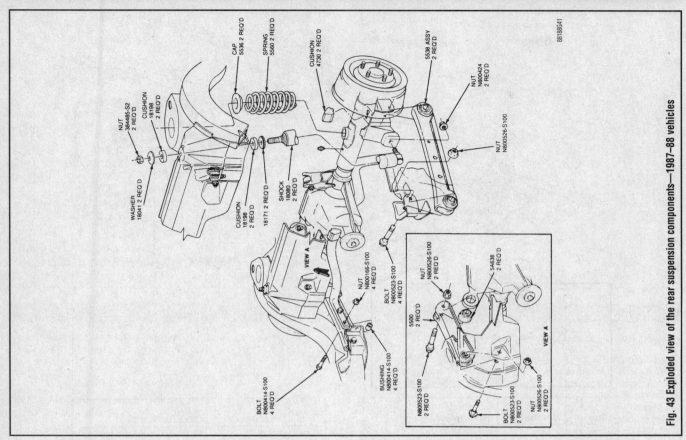

Fig. 43 Exploded view of the rear suspension components—1987–88 vehicles

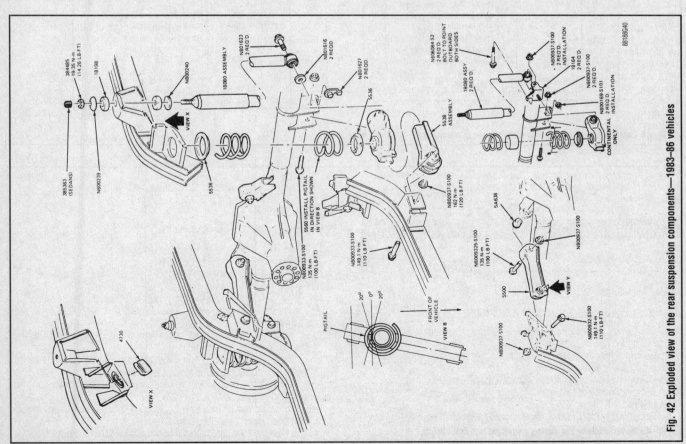

Fig. 42 Exploded view of the rear suspension components—1983–86 vehicles

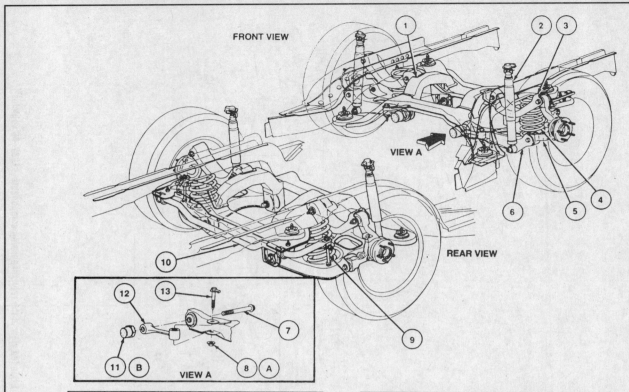

Item	Part Number	Description
1	—	Sub-Frame Assy
2	18125	Rear Shock Absorber
3	5500	Upper Rear Suspension Arm and Bushing
4	5560	Rear Spring
5	5A969	Rear Wheel Knuckle
6	5500	Rear Suspension Arm and Bushing
7	N805467-S160	Bolt (2 Req'd)
8	N805479-S1050C	Nut

Item	Part Number	Description
9	5C488	Rear Stabilizer Bar Link and Bushing
10	5A772	Rear Stabilizer Bar
11	N805646-S161	Nut (w/Cap) (2 Req'd)
12	5A972	Rear Suspension Compensator Link
13	N806066-S160	Bolt (2 Req'd)
A	—	Tighten to 149-201 N·m (110-148 Lb-Ft)
B	—	Tighten to 225-275 N·m (166-202 Lb-Ft)

88188G42

Fig. 44 Exploded view of the rear suspension components—1989–97 vehicles

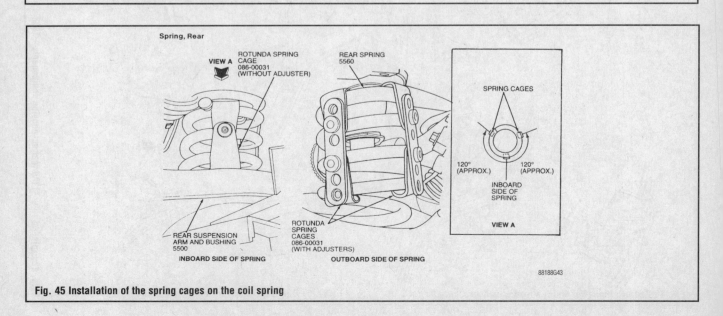

88188G43

Fig. 45 Installation of the spring cages on the coil spring

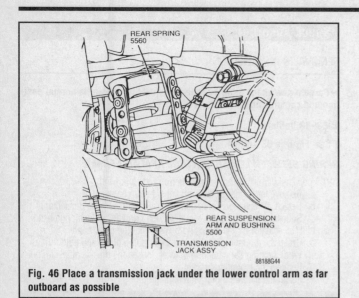

Fig. 46 Place a transmission jack under the lower control arm as far outboard as possible

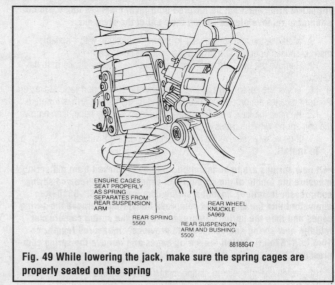

Fig. 49 While lowering the jack, make sure the spring cages are properly seated on the spring

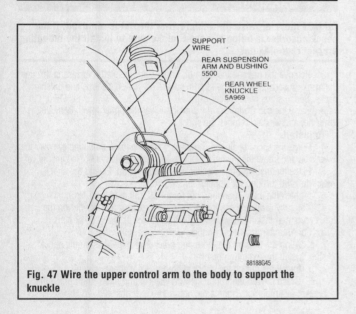

Fig. 47 Wire the upper control arm to the body to support the knuckle

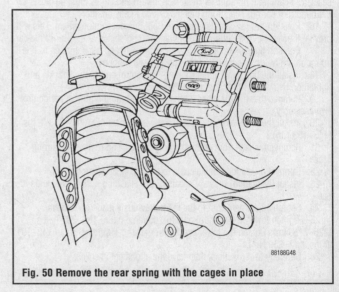

Fig. 50 Remove the rear spring with the cages in place

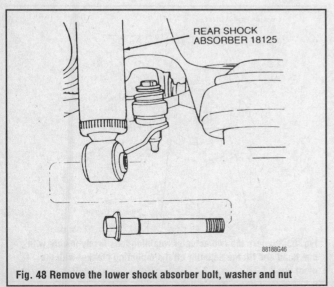

Fig. 48 Remove the lower shock absorber bolt, washer and nut

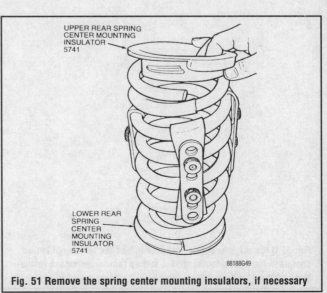

Fig. 51 Remove the spring center mounting insulators, if necessary

➡**Control arms must not be lowered until pivot bolts are loose. Do not attempt to remove plastic cap on the front of the pivot nut.**

9. Mark the toe adjustment cam-to-subframe position with a suitable marker. Loosen both inboard pivot bolts on lower control arm.

10. Remove the two bolts and nuts attaching the lower control arm to the knuckle.

11. Lower the control arm by carefully lowering the support jack. Make sure the spring cages are properly seated on spring as the control arm is lowered.

12. Remove the jack, pull the control arm down fully by hand, then remove the coil spring with the cages in place.

13. If necessary, remove the spring center mounting insulators.

To install:

➡**If new springs are to be installed, or cages removed from old spring, measure the length of the spring (with cages still installed and spring compressor installed), install a spring compressor D78P–5310–A or equivalent into the spring and compress the spring. Remove the spring cages and then the spring compressor. Install the spring compressor into the new spring and compress to previously measured length, or 10.5 in. (267mm). Install the spring cages and remove the spring compressor.**

14. Install spring center mounting insulators, if removed.

15. Place spring, with cages installed, onto upper and lower control arm seats. The cage with no adjuster must face inward and cages must be closer to the bottom of spring. The spring pigtails can be in any position.

16. Position two jackstands under the front bumper reinforcement. This will prevent the vehicle from lifting off of the supporting stands at the rear of the car.

17. Position the jack under the lower control arm and raise enough to line up mounting holes, ensuring that the spring seats properly.

18. Install the bolts and nuts attaching the control arm to the knuckle and tighten bolts to 110–148 ft. lbs. (149–201 Nm).

19. Remove the wire, or other means of support, holding the upper control arm assembly.

20. Install the lower strut/shock bolt and nut, tighten nut to 83–113 ft. lbs. (113–153 Nm).

21. Remove the jack from under the control arm, and remove the spring cages.

22. Connect the parking brake cable to brake caliper assembly.

23. Install the stabilizer (sway) bar links and attaching nuts at both ends of bar.

24. Set toe adjustment cam to the mark previously made on removal.

25. Tighten lower front control arm-to-subframe nut to 166–202 ft. lbs. (225–275 Nm). Tighten the lower rear control arm-to-subframe nut to 142–191 ft. lbs. 192–259 Nm).

26. Carefully lower vehicle, then have the alignment checked.

Shock Absorber

REMOVAL & INSTALLATION

➡**Purge a new shock of air by repeatedly extending it in its normal position and compressing it while inverted.**

1983–88 Vehicles

▶ **See Figures 53 and 54**

SPRING BETWEEN LOWER CONTROL ARM AND FRAME

1. For Thunderbird Turbo Coupes, perform the following:
   a. Remove the luggage compartment side trim panel.
   b. Detach the actuator wiring connector from the harness connector.
   c. Squeeze the two actuator retaining tabs firmly inward with one hand and lift the actuator off the mounting bracket with the other hand.
   d. Grasp the mounting bracket with water pump pliers and hold firmly.
   e. While holding the mounting bracket, loosen the bracket attaching nut.
   f. Remove the mounting bracket.
   g. Install the mounting bracket retaining nut.

❊❊ WARNING

Do NOT move or raise the vehicle after the nut is removed. If the shock absorber is being removed, make sure to install the mounting bracket retaining nut.

2. Remove the upper attaching nut, washer, and insulator. Access is through the trunk on sedans or side panel trim covers on station wagons and hatchbacks. Sedan studs have rubber caps.

3. Raise the car. Compress the shock to clear the upper tower. Remove the lower nut and washer; remove the shock.

To install:

4. Purge the shock of air and compress. Place the lower mounting eye over the lower stud and install the washer and a new locking nut. Do not tighten the nut yet.

5. Place the insulator and washer on the upper stud. Extend the shock, install the stud through the upper mounting hole.

6. Tighten the lower mounting nut to 45–60 ft. lbs. (61–81 Nm).

7. Carefully lower the car. Install the outer insulator and washer on the upper stud, and install a new nut. Tighten to 19–27 ft. lbs. (26–37 Nm).

8. For Thunderbird Turbo Coupes, perform the following:
   a. Align the flats on the mounting bracket with the flats on the shock stud. Install the mounting bracket.
   b. Install the nut on the shock absorber, if not already done.
   c. Grasp the mounting bracket with water pump pliers and tighten the bracket retaining nut. Tighten the nut to 15–21 ft. lbs. (20–28 Nm).

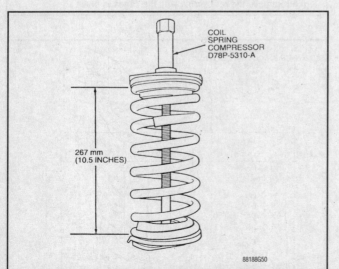

COIL SPRING COMPRESSOR D78P-5310-A

267 mm (10.5 INCHES)

88188G50

Fig. 52 If the original spring was broken and the length not known, compress the spring to about 10.5 inches (not including the insulators)

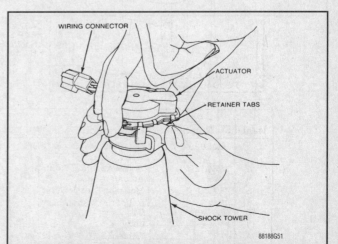

WIRING CONNECTOR

ACTUATOR

RETAINER TABS

SHOCK TOWER

88188G51

Fig. 53 Squeeze the two actuator retaining tabs firmly inward with one hand and lift the actuator off the mounting bracket with the other hand

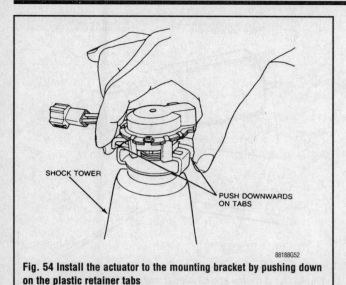

Fig. 54 Install the actuator to the mounting bracket by pushing down on the plastic retainer tabs

d. Grasp the actuator by the retaining tabs, then install the actuator on the mounting bracket by pushing down on the plastic retainer tabs.

e. Attach the actuator wiring connector.

9. Install the trim panel on station wagons and hatchbacks or the rubber cap on sedans.

SPRING BETWEEN AXLE HOUSING AND FRAME

1. Raise the vehicle and install jackstands.

2. Remove the shock absorber outer attaching nut, washer and insulator from the stud at the top side of the spring upper seat. Compress the shock sufficiently to clear the spring seat hole, and remove the inner insulator and washer from the upper attaching stud.

3. Remove the locknut and disconnect the shock absorber lower stud at the mounting bracket on the axle housing. Remove the shock absorber.

To install:

4. Position a new inner washer and insulator on the upper attaching stud. Place the upper stud in the hole in the upper spring seat. While maintaining the shock in this position, install a new outer insulator, washer, and nut on the stud from the top side of the spring upper seat.

5. Extend the shock absorber. Locate the lower stud in the mounting bracket hole on the axle housing and install the locknut.

1989–97 Vehicles

▶ See Figure 55

✳✳ WARNING

The rear shock/struts act as the rebound stops for the rear suspension. When the rear shock/struts are removed, the suspension arms must be restrained. The best method for rear shock/strut removal is to use a drive on hoist or an alignment pit. Portable car ramps can be substituted, But make sure the ramps are secure, the parking brake is set, and the front wheels are chocked properly before proceeding.

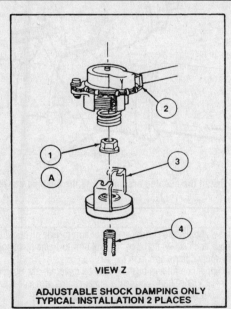

VIEW Z

**ADJUSTABLE SHOCK DAMPING ONLY
TYPICAL INSTALLATION 2 PLACES**

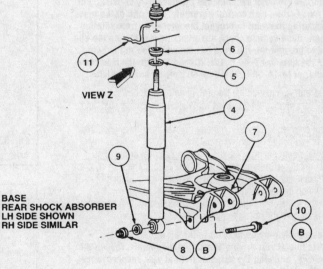

**BASE
REAR SHOCK ABSORBER
LH SIDE SHOWN
RH SIDE SIMILAR**

Item	Part Number	Description
1	N805828-S150	Nut (2 Req'd) (Super Coupe Only)
2	18B012	Shock Absorber Electronic Actuator
3	18A192	Mounting Bracket Assy
4	18125	Rear Shock Absorber
10	N805289-S150	Bolt
11	—	Body
A	—	Tighten to 37-54 N·m (27-40 Lb-Ft) (All Except Shock Damping)

Item	Part Number	Description
5	18177	Washer (2 Req'd)
6	18198	Insulator
7	5500	Lower Rear Suspension Arm and Bushing
8	N620484-S428	Nut
9	N805290-S36M	Washer
B	—	Tighten to 113-153 N·m (83-113 Lb-Ft)
C	—	Tighten to 60-80 N·m (44-58 Lb-Ft)

Fig. 55 Rear shock absorber mounting—1995 vehicle shown

1. Position the vehicle safely on a pit, hoist or ramps.

✳✳ WARNING

These vehicles are equipped with gas-pressurized shock absorbers which will extend unassisted. DO NOT apply heat or flame to the shock absorber tube during removal.

2. Remove the side trim panels from inside luggage compartment.
3. If equipped with an Automatic Ride Control, perform the following:
   a. Detach the actuator wiring connector from harness connector.
   b. Squeeze the two actuator retaining tabs firmly inward with one hand and lift actuator off with the other hand, if so equipped.
   c. Using water pump pliers, grasp the mounting bracket and hold firmly. loosen attaching nut and remove mounting bracket, if so equipped.
4. Remove top attaching nut washer and insulator.
5. Remove the lower shock/strut mounting bolt and remove shock/strut.

To install:

6. Properly prime the new shock/strut by inverting and collapsing, then releasing the shock/strut to its fully extended position.

➡**When replacing shock/strut on an Automatic Ride Control equipped vehicle, an exact replacement automatic adjustable shock/strut must be used. Failure to do so will result in a vehicle that will handle poorly, and could lead to a potentially dangerous situation.**

7. Place the inner washer and insulator on the upper retaining stud. Place the shock/strut up into position in upper mounting hole. Compress shock enough to install the lower mounting bolt and nut, then tighten the nut to 83–113 ft. lbs. (113–153 Nm).
8. With the upper end of the shock absorber protruding through the body shock tower hole, install the insulator, washer and nut on top of shock/strut, inside luggage compartment.

➡**Automatic ride control shock absorbers (Super Coupe and XR7) use a separate nut whereas the base vehicles use the assembly consisting of the crimped on nut. For the ride control assembly, hold one of the tags on the washer securing the joint to prevent the shock rod from rotating during installation. Base vehicle shock absorbers have a hex on the end of the piston rod to prevent the rod from turning while the nut is being torqued. Tighten the nuts to 27–40 ft. lbs. (37–54 Nm) on the ride control shock absorber or to 44–58 ft. lbs. (60–80 Nm) on base vehicles.**

9. If equipped with Automatic Ride Control, perform the following:
   a. Align the flats on mounting bracket with flats on the shock stud, and install mounting bracket.
   b. Install nut onto stud. Tabs on mounting bracket must be aligned in a fore and aft direction before tightening of nut.
   c. Using water pump pliers, grasp the mounting bracket firmly (if so equipped) and tighten the bracket retaining nut to 27–35 ft. lbs. (37–47 Nm).
   d. Grasp the actuator by the retaining tabs, install onto mounting bracket by pushing down on the retainer tabs.
   e. Connect the actuator wiring connector, and harness mating connector. Slide the connector onto the rail and push into secured position.

➡**The actuator assembly may be difficult to install if the plastic becomes eccentric to actuator driving shaft. If this happens; loosen the two mounting screws, allowing the actuator to float with respect to the locator and install onto the shock. Tighten the two screws, if so equipped.**

10. Install luggage compartment, and lower vehicle.

Upper Control Arms

REMOVAL & INSTALLATION

1983–88 Vehicles

▶ **See Figure 56 and 57**

➡**If one arm requires replacement, replace the other one also.**

1. Raise and safely support the vehicle at the rear crossmember.

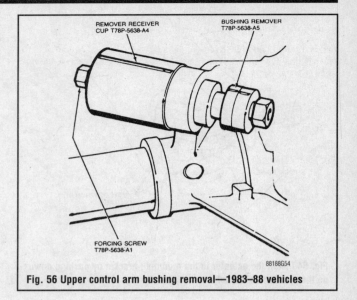

Fig. 56 Upper control arm bushing removal—1983–88 vehicles

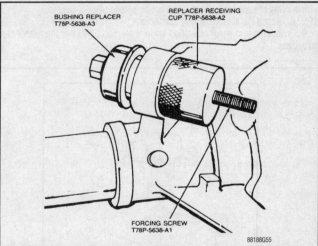

Fig. 57 Install the bushing assembly into the bushing ear of the rear axle

2. Remove and discard the upper control arm-to-axle pivot bolts and nut.
3. Remove and discard the upper control arm-to-frame pivot bolt and nut. Remove the upper control arm from the vehicle.
4. If the upper control arm bushing is to be replaced, use Bushing Remover and Installer Set T78P-5638-A place the upper control arm axle bushing remover tool in position, then remove the bushing assembly.
5. Use the installer tool, shown in the accompanying figure to install the bushing assembly into the bushing ear of the rear axle.

To install:

6. Place the upper control arm into the bracket of the body side rail. Insert a new control arm-to-frame pivot bolt and nut with the nut facing outboard. Do not tighten the nut yet.
7. Raise the suspension until the upper control arm-to-axle pivot hole is in position with the hole in the axle bushing. Install a new pivot bolt and nut with the nut facing inboard, but do not tighten yet.
8. Raise the suspension to curb height. Tighten the front upper control arm bolt to 70–100 ft. lbs. (95–135 Nm) and the rear bolt to 80–105 ft. lbs. (108–142 Nm).

1989–97 Vehicles

1. Raise and safely the support the vehicle with jackstands.
2. Remove rear wheel and tire assembly.

3. Using a wire, or other suitable means, support the knuckle and hub assembly so that it can not swing outward.

➡**It is of great importance to mark the position of the inner pivot bolt washer, relative to the frame mount, to ensure proper camber alignment upon reinstallation.**

4. Remove the inner and outer pivot bolts and nuts from the upper control arm.
5. Remove the upper control arm from vehicle.

To install:

➡**Inspect all fasteners for damage, pitting, corrosion, stretching, etc. Replace fasteners as necessary.**

6. Install the upper control arm into its position.
7. Install the inner pivot bolt and nut loosely.
8. Install the outer pivot bolt and tighten to 110–148 ft. lbs. (149–201 Nm). Remove the wire or other means of support used to hold knuckle and hub assembly.
9. Align the inner pivot bolt washer with the mark made prior to removal. Tighten nut to 81–98 ft. lbs. for vehicles through 1993. For 1994–97 vehicles, tighten the nut to 50–68 ft. lbs. (68–92 Nm).
10. Install the tire and wheel assembly.
11. Carefully lower the vehicle and have the alignment checked at a reputable repair shop.

Lower Control Arms

REMOVAL & INSTALLATION

1983–88 Vehicles

➡**If one arm requires replacement, replace the other one also. If the vehicle is equipped with a rear stabilizer bar, remove the bar.**

1. Raise the vehicle and safely support the body at the rear crossmember.
2. Lower the vehicle until the rear shocks are fully extended.

➡**The axle must be supported by a transmission jack or jackstands.**

3. Place a transmission jack under the lower control arm-to-axle pivot bolt. Remove and discard the bolt and nut. Lower the transmission slowly until the coil spring can be removed.
4. Remove and discard the lower control arm-to-frame pivot bolt and nut, then remove the lower control arm.

To install:

5. Position the lower control arm into the front arm bracket. Insert a new arm-to-frame pivot bolt and nut with the nut facing outwards. Do not tighten at this time.
6. Install the coil spring. Holding the spring into position, use the transmission jack under the rear of the lower control arm. Raise the jack until the arm is in position. Insert a new, arm-to-axle pivot bolt and nut with the nut facing outward. Do not tighten at this time.
7. Lower the transmission jack. Raise the axle with a suitable jack to curb height. Tighten the lower arm front bolt to 80–105 ft. lbs. (108–142 Nm) and the rear pivot bolt to 70–100 ft. lbs. (95–135 Nm).
8. If equipped, install the rear stabilizer bar.
9. Remove the crossmember supports, then carefully lower the vehicle.

1989–97 Vehicles

▶ **See Figure 58**

1. Raise and safely support vehicle on jackstands.
2. Remove the rear coil spring as outlined previously in this section.
3. Remove the inner control arm pivot bolts and nuts and remove arm assembly.
4. Remove the toe compensating link from control arm.

To install:

5. Inspect all fasteners for pitting, corrosion, stretching, thread conditioning, etc. Reuse fasteners only if in good condition.

➡**If the plastic cap on the large nut, used on the inner front part of control arm, is damaged, loose or missing, replace the nut.**

6. Install the toe compensating link on control arm.
7. Place lower control arm on subframe, install bolts and nuts loosely.
8. Tighten the toe compensating link nut to 110–148 ft. lbs. (149–201 Nm).
9. Install the coil spring and attach outer lower control arm as previously described.
10. Carefully lower the vehicle, then have the alignment checked.

Stabilizer Bar

REMOVAL & INSTALLATION

1983–88 Vehicles

▶ **See Figure 59**

1. Raise and support the rear end on jackstands.
2. Remove and discard the four bolts and stamped nuts attaching the stabilizer bar to the brackets in the lower control arms.
3. Remove the stabilizer bar from the vehicle.

To install:

4. Install four new stamped nuts on the stabilizer bar over each attaching hole.
5. Align the four holes in the stabilizer bar with the holes in the brackets in the lower control arms.
6. Install four new bolts. Tighten bolts to 33–51 ft. lbs. (45–71 Nm).
7. Visually inspect the installation to be sure there is adequate clearance between the stabilizer bar and the lower control arm.

➡**Make sure the stabilizer bar is not installed upside down. A color code is provided on the bar (passenger side only) as an aid for proper position.**

8. Carefully lower the vehicle.

1989–97 Vehicles

1. Raise and safely support vehicle on jackstands.
2. Remove both rear wheel and tire assemblies.
3. Remove both stabilizer bar link and bushing upper retaining bolts and nuts.
4. Remove both stabilizer bar bracket-to-frame bolts.
5. Remove the rear muffler hanger retaining nuts.
6. Remove the stabilizer bar from vehicle. Remove the bushings/insulator if necessary.

To install:

7. If removed, install the stabilizer bar bushings/insulator.
8. Place the stabilizer bar into position on vehicle.
9. Install the stabilizer bar bracket bolts loosely.
10. Install the rear muffler hanger retaining nuts.
11. Position the bar ends onto the bar links and install the link retaining bolts and nuts.
12. Tighten the link retaining nuts to 35–47 ft. lbs. (46.7–63.3 Nm).
13. Tighten the stabilizer bar mounting bracket bolts to 25–34 ft. lbs. (34–46 Nm).
14. Install the wheel and tire assemblies.
15. Lower the vehicle.

Rear Wheel Bearings and Hub

REMOVAL & INSTALLATION

▶ **See Figures 60 thru 71**

❋❋ WARNING

Do NOT begin this procedure unless a new hub retainer nut is available. Once removed, this part cannot be reused during assembly. Its torque holding and/or retention capability is greatly diminished during removal.

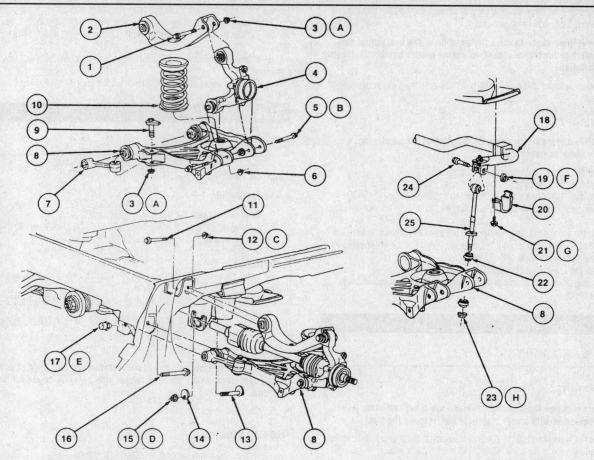

Item	Part Number	Description
1	N805618-S1050C	Bolt
2	5500	Upper Rear Suspension Arm and Bushing (2 Req'd Each Side)
3	N805479-S1050C	Nut
4	5A968	Rear Wheel Knuckle
5	N806365-S1050	Bolt (2 Req'd)
6	N806364-S1050	Nut (2 Req'd)
7	5A972	Rear Suspension Compensator Link
8	5A648	Lower Rear Suspension Arm and Bushing
9	N806066-S160	Bolt (1 Req'd Each Side)
10	5560	Rear Spring
11	N805678-S160	Bolt (2 Req'd)
12	N807144-S7	Nut (2 Req'd)
13	5K751	Rear Suspension Arm Adjusting Cam Kit (2 Req'd)

(Continued)

Item	Part Number	Description
14	5K751	Cam Assy (2 Req'd) (Part of 5K751)
15	N806082-S160	Nut (2 Req'd)
16	N805467-S160	Bolt (2 Req'd)
17	N805646-S161	Nut (2 Req'd)
18	5A772	Rear Stabilizer Bar
19	N805676-S150	Nut (2 Req'd)
20	5486	Stabilizer Bar Bracket
21	N805462-S160	Bolt (1 Req'd Each Side)
22	5493	Lower Suspension Arm Stabilizer Bar Insulator (2 Req'd)
23	N806001-S160	Nut (2 Req'd)
24	N805739-S150	Bolt (2 Req'd)
25	5C486	Link Assy
A	—	Tighten to 149-201 N·m (110-148 Lb-Ft)
B	—	Tighten to 113-153 N·m (83-113 Lb-Ft)

Item	Part Number	Description
C	—	Tighten to 68-92 N·m (50-68 Lb-Ft)
D	—	Tighten to 192-259 N·m (141-191 Lb-Ft)
E	—	Tighten to 225-275 N·m (166-202 Lb-Ft)

(Continued)

Item	Part Number	Description
F	—	Tighten to 46.7-63.3 N·m (35-47 Lb-Ft)
G	—	Tighten to 34-46 N·m (25-34 Lb-Ft)
H	—	Tighten to 10.2-13.8 N·m (8-10 Lb-Ft)

Fig. 58 Lower control arm (suspension arm) mounting—1995 vehicle shown

88188G56

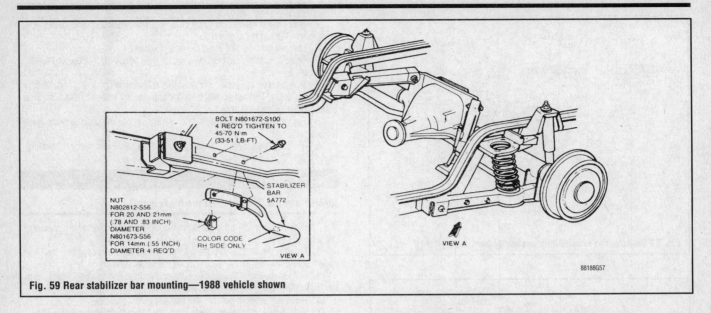

Fig. 59 Rear stabilizer bar mounting—1988 vehicle shown

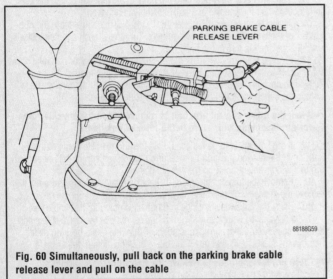

Fig. 60 Simultaneously, pull back on the parking brake cable release lever and pull on the cable

5. Remove parking brake cable from brake caliper (disc brakes only).

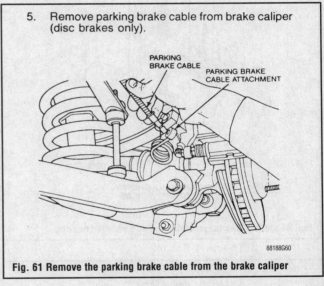

Fig. 61 Remove the parking brake cable from the brake caliper

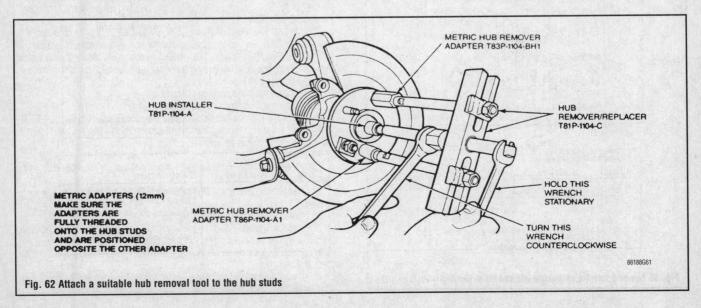

Fig. 62 Attach a suitable hub removal tool to the hub studs

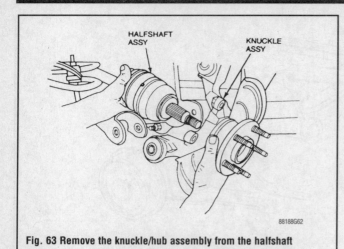

Fig. 63 Remove the knuckle/hub assembly from the halfshaft

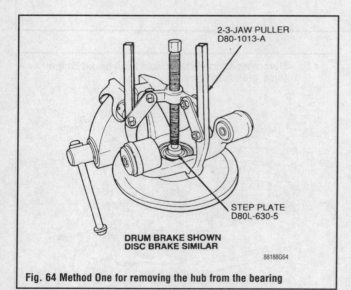

Fig. 64 Method One for removing the hub from the bearing

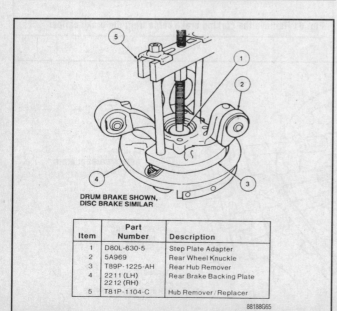

Item	Part Number	Description
1	D80L-630-5	Step Plate Adapter
2	5A969	Rear Wheel Knuckle
3	T89P-1225-AH	Rear Hub Remover
4	2211 (LH) 2212 (RH)	Rear Brake Backing Plate
5	T81P-1104-C	Hub Remover/Replacer

Fig. 65 Method Two for removing the hub from the bearing

1. Remove the wheel cover/hub cover from the wheel and tire assembly, then loosen the lug nuts.

2. Remove and discard the hub nut and washer.

3. Raise and safely support the vehicle, then remove the wheel and tire assembly.

4. Pull back on the parking brake cable release lever and, at the same time, pull on the cable. This action will relax the cable so it can be removed from the brake caliper or backing plate.

5. For vehicles equipped with disc brakes, remove the parking brake from the caliper.

6. For vehicles with disc brakes, remove the caliper and support from the brake junction bracket with a piece of wire.

❊❊ WARNING

Do NOT stretch, kink or twist the brake hose!

7. Remove the push-on nuts, then remove the brake rotor or drum assembly, as applicable.

8. For vehicles with disc brakes, remove the three bolts retaining the splash shield to the knuckle, then remove the splash shield.

9. For vehicles with drum brakes, disconnect the parking brake cable and disconnect the brake lines from the wheel cylinder.

10. Remove the upper control arm nut and bolt.

11. Wire the upper control arm to the body to prevent damage to the CV-joint boots when the knuckle and hub assembly is removed.

12. Attach Hub Remover/Replacer T81P-1104-C or equivalent to the hub studs, as shown in the accompanying figure. Turn the wrench counterclockwise until the halfshaft is free in the hub.

13. Using a paint marker, mark the position of the control arm in relation to the knuckle with the bushings in relaxed position. Failure to mark the position will cause bushing wind-up upon assembly and incorrect ride height. These conditions can cause misalignment and premature tire wear.

➡**When the upper control arm bolt is removed from the knuckle, the lower arm bushings will return to the relaxed position.**

14. If the knuckle is to be replaced, note the approximate angle of the knuckle in the relaxed position by measuring the distance from the upper bushing to any convenient point on the vehicle body.

15. Remove the lower control arm-to-knuckle retaining bolts and nuts, then remove the knuckle and hub assembly from the halfshaft.

16. Place the rear wheel knuckle and hub assembly into a suitable vise.

17. For vehicles equipped with drum brakes, remove the brake shoes and linings, shoe hold-down spring, and adjuster from the brake backing plate. Remove the four screws that retain the brake backing plate to the knuckle.

➡**There are two methods to remove the hub from the bearing.**

18. Method One: Position a 2–3 Jaw Puller D80L-1013-A and Step Plate Adapter D80L-630-5 or equivalent on the knuckle and press out the hub from the knuckle assembly.

19. Method Two: Position Rear Hub Remover T89P-1225-AH between the knuckle and the brake backing plate. Assembly Hub Remover/Replacer T81P-1104-C and Step Plate Adapter D80L-630-5 or equivalent. While forcing the nut below the crossbar, hold the forcing screw and turn the forcing nut to remove the hub from the knuckle.

20. Remove the brake backing plate.

21. Remove the bearing retainer snapring.

22. Place the knuckle and bearing on a press bed using Hub Support T89P-1104-A and Front Hub Bearing Remover/Replacer T83P-1104-AH2 and press the wheel bearing out of the knuckle.

To install:

23. Place the knuckle on the press bed and position the wheel bearing in the bearing bore of the knuckle.

24. Use Bearing Replacer T86P-1104-A3 to press the bearing into the knuckle.

25. Install the bearing retainer snapring.

26. Position the brake backing plate on the knuckle. Install the four retaining bolts and tighten to 44–60 ft. lbs. (59.5–80.5 Nm).

27. Place the knuckle on the Hub Support T89P-1104-A and position on the press bed plate.

28. If equipped with drum brakes, install the brake shoes and linings, brake shoe hold-down springs and adjuster to the backing plate.

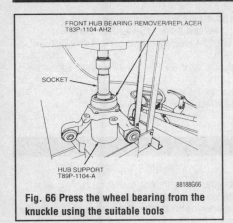

Fig. 66 Press the wheel bearing from the knuckle using the suitable tools

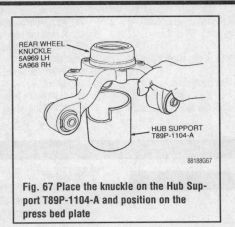

Fig. 67 Place the knuckle on the Hub Support T89P-1104-A and position on the press bed plate

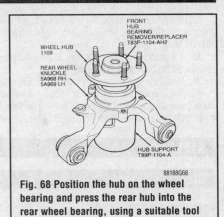

Fig. 68 Position the hub on the wheel bearing and press the rear hub into the rear wheel bearing, using a suitable tool

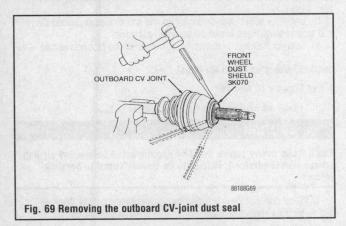

Fig. 69 Removing the outboard CV-joint dust seal

29. Position the hub on the wheel bearing and, using Front Hub Bearing Remover/Replacer T83P-1104-AH4, press the rear hub into the rear wheel bearing.

30. Prior to hub/bearing/knuckle installation replace the bearing dust seal on the outboard CV-joint with a new seal.

31. Install a new dust seal, making sure the seal flange faces outboard toward the bearing. Use Spindle/Axle Installer T83T-3132-A1 and Bearing Dust Seal Replacer T89P-1249-A or equivalent.

32. Place the knuckle and hub assembly on the halfshaft splines and install the lower control arm-to-knuckle bolts and nuts.

33. Position the knuckle so that the index marks on the bushing line up with the marks on the control arm. If a new knuckle is being installed, set the knuckle at the approximate angle noted during removal before tightening the bolts.

34. Push the knuckle and hub assembly firmly onto the halfshaft splines.

35. Install the upper control arm bolts and nut and tighten the nut to 118–148 ft. lbs. (160–200 Nm).

36. Install a new hub nut and washer assembly. Manually thread the nut onto the CV-joint shaft as far as possible.

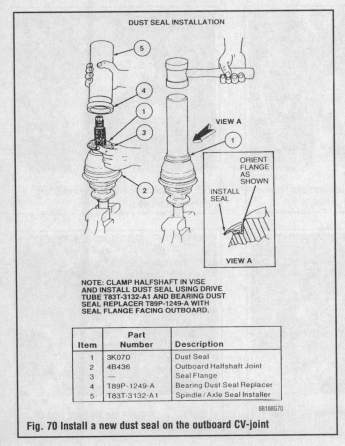

Item	Part Number	Description
1	3K070	Dust Seal
2	4B436	Outboard Halfshaft Joint
3	—	Seal Flange
4	T89P-1249-A	Bearing Dust Seal Replacer
5	T83T-3132-A1	Spindle / Axle Seal Installer

Fig. 70 Install a new dust seal on the outboard CV-joint

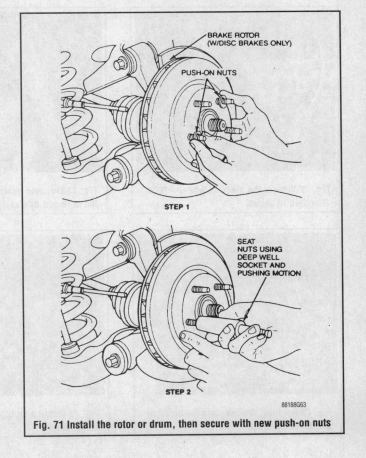

Fig. 71 Install the rotor or drum, then secure with new push-on nuts

37. If equipped, position the disc brake splash shield to the knuckle assembly and install the three retaining bolts. Tighten the bolts to 45–59 ft. lbs. (61–81 Nm).

38. If equipped with drum brakes, attach the brake tube to the wheel cylinder and install the parking brake cable.

39. Install the brake rotor or drum and secure with new push-on nuts.

40. If equipped with disc brakes, install the caliper over the rotor with the outer brake shoes against the rotor's braking surface. Install the caliper retaining bolts and tighten to 23–26 ft. lbs. (31–35 Nm).

41. Attach the parking brake cable to the brake caliper.

42. Adjust the parking brake as outlined in Section 9 of this manual.

43. For drum brakes, bleed the brake system, as outlined in Section 9 of this manual.

44. Install the wheel and tire assembly, then lower the vehicle and set the parking brake.

45. Tighten the hub retaining nut to 250 ft. lbs. (340 Nm).

46. Install the wheel cover/hub cover.

STEERING

Steering Wheel

REMOVAL & INSTALLATION

1983–93 Vehicles (Without Air Bags)

▶ **See Figures 72 thru 77**

1. Disconnect the negative battery cable.

2. Remove the horn pad and cover assembly by pulling it off or removing the attaching screws from the underside of the steering wheel spoke. Pull straight out on the hub cover. Disconnect the horn and speed control wires from the pad and cover assembly.

3. Remove and discard the steering wheel retaining nut from the end of the shaft.

4. Install Steering Wheel Remover T67L-3600-A or equivalent puller on the end of the shaft and remove the steering wheel.

☀ WARNING

The use of a knock-off type steering wheel puller or the use of a hammer on the steering shaft will damage the collapsible column.

To install:

5. Lubricate the upper surface of the steering shaft upper bushing with white grease. Transfer all serviceable parts to the new steering wheel.

6. Position the steering wheel on the shaft so that the alignment marks line up. Install a locknut and torque it to 23–33 ft. lbs. (31–45 Nm). Connect the horn wires.

7. Install the horn button or ring by turning it clockwise or connect the horn and speed control wires, install the horn pad and cover.

8. Connect the negative battery cable, then check for proper operation.

1994–97 Vehicles (With Air Bags)

▶ **See Figures 78 and 79**

1. Center the front wheels in the straight ahead position.

☀ CAUTION

The backup power supply must be disconnected before any air bag component is serviced. Failure to do so may result in personal injury

2. Disconnect the negative, then the positive battery cables. Wait one minute for the air bag diagnostic monitor to deplete its stored energy.

Fig. 72 View of the steering wheel—1990 Thunderbird shown

Fig. 73 On some vehicles, you can remove the horn pad by simply pulling it off

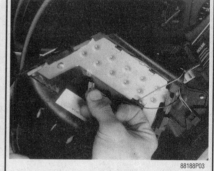
Fig. 74 Detach the electrical connectors from the horn pad

Fig. 75 Remove, then discard the steering wheel retaining nut

Fig. 76 Install a suitable steering wheel puller, then . . .

Fig. 77 . . . remove the steering wheel from the shaft

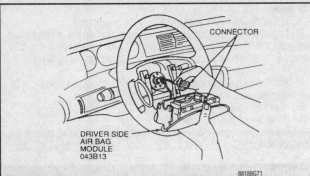

Fig. 78 Detach the air bag wiring, then remove the module from the steering wheel

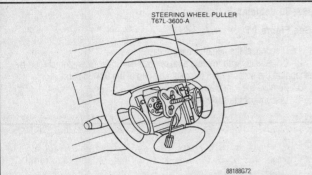

Fig. 79 Install a suitable steering wheel puller, then remove the wheel from the vehicle

3. Remove the two back cover side plugs, then remove the two air bag module retaining screws.

4. Disconnect the air bag wire harness from the driver's side air bag module, then remove the driver's side air bag module from the steering wheel.

5. Disconnect the speed control wiring harness from the steering wheel, if equipped.

6. Remove and discard the steering wheel retaining bolt.

7. Install Steering Wheel Puller T67L-3600-A and remove the steering wheel. Route the air bag sliding contact assembly wire harness through the steering wheel as the wheel is lifted off the steering gear input worm gear and rack.

To install:

8. Make sure the vehicle's front wheels are still in the straight ahead position.

☀☀ WARNING

Make sure the wiring does not get trapped between the steering wheel and air bag sliding contact, as damage to the sliding contact wiring may occur.

9. Route the air bag sliding contact wire harness through the steering wheel opening at the three o'clock position and position the steering wheel on the steering gear input worm gear and rack. The steering wheel and steering gear input worm gear and rack alignment marks should be aligned. Be sure the air bag sliding contact wire is not pinched.

10. Install a new steering wheel retaining bolt, then tighten to 23–33 ft. lbs. (31–48 Nm).

11. Attach the speed control wire harness to the steering wheel, then snap the connector assembly into the steering wheel clip.

12. Connect the air bag wire harness to the driver side air bag module, then position the module to the steering wheel. Tighten the air bag module retaining screws to 8–10 ft. lbs. (10–14 Nm).

13. Connect the positive, then the negative battery cables. Verify the air bag warning indicator.

Turn Signal Switch

REMOVAL & INSTALLATION

1983–88 Vehicles

1. Disconnect the negative battery cable.

2. For vehicles equipped with a tilt column, remove the upper extension shroud by unsnapping the shroud from the retaining clip at the 9 o'clock position.

3. Remove the two trim shroud halves by removing the attaching screws.

4. Remove the turn signal lever by pulling and twisting it straight out from the switch.

5. Peel back the foam sight shield from the turn signal switch.

6. Detach the two switch electrical connectors.

7. Remove the two self-tapping screws that attach the turn signal switch to the lock cylinder housing, then disengage the switch from the housing.

To install:

8. Align the turn signal switch mounting holes with the corresponding holes in the lock cylinder housing and install the two self-tapping screws until tight.

9. Stick the foam sight shield to the turn signal switch.

10. Install the turn signal lever into the switch manually by aligning the key to the lever with the keyway in the switch and pushing the lever toward the switch to full engagement.

11. Install the two switch electrical connectors to full engagement.

12. Install the steering column trim shroud(s).

13. Connect the negative battery cable, then test the switch.

Multi-Function Switch

REMOVAL & INSTALLATION

1989–93 Vehicles

1. Disconnect the negative ground cable.

2. Remove the lower left side finish panel retaining bolts.

3. Carefully pull the finish panel to disengage the retaining clips.

4. Remove the left side reinforcement panel retaining bolts and remove the panel.

5. Remove the steering column lower shroud retaining screws, then remove the lower shroud.

6. Remove the steering column retaining nuts.

7. Remove the steering column upper shroud.

8. Detach the multi-function switch electrical connector.

9. Remove the multi-function switch retaining bolts, then remove the switch.

To install:

10. Position the switch and install the retaining bolts.

11. Attach the electrical wiring connector to the switch.

12. Install the steering column upper shroud.

13. Position the steering column and install the retaining nuts.

14. Position the lower shroud and install the retaining screws.

15. Install the side reinforcement panel and secure with the retaining bolts.

16. Position the side finish panel and install the bolts.

17. Connect the negative battery cable, then check switch operation.

1994–97 Vehicles

▶ See Figure 80

1. Disconnect the negative battery cable.

2. Tilt the steering column to its lowest position, then remove the tilt steering column lock lever.

3. Remove the ignition switch lock cylinder, as outlined in this section.

4. Unfasten the shroud screws, then remove the upper and lower steering column shrouds.

5. Remove the two self-tapping screws retaining the multi-function switch to the steering column tube flange. Disengage the switch from the steering column tube flange.

6. Detach the two switch electrical connectors.

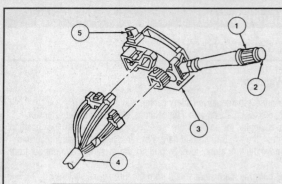

Item	Part Number	Description
1	—	Windshield Wiper Control Switch (Part of 13K359)
2	—	Windshield Washer Switch (Part of 13K359)
3	13K359	Multi-Function Switch
4	—	Part of 14401
5	—	Hazard Flasher Switch (Part of 13K359)

88188G75

Fig. 80 Multi-function switch and related components—1994–97 vehicles

To install:

7. Install the two electrical connectors to full engagement.

8. Align the multi-function switch mounting holes with the corresponding holes in the steering column tube flange. Install the two self-tapping screws, making sure to start the screws in the previously tapped holes. Tighten the screws to 18–26 inch lbs. (2–3 Nm).

9. Install the upper and lower steering column shrouds, then secure with the retaining screws.

10. Install the ignition switch lock cylinder.

11. Install the tilt steering lock lever.

12. Connect the negative battery cable, then check the steering column for proper operation.

Ignition Switch

REMOVAL & INSTALLATION

1983–88 Vehicles

▶ **See Figure 81**

1. Disconnect the negative battery cable.

2. On vehicles with tilt columns, remove the upper extension shroud by unsnapping the shroud from the retaining clip at the 9 o'clock position.

3. Remove the trim shroud halves.

4. Disconnect the switch wiring.

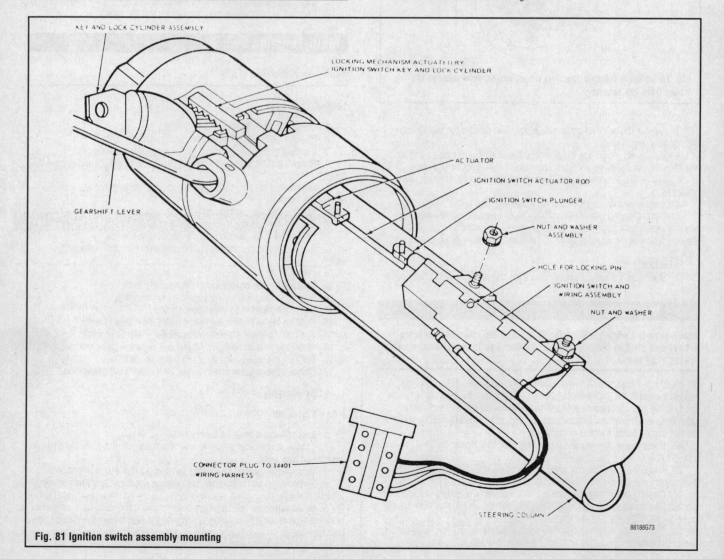

Fig. 81 Ignition switch assembly mounting

88188G73

5. On 1983–85 vehicles, drill out the break-off head bolts attaching the switch to the lock cylinder with a ⅛ in. (3mm) drill bit. Remove the remainder of the bolts with a screw extractor.

6. On 1986–88 vehicles, remove the bolts securing the switch to the lock cylinder housing.

7. Disengage the switch from the actuator pin.

To install:

8. Slide the switch carrier to the ON RUN position. New replacement switches will be in this position.

9. Turn the key to the ON RUN position.

10. Position the switch on the actuator pin. It may be necessary to move the switch slightly back and forth to align the switch mounting holes with the column lock housing threaded holes.

11. On 1983–85 cars, install new break-off bolts and hand tighten them.

12. On 1986–88 cars, install the bolts and tighten them to 50–60 inch lbs. (5.6–6.9 Nm).

13. Push the switch towards the steering wheel, parallel with the column, to remove any slack between the bolts and the switch slots.

14. While holding the switch in this position, tighten the bolts until the heads break off.

15. Remove the drill bit or packaging pin.

16. Connect the switch electrical wiring.

17. The remainder of installation is the reverse of the removal procedure.

1989–93 Vehicles

▶ **See Figure 82**

1. Disconnect the negative battery cable.

2. Remove the three steering column shroud screws and remove the lower shroud.

3. Remove the four nuts holding the steering column assembly to the column mounting bracket, and lower the column enough to reach the ignition switch retaining screws.

4. Remove the upper shroud.

5. Detach ignition switch electrical connector.

6. Rotate the ignition key lock cylinder to the run position.

7. Remove the two attaching screws retaining the switch-to-lock cylinder housing.

8. Disengage and remove ignition switch from the actuator pin.

To install:

9. Ensure the actuator pin slot in ignition switch is in the RUN position (a new switch assembly comes preset in the RUN position).

10. Check the ignition key lock cylinder to ensure that it is set approximately in the RUN position to properly locate lock actuator pin. The RUN position can be located by rotating the key lock cylinder approximately 90° from lock position.

11. Install the ignition switch onto actuator pin.

12. Install attaching screws and tighten to 50–70 inch lbs. (5.6–7.9 Nm).

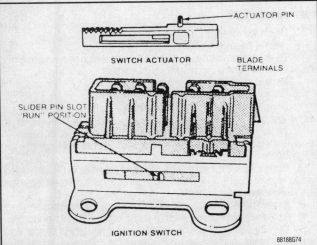

Fig. 82 If reinstalling an ignition switch, make sure it is set in the RUN position

➡ **It may be necessary to move the switch back and forth slightly in order to line up the mounting holes for the attaching screws.**

13. Attach electrical connector to the ignition switch.

14. Connect the negative battery cable.

15. Check ignition switch for proper operation, including the START and ACC positions.

16. Position the upper shroud onto the steering column.

17. Install the four nuts holding the steering column to the column mounting bracket.

➡ **Check the mounting bracket studs for retaining clips. Remove and discard them if present.**

18. Position the lower shroud to the column and upper shroud. Install the three attaching screws.

1994–97 Vehicles

1. Disconnect the negative battery cable. Remove the upper steering column shroud by removing the self-tapping screws.

2. Unfasten the four bolts retaining the lower steering column shroud, then remove the shroud.

3. Remove the lock screw, then detach the ignition switch electrical connector.

4. Rotate the ignition switch lock cylinder to the RUN position.

5. Remove the two screws retaining the ignition switch, then disengage the ignition switch from the actuator.

To install:

➡ **A new replacement switch will be set in the RUN position as received.**

6. Adjust the ignition switch by sliding the carrier to the ignition switch run position.

7. Check to make sure the ignition switch lock cylinder is in the RUN position. The RUN position is achieved by rotating the ignition switch lock approximately 90° from the LOCK position.

8. Install the ignition switch assembly into the column actuator hole. It may be necessary to move the ignition switch slightly back and forth to align the ignition switch mounting holes wit the lock cylinder housing threaded holes.

9. Install the retaining screws and tighten to 53–71 inch lbs. (6–8 Nm).

10. Attach the electrical connector to the ignition switch. Tighten the lock screw to 7–11.5 inch lbs. (0.8–1.3 Nm).

11. Connect the negative battery cable. Check the ignition switch for proper function, including the START and ACC positions. Also, make sure the column is in the LOCK position.

12. Install the upper and lower steering column steering shrouds.

Ignition Lock Cylinder

REMOVAL & INSTALLATION

Functioning Lock Cylinder

➡ **The following procedures apply to vehicles that have functional ignition switch lock cylinders. Lock cylinder keys are available for these vehicles, or the lock cylinder key numbers are known and the proper key can be made.**

1983–93 VEHICLES

▶ **See Figures 83 and 84**

1. Disconnect the negative battery cable.

2. On tilt columns, remove the upper extension shroud by unsnapping the shroud from the retaining clip at the 9 o'clock position.

3. Remove the trim shroud halves.

4. Unplug the wire connector at the key warning switch.

5. Place the shift lever in PARK and turn the key to RUN.

6. Place a ⅛ in. (3mm) wire pin in the hole in the casting surrounding the lock cylinder and depress the retaining pin while pulling out on the cylinder.

To install:

7. When installing the cylinder, turn the lock cylinder to the RUN position and depress the retaining pin, then insert the lock cylinder into its housing in

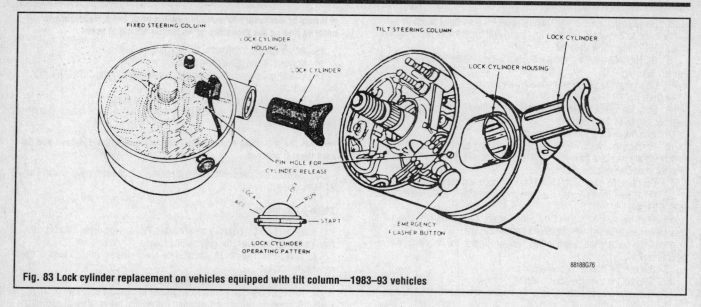

Fig. 83 Lock cylinder replacement on vehicles equipped with tilt column—1983–93 vehicles

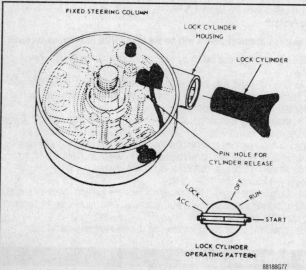

Fig. 84 Lock cylinder replacement on vehicles equipped with a fixed column—1983–93 vehicles

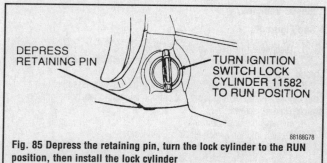

Fig. 85 Depress the retaining pin, turn the lock cylinder to the RUN position, then install the lock cylinder

the flange casting. Assure that the cylinder is fully seated and aligned in the interlocking washer before turning the key to the OFF position. This will allow the cylinder retaining pin to extend into the cylinder cast housing hole.

8. The remainder of installation is the reverse of the removal procedure.
9. Connect the negative battery cable and check for proper operation.

1994–97 VEHICLES

♦ See Figure 85

1. Disconnect the negative battery cable.
2. Turn the ignition switch lock cylinder to the **RUN** position.
3. Place a ⅛ in. (3.17mm) diameter wire pin or small drift punch in the hole in the upper steering column shroud under the ignition switch lock cylinder. Press the retaining pin while pulling out of the ignition switch lock cylinder to remove it from the steering column tube flange.

To install:

4. Install the ignition lock cylinder by turning it to the **RUN** position and pressing the retaining pin. Insert the ignition lock cylinder into the steering column tube flange. Make sure the lock cylinder is fully seated and aligned in the interlocking washer before turning the key to the **OFF** position. This will permit the cylinder retaining pin to extend into the steering column tube flange hole.

5. Rotate the ignition lock cylinder, using the ignition key, to ensure correct mechanical operation in all positions.
6. Connect the negative battery cable.

Non-Functioning Lock Cylinder

➡The following procedure applies to vehicles in which the ignition lock is inoperative and the lock cylinder cannot be rotated due to a lost or broken lock key, the key number is not known, or the lock cap is damaged and/or broken to the extent that the lock cylinder cannot be rotated.

1983–93 VEHICLES

1. Disconnect the battery ground.
2. Remove the steering wheel.
3. On tilt columns, remove the upper extension shroud by unsnapping the shroud from the retaining clip at the 9 o'clock position.
4. Remove the steering column trim shrouds.
5. Disconnect the wiring at the key warning switch.
6. Using a ⅛ in. (3mm) drill bit, mounted in a right angle drive drill adapter, drill out the retaining pin, going no deeper than ½ in. (13mm).
7. Tilt the column to the full down position. Place a chisel at the base of the ignition lock cylinder cap and using a hammer, break away the cap from the lock cylinder.
8. Using a ⅜ in. (9.5mm) drill bit, drill down the center of the ignition lock cylinder key slot about 1¾ in. (44mm), until the lock cylinder breaks loose from the steering column cover casting.
9. Remove the lock cylinder and the drill shavings from the housing.
10. Remove the upper bearing snapring washer and steering column lock gear.
11. Carefully inspect the steering column housing for signs of damage from the previous operation. If any damage is apparent, the components should be replaced.
12. Installation is the reverse of removal.

1994–97 VEHICLES

1. Disconnect the negative battery cable.

2. Remove the steering wheel, as outlined earlier in this section.

3. Using suitable locking pliers, twist the ignition switch cap or bezel until it separates from the lock cylinder.

4. Using a ⅜ in. drill bit, drill down the middle of the key slot approximately 1¾ in. (44mm) until the lock cylinder breaks loose from the breakaway base of the lock cylinder. Remove the lock cylinder and drill shavings from the steering column tube flange.

5. Remove the steering column upper bearing retainer, steering column lock housing and bearing, ignition switch lock cylinder and steering column lock gear. Thoroughly clean all drill shavings and other foreign materials from the casting.

6. Carefully inspect the steering column tube flange for damage. If there is damage, the steering column tube flange must be replaced.

To install:

7. If necessary, replace the steering column tube flange.

8. Install the steering column lock gear and ignition switch lock cylinder.

9. Install the trim and electrical parts.

10. Install a new ignition switch lock cylinder as outlined earlier in this section.

11. Install the steering wheel.

12. Connect the negative battery cable, then check the lock cylinder for proper operation.

Steering Linkage

REMOVAL & INSTALLATION

Tie Rod Ends

OUTER

1. Raise and safely support the front of the vehicle with jackstands.

2. Remove and discard the cotter pin and nut from the worn tie rod end.

3. Separate the tie rod end from the steering knuckle (spindle) using Tie Rod End Remover TOOL-3290-D or equivalent.

4. Holding the tie rod end with a wrench, loosen the tie rod end jam nut.

5. Note the depth to which the tie rod end was located by using the jam nut as a marker. Grip the tie rod end with a suitable pair of pliers, then remove the tie rod end.

To install:

6. Clean the tie rod end threads. Thread the tie rod ends to the same depth as the removed tie rod end.

7. Place the tie rod end into the steering knuckle (spindle). Make sure the wheels are in the straight ahead position.

8. Install a new nut on the tie rod end. Tighten the nut to 39 ft. lbs. (53 Nm), and continue tightening the nut to align the next castellation of the nut with the cotter pin hole in the stud. Install a new cotter pin.

9. Tighten the jam nut to 35–50 ft. lbs. (48–68 Nm).

10. Have the front end alignment checked at a reputable repair shop.

INNER

▶ **See Figures 86 and 87**

1. Disconnect the negative battery cable, and turn the ignition key to the **ON** position.

2. Raise and safely support the vehicle on jackstands.

3. Remove both wheels and tire assemblies.

4. Disconnect and remove the outer tie rod ends.

5. Remove the four clamps retaining the bellows (rubber boots) to the gear housing and the tie rods. Discard the clamps if damaged or corroded.

6. Remove the bellows along with the breather tube, using care not to damage the bellows.

7. Remove the coiled lock pins from inner tie rod ball joint, using a locknut pin removal tool D81P-3504-N or equivalent.

8. Turn the steering towards the right enough to expose a few rack teeth. Hold the rack with an adjustable wrench (on end teeth only), while loosening tie rod ball joints with a nut wrench T74P-3504-U or equivalent.

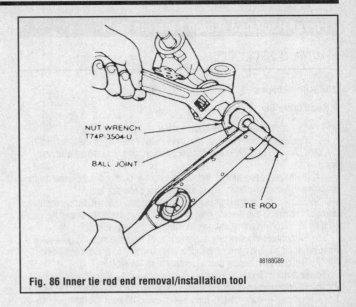

Fig. 86 Inner tie rod end removal/installation tool

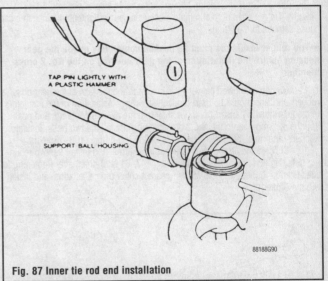

Fig. 87 Inner tie rod end installation

➡ **Some gear assemblies may contain one or two rack travel restrictors on each side of the rack. The restrictors are split nylon washers and, if required, can easily be removed from the rack following tie rod removal. Restrictors may be reused unless heavily worn.**

To install:

9. Turn the gear against or near left side stop and hold rack with an adjustable wrench nearest the rack end. Tighten each tie rod ball joint separately, using nut wrench T74P-3504-U or equivalent.

10. Thoroughly clean the rack and housing of any foreign material. Any abrasive material is extremely harmful to the high pressure oil seals in the rack.

➡ **Apply some gear grease to the groove on the tie rods where the bellows clamp to the rod. This allows for toe adjustments without damaging the bellows (rubber boots).**

11. Install the breather tube and the bellows into position on the housing and tie rods.

12. Install new clamps onto the bellows.

13. Install the jam nuts and place a small amount of grease on the threads of the tie rods.

14. Install the outer tie rod ends.

15. Install the wheels and tires assemblies.

16. Carefully lower the vehicle, connect the negative battery cable, and have the alignment checked at a reputable repair shop.

Power Rack And Pinion Steering Gear

REMOVAL & INSTALLATION

1983–88 Vehicles

▶ **See Figure 88**

1. Disconnect the negative battery cable.
2. Remove the one bolt retaining the flexible coupling to the input shaft.
3. Leave the ignition key in the **ON** position, and raise the vehicle on a hoist.
4. Remove the two tie rod end retaining cotter pins and nuts. Separate the studs from the spindle arms, using the ball joint separator tool.
5. Support the steering gear, and remove the two nuts, insulator, washers, and bolts retaining the steering gear to the No. 2 crossmember. Lower the gear slightly to permit access to the pressure and return line fittings.
6. Disconnect the pressure and return lines from the steering gear valve housing. Plug the lines and parts in the valve housing to prevent entry of dirt.
7. Remove the steering gear assembly from the vehicle.

To install:

8. Support and position the steering gear, so that the pressure and return line fittings can be connected to the valve housing. Tighten the fittings to 15–20 ft. lbs. (20–27 Nm). The design allows the hoses to swivel when tightened properly. Do not attempt to eliminate looseness by overtightening, since this can cause damage to the fittings.

➡ **The rubber insulators must be pushed completely inside the gear housing before the installation of the gear housing on the No. 2 crossmember.**

9. No gap is allowed between the insulator and the face of the gear boss. A rubber lubricant should be used to facilitate proper installation of the insulators in the gear housing. Insert the input shaft into the flexible coupling, and position the steering gear to the No. 2 crossmember. Install the two bolts, insulator washers, and nuts. Tighten the two nuts to 80–100 ft. lbs. (108–136 Nm).
10. Connect the tie rod ends to the spindle arms, and install the two retaining nuts. Tighten the nuts to 35–45 ft. lbs. (47–61 Nm), then, after tightening to specification, tighten the nuts to their nearest cotter pin castellation, and install two new cotter pins.

11. Lower the vehicle, and install the one bolt retaining the flexible coupling to the input shaft. Tighten the bolt to 18–23 ft. lbs. (24–31 Nm).
12. Turn the ignition key to the **OFF** position.
13. Connect the negative battery cable.
14. Remove the coil wire.
15. Fill the power steering pump reservoir.
16. Engage the starter, and cycle the steering wheel to distribute the fluid. Check the fluid level and add as required.
17. Install the coil wire, start the engine, and cycle the steering wheel. Check for fluid leaks.
18. If the tie rod ends were loosened, have the wheel alignment checked.

1989–97 Vehicles

▶ **See Figures 89 and 90**

1. Raise and safely support the vehicle with jackstands.
2. Remove both front wheel and tire assemblies.
3. Remove the cotter pins at the outer tie rod ends, then remove the castellated nuts from each end. Discard the cotter pins.
4. Separate the tie rod ends from the left and right side knuckle (spindle) using Tie Rod End Remover TOOL-3290-D or equivalent.
5. Place a suitable drain pan under the vehicle. Disconnect and plug the power steering return hose.
6. Disconnect the power steering pressure hose at the intermediate fitting and position out of the way.
7. Remove the steering shaft retaining bolt.
8. Remove the rack-to-subframe bolts and nuts. Access the nuts through the hole in the front crossmember.
9. Lower the power steering short rack as necessary, to remove the pressure line inlet tube. Remove and discard the plastic seal on the inlet tube.
10. Cut the tie strap securing the power steering pressure hose to each tube.
11. Remove the power steering short rack from the vehicle.

To install:

12. Install a new seal on the pressure line.
13. Install the steering gear insulator from the rear side of the steering gear housing, making sure they are fully seated. Use a suitable rubber lubricant to aid in installation.
14. Install and position the power steering short rack to the front crossmember.
15. Install the pressure line in the intermediate fitting.

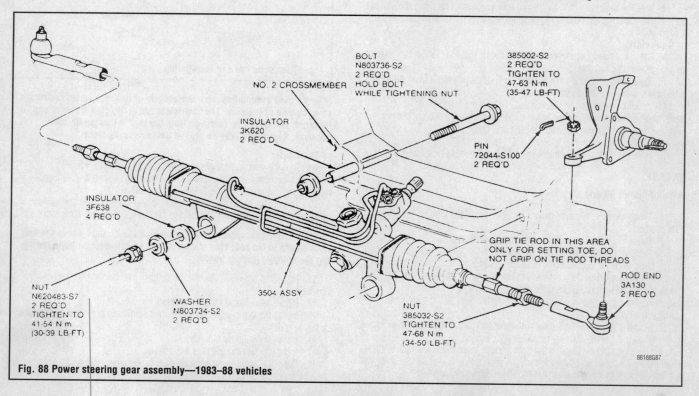

BOLT
N803736-S2
2 REQ'D
HOLD BOLT
WHILE TIGHTENING NUT

NO. 2 CROSSMEMBER

INSULATOR
3K620
2 REQ'D

INSULATOR
3F638
4 REQ'D

385002-S2
2 REQ'D
TIGHTEN TO
47-63 N·m
(35-47 LB-FT)

PIN
72044-S100
2 REQ'D

GRIP TIE ROD IN THIS AREA
ONLY FOR SETTING TOE, DO
NOT GRIP ON TIE ROD THREADS

ROD END
3A130
2 REQ'D

NUT
N620483-S7
2 REQ'D
TIGHTEN TO
41-54 N·m
(30-39 LB-FT)

WASHER
N803734-S2
2 REQ'D

3504 ASSY

NUT
385032-S2
TIGHTEN TO
47-68 N·m
(34-50 LB-FT)

88188G87

Fig. 88 Power steering gear assembly—1983–88 vehicles

16. Align the steering gear input shaft to allow the power steering short rack to completely seat on the front crossmember.

17. Install the steering gear input shaft retaining bolts and nuts. Tighten the bolts to 100–144 ft. lbs. (135–195 Nm).

18. Install the steering shaft flex coupling retaining bolt and tighten to 30–42 ft. lbs. (41–57 Nm).

19. Secure the power steering pressure hose to the power steering left turn pressure hose with a new tie strap.

20. Connect the power steering pressure hose.

21. Attach the power steering return hose, then tighten the clamp to 12–18 ft. lbs. (1.4–2.0 Nm).

22. Install the outer tie rod ends to the left and right knuckles and install castellated nuts at each ends. Tighten the nuts to 39 ft. lbs. (53 Nm). Continue to tighten the nuts until the castellations line up with the stud bores.

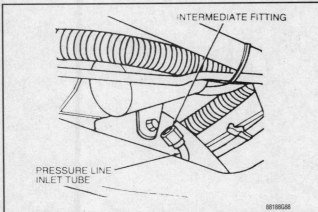

Fig. 89 Disconnect the power steering pressure hose at the intermediate fitting and position out of the way

23. Install new cotter pins through the stud bores at each tie rod end.

24. Install both wheel and tire assemblies. Tighten the lug nuts to 85–105 ft. lbs. (115–142 Nm).

25. Carefully lower the vehicle, then fill the power steering system with the correct amount and type of fluid.

26. Connect the negative battery cable, then have the alignment checked at a reputable repair shop.

Power Steering Pump

REMOVAL & INSTALLATION

Except 4.6L Engines

♦ See Figures 91, 92, 93, 94 and 95

➡On supercharged engines the intercooler/charge air cooler tubes must be removed to gain access to the power steering pump.

1. Disconnect the negative battery cable.

2. Drain as much fluid as possible from the pump reservoir by disconnecting the fluid return hose at the reservoir and draining the fluid into a suitable container.

3. Disconnect and cap the power steering pressure hose.

➡If vehicle is equipped with a serpentine belt, remove the belt at this time.

4. Remove the mounting bolts from the front of the pump. After removal, move the pump inward to loosen the belt tension and remove the belt from the pulley. Some 1989 and later models require the removal of the pulley from the pump. Remove the power steering pump from the vehicle.

To install:

5. Position the power steering pump on the mounting bracket and install the mounting bolts and nuts. Tighten the nuts to 30–45 ft. lbs. (40–62 Nm). If removed, install the pulley.

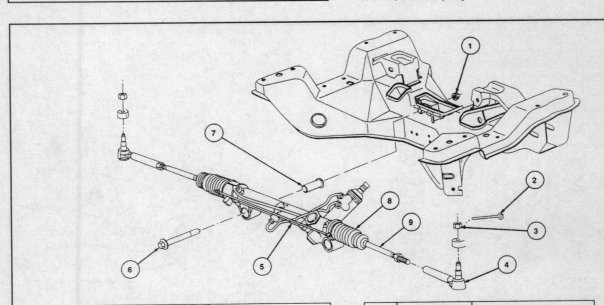

Item	Part Number	Description
1	N800237-S100	Nut (2 Req'd)
2	72044-S36	Pin
3	385002-S2	Nut (2 Req'd)
4	3A130	Tie Rod End
5	3L547	Power Steering Short Rack
6	N806254-S119	Bolt and Washer Assy (2 Req'd)

Item	Part Number	Description
7	3C716	Steering Gear Insulator (2 Req'd)
8	3332	Tie Rod Bellows (2 Req'd)
9	3280	Front Wheel Spindle Tie Rod (2 Req'd)

Fig. 90 Power steering gear assembly—1995 vehicle shown

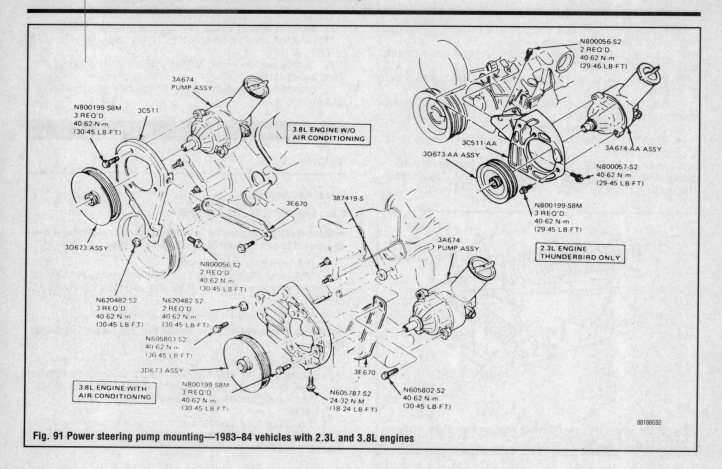

Fig. 91 Power steering pump mounting—1983–84 vehicles with 2.3L and 3.8L engines

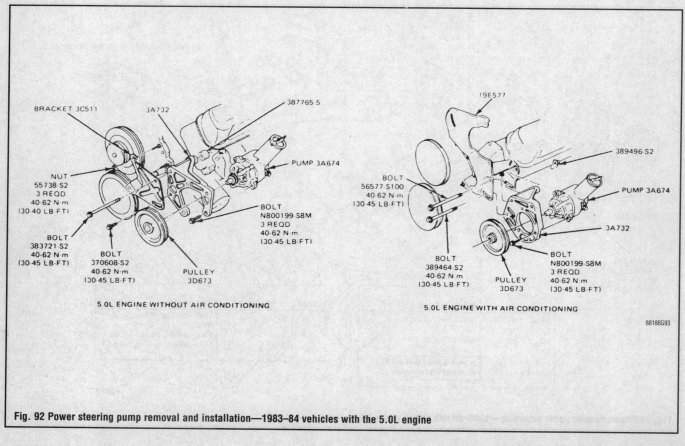

Fig. 92 Power steering pump removal and installation—1983–84 vehicles with the 5.0L engine

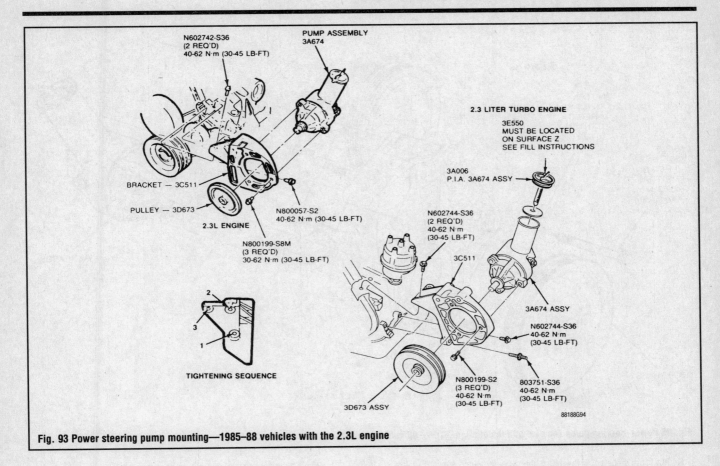

Fig. 93 Power steering pump mounting—1985–88 vehicles with the 2.3L engine

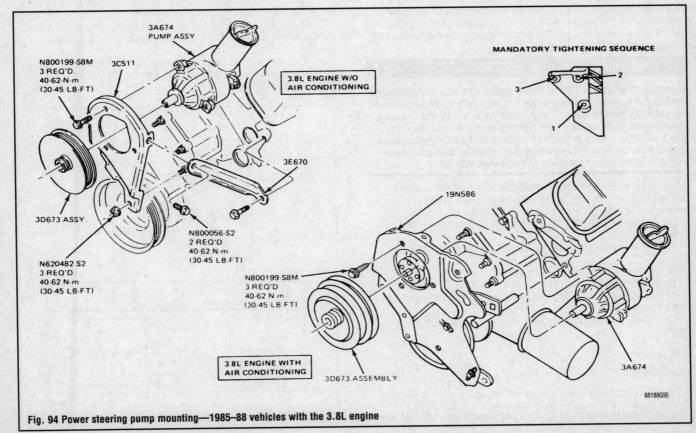

Fig. 94 Power steering pump mounting—1985–88 vehicles with the 3.8L engine

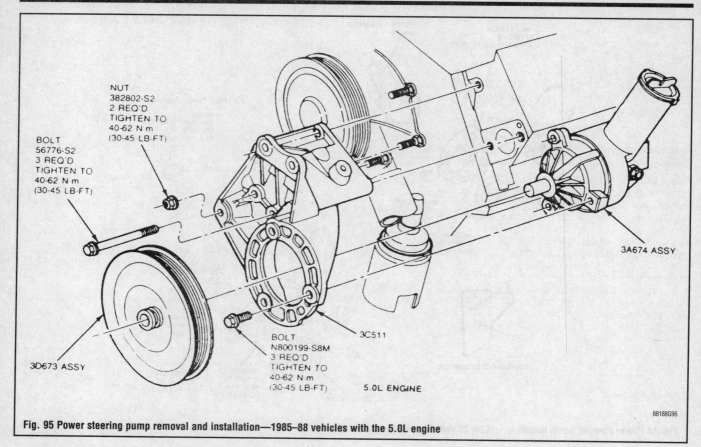

NUT
382802-S2
2 REQ'D
TIGHTEN TO
40-62 N·m
(30-45 LB·FT)

BOLT
56776-S2
3 REQ'D
TIGHTEN TO
40-62 N·m
(30-45 LB·FT)

BOLT
N800199-S8M
3 REQ'D
TIGHTEN TO
40-62 N·m
(30-45 LB·FT)

3D673 ASSY

3C511

3A674 ASSY

5.0L ENGINE

88188G96

Fig. 95 Power steering pump removal and installation—1985–88 vehicles with the 5.0L engine

6. Put the drive belt over the pulley and move the pump outward against the belt until the proper belt tension is obtained. Do not pry against the pump body. Measure the belt tension with a belt tension gauge for the proper adjustment. Only in cases where a belt tension gauge is not available should the belt deflection method be used.

✳✳ WARNING

Do not overtighten this fitting. Swivel and/or end play of the fitting is normal and does not indicate a loose fitting. Over-tightening the tube nut can collapse the tube nut wall, resulting in a leak and requiring replacement of the entire power steering pressure hose assembly. Use a tube nut wrench to tighten the tube nut. An open-end wrench may deform the tube nut hex which may result in improper torque and may make further servicing of the system difficult.

7. Uncap and install the power steering pressure hose on the pump or reservoir fitting, as applicable. Using a tube nut wrench adapter on your torque wrench, NOT an open-end wrench, tighten to 20–25 ft. lbs. (27–34 Nm).

8. Connect the power steering return hose to the pump, then tighten the clamp.

9. Fill the power steering reservoir with the correct amount and type of fluid.

10. Install the serpentine belt, if so equipped.

11. Install the supercharger intercooler, if so equipped.

12. Use the start-up procedure after power steering fluid reservoir or steering rack overhaul.

13. Connect the negative battery cable, then start engine and check for leaks.

4.6L Engine

▶ See Figure 96

1. To remove power steering fluid from the reservoir, disconnect the power steering return hose at the cooler return tube connection and drain the fluid into a suitable container.

2. Remove the power steering pressure hose from the power steering pump outlet, then drain the fluid into a suitable container.

3. Disconnect the drive belt from the power steering pump pulley, remove the four retaining bolts, then remove the power steering pump and pulley assembly.

4. Place the pump and pulley in a suitable vise, then separate the pulley from the pump using Steering Pump Pulley Remover T69L-10300-B or equivalent on the pulley hub.

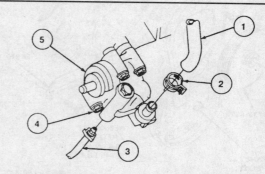

Item	Part Number	Description
1	3691	Power Steering Reservoir Pump Hose
2	3C750	Clamp
3	3A719	Power Steering Pressure Hose
4	N806176-S2	Bolt (4 Req'd)
5	3A674	Power Steering Pump

88188G97

Fig. 96 View of the power steering pump—4.6L engine

To install:

➡**Before installing the pump, remove the shipping tube nut from the housing, if equipped.**

5. Install the pulley to the power steering pump using Steering Pump Pulley Replacer T91P-3A733-A or equivalent.

6. Place the power steering pump on the mounting bosses of the engine block and install the bolts at the side of the pump. Tighten the bolts to 15–22 ft. lbs. (20–30 Nm).

7. Install the drive belt.

✴✴ WARNING

Do not overtighten this fitting. Swivel and/or end play of the fitting is normal and does not indicate a loose fitting. Over-tightening the tube nut can collapse the tube nut wall, resulting in a leak and requiring replacement of the entire power steering pressure hose assembly. Use a tube nut wrench to tighten the tube nut. An open-end wrench may deform the tube nut hex which may result in improper torque and may make further servicing of the system difficult.

8. Install the power steering pressure hose to the pump fitting. Tighten the nut with a tube wrench adapter on your torque wrench, NOT an open end wrench. Tighten the nut to 40–54 ft. lbs. (57–73 Nm).

9. Connect the power steering pump hose to the cooler return tube, and reposition the hose clamp to the pump inlet fitting.

BLEEDING

Fluid Level Top-Off Procedure

1. Check and fill the pump reservoir to the dipstick FULL COLD or remote reservoir center mark with the correct type of power steering fluid.

2. Disable the ignition by disconnecting the ignition coil wire.

3. Crank the engine for 30 seconds, check the fluid level, then add if necessary.

➡**Do NOT hold the steering wheel on the stops.**

4. Crank the engine for 30 seconds while cycling the steering wheel lock-to-lock.

5. Check the fluid level and add, if required.

Start-Up Procedure After Power Steering Pump or Gear Service

After engine start-up, follow these steps to eliminate excessive steering system noise due to air trapped in the system during service.

1. Disable the ignition by disconnecting the ignition coil wire.

2. Raise and safely support the front end of the vehicle.

3. Fill the power steering fluid reservoir with the correct type and amount of power steering fluid.

4. Crank the engine with the starter motor and add power steering fluid until the level remains constant.

➡**The front wheels MUST be off the ground during lock-to-lock rotation of the steering wheel.**

5. While cranking the engine, rotate the steering wheel from lock-to-lock.

6. Check the fluid level and add, if necessary.

7. Connect the ignition coil wire.

8. Start the engine and allow it to run for several minutes.

9. Rotate the steering wheel from lock-to-lock.

10. Turn the engine OFF, then check the fluid level and add, if necessary.

11. If air is still present, purge the system of air using the Air Purge With External Vacuum procedure.

12. Carefully lower the vehicle.

Air Purge With External Vacuum Source

▶ **See Figure 97**

Air trapped in the power steering system, which causes a whine or moaning noise, can be removed by using a power steering pump air evacuator assembly (devac tool). Use the Rotunda Vacuum Tester 021-98014 or equivalent.

1. Tightly insert the rubber stopper of the air evacuator assembly into the power steering pump reservoir.

2. Reattach the connection used to disable the ignition, then start the engine.

3. Apply 20–25 in. Hg (68–85 kPa) maximum vacuum for a minimum of three minutes at idle; maintain the vacuum with the vacuum source.

4. Release the vacuum, then remove the vacuum source.

5. Add fluid to the full warm or reservoir center mark.

6. Reinstall the vacuum source, then apply 20–25 in. Hg (68–85 kPa) vacuum.

➡**Do NOT hold the steering wheel on the stops.**

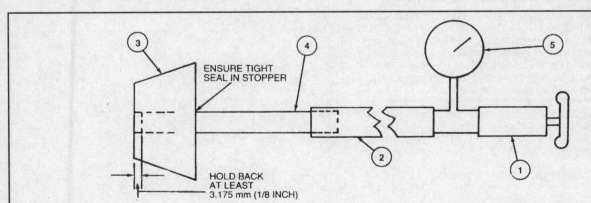

ENSURE TIGHT SEAL IN STOPPER

HOLD BACK AT LEAST 3.175 mm (1/8 INCH)

Item	Part Number	Description
1	021-00014	Rotunda Vacuum Source
2	—	Vacuum Hose
3	—	Rubber Stopper Cap No. 7 for CIII No. 11 for CII

Item	Part Number	Description
4	—	Tubing—Plexiglass, Steel or Copper (6.35-7.93 mm (1/4-5/16 inch))
5	—	Vacuum Gauge

88188G98

Fig. 97 Tightly insert the rubber stopper of the air evacuator assembly into the power steering pump reservoir

7. Cycle the steering wheel from lock-to-lock every 30 seconds for about 5 minutes.

8. Shut the engine off, release the vacuum, then remove the vacuum source.

9. Add fluid if necessary, install the dipstick or reservoir cap.

➡**Do NOT hold the steering wheel on the stops.**

10. Cycle the steering wheel from lock-to-lock every 30 seconds for about 5 minutes.

11. Check for oil leaks at all connections.

12. In severe cases, it may be necessary to repeat the air purge procedure.

BRAKE OPERATING SYSTEM 9-2
BRAKE LIGHT SWITCH 9-2
  REMOVAL & INSTALLATION 9-2
MASTER CYLINDER 9-2
  REMOVAL & INSTALLATION 9-2
POWER BRAKE BOOSTER 9-3
  REMOVAL & INSTALLATION 9-3
PROPORTIONING VALVE 9-4
BRAKE HOSES AND LINES 9-4
  REMOVAL & INSTALLATION 9-4
BLEEDING THE HYDRAULIC
  SYSTEM 9-5
  PROCEDURE 9-5
FRONT DISC BRAKES 9-6
BRAKE PADS 9-6
  REMOVAL & INSTALLATION 9-6
  INSPECTION 9-8
BRAKE CALIPER 9-8
  REMOVAL & INSTALLATION 9-8
  OVERHAUL 9-10
BRAKE DISC (ROTOR) 9-11
  REMOVAL & INSTALLATION 9-11
  INSPECTION 9-12
REAR DRUM BRAKES 9-12
BRAKE DRUM 9-12
  REMOVAL & INSTALLATION 9-12
  INSPECTION 9-13
  ADJUSTMENTS 9-13
BRAKE SHOES 9-14
  INSPECTION 9-14
  REMOVAL & INSTALLATION 9-14
WHEEL CYLINDERS 9-16
  REMOVAL & INSTALLATION 9-16
REAR DISC BRAKES 9-17
DISC BRAKE PADS 9-17
  REMOVAL & INSTALLATION 9-17
CALIPER 9-18
  REMOVAL & INSTALLATION 9-18
  CALIPER OVERHAUL 9-19
BRAKE DISC (ROTOR) 9-19
  REMOVAL & INSTALLATION 9-19
PARKING BRAKE 9-20
CABLES 9-20
  REMOVAL & INSTALLATION 9-20
  ADJUSTMENT 9-24
**TEVES MARK II 4-WHEEL
  ANTI-LOCK BRAKE
  SYSTEM (ABS) 9-25**
GENERAL INFORMATION 9-25
MASTER CYLINDER-BOOSTER
  UNIT/ACTUATION
  ASSEMBLY 9-25
  REMOVAL & INSTALLATION 9-25
HYDRAULIC ACCUMULATOR 9-26
  REMOVAL & INSTALLATION 9-26
HYDRAULIC PUMP MOTOR 9-26
  REMOVAL & INSTALLATION 9-26
RESERVOIR ASSEMBLY 9-27
  REMOVAL & INSTALLATION 9-27

ELECTRONIC CONTROLLER 9-28
  REMOVAL & INSTALLATION 9-28
PRESSURE SWITCH 9-28
  REMOVAL & INSTALLATION 9-28
WHEEL SPEED SENSORS 9-29
  REMOVAL & INSTALLATION 9-29
FRONT WHEEL SENSOR RING 9-30
  REMOVAL & INSTALLATION 9-30
REAR WHEEL SENSOR RING 9-31
  REMOVAL & INSTALLATION 9-31
BLEEDING THE ABS SYSTEM 9-31
  SYSTEM DISCHARGING
    (DEPRESSURIZING) 9-32
  FRONT BRAKE BLEEDING 9-32
  REAR BRAKE BLEEDING 9-32
  BLEEDING THE SYSTEM WITH A
    FULLY CHARGED
    ACCUMULATOR 9-32
  HYDRAULIC PUMP PRIMING 9-32
  CHECKING FLUID LEVEL AND
    REFILLING 9-32
**TEVES MARK-IV ANTI-LOCK BRAKE
  SYSTEM (ABS) 9-32**
GENERAL INFORMATION 9-32
HYDRAULIC CONTROL UNIT (HCU) 9-32
  REMOVAL & INSTALLATION 9-32
ANTI-LOCK BRAKE CONTROL
  MODULE 9-34
  REMOVAL & INSTALLATION 9-34
BRAKE PRESSURE CONTROL
  VALVE 9-34
  REMOVAL & INSTALLATION 9-34
WHEEL SPEED SENSOR 9-34
  REMOVAL & INSTALLATION 9-34
BLEEDING THE ABS SYSTEM 9-35
SPECIFICATIONS CHART
  BRAKES 9-36

9

BRAKES

BRAKE OPERATING SYSTEM 9-2
FRONT DISC BRAKES 9-6
REAR DRUM BRAKES 9-12
REAR DISC BRAKES 9-17
PARKING BRAKE 9-20
TEVES MARK II 4-WHEEL ANTI-LOCK
  BRAKE SYSTEM (ABS) 9-25
TEVES MARK-IV ANTI-LOCK BRAKE
  SYSTEM (ABS) 9-32

BRAKE OPERATING SYSTEM

Brake Light Switch

REMOVAL & INSTALLATION

▶ **See Figure 1**

1. Disconnect the negative battery cable.

➡ **The locking tab on the connector must be lifted before the connector can be removed.**

2. Raise the locking tab and unplug the wiring harness at the switch.
3. Remove the hairpin clip from the stud and slide the switch up and down. Remove the switch and washers from the pedal.

➡ **It is not necessary to remove the pushrod from the stud.**

To install:

4. Installation is the reverse of removal. Position the U-shaped side nearest the pedal and directly over/under the pin. Slide the switch up and down trapping the pushrod and bushing between the switch sideplates.
5. Connect the negative battery cable.

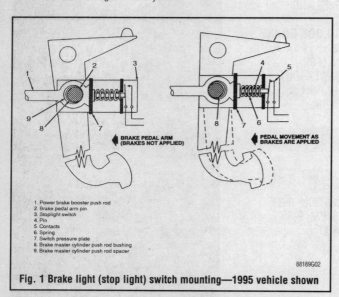

1. Power brake booster push rod
2. Brake pedal arm pin
3. Stoplight switch
4. Pin
5. Contacts
6. Spring
7. Switch pressure plate
8. Brake master cylinder push rod bushing
9. Brake master cylinder push rod spacer

88189G02

Fig. 1 Brake light (stop light) switch mounting—1995 vehicle shown

Master Cylinder

REMOVAL & INSTALLATION

Except Vehicles With ABS

▶ **See Figures 2, 3, 4 and 5**

1. Disconnect the negative battery cable.
2. Apply the brake pedal several times to exhaust all the vacuum in the system.
3. Detach and cap the brake lines from the master cylinder.
4. If equipped, detach the brake warning indicator connector.
5. Unfasten the two nuts and lockwashers that attach the master cylinder to the brake booster.
6. Remove the master cylinder from the booster by sliding it forward and upward from the vehicle.

To install:

7. Position the master cylinder assembly over the booster pushrod and onto the two studs on the booster assembly.
8. Install the retaining nuts, then tighten to 14–25 ft. lbs. (18–34 Nm).
9. Uncap and connect the brake lines to the master cylinder.

10. If equipped, connect the brake warning indicator.
11. Fill the master cylinder with Heavy Duty Brake Fluid C6AZ-19542-AA or equivalent DOT 3 brake fluid from a clean, sealed container. Bleed the entire brake system, as outlined in this section.
12. Connect the negative battery cable.
13. Operate the brake several times, then check for external hydraulic leaks.

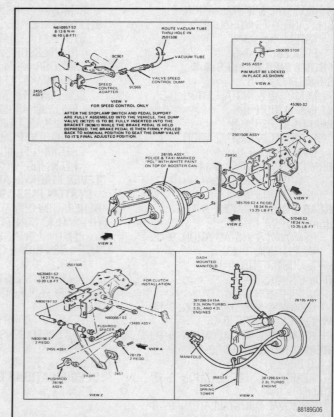

Fig. 2 Master cylinder mounting—1983 vehicle shown

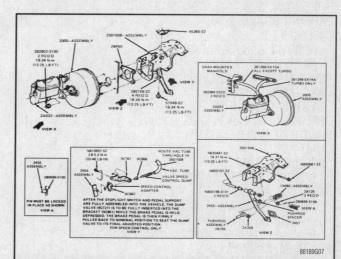

Fig. 3 Master cylinder removal and installation—1984–87 vehicle shown

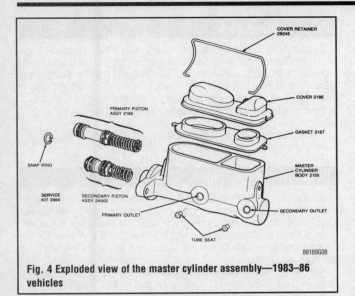

Fig. 4 Exploded view of the master cylinder assembly—1983–86 vehicles

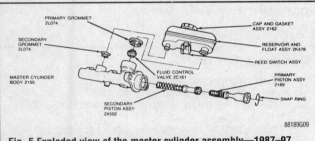

Fig. 5 Exploded view of the master cylinder assembly—1987–97 vehicles without ABS shown

Power Brake Booster

REMOVAL & INSTALLATION

Vacuum Booster

▶ See Figure 6

1. Disconnect the negative battery cable.
2. Detach the manifold vacuum hose from the booster check valve.
3. Disconnect and plug the brake tubes from the master cylinder.
4. Remove the master cylinder, as outlined in this section.
5. For 1993–97 vehicles, remove the windshield wiper motor.
6. Working inside the car below the instrument panel, remove the stoplight switch connector from the switch. Remove the hairpin retainer and outer nylon washer from the pedal pin. Slide the stop lamp switch off the brake pedal just far enough for the outer arm to clear the pin.
7. If equipped, remove the speed amplifier.
8. Remove the booster-to-dash panel attaching bolts/nuts. Slide the booster pushrod, bushing and the inner nylon washer off the brake pedal pin.
9. Inside the engine compartment, move the booster forward until the booster studs clear the dash panel. Rotate the front of the booster inward (toward the engine), then remove the booster by raising it up until it is clear.

To install:

10. Mount the booster and bracket assembly to the dash panel by sliding the valve operating rod in through the hole in the dash panel.
11. Install the booster-to-dash panel retaining nuts/bolts and tighten to 16–21 ft. lbs. (21–29 Nm).
12. Position the stoplight switch so it straddles the pushrod with the slot on the pedal pin and the switch outer frame holes just clearing the pin. Slide the stoplight switch onto the pin and pushrod. Slide the assembly toward the brake

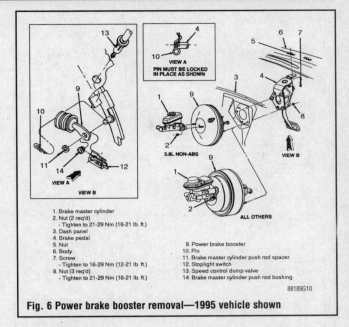

1. Brake master cylinder
2. Nut (2 req'd)
   - Tighten to 21-29 Nm (16-21 lb. ft.)
3. Dash panel
4. Brake pedal
5. Nut
6. Body
7. Screw
   - Tighten to 16-29 Nm (12-21 lb. ft.)
8. Nut (3 req'd)
   - Tighten to 21-29 Nm (16-21 lb. ft.)
9. Power brake booster
10. Pin
11. Brake master cylinder push rod spacer
12. Stoplight switch
13. Speed control dump valve
14. Brake master cylinder push rod bushing

Fig. 6 Power brake booster removal—1995 vehicle shown

pedal arm. Install the brake master cylinder pushrod spacer and the pushrod retainer. Lock the retainer securely. Attach the connector to the switch.

13. If equipped, install the speed control amplifier.
14. For 1993–97 vehicles, install the wiper motor.
15. Connect the manifold vacuum hose to the booster check valve.
16. Install the master cylinder, as outlined in this section. Tighten the retainers to 16–21 ft. lbs. (21–29 Nm).
17. Uncap and attach the brake line fittings into the ports. Tighten to 11–17 ft. lbs. (14–24 Nm).
18. Properly bleed the brake system.
19. Connect the negative battery cable.

Hydro-Boost Hydraulic Booster

▶ See Figure 7

A hydraulically powered brake booster is used on the Thunderbird Turbo Coupe models. The power steering pump provides the fluid pressure to operate both the brake booster and the power steering gear.

The hydro-boost assembly contains a valve which controls pump pressure while braking, a lever to control the position of the valve and a boost piston to provide the force to operate a conventional master cylinder attached to the front of the booster. The hydro-boost also has a reserve system, designed to store sufficient pressurized fluid to provide at least 2 brake applications in the event of insufficient fluid flow from the power steering pump. The brakes can also be applied unassisted if the reserve system is depleted.

Before removing the hydro-boost, discharge the accumulator by making several brake applications until a hard pedal is felt.

1. Disconnect the negative battery cable.
2. Working from inside the vehicle, below the instrument panel, disconnect the pushrod from the brake pedal. Disconnect the stoplight switch wires at the connector. Remove the hairpin retainer. Slide the stoplight switch off the brake pedal far enough for the switch outer hole to clear the pin. Remove the switch from the pin. Slide the pushrod, nylon washers and bushing off the brake pedal pin.
3. Open the hood and remove the nuts attaching the master cylinder to the hydro-boost. Remove the master cylinder. Secure it to one side without disturbing the hydraulic lines.
4. Disconnect the pressure, steering gear and return lines from the booster. Plug the lines to prevent the entry of dirt.
5. Remove the nuts attaching the hydro-boost. Remove the booster from the firewall, sliding the pushrod link out of the engine side of the firewall.

To install:

6. Install the hydro-boost on the firewall and install the attaching nuts.
7. Install the master cylinder on the booster.

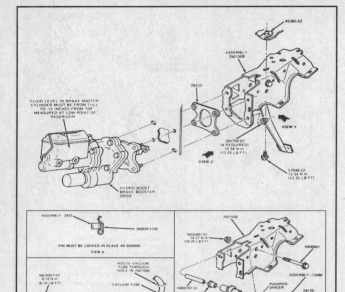

Fig. 7 View of the hydro-boost mounting and related components used on Thunderbird Turbo Coupes

8. Connect the pressure, steering gear and return lines to the booster.

9. Working below the instrument panel, install the nylon washer, booster pushrod and bushing on the brake pedal pin. Install the switch so that it straddles the pushrod with the switch slot on the pedal pin and the switch outer hole just clearing the pin. Slide the switch completely onto the pin and install the nylon washer. Attach these parts with the hairpin retainer. Connect the stoplight switch wires and install the wires in the retaining clip.

10. Connect the negative battery cable.

11. Remove the coil wire so that the engine will not start. Fill the power steering pump and engage the starter. Apply the brakes with a pumping action. Do not turn the steering wheel until air has been bled from the booster.

12. Check the fluid level and add as required. Start the engine and apply the brakes, checking for leaks. Cycle the steering wheel.

13. If a whine type noise is heard, suspect fluid aeration. Refer to the Power Steering bleeding procedure in Section 8.

Proportioning Valve

On vehicles equipped with front disc and rear drum brakes, a proportioning valve is an important part of the system. On cars through 1988, it is installed in the hydraulic line to the rear brakes. On 1989–97 cars, it is in the control valve assembly. Its function is to maintain the correct proportion between line pressures to the front and rear brakes. No attempt at adjustment of this valve should be made, as adjustment is preset and tampering will result in uneven braking action.

To assure correct installation when replacing the valve, the outlet to the rear brakes is stamped with the letter **R**.

Brake Hoses and Lines

Metal lines and rubber brake hoses should be checked frequently for leaks and external damage. Metal lines are particularly prone to crushing and kinking under the vehicle. Any such deformation can restrict the proper flow of fluid and therefore impair braking at the wheels. Rubber hoses should be checked for cracking or scraping; such damage can create a weak spot in the hose and it could fail under pressure.

Any time the lines are removed or disconnected, extreme cleanliness must be observed. Clean all joints and connections before disassembly (use a stiff bristle brush and clean brake fluid); be sure to plug the lines and ports as soon as they are opened. New lines and hoses should be flushed clean with brake fluid before installation to remove any contamination.

REMOVAL & INSTALLATION

◆ **See Figures 8, 9, 10 and 11**

1. Disconnect the negative battery cable.
2. Raise and safely support the vehicle on jackstands.
3. Remove any wheel and tire assemblies necessary for access to the particular line you are removing.
4. Thoroughly clean the surrounding area at the joints to be disconnected.
5. Place a suitable catch pan under the joint to be disconnected.
6. Using two wrenches (one to hold the joint and one to turn the fitting), disconnect the hose or line to be replaced.
7. Disconnect the other end of the line or hose, moving the drain pan if necessary. Always use a back-up wrench to avoid damaging the fitting.
8. Disconnect any retaining clips or brackets holding the line and remove the line from the vehicle.

➡ **If the brake system is to remain open for more time than it takes to swap lines, tape or plug each remaining clip and port to keep contaminants out and fluid in.**

To install:

9. Install the new line or hose, starting with the end farthest from the master cylinder. Connect the other end, then confirm that both fittings are correctly threaded and turn smoothly using finger pressure. Make sure the new line will not rub against any other part. Brake lines must be at least 1/2 in. (13mm) from the steering column and other moving parts. Any protective shielding or insulators must be reinstalled in the original location.

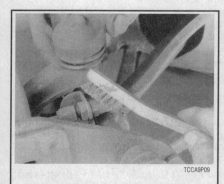

Fig. 8 Use a brush to clean the fittings of any debris

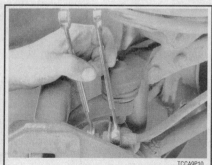

Fig. 9 Use two wrenches to loosen the fitting. If available, use flare nut type wrenches

Fig. 10 Any gaskets/crush washers should be replaced with new ones during installation

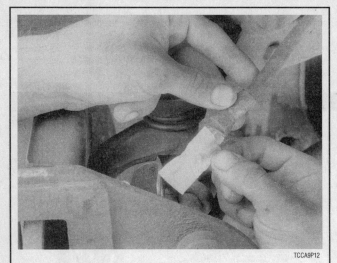

Fig. 11 Tape or plug the line to prevent contamination

Fig. 12 Submerge the free end of the brake tube in a container partly filled with clean brake fluid, then loosen the fitting about ¾ of a turn

❊❊ WARNING

Make sure the hose is NOT kinked or touching any part of the frame or suspension after installation. These conditions may cause the hose to fail prematurely.

10. Using two wrenches as before, tighten each fitting.
11. Install any retaining clips or brackets on the lines.
12. If removed, install the wheel and tire assemblies, then carefully lower the vehicle to the ground.
13. Refill the brake master cylinder reservoir with clean, fresh brake fluid, meeting DOT 3 specifications. Properly bleed the brake system.
14. Connect the negative battery cable.

Bleeding the Hydraulic System

➡**If equipped with ABS, see the appropriate section for ABS System Bleeding.**

When any part of the hydraulic system has been disconnected for service or replacement, air may enter the system causing a spongy pedal action. Bleed the hydraulic system, after it has been properly connected to ensure that all air has been expelled.

➡**Since the front and rear hydraulic systems are independent of each other, if it is known that only one system has air in it, only that system has to be bled.**

PROCEDURE

Manual Bleeding

♦ **See Figure 12**

1. Clean all dirt from the master cylinder filler cap.
2. If the master cylinder is known or suspected to have air in the bore, it must be bled BEFORE any of the wheel cylinders or calipers. To bleed the master cylinder, loosen the upper secondary left front outlet fitting approximately ¾ of a turn.
3. Have an assistant depress the brake pedal slowly through its full travel. Close the outlet fitting and let the pedal return slowly to the fully released position. Wait 5 seconds and then repeat the operation until all air bubbles disappear.
4. Loosen the upper primary right front outlet fitting about ¾ of a turn. Repeat Step 3 with the right front outlet fitting.
5. To continue to bleed the brake system, remove the rubber dust cap from the wheel cylinder bleeder fitting or caliper fitting at the right rear side of the vehicle. Check to make sure the wheel cylinder bleeder screw is positioned at the upper half of the front caliper. If not, the caliper is located on the wrong side.

Place a suitable box wrench on the bleeder fitting, then attach a rubber drain tube to the fitting. The end of the tube should fit snugly around the bleeder fitting.
6. Submerge the free end of the tube in a container partially filled with clean brake fluid, then loosen the fitting about ¾ of a turn.
7. Have an assistant push the brake pedal down slowly through its full travel. Close the bleeder fitting and allow the pedal to slowly return to its full release position. Wait 5 seconds, then repeat the procedure until no bubbles appear at the submerged end of the bleeder tube.
8. When the fluid is completely free of air bubbles, close the bleeder fitting, then remove the bleeder tube. Install the rubber dust cap on the bleeder fitting.
9. Repeat this procedure in the following sequence: left front, left rear and right front. Refill the master cylinder reservoir after each wheel cylinder or caliper has been bled, then install the master cylinder cover and gasket. When brake bleeding is completed, the fluid level should be filled to the maximum level indicated on the reservoir using clean brake fluid from a sealed container.
10. Always make sure the disc brake pistons are returned to their normal positions by depressing the brake pedal several times until normal pedal travel is established. If the pedal feels spongy, repeat the bleeding procedure.

Pressure Bleeding

For pressure bleeding, use Rotunda Brake Bleeder 104-00064 or equivalent. Always bleed the longest line first. The bleeder tank should contain enough new brake fluid to complete the braking operation. Use only DOT 3 brake fluid from a new, sealed container. Never reuse brake fluid that has been drained from the hydraulic system. The pressure bleeder tank should be charged with 10–30 psi (69–206 kPa) of air pressure.
1. Clean all dirt from the reservoir filler cap and surrounding area.

➡**NEVER exceed 50 psi (344 kPa) of air pressure to prevent system damage.**

2. Remove the master cylinder filler cap, then fill the reservoir with fluid to the MAX fill line. Following the manufacturer's instructions, install the pressure bleeder adapter tool to the master cylinder reservoir, then attach the bleeder tank hose to the fitting on the adapter.
3. If all wheel cylinders are to be bled, start with the right-hand rear brake wheel cylinder. Remove the dust cap from the right rear caliper bleeder fitting. Attach a rubber drain tube to the fitting, making sure the tube fits snugly.
4. Open the valve on the bleeder tank to admit pressurized brake fluid to the master cylinder reservoir.
5. Submerge the free end of the tube in a container partly filled with clean brake fluid, then loosen the wheel cylinder bleeder screw.
6. When the air bubbles cease to appear in the fluid at the submerged end of the bleeder tube, close the wheel cylinder bleeder screw, then remove the tube. Tighten to 7.5–8.9 ft. lbs. (10–12 Nm). Replace the rubber dust cap on the wheel cylinder bleeder screw.

7. Repeat Steps 3–6 at the left front disc brake caliper.

8. Next, repeat Steps 4, 5 and 6 at the left rear wheel cylinder or caliper, and then the right front disc brake caliper.

9. When the bleeding procedure is finished, close the bleeder tank valve, then remove the hose from the adapter fitting.

10. After disc brake service, make sure the disc brake pistons are returned to their normal positions and that the brake shoe and lining assemblies are properly seated. This is accomplished by depressing the brake pedal a few times until normal pedal travel is established.

11. Remove the pressure bleeder adapter tool from the master cylinder. Fill the master cylinder reservoir to the proper level using clean brake fluid from a sealed container.

FRONT DISC BRAKES

Brake Pads

✱✱ CAUTION

Some brake shoes contain asbestos, which has been determined to be a cancer causing agent. Never clean the brake surfaces with compressed air! Avoid inhaling any dust from any brake surface! When cleaning brake surfaces, use a commercially available brake cleaning fluid.

REMOVAL & INSTALLATION

1983–88 Vehicles

♦ **See Figures 13 and 14**

1. Disconnect the negative battery cable.

2. Remove the master cylinder cap. Remove brake fluid until the larger of the two reservoirs is half full. Discard this fluid.

3. Raise and safely support the vehicle.

4. Remove the wheel and tire assembly. Be careful to avoid damage to or interference with the caliper splash shield or bleeder screw fitting.

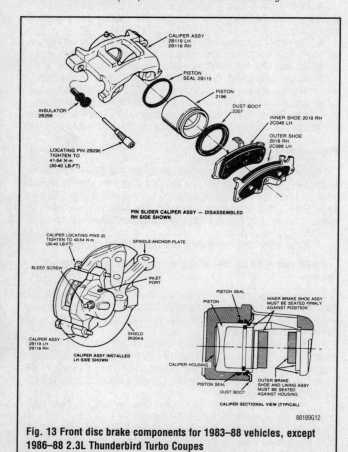

Fig. 13 Front disc brake components for 1983–88 vehicles, except 1986–88 2.3L Thunderbird Turbo Coupes

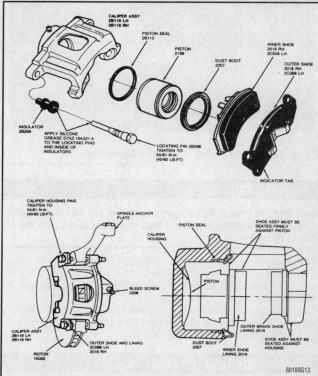

Fig. 14 Front disc brake components for 1986–88 Thunderbird Turbo Coupes

5. Lift the caliper assembly from the integral spindle/anchor plate and rotor. Remove the outer shoe from the caliper assembly.

6. Remove the inner shoe and lining assembly. This could require a force as high as 20–30 lbs. (90–135 N) Inspect both rotor braking surfaces. Minor scoring or building of lining material does not require machining or replacement of the rotor.

➡ **Never let the caliper hang from the brake hose.**

7. Suspend the caliper inside the fender housing with a wire hooked through the outer leg hole of the caliper. Be careful not to damage the caliper or stretch the brake hose.

8. Use a 4 in. (102mm) C-clamp and a block of wood 2¾ in. x 1 in. and approximately ¾ in. thick (70mm x 25mm x 19mm) to seat the caliper hydraulic piston in its bore. This must be done to provide clearance for the caliper assembly to fit over the rotor when installed. Remove the C-clamp from the caliper (the caliper piston will remain seated in its bore).

To install:

9. Install the inner shoe and lining assembly. All vehicles, have a separate anti-rattle clip and insulator that must be installed to the inner shoe and lining prior to their assembly to the caliper. The inner shoes are marked LH or RH and must be installed in the proper caliper. Also, care should be taken not to bend the anti-rattle clips too far in the piston or distortion and rattles can result.

10. Install the correct outer brake shoe and lining assembly (RH/LH), making sure that the clip and/or buttons located on the shoe are properly seated. The outer shoe can be identified as right hand or left hand by the war indicator which must always be installed toward the front of the vehicle or by a LH or RH mark.

✳✳ WARNING

Make certain that the two round torque buttons on all vehicles, are seated solidly in the two holes of the outer caliper leg and that the shoe is held tightly against the housing by the spring clip. If the buttons are not seated, a temporary loss of brakes may occur!

11. Install the caliper, as outlined later in this section.

12. Install the wheel and tire assembly; tighten the lug nuts to 80–105 ft. lbs. (108–142 Nm).

13. Carefully lower the vehicle, then connect the negative battery cable.

14. Pump the brake pedal prior to moving the vehicle to position the brake linings.

15. Road test the vehicle.

1989–97 Vehicles

▶ **See Figures 15, 16, 17, 18 and 19**

1. Remove the master cylinder cap. Remove brake fluid until the reservoir is half full. Discard this fluid.

2. Raise and safely support the vehicle. Remove the wheels. Be careful to avoid damage to, or interference with, the caliper splash shield or bleeder screw fitting.

➡ **It is not necessary to disconnect the hydraulic fluid line from the caliper to remove the brake pads.**

3. Remove the caliper, as outlined later in this section, but do not disconnect the fluid line.

4. For 1989–92 vehicles, remove the outer shoe from the caliper by pushing on the shoe to move the locating buttons from the caliper housing and slipping the shoe down the caliper leg until the clip is disengaged.

5. For 1989–92 vehicles, remove the inner shoe and lining assembly by pulling it straight out of the piston.

6. For 1993–97 vehicles, remove the outer brake shoe and lining from the caliper by sliding the brake shoe and lining in the front caliper anchor plate away from the outer leg to disengage it from the anchor plate.

7. For 1993–97 vehicles, remove the inner shoe and lining, sliding the brake shoe and lining in the front caliper anchor plate away from the caliper piston to disengage it from the anchor plate. Remove the brake shoe hold-down spring.

8. Inspect both rotor braking surfaces. Minor scoring of the lining material does not require machining or replacement of the rotor.

9. Suspend the caliper inside the fender housing with a wire hooked through the outer leg hole of the caliper. Be careful not to damage the caliper or stretch the brake hose.

10. Use a 4 in. (102mm) C-clamp and a block of wood 2¾ in. x 1 in. and approximately ¾ in. thick (70mm x 25mm x 19mm) to seat the caliper hydraulic piston in its bore. This must be done to provide clearance for the caliper assembly to fit over the rotor when installed. Remove the C-clamp from the caliper (the caliper piston will remain seated in its bore).

➡ **For 1993–97 vehicles, the caliper casting has the provision to allow the spring to be installed only one way. Right and left side springs are identical but installed in opposite directions.**

11. For 1993–97 vehicles, clean the caliper legs and shoe and lining abutments, as necessary. Make sure the brake pad anti-rattle clip is seated in the caliper lining inspection opening. The clip must installed from the lining side.

Fig. 15 View of the front disc brake assembly with the wheel and tire removed—1990 Thunderbird shown

88189P01

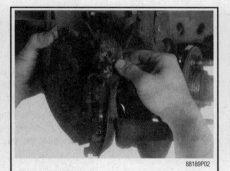

Fig. 16 Remove the outboard brake pad, then . . .

88189P02

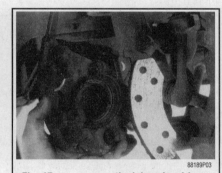

Fig. 17 . . . remove the inboard pad from the caliper—1990 Thunderbird with the rotor already removed

88189P03

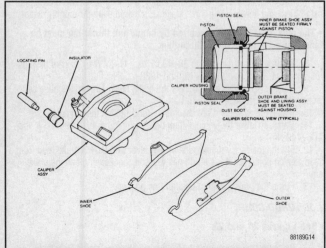

Fig. 18 View of the caliper and the brake shoe and lining assemblies—1989–92 vehicles

88189G14

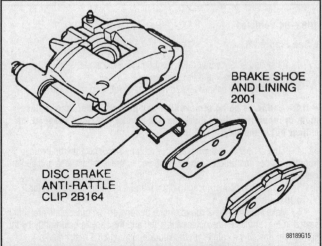

Fig. 19 Some vehicles are equipped with a disc brake anti-rattle clip—1995 vehicle shown

88189G15

12. If equipped, peel the protective paper from the insulator on the brake pad. The insulator is black when the paper has been removed. This pressure-sensitive adhesive insulator functions to reduce noise. Care should be taken to avoid contamination on the adhesive surface before installing the pad in the caliper.

13. For vehicles through 1992, place the inner shoe in the caliper. Take care to avoid bending the shoe clips during installation in the piston. If the clips are bent, rattles will occur.

✳✳ CAUTION

Damage to the boot and seal will occur if the 3-fingered clip is not visually verified to be resting on the inside rim of the piston prior to snapping it into place.

14. For vehicles through 1992, install the outer shoe, making sure that the clips are properly engaged.

15. For 1993–97 vehicles, engage the brake shoe and lining in the caliper anchor plate by first engaging the side opposite the caliper anti-rattle clip. Press the other end of the brake shoe and lining assembly to compress the anti-rattle clip and engage the brake shoe and lining in the anchor. Install the inner and outer shoe and linings (pads) in this manner.

16. Install the caliper, as outlined later in this section.

17. Install the wheel and tire assembly. Hand-tighten the lug nuts.

18. Carefully lower the vehicle, then tighten the lug nuts to 80–105 ft. lbs. (108–142 Nm).

19. Refill the master cylinder to the proper level with DOT 3 brake fluid from a fresh, sealed container.

20. Pump the brake pedal to seat the pads and position the piston.

INSPECTION

1. Raise the vehicle until the wheel and tire clear the floor. Place safety stands under the vehicle.

2. Remove the wheel cover, if equipped. Remove the wheel and tire from the hub and disc.

3. Visually inspect the shoe and lining assemblies. If the lining material has worn to a thickness of 0.030 in. (0.762mm) or less, or if the lining is contaminated with brake fluid, replace all pad assemblies on both front wheels. Make all thickness measurements across the thinnest section of the pad assembly. A slight taper on a used lining should be considered normal.

4. The caliper should be visually checked. If excess leakage is evident, the caliper should be replaced.

5. Install the wheel and hub assembly.

Brake Caliper

REMOVAL & INSTALLATION

1983–84 Vehicles

▶ See Figure 20

1. Raise and safely support the front end on jackstands.
2. Remove the wheel and tire assembly.
3. Matchmark the caliper and knuckle for installation reference.

➡️ **If the caliper is being removed for any purpose other than replacement or rebuilding, don't disconnect the brake line. Just suspend the caliper out of the way.**

4. If the caliper is being replaced or rebuilt, disconnect the brake hose from the caliper and plug or cap the hose end to prevent fluid loss and contamination.

5. Remove the caliper locating pins, then lift the caliper off the rotor.

To install:

6. Make sure that the 2 round torque buttons on the outer shoe are solidly seated in the 2 holes of the outer caliper leg and the shoe is held tightly by the spring clip. Install the caliper on the knuckle, aligning the matchmarks.

7. Lubricate the insulators with 5–7 grams of silicone grease and install them and the locating pins. Make sure the pins are thoroughly clean!

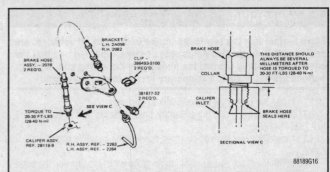

Fig. 20 Brake hose-to-front caliper attachment—1983–88 vehicles, except 2.3L Turbo Coupe

➡️ **The pins must be easily inserted by hand, and threading must be hand-started to avoid cross-threading.**

8. Torque the pins to 30–40 ft. lbs. (41–54 Nm).

9. If detached, uncap and connect the brake hose. Tighten the hose connection to 20–30 ft. lbs. (27–41 Nm).

10. Install the wheel and tire assembly. Hand-tighten the lug nuts.

11. Carefully lower the vehicle, then tighten the lug nuts to 80–105 ft. lbs. (108–142 Nm).

12. Fill the master cylinder to the proper level with DOT 3 brake fluid from a clean, sealed container. If the fluid lines were disconnected, bleed the brake system.

13. Pump the brake pedal to position the pistons.

1985–88 Vehicles

EXCEPT 2.3L TURBO COUPE

▶ See Figure 20

1. Raise and safely support the front end of the vehicle on jackstands.
2. Remove the wheel and tire assembly.
3. Matchmark the caliper and knuckle for installation reference.

➡️ **If the caliper is being removed for any purpose other than replacement or rebuilding, don't disconnect the brake line. Just suspend the caliper out of the way.**

4. If the caliper is being replaced or rebuilt, disconnect the brake hose from the caliper and plug or cap the hose end to prevent fluid loss and contamination.

5. Remove the caliper locating pins and lift the caliper off the rotor.

To install:

6. Install the caliper on the knuckle, aligning the matchmarks made during removal.

7. Lubricate the rubber insulators with 4–8 grams of silicone grease and install them and new locating pins. Make sure the pins are thoroughly clean!

➡️ **The pins must be easily inserted by hand, and threading must be hand-started to avoid cross-threading.**

8. Tighten the caliper pins to 30–40 ft. lbs. (41–54 Nm) on cars through 1987 or to 45–65 ft. lbs. (61–88 Nm) on 1988 models.

9. If detached, uncap and connect the brake hose. Tighten the hose connection to 20–30 ft. lbs. (27–41 Nm).

10. Install the wheel and tire assembly. Hand-tighten the lug nuts.

11. Carefully lower the vehicle, then tighten the lug nuts to 80–105 ft. lbs. (108–142 Nm).

12. Fill the master cylinder to the proper level with DOT 3 brake fluid from a clean, sealed container. If the fluid lines were disconnected, bleed the brake system.

13. Pump the brake pedal to position the pistons.

2.3L TURBO COUPE

▶ See Figures 21 and 22

1. Raise and safely support the front end of the vehicle on jackstands.
2. Remove the wheel and tire assembly.

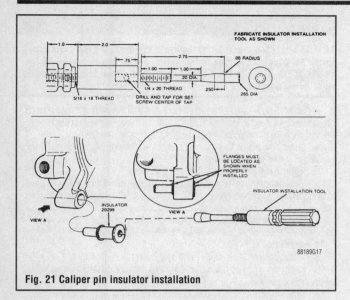

Fig. 21 Caliper pin insulator installation

3. Matchmark the caliper and knuckle for installation reference.

➡️**If the caliper is being removed for any purpose other than replacement or rebuilding, don't disconnect the brake line. Just suspend the caliper out of the way.**

4. If replacing or rebuilding the caliper, remove the hollow bolt and copper washers attaching the brake hose to the caliper. Discard the washers. Remove the brake hose from the caliper and plug or cap the hose end to prevent fluid loss and contamination.

5. Remove the caliper locating pins and lift off the caliper.

To install:

6. Install the caliper on the knuckle, aligning the matchmarks.

7. Lubricate the rubber insulators with 4–8 grams of silicone grease and install them and the locating pins. Make sure the pins are thoroughly clean!

➡️**The pins must be easily inserted by hand, and threading must be hand-started to avoid cross-threading.**

8. Tighten the caliper pins to 45–65 ft. lbs. (61–88 Nm).

9. Connect the brake hose using new copper washers. Tighten the bolt connection to 30–40 ft. lbs. (40–60 Nm).

10. Install the wheel and tire assembly. Hand-tighten the lug nuts.

11. Carefully lower the vehicle, then tighten the lug nuts to 80–105 ft. lbs. (108–142 Nm).

12. Fill the master cylinder to the proper level with DOT 3 brake fluid from a clean, sealed container. If the fluid lines were disconnected, bleed the brake system.

13. Pump the brake pedal to position the pistons.

1989–97 Vehicles

➡️ **See Figures 22, 23 and 24**

1. Raise and safely support the front end of the vehicle on jackstands.

2. Remove the wheel and tire assembly.

3. Matchmark the caliper assembly to be sure it is installed on the correct knuckle during installation.

➡️**If the caliper is being removed for any purpose other than replacement or rebuilding, don't disconnect the brake line. Just suspend the caliper out of the way.**

4. If the caliper is being replaced or rebuilt, remove the hollow bolt and disconnect the brake hose from the caliper. Plug the hose to prevent fluid loss and moisture contamination.

5. For vehicles through 1992, remove the caliper locating pins using Torx® Bit D79P-2100-T40 or equivalent. Lift the caliper off the rotor using a rotating motion.

6. For 1993–97 vehicles, remove the lower caliper locating pin. Rotate the caliper about 90° away from the caliper anchor plate. Slide the caliper away from the anchor plate until the caliper disengages from the upper caliper locating pin.

To install:

7. For vehicles through 1992, using a suitable C-clamp, retract the piston fully in its bore. Position the caliper above the rotor with the anti-rattle spring (if equipped) under the arm of the knuckle. Install the caliper over the rotor with a rotating motion. Make sure the inner and outer shoes are properly positioned.

➡️**Make sure the correct caliper assembly, as marked during removal, is installed on the correct knuckle. The caliper bleed screw should be positioned on top of the caliper when assembled on the vehicle.**

➡️**The pin threading must be hand-started to avoid cross-threading.**

8. For vehicles through 1992, lubricate the pins and insulators with a suitable silicone grease and install them. Using Torx® Bit D79P-2100-T40 or equivalent, tighten the locating pin to 19–25 ft. lbs. (25–34 Nm).

➡️**For 1993–97 vehicles, it is advised to use a new lower caliper locating pin during installation because of the thread locking compound provided on the threads.**

9. For 1993–97 vehicles, install the caliper by engaging the upper locating pin into the insulator. Rotate the caliper into place on the anchor plate. Install the lower caliper locating pin, then tighten to 60 ft. lbs. (81 Nm).

10. If detached, install the brake hose using new copper washers and hollow bolts. Tighten the bolts to 30–44 ft. lbs. (40–60 Nm).

11. Install the wheel and tire assembly. Hand-tighten the lug nuts.

12. Carefully lower the vehicle, then tighten the lug nuts to 80–105 ft. lbs. (108–142 Nm).

13. Fill the master cylinder to the proper level with DOT 3 brake fluid from a clean, sealed container. If the fluid lines were disconnected, bleed the brake system.

14. Pump the brake pedal to position the pistons.

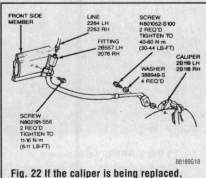

Fig. 22 If the caliper is being replaced, disconnect and cap the brake hose— 1987–88 2.3L and all 1989–97 vehicles

Fig. 23 On some vehicles, such as this 1990, you must use a Torx® bit to unfasten, then . . .

Fig. 24 . . . remove the caliper locating pins

OVERHAUL

▶ See Figures 25, 26, 27, 28 and 29

➡For this procedure, you will need new pressure fitting washers, as well as new caliper piston boots and seals.

1. Remove the brake caliper from the vehicle.
2. Position the caliper on a work bench and place clean shop towel or a piece of wood in the caliper opening. Using a small amount of compressed air, force the piston from its bore.

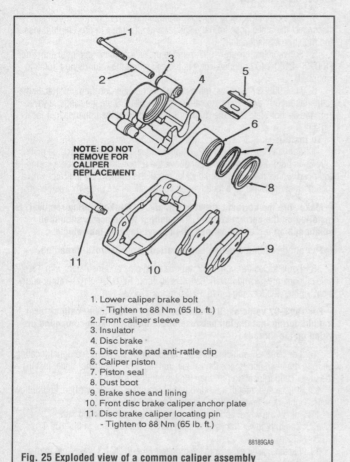

NOTE: DO NOT REMOVE FOR CALIPER REPLACEMENT

1. Lower caliper brake bolt
   - Tighten to 88 Nm (65 lb. ft.)
2. Front caliper sleeve
3. Insulator
4. Disc brake
5. Disc brake pad anti-rattle clip
6. Caliper piston
7. Piston seal
8. Dust boot
9. Brake shoe and lining
10. Front disc brake caliper anchor plate
11. Disc brake caliper locating pin
    - Tighten to 88 Nm (65 lb. ft.)

88189GA9

Fig. 25 Exploded view of a common caliper assembly

DO NOT apply too much air pressure to the bore, for the piston may jump out, causing damage to the piston and/or the operator. Be ABSOLUTELY SURE to keep your fingers away from the piston while air is being applied.

3. Remove and discard the piston boot and seal. Be careful not to scratch the bore. Use of a metal tool is NOT recommended when removing the boot and the seal because of the possibility of scoring and damaging the bore.
4. Inspect the piston and the caliper bore for damage or corrosion. Replace the caliper and/or the piston (if necessary).
5. Remove the bleeder screw and its rubber cap.
6. Clean all of the parts with non-mineral based solvent and blow dry with compressed air. All rubber parts should be replaced with those in the brake service kit.
7. Inspect the guide pins for corrosion. Replace them if necessary. When installing the guide pins, coat them with a silicone lubricant.

To assemble:

8. Lubricate the piston, caliper and seal with clean brake fluid.
9. Install the seal into the caliper bore making sure it is not twisted in the caliper bore groove.
10. Install the boot onto the piston, then position the piston into the caliper bore.

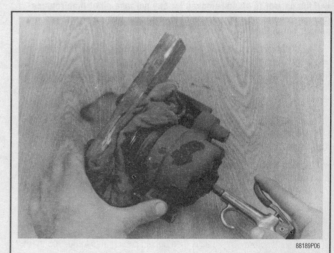

88189P06

Fig. 26 Apply a small amount of compressed air to push the piston out against a clean rag but KEEP YOUR FINGERS CLEAR

88189P07

Fig. 27 Grasp the piston and remove it from the caliper bore

88189P08

Fig. 28 Remove the boot from the caliper housing, taking care not to score or damage the bore

88189P10

Fig. 29 Use EXTREME caution when removing the piston seal; DO NOT scratch the caliper bore

11. Bottom the piston into the bore, then secure the boot using a suitable piston seal installer tool.

12. Install the caliper on the vehicle and properly bleed the hydraulic brake system.

Brake Disc (Rotor)

REMOVAL & INSTALLATION

1983–88 Vehicles

▶ See Figures 30 and 31

➡For vehicles through 1988, the rotor is removed with the hub as an assembly.

1. Raise and safely support the vehicle.
2. Remove the wheel and tire assembly.
3. Remove the caliper, as outlined earlier. Suspend the caliper with a suitable piece of wire. Do NOT disconnect the fluid line.
4. Remove the grease cap from the hub. Remove the cotter pin, nut lock, adjusting nut, and flat washer from the spindle. Discard the cotter pin.
5. Remove the outer wheel bearing cone and roller assembly from the hub.
6. Remove the hub and disc assembly from the spindle.

To install:

✳✳ WARNING

If a new disc is being installed, remove the protective coating with carburetor degreaser. If the original disc is being installed, make sure that the grease in the hub is clean and adequate, that the inner bearing and grease retainer are lubricated and in good condition, and that the disc breaking surfaces are clean.

7. Install the hub and disc assembly on the spindle.
8. Lubricate the outer bearing and install the thrust washer and adjusting nut.

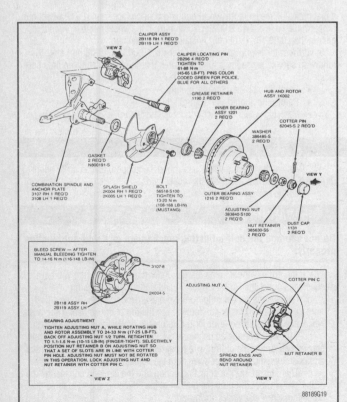

Fig. 30 View of the hub and rotor assembly—1983–88 vehicles, except 2.3L engine

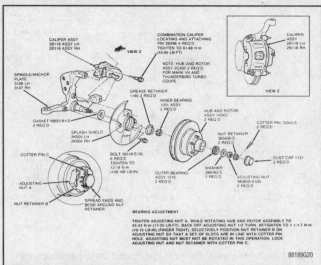

Fig. 31 On 1983–88 vehicles, the rotor and hub are removed as an assembly—2.3L Turbo engine shown

9. Adjust the wheel bearing, as outlined in Section 8.
10. Install the nut lock, a new cotter pin, and grease cap.
11. Install the caliper assembly, as outlined earlier in this section.
12. Install the wheel and tire assembly and hand-tighten nuts.
13. Carefully lower the vehicle, then tighten the lug nuts to 85–132 ft. lbs. (115–136 Nm).

1989–92 Vehicles

▶ See Figures 32 and 33

1. Raise and safely support the front end of the vehicle on jackstands.
2. Remove the wheel and tire assembly.
3. Remove the caliper and suspend it out of the way with a suitable piece of wire. DO NOT disconnect the brake line.
4. Remove the rotor from the hub.

➡On high mileage cars the rotor may be rusted to the hub. If so, squirt penetrating oil between the rotor and hub, let it work for a while, and strike the rotor between the lugs with a plastic hammer. If that doesn't work, a 3-jawed puller will be necessary. If excessive force is necessary, the rotor may become distorted.

5. Installation is the reverse of the removal procedure.

Fig. 32 Suspend the caliper with a piece of wire, then remove the rotor from the hub

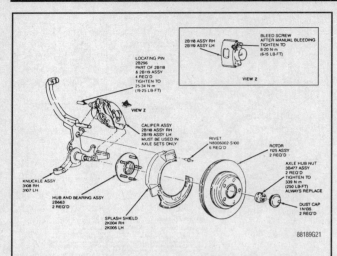

Fig. 33 Exploded view of the rotor and related brake system components

➡️If a new rotor is being installed, it will have a protective coating. Remove the coating with carburetor cleaner.

INSPECTION

▶ See Figures 34 and 35

➡️Whenever the rotor has been removed, clean any rust or foreign material from the mating surface on the wheel hub and rotor. Failure to do this may result in increased lateral runout of the rotor and brake pulsation.

1. Visually check the disc for scoring. Minor scores can be removed with fine emery cloth. If it is excessively scored, it must be machined or replaced.

2. Install the rotors, then hold in place using inverted lug nuts and washer to seat the rotors. Tighten the lug nuts to 85 ft. lbs. (115 Nm).

3. Using a suitable dial indicator, measure the rotor lateral runout as shown in the accompanying figure. Center the dial indicator on the braking surface. Rotate the rotor while measuring runout. If the runout is greater than 0.003 in. (0.08mm), reposition the rotor (index) on the hub to obtain the lower possible runout.

4. If the lateral runout of the rotor is above 0.003 in. (0.08mm) after repositioning (indexing), inspect the wheel hub assembly on 1993–97 vehicles. Using

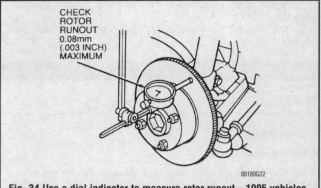

Fig. 34 Use a dial indicator to measure rotor runout—1995 vehicles shown

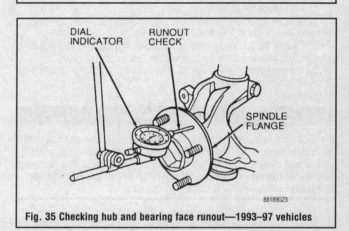

Fig. 35 Checking hub and bearing face runout—1993–97 vehicles

a dial indicator, measure the wheel hub and bearing face runout. The wheel hub runout must be less than 0.002 in. (0.06mm). If the wheel hub face runout is greater than 0.002 in. (0.06mm), install a new wheel hub.

5. If the rotor lateral runout is greater than 0.003 in. (0.08mm) after the following service procedures, this indicates that the brake lathe requires service:

- Front disc brake rotor machining
- Rotor repositioning (indexing)
- Verifying wheel hub face runout is less than 0.002 in. (0.06mm)

REAR DRUM BRAKES

▶ See Figure 36

✳️✳️ CAUTION

Brake shoes contain asbestos, which has been determined to be a cancer causing agent. Never clean the brake surfaces with compressed air! Avoid inhaling any dust from any brake surface! When cleaning brake surfaces, use a commercially available brake cleaning fluid.

Brake Drum

REMOVAL & INSTALLATION

▶ See Figures 37, 38, 39, 40 and 41

1. With the tires on the ground, break loose the lug nuts.
2. Make sure the parking brake is not on, then raise and safely support the rear of the vehicles with jackstands.
3. Remove the wheel cover/and or nuts covers, as applicable.

4. Remove the tire and wheel assembly. If equipped, use a pair of pliers to remove the Tinnerman nuts from the wheel studs.
5. Pull the brake drum of the axle shaft.

✳️✳️ WARNING

Do not damage the self-adjusting mechanism or it will not function properly.

6. If the drum will not come off, get under the car (make sure you have safety stands under the car to support it) and perform the following

a. Remove the rubber plug from the brake backing plate. Shine a flashlight into the slot in the plate. You will see the top of the adjusting screw star wheel and the adjusting lever for the automatic brake adjusting mechanism.

b. To back off on the adjusting screw, you must first insert a small, thin screwdriver or a piece of firm wire (coat hanger wire) into the adjusting slot and push the adjusting lever away from the adjusting screw.

c. Then, insert a brake adjusting spoon into the slot and engage the top of the star wheel. Lift up on the bottom of the adjusting spoon to force the adjusting screw star wheel downward.

d. Repeat this operation until the brake drum is free of the brake shoes and can be pulled off.

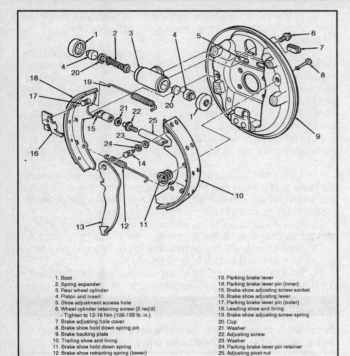

1. Boot
2. Spring expander
3. Rear wheel cylinder
4. Piston and insert
5. Shoe adjustment access hole
6. Wheel cylinder retaining screw (2 req'd)
   - Tighten to 12-18 Nm (106-159 lb. in.)
7. Brake adjusting hole cover
8. Brake shoe hold down spring pin
9. Brake backing plate
10. Trailing shoe and lining
11. Brake shoe hold down spring
12. Brake shoe retracting spring (lower)

13. Parking brake lever
14. Parking brake lever pin (inner)
15. Brake shoe adjusting screw socket
16. Brake shoe adjusting lever
17. Parking brake lever pin (outer)
18. Leading shoe and lining
19. Brake shoe adjusting screw spring
20. Cup
21. Washer
22. Adjusting screw
23. Washer
24. Parking brake lever pin retainer
25. Adjusting pivot nut

88189G26

Fig. 36 Exploded view of the drum brake assembly—1995 vehicle shown

To install:

7. If installing a new brake drum, remove the protective coating totally and lightly sand the inner brake drum surface.

8. If the brake adjustment was changed to remove the drum, adjust the brakes until the drum will just fit over the brakes. After the wheel is installed it will be necessary to complete the adjustment. See the Brake Adjustment procedure located earlier in this section.

9. Install the brake drum and secure with the retainer nuts, if equipped.

10. Install the tire and wheel assembly. Hand-tighten the lug nuts.

11. Carefully lower the vehicle, them tighten the lug nuts to 85–105 ft. lbs. (115–142 Nm).

INSPECTION

1. Clean the brake drums and remove any grease, brake fluid or other contaminants from the drum using denatured alcohol, or a suitable cleaner.

2. Inspect and measure the brake drum with Rotunda Brake Drum Micrometer 104-00046 or equivalent.

3. Measure the drums with a brake drum micrometer regardless of inspection. The brake drum micrometer is set to the drum diameter and measures the amount and type of ward. Measure the diameter at various point of 45 degrees around the circumference and at the bottom of the deepest groove to determine if the brake drum required replacement.

ADJUSTMENTS

▶ See Figure 42

The rear brakes are automatically adjusted while driving the vehicle. Manual brake adjustment is required only after the rear brake shoes and linings have been replaced, or if the adjuster has malfunctioned and has been repaired or replaced. Perform the manual adjustment with the brake drum removed, using Brake Adjustment Gauge D81L-1103-A or equivalent.

88189P12

Fig. 37 Remove the tire and wheel assembly, then . . .

88189P13

Fig. 38 . . . pull the drum off the axle shaft

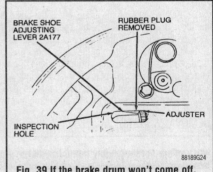

88189G24

Fig. 39 If the brake drum won't come off, remove the rubber plug from the inspection hole, then . . .

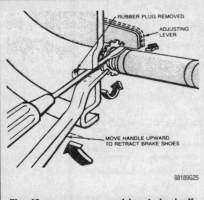

88189G25

Fig. 40 . . . use a screwdriver to back off the adjusting screw

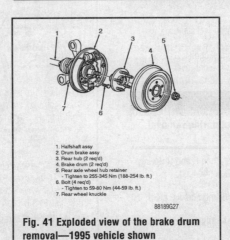

1. Halfshaft assy
2. Drum brake assy
3. Rear hub (2 req'd)
4. Brake drum (2 req'd)
5. Rear axle wheel hub retainer
   - Tighten to 255-345 Nm (188-254 lb. ft.)
6. Bolt (4 req'd)
   - Tighten to 59-80 Nm (44-59 lb. ft.)
7. Rear wheel knuckle

88189G27

Fig. 41 Exploded view of the brake drum removal—1995 vehicle shown

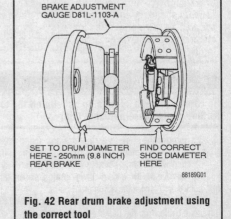

88189G01

Fig. 42 Rear drum brake adjustment using the correct tool

1. Raise and safely support the rear end of the vehicle on jackstands.
2. Remove the tire and wheel assembly, then remove the brake drum.
3. Apply a small quantity of Disc Brake Caliper Slide Grease D7AZ-19590-A or equivalent, to the points where the shoes contact the rear brake backing plate. Do NOT get any lubricant on the lining.
4. Determine the inside diameter of the brake drum braking surface using Brake Adjustment Gauge D81L-1103-A or equivalent.
5. Adjust the brake shoe and lining diameter to fit the gauge. Line up the brake shoes and linings vertically so that the flats on the bottom of the rear brake shoes and linings are aligned approximately 0.05 in. (1.5mm) above the bottom of the brake shoe and lining abutment plate before setting the gauge diameter. Hold the automatic brake shoe adjusting lever out of engagement while rotating the adjusting screw. If necessary, lubricate. Make sure the adjusting screw rotates freely.
6. Rotate Brake Adjustment Gauge D81L-1103-A or equivalent around the rear brake shoe and lining to ensure proper seating.
7. Install the brake drum, as outlined later in this section.
8. Install the tire and wheel assembly, then install the wheel cover and nut covers, as applicable.
9. After the rear brake shoes and linings have been properly adjusted, check the operation of the brakes by making several stops from varying forward speeds.

Brake Shoes

INSPECTION

1. Inspect the rear brake shoes and linings for excessive lining wear or shoe damage. If the lining is damaged or worn within 1⁄32 in. (0.79mm), it must be replaced. Replace any lining that has been contaminated with oil, grease or brake fluid. Replace the linings in axle sets only. Never replace just one rear shoe and lining of a brake assembly. Replace both leading and trailing shoes.

➡**Replace the brake shoe and lining in axle sets only. Never replace just one shoe of a brake assembly.**

2. Before replacing the lining, check the brake drum diameter to determine if the brake drum diameter is within specifications. If the braking surface diameter exceeds specifications, the drum must be replaced.
3. Check the condition of the brake shoes and linings, retracting spring, hold-down springs and brake drum for signs of overheating. If the brake shoes and linings have a slight blue coloring, this indicates overheating and retracting. Replace the hold-down springs. If not replaced, overheated springs could lose their tension and allow the new lining to drag and wear prematurely.

REMOVAL & INSTALLATION

➡**If you are not thoroughly familiar with the procedures involved in brake replacement, only disassemble and assemble one side at a time, leaving the other wheel intact as a reference.**

1983–88 Vehicles

▶ **See Figures 43, 44 and 45**

1. Raise and safely support the rear of the vehicle with jackstands.
2. Remove the tire and wheel assembly.
3. Remove the brake drum, as outlined earlier in this section.
4. Place Brake Cylinder Clamp D81L-1103-B or equivalent, over the ends of the brake cylinder.

✳✳ CAUTION

Be careful that the springs do not slip off the tool during removal, as they could cause personal injury.

5. Remove the shoe-to-anchor springs, using Brake Shoe R and R Spring BT-11, or equivalent, then unhook the cable eye from the anchor pin.
6. Remove the shoe guide (anchor pin) plate.
7. Remove the shoe hold-down springs, shoes, adjusting screws, pivot nut, socket and automatic adjustment parts.
8. Remove the parking brake link, spring and retainer. Disconnect the parking brake cable from the parking brake lever.

9. After removing the secondary brake shoe, disassembly the parking brake lever from the shoe by removing the retaining clip and spring washer.

To install:

10. The brake cable must be connected to the secondary brake shoe before the shoe is installed on the backing plate. To do this, first transfer the parking brake lever from the old secondary shoe to the new one. This is accomplished by spreading the bottom of the horseshoe clip and disengaging the lever. Position the lever on the new secondary shoe and install the spring washer and the horseshoe clip. Close the bottom of the clip after installing it. Grasp the metal tip of the parking brake cable with a pair of pliers. Position a pair of side cutter pliers on the end of the cable coil spring, and using the plier as a fulcrum, pull the coil spring back with the side cutters. Position the cable in the parking brake lever.
11. Apply a light coating of high temperature grease to the brake shoe contact points on the backing plate. Position the primary brake shoe on the front of the backing plate and install the hold-down spring and washer over the mounting pin. Install the secondary shoe on the rear of the backing plate.
12. Install the parking brake link between the notch in the primary brake shoe and the notch in the parking brake lever.
13. Install the automatic adjuster cable loop end on the anchor pin. Make sure the crimped side of the loop faces the backing plate.
14. Install the return spring in the primary brake shoe and, using the tapered end of the brake spring service tool, slide the top of the spring onto the anchor pin.

✳✳ CAUTION

Be careful to make sure that the spring does not slip off the tool during installation, as it could cause injury.

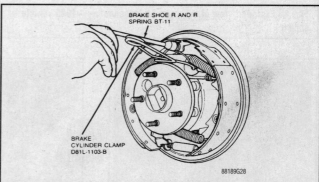

Fig. 43 Place the brake clamp tool over the ends of the wheel cylinder, then remove the shoe-to-anchor springs using the correct tool

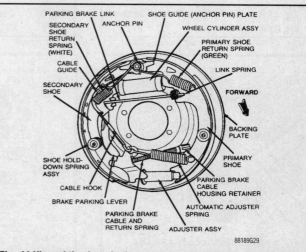

Fig. 44 View of the drum brake components—1983–88 9-inch brake shown

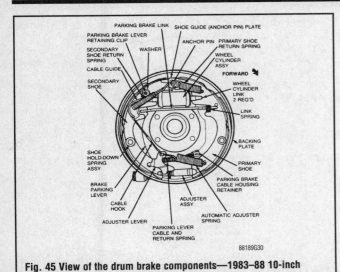

Fig. 45 View of the drum brake components—1983–88 10-inch brake shown

15. Install the automatic adjuster cable guide in the secondary brake shoe, making sure the flared hole in the cable guide is inside the hole in the brake shoe. Fit the cable into the groove in the top of the cable guide.

16. Install the secondary shoe return spring through the hole in the cable guide and the brake shoe. Using the brake spring tool, slide the top of the spring onto the anchor pin.

Fig. 46 View of the drum brake assembly with the drum removed

17. Clean the threads on the adjusting screw and apply a light coating of high temperature grease to the threads. Screw the adjuster closed, then open it ½ turn.

18. Install the adjusting screw between the brake shoes with the star wheel nearest to the secondary shoe. Make sure the star wheel is in a position that is accessible from the adjusting slot in the backing plate.

19. Install the short hooked end of the automatic adjuster spring in the proper hole in the primary brake shoe.

20. Connect the hooked end of the automatic adjuster cable and the free end of the automatic adjuster spring in the slot in the top of the automatic adjuster lever.

21. Pull the automatic adjuster lever (the lever will pull the cable and spring with it) downward and to the left and engage the pivot hook of the lever in the hole in the secondary brake shoe.

22. Check the entire brake assembly to make sure that everything is installed properly. Make sure that the shoes engage the wheel cylinder properly and are flush on the anchor pin. Make sure that the automatic adjuster cable is flush on the anchor pin and in the slot on the back of the cable guide. Make sure that the adjusting lever rests on the adjusting screw star wheel. Pull upward on the adjusting cable until the adjusting lever is free of the star wheel, then release the cable. The adjusting lever should snap back into place on the adjusting screw star wheel and turn the wheel one tooth.

23. Expand the brake adjusting screw until the brake drum will just fit over the brake shoes.

24. Install the brake drum and wheel and tire assembly, then adjust the brakes.

25. Carefully lower the vehicle.

1989–97 Vehicles

▶ **See Figures 46 thru 52**

1. Raise and safely support the vehicle.

2. Remove the rear wheel and tire assemblies, then remove the brake drum.

3. Install Brake Cylinder Clamp D81L-1103-B or equivalent, over the ends of the rear wheel cylinder.

4. Disconnect the parking brake cable from the parking brake lever.

5. Remove the 2 brake shoe hold-down retainers, springs and pins.

6. Spread the brake shoes over the piston shoe guide slots. Lift the brake shoes, springs and adjuster off the backing plate as an assembly. Be careful not to bend the adjusting lever.

7. Remove the adjuster spring. To separate the shoes, remove the retracting springs.

8. Remove the parking brake lever retaining clip and spring washer. Remove the lever from the pin.

To install:

9. Apply a light coating of caliper slide grease to the backing plate brake shoe contact areas.

10. Apply a light coat of lubricant to the threaded areas of the adjuster screw and socket. Assemble the brake adjuster with the stainless steel washer. Turn the socket all the way down on the screw, then back off ½ turn.

11. Install the parking brake lever to the trailing shoe with the spring washer and a new retaining clip. Crimp the clip to securely retain the lever.

12. Position the trailing shoe on the backing plate and attach the parking

Fig. 47 Use a commercially available brake spray to clean the components before removal

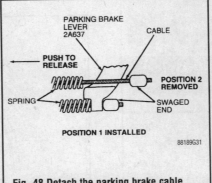

Fig. 48 Detach the parking brake cable and conduit from the parking brake lever

Fig. 49 Lift the brake shoes, springs and adjuster off the backing plate as an assembly

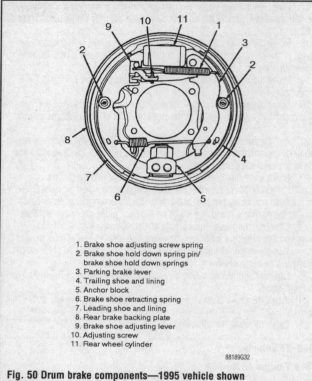

1. Brake shoe adjusting screw spring
2. Brake shoe hold down spring pin/
   brake shoe hold down springs
3. Parking brake lever
4. Trailing shoe and lining
5. Anchor block
6. Brake shoe retracting spring
7. Leading shoe and lining
8. Rear brake backing plate
9. Brake shoe adjusting lever
10. Adjusting screw
11. Rear wheel cylinder

88189G32

Fig. 50 Drum brake components—1995 vehicle shown

brake cable. Position the leading shoe on the backing plate and attach the lower retracting spring to the brake shoes.

13. Install the adjuster assembly to the slots in the brake shoes. The socket end must fit into the wider slot in the leading shoe. The slot in the adjuster nut must fit into the slots in the trailing shoe and parking brake lever.

14. Install the adjuster lever on the pin on the leading shoe and to the slot in the adjuster socket.

15. Install the upper retracting spring in the slot on the trailing shoe and the slot in the adjuster lever. The adjuster lever should contact the star and adjuster assembly.

16. Install the brake shoe anchor pins, springs and retainers. Remove the brake cylinder clamp tool

17. Install the brake drum, wheel and tire assemblies and lower the vehicle.

18. Apply the brakes several times while backing up the vehicle. After each stop, the vehicle must be moved forward.

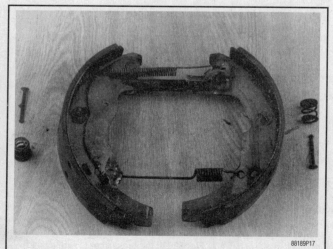

88189P17

Fig. 51 Exploded view of the drum brake components, removed from the vehicle

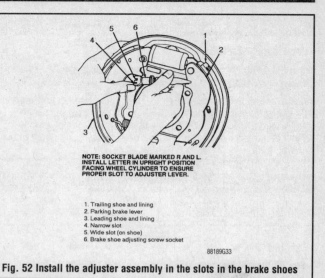

NOTE: SOCKET BLADE MARKED R AND L.
INSTALL LETTER IN UPRIGHT POSITION
FACING WHEEL CYLINDER TO ENSURE
PROPER SLOT TO ADJUSTER LEVER.

1. Trailing shoe and lining
2. Parking brake lever
3. Leading shoe and lining
4. Narrow slot
5. Wide slot (on shoe)
6. Brake shoe adjusting screw socket

88189G33

Fig. 52 Install the adjuster assembly in the slots in the brake shoes

Wheel Cylinders

REMOVAL & INSTALLATION

▶ See Figure 53

1. Raise and safely support the vehicle with jackstands.
2. Remove the tire and wheel assembly.
3. Remove the brake drum and shoes, as outlined earlier in this section.

➡**Do not let the brake fluid contact the brake linings or the linings must be replaced.**

4. Disconnect and plug the brake tube from the wheel cylinder at the backing plate. The tube will separate from the cylinder when it is removed from the backing plate.

5. Remove the wheel cylinder attaching bolts, then remove the wheel cylinder from the backing plate.

To install:

➡**Before making the fluid line connections, wipe the end(s) of the lines to remove any foreign matter.**

6. Position the wheel cylinder on the backing plate, then unplug and finger-tighten the brake line to the cylinder.

7. Secure the wheel cylinder to the backing plate, using the attaching bolts. Tighten the bolts to 10–20 ft. lbs. (14–27 Nm).

8. Tighten the tube nut fitting to 10–14 ft. lbs. (14–18 Nm) using Tube Nut Wrench 1112-144 or equivalent.

9. Install the links 10-inch brakes in the ends of the wheel cylinder, then install the shoes and adjuster assemblies.

10. Adjust the brakes. Install the brake drum and wheel and tire assembly.

11. Carefully lower the vehicle, then bleed the brake system.

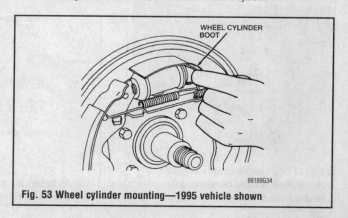

WHEEL CYLINDER
BOOT

88189G34

Fig. 53 Wheel cylinder mounting—1995 vehicle shown

REAR DISC BRAKES

▶ See Figures 54 and 55

❋❋ CAUTION

Some brake shoes contain asbestos, which has been determined to be a cancer causing agent. Never clean the brake surfaces with compressed air! Avoid inhaling any dust from any brake surface! When cleaning brake surfaces, use a commercially available brake cleaning fluid.

Disc Brake Pads

REMOVAL & INSTALLATION

1987–88 Vehicles

▶ See Figures 56, 57 and 58

1. Raise and safely support the vehicle on jackstands.
2. Remove the tire and wheel assembly.
3. Remove the screw retaining the brake hose bracket to shock/strut bracket.
4. Remove cable tension, and remove the retaining clip from the parking brake cable at the caliper. Remove the cable end from the parking brake lever.
5. Hold the slider pin hex-heads with an open-end wrench and remove the upper pinch bolt. Loosen, but do not remove the lower pinch bolt.

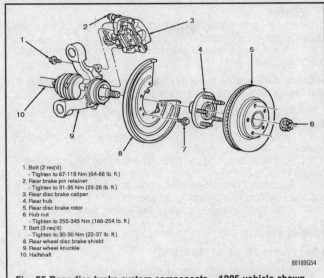

1. Bolt (2 req'd)
   - Tighten to 87-119 Nm (64-88 lb. ft.)
2. Rear brake pin retainer
   - Tighten to 31-35 Nm (23-26 lb. ft.)
3. Rear disc brake caliper
4. Rear hub
5. Rear disc brake rotor
6. Hub nut
   - Tighten to 255-345 Nm (188-254 lb. ft.)
7. Bolt (3 req'd)
   - Tighten to 30-50 Nm (22-37 lb. ft.)
8. Rear wheel disc brake shield
9. Rear wheel knuckle
10. Halfshaft

88189G54

Fig. 55 Rear disc brake system components—1995 vehicle shown

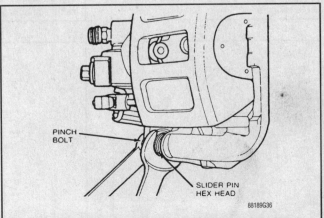

88189G35

Fig. 56 Detach the parking brake cable end from the lever

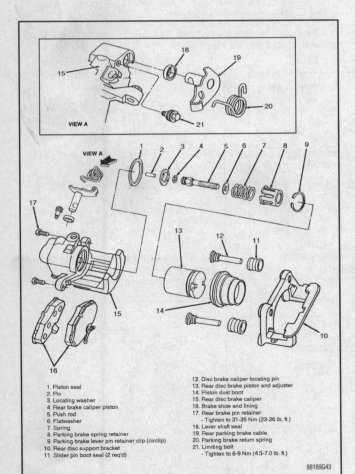

1. Piston seal
2. Pin
3. Locating washer
4. Rear brake caliper piston
5. Push rod
6. Flatwasher
7. Spring
8. Parking brake spring retainer
9. Parking brake lever pin retainer clip (circlip)
10. Rear disc support bracket
11. Slider pin boot seal (2 req'd)
12. Disc brake caliper locating pin
13. Rear disc brake piston and adjuster
14. Piston dust boot
15. Rear disc brake caliper
16. Brake shoe and lining
17. Rear brake pin retainer
   - Tighten to 31-35 Nm (23-26 lb. ft.)
18. Lever shaft seal
19. Rear parking brake cable
20. Parking brake return spring
21. Limiting bolt
   - Tighten to 6-9 Nm (4.5-7.0 lb. ft.)

88189G43

Fig. 54 Rear disc brake caliper and related system components—1995 vehicle shown

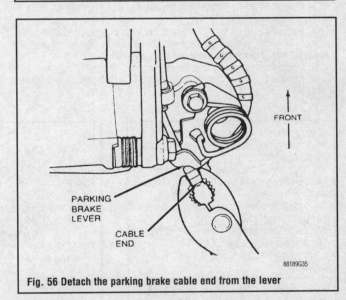

88189G36

Fig. 57 Remove the upper pinch bolt, while holding the pin hex-heads with an open-end wrench

6. Rotate the caliper away from the rotor.

7. Remove the inner and outer brake pads and the anti-rattle clips from the anchor plate.

To install:

8. Using a piston turning tool T87P–2588–A, or equivalent, rotate piston clockwise until it is fully seated.

9. Place the new inner brake pad on the anchor plate. Place the new outer pad in the caliper.

➡**Ensure that one of the two slots in the piston face is positioned so it will engage the nib on the back of the brake pad.**

10. Rotate the caliper assembly over rotor into position on anchor plate. Ensure that the brake pads are installed correctly.

11. Remove the residue from the pinch bolt threads and apply a threadlock sealer E0AZ–19554–A or equivalent.

12. Hold the slider pins with an open-end wrench, and tighten the pinch bolts to 30–35 ft. lbs. (40–47 Nm).

13. Attach the cable end to the parking brake lever. Install the cable retaining clip onto the caliper assembly and tighten screw to 30–37 ft. lbs. (41–50 Nm).

14. Install the tire and wheel assembly, then carefully lower the vehicle.

1989–97 Vehicles

♦ **See Figures 59, 60, 61, 62 and 63**

1. Raise and safely support vehicle on jackstands.

2. Remove the wheel and tire assembly.

3. Release the parking brake cable tension, and disengage parking brake cable end from the caliper.

4. Remove the rear brake pin retainers. For vehicles through 1992, hold the slider pin hex-heads with an open-end wrench. Remove the upper pinch bolt. Loosen but do not remove the lower bolt.

5. Rotate the caliper away from the rotor.

6. Remove the inner and outer brake pads and the anti-rattle clips from the anchor plate/rear support bracket.

To install:

➡**Ensure that one of the two slots in the piston face is positioned so it will engage the nib on the back of the brake pad.**

7. Using Rear Caliper Piston Adjuster T87P–2588–A, or equivalent, rotate piston and adjuster clockwise until it is fully seated.

8. Place the new inner brake pad on the anchor plate. Place the new outer pad in the caliper.

9. Rotate the caliper assembly over rotor into position on anchor plate. Ensure that the brake pads are installed correctly.

10. Remove the residue from the pinch bolt threads and apply a threadlock sealer.

11. Hold the slider pins with an open-end and tighten pinch bolts to 23–26 ft. lbs. (31–35 Nm).

12. Attach the cable end to parking brake lever. Install the cable retaining clip onto the caliper assembly and tighten screw to 16–22 ft. lbs. (22–29 Nm).

13. Install the tire and wheel assembly, then carefully lower the vehicle.

Caliper

REMOVAL & INSTALLATION

1987–88 Vehicles

♦ **See Figures 56, 57 and 64**

1. Raise and safely support the vehicle using jackstands.

2. Remove the wheel and tire assembly. Use care to avoid damage or interference with the splash shield.

3. Disconnect the parking brake cable from the lever. Use care to avoid kinking or cutting the cable or return spring.

➡**If the caliper is not being replaced or rebuilt, you do not have to disconnect the fluid line from the caliper.**

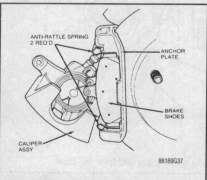

Fig. 58 Removing the brake shoes from the calipers

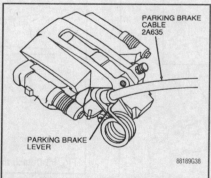

Fig. 59 Detach the rear parking brake cable end from the caliper

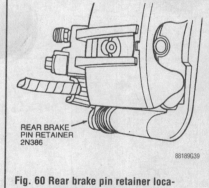

Fig. 60 Rear brake pin retainer locations—1995 vehicle shown

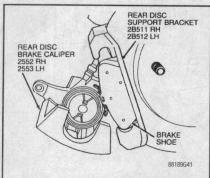

Fig. 61 Rotate the caliper from the rotor, then remove the brake pads

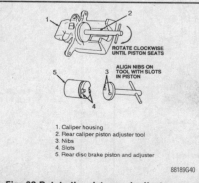

1. Caliper housing
2. Rear caliper piston adjuster tool
3. Nibs
4. Slots
5. Rear disc brake piston and adjuster

Fig. 62 Rotate the piston and adjuster clockwise until fully seated

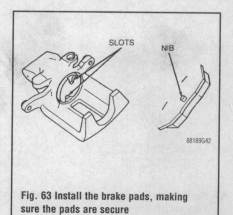

Fig. 63 Install the brake pads, making sure the pads are secure

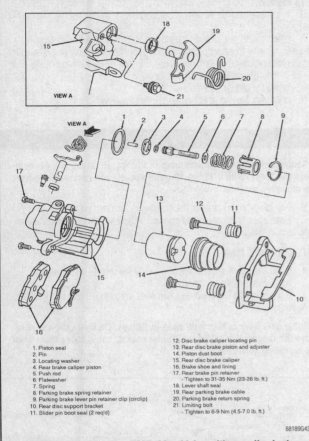

Fig. 64 Caliper removal on 1987–88 vehicles with rear disc brakes

1. Piston seal
2. Pin
3. Locating washer
4. Rear brake caliper piston
5. Push rod
6. Flatwasher
7. Spring
8. Parking brake spring retainer
9. Parking brake lever pin retainer clip (circlip)
10. Rear disc support bracket
11. Slider pin boot seal (2 req'd)
12. Disc brake caliper locating pin
13. Rear disc brake piston and adjuster
14. Piston dust boot
15. Rear disc brake caliper
16. Brake shoe and lining
17. Rear brake pin retainer
 - Tighten to 31–35 Nm (23–26 lb. ft.)
18. Lever shaft seal
19. Rear parking brake cable
20. Parking brake return spring
21. Limiting bolt
 - Tighten to 6–9 Nm (4.5–7.0 lb. ft.)

88189G43

4. If the caliper is being replaced or rebuilt, detach the brake hose from caliper assembly. Cap the hose to prevent fluid loss and contamination.

5. Hold the slider pin hex heads with an open-end wrench and remove the pinch bolts.

6. Lift the caliper assembly away from the anchor plate.

7. Remove slider pins and boots from the anchor plate.

To install:

8. Apply silicone grease to the inside of slider pin boots and slider pins. Position the slider pins and boots in anchor plate.

9. Position the caliper assembly onto the anchor plate, ensuring that the brakes are installed correctly.

10. Remove the residue from the pinch bolt threads and apply a thread-lock sealer E0AZ–18554–A or equivalent. Install the pinch bolts and tighten to 23–26 ft. lbs. (31–35 Nm) while holding the slider pin hex heads with an open-end wrench.

11. Attach the cable end to the parking brake lever. Install the cable retaining clip on the caliper. Tighten the screw to 16–22 ft. lbs. (22–29 Nm).

12. If detached, using new washers, connect the brake hose to the caliper and tighten bolt to 20–30 ft. lbs. (27–40 Nm).

13. Install the tire and wheel assembly and lower vehicle.

14. If the brake lines were disconnected, Bleed the brake system.

1989–97 Vehicles

▶ **See Figures 65, 66 and 67**

1. Raise and safely support the vehicle with jackstands.

2. Remove the wheel and tire assembly. Use care to avoid damage or interference with the splash shield.

➡ **If the caliper is not being replaced or rebuilt, you do not have to disconnect the fluid line from the caliper.**

3. If the caliper is being replaced or rebuilt, disconnect and cap the brake line from the caliper.

4. Release the rear parking brake cable tension. Detach the cable end from the caliper. Use care to avoid kinking or cutting the cable or return spring.

5. Hold the slider pin hex heads with an open-end wrench and remove the pinch bolts or remove the rear brake pin retainers, as applicable.

6. Lift the caliper assembly away from the anchor plate/support bracket.

7. Remove slider pins and boots from the anchor plate/support bracket.

To install:

8. Apply a silicone grease to the inside of slider pin boots and slider pins. Position the slider pins and boots in anchor plate/support plate.

9. Position the caliper assembly onto the anchor plate, ensuring that the brakes are installed correctly.

10. Remove the residue from the pinch bolt threads and apply a thread-lock sealer E0AZ–18554–A or equivalent. Install the pinch bolts and tighten to 23–26 ft. lbs. (31–35 Nm) while holding the slider pin hex heads with an open-end wrench, if necessary.

11. Attach the cable end to the parking brake lever and adjust the parking brake.

12. Using new washers, uncap and connect the brake flex hose to the caliper and tighten bolt to 30–45 ft. lbs. (40–60 Nm).

13. Install the tire and wheel assembly, then carefully lower vehicle.

14. If the brake hose was disconnected, bleed the brake system.

CALIPER OVERHAUL

Refer to Front Caliper Overhaul in this section.

Brake Disc (Rotor)

REMOVAL & INSTALLATION

1. Raise and safely support the vehicle. Remove the tire and wheel assembly.

2. Remove the caliper and support from the body with a piece of wire, as outlined earlier. Do NOT disconnect the fluid line.

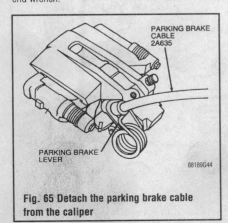

Fig. 65 Detach the parking brake cable from the caliper

PARKING BRAKE CABLE 2A635

PARKING BRAKE LEVER

88189G44

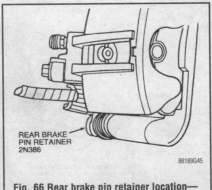

Fig. 66 Rear brake pin retainer location— 1995 vehicle shown

REAR BRAKE PIN RETAINER 2N386

88189G45

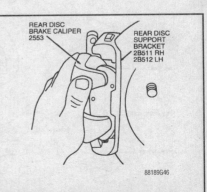

Fig. 67 Position the caliper on the anchor plate/support bracket

REAR DISC BRAKE CALIPER 2553

REAR DISC SUPPORT BRACKET 2B511 RH 2B512 LH

88189G46

3. Remove the two bolts that attach the anchor plate to the rear knuckle. Remove the anchor plate and brake pads.

4. If equipped, unfasten the two retainer nuts, then and remove the rotor from the hub.

➡ **Inspect the disc for excessive rust, scoring or pitting. A certain amount of rust on the edge of the disc is normal. Refer to the specifications chart and measure the thickness of the disc, using a micrometer. If the disc is below specifications, replace it. Clean the new rotor with a degreaser.**

To install:

5. Install the rotor on the axle shaft flange, and install the retaining nuts securely.

6. Clean the anchor plate and attaching bolt threads. Add one drop of a thread-lock sealer to each bolt and attach the anchor assembly to the knuckle. Tighten the bolts to 80–100 ft. lbs. (105–135 Nm) on cars through 1988 or to 45–65 ft. lbs. (61–88 Nm) on 1989–97 cars.

7. Install the caliper assembly.

8. Install the tire and wheel assembly, and lower vehicle.

PARKING BRAKE

Cables

REMOVAL & INSTALLATION

1983–88 Vehicles—Except Thunderbird Turbo Coupes

♦ **See Figures 68 and 69**

FRONT CABLE

1. Raise and safely support the rear end of the vehicle on jackstands.
2. Remove the adjusting nut at the equalizer and remove the equalizer from the cable.
3. Unfasten the clip that holds the cable to the frame or body bracket.
4. Remove the clip that retains the cable to the parking brake control, inside the car.
5. Disconnect the cable from the control assembly.

➡ **Some cars have cables with snap-in fittings. On these cables, compress the tangs, with a 13mm 12-point socket, and remove them from the mounting surface.**

6. Pull the cable up through the opening in the dash panel.
7. Installation is the reverse of removal. Adjust the parking brake, as outlined later in this section.

INTERMEDIATE CABLE

1. Raise and safely support the rear end of the vehicle on jackstands.
2. Remove the cable adjusting nut.
3. Disconnect the intermediate cable ends from the left rear and the transverse cables.

➡ **Some cars have cables with snap-in fittings. On these cables, compress the tangs, with a 13mm 12-point socket, and remove them from the mounting surface.**

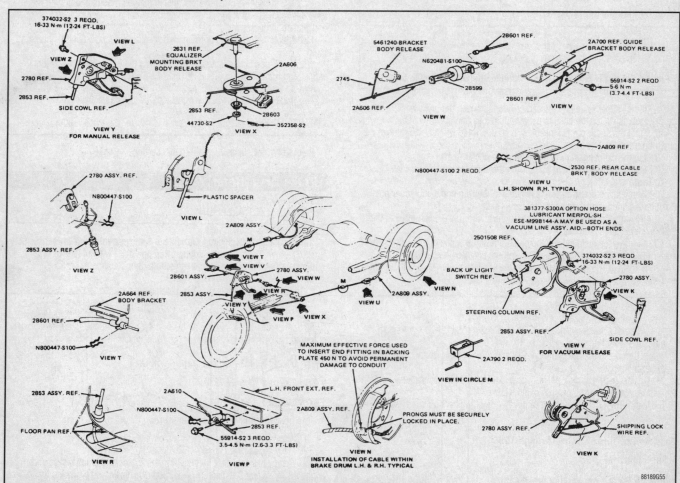

Fig. 68 Parking brake system components used on the 1983–85 Thunderbird, XR-7 and Cougars

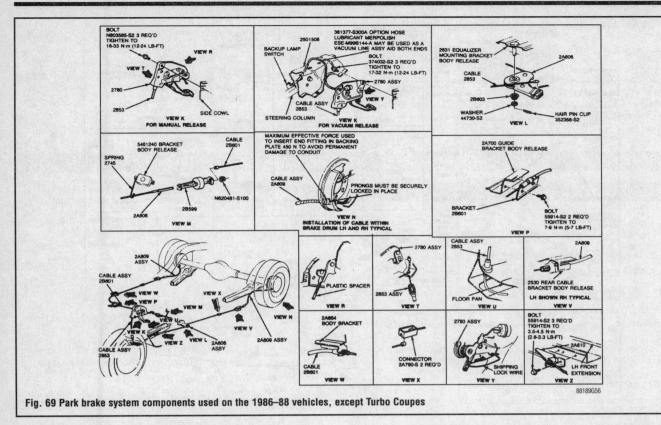

Fig. 69 Park brake system components used on the 1986–88 vehicles, except Turbo Coupes

4. Remove the cotter pin, washer and spring from the pin protruding from the equalizer assembly, and remove the lever.

➡**The intermediate cable cannot be separated from the lever.**

5. Installation is the reverse of removal. Adjust the parking brake, as outlined later in this section.

TRANSVERSE CABLE

1. Raise and safely support the rear end of the vehicle on jackstands.
2. Remove the adjusting nut.
3. Remove the transverse cable ends from the right rear and intermediate cables.
4. Remove the hairpin clips or conduit brackets and remove the cable.
5. Installation is the reverse of the removal procedure. Adjust the parking brake, as outlined later in this section.

REAR CABLES

1. Raise and safely support the rear end on of the vehicle jackstands.
2. Remove the equalizer adjusting nut and remove the equalizer.
3. Disconnect the rear cables from the right and left rear cable connectors.
4. Remove the cable from the retainer hooks.
5. Remove the hairpin clip retaining the cable housing to the side rail bracket.
6. On cars with rear drum brakes:
   a. Remove the brake drums.
   b. Remove the brake shoes and disconnect the cable end from the self-adjusting lever.
   c. Compress the pronged retainers and remove the cable assembly from the backing plate.
7. On cars with rear disc brakes, remove the clevis pin securing the cable to the caliper actuating arm, then remove the cable.
8. Installation is the reverse of removal. Adjust the parking brake, as outlined later in this section.

Thunderbird Turbo Coupe Through 1988

◆ **See Figure 70**

FRONT CABLE

1. Raise and safely support the rear end of the vehicle on jackstands.

2. Remove the adjusting nut at the equalizer and remove the equalizer from the cable.
3. Remove the clip that holds the cable to the frame or body bracket.
4. Remove the clip that retains the cable to the parking brake control, inside the car.
5. Disconnect the cable from the control assembly.

➡**Some cars have cables with snap-in fittings. On these cables, compress the tangs and remove them from the mounting surface.**

6. Pull the cable up through the opening in the dash panel.
7. Installation is the reverse of removal. Adjust the parking brake, as outlined later in this section.

REAR CABLES

1. Raise and safely support the rear end of the vehicle on jackstands.
2. Remove the adjuster nut.
3. Disconnect the parking brake release spring from the right cable at the equalizer.
4. Detach the right cable from the adjuster and the side rail bracket.
5. Remove all cable retaining brackets.
6. Disconnect the left cable from the equalizer and body side rail bracket.
7. Remove the clips retaining the cables to the calipers and remove the cable ends from the parking brake lever arm.
8. Installation is the reverse of removal. Note that the locating sleeve on the outboard side of the right cable must be tightened first!

1989–97 Vehicles—Except Super Coupe

◆ **See Figures 71 and 72**

FRONT CABLE

➡**This procedure requires two people.**

1. Raise and safely support vehicle on jackstands.
2. Fully release the parking brake.
3. Removal of the cable tension requires two people to disengage and reload the tensioner. One person is to unlock the tensioner by rotating the locking lever away from the threaded rod. While holding the tensioner unlocked, the sec-

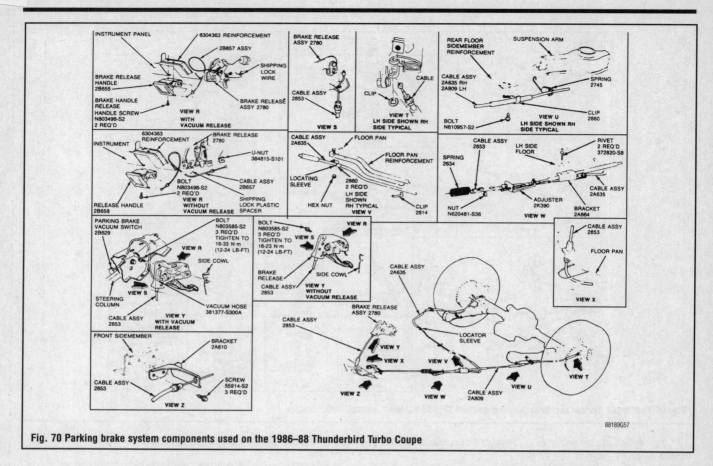

Fig. 70 Parking brake system components used on the 1986–88 Thunderbird Turbo Coupe

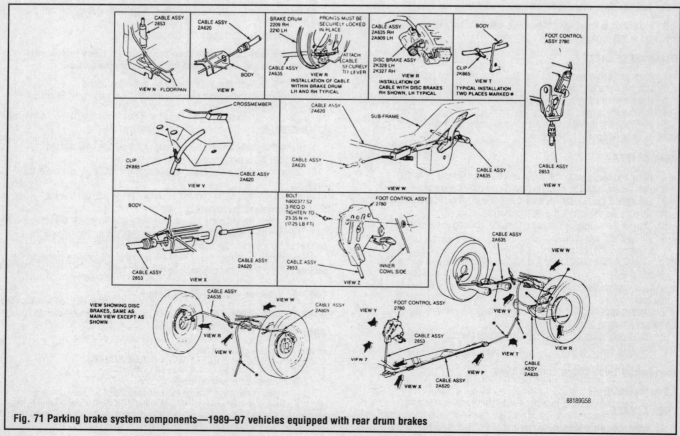

Fig. 71 Parking brake system components—1989–97 vehicles equipped with rear drum brakes

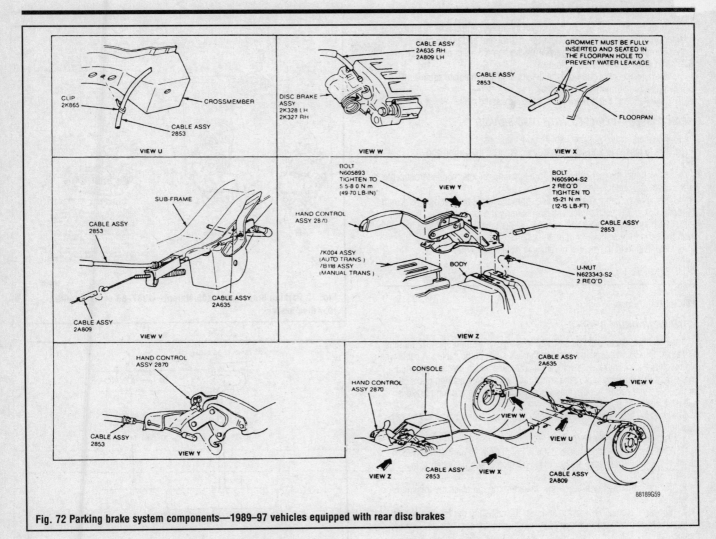

Fig. 72 Parking brake system components—1989–97 vehicles equipped with rear disc brakes

ond person is to apply the parking brake control fully to the last notch position. The tensioner spring will compress allowing cable slack to return. Next release the locking lever to lock the tensioner. Ensure that locking lever is secure by rotating it toward threaded rod. Wrap tape or wire around the locking lever and threaded rod, to prevent any accidental release. Release the brake control.

4. Disconnect the front cable from intermediate cable at the cable connector.
5. Remove the cable snap-in retainer from the cable bracket using a 13mm 12 point box end wrench to depress retaining prongs. Allow the cable to hang.
6. Lower the vehicle.
7. Remove the left side cowl trim panel.
8. Disconnect the cable from control assembly at clevis.
9. Remove the cable snap-in retainer from control assembly by depressing the retaining prongs with a 13mm wrench.
10. Pull the cable up through the floor pan.
11. Installation is reverse of removal. Adjust the cable, as outlined later in this section.

Super Coupe

FRONT CABLE

1. Loosen adjusting nut at the adjuster assembly.
2. Remove the floor console.
3. With hand control assembly in the released position, remove the slotted cable end from control assembly hook. Remove pronged cable retainer from the control assembly using a 13mm 12-point box end wrench.
4. Disconnect front cable from the right rear cable at the cable connector.
5. Remove the cable routing clip from body rear crossmember by squeezing the clip together with a pair of needle nose pliers, between the cable and crossmember. Allow the cable to hang.

6. Carefully lower the vehicle.
7. Remove the rear seat and console.
8. Disconnect cable from the control at clevis hook.
9. Remove the cable snap-in retainer from the hand control assembly by depressing the retaining prongs with a 13mm wrench.
10. Pull the cable and grommet up through the floor pan and out from under the carpet.
11. Installation is reverse of removal. Adjust the cable.

All Models, Except Super Coupe

INTERMEDIATE CABLE

1. Remove cable tension as outlined previously.
2. Disconnect intermediate cable from the right rear cable and the front cable at cable connector.
3. Remove the cable snap-in retainer from the tensioner housing and body bracket by using a 13mm 12-point box end wrench to depress retaining prongs.
4. Remove cable routing clips for the body side rails and rear crossmember by squeezing clip together with a pair of needle nose pliers between the cable and crossmembers, and remove the cable.
5. Installation is the reverse of removal. Adjust the cable.

REAR CABLES—VEHICLES WITH DRUM BRAKES

1. Remove the cable tension as described previously.
2. Remove the rear wheel and drum assembly.
3. Disconnect the brake cable end from the parking brake actuating lever. Using a 13mm 12-point box end wrench, depress the conduit retaining prongs and remove the cable end pronged fitting from the backing plate.

4. Remove the cable routing clips from the lower control arm by squeezing retainer prongs with pliers from under the control arm and pushing up.

5. Remove cable snap-in retainer from the frame bracket using a 13mm wrench to depress the retaining prongs.

6. Disconnect cable end from the tensioner or intermediate cable at the cable connector and remove rear cable.

7. Installation is the reverse of removal. Adjust the cable.

REAR CABLES—VEHICLES WITH DISC BRAKES

1. Raise and safely support vehicle on jackstands.

2. Grasp tensioner and pull forward to compress the spring and lock.

3. Disconnect the rear cable end from tensioner or intermediate/front cable at the cable connector.

4. Remove the cable snap-in retainer from the frame bracket using a 13mm 12-point box end wrench to depress the retaining prongs.

5. Disconnect rear cable end from the caliper housing and remove the cable from the parking brake lever arm on the caliper.

6. Installation is the reverse of removal. Adjust the cable.

ADJUSTMENT

1983–88 Vehicles

WITH REAR DRUM BRAKES

The parking brake should be adjusted for proper operation every 12 months or 12,000 miles and adjusted whenever there is slack in the cables. A cable with too much slack will not hold a vehicle on an incline which presents a serious safety hazard. Usually, a rear brake adjustment will restore parking brake efficiency, but if the cables appear loose or stretched when the parking brake is released, adjust as necessary.

The procedure for adjusting the parking brake on all pedal actuated systems is as follows:

1. Fully release the parking brake.

2. Depress the parking brake pedal one notch from its normal released position. On vacuum release brakes, the first notch is approximately 2 in. (51mm) of travel.

3. Taking proper safety precautions, raise the car and place the transmission in Neutral.

4. Loosen the equalizer locknut and turn the adjusting nut forward against the equalizer until moderate drag is felt when turning the rear wheels. Tighten the locknut.

5. Release the parking brake, making sure that the brake shoes return to the fully released position.

6. Lower the car and apply the parking brake. Under normal conditions, the third notch will hold the car if the brake is adjusted properly.

WITH REAR DISC BRAKES

◆ See Figure 73

Adjust the parking brake as shown in the accompanying figure.

1989–90 Vehicles

1. Apply the parking brake control fully on. Release the parking brake control. Repeat the application and release.

2. Place the transmission in **N**. Raise and safely support the vehicle by the axles.

3. With the parking brake control in the **OFF** position, release the tensioner by rotating the locking lever away from the threaded rod.

4. The tensioner spring will take up the cable slack and preload the cables.

5. Do not pull down on the locking lever for it will pull the cables down and cause the cables to have low tension.

➡ Lock the tensioner by releasing the locking lever. Make sure the locking lever is secure by rotating it toward the threaded rod.

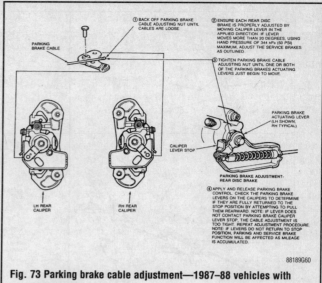

Fig. 73 Parking brake cable adjustment—1987–88 vehicles with rear disc brakes

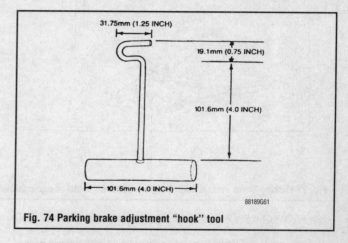

Fig. 74 Parking brake adjustment "hook" tool

6. Examine the tensioner for remaining cable take up capability. If none is present, check all cables, parking brake control and brackets for possible damage or deflection.

1991–97 Vehicles

◆ See Figure 74

1. Apply the parking brake control fully on. Release the parking brake control. Repeat the application and release.

2. Place the transmission in **N**. Raise and safely support the vehicle by the axles.

3. With the parking brake control in the **OFF** position, grasp the tensioner around the housing, then, using a hook tool, hook the end into the rounded end of the clip between the clip and the housing.

4. Unlock the clip by pulling downward with the tool and support tensioner; the tensioner spring will take up cable slack and preload the cables.

5. While holding the tensioner, lock the clip by pushing up on the bottom of the clip. If the clip does not slide up, move the assembly slightly to align the closest groove on the adjuster rod to the clip.

6. Examine the tensioner for remaining cable take up capability. If none is present, check all cables, parking brake control and brackets for possible damage or deflection.

TEVES MARK II 4-WHEEL ANTI-LOCK BRAKE SYSTEM (ABS)

General Information

▶ See Figure 75

The Teves Mark II 4 Wheel Anti-Lock Brake (ABS) system is a compact integral power brake system that uses brake fluid for both brake function and hydraulic boost. The system is used on 1987–88 Thunderbird Turbo Coupe and 1989–92 Thunderbird Super Coupe and Cougar XR-7 models.

The hydraulic pump maintains between 2,030 to 2,610 psi (13,997–17,996 kpa) pressure in the accumulator which is connected by a high pressure hose to the booster chamber and control valve. When the brakes are applied, a scissor/lever mechanism activates the control valve and pressure, proportional to brake pedal travel, enters the booster chamber. The pressure is transmitted through the normally open solenoid valve through the proportioning valve to the rear brakes. The same pressure moves the booster piston against the master cylinder piston, shutting off the central valves in the master cylinder. This applies pressure to the front wheels through the two normally open solenoid valves. The electronic controller monitors the electro-mechanical components of the system. Malfunction of the anti-lock system will cause the electronic controller to shut off or inhibit the anti-lock system. Normal power assisted braking remains if the anti-lock system shuts off. Malfunctions are indicated by one or two warning lamps inside the vehicle.

The 4-wheel anti-lock system is self-monitoring. When the ignition switch is placed in the Run position, the electronic controller will preform a preliminary self check on the anti-lock electrical system as indicated by a three to four second illumination of the amber Check Anti-Lock Brakes lamp in the overhead console. During vehicle operation, including normal and anti-lock braking operation is continually monitored. Should a problem occur, either the Check Anti-Lock Brakes or the Brake Warning Lamp(s) will be illuminated. The sequence of illumination of these warning lamps, combined with the problem symptoms, can determine the appropriate diagnostic tests to perform. However most malfunctions are stored as a coded number in the controller memory and pinpoint to the exact component needing servicing. Inspection of the system and any necessary repairs should be done before any further vehicle operation.

Individual front wheel brake circuits and a combined rear wheel brake circuit are used. Major components of the system are listed and outlined as follows.

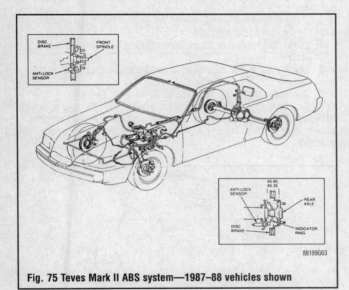

Fig. 75 Teves Mark II ABS system—1987–88 vehicles shown

88189G63

Master Cylinder-Booster Unit/Actuation Assembly

REMOVAL & INSTALLATION

1987–88 Vehicles

▶ See Figure 76

❉❉ **WARNING**

The Anti-lock Brake System must be depressurized before any service is performed. To depressurize the system, turn the ignition OFF and pump the brake pedal at least 20 times, until an obvious increase in pedal pressure is felt.

1. Disconnect the negative battery cable.
2. Tag and detach the electrical connectors from the fluid reservoir cap, main valve, solenoid valve body, pressure warning switch, hydraulic pump motor and the ground connector from the master cylinder.
3. Disconnect and plug the brake lines from the solenoid valve body.

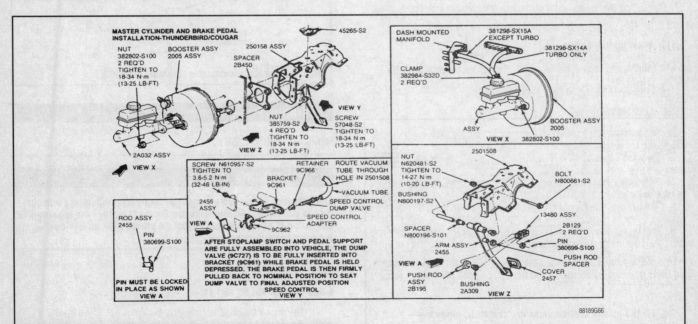

Fig. 76 Actuator assembly (master cylinder) removal—1987–88 vehicles

88189G66

4. Disconnect the booster pushrod from the brake pedal by first disconnecting the spotlight switch wires at the connector on the brake pedal. Then, remove the hairpin connector at the stoplight switch and slide the switch off the pedal pin until the large end of the switch (outer hole) is off of the pin. Remove the switch using a twisting motion. Remove the unit's four retaining nuts at the firewall.

5. Remove the booster from the engine compartment.

6. Installation is the reverse of the removal procedure. Tighten the retaining nuts to 13–25 ft. lbs. (18–34 Nm).

7. Bleed the brake system using the proper procedure located later in this section.

1989–92 Vehicles

♦ See Figure 77

✳✳ WARNING

The Anti-lock Brake System must be depressurized before any service is performed. To depressurize the system, turn the ignition OFF and pump the brake pedal at least 20 times, until an obvious increase in pedal pressure is felt.

1. Disconnect the battery ground cable.
2. Remove the air cleaner and ductwork.
3. Tag and unplug the electrical connectors at the following components:
   • fluid level indicator
   • main valve
   • solenoid valve block
   • pressure warning switch
   • hydraulic pump motor
   • master cylinder ground
4. Disconnect the 3 brake pipes and immediately plug the openings to prevent fluid loss and contamination.

✳✳ WARNING

Do not allow brake fluid to come in contact with any electrical connection!

5. Remove the steering column trim panel.
6. Disconnect the actuation assembly pushrod from the pedal.
7. Remove the 4 attaching nuts holding the actuation assembly to the pedal support bracket and lift out the assembly.

To install:

8. If a new unit is being installed, transfer the attached parts.
9. Position the new assembly on the mounting bracket and loosely thread on the 4 nuts.
10. Connect the pushrod.
11. Install the trim panel.
12. Tighten the nuts to 13–25 ft. lbs. (18–34 Nm).
13. Unplug and connect the fluid pipes. Tighten the connections to 10–18 ft. lbs. (14–24 Nm).
14. Connect all wiring, as tagged during removal.

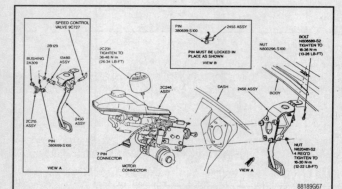

Fig. 77 ABS master cylinder (actuator assembly) mounting— 1989–92 vehicles

15. Install the air cleaner and ductwork.
16. Connect the negative battery cable.
17. Bleed the ABS system, as outlined later in this section.

Hydraulic Accumulator

REMOVAL & INSTALLATION

♦ See Figure 78

✳✳ WARNING

The Anti-lock Brake System must be depressurized before any service is performed. To depressurize the system, turn the ignition OFF and pump the brake pedal at least 20 times, until an obvious increase in pedal pressure is felt.

1. Disconnect the negative battery cable.
2. On 1987–88 models, detach the electrical connector at the hydraulic pump motor.
3. Using an 8mm hex wrench, loosen and unscrew the accumulator. Do not allow any dirt to enter the open port.
4. Loosen and remove the accumulator mounting block, if necessary.

To install:

5. Install in the reverse order using a new O-ring seal coated with clean brake fluid.
6. Tighten the accumulator assembly to 30–34 ft. lbs. (41–46 Nm).
7. Turn the ignition switch to the **ON** position for 1987–88 vehicles, or the **RUN** position for 1989–92 vehicles. Check that the BRAKE warning indicator and Anti-Lock lamps go out after a maximum of one minute. Fill the reservoir as necessary.

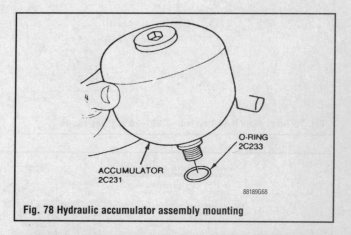

Fig. 78 Hydraulic accumulator assembly mounting

Hydraulic Pump Motor

REMOVAL & INSTALLATION

✳✳ WARNING

The Anti-lock Brake System must be depressurized before any service is performed. To depressurize the system, turn the ignition OFF and pump the brake pedal at least 20 times, until an obvious increase in pedal pressure is felt.

1987–88 Vehicles

♦ See Figures 79, 80 and 81

1. Disconnect the negative battery cable.
2. Detach the electrical connections at the hydraulic pump motor, reservoir cap, and pressure warning switch.

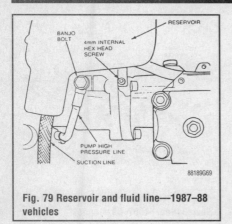

Fig. 79 Reservoir and fluid line—1987–88 vehicles

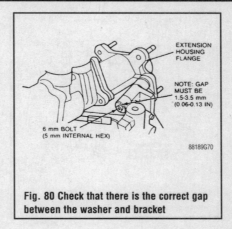

Fig. 80 Check that there is the correct gap between the washer and bracket

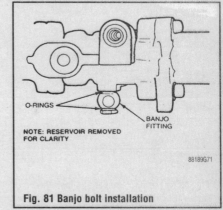

Fig. 81 Banjo bolt installation

3. Using a clean turkey baster or equivalent, drain as much fluid as possible from the reservoir.

4. Remove the suction line between the reservoir and the pump at the reservoir by twisting the hose and pulling.

5. Remove the return line from between the reservoir and master cylinder in the same manner.

6. Unfasten the 4mm hex headed reservoir mounting bolt.

7. Remove the reservoir by gently prying it off with a small prybar.

8. Remove the banjo bolt connecting the high pressure hose to the booster housing, at the housing. Be sure to catch and save the 2 sealing O-rings, one on each side of the banjo bolt head.

9. Using an 8mm allen wrench, remove the accumulator. Make certain no debris falls in the hole!

10. Remove the 6mm allen headed bolt attaching the pump and motor assembly to the extension housing which is located directly under the accumulator. A long extension and universal swivel socket will help reach the bolt.

11. Move the pump assembly toward the engine and remove the retainer pin on the inboard side of the extension housing. Remove the pump and motor assembly.

To install:

12. Position the pump and motor in place and install the bolt and spacer. Tighten the bolt to 60–84 inch lbs. (6.7–9.4 Nm).

➡There must be a gap of 1.5–3.5mm behind the washer on the bolt. If there is no gap, the pump will make a loud noise during operation.

13. Install the high pressure line, bolt and O-rings. Tighten the bolt to 12–15 ft. lbs. (16–20 Nm).

14. Install the reservoir mounting bracket, spacer and O-rings. Wet the grommets with clean brake fluid and push the reservoir into place as far as it will go. The reservoir should be held vertically in respect to the actuation assembly while pushing it into place.

15. Secure the mounting bracket to the booster with the allen screw. Tighten to 35–53 inch lbs. (3.9–5.9 Nm).

16. Connect the return and feed hoses.

17. Fill the reservoir with clean DOT 3 fluid from a fresh container.

18. Wet the O-ring with clean brake fluid and install the accumulator. Tighten it to 30–34 ft. lbs. (41–46 Nm).

19. Attach all the electrical connectors and the negative battery cable.

20. Bleed the ABS system, as outlined later in this section, and check that the brake warning lamps go out after a maximum of one minute.

21. Top off the fluid level.

1989–92 Vehicles

▶ See Figure 82

1. Disconnect the negative battery cable.

2. Using a clean turkey baster or equivalent, drain as much fluid as possible from the reservoir.

3. Remove the suction line between the reservoir and the pump at the reservoir by twisting the hose and pulling.

4. Using an 8mm allen wrench, remove the accumulator. Make certain no debris falls in the hole!

5. Loosen the pipe fitting connecting the high pressure hose to the pump

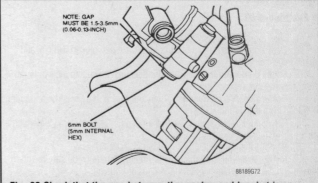

Fig. 82 Check that the gap between the washer and bracket is correct

housing. Take care to avoid bending the pipe! Disconnect the low pressure line from between the reservoir and suction port.

6. Disconnect the electrical connector from the pump motor and warning switch.

7. Remove the 6mm allen headed bolt attaching the pump and motor assembly to the actuation unit. Slide the pump and motor to the left to clear the retainer and pin and remove it.

To install:

8. Position the pump and motor in place and install the bolt and spacer. Tighten the bolt to 60–84 inch lbs. (7–9 Nm).

➡There must be a gap of 1.5–3.5mm behind the washer on the bolt. If there is no gap, the pump will make a loud noise during operation. See the accompanying figure.

9. Tighten the high pressure line fitting to 9–12 ft. lbs. (12–16 Nm).

10. Install the low pressure line.

11. Wet the O-ring with clean brake fluid and install the accumulator. Tighten it to 30–34 ft. lbs. (41–46 Nm).

12. Connect all electrical lines, bleed the system and check that the brake warning lamps go out after a maximum of one minute.

13. Top off the fluid level.

Reservoir Assembly

REMOVAL & INSTALLATION

☀☀ WARNING

The Anti-lock Brake System must be depressurized before any service is performed. To depressurize the system, turn the ignition OFF and pump the brake pedal at least 20 times, until an obvious increase in pedal pressure is felt.

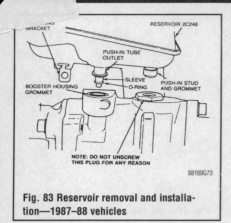

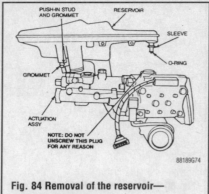

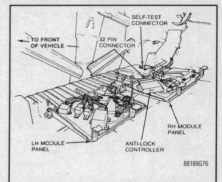

Fig. 83 Reservoir removal and installation—1987–88 vehicles

Fig. 84 Removal of the reservoir—1989–92 vehicles

Fig. 85 Electronic controller removal and installation—1987–88 vehicles

1987–88 Vehicles

♦ See Figure 83

1. Disconnect the negative battery cable.
2. Detach the electrical connectors from the reservoir cap. Unlock and remove the cap.
3. Empty the reservoir of as much fluid as possible using a clean large rubber syringe or suction gun.
4. Remove the line between the pump and reservoir by twisting and pulling the hose from the reservoir fitting.
5. Remove the return line between the reservoir and master cylinder at the reservoir in the same manner as Step 4.
6. Remove the 4mm allen head reservoir mounting screw.
7. Pry the reservoir from the booster housing carefully. Be sure the short sleeve and O-ring are removed from the booster housing.

To install:

8. Install the reservoir mounting bracket in its guide on the bottom of the reservoir. Check to be sure that the short sleeve and O-ring are in position at the bottom of the reservoir. Wet the mounting grommet with brake fluid.
9. Insert the reservoir into the grommets on the booster housing, as far as it will go. Make sure the short sleeve and O-ring are in place. The reservoir should be held vertically during installation.
10. The rest of the installation is in the reverse order of removal.
11. Fill the reservoir to the correct level with a charged accumulator. Bleed the system, as outlined later in this section.

1989–92 Vehicles

♦ See Figure 84

1. Disconnect the negative battery cable.
2. Remove the electrical connectors from the fluid level indicator.
3. Empty the reservoir of as much fluid as possible using a large rubber syringe or suction gun.
4. Remove the line between the pump and reservoir, from the reservoir by twisting and pulling the hose from the reservoir fitting.
5. Remove the 2 roll pins retaining the reservoir to the master cylinder.
6. Using a small prybar, gently pry the reservoir from the master cylinder.

To install:

7. Lubricate the O-rings, grommets and seals with clean brake fluid.
8. Align the reservoir with the 3 mounting holes and push it firmly into place as far as it will go. Install the roll pins.
9. Connect the hose, wire and battery ground.
10. Fill the reservoir and bleed the system.

Electronic Controller

REMOVAL & INSTALLATION

♦ See Figures 85 and 86

The controller is located in the luggage compartment in front of the forward trim panel.

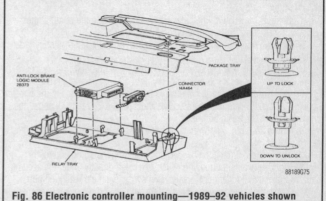

Fig. 86 Electronic controller mounting—1989–92 vehicles shown

1. Disconnect the negative battery cable.
2. Detach the 32 pin connector from the controller.
3. Remove the three retaining screws holding the controller to the seat back brace and remove the controller. For 1989–92 models, pull the two plastic tabs to remove controller.

To install:

4. Position the controller, then secure with the retaining screws or tabs, as applicable.
5. Attach the 32-pin connector to the controller.
6. Connect the negative battery cable.

Pressure Switch

REMOVAL & INSTALLATION

♦ See Figures 87 and 88

✳✳ WARNING

The Anti-lock Brake System must be depressurized before any service is performed. To depressurize the system, turn the ignition OFF and pump the brake pedal at least 20 times, until an obvious increase in pedal pressure is felt.

1. Disconnect the negative battery cable.
2. Detach the valve body electrical connector. Failure to disconnect the connector can result in damage to the connector if struck by removal tool.

➡ **On 1989–92 vehicles, the switch can best be accessed from underneath.**

3. Remove the pressure switch with special socket T85P-20215-B or equivalent.

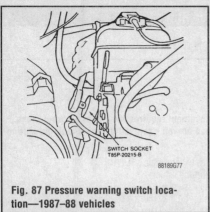

Fig. 87 Pressure warning switch location—1987–88 vehicles

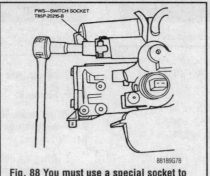

Fig. 88 You must use a special socket to remove the pressure switch—1989–92 vehicles

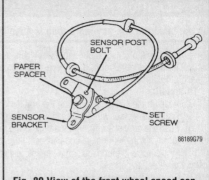

Fig. 89 View of the front wheel speed sensor—1987–88 vehicles

➡️If a new pressure switch is installed, the pump motor relay must be replaced.

4. Inspect the mounting O-ring and replace if necessary. Install the switch in the reverse order of removal. Tighten to 15–25 ft. lbs. (20–34 Nm).

Wheel Speed Sensors

REMOVAL & INSTALLATION

Front Sensor

1987–88 VEHICLES

♦ See Figure 89

1. Disconnect the negative battery cable.
2. Detach the harness connector on the inside of the engine compartment for either the right or left sensor.
3. Raise and safely support the front end on jackstands.
4. Remove the wheel and tire assembly.
5. Remove the caliper and disc rotor assemblies, as outlined in this section.
6. Disengage the wire grommet at the shock tower and draw the sensor cable carefully through the grommet mounting hole. Remove the harness from the mounting brackets.
7. Loosen the 5mm set screw that holds the sensor to the mounting bracket. Remove the sensor through the hole in the disc brake splash shield.
   To install:
8. Clean the sensor face, if reusing the original sensor. Install in the reverse order of removal.
9. Place a new 1.3mm thick paper spacer on the sensor mounting flange before installation.
10. Tighten the post retaining bolt and splash shield bolts to 10–15 ft. lbs. (14–20 Nm). The steel sleeve around the post bolt must be rotated to provide a new, clean surface for the setscrew to indent.
11. Tighten the sensor retaining bolt to 21-26 inch lbs. (2.3–2.9 Nm).
12. Connect the negative battery cable.

1989–92 VEHICLES

♦ See Figure 90

1. Disconnect the negative battery cable.
2. Raise and safely support the front end on jackstands.
3. Detach the sensor connector for either the right or left sensor, located near the radiator support
4. Remove the wiring harness routing clips.
5. Unbolt and remove the sensor from the spindle. If the toothed speed indicator ring appears damaged, replace it.
   To install:
6. Position the sensor on the spindle and torque the bolt to 40-60 inch lbs. (4.5–6.7 Nm).
7. Route the wires using the clips, then attach the connectors.

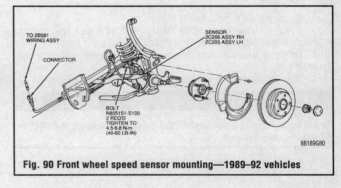

Fig. 90 Front wheel speed sensor mounting—1989–92 vehicles

8. Carefully lower the vehicle.
9. Connect the negative battery cable.

Rear Sensor

1987–88 VEHICLES

♦ See Figure 91

1. Disconnect the negative battery cable.
2. Detach the sensor connector for the side requiring service. The connector is located on the inside of the luggage compartment behind the forward trim panel.
3. Lift the carpet and push the sensor wire mounting grommet through the mounting hole.
4. Raise and support the rear of the vehicle. Remove the wheel from the side on which you are working.
5. Remove the wire harness from the retaining brackets and C-clip. Pull rearward on the clip to disengage.

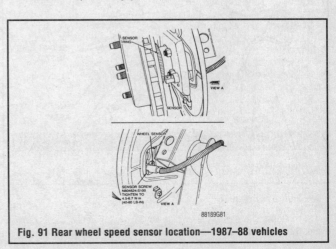

Fig. 91 Rear wheel speed sensor location—1987–88 vehicles

✷✷ CAUTION

Do not bend the clip any more than is absolutely necessary!

6. Remove the sensor mounting bolt. At this point, inspect the sensor bracket for damage, and replace it if necessary. Inspect the toothed ring and replace it if it appears damaged.

To install:

7. Position the sensor and tighten the bolt to 40-60 inch lbs. (4.5–6.7 Nm).

8. Install the sensor wire in the retainers along the axle housing.

9. Push the connector through the hole in the luggage compartment and seat the grommet in the luggage compartment floorpan.

10. From inside the luggage compartment, attach the wiring connector. Install the carpet as necessary.

11. Connect the negative battery cable and check system operation.

1989–92 VEHICLES

▶ **See Figure 92**

1. Disconnect the negative battery cable.

2. Detach the sensor connector for the side requiring service. The connector is located on the inside of the luggage compartment rearward of the wheelwell.

3. Lift the carpet and push the sensor wire mounting grommet through the mounting hole.

4. Raise and safely support the rear of the vehicle.

✷✷ WARNING

Do not bend the clip open beyond the amount necessary to remove it from the axle housing.

5. Remove the wire harness from the plastic clip.

6. Remove the mounting bolt and sensor.

To install:

7. Align the sensor locating tab and bolt hole with the axle housing and push into position.

8. Position the sensor on the axle, pushing the mounting tab into place. Tighten the bolt to 14–20 ft. lbs. (19–27 Nm).

9. Install the plastic clip retaining the sensor wire to the axle carrier housing and push the connector through the hole in floor into the luggage compartment. Make sure the rubber grommet is proper seated in the hole in the floor.

10. Carefully lower the vehicle.

11. Install and connect the wiring.

12. Connect the negative battery cable, then check the system for proper operation.

Front Wheel Sensor Ring

REMOVAL & INSTALLATION

1987–88 Vehicles

▶ **See Figure 93**

➡ **Toothed sensor ring replacement requires the use of an arbor press. An automotive machine shop or well equipped garage should be able to handle the job.**

1. Disconnect the negative battery cable.

2. Raise and safely support the vehicle.

3. Remove the brake rotor assembly.

4. Position the rotor face up on the arbor press bed.

5. Using the proper adapters, press each stud down just until they contact the sensor ring.

6. Position an adapter, T85P-20202-A, or equivalent, on the top of all of the studs and press the studs and sensor ring from the rotor.

To install:

7. Install the studs into the rotor, one at a time, using the press.

8. Using the adapter, install the sensor ring with the press until the ring bottoms in position. MAKE SURE IT IS STRAIGHT!

9. Install the rotor.

10. Carefully lower the vehicle, then connect the negative battery cable.

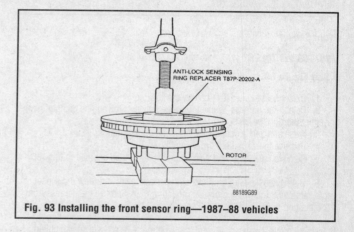

Fig. 93 Installing the front sensor ring—1987–88 vehicles

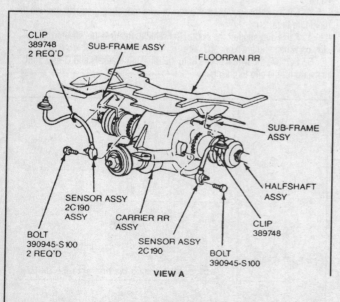

Fig. 92 Rear wheel speed sensor location—1989–92 vehicles

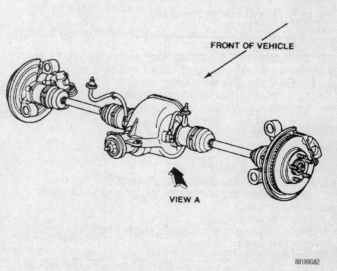

1989–92 Vehicles

1. Raise and safely support the vehicle.
2. Remove the tire and wheel assembly.
3. Remove the brake caliper, rotor and hub assemblies.
4. Using a suitable 3-jawed puller, remove the sensor ring from the hub.

To install:

5. Support the center of the hub so the wheel studs do not rest on the work surface.
6. Position the hub on an arbor press bed, and using a flat plate, press the ring on the hub. MAKE SURE IT IS STRAIGHT!
7. Install the hub, rotor and caliper.
8. Install the wheel and tire assembly, then carefully lower the vehicle.

Rear Wheel Sensor Ring

REMOVAL & INSTALLATION

1987–88 Vehicles

▶ **See Figures 94 and 95**

1. Raise and safely support the vehicle.
2. Remove the rear axle shaft, as outlined in Section 7.
3. Install a bearing cone remover adapter, such as T71P-4621-B, or equivalent, between the axle shaft flange and sensor ring.
4. Position the axle in an arbor press and remove the sensor ring.

To install:

5. Press the sensor ring into position until a gap of 65.35–85mm between the sensor ring and face of the axle flange is obtained.
6. Reinstall the axle shaft and removed components.

1989–92 Vehicles

▶ **See Figures 96, 97, 98 and 99**

1. Raise and safely support vehicle on jackstands.
2. Remove the axle halfshaft. Remove the CV-joint assembly from the shaft. See Section 7 for details.
3. Position a 2-jaw puller on the CV-joint inner stub shaft, with the puller jaws under sensor ring. Turn wrench until the ring pulls off.

➥ **Brake sensor rings must not be reused. Discard ring after removal and replace with a new one.**

To install:

4. Position sensor ring installer T89P-20202-A, or equivalent, on an arbor press bed, with the pilot up.
5. Place the new sensor ring on the installer.
6. Position the CV-joint stub shaft through the sensor ring and allow the joint to rest on the sensor ring.
7. Bottom the press ram in the CV-joint race and press the ring on until it contacts the CV-joint step.

Bleeding The ABS System

✳✳ **CAUTION**

The 4-Wheel Anti-Lock brake system is under high accumulator hydraulic pressure most of the time. Before servicing any component which contains high pressure, it is mandatory that the high pressure in the system be discharged.

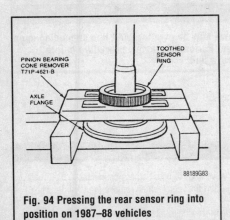

Fig. 94 Pressing the rear sensor ring into position on 1987–88 vehicles

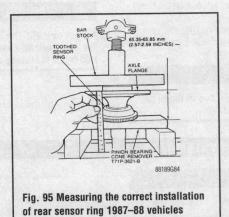

Fig. 95 Measuring the correct installation of rear sensor ring 1987–88 vehicles

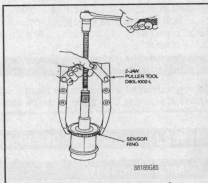

Fig. 96 Removing the rear sensor ring from the CV-joint—1989–92 vehicles

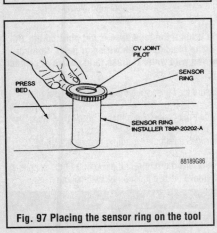

Fig. 97 Placing the sensor ring on the tool

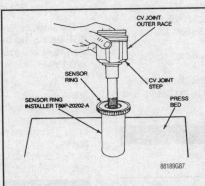

Fig. 98 Positioning the CV-joint through the ring and into the tool

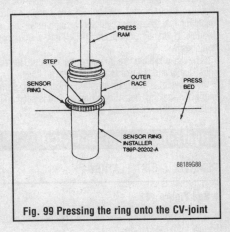

Fig. 99 Pressing the ring onto the CV-joint

SYSTEM DISCHARGING (DEPRESSURIZING)

Turn the ignition to the **OFF** position. Pump the brake pedal a minimum of 20 times until an increase in pedal force is clearly felt.

FRONT BRAKE BLEEDING

The front brakes can be bled in the conventional manner, with or without the accumulator being charged. Refer to the previous brake bleeding section at the beginning of this Section for instructions.

REAR BRAKE BLEEDING

A fully charged accumulator is required for successful rear brake system bleeding. Once accumulator pressure is applied to the system, the rear brakes can be bled by opening the rear caliper bleeder screw while holding the brake pedal in the applied position with the ignition switch in the Run position. Repeat the procedure until an air-free flow of brake fluid comes from the bleeder screw. Close the bleeder screw. Add fluid to the master cylinder reservoir until required level is reached.

**** CAUTION**

Care must be used when opening the bleeder screws. The fluid is under high pressure and could cause injury if splashed into eyes, etc.

BLEEDING THE SYSTEM WITH A FULLY CHARGED ACCUMULATOR

1. Remove the dust cap from the right side rear caliper bleeder fitting. Attach a rubber drain tube to the fitting making sure the end of the tube fits snugly around the fitting.
2. Turn the ignition switch to the **RUN** position. This will turn on the electric pump to charge the accumulator as required.
3. Hold the brake pedal in the applied position. Open the right side rear caliper bleeder fitting for 10 seconds at a time until an air-free stream of brake fluid is observed.

**** WARNING**

Be very careful when opening the bleeder screws due to the high pressure available from a fully charged accumulator.

4. Repeat the procedure at the left side rear caliper.
5. Pump the brake pedal several times to complete the bleeding procedure and to fully charge the accumulator.
6. Adjust the fluid level in the reservoir to the MAX mark with a fully charged accumulator.

➡If the pump motor is allowed to run continuously for approximately 20 minutes, a thermal safety switch inside the motor may shut the motor off t o prevent it from overheating. If that happens, a 2–10 minute cool down period is typically required before normal operation can resume.

HYDRAULIC PUMP PRIMING

1. Remove the dust cap from the right side rear caliper bleeder fitting. Attach a rubber drain tube to the fitting making sure the end of the tube fits snugly around the fitting.
2. Turn the ignition switch to the **RUN** position. This will turn on the electric pump.
3. Hold the brake pedal in the applied position. Open the right side rear caliper bleeder fitting for 10 seconds at a time until an air-free stream of brake fluid is observed.
4. Repeat the procedure at the left side rear caliper.

CHECKING FLUID LEVEL AND REFILLING

1. With the ignition switch **ON**, pump the brake pedal until the hydraulic pump motor starts.
2. Wait until the pump shuts off and check the brake fluid level in the reservoir. If the level is below the MAX fill line, add fluid until the line is reached.

**** WARNING**

Do not overfill! The level may be over the MAX line depending upon the accumulator charge. Perform the above procedure before adding or removing brake fluid.

TEVES MARK-IV ANTI-LOCK BRAKE SYSTEM (ABS)

General Information

➧ See Figures 100 and 101

The Teves Mark-IV Anti-lock Brake System (ABS) is used on 1993–97 models is an electronically operated, all wheel brake control system. Major components include the master cylinder, vacuum power brake booster, ABS Control Module, Hydraulic Control Unit (HCU) and various control sensors and switches.

The brake system is a three channel design. The front brakes are controlled individually and the rear brakes in tandem.

The system is designed to retard wheel lockup during periods of high wheel slip when braking. Retarding wheel lockup is accomplished by modulating fluid pressure to the wheel brake units.

Hydraulic Control Unit (HCU)

REMOVAL & INSTALLATION

➧ See Figure 102

1. Disconnect the negative, then the positive battery cables and remove the battery from the vehicle.
2. Unfasten the power distribution box-to-battery tray attaching bolt, then remove the battery tray.
3. Detach the 16-pin valve body to wire harness connector.
4. Raise and safely support the vehicle, then remove the left front wheel and tire assembly.
5. Remove the left side inner fender splash shield.
6. Detach the 3-pin fluid level switch connector, 4-pin pump motor connector and the 55-pin ABS control module connector.

➡The master cylinder will drain if the feed hose is not pinched off. DO NOT allow brake fluid to come in contact with wiring or paint. Immediately rinse any paint or wiring with water if brake fluid comes in contact with them.

7. Remove the low pressure feed hose from the hydraulic control unit reservoir.
8. Disconnect the left side front brake tube from the hose at the hose mounting bracket.
9. Remove the two lower ABS assembly mounting bracket attaching screws.
10. Carefully lower the vehicle and disconnect the five brake tube connections at the junction block. Remove the two junction block retaining nuts.

**** WARNING**

Do not allow the two upper bushings to turn in the bracket while loosening the two upper mounting bolts. Hold the bushings with a pair of vise grips if necessary. If the bushings turn in the bracket, they must be replaced with new parts before installation.

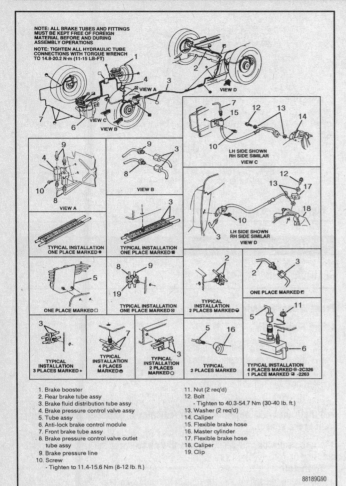

NOTE: ALL BRAKE TUBES AND FITTINGS MUST BE KEPT FREE OF FOREIGN MATERIAL BEFORE AND DURING ASSEMBLY OPERATIONS

NOTE: TIGHTEN ALL HYDRAULIC TUBE CONNECTIONS WITH TORQUE WRENCH TO 14.8-20.2 N·m (11-15 LB-FT)

1. Brake booster
2. Rear brake tube assy
3. Brake fluid distribution tube assy
4. Brake pressure control valve assy
5. Tube assy
6. Anti-lock brake control module
7. Front brake tube assy
8. Brake pressure control valve outlet tube assy
9. Brake pressure line
10. Screw
 - Tighten to 11.4-15.6 Nm (8-12 lb. ft.)
11. Nut (2 req'd)
12. Bolt
 - Tighten to 40.3-54.7 Nm (30-40 lb. ft.)
13. Washer (2 req'd)
14. Caliper
15. Flexible brake hose
16. Master cylinder
17. Flexible brake hose
18. Caliper
19. Clip

88189G90

Fig. 100 Exploded view of the Anti-lock Brake System (ABS) components and their locations—1995 model shown

DTC	CAUSED BY	PINPOINT TEST STEP
11	Generated by a disturbed or defective redundancy channel.	AA1
17	Generated by reference voltage failure, caused by high/low battery voltage, main power relay, main fuse, wire harness.	BB1
18	Generated by open or short circuit-isolation valve #1, wire harness.	BB26
19	Generated by open or short circuit-isolation valve #2, wire harness.	BB29
22	Generated by open or short circuit-LH front inlet valve, wire harness.	BB2
23	Generated by open or short circuit-LH front outlet valve, wire harness.	BB5
24	Generated by open or short circuit-RH front inlet valve, wire harness.	BB8
25	Generated by open or short circuit-RH front outlet valve, wire harness.	BB11
26	Generated by open or short circuit-RH rear inlet valve, wire harness.	BB14
27	Generated by open or short circuit-RH rear outlet valve, wire harness.	BB17
28	Generated by open or short circuit-LH rear inlet valve, wire harness.	BB20
29	Generated by open or short circuit-LH rear outlet valve, wire harness.	BB23
31	Generated by open or short circuit-LH front sensor, wire harness.	CC1
32	Generated by open or short circuit-RH front sensor, wire harness.	CC8
33	Generated by open or short circuit-RH rear sensor, wire harness.	CC15
34	Generated by open or short circuit-LH rear sensor, wire harness.	CC22
35	Generated by open or short circuit-LH front sensor, wire harness, damaged teeth on indicator ring, sensor air gap too small/large.	CC1
36	Generated by open or short circuit-RH front sensor, wire harness, damaged teeth on indicator ring, sensor air gap too small/large.	CC8
37	Generated by open or short circuit-RH rear sensor, wire harness, damaged teeth on indicator ring, sensor air gap too small/large.	CC15
38	Generated by open or short circuit-LH rear sensor, wire harness, damaged teeth on indicator ring, sensor air gap too small/large.	CC22
41	Generated by missing sensor signal LH front sensor (missing indicator ring).	CC1
42	Generated by missing sensor signal RH front sensor (missing indicator ring).	CC8
43	Generated by missing sensor signal RH rear sensor (missing indicator ring).	CC15
44	Generated by missing sensor signal LH rear sensor (missing indicator ring).	CC22
55	Generated by missing sensor signal LH front sensor (long term failure).	CC1
56	Generated by missing sensor signal RH front sensor (long term failure).	CC8
57	Generated by missing sensor signal RH rear sensor (long term failure).	CC15
58	Generated by missing sensor signal LH rear sensor (long term failure).	CC22
61	Generated by short circuit to ground-FLS #2 or wire harness.	DD1
62	Generated by short circuit to ground-pedal travel switch or wire harness.	DD1
63	Generated by no pump motor speed sensor signal during initial check@ 31 km/h (19 mph), wire harness or faulty electronic controller.	DD7 FF1
64	Generated by pump unable to build pressure during an ABS stop.	DD22
67	Generated by pump motor running not triggered by ECU.	E1
75	Generated by intermittent missing LH front sensor signal at speeds < 40 km/h (25 mph).	CC1
76	Generated by intermittent missing RH front sensor signal at speeds < 40 km/h (25 mph).	CC8
77	Generated by intermittent missing RH rear sensor signal at speeds < 40 km/h (25 mph).	CC15
78	Generated by intermittent missing LH rear sensor signal at speeds < 40 km/h (25 mph).	CC22

88189G94

Fig. 101 ABS Diagnostic Trouble Code List

11. Remove the two upper ABS/HCU assembly mounting bracket attaching bolts, then remove the assembly from the vehicle.

To install:

12. Position the ABS/HCU assembly and place the mounting bracket hook through the slot in the outer frame rail. Hand-start the two lower mounting screws.

13. Carefully lower the vehicle, then install the two upper mounting bolts. Tighten the bolts to 8.5–11.5 ft. lbs. (11.4–15.6 Nm).

14. Raise and safely support the vehicles and tighten the two lower mounting screws to 8.5–11.5 ft. lbs. (11.4–15.6 Nm).

15. Attach the lower pressure feed hose to the HCU reservoir.

16. Attach the 55-pin control module connector, the 4-pin pump motor relay connector and the 3-pin fluid level switch connector.

17. Carefully lower the vehicle and install the two junction block retaining nuts and tighten to 1.7–2.4 ft. lbs. (2.3–3.3 Nm).

18. Reattach the five tube connections at the junction block. Tighten to 10–18 ft. lbs. (14–247 Nm).

19. Attach the 16-pin valve body-to-wire harness connector. Install the battery tray.

20. Install the power distribution box on the battery tray attaching bolt.

21. Install the battery, then connect the positive, then the negative battery cables.

22. Raise and safely support the vehicle. Install the fender splash shield and the tire and wheel assembly.

23. Carefully lower the vehicle. Bleed the brake system as outlined in this section.

24. Test drive the vehicle and test for proper brake operation.

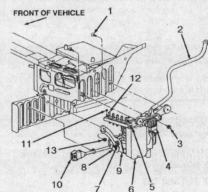

FRONT OF VEHICLE

1. Bolt (2 req'd)
 - Tighten to 11.4-15.6 Nm (8.5-11.5 lb. ft.)
2. Low pressure feed hose
3. Pump motor relay screws (2 req'd)
 - Tighten to 7-9 Nm (5-7 lb. ft.)
4. Pump motor relay
5. ABS module mounting screws (3 req'd)
 - Tighten to 7-9 Nm (5-7 lb. ft.)
6. Anti-lock brake control module
7. HCU to mounting bracket bolts (3 req'd)
 - Tighten to 7-9 Nm (5-7 lb. ft.)
8. 4 pin pump motor connector
9. ABS assy
10. 19 pin valve block connector
11. Nuts (2 req'd)
 - Tighten to 2.3-3.3 Nm (1.7-2.4 lb. ft.)
12. Thread savers (5 req'd)
 - Tighten to 12-14 Nm (9-10 lb. ft.)
13. Screws (2 req'd)
 - Tighten to 11.4-15.6 Nm (8.5-11.5 lb. ft.)

88189G96

Fig. 102 View of the HCU and related components mounting—1995 vehicle shown

Anti-Lock Brake Control Module

REMOVAL & INSTALLATION

▶ **See Figure 103**

1. Disconnect the negative battery cable.
2. Raise and safely support the vehicle.
3. Remove the wheel and tire assembly and the inner fender shield.
4. Remove the pump motor relay.
5. Detach the 55-pin connector.
6. Unfasten the three screws attaching the control module to the mounting bracket, then remove the module.

To install:

➡**If all three mounting holes in the control module do not line up with the holes in the mounting bracket, the module is incorrectly aligned with the bracket.**

7. Align the anti-lock brake control module with the bracket so the connector faces the rear of the vehicle and the locking lever faces up and the side with two mounting holes is flat against the bracket at the top.
8. Install the three retaining screws and tighten to 5–7 ft. lbs. (7–9 Nm).
9. Attach the 55-pin connector by installing the bottom part of the connector into the slots in the control module and pushing the top portion of the connector into the anti-lock brake control module. Then, pull the locking lever completely down to ensure proper installation.
10. Install the pump motor relay. Tighten to 5–7 ft. lbs. (7–9 Nm).
11. Install the inner fender splash shield and the wheel and tire assembly.
12. Carefully lower the vehicle.
13. Test drive the vehicle and verify proper brake operation.

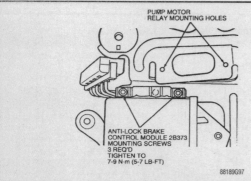

Fig. 103 Anti-Lock Brake Control Module mounting—1995 vehicle shown

Brake Pressure Control Valve

REMOVAL & INSTALLATION

▶ **See Figure 104**

1. Disconnect the negative battery cable.
2. Raise and safely support the vehicle.
3. Remove and cap the four brake tubes from the brake pressure control valve.
4. Unfasten the brake pressure control valve mounting screw, then remove the brake pressure control vale.

To install:

5. Position the brake pressure control valve and install the mounting screw.
6. Uncap and connect the four brake tubes to the brake pressure control valve. Tighten the brake tube nuts to 10–18 ft. lbs. (14–24 Nm).
7. Carefully lower the vehicle.
8. Connect the negative battery cable, then bleed the brake system, as outlined in this section.

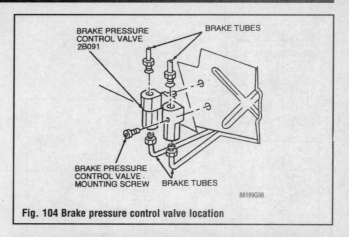

Fig. 104 Brake pressure control valve location

Wheel Speed Sensor

REMOVAL & INSTALLATION

Front Wheel Sensor

▶ **See Figure 105**

1. Disconnect the negative battery cable.
2. Raise and safely support the vehicle with jackstands.
3. Detach the sensor electrical connector for the right or left front sensor (located near the radiator support).
4. Remove the routing clips along the wiring harness.

➡**If the front brake anti-lock sensor indicator is damaged, replace the front brake sensor.**

5. Unfasten the bolt securing the anti-lock sensor to the front wheel spindle.

To install:

6. Install the sensor into the hole in the front wheel spindle. No adjustment is necessary. Install the bolt and tighten to 40–60 inch lbs. (4.5–6.8 Nm).
7. Route the wiring using the clips previously removed. Make sure the wiring is routed proper.
8. Carefully lower the vehicle.
9. Attach the sensor wiring connector to the harness connector.
10. Connect the negative battery cable.

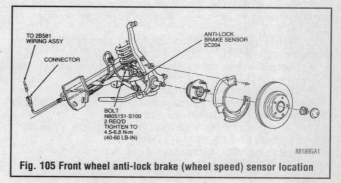

Fig. 105 Front wheel anti-lock brake (wheel speed) sensor location

Rear Sensor

▶ **See Figure 106**

1. Disconnect the negative battery cable.
2. From inside the luggage compartment, detach the wheel sensor electrical connector located rearward of the wheel well, behind the carpeting on the sides of the luggage compartment.
3. Lift the luggage compartment carpet and push the sensor wire grommet through the hole in the luggage compartment floor.

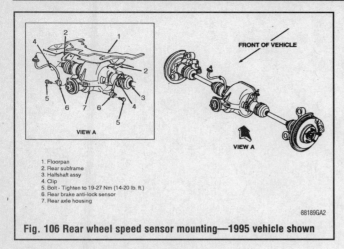

1. Floorpan
2. Rear subframe
3. Halfshaft assy
4. Clip
5. Bolt - Tighten to 19-27 Nm (14-20 lb. ft.)
6. Rear brake anti-lock sensor
7. Rear axle housing

88189GA2

Fig. 106 Rear wheel speed sensor mounting—1995 vehicle shown

4. Raise and safely support the vehicle with jackstands.

➡**Do NOT bend the clip beyond the amount necessary to remove the clip from the axle housing.**

5. Remove the plastic clip holding the sensor wire to the rear axle housing.
6. Unfasten the wheel sensor retaining bolt, then remove the sensor from then vehicle.

To install:

7. Align the sensor locating tab and bolt hole with the rear axle housing, then push into position.
8. Install the sensor retaining bolt and tighten to 14–20 ft. lbs. (19–27 Nm).
9. Install the plastic clip retaining the sensor wire to the rear axle housing and push the electrical connector through the hole in the luggage compartment. Make sure the rubber grommet is properly seated in the hole in the floor.
10. Carefully lower the vehicle.
11. Attach the sensor electrical connector to the connector on the harness.
12. Connect the negative battery cable.

Bleeding The ABS System

The brake system must be bled any time air is permitted to enter the system through loosened or disconnected lines or hoses, or anytime the modulator is removed. Excessive air within the system will cause a soft or spongy feel in the brake pedal.

When bleeding any part of the system, the reservoir must remain as close to full as possible at all times. Check the level frequently and top off fluid as needed.

➡**When any part of the hydraulic system has been disconnected for service, air may enter the system and cause spongy pedal action. Bleed the system after it has been opened to be sure that all air is expelled.**

The anti-lock brake system must be bled in 2 steps; both the master cylinder and hydraulic control unit reservoir must be bled using Rotunda Anti-Lock Brake Breakout Box/Bleeding Adapter tool No. T90P–50–ALA or equivalent. If this procedure is not followed, air will be trapped in the hydraulic control unit, and will eventually lead to a spongy brake pedal.

1. Disconnect the 55-pin plug from the electronic control unit/ABS control module, then install Anti-Lock Brake Breakout Box/Bleeding Adapter tool No. T90P-50-ALA or equivalent to the wire harness 55-pin plug.
   a. Place the Bleed/Harness switch in the **BLEED** position.
   b. Turn the ignition to the **ON** position. At this point the red **OFF** light should come **ON**.
   c. Push the motor button on the adapter down to start the pump motor. The red **OFF** light will turn **OFF**, and the green **ON** light will turn **ON**. The pump motor will run for 60 seconds after the motor button is pushed. If the pump motor is to be turned off for any reason before the 60 seconds have elapsed, push the abort button to turn the pump motor off.
   d. After 20 seconds of pump motor operation, push and hold the valve button down. Hold the valve button down for 20 seconds, then release it.
   e. The pump motor will continue to run for an additional 20 seconds after the valve button is released.
2. The brake lines can now be bled in the normal fashion. Bleed the brake system by removing the rubber dust cap from the caliper fitting at the right rear of the vehicle. Place a suitable box wrench on the bleeder fitting and attach a rubber drain tube to the fitting. The end of the tube should fit snugly around the bleeder fitting. Submerge the other end of the tube in a container partially filled with clean brake fluid and loosen the fitting ¾ turn.

➡**Brake fluid absorbs moisture from the air. Don't leave the master cylinder or the fluid container uncovered any longer than necessary. Be careful handling the fluid—it will damage the vehicle's paint.**

Check the level of the fluid often when bleeding, and refill the reservoirs as necessary. Don't let them run dry, or you will have to repeat the process.

3. Have an assistant push the brake pedal down slowly through its full travel. Close the bleeder fitting and allow the pedal to slowly return to its full release position. Wait 5 seconds and repeat the procedure until no bubbles appear at the submerged end of the bleeder tube. Secure the bleeder fitting and remove the bleeder tube. Install the rubber dust cap on the bleeder fitting.
4. Repeat the bleeding procedure at the left front, left rear and right front (in that order). Refill the master cylinder reservoir after each caliper has been bled, and install the master cylinder cap and gasket. When brake bleeding is completed, the fluid level should be filled to the maximum level indicated on the reservoir.
5. Always make sure the disc brake pistons are returned to their normal positions by depressing the brake pedal several times until normal pedal travel is established. If the pedal feels spongy, repeat the bleeding procedure.

After finishing, there should be no feeling of sponginess in the brake pedal. If there is, either there is still air in the line, in which case the process must be repeated, or there is a leak somewhere, which, of course, must be corrected before the vehicle is moved. After all repairs and service work is finished, road test the vehicle to verify proper brake system operation.

BRAKE SPECIFICATIONS
All measurements in inches unless noted

Year	Model		Master Cylinder Bore	Brake Disc Original Thickness	Brake Disc Minimum Thickness	Maximum Runout	Brake Drum Diameter Original Inside Diameter	Brake Drum Diameter Max. Wear Limit	Brake Drum Diameter Maximum Machine Diameter	Minimum Lining Thickness Front	Minimum Lining Thickness Rear
1983	Cougar	①	0.875	NA	0.810	0.003	9.00	9.09	9.06	0.125	0.030
		②	0.875	NA	0.810	0.003	10.00	10.09	10.06	0.125	0.030
	Thunderbird	①	0.875	NA	0.810	0.003	9.00	9.09	9.06	0.125	0.030
		②	0.875	NA	0.810	0.003	10.00	10.09	10.06	0.125	0.030
1984	Cougar	①	0.875	NA	0.810	0.003	9.00	9.09	9.06	0.125	0.030
		②	0.875	NA	0.810	0.003	10.00	10.09	10.06	0.125	0.030
	Thunderbird	①	0.875	NA	0.810	0.003	9.00	9.09	9.06	0.125	0.030
		②	0.875	NA	0.810	0.003	10.00	10.09	10.06	0.125	0.030
1985	Cougar	①	0.875	NA	0.810	0.003	9.00	9.09	9.06	0.125	0.030
		②	0.875	NA	0.810	0.003	10.00	10.09	10.06	0.125	0.030
	Thunderbird	①	0.875	NA	0.810	0.003	9.00	9.09	9.06	0.125	0.030
		②	0.875	NA	0.810	0.003	10.00	10.09	10.06	0.125	0.030
1986	Cougar	①	0.875	NA	0.810	0.003	9.00	9.09	9.06	0.125	0.030
		②	0.875	NA	0.810	0.003	10.00	10.09	10.06	0.125	0.030
	Thunderbird	①	0.875	NA	0.810	0.003	9.00	9.09	9.06	0.125	0.030
		②	0.875	NA	0.810	0.003	10.00	10.09	10.06	0.125	0.030
1987	Cougar	①	0.875	NA	0.810	0.003	9.00	9.89	9.06	0.125	0.030
		②	0.875	NA	0.810	0.003	10.00	10.89	10.06	0.125	0.030
	Thunderbird	③	0.875	NA	0.810	0.003	9.00	9.89	9.06	0.125	0.030
		④	0.875	NA	0.810	0.003	10.00	10.89	10.06	0.125	0.030
		⑤	0.875	NA	0.972	0.003	9.00	9.89	9.06	0.125	0.030
		⑥	0.875	NA	0.895	-	-	-	-	0.125	0.030
1988	Cougar	①	0.875	NA	0.810	0.003	9.00	9.89	9.06	0.125	0.030
		②	0.875	NA	0.810	0.003	10.00	10.89	10.06	0.125	0.030
	Thunderbird	③	0.875	NA	0.810	0.003	9.00	9.89	9.06	0.125	0.030
		④	0.875	NA	0.810	0.003	10.00	10.89	10.06	0.125	0.030
		⑥ F	0.875	NA	0.972	0.003	9.00	9.89	9.06	0.125	0.030
		⑥ R	0.875	NA	0.895	-	-	-	-	0.125	0.030
1989	Cougar	①	0.875	NA	0.810	0.003	9.00	9.89	9.06	0.125	0.030
		②	0.875	NA	0.810	0.003	10.00	10.89	10.06	0.125	0.030
	Thunderbird	⑦	0.875	NA	0.810	0.003	9.00	9.99	9.86	0.125	0.030
		⑧	0.875	NA	0.900	0.003	-	-	-	0.123	0.123
1990	Cougar	⑦ F	0.938	1.025	0.974	0.004	-	-	-	0.125	0.030
		⑧ R	-	0.945	0.896	0.003	9.80	9.89	9.86	0.123	0.030
	Thunderbird	⑦ F	-	NA	0.935	0.003	9.80	9.89	9.86	0.123	0.123
		⑧ R	0.875	NA	0.900	0.003	-	-	-		0.030
1991	Cougar	⑦ F	0.938	1.025	0.974	0.004	-	-	-	0.125	0.030
		⑧ R	-	0.710	0.657	0.003	9.80	9.90	9.86	0.123	0.123
	Thunderbird	⑦ F	0.875	NA	0.935	0.003	9.80	9.89	9.86	0.123	0.030
		⑧ R	-	NA	0.900	-	-	-	-		0.123

91339C01

BRAKE SPECIFICATIONS
All measurements in inches unless noted

Year	Model		Master Cylinder Bore	Brake Disc Original Thickness	Brake Disc Minimum Thickness	Maximum Runout	Brake Drum Diameter Original Inside Diameter	Brake Drum Diameter Max. Wear Limit	Brake Drum Diameter Maximum Machine Diameter	Minimum Lining Thickness Front	Minimum Lining Thickness Rear
1992	Cougar	⑦	0.938 ⑨	1.025	0.974	0.003	-	-	-	0.125	0.030
		⑧		0.710	0.657	0.003	-	-	-	0.123	0.123
	Thunderbird	⑦ F	0.938	1.024	0.974	0.003	9.80	9.90	9.86	0.125	0.030
		⑧ R		0.945	0.896	0.003	9.84	9.90	9.86	0.123	0.123
1993	Cougar	⑦	0.938 ⑨	1.025	0.974	0.003	-	-	-	0.125	0.030
		⑧		0.710	0.657	0.003	-	-	-	0.123	0.123
	Thunderbird	⑦ F	0.983	1.025	0.974	0.003	9.80	9.89	9.86	0.125	0.030
		⑧ R		0.945	0.896	0.003	9.84	9.89	9.86	0.123	0.123
1994	Cougar	⑦ F	0.938	1.025	0.974	0.003	9.80	9.89	9.89	0.040	0.030
		⑧ R		0.710	0.657	0.003	-	-	-	0.123	0.123
	Thunderbird	⑦ F	0.938 ⑨	1.025	0.974	0.003	9.84	9.89	9.89	0.040	0.030
		⑧ R		0.709	0.657	0.003	-	-	-	0.123	0.123
1995	Cougar	⑦ F	0.938	1.025	0.974	0.003	9.98	NA	9.90	0.040	⑩
		⑧ R		0.710	0.657	0.003	9.84	NA	9.86	0.040	0.030
	Thunderbird	⑦ F	0.938 ⑨	1.025	0.974	0.003	9.84	NA	9.86	0.040	0.030
		⑧ R		0.709	0.657	0.003	-	-	-	0.123	0.123
1996	Cougar	⑦ F	0.938	1.025	0.974	0.003	-	-	-	0.125	0.125
		⑧ R		0.710	0.657	0.002	9.80	NA	9.90		
	Thunderbird	⑦ F	0.938	1.025	0.974	0.002	-	-	-	0.125	0.125
		⑧ R		0.710	0.657	0.002	9.80	NA	9.90		
1997	Cougar	⑦ F	0.938	1.025	0.974	0.003	-	-	-	0.125	0.125
		⑧ R		0.710	0.657	0.002	9.80	NA	9.90		
	Thunderbird	⑦ F	0.938	1.025	0.974	0.002	-	-	-	0.125	0.125
		⑧ R		0.710	0.657	-	9.80	NA	9.90		

NOTE: Follow specifications stamped on rotor or drum
if figures differ from those in this chart
NA - Not Available
F - Front
R - Rear
1: 9 inch rear
2: 10 inch rear
3: 9 inch rear, except Turbo
4: 10 inch rear, except Turbo
5: Turbo without rear disc
6: Turbo with rear disc
7: Except rear disc
8: With rear disc
9: Without ABS
10: Riveted lining: 0.123
    Bonded lining: 0.030

91339C02

EXTERIOR 10-2
DOORS 10-2
    REMOVAL & INSTALLATION 10-2
    ADJUSTMENT 10-2
HOOD 10-3
    REMOVAL & INSTALLATION 10-3
    ALIGNMENT 10-3
TRUNK LID 10-3
    REMOVAL & INSTALLATION 10-3
    ALIGNMENT 10-3
GRILLE 10-3
    REMOVAL & INSTALLATION 10-3
OUTSIDE MIRRORS 10-5
    REMOVAL & INSTALLATION 10-5
ANTENNA 10-6
    REMOVAL & INSTALLATION 10-6
FENDERS 10-7
    REMOVAL & INSTALLATION 10-7
INTERIOR 10-8
INSTRUMENT PANEL 10-8
    REMOVAL & INSTALLATION 10-8
FLOOR CONSOLE 10-10
    REMOVAL & INSTALLATION 10-10
DOOR PANELS 10-11
    REMOVAL & INSTALLATION 10-11
DOOR GLASS 10-13
    REMOVAL & INSTALLATION 10-13
WINDOW REGULATOR 10-14
    REMOVAL & INSTALLATION 10-14
ELECTRIC WINDOW MOTOR 10-15
    REMOVAL & INSTALLATION 10-15
WINDSHIELD AND FIXED GLASS 10-16
    REMOVAL & INSTALLATION 10-16
    WINDSHIELD CHIP REPAIR 10-16
INSIDE REARVIEW MIRROR 10-18
    REMOVAL & INSTALLATION 10-18
SEATS 10-18
    REMOVAL & INSTALLATION 10-18
POWER SEAT MOTOR 10-20
    REMOVAL & INSTALLATION 10-20

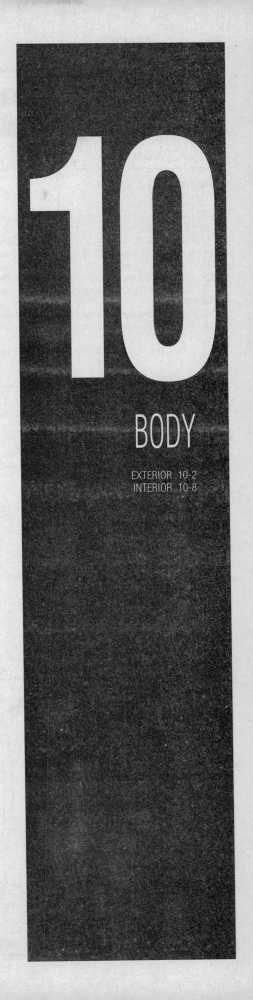

10

BODY

EXTERIOR 10-2
INTERIOR 10-8

EXTERIOR

Doors

REMOVAL & INSTALLATION

♦ **See Figures 1, 2, 3 and 4**

1. Remove the door trim panel.
2. Remove the watershield, and, if a new door is being installed, save all the molding clips and moldings.
3. Remove the wiring harness, actuator and speakers.
4. If a new door is being installed, remove all window and lock components.
5. Mark the location of the hinges on the door and pillar.
6. Support the door and unbolt the hinges from the door.

To install:

7. Position the upper and lower hinges on the door if removed.
8. Position the hinges on the door pillar and partially tighten the hinge bolts.
9. Align the door and tighten the hinge bolts to 18–26 ft lbs. (25–37 Nm).

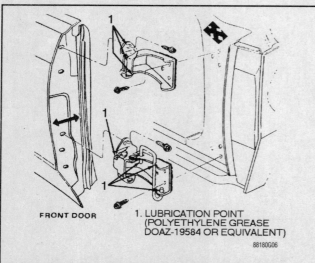

1. Front door
2. Front door trim panel
3. Nut (2 req'd each side)
4. Screw (2 req'd each side)

88180G02

Fig. 1 Assemble the homemade tool as shown

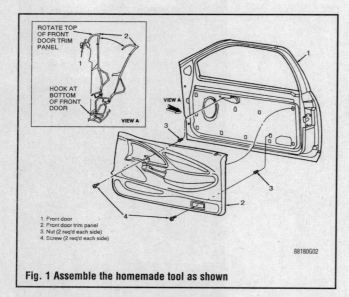

1. LUBRICATION POINT (POLYETHYLENE GREASE DOAZ-19584 OR EQUIVALENT)

FRONT DOOR

88180G06

Fig. 2 Exploded view of the door hinges on the 1983–84 models

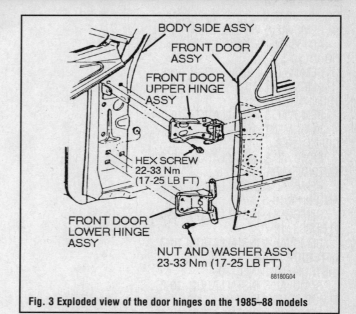

BODY SIDE ASSY

FRONT DOOR ASSY

FRONT DOOR UPPER HINGE ASSY

HEX SCREW 22-33 Nm (17-25 LB FT)

FRONT DOOR LOWER HINGE ASSY

NUT AND WASHER ASSY 23-33 Nm (17-25 LB FT)

88180G04

Fig. 3 Exploded view of the door hinges on the 1985–88 models

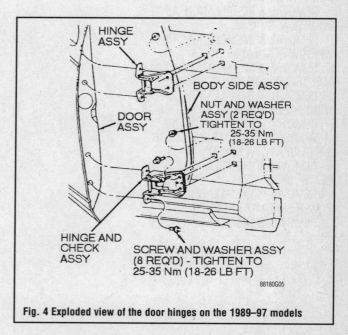

HINGE ASSY

BODY SIDE ASSY

NUT AND WASHER ASSY (2 REQ'D) TIGHTEN TO 25-35 Nm (18-26 LB FT)

DOOR ASSY

HINGE AND CHECK ASSY

SCREW AND WASHER ASSY (8 REQ'D) - TIGHTEN TO 25-35 Nm (18-26 LB FT)

88180G05

Fig. 4 Exploded view of the door hinges on the 1989–97 models

10. Attach the electrical harness. Install any remaining components if removed.

ADJUSTMENT

1. Determine which door hinge screws must be loosened to move the door in the desired direction.
2. Loosen the hinge screws enough to allow movement of the door with a padded prybar.
3. Move the door the necessary distance. Tighten the hinge screws to 18–26 ft. lbs. (25–35 Nm). Check the door fit ensuring that there is no binding or interference with the adjustment panel.
4. Repeat the procedure until the desired fit is obtained. Check that the door latch striker tapping plate alignment for proper door closing.

Hood

REMOVAL & INSTALLATION

▶ See Figures 5, 6 and 7

1. Open and support the hood.
2. Matchmark the hood-to-hinge positions.

➡It is a good practice to cover the fenders with an appropriate covering so as not to scratch or damage the body and paint while removing or installing the hood.

3. Have an assistant support the hood while you remove the hinge-to-hood bolts and disconnect the hood lift/gas supports.
4. Remove the hood, but rest the hood on its side, not on the rear corners.
To install:
5. Position the hood on the hinges.
6. Install the retaining bolts to attach the hood to the hinges. Tighten the bolts to 7–10 ft. lbs. (9–14 Nm).
7. Install the hood lift/gas supports.
8. Install the retaining clip the hood lift/gas supports.
9. Adjust the hood and hood latch.

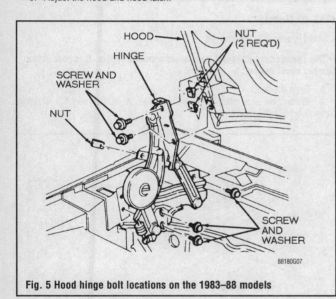

Fig. 5 Hood hinge bolt locations on the 1983–88 models

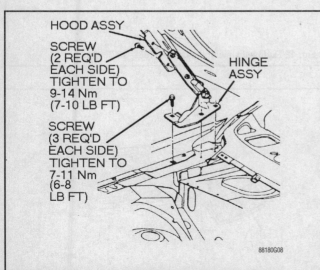

Fig. 6 The hinge type is slightly different on the 1989–97 models

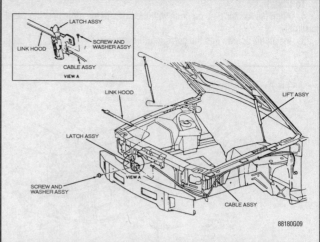

Fig. 7 When installing the hood, make sure the latch works properly prior to closing the hood

ALIGNMENT

1. Side-to-side and fore-aft adjustments can be made by loosening the hood-to-hinge attachment bolts and positioning the hood as necessary.
2. Hood vertical fit can be adjusted by raising or lowering the hinge-to-fender reinforcement bolts.
3. To ensure a snug fit of the hood against the rear hood bumpers, it may be necessary to rotate the hinge around the 3 attaching bolts.
4. Front level adjustment is done by adjusting the two front mounted rubbers on the radiator support, either up or down for proper alignment.

Trunk Lid

REMOVAL & INSTALLATION

1. With the aide of an assistant, remove the hinge-to-trunk lid screws and lift off the lid.
To install:
2. Position the lid on the hinges and loosely tighten the mounting screws.
3. Adjust the trunk lid and tighten the mounting screws to 4–6 ft. lbs. (5–9 Nm).

ALIGNMENT

Trunk Lid

1. Fore-aft fit may be adjusted by loosening the hinge to trunk lid bolts and positioning the lid as necessary.
2. Vertical fit can be adjusted by loosening then tightening the lid hinge screws. Tighten them to 4–6 ft. lbs. (5–9 Nm).

Grille

REMOVAL & INSTALLATION

1983–88 Models

▶ See Figures 8, 9, 10, and 11

1. Open the hood.
2. Remove the screws from front of grille.
3. Separate the grille from the vehicle.

To install:
4. Align the locator pins on grille with the holes in the grille opening panel assembly.
5. Install the screws into the holes in grille assembly.

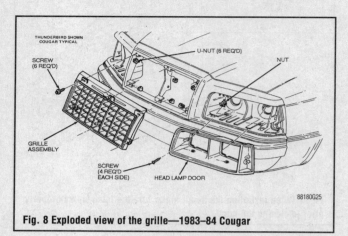

Fig. 8 Exploded view of the grille—1983–84 Cougar

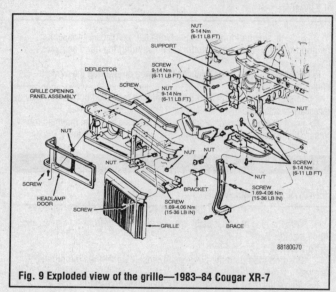

Fig. 9 Exploded view of the grille—1983–84 Cougar XR-7

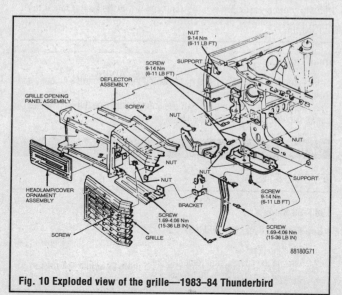

Fig. 10 Exploded view of the grille—1983–84 Thunderbird

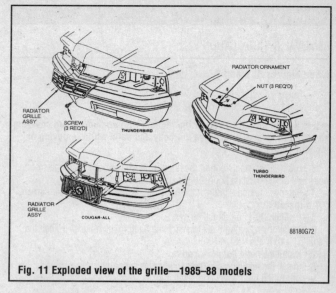

Fig. 11 Exploded view of the grille—1985–88 models

1989–97 Models

▶ See Figures 12, 13 and 14

➡The Thunderbird does not have a conventional grille. It is part of the bumper cover assembly.

1. Open the hood.
2. Remove two side retaining screws on 1989–90 models; four top retaining screws on 1991–97 models.

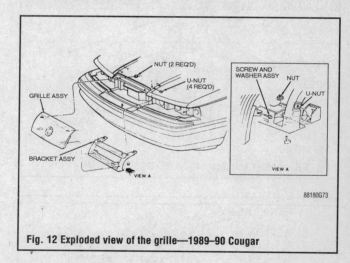

Fig. 12 Exploded view of the grille—1989–90 Cougar

Fig. 13 Exploded view of the grille—1991–93 Cougar

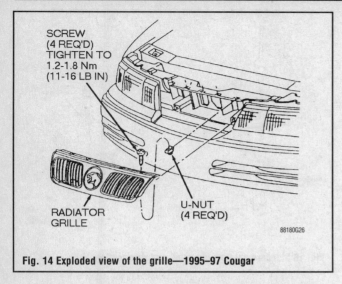

Fig. 14 Exploded view of the grille—1995–97 Cougar

3. Depress clips and pull grille forward releasing the grille at bottom from bracket assembly.

4. Remove the nut from bolt and retainer attached to the grille from underside of hood if equipped. Remove the grille.

To install:

5. Close the hood, then line up the bolt and retainer on the grille.

6. Attach the grill to the vehicle. Tighten the retaining screws to 89–123 inch lbs. (10–14 Nm).

Outside Mirrors

REMOVAL & INSTALLATION

Standard Manual

COUGAR

▶ See Figure 15

1. Remove the two screws from outside of mirror.
2. Remove the mirror, and gasket. Repeat this for the other side.

To install:

3. Place the gasket on the mirror and attach the mirror to the door.
4. Tighten the mirror screws.

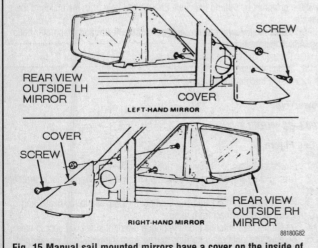

Fig. 15 Manual sail mounted mirrors have a cover on the inside of the vehicle

THUNDERBIRD AND XR-7

▶ See Figure 16

1. Remove the inside door trim panel.
2. Remove the two nuts from inside door retaining mirror to the door.
3. Remove the mirror and gasket. Repeat for other side.

To install:

4. Place the gasket on the mirror and attach to the door with the mounting nuts.

5. Install the door interior panel.

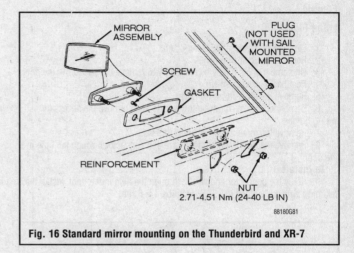

Fig. 16 Standard mirror mounting on the Thunderbird and XR-7

Manual Remote

▶ See Figure 17

1. Disconnect the negative battery cable.
2. Remove the inside trim cover retaining screw.
3. Loosen the allen set screw retaining the control to the cover, then remove the cover.
4. Remove the mirror retaining nuts and the mirror.
5. On the instrument panel mounted remote mirror, remove the bezel nut from panel.

    a. Disengage the actuator and cable from the instrument panel.

    b. Remove the door trim panel.

    c. Disengage the cable guide grommets from the door and door pillar.

    d. Remove the two mirror retaining nuts and remove the mirror, guiding the control actuator through the holes in the pillar and door.

➡ **If the remote assembly is to be replaced it may be easier to cut the cable at the control to remove control.**

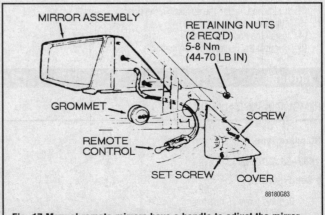

Fig. 17 Manual remote mirrors have a handle to adjust the mirror from inside the car

To install:

6. Attach the mirror to the bezel and tighten the mounting nuts.
7. Install the door trim panel.
8. On the instrument panel mounted mirror, guide the control actuator through the holes in the pillar and door.

    a. Attach the mirror by the two mounting nuts.
    b. Engage the cable guide grommets to the door and door pillar.
    c. Install the door trim panel.
    d. Engage the actuator and cable to the instrument panel.

9. Connect the negative battery cable.

Electric

▶ **See Figure 18**

1. Disconnect the negative battery cable.
2. Remove the door trim panel.
3. On some models it may be necessary to remove the speaker in the door.
4. Peel back the watershield.
5. Remove the snap-in mirror cover.
6. Disconnect the mirror assembly wiring, then remove the necessary wiring guides.
7. Remove the three mirror retaining screws.
8. Remove the mirror, guiding the wire and connector through the hole in the door.

To install:

9. Route the connector and wiring through the hole in the door. Install the retaining nuts and tighten to 35–53 inch lbs. (4–6 Nm).

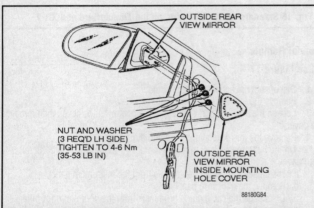

Fig. 18 Electric remote control mirror sail mounted is basically the same design as the manual remote

10. Connect the mirror wiring and install the wiring guides.
11. Install the watershield.
12. If removed, install the speaker in the door.
13. Attach the mirror hole cover.
14. Install the door trim panel.
15. Connect the negative battery cable.

Antenna

REMOVAL & INSTALLATION

Standard Type

1983–88 MODELS

▶ **See Figure 19**

1. Remove glove compartment.

➡**On Thunderbird and XR-7 models, drop the glove compartment by detaching holding straps from the instrument panel.**

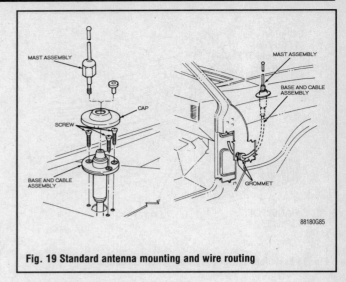

Fig. 19 Standard antenna mounting and wire routing

2. Remove the right side cowl trim panel.
3. Remove the antenna cable clip holding antenna lead to the heater and A/C plenum and disconnect antenna from the rear of radio.
4. Remove the antenna cap and antenna base attaching screws and pull the cable through holes in the door hinge pillar and fender, remove the antenna assembly.

To install:

5. Installation is the reverse of removal. Start with the passenger side door in the opened position before routing antenna cable through door pillar.

1989–97 MODELS

1. Drop glove compartment by detaching the holding straps from instrument panel.
2. Remove the right side cowl side trim panel.
3. Remove the antenna cable clip holding antenna lead to the heater and A/C plenum and disconnect from radio.
4. Disconnect the antenna motor wiring at the right side cowl access hole.
5. Remove the inner rear attaching screws of the right front wheel opening splash shield for access to the antenna, if necessary.
6. Remove the antenna cap and the antenna base retaining screws. Pull the cable through the holes in the door hinge pillar and fender and remove the antenna assembly.

To install:

7. With the right front door opened, position the radio antenna base and cable assembly in the fender opening. Place the gasket into position, then install the antenna base to the fender.
8. Pull the antenna lead in cable through the door hinge pillar opening. Seat the grommet by pulling the cable through the hole from the inside of the vehicle.
9. Route the antenna lead in cable behind the heater and evaporator housing. Attach the locating clips.
10. Connect the rear of the radio chassis.
11. Install the cowl side trim panel
12. Install the glove compartment.

Power Type

1983–88 MODELS

▶ **See Figure 20**

1. Lower antenna and remove the right side cowl trim panel.
2. Drop glove compartment by detaching the holding straps from instrument panel.
3. Remove the antenna cable clip holding antenna lead to the heater and A/C plenum and disconnect from radio.
4. Disconnect the antenna motor wiring at the right side cowl access hole.
5. Remove the inner rear attaching screws from the right front wheel opening splash shield for access to the antenna lower attaching bolt.
6. Remove the bolt located at the bottom of motor.

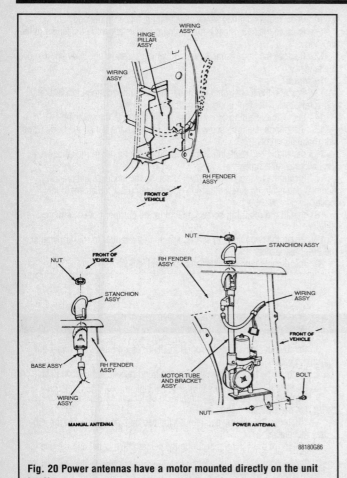

Fig. 20 Power antennas have a motor mounted directly on the unit itself

7. Remove trim nut from the top of motor tube and remove the antenna through fender/splash shield opening.
To install:
8. Installation is the reverse of removal.

1989–97 MODELS

♦ See Figure 21

1. Lower antenna and remove the right side cowl trim panel.
2. Remove the inner rear attaching screws from the right front wheel opening splash shield for access to the antenna lower attaching bolt.
3. Remove the bolt located at the bottom of motor.
4. Remove trim nut from the top of motor tube and remove the antenna through fender/splash shield opening.
5. Disconnect the signal cable and motor wire connector.
To install:
6. Reverse to install. Tighten the top antenna nut to 54–70 inch lbs. (6–8 Nm) and the lower retaining bolt to 31–48 inch lbs. (4–6 Nm).
7. Check the operation of the antenna.

Fenders

REMOVAL & INSTALLATION

♦ See Figures 22 and 23

1. Remove the retainers for the splash shield to the body.
2. Remove the screws attaching the bumper cover to the splash shield.
3. Remove the two retaining screws attaching the splash shield to fender and remove the splash shield.

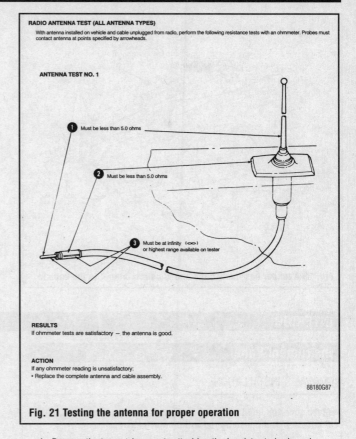

Fig. 21 Testing the antenna for proper operation

4. Remove the two push-on nuts attaching the insulator to body and remove the insulator.
5. Remove the two retaining nuts attaching the parking lamp.
6. Remove the retaining screws attaching the bumper cover to the fender.
7. Remove the two retaining screws attaching the fender to the brace. Remove one retaining screw attaching grille opening reinforcement to the fender.
8. Remove the two retaining screws attaching the fender to rocker panel at the lower rear attachment.
9. Remove one retaining screw attaching fender to the tab on the body (lower horizontal attachment).

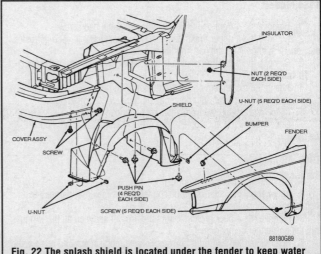

Fig. 22 The splash shield is located under the fender to keep water from rusting the fender

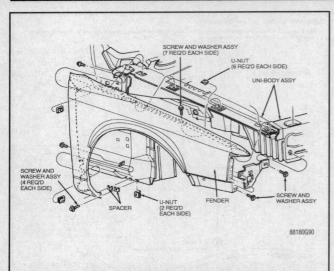

SCREW AND WASHER ASSY
(7 REQ'D EACH SIDE)

U-NUT
(6 REQ'D EACH SIDE)

UNI-BODY ASSY

SCREW AND
WASHER ASSY
(4 REQ'D
EACH SIDE)

SPACER

U-NUT
(2 REQ'D
EACH SIDE)

FENDER

SCREW AND
WASHER ASSY

88180G90

Fig. 23 A fender has many bolts and clips retaining it to the vehicle

10. Remove the retaining screw attaching the fender to the body tab.

11. Remove the four under hood retaining screws attaching the fender to the uni-body.

12. Remove the hood hinge forward retaining screw to uni-body and remove the fender.

To install:

13. Position the fender onto the body, install the hood hinge forward retaining screw, install the four under hood attaching screws.

14. Install the retaining screw attaching the fender to the body tab.

15. Install one retaining screw attaching fender to the tab on the body (lower horizontal attachment).

16. Install the two retaining screws attaching the fender to rocker panel at the lower rear attachment.

17. Install the two retaining screws attaching the fender to the brace. Remove one retaining screw attaching grille opening reinforcement to the fender.

18. Install the retaining screws attaching the bumper cover to the fender.

19. Install the two retaining screws attaching the fender to rocker panel at the lower rear attachment.

20. Install the sound insulator and splash shield.

INTERIOR

Instrument Panel

REMOVAL & INSTALLATION

➡**Make sure you label all wiring and hoses that you disconnect. This will ensure that the installation will be much easier.**

1983 Models

1. Remove the cluster and finish panel retaining screws.

2. Remove the instrument panel pad retaining screws in the front and on the ends of the panel.

3. Remove the instrument panel pad retaining screws in the top defroster openings and lift off the pad.

To install:

4. Install the instrument panel pad with the retaining screws, then tighten.

5. Install and tighten the cluster and finish panel retaining screws.

6. Once installation is complete, check the operation of all components in the dash.

1984 Models

1. Remove the 4 front and 2 side instrument panel pad screws.

2. Remove the 4 upper finish panel retaining screws, 2 in each defroster duct opening and lift off the pad and finish panel.

3. Remove the 5 pad-to-panel nuts and separate the pad from the panel.

To install:

4. Attach the instrument pad with the mounting nuts.

5. Install the defroster duct openings on the pad and finish panel.

6. Install and tighten the front and side panel pad screws.

7. Once installation is complete, check the operation of all components in the dash.

1985–88 Models

1. Disconnect the battery ground.

2. In the engine compartment, disconnect all main wiring harness-to-instrument panel connectors.

3. Remove the rubber grommet from the firewall and feed all the wiring into the passenger compartment.

4. Remove the left and right finish panel retaining screws and remove the panels by pulling down on the upper edges.

5. Remove the steering column opening trim cover.

6. Remove the left and right sound insulator assemblies from under the instrument panel.

7. Remove the two screws attaching the hood release to the cowl panel.

8. Remove the left and right cowl trim panels.

9. Remove the 10 cluster opening finish panel retaining screws.

10. On cars without a console:

a. Remove the ashtray and remove the two outboard screws in the ashtray receptacle.

b. Remove the 4 screws securing the center finish panel and remove the panel.

11. On cars with a console:

a. Remove the console front finish panel.

b. Remove the 4 screws securing the center finish panel and remove the panel.

12. Remove the steering column brace assemblies and disconnect all steering column wiring connectors.

13. Remove the speaker and headlamp dimmer sensor grilles.

14. Remove the 3 upper instrument panel-to-cowl retaining screws.

15. Open the glove compartment door and bend the flexible stops on the sidewalls to allow the liner to swing out.

16. Remove the to lower cowl side retaining screws.

17. Move the instrument panel away from the cowl and disconnect any remaining air conditioning controls and wire connectors.

18. Installation is the reverse of removal.

19. Once installation is complete, check the operation of all of the components.

1989–92 Models

➡**Make sure you label all wiring and hoses that you disconnect. This will ensure that the installation will be much easier.**

1. Disconnect the battery ground cable.

2. Disconnect the underhood wiring at the left side of dash panel.

3. Disengage wiring connector from dash panel and push wiring harness into passenger compartment.

4. Remove steering column lower trim cover by removing three screws at bottom, one screw on left side, and pull to disengage five snap-in retainers across top.

5. Remove six screws retaining steering column lower opening reinforcement, and remove from instrument panel.

6. Remove steering column upper and lower shrouds, and disconnect wiring from steering column.

7. Remove shift interlock switch.

8. Disconnect steering column lower universal joint.

9. Support steering column and remove four nuts retaining column to support bracket. Remove column from vehicle.

10. Remove one screw retaining left side of instrument panel to parking brake bracket.

11. Reinstall steering column lower opening reinforcement using only four screws (one in each corner).

➡️**Reinforcement prevents instrument panel from twisting when being removed from vehicle.**

12. Remove right and left cowl side trim panels.

13. Remove console assembly from vehicle. Refer to Floor Console removal and installation.

14. Remove two nuts retaining center of instrument panel to floor (tunnel).

15. Open glove compartment, squeeze sides of bin and lower to full open position.

16. From underneath the instrument panel and through glove compartment opening, disconnect wiring, heater, A/C vacuum lines and control cables.

➡️**Make sure that the vacuum line is disconnected for the boost gauge on supercharged models.**

17. Remove two screws at the right and left side retaining the instrument panel to the cowl sides.

18. Remove right and left upper finish panels by pulling up to disengage the snap-in retainers. Three on the right and four on the left sides.

19. Remove four screws retaining the instrument panel to the cowl top. Remove the right and left roof rail trim panel and remove door frame weatherstrip.

20. Carefully pull instrument panel away from the cowl. Disconnect any remaining wiring controls and remove from vehicle.

➡️**If instrument panel is being replaced, transfer all components, wiring and hardware to new panel.**

21. Installation is reverse of removal

22. Once installation is complete, check the operation of all of the components.

1993–97 Models

▶ **See Figures 24, 25 and 26**

➡️**You will need the help of an aid to perform the following procedure.**

➡️**Make sure you label all wiring and hoses that you disconnect. This will ensure the installation will be much easier.**

1. Disconnect the negative battery cable.

2. Disconnect the positive cable and wait one minute for the air bag diagnostic monitor to deplete the airbag back-up power supply.

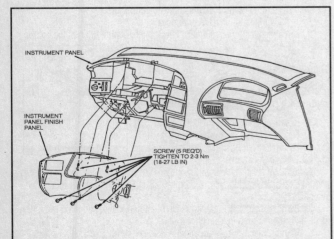

Fig. 24 Exploded view of the instrument panel finish panel mounting screws for the cluster—1995 shown

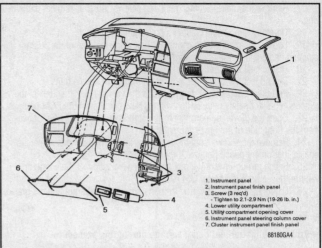

Fig. 25 Exploded view of the instrument panel finish panel center—1995 shown

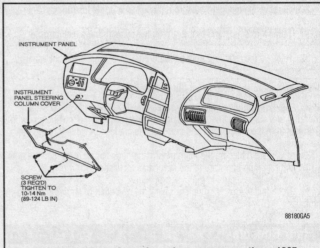

Fig. 26 Instrument panel steering column cover mounting—1995 shown

3. Loosen the main wiring connector bolt in the engine compartment on the left side of the dash panel, then separate the connectors.

4. Remove the antenna stanchion and disconnect the antenna lead in cable from the lead base of the antenna stanchion.

5. Remove the right and left windshield side garnish moldings.

➡️**Do not remove the safety belt retaining bolts.**

6. Remove the left and right scuff plates, then remove the door opening weatherstrips from the body flanges.

7. Remove the cowl side trim panels.

8. Remove the screws along the bottom of the steering column cover. Pull on the instrument panel steering column cover to unsnap the clips across the top of the instrument panel steering column cover. Remove the cover.

9. Remove the ignition lock cylinder.

10. Unscrew the steering column shrouds and remove.

11. Install the lock cylinder to prevent the steering wheel from turning.

12. Disconnect the wiring at the multi function switch.

13. Remove the screw and the A/C evaporator register duct from under the column tube.

14. Disconnect the wiring from the bottom of the column tube.

15. Remove the pinch bolt retaining the column tube to the steering column lower yoke, then slightly spread the column lower yoke with a flatbladed tool.

16. While supporting the column tube, remove the four retaining nuts.

17. Remove the interlock cable retaining screws and shift actuator cable fitting.

18. Carefully remove the column tube from the vehicle.

19. Loosen the main wiring connector bolt at the left side of the column opening and separate the connectors.

20. Disconnect the stoplight switch.

21. Disconnect the clutch pedal position switch. (manuals trans.)

22. Pull the carpet back on both sides of the vehicle, then disconnect the window regulator safety relay switch wiring. Next disconnect the PCM harness.

23. Open the glove compartment to the stop, then unsnap the door check from the right side of the glove compartment.

24. Remove the screws from the bottom of the glove box door hinge and box-to-instrument panel. Remove the glove box.

25. Reach through the glove box opening and disconnect the wiring and vacuum hoses from the heater and A/C.

26. Disconnect the main wiring from the speed control amplifier and bracket assembly.

27. Remove the floor console panel.

➡ **Protect the instrument panel surface during this procedure.**

28. Using a putty knife or similar tool, insert it under the left and right corner of the instrument panel upper finish panel. Pry up on the panel upper finish panel to release the one snap clip.

29. Unsnap the remaining clips by pulling up by hand, then working towards the opposite side of the vehicle.

30. Remove the retaining nuts from the left side of the instrument panel-to-cowl side.

31. Remove the nuts and bolt retaining the panel to the panel console bracket.

32. Remove the retaining nuts on the right side of the instrument panel-to-cowl side.

➡ **You will need the help of an aid to proceed.**

33. Carefully pull the instrument panel away from the windshield while checking and disconnecting any remaining wiring. Disengage the antenna wire grommet from the sheet metal and pull the antenna lead in cable through the dash panel.

34. If you are replacing the instrument panel, transfer all of the components, wiring and retaining hardware to the new panel as needed.

35. To install, reverse the removal procedure.

36. Once installation is complete, check the operation of all of the components.

Floor Console

REMOVAL & INSTALLATION

1983 Models

1. Open the console glove box door and remove the retaining screws from the bottom of the glove box and the top finish panels.

2. Lift the finish panel and disconnect all wiring at the console.

3. Through the 2 access holes in the front of the console, remove the nuts which attach the console to the instrument panel.

4. Lift up on the back end of the console and slide the console rearward enough to gain access to the wire connectors. Disconnect these wires and ground leads and remove the console.

To install:

5. Attach the wiring to the correct locations.

6. Install the console and tighten the mounting screws.

7. Attach any wring that may still need to be connected.

8. Install the screws to the bottom of the glove box and top finish panels.

1984–88 Models

1. Open the console door and remove the 4 console retaining screws.

2. Remove the ashtray receptacle and the 2 rear finish panel screws.

3. Remove the finish panel and unplug the wiring connectors.

4. Remove the 2 front finish panel screws and lift off the panel.

5. Remove the 2 screws that secure the console to the instrument panel.

On cars with column mounted automatic transmission, remove the two console front support bracket screws and remove the support bracket.

On cars with manual transmission, remove the shifter knob and slide the boot and finish panel up and off of the shifter.

6. Remove the 4 center panel attaching screws: 2 at the top of the panel and 2 under the ashtray receptacle door. Lift off the finish panel and disconnect all wiring.

7. On cars with a manual transmission, remove the support bracket at the ashtray receptacle (4 screws).

8. Pull the two front edges of the console away from the instrument panel to disengage the Velcro® fasteners, and, at the same time, slide the console rearward and upwards to remove it.

To install:

9. Position and attach the console.

10. On cars with a manual transmission, install the support bracket at the ashtray receptacle.

11. On cars with an automatic transmission, attach the console front support bracket.

12. Tighten the console retaining screws to the instrument panel.

13. Attach the front finish panel.

14. Install the ashtray receptacle.

15. Install the screws in the glove box.

1989–92 Models

1. Open console door and remove container and mat to gain access to the two console-to-floorpan retaining screws. Then remove screws.

2. Remove the gear shift knob on manual transmissions only.

3. Remove the two rear finish panel retaining screws. Tilt finish panel forward, disconnect and label the electrical connectors, then remove the panel.

4. Remove the two front console-to-instrument panel retaining screws and remove the console.

To install:

5. Place the console into position, then tighten the two front console-to-panel retaining screws.

6. Attach the electrical connections. Install and tighten the two rear finish panel retaining screws.

7. On cars with a manual transmission, install the gear shift knob.

8. Tighten the remaining screws for the console-to-floor pan, then install the mat and container.

1993–97 Models

▶ **See Figures 27 and 28**

1. Open the glove compartment door to access the screws for the console finish panel.

2. Remove the screws and lift the rear of the console finish panel to unsnap the snap-in retainers.

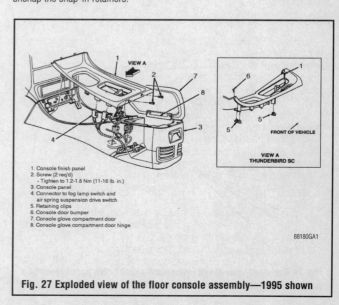

1. Console finish panel
2. Screw (2 req'd)
   - Tighten to 1.2-1.8 Nm (11-16 lb. in.)
3. Console panel
4. Connector to fog lamp switch and air spring suspension drive switch
5. Retaining clips
6. Console door bumper
7. Console glove compartment door
8. Console glove compartment door hinge

88180GA1

Fig. 27 Exploded view of the floor console assembly—1995 shown

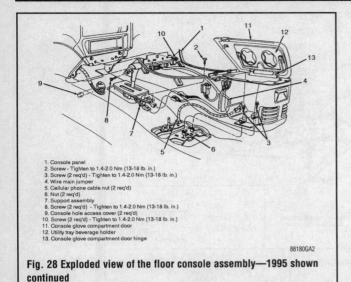

1. Console panel
2. Screw - Tighten to 1.4-2.0 Nm (13-18 lb. in.)
3. Screw (2 req'd) - Tighten to 1.4-2.0 Nm (13-18 lb. in.)
4. Wire main jumper
5. Cellular phone cable nut (2 req'd)
6. Nut (2 req'd)
7. Support assembly
8. Screw (2 req'd) - Tighten to 1.4-2.0 Nm (13-18 lb. in.)
9. Console hole access cover (2 req'd)
10. Screw (2 req'd) - Tighten to 1.4-2.0 Nm (13-18 lb. in.)
11. Console glove compartment door
12. Utility tray beverage holder
13. Console glove compartment door hinge

Fig. 28 Exploded view of the floor console assembly—1995 shown continued

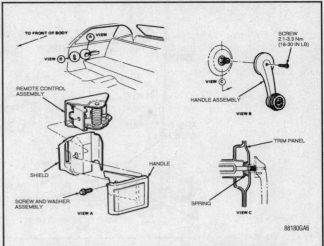

Fig. 29 Door handle removal on the 1983 Thunderbird and XR-7 models

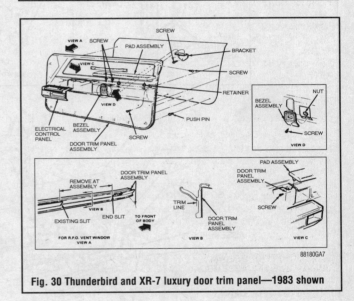

Fig. 30 Thunderbird and XR-7 luxury door trim panel—1983 shown

3. Reach under the finish panel and disconnect the wiring leading to the fog lamp switch, air spring suspension switch and lighter socket and retainer.

4. Lift the rear of the console panel, then slide it rearwards to release the front locating tabs. Remove the console finish panel.

5. Remove the center screws from the console glove compartment, then lift the compartment from the console panel. Disconnect the luggage compartment remote control lock switch and fuel filler door lock switch.

6. Remove the screws from the bottom of the console glove compartment to the front floor pan.

7. Remove the two caps and screws, then the floor console panel.

8. Remove the retaining screws from the front of the floor console panel to the instrument panel.

9. Disconnect the main jumper wire and the main wiring. Lift the console from the vehicle.

10. Reverse the procedure to install, tighten all of the components.

11. Check the operation of the switches involved from disconnecting the wiring.

Door Panels

REMOVAL & INSTALLATION

1983 Models

▶ **See Figures 29, 30 and 31**

1. Remove the window handle retaining screw and remove the handle.

2. On the Cougar, remove the door latch handle cup retaining screw and remove the cup. The screws are covered by removable appliques.

3. On the Thunderbird and XR-7, remove the inside door handle attaching screw and remove the handle and shield.

4. On the Thunderbird and XR-7, remove the screws from the armrest door pull cup area.

5. On the Cougar, remove the retaining screws from the armrest.

6. On the Thunderbird and XR-7 with power door locks and/or power windows, remove the retaining screws and power switch cover assembly. Remove the screws holding the switch housing.

7. Remove the mirror remote control bezel nut.

8. On the Thunderbird and XR-7, remove the door trim panel retaining screws.

9. With a flat, wood spatula, pry the trim retaining clips from the door panel. These clips can be easily torn from the trim panel, so be very careful to pry as closely as possible to the clips.

10. Pull the panel out slightly and disconnect all wiring.

11. If a new panel is being installed, transfer all necessary parts.

12. Installation is the reverse of removal.

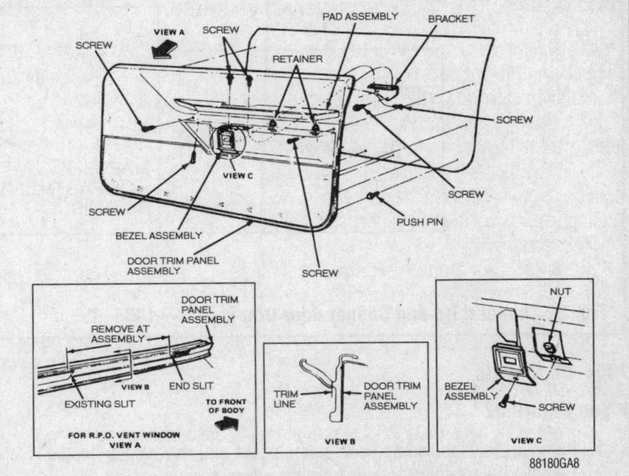

Fig. 31 Thunderbird and XR-7 standard door trim panel—1983 shown

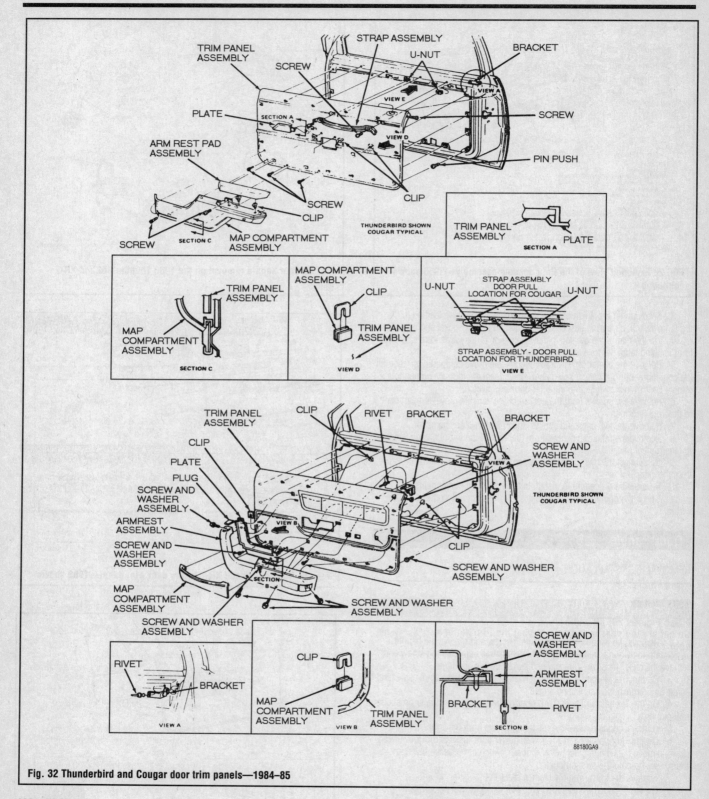

Fig. 32 Thunderbird and Cougar door trim panels—1984–85

1984–88 Models

▶ **See Figure 32**

1. Remove the window handle retaining screw and remove the handle.
2. Remove the retaining screws from the armrest.
3. Remove the mirror remote control bezel nut.
4. Remove the door trim panel retaining screws.

5. With a flat, wood spatula, pry the trim retaining clips from the door panel. These clips can be easily torn from the trim panel, so be very careful to pry as closely as possible to the clips.
6. Pull the panel out slightly and disconnect all wiring.
7. If a new panel is being installed, transfer all necessary parts.
8. Installation is the reverse of removal.

1989–92 Models

▶ **See Figure 33**

1. Remove window regulator switch housing.
2. Remove the door inside handle cup (snaps out).
3. Remove the self tapping screw retaining door trim panel upper front extension assembly, and remove assembly.
4. Remove the two self tapping screws retaining door trim panel to the door inner panel.
5. Lift the door trim panel upward and snap out trim panel.
6. Disconnect the wire harness for courtesy lamp.

To install:

7. Attach the wiring harness to the courtesy lamp.
8. Place the door panel into position, then tighten the panel to the inner panel.
9. Attach the upper front extension assembly.
10. Snap the door handle cup on the door assembly.
11. Install the window regulator switch housing.

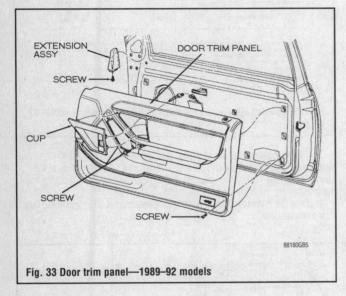

Fig. 33 Door trim panel—1989–92 models

1993–97 Models

▶ **See Figure 34**

✳✳ WARNING

Do not pry the door trim panel. Prying the trim panel may break the hook retainers.

1. Disconnect the negative battery cable.
2. Carefully pull the door trim finish panel away from the door trim panel.
3. Disconnect the wiring from the lock switches, outer rear view mirror controls, and regulator controls.
4. If equipped, remove the door trim panel finish panel.
5. Remove the trim panel retaining screw through the door trim panel finish panel opening.
6. Remove the interior lamp lens cover.
7. Remove the screw through the interior lamp opening.
8. Slide the door trim panel upwards to disengage the hooks.
9. Rotate the top of the trim panel away from the door, then lift the bottom hooks from the front door.
10. Disconnect the window regulator jumper wire.
11. Remove the trim panel.
12. Reverse the procedure to install the components.
13. Connect the wiring, then check the operation of all the components involved.

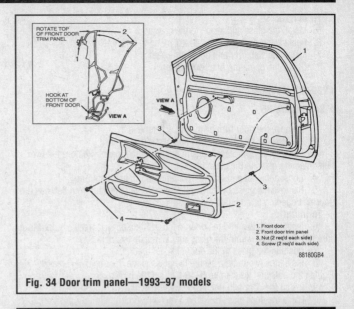

Fig. 34 Door trim panel—1993–97 models

Door Glass

REMOVAL & INSTALLATION

1983 Models without Pivot Type Vent Windows

1. Remove the door panel and watershield.
2. Raise the glass sufficiently to gain access to the 3 glass bracket retaining rivets and drill them out. Never try to pry out the rivets!

✳✳ WARNING

Before removing the rivets you should insert a suitable block support between the door outer panel and the glass bracket, to stabilize the glass during rivet removal.

3. Remove the glass.
4. Installation is the reverse of removal.

1983 Models with Pivot Type Vent Windows

1. Remove the door trim panel and watershield.
2. Raise the glass to the full up position.
3. Remove the rubber downstop from the glass bracket and lower the door glass to the full down position.
4. Remove the 3 screws securing the vent window frame to the door assembly.
5. Tip the vent window rearwards and remove it.
6. Raise the glass sufficiently to gain access to the 3 glass bracket attaching rivets and drill them out. Remove the glass.

To install:

7. Install the spacer and retainer assemblies into the glass retention holes and assure that each is securely fastened.
8. Insert the glass into the door between the door belt weatherstrips.
9. Position the regulator arm slide assembly into the C-channel of the glass bracket.
10. Position the glass in the glass bracket and use three ¼–20 x 1 in. bolts, flatwashers and nuts in place of rivets. Tighten the bolts to 36–60 inch lbs. (4–7 Nm)

1984–88 Models

1. Remove the door trim panel.
2. Remove the door glass stabilizer.
3. Drill out the two rivets attaching the glass to the glass bracket.
4. Remove the glass. Don't lose the spacers.

To install:

5. Install the glass and attach to the bracket.
6. Replace the rivets with ¼–20 x 1 in. bolts and nuts.
7. Install the stabilizer and door trim panel.
8. Check the operation of all components.

1989–97 Models

▶ **See Figure 35**

1. Remove the door trim panel and watershield.
2. Remove the inside door belt weatherstrip assembly.
3. Lower glass to access holes in the door inner panel. Remove the two nuts retaining glass to the glass bracket.
4. Loosen the nut and washer retaining door glass stabilizer.
5. Remove the glass by tipping it forward then removing from between the door belt opening to outboard side of door.

To install:

6. Install the glass into the door at the belt line outside weatherstrip. Make sure the glass is set within the glass run latch side retainers.
7. Position the glass to the door channel bracket.
8. Install the two nuts to secure the glass to the door channel bracket. Tighten the nuts and washers to 8–10 ft. lbs. (10–14 Nm).
9. Install the door belt line inside weatherstrip.
10. Raise the door glass to within 3 inches (75mm) of full-up position, then adjust the door window glass as necessary.
11. Install the door trim panel and door trim shield.

Window Regulator

REMOVAL & INSTALLATION

1983 Models

▶ **See Figure 36 and 37**

1. Remove the door trim panel and watershield.
2. Support the glass in the full up position.

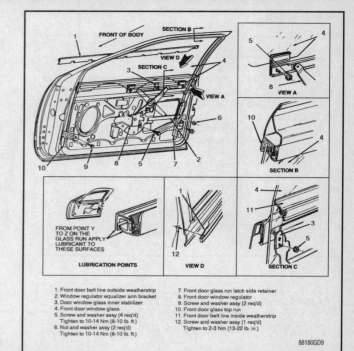

1. Front door belt line outside weatherstrip
2. Window regulator equalizer arm bracket
3. Door window glass inner stabilizer
4. Front door window glass
5. Screw and washer assy (4 req'd)
   Tighten to 10-14 Nm (8-10 lb. ft.)
6. Nut and washer assy (2 req'd)
   Tighten to 10-14 Nm (8-10 lb. ft.)
7. Front door glass run latch side retainer
8. Front door window regulator
9. Screw and washer assy (2 req'd)
10. Front door glass top run
11. Front door belt line inside weatherstrip
12. Screw and washer assy (1 req'd)
    Tighten to 2-3 Nm (13-22 lb. in.)

Fig. 35 Exploded view of the regulator and window glass—1989–97 models

3. On Cougars with power windows, drill out the motor bracket-to-inner panel attaching rivet and remove the rivet. Disconnect the motor wires at the connector. On the Thunderbird and XR-7 with power windows, drill out the regulator attaching rivets and remove the rivets.
4. Disengage the regulator arm from the glass bracket and remove the regulator from the door.

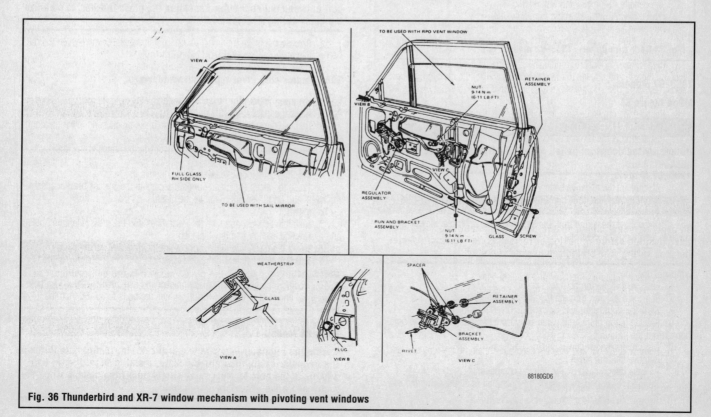

Fig. 36 Thunderbird and XR-7 window mechanism with pivoting vent windows

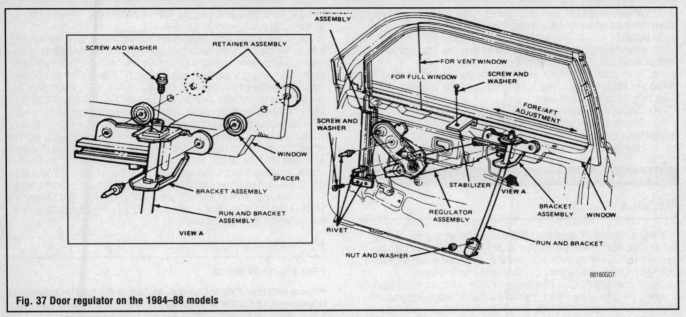

Fig. 37 Door regulator on the 1984–88 models

5. If equipped with power windows, secure the regulator in a vise and drill a 5/16 in. (8mm) hole through the regulator sector gear and the plate. Install a 1/4 in. (6mm) bolt and nut in the hole to prevent the sector gear from moving when the motor and drive assembly is removed.

6. Remove the motor assembly from the regulator and install it on a new regulator.

7. Installation is the reverse of removal. Replace the rivets with 1/4 –20½ in. machine screws. Remove the regulator restraining bolt and nut if the old regulator was re-used.

1984–88 Models

1. Remove the trim panel and watershield.
2. Prop the window glass in the full up position.
3. Disconnect the window motor wiring if so equipped.
4. Drill out the 3 rivets (manual windows) or 4 rivets (electric windows), attaching the regulator to the inner door panel.
5. Remove the upper screw and washer and the lower nut and washer, attaching the run and bracket to the inner door panel. Slide the run tube up between the door belt and glass. It's a good idea to cover the glass with a protective cloth.
6. Remove the regulator slide from the glass bracket and remove the regulator through the door access hole.
7. Installation is the reverse of removal. Replace the rivets with 1/4 –20–1 in. bolts and nuts.

1989–97 Models

> **❄❄ CAUTION**
>
> **To avoid personal injury, ensure that the regulator arms are in a fixed position before removing or replacing the regulator counterbalance spring. The spring can unwind violently.**

1. Remove the door trim panel and water shield.
2. Lower the glass to access the holes in the door inner panel. Remove the 2 nut and washer assemblies retaining the glass to the glass bracket.
3. Prop the glass in the full-up position.
4. Disconnect the negative battery cable.
5. Disconnect the electric motor wiring.
6. Remove the 2 nut and washer assemblies retaining the regulator equalizer bracket.
7. Remove the 4 rivets attaching the regulator to the door inner panel, drilling the rivets with a 6mm drillbit.
8. Remove the regulator through the access hole.

To Install:

9. With the glass in the full-up position, install the window regulator through the access hole.
10. Position the regulator base plate to door inner panel and install the 4 rivets.
11. Install the regulator equalizer bracket on the regulator and loosely assemble with the nut and washer assemblies.
12. Install the regulator glass bracket drive channel on the glass and secure with the nut and washer assemblies, torquing to 7–10 ft. lbs. (9–14 Nm).
13. Connect the motor wiring.
14. Connect the negative battery cable.
15. Lower the glass about 3 inches from the full-up position.
16. With the door open, place hands on each side of the glass and pull the glass fully into the door glass run assembly at the B-pillar.
17. Apply a downward pressure on the equalizer bracket and tighten the nut and washer assemblies to 7–10 ft. lbs. (9–14 Nm).
18. Cycle the door glass to ensure proper operation.
19. Install the door trim panel and the watershield.

Electric Window Motor

REMOVAL & INSTALLATION

1. Remove the trim panel and watershield.
2. Remove the speakers.
3. Disconnect the negative battery cable.
4. Disconnect the motor wires and the connector.
5. Using the dimples located on the inner door panel, drill 3/4 in. (19mm) holes for access to the motor.

> **❄❄ WARNING**
>
> **When drilling the holes, the glass must be in the up position. The hole saw pilot must not extend more than 1/4 in. (6mm) beyond the hole saw.**

> **❄❄ CAUTION**
>
> **Secure the regulator in a vise and drill a 5/16 in. (8mm) hole through the regulator sector gear and the plate. Install a 1/4 in. (6mm) bolt and nut in the hole to prevent the sector gear from moving when the motor and drive assembly is removed.**

6. Working through the holes, remove the 3 motor and drive-to-regulator attaching bolts. Remove the motor and drive from the door.

To install:

7. Clean the chips of metal from the surrounding area. Then coat the bare metal to avoid rust.

8. When installing the motor and drive to the regulator and install the 3 screws just snugly enough to hold it. Remove the regulator restraining bolt and nut if the old regulator was re-used.

9. Connect the negative battery cable.

10. Connect the wires and cycle the glass through its run to ensure gear engagement. Then, tighten the attaching screws to 50–85 inch lbs. (6–10 Nm).

11. Install the speakers and door trim panel with watershield.

Windshield and Fixed Glass

REMOVAL & INSTALLATION

If your windshield, or other fixed window, is cracked or chipped, you may decide to replace it with a new one yourself. However, there are two main reasons why replacement windshields and other window glass should be installed only by a professional automotive glass technician: safety and cost.

The most important reason a professional should install automotive glass is for safety. The glass in the vehicle, especially the windshield, is designed with safety in mind in case of a collision. The windshield is specially manufactured from two panes of specially-tempered glass with a thin layer of transparent plastic between them. This construction allows the glass to "give" in the event that a part of your body hits the windshield during the collision, and prevents the glass from shattering, which could cause lacerations, blinding and other harm to passengers of the vehicle. The other fixed windows are designed to be tempered so that if they break during a collision, they shatter in such a way that there are no large pointed glass pieces. The professional automotive glass technician knows how to install the glass in a vehicle so that it will function optimally during a collision. Without the proper experience, knowledge and tools,

installing a piece of automotive glass yourself could lead to additional harm if an accident should ever occur.

Cost is also a factor when deciding to install automotive glass yourself. Performing this could cost you much more than a professional may charge for the same job. Since the windshield is designed to break under stress, an often life saving characteristic, windshields tend to break VERY easily when an inexperienced person attempts to install one. Do-it-yourselfers buying two, three or even four windshields from a salvage yard because they have broken them during installation are common stories. Also, since the automotive glass is designed to prevent the outside elements from entering your vehicle, improper installation can lead to water and air leaks. Annoying whining noises at highway speeds from air leaks or inside body panel rusting from water leaks can add to your stress level and subtract from your wallet. After buying two or three windshields, installing them and ending up with a leak that produces a noise while driving and water damage during rainstorms, the cost of having a professional do it correctly the first time may be much more alluring. We here at Chilton, therefore, advise that you have a professional automotive glass technician service any broken glass on your vehicle.

WINDSHIELD CHIP REPAIR

▶ See Figures 38 thru 52

➡ Check with your state and local authorities on the laws for state safety inspection. Some states or municipalities may not allow chip repair as a viable option for correcting stone damage to your windshield.

Although severely cracked or damaged windshields must be replaced, there is something that you can do to prolong or even prevent the need for replacement of a chipped windshield. There are many companies which offer windshield chip repair products, such as Loctite's® Bullseye™ windshield repair kit. These kits usually consist of a syringe, pedestal and a sealing adhesive. The syringe is mounted on the pedestal and is used to create a vacuum which pulls the plastic layer against the glass. This helps make the chip transparent. The adhesive is then injected

TCCA0P00

Fig. 38 Small chips on your windshield can be fixed with an aftermarket repair kit, such as the one from Loctite®

TCCA0P01

Fig. 39 To repair a chip, clean the windshield with glass cleaner and dry it completely

TCCA0P02

Fig. 40 Remove the center from the adhesive disc and peel off the backing from one side of the disc . . .

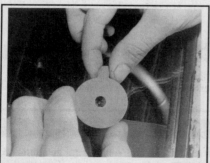

TCCA0P03

Fig. 41 . . . then press it on the windshield so that the chip is centered in the hole

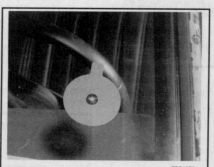

TCCA0P04

Fig. 42 Be sure that the tab points upward on the windshield

TCCA0P05

Fig. 43 Peel the backing off the exposed side of the adhesive disc . . .

Fig. 44 . . . then position the plastic pedestal on the adhesive disc, ensuring that the tabs are aligned

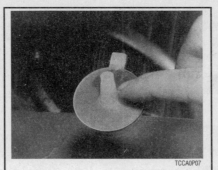

Fig. 45 Press the pedestal firmly on the adhesive disc to create an adequate seal . . .

Fig. 46 . . . then install the applicator syringe nipple in the pedestal's hole

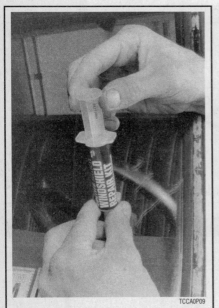

Fig. 47 Hold the syringe with one hand while pulling the plunger back with the other hand

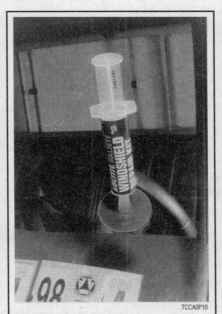

Fig. 48 After applying the solution, allow the entire assembly to sit until it has set completely

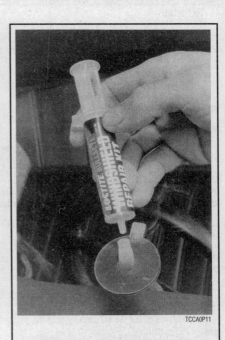

Fig. 49 After the solution has set, remove the syringe from the pedestal . . .

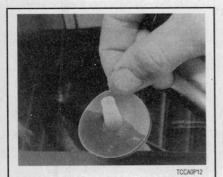

Fig. 50 . . . then peel the pedestal off of the adhesive disc . . .

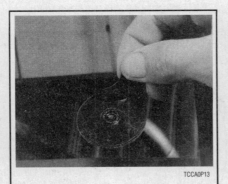

Fig. 51 . . . and peel the adhesive disc off of the windshield

Fig. 52 The chip will still be slightly visible, but it should be filled with the hardened solution

which seals the chip and helps to prevent further stress cracks from developing. Refer to the sequence of photos to get a general idea of what windshield chip repair involves.

➡**Always follow the specific manufacturer's instructions.**

Inside Rearview Mirror

REMOVAL & INSTALLATION

Non Breakaway

1. Loosen the mirror assembly to mounting bracket setscrew.
2. Remove mirror assembly by sliding upward and away from the mounting bracket.
3. If the bracket vinyl pad remains on the windshield, apply low heat from a heat gun until the vinyl softens. Peel vinyl off the windshield and discard.
To install:
4. If necessary, to install a new mounting bracket to windshield, a rearview mirror adhesive kit D9AZ–19554–CA, or equivalent must be obtained. Follow the instructions in the kit for gluing the mounting bracket vinyl to the windshield.
5. Attach the mirror to the mounting bracket.
6. Tighten the mirror mounting bracket setscrew.

Breakaway

◆ **See Figures 53, 54 and 55**

These breakaway mounts are designed to detach from the rearview mirror bracket during air bag deployment. Any excessive force or excessive up/down, side-to-side adjustment can cause the mirror to detach from the windshield.

➡**It may be necessary to obtain a special service tool to replace the mirror such as T94–17700–AH or equivalent to complete the job.**

1. Disconnect the wiring assembly, if equipped with automatic diming outside rearview mirror.
2. Grasp the inside mirror firmly. Use one hand to support one end of the mirror against the windshield. Use the other hand to pull the mirror away from the glass using a sideways movement.
To install:
3. Center the bottom of the mirror mount against the windshield at the top of the mirror bracket.
4. Slide the mirror mount partially onto the bracket, keeping the mount parallel to the windshield.
5. With the use of a special mirror installation tool, T94–17700–AH, complete the installation onto the mirror bracket.

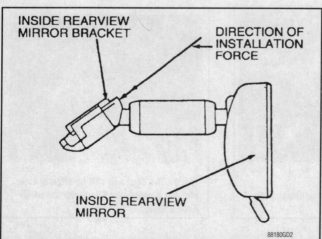

Fig. 53 The breakaway rear view mirror looks the same as a non-breakaway mirror

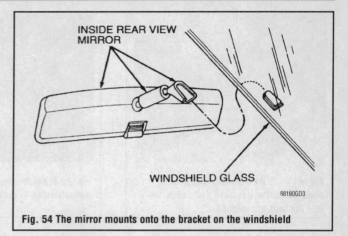

Fig. 54 The mirror mounts onto the bracket on the windshield

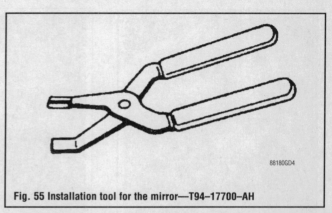

Fig. 55 Installation tool for the mirror—T94–17700–AH

Seats

REMOVAL & INSTALLATION

Front

◆ **See Figures 56, 57 and 58**

1. Remove the seat track to floor insulators.
2. Remove the seat track bolts and seat belt anchor bolts.
3. On power seats, tilt the seat backward and disconnect the motor wiring prior to lifting the seat from the car.
4. Remove the seat from the vehicle.
To install:
5. Place the seat into position and tighten the seat track and seat belt anchor bolts to 21–31 ft. lbs. (30–43 Nm).
6. Attach the wiring if disconnected.
7. Install the seat track to floor insulators.–

Rear Bench

◆ **See Figure 59**

1. Bearing down with your knee on the rear seat cushion, push the cushion rearward and disengage it from the retaining brackets.
2. Remove the rear seat armrests if applicable.
3. Remove the seatback lower retaining screws and seat belt bolts.
4. Grasp the seatback at the bottom and lift it up to disengage the hanger wire from the retainer brackets.
To install:
5. Position the seat back assembly so that the hanger wire is fully engaged in the package tray slots.
6. Install the lower retaining screws and tighten to 13–19 ft. lbs. (17–37 Nm).
7. Position the seat cushion assembly into the vehicle.

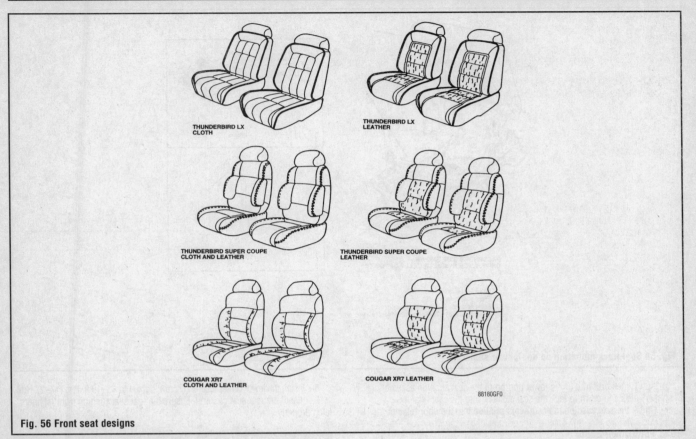

Fig. 56 Front seat designs

THUNDERBIRD LX
CLOTH

THUNDERBIRD LX
LEATHER

THUNDERBIRD SUPER COUPE
CLOTH AND LEATHER

THUNDERBIRD SUPER COUPE
LEATHER

COUGAR XR7
CLOTH AND LEATHER

COUGAR XR7 LEATHER

88180GF0

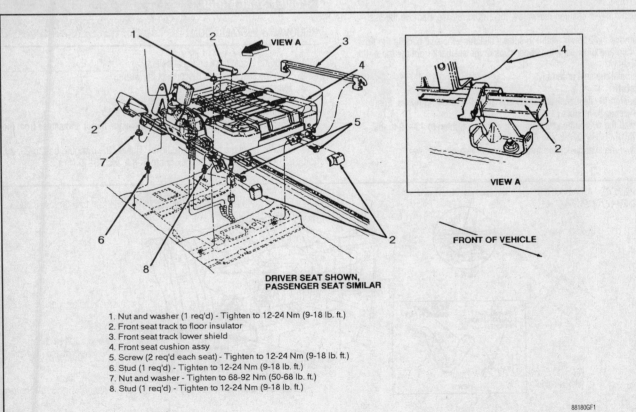

VIEW A

VIEW A

FRONT OF VEHICLE

DRIVER SEAT SHOWN,
PASSENGER SEAT SIMILAR

1. Nut and washer (1 req'd) - Tighten to 12-24 Nm (9-18 lb. ft.)
2. Front seat track to floor insulator
3. Front seat track lower shield
4. Front seat cushion assy
5. Screw (2 req'd each seat) - Tighten to 12-24 Nm (9-18 lb. ft.)
6. Stud (1 req'd) - Tighten to 12-24 Nm (9-18 lb. ft.)
7. Nut and washer - Tighten to 68-92 Nm (50-68 lb. ft.)
8. Stud (1 req'd) - Tighten to 12-24 Nm (9-18 lb. ft.)

88180GF1

Fig. 57 Seat track mounting on power seats

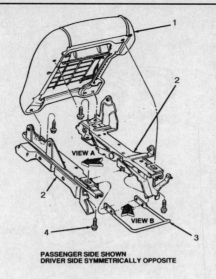
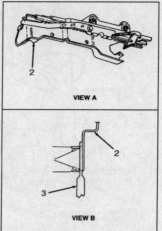

PASSENGER SIDE SHOWN
DRIVER SIDE SYMMETRICALLY OPPOSITE

1. Front seat cushion
2. Front seat track
3. Front seat cushion extension handle
4. Screw (4 req'd) - Tighten to 12-24 Nm (9-18 lb. ft.)

88180GF2

Fig. 58 Seat track mounting on non-power seats

8. Apply knee pressure to the lower portion of the seat cushion assembly. Push rearwards and down to lock the seat cushion into the seat retainer.

9. Check the seat cushion to ensure it is secured into the floor retainer.

Rear, Fold-Down Seats

1. Push the rear cushion rearwards, then lift to release. Remove the cushion.

2. Remove the 2 lower retaining screws attaching the seat back to the floor.

3. Lift up and disengage the upper clips of the seatback from the top of the folding floor.

4. Remove the seat assembly.

To install:

5. Position the seat back assembly and align the retaining hooks. Ensure hooks fully engage in slots.

6. Install the two outboard retaining bolts, then tighten to 13–19 ft. lbs. (17–27 Nm).

7. Lower the seat backs and install the upper retaining screws.

8. Install the lower center retaining screw, tighten to 13–19 ft. lbs. (17–27 Nm).

9. Install the rear seat cushion. Ensure the rear seat cushion front retainers latch properly.

Power Seat Motor

REMOVAL & INSTALLATION

1. Unbolt the seat track and seat belts.
2. Turn the seat over and disconnect the wiring.
3. Remove the seat from the car.
4. Remove the 3 motor mounting bolts.
5. Remove the cable-to-seat track clamps.
6. Open the wire retaining straps and remove the motor and cables from the seat.

7. Installation is the reverse of removal. Tighten the retaining bolt to 23–29 ft. lbs. (31–39 Nm). Tighten the hex nut to 5–8 ft. lbs. (6–10 Nm).

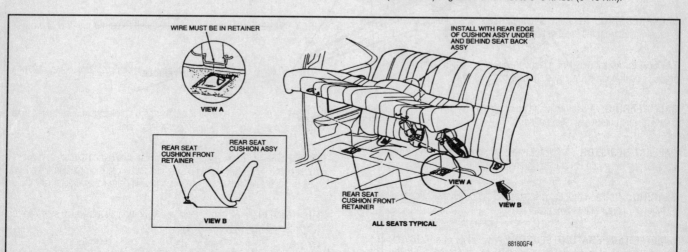

Fig. 59 Pull the bottom of the seat upwards and pull out

GLOSSARY

AIR/FUEL RATIO: The ratio of air-to-gasoline by weight in the fuel mixture drawn into the engine.

AIR INJECTION: One method of reducing harmful exhaust emissions by injecting air into each of the exhaust ports of an engine. The fresh air entering the hot exhaust manifold causes any remaining fuel to be burned before it can exit the tailpipe.

ALTERNATOR: A device used for converting mechanical energy into electrical energy.

AMMETER: An instrument, calibrated in amperes, used to measure the flow of an electrical current in a circuit. Ammeters are always connected in series with the circuit being tested.

AMPERE: The rate of flow of electrical current present when one volt of electrical pressure is applied against one ohm of electrical resistance.

ANALOG COMPUTER: Any microprocessor that uses similar (analogous) electrical signals to make its calculations.

ARMATURE: A laminated, soft iron core wrapped by a wire that converts electrical energy to mechanical energy as in a motor or relay. When rotated in a magnetic field, it changes mechanical energy into electrical energy as in a generator.

ATMOSPHERIC PRESSURE: The pressure on the Earth's surface caused by the weight of the air in the atmosphere. At sea level, this pressure is 14.7 psi at 32°F (101 kPa at 0°C).

ATOMIZATION: The breaking down of a liquid into a fine mist that can be suspended in air.

AXIAL PLAY: Movement parallel to a shaft or bearing bore.

BACKFIRE: The sudden combustion of gases in the intake or exhaust system that results in a loud explosion.

BACKLASH: The clearance or play between two parts, such as meshed gears.

BACKPRESSURE: Restrictions in the exhaust system that slow the exit of exhaust gases from the combustion chamber.

BAKELITE: A heat resistant, plastic insulator material commonly used in printed circuit boards and transistorized components.

BALL BEARING: A bearing made up of hardened inner and outer races between which hardened steel balls roll.

BALLAST RESISTOR: A resistor in the primary ignition circuit that lowers voltage after the engine is started to reduce wear on ignition components.

BEARING: A friction reducing, supportive device usually located between a stationary part and a moving part.

BIMETAL TEMPERATURE SENSOR: Any sensor or switch made of two dissimilar types of metal that bend when heated or cooled due to the different expansion rates of the alloys. These types of sensors usually function as an on/off switch.

BLOWBY: Combustion gases, composed of water vapor and unburned fuel, that leak past the piston rings into the crankcase during normal engine operation. These gases are removed by the PCV system to prevent the buildup of harmful acids in the crankcase.

BRAKE PAD: A brake shoe and lining assembly used with disc brakes.

BRAKE SHOE: The backing for the brake lining. The term is, however, usually applied to the assembly of the brake backing and lining.

BUSHING: A liner, usually removable, for a bearing; an anti-friction liner used in place of a bearing.

CALIPER: A hydraulically activated device in a disc brake system, which is mounted straddling the brake rotor (disc). The caliper contains at least one piston and two brake pads. Hydraulic pressure on the piston(s) forces the pads against the rotor.

CAMSHAFT: A shaft in the engine on which are the lobes (cams) which operate the valves. The camshaft is driven by the crankshaft, via a belt, chain or gears, at one half the crankshaft speed.

CAPACITOR: A device which stores an electrical charge.

CARBON MONOXIDE (CO): A colorless, odorless gas given off as a normal byproduct of combustion. It is poisonous and extremely dangerous in confined areas, building up slowly to toxic levels without warning if adequate ventilation is not available.

CARBURETOR: A device, usually mounted on the intake manifold of an engine, which mixes the air and fuel in the proper proportion to allow even combustion.

CATALYTIC CONVERTER: A device installed in the exhaust system, like a muffler, that converts harmful byproducts of combustion into carbon dioxide and water vapor by means of a heat-producing chemical reaction.

CENTRIFUGAL ADVANCE: A mechanical method of advancing the spark timing by using flyweights in the distributor that react to centrifugal force generated by the distributor shaft rotation.

CHECK VALVE: Any one-way valve installed to permit the flow of air, fuel or vacuum in one direction only.

CHOKE: A device, usually a moveable valve, placed in the intake path of a carburetor to restrict the flow of air.

CIRCUIT: Any unbroken path through which an electrical current can flow. Also used to describe fuel flow in some instances.

CIRCUIT BREAKER: A switch which protects an electrical circuit from overload by opening the circuit when the current flow exceeds a predetermined level. Some circuit breakers must be reset manually, while most reset automatically.

COIL (IGNITION): A transformer in the ignition circuit which steps up the voltage provided to the spark plugs.

COMBINATION MANIFOLD: An assembly which includes both the intake and exhaust manifolds in one casting.

COMBINATION VALVE: A device used in some fuel systems that routes fuel vapors to a charcoal storage canister instead of venting them into the atmosphere. The valve relieves fuel tank pressure and allows fresh air into the tank as the fuel level drops to prevent a vapor lock situation.

COMPRESSION RATIO: The comparison of the total volume of the cylinder and combustion chamber with the piston at BDC and the piston at TDC.

CONDENSER: 1. An electrical device which acts to store an electrical charge, preventing voltage surges. 2. A radiator-like device in the air conditioning system in which refrigerant gas condenses into a liquid, giving off heat.

CONDUCTOR: Any material through which an electrical current can be transmitted easily.

CONTINUITY: Continuous or complete circuit. Can be checked with an ohmmeter.

COUNTERSHAFT: An intermediate shaft which is rotated by a mainshaft and transmits, in turn, that rotation to a working part.

CRANKCASE: The lower part of an engine in which the crankshaft and related parts operate.

CRANKSHAFT: The main driving shaft of an engine which receives reciprocating motion from the pistons and converts it to rotary motion.

CYLINDER: In an engine, the round hole in the engine block in which the piston(s) ride.

CYLINDER BLOCK: The main structural member of an engine in which is found the cylinders, crankshaft and other principal parts.

CYLINDER HEAD: The detachable portion of the engine, usually fastened to the top of the cylinder block and containing all or most of the combustion chambers. On overhead valve engines, it contains the valves and their operating parts. On overhead cam engines, it contains the camshaft as well.

DEAD CENTER: The extreme top or bottom of the piston stroke.

DETONATION: An unwanted explosion of the air/fuel mixture in the combustion chamber caused by excess heat and compression, advanced timing, or an overly lean mixture. Also referred to as "ping".

DIAPHRAGM: A thin, flexible wall separating two cavities, such as in a vacuum advance unit.

DIESELING: A condition in which hot spots in the combustion chamber cause the engine to run on after the key is turned off.

DIFFERENTIAL: A geared assembly which allows the transmission of motion between drive axles, giving one axle the ability to turn faster than the other.

DIODE: An electrical device that will allow current to flow in one direction only.

DISC BRAKE: A hydraulic braking assembly consisting of a brake disc, or rotor, mounted on an axle, and a caliper assembly containing, usually two brake pads which are activated by hydraulic pressure. The pads are forced against the sides of the disc, creating friction which slows the vehicle.

DISTRIBUTOR: A mechanically driven device on an engine which is responsible for electrically firing the spark plug at a predetermined point of the piston stroke.

DOWEL PIN: A pin, inserted in mating holes in two different parts allowing those parts to maintain a fixed relationship.

DRUM BRAKE: A braking system which consists of two brake shoes and one or two wheel cylinders, mounted on a fixed backing plate, and a brake drum, mounted on an axle, which revolves around the assembly.

DWELL: The rate, measured in degrees of shaft rotation, at which an electrical circuit cycles on and off.

ELECTRONIC CONTROL UNIT (ECU): Ignition module, module, amplifier or igniter. See Module for definition.

ELECTRONIC IGNITION: A system in which the timing and firing of the spark plugs is controlled by an electronic control unit, usually called a module. These systems have no points or condenser.

END-PLAY: The measured amount of axial movement in a shaft.

ENGINE: A device that converts heat into mechanical energy.

EXHAUST MANIFOLD: A set of cast passages or pipes which conduct exhaust gases from the engine.

FEELER GAUGE: A blade, usually metal, or precisely predetermined thickness, used to measure the clearance between two parts.

FIRING ORDER: The order in which combustion occurs in the cylinders of an engine. Also the order in which spark is distributed to the plugs by the distributor.

FLOODING: The presence of too much fuel in the intake manifold and combustion chamber which prevents the air/fuel mixture from firing, thereby causing a no-start situation.

FLYWHEEL: A disc shaped part bolted to the rear end of the crankshaft. Around the outer perimeter is affixed the ring gear. The starter drive engages the ring gear, turning the flywheel, which rotates the crankshaft, imparting the initial starting motion to the engine.

FOOT POUND (ft. lbs. or sometimes, ft.lb.): The amount of energy or work needed to raise an item weighing one pound, a distance of one foot.

FUSE: A protective device in a circuit which prevents circuit overload by breaking the circuit when a specific amperage is present. The device is constructed around a strip or wire of a lower amperage rating than the circuit it is designed to protect. When an amperage higher than that stamped on the fuse is present in the circuit, the strip or wire melts, opening the circuit.

GEAR RATIO: The ratio between the number of teeth on meshing gears.

GENERATOR: A device which converts mechanical energy into electrical energy.

HEAT RANGE: The measure of a spark plug's ability to dissipate heat from its firing end. The higher the heat range, the hotter the plug fires.

HUB: The center part of a wheel or gear.

HYDROCARBON (HC): Any chemical compound made up of hydrogen and carbon. A major pollutant formed by the engine as a byproduct of combustion.

HYDROMETER: An instrument used to measure the specific gravity of a solution.

INCH POUND (inch lbs.; sometimes in.lb. or in. lbs.): One twelfth of a foot pound.

INDUCTION: A means of transferring electrical energy in the form of a magnetic field. Principle used in the ignition coil to increase voltage.

INJECTOR: A device which receives metered fuel under relatively low pressure and is activated to inject the fuel into the engine under relatively high pressure at a predetermined time.

INPUT SHAFT: The shaft to which torque is applied, usually carrying the driving gear or gears.

INTAKE MANIFOLD: A casting of passages or pipes used to conduct air or a fuel/air mixture to the cylinders.

JOURNAL: The bearing surface within which a shaft operates.

KEY: A small block usually fitted in a notch between a shaft and a hub to prevent slippage of the two parts.

MANIFOLD: A casting of passages or set of pipes which connect the cylinders to an inlet or outlet source.

MANIFOLD VACUUM: Low pressure in an engine intake manifold formed just below the throttle plates. Manifold vacuum is highest at idle and drops under acceleration.

MASTER CYLINDER: The primary fluid pressurizing device in a hydraulic system. In automotive use, it is found in brake and hydraulic clutch systems and is pedal activated, either directly or, in a power brake system, through the power booster.

MODULE: Electronic control unit, amplifier or igniter of solid state or integrated design which controls the current flow in the ignition primary circuit based on input from the pick-up coil. When the module opens the primary circuit, high secondary voltage is induced in the coil.

NEEDLE BEARING: A bearing which consists of a number (usually a large number) of long, thin rollers.

OHM: (Ω) The unit used to measure the resistance of conductor-to-electrical flow. One ohm is the amount of resistance that limits current flow to one ampere in a circuit with one volt of pressure.

OHMMETER: An instrument used for measuring the resistance, in ohms, in an electrical circuit.

OUTPUT SHAFT: The shaft which transmits torque from a device, such as a transmission.

OVERDRIVE: A gear assembly which produces more shaft revolutions than that transmitted to it.

OVERHEAD CAMSHAFT (OHC): An engine configuration in which the camshaft is mounted on top of the cylinder head and operates the valve either directly or by means of rocker arms.

OVERHEAD VALVE (OHV): An engine configuration in which all of the valves are located in the cylinder head and the camshaft is located in the cylinder block. The camshaft operates the valves via lifters and pushrods.

OXIDES OF NITROGEN (NOx): Chemical compounds of nitrogen produced as a byproduct of combustion. They combine with hydrocarbons to produce smog.

OXYGEN SENSOR: Use with the feedback system to sense the presence of oxygen in the exhaust gas and signal the computer which can reference the voltage signal to an air/fuel ratio.

PINION: The smaller of two meshing gears.

PISTON RING: An open-ended ring with fits into a groove on the outer diameter of the piston. Its chief function is to form a seal between the piston and cylinder wall. Most automotive pistons have three rings: two for compression sealing; one for oil sealing.

PRELOAD: A predetermined load placed on a bearing during assembly or by adjustment.

PRIMARY CIRCUIT: the low voltage side of the ignition system which consists of the ignition switch, ballast resistor or resistance wire, bypass, coil, electronic control unit and pick-up coil as well as the connecting wires and harnesses.

PRESS FIT: The mating of two parts under pressure, due to the inner diameter of one being smaller than the outer diameter of the other, or vice versa; an interference fit.

RACE: The surface on the inner or outer ring of a bearing on which the balls, needles or rollers move.

REGULATOR: A device which maintains the amperage and/or voltage levels of a circuit at predetermined values.

RELAY: A switch which automatically opens and/or closes a circuit.

RESISTANCE: The opposition to the flow of current through a circuit or electrical device, and is measured in ohms. Resistance is equal to the voltage divided by the amperage.

RESISTOR: A device, usually made of wire, which offers a preset amount of resistance in an electrical circuit.

RING GEAR: The name given to a ring-shaped gear attached to a differential case, or affixed to a flywheel or as part of a planetary gear set.

ROLLER BEARING: A bearing made up of hardened inner and outer races between which hardened steel rollers move.

ROTOR: 1. The disc-shaped part of a disc brake assembly, upon which the brake pads bear; also called, brake disc. 2. The device mounted atop the distributor shaft, which passes current to the distributor cap tower contacts.

SECONDARY CIRCUIT: The high voltage side of the ignition system, usually above 20,000 volts. The secondary includes the ignition coil, coil wire, distributor cap and rotor, spark plug wires and spark plugs.

SENDING UNIT: A mechanical, electrical, hydraulic or electro-magnetic device which transmits information to a gauge.

SENSOR: Any device designed to measure engine operating conditions or ambient pressures and temperatures. Usually electronic in nature and designed to send a voltage signal to an on-board computer, some sensors may operate as a simple on/off switch or they may provide a variable voltage signal (like a potentiometer) as conditions or measured parameters change.

SHIM: Spacers of precise, predetermined thickness used between parts to establish a proper working relationship.

SLAVE CYLINDER: In automotive use, a device in the hydraulic clutch system which is activated by hydraulic force, disengaging the clutch.

SOLENOID: A coil used to produce a magnetic field, the effect of which is to produce work.

SPARK PLUG: A device screwed into the combustion chamber of a spark ignition engine. The basic construction is a conductive core inside of a ceramic insulator, mounted in an outer conductive base. An electrical charge from the spark plug wire travels along the conductive core and jumps a preset air gap to a grounding point or points at the end of the conductive base. The resultant spark ignites the fuel/air mixture in the combustion chamber.

SPLINES: Ridges machined or cast onto the outer diameter of a shaft or inner diameter of a bore to enable parts to mate without rotation.

TACHOMETER: A device used to measure the rotary speed of an engine, shaft, gear, etc., usually in rotations per minute.

THERMOSTAT: A valve, located in the cooling system of an engine, which is closed when cold and opens gradually in response to engine heating, controlling the temperature of the coolant and rate of coolant flow.

TOP DEAD CENTER (TDC): The point at which the piston reaches the top of its travel on the compression stroke.

TORQUE: The twisting force applied to an object.

TORQUE CONVERTER: A turbine used to transmit power from a driving member to a driven member via hydraulic action, providing changes in drive ratio and torque. In automotive use, it links the driveplate at the rear of the engine to the automatic transmission.

TRANSDUCER: A device used to change a force into an electrical signal.

TRANSISTOR: A semi-conductor component which can be actuated by a small voltage to perform an electrical switching function.

TUNE-UP: A regular maintenance function, usually associated with the replacement and adjustment of parts and components in the electrical and fuel systems of a vehicle for the purpose of attaining optimum performance.

TURBOCHARGER: An exhaust driven pump which compresses intake air and forces it into the combustion chambers at higher than atmospheric pressures. The increased air pressure allows more fuel to be burned and results in increased horsepower being produced.

VACUUM ADVANCE: A device which advances the ignition timing in response to increased engine vacuum.

VACUUM GAUGE: An instrument used to measure the presence of vacuum in a chamber.

VALVE: A device which control the pressure, direction of flow or rate of flow of a liquid or gas.

VALVE CLEARANCE: The measured gap between the end of the valve stem and the rocker arm, cam lobe or follower that activates the valve.

VISCOSITY: The rating of a liquid's internal resistance to flow.

VOLTMETER: An instrument used for measuring electrical force in units called volts. Voltmeters are always connected parallel with the circuit being tested.

WHEEL CYLINDER: Found in the automotive drum brake assembly, it is a device, actuated by hydraulic pressure, which, through internal pistons, pushes the brake shoes outward against the drums.

ADJUSTMENT (CLUTCH) 7-4
ADJUSTMENTS (AUTOMATIC TRANSMISSION) 7-10
   AOD IDLE SPEED ADJUSTMENT 7-14
   BAND ADJUSTMENTS 7-10
   DOWNSHIFT (THROTTLE) LINKAGE ADJUSTMENT 7-14
   SHIFT LINKAGE ADJUSTMENT 7-10
ADJUSTMENTS (MANUAL TRANSMISSION) 7-2
   LINKAGE 7-2
AIR BAG DIAGNOSTIC MONITOR 6-10
AIR CLEANER ELEMENT 1-12
   REMOVAL & INSTALLATION 1-12
AIR CONDITIONING COMPONENTS 6-18
   REMOVAL & INSTALLATION 6-18
AIR CONDITIONING SYSTEM 1-31
   PREVENTIVE MAINTENANCE 1-32
   SYSTEM INSPECTION 1-32
   SYSTEM SERVICE & REPAIR 1-31
AIR INTAKE THROTTLE BODY 5-14
   REMOVAL & INSTALLATION 5-14
ALTERNATOR 2-17
   REMOVAL & INSTALLATION 2-18
   TESTING 2-17
ALTERNATOR PRECAUTIONS 2-17
AMPLIFIER 6-19
   REMOVAL & INSTALLATION 6-19
ANTENNA 10-6
   REMOVAL & INSTALLATION 10-6
ANTI-LOCK BRAKE CONTROL MODULE 9-34
   REMOVAL & INSTALLATION 9-34
AUTOMATIC TRANSMISSION 7-10
AUTOMATIC TRANSMISSIONS (FLUIDS AND LUBRICANTS) 1-40
   DRAIN AND REFILL 1-41
   FLUID RECOMMENDATIONS 1-40
   LEVEL CHECK 1-40
AUXILIARY SHAFT 3-55
   REMOVAL & INSTALLATION 3-55
AVOIDING THE MOST COMMON MISTAKES 1-2
AVOIDING TROUBLE 1-2
AXLE HOUSING ASSEMBLY 7-32
   REMOVAL & INSTALLATION 7-32
AXLE SHAFT, BEARING AND SEAL 7-29
   REMOVAL & INSTALLATION 7-29
BACK-UP LIGHT SWITCH (INSTRUMENTS AND SWITCHES) 6-29
   REMOVAL & INSTALLATION 6-29
BACK-UP LIGHT SWITCH (MANUAL TRANSMISSION) 7-2
   REMOVAL & INSTALLATION 7-2
BAROMETRIC/MANIFOLD ABSOLUTE PRESSURE SENSORS 4-16
   OPERATION 4-16
   REMOVAL & INSTALLATION 4-17
   TESTING 4-16
BASIC ELECTRICAL THEORY 6-2
   HOW DOES ELECTRICITY WORK: THE WATER ANALOGY 6-2
   OHM'S LAW 6-2
BASIC FUEL SYSTEM DIAGNOSIS 5-2
BATTERY 1-18
   BATTERY FLUID 1-18
   CABLES 1-19
   CHARGING 1-20
   GENERAL MAINTENANCE 1-18
   PRECAUTIONS 1-18
   REPLACEMENT 1-20
BATTERY CABLES 6-8
BELT-DRIVEN COOLING FAN 3-30
   REMOVAL & INSTALLATION 3-30
BELTS 1-20
   ADJUSTMENTS 1-20
   INSPECTION 1-20
   REMOVAL & INSTALLATION 1-22
BLEEDING THE ABS SYSTEM (TEVES MARK-IV ANTI-LOCK BRAKE
  SYSTEM) 9-35

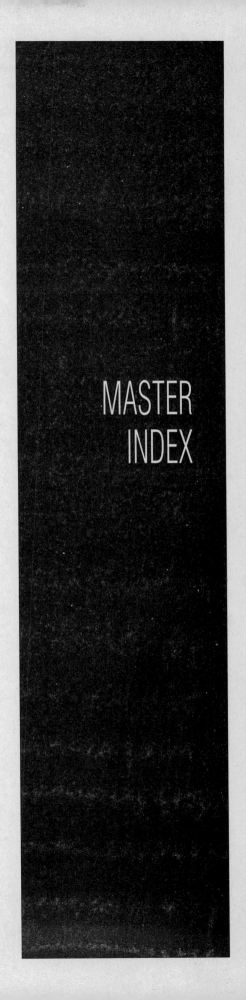

MASTER
INDEX

BLEEDING THE ABS SYSTEM (TEVES MARK II 4-WHEEL ANTI-LOCK
  BRAKE SYSTEM) 9-31
    BLEEDING THE SYSTEM WITH A FULLY CHARGED
      ACCUMULATOR 9-32
    CHECKING FLUID LEVEL AND REFILLING 9-32
    FRONT BRAKE BLEEDING 9-32
    HYDRAULIC PUMP PRIMING 9-32
    REAR BRAKE BLEEDING 9-32
    SYSTEM DISCHARGING (DEPRESSURIZING) 9-32
BLEEDING THE HYDRAULIC SYSTEM 9-5
    PROCEDURE 9-5
BLOWER MOTOR 6-11
    REMOVAL & INSTALLATION 6-11
BLOWER SWITCH 6-17
    PRESET & ADJUSTMENT 6-17
    REMOVAL & INSTALLATION 6-17
BODY LUBRICATION AND MAINTENANCE 1-44
    BODY DRAIN HOLES 1-45
    CARE OF YOUR VEHICLE 1-44
    DOOR HINGES & HINGE CHECKS 1-45
    LOCK CYLINDERS 1-45
    TRUNK LID 1-45
BOLTS, NUTS AND OTHER THREADED RETAINERS 1-5
BRAKE CALIPER 9-8
    OVERHAUL 9-10
    REMOVAL & INSTALLATION 9-8
BRAKE DISC (ROTOR) (FRONT DISC BRAKES) 9-11
    INSPECTION 9-12
    REMOVAL & INSTALLATION 9-11
BRAKE DISC (ROTOR) (REAR DISC BRAKES) 9-19
    REMOVAL & INSTALLATION 9-19
BRAKE DRUM 9-12
    ADJUSTMENTS 9-13
    INSPECTION 9-13
    REMOVAL & INSTALLATION 9-12
BRAKE HOSES AND LINES 9-4
    REMOVAL & INSTALLATION 9-4
BRAKE LIGHT SWITCH 9-2
    REMOVAL & INSTALLATION 9-2
BRAKE MASTER CYLINDER 1-43
    FLUID RECOMMENDATIONS 1-43
    LEVEL CHECK 1-43
BRAKE OPERATING SYSTEM 9-2
BRAKE PADS 9-6
    INSPECTION 9-8
    REMOVAL & INSTALLATION 9-6
BRAKE PRESSURE CONTROL VALVE 9-34
    REMOVAL & INSTALLATION 9-34
BRAKE SHOES 9-14
    INSPECTION 9-14
    REMOVAL & INSTALLATION 9-14
BRAKES 9-36
BULB SPECIFICATIONS 6-36
BUY OR REBUILD?* 3-60
CABLES 9-20
    ADJUSTMENT 9-24
    REMOVAL & INSTALLATION 9-20
CALIPER 9-18
    CALIPER OVERHAUL 9-19
    REMOVAL & INSTALLATION 9-18
CAMSHAFT 3-51
    INSPECTION 3-55
    REMOVAL & INSTALLATION 3-51
CAMSHAFT POSITION (CMP) SENSOR (DISTRIBUTORLESS IGNITION
  SYSTEM) 2-17
    REMOVAL & INSTALLATION 2-17
CAMSHAFT POSITION (CMP) SENSOR (ELECTRONIC ENGINE
  CONTROLS) 4-15

OPERATION 4-15
    REMOVAL & INSTALLATION 4-16
    TESTING 4-15
CAMSHAFT SPECIFICATIONS 3-3
CAMSHAFT SPROCKET 3-50
    REMOVAL & INSTALLATION 3-50
CAPACITIES 1-53
CARBURETED FUEL SYSTEM 5-3
CARBURETORS 5-4
    ADJUSTMENTS 5-4
CENTRAL FUEL INJECTION 5-7
CHARGING SYSTEM 2-17
CHASSIS GREASING 1-44
    AUTOMATIC TRANSMISSION LINKAGE 1-44
    BALL JOINTS 1-44
    CLUTCH LINKAGE 1-44
    PARKING BRAKE LINKAGE 1-44
    TIE ROD ENDS 1-44
CIRCUIT PROTECTION 6-38
CLEARING CODES 4-24
    KEEP ALIVE MEMORY (KAM) RESET 4-24
    PCM RESET 4-24
CLUTCH 7-4
CLUTCH CABLE ASSEMBLY 7-4
    REMOVAL & INSTALLATION 7-4
CLUTCH MASTER CYLINDER 1-44
    FLUID RECOMMENDATIONS 1-44
    LEVEL CHECK 1-44
COIL SPRINGS (FRONT SUSPENSION) 8-2
    REMOVAL & INSTALLATION 8-2
COIL SPRINGS (REAR SUSPENSION) 8-16
    REMOVAL & INSTALLATION 8-16
CONTROL PANEL 6-15
    REMOVAL & INSTALLATION 6-15
CONTROL SWITCHES 6-18
    REMOVAL & INSTALLATION 6-18
COOLING SYSTEM 1-42
    CHECKING SYSTEM PROTECTION 1-43
    DRAIN, FLUSH AND REFILL 1-42
    FLUID RECOMMENDATIONS 1-42
    LEVEL CHECK 1-42
    SYSTEM INSPECTION 1-43
CRANKCASE VENTILATION SYSTEM 4-2
    COMPONENT TESTING 4-2
    OPERATION 4-2
    REMOVAL & INSTALLATION 4-3
CRANKSHAFT AND CONNECTING ROD SPECIFICATIONS 3-4
CRANKSHAFT DAMPER 3-43
    REMOVAL & INSTALLATION 3-43
CRANKSHAFT POSITION (CKP) SENSOR 2-17
    REMOVAL & INSTA17LLATION 2-17
CRANKSHAFT POSITION (CP) SENSOR 4-17
    OPERATION 4-17
    REMOVAL & INSTALLATION 4-17
    TESTING 4-17
CRUISE CONTROL 6-18
CV BOOTS 1-26
    INSPECTION 1-26
CYLINDER HEAD (ENGINE MECHANICAL) 3-32
    REMOVAL & INSTALLATION 3-32
CYLINDER HEAD (ENGINE RECONDITIONING) 3-62
    ASSEMBLY 3-68
    DISASSEMBLY 3-62
    INSPECTION 3-65
    REFINISHING & REPAIRING 3-67
CYLINDER HEAD COVER 3-15
DASHBOARD 10-8
DATA LINK CONNECTOR (DLC) 4-23

DETERMINING ENGINE CONDITION   3-59
  COMPRESSION TEST   3-59
  OIL PRESSURE TEST   3-59
DIAGNOSIS AND TESTING (DISTRIBUTORLESS IGNITION SYSTEM)   2-15
  REMOVAL & INSTALLATION   2-15
DIAGNOSIS AND TESTING (DURA SPARK II IGNITION SYSTEM)   2-5
  CYLINDER DROP TEST   2-5
  SECONDARY SPARK TEST   2-5
DIAGNOSIS AND TESTING (EEC-IV THICK FILM INTEGRATED IGNITION SYSTEM)   2-10
DIFFERENTIAL CARRIER   7-32
  REMOVAL & INSTALLATION   7-32
DIS IGNITION MODULE/IGNITION CONTROL MODULE (ICM)   2-16
  REMOVAL & INSTALLATION   2-16
DISC BRAKE PADS   9-17
  REMOVAL & INSTALLATION   9-17
DISTRIBUTOR (DURA SPARK II IGNITION SYSTEM)   2-7
  INSTALLATION   2-8
  REMOVAL   2-7
DISTRIBUTOR (EEC-IV THICK FILM INTEGRATED IGNITION SYSTEM)   2-13
  REMOVAL & INSTALLATION   2-13
DISTRIBUTOR CAP AND ROTOR (DURASPARK II IGNITION SYSTEM)   2-7
  REMOVAL & INSTALLATION   2-7
DISTRIBUTOR CAP AND ROTOR (ROUTINE MAINTENANCE AND TUNE-UP)   1-29
  INSPECTION   1-29
  REMOVAL & INSTALLATION   1-29
DISTRIBUTORLESS IGNITION SYSTEM (DIS)   2-14
DO'S   1-4
DON'TS   1-5
DOOR GLASS   10-13
  REMOVAL & INSTALLATION   10-13
DOOR PANELS   10-11
  REMOVAL & INSTALLATION   10-11
DOORS   10-2
  ADJUSTMENT   10-2
  REMOVAL & INSTALLATION   10-2
DRIVE AXLE (FLUIDS AND LUBRICANTS)   1-41
  DRAIN AND REFILL   1-42
  FLUID RECOMMENDATIONS   1-41
  LEVEL CHECK   1-41
DRIVE AXLE (SERIAL NUMBER IDENTIFICATION)   1-12
DRIVELINE   7-25
DRIVEN DISC AND PRESSURE PLATE   7-4
  REMOVAL & INSTALLATION   7-4
DRIVESHAFT AND U-JOINTS   7-25
  REMOVAL AND INSTALLATION   7-25
  U-JOINT REPLACEMENT   7-28
DURA SPARK II IGNITION SYSTEM   2-3
EEC-IV THICK FILM INTEGRATED (TFI) IGNITION SYSTEM   2-8
EEC-IV TROUBLE CODES   4-18
EEC-V TROUBLE CODES   4-23
EGR VALVE POSITION (EVP) SENSOR   4-17
  OPERATION   4-17
  REMOVAL & INSTALLATION   4-18
  TESTING   4-18
ELECTRIC COOLING FAN   3-29
  REMOVAL & INSTALLATION   3-29
ELECTRIC FUEL PUMP (CENTRAL FUEL INJECTION)   5-7
  REMOVAL & INSTALLATION   5-7
  TESTING   5-11
ELECTRIC FUEL PUMP (MULTI-POINT INJECTION (EFI) AND SEQUENTIAL FUEL INJECTION)   5-12
  PRESSURE TESTING   5-12
  REMOVAL & INSTALLATION   5-12

ELECTRIC WINDOW MOTOR   10-15
  REMOVAL & INSTALLATION   10-15
ELECTRICAL COMPONENTS   6-2
  CONNECTORS   6-4
  GROUND   6-3
  LOAD   6-4
  POWER SOURCE   6-2
  PROTECTIVE DEVICES   6-3
  SWITCHES & RELAYS   6-3
  WIRING & HARNESSES   6-4
ELECTRONIC CONTROLLER   9-28
  REMOVAL & INSTALLATION   9-28
ELECTRONIC ENGINE CONTROL (EEC)   4-11
ELECTRONIC ENGINE CONTROLS   4-11
EMERGENCY BRAKE   9-20
EMISSION CONTROLS   4-2
EMISSION SERVICE LIGHTS   4-10
  RESETTING   4-10
ENGINE (ENGINE MECHANICAL)   3-7
  REMOVAL & INSTALLATION   3-7
ENGINE (SERIAL NUMBER IDENTIFICATION)   1-10
ENGINE BLOCK   3-69
  ASSEMBLY   3-72
  DISASSEMBLY   3-69
  GENERAL INFORMATION   3-69
  INSPECTION   3-70
  REFINISHING   3-72
ENGINE COOLANT TEMPERATURE (ECT) SENSOR   4-12
  OPERATION   4-12
  REMOVAL & INSTALLATION   4-13
  TESTING   4-12
ENGINE IDENTIFICATION   1-10
ENGINE MECHANICAL   3-2
ENGINE OVERHAUL TIPS   3-60
  CLEANING   3-60
  OVERHAUL TIPS   3-60
  REPAIRING DAMAGED THREADS   3-61
  TOOLS   3-60
ENGINE PREPARATION   3-62
ENGINE RECONDITIONING   3-59
ENGINE START-UP AND BREAK-IN   3-74
  BREAKING IT IN   3-74
  KEEP IT MAINTAINED   3-74
  STARTING THE ENGINE   3-74
ENTERTAINMENT SYSTEMS   6-20
EVAPORATIVE CANISTER   1-18
  SERVICING   1-18
EVAPORATIVE EMISSION CONTROLS   4-3
  OPERATION   4-3
  REMOVAL & INSTALLATION   4-3
  SYSTEM INSPECTION   4-3
EXHAUST GAS RECIRCULATION SYSTEM   4-7
  OPERATION   4-7
  REMOVAL & INSTALLATION   4-8
EXHAUST MANIFOLD   3-22
  REMOVAL & INSTALLATION   3-22
EXHAUST SYSTEM   3-57
EXTENSION HOUSING SEAL   7-2
  REMOVAL & INSTALLATION   7-2
EXTERIOR   10-2
FASTENERS, MEASUREMENTS AND CONVERSIONS   1-5
FENDERS   10-7
  REMOVAL & INSTALLATION   10-7
FIRING ORDERS   2-2
FLASHERS   6-39
  REPLACEMENT   6-39
FLOOR CONSOLE   10-10
  REMOVAL & INSTALLATION   10-10

FLUID DISPOSAL   1-35
FLUID PAN   7-10
FLUIDS AND LUBRICANTS   1-35
FLYWHEEL/FLEX PLATE AND RING GEAR   3-56
   REMOVAL & INSTALLATION   3-56
FRONT DISC BRAKES   9-6
FRONT HUB AND BEARING   8-14
   REMOVAL & INSTALLATION   8-14
FRONT SUSPENSION   8-2
FRONT WHEEL BEARINGS (FLUIDS AND LUBRICANTS)   1-45
   ADJUSTMENT   1-46
   REMOVAL, REPACKING, & INSTALLATION   1-45
FRONT WHEEL BEARINGS (FRONT SUSPENSION)   8-13
   REMOVAL & INSTALLATION   8-13
FRONT WHEEL SENSOR RING   9-30
   REMOVAL & INSTALLATION   9-30
FUEL AND ENGINE OIL RECOMMENDATIONS   1-38
   FUEL   1-38
   OIL   1-38
   OIL AND FILTER CHANGE   1-39
   OIL LEVEL CHECK   1-39
FUEL FILTER   1-14
   REMOVAL & INSTALLATION   1-14
FUEL INJECTOR   5-15
   REMOVAL & INSTALLATION   5-15
FUEL INJECTOR MANIFOLD ASSEMBLY   5-13
   REMOVAL & INSTALLATION   5-13
FUEL LINES AND FITTINGS   5-2
FUEL PRESSURE REGULATOR   5-12
   REMOVAL & INSTALLATION   5-12
FUEL TANK   5-17
   REMOVAL & INSTALLATION   5-17
FUSE PANEL DESCRIPTION   6-39
FUSES   6-38
   REPLACEMENT   6-38
FUSIBLE LINKS AND CIRCUIT BREAKERS   6-38
   REPLACEMENT   6-38
GAUGE CLUSTER   6-25
GAUGE PANEL   6-25
GAUGES   6-28
   REMOVAL & INSTALLATION   6-28
GENERAL ENGINE SPECIFICATIONS   1-11
GENERAL ENGINE TUNE-UP SPECIFICATIONS   1-31
GENERAL INFORMATION (CENTRAL FUEL INJECTION)   5-7
GENERAL INFORMATION (CHARGING SYSTEM)   2-17
GENERAL INFORMATION (DISTRIBUTORLESS IGNITION SYSTEM)   2-14
   SYSTEM COMPONENTS   2-15
   SYSTEM OPERATION   2-14
GENERAL INFORMATION (DURA SPARK II IGNITION SYSTEM)   2-3
   PRIMARY CIRCUIT   2-3
   SECONDARY CIRCUIT   2-3
GENERAL INFORMATION (EEC-IV THICK FILM INTEGRATED IGNITION SYSTEM)   2-8
   SYSTEM OPERATION   2-10
GENERAL INFORMATION (EEC-IV TROUBLE CODES)   4-18
   VEHICLE PREPARATION   4-18
   CLEARING CODES   4-19
   READING CODES   4-18
GENERAL INFORMATION (MULTI-POINT INJECTION (EFI) AND SEQUENTIAL FUEL INJECTION)   5-11
GENERAL INFORMATION (STARTING SYSTEM)   2-21
GENERAL INFORMATION (SUPPLEMENTAL RESTRAINT SYSTEM)   6-8
   SYSTEM COMPONENTS   6-9
   SYSTEM OPERATION   6-8
GENERAL INFORMATION (TEVES MARK II 4-WHEEL ANTI-LOCK BRAKE SYSTEM)   9-25
GENERAL INFORMATION (TEVES MARK-IV ANTI-LOCK BRAKE SYSTEM)   9-32

GENERAL INFORMATION   4-23
GRILLE   10-3
   REMOVAL & INSTALLATION   10-3
HEADLIGHT SWITCH   6-29
   REMOVAL & INSTALLATION   6-29
HEADLIGHTS   6-30
   AIMING   6-31
   REMOVAL & INSTALLATION   6-30
HEATED AIR INTAKE SYSTEM   4-6
   COMPONENT TESTING   4-6
   OPERATION   4-6
   REMOVAL & INSTALLATION   4-7
HEATER   6-11
HEATER CORE   6-12
   REMOVAL & INSTALLATION   6-12
HOOD   10-3
   ALIGNMENT   10-3
   REMOVAL & INSTALLATION   10-3
HOSES   1-25
   INSPECTION   1-25
   REMOVAL & INSTALLATION   1-25
HOW TO USE THIS BOOK   1-2
HYDRAULIC ACCUMULATOR   9-26
   REMOVAL & INSTALLATION   9-26
HYDRAULIC CONTROL UNIT (HCU)   9-32
   REMOVAL & INSTALLATION   9-32
HYDRAULIC PUMP MOTOR   9-26
   REMOVAL & INSTALLATION   9-26
IDLE AIR CONTROL (IAC) VALVE   4-12
   OPERATION   4-12
   REMOVAL & INSTALLATION   4-12
   TESTING   4-12
IDLE SPEED AND MIXTURE ADJUSTMENTS   1-31
IGNITION COIL (DURA SPARK II IGNITION SYSTEM)   2-6
   REMOVAL & INSTALLATION   2-7
   TESTING   2-6
IGNITION COIL (EEC-IV THICK FILM INTEGRATED IGNITION SYSTEM)   2-10
   REMOVAL & INSTALLATION   2-10
IGNITION LOCK CYLINDER   8-31
   REMOVAL & INSTALLATION   8-31
IGNITION SWITCH   8-30
   REMOVAL & INSTALLATION   8-30
IGNITION SYSTEMS   2-3
IGNITION TIMING   1-30
   GENERAL INFORMATION   1-30
   INSPECTION & ADJUSTMENT   1-30
INSIDE REARVIEW MIRROR   10-18
   REMOVAL & INSTALLATION   10-18
INSPECTION   3-57
   REPLACEMENT   3-58
INSTRUMENT CLUSTER   6-25
   REMOVAL & INSTALLATION   6-25
INSTRUMENT PANEL   10-8
   REMOVAL & INSTALLATION   10-8
INSTRUMENTS AND SWITCHES   6-25
INTAKE AIR TEMPERATURE (IAT) SENSOR   4-13
   OPERATION   4-13
   REMOVAL & INSTALLATION   4-13
   TESTING   4-13
INTAKE MANIFOLD   3-17
INTERIOR   10-8
JACKING   1-48
JACKING PRECAUTIONS   1-49
JUMP STARTING A DEAD BATTERY   1-47
JUMP STARTING PRECAUTIONS   1-47
JUMP STARTING PROCEDURE   1-47

KNOCK SENSOR (KS)   4-17
　OPERATION   4-17
　REMOVAL & INSTALLATION   4-17
　TESTING   4-17
LIGHTING   6-30
LOWER BALL JOINT   8-6
　INSPECTION   8-6
　REMOVAL & INSTALLATION   8-6
LOWER CONTROL ARM (FRONT SUSPENSION)   8-10
　CONTROL ARM BUSHING REPLACEMENT   8-11
　REMOVAL & INSTALLATION   8-10
LOWER CONTROL ARMS (REAR SUSPENSION)   8-23
　REMOVAL & INSTALLATION   8-23
MACPHERSON STRUT   8-5
　REMOVAL & INSTALLATION   8-5
MAINTENANCE OR REPAIR?   1-2
MAINTENANCE SCHEDULES   1-49
MANUAL TRANSMISSION   7-2
MANUAL TRANSMISSION (FLUIDS AND LUBRICANTS)   1-40
　DRAIN AND REFILL   1-40
　FLUID RECOMMENDATIONS   1-40
　LEVEL CHECK   1-40
MASS AIR FLOW (MAF) SENSOR   4-13
　OPERATION   4-13
　REMOVAL & INSTALLATION   4-14
　TESTING   4-13
MASTER CYLINDER (BRAKE OPERATING SYSTEM)   9-2
　REMOVAL & INSTALLATION   9-2
MASTER CYLINDER (CLUTCH)   7-7
　REMOVAL & INSTALLATION   7-7
MASTER CYLINDER-BOOSTER UNIT/ACTUATION
　ASSEMBLY   9-25
　REMOVAL & INSTALLATION   9-25
MECHANICAL FUEL PUMP   5-3
　REMOVAL & INSTALLATION   5-3
　TESTING   5-4
MULTI-FUNCTION SWITCH   8-29
　REMOVAL & INSTALLATION   8-29
**MULTI-POINT INJECTION (EFI) AND SEQUENTIAL FUEL
INJECTION (SEFI)   5-11**
NEUTRAL START SWITCH   7-16
　REMOVAL & INSTALLATION   7-16
O2 SENSOR   4-11
OIL PAN   3-38
　REMOVAL & INSTALLATION   3-38
OIL PUMP   3-42
　REMOVAL & INSTALLATION   3-42
OUTSIDE MIRRORS   10-5
　REMOVAL & INSTALLATION   10-5
OXYGEN SENSORS   4-11
　OPERATION   4-11
　REMOVAL & INSTALLATION   4-12
　TESTING   4-11
PARKING BRAKE   9-20
PCV VALVE   1-16
　REMOVAL & INSTALLATION   1-16
PINION OIL SEAL   7-30
　REMOVAL & INSTALLATION   7-30
PISTON RING SPECIFICATIONS   3-5
POWER BRAKE BOOSTER   9-3
　REMOVAL & INSTALLATION   9-3
POWER RACK AND PINION STEERING GEAR   8-34
　REMOVAL & INSTALLATION   8-34
POWER SEAT MOTOR   10-20
　REMOVAL & INSTALLATION   10-20
POWER STEERING   1-44
　FLUID RECOMMENDATION   1-44
　LEVEL CHECK   1-44

POWER STEERING PUMP   8-35
　BLEEDING   8-39
　REMOVAL & INSTALLATION   8-35
POWERTRAIN CONTROL MODULE (PCM)   4-11
　OPERATION   4-11
　REMOVAL & INSTALLATION   4-11
PRESSURE RELIEF VALVE   5-13
　REMOVAL & INSTALLATION   5-13
PRESSURE SWITCH   9-28
　REMOVAL & INSTALLATION   9-28
PROPORTIONING VALVE   9-4
QUICK-CONNECT FUEL LINE FITTINGS   5-2
　REMOVAL & INSTALLATION   5-2
RADIATOR   3-28
　REMOVAL & INSTALLATION   3-28
RADIO RECEIVER   6-20
　REMOVAL & INSTALLATION   6-20
READING CODES   4-23
REAR AXLE   7-29
REAR DISC BRAKES   9-17
REAR DRUM BRAKES   9-12
REAR MAIN OIL SEAL   3-55
　REMOVAL & INSTALLATION   3-56
REAR SUSPENSION   8-16
REAR WHEEL BEARINGS AND HUB   8-23
　REMOVAL & INSTALLATION   8-23
REAR WHEEL SENSOR RING   9-31
　REMOVAL & INSTALLATION   9-31
RELIEVING FUEL SYSTEM PRESSURE (CENTRAL FUEL
　INJECTION)   5-7
RELIEVING FUEL SYSTEM PRESSURE (MULTI-POINT INJECTION AND
　SEQUENTIAL FUEL INJECTION)   5-11
REMOVAL & INSTALLATION (ENGINE MECHANICAL)   3-17
RESERVOIR ASSEMBLY   9-27
　REMOVAL & INSTALLATION   9-27
REVERSE LIGHT SWITCH (INSTRUMENTS AND SWITCHES)   6-29
REVERSE LIGHT SWITCH (MANUAL TRANSMISSION)   7-2
RIM   8-2
ROCKER ARM (CAM FOLLOWER) AND HYDRAULIC LASH
　ADJUSTER   3-15
　REMOVAL & INSTALLATION   3-15
ROCKER ARM (VALVE) COVER   3-13
　REMOVAL & INSTALLATION   3-13
ROCKER ARM SHAFT/ROCKER ARMS   3-15
　REMOVAL & INSTALLATION   3-15
ROCKER COVER   3-15
ROUTINE MAINTENANCE AND TUNE-UP   1-12
SEATS   10-18
　REMOVAL & INSTALLATION   10-18
SENDING UNITS AND SENSORS   2-24
　REMOVAL & INSTALLATION   2-24
SENSORS   6-10
　ARMING THE SYSTEM   6-11
　DISARMING THE SYSTEM   6-10
　SERVICE PRECAUTIONS   6-10
SERIAL NUMBER IDENTIFICATION   1-7
SERVICING YOUR VEHICLE SAFELY   1-4
SERVO   6-19
　REMOVAL & INSTALLATION   6-19
SHIFT LEVER AND BOOT ASSEMBLY   7-2
　REMOVAL & INSTALLATION   7-2
SHOCK ABSORBER   8-20
　REMOVAL & INSTALLATION   8-20
SIGNAL AND MARKER LIGHTS   6-31
　REMOVAL & INSTALLATION   6-31
SLAVE CYLINDER   7-8
　HYDRAULIC SYSTEM BLEEDING   7-9
　REMOVAL & INSTALLATION   7-8

SPARK PLUG WIRES 1-28
   REMOVAL & INSTALLATION 1-29
   TESTING 1-28
SPARK PLUGS 1-26
   INSPECTION & GAPPING 1-27
   REMOVAL & INSTALLATION 1-27
   SPARK PLUG HEAT RANGE 1-27
SPEAKERS 6-22
   REMOVAL & INSTALLATION 6-22
SPECIAL TOOLS 1-4
SPECIFICATION CHARTS
  BRAKES 9-36
  BULB SPECIFICATIONS 6-36
  CAMSHAFT SPECIFICATIONS 3-3
  CAPACITIES 1-53
  CRANKSHAFT AND CONNECTING ROD
   SPECIFICATIONS 3-4
  ENGINE IDENTIFICATION 1-10
  FUSE PANEL DESCRIPTION 6-39
  GENERAL ENGINE SPECIFICATIONS 1-11
  GENERAL ENGINE TUNE-UP SPECIFICATIONS 1-31
  MAINTENANCE SCHEDULES 1-49
  PISTON RING SPECIFICATIONS 3-5
  TORQUE SPECIFICATIONS 3-6
  VALVE SPECIFICATIONS 3-2
  VEHICLE IDENTIFICATION CHART 1-8
SPEED SENSOR 6-19
   REMOVAL & INSTALLATION 6-19
SPINDLE/KNUCKLE 8-12
   REMOVAL & INSTALLATION 8-12
STABILIZER BAR (FRONT SUSPENSION) 8-7
   REMOVAL & INSTALLATION 8-7
STABILIZER BAR (REAR SUSPENSION) 8-23
   REMOVAL & INSTALLATION 8-23
STANDARD AND METRIC MEASUREMENTS 1-7
STARTER 2-21
   REMOVAL & INSTALLATION 2-21
   SOLENOID REPLACEMENT 2-23
   TESTING 2-21
STARTING SYSTEM 2-21
STATOR ASSEMBLY (DURA SPARK II IGNITION SYSTEM) 2-7
   REMOVAL & INSTALLATION 2-7
STATOR ASSEMBLY (EEC-IV THICK FILM INTEGRATED IGNITION
  SYSTEM) 2-12
   REMOVAL & INSTALLATION 2-12
STEERING 8-28
STEERING LINKAGE 8-33
   REMOVAL & INSTALLATION 8-33
STEERING WHEEL 8-28
   REMOVAL & INSTALLATION 8-28
STOP LIGHT SWITCH 9-2
STRUT 8-5
SUPERCHARGER 3-27
   REMOVAL & INSTALLATION 3-27
SUPPLEMENTAL RESTRAINT SYSTEM (AIR BAG) 6-8
SYNCHRONIZER ASSEMBLY 2-16
   REMOVAL & INSTALLATION 2-16
SYSTEM OPERATION 2-4
TEST EQUIPMENT 6-5
  JUMPER WIRES 6-5
  MULTIMETERS 6-5
  TEST LIGHTS 6-5
TESTING 6-6
  OPEN CIRCUITS 6-6
  RESISTANCE 6-7
  SHORT CIRCUITS 6-6
  VOLTAGE 6-6
  VOLTAGE DROP 6-7

TEVES MARK II 4-WHEEL ANTI-LOCK BRAKE
  SYSTEM (ABS) 9-25
TEVES MARK-IV ANTI-LOCK BRAKE
  SYSTEM (ABS) 9-32
TFI IGNITION MODULE 2-11
   REMOVAL & INSTALLATION 2-11
THERMACTOR® AIR INJECTOR SYSTEM 4-4
   OPERATION 4-4
   REMOVAL & INSTALLATION 4-6
   SYSTEM INSPECTION 4-5
THERMOSTAT 3-16
   REMOVAL & INSTALLATION 3-16
THROTTLE BODY 5-11
   REMOVAL & INSTALLATION 5-11
THROTTLE POSITION (TP) SENSOR 4-14
   OPERATION 4-14
   REMOVAL & INSTALLATION 4-15
   TESTING 4-14
TIMING BELT 3-46
   REMOVAL & INSTALLATION 3-46
TIMING BELT COVER 3-43
   REMOVAL & INSTALLATION 3-43
TIMING BELTS 1-24
   INSPECTION 1-24
TIMING CHAIN 3-47
   REMOVAL & INSTALLATION 3-47
TIMING CHAIN COVER AND SEAL 3-43
   REMOVAL & INSTALLATION 3-43
TIRES AND WHEELS 1-33
   INFLATION & INSPECTION 1-34
   TIRE DESIGN 1-33
   TIRE ROTATION 1-33
   TIRE STORAGE 1-34
TOOLS AND EQUIPMENT 1-2
TORQUE 1-6
  TORQUE ANGLE METERS 1-7
  TORQUE WRENCHES 1-6
TORQUE SPECIFICATIONS 3-6
TOWING 1-46
TOWING THE VEHICLE 1-46
TRAILER WIRING 6-37
TRANSMISSION (AUTOMATIC TRANSMISSION) 7-17
   REMOVAL & INSTALLATION 7-17
TRANSMISSION (MANUAL TRANSMISSION) 7-3
   REMOVAL & INSTALLATION 7-3
TRANSMISSION (SERIAL NUMBER IDENTIFICATION) 1-10
TROUBLE CODES 4-19
TROUBLESHOOTING CHARTS
  TROUBLE CODES 4-19
  TROUBLESHOOTING ELECTRICAL SYSTEMS 6-6
TRUNK LID 10-3
  ALIGNMENT 10-3
   REMOVAL & INSTALLATION 10-3
TURBOCHARGER 3-26
   REMOVAL & INSTALLATION 3-26
TURN SIGNAL SWITCH 8-29
   REMOVAL & INSTALLATION 8-29
UNDERSTANDING AND TROUBLESHOOTING ELECTRICAL
  SYSTEMS 6-2
UPPER BALL JOINT 8-6
   INSPECTION 8-6
   REMOVAL &INSTALLATION 8-6
UPPER CONTROL ARM (FRONT SUSPENSION) 8-9
   CONTROL ARM BUSHING REPLACEMENT 8-10
   REMOVAL & INSTALLATION 8-9
UPPER CONTROL ARMS (REAR SUSPENSION) 8-22
   REMOVAL & INSTALLATION 8-22
VACUUM DIAGRAMS 4-28

VACUUM DIAPHRAGM ASSEMBLY   2-7
    REMOVAL & INSTALLATION   2-7
VACUUM DUMP VALVE   6-19
    REMOVAL & INSTALLATION   6-19
VALVE COVER   3-13
VALVE LASH   3-15
    ADJUSTMENTS   3-15
VALVE SPECIFICATIONS   3-2
VEHICLE   1-7
VEHICLE CERTIFICATION LABEL   1-7
VEHICLE IDENTIFICATION CHART   1-8
VOLTAGE REGULATOR   2-20
    REMOVAL & INSTALLATION   2-20
WASHER PUMP AND RESERVOIR   6-25
    REMOVAL & INSTALLATION   6-25
WATER PUMP   3-30
    REMOVAL & INSTALLATION   3-30
WHEEL ALIGNMENT   8-15
    CAMBER   8-15
    CASTER   8-15
    TOE   8-15
WHEEL CYLINDERS   9-16
    REMOVAL & INSTALLATION   9-16
WHEEL LUG STUDS   8-2
    REMOVAL AND INSTALLATION   8-2

WHEEL SPEED SENSOR   9-34
    REMOVAL & INSTALLATION   9-34
WHEEL SPEED SENSORS   9-29
    REMOVAL & INSTALLATION   9-29
WHEELS   8-2
WHEELS   8-2
    REMOVAL & INSTALLATION   8-2
WHERE TO BEGIN   1-2
WINDOW REGULATOR   10-14
    REMOVAL & INSTALLATION   10-14
WINDSHIELD AND FIXED GLASS   10-16
    REMOVAL & INSTALLATION   10-16
    WINDSHIELD CHIP REPAIR   10-16
WINDSHIELD WIPER MOTOR   6-23
    REMOVAL & INSTALLATION   6-23
WINDSHIELD WIPER SWITCH   6-28
    REMOVAL & INSTALLATION   6-28
WINDSHIELD WIPERS   6-23
WINDSHIELD WIPERS (ROUTINE MAINTENANCE AND TUNE-UP)   1-32
    ELEMENT (REFILL) CARE & REPLACEMENT   1-32
WIPER BLADE AND ARM   6-23
    REMOVAL & INSTALLATION   6-23
WIRE AND CONNECTOR REPAIR   6-7
WIRING DIAGRAMS   6-43